LOST DOG

Real Life Rock

Also by Greil Marcus

Mystery Train: Images of America in Rock 'n' Roll Music (1975, 2015)

Lipstick Traces: A Secret History of the Twentieth Century (1989, 2009)

Dead Elvis: A Chronicle of a Cultural Obsession (1991)

In the Fascist Bathroom: Punk in Pop Music, 1977–1992 (1993, originally published as *Ranters & Crowd Pleasers*)

The Dustbin of History (1995)

The Old, Weird America: The World of Bob Dylan's Basement Tapes (2000, 2011, originally published as *Invisible Republic*, 1997)

Double Trouble: Bill Clinton and Elvis Presley in a Land of No Alternatives (2000)

"The Manchurian Candidate" (2002)

Like a Rolling Stone: Bob Dylan at the Crossroads (2005)

The Shape of Things to Come: Prophecy and the American Voice (2006)

When That Rough God Goes Riding: Listening to Van Morrison (2010)

Bob Dylan by Greil Marcus: Writings, 1968–2010 (2010)

The Doors: A Lifetime of Listening to Five Mean Years (2011)

The History of Rock 'n' Roll in Ten Songs (2014)

Three Songs, Three Singers, Three Nations (2015)

AS EDITOR

Stranded (1979, 2007)

Psychotic Reactions & Carburetor Dung by Lester Bangs (1987)

The Rose & the Briar: Death, Love, and Liberty in the American Ballad (2004, with Sean Wilentz)

Best Music Writing 2009 (2009)

A New Literary History of America (2009, with Werner Sollors)

Real Life Rock

■

The Complete
Top Ten Columns,
1986–2014

■

GREIL MARCUS

Yale

UNIVERSITY PRESS

New Haven and London

Published with assistance from the foundation established
in memory of Amasa Stone Mather of the Class of 1907, Yale College.

Yale University Press books may be purchased in quantity for educational,
business, or promotional use. For information, please e-mail sales.press@yale.edu
(U.S. office) or sales@yaleup.co.uk (U.K. office).

Designed by Sonia L. Shannon.
Set in Electra and Sans type by Westchester Publishing Services.
Printed in the United States of America.

Library of Congress Control Number: 2015935013
ISBN 978-0-300-19664-1 (cloth : alk. paper)

A catalogue record for this book is available from the British Library.

This paper meets the requirements of ANSI/NISO Z39.48-1992
(Permanence of Paper).

10 9 8 7 6 5 4 3 2 1

For Sleater-Kinney
and
the Mekons

two threads in this column

Contents

Introduction

A BOOK THIS LONG CANNOT SUFFER a long introduction. The work collected here began with a phone call at the beginning of 1986 from Doug Simmons, then the music editor of the *Village Voice*. In 1978, for *New West*, a magazine the late Clay Felker had launched as an outpost of his successful *New York*, I'd started a column called Real Life Rock. I took the title from Magazine's just-released album, *Real Life*. I loved the title, not the album. Calling a few songs slotted onto an LP real life seemed both ridiculous and like a challenge, or at least something to try to live up to: the notion that you could find real life anywhere, even on something shoved onto an LP or hidden away on it. It was an essay column, but each essay, through 1983, when it ended, closed with a top ten—songs, albums, commercials, ads, maybe a comment on a dress Bette Midler wore at an awards show. Anything.

Doug wanted to know if I'd turn that list idea into an actual column. He gave me the bottom third of a page once a month, about 700 words, which was room for anything: music, movies, fiction, critical theory, ads, television shows, remarks overheard waiting in line, news items, contributions from correspondents some of whom, under their column names or their real names, are still sending in items today, treating the column as a forum, or a good site for gossip, or the everyday conversation it has always wanted to be. I wrote the column every week until, in 1990, the *Voice* hired a new music editor who didn't like it. I moved it to *Artforum*, where I worked with Ingrid Sischy, David Frankel, Ida Panicelli, Jack Bankowsky, and Sydney Pokorny, off and on, with breaks to finish books, for nearly nine years, with more space, a page or sometimes two, for the magazine's ten issues a year. As in every following incarnation, the column changed according to the frame of reference of the publication and what I could presume the readership's frame of reference might be. The column began to take in more formal art, more politics, more novels, more critical absurdities. When finally I had to take a break and couldn't predict when it would end, the magazine offered a top ten to a different working artist every month. I kept writing for *Artforum* but in 1999 took the column to *Salon*, working with Gary Kamiya and Bill Wyman and publishing every other week—the online attention span, it was explained to me, was shorter than in the print world: "People forget what they've read more quickly"—and with no real word limit. At *Salon* the column was perhaps more ambitious than before—the work around it was thrilling, with the best coverage of the Clinton impeachment anywhere, wild humor, daring arguments—and more full of vitriol, because enemies were more plain. The column was killed in 2004 by David Talbot, the editor in chief, who said it was cut to save money. When I pointed out that given what I was being paid, doing away with it was not exactly going to make a measurable difference, he said that he didn't like the column anyway, and that since I always did whatever it was I did, there was no point in discussing it, thus allowing me to join the company of my friends Sarah Vowell, Steve Erickson, and Charles Taylor, who had lost columns at *Salon* before me. I went to *City Pages* in Minneapolis, which under the editorship of Steve Perry had become the best alternative weekly newspaper in the country—with the best reporting, the best criticism, the cleanest design, and the best editors. With my thousand or so words a month, I was lucky to work with Melissa Maerz. In 2005, after little more than a year, I went back to *Interview*, where I'd been writing an intermittent essay column, Days Between Stations (the title stolen from a Steve Erickson novel), since 1992, working again with Ingrid Sischy and with Graham Fuller and Brad Goldfarb. Ingrid wanted a new name for the column; "Elephant Dancing" popped into my head as the dumbest possible thing we could call it. "Fine," she said. She later asked me to switch the column to a top ten—but still under that terrible hoist-by-my-own-petard name, at about 750 words a month. This was the one time the column didn't work, because everything had to be music related, and I'd long since found the column was about anything under the sun or it was nothing. I didn't like writing it, Ingrid didn't like reading it, and we went back to an essay format—until Ingrid left in the middle of the night and the new editors killed all the criticism columns ("We're going more visual"). I tried for more than a year to find a home for Real Life Rock Top Ten, with no luck anywhere, until one good day Vendela Vida of the *Believer* called to say that Nick Hornby was taking a leave from his books column, and was there by any chance a column I'd like to write? I wrote one ten times a year, at any length I chose, working with Vendela Vida, Sheila Heti, Andi Winnette, and Andrew Leland, from 2008 to 2014, and in the best possible home, even under the crazy stricture that, in the *Believer*, which had begun as a publication abjuring all snark, you couldn't say anything mean about anybody, which made writing about Lucinda Williams a real challenge. I made it a game to sneak offending material into the column; sometimes I got away with it. When the *Believer* temporarily suspended publication in the fall of 2014, Bill Tipper of the *Barnes & Noble Review* took the column without hesitating, offering to publish it once a month at whatever length made sense.

Everything through *The Believer* is here. Whether that makes sense is for others to judge. I have corrected some errors, though some probably remain, and some, as when I misheard a song lyric, or cited what seemed to be a fact that later proved not to be, although that couldn't have been known at the time, remain on purpose. I haven't changed or softened any judgments. I had fun. I still do. I know I use variants of "black hole" and "heart on his sleeve" far too often.

The Village Voice

1986·1990

1 ■ Reducers, "Let's Go," from the sampler *Epic Presents the Unsigned* (Epic) Most of the stuff here is novelty-record cute; this pained, nervous stomp is part '56 rockabilly, part '64 British Invasion, part '77 punk—timeless. Chasing themselves out of their hometown of New London, Connecticut, to Paris to Texas to Munich, the Reducers just want to get out of here, and then get out of there. They only have to name a place to leave it.

2 ■ Billy Ocean, "When the Going Gets Tough, the Tough Get Going" (Jive/Arista) This piece of airwave fodder isn't "Billie Jean," but it's a beautifully layered conversation—after a hundred shots on the radio, the female chorus seems to be made up of real people. As for the line about "Your love is like a slow train coming"—is that what Bob Dylan meant?

3 ■ Godzilla (Takara, Japan) It was established long ago that all Japanese rock 'n' roll derives from Godzilla movies; at one and one-half inches high, this rubber monster spits fire when you rev its wheels, then runs flat out for 50 feet when you let it go, which is more than you can say for most Japanese rock 'n' roll. About $4 in better weird-toy, comix, or sci-fi stores.

4 ■ W. T. Lhamon Jr, "Little Richard as a Folk Performer," in *Studies in Popular Culture*, VIII:2, 1985 "One of the more obscuring claims critics make about the origins of rock music," Lhamon begins, "is that individual genius conceived it." Little Richard Penniman was not sui generis, Lhamon goes on: he was a product of the late '40s/early '50s "milieu of afternoon bars, minstrel shows, gay clubs, carny midways, folk patois, blues lyrics, road bonding, and the postwar leisure of Northern soldiers bored in Southern towns." Lhamon proves his case in frightening detail—at least, the way he traces Richard's "Miss Ann" to a 16th century British nursery rhyme frightens me—and he's just as strong making sense of the explosively new appeal of Richard's presumptively old story. On the originally ob-

scene "Tutti Frutti" in 1955: ". . . the puns on 'Sue' and 'Daisy' titilated uninitiated audiences simply as references to good opposite-sex partners. At another level in these days of desegregation, Daisy and Sue were racially moot names. . . . Was Little Richard probing the delights of miscegenated sex? At a third level, and to other audiences, Daisy and Sue were knowing referents to drag queens in the clubs where Little Richard had presented himself as Princess Lavonne. In seeming to sanitize 'Tutti Frutti,' [producer Bumps] Blackwell, [co-writer Dorothy] La Bostrie, and Penniman had instead sublimated it with small nodes of latent excitement. Most audiences probably did not suspect any of this . . . but the singer knew, Blackwell knew, and so did the musicians. . . . Their performance took on a licentious exuberance commensurate to their release from restraint." In other words, rock 'n' roll began as a code its new fans didn't know they were deciphering—a code that deciphered them.

5 ■ Lime, "Say You Love Me," from *Unexpected Lovers* (TSR) Shirley and Lee go disco—except this isn't Shirley and Lee. But Denyse Le Page has Shirley's impossibly high, quavering voice, and 30 years after "Let the Good Times Roll" or 11 after "Shame, Shame, Shame," it will do.

6 ■ Sam Cooke, "Just for You," from *The Man and His Music* (RCA reissue, 1956–1964) According to Joel Whitburn's *Top Pop 1955–1982*, this exquisitely syncopated 1961 ballad, Cooke's only release on his own S.A.R. label, never made the charts—which is either Whitburn's first documented mistake, or God's latest.

7 ■ The Costello Show (featuring Elvis Costello), "Brand New Hairdo" (CBS) Not on the new *King of America*, and nothing like it, either: fast, noisy, and nasty.

8 ■ Bette Midler, "You Belong to Me," in *Down and Out in Beverly Hills* (Buena Vista) Sweet.

9 ■ Sandy Denny, *Who Knows Where the Time Goes?* (Hannibal reissue, 1967–77) Four LPs in a box, much unreleased material, not all of it terrific—merely those mo-

ments ("Tam Lin," "Listen, Listen," "Autopsy") where all that "folk rock" was supposed to mean was put into play.

10 ■ Loyal Jones, *Minstrel of the Appalachians—The Story of Bascom Lamar Lunsford* (Appalachian Consortium Press, Boone, North Carolina) In 1928 a North Carolina lawyer named Bascom Lamar Lunsford (1882–1973) recorded a traditional mountain ballad called "I Wish I Was a Mole in the Ground"; six decades later, the marriage of fatalism and desire in his performance defines American mysticism, as it likely would have done six decades before. According to this book, everything Lunsford did was interesting, and so is everything in this book.

MARCH 18, 1986

1 ■ Richard Thompson, *Doom & Gloom from the Tomb* (Flypaper cassette) Eighteen unreleased performances, 1968–84, some demos, mostly live, better than the recent Sandy Denny box, and more playable than Thompson's own retrospective, *(guitar, vocal)*. The pairing of an '82 duet with then-wife Linda Thompson on "I'll Keep It with Mine" and an '84 "Calvary Cross" (fingering his guitar, Thompson seems to be fingering the timber, wondering what it would be like to be up there) shows how far this modest piece of tape can take the gnostic story Thompson has been telling for almost 20 years; the immodest price includes a four-issue subscription to *Flypaper,* the newsletter of the Richard Thompson fan club.

2 ■ Stan Ridgway, *The Big Heat* (I.R.S.) How to talk American—and not get caught. Whether or not Jim Thompson could have written these songs, his characters lived them out.

3 ■ Coin-operated Photo Booth, circa 1933, the first published photograph of Robert Johnson (*Rolling Stone*, 13 February 1986) Born in 1911, this titanic singer and guitarist at once summed up and exploded the Delta blues tradition when he recorded in 1936 and '37; he was killed in 1938. After that he became a legend, a ghost story, and was sub-

sumed into the tradition; in the 1960s he exploded out of it. In the early 1970s, blues archivist Steve La Vere tracked down the facts of his life; and his leavings, amongst which were three photographs, prizes sought for decades, the Grail of the blues. The two that remain unpublished are formal studio portraits: here, prehensile fingers snake over the neck of Johnson's guitar like hoodoo bone charms. You've got to see it.

4 ■ PiL, "Single (Rise)" (Elektra) Inside the rant ("anger is an energy," etc.) is a pause; John Lydon pulls back, thinks it over, almost croons to himself: "I may be wrong, I may be right." The tune is supposedly about the struggle against apartheid, but it segues as perfectly into "Pretty Vacant" as it does out of black South African Sipho Mabuse's "Burn Out."

5 ■ Luc Besson, director, *Subway* (Island Films) Punk flees blown blackmail plot into the Paris métro, and, having nothing better to do, decides to manage a really underground band.

6 ■ Margaret Atwood, *The Handmaid's Tale* (Houghton Mifflin) Not long into the future, when what was once the U.S.A. has become the Republic of Gilead, a theocracy that has replaced the Constitution with the Bible, a slave sings forbidden music to herself: "I feel so lonely, baby/I feel so lonely, baby/I feel so lonely, I could die." She doesn't know where it came from.

7 ■ Electric Light Orchestra, "Calling America" (CBS) Amazing how these portly gentlemen can still sound like addled teenagers, especially on an answer record to a 24-year-old hit. In 1962 the Tornadoes' "Telstar," commemorating the first communications satellite, became the first U.K. rock 'n' roll record to top the U.S. charts; now, the sci-fi "Telstar" sound still hanging in the background, Jeff Lynne finds his call suspended 20,000 miles up in space and he can't get it down. NASA is working on the problem.

8 ■ Firesign Theater, *Eat or Be Eaten* (Mercury) Probably written a few years ago—the premise is video games—but if the only true exemplars of multi-track dada

comedy have to spend the next decade catching up with themselves, everyone else will still be behind.

9 ▪ **Doug Hill and Jeff Weingrad, *Saturday Night—A Backstage History of "Saturday Night Live"* (Beech Tree/William Morrow)** A fine story, cleanly told, though the authors have no idea how good Laraine Newman was, or that her nose job represents a greater tragedy than John Belushi's death.

10 ▪ **Sam Cooke, "A Change Is Gonna Come," from *A Man and His Music* (RCA reissue, 1956–65)** When this performance was released as a posthumous single in 1965, a verse about the racism the 1964 Civil Rights Act was meant to abolish was omitted; you could only find it on the LP version, which you couldn't find. History has finally been corrected—though, given that a man who fought against that law is now responsible for enforcing it, history may be beside the point. Maybe RCA should have retitled the song "A Change Was Gonna Come."

APRIL 15, 1986

1 ▪ **T J. Clark, *The Painting of Modern Life—Paris in the Art of Manet and His Followers* (Princeton)** In the chapter "A Bar in the Folies-Bergère," named for the weird Manet painting, Clark takes you into the "café-concerts" of Paris in the 1860s and '70s, and captures nearly all that was up for grabs in the Roxy in London in 1977 with a clarity and drama that has escaped every writer who was there, if not the Clash, X-ray Spex, Wire, and the Adverts, who were there, too.

2 ▪ **Sonic Youth, *Walls Have Ears* (no label)** A deluxe two-LP bootleg, taken from a recent U.K. tour, and a map of where this downtown band can go. It meanders over a blurred terrain until flare-ups cause the music to contract past its surface of cryptic eschatology down to its unstable core: loathing, fatuity, confusion, smugness, play. The goal seems to be to turn amusement into dread, and to sustain dread long enough to turn it into a threat, which can be shaped into a song, which can be destroyed.

3 ▪ **Ted Nugent, Attempted Commercial Transaction** Westinghouse recently put its Muzak subsidiary up for sale, and the Detroit guitar hero tried to buy it—and kill it. "Muzak is an evil force in today's society," he announced, "causing people to lapse into uncontrollable fits of blandness. It's been responsible for ruining some of the best minds of our generation." Nugent's offer: $10 million. Westinghouse's response: the 101 Strings version of "Oh No, Not My Baby."

4 ▪ **Solomon Burke, "Love Buys Love," from *A Change Is Gonna Come* (Rounder)** Warm, knowing, perfectly rounded tones from a soul man who even in the heyday of the form never made the Top 20. Accompanied by a band whose touch is as light as it is firm, he sings with complete confidence, which isn't to say that doubt doesn't feed his every affirmation, either here or through the long reading of the title song. This is no revival, this is no comeback—this music is anchored, and the anchor goes to the bottom of the sea.

5 ▪ **James Robert Baker, *Fuel-Injected Dreams* (Dutton)** A unrelievedly hyped-up, luridly funny novel about a legendary '60s L.A. record producer who marries his Galatea and keeps her locked up in his mansion for years after. Not anyone you'd recognize, of course.

6 ▪ **Rosanne Cash, "Hold On" (Columbia)** She challenges a man to commit himself to her with such musky self-possession it's impossible to believe he's worth the trouble. Not as good as "Seven Year Ache," but what is?

7 ▪ **Hüsker Dü, *Candy Apple Grey* (Warner Bros.)** Finally—finally, Bob Dylan has recaptured his voice. Thuggish hillbilly drunk on books with a half-ton of plains dirt in his mouth shouting from inside a stampede of blue oxen driven by Paul Bunyans, and yet for all its fury the voice is lyrical, you can almost hear him thinking as he wails, damning the loss of everything that's left behind as he presses on to wherever it is he has to go.

8 ▪ **Mekons, *Crime and Punishment* (Sin EP, UK)** Without the suicidal tendencies of *Fear & Whiskey*, this lacks weight—the weight of the world. Let's call it "Fun and Games."

9 ▪ ***Sweet Beat,* directed by Ronnie Albert, 1958 (Silvermine Video)** One of the worst movies ever made, or anyway, one of the least—60 pallid British minutes of what the Angry Young Men were angry about. Then the insufferable heroine and her slime date walk into a nightclub where "Fred Parris and the Satins" (one of the Satins had left by this time, so they couldn't be "The Five" anymore) are trying to lip-synch "In the Still of the Nite." It's strange: they're so ordinary. Their hair isn't even conked, they all but bump into each other, and the music is still shocking.

10 ▪ **Asger Jorn and Guy-Ernest Debord, *Fin de Copenhague* (Editions Allia reprint, 1957)** Originally cut up, pasted, splattered, and printed (in an edition of 200) in 48 hours, this full-color little book at first seems like a slightly dated satire on advertising. With phrases and slogans from half a dozen tongues seeking whiskey bottles and models like feral orphans hunting for food, it becomes an attempt to extract secret codes from a language everyone understands and no one uses to think. "We have *ways* of making you talk," Jorn and Debord seem to say to the fetishized commodity, tied to a chair but still wearing a shit-eating grin—Jorn, Danish painter (1914–73) waving his brush; Debord, "French political thinker" (so says the April *Vogue*) brandishing his scissors—and the result is advertising transformed into free-floating graffiti. The book now reads as a harbinger of the punk flier, and as a testament to just how far short of its own possibilities that great common art project has stopped.

MAY 13, 1986

1 ▪ **The Costello Show (featuring Elvis Costello), "Sleep of the Just," from *King of America* (Columbia)** In a notably slow month, when such obvious critical hypes as Dwight Hokum seem possible until you have to listen, this deceptively quiet number is beginning to get airplay, and airplay is beginning to reveal its weight and complexity. Built around Mitchell Froom's "doctored piano," which has the shimmering sound of an old Leslie guitar, the song announces itself as a benediction; Jim Keltner's brushwork keys the end of a line with the feeling of dirt being tossed on a coffin. The dread that's been secretly building in the lyrics—images of black crows, a burning bus—doesn't surface until the third, turnaround verse, though Costello barely raises his voice to tell the tale of soldiers gang-banging a centerfold on their barracks wall. His music has never been harder, or more delicate—and the year itself will have to turn around to produce a better song.

2 ▪ **Bryan Ferry, "Is Your Love Strong Enough" (MCA)** Standard Ferry romanticism, which shows up Keith Richards's ballad on *Dirty Work* for the glop it is.

3 ▪ **Stephen Davis, *Hammer of the Gods—The Led Zeppelin Saga* (Ballantine)** Davis wildly overrates the music, digs up and then smooths out endless incidents of exploitation, sexism, and violence, and finally makes an ultimately meaningless story moving. Still, you've got to like the bit about drummer John Bonham placing below Karen Carpenter in the '75 *Playboy* music poll.

4 ▪ **Bryan Adams, "Summer of '69" (A&M)** It won't last. Why should it?

5 ▪ **28th Day, "I'm Only Asking," from *28th Day* (Bring Out Your Dead/Enigma)** Bassist Barbara Mannings takes this folk-rock trio into Robin Lane territory, where vulnerability leads to doubt, which might lead to trouble.

6 ▪ ***Desert Hearts,* directed by Donna Deitch (Goldwyn)** This movie about a free-spirited lesbian and her tightass divorcée love-object in 1959 Nevada has been predictably celebrated as a statement, but for the first half of the film, before F-S L Patricia Charbonneau gets what she's after, the atmosphere is irresistible. That's be-

cause Deitch has understood '50s music as a promise not of teenage lust but of pansexual desire: here, Johnny Ray's "Cry," Ferlin Husky's "Gone," Buddy Holly's "Rave On," and Elvis's "Blue Moon" take on a power they never had before. If Deitch's version of self-realization is old, she makes the music she uses to dramatize it new.

7 ■ **Chuck Berry, *Rock 'n Roll Rarities* (Chess/MCA)** Out-takes and oddities. Not great (the sterio remix of "Nadine" could be subtitled "Unhit Version"), but indispensable.

8 ■ **Jackson Browne, *Lives in the Balance* (Asylum)** Nothing could be easier than to dismiss this LP about U.S. atrocities in Central America; Reagan waves the bloody shirt, and Browne counters by wearing his bleeding heart on his sleeve. But the album is an act of real bravery—far more so than "Sun City"—and hearing "For America" on the radio, I pound the dashboard in time with my rage.

9 ■ **Fuzz Box, *We've Got a Fuzz Box and We're Gonna Use It!!* (Vindaloo UK 12-inch)** Four women who do what they say.

10 ■ **Jill Pearlman (writer) & Wayne White (illustrator), *Elvis for Beginners* (Writers & Readers/Norton)** The leftist "For Beginners" line of "documentary comic books" has produced superb work, but to find Elvis in the company of the likes of Marx, Freud, and Orwell is less shocking than Pearlman's heedless contempt for her subject. In contradistinction to the rest of the series, *Elvis* appears in a glossy color cover rather than in flat, serious grey or beige; the black-and-white interior design and illustration replaces the usual dense detail and wit with blaring caricatures; and the text, which must have taken Pearlman at least three hours to write, is riddled with errors: Marion Keisker, Sam Phillips's co-manager at Sun Records in Memphis in 1953, turns up as "Marion Tipler"—simply because Pearlman and White get her mixed up with one Gladys Tipler, noted on a nearby page as Elvis's '53 employer. The capper comes on the page between the Tipler/Keisker flub. Some years ago, in a review of Albert Goldman's *Elvis*, I wrote that Goldman's perversion of Phillips's early-'50s statement of his ambitions as a record producer (Goldman's transformation of "If I could find a white man who had the Negro sound and the Negro feel, I could make a billion dollars" into "If I could find a white boy who sang like a nigger, I could make a million dollars") would be cited in books to come, and pervert the history of rock 'n' roll itself; until *Elvis for Beginners*, I was wrong. No, this isn't the tenth best item to seek out in May 1986—but it ought to be at the top of anyone's bottom list.

JUNE 10, 1986

1 ■ **The Honeys, "The One That You Can't Have," from *Dream Babies—Girls and Girl Groups of the Sixties* (Capitol/EMI UK)** You have to slog through a lot of dross to get to this final cut—a '63 Brian Wilson composition/production for Marilyn Rovell (later Mrs. Brian), her sister Diane, and cousin Ginger Blake—but is it ever worth it. Save for "Wouldn't It Be Nice," nothing the Beach Boys ever touched came out half this warming. The sound is lightly Spectorish, anticipating and surpassing the BB's *Pet Sounds:* a perfect, lilting aura for the lead Honey's vocal, which has no parallels in rock. She's talking to herself, wondering over the paradoxes of life on earth as circumscribed by the mores of a suburban high school ("The one that you can't have/ Is the one that you want the most"). Cuteness that in a decade or so would harden into Valley-girl cliché is full of personality, a reach for the tones and elisions that might catch what one girl wants. The singing is displacingly amateurish—you can believe the style is being made up as the song is sung—and it holds a feeling of delight so patent you can almost see it in the air.

2 ■ **Robert Plant, "Far Post" (Esparanza/ WEA Japan)** Unavailable here as the B-side of the non-U.S. version of the '83 "Big Log" single, import copies have lately been turning up courtesy of Jem; loose and taut as a cowboy's rope spinning just before it's shot

out to catch a calf around the neck, this *swings*. Plant's laconic vocal rides over barroom piano into the smokiest, least pretentious music he's made since Led Zeppelin blew up; he actually sounds like a human being.

3 ■ **Dobie Gray, *From Where I Stand* (Capitol)** The follow-up to "Drift Away," a mere 13 years late. It's country soul, in the same way that Charlie Rich is soul country.

4 ■ ***Sweet Dreams,* directed by Karel Reisz (Thorn EMI/HBO Video)** What makes this Patsy Cline biopic work is Reisz's refusal to dramatize: both Jessica Lange (Cline) and Ed Harris (husband) give one-note performances, but they hit their notes. What makes the movie powerful is the use of Cline's recordings for Lange to lip-synch: as opposed to *Nashville* and *Coal Miner's Daughter*, where country music was judged such shit the actors were allowed to do their own singing, thus reducing the characters they played, in *Sweet Dreams* Lange's character becomes a mystery—an ordinary, exuberant woman with many worlds in her throat. The extraordinary fidelity in the remastering of Cline's tunes brings out subtleties of phrasing and motive that don't exist on record: you hear Cline aiming above her working-class status, not knowing how to get there, prettifying her passion, the passion swallowing the prettifying—and that's all the drama the movie needs.

5 ■ **Little Richard, *Early Studio Outtakes* (Sunjay)** Marvels from the '50s, highlighted by lines from "I Got It" that took years to make official vinyl, and then in a funk version that wiped off all their drool: "It ain't what you do it's the way how you do it/It ain't what you eat it's the way how you chew it."

6 ■ **Test Dept., *The Unacceptable Face of Freedom* (Ministry of Power/Some Bizarre UK)** English friends say this tape-collage LP captures the mood in Britain better than anything else, mainly by turning the loop on the sleeve into noise: "The State Forced to Concede the Empire Abroad, Finally Turns on Its Own People to Create a New Empire at Home. The Last Colony. The State Forced to—"

7 ■ **Heart, "Nothing at All" (Capitol)** Voices carry.

8 ■ **Radio commercial for Mercury Sable (Young & Rubicam)** It begins with the Four Tops' stirring "Reach Out." "I remember the first time I heard this song," says a man wistfully. "It was the night my first girlfriend *dumped* me . . ."

9 ■ ***O Love Is Teasin'* (Elektra)** It is of paramount importance that all people of good will avoid (if not invade record stores to burn) this three-LP boxed set of '50s retakes of ancient Appalachian ballads, unless such people harbor the irrepressible wish to hear "Barbara Allen" sung with the downhome charm of a public television station break.

10 ■ **"Lost Dog," street flyer (Berkeley, January 1986)** This stood out among a score of other punk handbills stapled onto a telephone pole; it's been bothering me ever since I ripped it down and tacked it over my desk. There's a sort of Mr. Bill putty animal, a few lines of type carefully inked over so you can't read them, a screaming "HAVE YOU SEEN THIS DOG??," the words "The noblest, most rational and most intelligent beast God ever made," and a cartoon of dogs and humans dressed for a fancy party taking place somewhere between Periclean Greece and prerevolutionary France. I thought I had it figured out as a cryptic record ad when a tune called "Fluffy," about a "lost dog," came on the local college station, but a call proved the song three years old. Is this a new band? A new philosophy? A new void?

JULY 15, 1986

1 ■ **Mekons, *The Edge of the World* (Sin, UK)** This lacks the insinuative potency of last year's *Fear and Whiskey*, that astonishing tale of termite rebels burrowing into dark times, but thanks to Rico Bell's accordion and Susie Honeyman's violin, it comes on stronger; the territory remains the same. Once more, you can follow real people struggling with real questions: how do we live when all we cherish has been buried in

the shit of power? Answers range from oblivion to good conversation. A cracked, impassioned cover of "Sweet Dreams" is cut off and you're plunged into "Dream, Dream, Dream" which is a joke and a nightmare; it leads to "Slightly South of the Border," an unhappy explanation of why small pleasures like shopping, strolling, and good conversation dry up when they're severed from a sense of the world-historical, a conviction confirmed by a hard and bitter Celtic fiddle piece that calls up Bob Dylan's "A Hard Rain's A-Gonna Fall," Richard Thompson's "Withered and Died," Wire's "I Am the Fly," and turns out to be Hank Williams's "Alone and Forsaken." *The Edge of the World* is a map of a secret time and place: here, now.

2 ▪ *Absolute Beginners*, **directed by Julien Temple (Orion)** For the moment in the race riot when the thug called Flikker (Bruce Payne) pours gasoline on a coloured family's piano, lights a match, and bangs out "Great Balls of Fire" as the keys go up in flames.

3 ▪ **Wilson Sisters, "1972" (flexi-disc in** *Monitor #6: Pop—Subversion and Surveillance*, **Oxford, UK)** They—whoever they are—make what's likely the least spooky year in rock history sound like the most.

4 ▪ **Joseph Ellroy,** *Blood on the Moon* **(Avon paperback)** Two decades after the Everly Brothers hit the charts with "Cathy's Clown," a mass murderer writes on a wall in the blood of his latest victim: "I'M NOT KATHY'S KLOWN." "Maybe it's a clue," says a cop, and it is—to this very gory mystery, and to the mysteries of pop metaphor.

5 ▪ *Zone 1/2*, **edited by Michel Feher and Sanford Kwinter, designed by Bruce Mau (Urzone/Johns Hopkins University Press)** This big, internationalist dramatization of urbanism is a map of a public time and place—here, now—a picture of the shit of power. The premise that "Productive space [is becoming] diffused throughout the urban fabric, while a new wave of puritanism subjects the household to the ethics of the factory" is shaped by 13 essays (most striking are Annie L. Cott's coolly horrifying "Neo-

conservative Economics, Utopia and Crisis" and Eric Alliez and Feher's inspired "The Luster of Capital"), nine art projects (see page 32 for John Baldessari's "Crowds With the Shape of Reason Missing"), and 19 replies to a what's-happening-with-the-city questionnaire, which take form as mini-essays and mini-art projects (go to page 456 for examples of Krzysztof Wodiczko's projection art)—all that's missing is a flexi of the Gang of Four's "At Home He's a Tourist" b/w "It's Her Factory." Ignoring pop music, *Zone* defines the social terrain that in ephemeral, everyday instants pop has to reveal for what it is, or could be: the temporal space new music will have to occupy if it is to be the sound of the city, not just sound in the city.

6 ▪ **Bob Dylan With the Heartbreakers, "Lonesome Town," Greek Theatre, Berkeley, June 13** "Ricky Nelson did a lot of my songs; I'd like to do one of his." A lovely gesture, and it worked. As for the rest of the show, Dylan traded emotional nuance for rote chanting so doggedly that when my seatmate wondered if the next number might not be "99 Bottles of Beer on the Wall," it was impossible to hear what followed as anything else. Two verses later, we deciphered it as a speeded-up "Rainy Day Women #12 & 35."

7 ▪ **Sonic Youth,** *Evol* **(SST)** By far their most pop, even rational, release, and still opening more doors to the void than the offerings of such putative allies as Big Black. I mean, if BB's *Atomizer* is flesh-eating, they ordered off a menu.

8 ▪ **Madonna, "Live To Tell" (Sire)** This is terribly contrived, and in a month or two it's going to sound like the luster of capital, if not the shit of power. For the moment, it's one more proof of her mastery.

9 ▪ **Rolling Stones, "Dirty Work," from** *Dirty Work* **(Rolling Stones)** Maybe the redundancy is a code, a clue: this kicks off like their ancient "Empty Heart," which is what it describes. Then it begins to fall apart, and Mick Jagger's recognition of the emptiness in his own heart keeps it going. What you're hearing is auto-cannibalism: Jagger feels

the remnants of "Salt of the Earth" in his heart, and so, dramatizing the neoconservative utopia, he eats it.

10 ▪ Mekons, Club DV8, San Francisco, June 26 Best oldie: their own eight-year-old "Where Were You?" Best performance: "Hard To Be Human Again." Best line: "Do you want to be part of the crime, or do you want to be part of the punishment?"

AUGUST 12, 1986

1 ▪ California Cooler, "Louie Louie" radio commercials (Chiat/DTV) Spots based on desiccated revisions of old rock songs (worst: "Runaround Sue" as a commercial for Zipwax—"I never thought I'd be singing about hair remover," says a breathless ms.) have become so ubiquitous that ads featuring the real thing now work as relief—and none more than these, which offer a measured voice recounting the history and etiquette of wine 'n' fruit juice consumption. The original buy traced the discovery of the beverage to California beaches, circa 1963—thus the Kingsmen, entering with a crash and tripping all over themselves—and provided a rundown on the drinking vessel de rigueur on the given beach (mayonnaise jar for Malibu, turkey baster for Santa Cruz). The latest argues that the stuff is appropriate to any setting—so, after the Kingsmen cover the beachfront, an opera singer essays "Louie Louie," a jazz combo plays it, and a mariachi band turns it into ethnic festival music. It's a true contribution to rock history: three more shots to add to college stations' "Louie Louie" marathons, whose annual accumulations have already unearthed more than a thousand versions of a song that wasn't even a hit for Richard Berry, its auteur.

2 ▪ Black Uhuru, Brutal (RAS) This sophisticated reggae combo lost a bit of soul with the departure of lead singer Michael Rose, but Junior Reid sounds enough like him to keep the story going; as always, the story is in the way chants, rhythms, and melodies are suspended, then stretched, broken, recreated. The story takes its power from the tension between the need to guard a secret and the wish to reveal it, the closest the group ever came to letting it loose was "Vampire," the closing cut on the 1980 Sinsemilla, and its mood of gnostic initiation is present on almost every track of Brutal.

3 ▪ Chris Furby and Slim Smith, God Crazy (Workforce Corporation, UK/Last Gasp) Imagine the Jehovah's Witnesses' tract factory taken over by graduates of the Richard Hamilton School of Advertising Collage— the result is a sustained example of post-punk dadaism, a little comic book pamphlet so winning it might deconvert David Thomas, if not Michael Jackson. Listen to Jesus, stretched out on the cross: "You, too, can have a body like mine!"

4 ▪ Teena Marie, Emerald City (Epic) The white funk queen's latest is being pushed as a breakthrough because it's got horrible ballads, pseudo-Brazilian folderol, and third-rate jazz on side two. The action is on side one, Prince country: as with "Kiss," you get pure sex without a single warning-label word. But "Kiss" was foreplay; this is the exchange of bodily fluids.

5 ▪ Moody Blues, "In Your Wildest Dreams" (Polydor) I spent two months trying to resist this soppy melody, and it can't be done.

6 ▪ Timex Social Club, "Rumors" (Jay) A smash because the sound captures the concept: to listen is to eavesdrop.

7 ▪ Mr. T Experience, street flyer (Berkeley, July 11) It's been said that "The moment of real poetry brings all the unsettled debts of history back into play"; this photocopy, just band name, gig info, and former Attorney General John Mitchell, is a moment of real poetry.

8 ▪ Alex Bennett Show, July 8 (6:30– 10 a.m. weekdays, KITS-FM, San Francisco) Bennett, who used to host Midnight Blue on New York cable TV, opens each day with "The Morning Obituaries"; regularly fighting for the mike with such motormouth comics as Bob Goldthwait, Steven Pearl, and Bobby Slayton, he runs the only wake-up show to carry an "Adults Only" disclaimer. Here, deferring to the random-drug-testing rules announced by Peters Ueberroth and Rozelle ("Commissioners of Urine"), Bennett inaugurated a new feature: a daily spin of the Peter Wheel to select a candidate from the world of pop. First winner, no surprise: Boy George.

9 ▪ **Paul Brady, "Steel Claw," from** *True for You* **(21/Atco)** Brady made his name with traditional Irish music; now, with a tune that had a tepid debut on Tina Turner's *Private Dancer*, he rocks out. It's irresistible guitar-based traditional late-'6os music; the rest of the LP is traditional sub-Van Morrison music.

10 ▪ **Anonymous,** *The International Battle of the Century—The Beatles vs the Third Reich* **(VE)** In the spirit of *Elvis' Greatest Shit!!*, an impeccably designed and produced bootleg parody of Vee-Jay's 1964 *The Beatles vs the Four Seasons*. Back then, "scoring by rounds," you were invited to rate "I Saw Her Standing There" against "Sherry"; now, you judge a muddy, previously unreleased 1962 Hamburg Star-Club tape against crowd noise. That is, "The Beatles Perform," "Till There Was You," "Where Have You Been All My Life," and "To Know Her Is to Love Her," and "The Audience Responds": "Ach Du Leiber," "Mach Shau," and "Arbeit Macht Frei"—the latter being the slogan that once adorned the gates of Auschwitz. Sharp.

SEPTEMBER 9, 1986

1 ▪ **Terry Clement & the Tune Tones, "She's My Baby Doll," from** *Sin Alley* **(Big Daddy)** Crammed with 1955–61 obscurities that make Carl Perkins sound like an accountant and Hasil Adkins seem like a craftsman, this is the most demented rockabilly compilation since *Juke Box at Eric's*. Clement leaps out of the pack, possessed by a thought the urgency of which stands undimmed by the passage of time: "Well, rich girl wears expensive perfume/Poor girl does the same/My girl don't wear none at all/But you can smell her just the same."

2 ▪ *Forced Exposure* **#10** Operating on the premise that "Extremism in the de-

fense of liberty is no vice—and fun, too," this thick punk-*maudit* quarterly has become the crucial music magazine in the U.S. That may be mainly due to Steve Albini, whose long "December Diary" is the high point of #10; his subject is candor, how it turns life into a war, and why it's worth fighting—at home, at work, in print, on stage. Albini's premise might be found in something the late Alexander Trocchi wrote: "We must do everything to attack the 'enemy' at his base, within ourselves."

3 ▪ **Charlatans,** *Alabama Bound* **(Eva, France/Performance Distributors, New Brunswick, NJ)** Killed by MGM in 1966, these addled folk-blues tracks by the first exemplars of the "San Francisco Sound" are historic; they're also a curio. But the last number—nine minutes 50 seconds of the title song, the band's signature tune—remains as rough and luminous as it was on the day it was performed: June 13, 1969, at the Charlatans' final show.

4 ▪ **Matt Mahurin, Sleeve photo for** *The Lover Speaks* **(Geffen)** Forget the record, which offers a U.K. translation of some of Phil Spector's pomposities with none of his desire; the cover portrait, a woman naked visible from her shoulders up, shot in the Victorian style of Julia Margaret Cameron and posed in a corrosive moment of (since *The Lover Speaks* claims influence by Barthes, we'll call it) "jouissance," is one of the sexiest things you'll ever see.

5 ▪ **Jamie Reid,** *(please wash your hands before) Leaving the 20th Century* **(Josh Baer Gallery, 270 Lafayette St., New York, September 12 through October 4)** I haven't previewed this exhibit of the Sex Pistols' art director's work from the early '70s on, just the catalogue/poster. But there should be wonders here, such as the pre-Pistols sticker Reid made up for clandestine posting in supermarkets: "LAST DAYS. *BUY NOW WHILE STOCKS LAST.* This store will be closing soon owing to the pending collapse of monopoly capitalism . . ."

6 ▪ **Lee "Scratch" Perry, "Grooving," from** *Battle of Armagideon (Millionaire Liquidator)* **(Trojan, UK)** What you slip into the

supermarket Muzak system after you've put up Reid's stickers.

7 ▪ **Neil Young, Advertisement for** *Landing on Water* **(Geffen), in** *New Musical Express,* **July 26** "A Return to Rock Roots," trumpets the copy, sweeping up after Young's recent commercial disasters; a photo-collage shows Neville Chamberlain brandishing his "piece of paper," now replaced by the sleeve of *Landing on Water.* The implication seems to be that Geffen, which sued Young to force him to produce salable music, is Chamberlain, and that Young is—Hitler? Who paid for this ad? What does it mean?

8 ▪ **Anna Paczuska (text) and Sophie Grillet (art),** *Socialism for Beginners* **(Writers and Readers)** A good comic strip survey, noted for the two-page spread on "les Enragés," fringe radicals of the French Revolution, presented as a punk band.

9 ▪ **Elvis Costello, "I Want You," from** *Blood and Chocolate* **(Columbia)** An anomaly on an LP that's a lot closer to *Nuggets* than *King of America*: with a nod to "Going Down Slow," a spare, determined, pitiless love song to a living corpse.

10 ▪ **Robert Shelton,** *No Direction Home—The Life and Music of Bob Dylan* **(Beech Tree)** Shelton published the first Dylan review, and it turned out to be a hook in his side. In the works for more than 20 years, his book finally arrives at a length of 578 pages, bleeding with incomprehension. Like Myra Friedman in *Buried Alive*, her Janis Joplin biography, Shelton falls helplessly into the role of village explainer. Any sense of play and discovery is banished; the endless search for sources and meanings doesn't open up the story, it narrows it. Still, Dylan's conversations with Shelton, from 1962 through 1985, all previously unpublished, are unparalleled in their sincerity and frankness: they make the book important. So cut this item out of the paper, take it to the bookstore, pull the book off the shelf, flip to pp. 14–18, 24–25, 38–40, 60, 63, 90–91, 109–10, 124, 129, 131, 188, 195, 279, 280–81, 287, 341–62, 479–81, 485–86, 491–92, and have a good time.

1 ▪ **Art Bears,** *The World As It Is Today* **(Re Records, UK, 1981)** This old LP, new to me, arrived in the mail courtesy of Chris Cutler, editor of *Re Records Quarterly*, disc 'n' magazine journal of radical pop theory; I threw it on, and played nothing else for days. "Out of town!" cried a man in a lugubrious voice. "My work takes me out of town!" Why was he so upset? His moans made the song into a statement of pure pathos; a displacing effect, given that the label said this was "The Song of Investment Capital Overseas." It was capital itself that was singing: like the slaver in Randy Newman's "Sail Away," it was capital, not its victims ("I burn the houses down/ . . . Lay out plantations/And bring prosperity/To the poorer nations"), who needed the listener's compassion, deserved it, was getting it. The whole album moved on that level, its gnomic parables full of screams, the sound suggesting the Weimar proto-rock of Kurt Weill and Hanns Eisler, or the doomy Futurism of Antonio Russolo. Eager to learn more, I opened the booklet of credits and lyrics, only to stop at the first line: "Play at 45 rpm." Uh-oh.

2 ▪ **Pussy Galore,** *groovy hate fuck* **EP (Shove)** Enough of that confusing Old World art music; here's some plain-speech New World raw meat—or, as one of the tunes has it, "Dead Meat." Particularly appealing is "Cunt Tease," and the way guitarist Julia Cafritz shouts "FUCK YOU!" every time vocalist Jon Spencer makes it to the title phrase.

3 ▪ **Roy Orbison, "In Dreams," as mimed by Dean Stockwell in** *Blue Velvet,* **directed by David Lynch (DEG)** Speaking of dead meat . . .

4 ▪ **Joel Whitburn,** *Pop Memories, 1890–1954* **(Record Research)** Chart chronicle of top pop records—except that in pre-Elvis eras, racial and cultural exclusion precluded any real surveys of extra-bourgeois American popular taste. Whitburn's response is heroic: collating countless forgot-

ten lists, he's created his own charts in retrospect, and the results change history. By placing, say, the Orioles' "It's Too Soon to Know" (an epochal "race music" hit that never made the official pop charts of its time) at #13 in late 1948, Whitburn rescues scores of performers from the ghettos to which phony charts once condemned them, allowing those artists to be seen in the context of mainstream popular culture for the first time. Expensive and essential.

5 ▪ Beat Farmers, "Riverside," from *Van Go* (Curb) Just a slight, descending figure, played on two guitars, which says all there is to say about what can happen when the bars close.

6 ▪ James Brown and Steven Wells, *Attack on Bzag/Molotov Comics* (Manchester, UK) A fanzine that can't decide if it likes the didacticism accessible through words better than the noise accessible through collage, though any reader/auditor is going to choose the noise.

7 ▪ Jacques Attali, *Noise—The Political Economy of Music* (Minnesota) At once a clear history of all post-Roman motivated Western noise ("music") and a delirious theoretical proof that, with a few breaks, such noise can transform, and thus save, the world. Originally published in French in 1977, *Noise* at once called for punk and proved its historical necessity; as with all good French critical theory, the clarity is inseparable from the delirium.

8 ▪ Steve Erickson, *Rubicon Beach*, a novel (Poseidon) It seems to begin in the future, but I'm not sure it does. In this no-future, "music" is banned, but it comes out of the ground, collapses buildings, and turns a police state into a question mark: "In a town where music is a topographical map, the music of the earth is legal and the music of men is not," says a cop. "I don't make the fucking laws. . . . Get rid of the radio, Cale." In the best novel I've read this year, there are a lot of red herrings and shaggy dog stories; what it is Cale might be hearing on his illegal radio is the one missing answer a reader can't imagine.

9 ▪ Beach Boys, *Be True to Your School* (Capitol reissue, c. 1963) Including the correct, 45 rpm, previously non-LP version of the title song; the perfectly generic "Surf Jam"; and the fabulously repressed (doo-wop, which was to say, in 1963, joked-up) "I'm Bugged at My Ol' Man" (i.e., Murry Wilson, whom son Brian once served a plate of stool).

10 ▪ Art Bears, *The World As It Is Today* (Re Records, UK, 1981) At 45 rpm, the pathos of the slow speed becomes hysteria. Screams become screeches; Weill and Eisler remain; Russolo disappears. The singer turns out to be a woman, Dagmar Krause, far more powerful here than on her new *Supply & Demand—Songs by Brecht/Weill & Eisler*, possibly because the tunes by percussionist Chris Cutler and guitarist/synthesizerist Fred Frith, composers for the Art Bears, say more about the world as it is today. I still like the record better at 33.

NOVEMBER 11, 1986

1 ▪ David & David, "Swallowed by the Cracks," from *Boomtown* (A&M) It wasn't Bob Dylan, it was Satchel Paige who said "Don't look back"—because "someone might be gaining on you," and whoever it was has long since passed the singer of this song. "This drunken old whore," David Baerwald half jokes, half snarls from a back table in some L.A. dive: "You see, we'd been swallowed by the cracks, fallen so far down/ Like the rest of those clowns, begging bus-fare back." Those lines are too cold, too unpleasant, to do anything but pull the string on a life, but as an overdubbed one-man-band David Ricketts has a feel for the light touch, strong melodies, good rhythms; his music and Davitt Sigerson's careful, anonymous production give Baerwald back the will he's mourning. A great song to listen to when you're miserable.

2 ▪ Cameo, "Word Up!" (Atlanta Artists) A piece of funk so imaginative and clean it'd fit on Prince's *Dirty Mind*; a trick vocal; and a lyric that starts off as if it's going to try to teach you a new dance ("The

Word," or something), turns into Ashton, Gardner & Dyke's "Resurrection Shuffle," the Trashmen's "Surfin' Bird," the Staple Singers' "Respect Yourself," and then gets complicated.

3 ■ Billy Bragg, "Levi Stubbs' Tears" (Go! 12-inch, UK) A knife in the heart—and, in the best of all possible worlds, the last song the Four Tops will sing before Levi Stubbs's promised retirement in 1990.

4 ■ Impotent Sea Snakes, *Too Cool for Rock & Roll* (Pravda) From Florida: leading off with "Pope John Paul Can Suck My Dick" (it's not anticlerical—the singer's doing Johnny a favor), moving on to "Missing Link" (i.e., black people) and "I Caught AIDS from a Dead Man," this set of cheap but extremely detailed slurs isn't especially shocking, and it isn't funny. What it is is pointlessly vicious and obscene, and listening to it in 1986—as opposed to, say, 1979—carries a certain charge: you wonder how long it might be before this sort of public speech is made illegal. (It already is in North Carolina; see "University Under Fire," James B. Meigs's report on that state's recent nullification of the First Amendment, *Rolling Stone*, September 25.)

5 ■ Eddie Money, "Take Me Home Tonight" (Columbia) Urgent, with a good idea: "Just like Ronnie sang," pleads the man to his one-night would-be, and then there she is, Ronnie of the Ronettes in the flesh, warbling "Uh-uh-uh-oh/Be my little baby . . ." She sounds terrible, hopeless— and she's right in your lap, when she should have been mixed back, emerging only as a radio ghost. The number still makes it.

6 ■ Stacey Q, "Two of Hearts" (Atlantic) Not as good as Madonna's "True Blue," better than anything on Cyndi Lauper's *True Colors*.

7 ■ Bangles, "Walk Like an Egyptian" (Columbia) Not as good as Steve Martin's "King Tut," better than the Pyramids' "Here Comes Marsha."

8 ■ Smokey Robinson, "The Star-Spangled Banner" (Fenway Park, Boston, October 23) Not as good as Marvin Gaye, better than José Feliciano.

9 ■ Del Shannon, "Runaway," theme song for *Crime Story* (NBC, Tuesdays, 9 p.m.) As lead cop Dennis Farina's wife, Darlanne Fluegel is the sexiest woman on TV.

10 ■ Unknown guitarist, "Apache" (Piazza Maggiore, Bologna, Italy, October 12) Throughout the weekend, the streets and plazas of central Bologna fill with citizens. Thousands and thousands of people, old and young, most of whom have taken the bus in from cheaper districts, gather together: they form groups and leave them, talk and argue, look for friends and find them. They're not shopping, or hanging out in cafés: they walk the streets and mill in the plazas as if they're on a pilgrimage to the place where, culturally, they were born. "I love my native city more than my own soul," Machiavelli wrote some four centuries ago; the people in Bologna seem to act out that sentiment as if it were the most obvious thing in the world. It's the pleasure of being part of something bigger than yourself; look for greed, resentment, or nervousness in these streets, and you won't find them. It was the most exuberant version of public life, of what used to be called "public happiness," I've ever witnessed.

In the midst of this ordinary festival— square in the middle of the biggest plaza in the city—was a guitar player with a mike and a little amp. There was something about the air, or the way the people baffled it, or the way the man played, that carried his notes hundreds of yards, and yet kept them from blaring at a distance of 10 feet: kept them from interrupting whatever anyone else might want to do. It struck me that there has never been a bad version of "Apache" (Jorgen Ingmann, 1961, first and last German surf instrumental); the melody is simply too sweet. But this was 10 in the morning; the guy was still there, as many people joyously listening as joyously ignoring him, 12 hours later.

November 13, 1986

Dear Greil Marcus
Re "Real Life Rock Top Ten" in November 11th issue of VV.

"10. Unknown Guitarist, 'Apache,' Piazza Maggione, Bologna, Italy."

. . . his name was Beppe. I too was in the square on that magical Sunday in October (the 12th). (He had written his name on the amp.)

Fantastico!

Tina Yagjian
Brooklyn, NY

DECEMBER 16, 1986

1 ▪ **John Lennon, *Menlove Avenue* (Capitol)** From the infamous "Lost Weekend" period: side 1 offers bad outtakes from the '75 oldies LP, while side 2, live studio rehearsals for tunes used on the '74 *Walls and Bridges*, contains the strongest music Lennon made from the '71 *Imagine* on down. With a small combo (led by guitarist Jesse Ed Davis), there's the feel of a private blues session, but it wasn't just the hysterical smear of strings and horns that ruined these songs on *Walls and Bridges*. It was their vocal mirror: the histrionics of "Steel and Glass," the portentous, self-consciously sensitive phrasing of "Nobody Knows You When You're Down and Out." Now there's a quiet, nihilistic confrontation with ugliness, lyrics just bitten, or chased out of control: "There you stand/With your toilet seat/And your Mickey Duck/And your Donald Fuck." "Fuuuu-uh-uh-uuuuck," that last word is actually sung; it's a chance for Lennon to say what he means, and he only finds out what he means as he happens upon the syllable, bends it, stretches it, breaks it, swallows it.

2 ▪ **Mel McDaniel, "Stand on It" (Capitol)** A country hit, and the best Springsteen cover since "Spirit in the Night" by Manfred Mann's Earth Band: full-throated middle-aged rockabilly glory.

3 ▪ **New Order, "Bizarre Love Triangle" (Factory U.K. 12-inch)** On LP, you get Gillian Gilbert's gorgeous synthesizer riff; here you get that plus the startling transformation of Bernard Sumner's perfunctory vocal into a vocoded chorale that, alone of all the elements in this recording, lives up to its title.

4 ▪ ***Merry Christmas from the Sonics/ Wailers/Galaxies* (Etiquette reissue, 1965)** This might have taken longer to record than it does to play (a half-hour); after all, with three bands, you have to figure in a few minutes for them to set up. Big theme is perfidy of Santa Claus ("Don't believe in Christmas/'Cause I didn't get nothin' last year," wail the Sonics; "Santa Claus/Won't you tell me please/What you're gonna put/Under my Christmas tree/And he just say/NOTHIN', NOTHIN', NOTHIN', NOTHIN'," sonicize the Wailers), but let's not forget the Wailers' touching "Maybe Next Year," a reverie so delicate and slow they have a real problem keeping the thing from coming to a complete stop.

5 ▪ **Coolies, *dig . . ?* (dB)** A precise and gleeful mutilation of Paul Simon hits. "Feelin' Groovy" as it might be played on the nod, a Duane Eddy-style instrumental version of "Mrs. Robinson"—by the end, there's little left of the songs but their vapidity, and it may be only copyright control that keeps the Coolies from taking on the townhouse jive of *Graceland* next, which deserves it more.

6 ▪ ***Sid & Nancy*, directed by Alex Cox (Goldwyn)** This is where a phrase like *mise-en-scène* helps; you need a concept that vague to pretend to know why songs contrived a decade ago, sung by actors who offscreen disclaim any feeling for them, can still terrify and thrill.

7 ▪ **Alice Yaeger Kaplan, *Reproductions of Banality—Fascism, Literature, and French Intellectual Life* (Minnesota)** The mass psychology of fascism is a cliché; this short, scholarly, jargon-free, almost conversational investigation of the aesthetic, utopian, avant-garde appeal of the movement in France from the '30s through the Occupation can be read as a study of fascist pop life.

8 ▪ **Marty Robbins, *Rock'n Roll'n Robbins* (Bear Family German reissue, 1954–58)** All the extremes of "rock" are missing here. The voice is supple, sensual, friendly (even on the morbid "Footprints in the Snow"); the guitar playing alternates cowboy cool-water with tumbling, tricky bluegrass runs; the whole is a comfortable, completely convincing account of white blues. It's what happened whan a singer who always

leaned to the western side of c&w tried to jump on a trend: a unique sound, not to mention a unique spelling.

9 ▪ Steven Gaines, *Heroes and Villains— The True Story of the Beach Boys* (NAL) Disgusting, repulsive, hateful—also pointless, save as the last word anyone will need on these cretins.

10 ▪ Alan Cranston, "Zschau's Greatest Hits" (Robert Shrum Associates) This TV spot was Cranston's last shot in his barely successful fight to hold his California U.S. Senate seat against the hard-right shift of "moderate" G.O.P. challenger Ed Zschau, already notorious for flip-flopping. It came on like a K-Tel ad, frantic and loud, lots of Zschau-faces pointing in different directions, a type overlay blaring song titles as a Wolfman Jack imitator growled them: "How Many Times can a Man Change His Mind," "Zschau Bop Flip Flop," and, sealing the package, "Both Sides Now."

JANUARY 13, 1987

1 ▪ Wire, *Snakedrill* (Mute U.K. 12-inch) Active in London from '77 to '80, this foursome sometimes played songs lasting under a minute, but even the longest were as gnomic as that gesture. A wash of repetition disguised careful sonic choices, and the edge of the music, and the moment, was never reduced, merely removed from the obvious: "I am the fly—the fly in the ointment" was Wire's version of "I am an antichrist." On *Snakedrill*, the band's first recording in years, neither the sound nor the role-playing has changed. " 'A Serious of Snakes,' " the best of the four tracks, starts off with some punning on "In-A-Gadda-Da-Vida," and the title tells you who the Gardener is; weaving a dramatically modulated melody around the conceit, Wire seems as implacable, as mysterious, and as new as it did a decade ago. I take this to mean not that Wire was ahead of its time, but that Wire caught its time, and that time has stood still—that the chiliastic voice found in London in the first year of punk has hardly been answered, let alone superseded.

2 ▪ Coolies, "Having My Baby," from *dig..?* (dB) After the singer professes his devotion to the point of delirium, there's a spoken passage: the father to be lets it slip that, well, you may be having my baby, but, you know, "I still got two weeks left on my Greyhound card," gotta go now, and, anyway, "You ain't the only woman in town. Come to think of it, you ain't the only woman in town who's—"

3 ▪ Communards, "Disenchanted" (MCA) An LP's worth of Jimmy Somerville's falsetto gets irritating; here, his spirit goes as high as his pitch.

4 ▪ Sylvester, "Sooner or Later," from *Mutual Attraction* (Warner Bros.) A desanctified gospel stomp, until the last choruses, when instrumentation drops away and Sylvester begins to harmonize with two women. They reach a state of ecstatic distraction, words coming loose from prayers and functioning only as signals of sexual abandon. What you're hearing isn't just church singing, but an altar call.

5 ▪ George J. Sowden, "American, 1983" (Memphis Milano) In 1956, Ettore Sottsass signed a manifesto affirming that "creation can now be nothing less than a synthesis aiming at an integral construction of an atmosphere"; in 1981 he and others, including Sowden, formed the Memphis design group in Milan, naming it after Bob Dylan's "Memphis Blues Again." The group has lived up to that old manifesto with certain endlessly suggestive everyday objects, and this is one of them: it looks like a '50s movie robot, tells time, and rocks around itself.

6 ▪ Alphaville, "Jerusalem," from *Afternoons in Utopia* (Atlantic) German trio heads back to the '60s to ask the musical question, "What's so funny 'bout peace, love, and understanding?"

7 ▪ Jay Cotton & Gary Panter, *Pee Dog #2* (Spooky Comics) This is what's so funny. "Blasphemy? Yeah, I guess you could say . . . 'we're into it,' " runs the intro to Cotton and Panter's coprophiliac comic book—a visual equivalent of the Butthole Surfers—which begins with an exotic dancer emitting the Main Course of the

Last Supper and ends with Jesus lugging his Cross up to Golgotha while reciting the complete text of "I Want to Know What Love Is."

8 ▪ **Beastie Boys, "I'm Down" (tape)** The old Beatle screamer, scheduled for *Licensed to Ill* but chilled by new copyright owner Michael Jackson because of supposed bad language, this is circulating, even on the radio. On one hearing, it sounds more like the Beach Boys having fun with "Barbara Ann" than the bloody killer rape job you might expect.

9 ▪ **Blind Boy Grunt & the Hawks, *The Basement Tapes*, Vols. 1 & 2 (Surprise bootlegs)** A few finished numbers missing from the official or common bootleg version of the fabled '67 Dylan and Band sessions (the eerie "I'm Not There," the corny "Sign on the Cross")—otherwise, over two double LPs, lo-fi fragments and rejects. It's all what it claims to be, save for four tracks the Hawks cut with Tiny Tim in rehearsal for the '68 film *You Are What You Eat* ("Be My Baby," "I Got You Babe," etc.), and they're the high point.

10 ▪ **WFMU-FM, *Lowest Common Denominator*, Fall '86 (Upsala College, East Orange, NJ)** Fanzine from the left-side dial spot (91.1) already described in these pages as "The #1 Choice of Lowlife Scum." There's an homage to Bobby Sherman, a poem about Vince Everett (Elvis in *Jailhouse Rock*), serious analysis of pop trends, and, completing our survey of contemporary religion, a summation of what it means to live in a world where God is dead, "JEAN-PAUL SARTRE FOR DODGE DARTRE," a flyer apparently scavenged from a telephone pole in Seattle, which plumbs the black hole of existential vertigo even better than Wire. Sartre: "In my journey to the end of the night, I must rely not only on dialectical paths of reason. I must have a good solid automobile, one that eschews the futile trappings of wordly ennui and asks only for the most basic maintenance. My Dodge Dartre offers me this basic solace, and as interior parts fall off I am struck by the realization of their pointlessness. I may not know if the window is up or down. It is of no consequence."

FEBRUARY 10, 1987

1 ▪ **Minutemen, *"ballot result"* (SST retrospective, 1980–85)** This is what was left after guitarist D. Boon lost his life in late '85: two LPs worth of demos, outtakes, stage tapes, audience cassettes, radio checks, and Mike Watt's bloody charge into Roky Erickson's "Bermuda." A few album cuts have been thrown in for continuity, and the upshot is, if not the best Minutemen set, the most accessible and the most fun. Yes, they really were the Grateful Dead of punk (replacing karma with politics, faith with irony, boogie with rage, folkiness with artiness), and also the Beach Boys, and also their fans.

2 ▪ **Bruce Springsteen & the E Street Band, "Two Hearts," from *Live/1975–85* (Columbia)** This ought to be a single—with a live "I'm Goin' Down" on the flip.

3 ▪ **Pauline Murray and the Storm, "New Age" (Polestar, UK)** Murray sang Penetration's generic punk manifesto "Don't Dictate" ten years ago, and she's been chasing her own voice ever since: dreamy, sweet, playful, confused, lyrical, above all naïve. It's all in her tone; from "Dream Sequence" in 1980 to now, she's answered questions no one else is even asking.

4 ▪ **Larry Speakes, White House Press Briefing, January 8** Which he opened by playing a tape of "That's All Right (Mama)." And continued by announcing that while he had no new information on the president, reporters could ask him "anything at all about the King."

5 ▪ **Sun Records, *The Country Years, 1950–1959* (Sun/Bear Family, W. Germany)** Unlike the Sun *Blues Years* box, which was an epic, this spectacularly packaged, overpriced ten-LP set is an ordinary story; its deepest themes aren't refusal and desire, but acceptance and routine. So you reduce your expectations, and notice small but gleaming anomalies, the product of an ordinary story being pushed just beyond itself,

or given perfect shape. This might be Howard Seratt's quiet folk-gospel, the rare sound of a man at peace with himself, or Cash King and the Miller Sisters' "Can't Find Time to Pray," so delicate it almost hides its sting: "You must find time to die."

6 ■ Eddie Money, "Bring on the Rain," from *Can't Hold Back* (Columbia) Gene Pitney lives.

7 ■ Julee Cruise, "Mysteries of Love," from *Blue Velvet: Original Motion Picture Soundtrack* (Varèse Sarabande) Sort of like Laurie Anderson's "O Superman"—as composed by David Lynch and Angelo Badalamenti, and performed by Rosie and the Originals.

8 ■ Muslim Gaze, *Hajj* (Limited 4, UK) This may be the first disc inspired by the Iran debacle, and simply as an artifact, it has an ominous power. The combination of the all-knowing face of Khomeni on the front cover, what seems to be the baffled, scared face of Reagan on the back, and the title—as Mike Watt says on *"ballot result,"* "one title is worth a million lyrics," and *Hajj* doesn't have any.

9 ■ Los Lobos, *By the Light of the Moon* (Slash) Fine. But not superfine.

10 ■ Malcolm Bradbury, *Eating People Is Wrong* (Academy Chicago reprint, 1959) As author of *The History Man* and *Rates of Exchange*, Bradbury has become increasingly impressed with his own sense of humor since publishing this rather chilling comic novel about the wasteland of postwar British liberal culture. Here the humor cuts, and it never claims the page merely for the sake of a joke. Bradbury understands that sometimes the gift of humor is to ease the way to seriousness, as in the following passage, just the musings of one of his characters, and also a eulogy appropriate to any person, at any time, in any place: "But the life one leads cuts out all the lives one might have led; one is never a virgin twice; events engrave themselves. Life is a unity to the soul. We meet events halfway; they are part of us, and we are part of them; nothing is incidental. Ahead comes the point where all events exist at once, and no

new ones are in sight, the point on the edge of death, which is a reckoning point." Play that dead band's song again.

MARCH 10, 1987

1 ■ Chris Isaak (Warner Bros.) Neorockabilly as received will and idea: formal almost to the point of abstraction. In print it sounds sterile, and in a year it may sound that way on record, but for the moment, shaped by Roy Orbison's "Only the Lonely" and Jody Reynolds's "Endless Sleep," it sounds like the last breath of true, which on Isaak's terms is to say lost, romance.

2 ■ Peter Davies, *The Last Election* (Vintage) At first, a rather obvious black-humor novel about England as Margaret Thatcher heads into her fifth (fourth?) (third?) term; then it gets ugly. Then it gets uglier. Then the worst happens: you start taking it seriously.

3 ■ Age of Chance, "Kiss" (Fon, UK) Here's Prince's elegant masterpiece, turned into a trash masterpiece; ripped to shreds, beer poured all over the pieces, which are then lapped up and spewed out all over again. Instant party, with an edge of menace—the Beastie Boys should be half so tough, or so touching.

4 ■ Ben E. King, *Stand by Me—The Best of Ben E. King and Ben E. King and the Drifters* (Atlantic reissue, 1960–75) Craven cash-in on the second appearance of the title tune in the Top Ten (1961 and '86), shamefully omitting "Tippin," a mature and measured '78 comeback bid. Great anyway—notably for the way King's singing on the Drifters' 1960 "This Magic Moment" now stands out as one of the most commanding performances in rhythm & blues.

5 ■ James Brown, "How Do You Stop?" (Scotti Bros. 12-inch) It's hip to dismiss Dan Hartman's productions of the Godfather of Soul as white-flour makeup, but this dance-floor ballad is something new for Brown: full-toned, emotionally generous. It brings to mind the Brook Benton of "Rainy Night in Georgia," or Van Morrison, who thinks soul music came from

"Caledonia"—i.e., Scotland, when whiteness was in flower.

6 ■ **Not Bored #11** A critical-theory fanzine dedicated to the proposition that not all received ideas are bad, especially if you can play with them. Highlight: inside dope on recent graffiti wars at SUNY Buffalo, based on an article about undergraduate negation that appeared in *Internationale Situationniste* #11, a critical-agitation journal published in Paris in 1967. Numbers of serendipity, or serendipity of numbers?

7 ■ **Scotch, "Take Me Up" (zyx 12-inch, West Germany)** What New Order would sound like if they went bubblegum—which they may yet.

8 ■ **Alvis Wayne, "Sleep, Rock-a-Roll, Rock-a-Baby," from *Texas Rockabilly* (RR reissue, c. 1956, France)** With Presleyish fervor filtered through a shimmering rain of steel guitars, the result is a reverie: a curio as gorgeous as it is unique.

9 ■ **Bill Flanagan, *Written in My Soul— Rock's Great Songwriters Talk About Creating Their Music* (Contemporary)** Given his stated limits—the rock tradition that can be traced to message-mongering folk music—Flanagan's interviews seek out clichés and turn up revelations. Willie Dixon (a token ancestor) damns gospel music as a means of social control; Neil Young (a typical inheritor) argues that while as form blues and country preceded rock 'n' roll, as spirit rock 'n' roll preceded blues and country—rock 'n' roll, Young says, is what blues and country emerged to control. Flanagan is prissy about music in the marketplace, and time and again he tries to get his subjects to buy into his equally prissy brand of ethics, but they won't do it. As always, dumb questions provoke the best answers.

10 ■ **Chuck Berry, "Rock 'n' Roll Music," from *More Rock 'n' Roll Rarities From the Golden Age of Chess Records* (Chess/MCA reissue, 1956)** In Richard Meltzer's *The Aesthetics of Rock* (first published in 1970, soon to be reissued by Da Capo), one can read that "Chuck Berry's 'Rock and Roll Music' predicts in 1957 the later outbreak of Afri-

can nationalism, 'It's way too early for the *congo*/So keep a-rockin' that piano.'" This sort of absurdist connection is a good part of what listening to rock 'n' roll is all about: the immediacy of the music transposing itself into an epistemology of simultaneity. Still, reading Meltzer, you automatically think: Berry must have meant "the *conga*," the dance, meaning "too early" as too-early-in-the-evening-for-such-a-stomp. Here, with the original demo of "Rock 'n' Roll Music," one discovers that Berry did say, did mean, "conga"—which is to say that one must base a whole way of understanding rock 'n' roll on a slip of the tongue.

APRIL 7, 1987

1 ■ **Lonnie Mack, "Why," from *The Wham of That Memphis Man!* (Alligator reissue, 1963)** This tune offers a false choice: listening to the most stately ballad in the annals of white blues, or listening to a man kill himself. The choice is false because in the last verse you don't get to choose.

2 ■ **Tina Turner, "What You Get Is What You See" (Capitol)** Not the track from the conformist *Break Every Rule*. Here, producer Terry Brittan takes a melody with the fervor of Graham Parker's "Nobody Hurts You," orchestrates it with the guitar-hero momentum of Dire Straits' "Expresso Love," explodes it with the kinetic release of the Rolling Stones' "Shattered," then challenges the singer to beat the band.

3 ■ **Pussy Galore, *Pussy Gold 5000* (Buy Our Records EP)** I hate the way language is corrupted by people who use born-dead neologisms as if they were alive, as if they were more than shortcuts for dopes too lazy or hip to say what they mean, as with "take," putatively a noun signifying one's perspective on a given phenomenon, the pervasive employment of the word hiding its reduction of all perspective to an effete glance, as if nothing were worth more, as in "Holden Caulfield's takes on the world" (*Voice*, March 17), or "Marx's take on political economy" (my paranoid fantasy, until I saw a version of it in these pages), or, you

know, Noah's take on the Flood: "Big, isn't it?" Fuck off and die, cretins.

4 ▪ Mickey Rourke, *Angel Heart* (Tri-Star) Mouthing Bob Seger's "Feel Like a Number," Rourke came up with the only emotionally credible moments in *Body Heat*; he's had lead roles ever since, but this is the first time he's sustained the nervous, slimy, nihilistic tension of that performance for a whole movie.

5 ▪ Siouxsie and the Banshees, "Scrap-heap," from *Track Rehearsals 1977* (KO boot-leg EP, UK) They swallowed a lot of what made a difference in the Sex Pistols' England; save for "Nicotine Stain" on *The Scream*, their first album, this is the only piece they were able to spit out.

6 ▪ Elvis Costello, aka Various Artists, "Blue Chair" from *Out of Our Idiot* (Demon, UK) A blur on *Blood and Chocolate*, this version is pure pop craft. It's in the lift of the chorus—which, every time it comes around, seems to come out of nowhere.

7 ▪ Richard Krawiec, *Time Sharing* (Penguin) In this sickeningly convincing novel about a white couple so economically marginal they have become almost socially illiterate, when the woman turns on her transistor, "She swore she knew the words to the ads better than she knew the songs"—but so do most of us, and thus for a moment this fact makes easy sense. What doesn't make easy sense is a larger fact, which Krawiec gets across on every page: the country has established enclaves of material and spiritual deprivation—black holes of possibility—that are so absolute pop messages cannot enter them, save as the tawdry beats against which a woman without money stands before a roomful of drunks and takes off her clothes.

8 ▪ *San Francisco Chronicle:* Entertainment listing, March 1 "Reno, El Dorado Hotel: Bill Haley and the Comets." *Ars brevis, vita longa?*

9 ▪ Crime Story, (NBC, February 27) "Paulie," says mob boss Ray Luca (a pompadoured Elvis-from-hell) to his gofer/hitman, "what you lack in intelligence, you make up in stupidity." As this show was rock 'n' roll from its Del Shannon theme song to its buried, fannish asides ("Let's *all* get Dixie fried," crows another Luca goon after a good bombing), that line is a perfect example of a form revealing its spirit.

10 ▪ Andrew Britton, "Blissing Out—The Politics of Reaganite Entertainment" (*Movie* 31/32) After defining the hegemonic significance of two mystifications—the everyday notion that a work of popular culture can be "just entertainment," and the "academic fiction" of autonomous textuality—Britton goes on, through more than 30,000 words, to investigate the American movies of the last several years as a reactionary project that has implicated its audience—gained its assent—in ways far more complex than the concurrent political project the cultural version at once trivializes and deepens. The extraordinary weight and determination of Britton's essay has a side effect: the exposure of the impoverishment of what, in every realm of discourse, music no less than movies, politics no less than music, passes for criticism in the pages you and I read and write.

MAY 5, 1987

1 ▪ Michelob TV commercial, "I Move Better in the Night" (Needham Harper/Jeremiah Chechik, director) In this best of all possible music videos, every situation is infinitesimally developed, and then left completely open. A blond woman turns her head after kissing her boyfriend; there's a blithe, irreducibly autonomous sensuality in her face that will never have anything to do with beer. In fact, it doesn't seem to have anything to do with her boyfriend.

2 ▪ Slits, "New Town," from *The Peel Sessions* (Strange Fruit, EP, UK, 1977) Cute—until you realize it's about heroin.

3 ▪ Oingo Boingo, "Not My Slave" (MCA) Pointless old "new wave" group finally devolves into the new Raspberries. I guess it was worth the wait.

4 ▪ **77's, "I Can't Get Over It" (Island)** Faceless: words and music just this side of absolutely nothing, but the band finds a tough groove, and the guitarist knows just what to do with it, and what not to.

5 ▪ **Nike TV commercial, "Revolution" (Beatles/Wieden & Kennedy)** "Poetic justic," says Howard Hampton. "The song's essential mealiness of mouth comes home to roost." Licensing by Michael Jackson, with the approval of Yoko, who says (by permission of Michael Jackson), "You know it's gonna be/Alright."

6 ▪ **Fleetwood Mac, *Tango in the Night* (Warner Bros.)** Some people find this kind of dull, but it's saving dentists millions on novocaine, the American Association of Anesthesiologists is sponsoring the tour, and Wizard won a furious bidding war for the air freshener rights—in a month or so, when you spray your room with "Evergreen" or "Floral," you'll hear FM's new melodies at the very same time. Of course, some people think they already do.

7 ▪ **Joyce Milman and Mark Moses, "You Read It Here April First" (*Boston Phoenix,* April 3)** Gossip columns are boring because they try to make you care about what boring people actually do. The one-step-beyond approach turns up the real inside dope, as in this notably sustained effort, where "Paul Simon's next album promises to be another eclectic trendsetter. The multi-Grammy winner is recording an album in faraway Minneapolis with a local musician named 'Prince' who plays what the natives refer to as 'funk.' Says Simon, 'I heard a tape of this wonderfully joyous music at Sting's. . . . He said it was simply titled 1999, and I went crazy trying to track down the artist. . .'"

8 ▪ **Culturcide, "Industrial Band," from *Tacky Souvenirs of Pre-revolutionary America* (no label)** Citing Lautréamont on the necessity of plagiarism, these Houston illegals bent on the exposure of pop as a false consciousness machine play other people's hit records and sing their own words over them. They can't get here from there—can't get off the records and into the social milieu

they want to talk about—but that leaves one small classic, which underneath is still Grand Funk's "We're an American Band": "Now, these fine ladies, they had a plan/ They was out to meet the boys in the band/ They said, 'C'mon, dudes, let's have sex!'/ But we just talked about child abuse and Hitler's SS . . ."

9 ▪ **Wim Mertens, *Educes Me* (Crepuscule, Belgium)** On a day so bad it seemed every other person I saw deserved to die, I walked into a record store that was playing this piano-and-incomprehensible-vocal item by the man who also works as Soft Verdict. It sounded like 17th century cathedral music, composed after the mass had been celebrated and everyone had gone home—though it turns out the melodies are cheap pop spun into a web of preciosity. It calmed me down like cold medicine kicking in.

10 ▪ **Elvis Costello, "I Want You" (San Jose Civic Auditorium, April 16)** Quietly diseased on disc, performed solo this is a horror movie that doesn't need special effects: *The Servant,* maybe, or *M.* The words, "I want you" alternate every other line with collapsing scenes of torture, flagellation, remorse, bloody glee; at first you're convinced it's all happening in the singer's mind, next that it's happening in the flesh. "I want you/And when I *wake up,*" Costello sang, just as he does on *Blood and Chocolate*—and then he pulled the string. Hanging onto the end of it were Dionne Warwick and Aretha Franklin, who came tumbling into the song like new victims: "—and put on my *makeup*/I say a little prayer for you/ Because I *want* you . . ."

JUNE 2, 1987

1 ▪ **The Mad Peck, *Mad Peck Studios—A Twenty-Year Retrospective* (Doubleday)** The adventures of a band of comic-strip rock critics whose watchword is "It don't mean a thing if it ain't headed straight to cut-out heaven" (typical subjects include Donny Iris, the *Idolmaker* soundtrack, and the second Human Sexual Response LP), this picks up where Richard Meltzer's *The Aes-*

thetics of Rock left off. Best concept: the "Inflatable Meat Loaf Love Doll." Best plot: faced with sky-rocketing doo-wop prices, a former member of the Five Royal-Keys hijacks a plane to come up with the money to buy a copy of his own 45.

2 ▪ **Suzanne Vega, "Luka" (A&M)** Despite her insufferable recitations and her coy way with words (tunes published by Waifersongs, Ltd.), this woman isn't merely a wilting flower to be pressed between pages of Tennyson. She's also a natural hitmaker, Janis Ian '87, and "Luka" does for wife-beating what "Society's Child" did for racism. Better, Vega can make her singing seem like real talk: skirting a good melody and ignoring a bell-ringing guitar solo, her phrasing is so naturalistic it sounds as eerie as the female vocal in Human League's "Don't You Want Me."

3 ▪ **Elko Ishioka and Arata Isozakl, "Performance" installation, *Tokyo: Form and Spirit* (San Francisco Museum of Modern Art)** Sixty video monitors were playing a loop of Japanese TV commercials in a mock-up of a Shinto temple ("Church of the Media," or "Shrine of the Commodity," or something). On came two pastel Godzillas, apparently a happily married couple, carrying coffee cups on a stroll through the suburbs, over which they towered like upright dirigibles, and then Debbie Reynolds poked her head out of the soundtrack: "I hear the cottonwoods whisperin' above/Tammy, Tammy, Tammy's in love." It turned out to be an ad for Live Beer.

4 ▪ **Mud Boy & the Neutrons, "Memphis Blues Again," from *Known Felons in Drag* (New Rose, France)** Actually, Jim Dickinson, lately producer of the Replacements' new LP, in drag, offering a brand of Memphis craziness the Replacements' "Alex Chilton" doesn't hint at.

5 ▪ **Darius Smith, *I Can't Explain #3* (Shred cassette)** Ohio bands of the so-you-fell-down-why-not-get-up stripe, notably the female Manwich, plus the Prom Sluts from Florida and Pussy Galore live in Cincinnati. "Mystery train issue/dedicated to the 1966 Beatles," though both the Beatles and Elvis would be surprised.

6 ▪ **Oliphant, Editorial cartoon, May 9 (Universal Press Syndicate)** "FCC RADIO POLICE TODAY ARRESTED SURGEON GENERAL KOOP FOR BROADCASTING AIDS WARNINGS WHICH CONTAINED SEXUAL INNUENDO."

7 ▪ **Age of Chance, *Crush Collison* (Virgin EP)** In 1920, in Berlin, dadaist Richard Huelsenbeck called for an "art which has been visibly shattered by the explosions of last week, which is forever trying to collect its limbs from yesterday's crash." These guys don't know from art; they're working on the crash.

8 ▪ **Robert Hewison, *Too Much—Art and Society in the Sixties, 1960–75* (Oxford)** What's remarkable about this analysis of convulsed British culture is Hewison's determination to take its most absurd manifestations seriously, and on their own terms. At a distance of two decades, such an approach necessarily misses the spirit of the era, and the book's weakness is that it sometimes makes the still-incredible almost obvious. Overpriced, but essential; watch for the paperback.

9 ▪ **Beverly Paterson, *Voices Green and Purple—A Comprehensive Guide of California's Amazing Garage and Freakbeat Bands of the Sixties* (Skylark Press)** If you get enough records together, all of social history falls into place—or anyway in your lap. Remember the Velvet Illusions' "Acid Head"/"Velvet Illusions," where the band, which included one Steven Weed, "sang about how cool and admired they were"? No? Well, how about Patti Smith's "Piss Factory," backed with her rewrite of "Hey Joe," where she celebrated the kidnapping of Patti Hearst by the Symbionese Liberation Army, which had to beat up Steven Weed to get Patty out the door and into the trunk? Does Steven Weed remember?

10 ▪ **Loudon Wainwright III, *More Love Songs* (Demon, UK)** Tired, but a far more believable account of the compromises demanded by feminism than Alix Kates Shulman's gooey *In Every Woman's Life* . . . Top cut: "The Back Nine," a why-go-on ballad built out of golf metaphors. He's still the only person who can make "whom"

work as rock 'n' roll, and perhaps the first to try "middle-aged."

JUNE 30, 1987

1 ■ Tapps, **"Hurricane"** (JDC 12-inch) Released about a year ago, this dance track has a light rhythm, a fast beat, a pleasantly Stacey Q-style vocal, and an ordinary lyric: "You knock me down like a hurricane," etc. But just when you think you've heard it all before, the singer pulls back, and returns with a stutter—a fluid, wordless "yip yip yip yip" so sustained, intricate, and erotically complex it makes the Silhouettes seem clumsy. I know, it was done with electronics—but it feels like a tongue.

2 ■ Catherine McDermott, *Street Style—British Design in the 80s* (Rizzoli) In 1953, a 19-year-old named Ivan Chtcheglov wrote a visionary manifesto, "Formula for a New Urbanism." "We are bored in the city," he began, "there is no longer any Temple of the Sun . . . the hacienda *where the roots think of the child and the wine is finished off with fables from an old almanac.* Now that's finished. You'll never see the hacienda. It doesn't exist. *The hacienda must be built.*" Mediated through the '60s generation of U.K. art-school radicals, this document became an almost secret inspiration for punk; in 1982, Tony Wilson of Factory Records commissioned designer Ben Kelly to build the Hacienda—as a nightclub in Manchester. The pages McDermott devotes to Wilson's attempt to answer Chtcheglov's challenge leap out of this full-color paperback like a moment of silence in a roomful of noise.

3 ■ Mason Ruffner, **"Gypsy Blood,"** from *Gypsy Blood* (CBS) Strong, heedless, grinning, violent rockabilly, played the way Jimi Hendrix would have played it, if he'd played rockabilly: with the tremolo arm.

4 ■ Misow, **"When it All Comes Down (Catechism)"** (Factory 12-inch) When the going gets tough, the smart get cryptic.

5 ■ Rolling Stones, *Beggars Banquet* (London reissue, 1968) With the once-banned bog-graffiti sleeve: the scrawled "Ronald Reagan is a *sissy*" reminds you how little has changed, the lyricism of the music how much.

6 ■ Rice-Armandt-Hart-Broadhurst Band, **"Twist and Shout"** (Compleat Angler Bar, Bimini, March 28) It would be poetic justice—some kind of justice, anyway—if the Isley Brothers turned out to have a greater effect on the next presidential election than Bruce Springsteen did on the last one.

7 ■ Big Black, *Headache* (Touch and Go EP) A cold, hard rhythm, when Steve Albini can manage to stay out of his own way.

8 ■ Peter and the Test Tube Babies, **"Louise Wouldn't Like It"** (Profile) But Wire fans would.

9 ■ Camille Peri, **"Our Shirelle—Doris Jackson's Life in Rock and Roll"** (*Image* magazine, *San Francisco Examiner,* May 31) A sensitive profile of a woman who now lives in Sacramento and still performs with her own "Shirelles," but the highlight comes with a story Jackson tells about a tour the original group made with Little Richard: "Things had just opened up in Washington, D.C., in about 1962 to the point where black acts could stay downtown. Well, we were all playing at the Howard and Little Richard decided he was going to stay at one of the downtown hotels. At the time he was traveling with eight uniformed guards, gorgeous guys, and as part of his act they would roll out a red carpet and he would walk on it, wearing a robe, the whole bit. When his limo pulled up at the hotel his guards rolled out his carpet and stood at attention and Richard in his robe came out and was greeted by the management. But as the week went on and his bills started to mount, they called up to his room and said, 'Sir, we're so happy you've chosen to stay at our hotel, but could you please tell us what country you're king of?'"

10 ■ Dr. Sanford Kellman, advertisement (*San Francisco Chronicle,* May 10) The rock 'n' roll "door policy" was something new in San Francisco when it arrived in "SoMa" (South of Market, the city's imita-

tion SoHo) a year or so ago; now hardly an art-dollar venue is complete without an authentic New York attitude cop. Kellman, owner of the I-Beam, long among the most congenial and adventurous local clubs, bought space to say no: "This admission process is illegal according to city business codes, state licensing regulations and nationally accepted civil rights standards, to say nothing of its moral bankruptcy. Neither the public nor the licensing authorities would tolerate these admission practices in any other form of business." And people used to complain about Bill Graham.

JULY 28, 1987

1 ▪ Fastbacks, . . . *and his Orchestra* (Popllama) and *Everyday Is Saturday* (No Threes EP) No gimmick here, no persona, no concept: just the will to communicate. With early-'70s trash as a first cause and '77–'80 U.K. punkpop (X-ray Spex, Revillos, Girls at Our Best) as the end of history, singers Kim Warnick (bass) and Lulu Gargiulo (guitar) and writer Kurt Bloch (lead guitar) make old sounds and gestures seem like the only language they'll ever need to say everything there is to say. The flattened vocals produce an overwhelming sense of realism, the rave-ups and hidden rhythm-jumps the kind of drama real life seeks and usually doesn't find—especially, these days, on records. I love this band.

2 ▪ Hank Williams, "Ramblin' Man," from *Hey Good Lookin'—December 1950–July 1951* (Polydor reissue, 1951) Chilling. Chill-out. Why he froze to death.

3 ▪ Bernard Lewis, *The Assassins—A Radical Sect in Islam* (Oxford reissue, 1967) The emergence of punk was so epistemologically disruptive it brought forth ancestors few of its adherents could have suspected existed. Among them was Hasan-i Sabbah, who in 11th-century Iran founded a murderous, gnostic Shi'a (or "Shi'ite," or "Chi-Lite") cult that survives today in the Hezbollah group, Shi'as who take hostages in Lebanon. Hasan was supposedly as well the author of the nihilist maxim punk grasped almost as soon as it learned to read: "Nothing is true; everything is permitted." The high point of Lewis's scholarly, unfailingly lucid story comes in 1164, when, after the death of Hasan-i Sabbah, a second Hasan announced the millennium and "the end of the law," putting Hasan-i Sabbah's purported slogan into practice: "'they spoke of the world as being uncreated and Time as unlimited'"; because in the "'world to come there is no action and all is reckoning,'" it was declared that on earth "'all is action and there is no reckoning.'" That sentiment survived in the Sex Pistols.

4 ▪ Cruzados, "Bed of Lies," (Arista) The tune comes off the radio with the force of a bad dream you don't want to wake from. "I'm drinking my way back into your heart," Tito Larriva snarls at himself; guitarist Marshall Rohner knows how to hold a note just past the crucial split-second that has you begging for it.

5 ▪ Sonic Youth, *Sister* (SST) Corrosive.

6 ▪ Peter Laughner, "Cinderella Backstreet" (Forced Exposure) An incandescent little piece from a man who founded Cleveland's Rocket from the Tombs and Pere Ubu, and died in '77; a bit like Bob Dylan's "I'm Not There" in theme, closer to Mick Jagger's "Cocksucker Blues" in feeling.

7 ▪ Darden Smith, "Bus Stop Bench" and "Stick and Stones," from *Native Soil* (Redi Mix) Smith is a folkie, and he has a folkie's smugness, but sometimes it fails him.

8 ▪ Adam Parfrey, "The Book of Charlie" (*Exit #3*) As a graphics magazine, *Exit* is a sort of pagan-fascist version of *RAW*. Halfway through its celebration of Charles Manson is a collage that combines Mansonoid graffiti with the famous photo of Hitler and his advisors studying war maps, except that the heads of the advisors have been replaced by those of the Beatles—"vulgar simpletons," says the artist, but nevertheless unwitting "messengers of the Gods," "harbingers of Helter-Skelter." Take a look.

9 ▪ Ted McKeever, *Eddy Current* (Mad Dog Graphics) In this unfolding comic-book

series, a good-hearted schizophrenic escapes from his asylum in order to save the world (he's got to be back in 12 hours, so there'll be one book for each hour). Problems: the world he wants to save tilts like the rooms in *The Cabinet of Dr. Caligari*, punks mug him, and a nun who thinks he's Jesus Christ kidnaps him. Also—he hasn't the vaguest idea of what he has to save the world from, though it'll turn out to be a mind-control plot by a version of the PMRC.

10 ▪ **Rosanne Cash,** *King's Record Shop* **(Columbia)** Cash is looking for a subject. "Rosie Strike Back" takes off from Graham Parker's "Nobody Hurts You" for its sound, and it sounds good, until you can no longer deny it's didactic enough to serve as a public service announcement for battered women's shelters; that takes about a minute. But "The Real Me," a ballad, may stand up: it's slow, warm, open, naked, and hard. "I want to crawl inside you, baby/But I don't want you near."

AUGUST 28, 1987

1 ▪ **Jim Dodge,** *Not Fade Away,* **a novel (Atlantic Monthly Press paperback)** Summer '87: in a season of Real Death Rock, reaching a head on August 16 with the 10th Annual Graceland Wake 'n' Family Picnic, the true auteur of the moment may be not Elvis Presley but Roger Petersen—who on February 3, 1959, took his single-engine Bonanza off the ground and almost immediately returned to it, along with Buddy Holly, the Big Bopper, and Ritchie Valens. Elvis remains buried beneath his own clichés; the plane crash is still turning up surprises.

The plane crash has its own clichés. The big one is Luis Valdez's lifeless film *La Bamba,* a goody-goody account of The Ritchie Valens Story redeemed only by **Danielle von Zerneck's** touching, sunny performance as Valens's real-life girlfriend Donna Ludwig (#3 on this month's chart) and **Marshall Crenshaw's** quick but revelatory portrayal of Buddy Holly as a hipster (#4). More promising (if unread) is **Beverly**

Wendheim's *Ritchie Valens: The First Latino Rocker,* a biography due later this month (Bilingual Review Press); it rates an easy #5 merely for its 23 pages of pictures. Maybe the radio will even drown out Los Lobos's folkie Valens covers with **Led Zeppelin's** unhinged version of his "Ooh, My Head"; ripped off and retitled (as "Boogie With Stu," on *Physical Graffiti*), it'd still come in at #6. All of which pales against the big surprise, Jim Dodge's *Not Fade Away.* Despite taking its title from a Holly tune, this is The Big Bopper Story—on a level no movie or biography will ever reach.

In San Francisco, in 1965, a young ex-trucker named George Gastin is hanging on to what's left of the Beat scene, making his rent smashing up expensive cars so their owners can collect on inflated insurance policies. Then his life begins to fall apart; faced with a cherry '59 Cadillac a client wants torched, Gastin hesitates. In the glove compartment, he discovers a letter from the original owner, a rich spinster three years dead. "I am a 57-year-old virgin," it begins. "I've never had sex with a man because none has ever moved me." But the man to whom the letter is addressed moved her; one night, dialing for a classical station, the woman chanced upon "Chantilly Lace," and had her life changed. The car, the letter says, is her way of returning the gift; it belongs to the man on the radio, the Big Bopper. But the letter is dated February 1, 1959.

Gastin decides to take the car where it belongs—to the Big Bopper's grave, at first, then to the site of the plane crash. A skimpy plot is hung on the premise, but the life of the novel is in Gastin's adventures along the way: a series of hilarious and ultimately mystical encounters with phantom characters as strange and believable as the 57-year-old virgin fan of "Chantilly Lace." There's a mad scientist testing theories that later showed up in Jacques Attali's *Noise,* the world's greatest traveling salesman, the 97-year-old woman who owns the land where the plane went down, others less easy to describe, all of them cut from the same vein of American fiction first mined by Melville in *The Confidence-Man*. What drives *Not Fade Away* is Gastin's growing suspicion that he's destined to join this company—to lose his status as a man with a place in time and become a road-spirit, no more and no less than a song half-heard at 3 a.m. in the middle of the Nevada desert, or in a rich woman's house in San Francisco.

2 ▪ **Lucy de Barbin and Dary Maters, *Are You Lonesome Tonight? The Untold Story of Elvis Presley's One True Love—and the Child He Never Knew* (Villard)** In a month glutted by such corpse-in-your-mouth Elvis product as **Jane and Michael Stern**'s all-filler *Elvis World* (Knopf, #9 on the level of Stay Away, Joe), **Lee Cotten**'s shoddy *Elvis Catalog* (Doubleday, #10, ditto), and **RCA**'s repackagings of the '54–'55 Sun and '69 Memphis comeback recordings (for the insensate every-instrument-in-its-place re-mastering of the '69 stuff, a combined #7 'n' #8), this bizarre memoir will supersede Dodge's fantasy of a woman who bought a Cadillac for a man she never met—not in the annals of rock, but in those of psychopathology. That is: Lucy de Barbin claims to remember every telling detail of her more than two-decade affair with Elvis, which resulted in two pregnancies and one child, and I believe she does remember. One day, a woman heard a song on the radio, and it sparked a fantasy, shared by millions, that the song was sung to her. Rather than accept the cruelty and degradation of her real life, unlike the rest who heard the song, this woman lived out the fantasy, and she is living it out today. In other words: the same radio that in *Not Fade Away* made a woman happy made Lucy de Barbin pregnant in *Are You Lonesome Tonight?*

SEPTEMBER 22, 1987

1 ▪ **John Mellencamp, *The Lonesome Jubilee* (Mercury)** This time out of the box, even a number called "We Are the People" makes it.

2 ▪ **Kim Wilde, "You Keep Me Hangin' On" (MCA 12-inch)** Holland-Dozier-Holland

built a terrible inexorableness into this tune, a no-way-out that Vanilla Fudge found by slowing the melody down and Wilde (Kim, or producer Ricki) gets by speeding it up. What's new is the extraordinary sense of desperation the song calls forth from a nakedly ordinary voice: the way K.W., in pursuit of high notes she'll never reach, throws herself off the cliff of ". . . and let me find somebody ELSE" is rock 'n' roll art if anything is.

3 ▪ **Einstürzende Neubauten, *Feunf auf der nach oben offenen Richterskala* [Five on the Richter Scale] (Relativity)** A tone poem about the progress of entropy; with surges of Romantic, classical themes, an accounting of what's already been lost.

4 ▪ **KALX, Station I.D. (90.7 FM, Berkeley)** "THIS IS ATTORNEY GENERAL ED MEESE! YOU'RE LISTENING TO THE NEWS ON KALX, BROADCASTING FROM THE UNIVERSITY OF CALIFORNIA! IT'S A CRIME IF YOU DON'T STAY TUNED!" And it may be a crime if you do—if UC alumnus Meese, whose voice this truly is, catches KALX airing Pussy Galore's "Cunt Tease" again.

5 ▪ **Contras, *Ciphers in the Snow* (Whittier Records)** "The name, of course, is not a reflection of our political views but our musical vision, to be rock's counter-revolutionaries"—whatever that means. Since the real contras are Reagan's Rasputins, and just as hard to kill, these "Contras" are probably even dumber than their little disclaimer. The music is smart: rangy punk with lots of room in the sound for cowboy-ballad guitar and a singer who, no matter how fast the tempo, settles all questions with a deadpan drawl, most notably on "Dead Guy," probably the best ever why-I-didn't-do-my-homework song (are there any others?).

6 ▪ **Five Jones Boys, Four Blackbirds, Three Peppers, Five Breezes, etc., *The Human Orchestra—Rhythm Quartets in the Thirties* (Clanka Lanka reissue, 1932–40, Sweden)** This is a very entertaining collection of formally ambitious performances that now seem like novelty records. It shouldn't be that way: the "human orchestra" of, say, the

Jones Boys Sing Band's "Pickin' a Rib" is likely a direct (if forgotten) ancestor of today's human beatboxes. In any larger context, though, this music is stranded in time: most of all, evidence that the theory of musical evolution cannot account for the shift from the pre-war black group sound to the doo-wop rock 'n' roll style that first gained shape in 1948 with the Orioles' "It's Too Soon to Know." The shift was a breach, and it was social.

7 ▪ **Residents, *Stars & Hank Forever!—The American Composer Series, Volume II* (Ralph Records)** One side of John Philip Sousa, as "The Stars and Stripes Forever" and "Semper Fidelis" might have worked on the *Eraserhead* soundtrack, and one of Hank Williams, whose "Ramblin' Man" no longer lusts for the other side, but comes from it.

8 ▪ **Richard Berry, *"Louie, Louie"* (Earth Angel reissue, 1953–58, Sweden)** Lacking the crucial legal-jeopardy discs ("Riot in Cell Block #9" with the Robins', "The Big Break," "Next Time"), this is solid L.A. doowop, which was greasier than the East Coast version. Plus more proof that if there's a hell the composer of "Besame Mucho" belongs in it.

9 ▪ **John Carman, review of Martin Scorsese's video for Michael Jackson's "Bad" (*San Francisco Chronicle*, September 2)** Good rock criticism from a TV columnist: "Scorsese's film turned out to be the longest build-up to one bad song since the conception, birth, and early life of Debby Boone."

10 ▪ **Mick Jagger, "Let's Work" (Columbia)** There are moments when you find yourself responding, yes, there is a reason, a reason beyond a love of one's own celebrity, even beyond the fear of losing it, that this song was written and sung . . . not that Jagger's words, which in the course of his long and distinguished career have often impinged on a world inhabited by persons other than himself, provide a clue as to what that reason might be.

OCTOBER 20, 1987

1 ▪ **Chuck Berry, *The Autobiography* (Harmony)** "I adjusted swiftly back to the general trends of society's majority," he says of his release from prison in 1963, "and settled down with friends in the subtle minority." There are volumes in that line, whole sociologies and poetics, and it's altogether emblematic of this remarkable testament: if the controlling theme of the book is racism (just overshadowing sexual adventurism, family love, and money-wit), its heart is in its language. What at first seems like doggerel ("Speaking of beauty, she had little to share, but if charms were hours, she had years to spare") turns into a unique and open voice, which only occasionally calls up the voice Berry used in his songs. (That voice, it's now clear, was not his at all, but his rendering of a fantasized conversation between audience and performer, crowd and observer: a pop construct.) Berry leaps past such categories as "prose style," demanding older, more ambiguous locutions: "phraseology," "cacology," "conjure." And of course there are countless good stories, none quite exhausting its facts, most sealed with a touch of bile: "I remember having extreme difficulty while writing 'Promised Land' in trying to secure a road atlas of the United States to verify the routing of the Po' Boy from Norfolk, Virginia, to Los Angeles. The penal institutions were not then so generous as to offer a map of any kind, for fear of providing the route for an escape."

2 ▪ **Big Black, *Songs About Fucking* (Touch and Go)** As with Sonic Youth's *Sister*, a slight move towards accessibility makes the void this now-defunct band tried to map more believable than ever before. With great sleeve art, a drum machine with a personality, and a cover of Kraftwerk's "Model" as a Rosetta Stone, the songs—events, really—quickly open into the terrain once occupied by PiL's "Poptones," and then dig in.

3 ▪ **Pussy Galore, *Pussy Galore, Right Now!* (Caroline)** A little vague, maybe—

nothing so arresting as "Pretty Fuck Look." Still, if when the Rolling Stones made *The Rolling Stones, Now!*, they'd also cut a secret version, this is what it might have sounded like.

4 ▪ **Jonathan Valin, *Fire Lake* (Delacorte)** The theme of the seventh Harry Stoner mystery is that of a thousand feature stories now lining birdcages: "The '60s Revisited— The Music! The Drug Culture! The Free Love Generation!" The difference is that for ex-junkie Karen Jackowski, time stopped when the '60s ended; for time to start again only means that the '60s are catching up with her.

5 ▪ **The Jesus and Mary Chain, *Darklands* (Warner Bros.)** Car music.

6 ▪ **Van Morrison, *Poetic Champions Compose* (Mercury)** And when the going gets tough, the tough get down on their knees and pray. The sound is close enough to New Age to appear on Windham Hill (each side opens with a vapid instrumental), but as on all of Morrison's recent albums, there are a lot of dead flies trapped in the gossamer threads, and sometimes the threads don't even need the flies.

7 ▪ **Billy Lee Riley, "Trouble Bound," as used on *Private Eye* (NBC, Fridays at 10 p.m.)** Running behind bad news in this Eisenhower-era corpse opera, Riley's brooding '56 rockabilly ballad made as perfect a moment as I've seen on TV this year. But such contrivances define the show's limits— even with a recent script based on President (of the Screen Actors Guild) Ronald Reagan's notorious deal with MCA, it's all concept, no fire.

8 ▪ **Vivien Vee, "Heartbeat" (TSR 12-inch)** Italian disco with every rhythm trick known to Western man ("good for aerobics," it says), a little-girl vocal reminiscent of Claire Grogan of Altered Images, and an extraordinarily warming upsurge every time the melody peaks for the apparently deathless couplet, "One-two-three/Baby what you do to me."

9 ▪ **Fearless Iranians from Hell, *Die for Allah* (Boner)** Speaking of death, or numerology, the noise here doesn't exactly transcend itself, but "1,2,3,4,5,6,7,8,9,10/See I can count to ten" does.

10 ▪ **PiL, "Open and Revolving," from *Happy?* (Virgin)** Yes—but everywhere else on this record, the door has closed.

NOVEMBER 17, 1987

1 ▪ **Pet Shop Boys, *actually* (Manhattan)** Thatcherism is now a pop tradition, and this exquisite album measures the costs of "People's Capitalism" as subtly as Springsteen's *Nebraska* exposed the nihilism of our own "National Renewal." Casting back no farther than Soft Cell's "Tainted Love," Human League's "Don't You Want Me," and Alphaville's "Forever Young," the music is almost subliminally affecting; the singing is full of doubt—consciousness. The theme of love and money—the impossibility, now, of telling one from the other—comes into deep focus with "Rent," the smooth, bitter tale of a kept man, singing for a kept country.

2 ▪ **Elvis Presley, Jerry Lee Lewis, Carl Perkins, *The One Million Dollar Quartet* (S bootleg reissue, 1956)** Not like the dim, truncated artifact-for-artifact's-sake that surfaced some years ago, but uncut, the sound so bright and present the legends might be setting up in your living room. Despite a dozen spirituals, what's startling is the patent lack of religious feeling: this is a celebration of worldly stardom and its loosening of all constraints ("Well, it's Saturday night, and I just got laid . . . ah, paid"). Elvis dominates, most notably trying once, twice, three times to top Jackie Wilson's Las Vegas version of "Don't Be Cruel," because he's sure it topped his. Available for a short time only at a record store not far from where John Fogerty went to high school.

3 ▪ **Bruce Springsteen, *Tunnel of Love* (Columbia)** For the mood of "Tougher Than the Rest."

4 ▪ ***Rolling Stone*, XX Anniversary Issue (#512, November 5–December 12)** "By the time the Labour party came into power in Britain in 1964, youth culture was already a *fait accompli*. That is, youth had already

benefited from the prosperous inflationary period of the early sixties—that whole period of teenage consumerism that Colin MacInnes wrote about in books like *Absolute Beginners.* . . ." So says Professor Michael Philip Jagger in this extraordinary compendium of new interviews with 34 traditional *RS* favorites: three blacks, three women, one twofer, and no punks. The leading questions emphasize "The Sixties" as concept and legacy; the answers are usually thoughtful, honest, hard-nosed, and sometimes (the first paragraph of the Keith Richards entry) pure poetry.

5 ▪ Jovan Acin, *Hey, Babu Riba* (Orion Pictures) A bizarre twist on the "L. O. V. E. across the knuckles of his right hand/ H. A. T. E. across the knuckles of his left" motif—not to mention proof that rock 'n' roll was invented in Yugoslavia, in 1953, by fans of Lionel Hampton's "Hey, Bop-a-Re-Bop," as a protest against Titoism.

6 ▪ AT&T, "Operator" radio commercial, with Jim Croce (1943–73) impersonator (NW Ayer) It's creepy (that's the hook), but also primitive (they didn't even have to hire the soundalike), because it's the wave of the future (or whatever tense applies): digital sampling now permits the rearrangement of any dead singer's phonemes into an endorsement of absolutely anything. Imagine, say, Janis Joplin: "I'm sorry, babe/I had to go/But you don't have to/'Just say no.'"

7 ▪ Wilfrid Mellers, *Music in a New Found Land—Themes and Developments in American Music* (Oxford paperback reissue, 1964) Strongly influenced by D. H. Lawrence's *Studies in Classic American Literature*, this study, unprecedented when first published and hardly superseded today, locates artists from Ives to Bessie Smith, Cage to Ellington, Copland to Robert Johnson just outside the gates of a Transcendentalist utopia—where, Mellers says, "We shall know at last that there is no differentiation between the genres."

8 ▪ Sisters of Mercy, "Gimme Shelter" (Brain Eater 12-inch, UK, 1983) The band is from Leeds, the record the flip of "Temple of Love," the composition by Jagger and

Richards, but punched up on the radio at night, about a minute into the drone, this Gothic performance sounds like a ritual from some pre-Christian Germanic forest—where, for the past thousand years, its cultists have been biding their time, waiting for the moment when the world will be ready to hear their terrible message.

9 ▪ Randy Shilts, *And the Band Played On—People, Politics, and the AIDS Epidemic* (St. Martin's) The lit-crit dismissal Shilts received in a recent VLS should not dissuade anyone from reading this tremendous book—overstated as a thriller, understated as a tragedy, realized as both—or from remembering that pop music has had less to say about AIDS than Ronald Reagan.

10 ▪ New Monkees, *New Monkees* (Warner Bros.) Not terrible, even if they do play their own instruments; at least they don't write their own songs.

DECEMBER 15, 1987

1 ▪ Creedence Clearwater Revival, "Effigy," from *Willie and the Poor Boys* (Fantasy CD reissue, 1969) Most classic-rock CDs vitiate the original sound with separation, and sabotage it with exaggerated percussion so intrusive it turns performances that survived reprocessed stereo into blackboard-scratching parodies. (But you can hear the grain of the nails!) With Creedence CDs, the sound is heightened but not changed. "Effigy" was a plodding, earnest rerun of Neil Young's "Cowgirl in the Sand" on LP; now, like a shell left over from a forgotten war, it explodes as a piece of absolute nihilism, for a moment silencing the records it prefigured: the Sex Pistols' "Anarchy in the U.K." in John Fogerty's cold words, Gang of Four's "At Home He's a Tourist" in the irrationalism of his cutup guitar.

2 ▪ Adverts, *The Peel Sessions* (Strange Fruit EP, UK, 1977) T. V. Smith seemed to scare himself with this version of "Gary Gilmore's Eyes." Why haven't Scott and Beth B. made a movie out of it?

3 ▪ Terence Trent D'Arby, "(Ain't Gonna Play) Vienna" (refusal to honor contract for

concert in Austria, November 10)** I like the cool, spare "Santayana Mix" best: "I cannot in good conscience allow money being made off my back to go into the government coffers of a country that has, in its own superior judgment, elected a known Nazi conspirator to head its nation"— somehow, the sound of a major-label rock 'n' roll singer making a political statement without 50 superstars in attendance is refreshing, bracing. But the "Atrocity Mix" is almost as good (lots of crowd noise, recorded live in Munich): "I DON'T WANT TO PLAY IN A COUNTRY THAT VOTED FOR A FUCKING NAZI."

4 ■ Crickets, *The "Chirping" Crickets* (MCA reissue, 1958) Buddy Holly as the Beatles.

5 ■ Anonymous headline writer, "SERGEANT BILKO MISTAKEN FOR DALAI LAMA IN TIBET" (*San Francisco Chronicle*, November 14) Somewhere, Phil Silvers is smiling.

6 ■ Pet Shop Boys, "Rent," from *actually* (Manhattan) You can hear this song as the testament of a man being kept by a woman; in England it's obvious the rent is paid by another man. So the tune begs the question of how much room there is in it, which only a female singer can answer. Marianne Faithfull? Rosanne Cash? Kim Gordon? Syd Straw? Where is Lesley Woods?

7 ■ Keith Abbott, "Spanish Castle," from *The First Thing Coming* (Coffee House Press, Minneapolis, MN) The action in this short story begins in the early '60s dance hall pictured on the sleeve of *The History of Northwest Rock, Vol. 4*, during a battle of the bands between the Checkers and the Wailers ("Losing band to have heads shaved on stage"); it's resolved in the front seat of a '57 Oldsmobile. Nobody writes about high-school sex as well as Abbott. He does it all in a line, which you read over and over, as if one more reading will put all the details he's led you to imagine on the page.

8 ■ George Michael, *Faith* (Columbia) SWM, friends call me a hunk, confused, repressed, into Prince, has put teenybopper idol past behind with "confused, repressed,

first-rate white Prince album" (*Voice*, December 15). If you want my sex, write my fan club.

9 ■ Talulah Gosh, "Talulah Gosh" (53rd & Third, UK, also on *Indie Top 20, Vol. II*, Revolver/Cartel, UK) Sounds like Pauline Murray—and even though she's not on it, you have to take her sound where you can find it.

10 ■ Paul Grushkin, *The Art of Rock—Posters from Presley to Punk* (Abbeville) This high-gloss, $85, 516 pp. book is unfortunately not for browsing. First of all, at 12 lbs. it's too heavy. Second, more than three-fifths of it is taken up by hundreds of tiny reproductions of '65–'87 psychedelic or postpsychedelic items (many masterpieces, many turkeys) that need a full-page format to communicate with any immediacy at all. You need to spend hours with this monster, picking out the thousands of stray, telling ephemera, be they legends on James Brown broadsides ("A Show for the Entire Family," says a '66 Apollo announcement; "SEX POWER AND LOVE," reads a poster from '71), or lines from one of Grushkin's interviews ("I've never gotten the same thrill out of having one of my cartoons printed in a magazine as much as seeing one of my old fliers—something I did for a punk gig the week before—laying in the gutter," says Shawn Kerri), or the picture of my brother on p. 412, or the skull handbills for my niece's husband's former band on pp. 478–79.

JANUARY 19, 1988

1 ■ Absolut Vodka ad, (*New Yorker*, December 21) You open the four-page insert, pull the strip at the fold, and out comes the melody of "We Wish You a Merry Christmas." Taking the pages apart, you find a sort of music box, about the size of a hearing aid, but much thinner; while the sound it makes isn't loud, it seems to travel through floors. The machine is efficient: mine has been playing for more than 48 hours now.

There are here possibilities for the creation of disturbance, for the promulgation of aesthetic displacement and social uncertainty, far beyond the obvious brutalism of beat boxes or the street-art critiques of Barbara Kruger and Jenny Holzman. "My ultimate vocation is to be an irritant," Elvis Costello once said. "Not something actively destructive, but someone who irritates, who disorientates. Someone who disrupts the daily drag of life just enough to leave the victim thinking there's maybe more to it all than the humdrum quality of existence." And that's what this device can do. The mechanics can't be that complicated; it ought to be easy to copy, program, and disseminate. Imagine tens of thousands of undetectable music boxes, coded with "Summertime, Summertime," "Come On in My Kitchen," "Jump," all secreted in the crevices of skyscrapers, in the cracks of telephone poles, stuck under bus seats, rugs, desks (in your office, in the Office of Management and Budget, behind the presidential seal the next time there's a televised White House news conference). Imagine "You Are My Sunshine" and "When a Man Loves a Woman" turning the whole country into one vast theater for the aural itch of a song you can't get out of your head, but now *every* song, a different one every few minutes, every few steps, people saying, "God, what *is* that, I know it, I just can't—"

Who knows, there might be a lot of interesting new conversations. There might be rioting in the streets. It might be the end of civilization as we know it. You read it here first.

2 ■ Charlie Haas, Bob Roe, et al., "Lost Documents of 1987" (*California Magazine*) Including a suppressed decision by Judge Ginsburg, written under the influence, a paste-up for *Roiling Stone's* junked special issue celebrating the 20-week anniversary of the 20-year anniversary of the Summer of Love ("One thing is certain: there will never be nostalgia for the sixties like that again"), and William Casey's last letter to Bob Woodward: "I want to apologize for drifting off in the middle of our last chat. . . . Anyway—to answer your question

from last time, let me say again that I believed, and I *still believe*, that 'Dark Side of the Moon' is Pink Floyd's best album . . ."

3 ■ Neil Young, "Hey Hey My My (Into the Black)" (*Rolling Stone Magazine's 20 Years of Rock 'n' Roll*, November 24, ABC-TV) After two hours of lulling performance clips, this was a shock—as music, terrorism; in context, the abyss.

4 ■ Prince, "I Could Never Take the Place of Your Man," (Paisley Park) But in the last minute he takes the place of Duane Allman.

5 ■ Mekons, *New York* (ROIR) Proof that "Hard To Be Human" is their best moment on stage.

6 ■ Jonathan King, "He's So Fine" (Rhino) Proof that *all* of George Harrison's songs were written by one Ronald Mack.

7 ■ Prince Buster, *Judge Dread* (Melodisc) The only LP I've ever found with all three parts of the Coasters cum-rock-steady saga of the Ethiopian judge who knows how to dance.

8 ■ The Johnnys, *Highlights of a Dangerous Life* (Enigma) Australian cowboy rock with a better beat than the Beat Farmers.

9 ■ Foreigner, *Inside Information* (Atlantic) What the hell—there's a hit here somewhere.

10 ■ Artemy Troitsky, *Back in the USSR: The True Story of Rock in Russia* (Omnibus Press) As a history of an imitation and a paean to *glasnost*, this survey by the Soviet Union's top rock networker can only be prelude. The prehistory is full of mystery and wonder: early bootlegs of Western pop cut "on ribs" (used X-ray plates), tales of the late '40s *stilyagi* ("stylists," USSR approximations of zoot-suiters and Teddy Boys), or Leningrad fan Kolya Vasin's discovery of "meaning in life": "A friend came to me and asked if I'd heard about the new sensation, the Beatles, and put on a tape recorded from a BBC broadcast. It was something heavenly, I felt blissful and invincible. I understood that everything other than the Beatles had been oppression." Kim Philby, eat your heart out.

1 ▪ **James Burton & Bruce Springsteen, "Oh, Pretty Woman," from** *Roy Orbison and Friends: An Evening in Black and White* **(Cinemax, or MTV clip)** What you don't get anymore: two guitarists trading a riff, making it into a phrase, and then, taking all the time in the world, writing a book. The moment was so invisibly sustained, suspended even out of the time of the song, that when MTV followed with Pink Floyd's "On the Turning Away," and David Gilmour stood still and played an endless, stately, perfectly generic late-'60s cosmic solo, even that sounded inspired.

2 ▪ **Terence Trent D'Arby, "Wonderful World" (Columbia 12-inch)** There are only three kinds of rock fans: those who think Sam Cooke's "A Change Is Gonna Come" is better than his "Wonderful World," those who think the opposite, and those who can't decide. D'Arby must fall in the latter camp. The complexity of his own music can be traced back to the consciousness of "Change," but so far that complexity exposes too much self-consciousness— "Wishing Well," the A-side of this disc, dies when you start hearing how many times he had to rehearse his laughter. The easy melody of "Wonderful World" gives D'Arby a chance to be a soul singer, not just a genius. When he covers the verse Paul Simon added to Cooke's version, "Don't know much about the Middle Ages/Look at the pictures I just turn the pages," he lets you see him squirming at his school-room desk, confused, wishing he did know about the Middle Ages—which, off the record, D'Arby surely does.

3 ▪ **Larks,** *When I Leave These Prison Walls* **(Apollo reissue, 1950–54)** Very smooth, professional, almost supper-club doo-wop; when a blues sensibility surfaces, it's a shock.

4 ▪ **Peter Sloterdijk, "Dada Chaotology" from** *Critique of Cynical Reason* **(Minnesota paperback)** "A subterranean line leads through the culture of hatred in our century—from Dada to the punk move-ment," says the 40-year-old author of this hit West German study of "enlightened false consciousness" (what's left when revolutionary consciousness goes to sleep). Dada/punk is an old argument, but it has force here. That's because, working with documents previously innocent of English translation, Sloterdijk is talking about Berlin dada, less an art movement than a free speech movement—an explosion of spleen that produced a language so cruel and self-contradictory ("We were for the war and today Dadaism is still for war," draft-dodger Richard Huelsenbeck announced in early 1918) it burned off all irony, leaving behind nothing but words that dared the listener to believe they meant what they said. Sloterdijk is one of the first to try.

5 ▪ **Bar-Kays, "Certified True" (Polygram 12-inch)** Certified Cameo, anyway.

6 ▪ **John Crawford,** *Baboon Dooley— Rock Critic!* **(Popular Reality Press Ann Arbor, MI)** First full-length book on the subject— even if it is all comic strips, even if the highlight is the flashback "Witness to Beat-nik Glory."

7 ▪ *Swellsville: A Critical Guide for Consumer Deviants* **(Winter of Our Discontent 1988 issue)** Fanzine with '60s UK would-be teen idol Heinz on the cover (I never heard of him either) and lots of words inside: "The inescapable truth is that avoiding critical thought doesn't dispel the need for it—it only submits you to somebody else's."

8 ▪ **Jonathan Richman and the Modern Lovers, "I Have Come Out to Play," from** *Modern Lovers 88* **(Rounder)** Much of the LP is vague, but the emotion is specific here, chased down till it gives up its own momentum; when Richman muffles the instruments and breaks out with "Rover, red Rover, come on over," his whole career finds a home in the line.

9 ▪ **Byrds,** *Never Before* **(CBS Special Prodcuts/Re-Flyte/Murray Hill/Outlet Book Co. archaeology, 1965), and T Bone Burnett:** *The Talking Animals* **(Columbia)** Dullest records of the month.

10 ▪ **Joni Mabe, "Love Letter to Elvis" (Primitivo gallery, San Francisco)** The show

was called *Elvis the King, a Folk Hero*; amidst Howard Finster's suspect tributes and a *Rock Dreams* ripoff, Mabe's collages stood out. In this giant handwritten valentine, you couldn't tell the dementia from the parody (if there was any)—reading along with "You could have discovered that sex and religion could be brought together in your feelings for me," pulled up short by the closing "confession": "I'm carrying your child. The last Elvis imitator I fucked was carrying your sacred seed. Please send money. Enclosed are photographs of myself and the earthly messenger you sent." That was an ugly ceramic Elvis doll; all around the letter, snapshots showed Mabe rubbing her bare breasts against it, grinning.

MARCH 29, 1988

1 ▪ **Roddy Doyle, *The Commitments* (Heinemann, London)** Finally, a novel about a band—a white band in contemporary Dublin dedicated to '60s soul music—that's not about success and failure, rise and fall. What it's mostly about is rehearsing, but no one has ever gotten more music on the page simply by turning up the volume: putting lyrics in caps and dramatizing the way a song resists the people who want to play it, the way they can make that song their own. The story is small, and it has room for an infinity of readers: here, listeners.

2 ▪ **Billy Stewart, "Baby, You're My Only Love," on *Okeh Rhythm & Blues* (Epic reissue, compiled 1982)** Startling—though the arrangement is a doo-wop cliché and Stewart's addled vocal style (which produced a single pop smash, "Summertime," 1966) is only marginally off-market. What gives this '57 nonhit its flesh-crawling power is the guitarist—Bo Diddley, maybe—who, every few lines, strips a low, corrosive run down the strings, revealing doo-wop courtly love as a high-wire act by making the sound of someone cutting the net.

3 ▪ **Beat Happening, *Jamboree* (Rough Trade)** As if the last 13 years never happened, this little band from Olympia, Washington, invents punk rock—more or less the way the

Marine Girls, with their homemade *Beach Party* cassette, invented it in 1981 in Hatfield, England.

4 ▪ **Jesse Belvin, "Hang Your Tears Out To Dry" (Earth Angel reissue, Sweden 1951–57)** There's a book to be written on '50s Los Angeles r&b: a sober history, tracing artists and businessmen, or a James Ellroy splatter-mystery, with the records appearing only as instants of impossible respite. Made out of the paradox of sun and confinement, the music was at once far more frankly pessimistic, clowning, and casual than the East Coast group sound or Southern band-based black rock. Belvin was perhaps the best pure singer of his place and time; leading off with the ineffable "Dream Girl," a labyrinth of blocked escape routes from the smooth prison of West Coast racism, this is the best collection of his work.

5 ▪ **Little Richard, Presentation of Best New Artist at the 30th Annual Grammy Awards (CBS-TV, March 2)** To himself, as everyone knows—an announcement that got the self-described "born-again black Jew" a nomination to fill the vacant cantor's post at San Francisco's Temple Beth Sholom. Let's see Jesse Jackson match that.

6 ▪ **Pamela Rose, "Hello, Hello, Taco Bell" (Tracy-Locke)** Rose normally reserves her florid belting for the Zazu Pitts Memorial Orchestra, a camp 'n' Motown outfit; what makes this radio commercial pornographic is her hysterical attempt to convince you she's never wanted another human being as much as she wants Taco Bell's current 99¢ (plus tax) special. There's talk Rose may even get a contract out of it—if the one numerous listeners have pledged to take out on her doesn't go through first.

7 ▪ **Nick Lowe, *Pinker and Prouder Than Previous* (Columbia)** An almost perfect Nick Lowe album: madly idiosyncratic tunes that sound so generic they'd be all but anonymous on the radio.

8 ▪ **Alan Leatherwood, "Preservation Halls: The Rock and Roll Hall of Fame" (*Option*, March/April)** A Cleveland report on a boondoggle worthy of the Pentagon.

9 ▪ **Jerry Lee Lewis, *Keep Your Hands Off It!* (Zu-Zazz reissue, UK, 1959–62)** Sun-label songs and instrumentals, loose and rangy and fine, with Jerry Lee and teen bride Myra on the cover. Proof that there's no bottom to the Lewis vault—which means his next album has to be a bootleg, a half-dozen outtakes of the drooling "Big Legged Woman" intercut with the sermon on Lewis-sins that first cousin Jimmy Swaggart made Nick Tosches cut out of his Lewis bio *Hellfire*. The cover should be fabulous.

10 ▪ **John Waters, *Hairspray* (New Line Cinema/MCA soundtrack)** The real, forgotten Toussaint McCall stands on a ghetto dance-hall stage and sings "Nothing Takes the Place of You" (it was a hit in '67, this is '62, but who cares); four kids leave the room. As they huddle in doorways on the street, making out, a bum walks by, picks up the song, and drowns out the artist: in this moment the song belongs to the derelict as if he wrote it. There hasn't been as true a rock 'n' roll event on screen since the garbage-can pounding of the would-be Little Richard at the end of Floyd Mutrux's '78 *American Hot Wax*.

APRIL 26, 1988

1 ▪ **Primitives, "Crash" (RCA UK)** The bounce of the Jamies' '58 "Summertime, Summertime," toughened up with '88 cynicism and doubt: from its first bars, a natural hit.

2 ▪ **Del-Lords, "Judas Kiss," from *Based on a True Story* (Enigma)** Eric Ambel's singing may be too open, too faceless, to make this explosive cut last, though Syd Straw's edgy backing vocals help—but it doesn't matter. Seventeen years ago the Rolling Stones' "Dead Flowers" was a good idea; now it's great rock 'n' roll.

3 ▪ **Eric Clapton, *Crossroads* (Polygram reissue, '63–'88, six LPs, four CDs)** This is overkill—disturbing, desperate moments lost in a 73-cut assemblage of dross and dates, confusion and careerism. It's got that acrid digital sound, complete with jumps

and drop-offs, lacking all warmth and presence, turning what once were shocks into lifeless exercises in remix. "Layla" is a horror: what you get, along with all the words, as if they were the point, is a man singing to a backing tape.

At its most distinctive, there was something heroic, something tragic, about Clapton's playing—you don't sense self-expression so much as struggle: the resistance of the music in the guitarist's mind to his will to realize that music, his resistance to losing himself in the sound he can make. What's being transcended is a kind of neurotic distance, a wish to disappear, to cease to be; the result is focus, elegance, balance—not blues. It's there in the solo in Cream's '66 "Spoonful," especially the three final notes; most of all, it's in the long, unsatisfied, unsatisfiable solo that ends Dave Mason's "Look at Me Look at You," which closed his '70 Blue Thumb LP, *Alone Together*. That performance is not on *Crossroads*, and I'm glad.

4 ▪ **Reverend Lonnie Farris, *Vocal and Steel Guitar* (Eden Records)** Walk into a room where this is playing and you'll ask what it is before you say hello. What it is is (a) what Eric Clapton wanted on the Bluesbreakers' '66 "All Your Love," and (b) an L.A. minister in 1962 with a steel guitar that sings like a Leslie. The shimmering, liquid chords are so evanescent you see them more than you hear them; Farris's guitar doesn't talk, it paints.

5 ▪ **Alex Bennett, a so-far undenied report, in two parts (Alex Bennett Show, KITS-FM, San Francisco, April 4)** Part one: Yoko Ono is married. Part two: she got married four months after John Lennon was shot.

6 ▪ **Deficit des Années Antérieures, *When a Cap Is Rising* (Big Noise/Red Rhino 10-inch LP, UK)** Tape collages with song overlays, '82–'86, from a Belgian outfit: what Wire would be if it were a little more arty, but no less sly.

7 ▪ **Coolies, "Coke Light Ice," from *Doug* (DB)** *Doug* is a "rock opera" tripping on its own parodies, but this tune may emerge in years to come as a classic of redeemed triv-

iality, which in some times (these) is at least half of what pop is for: a full-length song, driven by undifferentiated paranoia, about one man's inability to get more Coke than ice out of his favorite hamburger joint.

8 ▪ **Rykodisc, press release for** *The Atmosphere Collection: 8 Hours in the Big Apple* **(April 1)** Including "Gowanus Canal," "Busy Office," and "Haitian Taxi Driver," this eight-part ambient CD set is "intended for 'passive' listening," "designed to pummel the listener into resigned desperation," and "can be programmed to play all day . . . thus inducing a low-range psychosis in most listeners." It's just a joke—but why? Folkways once put out *Sounds of the Junkyard*, featuring "Burning Out an Old Car." And the fidelity today would be so much better . . .

9 ▪ **House of Schock, "Middle of Nowhere" (Capitol)** Best post-Go-Go's record, by the drummer, who had the only good smile in the band.

10 ▪ **Henry Silva, in** *The Manchurian Candidate,* **(1962, MGM/UA) and** *Above the Law* **(Warner Bros.)** The linkage between the villains Silva plays in the new *Above the Law* (a sort of Chuck Norris-bloodbath for leftwingers) and the re-released *Manchurian Candidate* (the best American movie made between *Citizen Kane* and *The Godfather*) is a nice twist. It half implies that after the failure of the Soviet-Chinese Communist-American fascist Manchurian Candidate plot, the Silva character went over from the KGB to the CIA, found work as a torturer in Vietnam, made his pile with Company cocaine, and then—

MAY 31, 1988

1 ▪ **Clash, "Complete Control," from** *The Story of the Clash, Volume I* **(Epic reissue, '77)** The purpose of this conventional double-LP, complete with unreadable life-on-the-road notes by the group's "valet," seems to be to certify the Clash as a conventional rock band. The fact that there was something more at stake in the Clash's career than a career is suppressed by the exclusion

of idiosyncrasy, playfulness, and despair ("The Right Profile," "Brand New Cadillac," the broken, empty-handed '85 "This Is England," what was left after Thatcherism erased the last traces of the white riot) in favor of rebel-rock shtick and chart hopes ("The Guns of Brixton," "Lost in the Supermarket," "Stay Free," "Should I Stay or Should I Go").

Given the shape of the package, the numbers on side three—all from '77–'78, when punk was still an idea seeking its field—send a nearly incomprehensible message of disruption, desire, and fear. Even less explainable, now, is that at the heart of this side is a performance that as pure sound stands as the greatest rock 'n' roll recording ever made. Oddly, it's about the Clash's career, at least on a literal, lyric-sheet level: their label-sanctioned protest single about their label committing the atrocity of releasing an earlier single without the band's permission. Big deal. Yet from this flimsy soapbox they leap musically to a dramatization of autonomy, community, personal identity and social contestation, and with a few scattered slogans ("THIS MEANS YOU!") make those usually abstract notions as real, as dangerous, as any moment governed by love or money, hate or war. Across more than 10 years of listening to "Complete Control," one reaction has always come first: disbelief. Disbelief that mere human beings could create such a sound, disbelief that the world could remain the same when it's over.

2 ▪ **Monty Python,** *The final rip off* **(Virgin reissue)** The same stuff that's been on all the other records, but not in the same order.

3 ▪ **Pet Shop Boys, "Always on My Mind" (Manhattan)** Now they say they meant no harm to either Elvis or the song. Trust the tale, not the teller.

4 ▪ **Jimmie Davis, "Down at the Old Country Church," from** *Barnyard Stomp* **(Bear Family reissue, '31, West Germany)** A two-time racist governor of Louisiana (elected on the basis of his purported authorship of "You Are My Sunshine"), Davis had a lot of alter egos way back when: Jimmie Rodgers

imitator, dirty songster, white Negro. Here the latter combines a rewrite of "When the Saints Go Marching In" with the bottleneck of black guitarist Ed Shaffer, a/k/a "Dizzy Head," and the result is dreamy, sensual—humid.

5 ▪ Bruce Springsteen and the E Street Band, "She's the One" (Shoreline Amphitheatre, Mountain View, CA, May 2) This time around, this is the one.

6 ▪ *Critical Texts*, v. V. #1 For C. O'Brien's "At Ease in Azania"—which, because it's fundamentally sympathetic, turns out to be the most convincing rejection of Paul Simon's bid for the Nobel Peace Prize. "*Graceland* was free to say anything it liked about what it engaged except what it did say: nothing."

7 ▪ Beach Boys, (TV commercial—sorry, I was too mesmerized to catch what for) As Mike Love jerks around the stage imitating a puppet with steel strings, you realize his longtime support for George Bush is no affectation—as a pop star, Mike Love *is* George Bush.

8 ▪ Jackie Collins, *Rock Star* (Simon & Schuster) I figured this would be a good excuse to get a fix on Ms. Collins. I was wrong.

9 ▪ Forgotten Rebels, "Surfin' on Heroin," from *Surfin' on Heroin* (Restless reissue) Madness from Ontario. The line "I'm surfin' on a sea of puke" (delivered with such fervor you could see the singer doing it) thrilled any number of college radio listeners in '83; in the tradition of Minnesota's Trashmen ("Surfin' Bird," '63), the first band to prove that only the ocean-deprived can realize the boundless possibilities of stupidity that lie behind the hedonism of California surf music, it closed out the *New Grove Dictionary of American Music* entry on the genre three years later. For that single slice of ineradicable miasma, this bunch will live forever.

10 ▪ Ronald Fraser, editor: *1968: A Student Generation in Revolt—An International Oral History* (Pantheon) The story behind side three of *The Story of the Clash*: slanted, riddled with errors and omissions (i.e., Czechoslovakia, Mexico, Japan), but graced with the genius for synthesizing testimony with narrative that made Fraser's *Blood of Spain* irresistible. What comes through is not sentiment but passion.

JUNE 21, 1988

1 ▪ Benny Spellman, "Life Is Too Short," from *Fortune Teller* (Charly r&b reissue, '59, UK) The seeker after deep soul usually bypasses New Orleans, even though it produced Irma Thomas's "Wish Someone Would Care." This is on the same level. The slow, quiet vocal is accompanied only by piano triplets, acoustic bass, brushes; when genre mannerisms surface in the singing, a sense of isolation so strong it is very nearly mystical wipes them away.

2 ▪ David Kennedy, "Debbie Does Swaggart" (*Penthouse*, July) These black and white reenactments of "poses" Debra Murphree struck for the Rev. Jimmy Lee Swaggart are not what one might have expected: grimy and cold, Kennedy's photographs carry a hint of Larry Clark's *Tulsa*, and an echo of Michael Lesy's *Wisconsin Death Trip*. They ought to be turned into punk flyers and stapled on telephone poles all over America, and they probably will be.

3 ▪ Wire, *A Bell Is a Cup Until It Is Struck* (Enigma/Mute) Dreamy, smart, and vague. In two years they'll be on Windham Hill.

4 ▪ Jamie Reid and Jon Savage, *Up They Rise—The Incomplete Work of Jamie Reid* (Faber & Faber) From the sly early '70s Suburban Press posters and stickers ("THIS WEEK ONLY. THIS STORE WELCOMES SHOPLIFTERS") through his Sex Pistols sleeves and ads, Reid practiced as a media alchemist, certain he could change critical theory into a threat and irony into violence.

5–6 ▪ Squeeze and Dave Edmunds Band, Budweiser commercials (AM radio) What's sold here is not name or personality but style. The familiar but chart-poor groups are not announced, and that anonymity provides an aural itch that you scratch when you remember the product with which the style is associated. The spots take the language of a performer and reduce it to two or three constituent elements; the result is that the performer's language—made of incipient clichés that, by means of a confrontation with a specific occasion of performance, are sometimes dissolved into an efflorescence that transcends cliché and extends language—is now reified into a single cliché hard enough to dominate any mere occasion. From now on, this is all the performer will have to say. His performance will communicate in terms of how well it approximates the reification of the commercial, not necessarily because the commercial will have been more widely or intensely heard than any other work by the performer (though it probably will have been), but because the commercial will now have completed—in fact, realized—the performer's career. When one hears an old Squeeze or Dave Edmunds record, it will sound like an attempt to formulate a cliché—to produce a style so recognizable and narrow that it can be marketed as an object, as a thing—which is what that record will have been.

7 ■ **Bob Dylan, "Silvio" (Columbia)** A tune by Robert Hunter, the Grateful Dead's writer, but the story isn't that the Dead rejected it first. The story is the arrangement, which goes back to Bill Haley for its suppression of elision or surprise. Dylan has always sung in country time, with an idiosyncrasy of rhythm and meter only certain musicians could keep up with: when he sings, he invents or he does nothing, but this is far less than nothing. "Silvio" suggests he has so little left of his style he couldn't even make a convincing Budweiser commercial—there's more musical freedom in the average Budweiser commercial than there is here. Dylan's music now has meaning only as neuroticism.

8–10 ■ **Larry Williams, "She Said 'Yeah'"** **(Specialty, '59)** I went into an oldies store looking for a copy of "Bony Moronie" and saw this on the flip of "Bad Boy." The clerk said it wasn't the same song the Rolling Stones used on *December's Children* in '65, but it was, and that made sense: the Beatles cut "Bad Boy," the Stones turn the record

over. But the change is curious. Williams enunciates clearly, almost trips over the broken beat, and takes 1:50 to make a nonevent out of a nonsong. Jagger takes a deep breath and spews; dropping the internal quotation marks, the band crashes through in 1:30, setting a personal speed record, and more or less accidentally leaving behind one of their five or six most exciting performances. The song is now even less of a song, but the nonevent becomes an event—which is why, more than two decades later, it can still overturn the numbers surrounding it on Pussy Galore's 1 Yr Live. There was, it turns out, a certain momentum built into that broken beat; absent either style or genre, it found a language and made history.

1 ■ **Prince, Lovesexy tour opening, Bercy, Paris (July 8)** A million-dollar set that does everything but shoot baskets into the on-stage hoop, enough hardware to fill two 747 cargo jets or 14 trucks, record-quality sound, the most sophisticated lighting in the history of mass entertainment, countless costume changes, skits, and dances in the course of a three-hour show, a nine-piece ensemble with every step blocked out, every gesture scripted, not a drop of sweat left to chance, the whole contained in one man's head, rehearsed past the point of role and into the theatrical realm where artifice and routine communicate as necessity and will, like a 50-year-old soul legend singing her greatest hit last week at the Lone Star with more passion than it brought from her when it topped out at number three in 1964—this is Prince in 1988.

The show is backed up musically, and it transcends itself when sound supersedes merely physical movement, merely electronic color; though people gasped at certain shifts in staging, this was the real shock. "When You Were Mine" caught it, opening on Prince's guitar with the heroic confusion of the first seconds of Claudine Clark's "Party Lights," but sustaining the excitement of that opening through three, five, six minutes, the guitar shaping the singing to ring changes of wit on regret, seduction on defeat, maturity on adolescence, blues on rock 'n' roll. It was one of those moments when, confronted with the distant figure on the stage, with the huge noise that years of concert-going cannot quite connect to the performer's body, you almost shudder at the reaction building inside you, asking, "Is this real? Is this happening?" You shut your eyes, trying to commit a thousand nuances to memory, but memory will barely hold a few—and you know that for all the rehearsals, all the effects, for every detail of the perfect script, the song can never be played precisely this way again. Like a fan who won't wash the hand that's touched the star, you're afraid to go to sleep, in fear of what you might forget.

2 ▪ Lee Maynard, *Crumb* (Washington Square paperback) Set in a nowhere West Virginia town a few years after the war, this novel about teenagers and sex could have been called "Country Without Music."

3 ▪ Terri Sutton, "Women in Rock—An Open Letter," *Puncture* #15) Why the Bangs (the Fucks) turned into the Bangles (the Glitter). "Biased critics aren't doing music reviewing. They're doing police work."

4 ▪ Reggie Jackson Chevrolet, (Berkeley, CA) In the showroom, the man's black-cherry '55 Bel Air and a bubbling Wurlitzer with pristine tone. Number one on the jukebox: Chuck Berry, "No Money Down."

5 ▪ Van Morrison & the Chieftains, *Irish Heartbeat* (Mercury) Not as good as *Into the Music*, but close.

6 ▪ Brian Wilson, *Brian Wilson* (Sire CD) The music is chirpy Beach-Boys Spector retread; the flat vocals grow flesh with every playing. But the sanctity of David Leaf's therapeutic liner notes (like that attending Patti Smith's gruesome "People Have the Power," or Tracy Chapman's stutters on "Fast Car") is disgusting. If you want Brian to get well, send him a get-well card: c/o Traubner and Flynn, 1849 Sawtelle Blvd., Suite 500, Los Angeles, CA 90025.

7 ▪ Happy Flowers, "They Cleaned Out My Cut With a WIRE BRUSH" (Homestead) Flipper lives.

8 ▪ Joe Higgs, *Family* (Shanachie) Cool walking.

9 ▪ Elvis Presley, for Blue Tana Lawn Shoes (advertisement in *Harpers & Queen*, London, June) "ABUNDANCE" it says, "by ELVIS PRESLEY." "Not a barn dance," it says. He's wearing blue and red "19th century floral design" shoes. They look great.

10 ▪ Pavel Büchler, *Untitled Portraits* (exhibition at Third Eye Centre, Glasgow, catalogue from Third Eye Centre, Glasgow, UK) Büchler takes a wire-service crowd photo, blows it up, and isolates various individuals: from dress and manner, the time seems to be the '50s, the place Europe. Close up, the now-huge wire-service dots print out into nearly complete abstraction; from a distance, each picture fingers a victim, matched in police files and then tracked, caught, and executed. Is the picture Büchler worked from specific, or could he have made a concert photo just as creepy?

SEPTEMBER 13, 1988

1 ▪ Muriel Gray, "Boxing Clever," interview by Alistar McKay in *Cut* (July) In Thatcherland you immediately notice a level of public discourse altogether different from our own. Despite the UK's lack of a Bill of Rights, the place has generated an intensity, a shamelessness, a sense of absolute stakes, that in the U.S. is muffled by calculation and strategy, by the realization that the American people are now an audience, not a polity: by the belief that Americans can now be addressed only through the sort of discourse that measures which sitcoms will stay on the air and which will get dumped. So it's a shock to pick up this Scottish culture magazine and read what Gray, a TV personality students recently elected rector, i.e., official spokesperson, of Edinburgh University, has to say. "If I could advise the Scottish people to do anything, I'd advise them to get down to the plant

where the *Sun* is printed and firebomb it. Seriously, if I had to have any terrorism in this country I would aim it at Murdoch. I'd like to see journalistic terrorism where they'd just keep setting fire to his newspaper printing plants, all over the country, all the time."

2 ▪ **Primitives, "Crash" (RCA)** A review of the band's album compared it favorably to a Peanut Butter Conspiracy LP—any one of which is a good bet for the worst psychedelic LP of the '60s—and that's what the Primitives *Lovely* is like. But their single, just now getting U.S. airplay after a few months floating around the margins, is the single of the year, guaranteed to sound as loud in 2005 as it would have in 1956.

3 ▪ **Brian Wilson, "Goodnight, Irene,"** from *Folkways: A Vision Shared—A Tribute to Woody Guthrie and Leadbelly* **(Columbia)** Irene becomes a California girl. This is what post-postmodernist critics would call "the music of transgression," if they could understand you can transgress to the right as well as to the left.

4 ▪ **Book of Love, "Lullaby," from** *Lullaby* **(Sire)** A tune to dream to—too good for sleep.

5 ▪ **John Mellencamp, "Rave On," from** *Cocktail* **(Elektra soundtrack)** A lot of Mellencamp falls between the tracks: acoustic B-sides, his grandmother warbling on *Scarecrow*, the heavenly "Colored Lights" he wrote and produced for the Blasters, and now this straight shot at Buddy Holly on an album filled up by hip, lousy artists.

6 ▪ **Philip Roth, *The Facts* (Farrar Straus)** There was more rock 'n' roll in Lyndon Johnson than in Bobby Kennedy; in this autobiography Roth, who in 1962 fashioned perhaps the most perfect integration of a rock song ("Earth Angel") into fiction (*Letting Go*), names Johnson the muse behind *Portnoy's Complaint*. As a book, *The Facts* is trivial; this claim is not.

7 ▪ **Aroma Disc, (Romance Division of Environmental Fragrance Technologies)** Lester Bangs once predicted rock would someday be no more than room spray; he couldn't have imagined records playing (on your special Aroma Disc Player) "Oriental Mystery," "Seduction," "Gourmet," "Candlelight Dinner," and "After Dinner Mint." But this isn't rock. Where's "Baby Let Me Bang Your Box," "Burn On," "Incense and Peppermints," "Hair Pie: Bake 1," or "Cold Sweat"? Not that it would make any difference.

8 ▪ **Joe Strummer, "The Return of Smokin' Joe," interview by Matthew Colin in** *Cut* **(July)** "I wish we hadn't taken it so seriously. . . . It said, 'Let's sweep away everything and start again,' but after a few years when all the old buzzards came back, it obviously hadn't swept away anything. It was a hiccup rather than a complete change." "Didn't you realise that was inevitable all along," says the recuperative voice of the interviewer. "Well, I should have. I'd seen all that before when I was taking my O levels, all that Vietnam protest stuff and Paris raging in '68 . . . then again, maybe we wouldn't have gotten into it without being so completely fanatical." The key word here is not "fanatical," it's "we."

9 ▪ **Pat Benatar, "All Fired Up" (Chrysalis)** In the sound and feel the record's reaching for, it's a lot like Patti Smith's "People Have the Power," and there's nothing to that record but its reach. But "All Fired Up" is twice as convincing, many times more exciting, and Benatar hasn't had a hit for years. How come no one's raving about *her* comeback?

10 ▪ **Albert Goldman, *The Lives of John Lennon* (Morrow)** Imagine it's all true; a lot of it is. Then connect the music to the truth. There you have a paradox, which the author doesn't want you to solve.

OCTOBER 4, 1988

1 ▪ **Randy Newman, "Dixie Flyer" and "New Orleans Wins the War" from** *Land of Dreams* **(Reprise)** Whether or not these songs are simple autobiography, they're presented as such, and for a man who's always sung as a character actor, it's a shock. As the tunes roll easily on a piano that communicates socially, that sets a mood of shopping,

banter, strolling, a mood so commonplace it validates every personal detail, Newman is singing about being Jewish in a gentile world, about late '40s racism as a natural fact, about the skewed, impossible, utterly concrete memories of childhood: his father coming back from the war to tell the people of New Orleans they'd won, and so sparking a citywide celebration—in 1948. "Maybe they'd heard it, maybe not," Newman remembers. "Probably they'd heard about it, just forgot"—and the way he sings the last two words of each line is as profound as anything in "Sail Away."

2 ■ **White of the Eye** (dir. Donald Cammell, Paramount video) For Cathy Moriarty, who uses obscenity with more conviction than anyone else in the movies.

3 ■ **Midnight Oil, "The Dead Heart"** (Columbia) The title plays against the singsong: "We carry in our hearts the true country/And that cannot be stolen." In other words, the country (in their case, Australia, and it doesn't matter that they're singing as Aborigines; in your case, as you listen, your country) is up for grabs. This band is not kidding—not, like others on the charts, making political music out of populist pieties. They're in the game for the wisdom their music can be made to give up.

4 ■ **The Sun** "STATUE OF ELVIS FOUND ON MARS—Satellite Beams Back 'All Shook Up'" (September 20) Let's see *Doonesbury* and *Bloom County* top that.

5 ■ Simon Frith, *Music for Pleasure—Essays in the Sociology of Pop* (Routledge) Eighties daily journalism and the footnoted scholarship it provoked: a collection in which each piece is engaged in a conversation with every other.

6 ■ Bo Diddley, *Bo Diddley's Beach Party* (Chess reissue, 1963, Japan) Recorded live in Myrtle Beach, South Carolina, when it cost a buck or two to get in. It costs $20 now, but if you were there, or ever wished you were, it might be worth it.

7 ■ **David Lindley & El Rayo-X, *Very Greasy*** (Elektra) Even the bad covers ("Papa Was a Rolling Stone," "Werewolves of London") echo the misanthropic wit (in the

singing) and the love of the world (the guitar playing) that made Lindley's 1981 *El Rayo-X* as personal in its way as *Astral Weeks*. Don't wait for the next one, David—the feeling is back, the momentum is there.

8 ■ **Four Tops, "Reach Out I'll Be There (Remix)"** (Motown '88/'66 12-inch) First, a remarkable atrocity: no crisp drum machine, no sharp synth sound, just poorly oiled disco machinery plugging on to nowhere, forever, a now-defeated Levi Stubbs reaching out to—his old song, maybe. But then, no doubt as a sop to moldy figs unhip to what the new breed breed, is the song as it hit number one 22 years ago, and in an instant, before the singing even begins, there's tension, drama, *suspense*. "I'm horny already," the woman next to me said.

9 ■ Gary Stewart, *Brand New* (Hightone) Drunk again, as he says, but the old stuff is fine, and what's new is "Lucretia," which owes more to Lynyrd Skynyrd's "That Smell" than to anything by George Jones or Jerry Lee Lewis.

10 ■ Sut Jhally and Ian Angus, "Introduction" to *Cultural Politics in Contemporary America* (Routledge) The editors of this wishfully "interventionist" academic anthology of no one's best work tip their hand straight off: dedication to Joe Hill, "genius of cultural politics," "Murdered by the Authorities of the State of Utah"; acknowledgement note re the "fruitful experience of collaborative work, which is at the very heart of socialist practice" (fascists always work alone, that's why they never get anywhere); the *"alternate* sphere" of cultural politics defined as "the 'sixties' tradition of Joe Hill, Woody Guthrie, Leadbelly, Joan Baez, Phil Ochs, the Weavers, Pete Seeger"—you know, all those people who later formed the Rolling Stones. But it's the discussion of Bruce Springsteen and John Lennon, "the two most important figures in mainstream culture, from a left perspective"—thank you—"in the last twenty years," that rings the bell: though Springsteen allowed people to misinterpret "Born in the U.S.A.," Lennon "suffered

from: no such ambiguity"—"there being no possible misunderstanding of his art." Forget that when there is no possibility of misunderstanding, there is no art—the privileging of Lennon leads straight to a bemoaning of the fact that "in the postmodern context," even Lennon's "Revolution" can be turned into a commercial and stripped of its revolutionary message, which of course it never had, since the song was against revolution, not for it. Well, socialist realists never did know what to make of rock 'n' roll ("it is too early, or too late, to throw out Pete Seeger," Jhally and Angus say, summing up), though rock 'n' roll has always known what to make of them.

NOVEMBER 1, 1988

1 ▪ **Shinehead, *Unity* (Elektra)** As a Jamaican toaster in a hip-hop milieu he's a motormouth, and as a motormouth he's a Porsche: words tumble by so fast it's a thrill not to keep up. He's also a joker, he wants to know what's so funny about peace, love, and understanding, and as a ballad singer ("Golden Touch"), he's Shep and the Limelights.

2 ▪ **Quartzlock, "No Regrets" (Reflection/Pinnacle 12-inch, UK)** Aerobic disco, with a thick, exuberant sound—and a showcase for an unnamed female singer. She might be Tina Turner recording for Motown in 1966: her voice is all pleasure, warmth, knowledge.

3 ▪ **King Butcher, "Spud-U-Like" (King 12-inch)** Jon King (late of Gang of Four) resurfaces with new partner Phil Butcher and a cutting, expert noise based on "One Potato, Two Potato." Songs should follow.

4 ▪ **Nigel Fountain, *Underground—The London Alternative Press, 1966–74* (Comedia/Routledge) and Jonathon Green: *Days in the Life—Voices From the English Underground, 1961–1971* (Heinemann, London)** Two good books—Green's a long, hundred-headed oral history set without commentary in the manner of *Edie*, Fountain's a conventional narrative. The adventure and cruelty of the time come through, especially

in Green, but what's odd is the unity of the story. "[It was] as if we had rubber bands stretched all over England and we could just pull one," Spike Hawkins says in Green of the first stirrings of new culture—yet both books are fundamentally about the same small group of people, the same few legendary scenes, events, pranks, and disasters. The books make it plain how much a small group of people can do—or how small the U.K. really is.

5 ▪ **Keith Richards, *Saturday Night Live* (NBC, October 8)** Mesmerizing, the way tricky melodies slowly crept out of the blur of rhythm and rasp; as for *Talk Is Cheap* (Virgin), a few numbers suggest a tune you heard on the radio once, 10 years ago, forgot the next day, and spent the next decade trying to remember.

6 ▪ **Michael Cormany, *Lost Daughter*, a detective novel (Lyle Stuart)** New twist on generically requisite cop/dick banter: "He picked at the cassettes on the seat between us. 'Replacements? Hüsker Dü?' He pronounced it Husker instead of Hoosker. I let it go."

7 ▪ **Abiezer Coppe, *Selected Writings* (Aporia Press, London)** Coppe was a Ranter preacher who with the fantastic *A Fiery Flying Roll* (1649) defined the limits of heresy during the English Revolution; the still-shocking tones of his blasphemies precisely capture the mood Johnny Rotten brought to bear in "Anarchy in the U.K."—which is why Coppe is now back in print.

8 ▪ **Susan Sontag, *Time* profile (October 24)** Preview of the coming cultural inquisition: "As for equating high and popular culture, she explains: 'I made a few jolly references to things in popular culture that I enjoyed. I said, for instance, one could enjoy both Jasper Johns and the Supremes. It isn't as if I wrote an essay on the Supremes.'"

9 ▪ **Cellos, *Rang Tang Ding Dong* (Apollo/Relic reissue, 1957–58)** Remembered only for their Mr. Bass-man-goes-to-Heaven classic, "Rang Tang Ding Dong (I Am the Japanese Sandman)"—and arcanely notable because the young engineer who discovered them, one Lewis Merenstein, went on to produce

Van Morrison's *Astral Weeks*. Who says there're no second acts in American lives?

10 ■ Julie Burchill, "Burchill on Thatcher" (*The Face*, September) In this short, sharp celebration ("there is really no alternative") of the *Führerprinzip* (sorry, Julie—it means leadership as the first principle of national life, which is exactly what you're talking about), the former punk critic and present-day media icon comes up with a snappy line: "Voting for [Thatcher] was like buying a Vera Lynn LP, getting it home and finding 'Never Mind the Bollocks' inside the red, white and blue sleeve." Except that one was singing about liberation, one about domination; one offering the paradoxes of "Bodies," the other the straight lines of Section 28. With the chant of "10 MORE YEARS!" rising, Burchill has her bread buttered.

NOVEMBER 29, 1988

1 ■ Randy Newman, "It's Money That Matters" (Reprise) Every review of Newman's *Land of Dreams* has made a point of dismissing this track as a rewrite of the '83 "It's Money That I Love." But at No. 70 with a small caliber bullet it's a radio natural—and it's a thrill to hear Newman working in an entirely commercial musical context, his voice mixed down, the harsh guitar guiding the car through traffic, the big beat always demanding more volume. In this context, and in the context of this historical moment, the song reveals itself: it's nothing like the other one. That was a joke, and this is not. This is painful, a no, a dead horse come to life and prancing: a protest song.

2 ■ Art of Noise featuring Tom Jones, "Kiss" (Polydor/China 12-inch) First Duane Eddy, now this—who's next, Connie Francis? Weighting the tempo with his own bulk, Jones comes up with a bullish, completely convincing performance, especially when he announces "Think I'd better *dance*, now" as if he's just remembered he's always wanted to be James Brown.

3 ■ Daniel Johnston, *Hi, How Are You— The Unfinished Album, Sept 83* (Homestead) Originally launched into the ether as one of Austin songwriter Johnston's various homemade cassettes, 10 years ago this would have sounded almost obvious. "Suddenly we could do anything," the motto of *Streets*, the first U.K. collection of punk singles, meant that suddenly you could hear anything; now the insistent individuality of Johnston's half-songs, orchestrated through found noise and found cadences, communicates weirdness, not speech, privacy, not a public space. Someone actually made this, with the idea that someone else would actually listen to it? When I try to picture the singer all I see is the puff-cheeked woman who lives in the radiator in *Eraserhead*.

4 ■ Five Satins, "In the Still of the Nite," in *Dead Ringers*, dir. David Cronenberg (Fox Pictures) In the shiny, ultrasuede apartment shared by the twin gynecologists Jeremy Irons plays, the one currently clinging to sanity puts a record on their $10,000 stereo; the other rises, and together they drape themselves around the first man's girlfriend. The pristine clarity of the sound and the desire it carries nearly makes the scene a match for the black hole "In Dreams" digs in *Blue Velvet*—the tune throws the whole movie off kilter, raising the specter of a life neither man has ever touched.

5 ■ Richard Thompson, "Turning of the Tide," on *Amnesia* (Capitol) Just a run-through, an attempt to teach the number to the band, and it opens up a sense of fate and dread everything else here seems to cover up with good humor and fast fingers. By the way, what's Christopher Reeve doing on the sleeve?

6 ■ Pet Shop Boys, "Always On My Mind," on *Introspection* (Manhattan) A nine-minute remake of their worldwide smash remake of the old Elvis hit—this time done as Elvis would have done it in Las Vegas, the orchestra up there sawing away, the female chorus washing up through the strings. It's all in place, except for the disruption of the drum machine and the wrong singer, who for a spoken passage has his thin voice twisted from near-Chipmunks levels down to 16 rpm bass, and then comes back as a real person full of bile and revenge. Neat.

7 ▪ **Lloyd Bentsen, Springsteen quote, campaign speech (November 7)** "No retreat, baby, no surrender," he said. Credit him for not backing off from "baby."

8 ▪ **Eskimo, song title (unrecorded)** As in "An Historical Perspective, or, Neil Sedaka Never Instituted Fascist Policies." Which is right up there with "Neil Sedaka, Horseman of the Apocalypse," a chapter title in Richard Meltzer's *Gulcher.*

9 ▪ **Traveling Wilburys, *Volume One* (Wilbury/Warner Bros.)** A/k/a Roy Orbison, George Harrison, Tom Petty, Jeff Lynne, and Bob Dylan, and not bad, even if the Masked Marauders (Dylan, Mick Jagger, Paul McCartney, John Lennon, and Chuck Berry) had more fun with the concept—Dylan's "Tweeter and the Monkey Man" is the first piece he's cut in ages that sounds as if he's having fun with words and music.

10 ▪ **John Carpenter, *They Live* (Universal Pictures)** As critic Michael Covino put it, an E.C. comics version of *The Society of the Spectacle.*

DECEMBER 27, 1988

1 ▪ **Cowboy Junkies, *The Trinity Session* (RCA)** Don't be fooled by the punk name or the "Sweet Jane" cover—or for that matter the "Sweet Jane" endorsement by Lou Reed. Margo Timmins has the pristine voice of so many early '60s Joan Baez imitators, a timbre wholly uncorrupted by personality. Beginning with an insufferable a cappella reading of the traditional ballad "Mining for Gold," she turns the wretched of the earth into art (to borrow a phrase from Alice Walker): in the matrix of Timmins's sensibility that's all the redemption the wretched need. The folk-music revival has got to be stopped before all ambitious pop music dissolves into a contemplation of its own piety. There's no better place for it to stop than here.

2 ▪ **Johnny Winter, "Stranger Blues," from *The Winter of '88* (MCA)** The Elmore James tune, and an overdue reminder that the '69 *Second Winter* remains one of the most exciting claims anyone has made on the rock tradition. With drums and bass behind him, Winter jumps his sinewy, snaking lines across the piece, refusing, as he did on *Second Winter*, both Clapton elegance and Hendrix grandeur. What you hear is smash, twist, high-stepping, every riff cutting itself short and then leaping forward. The pleasure is in the tension: knowing everything will turn out alright, as the guitarist scares you into sensing it just might not.

3 ▪ **Herman's Hermits, "I'm Into Something Good," in *The Naked Gun* (Paramount)** Postmod self-referentiality in a great trash film: after the song plays behind a falling-in-love sequence, its MTV credit appears on the screen.

4 ▪ **Herschel B. Chipp, *Picasso's Guernica— History, Transformations, Meanings* (California)** Someday, when a writer has had the time to live with the right disc as long as Chipp has lived with *Guernica*, I'd like to read a book about a single record as vitally detailed, as richly contextualized, as completely realized, as this book about a single painting. Submit titles and rationales now; the winner runs here, and the prize is a copy of Chipp—a good deal, since it goes for $37.50.

5 ▪ **Jewels, "Hearts of Stone," from *Oldies But Goodies* Vol. 5 (Original Sound reissue, 1955)** The LP itself is ancient; the cut sounds new. Still unknown compared to the hit version made in the same year by Otis Williams and the Charms, this L.A. doo-wop explosion sums up the freedom unleashed in the first flush of rock 'n' roll, and proves that the music was anything but a linear development out of r&b (even if "R&B" was the name of the label on which the Jewels' record was originally released). In the unstable chanting of the chorus you can hear the thrill of making secret music public, and also the thrill of discovering that such an act makes old secrets ("BADDA WADDA BADDA WAH," in this case) into a language not even the singers can under-

stand. The momentum is so strong, and so confused, you can't believe there's an ending to it, and when the performance does end, there's only one appropriate reaction: disbelief. Disbelief that it ended, and disbelief that it ever began.

6 ■ Emily Listfield, *It Was Gonna Be Like Paris* (Bantam reprint, 1984) Cool and touching—a Downtown novel already looking back to a time "when punk was punk."

7 ■ Michael Barson, *Lost, Lonely, & Vicious—Postcards From the Great Trash Films* (Pantheon) Old movie posters, topped by Roger Corman's '58 *Teenage Caveman* ("PREHISTORIC REBELS against PREHISTORIC MONSTERS"), featuring Robert Vaughn, looking at least 35, drawing his bow against some kind of swamp thing, which presumably represents his father. He can't really be rebelling against dinosaurs, can he?

8 ■ *Almost Grown,* premiere (CBS, November 27) This generational drama (the generation being the one supposed to respond to rock-sourced commercials) kicks off in 1962, though the dialogue says it's 1988: "Gimme a break," says one character. "I'm outta here," says another. While nobody says "It's history," there's a moment where the marketing strategy is coded into the storyline—thus rewriting history as mere hindsight, sealing the superiority of the present over the past. "Turn it down," Dad says over James Brown. His teenage son doesn't sulk, or run away, or get his bow out of the closet: he makes a rational argument. "Dad, it's a *force*. Rock 'n' roll could even become like—a huge business!" Dad: "Son, in this country, it doesn't mean anything unless it can sell products. Can you imagine this stuff selling cars?"

9 ■ Bangles, "In Your Room" (Columbia) Sexy, if you're a 16-year-old boy, or ever were.

10 ■ *All Things Considered,* segment on the death of Roy Orbison (National Public Radio, December 7) Here's a man whose music has never left the radio, who's in the midst of a major comeback, and on the day the news breaks only this station, of all

those monitored by a select group of dumbfounded listeners, bothered to follow the announcement with a song.

1 ■ Donald Hall, "Prophecy," from *The One Day* (Ticknor & Fields) The voice in this section of Hall's great book-length poem ("Your children will wander looting the shopping malls/for forty years, suffering from your idleness,/until the last dwarf body rots in a parking lot . . . the sky will disappear like a scroll rolled up") shares cadences Bob Dylan once used, and Johnny Rotten and Grandmaster Flash and in his yea-saying way even Chuck Berry. Like them, Hall-as-Isaiah is all too conscious of the absurdity of his powerless, fire-bringing voice, and like them he triumphs over that absurdity by merging his love of language with a loathing only language can make real, defining what rock 'n' roll no longer dares to say.

2 ■ Keith Richards, Henry J. Kaiser Auditorium, Oakland (December 13) Utterly personal in sound and feeling, with a stretched, uncertain sense of determination focusing guitar lines, melodies, words, vocal textures, the songs from *Talk Is Cheap* were in every case more unsettling, more exciting, than the Stones tunes Richards chose: "I Wanna Be Your Man," "Connection," "Time Is on My Side."

3 ■ Jane Kramer, "Letter from Europe" (*New Yorker,* November 28) Fans of Missing Foundation should note this cool and disturbing report on bohemia armed: the post-'60s, postpunk antimovement Autonomen as a ruling force in the Kreuzberg section of West Berlin. If the boys and girls in Godard's *Masculin-Féminin* were the children of Marx and Coca-Cola, the people Kramer writes about are the children of Fassbinder and amphetamine, except that they're not children.

4 ■ Don Julian and the Meadowlarks, et al., *The Dootone Story Volume One* (Ace reissue, '55–'61, UK) Regarding Vernon Green, lead singer of the Medallions, the

strangest doo-wop group to come out of Los Angeles or anywhere else (represented here not by their hit, "The Letter," but by its flip, "Buick '59," recorded 1954—Green chose the title because he thought it would keep the disc "current for at least five years"): "a polio victim . . . [he] attributed his musical ambition to a time in 1945 when Franklin D. Roosevelt, himself a survivor of polio, visited Green's crippled children's school and presented him with a set of leg braces. 'It was then I realized I could be somebody important,' Green said." He's still performing, as is, amazingly, almost every other principal musician featured on this good record.

5 ▪ Joel Whitburn, *Top R&B Singles 1942–1988* (Record Research) More than ever before, the numbers tell stories.

6 ▪ Richard Huelsenbeck, "Four Poems from *Phantastische Gebete*" (Fantastic Prayers), on *Audio by Visual Artists* (Tellus Audio Cassette Magazine No. 21) Park Avenue psychoanalyst, Berlin dadaist, and co-founder of the Cabaret Voltaire in 1916 in Zurich (where these poems were composed; they were recorded in New York in '67), Huelsenbeck was not a visual artist. More than any of his dada comrades he was a "bruitist," a noisemaker, and more so in his dada manifestos and histories than in his occasional poems. There's little of his mad-dog spirit left in this reading, but a bit in the contributions of some of the tape's other 29 performers. Top cut: Joseph Beuys's '70 "Ja Ja Ja Ne Ne Ne."

7 ▪ Peppermint Harris, et al., *'Black' Rock 'n' Roll* (Savage Kick) Hear black singers get just as confused by Little Richard as country singers did.

8 ▪ "Quarrymen," *Quarrymen Rehearse With Stu Sutcliffe Spring 1960* (Pre-Beatle bootleg) Possibly. Also possibly outtakes from *Let It Be*.

9 ▪ Nancy J. Holland, "Purple Passion: Images of Female Desire in 'When Doves Cry,'" in *Cultural Critique* #10, Fall 1988 "Textuality is all you really need," is Holland's punning motto, and her reading doesn't betray her text. But watch out for "Rock Music and the State: Dissonance or Coun-

terpoint?" by Katrina Irving, who doesn't understand the meaning of the word "state," let alone "rock."

10 ▪ "Louie," *Louie's Limbo Lounge (Las Vegas Grind Vol. 2)* (Strip) Preternaturally crude and worthless go-go rock recorded at a syphilitic dive ("Featuring the world's loveliest buxotics!") between '55 and '65. It's a version of the primeval sink from which sometimes emerge crazed masterpieces— the chord changes in Art Roberts's "Give Her the Axe, Max!" might be signals from outer space—though not this time. Still, there is "Louie Oversees a Recording Session With One of His Artists"—that being "Wiggles," a "retired burlesque singer" an armed Louie shoots halfway through the date because "Wiggles," who according to the liner photos was Adlai Stevenson, sings too clearly.

FEBRUARY 21, 1989

1 ▪ Elvis Costello, "Tramp the Dirt Down," from *Spike* (Warner Bros.) This ode to the death of Margaret Thatcher— Costello names her—recalls his "Pills and Soap," "Little Palaces," and "Sleep of the Just" in its arrangement. Anchored in regret and hatred, it also begins in Bob Dylan's "Masters of War," "With God on Our Side," and "The Lonesome Death of Hattie Carroll." There's a lot of death here, in the deliberate cadence of the first verse, in the rage that follows, in the way Costello forms the words "cheap," "maimed," "pitiful," and especially the phrase "subtle difference"— the "subtle difference," in Thatcher's England, "between justice and contempt." To make true political music, you have to say what decent people don't want to hear; that's something that people fit for satellite benefit concerts will never understand, and that Costello understood before anyone heard his name.

2 ▪ Ciccone Youth, *The Whitey Album* (Blast First/Enigma) More fun than their cover of the White Album would ever have been—and, finally, Kim Gordon's show, from the bad-dream "G-Force" (hers, yours)

to a version of "Addicted to Love" that makes slick pop into everyday speech and, after all his worthless years, really ought to send Robert Palmer back where he came from.

3 ▪ Drifters, *Let the Boogie-Woogie Roll: Greatest Hits 1953–1958* (Atlantic CD) Forty cuts to match the label's 40th anniversary, mostly the ethereal, playful, deep soul meanders of Clyde McPhatter, but highlights too from Gerhart Thrasher: "Your Promise To Be Mine," pressing hard, histrionic, almost a threat. With the first notes of McPhatter's "Lucille," the opening cut here, an obscure B-side, the intensity, the directness of feeling, is staggering, and you don't know where it comes from—it's as if centuries of emotion could be called up and shaped at will. You can hear the Orioles, and also Hoagy Carmichael, a hint of Fred Astaire, more of Billie Holiday. Making McPhatter into an actor in plays of his own device, the CD sound is perfect for the ballads; with the big tempo numbers, "Money Honey" and "What'cha Gonna Do," it can't find the rock. But you can find the big tempo numbers anywhere else.

4 ▪ James C. Faris, "Comment on 'The Origins of Image Making' by Whitney Davis" (*Current Anthropology*, June 1986) "Can we predict from Davis's generative approach the images that came to characterize the Upper Paleolithic? Why *these* images rather than others . . . ? Nor will this approach to capacities account, in any non-trivial sense, for fascism, belief in afterlife, the periodic table, rock and roll, or the incest prohibition." And they said it wasn't world-historical.

5 ▪ When People Were Shorter and Lived Near the Water, *Timothy* (Shimmy Disc) A triumphant cacophony riding an against-all-odds melody, the last sound you hear before every barrier falls and liberty reigns forever—and an oddity on an EP that includes covers of Herb Alpert's "This Guy's in Love With You" (1968), Eric Burdon's "Girl Named Sandoz" (1967), and the Singing Nun's "Dominique" (1963), all of which are better remembered than the Buoys' "Timothy" (1971).

6 ▪ Alphaville, *The Singles Collection* (Atlantic) "Big in Japan" is still chilling; the fast mix of "Forever Young" is still the best Eurodisco ever made.

7 ▪ David Feldman, "Astonishing Similarities Between the Death of Elvis Presley and the Death of John F. Kennedy," (Alex Bennett Show, January 24, KITS-FM, San Francisco) Not that astonishing: "Presley slept with Priscilla Presley; *Kennedy* slept with Priscilla Presley . . ."

8 ▪ Marshall Berman, "Why Modernism Matters" (*Tikkun*, January/February) And why postmodernism never did.

9 ▪ Fall, "Kurious Oranj" (BMG/Beggars Banquet) Pointlessness as its own reward.

10 ▪ Lee Atwater, Bo Diddley, Willie Dixon, Percy Sledge, et al., "Celebration for Young Americans" (George Bush inaugural, January 21) In which, led on guitar by the chairman of the GOP national committee, various black Americans took the stage to validate the institutionalization of their exclusion from their own society, simultaneously suggesting that political parties will soon sign up musicians just like corporations do. Best commentary: John Rockwell, *New York Times* (January 22); Ed Ward, *Austin Chronicle* ("The Ward Report," January 20); and Thomas Schlegel, in a letter to the *San Francisco Chronicle* (February 2): "According to Atwater, 'There is a place for black people in the Republican Party' . . . the same place that has been offered by the white establishment since Reconstruction, singing and dancing for the rich and scaring poor whites at election time."

MARCH 31, 1989

1 ▪ Fine Young Cannibals, "She Drives Me Crazy" (I.R.S. 12-inch) General Johnson ("It Will Stand," with the Showmen, "Give Me Just a Little More Time," with the Chairmen of the Board) fronting Hot Chocolate ("You Sexy Thing," "Every 1's a Winner")—well, not exactly, but they have HC's feel for rhythms that disguise their hardness, and like GJ Roland Gift has a

voice so determinedly eccentric he could never be mistaken for anyone else. This moves slowly, all muscle, until after a minute or two every change signals a release that Gift always returns to half-deny, a sweetness he can't accept. There are more words to this song than "She drives me crazy [doot-doot]/Like no one else/She drives me crazy [doot-doot]/And I can't help myself," but there don't seem to be, and there don't have to be.

2 ▪ Elvis Costello, **"Leave My Kitten Alone," on** *Late Night* **(NBC, March 3)** Who else would be so unprofessional as to waste three minutes of network time with a Little Willie John tune when he could have been advertising his new single? Who else would be so professional as to respond to "How do you write your songs?" with an answer that nailed a *Spike* track in your mind more surely than the song itself?

3 ▪ Saints, **"Grain of Sand," on** *Prodigal Son* **(Mushroom/TVT)** A new wrinkle on Demosthenes: after 12 years, Chris Bailey sings as if that sand is in his throat, as if singing is the only way to keep it from turning into a pearl. He was a punk, after all.

4 ▪ Chuck Russell, director, *The Blob* **(RCA-Columbia video)** For the scene where the yo-yo spinning projectionist gets blobbed. Someone comes into the booth to find out why the film has broken, then he looks up at the ceiling and sees a hideous face screaming silently out of the slime—and the yo-yo, dangling from what used to be a hand, still running up and down, perfectly.

5 ▪ Henry S. Kariel, *The Desperate Politics of Postmodernism* **(Massachusetts paperback)** Most books with "postmodernism" in their title are once-removed frog-speak: Americans trying to squeeze a drop of insight or prestige not out of the world but out of Lyotard or Baudrillard, and with all the charge of a bad game of Scrabble. Kariel, of the University of Hawaii, writes in his own voice, and the desperate politics of his title are his politics. His arguments seek a thin cultural margin where he believes the possibilities for new kinds of speech and action

are still alive. Whether or not Laurie Anderson, among others he talks about, is mapping that line, this book, as Charles Perry once wrote about what I don't remember, is like finding a hamburger in a medicine cabinet.

6 ▪ Eddie Murphy, producer, Thomas Schlamme, director, *What's Alan Watching?*, pilot **(CBS, February 27)** Alan is a teenager with a TV in his room; the show is based on the premise that changing channels is the primary cultural—no, social—experience of our time. Of all the wonders Alan turned up this night, most bizarre was footage on James Brown's incarceration: not, it seemed, as news, but as instant movie-of-the-week. Murphy played Brown, of course (also a "Free James Brown" James Brown clone); the bit was shocking both as a violation of decency and as a violation of media temporality. Alan didn't seem to know who James Brown was; I can't wait to see how *Almost Grown* follows up. On TV, generational fiction is now the milieu that counts; any real TV movie on James Brown is already irrelevant.

7 ▪ Tone-Loc, **"Funky Cold Medina," on** *Loc-ed After Dark* **(Delicious Vinyl/Island)** There's more to this L.A. rapper than "Wild Thing." His timbre is odd, and it can tell a story.

8 ▪ Bobbie Ann Mason, *Love Life—Stories* **(Harper & Row)** Tales of mall-dwellers, in which changing channels is only apparently the primary social experience of our time.

9 ▪ Johnny O, **"Fantasy Girl" (Micmac 12-inch)** Dream lover, where are you?

10 ▪ Jerry Garcia, guitar on **"Slow Train," on** *Dylan and the Dead* **(Columbia)** This is a horrible album. When "All Along the Watchtower" starts, even though the backing is country-thin (listen to what the Band did with it on *Before the Flood*), you think the melody is so dramatic nothing could break it; then Dylan, sounding too much like Elvis in his final "Are You Lonesome Tonight?," does the impossible. But there's an uncanny splendor in Garcia's rote "Slow Train" break; I know I'll never play the rec-

ord again to hear it, and smile every time the radio gives it back.

1 ▪ Gérard de Thame, video for Tanita Tikaram's "Twist in My Sobriety" (Warner Bros) On record, the number is an elliptical folkie conceit, and the seductiveness of the piece dries up before it's over. The video makes the song rich, confusing, scary. In a green-yellow wash over black-and-white footage of Mayan peasants smiling (Guatemalan peasants? Mexican? Hollywood extras?), or standing in mud—the mud crusting around their feet like leprosy—or staring straight ahead as if the only thing to do about death squads is wait for them, a view from the inside of a battered worker's car focuses on a revolver dangling from the rearview mirror. "Twist in My Sobriety," Tikaram sings again and again—what does it mean? A break with the monotony of ordinary life, she says in an interview, which doesn't speak for the people you're watching. Or does it? The phrase rises out of the video, malevolent and impenetrable, on MTV destroying everything around it, except for Metallica's "One."

2 ▪ Guadalcanal Diary, "Always Saturday" (Elektra) "I want to live where it's always the same . . . I wish I lived in a shopping mall"; it's the Beach Boys in hell, "I Get Around" as "I Don't Wanna Get Around." "So many choices, it's not fair/I hop in the car, and I just sit/There." The melody snaps, the performance seems to have no real stops in it, the sound is irresistible; you resist the message before you've quite grasped it. The strategy is old, and it will never wear out: take a negative idea and put it across with all the positive energy you can.

3 ▪ Janice Benally, Harman Yellowman, Toby Topaha, et al., "I Think We're Alone Now," theme from *Have You Ever Seen a Rainbow at Midnight?*, video on Navajo children's art by Bruce Huck (Wheelwright Museum of the American Indian, Santa Fe, New Mexico) The kids in Huck's class made good art;

what I can't get out of my mind are the harmonies they put on the old Tiffany song.

4 ▪ Joe Grushecky and the Houserockers, *Rock and Real* (Rounder CD) Bleeding-heart, guitar-led small-combo rock from the man whose Iron City Houserockers made the best mainstream rock 'n' roll of the early '80s with *Have a Good Time But Get Out Alive*. This isn't on that level, but "Freedom's Heart" and "How Long" (with the only good lyrics anyone's produced on the Iran-contra crimes) say the next one might be. For there to be a next one a few people will have to buy this one.

5 ▪ Monotones, "Book of Love" on *The Newlywed Game* (Barris Entertainment) Intro: in a montage of ancient photos of just-marrieds, the lips of the frozen brides and grooms mouth the song like a Terry Gilliam *Monty Python* mock-up.

6 ▪ Minneapolis Institute of the Arts, "SEE THE REVOLUTIONARY WORKS OF A '60s RADICAL" (ad copy for *Courbet Reconsidered*) "He was a firebrand, assailed by critics as an upstart in muddy boots. He was a rebel who challenged the preconceptions of the '50s establishment, leading his radical movement into the '60s. The 1860s."

7 ▪ James Brown, "I Got You (I Feel Good)" (wake-up call, *Discovery* space shuttle, March 14) Did JB?

8 ▪ Nick Kent, "Roy Orbison: *The Face* Interview" (*The Face*, February) "I first saw Elvis live in '54. It was at the Big D Jamboree in Dallas and first thing, he came out and spat on the stage. . . . It affected me exactly the same way as when I first saw that David Lynch film. I didn't know what to make of it. There was just no reference point in the culture to compare it."

9 ▪ Elvis Costello, "You're No Good" on "Veronica" maxi-single (Warner Bros. four-track CD) Maybe the dank, drum-machined version of the Linda Ronstadt hit was vengeful payback for the guilt Costello felt collecting checks for the Ronstadt covers he says he hated; that's what it was on the radio. My CD had an apparently jokey opening: a few seconds of "Whole Lotta Love." But the tune went on to its conclusion, to be followed by "Rock & Roll," which was followed by . . . a whole disc's worth of the best of Led Zeppelin. So much for futurism.

10 ■ **Untouchables, "Agent Double O Soul" (Twist/Restless)** Not as good as Edwin Starr's '65 original, better than the last nine James Bond movies.

MAY 30, 1989

1 ■ **Chet Baker, *Chet Baker sings and plays from the film "Let's Get Lost"* (RCA)** For a listener who knows nothing about jazz, Baker's art was in his face: the way the golden boy pan of the '50s already implied the lizard grimace of the '70s and '80s, the way the junkie ruin still contained what was destroyed. That double reflection is one of the stories told in Baker's singing on these nine end-of-the-road tracks: a caress, beautiful and revolting, a spider kiss. The only tune that doesn't hurt is Elvis Costello's "Almost Blue"; it's as if Baker had to live with a song for an age before he could bring it to life.

2 ■ **Madonna, "Like a Prayer" video (MTV)** Her defenders ought to stop pretending this isn't blasphemous; of course it is, at least according to the strictures of any above-ground Christian sect. What's "like" a prayer here is like the sensuality of pissing drunk as caught in Henry Bean's novel *False Match* ("the closest I ever came to prayer," says the narrator): it's sex, specifically Madonna's fantasy of resurrecting Jesus by taking him into her mouth. Probably Salman Rushdie would understand; I imagine him somewhere in England, bent over his desk, an I AM MADONNA button pinned to his lapel.

3 ■ **Pauline Kael, *Hooked* (Dutton)** On *Something Wild*: "The movie gives you the feeling you sometimes get when you're driving across the country listening to a terrific new tape, and out of nowhere you pull into a truck-stop and the jukebox is playing the same song."

4 ■ **Mark Ribowsky, *He's a Rebel: The Truth About Phil Spector—Rock and Roll's Leg-**

endary Madman **(Dutton)** Nothing like the whole truth, but some strong lines, the worst high school reunion story you've ever heard, and good depth perception, as in Teddy Bear Marshall Lieb's analysis of the Wall of Sound: "It was more air than sound."

5 ■ **Stan Ridgway, "Goin' Southbound," on *Mosquitos* (Geffen)** Ridgway has a way of twisting his voice around a lyric as if the effort is the only way to dull a toothache; this cut lets you hear more twist than effort, which is to say, mannerism.

6 ■ **Frank Zappa & Captain Beefheart, *Bongo Fury—Live in Concert at Armadillo World Headquarters, Austin, Texas, May 20th & 21st, 1975* (Rykodisc CD)** Beefheart sings like his clothes are unraveling; then Zappa takes out the trash.

7 ■ **Jon Wozencroft, *The Graphic Language of Neville Brody* (Rizzoli)** This premature enshrining of the 31-year-old UK designer, celebrated for his album jackets and alphabets, catches Brody's perspicacity, from his words on Andy Warhol ("his art was subversive for about fifteen minutes") to handwritten restaurant menus ("Distant utopias. It's also a class distance, it's offering the promise that for a short period of time you can be 'one of us'"). Most striking is the way his record work signifies a transfer of unfettered, world-historical design (the sense that the future is riding on the success or failure of a design) from books to records. In the '20s and '30s, John Heartfield, Vavara Stepanova (see Alexander Lavrentiev, *Vavara Stepanoua*, MIT), and other Europeans made books explode out of their covers, turning them into objects that almost talked like people, or nations, or events, or history as such. Brody doesn't do that, but sometimes he seems to be trying.

8 ■ **Marc Eliot, *Rockonomics—The Money Behind the Music* (Franklin Watts)** "Nowhere," Eliot writes in this shocking exposé, which comes in a first printing of 50,000 copies, most of which will soon be selling for $4.95, "was there any obvious R&B influence or direction in Elvis's career. Whenever he was asked about how he developed

his singing style, he was always careful to
avoid any mention of black music."

9 ■ Ex, *Aural Guerrilla* (Homestead)
One of the atrocity posters included with
this Test Department-does-it-better noise 'n'
politics LP matches photos of people being
marched off under guard: "GERMANY—'44"
paired with "ISRAEL—'88." That the first
shot (which looks more like '39 than '44, but
the two sets of double digits make the point
more neatly, so what the hell) is of Jews being marched to extermination and the second is of Palestinians being marched to
detention or brutalization is the kind of political distinction the Ex's noise so blithely
transcends.

10 ■ Moonglows, "Come Back Baby"
(presumed title) Heard this on NPR: sounds
like a house party. Can't find it. Reward.

JUNE 20, 1989

Zero "By 3:15 a.m., students, chanting,
'Fascist, fasbeast, beast,' faced a line of helmeted soldiers sitting in the street in front
of the Museum of Revolutionary History.

"Suddenly, a woman of about 20, wearing a light-colored summer dress, jumped
up from her place on the ground, and ran
toward the soldiers, her arms in the air. She
was followed by about six more students. All
were cut down by bullets."—Mary Ganz,
San Francisco *Examiner*, Beijing, June 4

JULY 18, 1989

1 ■ Pulnoc, tape of performance at the
Kennel Club, San Francisco (May 5; thanks to
Adam Block) The Czech band, leavings of
the Plastic People: in "Dopis" (Letter)—in
the slow pace, in the way the group shifts
lyrical readymades into mysticism—there's
a hint of Joseph Skvorecky's "Emöke" from
The Bass Saxophone, the tale of a Hungarian woman who somehow contains an in-
eradicably pagan, pre-Christian soul. That
sense of the ineradicable may be at the root
of the current rediscovery of free speech in
parts of Central and Eastern Europe; to
Westerners it may sound like resurgent nationalism, but if it is, "Dopis" says we
haven't begun to understand the borderless-
ness of the idea.

2 ■ My Sin, "My Sin" (Endless Music cassette single) A one-man "not a BAND but a
living breathing thing" takes a buttoned-up
suburban gospel singer off the radio, adds
synthesized drums, bass, and a terrific, rising guitar line that turns the singer into an
avatar; Jimmy Swaggart enters, preaching,
his every line followed by a pounding Spanish translator; then the not-a-BAND jumps
on the vocals and matches Swaggart's fervor—no easy trick. It's the best single of the
half-year; the sleeve art (or whatever you
call it on a cassette) won't be topped.

"Zero" (AP/Wide World)

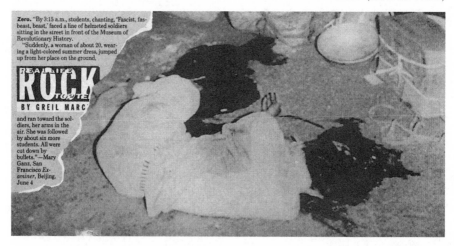

Zero. "By 3:15 a.m., students, chanting, 'Fascist, fasbeast, beast,' faced a line of helmeted soldiers
sitting in the street in front of the Museum of
Revolutionary History.
   "Suddenly, a woman of about 20, wearing a light-colored summer dress, jumped
up from her place on the ground,

REAL LIFE
ROCK
TOP TE
BY GREIL MARC

and ran toward the sol-
diers, her arms in the
air. She was followed
by about six more
students. All were
cut down by
bullets."—Mary
Ganz, San
Francisco *Ex-
aminer*, Beijing,
June 4

3 ▪ Dr. Licks, *Standing in the Shadows of Motown—The Life and Music of Legendary Bassist James Jamerson* (Dr. Licks Pub., Wynewood, PA) Born in 1936, Jamerson died of alcoholism in 1983. This big, spiral-bound tribute combines an illustrated biography ("I used to go out behind the house where there were all these ants on the ground, and I would take a stick and stretch a long rubber band across it and play for the ants. I would make the ants dance"), a musical analysis complete with scores, and two hour-long cassettes of raucous interviews and various bassists recreating Jamerson's art on instrumental versions of Motown hits, with the bass on its own channel. Most effective is Phil Chen, with the intro to "Reach Out I'll Be There"—heart-stopping, even secondhand.

4 ▪ Tom Petty, "Runnin' Down a Dream" on *Full Moon Fever* (MCA) Nothing, until guitarist Mike Campbell takes over for the long finish, the perfect fade.

5 ▪ Charles Burns, "Teen Plague," in *RAW*, Vol. 2, No. 1 (Penguin) The burning comic strip that, as it ran in various alternative weeklies last year, caused countless decent folk who would never shake hands with the Reverend Donald Wildmon to demand the thing be, well, you know, not "censored," exactly, but, say, published somewhere *else* . . .

6 ▪ John Mellencamp, "Big Daddy of Them All," on *Big Daddy* (Mercury) The LP gets dull fast; the lead cut, so loose it's nearly abstract, is undeniable: a modal folk sound that says, "Louder! Play me louder!"

7 ▪ Lara Stapleton, "Butthole Surfers," in *BigFire-ProofBox* #2 Stapleton goes to hear the band and sees a naked woman onstage as part of the act, finally as the whole show: "She squirms, heroin stupor smile. 'Fuck the bitch!' this guy behind me yells. I turn around, look him in his barren skinhead eyes. He towers over me, and I'm a big girl. I'm a big girl." It gets worse, and she runs: "We'll smash bottles and hold them against throats and take money and we'll be gone." It's punk a hundred steps over the line it erases.

8 ▪ McKenzie Wark, "Elvis: Listen to the Loss," in *Art & Text* #31 (City Art Institute, Paddington, Australia) An argument that Elvis destroyed his career with his '68 comeback TV special, because he could never match it.

9 ▪ Jon Savage, interview with Tom Vague, in *Vague* #21 (London) The British critic on rage as an essential part of criticism.

10 ▪ Moonglows, "I Was Wrong" (Lost-Nite reissue, 1953) Misidentified in May as "Come Back Baby," provided by Donn Fileti of Relic Records, and taken so slowly it sounds like the turntable's jamming. But twice the group breaks out in shouts and moans and stomps, leaving behind a doo-wop aesthetic that makes no sense whatsoever.

AUGUST 15, 1989

1 ▪ Don Henley, *The End of the Innocence* (Geffen) THIS ALBUM *I really do wish Don Henley would stop addressing all his songs to the same hapless frail Cat Stevens so gently sneered at in "Wild World." If you listen to the title tune more than once (and if you listen to the radio for more than 10 minutes you will), you might catch just a hint of rape* IS SO GOOD *or anyway a theft of virginity, in "Offer up your best defense," even though the line is likely meant to sound, not mean* IT'S RIDICULOUS.

2 ▪ Priscilla Harris, in *Great Balls of Fire!*, dir. Jim McBride (Orion) I think she's the one who does the shimmy when Dennis Quaid plays "Whole Lotta Shakin'" behind the chicken wire—whoever it is, she burns a hole in the screen. On the other hand, the short fat fanny who kicks off the bop, on-camera for about a second, isn't exactly waiting in line at the bank.

3 ▪ Diamonds, "Think About It," on Lee "Scratch" Perry and friends, *Open the Gate* (Trojan 3-LP box reissue, mid-'70s) Trojan's current 30-album-plus reissue series forces you to buy nearly blind, so you keep the records playing until they give up their many ghosts. With a feeling close to any cut on

the Melodians' unsurpassed *pre-meditation*, this is one, a very quiet heartbreaker stepping up to the ineffable on a melody that's a surprise every time it lifts.

4 ▪ **Don Henley, "I Will Not Go Quietly," on** *The End of the Innocence* **(Geffen)** The title phrase promises a track as clunky as "Dirty Laundry." How's he going to make those stiff words swing? Pump up the volume, rock the house.

5 ▪ **Gina Arnold, "Fools Rush In" (***East Bay Express,* **Berkeley, CA)** No more appalled or less snotty work on the Who's $2000-a-seat *Tommy* revivals has appeared than in Arnold's weekly column: a few phone calls produced the interesting fact that the shows were anounced as "benefits" well before anyone had troubled to figure out who'd get the money. Polling her readers on what concert might be worth such a tab, she got a more or less final answer from Martin Buonochristiani: "the Clash, circa 1977, the Rolling Stones ('before they got bored, say around '68, '69), and Bob Dylan ('before he got born, say 1966 . . .') all on the same bill and all opening for Robert Johnson."

6 ▪ **Gentlemen, "Don't Leave Me, Baby," on** *The Golden Groups, Vol 48* **(Relic reissue, 1954)** What sets this otherwise merely fine piece of black vocal music apart is the graceful, deepening blues guitar bridge. Why wasn't there more of this in doo-wop? It's too late to know.

7 ▪ **Don Henley, "How Bad Do You Want It?" on** *The End of the Innocence* **(Geffen)** Not bad enough, he says convincingly—she'll never learn.

8 ▪ **Rolling Stones,** *Get Satisfaction . . . If You Want! The Best of BBC Radio Recordings 1963–65* **(Swingin' Pig bootleg CD)** Eighteen shots from the stage and the studio, highlighted by Bo Diddley's "Cops and Robbers," Buster Brown's "Fannie May," and a snatch of ancient interview: "Mick, you've achieved so very much on the international scene. What is there left to make you want to go on?"

9 ▪ **Beijing University, "First Student Protest" (***San Francisco Chronicle,* **July 26)** "In the first known revival of student protests here since the army crushed a pro-democracy movement last month, about 300 Beijing University students gathered Sunday night at a campus courtyard and sang Communist songs. . . . 'We are forced to endure hours of political study every day, telling us that the soldiers killing our classmates was a glorious victory,' [one student said]. 'Sarcasm is our only means of dissent.'"

10 ▪ **Don Henley, "The End of the Innocence" (Geffen)** "This titled man that we elected king," he says, and you can hear how plainly felt the idea was, how carefully he constructed the line, and how contrived it seems. But the way he sings the word "king," letting it break, is like the way Bob Dylan and Johnny Cash sing the last "remember" in the *Nashville Skyline* version of "Girl From the North Country," 20 years gone.

SEPTEMBER 19, 1989

1 ▪ **Natural Spiritual Orchestra, incidental music composed and conducted by William J. E. Lee, in Spike Lee's** *Do the Right Thing* **(Universal)** Sometimes suggesting Aaron Copland, sometimes Randy Newman—but more urgent, more confusing—Lee's (Spike's father) half-buried work is seemingly as foreign to its Brooklyn setting as modern African sounds would be; in a movie where every actor is immediately questioned by another, the music plays as the film's second mind. It's not on the soundtrack album.

2 ▪ **Hüsker Dü, "Diane," on** *Metal Circus* **(SST, 1983)** Guy hits on a girl. He says he loves her. He proves it by pulling out his heart with his hands.

3 ▪ **Lee Cotten,** *Shake Rattle & Roll—The Golden Age of American Rock 'n Roll, Volume 1: 1952–1955* **(Pierian Press/Popular Culture, Ink., Ann Arbor, Michigan)** This big, day-by-day log of shows and record releases— "an intellectual feast," to borrow Robert Bork's phrase—exposes the anomaly of Living Colour's "black rock" for the racist construction the last 20 years have made it, demonstrating that, once, "rock 'n' roll" was

a black name, a black idea, embraced and pursued by black musicians and hustlers not as a compromise but on its own new terms, even if Cotten does cheat a bit: here, rockabilly is barely "rock n' roll." Call it affirmative action.

4 ▪ **Fine Young Cannibals, "Don't Look Back" (Sire)** Has this title ever been on a bad record?

5 ▪ **David Fincher, video for Don Henley's "The End of the Innocence" (Geffen)** From Walker Evans's 1935–38 FSA photos to Robert Franks's 1959 *The Americans* (one of Fincher's shots is an almost exact recreation of Franks's "View from a hotel window—Butte, Montana") to something more: a bride, turning in an empty room with her new husband, trying to hide a smile so shy and full of promise neither Evans nor Franks would have known what to do with it. Whether it's the same woman who later appears as a prostitute, or as a mother whose eyes have given up their life wholly to a movie screen, is uncertain.

6 ▪ **Link Wray, *Rumble Man* (Ace, UK)** Wray cut "Rumble," a guitar instrumental described by its title, in 1957; he was in his middle or late twenties. Now, near 60, with undiminished flash and conviction, he becomes the oldest rocker to make a good record, lining out the who-cares stomp the Rolling Stones have pledged for their fifties since they were in their thirties. It'll be a surprise if anything on *Steel Wheels* outlives Wray's "Draggin'" or "Aces Wild."

7 ▪ **Louise Brooks, in Barry Paris's *Louise Brooks* (Knopf)** The woman in G. W. Pabst's 1929 silent film *Pandora's Box*, more than 40 years later, to "one of her last lovers": "If I ever bore you it'll be with a knife."

8 ▪ **Julee Cruise, *Floating Into the Night* (Warner Bros.)** Ten variations on *Blue Velvet*'s "Mysteries of Love," produced by David Lynch, who would have known how to direct Louise Brooks (1906–85): a bore in the daytime, visionary at 3 a.m.

9 ▪ **Monte Moore, comment during A's-Yankees telecast, on spotting a man in an Elvis mask sitting in Yankee Stadium, August 28 (KICU, San Jose)** "The next manager."

10 ▪ **Sonic Youth, Henry Kaiser, Soul Asylum, and others, *The Bridge—A Tribute to Neil Young* (Caroline)** Dedicated to "physically challenged children everywhere" (not a term Sonic Youth would use for a song—"Crips Galore" would be more like it), with "a portion of the proceeds" to the Bridge School, where Young's two handicapped kids go, but lest we forget, the man himself, in 1984, endorsing Ronald Reagan: "You can't always support the weak. You have to make the weak stand up on one leg, or half a leg, whatever they've got."

OCTOBER 17, 1989

1 ▪ **Elvis Costello, "Tramp the Dirt Down" (Greek Theatre, Berkeley, September 15)** Who else could toss off cheap Reagan jokes ("Do you really think it was only *last* week he needed brain surgery?") without cheapening a song about—well, there's no word equivalent to "regicide" for elected rulers ("You can change the names if you like"), so "regicide" will have to do. Taken far beyond its recorded version, the tune was vicious and sensual; the next day, when Reagan appeared in every paper with his head half-shaved, he somehow looked like Zippy the Pinhead—who once shared a White House bed with Ron and Nancy, Ron questioning him about the fall of Yugoslavia to the Neosurrealists in 1963.

2 ▪ **Public Enemy, *Protocols of the Elders of Zion* (unreleased)** Controversial, of course; disturbing (samples from Steely Dan's "Pretzel Logic," the *Shoah* soundtrack, tapes of Bilderburg conferences); and, given the powers that be, not commercial, not even recordable, altogether apocryphal, but nevertheless anguished, passionate, shot through with rage and ambiguity. Face it: it doesn't matter if these artists don't always know what they're talking about, though few have the right to gainsay tracks like "Socialism of Fools/ Fools of Socialism," "Peace Ship," or Professor Griff's 11-minute silent rap over a Dr. Seuss LP, "How the Jews Stole Christmas." Their business isn't answering questions, it's raising them. As they say in "Little Flower," every few lines cut up with pieces of an old Father Coughlin broadcast: "He may be right/He may be wrong/I just want to bang the gong."

3 ▪ Charlotte Greig, *Will You Still Love Me Tomorrow—Girl Groups From the 50s On* (Virago/Random House) She gets Arlene Smith of the Chantels right, brings her to life, and anyone who does is halfway home, even if the road goes all the way to Salt-n-Pepa. She covers the hits, but also scores of strange obscurities, and always with spirit. The "songs are a fascinating and accurate expression of the changing aspirations and preoccupations of women over three decades . . . [and] for that reason I have given the song lyrics more space than is usually accorded them," Greig writes in an untypically dry passage, then pulling the string: "The other reason I have quoted so extensively from them is because I like them."

4 ▪ Neil Young, "Rockin' in the Free World," on *Saturday Night Live* (September 30) *SNL* bandleader G. E. Smith can play anything and communicate nothing; on guitar, Young raised the rock Smith belongs under.

5 ▪ Mick Jones, video for "I Just Wanna Hold" (Atlantic) As close as anyone has come to the good feeling of Van Halen's video for "Jump."

6 ▪ Phil Phillips With the Twilights, "Sea of Love" (1959), in *Sea of Love* (Universal) Why is Al Pacino so freaked to find this in Ellen Barkin's record collection? Didn't he see *Diner*? She got it in the divorce settlement.

7 ▪ Jonathan Richman, "Closer," from *Jonathan Richman* (Rounder) Lousy album, lousy song, except for one line: "Meanwhile, back in the bed . . ."

8 ▪ Bruce A and the Secular Atavists, "Tougher Than Jesus" (street flier) A Jehovah's Witnesses-style comic strip about "the weird Asian Death Cult!!" of a "SAVIOR ON A STICK." Also a band, offering "a cassette that will show the path of light and truth."

9 ▪ Jefferson Airplane, "Planes," from *Jefferson Airplane* (Epic) The FAA is investigating.

10 ▪ Howard Hampton, "Chinese Radiation," in *Artpaper,* September An essay on music as memory, taking in Tiananmen Square, student leader Chai Ling's elegy, and coverage of the event in the Western media (*"That couldn't happen here* go the reassuring passwords: the massacre or the uprising?"), Charlie Haden's 1969 *Liberation Music Orchestra* LP, Pere Ubu's 1989 *Cloudland* ("deadpan and mercurial . . . a fire at your house viewed from a distant ridge"), and surrealist René Magritte's 1929 *On the Threshold of Liberty,* "where we remain. The cannon has not fired, the panels have not fallen, what is on the other side is either our collective mystery or our collective amnesia."

William J. E. Lee's music for Do the Right Thing, *noted here last month, has been released as the film's* Original Score *(Columbia).*

NOVEMBER 14, 1989

1 ▪ Neil Young, "Rockin' in the Free World" (acoustic), from *Freedom* (Reprise) It's a horror story, Young onstage wailing his lament for dead values as the distracted, drunken crowd shouts him on, barely able to catch the "free world" buzzword and cheer, all irony as wasted as the fans. The performance also seems like a setup: with even a harmonica rack in place, the persona of the folk-prophet without honor is too complete, the crowd too cretinous to be anything other than an audience tape cut up and mixed in like a laugh track on a sitcom. Then you might read the credits—"Recorded at Jones Beach"—and then you can hear why the crowd gathers itself for its biggest ululation: it's tossing a beach ball back and forth.

2 ▪ Bryan Ferry/Roxy Music, *Street Life/20 Great Hits* (Reprise, 1972–85) The story of a style, not an attitude, distilled to its essence in "More Than This" (Roxy

Music, '82), where the guitar solo is just a phrase, so evanescent and so much a part of a whole you can't remember precisely how it sounds any more than you can forget you heard it. But with "A Hard Rain's A-Gonna Fall" (Ferry, '73), who needs essence?

3 ▪ **Lemonheads, "Luka," from** *Lick* **(Taang!)** Depending on your mood, this thrilling fuzztone job on Suzanne Vega's Walter Keane klassic is proof her melody can't be smashed, a camp destruction of neofolkie piety (suggesting, say, a version of "Fast Car" by Lee Atwater, recently signed to Curb Records), or a reversal as tough as Ferry's "Hard Rain": a joke that ends up as moving as the original. Whatever it is, it grabs your attention like a mugging—as does the sleeve of *Lick*, a Jesse Peretz photo so erotic it's painful.

4 ▪ *NBC Today*, **"Robert Johnson" (October 15)** "Me and the Devil Blues" on national TV, and never stranger.

5 ▪ **Steve Erickson,** *Leap Year—A Political Journey* **(Poseidon Press)** For the scene with Tipper Gore in the New York bar, the night before the 1988 presidential primary: "'Purple haze! Is in my brain!' She says over and over, angrily, 'I was *there*, I was there, man. I was a child of the Sixties.'"

6 ▪ **Bo Jackson and Bo Diddley, "Cross Training" (Nike TV commercial)** Jackson on the diamond, gridiron, basketball court, and hockey ice: unstoppable, until he straps on Diddley's cigar-box guitar and hits a bum note. Next installment: Jackson meets Derek.

7 ▪ **Michael Barson,** *Rip It Up!— Postcards From the Heyday of Rock 'n' Roll* **(Pantheon)** Made from movie posters, sheet music, concert programs, and fan magazines, notably *Tommy Sands vs. Belafonte and Elvis*. Barson's I.D.: "Sands had one fairly huge hit early in 1957, 'Teen-Age Crush,' and never saw the Top Ten again, though he did marry Nancy Sinatra. Brooklyn-born Harry Belafonte fared better, with several calypso-flavored hits in 1956 and '57, and a long life as an LP artist who appealed to an older audience. Elvis had a few hits, was drafted, then returned

to driving a truck for Crown Electric in Memphis and was never heard from again."

8 ▪ **Rolling Stones,** *Detroit* **(bootleg, 1969)** The songs are slowed down, cut to cadence almost like marches; they hover, like prophecies remembered generations after they were delivered; you hear only the singer, who seems scared of his own power, and the guitarists, who revel in theirs, "'We Didn't Really Get It On Until Detroit'— M. Jagger," it says on the sleeve—which, 20 years later, sort of begs the question.

9 ▪ **Bob Dylan,** *Oh Mercy* **(Columbia)** Producer's record, shapely and airless. Featuring Daniel Lanois as the director who likes to chalk marks on the floor and Dylan as the actor who has to hit them.

10 ▪ **Neil Young, "Rockin' in the Free World" (electric), from** *Freedom* Well over 40, like most of the people starring in this column, Young alone among them uses his past for context, not careerism. Mick Jagger sings "Satisfaction" today because there's money in it, and no doubt; at his best Young always sounds as if he's ready to blow every dollar on what he has to say. Here, with lyrics left out of the Jones Beach version, he erases Ronald Reagan and lets George Bush be his own man: the cadaverous face of his silent crimes. More to the point, it's Young's best ride since "Surfer Joe and Moe the Sleaze" on *Re·ac·tor* eight years ago, which in the time frame Young creates means nothing at all.

DECEMBER 12, 1989

1 ▪ **Howlin' Wolf, "Rollin' and Tumblin'," from** *Killing Floor* **(Chess, Japan, out of print)** One minute of the primeval from the great electric bluesman. The only accompaniment here is acoustic guitar; no band could match the broken country time. The guitarist is unnamed, the date unlisted, there's no other known Wolf recording like it, but there must be more. Where?

2 ▪ **KALX, pledge-drive spots (FM 90.7, University of California at Berkeley, November 10)** "Hello," says a creamy phone-sex voice. "I'm your *Pledge Mistress*. . . . If

you'd like to make a *donation*, press one. If you need *encouragement* to *leave your deposit*, press. . . ." Even better was an evangelist, droning on and on in plummy, pukey tones about the final struggle between the Mammon of "Commercial Radio" and the holiness of "Listener-Supported Radio," his syntax impossibly garbled by insensate repetition and the slow train of his mind.

3 ▪ **David Remnick and Marc Fisher, dispatch on the resignation of the Czechoslovakian Communist Party presidium (*Washington Post*, November 25)** "Taxi drivers led a manic procession through Wenceslas Square, honking their horns. A man carried a victory cake to the center of the celebration. All around, people were lighting firecrackers and sparklers. A single trumpeter, like the leader of a New Orleans jazz wedding, led a few hundred people up the promenade."

4 ▪ **MTV, graphic (November 12)** Picture: the Berlin Wall. Soundtrack: electric version of Neil Young's "Rockin' in the Free World." Title: "ANOTHER BAD IDEA BITES THE DUST." And another irony buried under it.

5 ▪ **Elizabeth Shogren, "A New Political Generation" (*San Francisco Chronicle*, November 25)** "Anne-Kathrin Pauk, 23, an elementary school teacher and publicist for the Berlin branch of a fledgling political party, exemplifies the role played by the younger generation in East Germany's fast-paced reforms. 'A lot of my friends already left, but now my friends are deciding to stay and try to change our country,' said Pauk. . . . Pauk has brought her own style into her classroom. At the start of each class period in East Germany, pupils stand erect and report to their teacher in military fashion. The first day of her class, Pauk made it clear that she was different. After the pupils reported in their usual way, she stood at attention and sang the American song 'We're in the Army Now.' Then she translated the words for her astonished, giggling pupils. Her students no longer report at the beginning of class."

6 ▪ ***Actuel,* sponsorship of pirate radio station off the coast of the People's Republic of China** Yes, they'll probably be playing "Rockin' in the Free World," but as the sound of the Beatles' "Revolution" said "rise up" even when the words said "don't," the sound of Young's attack on our version of the Free World may simply say that when you can bring sound to this level, you're free.

7 ▪ **Vulgar Boatmen, *You and Your Sister* (Independent Label Alliance CD)** From Gainesville, Florida: insinuating songs orchestrated by a quiet band and sung in a reedy voice, the tunes very '50s in their casualness, present-day in their insistence on doubt. The best tunes center on girl's names ("Mary Jane," "Margaret Says," "Katie") or on the way metaphors of unrequited love can turn into politics: "Change the World All Around," a subtle retrieval of the momentum in "Heroin."

8 ▪ **Syd Straw, *Surprise* (Virgin)** More surprising on the radio than on the turntable, where too many words on one track after another trip up the autonomy of the songs. Still, proof that sometimes sweet dreams are made of sweetness.

9 ▪ **Mekons, "Memphis, Egypt," from *Rock'n'Roll* (Twintone/A&M)** In the annals of rock epistemology, this account of the struggle between, more or less, commercial radio and listener-supported radio, as one band fought not to be "consumed by rock 'n' roll," at least corrects Talking Heads' "Cities," where David Byrne sang of "Memphis—home of Elvis, and the ancient Greeks."

10 ▪ **Grace Catalano, *New Kids on the Block* (Bantam)** You can laugh at fan-bios, but it's all Creedence Clearwater ever got. There are still no books on Jackie Wilson, the Band, Martha Reeves, Sly Stone, Alan Freed, Fats Domino, or the Monotones.

JANUARY 9, 1990

1 ▪ **Alison Krauss and Union Station, "Two Highways," from *Two Highways* (Rounder)** A shining bluegrass tune, moving fast, but seemingly coming very slowly,

maybe because of the lifetimes in Alison Krauss's young voice. "Only time will tell if I have made a loser's choice"—there's a memory of a road Dolly Parton might have taken, but no mannerisms or borrowings are audible. This is a song where even bad lines are suggestive: "Will I hear the melody I searched for oh so long," Krauss sings. If this isn't it, what is?

2 ▪ Carl Hiaasen, *Double Whammy* **(Warner Books)** Inside this terrific mystery about bass fishing is a tiny novel—not screaming to get out, but happy right where it is. Sometime in the '70s a reformist governor of Florida subverted on all sides by developers' money quits, disappears, and turns up years later as a swamp rat known as Skink. He's a saint but he doesn't talk like one: speeding down the road in a villain's top-down Corvette he rips Whitney Houston out of the tape deck, throws it in the air, and growls. "Got any Creedence?"

3 ▪ Little Richard, *The Specialty Sessions* **(Ace/Specialty reissue, 1955–64, UK)** Given Richard's nearly monolithic attack, this is nowhere near so playable as boxes devoted to Jerry Lee Lewis or Buddy Holly; the remastering is often scholastic, bringing up the voice and losing the sound. But halfway into the eight LPs or six CDs a story emerges: songs carried over from session to session, months between attempts to get it right, a saga of a refusal to settle for anything less than a division of history: the division, say, between the first take of "I Got It" and the ninth.

4 ▪ Steve Propes, et al, liner notes to Los Angeles reissues on Mr. R&B labels, Sweden **(Jaguars,** *The Way You Look Tonight,* **1955–61, Earth Angel; Hollywood Flames,** *The John Dolphin Sessions,* **1951–56, Earth Angel; and Jimmy Wright,** *Let's Go Crazy Baby,* **1953–56, Saxophonographic)** The music is not great; the tale it tells, of the hustle and miscegenation of early L.A. rock, is. The notes to the LP by the Jaguars (two blacks, an Italian, a Chicano—their "Charlene" was redone by Los Lobos on the *La Bamba* soundtrack) trace a line that began with

backing on a worthless Walt Disney-Davy Crockett-craze number and ended in failure: a line that connects Buddy Ebsen to Richard Berry to the Lettermen to the Penguins to David Lee Roth.

5 ▪ Georgia Satellites, "It's All Over But the Cryin'," from *In the Land of Salvation and Sin* **(Elektra)** In the vein of Lynyrd Skynyrd's *Street Survivors,* and good enough to be on it.

6 ▪ Dave Marsh, *The Heart of Rock & Soul* **(Plume)** A close reading of 1001 singles, Scheherazade at the jukebox—the longest book of rock criticism ever published, one that every reader will rewrite, and far and away my friend's top work. As a skeptic about punk his entries on the Sex Pistols are profound; as a fan who finds the high point of rock in the mid-'60s he offers a double-slap in the face that has Chuck Berry on one cheek and *Sgt. Pepper* on the other.

7 ▪ Bob Black, "On the Art Strike" **(Art-paper, December)** Black takes bad ideas seriously. "On January 1, 1990—if they comply with the directives of the PRAXIS Group—all artists will put down their tools for three years," he begins. Then he imagines the result of this "ostentatious renunciation," promoted as a utopia where "plebian masses, no longer cowed by 'talented bullies,' are in turn expected to rush into art like fresh air into a vacuum": "Not, as is pretended, the general strike of the proletariat, but rather something already depicted in a work of art—the general strike of the capitalists in Ayn Rand's *Atlas Shrugged.*"

8 ▪ MTV, *Decade—1980–1989* **(December 24)** A two-hour tribute to digital editing, with talking heads both stupid (John Mellencamp, Tina Turner, and most of all Linda Ellerbee) and not (Frank Zappa, David Byrne, Roseanne Barr). Best line, Don Henley: "Reagan had a bedside manner for a dying nation."

9 ▪ Album of the Decade, Mekons, *Fear & Whiskey* **(Sin, 1985, UK)** Take your choice.

10 ▪ Single of the Decade, Foreigner, "I Want To Know What Love Is" **(Atlantic, 1984)** Because in the last minute, you find out.

1 ▪ **David Acomba, director; Maynard Collins, writer, *Hank Williams—The Show He Never Gave* (Drifter Films, Canada, 1982, the Nashville Network, January 1)** Aired on the 37th anniversary of Williams's death and set in a bar the night before: December 31, 1952. Playing Williams, country singer Sneezy Waters doesn't look like him, doesn't necessarily sound like him, but within minutes he is him, running through the hits and making each one into an event the people in the crowd will never forget. They mill around the foot-high platform that serves as a stage, as close to Williams as pogo dancers were to Johnny Rotten, but without starlust, as if it's just one more night in a long life. After jokes about alcoholism and divorce—after lead-in stories as complex, scripted, and seemingly spontaneous as those Bruce Springsteen tells—Williams/Waters ends his first set with "Alone and Forsaken." It's a number as awful and anomalous in the Williams catalogue as "Hellhound on My Trail" is in Robert Johnson's. The words fail to fit into "Cold, Cold Heart" as the messy structure of "Hellhound" breaks up the order of even "Me and the Devil Blues"; the cadence damns the melody of "I'm So Lonesome I Could Cry" as the antibeat of "Hellhound" destroys the rhythm of "Terraplane Blues." It seems clear, after Waters's "Alone and Forsaken"— listen to the Mekons' version on *The Edge of the World*—that nothing could follow it, but after a short time in his dressing room Williams comes back for his second set, and it's time to pay the piper: in blood (Williams's), sweat (his and the audience's), and tears (his, theirs, yours).

2 ▪ **Andrew Baumer, former bassist for Minimal Man, history lesson, on the occasion of his 38th birthday (January 6)** "When I woke up this morning, to celebrate I put on my favorite record: the Sex Pistols. But when 'Holidays in the Sun' came on, it struck me—someday, when I have a child, and I want to tell my son or daughter about my favorite record, I'm going to have to explain what the Berlin Wall was."

3 ▪ **Kinks, "The Way Love Used To Be" (Reprise, 1971)** Save for Duncan Browne's forgotten 1968 *Give Me Take You*, the sole exemplar of an unknown genre: Pre-Raphaelite rock.

4 ▪ **Warren Zevon, "Run Straight Down," from *Transverse City* (Virgin)** Once he gets the orchestration up, he doesn't have to do much more than chant the title to bring on the night.

5 ▪ **Gang of Four, "History's Not Made by Great Men," from *At the Palace* (Mercury, 1984)** As covered by CBS *Evening News*, December 1, with new lyrics: "Even world leaders, it would seem, no longer make history. All they can do is cope with history in the making."

6 ▪ **Dangermice, *Sound Session* (Sounds! EP)** A band centered on Marlene Marder (writer and guitarist for Kleenex and Liliput, 1978–84): straight stuff, except for "There's a Light," as harshly utopian as Liliput's "Split."

7 ▪ **Associated Press, worst news of the month (January 9)** "Don Henley and Glenn Frey have settled their decade-old feud and will reunite the Eagles . . ."

8 ▪ **Andrew Goodwin, worst news of the month before (*East Bay Express*, December 29)** Rock critic Goodwin reports on a conversation with *Nightline* correspondent James Walker, in Berkeley to research a show about bigotry in popular music: "Walker's next stop is L.A., where he will interview NWA. Walker wants to know if NWA's members speak English."

9 ▪ **Los Angeles Times, news story (January 10)** "Designers of Richard Nixon's presidential library say that visitors will be able to question the former president and get an answer from his own lips—through the miracle of video. With the latest in computer wizardry and more than 400 video clips, the questioner will touch a screen and get an answer from Nixon's video image. 'It's as if by some form of fortune, you actually meet the president,' said designer Alex Cranstoun"—no doubt a fan of the Firesign Theater's 1971 *We're All Bozos on This Bus*, which featured the same psuedo-Nixon, and also detailed how to blow its fuse.

10 ▪ Warner Bros., radio ad (January) For Laurie Anderson's *Strange Angels*: "It has music you can listen to." What'll they think of next?

1 ▪ Laurie Anderson, *Strange Angels* (Warner Bros.) Julee Cruise armed. Or David Lynch's next movie.

2 ▪ Wim Wenders, *Emotion Pictures— Reflections on the Cinema*, translated from the German by Sean Whiteside with Michael Hofman (Faber & Faber) Between 1968 and '71 the German director was a film student, and also a critic, tossing out pieces on rock as film and film as rock ("The 10th Kinks LP—The 51st Alfred Hitchcock Film—The 4th Creedence Clearwater LP—The 3rd Harvey Mandel LP"); free-associating between records and movies, in almost every case essaying a page or two of nothing on his way to the image he's looking for (on rock cinema, "A Non-Existent Genre": a "close-up of a screaming girl is really only a reverse angle of a cameraman screaming with disgust"). The book ends with later, more conventional, and very angry articles, and with "The American Dream," an endless 1984 poem. After 10 pages or so, if you last that long, its insistent banality begins to work as a set-up for occasional moments of vehement clarity ("The more impossible and unthinkable wars become/ . . . the more evident world-wide entertainment will appear/as the 'continuation of politics by other means'"); farther on is as heartbreaking an account of the liberating effects of early rock 'n' roll as one will ever read.

3 ▪ Sinéad O'Connor, "Nothing Compares 2 U" (Chrysalis 12-inch) The principal difference between O'Connor's immersion in this Prince tune and classic '60s deep soul ballads is that this runs five minutes and they didn't go past three.

4 ▪ B-52's, "Roam" (Reprise) A good sound, thanks mainly to the absence of Fred Schneider's smirking anti-singing, plus a double entendre on "around the world" worthy of ZZ Top, or Bullmoose Jackson's 1952 "Big Ten Inch (Record of the Blues)." But if the song is suggestive it's in terms of the video you automatically run in your head. The group settled for cutting the performance in half with a cheap travelogue of exotic places; that's why they'll never be more than a decent joke.

5 ▪ Mötley Crüe, "Kickstart My Heart" video and Paula Abdul: "Opposites Attract" video Two proofs that the current ruling MTV aesthetic is nearly indistinguishable from soft-core porn: action shots (Mötley Crüe's stage moves, Abdul's all-promising grin) so brief they verge on the subliminal, so out of reach the only feeling they leave behind is frustration.

6 ▪ Electric Eels, *Having a Philosophical Investigation With the Electric Eels* (unreleased recordings from 1975, Tinnitus) As in *Having a Rave Up With the Yardbirds*; on "Agitated" and "Jaguar Ride," these progenitors of Cleveland's Rocket from the Tombs and Pere Ubu almost do.

7 ▪ Filippo Marinetti, *The Futurist Cookbook*, translated from the Italian by Suzanne Brill, edited by Lesley Chamberlain (Bedford Arts reissue, 1932) As a committed Fascist, the enemy of all passéism takes his crusade to the ultimate enemy: pasta ("originated by the Ostrogoths"). Thus, popping up throughout this hilarious, delirious masterwork, the likes of " 'The Excited Pig'—A whole salami, skinned, is served upright on a dish containing some very hot black coffee mixed with a good deal of eau de Cologne," and realization, now, that cuisine à la Zippy the Pinhead (tacos with Liquid Paper sauce) fixes Bill Griffith's hero not as a dyslexic for all seasons but as a professor paying polite homage to the great days of the avant-garde.

8 ▪ Rolling Stones, "Fancy Man Blues," from *After the Hurricane: Songs for Montserrat* (Chrysalis CD) Rote and soulless, but a dozen similar rehearsals, bootlegged as *Blues by the Numbers*, might be a way out of the "How to Write Pop Songs" slime of "Mixed Emotions" and the rest of *Steel Wool*. Dream on, as the Five Keys once put it.

9 ▪ **Ronnie McDowell (voice) and Michael St. Gerard (mime), "My Happiness," in** *Elvis* **(ABC-TV, February 6)** The original for-his-mother's-birthday recording, here dramatized as bereft of everything but heart. The actual artifact, lost since 1953, turned up recently; McDowell must have heard it.

10 ▪ *Super Hits of the 70s: Have a Nice Day,* **Vols. 1–5 (Rhino CDs)** Checking out this series of horrors (Sugarloaf's "Green Eyed Lady," Ocean's "Put Your Hand in the Hand," so many more), you ask why Rhino stopped short of the bottom: Five Man Electrical Band's "Signs," wherein the hippie rebel pulls off his disguise to reveal the true face of the age—the Jesus Freak. Rhino says it's on the way.

APRIL 3, 1990

1 ▪ **Pete Seeger, "A Hard Rain's A-Gonna Fall," from** *We Shall Overcome—The Complete Carnegie Hall Concert, June 8, 1963* **(Columbia double CD)** I first heard Bob Dylan's song as Seeger sang it, just days before the March on Washington, where Martin Luther King replaced Dylan's armageddon ("hard rain" meant, among other things, nuclear fallout) with a vision of liberation. But both King and Dylan spoke the same, apocalyptic language; it was never Seeger's. His version of the song seemed like a final statement 27 years ago, in the flesh or on the original, one-LP Carnegie Hall recording, but today it's plain the moment made the music. Seeger notoriously lacked any blues feeling, and "Hard Rain" is proof he had none for country, not even for Child ballads; as Woody Guthrie or Big Bill Broonzy he was Henry Ward Beecher, Yankee abolitionist to his toenails. This performance documents one of the great musical events of the American postwar period, but the event is no longer musical; to hear how scary the song can be, you have to listen to Bryan Ferry sing it.

2 ▪ **Midnight Oil,** *Blue Sky Mining* **(Columbia)** As with U2, there's good guitar in the storm of politics and morals, but the hooks are not smothered in a personification of universal humanism, perhaps because singer Peter Garrett doesn't seem very impressed with himself. He doesn't even necessarily write the songs, which frees him to function as just another instrument.

3 ▪ **Robert B. Ray, "The ABC of Visual Theory," in** *Visible Language* **(Autumn 1988)** Playing within the strictures of the self-referentiality of current critical theory, Ray (of the Vulgar Boatmen and the University of Florida at Gainesville) takes on the hegemonic artificiality of the alphabet, picking up, among other items, "Barthes," "Rochefort, Joseph," "Vertov, Dziga," and "Louie, Louie." The last is discussed as happenstance, an incident interesting on its own terms: the supposedly obscene lyrics of the Kingsmen's '63 single working on millions of people like Poe's purloined letter, hidden in plain sight.

4 ▪ **KALX-FM, two-and-a-half hours of Lou Reed, on the occasion of his 47th birthday (March 2, Berkeley)** Upsetting, since these days if you hear two songs in a row from the same performer you figure he or she just died.

5 ▪ **Robert Plant, "Hurting Kind (I've Got My Eyes on You)," from** *Manic Nirvana* **(Es Paranza)** Inside the familiar noise is humor, the thrill of discovery, maybe the hint of a quest. After 20 years on the assembly line attaching the hysterical to the frantic, he still can't deliver mere product.

6 ▪ **Aaron Neville, "For Your Precious Love," from** *Midnight Orchid* **(Rhino CD, recorded 1981)** Neville's trademark is overworrying, getting so many syllables out of a phrase (none of them melismatic, all of them clipped) he makes Otis Redding sound like Sam Cooke. Thus on most of this five-song oldies disc Neville barely gets started, hacking so much angst into the verses you lose track of what he's singing about—but with his embrace of Jerry Butler's 1958 hit, you wonder why he has to stop.

7 ▪ **Rolling Stones, "You Can't Always Get What You Want," from** *25×5* **(CBS video)** An edit of a clip from an unreleased '69 TV special, which replaces the regret and nos-

talgia of the *Let It Bleed* cut with a definite lack of charity.

8 ▪ **Bruce Sterling, "Dori Bangs," in** *Isaac Asimov's Science Fiction* **(September 1989)** What if rock critic Lester Bangs hadn't died in 1982 and comix artist Dori Seda five years later, but rather met, got married, and lived on? Sterling's story is compelling because it reads like gossip.

9 ▪ **George Harrison, discourse on karma, in "The Quiet Wilbury," interview by Mark Rowland (***Musician,* **March)** "It was such a waste, some stupid person. If John had been killed by Elvis, it would have at least had meaning!"

10 ▪ **Jacob Weisberg, "Washington Diarist," in the** *New Republic* **(March 5)** An argument that the Velvet Underground played no small role in naming and even making what Czech president Václav Havel calls the country's "Velvet Revolution"— through the agency of the Plastic People of the Universe, Velvets followers who once recorded and performed at Havel's farmhouse. On the other hand, since Frank Zappa (recently made adviser to the Czech minister of culture) reports Havel is a big fan of Zappa's own *Bongo Fury,* maybe one ought to be thankful Havel didn't announce the "Bongo Revolution." That would have really confused people, especially future historians, who would likely conclude that the Czech victory over Stalinism had its roots in dubbed Hollywood exploitation movies about beatniks— which, to some degree, it probably did.

MAY 1, 1990

1 ▪ **Herb Ritts, Marianne Faithfull, Gap ad (***Vanity Fair,* **April)** "What were once vices are now habits," the Doobie Brothers smirked for an album title in 1974. Ritts's portrait, almost unrecognizable without a caption, says that what were once scars are now features: a junkie tattoo and a Pre-Raphaelite face.

2 ▪ **Lisa Shrage, as Mary Lou Mahoney in** *Hello Mary Lou—Prom Night II* **(Virgin Vision Video, 1987)** In a movie sharp enough to favor Ronnie Hawkins's "Mary Lou" over

Ricky Nelson's title song, Shrage is a murdered '57 prom queen back from the dead 30 years later: the human equivalent of Christine, Stephen King's demonic '58 Plymouth. Where's Shrage been since?

3 ▪ **Chris Thomas,** *Cry of the Prophets* **(Sire/Hightone)** He's the son of '50s Louisiana bluesman Tabby Thomas, and if this LP had been released in the mid-'60s, in the heyday of deep feeling deep South r&b, it would have seemed like a curio: too eclectic. Today it's a shock, because deep soul has hardly been heard in public since Al Green's *The Belle Album,* and because nobody's heard deep soul guitar or deep soul crying applied to crack and Uzis. Up against the likes of N.W.A., Thomas sounds pathetic—but also real.

4 ▪ **Don Letts, director,** *The Punk Rock Movie* **(1979, Rhino Home Video)** England, 1977. The Slits are fierce (drummer Palmolive seems to care the most); so is X-ray Spex (with Lora Logic). Eater plays with a pig's head on the stage, a huge cleft cut into its skull. When the song ends the bandmembers hack at the head, stab it, then throw what's left to the crowd. They are acting out (a) the seventh verse of the Eagles' "Hotel California"; (b) Margaret Murray's 1921 *The Witch-Cult in Western Europe,* which holds that even after nearly 2000 years Christianity remained threatened by the devil worship of the lower orders; or (c) a rite secretly passed down through the centuries by British pagans masquerading as Christers. But the Sex Pistols, with Johnny Rotten in a suit coat and bow tie looking a lot like Baudelaire, make Eater's ritual seem secondhand, because it is so literal; with the Pistols, (c) is the only answer, and the only question. Their "no future" means the whole of the past, a tidal wave.

5 ▪ **Silos,** *The Silos* **(BMG/RCA)** Folk rock, pursuing the thin sound of Prince's "When You Were Mine" into its rhythms, all coolness and regret: "Picture of Helen" and "I'm Over You," the latter taking two minutes to essay a classic driving song, only to pull up short and admit it's about immobilization and loss.

6 ▪ Sinéad O'Connor, "Black Boys on Mopeds," from *I Do Not Want What I Haven't Got* (Chrysalis) "Margaret Thatcher on TV/ Shocked by the deaths that took place in Beijing/It seems strange that she should be offended." The lifetime O'Connor invests in the word *offended* is, as singing, a match for the gestures of the man who, a year ago, played chicken with the tanks of the ruling class.

7 ▪ Virginia Madsen, as Dixie Lee Boxx in *Long Gone* (HBO movie, 1987) Though she's in the tradition of big American blonds (as aerobic Madonna is not), if Madsen had taken Mamie Van Doren's role in *High School Confidential* it would have been a different movie: everything Madsen does radiates intelligence and will. This good flick about a '50s Florida minor-league baseball team has a superb rockabilly/doo-wop soundtrack; Madsen seems to be the only character who knows what the songs are about.

8 ▪ Heart, "All I Wanna Do Is Make Love to You" (Portrait) Since "Magic Man," Ann Wilson's theme has been lust and loss—loss of control. She'll have to push to take the story any farther.

9 ▪ Smithereens, "Behind the Wall of Sleep" from *Especially for You* (Enigma, 1986) As good as Richard Thompson's "Wall of Death."

10 ▪ Jerry Roberts, on California gubernatorial candidate John Van de Kamp's address to the state Democratic Party convention (*San Francisco Chronicle*, April 9) "The straitlaced Van de Kamp's appearance was most memorable for the music selected for his introduction to the delegates—the rock and roll classic 'Johnny B. Goode.' Van de Kamp spent part of the weekend laid up in a back brace . . . aides denied speculation that he hurt his back practicing a Chuck Berry-style duck walk." Lee Atwater rocks on.

MAY 29, 1990

1 ▪ Babes In Toyland, *Spanking Machine* (Twin/Tone) Three women who take up the challenge the Slits laid down in 1977. As if

no more than a minute has passed, they shout back: harridan shouts, bloody laughter.

2 ▪ Marianne Faithfull, at Slims, San Francisco (April 17) There was a searing, anti-art ending on the arty "Sister Morphine"; with "Broken English," the lyric's insistence that the singer didn't know what the Baader-Meinhof terrorists were talking about was now an insistence that she understood every word.

3 ▪ Chai Ling, on *Nightline* (ABC, April 17) A few days after the killings in Tiananmen Square last year, Chai Ling, a leader of the demonstrations, smuggled a tape from her hiding place: "I am still alive," she began. Those words were a stoic anticipation and refusal of the quick death she was facing as she spoke. This night, just a few days escaped from China, she appeared from Paris on a screen talking in voice-over translation to Ted Koppel, who ignored her amazing smile in favor of asking her if she intended to meet with George Bush; better he should have asked if she wanted to meet with Sinéad O'Connor.

4 ▪ Surreal Estate, *La Revolution Surrealiste* (Salvador, 1985) Up against a dozen discs, including A Tribe Called Quest's smart backing track and dead vocals, this defunct Ann Arbor trio's precious, postpunk affectations gave something back: mainly Detroit's 1967 Spike Drivers, their uncollected "Strange Mysterious Sounds."

5 ▪ Bobby "Blue" Bland, Junior Parker, Earl Forest, and Johnny Ace, *The Original Memphis Blues Brothers* (Ace reissue, 1951–53) The title refers less to Bland et al. than to Matt Murphy, guitarist on these sessions, who later turned up in *The Blues Brothers*, where he walked out on Aretha Franklin to play with his soul brothers John Belushi and Dan Ackroyd; the music is on side one, Bland wailing "Drifting from Town to Town" three times. His singing is so saxophonic it suggests that if an instrument can talk, to truly communicate a singer has to get past words.

6 ▪ Joel Selvin, *Ricky Nelson—Idol for a Generation* (Contemporary Books) A moderately compelling biography of a moderately compelling singer, whose moderately awful end was coded in his moderate rebellion against the moderately repressed life he was supposed to live.

7 ■ **Richard Beymer, on** *Twin Peaks* **(ABC, May 3)** In bed with Piper Laurie, the town Slime King gets up, brandishing one of the non sequiturs the script piles on its red herrings: a tiny Elvis whiskey decanter. "Going to give Little Elvis a shower," he says. But what's in the bottle?

8 ■ **Lou Reed and John Cale,** *Songs for Drella* **(Sire)** Good guitar.

9 ■ **Mark Kitchell, director,** *Berkeley in the Sixties* **(Kitchell Films) and Richard Lester, director:** *Paul McCartney in His Times* **(Memorial Stadium, Berkeley, April 1, short film introducing McCartney tour)** Combining documentary footage and now-interviews with the then-participants, Kitchell's movie replaces history with highlights: there's no texture, no sense of lived time. There are moments when the forgotten comes back as shock, notably then-governor Ronald Reagan, not the "easygoing monster" (Robert Christgau's perfect words) of the presidential years, but hawk-faced and harsh, matching the Mr. Big he played in Don Siegel's *The Killers*. Ultimately the picture is tinged with a condescending sentimentality; when it ended with Pete Seeger singing "We Shall Overcome," the *we* seemed smugly narrow. I took part in most of what I was looking at, but I was far more moved by Lester's little triptych: "history" on the sides, Paul in the middle. At first it was an ordinary collage, Beatles surrounded by Kennedys and miniskirts and missile crises—with the soundtrack Beatle music more vivid than any of the images. Then Lester broke the formula: four unrelieved minutes of the Vietnam War, no Beatles and no Paul, simply tripled horror, all to "The Long and Winding Road," which against what one was seeing was almost silent, sucked into the air. When the film ended with red, lurid night footage of the massacre in Tiananmen Square, it didn't seem cheap. Paul McCartney had been reduced

to one person doing his work in times that overtook him. Then he came out and sang his songs as best he could.

10 ■ **Eddie Money, "Peace in Our Time" (Columbia)** Along with the title phrase, the lyric includes "heaven on earth," "turning water into wine," "streets of shame," "cities of dust," "phoenix from the flames," "break down the walls," "wheels of fortune," "keep on keepin' on," "on a wing and a prayer," and "a song in our hearts," encapsulating better than a hundred academic papers the poststructuralist refutation of "the original." Or a dogged refusal to shut up.

JUNE 26, 1990

1 ■ **Madonna, "Blond Ambition Tour" (Oakland Coliseum Arena, May 20)** It doesn't matter how cool you are: this great production showcases gestures as shocking now as any Elvis Presley put on television in 1956, and it's a prissy myth that only those who disapproved of Elvis were shocked. Here, the interracial hermaphroditic porn of "Like a Virgin" was merely a warm-up for the blasphemies of "Like a Prayer," which as a dance raised the music to the level of Foreigner's "I Want To Know What Love Is," cut in with Ray Charles's "What'd I Say." "This," Madonna said on May 31 in Toronto, when police arrived with an order that she alter her performance, "is certainly a cause for which I am willing to be arrested."

2 ■ **Dorothy Wade and Justine Picardie,** *Music Man—Ahmet Ertegun, Atlantic Records, and the Triumph of Rock 'n' Roll* **(Norton)** Engaging, seductive writing that never calls attention to itself, first-class business reporting—a music book you can actually read, not simply glean for gossip, though there's plenty of that, from Jerry Leiber and Mike Stoller's attempt to get Red Bird Records back from the Mafia to Mick Jones's pre-Foreigner bid to take over the corpse of Stax. The book is strongest as a shadow biography of Morris Levy—mobster, bad conscience of pop laissez-faire capitalism, and imp of the perverse—who talked his head off.

3 ▪ Clancy Eccles, et al., *Clancy Eccles Presents His Reggae Revue* (Heartbeat CD reissue, 1967–72) Rock steady, and never steadier—not a single twitching nerve.

4 ▪ Wedding Present, *Bizarro* (RCA CD) As a singer, David Gedge sounds like John Cale on his obscure 1969 *Vintage Violence* LP; as a guitarist he fronts a Leeds band whose influences seem to begin and end with the Velvet Underground's 8:47 1969 live version of "What Goes On"—and what goes on on *Bizarro* is a fanatical argument that true rock 'n' roll, or music, emerges only at that point where repetition takes on a charge so powerful not even rhythm can be heard. Listen to "What Have I Said Now?"—Fairport Convention's "A Sailor's Life" as redone by Joy Division—and tell Gedge he's wrong.

5 ▪ Sinéad O'Connor, green T-shirt (Berkeley Community Theater, June 4) "PWA," it read; her publicist said it meant "Paddies With Attitude," not "Person With AIDS." I don't know what the ACT UP sticker on the sleeve meant.

6 ▪ Catherine Adams, dispatch on Romanian elections (UPI, May 20) "More than 80 political parties are participating in the elections," Adams reported. "The Laughter Party, the Barking Dog Party, the Gypsy Home Decorators Party . . . More than 1000 foreign observers have begun traveling to some of the 3000 polling stations around the country to monitor the balloting. 'I'm overwhelmed by the enthusiasm for democracy,' said Roy Hattersley, a British Labor Party deputy." "Me, too," said Monty Python.

7 ▪ Fleetwood Mac, "Save Me" (Warner Bros.) Rock economics: the guitar solo costs nobody anything; the way Christine McVie sings "Is it one or the other, baby?" was paid for a long time ago.

8 ▪ Rod Stewart and Ronald Isley, "This Old Heart of Mine (Is Weak for You)" (Warner Bros.) Flying back from the U.K. in 1966, I found the Isley Brothers' original on the audio; for the next 14 hours Swinging London dissolved as I waited for the headset to give up the tune again and again. As a 1990 video it's a period piece: ignoring Holland-Dozier-Holland's sweetest melody, the slowly vamping go-go girls have that ultra-'60s Edie Sedgwick coldness down pat, and they're hard to resist. But on the radio, where it's just as hard to tell feathered Rod from pony-tailed Ron, the music is flooded with a new warmth, probably because Rod and Ron are riding the melody, and toward the same goal: their shared past.

9 ▪ The Ghost of Gene Chandler, "Duke of Earl," on *Billboard Top Rock 'n' Roll Hits—1962* (Rhino CD) Digital displacement No. 7891: did you know this featured organ, guitar, *clarinet*? It does now—and if you believe that sound converted into numbers tells the truth, what once seemed a primarily casual piece of singing has now been revealed as a precise, professional, altogether constructed piece of orchestration. I'm not sure we're richer for this information.

10 ▪ Charles Freeman, proprietor, E. C. Records, arrested on charges of distributing obscene material for selling copies of 2 Live Crew's *As Nasty As They Wanna Be* (Fort Lauderdale) "America is free, free for everybody," he said two days after federal judge Jose Gonzalez found the music "as much against the law as assault, rape, [or] kidnapping." "I'll go to jail, and I'll come back and sell it again."

JULY 24, 1990

1 ▪ Alexander Brodsky and Ilya Utkin, *Site Specific Installation*, in "Between Spring and Summer: Soviet Conceptual Art in the Era of Late Communism" (Tacoma Art Museum, through September 9, at the Institute of Contemporary Art in Boston, November 1 through January 6, 1991) Over your head is a labyrinth—or spiderweb—of household detritus. Below is a clear pool with hundreds of scissors, batteries, rags, broken toys; the pool is layered and infinitely deep. Crumbling Greek columns connect the pool to what seems like its overhead reflection. But the stuff overhead is real; the stuff below is just imagery. It feels like the opposite. The piece has a room to itself, and it makes a world; it should be called "The Archaeology of Everyday Life," or "The Ruins."

2 ■ Sonic Youth, "Tunic (Song for Karen)," from *Goo* (Geffen) Dressed up as Karen Carpenter in heaven—or stripped naked—Kim Gordon insists on the edge that was almost always cutting in Carpenter's singing, the edge Carpenter did everything she could to hide, failing only with "Superstar," "Merry Christmas Darling," her life, and this song.

3 ■ Romantics, "What I Like About You" (Diamond Vision reissue, 1980) Once the Oakland A's took Kool and the Gang's "Celebration" as a theme song, and had a Coasters' hit rewritten as "Billy Ball." Now, at the Oakland Coliseum, you hear the Romantics every time the A's win, except when the Diamond Vision archivists program Michael Morales's version. It's not as good, but you won't hear it anywhere else.

4 ■ Jon Wiener, on Albert Goldman's *Life* cover story, "Thirteen Years After the Death of ELVIS PRESLEY New Evidence Points to an Inescapable Conclusion—SUICIDE" (June) "When Goldman brings out a new paperback of his Lennon book, he will discover that he was wrong; Lennon committed suicide. People told him, it was there in his notes, but he missed it."

5 ■ Van Morrison, "Almost Independence Day," from *Saint Dominic's Preview* (Warner Bros, 1972) and X: "4th of July," from *See How We Are* (Elektra, 1987) It's right that flag burning is legal, but I could never do it; to say that the flag is only a symbol is to trivialize the diversion of religious epistemology into secular Western culture since Jehovah forbade images of himself, which is to say that to burn the flag is to make a kind of exile. If you want confirmation that the flag contains betrayal as well as promise, you can listen to these songs. X asks the promises of the Fourth of July to redeem the betrayals of a marriage; the conflation of the personal and the political is insensate and inevitable because the promises are boundless. Morrison watches from Marin as fireworks explode over San Francisco Bay. The lights are shrouded in the fog that rolls in over the Marin hills, and very nearly the whole of the instrumentation is in the Moog synthesizers of the late Bernie Krause and Mark Naftalin, who make a foghorn sound—a fog sound. But if fireworks are already exploding, why is it "almost" Independence Day?

6 ■ Gang of Four, *The Peel Sessions Album* (Strange Fruit, UK, 1979–81) The most exciting account available of the discovery that everything we understand as natural is someone else's project.

7 ■ Social Distortion, "Ball and Chain," from *Social Distortion* (Columbia) The Rolling Stones' "Dead Flowers" without humor, but that lack, perhaps forcing you to take the singer's self-pity seriously, could be what's kept this crude number sneaking around the radio for months. What's simple—simplistic—about the tune, and that includes the blurry guitars, the fourth-hand lyrics, the worn-out voice (which senses a hit), is also what's irreducible about it. Verdict: a classic.

8 ■ Gene Pitney, the Embers, the 5 Belairs, etc., *Unreleased Gems of the 1950s—The Hartford Groups* (Relic, 1957–59) Doo–Wop looking for a way out of itself, topped by Pitney's "Victory" and "Darkness." Yep, he was weird from the start.

9 ■ Guns N' Roses, "Knockin' on Heaven's Door," from *Days of Thunder* soundtrack (Paramount) Little Richard cut the answer record in 1957.

10 ■ Anonymous, "The Insult That Made a Stiff Out of a Stooge!" in *Skels Life #7* (March) The old Charles Atlas wimp-who-gets-sand-kicked-in-his-face comic-strip ad, fanzined. The creep sits on the beach listening to Guns N' Roses' "immigrants and faggots. . . . police and niggers," gets dog shit kicked in his face, goes home, and kicks his dog: "I'm sick and tired of being a piece of human refuse!" Next panel: he's hanged himself. Dog, thinking: "Cool."

AUGUST 28, 1990

1 ■ Cetu Javu, "A Donde," B-side of "So Strange" (ZYX, West Germany, 1989) Erasure as Alphaville, in excelsis.

2 ▪ Charles Shaar Murray, *Crosstown Traffic—Jimi Hendrix and the Post-War Rock 'n' Roll Revolution* **(St Martin's)** Criticism, not bio, magically combining irreverence with utter seriousness.

3 ▪ Odds, "Truth or Dare," from *By the Seat of Our Pants* **(demo cassette)** From Vancouver, postpunk but also post-Beatles: full-throated, nothing-held-back singing so bent on its own epiphanies it cuts loose from its own band. Not as simple as it sounds.

4 ▪ Alice Donut, "My Boyfriend's Back," B-side of "Demonologist" **(Alternative Tentacles, San Francisco, CA)** The 1963 No. 1 hit by the Angels, redone as a grunge-fest, almost a disease, sung by a guy, of course, with horrible new lyrics, which is why some sort of milestone in the new (rock) historicism is reached with the author's credit: "Traditional."

5 ▪ Two Nice Girls, *Like a Version* **(Rough Trade US)** Among five covers, a faithful reprise of the Carpenters' "Top of the World" and an angelic reading of Sonic Youth's "Cotton Crown" (the pairing anticipated Sonic Youth's Karen Carpenter tribute, "Tunic," and very naturally—real fans don't hear the genre boundaries record companies think sell records), plus TNG's own "I Spent My Last $10.00 (On Birth Control and Beer)"—"My life was so much simpler/ When I was sober/And queer."

6 ▪ Dave Ray and Tony Glover, "HIV Blues," from *Ashes in My Whiskey* **(Rough Trade US)** In the early '60s (John) Koerner, Ray & Glover were folkie blues players, and what they did then Ray (guitar) and Glover (harmonica) do now, except on this cut, which is blues without modifiers. Glover doesn't so much sing as let his voice break over the words; the fluttery harp and the shuddering electric guitar (there's a touch of Lowell Fulson's "Tollin' Bells") make a sound that seems to dissolve as soon as you hear it; they take the song where Glover's vocal can't, or won't.

7 ▪ John Densmore, *Riders on the Storm—My Life With Jim Morrison and the Doors* **(Delacorte)** The drummer writes as a man still trying to get the echo of an ex-

plosion 20 years gone out of his head, and thus addressing the better parts of his modest book to Morrison in heaven, hoping Jim will get the joke that the echo now likely has more fans than the explosion ever did: *"Cigar-Pain, remember him? The young bum (and there weren't as many young ones then) who used to hang around our rehearsal studio and burn his tongue with a lit cigar in order to acquire a singing voice like you . . . news came recently that he killed his mother and then himself. . . . He got our lyrics all wrong; he was supposed to kill his father and fuck his mother!"*

8 ▪ Sonic Youth, "Mary-Christ," from *Goo* **(Geffen)** Nothing close to it since Captain Beefheart, 1969: "Tits tits the blimp the blimp/The mother ship the mother ship/The brothers hid under their hood/From the blimp the blimp."

9 ▪ Guns N' Roses, "Civil War," from *Nobody's Child—Romanian Angel Appeal* **(Warner Bros.)** Closing out a set of unbearable piety (the "angels" are orphans, like fetuses are "innocent human life"), this titanic slab of hard rock is staggeringly powerful, at least until Axl Rose's whining chant of "I DON'T NEED YOUR CIVIL WAR" cuts against both the music and its context. The Romanians certainly needed the civil war the music dramatizes—but then Axl doesn't look beyond number one, and not just on the charts.

10 ▪ Colin Hughes, "Search for Antichrist leads soldiers astray" **(London Independent/San Francisco Examiner, July 23)** "Five men and one woman, all of whom worked with the 701st Military Intelligence Brigade . . . [and] belonged to the End of the World Group . . . went AWOL on July 9 from their station in Augsburg, West Germany . . . The soldiers set off for Florida in search of the Antichrist but apparently failed to find the biblically prognosticated evil one before being arrested last Sunday in Gulf Breeze, Fla. Now they are awaiting court-martial on desertion charges." Reached in Los Angeles, John Lydon, former singer for the rock group the Sex Pistols and one-time self-professed "Antichrist" had "No comment. Probably they just wanted to go to Disneyworld. The media always lie. Anyway, I wasn't in Florida. Ha ha ha ha ha."

My apologies to Bernie Krause, who I killed off in last month's entry on Van Mor-rison's "Almost Independence Day"; he isn't dead, though this column is, at least in these pages. It will reappear in Artforum, beginning with the November issue. My thanks to Doug Simmons for 57 months of friendly editing and good talk.

Artforum

1990·1998

1 ■ **W. T. Lhamon, Jr.,** *Deliberate Speed— The Origins of a Cultural Style in the American 1950s* **(Smithsonian Institution Press)** Lhamon's thesis that the American '50s were culturally rich is not so novel as it might have been when he began his book, ten years ago, but his set pieces are shockingly original. On Chuck Berry's "Promised Land," for instance, heard since 1964 as Berry's "poor boy's" happy odyssey from Virginia to California—"but that," Lhamon says, "is its minstrel mask." Noting that the song was written in prison, Lhamon redescribes it—so vividly and with such historical detail you could say he reinscribes it—as a coded but insistently specific parable of the early civil rights movement, reconnecting Rock Hill, South Carolina, to the Freedom Rides, Birmingham to its bombed church, and the poor boy's "broke down" Greyhound to the Freedom Riders' torched bus. Safe in Los Angeles, the singer calls home, Tidewater 4-1009: "He achieves the promised land only after a hell of a trip; everyone the poor boy cares about is still in hell."

2 ■ **Luther Campbell and 2 Live Crew,** *Banned in the U.S.A.* **(Luke/Atlantic)** Bruce Springsteen got as much as he gave when he let the former Luke Skyywalker (the name banned by George Lucas, not the sheriff of Broward County, Florida, or the federal judiciary) redo his "Born in the U.S.A." for this celebration of free speech. Not only is it as stirring as the first version, it replaces the dead patriotism that fans from Ronald Reagan to millions of audience fist-thrusters loaded onto the song with the ironies Springsteen wrote but could never get heard.

3 ■ **Fastbacks, "In the Summer" et al. (No Threes/Steve Priest Fan Club)** A band that's wandered for nearly a decade in the pop wilderness plays like it's ready for another thirty. For two numbers the wilderness is all you hear—doubt, fatigue, and holding back—and then comes "Everything That I Don't Need," written by guitarist

Kurt Bloch, sung by Kim Warnick. In the ep's sleeve photos, both of them look too old and beaten for the glory of this small refusal: rock simple, rock treasure.

4 ■ **Patrick Wright, "Gesture Politics,"** in *New Statesman & Society* **(vol. 3 no. 103, June 1)** On Jan Budaj, a Slovakian "stoker-intellectual" from Bratislava, who "spent the seventies pursuing a cultural civil war against the Communist regime. . . . Drawing on such sources as Conceptual Art, Duchamp and Dada, Budaj set out to demonstrate the lies on which Communist 'reality' was built. He hung his own renegade version of the conventional slogan-ridden red banner on a prominent public building in Bratislava: it bore the obligatory red star and a completely meaningless jumble of letters, and the success with which it proved its point could be counted through the many weeks that passed before the authorities recognized it as a fake. . . . He produced highly realistic official posters advertising cultural events which could never happen in Bratislava—a concert by Abba and Bob Dylan, or the coming of Ingmar Bergman's latest film. Box offices were inundated."

5 ■ **Lonnie Mack, "Stop," from** *Live!— Attack of the Killer V* **(Alligator)** Mack—a 49-year-old guitarist with a Flying V Gibson—once told a story about a mouse that crossed his stage in the middle of a tune; when Mack hit his "highest, most soulful note," he said, the mouse dropped dead, and on those terms this nine-minute blues is a massacre: loud no matter how low you play it, containing an irreducible quietness no matter how high you crank it up.

6 ■ **Allan Moyle, writer and director,** *Pump Up the Volume* **(New Line Cinema)** The full weight of this film about a teenager's pirate radio station is the realization that the obscene idiosyncrasy of his nightly broadcasts is utterly right and proper, the First Amendment alive to itself, and under the law today completely impossible (as it wouldn't have been during the early Reagan years, when free-market libertarians were running the FCC). Always threatening

to turn into an already-made lousy movie—
Footloose, Rock 'n' Roll High School, Network, Heathers—it never does, thanks mostly to Christian Slater. In the end it can leave a smile on your lips and pain in your heart.

7 ▪ Gang of Four, *Money Talks* (Scarlett, U.K.) The Leeds postpunk band, reformed as a gang of two: singer Jon King and guitarist Andy Gill, plus hired musicians and vocalist Louise Goffin, daughter of Brill Building songwriters ("Will You Love Me Tomorrow") Gerry Goffin and Carole King. The music takes its cue from King's deeply layered sleeve collage on Pax Americana, which borrows as surely from Art & Language as from London's Imperial War Museum and recent news photos of George Bush and Manuel Noriega—who appear here as twins, their arms raised together in comradeship.

8 ▪ Birney Imes, *Juke Joint* (University Press of Mississippi) These blazing pictures of crudely, seriously decorated black bars and nightclubs in the Mississippi Delta may be the first successful transference of Walker Evans' style to color photography. Imes' use of red yellow and blue is as extreme and unnatural as Evans' somber framing, and as convincing. You page through the book spellbound, dizzy with its light; then you go into it again and again, picking out the ads made into art, the slogans of good times and gentility ("BE NICE OR LEAVE—THANK YOU"). Docked a notch for a cretinous introduction by novelist Richard Ford.

9 ▪ Eric Bogosian, "Benefit," from *Sex, Drugs, Rock & Roll* (SBK) The record of the performance piece: cheap shots, but with a We-Are-the-Worlder U.K. rocker on a talk show condemning drugs while stoned out of his mind, worth a few bucks.

10 ▪ David Robbins, editor, *The Independent Group: Postwar Britain and the Aesthetics of Plenty* (MIT Press, catalogue of exhibition: 4 November–13 January 1991, Museum of Contemporary Art, Los Angeles; 6 February–21 April, University Art Museum, Berkeley; 8 June–18 August, Hood Museum of Art, Dartmouth College, Hanover, N.H.) Given that the Independent Group—Richard Hamilton, Reyner Banham, Lawrence Alloway, Eduardo Paolozzi, Peter and Alison Smithson, and a few more—brought Futurism and Dada into British art schools, thus inspiring everyone from John Lennon to Johnny Rotten, it's odd that pop music is hardly mentioned in this book. In another sense it's not surprising: the IG was always engaged in a kind of slumming, a condescension carried through and confessed to in these pages. "We deliberately crossed up the borders of fine and popular art," Alloway says, but Peter Smithson is more honest: "'isn't that a handsome picture or a handsome layout which I could parody for a fine art picture?'" The collage work of the IG was never so free as Kenneth Halliwell and Joe Orton's brutal alterations of library books, which sent them to prison. Finally the group's embrace of the popular emerges less as appropriation than as droit du seigneur. Pick to click: from the 1956 "This Is Tomorrow" show, Banham's still-thrilling dada poem "Marriage of Two Minds," even if they were divorced in advance.

1 ▪ Neil Young & Crazy Horse, "Over and Over," from *Ragged Glory* (Reprise CD) Once upon a time Neil Young and a trio named Crazy Horse cut a tune called "Cowgirl in the Sand," three verses serving as an excuse for three guitar breaks. On the first of those, Young made four stabs at a leading theme. He tried it as flamenco, screech, fuzztone; finally he gave up and played scales. Only second guitarist Danny Whitten, playing around the beat, held the sound together. Then Young sang the next verse and came off it so fast the expectations a listener brought to the second break never had a chance. With bassist Billy Talbot and drummer Ralph Molina pushing the rhythm and Whitten somehow anticipating the explosions going off in Young's heart, the music changed into something there's no word for: by split seconds it grew bigger, too big, blew away the room. That was in 1969; Whitten died in 1972 of a heroin overdose, his place taken by Frank Sampedro. The other difference is that this time Young gets it all on his first try.

2 ■ **Memphis Slim, Big Bill Broonzy, and Sonny Boy Williamson, as recorded by Alan Lomax, *Blues in the Mississippi Night* (Ryko-disc CD with transcript)** In 1946 three black men sat in a small studio with a folklorist and described and sang their music. Their subjects were peonage, violence, white supremacy, and death. The language they spoke summoned up an ancient world that promised mostly it would never change: mentioning a holster, Memphis Slim (Peter Chatman, 1915–88) referred to it as a scabbard. The men were certain their families would be killed if their talk were made public, and when the session was released, in the late '50s, their names stayed missing. Now it's history—meaning not that you can forget about it, but that once you've heard it you cannot.

3 ■ **Simon Reynolds, *Blissed Out—The Raptures of Rock* (Serpent's Tall)** Drunk on good French wine (mouth-filling Bataille red, astringent Kristeva white), a self-described "acolyte of obliteration" and "sucker-ass liberal" claims the pop present of A. R. Kane and Metallica over what anyone else cares to make of its past or future. "'Bliss' and 'noise' are the same thing," this young British critic insists, as he grasps contradictions with both hands: "To embrace both decency and pop . . . to be a socialist by day and a hip hopper by night after a hard day's campaigning, are quite feasible options, but only in a rotten, free-market society such as our own." Thus Reynold's credo, "Pop or a better world. The choice is yours!"—a good joke when he first flips it at you, a true riddle by the time you close his book.

4 ■ **Danzig, *Danzig II—Lucifuge* (Def American)** What might happen if Jim Morrison reappeared fronting a mean, very efficient hard rock band: all those years in the grave would have turned his psychedelic shamanism into satanism, at least as a convincing career move. They would have also left him more ordinary, more passionate, and shameless, finally ready to admit how much he admires Gene Pitney.

5 ■ **Bob Dylan, "10,000 Men," from *Under the Red Sky* (Columbia)** His voice seems to drift away from him, all the way back to the way he sang "Trail of the Buffalo" 29 years ago, which may be where he left it.

6 ■ **Sidra Stich, curator, "Anxious Visions—Surrealist Art" (University Art Museum, Berkeley, through December 30; catalogue by Stich and others, Abbeville Press)** Stressing the realism in Surrealism, arguing for its objects as versions of experience directly lived—the cataclysm of World War I and the political chaos of the next two decades—the show uses blowups of contemporaneous news photos as a frame. Most striking is "The Union of Bashed Faces," ten formally dressed, hideously disfigured French veterans: "what," Stich says, "the surrealists saw when they walked down the street" (and what, had this show been up 12 years ago, we would have seen—on punk flyers). Reflected off this item, the likes of Dora Marr's uncanny photograph *Père Ubu* (1936: a fetal armadillo that looks a thousand years old) don't seem precious, or in any manner fantastic. They seem most of all unfrivolous.

7 ■ **Boogie Down Productions, *Edutainment* (RCA)** Hip-hop as lecture, thin and echoing—a great lecture, sometimes, as with "Love's Gonna Get 'Cha (Material Love)," a dope-dealer parable that with its tinny toy-Uzi sound effects falls not far short of the empathy and fright of Grandmaster Flash and the Furious Five's "The Message."

8 ■ **Anonymous, *Fascist*—"Life Affirmation" issue** A Xeroxed collage journal, highlighted by an Archie comic with new speech balloons, wherein meliorist Veronica and CIA plant Archie outpoint commie

dupe Betty in a dispute over Gramsci's concept of hegemony, then call for violins to be dubbed in on every Replacements lp.

9 ▪ Spoc, "I Fought the Law" (wedding in Corunna, MI, 21 September, as reported by the AP) The groom was a major drug buyer fronting for a crime boss, or so the guests, all of them dealers, had been led to believe; when the band—COPS spelled backward—broke into the old Bobby Fuller Four hit, the bride pulled a gun from under her gown, and she and the rest of the wedding party busted everybody else. Whether it was a fitting homage to Fuller may depend on whether you believe his death in 1966 was due to accidental asphyxiation or, as rumor had it, gasoline poured down his throat.

10 ▪ Great Balls of Fire, Inc., Nampa, ID, Great Balls of Fire® Strike a match to one of these little gray spheres (six per box) and your charcoal or firewood starts up slow and steady, no flare, no smell. In a year or so they'll have figured out how to make the things play the song while they burn.

JANUARY 1991

1 ▪ Susan McClary, "Living to Tell: Madonna's Resurrection of the Fleshly," in *Feminine Endings: Music, Gender, and Sexuality* (University of Minnesota Press) McClary, a professor in the School of Music at the University of Minnesota, writes that her certification as a guardian of the highest and purest of Western art traditions demanded only a single sacrifice: "that I never ask what any of it means." Thus McClary moves from female characters in 17th-century opera to Laurie Anderson as an apostate, but also as a teacher who's found her own voice, a critic empowered by feminist theory and the thrill of fandom. "The strategies of Madonna's songs are those of one who has radically conflicting subject positions—one who has been taught to cheer for resolutions in cultural narratives, but who also realizes that she is of the sort that typically gets purged for the sake of that resolution"—this is the ordinary language version of McClary's formal, precisely musi-

cological reading of the uncanny reversals and suspensions in Madonna's "Live to Tell," a reading as intense and lucid as the record itself.

2 ▪ Roxy Music, *Heart Still Beating* (Reprise/EG) A concert recorded in 1982 in Fréjus, France, by the remains of the best band of its time. Exquisite, though only fans will care; one day, some may even claim to have been there.

3 ▪ Robert Johnson, *The Complete Recordings* (Columbia reissue, 1936–37); Hindu Love Gods (Warren Zevon with members of R.E.M.): "Travelin' Riverside Blues," from *Hindu Love Gods* (Reprise/Giant); Led Zeppelin: "Travelling Riverside Blues," from *Led Zeppelin* (Atlantic four-CD reissue, 1969) Mississippi bluesman Robert Johnson finally made the pop charts last fall, 52 years after his death. The occasion was the release of a 41-track boxed set—marred by scholastic programming, dumbly cropped photos, erroneous lyric transcriptions, and an illiterate, coyly racist biographical essay by coproducer Stephen C. LaVere. Two noisy, scattershot versions of one of Johnson's shapeliest songs—both natural singles—erase LaVere's garbage with pop trash.

4 ▪ Blake Babies, *Sunburn* (Mammoth) A Boston trio (Freda Boner, drums; Juliana Hatfield, bass & vocals; John Strohm, guitar & vocals) that hints at the heedless negations of Minnesota's Babes in Toyland, though ultimately Hatfield's teenage voice shies away back to Clare Grogan of Altered Images, and Strohm's plain-talk "Train" harks back much farther than that: "I know that train you're riding on / It's 16 coaches long / My baby's on that train and gone." It speaks perfectly to

5 ▪ Alison Krauss, "Steel Rails," from *I've Got That Old Feeling* (Rounder) She's a teenage bluegrass fiddler with hundreds of years in her throat. The voice is small, always reaching for melody, somehow always slow within quick tempos, but her knowledge doesn't hold against

6 ▪ Rosanne Cash, *Interiors* (Columbia) She may stand as the greatest of the Cash family. Seduced by rock 'n' roll but unable to trust it, again and again she's reembraced country, even waved at Las Vegas, but her touch betrays the fear that someday, in her career or in her private life, she could end up just like anybody else.

7 ▪ **Marcia Ball, Lou Ann Barton & Angela Strehli, *Dreams Come True* (Antone's)** Hot stuff from white Texas soul singers who define their genre at the ends of certain lines, where words fray into instinctive melisma; thick, weathered voices that go clear in moments of surprise; and, with Barton's "Bad Thing," a last-call rocker written by bassist Sarah Brown, the sound of a whip hitting flesh, mainly to keep time.

8 ▪ **Mick Fleetwood with Stephen Davis, *Fleetwood: My Life and Adventures in Fleetwood Mac* (Morrow)** For 23 years drummer for a group that today bears no resemblance to the drunken, obscene, blues-purist ensemble as which it began, Fleetwood's pop history cum autobiography ("too stupid to do anything else") is irrepressibly engaging and happily shallow—profoundly shallow, maybe. Fleetwood is ordinary and he treasures his ordinariness; his tale is shadowed by the early departures of his first three guitarists, all victims of one or another kind of madness. The term "deep blues" is rightly reserved for black artists, but Fleetwood Mac founder Peter Green—born Peter Greenbaum, a Jew who became a solitary, sackcloth Christian—deserves it as Duane Allman never did and Eric Clapton never has. Listening today, Green's late-'60s Fleetwood Mac blues—more than any, "Love that Burns," inspired by Chicago bluesman Otis Rush's "Double Trouble" and perhaps outreaching it—are shockingly cruel, romance caught at just that pass where it turns into nihilism. Mick Fleetwood has played on a dozen memorable pop hits, but once he touched genius; his book is about how pleasant it is to be free of it.

9 ▪ **Pet Shop Boys, "Being Boring," from *Behavior* (EMI)** Bohemian life as lived by British art students—very distant, flattened words, the joys of insularity, and the first true follow-up to the duo's 1987 "Rent," a

tale of expensive male prostitution, though from which side you were never sure, as you're not here.

10 ▪ **Edwin Heaven, writer & director, trailer for 13th Annual Mill Valley Film Festival (Act One theater, Berkeley, 6 October 1990, preceding *Henry & June*)** It was hilarious: a celebration of the Art of Film by means of an impossibly rushed montage of super-pretentious silent-movie clips. Oddly, the audience didn't laugh. After the credits rolled, there was a final title card: "FREE JAMES BROWN!" The house roared as one, as if the director's sole real homage was some kind of joke; then, when the last title to *Henry & June* came up, with the information that, after Paris, June Miller became a social worker, the crowd responded with the same mass titter. Talk about "High & Low" . . .

1 ▪ **ZZ Top, "My Head's in Mississippi," *Recycler* (Warner Bros.)** Mick Jagger may have achieved union with the map of the South in "Parachute Woman," but Billy Gibbons, with his feet in Texas, is probably the first to eat it. The lurching beat and the voice he can't quite pull out of his throat describe what it means to remember a ten-day drunk in the middle of another one: you see God in a toilet bowl. "I keep thinking 'bout that night in Memphis," Gibbons testifies. "Lord, I thought I was in heaven / I keep thinking 'bout that night in Memphis / I thought I was in heaven / But I was stumblin' through the parking lot / Of an invisible 7-Eleven." This will have been up and down the charts by now, but it'll be back.

2 ▪ **Sharyn McCrumb, *If Ever I Return, Pretty Peggy-O* (Scribner's)** A chilly, carefully paced murder mystery about the return of Vietnam ghosts to a small Tennessee town that seems to have spent the last twenty years looking over its shoulder. The story revolves around three kinds of music: the sheriff's "internal Muzak," the radio that plays in his head according to the clues

everyday life kicks up; the hit parade of his Viet-vet deputy, mostly lurid sounds of Hendrix, the Doors; and the traditional Appalachian tunes of the famous-long-ago '60s folksinger who's lately moved into town. In every case, music is compulsively mnemonic, never utopian, enclosing, never liberating. The strands come together when, according to the archaic ballad "The Knoxville Girl," a girl is found floating in the song's river, and the sheriff's radio turns on "Moody River," sung by Pat Boone, "almost mindlessly cheerful," the sheriff thinks, but then he's not the DJ, just the receiver. Finally the killer comes back from the war: "Sex is good, but killing is better. You can *remember* killing clearer." And music even more clearly than that.

3 ■ **Sisters of Mercy,** *Vision Thing* **(Elektra)** Gloom and doom from Leeds, England, with a brutal title song about George Bush and a hit, "More," produced by notorious Meat Loaf-meister Jim Steinman: very pretentious, and convincing from beginning to end.

4 ■ *Geraldo,* **"The Women They Sang About," 28 November 1990 (CBS)** Featuring Angela Bowie ("Angie," Rolling Stones, 1973), Barbara Ann Rizzo ("Barbara Ann," Regents, 1961, Beach Boys, 1965), Peggy Sue Rackham ("Peggy Sue," Buddy Holly, 1957), and Donna Fox ("Donna," Ritchie Valens, 1958). The Regents were present to sing "Barbara Ann" as its namesake danced with Geraldo, but the real action was with Fox. Geraldo asked her if it was true, as shown in the film *La Bamba,* that Valens wrote "Donna" for her because her father wouldn't let her go out with a Hispanic. It was certainly true, Fox said: "My dad wasn't a very nice man. I haven't seen my father since I was 18. . . . I snuck out. I climbed out the window." "Was your dad waiting for you?" "No, he was usually passed out." No songs about that, then, but another exchange was mythical even if it happened, a novel in a day. When *La Bamba* was released, Rackham read in the paper that Fox lived in Sacramento, as does she. She called her up. "Are you the Donna in the song?" *Oh no,* thought Fox, who'd been inundated by calls from '50s cultists, *another one.* "Yes," she said. "Well," said Rackham, "I'm Peggy Sue."

5 ■ *Nightline,* **"Justify My Love" video plus interview with Madonna, 3 December 1990 (ABC)** For all the press this show got, no one seems to have mentioned the most shocking moment: at the end of a Rock the Vote anticensorship commercial, Donny Osmond in an SS uniform, grinning madly.

6 ■ **Van Morrison,** *Enlightenment* **(Mercury)** After twenty-five years his voice has turned thick; in another twenty-five it may still float, even if it's on *Van Morrison Sings John McCormack,* who can be heard in

7 ■ **Ethan and Joel Coen,** *Miller's Crossing* **(20th Century Fox)** What lifts this academically severe version of Dashiell Hammett (*Red Harvest,* "The Big Knockover") out of its homage is the face of Gabriel Byrne's Irish gangster. He has the malevolent intelligence you once saw in Bob Dylan, a look—and it's far too complex to be a single look—that Sting, Chuck D., Ice Cube, and Sinéad O'Connor will be working on for years.

8 ■ *Twin Peaks,* **17 November 1990 (ABC)** With Benjamin Horne briefly jailed for the murder of Laura Palmer (I still think he did it), his lawyer brother notices the cell's metal bunk beds, thinks of the nice wooden bunks he once shared with Ben, then remembers something else from their bedroom: the two of them, 10 or 12, sitting wide-eyed in the dark as an older Louise Dombrowski danced for them with a flashlight, swaying magically to Angelo Badalamenti's generically obvious version of the corniest piano-triplet doo-wop. The scene caught the feel of teenage sex you can find in fiction by Keith Abbott and Jill McCorkle and not often elsewhere: the mystery of an unfamiliar body, the other's, yours, desire that breaks no rules because it dissolves them—desire that, unsatisfied, decades later, can make new sense as death. "I knew I was going to lie there with him on that sleeping bag and

I was going to look through the slit in the drapes to that empty room, the windows there, beyond which the trees were lush and green," McCorkle's Kate remembers in *Ferris Beach* (Algonquin, 1990), prettifying, then not: "I was going to pretend that there was no day other than this one, no world beyond those trees; there was no future, no guarantee that I would turn sixteen, this was it."

9 ▪ **Paris, *The Devil Made Me Do It* (Tommy Boy)** A flat San Francisco rapper celebrated for his bring-back-the-Black-Panthers rhetoric (you won't hear it anywhere else), his disc appropriately packaged with bios of Nat Turner, Elijah Muhammad, Malcolm X, and Huey Newton, ignoring what Malcolm X found out about Elijah Muhammad and sadly noting that in 1989 Newton was murdered by "unknown assailants," as opposed to the Oakland crack dealer who confessed to the killing. In other words, pop Stalinism, or the kind of revisionism you can find in most textbooks on American history.

10 ▪ **Students in Biology and Society 451, AIDS and Society, 6 December 1990 (Cornell University student union)** Having taped "Justify My Love" off *Nightline*, the class ran the video nonstop as part of AIDS Awareness Week, handing out condoms to the hundreds who came to watch—most of whom, the *Cornell Daily Sun* reported, "laughed self-consciously." One condemned the clip as "warped." " 'You should have to pay a quarter to see this video in an adult book store,' said Alex C. Smith, '92." Wake up: Jesse Helms is not the enemy. The enemy is nice people you have to argue with.

MARCH 1991

1 ▪ **Various radio stations, format violation, January 15** After so many years devoted to erasing the notion that in the mix of radio sounds one might expect a subject, it was a shock, on this strange, suspended day, to find the medium talking to you, in a kind of celebration of dread. No matter

what button you pushed you were faced with the same conversation, the pressure drop of Edwin Starr's "War," or Bruce Springsteen's cover of it, or Freda Payne's "Bring the Boys Home," Country Joe and the Fish's "I-Feel-Like-I'm-Fixin'-to-Die Rag," Gang of Four's "I Love a Man in a Uniform," Creedence Clearwater's "Bad Moon Rising," Peter Gabriel's "Here Comes the Flood," an unidentified woman's "Will Jesus Wash the Blood from Your Hands," the Beatles' "I Wanna Be Your Man" (relief, violation of the new format within the old format; it felt fabulous). Bob Dylan's "Masters of War" and Plastic Ono Band's "Give Peace a Chance" seemed thin and arch, too far above the mess of confused, violently random emotion, morally insulated (though not so much as Sean Lennon and Lenny Kravitz's Peace Choir smile-button video for their new version of the tune, so removed from fear its basic message might have been that Cyndi Lauper had found a way to get back on MTV). Cutting through the many voices, even those of songs only playing in your head—Elvis Costello's "(What's So Funny 'bout) Peace, Love and Understanding," maybe, or Metallica's "One," or Laurie Anderson's "O Superman" ("Your military arms," so softly, "your petrochemical arms")—was the Pogues' "And the Band Played Waltzing Matilda." It's a long, slow, unbearably bitter first-person account of a mutilated Australian soldier who came back from Gallipoli; Shane MacGowan collapses 70 years to make the man explain why he wishes he hadn't come back, self-hate and wonderment dripping from every line. When the war began the next day HBO had *Top Gun* scheduled and the radio was back to normal.

2 ▪ **Blue Sky Boys, "Where the Soul of Man Never Dies," from *Something Got a Hold of Me—A Treasury of Sacred Music* (RCA reissue, 1936)** This modest white-gospel embrace of the unknowable says it's the Holy Land; Sam Phillips once said it was Howlin' Wolf.

3 ▪ **Ed Sanders, *The Family—The Manson Group and Its Aftermath* (Signet/NAL**

reissue, 1971) Twenty-two years later it still sits there, right in the middle of the Beach Boys' 20/20, "Never Learn Not to Love." "A disturbing lyric and an hypnotic sound," read the liner notes to the CD reissue. No kidding: credited to Dennis Wilson, in truth the song was written by Charles Manson. He titled it "Cease To Exist," and that's what it says, even now. Even now: "Out there somewhere," Sanders says at the end of this extensively updated edition of one of the few great books on and from the '60s, "are the scattered handful of foreheads with faint fading X's. . . ." If that doesn't make your flesh creep maybe the book won't scare you. Here sex can seem uglier than murder, murder more casual than sex, sex so often ritual, dog blood poured on copulating bodies a logical extension of the standard Family initiation or its everyday, California, do-your-own-thing version of Adamite and Free Spirit beliefs and practices that went back almost a thousand years. Even without the material on the Process Church of the Final Judgment and the Solar Lodge of the Ordo Templi Orientis, removed after the first edition because of lawsuits (but that's what libraries are for), Sanders' narrative casts a spell so strong it can suck in almost anything. I saw the Shangri-Las in a TV nostalgia clip doing "Give Him a Great Big Kiss" and in their blithe teenage nihilism they could have been from Manson's harem; I heard Neil Young singing about an old man with a kind voice and wild eyes in "Mansion on the Hill"—the one with the creaky psychedelic music drifting out of the windows— and who else could it be? "He was different," Young remembered a few years ago. "Something about him that's . . . I can't forget it. I don't know what you would call it, but I wouldn't want to call it anything in an interview."

4 ▪ Sydney Youngblood, *Sydney Youngblood* (Arista) The shift from the classically arranged soul misery of "I'd Rather Go Blind" to the dance of hooks in the following "Sit and Wait" indicates this young singer could take Roland Gift's place in

Fine Young Cannibals if he had to, but he won't have to.

5 ▪ Robert Klein, "Fabulous 50's," from *Child of the 50's* (Rhino reissue, 1973) The comic throws every trick of the genre into this doo-wop parody, and every one shines, especially the recitation, "And so/I wrote a letter/To Joe McCarthy/In the sky"— "*Joe McCarthy/In the sky,*" echoes the falsetto chorus—"I said, 'My teacher is a Communist. . . .'"

6 ▪ Tony Scherman, "The Hellhound's Trail—Following Robert Johnson" (*Musician,* January) The best result of the botched release of Johnson's *Complete Recordings* is this set of interviews with 11 contemporary musicians on the '30s country bluesman. Vernon Reid presses the tension between the existential and the social, Robert Plant the thrill of the unexplainable, Ry Cooder impossibility ("It is *very hard to do* . . . I don't play Robert Johnson's music, 'cause I just can't get in the door"), Jim Dickinson talks about madness, and Billy Gibbons about "why the Mississippi Delta blues— the work of just a few people, who were black, illiterate, who were from a whole other world than urban people in the '90s— can still affect us so deeply": because "there was no reason, ethnically or politically or spiritually, for these guys to hold back."

7 ▪ Chumbawamba, "Ulrike," from *Slap!* (Agit-Prop) As a reggae horn section kicks up dust, a duet from beyond the grave: a pseudo-Meinhof, insisting in a clear, unsolemn pop voice that she's not sorry ("Don't think I walked into banks to stand in the queue"—Raymond Chandler wouldn't have minded having written that); then Elvis, not pseudo but sampled (credited as a band member doubling on Quaaludes and Placydil), aiming "Can't Help Falling in Love" right back.

8 ▪ David Lee Roth, *A Little Ain't Enough* (Warner Bros.) It's been seven years since "Jump" but he can still rewrite "Back Door Man" and call it "Hammerhead Shark."

9 ▪ California State Department of Motor Vehicles, radio public-service announcement (1991) 800 number to call for newly mandated training required for minor's motorcycle operator's license: 227-4337— or, as the ad put it, "CCR-IDER." And you thought bureaucrats couldn't sing the blues.

10 ▪ **Ice Cube, "Dead Homiez," from** *Kill at Will* **(Priority)** In naked mourning, the L.A. rapper gives up his armed 'n' dangerous pose to wear his heart on his sleeve— the sleeve of his DEAD HOMIEZ T-shirt, *which can be yours* for only $12.95. Add $3 for shipping and handling.

APRIL 1991

1 ▪ **Pamela Page and Patrick Montgomery,** *Rock and Roll the Early Days* **(Archive Films, 1985, running occasionally on VH-1)** Of all the documentaries on the subject—each one picking up much of the same stock footage of Elvis, of DJs breaking barbaric records on the air or White Citizens Council spokesmen denouncing animal music—none touches this one. That may be because it focuses so sharply on black artists and dancing. White zoot-suiters turn "Roll Over Beethoven" into Roll Over Isaac Newton; then black teenagers rise out of their seats in some Tropicana hotel ballroom and explode into a kicking line that's plainly not of this world—not *this* world, anyway. Clips of a shockingly cloddish Bill Haley are cut away into performances by Little Richard, Fats Domino, the Treniers— and Bo Diddley, who even in this company seems most of all strange, the Alien King. Poker-faced, riding that underwater guitar sound that simply does not connect to anyone else's rhythms, he negates the genre even as it's forming. He's at once primeval, inescapably African, and almost formally avant-garde, anticipating and then leaping past the Fluxus music of the years to come and back to Dada, which in certain moments thought it was African too. Throughout the production there's a controlling sense of novelty coming off the singers and dancers—the bounce of the new, an apprehension of the never before. It's so strong

that, as you watch, it can produce an unwanted corollary: never again.

2 ▪ **Eleventh Dream Day,** *Lived To Tell* **(Atlantic)** Made by a four-piece Chicago band, this is a record to get lost in, with vocal action that's hard to catch hovering over grinding, growling guitar noise like a heat mirage on a highway no one's driven for years. Guitarist Rick Rizzo does most of the singing, but it's drummer Janet Bean, rushing in at the end of a verse like Exene Cervenka ambushing John Doe in X, who nails song after song. Words emerge in fragments in a seamless aural setting; the whole, once you glimpse it, is exhilarating and bleak, the exhilaration of people saying what they mean even if they wish they could talk about something other than their fear of loss, defeat, and hiding. The music holds an inner drama, summed up in lines by Bean: "There's this thing, lately/Where the sound of tearing fabric/Is louder than the traffic."

3 ▪ **a-ha,** *East of the Sun, West of the Moon* **(Warner Bros)** Meaningless pop songs from a Swedish boy group.

4 ▪ **Book of Love,** *Candy Carol* **(Sire)** Dreamy, mysterious pop songs from a New York girl group. More or less meaningless, though not, were it to hit the radio, the muscular dance track "Quiver," as in "She/ Makes me. . . ."

5 ▪ **Randy Newman, "Lines in the Sand" (Reprise)** Not for sale, distributed only to DJs, and no surprise most didn't play it. Against the piety of "Voices That Care," the Hollywood tribute-to-the-troops number (they should have called it "We Are the War"), this was an elegy in advance: a cold, defeatist funeral march.

6 ▪ **Sport,** *Skels Life* **#10 (Mystery Fez)** Skels is a decent rock 'n' roll outfit but *Skels Life* is a great rock 'n' roll comic book, a 12-page collage of '60s underground styles, pornography, and male girdle ads that usually operates on the level of Jess's '50s Dick Tracy revisions. I keep coming back to one of the artworks that beat out Sport's latest bid for a government grant: Sinéad O'Connor as painted by "Walter Keen."

7 ▪ Bob Marley & the Wailers, *Talkin'
Blues* (Tuff Gang/Island) An impeccable live
set cut in 1973; when Marley sings "I remember / On the slave ship," "the mystic
chords of memory" is no metaphor.

8 ▪ Rolling Stones, "Gimmie Shelter" (as
licensed for a PSA for the American Red Cross)
What a fine conceit: a paramedic squad as
a band, with, among others, Paul Shaffer
"on keys" (at a blood-drive computer) and
Carly Simon "on lead," heroically guiding
some kids to safety with the same expression of celebrity noblesse oblige that Jean-
Luc Godard and Jean-Pierre Gorin spent a
whole film critiquing with the 1972 *Letter
to Jane: Investigation of a Still*. It's no use
saying the song deserves better; a commercial for home insurance would be better.

9 ▪ R.E.M., "I Walked with a Zombie,"
from *Where the Pyramid Meets the Eye—
A Tribute to Roky Erickson* (Sire) This is a
metaphor—for R.E.M. It's also their best
recording.

10 ▪ Richard Huelsenbeck, *Memoirs of a
Dada Drummer*, edited by Hans J. Klein-
schmidt (University of California Press reissue, 1974) Hulsenbeck (1892–1974) was the
Dada African (also a bourgeois German
medical student), pounding his big drum
and chanting "Negro poems" on the stage
of the Cabaret Voltaire in Zurich in 1916.
Perhaps because he wasn't an artist but
a noisemaker, a troublemaker, Herr Bad
News, he became Dada's most unapologetic chronicler and least evasive storyteller. Top tale in *Memoirs*: Richard meets
a girl from a nice family who appreciates his
promising future but not the embarrassing
stuff he does on stage—in other words, she
won't sleep with him unless he agrees to
give up Dada. He's in agony, he feels the
zeitgeist in his heart every night in the cabaret. On the other hand . . . Thus he gives
in—but, as he would later write, "Dada was
a creature which stood head and shoulders
above all present," and when the big night
comes he turns up impotent. So he went
back to the nightclub.

1 ▪ Bob Dylan, at the Grammy Awards
(CBS, 20 February) Thirty years after arriving in New York from Minnesota, Bob
Dylan stepped forward to be honored with
a Lifetime Achievement Award. The blanket of acceptance that had been draped over
the show was so heavy the WAR SUCKS
T-shirt New Kid on the Block Donnie
Wahlberg wore to the American Music
Awards a few weeks earlier would have
been forbidden here; maybe that's why
Dylan sang "Masters of War," and maybe
that's why he disguised it, smearing the
verses into one long word. If you caught on
to the number, the lyrics did emerge—
"And I'll stand o'er your grave/'Til I'm sure
that you're dead"—but lyrics were not the
point. What was was the ride Dylan and his
band gave them. With hats pulled down
and dressed dark, looking and moving like
Chicago hipsters from the end of the '50s,
guitarists Cesar Diaz and John Jackson,
bassist Tony Garnier, and drummer Ian
Wallace went after the song as if it was
theirs as much as Dylan's: a chance at revenge, excitement, pleasure. You couldn't
tell one from the other, and why bother?

With this career performance behind
him, Dylan took his trophy from a beaming Jack Nicholson; he squinted, as if looking for his mother, who was in the audience.
"Well," he said, "my daddy, he didn't leave
me much, you know, he was a very simple
man, but what he tell me was this, he did
say, *son*, he said"—there was a long pause,
nervous laughter from the crowd—"he say,
you know it's possible to become so defiled
in this world that your own mother and
father will abandon you and if that happens, God will always believe in your ability to mend your own ways."

Then he walked off. He had managed to
get in and out without thanking anybody,
and this night it really did seem as if he
owed nobody anything.

2 ▪ Rolling Stones, "Highwire" (Rolling
Stones Records) There's a helplessly celebratory cast to the flabby, crowded, let's-hope-

for-the-best closing choruses of this Desert Storm disc, but the action is up front, in the open sound that drives the verses (built around "Get up, stand up" and "Catch a fire," old revolutionary phrases from Bob Marley and the Wailers), in the amazingly cynical snap Mick Jagger uses to break up every line. Recorded just before the air war began, hitting the radio just as the ground war was ending, the song's timing made it simultaneously moot and dangerous: it came off as a cheap exploitation of the last war and a set-up for the next one.

3 ▪ **Enigma, *MCMXC a.D.* (Charisma)** For the nearly 12 minutes of "Principles of Lust," which includes the world-wide Gregorian chant-hit "Sadeness," probably the best heavy-breathing number since Jane Birkin and Serge Gainsbourg's 1969 "Je t'aime (moi non plus)"—which enjoyed a certain revival after Gainsbourg's March 2 death in Paris, though Conservative leader Jacques Chirac said it was Gainsbourg's song "Harley-Davidson" that was "engraved on my heart."

4 ▪ **Oliver Stone, director, *The Doors* (Tri-Star)** Nothing could be easier than to write this movie off, but there are currents of empathy at work throughout that bring you face to face with "the '60s" as a true curse: no grand, simple, romantic time to sell to present-day teenagers as a nice place to visit, but a time that, even as it came forth, people sensed they could never really inhabit, and also never leave. Stone catches this displacement in the concert sequences near the end of the Doors' career. He makes a terrific noise out of instruments, fans, booze, nudity, fire, feedback, and history, but as he moves the show on he makes the sound stop. All you can fix on is Val Kilmer's Jim Morrison, in a moment of complete suspension, caught between wondering how he got where he is and accepting that he can't go forward and he can't go back. It may not be the story the band set out to tell, but it's what the movie has done to

5 ▪ **The Doors, *The Doors* (Elektra, 1967)** It didn't cost much to listen to "Take It As It Comes" ("Time to laugh/Time to live/

Time to die," etc.), "The Crystal Ship," or the last, quiet minute of "The End" when they were new, but now you can hear an ugly momentum in the music, the music's urge to catch up with the people who made it. Forget the soundtrack album, forget best-of's and greatest hits; this is all you need, and, maybe, all there ever was.

6 ▪ **Fastbacks, *Very, Very Powerful Motor* (Popllama)** Unreconstructed punk with a lot of melody, no apologies (though there is a tune called "Apologies," along with "Trouble Sleeping," "What To Expect," "I Won't Regret," and "I Guess"), and Kim Warnick, for whom singing flat is just a form of realism.

7 ▪ **Gang of Four, *Mall* (PolyGram)** Where you don't pick up pennies because you don't want anyone to think you have to.

8 ▪ **H. L. Goodall, Jr., *Living in the Rock N Roll Mystery—Reading Context, Self, and Others as Clues* (Southern Illinois University Press)** An argument that "interpretive ethnography is to cultural studies what rock n roll is to social life," though the real questions here have to do with what "rock n roll" is, and the balance between social life and one's own life, finally unshareable no matter how loudly one shouts the awful facts. "In addition to the lives we lead we also live lives we don't lead," Goodall says; now on stage with his band, now following realtors around as they inspect properties, he makes himself his own test case, switching sides as self and other, musician and fan, detective and dupe, social scientist and impostor.

9 ▪ **Charles Reagan Wilson and William Ferris, editors, *Encyclopedia of Southern Culture* vols. 1–4 (Anchor)** Speaking of impostors . . .

10 ▪ **Pink Floyd, Julie Christie, the Small Faces, David Hockney, the Marquess of Kensington, etc., *Tonite Let's All Make Love In London* (See for Miles reissue, 1968)** To end our mini-'60s survey, this weird artifact: the augmented soundtrack to a forgotten Swinging London movie by Peter Whitehead. Pink Floyd offers nearly half an hour of intriguingly vague psychedelic music;

one Vashti sings bits of the charmingly innocent "Winter Is Blue"; and various people
talk about various aspects of the New
World, from Edna O'Brien on sex to Mick
Jagger on his plans to go into politics to Michael Caine and Lee Marvin (what's he
doing here?) on miniskirts: Marvin is pro,
Caine is con. It's a lot of fun, and patheti-
cally trivial: people trying to describe the
enormous energies of change and having a
hard time thinking of anything to say. But
then you run into Whitehead's 1990 liner
notes: "Never forget that what that time
meant to the people who were responsible
for creating that whole period and mood . . .
was the love of freedom, in the profound
sense, the hatred of fascism, in every
sense . . ." He goes on: "It was a time of anarchy, yes, but also a time of sowing . . .
seeds of hope and the future. Those seeds
are continuously sprouting in the most unexpected places, and there are a lot of them
still under the soil. . . . Keep an eye on
those verges at the side of the concrete
road . . . those margins at the side of that
colossal text, that thrust of rationality and
falsification. . . . Be ready when it comes—
the flood—Salome dancing again—the demise of history."

I found it hard to gainsay a word; I put
the disc back on and tried to make it give
up even a hint of what Whitehead was talking about. It didn't. Someone was crazy, but
I don't know who.

SUMMER 1991

Bob Dylan's *the bootleg series, volumes 1–3
(rare & unreleased) 1961–1991* (Columbia)
contains a shadow version of his entire
career, embedded within 58 performances.
They range from a tune taped in a Minnesota hotel room in 1961 to an outtake from
the 1989 album *Oh Mercy*; along the way,
three CDs collect concert recordings, alternate takes, rehearsals, and publishing
demos, programmed roughly year by year.
A lot of it is dross, a history of unfinished
ideas or un-transcended clichés, a book of
footnotes. Other parts work as a series of in-

terruptions—of the whole, of whatever you
happen to be doing—moments that leap
out of the chronology and stop it cold, turn
it back on itself. Some seem to need no context, and to make none; some seem to fall
together and make a story.

Beginning with the fourth track:

**1 ■ "No More Auction Block," from a
show at the Gaslight Café in Greenwich Village, late 1962** The song was composed in
antebellum times by escaped slaves who
had reached the end of the Underground
Railroad, in Nova Scotia. As "Many Thousands Gone," it was probably first taken
down from black Union soldiers in the
middle of the Civil War, in 1862, precisely
a century before Bob Dylan mixed it into
an otherwise undistinguished set compris-
ing mostly New York folk-scene com-
monplaces: "Barbara Allen," "Motherless
Children," "The Cuckoo," and so on.

The number opens here with a few hurried but isolated guitar notes, which instantly promise a weight no other song
sung this night will achieve. Throughout,
the guitar sound suppresses melody (though
the melody Dylan sings is the one he took
for "Blowin' in the Wind," a piece as ersatz
and clumsy as this is real and shaped); instead it produces a strange hum, maybe the
sound history makes when for a few minutes it dissolves. Not the acting a singer
might do, or impersonation, but a transforming empathy breaks down all distance, not of persona, or race, but of time.
When Dylan sings, "No more/ Auction
block/ For me"—and then, much more
slowly, "No more/ No more"—there's no reference to any symbol. The auction block is
a thing, you can touch it, people are standing on it: "Many thousands gone." The
hesitations in the singing are so eloquent,
so suggestive, that they generate images far
beyond these of the "driver's lash" or "pint
of salt" in the lyric. I thought of Tommie
Smith and John Carlos, black members of
the 1968 U.S. Olympic team, standing
on the victory blocks in Mexico City after
taking gold and bronze medals in the
200-meter dash, each with bowed head and

a raised fist in a black glove. A small protest against racism, a silent no to the assassination of Martin Luther King, and it caused a firestorm: the men were all but arrested, then sent back. The picture of the two of them that was flashed around the world seemed to terrify the nation; listening now to a 21-year-old Jewish folkie as he sang "No More Auction Block" six years before, you can feel the reason why. In the symbolic matrix their gestures made, Smith and Carlos suddenly knew, and everyone just as suddenly understood, what they were standing on.

Skipping 12 tracks:

2 ▪ **"Who Killed Davey Moore?," from a concert at Carnegie Hall, 26 October 1963** Fashionable bleeding-heart pieties about a boxer who died after a fight with Sugar Ramos—in 1971 Dylan himself would be present for the first Ali-Frazier match—but also songwriting as intricate and satisfying as Neil Sedaka and Howard Greenfield's "Calendar Girl." With referee, fans, manager, gambler, sportswriter, and opponent each stepping forward in ritual denial, the lyric is almost all dialogue; the filler between rhymes ("'It's hard to say, it's hard to tell'") can seem like genius. You can sense a new energy here: the thrill of getting it right.

Skipping one track:

3 ▪ **"Moonshiner," outtake from *The Times They Are A-Changin'*, 12 August 1963** "I hit all those notes," Dylan said in 1965, in reply to an interviewer's mention of Caruso, "and I can hold my breath three times as long if I want to." This ancient Appalachian ballad—five minutes of suspension, single notes from the singer's throat and harmonica held in the air as if to come down would be to bring death with them—must have been what he meant.

Skipping one track:

4 ▪ **"The Times They Are A-Changin'," piano demo, 1963** Dylan presses hard, right through the song's instant clichés. Times are changing; events are physically present; the force of history is driving this performance, and you might feel like getting out of the way.

Skipping one track:

5 ▪ **"Seven Curses," outtake from *The Times They Are A-Changin'*, 6 August 1963** A horse thief is caught, his daughter tries to buy his life, the judge demands a night with her instead, she pays, her father hangs anyway—seemingly set in feudal Britain (that's where the melody comes from), this is a simpler, more elemental version of "The Lonesome Death of Hattie Carroll," perhaps Dylan's greatest protest song, but with the position of the narrator impossible to place. The resentments and hopes in the preceding tunes of oppression and rebellion, "No More Auction Block," "Who Killed Davey Moore?," "Moonshiner," "The Times They Are A-Changin'," or others someone else might choose from *the bootleg series*, all are present here, but with an ending: there is no such thing as change. That old melody turns out not to be the skeleton of the song, but its flesh; it carries its own, unspoken words, which are "there is nothing new under the sun."

Skipping six tracks:

6 ▪ **"Sitting on a Barbed Wire Fence," outtake from *Highway 61 Revisited*, 15 June 1965** Chicago blues with a Howlin' Wolf laugh. All rhythmic hipness, especially the first time Dylan says "All right," investing the words with more meaning—more stealth, more motionless Dean-Brando menace—than any of the number's real lyrics.

Skipping one track:

7 ▪ **"It Takes a Lot to Laugh, It Takes a Train to Cry," *Highway 61 Revisited* alternate, 15 June 1965** As if he'd waited one year too many to shake it up and put the Beatles in their place, a headlong rush. And after a minute or so, a heedless extremism, as with the last minute of the Velvet Underground's "Heroin"—which, when it was released in 1967, sounded too much like Bob Dylan was singing it.

Skipping one track:

8 ▪ **"She's Your Lover Now," outtake from *Blonde on Blonde*, 21 January 1966** An unforgiving, barely coherent rant, but less about the unnamed she than the rumble

that repeatedly builds up to an explosive convergence of guitar, piano, bass, drums, organ, lyric, and vocal—a convergence that never arrives in the same place twice. As for the piano, liner notes credit both Paul Griffin (who played on "Like a Rolling Stone" and Don McLean's "American Pie") and Richard Manuel (of the Hawks, Dylan's touring group in 1965 and '66, later of the Band), but it must be Dylan. No other pianist could follow his singing; no singer could follow this piano without playing it.

Skipping 21 tracks:

9 ▪ **"Blind Willie McTell," outtake from** *Infidels*, **5 May 1983** Between "No More Auction Block" and "She's Your Lover Now" there are barely 3 years; between "She's Your Lover Now" and this song, more than 17. Seventeen years of great work, bad work, endless comebacks, divorce, musical confusion, a terrible search for a subject producing hopeless songs about Legionnaires' disease and Catfish Hunter, a retreat into simple careerism, and, most shockingly, conversion to a particularly self-interested, middle-class, Southern California suburban version of fundamentalist Christianity, and then reemergence as a Full Gospel preacher with God on his side. "You came in like the wind," he sang to Jesus in 1981, on "You Changed My Life," a *bootleg series* number: "Like Errol Flynn." And went out like him too, maybe; with three explicitly born-again albums behind him and sales plummeting, Dylan seemed to come back to the world with *Infidels*, and critics climbed on for another comeback, a return to form: "License to Kill," "Neighborhood Bully," and "Union Sundown" sounded like . . . protest songs!

Perhaps they were, but "Blind Willie McTell"—left off the album, one can imagine, because it would have upended it—is much more. It turns all the old, sainted rebels and victims parading across *Infidels* as across Dylan's whole songbook to dust, then blows them away. Led by Dylan on piano, with Mark Knopfler in his steps on guitar, this piece claims the story: the singer finds not evil in the world but that the world is

evil. The whole world is an auction block; all are bidders, all are for sale: "Smell that sweet magnolia bloomin'/See the ghost of slavery still."

The song is detailed, the language is secular, the mood is final. It's the last day before the Last Days, except for one thing, one weird, indelible non sequitur closing every verse, every scene of corruption and failure, like a gong: "Nobody can sing the blues/Like Blind Willie McTell." So the prophet answers his own prophecy with a mystery not even he can explain; the singer sums up and transcends his entire career; and the listener, still in the world, turns off the stereo, walks out of the house, and goes looking for an answer.

10 ▪ **Blind Willie McTell,** *Last Session* **(Prestige Bluesville)** Willie McTell was born in Georgia in 1901; he died there in 1959. He first recorded in 1927, and ended his life frequenting a lot behind the Blue Lantern Club in Atlanta, where couples parked to drink and make love; McTell would walk from car to car, trying to find someone to pay him for a tune. In 1956 a record store owner convinced him to sit down before a tape recorder, and he talked and sang his life and times.

SEPTEMBER 1991

1 ▪ **Gordon Burn,** *Alma Cogan* **(Secker & Warburg, U.K.)** This first novel by a London journalist has an odd premise and a strangely naturalistic follow-through. Alma Cogan was Britain's most popular female singer of the pre-Beatle '50s; she died of cancer in 1966 at 34. But here, with Burn taking Cogan's voice and writing in her first person, she has simply lived on in oblivion, in the nowhere of forgottenness Beatlemania would have ensured her in any case. In 1986, having had enough of it, she looks back and tells her story—and it's an enchantment, full of rise-and-fall, namedropping ("When Cary Grant . . ."), and reflection. The "chuckle in her voice" Cogan was loved for sounds throughout the monologue, though less comfortable sorts

of laughter often drown it out; from the first page, you don't need to have ever heard of Cogan to need to know what comes next. Burn's real concern, though—I almost said "Cogan's"—is not my-life but fame-death. Often the narrative, moving smoothly through an incident, tilts, tears, as Cogan, with perfect reserve, tries to explain: "To be the owner of a famous face, even in the days when mine was famous, in an age when the advertising and publicity industries were in their infancy, was an enlivening thing. You felt invigorated, extra-alive, knowing that you were out there somewhere, circulating, multiplying, reproducing, like a spore in the world, even when you were sleeping. . . . What's happening [now] is like a real-life enactment of those television title sequences where on atomised image shinily reassembles itself, like an explosion in reverse." This is spooky. It's spookier, maybe, than the formal, bloody mystery that Burn has brought Cogan back from the dead to solve—and that turns out to be the kind of detective story one might write if one took Guy Debord's *Society of the Spectacle* rather than the usual mean streets as a setting.

2 ▪ **Type O Negative, *Slow, Deep and Hard* (RoadRacer)** Self-conscious heavy metal that matches its song titles ("Glass Walls of Limbo [Dance Mix]," "Prelude to Agony," "The Misinterpretation of Silence and Its Disastrous Consequences") only with the 12 minutes plus of "Unsuccessfully Coping with the Natural Beauty of Infidelity." The singer's self-hatred builds to a fury, a woman's languorous moans wipe it away, the melody of "(I'm Not Your) Stepping Stone" refuses to die, but finally a pounding male chorus rides in for the rescue. "I know you're fucking someone else," the singer cries, and his brothers answer: *"He knows you're fucking . . . "* "I know . . ." *"He said he knows!"* "I know!" "HE KNOWS!" She doesn't care.

3 ▪ **Alexander "Skip" Spence, *Oar* (Sony Music Special Products reissue, 1969)** Spence was the original drummer for the Jefferson Airplane, then leader and guitarist of Moby Grape, a band that dissolved when commercial hype destroyed its Haight-Ashbury cachet. After 22 years, Spence's first and last solo album sounds like an autopsy performed on a bohemia that, if not quite dead, was ready to die—with the coroner in no better shape. *Oar* (with some numbers now extended and five cuts added) doesn't equal the unholy horror of Dave Van Ronk's 1966 MacDougal Street tribute, "Zen Koans Gonna Rise Again," but Van Rank was playing from at least a few steps away ("Enough time on that street would disintegrate anyone"), and Spence wasn't.

4 ▪ **Michael Madsen, as Jimmy (Louise's boyfriend) in *Thelma and Louise* (MGM/Pathé)** The best Elvis sighting of the season.

5 ▪ **Aaron Neville, *Warm Your Heart* (A&M)** Lovely shlock, with a cover of Main Ingredient's goopy "Everybody Plays the Fool" better than one of Randy Newman's exquisite "Louisiana 1927," probably because it gave Neville more to work with.

6 ▪ **X-ray Spex, *Live at the Roxy Club* (Receiver, U.K.)** In 1977 in this London basement, teenage saxophonist Lora Logic meanders through Poly Styrene's songs as if she's never played before and probably won't again. She drifts, but pushes the edges of the music into its center; she sounds at once completely lost and completely confident.

7 ▪ **Michael Mann, producer, *Crime Story*, 1986–88 (now running on USA cable)** Chicago, 1963: cops track mobsters. As soon as a tune appears on the soundtrack—Bobby Bland, buried deep beneath nightclub noise for "I Pity the Fool," or a killer twisting the dial to bring up just a primitive taste of Jimmy Reed's "Bright Lights, Big City"—you believe the characters you're watching are listening, and understanding every note.

8 ▪ **G-Clefs, Cleftones, Schoolboys, Students, etc., *Street Corner Serenade* (Time-Life Music reissue, 1954–63)** Doo-wop so self-referential (the Cellos' "Rang Tang Ding Dong [I Am the Japanese Sandman]"),

heedless (the Jewels' "Hearts of Stone"), or confused (the Gladiolas' "Little Darlin'") that it never became classic, and now seems most of all unlikely.

9 ▪ **Siouxsie and the Banshees, "Overload," from** *The Peel Sessions* **(Dutch East India reissue, 1978) and Mecca Normal, "Taking the Back Stairs," from** *Water Cuts My Hands* **(K/Matador)** With 12 years in the middle, the same shout at both ends.

10 ▪ **Mekons,** *The Curse of the Mekons* **(Blast First, U.K.) and Wallace Shawn,** *The Fever* **(Farrar, Straus and Giroux)** Their 14 years as a transhistorical punk band have become the Mekons' subject, but not in terms of career. Rather the Mekons' subject is their quarrel with history, and their growing conviction that it means to leave them behind; Sally Timms, so quietly soulful she can make Rosanne Cash seem strident, sometimes makes this story feel fated, but it always hurts. In Wallace Shawn's one-person perform-anywhere play, the subject is the impossibility of escaping from history, and there is no relief, no humor. There is simply the scream of a bourgeois sorcerer (to quote Marx, and the Mekons quoting Marshall Berman quoting Marx) who cannot get free of his magic, cannot break the contract that ties his comfort to torture, his priceless individuality to the facelessness of the poor, who must be made to "understand that the dreamers, the idealists, the ones who say that they love the poor, will all become vicious killers in the end, and the ones who claim they can create something better will always end up by creating something worse. The poor must understand these essential lessons, chapters from history. And if they don't understand them, they must all be taken out and shot."

The Mekons are always exuberant, whistling in the dark, but this is tough stuff, no fun, sleepless nights: to be left behind by history is to have never existed at all. "Funeral," about the collapse of Marxism—which on *The Curse of the Mekons* means any resistance to capitalism as the measure of all things—is "a dinosaur's confession":

"This funeral is for the wrong corpse." Shawn's nameless tourist enjoying his cheap holiday in other people's misery has a ticket to the funeral, but he doesn't want to go: "Cowards who sit in lecture halls or the halls of state denouncing the crimes of the revolutionaries are not as admirable as the farmers and nuns who ran so swiftly into the wind." Listen as you read, read as you listen, and you might be back in Bob Dylan's "Memphis Blues Again": "Now people just get uglier/And I have no sense of time."

1 ▪ **Ice Cube, as Dough Boy in** *Boyz N the Hood,* **directed by John Singleton (Columbia Pictures)** On the covers of *Amerikkka's Most Wanted* and *Kill at Will*, Ice Cube flaunts a death stare—sort of daring you to buy his records, it can seem. But his eyes contain almost all of the credibility in this very Hollywoodish low-budget film-from-the-heart about a black L.A. neighborhood. Plainly the most intelligent character in the movie, Dough Boy has less of a chance than any other to do anything with his life but wait for it to end. In his face, from shot to shot, scene to scene, is the dilemma of what it means to act in a world where you've consciously given yourself over to a fate that no one around you has even imagined that—unlike the football player or the studious kids—*you* could ever escape. And there's worse than that in Ice Cube's eyes: the wish to take at least some of the blame off himself, and the knowledge that he can't, because no one would listen to talk like that from a man with eyes like his.

2 ▪ **Robbie Robertson,** *Storyville* **(Geffen)** As point-man for the Band—guitarist, songwriter, spokesman—Robertson rarely sang. When he released his first solo album, in 1987, it came draped in curtains of overproduction, themes so elaborated and vocals so disguised it was hard to discern an actual human being behind any of it. But this clean, cool record—vaguely set in New

Orleans and cut with such Crescent City flyers as the Meters, Aaron Neville, the Rebirth Brass Band, Chief Bo Dollis of the Wild Magnolias, plus subtle contributions from Band keyboardist Garth Hudson—is alive. Horns carry melody, but lightly; the sound is full of room. Robertson's voice is smoked, airy, pinched, ranging from a whisper to a rasp, but most of all it is unprotected. Very quickly, you can understand the story the voice is telling: a story too spectral for plot or anecdote, let alone any kind of shout. There's no travelogue in the lyrics, no dead references to gumbo or second-line; the music kicks off with a "Night Parade" and follows it.

3 ▪ **Muzak, in Virginia Cleaners (Berkeley, June 24)** The—yes, I think "strains" is the only word—were distantly familiar, teasing. The tune got better by the second, then better than that. It turned out to be "Double Shot (Of My Baby's Love)," perhaps the only Top 40 record that makes the Kingsmen's "Louie Louie" seem elegant and Bob Dylan's "Rainy Day Women #12 and 35" sober—and even beneath Muzak's polka accordions and the huffing, middle-aged beat, you could hear the Swingin' Medallions, way back in '66, somewhere in South Carolina, laughing at history and time.

4 ▪ **Charlie Feathers, *Charlie Feathers* (Elektra Nonesuch)** Feathers hung around Sun Records in Memphis the same time Elvis did, and has claimed ever since that, in essence, *he* is Elvis; scores of records on more than a score of tiny labels have not proved his case. In fact he is a quirky, sometimes doggedly weird rockabilly survival, now lapsing into birdcalls and animal noises, now pumping his legend, and then (as, here, on "A Long Time Ago") shifting without warning into a reverie—loose, spooky, wailing, and more than anything emotionally *unclear*—of the way things never were, of the man he never was. In moments like this there's nobody like him.

5 ▪ **Chin-Chin, "Stop! Your Crying"/ "Revolution"/"Cry in Vain" (Farmer Records,** **Zurich, Switzerland, 1986)** Three Swiss women who sound like a whole batallion of Lesley Gores. The spirit of Lilliput lives, as it does also on.

6 ▪ **UnknownmiX, "Sincerely"/"Habibi" (RecRec Vertrieb, Zurich, Switzerland)** Two women and two men who program their 7-inch like an "Oldies but Goodies" LP: a "Rockin' Side," all chirps and gulps, and a "Dreamy Side," dark, Catholic, guilty, and forgiven.

7 ▪ **Jimmy Guterman and Owen O'Donnell, *The Worst Rock-and-Roll Records of All Time* (Citadel)** A book that recognizes it's as much fun to hate certain records and performers as it is to love others (or the same ones), and that insensate bigotry is the most fun of all. A lot of pages here get by on mere glee (on the 1984 Michael Jackson-Mick Jagger duet, "State of Shock": "it seems as if the song takes longer to listen to than it did to record"), but there's also rage, even paranoia—which can be even more satisfying than bigotry. On Bryan Adams' 1985 "Summer of '69": "The sixties nostalgia that sprung up in the mid-eighties was a fraud by industry leaders who refused to divulge to a new generation that the unmatchable music was inextricable from the horrible events that split this country in two as nothing had since the Civil War. Instead, culturally uneducated kids were made to hear songs like Martha and the Vandellas' 'Dancing in the Street' . . . as no more than party ditties. It's this imagined sixties— one without Vietnam, one without James Earl Ray, one without Altamont—that 'Summer of '69' memorializes." Yeah, but I still like it.

8 ▪ **Hole, *Pretty on the Inside* (Caroline)** Coproduced by Kim Gordon of Sonic Youth, this debut set from an L.A. combo could pass for a Kim Gordon solo album, if you didn't miss her wit. Somehow every song would jump a notch in flair if singer Courtney Love—who has a deep, harsh voice that without a stage is just too theatrical to wound—had changed her name to Courtly.

9 ■ **Marc Cohn, *Marc Cohn* (Atlantic)** The hit "Walking in Memphis" is a sentimental version of the quest made by the young Japanese couple in Jim Jarmusch's *Mystery Train*—corny, but also more vivid. The hit "Silver Thunderbird" is a mystified version of, oh, the Beach Boys' "409," but it carries a lift and it leaves an echo. Cohn has a thick voice with little play in it, and uses heavy, portentous piano notes without any humor. He can be written off as a decent Springsteen acolyte or an improvement on Billy Joel, which would still be second-rate; maybe he's the new Bruce Hornsby. But his songs have shape and heart; one more hit— which I don't hear on this first album—and he might turn his own corner.

10 ■ **Public Image Ltd., *Metal Box* (Virgin U.K. reissue, 1979)** Then as now, this unsuperseded miasma of loathing and dub comes in a can—though now instead of three 12-inch 45s there's one CD, and the container is only four-and-three-quarter inches across. It's so *cute*.

NOVEMBER 1991

1 ■ **John Lee Hooker, "I Cover the Waterfront," from *Mr. Lucky* (Charisma/Point Blank)** At 74, the bluesman records with devotees gathered at his feet (here, Keith Richards, Albert Collins, Robert Cray, Johnny Winter, etc.), but he is not relaxed. With "I Cover the Waterfront" (not the standard, not exactly even a song), he takes the title phrase and for six minutes drifts through it, now a night watchman, now a night crawler. Booker T. Jones quietly vamps on organ, Van Morrison flicks brittle notes off a guitar, and Hooker seems to hold still, hovering over the docks and the water; there's great calm in his voice, and certain death. It's as if he died a long time ago, long since came to terms with that fact, but wants another look.

2–3 ■ **James Carr, "The Dark End of the Street," on *You Got My Mind Messed Up* (Goldwax/Vivid Sound reissue, 1966, Japan) and the Commitments: "The Dark End of the Street," in *The Commitments*, directed by Alan Parker (20th Century Fox)** Carr was only about 24 when he recorded this ballad about adultery that makes "(If Loving You Is Wrong) I Don't Want to Be Right" seem like Whitney Houston material—but he sounded much older, or maybe ageless. He's been called "The World's Greatest Soul Singer," but if his style is the essence of the genre he's also defined by it, and never escapes it. There's terrible fright when he almost stops "The Dark End of the Street" to call out, "They gonna find us, they gonna find us," but then he's rescued by the very classicism of his own performance.

A quarter-century later the tune shows up in a movie about a fictional, present-day white Dublin band, a bunch of kids who want to play soul music—to carry the torch of freedom it once symbolized—or maybe just get heard, get around. So the musicians, backup singers, and lead singer Andrew Strong, 16 (looking 30, sounding 24?), haul the song onto the stage of their first-ever gig as if it's a dead man's corpse and it's up to them to bury it, hide it, or bring it back to life. They're amateurs, we've seen that their passion most often produces only bum notes, but this time Strong gets his hands around the dead man's throat and begins to strangle air into him. Not even a memory of Carr's restraint, his knowledge, remains in the song; the people on the screen seem to get bigger as the music seems to rise in volume. The performance is crude, noisy, sweaty, confused, a mess, and there were tears on my face before it was half through.

4 ■ **Duncan Browne, *Give Me Take You* (Immediate/Sony Music Special Products reissue, 1968)** Pre-Raphaelite rock, and one of a kind.

5 ■ **Geto Boys, *We Can't Be Stopped* (RAP-A-LOT/Priority)** The Geffen label dropped this Houston outfit's first disk for excessive violence, misogyny, and necrophilia, and there's plenty of ho'-bitch spew on number two. But spinning hard at the center, so hard it throws off almost everything else, is "Mind Playing Tricks on Me," something between a bad dream and

a reverie—the sort of confession that has to be made to the whole world, never to a friend, because a friend might see you differently but the world won't see you at all. Socially sanctioned (or anyway genre sanctioned) rage dissolves into a doubt that has no support outside of its own reality, its own vertigo; it calls up shades of empathy and regret that vanish before they can be named. Plus there's "Trophy," an anti-Grammy rant that scores with Elvis' award for "Most Appearances Made After Death." He can't be present, "due to illness," so accepting instead is—the Grateful Dead.

6 ▪ **Tom Petty and the Heartbreakers, "Out in the Cold" (MCA)** You need ten random seconds on the radio to know you have to hear it again, two or three the next time around to know that you are. It's nothing new: Petty's been a hit machine since 1977, playing a loner sensitive enough to whine about being tough. Save for those rare exceptions when his songs are about someone else ("American Girl," "Refugee"), his music has zero content, just rockabilly formalism. All that's formally different this time is the breakup of the number by drums, not guitar—and yet the urgency is unstoppable. It's by the book but it can sound like Petty's got the only copy.

7 ▪ **Private Joke, "Back in the U.S.S.R.," on *All Things Considered* (National Public Radio, August 29)** As sung by Mikhail Gorbachev with postcoup lyrics, the closing shouts of "Hey, I'm back! I'm back!" echoing as if no one is listening.

8 ▪ **Negativland, "U2" (SST)** The California collage unit makes fun of "I Still Haven't Found What I'm Looking For," and so comprehensively you might begin to feel sorry for Bono. Among numerous interjections and found aural objects, the hook is a sample of D.J. Casey Kasem chirping "That's the letter *U*—and the numeral *two!*" so many times he turns into Mr. Rogers. Squelched just weeks after release by U2's label—if the band has a sense of humor they'll put it out themselves.

9 ▪ **Van Morrison, *Hymns to the Silence* (Polydor)** An ambitious career survey by means of 21 new songs, and finally flat, too clean, well-crafted, and lifeless. But there are moments, as when Morrison chants "Take me back" five times, and then, with complete disregard for rhythm or timing, caring for nothing but bitterness and exile, just says what he means: "To when the world made more *sense.*"

10 ▪ **Avengers, *The Avengers* (Target Video, 1978—try used-video or -music stores)** The tape is dim and smudgy, the right tone for eight live shots from San Francisco's best punk band. Target gets a little arty with "Car Crash," intercutting a lot of stock car-crash footage and a highway patrolman setting up a roadblock. It takes a few seconds to realize it's Ronald Reagan—in 1964, in Don Siegel's version of *The Killers*, in his last and best role, as Mr. Big.

DECEMBER 1991

1 ▪ **Buzzcocks, *Spiral Scratch* (Document CD or 12", U.K.) and *Time's Up* (Document CD, U.K.)** In the summer of 1976, in Manchester, the Buzzcocks formed on the model of the Sex Pistols; in October, with Howard Devoto as singer, they went into the local Revolution studio and for something under $100 of mike time cut their songs. Released in February 1977, the EP *Spiral Scratch* was only the third U.K. punk disk to be issued; more than that, it was the first independent, do-it-yourself U.K. punk record; and more than that, it was definitive. "Boredom" ("I'm living in this, uh, movie," Devoto snapped, "But it doesn't move me") was an instant anthem, or rather a fragment of an anthem floating away to be caught by its listeners. It set the tone: sarcastic (many of the tunes had their genesis in a notebook where Devoto had set down all-purpose, lumpen-surrealist insults), distracted, thin, spidery, and most of all in a hurry. Carl Perkins' "Blue Suede Shoes" was about taking a stand; "Breakdown," "Friends of Mine," and the rest (bootlegged as *Time's Up* again and again over the years) were about evading an enemy more sensed than defined, and then turning up at his

back, then disappearing. The feeling was anonymous—a dare taken and won.

Devoto went on to more ornamented music with his groups Magazine and Luxuria; led by guitarist Pete Shelley, the Buzzcocks made sharp, poppy punk through the decade (re-formed, they tour the clubs even now). But October 1976 was their moment. With "Lester Sands (Drop in the ocean)" they caught an ancient snarl, blindly retrieving the voice of the Ranters along with echoes of their cosmology ("Every creature is God," it was written in 1646, "every creature that hath life and breath being an efflux of God, and shall return to God again, be swallowed up in him as a drop is in the ocean"). Blasphemy edged out of their blank complaints; ambition rose from the songs and came down as vengeance.

"History is made by those who say 'no,'" Jon Savage writes at the close of *England's Dreaming*, his recreation of the Sex Pistols' era, "and Punk's utopian heresies remain its gift to the world." On *Spiral Scratch* and *Time's Up* that gift was offered as ordinary, unspectacular, everyday life; since the music was made the world has changed enough that, putting on the disks today, it can seem as if the gift is being opened for the first time.

2 ▪ Bruce Thomas, *The Big Wheel—Rock & Roll and Roadside Attractions* (Faber and Faber) Elvis Costello's former Attractions bassist on the road, living in a dream, remaking it on the page with a born writer's love of the right phrase and a loathing for cliché, and, finally, trying to break away: "There were times when it all made sense. After all, nobody plays a piece of music just to get to the last note. There were some nights when everything went with that effortless kind of swing that requires a certain kind of effort to allow. Nights like those were never the same and could not be repeated; they contained a feeling of being a spectator as well as a participant."

3 ▪ Nirvana, video for "Smells like Teen Spirit" (directed by Samuel Bayer, DGC Records) Lear to Gloucester: "There's hell,

there's darkness, there is the sulphurous pit, burning, scalding, stench, corruption"—all this when the visual setup is no more than a small crowd and a furious Seattle three-piece in a high school gym.

4 ▪ Ashtray, "Trailer"/"Riding on the Train" (Shoe Records) A nothing day in the present on the A side wars against a timeless, lyrical chorus shared by guitarist Joe Leifheit and bassist Sarah Howells on the B; the balance tips to the past and into it.

5 ▪ Erasure, *Chorus* (Sire) Dance music you can use sitting still, at 3 A.M.

6 ▪ Brian Morton, *The Dylanist* (Harper-Collins) In this novel about a young woman growing up through the lives lived and surrendered by her parents, ex-Communists who still believe, what begins in mildness turns graceful and then quietly hard. Bob Dylan is Sally Burke's talisman—she's a Dylanist, a young union man tells her as she revels in a bootlegged copy of the incomprehensible, never released Basement Tapes tune "I'm Not There" ("This," she says, "may be the greatest song ever written," and she's right); she's "too hip to believe in anything but [her] own feelings." But she grows past Dylan, too—in her late 20s, "when she looked at his records, she could never find anything she wanted to hear." In the end who she is is more fated, a life made of a contradiction Dylan might have escaped but she can't: "She would never find a home, as [her parents] had, in the effort to transfigure the world. But in her belief that she lived in a world that needed to be transfigured, she'd probably always feel homeless."

7 ▪ Roxy Music, *Total Recall—A History, 1972–1982* (Virgin Music Video) TV appearances, concert footage, and primitive videos: madly outré in the beginning, when Bryan Ferry and the band would do anything for a thrill, pathetic in the middle, when they'd do anything for a hit, and exploding off the screen with Ferry's 1976 solo "Let's Stick Together"—where, as he emotes in his stiff-legged way, then-girlfriend Jerry Hall sticks a long leg into the frame and then vamps across it with a bombshell grin

so self-absorbed you can already feel Ferry's heart breaking.

8 ▪ **Guy Debord,** *Panegyric—Volume I,* **translated from the French by James Brook (Verso)** From the author of *The Society of the Spectacle,* a brief and elegiac memoir of a life lived in its shadows and cracks. With a notable chapter on drunkenness as part of Debord's lifework, and a comment on the loss of taste imposed on alcohol by mass production: "No one had ever imagined that he would see drink pass away before the drinker."

9 ▪ **Cargo Records, advertisement (***Option,* **September/October)** "This young band," reads the copy for *First of Many,* the debut disk from a duo calling themselves the Future, "dares to capture 60's folk-rock music, and blend it with the 70's revival, to create a new sound for a new generation." "NO FUTURE FOR YOU/NO FUTURE FOR ME"—this must be the payoff.

10 ▪ **First Presbyterian Church, Yellow Springs, Ohio, sermon announcement (September 1991)** "What kind of country is it in which people believe God is Dead but Elvis is Alive?"

JANUARY 1992

1–3 ▪ **Fastbacks,** *The Answer Is You* **(Sub Pop double 45);** *In America* **(Lost & Found CD, Germany, recorded 1988); . . .** *and his Orchestra/Everyday Is Saturday/Play Five of Their Favorites* **(Popllama CD reissue, 1987, 1984, 1982)** Seattle's Fastbacks must be the most time-defying band in the world. Their very first, 1981 recordings (available on the hard-to-find LP *never fails, never works,* Blaster! Records, 3 Dove Lane, Bristol BS2 9HP, UK) represented their only real brush with fame—the drummer was Duff McKagan, now bassist in Guns N' Roses. From then to now the Fastbacks have hammered at the door of an imaginary audience, the millions who could care less about their heart-on-their-sleeve punk, as if it were most of all the fact that the door is locked that keeps them talking. Their sound—Kim Warnick's eager, no-range vocals set against

Kurt Bloch's sometimes raging, sometimes questioning guitar—has never changed, or even exactly improved. They can still play as if the notion had just occurred to them, and there are small, perfectly realized tunes—on the radio, odd ambushes of anyone's pop expectations—scattered all across their decade.

The four songs on *The Answer Is You,* though, might be their most free-swinging—one great, self-sustaining, all-night argument, with flashbacks of the Buzzcocks in "Impatience" and of the Safaris' gentle 1960 "Image of a Girl" in "Above the Sunrise." . . . *and his Orchestra* is the band's best album. *In America* is live ("Thanks for staying," Warnick ends it, without attitude)—and proof that, six years after, the title number was still one of *Their Favorites.*

The song "In America" sums up the warmth and the fear that seem to lurk behind the Fastbacks' music. It opens hard, like a Sex Pistols outtake; in Warnick's voice is the permission to speak that punk gave to everyone who couldn't sing. But the theme is a big one, what someone thinking seriously for the first time in her life might think about: whether the country is too much of a lie to take. The answer is that the lie will kill you only if you let it. "Who said the government's on your side?" Warnick snaps—and the liberation in that line, the exile and the isolation, so much given up and so much claimed, is more than most bands will ever think of wanting.

4 ▪ **Pulnoc,** *City of Hysteria* **(Arista)** Led by Milan Hlavsa of the Plastic People of the Universe, from which Pulnoc derives, this Czech band making its major-label debut has more than 20 years of persecution and fandom behind it, and, as Vaclav Havel says in the sleeve notes, something more. The secret of the Plastic People, Havel wrote in 1984, had to do with "a certain, specific experience of the world that has been formed here by history not just over decades, but over the centuries, a spiritual and emotional atmosphere that belongs to this

place and no other." You can hear hints of that on what at first seems mostly a lively, aggressive piece of '60s-rooted art rock that suggests Eric Ambler's pre-WWII Central European espionage thrillers as distantly as it does the prayers of pre-Christian religion, or the guitar break in Christie's 1970 "Yellow River" as precisely as it does the light touch of Merrilee Rush's 1968 "Angel of the Morning." Repetition, pushed hard for truths it will give up only after one more time, underpins a sound where the instrumental doo-wop intro to "City of Hysteria" ("city of history," singer Michaela Nemcová seems to make it) is as right as the jerky, trailing beat of "End of the World." The group's style is altogether its own, and also plainly unfinished; most of the faces in this band are lined and puffy, their eyes have too much knowledge in them, but still they're just starting. As for Havel's insistence that "encoded" in the music of the Plastic People is "an important warning . . . [from] a place where the knots of history are tied and unraveled" (that really has to be an epigraph for the next reissue of Ambler's *Background to Danger*), such praise for a dead band is now the treasure a living band could spend the next 20 years seeking.

5 ▪ **Nancy Savoca, director, *Dogfight* (Warner Bros.)** This modest, very believable film about a young soldier (River Phoenix) and the folksinger-worshiping "dog" (Lili Taylor) he meets the night before shipping out for Vietnam (November 21, 1963) uses a lot of period music, but it comes off the screen with its conventional signifiers reversed. Joan Baez's pristine rendition of the ancient ballad "Silver Dagger" now communicates, or fails to communicate, the way bad pop is supposed to—it's brittle, self-conscious, and completely timebound. But Claudine Clark's "Party Lights" and other putatively disposable commodities seem like events—chants of flesh, will, and endless echo.

6 ▪ **Bob Marley and the Wailers, *One Love at Studio One* (Heartbeat reissue, 1963–71)** The rude–boy ska–beat Wailers, back

when Marley, Peter Tosh, and Bunny Wailer (now the only one not dead) lived from disk to disk. It's a thrill to hear their first, not because "Simmer Down" is a classic but because it's so inescapably a smash (this song *can't wait* to get released and be a hit). The group covers everyone in sight (Dion and the Belmonts, Jimmy Clanton, Junior Walker, the Beatles) in quest of the same success, then stumbles into Bob Dylan's "Like A Rolling Stone." Bunny Wailer sings a quiet, mournful lead; the opening beat is textbook "Louie Louie"; the chorus remains as Dylan wrote it; the verses are new, Old Testament imagery Dylan would have used if he'd thought of it: "Time like a scorpion/Stings without warning." Oh, this is so good.

7 ▪ **Strawberry, *Smash-Up—Story of a woman* (Endless Music CD)** Bits of monologue orchestrated out of a song or two and a lot of bad-dream electronics (the musician goes by Ursula, the producer by My Sin) finally take over in Strawberry's long account of incest, prostitution, heroin, cocaine, living homeless in a cemetery, and epiphany ("I knew I couldn't fuck another man for money"). Every line of the tale is affectless, unimpressed with its own pathos—on *Oprah* or *Geraldo* this wouldn't do at all—and somehow validated by the soul Strawberry puts into the first cut of the set, a simple version of George Jones' "He Stopped Loving Her Today."

8 ▪ **Neil Young and Crazy Horse, *Arc* (Reprise)** The two *Weld* CDs make a conventional live album, mostly redundant footnotes to songs prv. rl. Advertised as a random collage of onstage feedback, *Arc* seems almost composed, and sadistically so: a giant body of noise that for 35 minutes edges toward release and then gets distracted.

9 ▪ **John Helleman, "Rouble without a Cause," in *The Modern Review* (Autumn 1991, UK)** "It's past midnight, 20 August, and Boris Yeltsin is hunkered down in the bowels of the Russian White House in Moscow. Outside, several hundred members of the resistance militia man the hastily assem-

bled barricades. Three of them will die later in the night. In his sanctuary, Yeltsin sits alone, pondering that time, for him, is running out. . . . He puts on 'Are you Lonesome Tonight?'"

Think about it. Here is this man, at the crossroads of history, and he wants to know what Elvis Presley has to say about it. This is what he has to say about it: "You know, someone said, the world's a stage, and each must play a part . . ." Is that what Yeltsin was listening for? Or was it the high-lonesome catch in Elvis's voice as he traced the verses like a man running his fingers over the pages of an old book, over words that no longer make sense?

10 ■ **Phil Spector, *Back to Mono (1958–1969)* (ABKCO 4-CD box)** Girl groups, Bob B. Soxx and the Blue Jeans, the Crystals, Darlene Love, the Christmas album, lost treasures from Love's "Strange Love" to the Ronettes' "Paradise," the *legacy*—and, even "mastered in analog," as it says here (with the information still stored and transmitted digitally), not the real thing, not even close. Spector's "Wall of Sound," Marshall Lieb, the producer's first collaborator, once said, "was more air than sound," and there's no air here. What's left is self-evidently a replica of a sound, a sheen without lungs or sweat: pinched, cold, not human.

Don't go near it. Look for the out-of-print LPs, especially the U.K. *Rare Masters* series; look for the singles, or wait for the vinyl bootlegs. "The mind has been tricked, but the heart is sad," Neil Young recently said of digital reissues. "It doesn't know why it can't feel the music."

FEBRUARY 1992

1 ■ **Otis Rush, "Double Trouble" (1958), on *Groaning the Blues* (Flywright LP, UK) or *1956–58: His Original Cobra Recordings* (Flywright CD, UK)** A year or so ago you could have heard Rush's song as a personal statement or a Chicago blues classic, but not today. Now, bad times have expanded the music, blown it up: there are countless people traversing its two and a half minutes, and they grow smaller, more indistinct, as Rush's voice gets bigger and his guitar moves like a virus. Sagging horns bring images of men and women walking the streets with their shoulders slumped; in the slow, hesitating drift of the main theme to the end of each chord progression, you can almost hear feet shuffling. "Some of this generation is millionaires," Rush sings in bitter wonder, breaking the last word into three parts, "million-air-es," making it fit the rhythm, but also making the word strange. The horns, guitar, and piano converge on the beat in a fury, but only for a phrase; then they separate, muted, as if they have nothing to say to each other. From line to line rage turns into embarrassment, oppression into shame. "You laughed at me walkin', baby," Rush shouts, then steps back like Paul Muni in *I Am a Fugitive from a Chain Gang* dropping into the shadows of the film's last shot, the voice quiet now: "But I have no place to go / Bad luck and trouble have taken me / I have no money to show." By this time there is no place in the city the music doesn't touch, or anyway no closed door it isn't knocking on.

2 ■ **Gambang Kromong Slendang Betawi, "Stambul Bila," from *Music of Indonesia 3: Music from the Outskirts of Jakarta* (Smithsonian Folkways/Rounder)** Nine minutes and 12 contemporary seconds in which you might imagine anything from a late-'30s Southeast Asian jazz band that got it all wrong to a troupe of original Dadaists who recorded underwater. At first the apparent complete disassociation between the drums, flute, stringed instruments, male singer, and female singer is funny; then boring; then it begins to make sense, and then you just barely miss the connection, just as Sydney Greenstreet puts the wrong piece of paper into Hugo Ball's pocket in the weird nightclub of this song.

3 ■ **Kid Balley, Tommy Johnson, Bukka White, Willie Brown, Ishmon Bracey, Louise Johnson, Son House, and Bertha Lee, *Masters of the Delta Blues—The Friends of Charlie Patton* (Yazoo reissue, late 1920s/early 1930s)** Twenty-three cuts—and with both founder

Patton (as a singer) and legatee Robert Johnson absent, this may still be the best country blues anthology ever assembled. The two guitars (House and Patton or Brown) on Son House's original "Walking Blues" sound as clearly in the guitar line snaking behind John Mellencamp's vocal in his new "Get a Leg Up" as they do in Johnson's he-must-have-three-hands playing: there's no distance from here to there. But on some tunes—Kid Bailey's whispery "Rowdy Blues," anything by Tommy Johnson— music that in fact opened into the future, into our present, seems to close in on itself, to shut its own door. The echo that remains leaves you wondering: if these dead people are in some way my ancestors, who am I?

4 ■ Henri Lefebvre, *Critique of Everyday Life—Volumé One* (1947/1958), translated by John Moore (Verso) In English for the first time (the 1971 *Everyday Life in the Modern World* was a tepid finale by comparison), this seductive, noisy, always querulous, always open text had its roots in the '20s, in Marxism and Surrealism—which is to say that Marx is the judge, alienation is the crime, the commodity is the defense, Surrealism is the prosecutor, and you are both the victim and the accused.

5 ■ Howlin' Wolf, *The Chess Box* (Chess/ MCA 3-CD reissue, 1951–73) A good sampler of the work of one of the major American artists of the postwar period, but the revelation of the digital transfer, which dulls the edge of guitarist Willie Johnson, is to foreground Hubert Sumlin, who replaced Johnson in 1954, as one of the great mysteries of the blues. Huge sheets of sound break off the performances like sheets of ice breaking off an iceberg; on the way to the sea they change into sheets of glass and the sea turns into pavement. The man behind Robbie Robertson's most explosive music, from Ronnie Hawkins' 1963 "Who Do You Love" to Bob Dylan's 1966 "Albert Hall" version of "Ballad of a Thin Man," Sumlin doesn't seem to know where the beat is, or need to know. He's an abstractionist; he could have played with Pollock.

6 ■ Chuck Berry, the Willows, Betty Boo, et al., *Music from the Film "A Rage in Harlem"* (Sire) Except for Robin Givens the movie's a dud, and the music drowned out by gunfire and heavy breathing. But here new La Vern Baker bumps old Lloyd Price, Johnny Ace pleads for deliverance from Bo Diddley, James Brown meets Tommy Johnson in the form of Howlin' Wolf, and it's too bad there isn't at least some Robin Givens dialogue . . .

7 ■ FSK (German-American Sextet), "Hitler Lives," from *Son of Kraut* (Sub Up Records, Germany) Founded in 1980, FSK now resembles the Mekons with a lot more yodeling and a frame of reference that frequently tunes into Armed Forces Radio. "Hitler Lives" was an AFR hit in 1947, a warning that the ideas had to be buried with the man; today, as HITLER LEBT! is proud graffiti and purification follows unification, FSK's cool, country rendition is almost wistful, until it turns into a rave-up.

8 ■ Wir, *The First Letter* (Mute/Electra) and Kevin S. Eden, *Wire . . . everybody loves a history* (SAF Publishing Ltd., Wembley, UK) On disc, England's original art punk band loses a letter, a member (Robert Gotobed, one of the all-time punk names, even if it was real), and comes back to life, unpredictable and nervy; in endless interviews, punctuated with photos of them dressing up like Sydney Greenstreet's contact in the Cabaret Voltaire in 1916, they sound like anybody else.

9 ■ Clash, *Clash on Broadway* (Epic/Legacy 3-CD reissue, 1977–82) From "White Riot" to "Ghetto Defendant," it takes them five years to get from Rasta London to the Paris Commune. It's an interesting trip.

10 ■ Daniel M. Pinkwater, *Young Adults* (Tor paperback reissue, 1982/85) This really is a "young adult novel"—in which five high school washouts reform as the Wild Dada Ducks, levy fines on each other for such crimes as uttering the word "life-style," and foment a prank that leads to the election of the school's least-known student to all student offices, his transformation into a dictator with absolute power, and the defeat of

Dada by Heroic Realism. In other words, a parable of the 1918 Berlin Dada club as a crucible for Nazism.

MARCH 1992

1 ■ **Eleventh Dream Day, *Lived to Tell* (Atlantic)** Last April in these pages this fourth album from a Chicago four-piece seemed like a strong record; now it seems to cut loose from its time. And yet it is also exactly of its time: in its bitter, shamed embrace of exile and retreat, nailed again and again by Janet Beveridge Bean's loud, stoic drumming—she's learned something from Maureen Tucker, and something from Al Jackson. I come back to "It's Not My World" every week or so, when there's a need to redeem the ugliness of the news, to hide in the sound—to be stretched out on Rick Rizzo's long, tensed guitar passages as if they were a rack. Slipping into the lyrics that establish the song as just a set of stray fragments about how people are failing, are falling through the cracks, are finding that all doors open onto blank walls, you hit a chorus with no narrative connection to the bar talk you've been overhearing, but an absolute spiritual connection. The lyric jumps from third person to first, the singing is no longer conversational but stately, heavily cadenced, a curse read from some ruined pulpit: "Over and over / By and by / Living by habits / To get by," the chorus begins, two people singing, but separately, as if they'll never meet, don't need to, don't want to. "The world might be changing / Outside my door / But that's not my world / Anymore."

2 ■ **Gordon Legge, *The Shoe* (Polygon, Edinburgh, Scotland, 1989)** An expert, naturalistic novel about fandom as everyday life, nearly all of it: a few friends and their music in a nowhere town between Glasgow and Edinburgh. In their early 20s, querulous, trying to fend off cynicism and resignation, without real money or work, they talk about the radio, records, the pop press. They talk so intensely that if Jesus and Mary Chain's "Never Understand" is "the spirit of

the good," another disk reflects the human spirit as cesspool. For all that's shared, though—the attempt to act out in public the extreme feelings music provokes—fandom finally leaves each person a solitary, ruler of the kingdom of one's own taste, and prisoner of it too. "I played *Slippery People* and *Lady Marmalade* three times each," one character says to another. "The thing that bugs me about listening to my records is that nobody ever sees me when I'm that happy, and if they did they wouldn't understand."

3 ■ **Gabriel Sibusi, "Call Me Mister!" from *Flying Rock—South African Rock 'n Roll, 1950–1962* (Global Village cassette)** An anthology of black South Africans reworking Elvis, Gene Vincent, the Drifters, Buddy Holly, etc., and surprising partly because it so precisely parallels the efforts of second-rank white American performers to do the same thing—from hopeless shouts of "Rog, rog, rog, everybody rog" (King's Brothers' "Zulu Rock") to highly individualized attempts to shift steel-guitar phrasing into rockabilly (the Bogard Brothers' "She Keeps on Knocking"). But Sibusi's testament, recorded in the early '60s, works on another level. As on a lot of the cuts, the instrumentation is only strummed acoustic guitar. The insinuating melody anticipates Desmond Dekker and the Aces' 1969 reggae hit "Israelites" even as the vocal can recall New Orleans bluesman Rabbit Brown's 1927 attack on "The Sinking of the Titanic"—a smoldering, gloating attack, because the *Titanic* advertised itself as for Caucasians only. Sibusi's subject is race, and the *Titanic* of his own country, and though he sings from the shadows, his bare affirmation today reverberates so powerfully you hope he's alive to feel it: "I will never be as ashamed as much / As you think."

4 ■ **Carter the Unstoppable Sex Machine, *101 Dalmatians* (Chrysalis)** This first album by two former London buskers is the noisiest and smartest record I've heard since early Wire—and more hysterical, in both senses of the word. It begins slowly; after

five cuts the subject matter burns off its satire ("A Perfect Day to Drop the Bomb") and the singing, or ranting, or insane critical recycling of pop references, leaves the world behind. Chuck Berry's "Memphis" is smeared into "Long distance information get me Jesus on the line," there's a dialogue sample from (I think) Stan Freberg's 1960 "The Old Payola Roll Blues," and then a quote from Grandmaster Flash and the Furious Five's "The Message" so bloody and convincing ("DON'T / PUSH ME / 'CAUSE—") you can't believe the disk keeps spinning. I hope these guys stay healthy; they could change a lot.

5 ▪ Nirvana, *Bleach* (Sub Pop, 1989) A close call between this debut lp and the chart-topping *Nevermind*, but here there's less of a stagger, more inexplicable leaps. And whatever *Nevermind* has, it doesn't have anybody ending a song called "School" with terrorized shouts of "NO RECESS! NO RECESS!" And neither does anything else in the history of rock 'n' roll.

6 ▪ Lou Reed, guitar solo, "Magic and Loss: The Summation," on *Magic and Loss* (Sire) The talk-singing is no more pungent than elsewhere on this elegy, the lyrics are sticky ("There's a bit of magic in everything / And some loss to even things out"), but there's also a rising, hovering fuzztone that—to paraphrase Skip James on himself—has been and gone from places most music never gets to.

7 ▪ Termites, *Do the Rock Steady* (Heartbeat reissue, 1967) With this on you could do it underwater.

8 ▪ Bob Seger, "Like a Rock," in a commercial for Chevy trucks (NFL playoffs, NBC and CBS, December and January) I'm not sure why the running of this 1986 single over glowing slo-mo shots of blue-collar folk sweating, hugging, and high-fiving is so much more depressing than anything else of its kind. It's not simply the use of Seger's "I was 18, didn't have a care, workin' for peanuts" reverie to drive home the message that in hard times, low wages+uncomplaining labor=patriotism—or "*TRAVAIL, FAMILLE, PATRIE*," as the Gang of Four put

it on the cover of *A Brief History of the Twentieth Century*, reproducing a coin from Vichy France. It may have more to do with the fact that Seger sings so insistently in the first person. This is a voice you don't often hear in commercials, the soulfully privileged "I"—though when you come down to it, it's unclear whether it's the worker or the truck that's singing.

9 ▪ Little Jack Melody with His Young Turks, *On the Blank Generation* (Four Dots Records) There are moments here—mainly in "Happily Ever After (West of Eden)," a nightclub fantasia in which Frank Sinatra is both Adam and Eve and gives birth to all culture—where this would-be Weimar combo (banjo, harmonium, tuba) actually comes close to its ambition of realizing George Grosz in sound. But you probably wouldn't want to make too much of it.

10 ▪ Nedra Olds-Neal and Michael Brooks, producers: *The Words and Music of World War II* (Columbia/Legacy double CD) This two-hour 23-minute documentary includes the expected words—excerpts from speeches by FDR, Neville Chamberlain, Churchill, plus copious Edward R. Murrow broadcasts and Axis propaganda from Tokyo Rose and Lord Haw-Haw. The shock is in the songs, from "Remember Pearl Harbor" ("We'll die for liberty") to "Joltin' Joe DiMaggio" to "The Deepest Shelter in Town" to "Wonder When My Baby's Coming Home"—if you ever wondered if rock 'n' roll was really necessary, the answer is here. Save for a few numbers by the black a capella Golden Gate Quartet (especially "Comin' in on a Wing and a Prayer," seemingly based on Blind Lemon Jefferson's "See That My Grave Is Kept Clean"), there is not simply an absence but a negation of any true emotion, be it fear, pride, anger, excitement, love, pain. The exclusion of subjectivity is too complete to be explained by the propaganda needs of the Home Front—the Home Front didn't need a version of "When the Lights Go On Again" that makes Barry Manilow sound like James Brown. After two hours, it's hard to feel anything but dis-

gust, and confusion: how could any country win a war on music like this?

But the narration—credited to Michael Brooks, script, and Gary Nunn, commentary—has all along been shifting, from stalwart to acrid, embattled to cynical. As General MacArthur announces the Japanese surrender, it shifts once again, into the real, which in the context that has been created is weird beyond weird: "The ghastly death and destruction, the broken promises, the men and the women physically and mentally destroyed by the war do not concern us here. For this is a fairy tale, and fairy tales must end happily. So let us relive that build-up to everlasting love, peace, and happiness, in the bright new world of 1945." And then into one Ginny Simms belting out "I'm Gonna Love That Guy." And then enter the Firesign Theater.

APRIL 1992

1 ▪ **Vulgar Boatmen, *Please Panic* (Caroline/Safehouse)** I left town two days after first playing this light, irreducible set of songs about falling into ordinary love affairs and getting into your car and driving away; for four days "Calling Upstairs," "You Don't Love Me Yet," "You're the One," and "Allison Says" drew in Buddy Holly's "Well All Right," the Young Marble Giants, John Cale, the Fleetwoods, General Johnson and beach music, and spun them all off. The numbers played so casually in my head, the drift of one tune breaking off only to be picked up by the melody of another, and the songs seemed not made but found—but if it were that easy the songs would be faceless, and the people in them come to life as soon as they're named. More next month.

2 ▪ **Malcolm McLaren, director, *The Ghosts of Oxford Street*, 25 December 1991 (BBC4, UK)** This TV fantasia (with Happy Mondays, Sinéad O'Connor, Shane McGowan, and others) was conceived by McLaren in art school in the '60s, and its nostalgia is less for the London shopping street than for the idea of the film itself.

Planned as a history of the street, it is realized as a Christmas special, with McLaren as Anticlaus. But while he appears all over the place—as Fagin, as interlocutor, as a little (bad) boy—he may be most present in Tom Jones' Gordon Selfridge, the American entrepreneur who drew a million people to his great Oxford Street department store in the week it opened in 1909. It's funny to have "Selfridge" cover Barrett Strong's "Money (That's What I Want)" before the fact, though the joke goes on too long without getting any better. But then McLaren explains how Selfridge looted his own company, how at 84 he was forced out, how every day he returned to stand in front of his store in shabby clothes, wondering, like any shopper, at the marvel he'd built. With real heart, Jones sings "Nobody Knows You When You're Down and Out," and the scene runs aways from its story, and into McLaren's: the agony of victory, the thrill of defeat.

3 ▪ **Wedding Present, *Seamonsters* (RCA)** As always, as a guitarist David Gedge of Leeds seeks that faraway margin where repetition doesn't repeat but doubles back on itself, when sound turns into a snake, swallows its own tail, and comes out the other end, the listener still looking in the wrong direction. But as a singer he now refuses to budge: his voice is rough, pebbled, grinding, all fatalism. He pulls against his own music; he loses.

4 ▪ **Digital Underground, "No Nose Job," on *Sons of the P* (Tommy Boy).** Oakland rapper Eddie Humphrey III has a lot of people bouncing around in his voice, among them a stunned '50s hipster and Alfred E. Neuman—but instead of big ears he's got a big nose. He insists on its social function in the context of stardom: trimming the bone for better video presence really means "bailing out of the community and place where you come from." Is that why so many faces on MTV seem to come from nowhere?

5 ▪ **Burning Spear, *Marcus Garvey/Garvey's Ghost* (Mango CD reissue, 1976)** As a tribute to the founder of the Jamaican/

American Back-to-Africa Movement—
Garvey was born in 1887 and died in 1940;
I don't know why the set proclaims "SPE-
CIAL RELEASE TO CELEBRATE THE 100TH
ANNIVERSARY OF MARCUS GARVEY'S
BIRTH"—the first disk, with Winston Rod-
ney's singing, convinces you he's still dead.
The second, the coolest dub album ever
made, is proof he's still waiting.

6 ■ Scarface of the Geto Boys, *Mr. Scarface Is Back* (Rap-A-Lot/Priority) Houston
gangster rap: sex 'n' death as rape 'n' murder. It's ugly, even evil, disgusting—yet
pushed to such extremes of cynicism, self-
loathing, and shame that hesitation rises up
in the midst of every act.

7 ■ All-Star Band with Special Musical
Guest Bob Dylan, "Like a Rolling Stone," *Late
Night with David Letterman 10th Anniversary
Special*, February 6 (NBC) Carole King, piano, lit up the screen; guitarist Chrissie
Hynde and organist Paul Shaffer played
their instruments for percussion; after
standing in for the devil in the film *Crossroads*, guitarist Steve Vai looked thrilled to
have God on his side; and Dylan was merely
along for the ride that, by this time, in these
hands, the song could produce by itself.

8 ■ Londonbeat, "I've Been Thinking
About You" (Radioactive/RCA) A multicul-
tural groove patched together from a little-
note South African rhythm guitar, a
guitar solo left over from Marty Robbins'
"El Paso," and a vocal that might as well be
by Billy Ocean—the sound the Fine Young
Cannibals would be making, if they were
still making sound.

9 ■ Harry Connick, Jr., "The Star-
Spangled Banner," at the Super Bowl, January 26 (CBS) His hair was raised so high he
looked like he was wearing the Statue of
Liberty on his head. Too bad it wasn't last
year; he could have tied a yellow ribbon
around his neck.

10 ■ Elvis Presley, *Collectors Gold* (RCA 3-
CD set, 1960–69) This set of rehearsals
and outtakes has been rightfully dismissed,
but it has its moments, and the most suggestive comes with a warm-up for "Going
Home," a throwaway ballad from 1968.

"PAPA OO MAU MAU *papa oo mau mau* papa
oo mau mau," Elvis announces. "Be talkin'
in unknown tongues here in a minute." Before the band can stop him he slides into a
distant second of "I Got a Woman," and you
can imagine he is going to take the song
home, back to the glossolalia from which
both he and it came, the primal swamp
of deliverance and revelation— Well, of
course not.

MAY 1992

1 ■ UnknownmiX, *DominaDea* (ReeDee
Distribution) Magda Vogel sings in Spanish,
English, Italian, French, and Dada. The
whole brings up the spirit of a dubbed 1930s
Czech spy movie, or the enchanting, disturbing tones of Ildiko Enyedi's 1989 *My
20th Century*, a film from Hungary—
borders slipping around a center hard with
consequence and danger. This precise, experimental quartet, which can ride a good
beat when it finds one, shares a field with
Pulnoc; as Central Europe returns to history, a new music is perhaps a half-step
ahead.

2 ■ Jimmie Rodgers, *Last Sessions,
1933* (Rounder) "The Father of Country
Music"—and the first great white
bluesman—made these recordings just days
before his death from tuberculosis, and in
moments they are wrenching, with no parallels I know of. On "Blue Yodel No. 12,"
Rodgers fades the word "home" in the line
"I know she's never coming home." He's trying to disguise the rasp in his chest, but his
technique and his commitment to the song
are such that he produces something very
different: an instant of absolute blues, where
a certain word, a certain signifier, is so hurtful it can't be borne. The conventional
blues device is to drop the word and play up
its absence on guitar. Rodgers lets the word
surface—and then, as if by hoodoo, he
makes it disappear.

With "Yodeling My Way Back Home"
he can make nothing disappear. His wails
build between the verses, until very soon he
is plainly going too far. Neither his formal

structures nor his persona can contain the fear and acceptance in the death sound he's making. It's not easy to listen to; the vibrations of his voice unbalance the room. It's like the last shots of F. W. Murnau's *Tabu*, with Matahi swimming to his death against the tides, chasing the skiff that has taken Reri—which, as Pauline Kael has written, "is headed for nothing so commonplace as land."

3 ▪ **Jess Mowry, *Way Past Cool*, a novel (Farrar Straus Giroux)** In Oakland, "the Friends"—a tiny gang of 12-and 13-year-old black boys—try to create comradeship and enforce decency on their few blocks of turf, in "a blind fight for a freedom they *knew* existed but saw only as secondhand shadows behind a TV screen. It was like the ancient cartoon where a starving wolf tried to eat a picture of a Thanksgiving turkey." The threat of murder and the temptation of addiction, of oblivion, are constants; no one has any reason to expect to grow up. Again and again, you have to remind yourself how young the characters are. From the kids to the 16-year-old dope dealer who functions as the devil to his tortured bodyguard—the real focus of the story—each can believe he's seen or done too much for adulthood to promise any mysteries. Not having enough to eat is a leitmotiv, and so is the closed nature of the society the Friends inhabit, where "San Francisco" and "cable cars" are references to another planet. As are stray mentions of Oakland's rap heroes. Hammer, Too Short—their hits have been sucked out of this vacuum, leaving only a vague sound of mockery, an Oakland without music.

4 ▪ **Vulgar Boatmen, *Please Panic* (Caroline/Safehouse)** The insinuating power of this combo has a lot to do with the lightness with which it approaches almost every tune—and the nearly subliminal weight provided by Helen Kirklin's viola. Just as central is an odd sense of distance. The emotional economy is almost always teenage—the people in the songs react with the confusion, woundedness, and pride of teenagers—but the guitarist and lead singer,

Robert Ray, is the 48-year-old director of film and media studies at the University of Florida. He doesn't remember, and he doesn't relive. Like the couple in *Almost Grown*, a TV series of a few years back where the same actors played themselves from their teenage 1960s to their middle-aged '80s in constant flashbacks and flashforwards, Ray feels for the contours of the present and discovers an unresolved past.

5 ▪ **Barrington Levy, *Turning Point* (Profile)** Old-fashioned reggae, full of petty musical theft, heart-stopping dub piano, lunatic dance-hall rock, strange effects (what is that chirping bird doing on "Lipstick"?), and, on the back cover, an outfit that could bring back the zoot suit.

6 ▪ **Harold Meyerson, "Then There Were Two?," review of unreleased Bill Clinton video (*LA Weekly*, March 20–26)** "The next church is Union Missionary Baptist on Chicago's Westside . . . with a congregation that is black working class and poor and that practices religious rituals not far removed from the members' Mississippi roots. The music, though, is pure Chicago: organ, piano, electric guitar, and drum kit. . . . 'The church is not a place for saints, but for sinners,' [Clinton] begins, 'but all of us are called to do the Lord's work.' Amens echo again—and the organ and drums, too; apparently, they will accompany Clinton throughout. . . . He omits his statistics on rising income inequality and conveys his sense in short rhythmical sentences: 'It is honestly true, more people are working harder for less.' He cites experiments in tenant-managed projects, model schools, community development banks. After each, he says 'If it can be so, why can't it be so everywhere else?' The drums roll, the guitar and organ riff for a second, the amens rise. 'We are tired of being divided by race!' (Music and amens.) 'We are tired of being divided by gender!' (Music and amens.) 'We are tired of being divided by income!' (Music and amens.) And then, raising his voice, he closes with scriptural passages about faith and redemption: he

shouts it over the music and the congregation's own shouts, and he leaves the crowd in ecstasy."

7 ■ PiL, *That What Is Not* (Virgin) With the Sex Pistols, as a great ranter John Lydon was also a great singer: grabbing words with his teeth, he twisted them into new shapes before he swallowed them. But for years now he's merely chanted, forcing his lyrics and his bands into the same square boxes. Here there are hints of jailbreak by both the musicians and Lydon himself. Sometimes it almost seems as if you're listening to a real person.

8 ■ The Jesus and Mary Chain, "Reverence"/"Heat" (Blanco y Negro/Warner Music, UK) The top spin is a dull grind on hero fetishism ("I want to die like JFK," etc.): the buried cut breaks in all directions with the wah-wah of the gods.

9 ■ Nymphs, *Nymphs* (DGC) Hellfire from Los Angeles. In concept.

10 ■ Jon Wayne, *Texas Funeral* (Fist Puppet/Cargo reissue, 1985) A guy who's been listening to too much Beat Farmers breaks into a radio station just over the Mexican border and turns on the transmitter, but he's deep in his second bottle and he can't keep the microphone in focus. "Officer," he warbles from his "Texas Jailcell" (along with the title cut there's also "Texas Cyclone," "Texas Wine," "Texas Polka," and so on), "this Indian says he needs some sexual healing." Play this next time somebody brings up the Cowboy Junkies; it'll drive them right out of the room.

SUMMER 1992

1 ■ Stanley Booth, *Rythm Oil—A Journey Through the Music of the American South* (Pantheon) "After nearly three hours, with the audience so bored that it was on the point of having a religious experience"— the line is typical of the sparks that fly in Booth's chronicle, a collection of portraits published over the last 25 years but running, as he puts it, "from slavery in 1940s south Georgia to murder in 1960s Memphis and back again to savagery in 1990s Georgia,

with many laughs along the way," and many casualties, too. The book is bitter ("Watching Memphis's most brilliant products die out of work had made me fervent"), shifting from experience to nostalgia, wonder to elegy, and carried by a certain sense of mission: Booth saw remarkable things, and he has a duty to pass them on. His ruling theme is the struggle of the performer to move an audience. A 1968 piece has B. B. King fighting the same battle in the Fillmore Auditorium in San Francisco and the Club Paradise in Memphis—the crowds are different, so are the tactics, but the stakes are the same.

Rythm Oil was published in London in 1991 by Cape, complete with a quiet portfolio of color photos by William Eggleston that opens the book cold. All are missing from the 1992 Pantheon edition—even the gorgeous red-black-and-yellow label from the bottle of LUCKY MON-GOL RYTHM OIL, which you can still buy at Schwab's on Beale Street. Too bad that like so many of his blues heroes, Booth had to go abroad to find a decent welcome.

2 ■ Love Battery, *Day Glo* (SubPop/Caroline) This Seattle four-piece has a knack for song titles: "Foot" is good, "Side (With You)" is inspired. They also have a sound that chases noise, folk-rock lyricism, and everyday dread into a sensation of expansion, a lifting-off. The music gets bigger, the room gets smaller, and whatever's happening it isn't on the ground.

3 ■ Tom Waits, "Back in the Good Old World (gypsy)," from *Night on Earth—Original Soundtrack Recording* (Island) As Jim Jarmusch's new movie shifts from L.A. to New York to Paris to Rome to Helsinki, the atmospheres are so strong, precisely establishing the clichés of a given city before letting the action in a taxi moving through it dissolve those clichés, that Waits' occasional vocals barely register. They may not even be needed. But I heard the sound track before seeing the film, and on its own the clanking, generous opening tune, so happy with its sprung Kurt Weill rhythms, seems to reveal a childhood secret behind

Waits' twenty years of low-life dramaturgy: Wallace Beery as Long John Silver, "Yo ho ho and a bottle of rum."

4 ▪ **Béatrice Dalle, as the Blind Passenger (Paris segment) in *Night on Earth* (Fine Line Features)** Probably the main reason the picture doesn't need Tom Waits; he couldn't keep up with her any more than her cabdriver can.

5 ▪ **Melvins, *Bullhead* (Tupelo)** The Melvins formed about ten years ago in Aberdeen, Washington, where leader Buzz Osborne was mentor to Kurt Cobain and Chris Novoselic of Nirvana. Now they play really underground music: slow, disconnected, almost always seeking the longest distance between two points. They play like moles, occasionally poking their heads into the air, usually avoiding it.

6 ▪ **Christopher Münch, writer and director, *The Hours and Times* (Antarctic Pictures)** Maybe this is the way to shoot rock 'n' roll history: by reimagining small, almost forgotten turning points. Here Münch, in black and white, with the simplest sets (mostly hotel rooms) and cast (a few people practicing naturalism), takes John Lennon and Brian Epstein back to Barcelona in the spring of 1963, where they spent a few days among the Gaudís and did or did not make love. John (Ian Hart) has the upper hand but he's not sure he wants it; Epstein wants John so badly, and with such self-loathing, he's not sure he could survive getting him; and a stewardess John picks up on the flight over (Stephanie Pack—presumably hers is an invented character, but just because Münch made her up doesn't mean she wasn't there) may stay with you longer than either John or Brian. Hell, she might still be alive.

7 ▪ **Body Count, *Cop Killer* (Sire)** To Rapper Ice-T and the other thrash 'n' metal fans in Body Count the kind of racism that makes black rock an oxymoron is a fraud on their taste. Thus guitarist Ernie C. proves he doesn't care if Pink Floyd is less hip than Funkadelic, drummer Beatmaster "V" offers a pulse so tough and quick he can make the musicians around him seem irrel-

evant, and Ice-T will need at least another album to catch up with his band.

8–9 ▪ **Bruce Springsteen, *Human Touch* and *Lucky Town* (Columbia)** Springsteen's last record, the 1987 *Tunnel of Love*, may have come out of his first marriage, but you didn't have to hear it that way; you do have to hear most of his new songs as celebrations of his second marriage. There are exceptions, escapes from this prison of literal meaning and transparent metaphor— the musical reach in "Human Touch," the gritted-teeth abandon in "Lucky Town," the measured pace of "If I Should Fall Behind"—but in sum these numbers have little room for other people in them. Which raises a political question I imagine Springsteen will find ways to address after these two most commercially successful transitional albums of all time are more or less forgotten: people may care whether or not you're happy, Bruce, but why should they?

10 ▪ **Patricia Kennealy, *Strange Days— My Life With and Without Jim Morrison* (Dutton)** Kennealy married Morrison in a Celtic handfasting ceremony in 1970; she writes as if she took a deep breath the day she heard he'd died and is only now letting it out.

SEPTEMBER 1992

1 ▪ **The Earliest Negro Vocal Quartets, 1894–1928, (Document, Austria)** One day in 1894, in Washington, D.C., the Standard Quartette—H. C. Williams, Ed De Moss, R. L. Scott, and William Cottrell— cut a number of cylinders for Columbia. Only one survives—"Keep Movin'," the earliest recording of African-American music yet discovered. It's just as spooky as its distant provenance suggests. Emerging now out of a wash of distortion and surface noise is a single, strong tenor, then a full, closely shaped chorale; what you hear, first, is the nearly ten decades that separate you from them. But there is nothing foreign here. If formally the unaccompanied singing seems primarily genteel, the passion is at odds with its bounds, and soon you're hearing

church sermons, street preachers, gospel choruses, marching bands, Walt Disney's *Song of the South*, Paul Robeson's "Old Man River," the national anthem, funeral lamentations, folk tales told in the rounded, plummy tones of the Carolinas . . .

The other 22 recordings collected here can't match the power of this stray artifact, though there is not a completely obvious moment among them. The a cappella Dinwiddie Colored Quartet (1902) was clearly in the crowd-pleasing business, mixing animal tales and black-to-white-to-black Stephen Fosterish arrangements into a flat, effective formula. The Male Quartette's "The Camp Meeting Jubilee" (1910) is exactly that: a little play. As up-to-date as Marky Mark and the Funky Bunch (not to mention David Byrne, Paul Simon, Sting, and dozens more), Polk Miller and His Old South Quartette (1909–10) featured a white singer and his black backing group. They played Carnegie Hall, flogging a sort of antebellum nostalgia act about the good old days before the Yankees came: "The Watermelon Party" plus "The 'Old Time' Religion." Mark Twain called two of their numbers "musical earthquakes"—though perhaps not these.

In sum, more sociology than music, leading off with a fact of history that also transcends it: "the mystic chords of memory."

2 ▪ X-Tal, *Everything Crash* (Alias) Fronted by J Neo, who has a lot of heart and no attitude in his thin punk voice, and sparked by bassist Allison Moseley and violinist Carrie Bradley, this small-time San Francisco combo wears their defeated leftist politics on their sleeves and can open for the Mekons without letting you forget them when the headliners come on. They write good songs, but much better than good are Moseley's cover of Fairport Convention's "Genesis Hall" and Neo's despair-hate-grief-and-rage cocktail "Black Russian," which ends with the meanest Elvis tribute I've ever heard: "So pour me another Black Russian," Neo says to the bartender, "and let's get real, real *gone* for a change."

3 ▪ **Carter the Unstoppable Sex Machine,** *1992—The Love Album* (Chrysalis) More exciting, overwrought, high-pop songs about power, corruption, and lies, not to mention AIDS, child abuse, alcoholism, poverty, rape, and heretic-burning, keyed by "The Only Living Boy in New Cross"— which is sort of based on the Trade Winds' 1965 "New York's a Lonely Town" ("When you're the only surfer boy around")—and topped off by a straight version of "The Impossible Dream." Heard in the right mood, this can be very depressing.

4 ▪ **Anonymous performance, downtown Manhattan subway (May 12)** Two young black men, one short, the other tall, moved fast through the car and stopped in front of two women, one white, one black, both in their 20s. "CAN WE ASK YOU A QUESTION?" they shouted at the black woman. When she didn't answer they jacked up the pace: "CANWEASKYOUAQUESTION-CANWEASKYOUAQUES—" As she sat stone-faced they fell silent, struck a pose, and then, slowly, asked anyway: "What's your name / Is it Mary, or Sue?"—and then went on through almost the whole of Don & Juan's 1962 doo-wop hit. As the black woman broke into embarrassed smiles and the white woman got out a dollar, I wondered why the guys, already heading for the next car, had left off the song's kicker, "Shooby doo-waht do wha." The tall one looked over his shoulder: "Shooby doo-waht do-WHAHHHHHH," he and his pal sang, giving the last syllable a fabulous lift, and they were through the doors.

5 ▪ **EMF, "Search and Destroy," on** *unexplained EP* (EMI) A superhot cover of Iggy Pop's hottest song, all keening melody, guitar like bad weather, drooling glee. Maybe payback for last year's horrible, inescapable "Unbelievable"—you may not believe in censoring music for content, but what about for form?

6 ▪ **Valerie Buhagiar, in** *Highway 61*, **dir. Bruce McDonald** (Skouras Pictures) As the can't-take-your-eyes-off-her-bad-girl-on-the-run, Jackie Bangs—Lester's sister?

7 ▪ **Walter Karp,** *Buried Alive—Essays on Our Endangered Republic* **(Franklin Square Press)** Karp, who died in 1989, was a brave and finally ranting political critic best known for his work in *Harper's*. He left behind a brutal, point-by-point account of what's at stake in this year's election: a choice between betrayal and tyranny. Seems easy enough to me.

8 ▪ **Sadie Plant,** *The Most Radical Gesture—The Situationist International in a Postmodern Age* **(Routledge)** A clear, engaged explication of the least obscure Situationist texts (notably Guy Debord's *Society of the Spectacle* and Raoul Vaneigem's *The Revolution of Everyday Life*), along with a long, cool look at how the likes of Baudrillard and Lyotard got famous enough not to need first names by reducing such texts to fashionable mush.

9 ▪ **Jim Dickinson, liner notes to Howlin' Wolf,** *Memphis Days—The Definitive Edition,* **vol. 2 (Bear Family, Germany)** Releases and outtakes from 1951–52, ranging from the breathtaking to the merely heroic. Memphian Dickinson, who likes to talk about his town's culture as a Dada subspecies, nails the legend of the man who, when born of woman, was just Chester Burnett: "He was a primitive-modernist . . . [whose] contribution to the blues goes beyond musical phrases. The 'idea' of Howlin' Wolf makes blues history somehow deeper and richer."

10 ▪ *New York Times,* **"A Scholar Finds Huck Finn's Voice in Twain's Writing about a Black Youth,"** re Professor Shelley Fisher Fiskin's *Was Huck Black? Mark Twain and African-American Voices,* **Oxford University Press, forthcoming 1993 (July 7)** While it's tempting to claim Twain as the founder of rock 'n' roll, or the first good white blues singer (or anyway the inspiration for Polk Miller), I doubt that Ishmael Reed, Greg Tate, or Henry Louis Gates, Jr., were surprised by Fiskin's thesis that the voice of Huckleberry Finn was rooted in that of a black person (Twain: "the most artless, sociable, and exhaustless talker I ever came

across"). Sorry, but given the setting Twain chose and his commitment to vernacular realism, how, at least to a good degree, could it *not* have been? (As George Carlin used to say, lock five kids from Harlem and five from Scarsdale in a room for a week and see who comes out talking like who.) But Reed, et al., would probably not be surprised that the Fiskin newsbreak has already produced the sort of happy talk to which no American racial paradox is immune: the argument that black people (or anyone else) need no longer be troubled by Huck's use of the word "nigger" in reference to Jim, since now it's really two brothers getting down.

OCTOBER 1992

1 ▪ **Heavens to Betsy, "My Red Self," on** *Kill Rock Stars* **(Kill Rock Stars) and "Baby's Gone," on** *Throw: The Yoyo Studio Compilation* **(Yoyo Recordings)** The two stray tracks on various artists' anthologies by this Olympia combo (Corin Tucker, guitar and vocals, Tracy Sawyer, bass and occasional drums) are as fierce—as unforgiving, and as unforgiven—as anything I've heard in ages. These songs sound anonymous, almost found; appearing alongside tracks by the likes of Nirvana, Bikini Kill, Unwound, Mecca Normal, Bratmobile, 7 Year Bitch, and Kreviss, the music simply seems part of an ordinary rock 'n' roll conversation, at least in Olympia. ("The birthplace of rock," it says on the back of the *Kill Rock Stars* CD, as if rock 'n' roll could be born anywhere, again and again, as if for the first time, and of course it can.)

"My Red Self," about menstruation, is modest and strong; "Baby's Gone" is riveting. A single, naked fuzztone makes a backdrop for what you might call testifying, if you can merge the old meaning of testifying in church with testifying in court. The same absolute need to be heard that drives the Mekon's voice-and-stamping-foot "The Building" powers this performance, which doesn't seem minimalist in any way; rather, it gets bigger as it goes on, until, near the end ("I did what you told me to/Now I'm dead"), it seems to try to explode but can't. The pressure is enormous, and passed on straight.

2 ■ Heavenly, "She Says"/"Escort Crash on Marston Street" (K Records) A four-person band from Oxford, England, led by singer Amelia Fletcher, late of Talulah Gosh and still playing with the sweetest, most barbed warble in pop: her heaven is not for the innocent. An album, *Le Jardin de Heavenly*, is due, but for the moment this single spins on and on.

3–4 ■ Walter Mosley, *White Butterfly* (Norton) and John Lee Hooker: "This Land Is Nobody's Land," from *More Real Folk Blues— The Missing Album* (Chess/MCA) In Mosley's Easy Rawlins mysteries—*White Butterfly*, set in 1956 and the third in the series, is the most effective so far—what's at stake is the unwritten history of postwar Los Angeles. Mosley, a man in his 30s writing in the voice of a retired black detective who would now be past 70, is writing this history from the inside out: from inside Watts. First appearing in the '40s, Easy Rawlins is Ralph Ellison's Invisible Man as private eye; his skin and shuffle may be cover, but the wariness of his movements carries a greater charge than any scene of violence. Pages can curl with tension even when nothing is happening. Mosley isn't much of a plotter, or even a storyteller; the books work in moods that shift like weather, on the glacial but certain apprehension of a society changing, though not in any direction anyone can control, or that anyone is necessarily going to like. Perhaps more than in the most extreme and Afrocentric rap, white people are foreigners in these books, and in Rawlins' L.A., and black people are exiles. "This land is no one's land," John Lee Hooker sang in 1966, a year after the Watts riots— the tune was a slow, improvised blues, a blunt reply to Woody Guthrie, and it remained unreleased until 1991—"This land/ Is your burying ground." Easy Rawlins' next appearance should place him in just about that year, if not that territory.

5 ■ Steely & Clevie, *Play Studio One Vintage* (Heartbeat) Classic late-'60s reggae, cut last year by the leading dance-hall producers and rhythm section, backing Theophilus Beckford, Alton Ellis, the Clarendonians, and more. The music is all definition, like a perfect black and white print of a '40s film noir following the dead video color of the nightly news.

6 ■ Sonic Youth, *Dirty* (DGC) I like the way Thurston Moore snaps "I believe Anita Hill/That judge'll rot in hell" on "Youth Against Fascism." It's so peremptory. It's so convincing.

7 ■ Tori Amos, *Little Earthquakes* and *Crucify* (Atlantic) In a year or so, Amos' attempt to find her own voice somewhere between those of Donovan and Kate Bush may sound impossibly arch and contrived; her version of Nirvana's "Smells Like Teen Spirit," on the *Crucify* EP, already does. But that's also what's compelling about it. Breathy, precious, arty, and cool, Amos can get under your skin, and then rip.

8 ■ Ashtray, *Ashtray* (Shoe Records) Bare-bones lyricism, crude male and female vocal leads, and a guitarist who can play his string all the way out.

9 ■ Chris Hunt, director, *The Search for Robert Johnson* (Sony Music Video) Willie Mae Powell was Johnson's lover in the '30s; the look on her still-beautiful face when she listens to Johnson's "Love in Vain," which mentions her, is worth a lot, as is blues researcher Mack McCormick's highly sophisticated analysis of Johnson's psyche. They may even be worth sitting through a lot of stilted, overrehearsed interviews and endless takes of narrator John Hammond, Jr., strangling Johnson's songs.

10 ■ Bono, "Can't Help Falling in Love," from *Honeymoon in Vegas—Music from the Original Soundtrack* (Epic Soundtrax) This set mixes by-the-numbers Elvis covers (Billy Joel's "All Shook Up," Ricky Van Shelton's "Wear My Ring Around Your Neck") with surprises: a thrilling ride through "Suspicious Minds" with Dwight Yoakam and an uncredited Beth Anderson, a torchy, Mary Lou Barton–styled "(You're The) Devil in

Disguise" by Trisha Yearwood, a hipster "Jailhouse Rock" from John Mellencamp. The stunner is Bono's twisted reading of the ultimate Big E show-closer, here accompanied principally by an old Elvis interview running in the background. As Bono climbs the golden ladder of the song toward a falsetto so desperate it's all too obvious who he can't help falling in love with, the man himself—or the boy; Elvis sounds very young, and completely guileless—talks about a book called *Poems That Touch the Heart.* After two minutes, Bono fades into the ether, and from out of it comes that familiar voice: "Yessir, I'll be looking forward to coming back. Yessir, I'm looking forward to it."

NOVEMBER 1992

1 ▪ Lucious Curtis, "High Lonesome Hill," on the various-artists anthology *Mississippi Blues—Library of Congress Recordings 1940–1942* (Travelin' Man) With the national music companies no longer digging up the South, folklorist John Lomax came to Natchez in 1940 to make field recordings. Among those whose songs he cut into his 12-inch acetates one Saturday was singer-guitarist Curtis, working with second guitarist Willie Ford. Curtis never recorded again, and if there is another country blues performance quite like "High Lonesome Hill" I haven't heard it.

The tone is light, melodic, the vocal sly. The two guitarists find the pulse they will push and twist through the long instrumental passages of this four-minute-31-second sun shower, and the dynamics of the instrumentation are completely open, the excitement jumping ahead thirty or fifty years to prophesy the Allman Brothers' "Blue Sky" and R.E.M.'s "Losing My Religion." You can get lost in this music, wonder what became of Lucious Curtis. But it's the opening lines of the song that echo—again with that glancing attack, yet delivering a statement so weighted it can make you wonder where Lucious Curtis came from. The first line is broken up with hesitations, the sec-

ond line is rushed, and the third line is a deep breath:

> Babe, I went, and I stood up, on some high old lonesome hill
> Babe I went and I stood up on some high old lonesome hill
> And looked down on the house where I used to live

These are the words of a man who has seen all around his life, and is about to tell you everything he's seen.

2 ▪ Alison Krauss & Union Station, *Every Time You Say Goodbye* (Rounder) Bluegrass fiddler Krauss sings in a warble that sounds first of all small. A second listen turns plaintiveness into toughness, and after that—well, her voice becomes a thing of real complexity, to the point where you can locate the soul in "Who Can Blame You" in the way she communicates that she doesn't believe a word she's singing.

3 ▪ Bill Buford, *Among the Thugs* (Norton) This is a book about crowd violence and English football fans: a milieu that caught up American-in-Britain Buford for eight years. His conclusion is extreme: "This bored, empty, decadent generation consists of nothing more than what it appears to be. It is a lad culture without mystery, so deadened that it uses violence to wake itself up. It pricks itself so that it has feeling, burns its flesh so that it has smell." Buford's prose is almost unique these days: first-class, yet seemingly ordinary, straight, and never calling attention to itself (try reading P. J. O'Rourke after Buford—it can't be done). The result is a noisy book about the fascist possibilities of Western democracy: "A crowd had been made by the people who had stepped into the street, and everyone was aware of what they had done; it was a creative act." And what was created? "They were all strangers. This march was a march of strangers. More to the point: this march was a march. It recalled not football crowds, but demonstrations or protest rallies. You could see the surprise in the faces of the people near me; they had created something big, but weren't sure how they'd done it."

4 ▪ Ramones, "Poison Heart," from *Mondo Bizarro* (Radioactive) The Ramones began as kings of irony, but Joey Ramone is most present when his heart is bleeding all over his sleeve. As on "Bonzo Goes to Bitburg"; the touching he-doesn't-wanna-be-buried-in-a "Pet Sematary" (given Joey's ruling pinhead persona, his fear is credible); and this ditty, all cornball angst and thrilling negative uplift.

5 ▪ Hopey Glass, "Great Lost Recordings," in *The Wire* #102, September 1992 Glass on "My Happiness," Elvis' first, for-his-mother recording, as it surfaced 37 years after the fact, and why no one paid attention: "Sung to Gladys or himself, or the young Gladys in himself, [it] says quiet gentleness can also be an unearthly force." At full length, as Glass seeks to understand Elvis not as a rebel but as a mother, a cultural mother, this is the most sophisticated and risky music criticism I've read in a long time, and a match for William Carlos Williams on Abraham Lincoln: "The Great Rail-splitter's 'All I am or ever hope to be I owe to my angel mother'; the walking up and down in Springfield on the narrow walk between the two houses, day after day, with a neighbor's baby, borrowed for the occasion, sleeping inside his cape on his shoulder to give him stability while thinking about coming speeches. . . . The least private would find a woman to caress him, a woman in an old shawl—with a great bearded face and a towering black hat above it, to give it unearthly reality."

6 ▪ Fred Bronson, *The Billboard Book of Number One Hits* (Billboard/Watson-Guptill) The third edition ("Rock Around the Clock" through Vanessa Williams' "Save the Best for Last") of one of the most entertaining and informative books ever written about pop music. The format is strict—one page with pic per disc—and depending on whether he's writing about one-hit wonders Maurice Williams & the Zodiacs or four-time chart-topper Roxette, Bronson can cram the whole of a singular career into less than 1,000 words or stretch a pointless one over several pages without ever seeming bored. Exasperated, that's another story.

7 ▪ Lynn Hope, *"Morocco"* (Saxophonograph reissue, 1950–55, Sweden) Hope—a.k.a. Al Hajj Abdulla Rasheed Ahmed—had a national hit in 1950 with "Tenderly," a sweet, snazzy sax instrumental typical of his relaxed style. Though you can imagine Big Red Little in the audience, you don't hear Hope's faith in Islam in his music—he led the only all-Muslim band in the country, turban on his head, fezzes for the rest—you hear rhythm & blues on the verge of taking shape, and then taking one step back.

8–9 ▪ Johnny Shines, Henry Townshend, Lonnie Pitchford, Honeyboy Edwards, Railroad Maintenance Crew, et al., *Roots of Rhythm and Blues—A Tribute to the Robert Johnson Era* (Columbia) and George Thorogood, "I'm a Steady Rollin' Man," from *The Baddest of George Thorogood and the Destroyers* (EMI) Proof of Robert Johnson's genius: there's more of his spirit in Thorogood's trash bonus track for a greatest-hits package than there is in a reverent tribute by the Smithsonian Folklife Festival.

10 ▪ Paul Schrader, writer and director, *Light Sleeper* (Fine Line Features) Lousy as they almost always are, Schrader's films almost always contain elements of obsession that cough up incidents so intense they all but come loose from their own movies. This time not even Michael Been's obese soundtrack songs can filter what goes on in Dana Delany's face. There's a look in her eyes as she sits in bed with Willem Dafoe—a fluttering anticipation of ecstasy unto oblivion—that might have satisfied Louise Brooks. And too soon after that a look of such abasement and self-loathing even Brooks might have flinched at it.

DECEMBER 1992

1 ▪ Sinéad O'Connor, "War," on *Saturday Night Live* (NBC, October 3) For the record: live TV, O'Connor in a long formal gown, Star of David necklace, nose stud, chanting her rewrite of Bob Marley's "War" a cappella, her face shifting by imperceptible degrees from saint to thug, rat to Hedy

Lamarr. Then for the last line, "The victory of good over evil," she produces a picture of Pope John Paul II, rips it into pieces: "Fight the real enemy!" On audiotape, no visuals, it's so suggestive: "Good . . . over *evil*," then just *switch, switch*, the sound loud in its oddity.

This was a classic media shock. Even if you were with her all the way—after the fact—you had to realize that someone this intransigent will sooner or later put you on the other side. And if the act itself seems cheap, a setup, self-aggrandizing, ask yourself this: given the chance to say what I wanted to the whole country, would I have had the nerve?

2 ▪ Bob Marley & the Wailers, "War" (1976), on the 4-CD Bob Marley reissue *Songs of Freedom* (Tuff Gong) Originally the highlight of the mostly boilerplate LP *Rastaman Vibration*, and in fact Marley's rewrite of a speech delivered in California in 1968 by Haile Selassie—then still Emperor of Ethiopia, and also "King of Kings, Lord of Lords, the Conquering Lion of the Tribe of Judah." With Aston "Familyman" Barrett leading the way with bass notes more ominously confident than anyone's found since, and a chorus of closely gathered horns following at a distance, the speech is turned into music, and the politics changed from one man's statement into a common rite.

3 ▪ Darcey Steinke, *Suicide Blonde* (Atlantic Monthly Press) Very catchy jacket: nude blonde woman on rumpled bed lights cigarette. There's not a moment in this increasingly tense short novel when the first-person narrator the cover girl's standing in for is half so cool. As with most bohemias, punk slowly devolved toward oblivion and small-time criminal trade; set in San Francisco bad-news neighborhoods, this report on that milieu escapes the confines of genre. Near the end there's a voyeuristic scene so fast, blunt, and cruel that when you're told "her eyes were dead" there's no surface to go beneath; Steinke works with blood, sweat, and semen, not metaphors.

4 ▪ Carter the Unstoppable Sex Machine, at the Quake, San Francisco (October

6) Singer/guitarist Jim Bob and lead guitarist Fruitbat play with tapes carrying synthesized orchestrations that are at once huge and conveniently sized: they seem to fill a room precisely. That's because lead actor Jim Bob's physical and vocal timing is perfect, yet still comes off as no less spontaneous than any other rock performer's moves. The drama, though, is unique. Fruitbat plays bemused sidekick—but after a few tunes his Faith No More T-shirt no longer seems to refer to that band. Jim Bob might be playing someone dying of AIDS who's just realized Judgment Day is a con. Tall, thin, beaky, wearing a shirt covered with cartoon faces of the Big Bad Wolf, with just a buzz of brown hair save for a foot-long forelock he can shake for emphasis, Jim Bob has as evil a grin as you'll ever see, and this night the music was so thrilling he only had to use it once.

5 ▪ Bushwick Bill, *Little Big Man* (Rap-A-Lot) To be young, four feet two inches tall, black, and conscious—a solo shot by the lead bad dream of Houston's Geto Boys. "Where I'm from is a modern-day motherfuckin' Vietnam," he says plainly; movie suspense music keeps you hooked as crossing vocals trade violent fantasies and laments over how little is left of a chance for a decent life. The two sides come together with a true-crime track: "Ever So Clear," the tale of how Bushwick, drunk on Everclear, tried to force his girlfriend to shoot him. She missed his brain but took an eye.

6 ▪ Brenda Kahn, *Epiphany in Brooklyn* (Chaos/Columbia) So you're at this party and this woman with great legs has you backed into a corner with how much she's talking, she's smart, she's really smart, she's so smart and she talks so fast she sucks the air right out of the room. You were having fun till that happened.

7–8 ▪ Beat Happening, *You Turn Me On* (Sub Pop/K Records) and Roger Corman, director: *Teenage Caveman* (Columbia TriStar video) Yea, verily, and how weird. T'was with producer Jerry Dennon of Beat Happening's own Great Northwest that English pop star Ian Whitcomb recorded his horri-

ble 1965 international smash "You Turn Me
On." Thus you can chalk up Beat Happening's new album title—anomalous for this
doggedly we're-flat-and-we're-proud trio—
to cultural memory. But it's unlikely their
Olympia, Washington, hometown provides
the connections that would have tipped
them off that their tune "Teenage Caveman" would hit the stores the same season
as the reissue of its namesake: an unbelievable 1958 oedipal drama starring a
loin-clothed Robert Vaughn and a lot of
dinosaurs. That convergence you have to
credit to serendipity, or the fact that Beat
Happening singer Heather Lewis' heart is
always in the right place. For more information, see *Beat Happening 1983–85* (K/Feel
Good All Over), *Jamboree* (Sub Pop/K,
1988), and *Dreamy* (Sub Pop, 1991).

9 ▪ **Peter Gabriel, *US* (Geffen)** When
he's on—as with "Come Talk To Me," with
Sinéad O'Connor making trouble in the
background—he's beginning to sound like
Richard Harris looks.

10 ▪ **Dave Morey, "10 at 10," KFOG-FM
104.5, San Francisco (September 23).** Running since 1982, Morey's every-weekday
show contextualizes "ten great songs from
one great year" by combining often forgotten hits with audio documentary far richer
than radio news ever offered in its own
time. Morey creates the instant history the
radio should have delivered, and the results
are often startling, as with his Barry Goldwater montage from the 1964 election. He
opened with a soundbite from Goldwater's
speech accepting the Republican nomination, cut to the candidate's response to a student's question about avoiding war ("Peace
through strength"), to the Goldwater slogan
that made so many people nervous, "IN
YOUR HEART YOU KNOW HE'S RIGHT"—and
then, with no pause whatsoever, Morey hit
you in the face with the brittle opening
chords of the Rolling Stones' "Not Fade
Away," the Buddy Holly cover that introduced them to the U.S.A. Bomp budda
BAH—it was no contest. This was a discourse contradiction, a discourse warp; the
previous forms of speech disappeared, were

rendered incomprehensible, turned into
babble by the emotional clarity of a few
harsh seconds of true rock 'n' roll—a language that didn't translate back. That this
event—this imaginary event?—was anything but inevitable was proven by Morey's
next segue, into the Temptations' "The
Way You Do the Things You Do." It made
no breach; it translated into the political
speech around it with ease.

1 ▪ **Lou Reed, "Foot of Pride," at "Columbia Records Celebrates the Music of Bob
Dylan," Madison Square Garden, NYC, October 16 (radio and pay-per-view TV broadcast)**
In Bob Dylan's version, from 1983, this long
and muscular song sounds vaguely influenced by Lou Reed. In Reed's version
Judgment Day looms and—backed by
Booker T., Duck Dunn, and Steve Cropper,
the MGs minus the late Al Jackson—Reed
leads its charge. All debts are paid before
the first line closes; from then on the tune
is Reed's more than it was ever Dylan's. All
those years of clunky talk songs, good ones,
bad ones—here Reed grabs a note, rings it,
wrings it: like Jimi Hendrix said, he'll kiss
the sky. For the first time in an era Reed
sings, heading into each chorus like Jan
Berry, if Jan Berry were to finally solve
Dead Man's Curve—and as written the
chorus is so strong each one seems as if it
has to be the last, as if nothing could follow
it. Lou, you've got to put this out.

2 ▪ **Larry Doyle, writer, Alan Kupper-
berg, illustrator, *The Fantastic Foursome*
(comic book insert to *Spy*, October)** Sure to
be a valued artifact of the '92 election, and
the story line is wickedly consistent: the
opening panel has superheroes Bill ("The
Golden Doughboy"), Hillary ("Sweet-
and-Sour Girl"), Al ("The Wooden Wonder"), and Tipper ("The Hearth Keeper")
campaigning as a band ("Born to Run
the U.S.A."), and the drama reaches its apex
when Barbara Bush ("Silver Ox") calls Tipper a bitch and Tipper slaps her mouth
shut with a PMRC parental-advisory label.

3 ▪ **Soul Asylum, *Grave Dancers Union* (Columbia)** A balanced, lyrical, commercial album from an outsider combo a lot of people thought had seen its day—but if you want your heart broken in the middle of a laugh, go right to "Without a Trace." A little detail like "Don't forget your mace/If you're out walking late" slips through this slapstick chronicle of no-future almost before you have a chance to realize that's not the way it has to be.

4 ▪ **Chuck Berry, et al., *Stoned Alchemy—27 Original Blues and R & B Hits That Inspired the Rolling Stones* (Instant/ Charly reissue, 1948–64, UK)** A collection based on obscure Stones numbers, from odd singles to ancient rehearsal tapes, and topped by Bo Diddley's bizarre 1956 miniplay "Cops and Robbers." "Yeah," the cop says after the robber's been collared, "we gonna put him so far back in jail this time, they gonna have to pump *air* in to him." I wonder if Mick still has a copy.

5 ▪ **International Secular Atavism, stickers** The Traditional Family Values set, highlighted by a loving heterosexual couple in a prayerful if sodomitic position, a collage of headlines on clerical pedophilia, and "'Jesus Christ' Threw Up in My Car." "He was wearing a yellow rented party dress which was wrecked," the sticker continues. "He was heard saying 'I don't fucking care . . . *It's not fucking mine.*'" If you think it's easy to think up stuff like that, try it yourself.

6 ▪ **Heavenly, *Le Jardin de Heavenly* (K/ Cargo)** Beatle echoes cut with a present-day cynicism so light it merely seems like doubt. There hasn't been a vocal smile as good as Amelia Fletcher's since Claire Grogan broke up Altered Images.

7 ▪ **Robbie Robertson, "Canon" (Part 2) (includes "Playing Chess with Bobby Fischer in Bellevue Reverie) from *Beneath The Underdog*," on *Hal Willner Presents Weird Nightmare—Meditations on Mingus* (Columbia)** Reading from Charles Mingus' autobiography on this mostly-musical tribute album, Robertson catches one border station of '60s Manhattan bohemia, like a

narrator for an episode of *The Twilight Zone*, or maybe *Peter Gunn*.

8 ▪ **Blue Blouse, postcards** Eight proofs that the '20s Soviet agit-prop collective Blue Blouse—a 100,000-strong perform-anywhere "living newspaper"—actually existed: group poses of the stolid "Physical Culture Dance," the Arthurian "Strengthen the Might of the Red Army," the grinning roundelay of "Revolt of the Toys," and the flirtatious "Five Year Plan." With tableaux that make production sexy, these postcards from a vanished time truly speak from a new world, albeit not quite a real one.

9 ▪ **Frederick Pollack, "Theses on Intellectuals," in *Representations* #39, Summer 1992** A rollercoaster that only goes down: 161 sentences on why intellectuals underestimate the will to power, the pleasures of scapegoating, and the joy of inflicting pain. Extra-credit reading: The Old Testament. Soundtrack: anything by Guns N' Roses.

10 ▪ **Terry Gross, interview with Neil Young, on *Fresh Air*, November 5 (NPR, originating from WHYY-FM, Philadelphia)** This rare audio interview with Young featured direct answers that came to flat stops, silences that left the air not dead but surprised, a tone that at first sounded like impatience and soon came across as authority, plus an exchange on how easily Young might fit into Nirvana. Gross: "Most of the people who play that kind of loud, grunge sound are much younger. I wonder how you felt as somebody in your 40s who's been playing since the mid '60s, playing a music that mostly people who are a generation younger than you—" Young: "None of these old guys around know how to do it." "None of the old guys around know how to do it?" "No, they don't. They can't do it, you know, so they don't do it. That's why I'm still doing it, 'cause I know how. If they were as lucky as me, they'd be doing it too. I mean, it's fantastic. There's no sensation like it."

FEBRUARY 1993

1 ▪ **Jonathan Richman, *I, Jonathan* (Rounder)** Good news: from the premier

regressive in pop music, his best album since the '77 *Rock 'n' Roll with the Modern Lovers*. The sound is living room pristine, the technique a wave at second-rank '50s rockabilly and particularly unaccomplished '20s country blues, and the instrumentation is extant, barely: that is, Richman and friends can make a guitar, tambourine, and handclaps feel like a whole band. Material includes a rediscovery of surf music ("Grunion Run"), a rewrite of "Gypsy Woman" into "I Was Dancing in the Lesbian Bar" ("Well, the first bar, things were stop and stare/But in this bar, things were laissez-faire"—he pronounces it two different ways, both correct), a heartwarming tribute to the Velvet Underground ("America at its best"—now that Richman's transcended his influences he can wallow in them), and the hysterical "Rooming House on Venice Beach." Starting with a normal beat, Richman is soon falling over himself with the gross *hippieness* of the place; he sings as if he still can't believe he was ever there. "The ancient world was at my reach," he chants, but he means people who were '60s relics long about, oh, 1970: "The ancient drunk guys/Passing the cup," or "The weirdo weird guys/Passing the hat." As social history this ranks with the fabled "Dodge Veg-O-Matic," the Modern Lovers' number about the worst car ever made. Bad news: title is sort of dumb.

2 ▪ **Bob Dylan, *Good As I Been to You* (Columbia)** Solo versions of very old ballads and prewar blues standards—"other people's songs," but these songs are as much Dylan's as anyone else's, and he sings them with an authority equal to that he brought to Blind Lemon Jefferson's "See That My Grave Is Kept Clean" in 1962. The authority is not the same, though; there's more freedom in it now. "Little Maggie" is always played for its melody, but Dylan goes for its drama, the drama of a weak, scared man in love with an unfaithful drunk. The music is cut up, stretched, snapped back: each line opens with a stop, and at its end just fades out. The more historical numbers—18th- and 19th-century tales of, to be blunt, im-

perialist class war and primitive capitalist exploitation—are personalized, Dylan inhabiting the first-person narratives as if he lived them twice. It's only after a time, when the melancholy and bitterness seem too great for one voice, that you hear them as history, as more than one man's plight. Finally all of the story is shared, the singer only its mouthpiece, medium for private miseries within the great sweep of disaster; these songs are yours as much as anyone else's. As for the guile, the slyness, the pleasing cynicism in the singer's voice—he gets to keep that.

3 ▪ **Bikini Kill, *Bikini Kill* (Kill Rock Stars 12" e.p.)** Singer Kathleen Hanna on her influences: "Fourteen women in Montreal." This disc—the first generally available release from this hard, cruelly funny band—offers five rumbling tales of sex and violence, plus the live "Thurston Hearts The Who," in which roiling noise accompanies the onstage reading of a review Bikini Kill didn't like. Sounds stupid, but it's like a house burning down.

4 ▪ **Gabriel Yared, music in *The Lover*, dir. Jean-Jacques Annaud (MGM)** In the sex scenes, which are severe and modest, avoiding both high theater and porn pomp, Yared's synthesized soundtrack produces depth: the epic passion Annaud can't show. The music is mechanical, slowed down— *Clash of the Titans* stuff.

5 ▪ **Dada, "Dizz Knee Land" (I.R.S.)** "I just ran away from home," begins a laconic, bored voice. "Now I'm going to Disneyland . . ." It seems little remembered that when Ronald Reagan left the White House, he had it in mind to set a plant in the crowd of reporters lined up to shout at him as he boarded the helicopter. "What are you going to do now?" the plant was supposed to yell, and of course Reagan would flash the grin: "I'm going to Disneyland." Hey, it was an easy 50 grand—but killjoys like James Baker squelched the move as "unpresidential," not understanding that Ronald Reagan took power from the great cliché, hiding in its light.

Well, it's an old story. It almost hides the true horror of the "I'm Going to Disneyland" buy, as the likes of Joe Montana rush off the field after winning a national championship, all pumped up to say the right thing when the plant gives out with "Whaddaya gonna do now?" The horror is in the way Disney now nails down rights to what had previously been understood as subjective responses to unrepeatable moments. The little exchange of set phrases, accompanied by the exchange of a large but not *that* large amount of money (the real payoff is in being selected to say the magic words), signals the ability of a corporation to completely commodify individual emotion—to destroy, symbolically, any realm of privacy.

Dada, an L.A. trio whose sound is as dulled as its singer's tone, forces the Disney conspiracy to accept the subjectivity it means to deny. The song turns "Disneyland" (the "Dizz Knee Land" titling obviously meant to protect Dada from Disney's notorious trademark cops) into a perfect blank: the place you go when you can't think of anything else to do, when you haven't got the energy to choose one road over another. "I just crashed my car again/ Now I'm. . . ." "I just robbed a grocery store. . . ." "I just tossed a fifth of gin. . . ." The song was released late in 1992, and by now people ought to be singing it on Main Street.

6 ▪ **Television fairy, serendipitous Beatle night, U.S. TV, 4 December 1992** If you ever get the feeling that there is a momentum, or inertia, in our more or less official cultural industries to fix a single point of reference, this evening—or rather simply a single 10–11 P.M. slot—would have done for proof. On CNN, Larry King: "Good lineup next week—Mark David Chapman, who assassinated John Lennon 12 years ago, is with us next week!" But switch to ABC, to Barbara Walters and 20/20, and Chapman was already there, his devil-made-me-do-it responses intercut with home movies of John and Yoko mugging and trying to look gay. Click to NBC, and there's Linda Mc-

Cartney, explaining that fans resent her even now for taking their Paul away and, my god, enough of that, zip zip zip and here's the Disney Channel, "The Making of Sgt. Pepper." It was enough to make you wish the Beatles had never been—but the next night Disney was running *A Hard Day's Night*. In that magical scene when the foursome escape their evil manager and settle in at a nightclub, with the dark mood of "Don't Bother Me" in the background, you got to see Ringo and the tall, beaky blond guy invent the Pogo, and for an instant there was a sense that all was right with the world: that Barbara Walters and Larry King would end up in the same hell as Mark Chapman.

7 ▪ **Nirvana, "In Bloom" video, dir. Kevin Kerslake (DGC)** For a tune about people who don't understand what they're listening to, three early-'60s nerds appear on some local imitation Ed Sullivan Show. (The costumes are fabulous: drummer David Grohl's short-hair wig looks like it's made out of carpet remnant.) As they dribble out the song, they change into pinheads in dresses, trashing the set and the music, then back again. It's geeks to freaks—Tod Browning's *Freaks*. As Kurt Cobain writes in the notes to *Incesticide* (DGC), a collection of fugitive Nirvana recordings, "If any of you in any way hate homosexuals, people of different color, or women, please do this one favor for us—leave us the fuck alone! Don't come to our shows and don't buy our records."

8 ▪ **Kathleen H., "Rockstar" (Kill Rock Stars Wordcore)** A woman in the audience hears Prince's "Sister" and goes home to make a spoken-word 45 about the same story—incest from her side. Her boyfriend, listening, throws up.

9 ▪ **Hal Hartley, writer, director, coproducer, *Simple Men* (Fine Line Features)** In a roadhouse, three people high-step to Sonic Youth's "Kool Thing" as two others appear to waltz to it. Then a cut to the next scene: hours later, everybody drunk and delving into the Madonna mystery, weighty issues of control, gender, domination, how to

avoid passing out ("Hey," one person says, "I thought we were talking about *music*"), until finally it is resolved that, yes, Madonna *is* the owner and producer of her own self, product, image, body, signifier, and then a killjoy asks, "What about the audience?" Answer: "Well, what about it?"

10 ■ **Bob Dylan, "Froggie Went A-Courtin'," on** *Good As I Been to You* If it seems as if this little children's ditty doesn't fit with the accounts of betrayal and loss that make up the rest of the album, listen again. Especially to the last two verses, when the wedding party ends in the massacre of the bride and groom.

MARCH 1993

1 ■ **Sarah Shankman,** *The King Is Dead* **(Pocket Books)** Set in Tupelo in the midst of an international barbecue cook-off, this entrancing murder mystery—a combination of Carl Hiaasen's *Double Whammy* and Elaine Dundy's *Elvis and Gladys*—is Shankman's fifth featuring amateur sleuth Sam (Samantha) Adams, and the first in which the prose isn't held back by tedious plotting. A web of full-blown Southern characters trailing hazy pasts moves the story on with slap-back dialogue ("'Do you think y'all are related?' 'Only if you think sleeping with the same man makes women kin'"); Sam Adams, functioning less as private eye than as catalyst, stays out of the way and lets a biting, felt critique of the Southern class system emerge alongside a progressively creepy Jesse Garon Presley impersonator. Like Bobbie Ann Mason or Jill McCorkle with a more convincing sense of humor, or anyway less to worry about, Shankman communicates a joy in making words dance on the page that's rare in the best fiction: "The second bullet flew like a little bird right into Obie's open mouth and out the back of his head." This is a book of pleasures; it only made me nervous when I realized the pages were running out.

2 ■ **Eleventh Dream Day,** *El Moodio* **(Atlantic)** Singer/drummer Janet Beveridge Bean throws bar talk in your face like cold water with "Making Like a Rug" (you lie), domestic quarrels fade as windows open onto the trouble in the streets outside, and on "Rubber Band," singer/guitarist Rick Rizzo asks the musical question, How far can a phrase be stretched before every trace of the meaning it began with is gone?, and doesn't answer it.

3 ■ **Michael Jackson, Aretha Franklin, Kenny Rogers, Bill Clinton, James Ingram, Stevie Wonder, Tony Bennett, Dionne Warwick, Michael Bolton, children's choruses, adult choruses, and more, more, more, "We Are the World," An American Reunion (HBO, January 17)** It may be that behind the great good feeling of this performance lies only propaganda, a fabulous sheen of communitarian self-recognition disguising a new government that means to leave the country as it found it. But as John F. Kennedy proved against his own will, or for that matter his thoughtlessness, false promises can be taken up by those who only hear the tune and don't care about the copyright. If, as Robert Ray of the Vulgar Boatmen puts it, "The *sound* of Dylan's voice changed more people's ideas about the world than his political message did," then the same can be said of the sound of Kennedy's voice and his political acts. The same may prove true of Bill Clinton's demeanor and his political instinct—as opposed to his personal instinct—to pull back at the first sign of trouble. The double-hearted rule but do not govern; desires have been loosed in the air and there's no telling where they'll light.

4 ■ **Peter Blegvad, Roman Bunka, Holger Czukay, Raymond Federman, John Greaves, Jon Sass, Stefan Schwerdtfeger, with special appearances by Richard Huelsenbeck and Hans Richter, and produced by Herbert Kapfer and Regina Moths,** *dr. huelsenbeck's mentale heilmethode* **(Rough Trade Rec, Germany)** A free-swinging, altogether unpredictable tribute to the Cabaret Voltaire Dadaist and New York psychoanalyst, this radio-play version of Huelsenbeck's "psychological salvation system" explodes all over the place: in the six-and-a-half-minute

Berlin Dada donny-brook *"röhrenhose rokoko-neger-rhythmus,"* in the weird *"hottentotten-kral new york,"* in the ghostly occasional samples from lectures and interviews by Huelsenbeck himself, and especially with American Peter Blegvad's rendition of the old Dada hit *"Ende der Welt,"* which is here performed in English, as a blues. Huelsenbeck, who always thought his act was "Negro poetry," a kind of German ragtime, would be—well, who knows what he'd be?

5 ■ Social Distortion, "Cold Feelings" (Epic) The subjectivity—the passion and flair—in this well-scarred L.A. punk combo's songs is easy to miss, because the thrash 'n' burn sound and Mike Ness' flagellant vocals—he might as well have "Born to Lose" tattooed on the inside of his throat—are so utterly generic. Every tune begins with a promise that you've heard it all before. But there's a weariness here, a fury reduced to a twitch, that puts you in touch with a particular person, the singer, not someone you'd meet anywhere else. Ness throws his words over his shoulder as if that way he could actually get rid of what they say; the band throws them back. "Try to separate my body from my mind," he says, having long since seen through the paradox and still not caring that what he wants can't be done. He keeps saying it, and after a minute or two everything our nation's film critics say happens in *Bad Lieutenant* happens here. Not only do you look all the way into someone else's broken mirror, you care what you see.

6 ■ On the Wall, Inc., *Scream* giant inflatable Yes, 50 multicolored vinyl inches of Edvard Munch's all-time chart topper, "The timeless work of art that sums up all the stress, tension, frustration, and just plain AUUGGHH! that we all feel now and then." If you hate Jeff Koons this'll have you sweating blood, but I imagine some people take theirs to bed with them.

7 ■ Jimi Hendrix, "Star Spangled Banner," in a TV public service announcement for Children Now/California (KTVU, Oakland, December 18) The shattered Woodstock in-strumental, running under a black and white, documentary-style montage of children writhing on the floor in gas-station bathrooms, picking through dumpsters, smiling, huddling together, looking scared, as if they were listening to the dead man: "He's playing our song!" An obvious idea, with a complete follow-through.

8 ■ Bob Dylan, "Chimes of Freedom," An American Reunion (HBO, January 17) Yeah, he sounded terrible, but did you see that jacket? Purple, with black appliqué? On a night when Michael Jackson looked less human than the Mickey Mouse-men in Disneyland commercials, Dylan looked like he'd just bought a Nashville haberdashery.

9 ■ David Lynch, director, *Twin Peaks—Fire Walk with Me* (New Line Home Video) Though nobody needed the subtitled dwarf, this much-maligned film is a lot tougher than *Wild at Heart*, and also probably the greatest teen-jeopardy flick ever made. It opens on the corpse of Teresa Banks, the fiend's first victim, then focuses on the surprise and despair around her mouth, frozen by rigor mortis; the movie sheds its conceits when Laura Palmer, in a heedlessly extremist performance by Sheryl Lee, finds the same expression in life. Now the most ordinary situation is the worst: Laura's father taunting her at the dinner table because she hasn't washed her hands. You know he'll get rid of the dirt by the end, and in this sudden moment so does Laura. The disbelief in her face as he rails at her is awful, but not as bad as the belief that replaces it.

The composition of many shots is arty, the efficient production of effects that mostly call attention to themselves; the composition of others is so fine they all but leave the picture. Near the beginning, the FBI agent played by Chris Isaak stands in a trailer park, his feet on wet ground, a trenchcoat on his shoulders, mountains in the background: a last moment of contemplation and puzzlement before he disappears from the film like Bulkington from *Moby-Dick*. I rewound the tape, hit the pause button, and stared into a perfect picture of the loneliness, the possibility of abandonment, implicit in American open spaces—where, as Lynch says here, anything can happen, and will.

10 ■ **Calvin Klein underwear ads, with Kate Moss,** In her uncanny impersonation of a brain-dead tadpole, you can see her future: supermodel for legal euthanasia. "WOULD YOU WANT *YOUR* CHILD TO LIVE LIKE THIS?"

APRIL 1993

1 ■ **Popinjays, *Flying Down to Mono Valley* (Epic/One Little Indian)** A snazzier, more expert Fastbacks goes to the circus, where the women run the trapezes like hopscotch squares, get harmonies selling popcorn and hot dogs in the stands, and make a quick exit: who were those girls, anyway? In this case, Wendy Robinson and Polly Hancock of London.

2 ■ **Elizabeth Armstrong & Joan Rothfuss, curators, and Janet Jenkins, editor, "In the Spirit of Fluxus," exhibition (Walker Art Center, Minneapolis, until June 6, and traveling in the U.S. and Europe until January 1995) and catalogue** The best art out of Fluxus—a sort of ur-'60s conspiracy of minimalist careerists—was gestural: the discovery and performance of severe and extended gestures of (supposedly) enormous symbolic and (absolutely) no practical significance. It was the performance of life as a joke we play on ourselves. At the time, Fluxus struck me as an exercise in pose, the worst sort of bohemian condescension: a bet that the audience wouldn't get the joke. But in the Walker, among various not-overworried reconstructions of Fluxus sites and events (the founding performances of Nam June Paik and others at Wiesbaden in 1962; the week Ben Vautier spent in the window of a London art gallery in the same year), the feeling was stirring. You could catch the desire of disparate people from all over the world to do things that had never been done before, no matter how dumb they might appear at first, or ever after.

That spirit gets codified and ossified as the exhibit moves on from its first rooms; then it breaks out again in odd places. When you reach the *Flux-Labyrinth*, a full-size recreation of the fun-house-as-punishment contraption Larry Miller and the late George Maciunas built in Berlin in 1976 (Miller was at the Walker fine-tuning the monster), the spirit the Flux folk might have loved best is passed on, especially when you're stuck in the room with the piano. As Kristine Stiles puts it in her fine catalogue essay, "Between Water and Stone," the "ostensible inability to do or to get things right is the source of amusement and release."

3 ■ **Arthur Flowers, *Another Good Loving Blues*, a novel (Viking)** In Mississippi, in 1918, Luke Bodeen, a bluesman, meets Melvira Dupree, a conjure woman. She seeks the mother who abandoned her, he seeks the "'blues that will still be here touching folk long after I'm dead and gone,'" and together they seek each other. There's a great sweep of history in this peaceful, steady-rolling tale: as Dupree struggles with the modern disbelief that saps her powers, Bodeen can remember a time, right about the turn of the century, "when there wasn't no such thing as the blues," and he can remember when he first picked up hints of the new sound, as a riverboat piano man hired onto the *Stacker Lee*. Flowers never overplays a scene, not when Bodeen ends up a begging drunk in a public park, bereft of the dignity and moral purpose he'd discovered in the blues, and not when Dupree puts the hex on. "'St. Louie Slick Miz Melvira. A lowlife pimp and gambling man,'" says the mother of a girl seduced into prostitution. "'Hurt him before he hurt our baby.'" Dupree finds him in a barbershop. "'St. Louie Slick?'" she asks.

Slick stared impassively from behind silvered shades. He saw a good-looking woman with an open-necked jar in one hand and a cork in the other.

He smiled his professional approval. "Yeah baby, thats me, what can I do for a fine young thing like you?"

Melvira corked the jar as soon as he answered her and walked out of the barbershop.

She's taken his soul—and with no more fuss than if she were serving a subpoena.

4 ▪ **The Troggs, *Archaeology (1966–1976)* (Fontana 3-CD box)** In John Duigan's lovely film *Flirting*—Beatle-era teenage love in Australia—there's a moment when a wispy, insistently affectionate piece of music comes on the soundtrack. It's "With a Girl Like You," a highlight of this collection. Here "Wild Thing" is just an immortal anomaly in a crude ten-year struggle to find the charts, and "I Just Sing," "I Can't Control Myself," "Gonna Make You," and 10 or 20 others, the real, ordinary story. The immortal and the ordinary come together on the last disc, "The Troggs Tape," 11 minutes 45 seconds of argument accidentally salvaged from a wasted session in 1970.

By then the Troggs hadn't hit the American Top 100 for two years—an eternity in those days—and you can hear plain desperation straight off. "It's a fucking number one! It is!" moans a young voice. "This is a fucking number one and if, if that doesn't go, I fucking retire. I fucking do." "It is a good song," says an older, much-too-relaxed voice. "I agree—" "But it fucking well *won't be*," says the first voice, at once a general rallying his troops and a condemned man begging for one more day, "unless we spend a little bit of fucking thought and imagination to *make it* fucking number one!" And it goes on like that, the most profane pop document ever to surface, scared, hopeful, disgusted, doors slamming, instruments hurled to the floor, fights breaking out, a panorama of frustration, and aside from anyone's everyday life there's nothing like it anywhere.

5 ▪ **Cynthia Rose, *Design after Dark—The Story of Dancefloor Style* (Thames & Hudson)** At first it looks like a particularly well-set-up picture book, covering clothes, record sleeves, posters, videos, faces, plus captions—but in Rose's text you'll find not gloss but an animating sense of detail and adventure. She gives style weight without letting it weigh down her subjects—the tribes of black and white Britons, some

anonymous, some now famous, who in the 1980s remade leisure culture sideways—and the result is a little depressing. So much flair, so much energy, so many ideas, so many good smiles, and, finally, no power. Style changed but not society; no-future didn't move an inch from where it stood in 1977.

6–7 ▪ **Sonic Youth, "Ça Plane pour Moi," on *Freedom of Choice—Yesterday's New Wave Hits as Performed by Today's Stars* (Caroline) and Dave Markey, director: *1991: The Year Punk Broke* (DGC Home Video)** The bigger Sonic Youth have gotten the lower they've stooped—which is to say they'll still pump out a track for fun or the betterment of humanity as readily as a nowhere band that only wants to get its name in print. "Ça Plane pour Moi," by one Plastic Bertrand, was a near embarrassment in 1977—proof, from Belgium of all places, that a merging of punk and the Beach Boys might produce no contradictions whatsoever. On *Freedom of Choice* (all proceeds to Planned Parenthood) Thurston Moore rides the joke hard enough to prove that "guilty pleasure" is an oxymoron. *1991* is, offstage anyway, an embarrassing handheld *Don't Look Back* imitation covering Sonic Youth on tour in Europe, with then-smaller-fry (Nirvana, etc.) in tow. Onstage it's the strongest documentation of how hard Sonic Youth can push their own music you can get without breaking the law.

8–9 ▪ **Quentin Tarantino, director, *Reservoir Dogs* (Miramax) and Abel Ferrara, director, *Bad Lieutenant* (Aries Film)** Evidence that pop tunes say far more as part of a film's soundtrack than in their own videos is all over these movies. In *Bad Lieutenant*, a dark-night-of-Harvey Keitel's-soul number that's about as liberating as a sermon on homosexuality by John Cardinal O'Connor, the only moments that don't seem like a total crock come when Schoolly D's "Signifying Rapper" and Johnny Ace's "Pledging My Love" are playing—with Keitel slow death-dancing to the latter, just as he did almost 20 years before in *Mean Streets*. In *Reservoir Dogs*, a truly cruel picture where the shocks in the action hurt the viewer, the most perverse theme has to do with what the characters are listening to and talking about as their dishonor-among-thieves roundelay breaks up: a horrible, kind-of-catchy "Sound of the Seventies" retrospective on the local classic-rock station, with Stephen Wright in a perfect impersonation of what a classic laid-back '70s DJ would sound like after two decades of Quaaludes. "Stuck in the Middle with You," by Stealers Wheel, the Village People's "Y.M.C.A.," and more, more, to the point where you dread what song might be up next as much as what atrocity you might have to watch, which brings us to—

10 ▪ Billy Ray Cyrus, "Achy Breaky Heart (Dance Mix)" (Mercury) Yes, he might be a walking score in some future edition of Trivial Pursuit, he may never have another mass hit, but he's not going to be forgotten anymore than the world has yet escaped the specter Debby Boone raised with "You Light Up My Life," which in 1977 was number one for ten weeks. There is an elemental stupidity in "Achy Breaky Heart," a phrase so dumb it's humiliating to say out loud; in the dance mix, over 7 minutes long but it might as well be 17 or 70, with some guy hee-hawing in the background over and over, as if to say "WE FOOLED YOU! AND WE'RE DOING IT AGAIN!," stupidity becomes a sort of blessedness, a form of pop grace. Like Sheb Wooley ("The Purple People Eater," number one for six weeks in 1958) or Ross Bagdasarian (as the Chipmunks, with "The Chipmunk Song," number one for four weeks in that same weird year) before him, for as long as his song lasts—*as long as he wants*—Billy Ray Cyrus can get away with anything.

SUMMER 1993

1 ▪ Andre Braugher, in *Homicide—Life on the Street* "Three Men and Adena" (NBC, March 3) For decades now, scripts of one version or another of "The Robert Johnson Story" have bounced around Hollywood (though the closest anyone's gotten to an actual movie was John Fusco's putrid *Crossroads*, shot in 1986 by Walter Hill). Every conceivable black actor or singer has been mentioned for the role of the '30s Mississippi bluesman, but the search can stop now. It's not only that Andre Braugher, playing a Baltimore homicide detective, looks enough like Johnson to be his son. It's not that when Johnson's trail (cold since his death in 1938) was finally picked up in the '70s it led to Maryland, where Johnson's sister lived—thus making it possible that Braugher's detective could be, in character, Johnson's great-nephew. (I know he says he's from New York in this episode; that's just to confuse the suspect.) As an actor, Braugher draws on the qualities of restraint, thoughtfulness, and jeopardy that animate Johnson's greatest songs. Were "Come On in My Kitchen" playing on the soundtrack as Braugher tries to lead the suspect into a trap, no one would notice that the dates of the recording and the drama were 57 years apart.

2 ▪ Joe Dante, director, Charlie Haas, writer, *Matinee* (Universal Home Video) With John Goodman having a great time impersonating '50s/'60s movie shlockmeister William Castle opening a new horror flick in South Florida during the Cuban Missile Crisis (it's "*Mant*—Half Man, Half Ant"; bits are featured in *Matinee* proper, but the video will include the complete, 20-minute version shot for continuity), you get A-bomb radiation coming at you from both sides. The movie's tremendous fun. What's most interesting, though, are the tendrils of alien culture nibbling at the corners of the frame. A Beat couple arguing about the First Amendment, their Ban the Bomb daughter busting up a high school air raid drill, a clean-cut kid with a secret Lenny Bruce record, a J.D. with a D.A. and a switchblade he'll hold to your neck to make you listen to his poetry, and the weird question that hangs in the air, "Where are the Negro kids?"—in every case, portents of a culture, in both senses of the word, that the all-white world of Key West can't completely stop. But if this is subversion, where is rock 'n' roll? Back home in the bungalow,

just keeping time (it's the Tokens, doing "The Lion Sleeps Tonight")—no more threatening than a metronome.

3 ▪ **Bobby Bland, *I Pity the Fool—The Duke Recordings, Vol One* (MCA 2-CD reissue, 1952–60)** The coolest blues singer who ever was, and one of the deepest.

4 ▪ **Melodians, *Swing and Dine* (Heartbeat reissue, 1967–75)** Jamaica's finest: a floating sound, kicking off with a tune about Expo '67, a search for a smile, but with an undertone of regret over something far too great to put into words.

5 ▪ **Rosanne Cash, *The Wheel* (Columbia)** In the last few years it's been incumbent upon female singers even one step away from punk to expose themselves if they want serious sales action. Posing in a bra will do, but a discreetly naked chest is better: witness Melissa Etheridge, Sade, and now Rosanne Cash, the Jennifer Jason Leigh of pop music—a supremely talented, dedicated artist who knows what trouble is worth. Why we need proof—as opposed to an until-proven-otherwise assumption— that a given singer has breasts is unclear, unless what's really going on is a need for proof that any female singer can be made to whore for her label or her listeners. Presumably it's working for Cash: *Entertainment Weekly* splashed *The Wheel*'s insert pic—Cash flat on her back, roses on her breasts, come-hither smile on her lips— over a full page.

You wouldn't deduce such a move from the music. As a singer, Cash retains a dignity that seems located more in her songs than in any persona; her fervor is undiminished. The title track, a mostly elegant composition, opens without warning into realms of delirium. Still, despite the slow, smoky "Seventh Avenue" and the off-the-beat realism of "The Truth About You," as the disc plays you can feel Cash holding more and more of herself back. By the time she reaches the last cut, "If There's a God on My Side," the music doesn't end, it just stops.

6 ▪ **Basehead, *Not in Kansas Anymore* (Imägo)** As on the 1992 *Play with Toys*, Michael Ivey redefines hip-hop philosophy, placing above all others the question of whether it's worth getting to one's feet and leaving one's apartment—and if it is, *why*. After an opening in a C&W club where Basehead, presumably booked by mistake, introduces its first number as "a song about the problems that the white male has to face in America today" (the song consists of about two seconds of fuzztone), Ivey meanders, drifts, and complains about sex, police harassment, racism, oblivion, girlfriends, boredom, and drive-by shootings, until each sounds most of all not fun and he sounds like someone you'd love spending time with. Who knows, maybe the whole thing's one long personals ad. So you play the record again, maybe wondering about the empty dog-muzzle on the cover. That is, if it's for Toto, where's the dog? But by then you can already feel the bite.

7 ▪ **Bob Dylan, on Guns N' Roses' cover of his "Knocking on Heaven's Door," in *The Telegraph* 42 (Summer 1992)** "Guns N' Roses is OK, Slash is OK, but there's something about their version of that song that reminds me of the movie *Invasion of the Body Snatchers*. I always wonder who's been transformed into some sort of clone, and who's stayed true to himself. And I never seem to have an answer."

8 ▪ **Ishmael Reed, *Japanese by Spring* (Atheneum)** A bitter, hilarious novel about multiculturalism, where a Japanese concern buys the failing Jack London College in California in order to, among other things, change Ethnic Studies to "Barbarian Studies," and one Chappie Puttbutt, a would-be Clarence Thomas who's just been turned down for tenure despite years of kissing white ass, suddenly finds himself fronting the show. Reed himself enters in the last pages to settle a few scores; like a retired gunslinger forced to take on some rough business before the big church social, he finds himself wondering if there was "no end to the sacrifices he would be called on to make on behalf of Western civilization." Given that this self-described "mongrel" ("African, French, Irish, Cherokee") has

made it his mission not so much to change that civilization as to lead others to see it for the crazy quilt it already is, the answer would have to be no. Reviewers would love Reed to keep to his supposed place as an African-American novelist, but it isn't his place and he's never stopped there long enough to do more than kick down the fences around the plot. He's an all-American writer now moving into world beat, and there's no telling what story he'll tell next, though I'd love to see him send Jean-Bertrand Aristide back to Haiti. The way things are going, that may be the only way Aristide'll get there.

9 ■ **Elvis Costello and the Brodsky Quartet, Davies Hall, San Francisco (March 15)** I had to drag myself back to *The Juliet Letters* (Warner Bros.), Costello's song cycle with the UK's version of our Kronos Quartet, and the live version revealed why: the Brodskys are not exciting. The songs disappear into predictable arrangements and bland orchestrations. But onstage, surrounded by a crowd alternately polite and hysterical—almost a Randy Newman crowd in its self-congratulatory enthusiasm—Costello the singer took over. He'd never given himself so much range; he'd never been more musically playful. On the encores, the Beach Boys' "God Only Knows" sounded just right next to Kurt Weill's "Lost in the Stars."

10 ■ **Rosey Golds, "Reader, I Married Him—Priscilla as Gothic Heroine," in** *Perfect Beat* 2 no 1 You got it—Priscilla Presley is Jane Eyre, but is Mrs. Rochester Gladys or Elvis? Originally delivered as a breathless talk in Sydney last year, Golds' essay ranges over the whole corpus of the genre for metaphors and familiars (Col. Parker turns up as Dr. Frankenstein), but from start to finish it soars with the extremism, the passion and fear, the corny apocalypse, of your favorite Gothic novel. Happy ending, too. Sort of.

OCTOBER 1993

1 ■ **REM video, conceived by Michael Stipe, directed by Peter Care, "Man on the Moon" (Warner Bros.)** This is the best video I've seen since Nirvana's "Smells Like Teen Spirit"—though formally there's nothing unusual about it, just the standard pillaging of the last forty years of American independent cinema. The piece starts off with Michael Stipe striding across a western desert in a cowboy hat, lip-syncing his song about illusion and reality, identity as fact or choice, and the late comedian Andy Kaufman, who at times thought he was a professional wrestler or Elvis Presley. In black and white, split screens, grainy textures, overlit figures, double exposures, fades even within frames, and of course super-fast cutting are used smartly. Not even the way the design matches words to images (when Stipe sings about an asp, you see a snake: when he mentions "Mr. Darwin," you see the pages of a human-evolution textbook flipping) is oppressive. A terrific feeling of empathy, of loss and regret, grows in the piece. The second time Kaufman rises up, like a ghost in the mix, in his Elvis outfit, you know Stipe loved the man.

Stipe hitches a ride on a truck, which drops him, at dusk, at the Easy-Rest Diner (the lyrics say "truck stop"). The way Peter Care brings Stipe to the door is pure Bruce Conner: flashes are piled onto flashes—seemingly hundreds of cuts to move a man a few steps—and it's as quietly thrilling here as it was in 1967, when Conner took you into Jay DeFeo's studio with his film *The White Rose*. Stipe sits down at the bar and signals for a beer. The expression on his face as he does so (his modesty, his happiness to be in this place) is striking, but no setup for what happens next. The camera begins to move around the bar, picking up old people, young people, men, women, pool players, drinkers, people just standing around in this nameless western place: where they're from. And every one of them is lip-syncing the words to "Man on the Moon."

There's nothing new about this device: as a trick of self-glorification ("I'd like to teach the world to sing—my song") it's as old as MTV. It was used perhaps most famously, and certainly most obnoxiously, by Talking Heads in "Wild, Wild Life," where a bunch of small-town types in David Byrne's vanity film *True Stories* were trotted onto a stage to mouth snatches of the tune like contestants on *The Gong Show*. "Man on the Moon" takes place in a different world. Face to face, line by line, what you're seeing and hearing comes across as ordinary conversation: somehow it seems as likely that the weathered old man in the cowboy hat would be saying "Man on the Moon" as "Gimme another one, Joe." The tableau expands—begins to construct itself as a feeling, something shared, the way a song on a jukebox can change a room—and suddenly you realize you don't want this to end. You begin to worry that it will—even though you're not sensing the song nearing its end, you're simply drawn into the bar, this intimate place, part of it.

The cuts are not so fast now. You get to know the faces, the people. The warmth in the room is as physical as the sensation of a cold lifting. The room seems to be swirling, though it's not, there are no more special effects; by this point it's emotion that's moving too fast to keep up with. And then in the midst of this fine conversation, this magical invocation of community in its smallest, most everyday dimensions, the camera gives up a second or two to a blonde woman, smiling to the person she's talking to—not at the camera. The knowledge in that smile, a knowledge that's superior to nothing, that assumes everyone in the room knows what she knows: the pleasure and confirmation as the woman puts her lips around "They put a man on the moon"— it's as perfect a moment as you'll find anywhere, though for you, watching this video, the moment will be somebody else saying the same thing.

2 ▪ **Heavenly, *P.U.N.K. Girl* (K Records)** A five-song ep that's stronger than last year's · lp *Le Jardin de Heavenly*, and more playful: you can imagine Emma Thompson fronting this English band, even if you know it's sweet-voiced Amelia Fletcher, joined by three men and one Cathy Rogers on vocals.

Heavenly's idea of play, though, is to pull the rug out from under you. "Hearts and Crosses" starts off in a lacy virgin's bedroom, and the air is filled with flowers, angels, fantasies of true love ("How would it feel to hold him for real? To whisper 'I love you' and lean on his shoulder?"). The tone is sunny, confident, friendly, cool— like the Jamies' 1958 hit "Summertime, Summertime." This is classic pop, you've heard it forever—but never, it seems in the moment, with such convincing delicacy. Then the tune breaks, and there's a flat, spoken, rhymed narrative about date rape. It's rough: "He bit her hard but never kissed her." Fletcher's voice never rises and when the tune comes back the tone hasn't altered a bit from the opening—just the story, which is now about ruin, not betrayal so much as memories that can't be erased.

3 ▪ **Garth Brooks, "That Summer" (Liberty)** Carefully written, arranged to highlight peaks and valleys, this country hit is recognizable in an instant even if you've only heard half of it once before. And as an entry in the hoary boy-loses-virginity-to-older-woman genre it doesn't hedge on passion: the singer doesn't learn how to be a man, he finds out there are things that can never be taken back. "I have rarely held another/When I haven't seen her face" is the sort of confession the genre took shape to suppress.

4 ▪ **Annie Ernaux, *Simple Passion*, translated from the French by Tanya Leslie (Four Walls Eight Windows)** In 1974, after Aleksander Solzhenitsyn won the Nobel Prize and was deported from the Soviet Union, *Punch* writer Alan Coren warned that despite the great man's popularity with Paris' revisionist intelligentsia, he would be unlikely to find a warm welcome in France. Reason: he had never written a novel that was (a) five million words long or (b) five thousand words long. Ernaux's tale of a grown-up, all-consuming love affair (all-consuming from the female narrator's point of view, anyway) comes in at the low end of the scale: about eight thousand

words. Yet in the short time she demands of a reader Ernaux can leave you as drained as an early Godard movie, and she shapes her story with Barthes-like notes sharp enough to start you thinking through the novels in your own life. As when the narrator speaks of "the cultural standards governing emotion which have influenced me since childhood (*Gone with the Wind, Phèdre* or the songs of Edith Piaf are just as decisive as the Oedipus complex)."

5 ▪ **John Heartfield, "Photomontages" (San Francisco Museum of Modern Art, 8 August, moving to Los Angeles County Museum, 7 October–2 January 1994)** "This makes me nervous," a friend said as we walked through a show dominated by Heartfield's late-'20–'30s antifascist agit-prop, most of it made in Berlin, some of it made in Prague, in exile. It wasn't hard to know what she meant. As Hitler, Goering, and Goebbels appeared in Heartfield's collages—shouting and preening, mocked and tossing off mockery like spittle—they were not art subjects, not then and not now. They escaped the museum just like that. This was real speech about real things that actually happened—or that, because of Heartfield's power, were actually happening. The pictures weren't safe and the past wasn't buried.

6 ▪ **Steve "Scarface" Williams, sound supervisor for *Menace II Society*, directed by the Hughes Brothers (New Line Cinema)** Here and there in this film about not growing up in black Los Angeles, the sound made by ordinary movements—a car pulling up to a curb, a door closing, words coming out of a father's mouth after he shoots a friend—is amplified all out of proportion to what's on the screen. The sound isn't merely loud, but slowed down, thickened, and inflated, as if it's coming from somewhere else, from some off-screen prophet-beast whose threats and warnings don't suffer language. The unnaturalness of the effect takes you right out of the movie, and what's dramatized is the unnaturalness of the social order the movie is about.

7 ▪ **George Michael and Queen, "Somebody to Love," from *Five Live* (Hollywood)** Recorded at the Freddie Mercury tribute in April 1992, and as complete a validation of professionalism as you'd ever want to hear: going strictly by the book, Michael rings glory out of every note.

8 ▪ **Shaver, *Tramp on Your Street* (Zoo/Praxis)** A drifter's record—as Billy Joe Shaver appears on the cover, weathered and road-beaten, with long, stringy gray hair, he's the tramp you see every day. Then he starts singing, taking the old outlaw-country voice away from its clichés; guitarist and son Eddy Shaver brings the songs as close to rock 'n' roll as he can without crossing over. The music is ambitious social realism under a rainbow of religion—in the end, no more than muscle and heart.

9 ▪ **Pet Shop Boys, *Very* (EMI)** Though Chris Lowe's airy, bohemian dance rhythms again seem to suggest a salon more than a disco (nothing wrong with that), there's a difference in Neil Tennant's voice, and in the cadences he builds his words around. His naïveté—the assumed, artificial, self-protecting naïveté of someone who could too easily have given himself over to cynicism—is gone. Tennant no longer pretends to be surprised by things he ought to understand; at 39, he sounds tested.

10 ▪ **Dan Graham, *Rock My Religion—Writings and Art Projects, 1965–1990*, ed. Brian Wallis (MIT)** This handsome compendium of essays, attempts at collage narrative, and *bonnes pensées* is rooted almost wholly in the obvious. Scattering bits of wisdom from Walter Benjamin or the Frankfurt School like alms to the poor, Graham digs for signs of life in commodity culture, finds them in rock 'n' roll, punk, and cinema, and trumpets his discoveries like the first white man pressing into the Dark Continent. Mixing blunt historical solecisms (the Puritans believed "the only possible way to overcome this Original Sin was through hard work"—sorry, it was predestination) with what might be called gestural criticism (faced with a subject, you wave at it), Graham

seems committed to establishing one truth beyond doubt: he's hip.

NOVEMBER 1993

1 ◾ **Otis Spann, "Hotel Lorraine" and "Blues for Martin Luther King," from the anthology** *Rare Chicago Blues, 1962–1968* **(Bullseye Blues/Rounder)** "On the fourth of April/In the year nineteen and sixty-eight/ Yes! On the fourth of April . . ." It's the next day, in a storefront church on 43rd Street in Chicago, the day after Martin Luther King was shot. Outside, the riots are beginning: "The world was all up in flames." Accompanied only by drummer S. P. Leary and some shouting from Muddy Waters, blues pianist Otis Spann is bringing the day into focus. He pulls his words out of the air; his piano opens "Hotel Lorraine" with the same unanswerable sense of foreboding he and others had found ten years before in Little Walter's "Blue and Lonesome." God is judging us as we speak, the sound says— so speak truly.

"Blues for Martin Luther King" was issued as a single on the Cry label, with profits going to the Southern Christian Leadership Conference; "Hotel Lorraine" remained unreleased until it appeared on a little-heard blues collection in 1977, seven years after Spann's death, at age 40. His voice is now desperate, now stoic; his piano traces familiar blues runs with such passion it's as if the blues came into being exactly in anticipation of the need to answer to this event. For this is no representation, not even a version: this is the event itself, a voice in a room made of walls that may not last the day. A quarter-century later, the performances reach out of the past like the hand that comes out of the ground at the end of *Carrie*.

2 ◾ **Pearl Jam, "Crazy Mary," on** *Sweet Relief—A Benefit for Victoria Williams* **(Chaos/Columbia)** Singer-songwriter Williams has MS and no health insurance. Thus this tribute album, featuring more or less neo-folk-rock folk from the Waterboys to Michelle Shocked to Evan Dando to

Matthew Sweet, and like a lot of the singers, Williams' songs have a fussiness about them—they're self-conscious, self-referential, often calling attention to themselves. That's as true of "Tarbelly and Featherfoot" (done here by Lou Reed) as of "Crazy Mary," which comes on like a college-class short story inspired by *Winesburg, Ohio*. But when Eddie Vedder wraps his voice around the chorus—the more melody this guy has to work with the tougher he gets— an ominousness rises out of the piece, and it begins to suggest something altogether more vulgar, and deeper: the last page of "The Lottery," maybe.

3 ◾ **J. T. Brown, saxophone solo on Elmore James' "Madison Blues," on the anthology** *Blues Masters, Volume 6: Blues Originals* **(Rhino)** It's Chicago again, 1960, and Brown is barely in the band—his long, lazy notes float so freely on clouds of happiness and pleasure he's barely on the record.

4 ◾ **Adam Green,** *What Were You in a Previous Life?* **(Thunder's Mouth Press)** Cartoons kin to Matt Groening's "Life in Hell" strip, but less detailed, more blank ("Yet Another Cartoon That Fails to Address Class Struggle"), with pretty much three stock characters: office-worker male, office-worker female, plus cat as living non sequitur. You have to be there.

5 ◾ **Lisa Germano,** *Happiness* **(Capitol)** A lot of melody, a lot of dissonance—the fiddle player in John Mellencamp's band gets her own thick, sensuous sound, drawing out her vocals with a tone that falls somewhere between sleep, a drawl, and a drunk. Having lowered expectations, she produces surprises all over the place: her "Sycophant" is the return of the Raincoats (whose post-punk gem *Odyshape* will be reissued next year on DGC), and her cover of "These Boots are Made for Walkin'" is better than Amy Tan's.

6 ◾ **Moby Grape, "Big," on** *Vintage— The Very Best of Moby Grape* **(Columbia Legacy reissue, 1968)** Compiler Bob Irwin has done a magnificent job reconstructing the leavings of this doomed band, which in the great days of the San Francisco Sound

shared little with the Grateful Dead, the Jefferson Airplane, or the Quicksilver Messenger Service other than a couple of stages and a certain feel for the Old West—though by looking at people on the streets of the Haight in 1967 you couldn't tell if their Old West came from the Gold Rush or *Have Gun, Will Travel.* Well, you can tell now, listening to this previously unheard, broken ramble: they go right back to the days of '49 and don't even try to make it home.

7–8 ■ **Hanif Kureishi, writer and director, *London Kills Me* (New Line Cinema Home Video) and Cornershop, *Elvis Sex-Change* (W111JA ep)** Screenwriter (*My Beautiful Laundrette*) and novelist (*The Buddha of Suburbia*) Kureishi released his first film last year—the tale of a loose band of misfits a couple of hours away from homelessness and a few days away from suicide. *London Kills Me* was mercilessly savaged by British critics, but it's hard to see why: not only is each character distinct, he or she makes claims on your attention at different times, and by the end of the movie the guy who at first seemed too stupid to bother with is more interesting than anybody else. A poor neighborhood where the mix of food smells is as confusing as the mix of languages on the street is captured with affection and a keen sense of the place as a dead end; the film almost asks you to feel superior to both its people and its milieu, but never does so itself, whether you do or not. Cornershop's songs (including "Hanif Kureishi Scene") are the tunes the people in *London Kills Me* would come up with if they weren't too busy getting lost in *Billy Liar* or trying to escape from it. They're all blocked gestures and creative exhaustion, stumbling stabs at anger or love. It's music completely defined by its limits, and touching for just that quality.

9 ■ **Cannanes, "Frightening Thing" (K Records)** Sunny, guiltless girl-boy punk from Australia, with good teenage advice on the sleeve and an even better instruction on the label: "PLAY LOUD & LEAVE THE ROOM."

10 ■ **Firesign Theater, *Shoes for Industry!—The Best of the Firesign Theater* (Columbia Legacy reissue, 1967–75)** If you've lost your old lps by the best comedy group in the history of the phonograph record, this is a road back to a rather more convincing account of '60s liberation than can be found in books. If you've never heard the most effective surrealists in the history of Dada, this is the place to start. But Peter Bergman, David Ossman, Phil Proctor, and Phil Austin are still around—why did they ever stop? "Our best albums," Bergman told Steve Simels, who wrote the notes to this set, "had a theme underneath them—the War. And when the War was over, we lost our theme." "There was something about the Eighties—the anti-surrealist politics of the Eighties—that was wrong for the Firesign Theater," says Ossman. The group promises a new record, *The Illusion of Unity*, in 1994: "Sure enough," Bergman says, "when we kicked the fascists out of office it was time for the Firesign Theater to come back." If the record is any good the return of the Firesign Theater won't make up for all of Bill Clinton's failings, but it'll make up for some of them.

DECEMBER 1993

1 ■ **Lee Smith, *The Devil's Dream* (Ballantine)** "One time years back, when she was sitting on the porch hooking a rug and singing one of these mournful old hymns, as she frequently did, little Ezekiel asked her, 'Aunt Dot, how come you to sing that old song? How come you don't sing something pretty?' For he knew full well how pretty his Aunt Dot could sing if she took a mind to, and how many songs she knew. She turned to look at him, pursing her mouth, and said, 'Honey, they is pretty singing, and then they is true singing.'" *The Devil's Dream* is about true singing. It's a spell-caster of a novel, with a family ghost wending its way from the 1830s into the present, from a hollow in Virginia to Nashville, from a young woman destroyed by God's curse on her fiddle to her great-great-

great-granddaughter with a Ph.D. in deconstruction from Duke. Along the way the ghost makes country music history, tossing up a rockabilly singer ("that dark dangerous look the women like, that's what Johnny's going for, kind of a cross between Porter Wagoner and an undertaker"), expecting no peace and finding none. Always, whatever music is found is framed by "The Cuckoo Song," an ancient, mystical tune about not being at home in the world, and "Blackjack Davey," an even older fable about a wife and mother who abandons her home to fuck a faithless lover—and the lives of Smith's men and women are framed by these songs, too. They can't get out of them—not because they are weak, or uneducated, or trapped in the prison of fundamentalist religion, but because the songs are so deep.

2 ▪ **PJ Harvey, 4-Track Demos (Island)** There's more freedom on these one-woman overdubs than on Harvey's group albums— more freedom as wish and realization, on guitar and in the voice. What sounded like contrived effects on *Dry* and especially *Rid of Me* are events here. "Oh, she fucked my memory," Harvey sings on the demo for "Yuri-G"; I can't make out what she's saying on the *Rid of Me* version, but it isn't that.

3 ▪ **Muddy Waters, licensed music in TV ads for Timberland waterproof clothing (W L. Gore & Associates, Newark, Delaware)** Beginning in a simple verbal/visual pun, these spots—people slogging through mud and rain while the late Chicago bluesman thunders on like a South Side Jeremiah—are weirdly unstable. It's media shock: you're not prepared for something this powerful in a television commercial. Uncontextualized, or miscontextualized, the music may for a fleeting moment seem stronger here than it ever has elsewhere. What were they selling again?

4–5 ▪ **Ted Levin and Ankica Petrović (recording, compilation, annotation): Bosnia—echoes from an endangered world—Music and Chant of the Bosnian Muslims (Smithsonian Folkways) and Ammiel Alcalay et al., Lusitania no. 5 (Fall 1993)—**

For/Za Sarajevo At the Miss Besieged Sarajevo pageant last May, it wasn't traditional Bosnian music that was played but "Eve of Destruction." On *Bosnia*, an anthology of 1984–85 field recordings plus a few popularized folk numbers, you don't hear desperation; most intensely you hear serenity ("*Ezan*," a Muslim call to prayer) or strength. PJ Harvey fans will have no problem with "*Ganga: Odkad seke nismo zapjevale*" (How long we sisters haven't sung), even if, in Ankica Petrović's words, "Urban dwellers tend to dismiss *ganga* as simply unorganized (or disorganized) sound." Here three women from the village of Podorašac in northern Herzegovina fill Levin and Petrović's tape less with voices than with hearts, lungs, stomachs—whole bodies. In Herzegovinian fact or Appalachian-American analogy, this is mountain music: melisma and flattened tones twist themes until the individual and the community, the present and the past, are both complete and indistinguishable. As Petrović writes, "Singers and their active listeners achieve maximal harmony through dissonance."

Though Serbs and Croats as well as Muslims practice *ganga*, Petrović's comment is obviously no metaphor for politics, and the *Bosnia* collection doesn't work as background music to *For/Za Sarajevo*, a living tombstone of essays and classic texts running in both English and Serbo-Croatian. The CD is from what was a country, the journal number is a cemetery map. There are no atrocity photos, just a few pictures of people, artworks, objects, architecture. Entries open with an almost biblical incantation from Meša Selimović's 1966 *The Dervish and Death* ("I begin this, my story, for naught—with no benefit to myself nor to others, from a need that is stronger than profit or reason, that my record remain") and move toward Tomaž Mastnak's enraged, incisive "A Journal of the Plague Years: Notes on European Anti-Nationalism," where the legacy of fascism meets the unfinished business of the Enlightenment (Voltaire, on Muslims:

"It is not enough to humiliate them, they should be destroyed"). "I would not call this a conspiracy," Mastnak says of Europe's acquiescence in the Bosnian genocide. "It is more like a dream coming true."

"DON'T LET THEM KILL US," read the banner, in English, carried by the 13 swimsuited contestants in the Miss Besieged Sarajevo contest. In a way, you can find them all in the most striking art in *For/Za Sarajevo*, Mustafa Skopljak's 1993 *Sarajevo 91' 92' 93' 94'*, from the OBALA Gallery's Witness of Existence project. Little terracotta faces with odd expressions are placed in holes on a bed of dirt; it's a graveyard, but all the graves are open and everybody, from whatever century or religion, is still alive and looking right at you.

6–8 ■ Mekons, "Millionaire" and *I ♥ Mekons* (both Quarterstick) and *The Mekons Story, 1977–1982* (Feel Good All Over reissue) *I ♥ Mekons*, which has been wandering in the desert of the music business since at least 1991, is muscular, confident, anguished—perhaps just right for a group that currently rotates on a Chicago–New York–London axis. Yet "Millionaire" (with three live tracks appended) all but floats over the rest of the music, Sally Timms' rich country vocal so soulful and Tom Greenhalgh's guitar such an upheaval the tune deserves its own disc. As for *The Mekons Story* (originally led by the pretitle *it falleth like the gentle rain from heaven*), it's a strange assemblage of scraps and shouts, broken promises and drunken regret: a stirring would-be suicide note from a time, now more than ten years gone, when the already-old band first tried to give up the ghost.

9 ■ Al Kooper, *Rekooperation* (MusicMasters/BMG) Blues and soul instrumentals—a jam on Richard Thompson's "When the Spell Is Broken" keeping company with "Soul Twist-ed" and "Honky Tonk"—but after hours, with the doors locked, somebody stealing the tape that wasn't supposed to be running anyway.

10 ■ CBS-TV, Philadelphia Phillies/Toronto Blue Jays, game two, World Series

(Toronto, October 17) Lest we forget: with the Phillies' John Kruk, the coolest guy what is what am this night, at bat, a camera panning the stands for celebrities zoomed in on the only man in the place whose hair could make Kruk's look good. In a just world this is what Michael Bolton would be remembered for.

JANUARY 1994

1 ■ Dramarama, *Hi-Fi Sci-Fi* (Chameleon) So smart and funny they could pass for American Kinks, this New Jersey guitar band wears its heart on its collective sleeve with a shamelessness beyond any upstanding Englishperson. In "Work for Food" lead singer John Easdale, singing as himself, is pushing a shopping cart with everything he owns down the street ("The records never sold and that was that"); he tells you exactly what's in it. He's pathetic, a joke, not quite heartrending, and completely believable. It's a great idea. But "Shadowless Heart" is a great song: slow, cool, disturbing, knowing, near death, like Social Distortion without the blood and guts—without the distortion. I play it over and over, and I still can't tell: "You got a shadowless heart," Easdale sings, but is that good or bad?

2 ■ John Irvin, director, Sam Resnick and John Mcgrath, writers: *Robin Hood* (Fox Video) With Patrick Bergin underplaying the Errol Flynn in Robin and Uma Thurman playing Maid Marian as a swan—and featuring Jeff Nuttal, author of *Bomb Culture* and longtime mainstay of British bohemia, as Friar Tuck—this 1991 ambush of the Kevin Costner vehicle of the same year is sexy, wisecracking, deliriously hip, and a shock. Throughout the film, Saxon anticlericalism builds as a counter to Norman power (Tuck peddles holy relics—he's got St. Peter's finger—made out of chicken bones), eventually turning into outright paganism: the Merry Men invade the baron's castle on All Fool's Day, with Tuck as Lord of Misrule and everyone else costumed as animals, spirits, shamans, trees. Druidic

ceremonies blast the Church like a hurricane blowing away a tract home. The Cross is toppled by the Golden Bough—and at the end, when Robin and Marian marry, it's as king and queen of nothing so transitory as a manmade kingdom, but of the May.

3 ■ **Bratmobile, *Pottymouth* (Kill Rock Stars)** Three young American women have fun and experience, as the Slits once put it, and get more mileage out of the word "fuck" than the Mamas & the Papas did out of the word "yeah." They're so fast they burn up their own tracks, barely leaving a trace; it's not individual tunes that stick in the mind but the thrill of making they all carry, sort of "Hey, Hey We're the Monkees" armed with humor and obscenity.

4 ■ **Denis Johnson, *Jesus' Son* (HarperPerennial)** In these linked tales of losers circling around a bar so far below the normal economy that people try to pay with money they've copied on Xerox machines, the narrator sometimes notices too much: "seeds were moaning in the gardens" is supposed to be dope talking, but it's Literature. Far more often, though, the holes that drugs and booze put in the narrator's memory fill up with gestures that grow into acts that are recreated as compulsions, small pictures of fate. "The Vine had no jukebox, but a real stereo continually playing tunes of alcoholic self-pity and sentimental divorce": using the cliché of the first description to disguise the unusualness of the second is real writing.

5 ■ **Bikini Kill, *Pussy Whipped* (Kill Rock Stars)** The original pointwomen (well, three women, one man) for riot grrrl, a movement now happily dismissed by the likes of *Newsweek* as last year's fad ("Young feminists," Jeff Giles wrote recently, "with RAPE and SLUT scrawled on their bellies"—sure sounds like a fad), prove they've only just begun to talk. They play the way good graffiti looks.

6 ■ **Counting Crows, "Mr. Jones," on *August and Everything After* (DGC)** "I want to be Bob Dylan!" Adam Duritz of Berkeley admits two-thirds of the way through this

irresistibly desperate, demented song about stardom, a song that could be about almost anything else—the emotion is that loose, that confused. As for Mr. Jones, presumably the same one Dylan was after in "Ballad of a Thin Man," he doesn't seem like anyone to be trusted, though the singer does trust him, which means the trouble the music constantly suggests on this track ought to pay off elsewhere on the album, which it doesn't.

7 ■ **Mary Lou Lord, "Some Jingle Jangle Morning" (Kill Rock Stars)** Airy, folky, but hard, too: a character out of one of Denis Johnson's stories escapes from Johnson's book, just like almost all the women in the book do, and then gives up on dope, as they probably don't.

8 ■ **Modern Lovers, *Live at the Long-branch Saloon* (Fan Club/New Rose, France)** Mostly from a 1971 Berkeley show, back when Jonathan Richman wasn't just odd but unbelievable: a pudgy world-class guitarist trumpeting naïveté as the fount of all values. The most perfect moment here, though, comes from a 1971 or '72 show at Harvard. "I think this song is one of the worst songs that I've ever heard in my whole life," guitarist John Felice says, introducing "Wake Up Sleepyheads." "Thank you, John," says Richman. "It's really disgusting," Felice continues, "and I really don't want to play on it, but they're making me." "You like the chord changes," Richman says. "I like the chord changes," Felice admits, "but the words are horrible." "That's OK," Richman finishes. "I sing the words, so it's alright." "But I hate the song—"

9 ■ **Frank Hutchison, et al., *White Country Blues (1926–1938): A Lighter Shade of Blue* (Columbia/Legacy)** Kicking off with "K.C. Blues" and "Cannon Ball Blues" (both 1929) by the uncanny West Virginia slide guitarist Hutchison, moving on to Charlie Poole with the North Carolina Ramblers' "Leaving Home" (1926) and "If the River Was Whiskey" (1930), the first disc of this two-CD set is an almost perfect backdrop to Bob Dylan's recent *World Gone*

Wrong. The second disc is dead, but you won't care.

10 ■ **Robert Altman, director, Altman and Frank Barhydt, writers,** *Short Cuts* Altman's characters have sometimes taken his sneer away from him (*McCabe and Mrs. Miller, Thieves Like Us, Come Back to the Five and Dime, Jimmy Dean, Jimmy Dean*), but the sneer does all the work in this film, though perhaps more economically than in the past. With *Nashville* Altman's contempt for his material was so vast he had actors playing country singers write and perform their own songs; here he merely posits a nightclub with an all-black clientele (save for Tom Waits and a party that wanders in by accident) and an all-white jazz band, led by a white singer. Yes, it's Annie Ross, who's supposed to have seen better days, but the only thing phonier than her singing is her patter.

FEBRUARY 1994

1 ■ **Andreas Ammer & FM Einheit,** *Radio Inferno* **(EGO/Rough Trade, Germany)** This astonishing radio play was written by Ammer, produced by Herbert Kapfer, and aired last year in Munich on Bayerischer Rundfunk. Here it's a single 34-track CD: Dante's *Inferno,* cantos I through XXXIV, recast in German, English, and Latin, with all time scrambled. Apt musical composition combines with inspired sampling (a bit of the Temptations' "Papa Was a Rolling Stone," gongs and bells in a background so deep the sounds don't seem to be coming from your speakers) and an even more inspired cast: Blixa Bargeld as Dante; Phil Minton as Virgil, his guide; Yvonne Ducksworth as Beatrice ("and characters from hell"); and John Peel, the great BBC dj, as *your* guide, the voice of authority, the man with the microphone, sardonic, entertaining, professional, surprised by nothing, so cool ice wouldn't melt in his mouth no matter what circle of hell he's covering.

It's an insane conceit, a shadow play with the 20th century plunged into the 14th and then locked up. Peel: "The surrender

to sin leads, by degradation, to solitary self-indulgence. Here, beatnik Burroughs has to read his own book, for all eternity." John Cage and Marcel Duchamp call out in their own voices; soon enough all are possessed by the spirit of Bosch, laughing at the tenth circle, which is filled with the Falsifiers, the Modern artists "stricken by hideous diseases," the Dadaists "covered in ulcers." "Welcome to the Terrordome," Peel announces with utter contempt. "We're coming to the countdown to Hell, our Eternal Hit Parade of Sin and Punishment—" It's funny at first. At the end, too. Strange things happen on the way.

2–3 ■ **Tara Key,** *Bourbon County* **(Homestead) & Funkadelic: "Maggot Brain," on** *Maggot Brain* **(Westbound reissue, 1971)** Key has been an effective lead guitarist for well over a decade, first with Louisville's Babylon Dance Band (not a name to leave behind), then with Antietam. Six or seven cuts into her first solo disc she lets loose with a twisting, uncertain exploration of heretofore hidden passages in her music, as if the likes of "V.O.B." were her Mammoth Cave and her guitar both torchlight and pickaxe, as if her terrain didn't exist until she opened it up. It's a thrilling, mysterious kind of tension she creates—the tension of self-discovery, so many years on. Twenty-three years ago the late Eddie Hazel, guitarist of Funkadelic, went farther without, so to speak, leaving his room, almost without moving. "Maggot Brain" begins where Peter Green's 1967 "Supernatural" left off, meandering slowly, always more slowly, over ten perfect minutes, toward a peace beyond words. Guess that's why the original *Maggot Brain* liner notes, crypto-Nazi cultspeak from the Process Church of the Final Judgment, are included with the new CD—just in case you get too confident, you know?

4 ■ **Janis Joplin, "Coo Coo," from** *Janis* **(Columbia/Legacy 3-CD reissue, 1966)** "We Americans are all cuckoos,—we make our homes in the nests of other birds," Oliver Wendell Holmes wrote in 1872, and no one who has recorded this scary Appalachian

ballad ever got more homelessness out of it than Joplin did. The leap she takes coming off the second line of each verse—a wail that's part abandonment to desire, half abandonment to death—was the promise her music, and her myth, almost always made, a promise she could almost never keep when tape was running.

5 ▪ **Mudboy & the Neutrons, "Land of 1000 Shotguns," from** *Negro Streets at Dawn* **(New Rose, France)** When this tune started life, as "Land of 1000 Dances," the Apache Dance was probably not one of those writer Chris Kenner had in mind. These days, on certain Negro streets, it may be the only one left.

6 ▪ **Kristin Hersh, "Cuckoo," from** *Hips and Makers* **(4 AD)** Wordsworth, 1804: "shall I call thee Bird, Or but a wandering Voice?" Why not a spell?

7 ▪ **Coup,** *Kill My Landlord* **(Wild Pitch/ EMI)** This non-gangsta Oakland rap trio— Boots, E Roc, Pam the Funkstress—is determinedly local. They don't care if when they mention "Moby D." you don't know they're referring to the Alameda County courthouse. They're conversationalists, not braggarts; moody, not melodramatic. But they play with irony both as a weapon and for fun. It's unnerving to realize the old Vietnam War chant "Hey, hey, how many kids did you kill today?" now refers not to LBJ but to a neighborhood shooter. And it's hilarious when a white reporter calls Boots for a comment on L.A.'s "tragic riots": "Not a riot, a rebellion," Boots snaps. "Well," says the reporter, "the, uh, tragic rebellion . . ."

8 ▪ **Lisa Rebecca Gubernick,** *Get Hot or Go Home—Trisha Yearwood: The Making of a Nashville Star* **(Morrow)** A solid account of a newcomer's attempt to turn a successful debut album into a career. Gubernick, a *Forbes* editor, plays fly on the wall with barely a hint of condescension or cynicism, but her story could have used a bit more of the latter. The people in her pages are theme-park nice, and not unbelievably so; the goals they struggle for so efficiently with such a clear sense of what the rules are, seem benign, pinched, and wholly self-ref-

erential. Gubernick's description of Nashville's Fan Fair, where stars sit in booths for five days signing autographs, as a "country-music petting zoo" stands out—for once, Lisa the fly turns back into a human being. The line strikes a discord, and it makes you wonder: did the presence of a New York reporter throughout the conception and recording of Yearwood's second album have no effect at all on the way the principals thought, spoke, acted?

9 ▪ **Jim Pollack, Nairobi Sailcat, Carrie Weiland,** *Slide to the Rhythm* **(Fitness Innovations/Dynamix Music Services)** An aerobics tape, 126 B.P.M., with every other of the 12 tracks building off a riff so suggestive, so determined, you can't think about anything but the rhythmic truth it's about to reveal before the following track sweeps it away.

10 ▪ **Betsy Bowden, English 393, fall 1993 (Rutgers at Camden)** Bowden, a Chaucer scholar who describes herself as "world famous among a very tiny group of people who truly care about obscene puns in 12th-century Latin," invented a Literature of Travel course to assuage her guilt over making full professor. Starting in 400 B.C. with Xenophon's *Anabasis,* she covered, among other highlights, *The Canterbury Tales, Piers Plowman, Pilgrim's Progress, Gulliver's Travels,* Twain's *Innocents Abroad,* and Steinbeck's *Harvest Gypsies* and *The Grapes of Wrath,* all arranged "such that the whole of Western literary culture culminates in Dylan's *Highway 61 Revisited.*" "On the last day of class, thus," Bowden wrote to friends last Christmas, "I was teaching the Nun's Priest Tale and 'Desolation Row,' and watching the Medieval Lit class put on the Second Shepherd's Play in Middle English. I more or less feel as if this is what I ought to be doing when I grow up."

MARCH 1994

1 ▪ **Heavens to Betsy,** *Calculated* **(Kill Rock Stars)** This two-woman band (voice, guitar, bass, drums, or less) has been making extremist music about girlhood on stray singles and compilation-album cuts since

1991. For the first half of their own album they could be imitating themselves—looking for a subject, for a metaphor to burn the riot grrrl ideology out of singer Corin's throat. But with the instrumental "Intermission," everything hurts, and every note rings true, especially on "Donating My Body to Science," which may be the coolest metaphor for sex in the history of riot grrrl, not to mention the history of Western civilization.

2 ▪ **Billy Ray Cyrus, "When I'm Gone,"** from *It Won't Be the Last* **(Mercury)** A completely convincing back-from-the-dead rewrite of "Are You Lonesome Tonight?," apparently Boris Yeltsin's favorite Elvis song. Will Boris cover this one? Has he already?

3 ▪ **John Zorn, "Never Again," from** *Kristallnacht* **(Eva)** For almost three minutes the sound of breaking glass is like a waterfall: that fast, that implacable. Then just the footsteps of someone running away; then Hebrew chanting; then a sort of Austro-Hungarian salon ensemble, discreetly summoning the dead soul of Central Europe. Despite the distant echoes, the true subject of this nearly 12-minute piece, recorded on 9 November 1992, seems as much the Germany of the present day as of 9 November 1938, when Nazis smashed the windows of Jewish shopkeepers all over the country. When the breaking glass comes back, and with it a mob unafraid of its own voice, you're sure of it. "Contains high frequency extremes, at the limits of human hearing & beyond, which may cause nausea, headaches & ringing in the ears," Zorn warns. "Prolonged or repeated listening is not advisable." Tell it to the thugs.

4 ▪ **Alison Krauss & Union Station, "Baby, Now That I've Found You," at the Grand Ole Opry (TNN, 27 November 1993)** A friend sent me a barely audible tape—Krauss' shimmering, preternaturally delicate warble of a 1967 hit by the Foundations, a not-forgotten British/Caribbean pop group. Their interracial arms now reach from the Sex Pistols (who began rehearsing with the Foundations' "Build Me Up Buttercup") to the quiet queen of bluegrass, singing like extra virgin olive oil pours in sunlight. Miss Krauss, meet Mr. Rotten. Oh, you've already met?

5–6 ▪ **Bob Dylan, notes to** *World Gone Wrong* **(Columbia) &** **Mike Kelley:** *Winter's Stillness #1* Reading Dylan as he explicates his album's old blues and Appalachian folk songs (on the ancient "Love Henry": "Henry-modern corporate man off some foreign boat, unable to handle his 'psychosis' responsible for organizing the Intelligensia, disarming the people, an infantile sensualist"), two thoughts struck me. First, by abandoning liner notes after his 1965 *Highway 61 Revisited*, Dylan invented rock criticism, or anyway called it into being, simply by making a vacuum for it to fill. Second, even today no critic would dare make half as much of a song as Dylan always has when he's taken to putting them into other words.

Since a verbal commentary would inevitably fall short of the one Dylan had already provided, I thought *World Gone Wrong* needed a visual commentary, by someone who could let the music spark a picture. Given the opportunity, I asked Mike Kelley; he demurred, suggesting Raymond Pettibone. But then, paging through *Mike Kelley—Catholic Tastes*, the catalogue Elisabeth Sussman edited for Kelley's recent retrospective at New York's Whitney Museum of American Art, I realized the picture was already there. *Winter's Stillness #1* is from 1985: a top border illustrates the title in Currier & Ives clichés; below it there's a rough drawing of the map of the U.S.A. The top two-thirds are blank; then Kelley's version of the Mason-Dixon line stretches from coast to coast, with the lower third of the country dark and dank, the word "Hillbillies" dripping excreta into a lake of slime. On that lake is a cabalistic symbol, seemingly named in Kelley's caption, a pun on hillbilly cliché and on the title of the piece itself: "A NEW KIND OF STILL—IT DISTILLS PURE INBRED EVIL. THE FOUL-SMELLING MASH SINKS TO THE BOTTOM—FIRE-BREWED. DOWN HERE IT IS.

UH UH." If that doesn't outdistance Dylan it sure as hell keeps up with him.

7 ▪ Folkes Brothers, Laurel Aitken, Owen Gray, Theophilus Beckford, et al., *Tougher Than Tough—The Story of Jamaican Music* **(Mango 4-CD reissue, 1958–93)** Sure, it's all great. But the first disc, covering 1958 through 1967, has the aura of people waking from a four-century sleep to take back their island from Columbus and all who came after him; only their skin color has changed.

8 ▪ ZZ Top, *Antenna* **(RCA)** REPAIRS COMPLETED. ROAD OPEN. SPEED LIMITS STRICTLY ENFORCED.

9 ▪ Rock and Roll Hall of Fame, induction ceremonies, Waldorf-Astoria Hotel Grand Ballroom (New York City, 19 January) Just think: in four years, Aerosmith will be eligible.

10 ▪ Ian Softley, director, *Backbeat* **(Gramercy Films)** As a movie about the Beatles in Hamburg in the very early '60s, this is perfectly adequate. As a movie about the love affair between then-Beatle bass player Stuart Sutcliffe and Hamburg photographer Astrid Kirchherr, which is what *Backbeat* wants to be, it's a blank. Sheryl Lee is wasted as Kirchherr; like her soulmates in Heavens to Betsy she goes to extremes or she goes nowhere, and her underwritten part gives her nowhere to go and nothing to do, save to sit around looking knowing and occasionally pull off her sweater.

What's most intriguing in *Backbeat* is its presentation of Kirchherr's world, the world of the Hamburg Exis, or existentialists: a flamboyant, costumed, forbidding, sexually ambiguous haute bohemia. The question the film begs is where this supremely self-confident outsider milieu came from, given the suppression of bohemian cultures under the Nazis and the privations of the postwar period. Did Kirchherr and her friends hark back to the Weimar Dadaists, or did they come together in the same spirit as their peers in Paris, London, San Francisco, and New York? What were their resources— and how different, really, was Liverpool's working-class beat-group scene, where *Un*

Chien Andalou was as familiar as Jimmy Reed and Muddy Waters, from Hamburg's bourgeois Beat scene, where Sartre was a hero and Chuck Berry arrived via Armed Forces Radio? Did worlds collide, or were they the same?

At least in the Beatle literature, this is a question no one has asked, let alone answered. Stuart Sutcliffe died in 1961, but Astrid Kirchherr, now in her mid 50s, is still living in Hamburg; it's unlikely she's forgotten a thing.

1 ▪ Rickie Lee Jones, "Rebel Rebel," on *Traffic from Paradise* **(Geffen)** One of the *really great* David Bowie songs, brought to life with the intimacy of two people off in the bathroom halfway through a concert, fixing their makeup and taking their heads off.

2 ▪ Jimmy Reed, the Spaniels, etc., *The Vee-Jay Story* **(Vee-Jay 3-CD reissue, 1953–65)** An imaginatively programmed assemblage of gritty, close-to-the-ground smashes and obscurities from the black-owned Chicago label that in 1963 brought America the Beatles ("Please Please Me" fell short of the charts; "From Me to You" struggled to #116) and went belly up three years later. For the paranoid inside story of the emergence and ruin of this pioneering company, see Joseph C. Smith's novel *The Day the Music Died*, from 1981; for the prosaic version, in which genius and genre coexisted in a state of exquisite tension, listen to the alcoholic prophecies of Jimmy Reed's primitive "High & Lonesome," the doo-wop swoon of the El Dorados' "At My Front Door," the doom-struck pop rhythms of Dee Clark's "Your Friends," and the overwhelming emotional striptease of Little Richard's greatest blues, "I Don't Know What You've Got But It's Got Me." The year is 1965; Richard, wailing, testifying, madly gesticulating, is the genius; an unknown Jimi Hendrix, on guitar, is the genre. And two years later they'd changed places.

3 ▪ Mike Leigh, writer & director, *Naked* This portrait of rape in present-day London may be a parable of the ruins of Thatcherism, but there are older echoes. Charming scum Johnny (David Thewlis) might be a time-traveler from the plague years; he seems almost to rot as the movie goes on. His exgirlfriend Louise (Lesley Sharp) has the sort of deep, heavy face that pretty much left the screen when talkies arrived. She can recall Gloria Swanson, or even Albert Dieudonné in Abel Gance's *Napoléon*. Still, no-future is what the film is always about: erasing the future as it comes into being, registering what's being left behind and letting it go. Desperate for company, a guard in an empty deluxe office building takes a homeless Johnny inside and guides him through the place; he clears locks with some sort of post-Modern security wand, a black baton with a white tip. "What's that," says Johnny, "a Dadaist nun?"

4 ▪ **Eugène Atget, *Atget Paris* (Hazan, Paris, and Gingko Press, Santa Rosa, CA)** Atget was a real street photographer—that is, he took pictures of streets, not of "street life"—and from the 1890s to about 1914 he mapped the Paris that had escaped the enormous hands of Baron Haussmann, from the Pont Neuf in the 1st *arrondissement* to the falling-down shacks at the farthest edges of the 20th. People who know—Louis Chevalier, for one, in his 1977 *The Assassination of Paris*—will tell you that Atget's city was destroyed in our own time, and that to reach for the smoky auras captured in the 840 photos collected here is sheer romanticism, no matter how seemingly familiar a lot of Atget's streets still look. Well, give it a test. Unlike so many other Atget volumes, this is no coffee table book. At 5½ by 7⅝ by 2½ inches, it's like an elegant brick; you can hold it in your hand, using the pictures as a map of the city, following where they lead, and see if the city is still there.

5–6 ▪ **Iris Dement, *Infamous Angel* (Warner Bros.) & Bratmobile: *The Real Janelle* (Kill Rock Stars)** The future of the past—the past being, respectively, the catch and curl of Dolly Parton's voice in "My Blue Ridge Mountain Boy" and the unaccompanied mountain ballads she harks back to, and the glee and resentment of old Blondie records like "Rip Her to Shreds" and old Au Pairs records like "It's Obvious." Plus just a hint of "Papa-Oom-Mow-Mow."

7 ▪ **Joyce Carol Oates, "Waiting on Elvis, 1956," in *Sweet Nothings: An Anthology of Rock and Roll in American Poetry*, ed. Jim Elledge (Indiana University Press)** Set in a café in Charlotte called Chuck's ("I was 26 married but still/waiting tables"), written in 1987, and the most convincing Elvis-Clinton sighting yet: "I slapped at him a little saying, You/sure are the one aren't you feeling my face burn but/he was the kind of boy even meanness turned sweet in/his mouth./Smiled at me and said, Yeah honey I guess I sure am."

8 ▪ **Band, "Remedy," on *The Tonight Show* (NBC, 22 February)** With drummer Levon Helm, organist Garth Hudson, and bassist Rick Danko accompanied by new guitarist, pianist, second drummer, and a four-man *Tonight Show* horn section, they were better than on their recent *Jericho*—John Hiatt's "Buffalo River Home," from his *Perfectly Good Guitar*, is probably a better Band imitation than anything on Helm & Co.'s first album since guitarist Robbie Robertson left and pianist Richard Manuel killed himself. But this night there was a spark in the sound, muscle and play—and a definite, appropriate ordinariness. In 1968, when these men first announced themselves as The Band, the emphasis seemed to be on the "The," as a statement of arrogance, which they proceeded to live up to. Now both capital letters might as well be gone. With a pretty good Diet Coke commercial based on "The Weight" running on TV, they played, sang, and carried themselves with a humility so complete it might not support any name at all.

9 ▪ **Juliana Hatfield Three, "My Sister" (Mammoth)** Nancy Kerrigan's soul sister, anyway.

10 ▪ **Tom Petty, "I Won't Back Down" (MCA, 1989)** How long before people here and there will be able to hear this without

thinking of Dr. David Gunn, shot to death last year as he arrived for work at a Pensacola abortion clinic? Not long before, Gunn, armed with a cassette machine, faced a crowd of protesters and blared the song right at them—not only because its message was right, you might imagine, but because the song made him feel more alive. Listening to it today, joined to the history it helped make, you can hear Petty take what on paper is no more than an exercise in the obvious past itself, or vice versa.

MAY 1994

1–2 ▪ **Mudboy & the Neutrons, *Negro Streets at Dawn* (New Rose, Paris) and "5" Royales: *Monkey Hips and Rice* (Rhino 2-CD reissue, 1952–62)** A big, noisy rumble; a testament to Memphis eccentricity; a revel that leaps from a growled, updated riff by the late bluesman Furry Lewis ("Our father who art in Washington/Slick Willie be his name/He taken me off Rabbit Track tobacco/Put me back on novocaine!") to the deep soul of "Dark End of the Street." Led by Rivertown favorite son Jim Dickinson, the set almost disappears into its own black hole with a deliriously cheesy white-boy trash version of the "5" Royales' bizarre "The Slummer the Slum." Released in 1958, the tune, Robert Ray of the Vulgar Boatmen recalls, "was always known in Memphis (where it was a huge hit, played by every high school garage band) as 'The Stompity Stomp' (which was the way it was always sung)."

The "5" Royales themselves—a dynamic, still obscure R&B vocal combo featuring Lowman Pauling, a guitarist unparalleled in his ability to wring surprise from a song—get their due on *Monkey Hips and Rice*, a model retrospective with sparkling liner notes by Ed Ward. Originally from North Carolina, the "5" Royales began in the 1940s, as a gospel group; by the early '50s they had found a protean rock 'n' roll style that combined tremendous excitement with open spaces in the sound, so that even in the midst of a rave-up their records always breathed. Their "Slummer the Slum" is no "Stompity Stomp," but a dance-floor mystery: "Don't try," chants Johnny Tanner off an extreme stop-time beat, "to figure out/Where I/Come from," instantly summoning thousands of years of heavenly interventions, divine portents, and unnatural catastrophes, along with a couple of the most unlikely guitar solos ever played.

3 ▪ **Elvis Costello, "Sulky Girl," on *Brutal Youth* (Warner Bros.)** A quiet, vaguely noirish lead-in on electric piano, and then these opening lines: "She wears a wedding ring her sister left to throw them off the scent/Just let them guess/It's what they expect. . . ." Wouldn't you keep listening?

4 ▪ **Tasmin Archer, *Shipbuilding* (ERG/SBK)** Archer is a classy young British singer with a voice she can take lower than you'd expect. Here she makes a better case than Elvis Costello did on *Spike* that "Deep Dark Truthful Mirror" is one of his best. She does real damage with her own "Lords of the New Church." Archer seems to sing around a song; then suddenly you realize she's singing straight from its heart. From her own heart: maybe not yet.

5 ▪ **Mekons, *Retreat from Memphis* (Quarterstick)** Yes, fans, it's that big fuzztone sound of the Mekons! Except that on the very first cut the guitar calls up Sergio Leone's elegiac *Once Upon a Time in the West*, and by the last the band is back in the 1640s, laughing at the church: "Never wanna work, always wanna play, pleasure, pleasure, every day."

6 ▪ **Charles Arnoldi, *Hound Dog*, in "The Architect's Eye," Frederick R. Weisman Art Museum, University of Minnesota, Minneapolis (November 1993–March 1994)** In the opening exhibition in Frank Gehry's fabulous new pile, a stunner: 120 inches by 104, acrylic on wood, black-gray-blue with slashes of red, though actually it bespoke less any sort of hound dog, or "Hound Dog," than a Texas chainsaw massacre of *Demoiselles d'Avignon*. Maybe Jonathan Richman can figure this one out.

7 ▪ **John Lydon, *Rotten—No Irish, No Blacks, No Dogs* (St. Martin's)** Whipped into shape by Keith and Kent Zimmerman, two record-business tip-sheet editors, and fleshed out in long stretches by interviews with various there-when's, from Chrissie Hynde to Lydon's father, this "authorized autobiography of Johnny Rotten of the Sex Pistols" is a terrible disappointment. If he'd forced himself to write the book himself, you can think, Lydon would have had to confront both his success and his failure; instead, he more or less denies everything.

And yet, near the end, there's a weird reminder of a passage from Umberto Eco's *Foucault's Pendulum*, his great pseudodetective story about the mystery of the Knights Templar. One character is expounding upon the difference between the "four kinds of people in the world: cretins, fools, morons, and lunatics." The lunatic, he explains, "is all idée fixe, and whatever he comes across confirms his lunacy. You can tell him by the liberties he takes with common sense, by his flashes of inspiration, and by the fact that sooner or later he brings up the Templars." After nearly 350 pages of insisting that the Sex Pistols were all about him, 350 pages in which he tries doggedly to keep the world-historical stopped up in its bottle, Lydon offers this: "The Royal family has been brought up to believe it's God's will for them to be where they are. That's what I find so disgraceful. . . . Think back. The only group of knights that did good were the Knights Hospitaller and the Knights Templar. They were all exterminated because they gave up money, power and position. They were like early Franciscans and that could not be tolerated by the British establishment and they were slaughtered to a man. What would you call them? Early Communists? Their love of humanity above the love of selfishness attacked the establishment by their very existence. They fought all their wars and were a pre-SAS, the top assassins of their day, but they gave up all worldly goods, too frightening for the powers that be to tolerate for too long. Now I'm certainly no Knights Templar and I'm

not out looking for the Holy Grail. . . . Which brings us back to the Royal family."

And which may leave us where we started: John Lydon may be a lunatic, but the punk syllogism remains intact—everyone else is a cretin, a fool, or a moron.

8 ■ **Howlin' Wolf, "Rollin' and Tumblin'," "I Ain't Gonna Be Your Dog No More," "Woke Up This Morning," "Ain't Going Down That Dirt Road," on *Ain't Gonna Be Your Dog* (MCA Chess 2-CD reissue, 1951–69)** In 1968 Howlin' Wolf was forced to record a psychedelic album eventually released as *This Is Howlin' Wolf's New Album. He Doesn't Like It.* ("Dogshit" is what he called it.) Perhaps as compensation, at the same sessions the tape ran when he picked up an acoustic guitar and battered out pieces of old blues like a man knocking branches off a tree with an axe, just for the hell of it.

9 ■ **Rob Wasserman, "Fantasy Is Reality/Bells of Madness," from *Trios* (MCA/GRP)** Bassist Wasserman's bit is that he plays with two additional, famous people (pairing Neil Young and Bob Weir, say); the results are not staggering. But the cut featuring famous nutcase Brian Wilson and his famous (ex-Wilson Phillips) daughter Carnie on his own tune—unlike the rest of the album, produced by Don Was—is disturbing. The melody contains a preternatural lift, Carnie Wilson's voice shimmers, and when she presses on the *hear* in "But when I hear the bells of madness" the effect is lovely and horrible precisely to the same degree.

10 ■ **th Faith Healers UK, *Imaginary friend* (Elektra)** Drone band with sense of humor makes what may turn out to be best album of year.

SUMMER 1994

1 ■ **Robert Cantwell, "When We Were Good: Class and Culture in the Folk Music Revival," in *Transforming Tradition*, ed. Neil V. Rosenberg (University of Illinois Press)** Starting with the Kingston Trio's long-scorned 1958 #1 hit "Tom Dooley" and ending with the "national seance" of the 1963 Newport Folk Festival, this plainspoken essay re-

writes history with music, and vice versa. Diffusing a perfectly sketched, generic, white, middle-class, suburban, postwar upbringing across the whole spectrum of American legend and experience, Cantwell pours old wine into a cruet that suddenly gleams with transparency: "the revival made the romantic claim of folk culture— oral, immediate, traditional, idiomatic, communal, a culture of characters, of rights, obligations, and beliefs, against a centrist, specialist, impersonal, technocratic culture . . . of types, functions, jobs, and goals."

As Cantwell begins to trace the roles played by his characters—those figures dancing on the surface of "Tom Dooley," or hiding in its grooves—he makes the wine new. Surrounding the youthful folk acolytes of the late '50s and early '60s he finds the outlaw Tom Dula (who murdered his exlover, Laura Foster, in North Carolina in 1866) and Dr. Tom Dooley (an American doctor whose work in Laos inspired the Peace Corps), Wild Bill Hickok and Clint Eastwood (early on, as a TV cowboy), Appalachian ballad singers of the '20s and Paris existentialists of the '40s, Dr. Spock and John Lomax, Doc Watson and the Coasters, Ichabod Crane and Laura Ingalls Wilder, Robin Hood and Theodore Roosevelt, Marlon Brando and of course James Dean—who, rather miraculously, Cantwell makes new along with everybody else, precisely by introducing him to everybody else. Tom Joad and Leatherstocking, Nicholas Ray (director of *Rebel without a Cause*, but also "closely associated as a radio producer in the 1940s with the left-wing folksong movement in New York") and Willa Cather, New Deal populists and blackface minstrels: all of them, in Dean's hesitant speech and broken, then furious gestures, make a seance of their own. The only problem with this generous essay is that it is available only in the sort of overpriced volume most libraries can no longer afford, and no paperback is planned. Short of an essay collection by Cantwell—the author of *Bluegrass Breakdown: The Making*

of the Old Southern Sound (1984, Da Capo) and the recent *Ethnomimesis: Folklife and the Representation of Culture* (University of North Carolina Press)—pray for remaindering.

2 ▪ th Faith Healers UK, *imaginary friend* (elektra) "Psychedelic" is the only word for this obsessive band, led by the buried but mesmerizing vocals of one Roxanne. Using repetition, distance, and the sort of indecipherable echoes that still make Moby Grape's "Indifference" feel unstable, the group works with negative space, creating it, filling it, then leaving it empty again. The sound can suggest George Grosz, Otto Dix—you sense an outraged innocence beneath a veneer of cynicism. The band bets the farm on the last cut, "everything, all at once, forever" (the complete lyric): for 19 minutes 58 seconds they try to turn bad news into transcendence, and the fact that the change never comes sustains the meandering, patient, fed-up performance to the end. It's a false ending, though: after 12 minutes 25 seconds of silence, your CD player visibly counting backward to keep you from removing the disc, the song returns for another 7 minutes 35 seconds. This is a little boring.

3 ▪ Richard Thompson, "You'll Never Walk Alone," live on *Fresh Air* (National Public Radio, 13 April) "In England it's a football song," he said, after singing his heart out.

4 ▪ Lewis Nordan, *Wolf Whistle* (Algonquin) A novel based on the 1955 Mississippi lynching of Emmett Till—but here, amateur bluesmen getting drunk in the morning and lining out old Robert Johnson songs recede in the face of Moby Dick rising out of dry land. Dead, Emmett Till turns into Pip the cabin boy, comes back to life "dressed in a heavy garment of fish and turtles," then dies for good; entering a courtroom to testify before an all-white jury, a black witness sees the whiteness of the whale—as Thomas Hobbes put it in 1651, *Leviathan, or the Matter, Forme and Power of a Commonwealth Ecclesiasticall and Civil.*

5 ▪ Iris Dement, *My Life* (Warner Bros.) In DeMent's voice you can hear bluegrass,

old-time country music, and the physical and moral tiredness of some of the people Bobbie Ann Mason writes about. In her own songs you can't always tell if DeMent is parodying clichés, exploiting them, or caught by them, but then she takes something extra from a too-familiar image, or dances over a line anyone could have produced, and she's gone.

6 ▪ Hole, **"Credit in the Straight World,"** from *Live Through This* **(DGC)** Good luck.

7 ▪ Red Alert, *DJ Red Alert's Propmaster Dancehall Show* **(Epic Street)** A compilation of delirious, irresistible tracks—the collection all but drowns in its own fluids with Patra's "Love All the Men"—pretending it's the best radio show in the world, heading your way from KISS-FM, New York. Too bad it's not.

8 ▪ Jonathan Coe, *What a Carve Up!* **(Viking, UK)** In this black comedy about the evil of Thatcherism, so extreme even Elvis Costello might be caught up short, cutbacks in funding for the Underground lead to hideously overcrowded cars and disastrous service failures. A train stops dead in a tunnel; then the lights go out. The air turns unbreathable. "I could sense fear, now, fear all around me whereas before there had only been boredom and discomfort," the narrator says. "There was desperation in the air, and before it proved contagious I decided to beat a retreat, as far as possible, into the privacy of my own mind. To start with, I tried telling myself that the situation could be worse: but there were surprisingly few scenarios which bore this out—a rat on the loose in the carriage, perhaps, or a busker spontaneously . . . treating us all to a few rousing choruses of 'Imagine.' No, I would have to try harder than that . . ."

9 ▪ NKOTB, *Face the Music* **(Columbia)** The presentation is all shame and guilt—for more than ten years, NKOTB were New Kids on the Block. They aren't giving the money back, but Danny Wood now looks exactly like Erik Menendez.

10 ▪ Pearl Jam, on *Saturday Night Live* **(NBC, 16 April)** On April 8, the day Kurt Cobain's suicide was announced, there seemed to be as much Pearl Jam on the radio as Nirvana; given the solemnity always present in Eddie Vedder's singing, every song sounded like a eulogy. Still, that was no preparation for the wake the band staged little more than a week later. On a program that takes Nirvana's audience as a given, but which over the course of two shows had found no way even to mention Cobain's death, Pearl Jam began with the unreleased "Not for You." It was an extraordinary number—led by the most rudimentary up-and-down guitar riff by Vedder, and only for a moment raised into the realm of myth by a modal passage from guitarist Stone Gossard—a song at once ordinary and mysterious, elemental and twisted, quiet and full of alarms, elegiac and damning. Later the group moved on to "Rearviewmirror," then closed, after another break for moronic skits, with "Daughter." Pointedly pulling back his jacket to display a *K* on his T-shirt, Vedder ended the tune with a few lines from Neil Young's *Rust Never Sleeps*—the album Cobain quoted in the suicide note his widow, Courtney Love, had publically denounced as "like a letter to the fuckin editor."

She was right. One of the horrors of the event, a small horror, maybe, but a horror nonetheless, was that a man who could speak so freely in his own songs could not in the end find his own words, or make someone else's words ("It's better to burn out than to fade away") sound like his own. Yet when Vedder sang, as if the thought or the quote had just occurred to him, "Hey, hey, my, my, rock and roll can never die" (the line has carried unpleasant ironies since Young first offered it; once again, as always, it had to fight off an audience's idiot whoops), Vedder could not have appeared more completely himself: a fan surprised to find himself on a stage but ready to push his chance to the limit.

1 ■ **Walter Hill, director, *Streets of Fire* (1984; A&E cable, MCA video)** I caught the last 20 minutes of this urban never-never-land rock fable on A&E one afternoon (cast: Diane Lane, Michael Paré, Willem Dafoe, Rick Moranis, Amy Madigan, Lee Ving, Bill Paxton, Ed Begley, Jr., the Blasters, Robert Townsend), waited out the plot for the final musical number, and had my memories of the film dissolved by the wonder of what goes on. There's tremendous unreality to the sound and staging of "Tonight Is What It Means to Be Young"—it's thrilling, but in a prickly, disturbing way. Music videos have never come within centuries of what Hill (and Jeffrey Hornaday, the choreographer) does here with every gesture. Contradictions are the medium: singer Lane's dress is at once tight and hanging on her like a piece of paper, slit all the way down in back—she's not thin. The perfection of every move, every cut, is scary, and the sense that this isn't happening is overpowering: it's as if this is no performance but a transmission to the stage, by unknown technology, of your deepest performance fantasies. The audience waves its arms, and you peer through them: at the way the drummer, shot from below, makes the beat, the way the guitarist frames Lane with his back to her, his zoot suit touching her skin, the way the black vocal quartet enters the ensemble, strolling and strutting as if they've been called forth to walk it like she talks it.

On-screen the music—by some faceless aggregation called Fire, Inc.—sounds a thousand times better than it would on a record. This is exactly right for what you know cannot be real: the many female and for all I know male voices coming out of Lane's mouth. There's no way in the world what you're seeing is making the sound you hear, but you can believe the performers, in character, know this as well as you do. As you, in the audience, watch, the performers are projecting their own fantasies onto themselves, desperately, happily, casually,

as a matter of life and death. Isn't this what happens in a real show?

2 ■ **Joan Jett and the Blackhearts, "As I Am," from *Pure and Simple* (Warner Bros.)** Jett is wildly overrated as a survivor (aren't they all?), but as she runs her hoarse plea through a small, delicate knockoff of a circa '65 Phil Spector arrangement, she could be making her first record.

3 ■ **Anonymous, *I, Spastic*** A deliriously tasteless and appallingly hilarious one-person fanzine about, among other things, Jesus ("probably the most influential figure in history before Aaron Spelling") and the Apostles as a teenage gang ("all wearing dark coats made from the skin of a cow. . . . 'My man!'" says Jesus to a leper, "'Give me three and a half!'"), the transmogrification of confessed Bosnian Serb war-criminal Borislav Herak into an Azerbaijani pop star (illustrated), an L.A. porn actress home in Waukesha, Wisconsin, for Thanksgiving and recruiting her teenage sister (though their little brother gets all the best lines), and the Kurt Cobain–like death of Barney the dinosaur (illustrated): "In potting soil near his body, a pen thrust into the dirt held his one-page suicide note, written in appropriately purple ink. It read, in part, 'I love you, and you love me, but I hate myself and want to die.'"

4 ■ **Neil Young & Crazy Horse, *Sleeps with Angels* (Reprise)** *Tonight's the Night* disguised as *Harvest*—some trick.

5 ■ **Erasure, *I Say I Say I Say* (Mute/Elektra)** A lift.

6 ■ **Wallace Berman, *Support the Revolution* (Institute of Contemporary Art, Amsterdam/D.A.P.)** Berman (1926–76) started out in the '40s as a Watts white Negro. By 1967 his presence at the center of the Bay Area collage and assemblage circle led Peter Blake to include him in the gallery of culture heroes on the sleeve of the Beatles' *Sgt. Pepper* (just to the right of Tony Curtis). This retrospective volume features dull text by a variety of writers, and a handsome, loose design. Scattered all through it, dating from at least 1964 to nearly the end of Berman's life, are scores of versions of his

most iconic construct: they always begin with the same photograph, of a hand holding up a tiny transistor radio, completed with a picture where the speaker ought to be. Presented in sets of 56, like a sheet of stamps; of five, spread like a poker hand; or solitary, the doubled images work as omens, judgments—Verifax collages in color or black and white, positive or negative, showing two men hugging, a man and a woman having sex, a watch, a snake, a basketball game, a pistol, Kenneth Anger in a teenager movie role, an Iron Cross, George and Ringo, nothing, a galaxy, Bob Dylan, ancient coins, a spider. Each image communicates a kind of blankness, the radio silenced by the picture that has, it seems, developed out of it. All together the pieces make a whole metaphysics, derived from the simplest notion: changing the station.

7 ■ **Junior Kimbrough and the Soul Blues Boys,** *Sad Days, Lonely Nights* **(Fat Possum)** Taped in Kimbrough's juke joint in Chulahoma, Mississippi, with the nightspot used as a cold room—no audience. The result is rough, fraying, introspective, so much so it's almost abstract.

8 ■ **Marshall Crenshaw,** *Hollywood Rock* **(HarperPerennial)** Former *Beatlemania* John Lennon and continuing dubious rockabilly impersonator, Crenshaw may have found his true calling with this rock-movie guide—though there are 26 reviewers besides Crenshaw, and one Ted Mico is credited as editor. Films are graded for "music," "attitude," and "fun"; *Streets of Fire* gets three, one, and two stars, *Hated: G. G. Allin and the Murder Junkies* gets five across the board. The book is a treasure, or anyway a treasure chest: unpredictable, full of bizarre (or made-up) facts, obsessive to the point of dementia, and if you've heard of every movie here—*Amor a Ritmo de Go-Go? Teenage Millionaire? The Wizard of Waukesha* (say, weren't we just talking about . . .)? *Blonde on a Bum Trip? The Amorous Sex* (I actually rented this once, under another title)?—you probably don't remember your own name.

9 ■ **Harvey Keitel & Madonna, in** *Dangerous Game,* **dir. Abel Ferrara (1993, MGM/UA Home Video)** Lionized in 1992 for *Bad Lieutenant,* Ferrara could easily have called this one (or that one) *Bad Director.* But here both Keitel, as a lionized film director, and Madonna, as his leading actress and meal ticket, come off with dignity, and they're fascinating to watch. Madonna's character—off the screen of the movie-within-the-movie—is believable as an actual person, quietly evading Madonna's own image factories. As a Ferrara stand-in, Keitel's character isn't there as such, but it's gratifying to realize how completely and how well Keitel has aged on the screen over the last two decades. He seems to carry all of his roles with him, somewhere in the back of his mind, in the fatigue or vehemence of his gestures—and also, in his eyes, our memory of those roles, as he connives with himself, playing what we haven't seen him do before against what we have.

10 ■ **Pale Saints,** *Slow Buildings* **(4AD)** Th faith healers meet Sonic Youth, spook the hell out of each other, and wake up from an arty swoon, satisfied.

OCTOBER 1994

1 ■ **Martina McBride, "Independence Day," from** *The Way That I Am* **(RCA)** Written by Gretchen Peters, this is one of those ultra-professional country songs where all craft is marshaled to burn a tune into your heart. McBride sings it rangy, loud, and hard, like Trisha Yearwood with more than a career on her mind. "Talk about your revolution," says a young girl of her drunken father and her beaten mother; by the time the story finds its ending, the number has joined Van Morrison's "Almost Independence Day" and X's version of Dave Alvin's "4th of July" in the thin folio of recordings that expose a legacy nearly too distant and demanding to think about. It's a legacy that still carries an echo of Herman Melville's version: "The Declaration of Independence makes a difference."

2 ■ **John McNaughton, director, Samuel Fuller & Christa Lang, writers,** *Girls in Prison*

(Showtime made-for-TV movie) By far the most intense entry in the "Rebel Highway" series of old-title/new-script remakes of '50s AIP teen-exploitation films—the author of "Endless Sleep" gets framed for murder. The film goes giddy with glee over its freedom to push old ideas to the point of explosion: to get its first two heroines into the slam, they're shown as driven literally berserk by McCarthyism. A famous liberal Hollywood actor and his playwright daughter rehearse a new script; then, as you see it tried out in a little theater, with the father as a witness fighting off his McCarthyist inquisitor, the members of the audience rise from their seats and, all barriers between art, life, and propaganda dissolving, beat the father to the edge of death. After that, in the hospital, he can only mumble "Are you a communist?" over and over; after shock therapy, he says nothing at all.

3 ▪ Juliette Lewis, "These Boots are Made for Walkin'," in *Natural Born Killers*, dir. Oliver Stone (Warner Bros.) Out on her feet from snakebite, finally captured, her stomach covered with blood from the criss-crossings of a cop's knife, she's got rhythm, just barely.

4 ▪ Bill Clinton et al., *Bill Clinton Jam Session—The Pres Blows* (Pres/Daybreak M.O.) Too many strange clues here to handle—the sneer of the subtitle, itself a homage to Lester Young, the first tenor saxophonist to take the name "Prez"; the Mark of the Beast in the 800 number—but in fact this 17-minute CD is straight cool school, with more soul than Clinton fave Kenny G. Cut at the Reduta Jazz Club in Prague on January 11, with Clinton playing an instrument handed him by Vaclav Havel and leading a small troupe of Czechs through "Summertime" and a ten-minute "My Funny Valentine," the music meanders at first, with more to hear as themes fade than as they try to take shape. At the end, Clinton gathers Jan Konopásek's baritone sax to his tenor, and there's a stirring moment of peace at the heart of a storm not long in the past. As for the concurrent release of brother Roger's debut disc, *Nothing*

Good Comes Easy, it's lounge music, and where was it when the KGB could have used it? Lock Havel back up in his old cell, pump this in for . . . oh, about five tracks, and he'd renounce Frank Zappa and the Velvet Underground too if that's what it took to get out.

5 ▪ Richard Huelsenbeck, editor, *Dada Almanac*, presented by Malcolm Green (Atlas Press, London) A long-overdue though not inspired translation, usefully if burdensomely annotated, of the still thrilling, still weird 1920 anthology. Almost three-quarters of a century of paranoid delusions of grandeur have not quite recovered the language (let alone the frame of reference) Walter Mehring found in Berlin for "Revelations": "Since [the] Balkan division [of the first Dada dynasty] began the Albanian interregnum in collaboration with the Viennese *Bankverein* and the Italian *Banca Commerciale*, and launched its missionary activities among the Shiite Bektashiyahs, even simple jobbers at the stock exchange are beginning to realize . . ."

6 ▪ Come, *"Don't Ask, Don't Tell"* (Matador) No matter what dustbin of history Clinton's gays-in-the-military policy ends up in, the phrase will live on. It's a work of genius, a perfect title for anything save what it stands for—including this moody, accessible album by a band that was previously a dirge factory for singer Thalia Zedek—the Avital Ronell of rock 'n' roll—and is now letting a little speed and light into its sound. The music gets stronger and more whole song by song, until you can almost believe that inside the Gothic clichés some kind of secret is waiting.

7 ▪ Prince 1958–93, *Come* (Warner Bros.) Currently on a supposedly permanent recording strike, The Artist Formerly Known As Prince has announced his intention to fulfill his huge Warner Bros. contract by dumping tapes out of his bottomless vaults for as long as it takes. The first fruit of this bizarre insult is his/its most elegant and idiosyncratic album since *Dirty Mind*, and that was 14 years ago. *Come* is superhigh concept: the careful, inventive, all but liq-

uid dramatization of a single 48-minute-46-second fuck. Except for the hokey last track, "Orgasm"—if you believe Prince when he promises "I love you" to the accompanying female vocalist, credited as "partner," he's got an old Warner Bros. contract you might be interested in—the music basks in a kind of ease and luxury that brings back Howlin' Wolf's opening brag in "Going Down Slow," lines you can imagine spinning off the end of the last tape the Kid retrieves from the last vault: *"Now, I did not say I was a millionaire/But I said, I have spent more money/Than a millionaire."*

8 ■ **Heavens to Betsy,** *Direction* **EP (Chainsaw)** Latest news from Tracy and Corin—who in pursuit of their next move ("Direction," "Get Out of My Head," "The Ones") complain themselves all the way back to an X-ray Spex show in London in early '77, at which point they climb out of the crowd, onto the stage, and call their own tune ("Driving Song").

9 ■ **Beck's Beer Commercial, "Sail Away" spot (Wensauer • D.D.B. Needham, Düsseldorf)** I once wondered what would happen if Randy Newman's greatest song, conceived as a slaver's recruiting pitch, were heard anytime, anywhere—part of the noise of any given day. Well, here's the answer. Though only the title phrase and a hint of melody are used, the song is instantly recognizable behind footage of tall ships and waves surging. Why? To catch a vague echo of its evil, to give the commercial just the subliminal edge it needs?

10 ■ **Fastbacks,** *"Answer the Phone, Dummy"* **(Sub Pop)** After 14 years of evading anything resembling professionalism—seemingly abandoning all craft to glance a tune off your heart—bassist Kim Warnick and rhythm guitarist Lulu Gargiulo are singing lead guitarist Kurt Bloch's songs with a new confidence, which doesn't hurt lines like "I learned something today/People don't think the way I do." As always, the smallest incidents of memory or present-day this-'n'-that rush forward with a sense of fate and consequence, practical joke and tragedy, puzzlement and wonder—for example,

the possibility of actually finding out "what it really was/An observatory does." And speaking of great titles . . .

1 ■ **Stuart Davis,** *The Back Room,* **1913, and Thomas Hart Benton,** *House in Cubist Landscape,* **ca. 1915–20, in "American Art, 1900–1940: A History Reconsidered" (San Jose Museum of Art, through October 1995)** Drawn from the vaults of New York's Whitney Museum of American Art, this survey show is full of surprises; these paintings leap out. In Davis' dank barroom hideaway there's a lone drummer standing in for a band, one couple dancing, others immobilized. Their roughed-out faces could be prototypes for the 1933 Charles Laughton classic *The Island of Lost Souls* ("Are we not men?"). It looks like a place you'd likely never get into—an aura of pleasure earned, bled for, rises out of the frame. The piece is just around a turn from Benton's watercolor, which is as white as Davis' sanctuary is black. Here is an Appalachian pastoral upended by shapes impossible in nature, trees and fields and rivers now a jumble of Cubist blocks; an arch into the sky could be two tree trunks fallen against each other or a direct route to a Primitive Baptist heaven. It's as if the liquid bodies and landscapes of Benton's later, celebratory Americana represented not only freedom but an attempt to escape the violence implicit in a once trendy, momentarily irresistible style. Soundtracks: for Davis, Memphis Jug Band, "Turpentine Blues" (1927), on *Memphis Jug Band—Volume One* (JSP/UK); for Benton, Carter Family, *My Clinch Mountain Home—Their Complete Victor Recordings, 1928–1929* (Rounder).

2 ■ **R.E.M., "Wall of Death," on** *Beat the Retreat—Songs by Richard Thompson,* **a tribute album (Capitol)** On Richard and Linda Thompson's 1982 *Shoot Out the Lights* and ever since, I'd heard "Wall of Death" (collected on *Watching the Dark—The History of Richard Thompson,* Rykodisc) as an affirmation by then-Sufi Thompson of some

sort of Islamic trial by endurance: you know, they hang you on the wall of death in the morning when it's 120 degrees and if you're still alive by sundown your heart is true. Thompson's guitar and the wispy vocals were suggestive before they were anything else; the only lines I ever caught were "I'll take my chances on the wall of death" and "Beware of the bearded lady," which meant who knew what. But on R.E.M.'s magic carpet of a cover version, with steel guitar making the strange familiar and Michael Stipe wanting everything and as close to being scared of nothing as he'll ever be, I found myself looking down from the ride and discovered that the song is about a carnival attraction. O.K., so you knew it all the time—but I still believe that if musicians cover songs by recutting them, listeners cover songs by mishearing them.

3 ▪ **Jimi Hendrix, *Woodstock* (MCA)** Astonishing. Everyone's heard of it, but for 25 years only the 30,000 or so who were left to sit out the festival's finest hour—63 minutes—actually heard it. Fifteen minutes into the performance, it seems impossible he could go farther than "Hear My Train A Comin'," but about halfway through, with "Voodoo Child (Slight Return)," the fervor and drive of Hendrix's playing goes over some edge, and it's as if he caught a glimpse of where his train was going. Whether he did or not, you do.

4 ▪ **Spice 1, "Strap on the Side" (Jive)** This is a mean, ugly Oakland rap about a big gun and using it; running in the background, sometimes alongside, is a meandering, intensely melodic, conversation-with-the-mirror reverie that, while reinforcing the threat of the dominant speech with its words, in its tone falls just short of calling the song's own bluff.

5 ▪ **The Cranberries, *No Need to Argue* (Island)** The confidence that can come from even a rather bland top ten hit like "Linger" has changed Dolores O'Riordan's voice. Now it's more ordinary, idiosyncratic, Irish, bitter, and most of all unpredictable.

6 ▪ **Quentin Tarantino, Lawrence Bender, and Karyn Rachtman, executive al-**bum producers, *Pulp Fiction—Music from the Motion Picture* (MCA) The music here comes off much weirder than it does in the movie, mainly because concept albums based in second-rate California surf instrumentals are uncommon these days. Dick Dale & His Del-Tones' 1963 "Misirlou" is relatively well-known, but the likes of the Revels' 1964 "Comanche" or the Tornadoes' 1962 "Bustin' Surfboards" are completely obscure. This stuff appeared right about the time *Pulp Fiction* director Tarantino was born, and disappeared soon afterward. On disc it's close to a foreign language, and also completely bracing; as a frame its very nearly heroic reach for a decent riff makes Dusty Springfield's "Son of a Preacher Man" feel like deep soul (it is) and Urge Overkill's "Girl, You'll Be a Woman Soon," their two-year-old cover of a 27-year-old Neil Diamond hit, sound like Elvis fighting over the song with the grittiest white street singer, Joe Grushecky in his Iron City Houserocker days, maybe—like heaven on the run from hell.

7 ▪ **Kurt Schwitters, *Ursonate* (WERGO Schallplatten GmbH, Mainz, Germany)** The sound of a very old radio playing a very old record (on this CD, you can hear the original shellac discs spinning): the legendary sound-poetry epic, here 41 minutes 29 seconds, by the legendary German Dada Merz-man, only recently discovered, and recorded in . . . nobody knows. The piece sounds overwhelmingly influenced by the far shorter letter-sound poems of Schwitters' 1920s Dada comrade Raoul Hausmann, except that the only Hausmann recordings one has to go on were made in the '50s and the sonically more ambitious Schwitters, also Hausmann's postwar partner, died in 1948. For the moment, let the puzzle rest with this: if you could stick your head all the way into the big end of one of the giant ear horns that served as amplifiers on the earliest phonographs, it's the blips and rushes of its ocean you might hear in *Ursonate*.

8 ▪ **Colin Escott with George Merritt and William MacEwen, *Hank Wilsons: The Bi-**

ography (Little, Brown) In earlier books on Sun Records, Escott wrote with a dogged academicism; now he's found both his style and his heart. Avoiding the Hunter Thompson–like sensationalism of Chet Flippo's harrowing 1981 *Your Cheatin' Heart*, Escott—facing down a figure who on the terms of conventional biography is a specter behind scandal and who yet remains "almost desperately real through his music"—ends up in a graveyard far more awful. "There's the notion that the writer or poet calms his troublous soul by reducing it to rhyme," Escott finishes, ready to seal the case he's made. "For Hank Williams, though, as he pulled off his boots and eased himself gingerly onto his bed, the little verses scratched out in his untutored spidery handwriting almost certainly offered no relief at all."

9 ■ Tom Jones, *The Lead and How to Swing It* (Interscope) He's 54; his last hit came in 1988, with "Kiss," and he still hasn't gotten over Prince. He has gotten better—on Yaz's "Situation," madly so.

10 ■ Sheryl Crow, *Tuesday Night Music Club* (A&M) It's fine for her to rip off Stealers Wheel's "Stuck in the Middle with You" for "All I Wanna Do"—Stealers Wheel is thankfully long gone. But since Ricki Lee Jones is very much around, it seems premature for someone to make the top ten by absconding with her entire act.

JANUARY 1995

1 ■ Allen Ginsberg, *Holy Soul Jelly Roll— Poems and Songs, 1949–1993* (Rhino Word Beat 4-CD box) I put this on out of curiosity; except for performances I had to repeat, I played it straight through to the end. It is, somehow, a monument without pretensions, a testament of ambition without hubris, a year's worth of lectures on the origins of language without pedantry. Like a long singing from the Haftorah, the 63-minute-plus "Kaddish" only explodes at the end, shuddering toward a dissolution that, here, is the only way to wholeness. The previously unreleased version of "America," live

in Berkeley in 1956, changes the solemn heart-breaker of Ginsberg's 1959 studio recording into a stand-up comedy routine not far from *Richard Pryor—Live in Concert*. The best album of 1994—no contest.

2 ■ Hole, Fillmore Auditorium, San Francisco (11 November) Fronting bass, drums, and lead guitar with her own guitar in her hands and one leg hoisted onto a monitor speaker, Courtney Love has a number she runs on the crowd between songs: a lot of casual-sounding talk about what she dislikes about the site of a given show, former sex partners (especially whoever might be present), a fair amount of undifferentiated loathing, and a few well-placed invocations of Kurt Cobain ("I wrote this with my husband"; "Will you just come back, dickhead!"). It's a punk version, or her version, of "HELLO, SAN FRANCISCO!"—which you usually hear bellowed out at the Oakland Coliseum. But as a standard routine her words come off as detritus she happened to find onstage, and the fact that her music has the same offhand, let's-get-it-over-with quality produces a strange effect. There are no divisions between patter and song, and rather than everything communicating like performance, nothing does. The shifts between talk and music, shifts that given the band's precision timing you don't have to notice, merely take a conversation to another level; the burr in Love's voice is the same whether she's insulting someone, negotiating the careful steps of her time-stopping "Asking for It," or tossing off half of "Hungry like the Wolf." The result reminded me more than anything of a recent all-acoustic, sit-down, no-smoking, mother-in-the-audience concert by Iris DeMent, baring her soul and everyone else's with her "No Time to Cry," reinventing country music by treating it like ordinary speech—except that Love was more believable.

3 ■ Libby Gelman-Waxner, *If You Ask Me* (St. Martin's) Collected columns from *Premiere* on what really matters in the movies—the way clothes determine attitude, and vice versa. Too bad no music critics

have figured out an equivalent approach, which allows for, or for that matter demands, the ability to comment on anything at any time—as when Gelman-Waxner blithely mentions, in the course of reviewing *Ghost* (or rather explaining the subtext of same to her seven-year-old), that "the Richard Nixon Library & Birthplace in Yorba Linda, California, is spoken of as the entrance to the underworld in the Dead Sea Scrolls."

4 ▪ Unnamed Dixieland Band, unnamed New Orleans Sanitation Department driver, encounter (19 November) In the French quarter, a small combo was churning out a tepid version of very old style for the Grand Opening of a nondescript bar. The musicians spilled out into the street, so when the garbage truck came up Dumaine and tried to turn onto Chartres the driver found the way blocked. He blasted his horn—and then, as if he'd just noticed the awfulness of the noise he'd failed to silence, picked up the band's half-dead riff and punched it out on the horn, once, twice, three times. He completed his turn and growled on down the street, still playing, leaving the band to its miseries.

5 ▪ Frontline, "Hillary's Class" (PBS, 15 November) In this examination of the women of Wellesley '69 and their devil's choice between career and family, the ground opened up straight off, at commencement ceremonies 25 years ago. Republican Senator Edward Brooke of Massachusetts, the main speaker, had just concluded his remarks on student protest ("a perversion of democratic privilege") when Hillary Rodham, the first Wellesley student ever chosen to address her own class, stepped up in turn. She put aside her speech and talked back: "As the French student wrote on the wall of the Sorbonne," she said, "'Demand the Impossible.' We will settle for nothing less." After the Republican victories of last November, Speaker-presumptive Newt Gingrich famously derided Hillary and Bill Clinton as "counterculture McGoverniks," and the unusual suffix was meant for automatic, sub-

conscious decoding: first back to beatnik, and from there to the source of that word in Sputnik, the first space satellite, launched by the Soviet Union in 1957, and thus the root translation—commie. But what Hillary Rodham quoted that day was Situationist graffiti, from the uprising of May '68. That event has been written out of history, and so, many times, has Hillary Clinton, but I doubt we've heard the last from her.

6 ▪ Nirvana, "Lake of Fire," from *MTV: Unplugged in New York* (DGC) Almost every tune the band did this night sounded ancient, but none more so than this Meat Puppets number. With its lyric constructed like an authorless folk ballad—each line at once a literal non sequitur and a poetic link to any other—the out-of-nowhere reference to "the Fourth of July" suggested that here, as in "The Coo Coo," in America the type case of this kind of song, the Fourth of July is a predestined date, waiting, deep in unknown traditions, to be found and used. In other words, the feeling the music gives off is that as a talisman the Fourth of July not only preceded the Declaration of Independence but called it into being.

7 ▪ Dave Marsh and James Bernard, editors, *The New Book of Rock Lists* (Fireside) The table of contents includes 27 chapters, 533 subsections, and no page numbers. This is very avant-garde.

8 ▪ Laurie Anderson, *Bright Red/Tightrope* (Warner Bros.) The archness in her voice that since the 1983 *United States* has left her disembodied is gone. Now she sounds at home in her own skin—given the current state of the United States, not a moment too soon. You take your prophets where you find them, if you can find them.

9 ▪ KABL-FM, bus advertisement (Berkeley, 15 November) "BIG 98.1," it read. "Biggest Hits of the '70s. If Keith Richards Were Alive Today, He'd Be Listening to Us." Could be; at the Voodoo Lounge show I saw, the best music of the night was Elmore James' "Madison Blues"—the record, playing in the dead time between the opening act and the headliners.

10 ▪ Guns N' Roses, "Sympathy for the Devil," in *Interview with the Vampire* **(Geffen Pictures)** At the film's close, as a car speeds across the Golden Gate Bridge, this most menacing of all Rolling Stones songs comes on. It is the most menacing less because of its themes than because of the impossible certainty in Bill Wyman's bass, taking your feet out from under you, hurling you toward a destination you can neither credit nor resist—I mean, it moves like nothing else. The performance is so rich Jean-Luc Godard could build an entire movie around the emergence of its arrangement (his 1968 *Sympathy for the Devil* has just been released on video by ABKCO). But here, at the end of a film that gets stronger—more menacing—as it goes on, instead of the thing itself there is, by Geffen Records' own, a horrible imitation: generic, cloddish, ham-fisted and, in Axl Rose's singing, hysterical, as if the end, the end of the vogue for his band, is all too plain. For the movie it's a major false note: Lestat would have better taste.

FEBRUARY 1995

1–2 ▪ Chieftains, *The Long Black Veil* **(RCA) and Sharyn McCrumb:** *She Walks These Hills: A Novel of Suspense* **(Scribner's)** Both album and detective story take their title from "Long Black Veil," a 1959 Lefty Frizzell hit revived by the Band for their first album—an "instant folk song," as co-composer Danny Dill described it, because it had the feel of a 200-year-old Appalachian ballad. On the latest version of the tribute album (you recruit the stars and back them up yourself), the song is the best thing Mick Jagger has put his name to in years. It's also the ghost in McCrumb's third "ballad book," the key less to her murders than to the mystery of the Tennessee mountains, where old crimes cling to the hills like smoke. Along the way, the Chieftains loosen up their revered Irish traditionalism, drawing luminous, self-realizing performances from Mark Knopfler (a wistful "Lily of the West"), Sinéad O'Connor

("The Foggy Dew" and "He Moved Through the Fair"), and Tom Jones ("Tennessee Waltz/Tennessee Mazurka")—and McCrumb, writing long before the fact, throws the national orgy of pious incredulity over Susan Smith's killing of her children into ordinary light. In McCrumb's pages, both the song and her characters let a reader understand that what most distinguished Smith from the countless other Americans who each year kill their children was her use of her crime momentarily to become, before the whole country, what she must have felt herself to be: a star, her own abandoned child.

3 ▪ Antietam, *Rope-a-Dope* **(Homestead)** Tim Harris (bass) and Tara Key (guitar) can't sing—not in the time-honored rock 'n' roll tradition of can't sing, but can't sing the way normally proportioned human beings, which they are, can't kiss their elbows. Yet every time you're about to give up on this music, Key summons a passage on her instrument that does sing: a twist around a corner that a second before wasn't there, a breakaway.

4 ▪ David Evans, *John Heartfield—AIZ: Arbeiter-Illustrierte Zeitung/Volks Illustrierte 1930–38* **(Kent)** Two-hundred-and-thirty-seven antifascist photomontages—for all the good they did the first time around, a language worth relearning.

5 ▪ James Marsh, director, *Highway 61 Revisited* **(Arena Television/BBC, UK, 1993)** Part of a "Tales of Rock 'n' Roll" series so far unseen in the U.S., this documentary focuses on one of Bob Dylan's most inspired recordings and the spine-of-the-nation highway it's named for. There are surprises everywhere: Dylan's great "Blind Willie McTell" orchestrates footage of the Civil Rights Movement, a specter dissolving the words of heroes; a rough, clanking piano demo of "Like a Rolling Stone" turns into the anthem everyone knows as New York City looms up; and on Dylan's old buddy John Bucklen's high school tapes, Bucklen and then–Bobby Zimmerman talk into the tape recorder self-consciously, as if they know someday we'll be listening, judging whether Dylan's claim that Johnny Cash is more boring than dirt, or that Elvis was a thief, sounds sincere (not completely). Dylan hammers out Little Richard's "Jenny, Jenny" on the piano. He sings "Little Richard"—the song. His song. Good, too.

6 ▪ Colin McGinn, **"Out of Body, Out of Mind,** *Lingua Franca* **(November/December 1994)** "From the fact that *we* cannot make sense of something it does not follow that *it* makes no sense. We know that consciousness exists and that it is robustly natural, though we cannot in principle produce the theory that would make its nature manifest. There is thus nothing mysterious about the existence of the mystery." A philosophy professor at Rutgers, McGinn has been named a "New Mysterian"—a member of a minischool of mind-body theory named for ? and the Mysterians, who in 1966 forever altered the consciousness of all too many people with their immortal "96 Tears." "What difference has being a mysterian made to my life?" McGinn asks, and answers: "It has released me from the uncomfortable sensation that philosophical problems have always stimulated in me—the feeling that reality is inherently preposterous, ill-formed, bizarre." Rudy Martinez, a.k.a. ?, who after an eight-year hiatus is again performing under his philosophical name, with the original Mysterians, should be proud.

7 ▪ **Juned,** *Juned* **(Up)** Four women from Seattle stick an old picture of ugly transvestites on their CD sleeve, then combine folkish, borne-upon-the-winds vocals with an attack that veers from the relentless to the casually experimental. The sense that they could go anywhere pops up again and again, but for the time being they just go from one place to another.

8 ▪ **Marianne Faithfull,** *A Secret Life* **(Island)** Her much anticipated collaboration with Angelo Badalamenti, and the perfect accompaniment to her recent autobiography: the tone of exasperated, imperious noblesse oblige is the same.

9 ▪ **Janet Lyon and Michael Bérubé "Living on Disability—The Upward Climb of**

Down Syndrome," *Voice Literary Supplement* **(December 1994)** English professors Lyon and Bérubé's breathtaking comment on their Down's syndrome son: "In the end, he's both like and unlike everyone else— part body, part discourse, part counterdiscourse." It's a stunning example of why so many find this sort of critical writing—flipping buzzwords like card tricks—an occasion for mirth, if not disgust.

10 ▪ **Albert Zugsmith, producer,** *Girls Town* **(or** *The Innocent and the Damned***), 1959, on** *Mystery Science Theater 3000* **(16 December 1994, Comedy Central)** The setting: a prison farm run by nuns. The star: Mamie Van Doren. The human and the two robots who trade wisecracks about the movies they watch in the *MST 3000* screening room might as well be lobbing spitballs for all the mileage they're getting out of this one—until escapee Cathy Crosby is caught, and boyfriend Paul Anka has to convince her to go back to the nuns without scratching her, or their, eyes out. "I'll visit you," says Paul. Cathy manages a weak smile. "You tell me what your favorite song is," Paul says, "and I'll come up and sing it to you." From the peanut gallery: "You know 'White Light/White Heat'?"

1 ▪ **Alison Krauss,** *Now That I've Found You—A Collection* **(Rounder, 1987–94)** Going pop, bluegrass thrush opens up far more roads than she found on her most luminous recording, which isn't even here. Some performances are from her own records, some are more inaccessible: covers of the Beatles' "I Will," and of Autry Inman's room-spinning "I Don't Believe You've Met My Baby." Krauss makes you hope you never will.

2 ▪ **Mark Merlis,** *American Studies* **(Houghton Mifflin)** In this unmannered novel, a 62-year-old man, Reeve, lies in a hospital bed, having been beaten nearly to death by a boy he'd picked up. He thinks about his old professor, one Tom Slater—a figure Merlis has based on F. O. Matthiessen, Harvard teacher, communist,

homosexual, suicide, and author in 1941 of the classic *American Renaissance: Art and Expression in the Age of Emerson and Whitman*, though here the book is called *The Invincible City*. All that Slater wanted from life—from love and politics made inseparable—is summed up in his affection for Whitman's magic word "camerado." As Reeve thinks through the past, he nails its every vanity—of the left, the university, the famous book, of the closeted professor and his salon of golden youths. But no matter how distant, or evanescent, or false, the image of utopia the long-dead professor raised before his eyes cannot be erased: "The seminar above all, that famous seminar of his, that he first had the audacity to call 'American Studies.' Nowadays that means dissertations on 'Gilligan's Island.' But that wasn't what Tom meant at all. . . . For him there were, perhaps, three hundred Americans in as many years. They dwelt together in a tiny village, Cambridge/Concord/Mannahatta, Puritans and Transcendentalists exchanging good mornings, and Walt Whitman peeping in the windows. . . . He had made a little country of his own. . . . As Jefferson thought it would take a millennium to settle the continent, so we thought it would take forever just to cut a few paths through the forest primeval of nineteenth-century letters. . . . Even I felt, with Tom and his real students, like a conquistador, staking my claim on the imagined America that lived in that little room."

For Reeve, this memory, as metaphor, can give meaning to any incident of sex or history, or can take away whatever meaning he might have found in such incidents: can find them wanting. And this is the meaning of his life. It's a terrible paradox, the essential paradox of art and criticism, and I have never seen it rendered with such flesh and spirit, in such a good story.

3 ▪ PJ Harvey, *To Bring You My Love* (Island) On her best album she rides a broomstick she hasn't used before: a thick, heavy, pansexual voice. On "I Think I'm a Mother" it can feel like a man's. The music is forbidding—*dare you enter these portals?*—but while the sound is never transparent, sometimes Harvey seems to sing through herself, and then the sound is opaque, almost open, ivory.

4 ▪ Martin Scorsese, *Who's That Knocking at My Door?* (1968, Warner Home Video) First feature for both Scorsese and Harvey Keitel, and the most violent sequences are typically shot silent but scored with a song—the Channels' slow doo-wop "The Closer You Are," say. At first this seems to make no sense: what's on the screen is a rape, physically vicious but emotionally even more so. It's as if the woman is against all reason holding onto the perfect promises the Channels made, that she thought the guy with her made—until, finally, long before the rape is over, she lets those promises go. Then, on the soundtrack, the song begins to break up, to shred.

5 ▪ Team Dresch, *Personal Best* (Chainsaw/Candy Ass) Fast, prickly, with screams ambushing lilts and an ineradicable feel for the beat in tunes that seem made to disguise it. A press release brags that this female four-piece "only play all ages shows and queer bars," but they could play anywhere they want.

6 ▪ Little Axe, *The Wolf That House Built* (Okeh/Epic) Little Axe is a group led by singer/guitarist Skip McDonald, Wolf is Chester Burnett, house is the music, and too often in this collage all is indistinct. There are small moments of sampled vision: the surging rhythm that begins with a brakeman announcing "All aboard, all aboard," which itself kicks up the riff Robert Johnson used to open "Preaching Blues," which never sounded so cool as it does here.

7 ▪ Pocket Fisherman, *Future Gods of Rock* (Sector 2) The bassist quit for a group called Jesus Christ Superfly. He was smart.

8 ▪ Clinton Bottling Works, "ClinTonic" (ca. 1870–1935, on display at the Lower East Side Tenement Museum, N.Y.C.) Raspberry soda bottle discovered at the site in 1993. Shouldn't this be in the White House? Maybe there's a drop left.

9 ▪ Birney Imes, *Whispering Pines* (Mississippi) Color photographs of a Mississippi bar—often, shots of mementos stored in cigar boxes, with one item sneaking out, a yellowed news clipping, likely from the late '50s, possibly from the early '60s: "Singer Charged in Mississippi—Negro Rock and Roll Star Denies He Asked For Date From Girl." "Charles 'Chuck' Berry" has been "jailed without bond" and transferred from the police station to the county jail "for his own safety"; a "20-year-old girl" is "near hysteria" after the incident; the dateline is Meridian, from where, in June 1964, came the news of the disappearance of civil rights workers James Chaney, Andrew Goodman, and Michael Schwerner, and later the news of the discovery of their bodies.

10 ▪ Alison Krauss & Union Station, "Two Highways," from *Two Highways* (Rounder, 1989) Her most luminous recording. I think.

APRIL 1995

1 ▪ Nicole Eisenman, *Alive with Pleasure*, 1992–94, installation, "In a Different Light" (University Art Museum, Berkeley, through April 9) In this big wall assemblage of ads, doll parts, and Eisenman's own cartoons, the famous 16th-century image of a naked Diana Poitiers pinching her sister's nipple stands out, mainly because Eisenman has printed "SLUT" on D. P.'s chest, thus introducing *l'École de Fontainebleu* to riot grrrl. "Early on," Simon Reynolds and Joy Press write in their new *The Sex Revolts: Gender, Rebellion, and Rock 'n' Roll* (Harvard), "some daubed slogans and words with lipstick on their bodies," and they quote Kathleen Hanna of Bikini Kill: "When you take off your shirt [onstage] the guys think, 'Oh, what a slut' and it's really funny because they think that and then they look at you and it says it." All of which is probably subsumed by the *Beavis and Butt-head* episode where the boys are watching Sheena Easton's video for "Sugar Walls." "She did Prince," Butt-head says. "And she dresses like a slut."

"Prince makes all his women dress like sluts," Beavis says. "That's why I like him," Butt-head says. "He has a vision."

2 ▪ Mike Seeger, *Third Annual Farewell Reunion* (Rounder) A long day's Appalachian picnic, with Seeger gathering 23 performances by fiddlers, banjoists, mouth-bow players, and singers he's worked with from the '50s to now—siblings Pete and Peggy Seeger, Bob Dylan, Jimmie Driftwood, Jean Ritchie, many more. The best music is mountain air, the weather shifting in an instant but never really changing, and in its cleanest moments—"Oldtime Sally Ann," with the late Tommy Jarrell on fiddle, Paul Brown on banjo, and Seeger on guitar—pointing toward paradise on earth. "I strive for really traditional-feeling sounds," Seeger writes, "some of which may have never previously existed."

3 ▪ Mazzy Star, "Halah" (Capitol) Escaping from the 1990 *She Hangs Brightly* album, an unlikely FM hit, and also weird—cool trash on the order of Joanie Sommers' 1962 "Johnny Get Angry," and it may hold up as well. Languorously negotiating the sand dunes of the verses, Hope Sandoval sounds like Elizabeth Wurtzel looks on the jacket of *Prozac Nation* ("a Playboy bunny as St. Sebastian," a friend put it), but on the tag-lines ("Baby won't you change your mind," which finally turns into "Baby I wish I was dead") she sounds like Julie Delpy looks anywhere.

4 ▪ Jerry Lee Lewis, interviewed on *The History of Rock 'n' Roll* (Time-Life Video & Television, 11 March) For his fabulous impression of William Burroughs.

5 ▪ Sleater-Kinney, Kaia, Eileen Myles, Tattle Tale, Ruby Falls, Azalia Snail, *Move Into the Villa Villakula* (Villa Villakula) Stumbles and bruised knees (punctuated by singer-songwriter Kaia finding the right riff in "Off," or the New York combo Ruby Falls investigating a small mystery in "Spanish Olive") cover most of this compilation, but Sleater-Kinney's Corin Tucker, formerly of Heavens to Betsy, may have the most distinctive, demanding voice in pop music today, and once you've learned to hear it, every

inflection, every silence, tells secrets and wrestles demons. As she muses over the words "When I hear that old song . . . ," you realize the old song is the song she's singing, but she's already put more than a feeling into Boston's "More Than a Feeling"—try theory, history, fortune-telling.

6 ■ **Red Krayola, *The Red Krayola* (Drag City)** Leader Mayo Thompson remains as dour as ever—this is a man who once called an album *The Parable of Arable Land*. But the beat is often so odd, and so impossible to shake, that you might find yourself trying to keep time well after a song is over, even into the next track, which really confuses things.

7 ■ **Fakes, *Real Fiction* (Chainsaw)** An artfully crude rock opera about child abuse, orchestrated by Kathleen Hanna but whip-cracked three times by the is-it-real-or-is-it-recovered-memory testimony of Billie Strain ("Held"), Sue Fox ("Burnt Girl"), and Angie ("Secret Weapon"), not to mention Phyllis, credited as the Voice of Reason. "Why do the indie boys like women who sing like angels or children?" asks a jacket note; these women sound like people you hear talking on the street, every day.

8 ■ **Bush, "Everything Zen," from *Sixteen Stone* (Trauma)** Inflamed. Less ugly and less elegant than Nine Inch Nails, but more convincing.

9 ■ **Shawn Colvin, "Viva Las Vegas," on *Till the Night Is Gone—A Tribute to Doc Pomus* (Forward/Rhino)** Sheryl Crow really is everywhere: as if she can't help herself, Colvin turns "Viva Las Vegas" into "Leaving Las Vegas." And comes out ahead of the song.

10 ■ **Guy Debord, *Mémoires* (Les Belles Lettres, Paris)** When Debord shot himself last November 30, he had completed the return to print of almost all his published work, including this legendary book: a collage of commonplace illustrations and text fragments, none containing a word Debord had written, all overpainted by Asger Jorn in bright colors, the result being an accurate and poetic account of Debord's life in Paris in 1952 and 1953: a time and a place, as he wrote elsewhere, "where the negative

held court." The drifting streaks of paint, the looming fields of white space, the half-sentences chasing their missing endings and being forced to settle for yet another sentence's beginning—the pleasure of nostalgia was already there in 1958, when the book first appeared, and it is present now, along with the cold wit that led Debord to disguise an altogether readable book as an unreadable antibook. " 'I wanted to speak the language of my century,' " Debord quoted the last line of *Mémoires* in his 1993 introduction to this 2,300-copy reissue, not quite quoting himself. "I wasn't so concerned with being heard."

SUMMER 1995

1 ■ **K. McCarty, "Walking the Cow," on *Dead Dog's Eyeball: Songs of Daniel Johnston* (Bar None)** Late of Austin's Glass Eye, Kathy McCarty here dedicates herself to a whole album's worth of compositions by the Austin *idiot sacré*. Most often the oddity of the tunes falls short of their length, but McCarty's breathless dive into "Walking the Cow" comes without warning, and for its 3 minutes 13 seconds no warning could catch her. The singer has escaped from the asylum. She has you by the throat, and the only thing more crazy than her eyes is her reasonableness. You can't even croak back, but her voice is full, her madness audible only in the farthest curves of a bending phrase; a true rock 'n' roll string section raises a wall of sound and puts your back up against it. *You don't know me, but right now we have to walk the cow. You do understand this, don't you?* If you don't understand this, you do understand that the singer has only a second to get her words out before she forgets what they mean.

2 ■ **Beatles, "Baby It's You," from *Live at the BBC* (Apple/Capitol, recorded 1963)** "Cheat, cheat"—they get as much into those two words as the world got out of "A Day in the Life."

3 ■ **Richard Candida Smith, *Utopia and Dissent: Art, Poetry and Politics in California* (University of California)** This chronicle of

the emergence of an avant-garde in California after World War II maintains a magical balance between empathy and skepticism; it is a very long book that never begins to suggest it is exhausting its subject. While not effacing the events or cultural movements of the world at large, the book, like its subjects (in greatest detail, Kenneth Rexroth, Joan Brown, Jay DeFeo, Wallace Berman, Michael McClure, Gary Snyder, and Robert Duncan), escapes them. What comes forth is a sense of an attenuated but vibrant public life—even if the circle of friends you showed your work to was your public, even if your public life was a public secret, a secret you weren't sure you wanted to make public and likely as not couldn't make public even if the desire was there. "What was left then was to operate as a dream substratum within American society, influencing without being recognized. . . . The rejection of the world as it is flings one into an otherworldly limbo between heaven and hell. By choosing retreat the avant-garde transformed themselves into a reservoir of pure tendentiousness that would become increasingly attractive and relevant as the mechanisms for extracting consensus in American society collapsed. Like [DeFeo's] *The Rose*, the avant-garde of the beat era was less a definable image than a response waiting to be activated."

4 ▪ **Sally Timms, *To the Land of Milk & Honey* (Feel Good All Over)** Except for a romantic, retitled cover of Jackie DeShannon's 1964 "When You Walk in the Room," the 35-year-old Mekons veteran less sings her songs than drifts through them, world-weary, expecting nothing from the future but time. When she calls up an afternoon in Central Park with "the Grateful Dead performing for the Czar," she sounds far better acquainted with the latter than with the former.

5 ▪ **Laurie Anderson, *The Ugly One with the Jewels and Other Stories—A Reading from "Stories from the Nerve Bible"* (Warner Bros.)** The Book of Revelation, retold in the voice of *Goodnight Moon*. To begin with. Her best album.

6–7 ▪ **Andreas Ammer, FM Einheit and Ulrike Haage, *Apocalypse Live* (Reine Ego/ Rough Trade Records, Herne, Germany) and Yabby U, *King Tubby's Prophesy of Dub* (Blood & Fire reissue, Ducie House, Manchester, UK, recorded 1976)** More Revelation remakes, this time formally so, complete with ancient woodcuts and portraits of prophets and saints. *Apocalypse* is an English-German radio play, by turns hilarious and Wagnerian, with music from '50s refrigerator commercials, Bible movies, and the sound of collapsing mountains alternating with the spiels of an American huckster and a continental theologian, both selling the end of the world. *Prophesy* is a Jamaican meditation, positing the end of the world because the composer, Vivian Jackson, seems already to have survived the great event. As such the music is the perfection of a form, or a perfect statement of redundancy: all dub is a version of Revelation.

8 ▪ **Violent Green, *Eros* (Up)** Offering homages to Laurie Anderson and Patti Smith and sounding like neither, this rough three-piece is interested more in drama than in sound, more in sound than in songs; track by track they seem interested less in music than in ritual. Singer-guitarist Jennifer Olay might have a soulmate in Come's Thalia Zedek, but while Come's recent gestures toward conventional rhythms suggest an acknowledgment that a band is completed by an audience, Violent Green's conventional rhythms seem like a setup: eliciting the conventional expectations of a listener, the band can then dissolve them. The rhythms don't disappear, they simply cease to matter. As the disc moves on, what at first was vague begins to feel dangerous. Olay's deep, burred voice erases whatever face you might have mentally attached to it. That is the rite—the removal of all ego, all personality, the merging of whoever's playing and whoever's listening into a single, pagan smear: "the long slow suck," as Camille Paglia once called it.

9 ▪ **Elastica, *Elastica* (DGC)** Like Veruca Salt, the Breeders, and Belly, they're female-dominated and photogenic—here

the guy plays drums and looks like David Byrne. The difference is that they're English and the vocals are less cute, though even more colorless. The album could be an A+ senior thesis—on Wire, the Buzzcocks, and other avatars of arty punk—by a student who's got her professor's number; there's not a moment that hasn't been calculated, fussed over, and bled dry. One spin and the music is used up.

Like their market-niche peers, Elastica know how to preen. Like Veruca et al. they might have been designed for cover stories, even if all they have to sell is attitude—which is short of posture, which is short of stance, which is short of position, which is short of action, which is short of blood on the floor, which is to say short of Heavens to Betsy. The attitude Elastica and the others are selling is that the last thing on their minds is a good pop song, like Veruca Salt's "Seether"—cool, disdainful, hip, those high, high voices instantly catching your ear and then refusing to let go. Within days (if not hours) the performance has turned into an irritation that reveals its genius: this was a jingle before it was a song, and so effective a jingle that it's as if the number had already been licensed to promote something else. "Seether" is its own commercial, and what it's advertising is commercial space for the likes of Elastica, the Breeders, Belly, or Veruca Salt—in other words, the bands are their own commercials.

10 ▪ **Anheuser-Busch, Cross Roads Beer ("Where Substantial Flavor and Easy Drinking Meet")** Or, where Robert Johnson meets yet another incarnation of the Devil: in the TV commercial, as white folk frolic over this insipid beer, a Cream-style version of the Mississippi bluesman's 1936 signature tune pounds the message straight out of the frame. Who gets the money?

JANUARY 1997

1 ▪ **Michael Ventura, *The Death of Frank Sinatra* (Henry Holt)** Ventura's third novel: a Las Vegas family detective story that's nervous and delicate even in its most brutal scenes. The tale moves from the Bugsy Sie-

gel days to the present, catching the emergence of a culture made out of mob murder, sex clubs, atom-bomb tests, the specter of JFK, and Dean Martin's last drink. America's highest ideals rest on the same moral plane as the grimiest sleaze, *Showgirls'* Elizabeth Berkley mouthing phrases from Lincoln as she goes through the motions. Near the end of the book, Sinatra comes onstage, an old man, and makes a miracle: "Then on a high note the voice cracked, and for an instant the music soured, and the audience flinched as one person, but instead of retreating from that bad sound Sinatra leaned into it . . ." There's the feeling that in the American desert two utopias were founded, two great, queer cities that in some irreducible way remain as they began, outside the law—the other place being Salt Lake City.

2 ▪ **Sheryl Crow, "On the Outside," from *Songs in the Key of X: Music from and Inspired by the X Files* (Warner Bros.)** Her voice is slow, heavy, and subtle—conscious, not self-conscious, which is appropriate for this sliver of a really bad dream, the sort of dream that, when you wake, is about only one thing: your inability to remember anything but dread.

3 ▪ **Sarge, *Charcoal* (Mud Records)** Women speak the harsh, desperate language of Denis Johnson's *Jesus' Son* in the songs of this Illinois punk trio ("I walked into the bar where you hung out/24 and I still hadn't figured it out/Eight months pregnant and sick with all these lies") but there's a will to speak a more commonplace language in Elizabeth Elmore's singing and guitar playing. There's as much old Van Halen in her sound as Gang of Four.

4 ▪ **Mystery Science Theater 3000, "The Sinister Urge" (Comedy Central)** The film that the human and two robots are watching has something to do with '50s smut peddlers and a mad killer on the loose. Everything is hesitant and stumbling and clumsy, to the point where a zero-IQ cop surveys a crime scene and says, "There is . . ." And with his pause seemingly a wait for someone, anyone, to throw him his next

line, robot number one pipes up, perfectly matching Eric Burdon's pause at the beginning of the Animals' first big hit: ". . . a house, in New Orleans . . ." "That's why Ed Wood gets final cut," says the other robot.

5 ▪ **Bob Dylan, "All Along the Watchtower," from** *The Concert for the Rock and Roll Hall of Fame* **(Columbia)** For the moment, the only licensed recorded proof that what Dylan and his shocker of a combo (Winston Watson, Tony Garnier, Bucky Baxter, John Jackson) were doing onstage in 1995 was more than an illusion; and, until they release *Having a Rave Up with Bob Dylan*, the only proof that reinventing yourself in your fifties as a lead guitarist embracing syncopation as the source of all values is a brilliant idea.

6 ▪ **Collins Kids,** *Rockin' on T.V.* **(Krazy Kat, UK)** Like most rockabilly outfits without hits in their time, Larry and Lorrie don't come near their pseudolegend. For that matter, Larry was a clod. These thirty-one 1957–61 transcriptions are just OK—until the Kids get to Buddy Holly's "Oh Boy!" and the world blows up. Larry sings—and Lorrie hiccups into an orgasmic frenzy so absolute and unstoppable it can suck you into your speakers.

7 ▪ **Ellen Lupton and Elaine Lustig Cohen,** *Letters from the Avant Garde: Modern Graphic Design* **(Princeton Architectural Press)** Stationery, most of it from between the wars. The best of it is De Stijl with a Dada touch, as in the '20s work of Piet Zwart, whose motto was, "The more uninteresting a letter, the more useful it is to the typographer." It certainly sums up the letterhead he designed for the Netherlands Cable Works.

8 ▪ **R. L. Burnside,** *A Ass Pocket Of Whiskey* **(Matador)** Mississippi bluesman who makes John Lee Hooker sound like Kenneth Tynan gets together with the Jon Spencer Blues Explosion, who make Canned Heat sound like the Kronos Quartet. The results make Jon Spencer Blues Explosion records sound like Jon Spencer Blues Explosion records.

9 ▪ **Sleater-Kinney,** *Call the Doctor* **(Chainsaw)** Then put this on; you'll never hear the doctor call back, but by the time she does you won't need her, or you'll be beyond help. A punk breakout of unparalleled ferocity, body, and balance, and the best album of 1996.

10 ▪ **M. Dolors Genovès,** *Europa de postguerra, 1945–1965 Art després del diluvi* **(Postwar Europe, 1945–1965 Art after the deluge), a documentary video included in** *"Europa de postguerra, 1945–1965. Art després del diluvi"* **(Fundació "la Caixa" and Televisió de Catalunya, Barcelona, 1995)** All Genovès does is orchestrate stock footage from the postwar period—or rather she orchestrates the social war that followed the shooting war, using pop culture to undercut the authority and pomposity of official culture. Top of the pops: On *The Ed Sullivan Show*, Elvis Presley is performing "Hound Dog," smiling through the tinny kinescope sound. Genovès cuts simultaneously into the hard fullness of the studio recording of "Hound Dog" and to footage of Soviet commissars filling a steep auditorium, wildly pounding their fists as if in a mad attempt to keep time. The line "You said that you was high class, well, that was just a lie" comes up; Genovès cuts to shots of Eisenhower, the Pope, de Gaulle. And then back to Elvis, who, mission accomplished, takes a bow.

FEBRUARY 1997

1 ▪ DJ Shadow, *Endtroducing . . . .* (Mowax/ffrr) This all-sampled reflection of a "lifetime of vinyl culture" is best heard as a double LP; it's more of a *thing* than the CD version, takes up more space, gets in the way, makes you interrogate it more physically. Musically, it's a throwback, straight to the beginnings of recorded hip-hop—to Grandmaster Flash's 1980 "The Adventures of Grandmaster Flash on the Wheels of Steel." It's also absolutely modern—which is to say ambient-dreamy and techno-abstract. Quite brilliant throughout, it resurrects the body only on the 9:21

"Stem/Long Stem," which combines a gorgeous, unspeakably beckoning riff from the ether with what sounds like dialogue from the opening pages of an old James Ellroy mystery, just before everything gets really bad. Not to be confused with DJ Spooky, one of the great bores of our time.

2 ■ **John Parish & Polly Jean Harvey, "Who Will Love Me Now" (Island)** A fourth track sliding off the single "That Was My Veil"—a slow ballad, as if from the end of a war, a woman bidding farewell to everything she ever cared about. Very European, very cinematic, and unlike anything else Harvey has done.

3–4 ■ **The Rolling Stones, "You Can't Always Get What You Want" & "Sympathy for the Devil," from *The Rolling Stones Rock and Roll Circus* (Abkco CD and video)** Mick Jagger may have gone farther into his music than on this night in 1968, but if he did the proof has not survived.

5 ■ **Wendy Brenner, "My Ex-Fiancé" (essay in *The Oxford American*, August/September, 1996)** Her ex-fiancé ran a comedy club/avant-garde theater in Chicago; he was odd, scary, beautiful, sexually ambiguous, needy, and alluring. When he decided to move to Arizona, "to get his act together," Brenner recalls, "for a while I made plans to follow him, but in the end I stayed in Chicago, and shortly thereafter I met a young prosecutor who offered all my ex-fiancé could not: idealism, clear skin and eyes, strict heterosexuality, and a graduate degree from an Ivy League school. . . . He worshipped Bruce Springsteen and often quoted from his songs. He fought for the little guy. *The world tries to beat you down,* he said. *You've gotta fight to keep the wolves at bay. C'mon Wendy, champs like us, etc.*"

"So I moved in with him and everything went fine until an argument we had one evening that started with me saying I thought 'Born in the U.S.A.' was a joke, and ended with him holding me by the throat with one hand and cracking the back of my head against the hardwood floor, over and over, alternately spitting in my face and shouting at me that I would never under-stand Bruce because I'd never suffered, never had to live in the *real world*," as Bob Dole so famously put it last summer, unless it was respectable fascist novelist Mark Helprin speaking through him. "I'd grabbed for order, for safety," Brenner says. "I'd somehow managed to invite the wolf right inside my door, without even knowing it."

6 ■ **Iris Dement, *The Way I Should* (Warner Bros.)** DeMent's third album revolves around "Wasteland of the Free," a protest song that if not for its drive and sincerity would drown in its own disgust, and the title song, a ditty about self-affirmation that after two or three plays feels as big as a house. "I'll tell you why we won't play this," a DJ said to DeMent's husband about a new DeMent single, speaking of his station's format. "It's too country. We only play Real Country." (From Nicholas Dawidoff's *In the Country of Country*, Pantheon.)

7 ■ **Social Distortion, *White Light White Heat White Trash* (550 Music/Epic)** The kind of punk Mike Ness and his band play is now so traditional it might be folk music. They're living up to their name, both as effect and cause, as fate and goal.

8 ■ **Nirvana, "The End," from *Complete Cover Versions* (bootleg)** A 2:17 onstage compression of the 11:35 1967 Doors classic, here featuring Krist Novoselic and set mostly in a Waffle House. Surrounded by tunes originally cut by Kiss, the Wipers, Led Zeppelin, the Who, and the Meat Puppets, it's a reminder that the trio's disdain was as funny turned outward as it was awful turned inward.

9 ■ **Pauline Kael, *Conversations with Pauline Kael*, ed. Will Brantley (Jackson: The University Press of Mississippi)** Criticism—not how, but why.

10 ■ **Lars Von Trier, *Breaking the Waves* (October Films)** This is the worst sort of art-house swill—sub-Ingmar Bergman infused with the spirit of Joan Osborne's "One of Us"—but the intertitles introducing each "chapter" are weird. Glowing, romantic landscapes worked up with painter Per Kirkeby unfold almost like blooming flowers in time-lapse photography; each one is

accompanied by a pop song, so glossy and bright on the soundtrack it might be a commercial. The songs have something to do with the heroine's holy madness: when asked by her church elders if outsiders have ever brought anything good to her isolated, blasted Scottish village, she shyly replies, "Their music." Just as Mott the Hoople's "All the Way from Memphis" almost upends the movie as it begins, David Bowie's exquisite "Life on Mars?" almost seals it at the end. But with Chapter 5 comes Leonard Cohen's "Suzanne," in its dreadful, preening vanity really the perfect song for this film, and the fact that it was chosen at all should have given the game away. Nobody seems to be getting the joke.

MARCH 1997

1 ▪ **Warren Zevon,** *I'll Sleep When I'm Dead (An Anthology)* **(Rhino)** The songs on this dauntingly solid two-CD retrospective—roughly crafted, built-to-last artifacts of a rounder's wasted life—come across as an unacknowledged pop anchor, a bad conscience, a refusal to go away. Across the years the bravado of muscled rhythm may yield to melody, to the hidden surges in "Looking for the Next Best Thing" or "Suzie Lightning," but the change is just lines on a face; the singer doesn't change. In 1976 with "Desperados Under the Eaves," Zevon asks you to listen to the air conditioner humming in his room in the Hollywood Hawaiian Hotel—humming "Dixie" and "The Battle Hymn of the Republic" at the same time; in 1995 "Mutineer" is as defiant and as lost. Along the way there is a magnificent "Mohammed's Radio," a 1980 live recording that becomes the ruined bohemians' drinking song the Rolling Stones' "Salt of the Earth" was meant to be; on this all-night show you can hear the future calling even as the past pulls you down. "Even Jimmy Carter's got the highway blues," Zevon cries, half laughing, half shocked, and you can see the president looking at the Ayatollah Khomeini over one shoulder and Ronald Reagan over the other, standing somewhere in the middle of Nevada, the radiator of his empty limousine boiling over, his thumb in the air.

2 ▪ **Oval,** *94Diskont* **(Thrill Jockey)** The claims this German techno trio make in their manifestos/PR copy read like parodies of Mike Meyers' *Saturday Night Live* Prussian hipster Dieter hosting his poststructuralist dance party "Sprockets." Their fave aesthetic categories seem to be "offensive" and "disobident" (read that as "disobedient" at your peril; it's probably a new concept), and the calming, vaguely threatening ambient fields they depict are steps ahead of contemporaneous anti-dance music. Still, rather than the intended proofs of the obsolescence of music as we know it, what Oval make are proofs of the existence of a realm where music has always done its work, the subconscious.

3 ▪ **Georgina Boyes,** *The Imagined Village—Culture, Ideology and the English Folk Revival* **(Manchester University Press/St. Martin's)** Unsentimental throughout, and startling when Boyes turns over the ideological stone of folk authenticity circa 1936 and forces the insects beneath it into the light. The genteel folk-dance summer camps of a movement born with John Ruskin and Morris dancing made common cause with Nazism; the search for the eternal Folk at the heart of a true England turned into an openly fascist precursor of the present day Men's Movement, with bands of brothers possessed of "The Secret of Memory" and dancing the Sword Dance, deep in the woods around their leaping fires. All "are consumed," Rolf Gardiner wrote in *The English Folk Dance Tradition*, "by one fluid, electric, purging, flame of ecstasy, an exaltation, a cathartic frenzy, impossible to convey in words to one who has not experienced it." And then it gets worse.

4–5 ▪ **Koerner, Ray & Glover,** *Blues, Rags & Hollers* **(Red House reissue, 1963) and** *One Foot in the Groove* **(Tim/Kerr)** Thirty-four years ago, a Twin Cities folk blues trio—guitarists John Koerner and Dave Ray, harmonica player Tony Glover—put out an album that today feels like ice breaking.

The follow-up, recorded live on home ground, sounds not late but patient, all practical humor ("France Blues," "Pick Poor Robin Clean") and, with "Shenandoah," a nostalgia beyond dreams.

6 ▪ **Waco Brothers, *Cowboy in Flames* (Bloodshot)** Deconstruct the signifiers in the group name, the record title, and the label and you're halfway through the music, British country without apologies. The only stuff not coded is the thrill, the ride.

7 ▪ **Mick Lasalle, "No Love Lost for Worst of '96" (*San Francisco Chronicle*, film wrap-up, 3 January)** On *The Evening Star*, "with Juliette Lewis, looking as fresh-faced and wholesome as a dead blues singer . . ."

8 ▪ **John J. Strauss and Ed Decter, Creators/executive producers, *Chicago Sons* (NBC, Wednesdays, 8:30 PM)** Speaking of dead blues singers, this sitcom about three bumbling brothers made me laugh a couple of times, but it hit home in one of the promos that aired earlier—where behind the it's-a-guy-thing antics you could hear someone turning Robert Johnson's 1936 "Sweet Home Chicago" into theme music indistinguishable from the Rembrandts' "I'll Be There for You" on *Friends*.

9 ▪ **Wieden and Kennedy, Ad for Nike's Air Penny Basketball Shoe (*The Times Magazine*, London, 23 November 1996)** "This is Penny Hardaway," it says next to a small picture of the Orlando Magic star. "He is not a marketing commodity and he is not a puppet"—i.e., *shut up*. Then the piece gets down to business: "LISTEN: If you have a toothache, you don't call an interior decorator. If you're dirty, you don't turn on the vacuum cleaner. If you make athletic shoes, you don't ask referees or podgy sports writers how to make them better. If this is not perfectly clear we can come to your house and spray paint it on your walls in English, French, Italian or Esperanto." In other words, if you don't understand this ad, call Nike and they'll send you an interior decorator?

10 ▪ ***New York Times* (national edition), Dada typesetting in article on Marcel Janco ("Bucharest Rediscovers Houses by a Mod-** ernist," by Jane Perlez, 14 January) "Tristan Tzara and Janco were among the founders of the anti-bourgeois Dada movement in 1916 when they were young art students in Zurich. (In Romanian, Dada movement in 1916 when they were young art students in Zurich. (In Romanian, Dada is 'yes' said twice Dada is 'yes' said twice . . .)."

APRIL 1997

1 ▪ **Annie Lennox, "Walking on Broken Glass," from *Diva* (Arista, 1992)** A decent hit the first time around, now resurfacing on the radio apparently in answer to some request from outer space, this is a perfect pop record, falling somewhere between Marc Cohn's "Silver Thunderbird" and Connie Francis' "Lipstick on Your Collar": a simple, increasingly impassioned arrangement that by the final chorus has all of its parts battling for the right to save the singer from the hell of her lost love. I don't think they do, though.

2 ▪ **Sleater-Kinney, *Dig Me Out* (Kill Rock Stars)** Dense and crowded, even if new drummer Janet Weiss' quickened beat lets the combo in on more conventional and more shapely rhythms than they've used before. Carrie Brownstein presses nagging guitar lines that match the nyah-nyah-nyahs of the counter-vocals she pits against Corin Tucker's leads; as a one-woman chorus Brownstein is half imperious Greek, half impatient Shangri-La, but on "The Drama You've Been Craving" she steps out of the background and she and Tucker leap into nameless wildness. The pressure the band has used to shock small clubs around the country is there in "One More Hour," "Turn It Up," and "Not What You Want," this time building from the inside, but pressure is far too one-dimensional a word to describe the attack that takes place in the last cut, "Jenny." By the end there seems to be nothing standing, not even the singer, not in the desert she's made of the house in which she began.

3 ▪ **Dennis Miller, rant on UFOs (*Dennis Miller Live*, HBO, January 31)** "In 1947, some-

thing crashed in Roswell, New Mexico. Some believe four aliens were discovered at the site, and that their remains, as well as their flying saucer, are being held in an Air Force installation a hundred miles north of Las Vegas known as Area 51. Ufologists insist that the four aliens and their manager Brian Epstein . . ."

4 ■ **Cliff Carlisle,** *Blues Yodeler and Steel Guitar Wizard* **(Arhoolie Folklyric)** 1930–37 recordings from a man who walked in the footsteps of Jimmie Rodgers (gone by 1933) and whose singing and lap slide guitar playing relaxed into a luxuriousness Rodgers himself could never afford.

5 ■ **Scottie Priesmeyer,** *The Cheaters— The Walter Scott Murder* **(Tula Publishing)** In 1966 in St. Louis, Walter Scott sang the lead on the weirdly named Bob Kuban and the In-Men's "The Cheater." It reached #12 on the national charts, and though it was catchy, even bouncy, there was something insinuating about it too—something disturbing. "Watch out for the cheater," Scott sang, and while the song played, cheaters seemed to be everywhere, sizing you up. The follow-up album died at #129. The In-Men broke up and went straight, Scott went solo, and nobody ever had another hit— until 1983, when Scott disappeared. Three years later, his body was pulled from a cistern on property owned by Scott's wife's new husband, a bullet in his back. What makes Priesmeyer's ill-written account of this story compelling is not its irony (after years of the case against Scott's accused killers going nowhere, Bob Kuban formed a band to play a benefit for Tim Braun's campaign for County prosecutor; Braun won, and then won the case), but its griminess, its low-rent drift away from even small-time glitz and back to the world where ordinary people commit murder for ordinary reasons, to get what they want, right now.

6 ■ **Chris Isaak,** *Baja Sessions* **(Reprise)** Never mind smalltime—playing the worst donkey-fuck emporium in Tijuana, Isaak would still give off the aura of lost millions.

7 ■ **TBWA/Chiat/Day, Jack's Jack in the Box commercials (all networks)** Dressed in

floppy clothes like a '90s Ozzie Nelson, the big white roundhead was everywhere as the year began, high-fiving with other dads at his kid's football game, etc., but he only came clean at the gate of Colonel Sanders' mansion, eager to get the Colonel (didn't he *die?*) to taste-test his new Spicy Chicken Sandwich. "The Colonel says go away," says a voice on the intercom, so Jack turns to go: "He says leave the sandwich." So Jack leaves the bag and palms the food. "Psyche!" he says, just like a twelve-year-old who's got it totally down, the smart-aleck comeback turning Jack's huge, bland grin smug and even slightly sinister. This is real subliminal advertising; in the same way that Joe Camel is a penis, Jack is Bill Gates.

8 ■ **Ray Charles, "I Don't Need No Doctor" (ABC Records, 1966/KPIX-FM, San Francisco)** Running the dial on the car radio, about once a week I can't believe my luck: tuning into the middle of this relentless, unanswerable plea to the gods of rhythm and love ("He gave me a medicated lotion/But it didn't *soooooooothe* my emotion!"), and then Dr. Nancy Snyderman comes on announcing her medical advice show, sounding as if she knows perfectly well one potential patient is out of her reach.

9 ■ **The Rickets, et al.,** *Yo Yo a Go Go* **(Yoyo)** There's good stuff on this double CD of live recordings from Yoyo's 1994 Olympia punk fest—Heavens to Betsy's primitive "Ax Men," Mecca Normal's scary "I Walk Alone"—but what moved me was a photo on the inside of the package. It shows Nikki McClure, dressed in a white shift and a funny hat, holding a big black guitar and squinting into the sun, Tae Won Yu of Kicking Giant, fingering his guitar and looking as at-home as anyone could, and Calvin Johnson of Beat Happening in shorts, staring off to one side. They're in the middle of main street, part of a parade, thirty yards or so up from the Vernor's float—and more than anything else I know, this picture of patient smiles captures punk: not as art or commerce but as appearance, as the pursuit of a public life on a human scale.

10 ▪ **Marianne Faithfull, *20th Century Blues* (RCA Victor)** In the immortal words of Bela Lugosi in Ed Wood's *Glen or Glenda*: "Bevare! Take care! Bevare!"

MAY 1997

1 ▪ **Eleventh Dream Day, *Eighth* (Thrill Jockey)** Chicago's most passionate rock 'n' roll trio on the city's most avant-garde label—it makes sense, because in its fourteenth year Eleventh Dream Day has moved off the stage and into the realm of a certain abstraction. Muscle and drums are still present, but as gestures and whispers; the pace is slowed. Timeless folk talismans—"salty dog," "She'll be comin' down the mountain, when she comes"—appear in the music like nearly meaningless fragments of an idea that lurks seductively behind them. The doubled voices of guitarist Rick Rizzo and drummer Janet Bean can be as bitter as an all-night argument in its last hour and as ordinary as a conversation overheard on the street, pursuing a realism beyond the reach or perhaps even the desire of anyone else currently making pop records; with bassist Douglas McCombs the whole of their music seems to revolve around a core of receding visions of honor and right, and to take its spirit from getting up in the morning and going to work.

2 ▪ **Susan Subtle Dintenfass, curator, *Hello Again! A New Wave of Recycled Art and Design* (Oakland Museum of California, through July 27)** There's anonymous tramp art from cigar boxes and generic third world unart from automobile tire sandals on up. There's Jan Yager's *American Breastplate*, 1995–97, fashioned from found crack vials and syringes, and Salvatore and Marie's *Alice*, 1996, a hilarious little walking clock made out of bent spoons and a pretty cat food can. And outstripping everything else is Nule Giulini's untitled wedding dress: classically lowcut, with a twenty-foot train, composed entirely of used underwear, which is to say the bride wore gray.

3 ▪ **Lush, "Last Night (Darkest Hour Mix)," on *City of Industry* soundtrack (Quango)** From a gangster movie starring the fearsome Timothy Hutton, praying mantis music: a complete '50s French film noir, as remade last year in Hong Kong. Second feature, same genre: Tricky's "Overcome."

4 ▪ **Charlatans, "Jack of Diamonds," on *The Amazing Charlatans* (Big Beat reissue, 1965–68)** They were a quintet of Edwardian gunslingers who came down from Virginia City to kick off San Francisco's psychedelic years, but their truest music was old-timey, from their epic revision of "Alabama Bound" to this crude, nervous, indelible 1965 rehearsal, a version of "The Cuckoo" that has all the art of a cowboy standing up at a campfire and giving a speech.

5–6 ▪ **Dan Bern, *Dog Boy Van* and *Dan Bern* (Work/Sony)** Bern doesn't want you to call him "The New Bob Dylan," and for good reason. "Talkin' Alien Abduction Blues" (which really ought to have been called "I Shall Be Free 10%") is "Talkin' World War III Blues" without wit or bite, while "Estelle," Bern's liveliest, most physical performance, is also a shameless rip-off of Dylan's "Brownsvile Girl"/"New Danville Girl." Otherwise "New Irritatingly Plain-Folks But Obnoxiously Self-Regarding Post-Generational Voice of His Generation" is more like it: Bern isn't afraid of big subjects like Kurt Cobain's suicide or the Oklahoma City bombing, and he isn't afraid of triteness or sententiousness.

7 ▪ **Shirelles, on *Homicide* (NBC, February 21)** Having their 1961 "Dedicated to the One I Love" playing in the background while Detective John Munch investigated the murder of his high-school crush Helen Rosenthal was an almost obvious touch, but the cleanness of Shirley Alston's voice cutting into the slack, middle-aged bodies that moved through the story was as cruel as life. It's unlikely anybody anticipated the girls popping up in the last fifteen minutes to apply "Mama Said" to a Pepto-Bismol commercial, though.

8 ▪ **Alison Krauss & Union Station, *So Long So Wrong* (Rounder)** Fine, with "It Doesn't Matter," a will o' the wisp in pitch

dark—and not far enough removed from the most frightening moment of this year's Grammy Awards show, beyond the android undulations of Celine Dion. That came when Krauss and her band joined Vince Gill and Patty Loveless for the gospel classic "Working on a Building." That is, Krauss was announced, but where was she? In place of the most soulful bluegrass singer of our day stood a pallid, rail-thin blonde, her voice a ghost. It was as if, after Krauss nailed the country charts last year with *Now That I've Found You*, somebody read her the riot act: Honey, you can go all the way, but only if you lose thirty pounds first.

9 ▪ **David Lynch, *Lost Highway* (October Films)** This movie has its flaws. Hank Williams' shadow title song is not acknowledged, the appearance of the "Lost Highway Hotel" is cheesy, as if the film is running its own ad, and the product placement is sloppy (Full Sail ale makes sense at the fancy party, not for Gary Busey's biker). But the self-loathing that never really leaves Bill Pullman's face—the look he perfected playing chump husbands in *Malice* and *The Last Seduction*—never leaves the picture, either. It's a grimace that somehow sums up American nihilism at the end of the American century, a sneer that contains knowledge of all the secrets that aren't worth telling.

10 ▪ **Richard Linklater, *SubUrbia* (Gramercy Pictures)** Based on Eric Bogosian's devastating portrait of lost youth trapped in the decaying wreckage of the modernity of our nation, or, as a patron put it as the credits rolled, "How many times have we seen this movie?"

SUMMER 1997

1 ▪ **Carter the Unstoppable Sex Machine, "Johnny Cash" on *A World Without Dave* (Cooking Vinyl America)** In the midst of a typically sour travelogue through the post-Thatcher, presumptively pre-Blair (or for that matter post-Blair) ruins of British social life, a pause in a bar. No matter how bitter the singer feels ("The people here should

be in a zoo," he mutters), nothing can rush him, nothing can shade the love he still feels for what life should be. The names this duo use—CUSM, "Jim Bob," "Fruitbat"—have always been there to disguise the fact that most of all they want to break your heart.

2 ▪ **Spice Girls, On *Saturday Night Live*, April 12 (NBC)** Yeah, sure. But this bad?

3 ▪ **John Sheinbaum, "Think About What You're Tryin' to Do to Me: Rock Historiography and Race-Based Dialectics," at "Re-pre-sent-ing Rock: An Interdisciplinary Conference on Rock Music and Culture" (Duke University, April 6)** In the midst of a passionate, carefully prepared presentation on the critical construction of Aretha Franklin's "Think" as craft and the Beatles' "Eleanor Rigby" as art, Sheinbaum, a graduate student at Cornell, noted that while Paul McCartney had asked producer George Martin for a string arrangement in the mode of Vivaldi, what he got "was a lot closer to a Bernard Herrmann film score." Sheinbaum played a few seconds of the Beatles record; the lights were on, but suddenly everyone in the room was watching *Psycho*.

4 ▪ **Tarnation, *Mirador* (Reprise)** There's something of Deborah Kara Unger's face as she appears in *Crash* in Paula Frazer's voice: a faraway coldness that's both alluring and repellent. Neither the singer nor the actress seems absolutely human. The difference is that the deaths Frazer has in her heart are versions of the Carter Family or Roy Orbison, while the deaths Unger's Catherine has in hers are just versions of herself.

5 ▪ **Big Red Ball, "Drown," on *Stuck on AM: Off the Record in Minneapolis* (TRG)** On a compilation of on-air recordings for the best college radio station imaginable—Radio K, 770 AM in the Twin Cities, daylight hours only—a harsh, accelerating chant from the 1994 "three-Lisa-lineup" of a defunct band who here fall somewhere between Grace Slick's Great Society in 1966 and the Gang of Four in 1978. I heard it on the radio, along with a solid hour's worth of

other knockouts I'd never heard on the radio, among them a Frank Zappa rant, an eerily distant Heavens to Betsy track, and a '50s pep talk on clean living.

6 ▪ Fleetwood Mac, "London Live '68" (Thunderbolt/Magnum) An audience recording, maybe even a bootleg, and a zero, until halfway in guitarist Peter Green locks into Willie Dixon's "I Don't Know Which Way to Go" and you realize he never will.

7–8 ▪ Bettie Serveert, Dust Bunnies (Matador) Cool. But their "I'll Keep It With Mine," from the I Shot Andy Warhol soundtrack (Atlantic), is not cool. It's sweet, but inside that sweetness Carol van Dijk is so defeated she's singing less to any lover than to all the now-dead souls in Mary Harron's movie, swaying back and forth so relentlessly that a song Bob Dylan wrote thirty-two years ago for Nico sounds like a song Liz Phair wrote for herself.

9 ▪ Paradisette (Stockholm), Diesel for Successful Living postcard (free postcard racks everywhere) In his day, Stalin had the heads of purged generals cut out of photos and new faces pasted in; now Diesel, for reasons of its own, offers the famous Yalta photo of Churchill, Roosevelt, and Uncle Joe, all smiling, and, through the magic of digital technology, with superleggy babes draped all over them. I think it's a subliminal ad for the Spice Girls—proof that along with the present, they rule the past.

10 ▪ Dana Bryant, et al., Time and Love: The Music of Laura Nyro (Astor Place) The '60s singer-songwriter received respectful notices when she died earlier this year, but don't let that fool you: as this tribute album insists, saint was always her shtick. "Her concerts were religious experiences," writes producer Peter Gallway. "Laura gowned, surrounded by roses, alone in purple light at the grand piano. Her style, her holiness, her reclusivity, her high standards became the stuff of legend. Her records were even more intimate, more natural"—and the world recoils almost as one: "'More natural?'" Many of those who wouldn't recoil are included on this pre-posthumous production: admirers from Jane Siberry to

Sweet Honey in the Rock, Rosanne Cash to Suzanne Vega. They all sound mannered and self-conscious (gosh, wonder why), all offering little encomiums of their own. Only Lisa Germano avoids embarrassment: "I thought it'd be refreshing to do a song about somebody else's boyfriend for a change."

SEPTEMBER 1997

1 ▪ John Cale, Eat/Kiss: Music for the Films by Andy Warhol (Hannibal) Chamber music that in the eleven-movement sequence for Kiss (1963) runs from the austere to the severely trashy. The four-part piece for Eat (1964) is deadly dull, but so much so you hardly notice it's there, or that the movies aren't.

2 ▪ Amy Sedaris, Incident at Cobbler's Knob, by the Talent Family (Lincoln Center Festival, New York City, July 8–11) Sedaris plays both a witch (Theresa from Flathurst) and an animal (Donkey) as hillbillies, and she plays hillbillies as creatures who have discovered that the quickest route to true communication is obscenity: as weary irony, as a wallow in the mud, it doesn't matter. Not only does the donkey prove Sedaris' case, unlike almost every other character in this little play, it lives.

3 ▪ Kenny Bill Stinson & the Ark-La Mystics, Festival of American Folklife (Washington DC, July 4) Performing as part of the "Mississippi Delta" subsection—along with Memphis legend Rufus Thomas and some pretty bad blues players—this loose and rangy rockabilly outfit had the right song for Independence Day: Chuck Berry's "Back in the U.S.A.," so full of longing you could almost feel you weren't home. With leader Stinson all ease and guitarist Kevin Gordon all effort, the band got where it meant to go every time. My favorite moment came not with Stinson's from-the-ground-up Jerry Lee Lewis covers or Gordon's own "Blue Collar Dollar," but when Stinson claimed drummer Paul Griffith's hometown as Waterproof, Louisiana—probably the last thing you could call any

town in Louisiana, let alone one in the delta. It's not on any map I've got, but maybe that's where the second part of the band's name comes in.

4 ▪ **Jonathan Lethem, As She Climbed Across the Table (Doubleday)** A third novel that starts slowly but turns out to be as good as its title—if not quite as sexy.

5 ▪ **Saints, "Messin' with the Kid," from The Most Primitive Band in the World (Hot/ Restless)** The Saints were Australia's original punk band; their 1977 *I'm Stranded* seemed definitive on release. This 1974 recording has more in common with what Peter Laughner was doing with Pere Ubu in Cleveland about the same time: striking matches in a self-created dankness, the dankness courtesy of the Rolling Stones' "Sway."

6 ▪ **Don Bolles, Don Bolles Presents "I'm Just the Other Woman," MSR Madness Vol. #4).** "Song-poem music," states producer Don Bolles of the results of the small-ad scam where frustrated small-ad readers are seduced into sending off their heartfelt scribblings to a concern that will "set them to music," for a very reasonable fee, "is one of the richest motherlodes of pure unfiltered glorious *wrongness* to be found in any field of human endeavor. I believe in that statement so firmly that I am willing to die for it." Now *that,* you might say to the former drummer of LA's by-now nearly mythical Germs, is *punk*—but only before you've played Bolles' compilation of what the MSR company did for its would-be George Gershwins and Neil Sedakas. Some of the numbers—mildly insane rambles sung as if they were Tony Bennett album filler—are charmingly odd. Then you come up against "The Will of God," written by Dan Ashwander, sung pleasantly enough by Keith Bradford. This, you accept some time after you've realized it, is God Himself's attempt to get Himself a hit record, while also stopping "the evil German race" and its plan for "a secret Nazi dictatorship," a pairing that as Bradford renders it could almost be "moon" and "spoon."

7 ▪ **Alan Lomax, producer, Southern Journey (Rounder)** A thirteen-volume reissue of Lomax's historic recordings of gospel, blues, breakdowns, etc., and the Heisenberg Principle was never more in effect: the sound is as sterile as the performances are formal.

8 ▪ **Guided by Voices, "I am a Tree," from Mag Earwhig! (Matador)** It'd be a step up.

9 ▪ **Midway Stadium/Ticketmaster, advertisement for upcoming concert (City Pages, June 18)** You know how in the ads for once-mighty rock heroes now reduced to playing local bars you've never heard of, the promoter always sticks the title of the one big hit under the marquee name, since you might remember the song even if you've forgotten who did it: *Every Mother's Son ("Come on Down to My Boat")*—Gino's No Cover One Nite Only? But this was a shock, and for a show at the Minnesota State Fair, no less:

> Featuring . . . IN PERSON
> "Sensational!!"
> BOB
> DYLAN
> "Blowing in the Wind"

Not to mention that it's "Blowin'," not "Blowing."

10 ▪ **Anonymous, altered Travel Guard International travel insurance vending machine (Oakland Airport, April 7)** As TRA ELVIS-URANCE, naturally. Or unnaturally.

OCTOBER 1997

1–2 ▪ **Daft Punk, Homework (Virgin) and Various Artists, KAOS Theory: 89.3 Olympia Community Radio (K)** Ages ago there was a record called something like "Radio KAOS!"—a satire of hysterical Top 40 DJs so on the mark it jumped like the best radio station on earth. Started in 1973, broadcasting out of Evergreen State College in Washington state, KAOS-FM, here represented in a compilation of on-air performances, is at least 89.3 percent for real. ("I was going out with Henry Ford/And you, you were seeing Henry Thoreau," Matthew Hattie Hein and Christine Denk recall on

"I'll Never Learn." "I said, 'We've got a lot in common.'") But it's Daft Punk who truly act out the broadcast of dreams. The best pop group in the history of Paris—not that there's been much competition since the days of Royer Collard and the Doctrinaires—this techno duo works with unparalleled muscle and depth. Their textures are thick, their sound all but bottomless, and unlike the currently more celebrated Prodigy and Chemical Brothers, musically they never preen. Listening, you feel as if you're tuning in to a broadcast that began long ago and will circle around long after you've forgotten how to find your way back to its unmarked spot on the dial.

3 ▪ Linda Scott, "Don't Bet Money Honey" (Canadian American, 1961, on various collections) For "You Don't Own Me," Lesley Gore is credited with the first breath of feminism in rock 'n' roll—the first female "fuck off." Coming off the pleasingly gooey "I've Told Every Little Star," this favorite of Arthur Godfrey, later a music teacher at the New York Christian Academy, had it down two years earlier, and with a cooler tone. With her small voice shaping the title phrase—"Don't bet money, honey/Our love will last"—it's as if she's just in it for the sex.

4 ▪ Bharati Mukherjee, Leave it to Me (Knopf) Mukherjee's last book, *The Holder of the World*, is a great visionary novel. Complete with a courtroom "That was no lady, that was my wife!" joke, this is more like a comic book—starring adopted Debby DiMartino as self-named Devi Dee, fearless wisecracking avenger bent on the unmasking and destruction of her birth parents. There's lots of cheap sex and violence, but what really inflames twenty-three-year-old Devi, prospecting in a Bay Area milieu dominated by her parents' generation, is sanctimony: that old '60s canard that anyone who wasn't there was born too late. Her parents abandoned her in India, on the old pot trail—how could they? "Think Vietnam," says Ham, a Berkeley film producer Devi has seduced because Jess, a woman who was Ham's lover before Devi was conceived and might be his lover

still, might also be Devi's mother. "Rent the *Apocalypse Now* video if you can't think. You made your life one continuous flying fuck or you didn't survive the times." "And how do you protest the war by doing dope on an alien continent?" Devi asks herself. "That didn't make sense." But "It had to Jess in her twenties; it still did. It made all the sense in the world to anyone her age, Ham's age . . . those who had survived and owned up to what war'd really done for them, how it'd freed them to be themselves, to curse and fuck and burn and loot, to kill or die, to feel superior while having fun."

5 ▪ Beezus, Lives of the Saints (Mud) This Champaign-Urbana female trio are fabulous complainers ("Buttercup") and world-class leapers. Witness their doubled version of "Rebel Girl," a strummed 1:14 on Joe Hill's Wobbly-era original and 2:34 worth of grunge on Bikini Kill's 1992 rewrite. Who else has realized both songs hinge on the question of the right clothes?

6 ▪ 10,000 Maniacs, "More Than This" (Geffen) Tiresias had been both man and woman; when asked which was capable of greater pleasure, he said woman. Less covering than joining Bryan Ferry's stilled and drifting erotic reverie—with Roxy Music in 1982, his highest moment—Mary Ramsey makes the case for perfect equality.

7 ▪ Starlet, From the One You Left Behind (Parasol) Very catchy Swedish boy pop that has no trouble rising to its titles: "Girlfriend," "Wendy," "Pin-up." Two steps away from the *Friends* soundtrack, but only one step away from the irresistible Norwegian boy pop of a-ha's "Take on Me."

8 ▪ Johnny Green and Garry Barker, with illustrations by Ray Lowry, A Riot of Our Own—Night and Day with the Clash (Indigo, London) The tour diary is not the richest music-book genre. This touching, angry, uproarious tale sustains 238 pages because it never lets go of the notion that as one day follows another something more than a pop group's career might be at stake.

9 ▪ Ani DiFranco, Dilate and Living in Clip (Righteous Babe) Alanis Morissette may have glommed her act from DiFranco. It'd be to DiFranco's credit if she made Morissette sound like an unwitting self-parody, but for that you have to go to the Morissette-sound-alike Sprite commercial.

10 ▪ Bob Dylan, *Time Out of Mind* (Columbia) A Western. It starts with Clint Eastwood's face at the end of *Unforgiven*, then turns around and heads back east like bad weather.

NOVEMBER 1997

1–2 ▪ Kelly Hogan, "The Great Titanic," on *Rudy's Rockin' Kiddie Caravan* (TNT) and William and Versey Smith: "When that Great Ship Went Down," 1927, on *Anthology of American Folk Music*, ed. Harry Smith (Smithsonian Folkways six-CD reissue) The Smiths' street-singer chant is one of the most primitive—or primeval—morality plays in a set that works as a map of Gothic America. But seventy years later lead vocalist Kelly Hogan, also credited with "barstool legs and folding chair," and "storytelling" vocalist and guitarist Andy Hopkins give no ground in their contribution to a *Rudy and Gogo World Famous Cartoon Show* collection of twenty-two old folk ditties ("This Old Man," "Home on the Range," etc.) rendered by a crew suspiciously loaded with Mekons types. "Le's do it," snarls a scratchy male voice to introduce Hogan's clear alto; with notes breaking up around her, she sets the stage for a staticky news report by Hopkins as Shine, according to legend the only black person aboard the officially whites-only *Titanic*, and the first off. "It was sad when the great ship went down," Hogan glows at the end, all roaring glee. With the rich passengers sinking to the bottom of the sea, it's as if she's discovered the one time trickle-down economics actually worked.

3 ▪ Christian Schad, *Marietta*, 1916, in "Christian Schad: 1894–1982," curated by Tobia Bezzola (Kunsthaus Zürich through November 9; Städtische Galerie, Munich, from November 26) The Zurich Dadaist and inventor of the photogram found his true calling as a portraitist, and he found it early, in

this devastatingly unstable picture of an archetypal Central European bohemian cabaret singer. Marietta was a real person, but here, with the painting's cubist fragments at once drawn to the center of the canvas by the force of Marietta's eyes and driven away from it by the threat her eyes carry, she is also her own twentieth century: born out of the brow of Hedda Gabler, crossing the bridge of the world war hand in hand with her contemporary Emmy Hennings, soon to fix the world in her gaze in the person of Louise Brooks.

4 ▪ Patsy Cline, *Live at the Cimarron Ballroom* (MCA) Cut July 21, 1961, at Cline's first show after a near-fatal auto accident. As her studio recordings couldn't do, the rough, brassy set catches the spirit of a woman who never got around to apologizing for anything.

5 ▪ Miranda July, *10 Million Hours a Mile* (Kill Rock Stars) This serious-looking woman comes up to you on the street and starts telling you about her philosophy of life and half an hour later you're still listening.

6 ▪ Waco Brothers, "Revolution Blues," on *Do You Think About Me?* (Bloodshot) In 1974 on Neil Young's *On the Beach* this Manson Family manifesto was lumbering, sardonic, even smug. Now, with the sound of time running out matching Jon Langford's race through scattered images of dune-buggy attack squadrons and dead dogs on million-dollar lawns, the reach for the end of the world in the music suggests a Waco Brother not credited here: David Koresh.

7 ▪ J. Walter Thompson agency, Alan Jackson's commercial for Ford Trucks (all networks) You've got the smarmiest country singer—and one of the richest—smiling down from under his Stetson with "If I had money/I'll tell you what I'd do" as the inescapable rhythm of K.C. Douglas' holy "Mercury Blues" pours out of the rewrite and Jackson promises he'd buy two Fords. The wrong singer for a song is one thing, but you can't use a car song for the wrong *car*.

8 ▪ Brown-Eyed Soul, The Sound of East L.A., Vols. 1–3 (Rhino) This smooth, warming, endlessly surprising project documents not a genre but a sensibility: less the records young people made in the barrio in the mid '60s, when the southern California Chicano community passed through the shock of self-recognition, than the records people liked—the music people used to tell each other who they were. So there's hot rock from the Olympics, cool soul from Peaches and Herb, jam-it-up stompers from local heroes Thee Midnighters and the Premiers, funk from War, searing blues from Johnny "Guitar" Watson, the still heartbreaking, still weird "Image of a Girl" by the Safaris (a surf group)—and what links almost everything here is a certain restraint, the sense that a whispered code word will travel further than a shout.

9–10 ▪ Lynne Dawson/Rolling Stones, September 6 (all networks/KFOG-FM, San Francisco) You chose your own moments at Diana's funeral, or they chose you, but on my day soprano Dawson's impassioned reading of Verdi's Requiem—as alarming for the way she turned the pages of the sheet music as for the faraway notes she hit as if they were speeches from *Wuthering Heights*—took on a new cast a few hours later, when the first, high, solo, female chorus of "You Can't Always Get What You Want" stepped off the radio. Whoever the song's first voice is, instantly it was inescapably Dawson; when Mick Jagger came in for the first verse, the song had already said what it had to say.

JANUARY 1998

1 ▪ Roger McGuinn, Jeff Tweedy, Jay Bennett, at "Revelations of Tradition: Harry Smith's *Anthology of American Folk Music* and Its Legacy" (Wolf Trap, Vienna, VA, October 25, 1997) To close a rather stereotypical folk revue, the former leader of the Byrds and two members of Wilco found the heart of Dock Boggs' implacable "Sugar Baby" in an instant; with Tweedy singing and McGuinn getting a pulse on his acoustic

twelve-string, it was as if the song had caught them, not the other way around. After a warm McGuinn vocal on "Springfield Mountain" ("1761," McGuinn said; "the first indigenous folk ballad to gain national currency," Alan Lomax writes), Tweedy took up Richard "Rabbit" Brown's "James Alley Blues." The Boggs and Brown originals, both dating to 1927, are among the most determined and idiosyncratic recordings ever made in this country; they ought to be uncoverable, and as far as I know up to this night they were. Tweedy's simple audaciousness in taking them on was admirable enough; to hear him make them his own, without apparent reach or guile, casually shifting lyrics to his liking, ignoring the hellfire of Boggs' cadence or Brown's flatly untouchable orchestration in favor of his own rhythms, his own pace, was like a dream, and it came off as a feat about as remarkable as collecting the mail.

2 ▪ Uncle Tupelo, "I Wish My Baby Was Born," from *March 16–20, 1992* (Rockville) On record, the only Jeff Tweedy performance that comes close to the haunts at Wolf Trap he grasped like brothers.

3 ▪ The Doors, *Box Set* (Elektra 4-CD) Hard, cruel, ridiculous, mostly unreleased, with a cold, thrilling "Crystal Ship" from a crummy 1967 nightclub tape and 1965 demo of "Hello, I Love You" that proves the awful no. 1 hit actually began life as a decent song.

4 ▪ Adam Green, *Adam Green's Book of Hollow Days* (Kensington Books) New Year's Day to New Year's Eve with Chicago's sourest cartoonist. Stops dead on Father's Day—Joseph: "Now Jesus, you be home by nine." "Shut up! You're not my real dad!"

5 ▪ Bardo Pond, *Lapsed* (Matador) The Cowboy Junkies pull a Heaven's Gate and then realize the only way to communicate from the other side is with forty-seven minutes of unrelieved feedback, fuzztone, and moaning; for the first time, they sound alive.

6 ▪ George Garrett, *The King of Babylon Shall Not Come Against You* (Harcourt Brace) Early in the first Clinton administration, a reporter goes home to Paradise Springs, Florida, to write a book about an inexplicable local sex-and-gospel double killing. It took place as Martin Luther King, Jr. was assassinated in Memphis and must somehow be the other side of the '68 coin. That the premise makes sense neither at the beginning nor the end of Garrett's novel doesn't stop him from letting a zoo of characters rant and cogitate their way through the mysteries of history and time. The Paradise Springs librarian was three in 1968, but what interests her is the way in her life "1968" might as well have been 1776: "Even though most of the cultural icons and artifacts of 1968, trash as well as treasure, persistently, indeed relentlessly continue to exist, and not in an antiquarian sense either, even so, it is surprising to contemplate a time when these things began and were *new*," she says. "I find it difficult to unlearn and imagine a world in which pop culture was not always at the very center of things." Along with many others she proves that the true curse of pop-cultural time is not transience, but permanence.

7 ▪ **Scott Ellis, director, *1776* (Roundabout Theater, New York City, October 15)** At the end of the musical all the singing members of the Continental Congress step up to sign the Declaration of Independence, and the Liberty Bell begins to toll. You expect an air of celebration, Ben Franklin pumping his fists and hissing "Yes!"—anything but the suspension and terror of a small band of men suddenly face to face with the history they've just made.

8 ▪ **Darcey Steinke, *Jesus Saves* (Atlantic Monthly Press)** And Elvis rapes little girls.

9 ▪ **Barry Levinson, producer, "Blood Ties," *Homicide: Life on the Street* (NBC, October 17, 24, 31)** This odd three-part teleplay about the murder of a young Haitian woman employed by a rich Baltimore family was all wrapped in a parable—the parable of Bob Dylan's 1963 "The Lonesome Death of Hattie Carroll." It was William Zantzinger, explains James Earl Jones, playing a millionaire businessman and com-

munity activist: Zantzinger, a rich man's son who at a Baltimore society ball thirty-four years ago casually beat a black barmaid to death with a cane, a crime for which he received six months in jail and a $500 fine—and who was last heard from in 1991, extorting rents from the black tenants of hovels he did not even own. "'In the courtroom of honor, the judge pounded his gavel, to show that all's equal and that the courts are on the level,'" Jones as guilty father quoted Dylan's song after his son confessed. "'The ladder of law has no top and no bottom,'" Jones went on, as if to say— what? That finally we too can get away with murder? Time flipped, history shrunk, and the song, read out so eloquently, only got bigger.

10 ▪ **Portishead, *Portishead* (Go! Beat)** Famous last words, again.

FEBRUARY 1998

1 ▪ **Yardbirds, "You're a Better Man Than I" on *BBC Sessions* (Warner Archives)** In HBO's recent Don King biopic, the Yardbirds' British-blues version of Bo Diddley's "I'm a Man" was used without a cut to orchestrate a restaging of the historic 1974 Ali-Foreman fight in Zaire. It was a reminder that nothing in rock 'n' roll can outrun that particular recording, a hit in October 1965, just two months before the band cut a live radio session and, for one performance anyway, topped themselves with a rather clumsily written antiwar, antiracism protest song. "You're a Better Man Than I" was always the Yardbirds' most heartfelt and formally experimental number; here, with a wash of feedback threatening to upend the piece just as the band heads into the last chorus before the instrumental break, the music is plainly terrifying, and so exciting you might have to play it over and over just to make sure you heard what you heard.

2 ▪ **Sleater-Kinney, "Big Big Lights" on *Free to Fight #1* (Candy-Ass)** A 7-inch disc plus a 12-page booklet on "Girls Fighting Girls," with instructions, reflections, and

letters, including one on the Spice Girls' "Girl Power": "Girlism is the step back to the sixties . . . As long as women think they are free to do whatever they want there's no reason to start a revolt against our men-oriented systems." Sleater-Kinney's contribution features a vocal that's extremist even by Corin Tucker's standards—a vocal so consumed, so nearly a body in jeopardy, that you can sense it beginning to break up. B-side highlight: "Everyday," a roundelay of overlaid voices that starts with "Every second a woman is called stupid, fat, crazy, a whore" and ends with "Every 15 seconds, a woman fights back . . ."

3 ▪ **Ivy, *Apartment Life* (Atlantic)** A trio led by chanteuse Dominique Durand that with light echoes of Nico lives up to a terrific album title. The more you listen, the more bite you feel, as if you're slowly realizing that the glossy shampoo commercial you're watching on TV is made out of a cut-up of Godard's *My Life to Live.*

4 ▪ **Darren Starr, creator, *Melrose Place* (Fox, November 24, 1997)** Dr. Brett Cooper, who has a real serial girlfriend-in-a-coma problem, attends comatose Megan. "Music can get through where nothing else can," Coop says over Megan. "I'm betting you love Joni Mitchell as much as I do." He slips a CD into a boom box, and as the camera comes in close on Megan's face you can barely hear "Big Yellow Taxi." "I'm awake! I'm awake!" screamed a sympathetic viewer. "Just turn off that horrible music!"

5 ▪ **Charles Brown, "Rising Sun" on *The Cocktail Combos* (Capitol 3-CD reissue)** R&B pianist Brown is a swaggering presence at shows around Berkeley and Oakland these days. In Los Angeles in 1948 he sang like an opium eater sleeping in the grooves of his own 78s, his dreams too sensual to allow a hurried word, and there's no sound quite like it anywhere.

6 ▪ **X, *Beyond & Back—The X Anthology* (Elektra 2-CD reissue)** Punk looking for the heart of Raymond Chandler's LA, and finding it—and also finding pure rock in the

twelve-second guitar and bass intro to the 1982 "The Have Nots," as perfect as the ten-second piano intro to the Falcons' 1959 "You're So Fine," but with so much more jump.

7 ▪ **44 Long, *Collect Them All* (Schizophrenic)** Brian Berg is at home in Richard Manuel territory—think of "Whispering Pines" on *The Band*—but more often he and his Portland bandmates are cowboys seeking a Western. They get it in "Undertaker" ("I lost my faith," Berg testifies, as if all good stories start right here), which could have inspired Jim Jarmusch's *Dead Man* if it isn't the other way around.

8 ▪ **Carl Hiaasen, *Lucky You* (Knopf)** Centering on two poisonous Florida losers who form their own Aryan militia, the White Rebel Brotherhood—which they soon discover is also the name of a mostly black hip-hop band beloved by half the people they meet, most notably their kidnap victim, Amber Bernstein, a Hooters waitress who keeps asking them what they think of WRB's "Nut Cutting Bitch," her favorite song.

9 ▪ **Alaine M. Labauve, "Louisiana Highway 1: Images" (Louisiana State Museum, Presbytere, New Orleans, through May 24, 1998)** From composition to printing LaBauve is a stunningly dull photographer, but in this gallery of roadside shots one stood out, oddness poking through the obviousness: a ruined bar, half-reclaimed by the wild growth around it and dominated by a huge ad, almost a mural, for Old Milwaukee Beer. It was testament to how quickly time can pass, with a beer that didn't even come on the market until the '70s appearing as far gone as a brand name in a WPA photo by Walker Evans.

10 ▪ **Patti Smith, *Peace and Noise* (Arista)** With an album dedicated to personal losses behind her, here Smith steps out as a universal mother of death, mourning among others Ginsberg, Burroughs, massacred Tibetans, the Heaven's Gate crew, and with such self-importance you get the feeling a death doesn't really count un-

til Smith has blessed it. And yet "Last Call," the Heaven's Gate number, has murmurs of danger; the 10:34 "Memento Mori" touches the Rolling Stones' "Goin' Home" and catches the momentum of a Jim Morrison rant. What remains is Smith's ability to get lost in a piece of music without losing it, to momentarily change into a strange woman before once again taking her shape as a saint.

Salon

1999·2003

1 ▪ **Slapp Happy, "Scarred for Life," on *Ça Va* (V2)** Inside an empty Middle European cabaret Dagmar Krause is singing. She's seen the whole of the century. She's not opening the door.

2 ▪ **She Mob, *Cancel the Wedding* (Spinster Playtime Records)** As with such modest, cutting 1980s U.K. punk combos as Delta 5, women singing like people having real conversations. Increasingly funny, vehement, distracted conversations. For example, "Why did I become a teacher? Why did I become a teacher?" For all the right reasons, but—

3 ▪ **James Marsh, director, *Wisconsin Death Trip* (BBC Arena/Cinemax)** In 1973 historian Michael Lesy, working from an 1890s archive left by the town photographer of Black River Falls, Wisconsin, published a book of this name. It was a study of morbidity replacing vitality in the conduct of everyday life, a chronicle of seven plagues—childhood epidemics, murder, suicide, insanity, drought, tramp armies and economic ruin—and the story of how the Depression of the 1890s all but dissolved the assumption that is the bedrock of ordinary affairs: that tomorrow will be like today. Using unbearably intense frame-enlargements of family pictures, Lesy focused on disassociation in eyes, on horror around mouths. The time seemed very far away.

In James Marsh's poetically cruel film—rumored to be set for its world premiere over Labor Day weekend at the Telluride Film Festival, which never announces its program in advance—the distance of then from now seems our conceit, and Marsh collapses it. Using a steely, low-contrast black and white for the 1890s, color for underplayed footage of Black River Falls in the 1990s, and working almost without faces, re-enacting incidents Lesy unearthed—the if-I-can't-have-you-nobody-can killings that in our newspapers seem like weather reports and here appear as parables scripted by Jim Thompson, or a 125-year-old Wisconsinite Susan Smith, peacefully waiting by the water after drowning her children—Marsh leaves only the quiet as an anomaly; salvation through vengeance seems not part of a time but part of the land.

Marsh uses very little music, and what he does use is extraordinary: at one point bluesman Blind Lemon Jefferson's "See That My Grave Is Kept Clean" from 1928, and, throughout, a variation of DJ Shadow's "Stem/Long Stem," the highlight of his epochal 1996 *Endtroducing…* Jefferson's profound song is an argument with death; the singer surrenders, but as a guitarist the same man backs away, circles around, almost dances, the arcs of sound young, supple, a dare. Shadow's piece—a purloined note layered until the theme constructed from it seems not made but found, always present, a reminder of something you just can't catch—is calming, comforting. But in the reassurance of the repetition there is a suggestion of no way out, and before long the music is sinister before it is anything else. It's always struck me as film noir—not film noir music, but a whole, generic film in the music itself—and now it is, with film noir backdated 50 years from the '40s, and set in a small town in the Midwest.

4 ▪ **Mark Pellington, director, *Arlington Road* (Sony Pictures)** For the scene where Jeff Bridges' Professor of Urban Terrorism stumbles into his terrorist neighbors' backyard cookout—bizarre not just because he doesn't even notice the Ruby Ridge Body Snatcher who murdered his FBI agent wife, or because the gathering is set up to match the closing ghoul-fest in *Rosemary's Baby*, but for the music that's playing. "Yes, after a hard day of smashing the state, we like to get down with the cool '70s sound of KC and the Sunshine Band—don't you?"

5 ▪ **Bonnie "Prince" Billy, *i see a darkness* (Palace)** Lots of people go back to the hills and say they've seen a darkness; Will Oldham of Louisville, who usually records as Palace, just asks you to trust him. He sings a lullaby that takes you to the edge of sleep, where you realize the music is saying you might not wake up. "Nomadic Reverie" is

just that—until terrible voices begin to echo from the hills Oldham keeps in his back pocket. "Woo-woo, woo-woo"—it's the sound Jeff Bridges can't get out of his throat.

6 ▪ Jonathan Van Meter, "The Tyranny of the Hit Single: What's a Record Exec to Do with Aimee Mann?" *New York Times Magazine,* July 11 Still whining after all these years, the former 'Til Tuesday voice continues her Harold Stassen act: she had a hit in 1985. Given that her principal talent is for converting self-deprecation into self-celebration, with luck and a lot of critical support she could become the next Lucinda Williams.

7 ▪ Kristin Hersh, *Sky Motel* (4 AD) The former Throwing Muses singer presses on as well. Wan ballads in a thin voice, Appalachian standards, her own tunes, it all comes out the same: air conditioning.

8 ▪ Tentacles, "Louie Louie Got Married" (K 7' single) He'd be 43, but the people at the wedding don't sound a day over 17.

9 ▪ ELVIS at UCSF Medical Center (Nuclear Medicine, basement, 505 Parnassus, San Francisco) A dirty white contraption in the middle of a corridor, 4 feet high, 3 feet wide—with a gorgeous black-and-white glossy of Elvis from *Loving You* laminated on the front. On the back is an Elvis tableau that, it turns out, changes with the holidays: On March 15 he's a leprechaun—why not Julius Caesar?—for St. Patrick's Day, an Easter bunny the next week. Signs on machine: "DO NOT BRING ELVIS INSIDE (CUDA) EVEN IF NOT WORKING" and "NO LAB SPECIMENS IN ELVIS." Two yellow headlights on the front look like eyes.

A technician comes up and starts to press buttons. "What's this?" he's asked. "It's a robot," he starts to explain, when a doctor passing by indignantly corrects him: "It's *Elvis!*" It turns out to be an autonomous refrigerated drug-delivery apparatus: i.e., it's full of drugs. You program it, it navigates the hallways to its destination. The eyes register obstacles; bumpers around the bottom protect the walls when the eyes don't work. You don't have to pay it and it doesn't get benefits.

ELVIS ("Some kind of acronym," a pharmacist says. "Evasion/Sensory . . . I don't know where the 'L' is") took off down the corridor, eyes blinking. "Be careful he doesn't hit you," the pharmacist said to a woman in the hall. "He's supposed to know better," she said. "Elvis wouldn't hit a woman." It just missed a wall, then smoothly turned a corner and disappeared.

10 ▪ Department of Yeah, Right, Death Trip Division, Midwestern Subsection, *San Francisco Chronicle,* July 27 "Heat advisories were posted yesterday from Kansas eastward through the Ohio Valley and over parts of the Southeast. Temperatures throughout the region hit the 90s and reached triple digits with the heat index.

"The weather was blamed on eight deaths in Cincinnati over the weekend, 11 deaths in Illinois in the past week and five in Missouri."

AUGUST 23, 1999

1 ▪ Atmosphere, "The Abusing of the Rib," on *Stuck on AM—Live Performances on 770 Radio K* (No Alternative) Drifting out of a studio at the University of Minnesota is a modest, unsettling, finally disturbing question: "What do you love?" The questioner is the earnest, smooth-voiced Slug, of the Minneapolis hip-hop collective Rhyme Sayers; off to the side is the gravelly, much older-sounding voice of Eyedea, a high school student. A piano runs a repeating, regretful line in the background, regretting that all questions were settled before the questioner arrived, but he doesn't buy it. Life has put him on the spot; he means to put you there, too. Still, he makes a beautiful reverie, and you can fall into it and forget yourself, until the very end. Somehow gathering up all the menace of Bo Diddley's "Who do you love" (God help you if it isn't him) and none of the flash, Slug's "What do you love?" becomes the hardest question he can ask. Now so much is at stake you can imagine that you or anyone might mumble, stammer, and then admit it: "Nothing."

2 ▪ *lunapark 0, 10* **(Sub Rosa)** Beginning with a ghostly, unbearably romantic minute from Apollinaire in 1912, then thunderbolts from Mayakovsky in 1914 and 1920, avant-garde poets read the century, which seems to have finished prematurely; by about 1960 they're mostly talking about themselves.

3 ▪ **Ad for** *Notting Hill* **(your daily newspaper)** Snuggled next to Julia Roberts', Hugh Grant's face takes you right back to the silent era, when leading men like Wallace Reid (king of the racing picture—*The Roaring Road, Double Speed*—before he became addicted to morphine) burst from their posters in unthreateningly fruity grins, mugs dripping with lipstick, rouge and the eyeliner that with Grant makes his eyes look like they were cut out of a magazine and pasted on. That's right, he's not human. He's not supposed to be.

4 ▪ **Dusty Springfield, "I Only Want to Be with You" (HBO, 9:30 p.m. Sundays)** I have no idea why Springfield's 35-year-old fluffy first hit is so thrilling as the kickoff to *Arli$$*, spreading warmth and delight over the montage of Robert Wuhl's sports agent suffering Bill Bradley's no-look hoop, Jesse Ventura's choke hold, Katerina Witt's kiss. Maybe it was just a perfect record; maybe the release is all in the editing.

5–6 ▪ **Captain Beefheart and His Magic Band, "Kandy Korn," on** *Grow Fins–rarities [1965–1982]* **(Revenant) and** *The Mirror Man Sessions* **(Buddah)** An L.A. band's guitar piece, live from 1968, from the studio the year before, in both cases arriving from a future still ahead of us, a future momentarily circling back to look for a spot in Mississippi in 1930, but missing.

7 ▪ **Nik Cohn,** *Yes We Have No—Adventures in the Other England* **(Knopf)** In this map of secret cultures hidden in plain sight—anarchistic and seeking cultures made by solitaries (a man requesting official recognition as the antichrist; Johnny Edge, now an old West Indian London hipster, in 1962 the Christine Keeler boyfriend who "detonated the whole Profumo affair, blew Harold MacMillan out of office, and so gave the Anglo club a whack from which

it never quite recovered") and groups (ravers, Odin worshippers, Elvis worshippers, travelers, Rastas, squatters, every form of contemporary heretic)—the novelist and pop chronicler has rewritten *The Pursuit of the Millennium—Revolutionary Millenarians and Mystical Anarchists of the Middle Ages*, Norman Cohn's soul-shaking 1957 study of medieval heretics. "The old religious idiom has been replaced by a secular one," Norman Cohn wrote, "and this tends to obscure what otherwise would be obvious": what we call the present is a bridge over an ancient pit, a bridge built out of wishful thinking. Nik Cohn is more sanguine, but he is more than four decades farther from Hitler than his father was.

8 ▪ **Old Time Relijun,** *Uterus and Fire* **(K)** A punk trio that believes in the past—and that running headlong down a path naked will get you somewhere you want to be. "Jail" echoes both the thrash Descendents of Redondo Beach and Chicago bluesman Magic Sam: desperate, a confession, weird moments of reflection in the noise. "I have a lot of time on my hands," the singer tells you. "I got a lot of good books to read."

9 ▪ **Magnetic Fields,** *69 Love Songs,* **Vols. 1–3 (Merge)** Stephin Merritt of this and other bands is running this show—writing all the songs, singing most of them in his cloying, sub-Morrissey voice, listing 90 instruments he plays, including not merely "jug" but "Paul Revere jug," which is to say that the preciousness of the project is all too apparent. (The voice is cloying on purpose, you fool.) But there's something intriguingly tentative and random about the words and the music, in the stupid puns and often slow, counted cadences. Just when you're ready to give up, a different singer will come in like someone on the street waving at the floats in a passing parade. You might find the radiant Shirley Simms hammering an old country vocal to a Bo Diddley beat on "I'm Sorry I Love You" ("It's a phase I'm going through"—you ought to hear that on *Sex and the City* before the season is out) or Claudia Gonson on "Yeah! Oh Yeah!"—though the exclamation points

are strictly postmodernist. A rough version of the guitar line from the Feelies' "Raised Eyebrows"—itself the inheritor of every great guitar melody from "Wild Weekend" to "Layla"—kicks off a very up-to-date version of Paul and Paula's horrid 1963 "First Quarrel." Gonson is flagellating herself over the possibility that her marriage has always been a joke no one bothered to tell her: "Did you dread every phone call, could you not stand me from the start?" "Yeah, oh yeaaaaaaah," Merritt moans in languid ecstasy. It's clear this is how the husband gets off; for the wife you can't tell, but I doubt it.

10 ■ **The Bad Seed, with Patty McCormack (Castro Theater, San Francisco, July 16)** In 1956 a 10-year-old McCormack played an 8-year-old serial killer in blond pigtails named Rhoda; the role was so perverse and her performance so fierce she burned up a whole career in advance. This night, with McCormack appearing after a screening of the film, the theater was packed with raucous gay men, but once the movie started the hooting part of the crowd was often shushed by those who didn't want to miss a word.

McCormack came out to be interviewed by *Village Voice* gossip columnist Michael Musto. Instead of the female female-impersonator you often get with half-forgotten mini-legends, she sat down as a fast, cool, completely alive woman in her 50s. She looked like a cross between Carol Lynley and Debbie Harry; Musto couldn't keep up with her. On her Catholic mother refusing to let her do the 1959 shocker *Blue Denim*: "[At 14] I thought about that and understood: I was allowed to kill people as long as I didn't sleep with them." (Lynley ended up getting pregnant and almost having an abortion instead.) Patty's little Rhoda dispatched whoever got in her way with whatever was handy—fire, blunt instruments, a staircase; the story's conceit was that it was all in the genes, because her grandmother was a homicidal maniac. "Did you play Rhoda as pure evil, or as cursed?" Musto asked. "I played her as

right," McCormack said without a smile, and nobody made a sound.

SEPTEMBER 7, 1999

1 ■ **The Best News of the Week,** *Denver Post,* **Aug. 22** "Universal Records has confirmed that Spin Doctors lead singer Chris Barron ['Little Miss Can't Be Wrong' etc.] has been diagnosed with a rare paralysis of his vocal cords. Barron is meeting with doctors who have indicated that he may never regain the full use of his voice. He now cannot speak above a whisper. All promotional activities for the band's new CD, 'Here Comes the Bride,' are on hold."

2 ■ **Trailer Bride,** *Whine de Lune* **(Bloodshot)** A small cowboy combo that plays as if it's not expecting more than the 10 people in the audience to show up, fronted by a woman who sings like she's wondering who she has to fuck to get out of going through everything twice. As if anybody knows.

3 ■ **Alison Krauss,** *Forget About It* **(Rounder)** For the title song, built around the way they say it and mean it not in mob-movie New York but in the rest of the country—not far from the way Bob Dylan said "Don't think twice," a whole lost world in three words. As always with Krauss, whose voice has the unsatisfiable yearning of her own bluegrass fiddle—unsatisfiable because the sound remembers a land of milk and honey—she needs hills and valleys in the melody to come to life, to pull away from the music and the listener, to get lost, then to come back just far enough to pull your string: to pull it right out of you. Songs on an even plane defeat her every time.

4 ■ **Marine Research,** *Sounds from the Gulf Stream* **(K) and "Parallel Horizontal"/"Angel in the Snow"/"I Confess" (K single)** Moving from Talulah Gosh to Heavenly to her new five-piece, Amelia Fletcher of Oxford, England, has lost a step each time. The fatigue now drawing her voice back still doesn't hide what makes that voice, all sweetness and worry, one of a kind.

5 ■ **Aspen Festival Orchestra, Kyoko Takezawa, soloist, Elgar's "Violin Concerto in**

B Minor" (Aspen Music Festival, Aug. 15) In "Allegro"—deliriously romantic and ominous—the whole first movement seemed to resolve itself into chase, run. The piece was the apparent source of all the high-class, high-gloss film noir music of the '40s (*Gilda*, *The Lady from Shanghai*, *Double Indemnity*, any production that could afford a real score)—so much so that the music, played now, isn't merely familiar, it's fabulously generic. You cannot attach, say, a certain gesture by Rita Hayworth or Orson Welles or Barbara Stanwyck to a given lift in the music, a particular door opening into a darkened room to a threatening slide on Takezawa's special "Hammer" Strat—I mean, *Strad*, her 1707 "Hammer" Stradivarius. But moment to moment the piece, read back on the films that plundered it, gives up near-images that stop the soundtracks as they play in your head. The plot rushes forward, breaking over the hesitations of the actors, smearing all of them into one.

6 ▪ Robert McNamara at Elgar's "Violin Concerto in B Minor" "The Architect of the Vietnam War"—or, if we give that honor to McGeorge Bundy, "The Contractor." "Do you remember Mr. McNamara?" said the woman next to me, who'd come in with McNamara, who was sitting next to her. "He's had such a hard time lately, what with all the criticism," she said, referring to the reception given the Kennedy/Johnson Secretary of Defense's recent I-Knew-It-Was-Folly-and-I-Wish-I'd-Mentioned-It-at-the-Time books. ("McNamara made a 'bad guess'/ 'Bad Guess' chorused the Reporters?/ Yes, no more than a Bad Guess, in 1962/ '8000 American Troops handle the/ Situation,'" Allen Ginsberg wrote in his great Vietnam poem "Wichita Vortex Sutra": "Your magic errandboy's/ Just made a bad guess again/ that's lasted a whole decade.") Now he looked old, fastidious, resolute: like an executioner-monk.

7 ▪ Howard Hampton, e-mail report (Aug. 13) "Wisecrack from the finale of *Mystery Science Theater 3000*, a few minutes into *Danger: Diabolik*, swinging '60s Italian-cum-Modesty Blaise send-up/rip-off, as a bunch of leather-boy motorcycle cops swarm by: 'If Hitler had won the war and hired Stu Sutcliffe as a fashion designer.' Besides summing up the dream life of *Scorpio Rising*, that line seems to have bottomless pop resonance, even if there are only six people in the world who got it, and I'm not even sure I'm one of them."

8 ▪ Bob Dylan, "Highlands," Madison Square Garden, July 27 An audience tape of just the second performance of the song since it appeared at nearly 17 minutes on the 1997 *Time Out of Mind*. In this 10-minute version the tone shifts from the original bitter weariness to something much sharper: sly, sinister, the sound of a scary old man whispering from a doorway. He could be a prophet; he could be trying to sell you dope. Only one way to find out.

9 ▪ David Lynch, director, *The Straight Story* (Disney) In a bar where they're the only patrons, two old men who have just met have told their awful stories of fighting Nazis in the Second World War—stories of what they saw, what they did, stories about their own guilt. Jo Stafford's "Happy Times" plays in the air; the young bartender stands in the half-light, trying to fade into the woodwork, trying not to hear, not to invade the privacy of the men speaking in this public place, shamed by his own youth.

10 ▪ David Bohrer/*Los Angeles Times* news photo (Aug. 10) The picture was carried in countless papers across the country: "Children from a Jewish Center in Los Angeles were escorted to safe ground yesterday by police officers after a gunman opened fire at the center," in the *New York Times*' caption. The shot was from above, with an officer in the middle of a line of 10 children, all holding hands; the curve in the line made it seem as if the police and the children were dancing. It was a rare instance of true déja vu. Framed by the photographer and then chosen by editors, by intent or by a common, silent memory, the shot was a match for the famous image from the end of Ingmar Bergman's 1957 *The Seventh*

Seal: men and women, holding hands, dancing off a hill, all led by Death.

SEPTEMBER 20, 1999

1 ▪ The Pale Orchestra conducted by David Thomas, *Mirror Man Act 1: Jack & the General* (Thirsty Ear) The centerpiece of the 1998 Diastodrome! Festival in London, with impresario/composer/performer Thomas moonlighting from his band Pere Ubu: a live recording of what could have been called "Route 66," because the journey the singers and musicians take across an America they're afraid of forgetting is that expansive. What's missing is that old Bobby Troup–Rolling Stones glee as the miles burn up and L.A. gleams in the distance. This is all backroads and, with Bob Holman's increasingly frantic monologues about how, no, no, no, don't you understand, that's not it—he's talking about gas prices and small towns and theme parks—panic. Then the tone shifts. A character something like Steve Martin's corrupt, dreaming traveling song-salesman in *Pennies from Heaven* emerges: Thomas, ready to sell you the Brooklyn Bridge, or whatever bridge takes you from here to there. He convinces you that he has the right to do it, because he doesn't take the bridge for granted and you do. Suddenly you want to leave the house and get in the car and see if you can find the same country this company is finding—leaving the disc on while you're gone.

2 ▪ Pere Ubu, *Apocalypse Now* (Thirsty Ear) A show from 1991, with David Thomas doing a stand-up comedy routine between songs ("I'm sure you'll be happy to know that one of our members onstage said to me right then, 'That was actually good'") and whispering the secrets of the universe into the ears of the audience as the songs themselves are played. With melodies rising out of the clattering sound like the modal themes of old folk songs, the effect is stirring, Cleveland punks more than 15 years down the road with no lessening of their conviction that they have been chosen to change the world, laughing at how little they've been changed by it.

3 ▪ Anonymous: altered billboard (Gilman Street at San Pablo Avenue, Berkeley, Calif., Sept. 8) A pair of red dice, one with a skull, and this message, in clean Times letters: "Just because you survived _____ doesn't mean your children will." The original word, still barely showing, was "drugs"; in the exact same typeface, it has been replaced by "Bush."

4 ▪ Jonathan Lethem, *Motherless Brooklyn* (Doubleday) A detective story where the hero's Tourette's Syndrome (unending waterfalls of tics, from the man's scrambled verbal outbursts to his fascinating need to straighten people's clothing) shapes the tale—allowing a rhythm in which the frenetic almost hides the islands of quiet where thinking gets done. Tourette's is a thing in itself here, a kind of invisible twin; thus Lethem (*Gun, With Occasional Music, Girl in Landscape, As She Climbed Across the Table*) writes in a double language, which opens up the mystery genre to the point that it's almost erased. As the hero tries to keep himself awake for an all-night stakeout, he recognizes "insomnia [as] a variant of Tourette's—the waking brain races, sampling the world after the world has turned away, touching it everywhere, refusing to settle, to join the collective nod. The insomniac brain is a sort of conspiracy theorist as well, believing too much in its own paranoiac importance—as though if it were to blink, then doze, the world might be overrun by some encroaching calamity, which its obsessive musings are somehow fending off." His favorite song: Prince, "Kiss."

5 ▪ Quickspace, *Precious Falling* (Hidden Agenda/Parasol) U.K. drone band derived from th faith healers. (Thee Headcoats won their "e" in a poker game, I think they said.) Not as demented as that great combo (their 1993 *Imaginary Friend* remains the most blithelessly extreme music of the decade), but with a neat trick: fast drone. Squealing and clicking in "Hadid," they appear as naked people in a field regressing as you listen: regressing not to a pre-verbal childhood but to a previous species.

6 ■ James Lee Burke, *Sunset Limited* (Island/Dell paperback) "St. Peters Cemetery in ten minutes," says a witness to cop Dave Robicheaux. "How will I recognize you?" "I'm the one that's not dead." Don't let your mouth write checks your ass can't cash, Robicheaux should say—but he doesn't use profanity. He won't even tolerate it unless it comes out of the mouth of his partner, Helen Soileau. ("I met Miss Pisspot of 1962 at the jail this morning," she says of an FBI agent.) It's not that he gives her a break because she's a lesbian; somewhere in the literary archetype Leslie Fiedler set out in 1948 in "Come Back to the Raft Ag'in, Huck Honey!" she's playing Jim to Robicheaux's Huck.

7 ■ Glad bags commercial (A&E, Sept. 9) A happy female gospel version of Mississippi bluesman Skip James' brittle, miserabilist 1931 "I'm So Glad" (famously redone in 1967 by Cream), and a travesty: not because it's being used to sell plastic bags, but because of the suggestion that it was originally used to sell God.

8 ■ Vanity Fair/Neutrogena party at the Telluride Film Festival (Sept. 3) The Neutrogena banner at the Skyline Guest Ranch was fairly modest, but against a backdrop of the Colorado Rockies, which were throwing up Matterhorns everywhere you looked, a big poster of the September *Vanity Fair* was like litter. It was the Bruce Weber shot of wistful, windblown, ridiculously blond Carolyn Bessette Kennedy—a face that, the setting revealed, was unmistakably slipping into camp, into that realm of the undead where "The Private Princess," as the magazine named its cover girl, had already joined not Princess Di but "America's people's princess"—as Patsy Ramsey calls her late daughter, JonBénet.

9 ■ Associated Press, "Music, the Universal Language," Sept. 13 "After a week of chaos and terror in East Timor, Indonesia's powerful military boss sang 'Feelings' yesterday to show why he can't walk away from the independence-minded province.

"To cheers from retired military officers at a party, Defense Minister Gen. Wiranto dedicated the song to foreign journalists: 'I hope you have the same feelings, like me, for East Timor.'

"His eyebrows arched in restrained emotion, Wiranto held the microphone in both hands and stood stiffly in a yellow batik shirt and crooned as a band played the 1975 hit popularized by Paul Williams:

"'Feelings, nothing more than feelings . . .'"

I can't go on. This is just too sick. You always knew the song was rotten, but evil?

10 ■ Fastbacks, *The Day That Didn't Exist* (Spinart) It's scary that Seattle's Fastbacks formed 20 years ago, that except for the drum spot the lineup has never changed, that they've never made it, that their music has never gotten better, only utterly failed to exhaust itself. Guitarist Kurt Bloch writes songs about the everyday that somehow contain the state of the union; bassist Kim Warnick sings them in a punk voice that's flat until you hear it as a form of address, as real talk; guitarist Lulu Gargulio keeps the other two honest. Here, one of the days that didn't exist can be found on "I Was Stolen": "We tried to save the world last fall," Warnick says in her high, girlish warble, as if nothing could be more obvious; when she follows with "You remember that we didn't save anything at all," the story seems to end before it's had a chance to begin. But the story goes on, it gets interesting, full of fury and good works, and by the time the story is over you're no longer convinced these people left the world as they found it—not 20 years ago, not last fall.

OCTOBER 4, 1999

1 ■ Fred Eaglesmith, *50-Odd Dollars* (Razor & Tie) Opening with a backwoods ballad drunk on Led Zeppelin's "When the Levee Breaks," a stolid-looking man says he knows his country when he sees it, especially in old cars. Listen to "Georgia Overdrive" and try to convince yourself that for two minutes you don't want to be in the driver's seat more than you want to be anywhere else.

2 ▪ Jay Mohr as Peter Dragon in *Action* (Fox, Sept. 16) Desperate, the producer runs to the house of his whore/script consultant, where he finds her with a client, who is down on his knees and cleaning her floor. Despite the bustier and black mask the guy is wearing, Dragon recognizes him as a Disney executive; "My name is Andri," the man insists. Dragon looks him in the eye: "My name is Luka," he says. "I live on the second floor . . ." You can't tell if the vicious glee in his face comes from having a rival where he wants him, or finally finding a use for the stupid lines that have been bouncing around in his head for more than 10 years.

3 ▪ Michael Ochs, *1000 Record Covers* (Taschen) At 7 inches by 5 inches and 768 pages, this dense object is not a typical album-cover-art book, where designs supposedly fashioned according to vision or genre are presented for your admiration. Opening with Hen Gates and His Gaters' 1957 *Let's Go Dancing to Rock and Roll* (happy white kids in red convertible, balding dad-like person at the wheel) and closing with Oasis' 1994 *Definitely Maybe*, this is stuff—the sort of stuff you'd find flipping LPs in a vinyl emporium, sleeves warped, images scratched or faded or gleaming with an eagerness hiding the truth that the people you're looking at are probably dead. Not looking at all dead, however, is the dead girlfriend on the cover of J. Frank Wilson and the Cavaliers' 1964 *Last Kiss*. There's been a car crash, but while her eyes are closed, her hair isn't even mussed. "Rumor has it that first printings of this cover actually had blood dripping from the girl's face but it was airbrushed out," Ochs says—but that would have only made the fact that the girl's arm resting on her skirt is plainly held there by still-functioning muscles even more weird. The boyfriend, in perfectly pomaded ducktail and gray business suit, looks at the girl's face as if he can't figure out why she's playing dead. But he's supposed to be about to bestow "our last kiss"—to act out the most convincing moment in the song. In 1964 and this year,

with Pearl Jam's stoic, anguished, unteenage version, the words are rushed—"I kissed her our last kiss." It's as if the singer can barely stand to remember what happened, and it catches you up. The burr in Eddie Vedder's voice, the labor you can feel from gestures you can't see, makes the quickness of the moment even more dramatic, almost secretly dramatic, than it was 35 years ago: You feel the moment, but you don't necessarily register it. The sour guitar note that closes the record says both you and the band know this dumb old song is a joke, but nobody told the singer, and that's why it's a hit. As for the cover of the album Pearl Jam's "Last Kiss" is on—*No Boundaries: A Benefit for the Kosovar Refugees* (Epic)—it shows a young man bent over, his hands gripping his neck, his whole body in a posture of despair. He's already learned about last kisses—the kind there's no time to give.

4 ▪ Tori Amos, *To Venus and Back* (Atlantic) Or rather the Twilight Zone. She walks through a deserted mansion, and there are mirrors everywhere: everywhere, she sees her own reflection. And then she sees it even when there aren't any mirrors.

5 ▪ Gino Washington, *Out of This World* (Norton) Detroit, early '60s, a time when only grunge and ridiculousness (the Flares' "Foot Stomping—Part 1," Jimmy Soul's "If You Wanna Be Happy") made the radio bearable. Now a black teenager with a white band steps up to the mike for his song "Out of This World." There's a dull little "All right, now" business, and then the music leaps and it never comes down. Mediocrity is all over this collection: life is hidden in the female backing singers, who sound like they were recruited out of the audience; in the way Washington loves his girl so much he actually doesn't care how he looks; in the twist of "Romeo": "Juliet was my first love / She won't be my last." And I'm not even mentioning what makes the set priceless.

6 ▪ David Johansen on soundtrack to *Burnzy's Last Call* (Ripe & Ready/Celsium) Johansen hasn't simply put ironic scare quotes around his music since he gave up trying to be a real rock 'n' roll hero with the

New York Dolls 70 years ago—he's put scare quotes around the scare quotes, to make it seem like he was, you know, playing a role right from the start. So now his songs might as well have titles like """"Hi There, Sucker!""""" I don't care, and you probably don't either, but when you're paying for something else it's creepy.

7 ■ **Nokia cell-phone ring menu** Cell phones are personal car alarms, and there's a problem when out of 35 rings—which include long, elliptical segments from "Ode to Joy," "The William Tell Overture" and Mozart—the least annoying choices are "Fly" and "Mosquito." I know it's not in the public domain, but I'd pay an extra buck for a "Louie Louie" option.

8 ■ **Goran Visnjic as Dr. Luka Kovac on *ER* (NBC, Sept. 30)** Incredibly handsome new "sub-doctor" from somewhere in Eastern Europe spies pouty little girl sitting alone in ambulance. "My name is Luka," he says endearingly—and that's all. What a letdown. But I'd bet money he'll get to the next line before the season is over—or someone will throw it in his face.

9 ■ **Daniel Wolff, "Elvis in the Dark" (*Threepenny Review*, Fall 1999)** As a review of Peter Guralnick's *Careless Love: The Unmaking of Elvis Presley*, this is an almost physical summoning of the singer himself to make the critic's argument against the biographer: that the singer was no innocent, but engaged throughout his career in a complex, cryptic argument with whoever might be listening to him. Wolff makes his case by taking the reader through a long, dizzyingly vivid walk through a song everybody who might care enough to read him will know: "Are You Lonesome Tonight?" The faithless woman in the song becomes the audience, but the penitent who begins the performance is not the same person who finishes it: That man, Wolff says, is much closer to the singer in Bob Dylan's "Ballad of a Thin Man," asking Mr. Jones if he knows what is happening, because he knows he doesn't. "'Fate,' Presley told us in an earlier section of the song," Wolff says, "had him 'playing in love,' just as fate made him an icon for mil-

lions of adoring fans. But it isn't fate, now. We've struck a bargain with the singer: a whole, complicated tangle we're not particularly willing to take apart."

10 ■ **Peter Boswell, Bruce Jenkins, Joan Rothfuss, "2000 BC: The Bruce Conner Story Part II" (Walker Art Center/D.A.P.)** This landmark show of work by the San Francisco artist opens Oct. 9 at the Walker in Minneapolis—but the catalogue of the same name is no fun. Read what Boswell and Jenkins have to say about Conner's pre- (and for that matter post-) MTV song film for Toni Basil's 1966 "Breakaway" (by 1982 she was No. 1 on the charts with "Mickey"). Basil is dancing through uncountable thousands of Conner cuts, forward and backward, in costumes and naked, and the writers sound like they're taking her blood pressure and measuring her lung capacity. But turn to the very back of the book, where an impish editor or designer has given Basil and Conner the last word: four double-page frame enlargements of a woman saying, in essence, "You know something's happening, and I just might tell you what it is."

OCTOBER 18, 1999

GUMSHOES AND OLD MEN EDITION.

1 ■ **Stan Ridgway, *Anatomy* (Ultra Modern/New West)** Coming out of the old L.A. punk scene with Wall of Voodoo, Ridgway has always peeked around corners as a kind of detective ("of the heart," I think you're supposed to add). Here the liner art plays off the '50s moderne credits of the 1959 movie *Anatomy of a Murder*. But unlike other detectives, Ridgway has all the time in the world. He's not going anywhere; he doesn't solve anything; he just takes notes. The slowness in his singing is like the slowness in the way Dwight Yoakam's trucker moves in *Red Rock West*. He misses nothing and he keeps his mouth shut. That's a hard trick for a singer, but that's the feeling you get: in Ridgway's songs, not a word is spoken out loud. They all take place in his thoughts as he tries to figure out what he's seen. The music is muscular, but all restraint: you

don't raise your voice if you're not really using it. "Wrong, so wrong, we're wrong," Ridgway says in "Mission Bell"; he winds the words around each other until the song they cast back to, a 20-year-old Elvis Presley's "I'm Left, You're Right, She's Gone," has risen up without ever announcing it's there at all.

2 ∎ **Heather Duby, *Post to Wire* (Sub Pop)** Seattle 25-year-old with a deeper voice than you'd put to her Juliette Binoche haircut pursues interesting project: take outsider cool and early-'80s synth bumps and echoes into Sarah McLachlan territory. It's a seductive journey, even though she may never get back.

3 ∎ **Chicago, "If You Leave Me Now," in *Three Kings*** On the day after the end of the Gulf War, the creamy 1976 No. 1 adult-contemporary hit is playing in the purloined Mercedes as Sgt. Ice Cube and an Iraqi rebel hairdresser pull up to the bunker where they're going to try to rescue Sgt. Mark Wahlberg from torture, the hairdresser silently mouthing the words as if they're a prayer.

4 ∎ **Robert Crais, *L.A. Requiem* (Doubleday)** P.I. Elvis Cole is riding with angry cop Samantha Dolan when her choice of L7's angry "Shove" on the radio inspires a critical meditation on the strategic use of pop music in everyday life. "'Too on the nose, Dolan,'" Cole says. "'The music should be counter to your character, and then the statement would be more dramatic. Try Shawn Colvin.'

"Dolan jerked the sedan around a produce delivery truck and blasted through an intersection that had already gone red. Horns blew. She flipped them off."

5 ∎ **Blank culture sighting (Oct. 1, 63rd St. & College Ave., Oakland, Calif.)** Street flyer glued to newspaper rack, black and white with vertical lines. Scrawled motto: "I eat fascist." Graphic: squared, elongated Hitler figure. On his sleeve: "Pez."

6 ∎ **Jacket of Raymond Chandler's *The Little Sister* as published in the U.K. by Hamish Hamilton, 1949 (Otto Penzler Books facsimile edition)** "I ought to have locked the door

and hid under the desk," L.A. dick Philip Marlowe says of his encounter with Orfamay Quest of Manhattan, Kan., a young woman with a "prim little narrow-minded smile." Here you see her entering his office for the first time, looking like the grammar-school teacher everyone's had and no one forgets. I mean, you're lucky if you've already read the book, because you may not want to open it.

7 ∎ **David Lynch, director, *The Straight Story* (Disney)** In Lynch's version of the adventure of the late Alvin Straight, who at 73 drove a lawn mower and a trailer across Iowa and into Wisconsin to visit a brother he hadn't seen in 10 years, people sometimes assume stiff, theatrical or uncomfortable postures; they occupy themselves with unique, seemingly obsessive, unexplained gestures. These incidents—Straight's next-door-neighbor fitting a pink SnoBall into her mouth; the fright in his daughter's eyes when she tries to push words through whatever it is that blocks them; a man at the end of a bar moving his hand (or a knife?) in a circular motion, making a distant, discomforting scratching sound—are no different from the way the Log Lady in *Twin Peaks* tries to get people to listen to her, or the way Kyle MacLachlan's Jeffrey says almost anything he says in *Blue Velvet*. As they are composed in Lynch's films, such events carry a displacing sense of the unnatural, yet once you've watched them, it's impossible to imagine the actors acting in any other way.

"I want to make films that occur in America, but that take people into worlds where they may never go," Lynch has said, and this America emerges not as a place, a history of deeds or a set of ideas. Instead it's a story people tell each other: a fable about how people can be expected to act, about how events can be expected to unfold. With *The Straight Story* this is a story about determination sliding into obsession—craziness, one could call it—and the persistence of the pioneer spirit, the faith that in America anything is possible, with the whole enveloped by decency on the part of every character present, a decency that seems brought forth by one man's expectation that he will find it. In *Blue Velvet*, *Twin Peaks: Fire Walk with Me* and *Lost Highway*, the story is about determination sliding into obsession—sociopathology, you could call it—and the persistence of the pioneer spirit, the dead certainty that in America anything can happen and probably will, with the whole wrapped in a storm of derangement, which some survive and some don't.

The language spoken to tell either story, though, is the same. People move and speak as if they are performing, for others and for themselves. They make gestures that are in some profound and casual way absolutely self-legitimating: gestures that say that those who wave their hands, stutter or proffer strange talismans have as much a right to speak, to tell the story, as anyone else. Sort of like the people on an old Randy Newman album.

8 ■ **Fleetwood Mac, *Shrine '69* (Rykodisc)** Live records by the original Fleetwood Mac, the all-English blues combo led by Peter Green, are all over the place. Legit, illegit—the cheesy cover art won't tell you which, or that, to bend a phrase Mississippi's Skip James once applied to himself, the band came and went from places its contemporaries never got to. The great guitarist Lonnie Mack used to tell a story about a ratty gig where a mouse crossed the stage "just as I hit my highest, most soulful note—and the mouse dropped dead." As Danny Kirwan finds his way into his Elmore James tribute "Something Inside of Me," you can kind of imagine that happening here.

9 ■ **Iggy Pop, *Avenue B* (Virgin)** The first, spoken track is Mr. "Search and Destroy" talking about growing older and facing death: "It was in the winter of my 50th year when it hit me . . ." (It would be the winter.) Funny thing is, the tone is exactly the same as in the Barbarians' 1965 "Moulty"—you can find it on Lenny Kaye's compilation *Nuggets: Original Artyfacts from the First Psychedelic Era*—where Moulty the drummer talks about how he lost his hand and now has to drum with a hook.

10 ■ **Stan Ridgway, *Songs That Made This Country Great: The Best of Stan Ridgway* (IRS, 1980–91)** Well, you never know. But "Lost Weekend" is one of those songs that describes the country as it is—a broken promise, with the whole of the nation present in a promise a couple make to each other.

NOVEMBER 1, 1999

1 ■ **Sally Timms, *Cowboy Sally's Twilight Laments for Lost Buckaroos* (Bloodshot)** Ever since she strolled coolly, coldly through "Millionaire" on *I ♥ Mekons*, Timms has been the last country singer you'd want to go up against in a staring contest. Her touch is light, and deceptive; her reserves of depth seem bottomless. But nothing she's done before suggests the exquisite balance of this disc, the way she makes both Robbie Fulks' "In Bristol Town One Bright Day" (which could be an ancient English ballad learned from a 1928 recording by Buell Kazee of Kentucky) and Johnny Cash's ditty "Cry Cry Cry" (the flip side of his first single, cut for Sun Records of Memphis in 1956) seem like old family stories: tales Timms might not have quite believed when she first heard them as a girl, but which, to her surprise, as a grown woman, she found she had lived out herself.

2 ■ **Pet Shop Boys, *Nightlife* (Sire)** Neil Tennant and Chris Lowe's *Very* and their remake of the Village People's "Go West" were the best album and single of 1993. In the years since it's been as if those records took all the two had to give. Here the group could be starting over from the beginning, in an '80s nightclub, dancing to the drum machine, all possibilities of love and fear present in the way your partner looks you in the eye or over your shoulder.

3 ■ **Bruce Bernard, editor, *Century* (Phaidon)** Of all the summing-up volumes currently clogging the bookstores, this 1,119-page, 25-pound, $50 photo collection is infinitely the most powerful. The brief captions (printed faintly, so you can ignore them and confront the pictures directly) sum up Bernard's response to the times: a sardonic face, held until it falls apart in horror and disgust. That happens even though Bernard's atrocity shots—even "Perhaps the worst photograph of all" (Page 421)—are, formally, mild. A little girl abandoned on the street in Berlin in 1920 is not bleeding; she is merely the void into which she has fallen, and she pulls you in. So for the single image from Bernard's century I would use to blot out all the others, I choose "Lily Brik, girlfriend of the poet Vladimir Mayakovsky," photographed by the great Constructivist Alexander Rodchenko in 1924, an image later made into a still-famous Soviet propaganda poster. With the photo here a thing in itself, though, you can hear what the happy woman with her hand cupped to her shouting mouth is saying: "Calling out around the world/ Are you ready for a brand new beat?" And the world answered: Yes, but not yours. Stalin walks across the facing page; turn it and Hitler is waiting.

4 ▪ Peter Lely, *Portrait of Louise de Keroualle, Duchess of Portsmouth*, 1671/74 (Getty Museum, Los Angeles)

Spy for Louis XIV, mistress of Charles II and a dead ringer for Rose McGowan—the unsurprisable face McGowan assumes in *Going All the Way*, stripping as the Orioles float through "It's Too Soon to Know."

5 ▪ Dr. Dre, Snoop Dogg & Eminem on *Saturday Night Live* (Oct. 23) Despite the two CDs of *Saturday Night Live: The Musical Performances* now in the racks, musicians rarely explode on the SNL stage: in all these years I count only Squeeze with "Annie Get Your Gun," Jackson Browne with "Running on Empty" and Snoop Dogg's first appearance (back when he had "Doggy" in the middle of his name). Rap summit meetings too often settle for self-celebration. But as Dre led the others through two segments, this was otherworldly from the start. With Snoop Dogg as gangly bodily as he was lithe verbally—he spoke the language as if he invented it—Dre provided drama, pathos, silence between the words, a preacher to Snoop Dogg's trickster. Finally the whole, possessed by the reach for abstraction that drives Snoop Dogg's best moments, seemed on the verge of swirling off into the sky. Half an hour later, when without a trace of black tongue Eminem began snapping off his syllables, piling each on the one before it, until his sound was a staircase he was too busy, too outraged to climb, Dre embodied experience and stoicism. He wasn't countering the younger man's impatience with the knowledge that this too shall pass away, but with the advice to save your strength: it'll be back. If a black man and a white man could make the Rodney King videotape into art, this was it.

6–7 ▪ Blind Alfred Reed, *Complete Recorded Works in Chronological Order: 1927–1929* (Document) and Del-Lords, *Get Tough: The Best of the Del-Lords* (Restless) From West Virginia, Reed (1880–1956) played a droning, sawing fiddle; along with Jimmie Rodgers and the Carter Family he first recorded at the fabled Bristol Sessions. He was a world-class complainer: he hated racism, feminism, alcohol, foolery and short hair on women ("Why Do You Bob Your Hair Girl"—it must have driven him nuts when a second version was mistakenly titled "Why Don't You Bob Your Hair"). No socialist, he hated capitalism most of all—for the way it promised that everyone could have everything, right now, including what a minute ago no one even thought of wanting, and produced instead worthless novelty, social division, ungodliness, inequality and poverty. So Reed struck back with his own songs, among them the remarkable "There'll Be No Distinction There" and "How Can a Poor Man Stand Such Times and Live."

The first, which as a piece of music could fit on Bob Dylan's *Time Out of Mind*, is a vision of heaven where the scourge of race and class will be erased in favor of a beloved community, because everyone will play on golden instruments and there will be no more colored people: "We'll all be white in the heavenly light." No drinking, no women flirting or bossing men around . . . the sweep of the performance is lovely and the sentiment irksome. Heaven is so obviously going to be exactly the way he wants it—and stay out of Old Man Reed's yard if you know what's good for you. "How Can a Poor Man Stand Such Times and Live" is a carefully written attack on every public institution except the church, from the police to the courts to public schooling to the high price of dry goods and meat and—everything else. It wasn't about the Depression—it hadn't happened yet—but inflation and the false values created by a runaway stock market. The sound is from another world, but you can feel the writer pressing down on his pencil, pushing right through from his time to now, where his words feel absolutely modern.

That hasn't gone unnoticed. The tune was covered by Ry Cooder in 1974, and 10 years after that, in a roughhouse rock 'n' roll version with new lyrics, by Scott Kempner (since then only coincidentally my son-in-law)—a number that leads off the recently released *Get Tough*. Alfred Reed would hardly have approved of Kempner's solution to their common predicament—a beer run—but could his bitterness and belief in right and wrong have inspired the Del-Lords' strongest number, "Judas Kiss"? "The radio kept playing the same rotten songs/ Every one reminded me of you/ All summer long," a guy says to his dead junkie girlfriend—that's Reed's voice if anything is. "Those roses in the closet/ Well, I took them from your grave"—backing singers Syd Straw and Pat Benatar are harder on her than lead singer Eric Ambel is, but that might be because they can sing harder than he can. Their vindictiveness is more effective than his frustration, but neither is as effective as the melody, which far more than any words convinces the singers that, unlike the song's subject, they're alive.

8 ▪ **Lindell Reeves, "Stagger Lee" (Berkeley Farmers Market, Oct. 19)** Recognizable from 30 feet, the tune rolled over and over. Playing guitar and singing for tips, songster Reeves had a light tone, sad and amused. For the words he followed Lloyd Price, up to the final "Go, go Stagger Lee," but without the glee Price gave the chant, a restraint

that set up Reeves' own close: "You have shot Billy/ Now your time is come." Aside from Reeves' particular variations, it was a scene that could have taken place almost anywhere in the country any time in the last hundred years. "Stag" Lee Shelton shot Billy Lyons in St. Louis in 1895; he died in 1912. When the last Americans then alive go out of the world, will the magic in the song go with them?

9 ▪ **Counting Crows, *This Desert Life* (DCG)** The heart-on-sleeve combo's *Across a Wire—Live in New York City* was a thrill; this has its moments. When Adam Duritz sings with, you know, naked emotion, the idea is a cliché, but the idea is real to him as an idea. He chases it and makes it give up a kind of self-exposure that nakedness only hints at. I couldn't explain what Duritz means in "I Wish I Was a Girl," and he doesn't even try. He simply tries to convince himself he means what he says, and, like Prince with "If I Was Your Girlfriend" and Ian Hunter in Mott the Hoople's shattering "I Wish I Was Your Mother," he can leave a listener scared.

10 ▪ **Bruce Jenkins, "3-Dot Lounge" (*San Francisco Chronicle* Sporting Green, Oct. 23)** "As baseball's managerial crew grows increasingly whiter, the Rockies made a particularly weak choice with Buddy Bell. Next up: The Orioles hire Johnny Winter."

NOVEMBER 16, 1999

1 ▪ **Teddy Morgan and the Pistolas, *Lost Love & Highways* (Hightone)** This trio starts in the country, and by the time they hit third gear they're not just in the city, they're so in love with their own momentum they grind right past the club where they're supposed to go on in 10 minutes. Grunge seeps out of the woods like a dead animal, then pulls the singer down by his feet and steals his guitar. The sound Morgan, drummer Chris Hunter and bass Jon Penner make as they take it back would have Hank Williams and Kurt Cobain high-fiving if they weren't so pissed they didn't see this coming.

2 ▪ Mark Sinker, "Concrete, So as to Self-Destruct: The Etiquette of Punk, Its Habits, Rules, Values and Dilemmas," in *Punk Rock: So What?—The Cultural Legacy of Punk*, edited by Roger Sabin (Routledge) In this complex and worried piece of criticism, Sinker wants to know how communities emerge out of nothing and then create a milieu in which individuals find each other and themselves, wants to know how such people then decide what to do in their shared space and time: "Imagine the ensuing centuries of Judeo-Christian moral debate had Moses returned from the mountain carrying not two stone tablets inscribed with five commandments each, but the first Siouxsie and the Banshees LP." And that's just the first sentence, on which Sinker builds a rickety heretics' church where all questions get asked in the right way. And no questions are closed, except whether or not it's OK to wear flares.

3 ▪ *Bob Marley: Chant Down Babylon* (Tuff Gong) "Bob Marley duets featuring today's hottest artists": wake up, dead man. For this necrophiliac gangbang, remixers fool with old Marley vocal tracks as Lauryn Hill drops her Laconic Goddess of Disdain routine all over "Turn Your Lights Down Low," MC Lyte makes a note to fire whoever got her into this, and a clueless Rakim croons like Crosby across a slowed-down "Concrete Jungle," which as the Wailers' greatest recording (once there were giants in the earth, and Marley was part of a band) was made out of equal parts despair, syncopation and menace. Out by the skin of their teeth: Aerosmith's Steven Tyler and Joe Perry on "Roots, Rock, Reggae," proving that trashiness can so conquer all.

4 ▪ Douglas Gordon, *Through a Looking Glass* (1999) at the Venice Bienalle (June 13–Nov. 7) Gordon ran a slightly fuzzy video of Robert De Niro's "You talkin' to me?" sequence from Martin Scorsese's 1976 *Taxi Driver* in a loop on two screens, with a stuttering echo on the soundtrack. Ten years old in Glasgow when *Taxi Driver* came out, Gordon removed the scene from its status

as a cliché in cultural discourse, a punch line without a joke, and allowed it to communicate on its own, a drama of absolute presence. At the same time, by means of repetition, Gordon isolated each word and gesture to the point where from second to second one could read De Niro's eyes flashing altogether different messages. You might have hit a mental pause button for the instant when the eyes were not taunting but mad, demanding revenge without regard to object—and you might have then seen the same eyes in De Niro's Rupert Pupkin in Scorsese's 1983 *The King of Comedy*. You might have seen the footage Gordon was playing with folding itself into the scene in which nowhere would-be stand-up comic Pupkin seats himself in his basement room in his mother's house, the room all made up as a set for the Jerry Langford Show, and Pupkin happily acting out his big break, his routine, his confident banter with the legendary host, his ease in the light of fame. You might have seen the scenes from the two movies as one and the same, two dangerous men rehearsing what they plan to do next, and the one without the gun infinitely the more terrifying.

5 ▪ Pipilotti Rist, "I'm a Victim of This Song," in *Himalaya* (Oktagon) Rist is a Swiss video artist; leading off *We Can't*, the CD included in the catalog for a recent exhibition, is her version of Chris Isaak's "Wicked Game." An insinuating guitar and a careful, Germanic male chorus take the performance away from karaoke; Rist lets the song draw her little-girl voice back to hopscotch days, lets it skin her knees, and then steps forward to sing with poise and balance—just as her alter ego, trapped in the locked room of any overplayed hit, begins screaming for her life.

6 ▪ Atmosphere, *Overcast!* (Rhyme Sayers) With voices Slug, Spawn, Beyond, Ant and Stress, this determinedly right-here-right-now Twin Cities hip-hop collective looks for the sound of thought. "In 200 years people will be studying Atmosphere," you hear, and there's such modest desperation in the way the line is spoken you can sense the singer reaching that far into the future, grabbing the first person he sees, shouting: "Why aren't you listening?"

7 ▪ **Nat Finkelstein, *Andy Warhol: The Factory Years, 1964–1967* (Cannongate)** One day in 1965 Bob Dylan and entourage arrive at the Factory for a screen test—or, really, in photographer Finkelstein's account, for a showdown in which hip is pitted against cool, and loses: "A Jewish potlatch commenced. Andy gave Bobby a great double image of Elvis. Bobby gave Andy short shrift." The real winner was Finkelstein, who came away with a perfectly framed back-shot of Warhol and Dylan facing each other as Warhol's *Flaming Star* Elvises, their guns drawn, aim blank-eyed at both—a concatenation of American iconography unmatched in this century. Dylan knew a curse when he saw one: he traded the picture to his manager Albert Grossman for a couch. The couch is probably long gone, the picture is worth millions, but guess who's still alive?

8 ▪ **Absinthe (74–75, rue Jean-Jacques Rousseau, Paris 1e)** On the way to the Picasso Museum, stop here and find yourself plunged into the turn-of-that-century haute bohemia of Barcelona, Picasso's first city. All the staff are in costume (you sort of hope): hair plastered to their skulls, black spit curls on their foreheads that a typhoon wouldn't dislodge, suits and dresses of outrageous and seductive design, the floor man and woman moving from customer to customer like tango dancers, the madame of the place sitting behind the counter like a madam, a dead ringer for an older, dissolute version of the woman in the Picasso Museum's 1918 *Portrait of Olga in an Armchair*, a magical painting of Olga Khokhlova, Picasso's first wife. The store is magical. But in the window, seen from the street, is something more magical still. On a brilliantly attired male mannequin is a peacock feather scarf, gleaming with gold and beads, but somehow subtle in its splendor. It was the essence of dandyism: if in the 1830s Paris poet Girard de Nerval took his pet lobster for walks on a leash, this was as close as you could come to wearing one around your neck.

9 ▪ **Sweetwater, *Cycles: The Reprise Collection* (Warner Archives/Rhino)** A recent VH1 film chronicled the Tragic Story of this band: adventurous hippies open at Woodstock, car crash sidelines lead singer and kills the group, the world turns, and 30 years later they reform for heroic comeback—reincarnated as, among others, Michelle Phillips of the Mamas and the Papas and Frederic Forrest of *The Rose*. This lovingly compiled set lets you hear the band as it really was: as Nansi Nevins makes a breakthrough to diffidence, her most passionate mode; as her sub–Grace Slick affectations give way to a shared aesthetic rooted somewhere in the final choruses of Marcia Strassman's "The Flower Children (Are Blooming Everywhere)"; as on the Woodstock stage one of the guys announces the band as "Sweetwawa" and is not immediately struck by lightning. These people were so bad it's embarrassing to be in the same room with them, and they're still resentful that they missed their "chance."

10 ▪ **Marianne Faithfull, *Vagabond Ways* (It/Virgin)** And when she gets it right, it can still be scary to be in the same room with her. Thanked, among others: Anita Pallenberg, Herman Melville, Kate Moss, and Elizabeth I.

NOVEMBER 29, 1999

1 ▪ **Macy Gray, *On How Life Is* (Epic)** An almost old-fashioned soul record, with tunes that draw from surprising sources ("Do Something" from the Wailers' "Kinky Reggae," "Caligula" from the Beatles' "Come Together," "Still" from the Rolling Stones' "Shine a Light") and a voice that recalls Eartha Kitt, Shirley Bassey and Tasmin Archer—for that matter, Gayl Jones—more than anyone on Atlantic or Motown. There's a thinness, a lack of glamour or costuming, in Gray's tone; you can imagine these songs as ordinary if acrid talk as easily as you can see them as performances. Soul music was about appearing to reveal

all, and Gray is plainly holding back, but that's part of what draws a listener in. It's as if something has been beaten out of the singer, and the real goal of the music is to get it back without giving up anything else. But that's just a notion; there are mysteries here. Momentum builds in "I've Committed Murder" until you can feel the sound won't escape the song; the last cut ends with a banjo, which is to say in the 19th century.

2 ■ **Nik Cohn & Guy Peellaert, 20th-Century Dreams (Knopf)** Like their 1973 *Rock Dreams*, cool fantasies of juxtaposition from writer Cohn, lurid realization from photo-collagist and painter Peellaert—as in Federal Agent at Large Elvis Presley smashing into a Yale dorm room to bust doper law student Bill Clinton.

3 ■ **Cellos, "Rang Tang Ding Dong (I Am the Japanese Sandman)," on Bringing out the Dead: Music from the Motion Picture (Columbia)** Doo-wop, and one of the most ridiculous records ever made. Plus, a backup singer revolts, stopping right in the middle of the song: "All you guys say the big things! All I ever get to say is, 'Ah he goes . . .'" A hit in 1957, and hard to find ever since.

4 ■ **ZZ Top, "(Let Me Be Your) Teddy Bear," on XXX (BMG)** Speaking of 1957, not to mention songs with parentheses, this cute Presley No. 1 was once described as Elvis "selling out to girls." Done here as a stripper blues, with new lyrics about cheetahs and rhinos, it's more like cash on the bed.

5 ■ **Laurie Anderson, "Songs & Stories from Moby-Dick" (Zellerbach Auditorium, Berkeley, Calif., Oct. 29)** My friend Andrew Baumer reports on a show I couldn't make: "If I were as self-consciously clever and downright arch as Laurie Anderson, I'd probably say something like 'How can a supposedly respectful and intelligent revision of *Moby-Dick* manage to be completely devoid of any reference to Freemasonry, castration or buggery?' The Edith Ann chair was silly and the much-vaunted Talking Stick was just a digital rehash of her magnetic-tape violin bow, but she's really hooked up with a killer bass player this time: Skuli Svernisson, who, despite his

birth in Iceland, not Kokovoko, played like he should be coated in full body tattoos and eat nothing but beefsteaks. The high point came 20 minutes in, when the astounding Thom Nelis, over a diabolical funk bass line, did a whirling peg-leg tarantella with and on crutches, all the time screaming, 'Have you seen the White Whale? He looks like NOTHING!'

"The oddest, and in retrospect most interesting, aspect of the whole performance was Anderson's unapologetically female take on this whale of a book. Maybe her ignoring the savage phallocentrism of it all in favor of celebrating the yearning, nurturing, healing elements I confess I'd ignored during my 20-plus rereadings throughout my adolescent and adult life might have been just a trifle disingenuous, and perhaps a teeny bit forced, in keeping with her elfin, ain't-I-clever persona, but so what. It never occurred to me that Melville's intention was to compose a meditation on the search for the secret love and beauty hidden within the human heart, but if Anderson sees it, it's obviously there."

6 ■ **Ann Hamilton, Myein (1999), at the Venice Bienalle (June 13–Nov. 7)** As you approached the American Pavilion, crossing a flagstone courtyard, you noticed the stones were stained red, as if someone had spilled paint. The neo-classical building was small and low, with two rectangular wings coming off a dome. The place, a sign in the entryway said, reminded Hamilton of Thomas Jefferson's Monticello, so she decided to orchestrate the place as an American metaphor. The sign explained further: the bumps you would see on the walls of the wings would be Braille renderings of poems from Charles Reznikoff's *Testimony*, which were drawn from court records, while the whispering voice you would hear emanating from the ceilings would be Hamilton reciting Lincoln's Second Inaugural Address in "International Phonetic Code."

In the wings the information dissolved into mere suggestion, like the title of a song standing in for words you can't make out.

The suggestion changed the dots on the walls from poems you couldn't read anyway into an abstract version of Lincoln's Second Inaugural as it's chiseled on a wall of the Lincoln Memorial—because it was now that building, not Monticello, that the Pavilion matched. Hamilton's voice-over was precisely a song where you can't make out the words, weirdly done in the style of one of these female heavy-breathing discs— Jane Birkin and Serge Gainsbourgh's 1970 "Je T'aime . . . Moi Non Plus" was probably the first—that's good for a hit every 10 years or so. The few identifiable words ("Oscar," "November," "Sierra," "uniform," "triumph") seemed not to belong to the Second Inaugural, even if one of them does. So there you were in this surrealist memorial, noticing the difference between Lincoln's and Hamilton's: her walls were alive.

Down every wall, streams of dark pink powder fell to the floor, sometimes in slivers, sometimes in gushes, like the bleeding walls in *The Shining*. The powder piled up on the floor, inches deep; as people walked through the rooms, causing drafts, the powder spread across the floor, and people picked it up on their shoes. When they left the U.S. Pavilion for those of other nations, they carried a trail of blood—not, you could think, the blood of conquest, but of crime and punishment: "Until every drop of blood drawn with the lash," as Lincoln said of slavery in his Second Inaugural, "shall be paid by another drawn with the sword." The sign explaining the piece was neat, balanced, and formal; the thing itself was almost vibrating.

7 ■ **Bryan Ferry, *As Time Goes By* (Virgin)** Bryan Ferry is a god. This is the most boring album of the year.

8 ■ **Rage Against the Machine, *The Battle of Los Angeles* (Epic)** They have a victory strategy: beat it to death.

9 ■ **Alanis Morissette in *Dogma* (Lion's Gate)** Typecast as God, she opens her mouth for a scream only dogs can hear and blows off Ben Affleck's head. As I recall, that's pretty much what happened every time "You Oughta Know" came on the air.

10 ■ **Levon Helm's Classic American Cafe (300 Decatur St., New Orleans)** Is this where the road ends? Here at this defunct restaurant-cafe, even the word "American" communicates like a lapsed trademark. A "Live at Levon's" poster has an insert of a Ronnie Hawkins & the Hawks poster and a design spelling out "BAND" to remind you; a spring 1999 calendar lists Levon and daughter Amy Helm with the Barn Burners, Levon Helm's Classic Blues Band, Levon Helm with Allen Toussaint, Levon Helm with James Cotton, Levon Helm with Cork, Levon Helm with the Dirty Dozen Blues Band. The creepy stuff is on the menu: "I'm a Lonely Boy . . . I Ain't Got No Home" Po' Boys; The Last Waltz Desserts; "Up on Cripple Creek" seafood—and, too perfectly, "King Harvest Has Surely Come" salads. After the big "FOR RENT" sign, a red and white sticker under the menu pages in the window seemed like the last word:

www.allmenaredogs.com
A Revenge Site for Women

DECEMBER 13, 1999

1 ■ **Beck, *Midnite Vultures* (Interscope)** This is embarrassing.

2 ■ **Gayl Jones, *Corregidora* (Beacon Press reprint)** Jones' first novel from 1975 about a blues singer singing a song no one's exactly heard before. "'Songs are devils. It's your own destruction you're singing. The voice is a devil.' 'Naw, Mama. You don't understand. Where did you get that?' 'Unless your voice is raised up to the glory of God . . . Where did you get those songs?' 'I got them from you.' 'I didn't hear the words.' Then let me give witness the only way I can. I'll make a fetus out of grounds of coffee to rub inside my eyes." On the other hand, Henry Louis Gates recently claimed the real significance of the book was that it introduced oral sex into fiction by black women.

3 ■ **Metallica, *S&M* (Elektra)** Recorded in April at the Berkeley Community Theater with the San Francisco Symphony Orchestra, conducted by Michael Kamen,

and glorious. On "Bleeding Me," Led Zeppelin's "Kashmir" comes into view, but it's a mirage: the real vision in the music is far more desperate, Ronald Colman clawing his way back to Shangri-La in the last shots of *Lost Horizon*. Across two discs, the band isn't lost for a second; they sound like they're on top of the mountain.

4 ▪ **Dolly Parton, *The Grass Is Blue* (Sugar Hill)** This is the best album Parton has made since *My Blue Ridge Mountain Boy* in 1969, and the killer is "Silver Dagger"—the pristine Appalachian ballad that in 1960 led off Joan Baez's first LP. Baez rarely again opened herself to a song so fully; Parton follows Baez like a girl following her mother through a field, wandering off the path, circling back, then disappearing into the woods. But now it's nightfall, everyone in town is searching and some people are already talking about haunts and ghosts. How it ends: the fiddler, Stuart Duncan, finds her.

5 ▪ **Martha Rosler, "Positions in the Life World" (retrospective at the Museu d'Art Contemporani de Barcelona)** In the 1967–72 series *Bringing the War Home*, Rosler made John Heartfield–like photocollages of disfigured Vietnamese waiting patiently on suburban patios; the images were disconcerting, but immediately obvious. At the end of the string, though, was *First Lady*, and real art: Pat Nixon posing proudly in a full-length formal gold gown, while over her shoulder in a gilt-framed mirror, Faye Dunaway was being shot to pieces at the end of *Bonnie and Clyde*. Not many thought that was a Vietnam movie when they walked out of the theaters, but, like Rosler, a lot of people knew.

6 ▪ **Bono on *Selections from the Book of Psalms* (*Los Angeles Times Book Review*, Nov. 28)** The way the U2 singer writes, King David might still rule and the psalms might still be in production. Or that's his argument: David "was forced into exile and ended up in a cave in some no-name border town facing the collapse of his ego and abandonment by God. But this is where the soap opera gets interesting: this is where David is said to have composed the first psalm—a blues. That's what a lot of the psalms sound like to me, a blues. Man shouting at God." Of course, Bono later calls David "the Elvis of the Bible," but that's just to set up his closer, a brief dissertation on authorship and authenticity: "It is not clear how many, if any, of these psalms David or his son Solomon actually wrote. Some scholars suggest the royals never dampened their nibs and that there was a host of Holy Ghost writers . . . who cares? I didn't buy Leiber and Stoller . . . they were just his songwriters . . . I bought Elvis."

7 ▪ **U.S. Postal Service, "1970s Celebrate the Century" stamps** Fifteen designs, every one ugly, and not one about anything worth remembering. "You mean," she said, "there was?"

8 ▪ ***Doo Wop 50* produced by T.J. Lubinsky/WQED/Rhino Entertainment (PBS, airing in December)** Last year, a high school teacher asked me to talk to her class about doo-wop. Drawing a blank on the concept, the students reacted tepidly to the bit of '50s-style harmonizing that opens Lauryn Hill's "Doo Wop (That Thing)," were tolerant of snatches of the Penguins' "Earth Angel" and the Five Satins' "In the Still of the Nite," and went absolutely crazy for the sequence in Floyd Mutrux's 1978 film *American Hot Wax* where the Planotones, standing in for the Del-Vikings, cut "Come Go With Me" in a studio crowded with fans, girlfriends and pizza delivery boys. I shudder to think what their reaction would have been if I'd hauled in this well-meant special, due soon enough on home video. Virtually every legend of the form living—and more than a few not, by the evidence of the singing—paraded out for the Greatest Hit: "Sincerely," "A Sunday Kind of Love," "There's a Moon Out Tonight," "The Great Pretender" and yes, "Earth Angel" and "Come Go With Me." But again and again the wine died on the vine; it was too late. It's not just love that, as so many of the old songs say, "makes the world go 'round"—it's also age and death.

There were exceptions: Tony Pasalaqua of the Fascinators with "Oh Rose Marie," a grandfather still living off the memory of a girl he never got to kiss, but getting another chance as he sang; the Cadillacs' outrageous minstrel-show act for "Speedo"; the dignity of Arlene Smith of the Chantels, probably the greatest voice rock 'n' roll has turned up, with "Maybe." The tears on her face recalled producer George Goldner's account of how he got Smith's heart in the grooves: cursing the teenager for her incompetence and stupidity until she would do anything to get away from this terrible man—including, with all her defenses gone, singing the song one last time. Best of all was the bassman for the Marcels, kicking off "Blue Moon" with a perfectly controlled avalanche of syllables, none seeking a word, each a symbol of pleasure and escape. Among all the fat men crossing the stage, he was gaunt; his hair hung down in rings. Dark glasses covered his eyes; the curl of his mouth as he waited for his moments said he'd never tell half of what he knew. He could have been Richard Belzer, or Dennis Rodman, but he was Fred Johnson, on stage in Pittsburgh PA, his hometown.

9 ▪ **Bob Neuwirth in "Hal Wilner's Harry Smith Project," Royal Festival Hall (London, July 2)** For a mass tribute to the compiler of *The Anthology of American Folk Music,* the old Dylan sidekick made a subtle shift in the lyrics of the impenetrable North Carolina ballad "I Wish I Was a Mole in the Ground," from "I wish I was a lizard in the spring" to "I wish I was a lizard in your spring." Sort of changed the meaning—or revealed it.

10 ▪ **Mango boutique, Plaga de Carles Pi I Sunyer, Barcelona (Nov. 24)** Found archaeology: A smooth-faced model was featured on a poster on the outside wall of the shop. The poster was so big it completely covered a still-functioning doorway, secured by a heavy lock and chain—which, appearing right in the middle of the model's cheek, made the whole tableau into a precise match for the most extreme examples of

London punk style, as it was almost a quarter century ago. The signifiers of domination and escape, control and refusal, of hiding in plain sight, swirled in the twilight; no tagger could have produced anything half so suggestive.

1 ▪ **Snakefarm, *Songs From My Funeral* (RCA)** For singer/guitarist Anna Domino and guitarist/programmer Michel Delory, the idea was irresistible: take the most commonplace folk ballads in the American tradition—all those deep, profound, death-soaked cornpone campfire singalongs from "John Henry" to "Tom Dooley" to "St. James Infirmary" to "Frankie and Johnny" to "The Streets of Laredo" to "House of the Rising Sun"—and take them away. Not make them their own, but make them perfect, distant, beckoning, resistant, irresistible in and of themselves. Other versions, by the '20s and '30s singers brought together on Harry Smith's *Anthology of American Folk Music,* by Bobby "Blue" Bland, the Kingston Trio, Bob Dylan, the Animals, or 100, 200 years' worth of street singers, might be convincing, down-home, inventive, scholarly, passionate, personal; for this project, every performance would be Garbo.

Domino's singing is cool, chilly, cold, funny and most of all unsurprised. She inhabits these songs—with the words of most of them radically extended, rewritten or recombined from the countless variants of each (have you ever heard "Seventeen coal-black horses/Are hitched to a rubber-tired hack" in "St. James Infirmary"?)—so completely you never question the techno aesthetic Delory has grafted onto them: electronic blips and beeps, a lot of wah-wah, the disembodiment of a drum machine and a synthesized chamber orchestra. Such effects are never effects at all, but merely the bleached, alkaline, Georgia O'Keeffe landscape in which the songs are now set. There's never a sense any song could have turned out any other way:

Domino's beyond-the-grave tones are matter-of-fact.

According to one account, Frankie Baker shot Allen Britt in St. Louis on Oct. 15, 1899, and ever since, as was said of Abraham Lincoln after John Wilkes Booth shot him, they've belonged to the ages, or whoever wanted them. No one cared about the facts; the story had room in it, and so singers, composers, playwrights, painters all took their places in the tale, changing names, faces, races, time and place. On *Songs From My Funeral*, the piece begins as if in some '50s nightclub in L.A., after hours, James Dean on the bongos, Chet Baker looking on, wondering whether to join in, wondering if he's Frankie or Johnny, wondering if he'd rather cheat and die or be wronged and kill. As Domino tells the story in this club—like someone pulling petals off a daisy: he loves me, he loves me not— it's a story everyone knows, something that happened back in the '20s, in New York, wasn't that it, Greenwich Village, didn't Edmund Wilson write something about this, something about him and Edna St. Vincent Millay? Or was it up in Harlem?

Domino is now coming out of *Anna Christie*, and as she fills in the details, the very perfection of her face—and, beneath the skin, the inhumanity perfection suggests—sexualizes the legend in a wholly new way. Suddenly, as Domino recites the necessary opening lines, "Frankie and Johnny were lovers/Oh lordy how they could love," you see Frankie's hands all over Johnny, unbuttoning his new suit, Johnny's hands under Frankie's dress, right on the street. When Frankie sees Johnny with Alice Fry, your heart goes into your throat, just as Frankie's goes into hers: No, no, you say, it can't end this way! But she has to shoot him—"Rooty toot toot," as Domino makes it happen, Frankie's last words before she gives up her life to myth.

Something this complex, unhurried and seemingly uncontrived—unfolded— happens with almost every tune. You can't get close to the bottom of any of them, even though you may have heard these songs all your life; Domino has, after all, and she hasn't gotten to the bottom of any of them, just dropped the false bottom of overfamiliarity out of each. As a result the old music comes back to a listener not like a ghost from the past, begging to be remembered, but as if from the future, certain nothing we do can change anything.

2–8 ▪ "America Takes Command—1950s into the 1960s," in "The American Century Part II, 1950–2000," Whitney Museum of American Art, Lisa Phillips, chief curator (New York, through Feb. 13) On the top floor, a moan from several galleries away took me to the section's "Culture Site," a collection of representative books, magazine covers, film stills and, in this moment, Hank Williams' 1950 "Ramblin' Man." Surrounded by ads for Cold War hysteria and the postwar boom, it sounded so old—older than any other object present on any of the floors, except, in the "Monochromatic Abstraction" mezzanine, from 1966, Brice Marden's pea-soup, prairie-flat *Nebraska*, which could have had a little radio playing the Bruce Springsteen song hidden behind it. Then Williams was followed by Muddy Waters' 1950 "Rollin' Stone," and then Elvis Presley's 1955 "Mystery Train." (Billboard for the whole "American Century Part II" show: Warhol's *Double Elvis* doubled, under the headline "GET HERE BEFORE ELVIS HAS LEFT THE BUILDING"—shouldn't it be "leaves"?) Contextualized like this, "Mystery Train" sounded exactly like "Rollin' Stone"—it was all in the rhythm, speeded up but also opened up—until Elvis hit his high notes, and Williams was back in the saddle. Then Elvis laughed, and he was on his own.

The picture Williams had taken me away from was Wallace Berman's 1964 *Papa's Got a Brand New Bag*, a fierce collage with a lot of story-untold empty space: Muhammad Ali in a cap, shouting, looking just like Elijah Muhammad; three Rolling Stones, in dark cutouts; a figure I couldn't recognize except generically, a type-case of the American drifter-killer, flanked by two detectives; people with swastikas on their foreheads; naked white women, from a sex magazine, probably, though in this unstable setting they looked as if they were on their way to the gas chambers. It all fit with a poster for the 1954 radioactive-ants movie *THEM!* On the far left, a fleeing man looked exactly like Ronald Reagan; in the center, a speech balloon coming out of a woman's mouth read, "Kill one and two take its place!" Well, isn't that the American way? Buy one, get one free?

9 ▪ **Handsome Family,** *Odessa* **(Carrot Top)** From 1994, this turned up in a bin: first, fully realized attempts by Chicagoans Brett and Rennie Sparks to transfer the fatalism of the old murder ballads into modern life. As in "Moving Furniture Around," a celebration of clinical depression.

10 ▪ **Bobby Fuller Four, "A New Shade of Blue," on** *Boys Don't Cry* **soundtrack (Koch)** The first sign the filmmakers are going to get Charles Starkweather country right comes right at the beginning, when Brandon and Candace, neither of whom will survive the film, pick each other up at a bar, and this gorgeous rockabilly crying song— altogether forgotten until now, it seems to have been made to be forgotten—is floating in the background. It was 1966, the Texas band had scored with "I Fought the Law," they filled up an album, this was on it, and then Fuller was found dead in an L.A. parking lot. Of "asphyxiation," the coroner ruled. Because someone had poured gasoline down Fuller's throat.

JANUARY 24, 2000

1 ▪ **Warren Zevon,** *Life'll Kill Ya* **(Artemis)** The old rounder borrows his old melodies, his old ideas and kicks over his own rocking chair: "I Was in the House When the House Burned Down" is "Excitable Boy" with humor intact, but no longer a joke, because when the house burned down the singer found he had nowhere else to go; he still lives in the ashes. So he blows his horn, gets syncopation out of his guitar, passes it off to the drummer and steps up to the mike. As Zevon imagines himself

back to the Crusades, back to Graceland ("He was an accident waiting to happen," he begins, speaking like a witness in court, a storm-warning guitar line hanging over his head. "Most accidents happen at home"), into the ground, the album takes on such a sweep that the house that burned down comes to seem less a place than Zevon's whole era, that time Billy Joel sings about in "We Didn't Start the Fire." Of course we did, Zevon says. Want a light?

2 ▪ **John Carman, "Mob Rule" (***San Francisco Chronicle***, Jan. 14)** *Saturday Night Live* ran a hysterical parody of *Sopranos* reviews on Jan. 15, but unlike most of the cream-in-their-jeans crowd—TV critics who sounded like nothing so much as the swells who take Tony to their golf club and treat him like an exotic pet—Carman has something to say. "There's a reason Tony can't find his bliss at home; at his strip-joint hangout; or in his psychoanalyst's office. He's a criminal; his life has rotted from the inside out." But that's just a warm-up. The code of the show is in its language, Carman writes, in all the variations of "fuck" except the one that takes a "Let's" in front of it: "The f-word as an adjective serves to demean the noun it modifies. As a nonsexual verb, it demeans the direct object. The language itself is life-negating, and the negation of life is the rampant disease corrupting Tony's two families, biological and criminal."

3 ▪ **Etta James, "A Sunday Kind of Love," on** *Her Best* **(Chess)** In 1960, "Miss Peaches" drifts around the old song as if it's "Since I Fell for You," as if she has all the time in the world.

4 ▪ **Bonnie Raitt voted into Rock & Roll Hall of Fame in first year of eligibility** I was complaining about this to another music writer. "I think her body of work is superior to Ruth Brown's," he said of the R&B pioneer inducted in 1993. But neither Brown nor Raitt has a body of work. Brown had a string of singles, Raitt has a bunch of albums; you flip through them, looking for a moment when you say, yes, this made a difference. If you place Brown's 1949

"Teardrops from My Eyes" against, say, Raitt's 1989 *Nick of Time*, you'll see that mannerism can never speak the language of style—and that Raitt, in her honest, dedicated way as false a singer as Michael Bolton (who really does love "When a Man Loves a Woman," you know), is being honored for her class. In the Marxist sense.

5 ▪ **Ed van der Elsken, *Love on the Left Bank* (Dewi Lewis)** This legendary photonovel, originally published in 1956, is set mostly in a small bar off St. Germaindes-Prés. It's the early '50s, and all the bohemian clichés are present—sex, drugs, violence, poverty, and bad art—but also movement, tension, the unknown. Looking at the way people stand, shout or pass out, you can feel the blank sense of freedom that followed the war all over the West now compressed into this one shabby cafe and nobody there having the slightest idea what to do with it. Or almost nobody. At one table, a few youthful megalomaniacs—among them Serge Berna, Michèle Bernstein, and Jean-Michel Mension, who are visible here, and Guy Debord, who isn't—were working on the problem. And you can feel that, too.

6 ▪ **Nan Goldin, *The Ballad of Sexual Dependency (1976–92)*, in "The American Century Part II, 1950–2000," Whitney Museum of American Art, Lisa Phillips, chief curator (New York, through Feb. 13)** "Generation to generation, nothing changes in bohemia," Nik Cohn wrote in 1968; that may be its allure. In 690 slides, Goldin takes the baton from van der Elsken, and while there's more sex, drugs and violence here—and, since the story goes on, death—the weightlessness of the boys and girls in *Love on the Left Bank* is missing. That's because the revolution those people counted on had, by Goldin's time, come and gone. The people in van der Elsken's book went on to make history; Goldin and her friends are stranded outside of it. In such a setting, it's fascinating, and heartbreaking, to discover which songs on Goldin's soundtrack emerge to take new power from photos of deadened lovers and defiant

casualties, and which are just wallpaper. The winners, somehow made pristine: Dionne Warwick's "Don't Make Me Over," Petula Clark's "Downtown" (equally alive as the liberation theme song in *Girl, Interrupted*) and "All Tomorrow's Parties" by Nico with the Velvet Underground. The first is a warning, the second a celebration. The third is a funeral: its strength is in its time shift, its elegy for what has not happened, its certainty that all tomorrow's parties have already taken place. And the last song is Dean Martin's "Memories Are Made of This"—which, following slides of cemeteries, coffins and a crude painting on a door of skeletons fucking standing up, can never have sounded so rich.

7 ▪ **Michael Lindsay-Hogg, director, *Two of Us* (VH1, premiering Feb. 1)** A fantasy: in 1976, after years of estrangement, Paul McCartney and John Lennon meet at the Dakota in New York. They walk, they talk, finally they get out their guitars and then—Yoko calls. From L.A. Where she's gone to sell a cow for half a million dollars.

8 ▪ **Degrees of believability in Paul Thomas Anderson's *Magnolia* (New Line Films)** 1. Fulfillment of Exodus 8:2. 2. Julianne Moore trying to kill herself because she feels so awful about being unfaithful to dying fossil Jason Robards. 3. The whole cast—sentient, OD'd, in a coma, it doesn't matter—reverently mouthing the words to Aimee Mann's "Wise Up."

9–10 ▪ ***Troxel vs. Granville* before the Supreme Court, Jan. 12, and *Come Softly to Me: The Very Best of the Fleetwoods* (EMI)** If you followed the coverage of this case, re the right of grandparents "to visit with a child over the objection of parents who have not been shown to be unfit," as Linda Greenhouse put it in the *New York Times*, you might have noticed one of the plaintiffs: a bald, stocky, tight-lipped man in glasses, Gary Troxel, 60. It was in 1958 that he joined with Gretchen Christopher and Barbara Ellis at Olympia High School to form the Fleetwoods—before Sleater-Kinney, the best band ever to come out of Olympia, Wash. Over the next three years, chasing

"Come Softly to Me" to "Mr. Blue" to "(He's) The Great Impostor," they would take the most obvious and commonplace sentiments and, floating them through doo-wop patterns, put them out of reach. "I saw him at an oldies concert about five years ago," Charles Taylor says of Troxel. "The 'Fleetwoods' were on the bill. (I have no idea if the two women were the same.) I fully expected it to be another depressing act. And he was wonderful. The voice was the same, and suddenly I was looking at a middle-aged man for whom none of the uncertainty of those songs had ever been settled." On the evening news shows, Troxel—whose son had killed himself in 1993, leaving two children with their mother, with whom Troxel and his wife were now in dispute—looked bitter, as if he had settled all questions in his heart and knew no one would ever feel as he did, as if he had nothing to say to anyone.

FEBRUARY 7, 2000

1 ▪ Mekons, *Journey to the End of the Night* **(Quarterstick)** An end-of-the—or anyway their—world album, maybe the best the intransigent Leeds-to-Chicago punk combo has made, with Morris dancing hiding inside reggae rhythms and inside of that "Neglect," which could be the Crests, climbing "Step by Step" in 1960, Rod Stewart in 1972 telling a woman he hasn't seen in years, "You Wear It Well," but has a twist nice songs like those were made to deny.

2 ▪ The Need, *The Need Is Dead* **(Chainsaw)** Olympians (as in Washington) Rachel Carns and Radio Sloan on a thrilling ride, down switchbacks in reverse. Freedom of speech is fine, but this is something else— in moments, as when they recapture the long-gone late-'70s London warble of Lora Logic's "Wake Up," freedom of throat.

3 ▪ Christina Aguilera **(Jan 30., ABC/MTV)** The blonde sensation's lip-sync job for the Super Bowl halftime show was creepy in a conventional, who-says-they-aren't-real? manner. It was no preparation at all for the low point of the two-hour biopic *Christina*

Aguilera: What a Girl Wants, which followed: in grainy footage of a little girl on a public stage, mike in her hand, singing an adult love song and making adult tease gestures, the 6- or 7-year-old Aguilera was the image of JonBenét Ramsey, and her mother, popping in to say, Oh, it wasn't ME, it was what SHE wanted, was the image of Patsy Ramsey. Running simultaneously on the USA network was *The Mary Kay Letourneau Story: All-American Girl*, but in this night's depravity sweepstakes it didn't have a chance.

4 ▪ Vue, *Vue* **(Sub Pop)** This young San Francisco band has rather bizarrely rediscovered the unrepentantly cheesy sound of the post-Beatles, pre-psychedelic San Francisco Bay Area—a sound perhaps summed up better by the name of one of its exemplars, Peter Wheat and the Breadmen, than any actual records, though "Little Girl," by San Jose's Syndicate of Sound, is close. Thanks to Jessica Graves' implacably poker-faced, two-fingered organ riff, Vue's "Girl" (principal lyric, ecstatically groaned by Rex Shelverton: "Oh, girl") is closer.

5 ▪ Robert Mugge, director, *Hellhounds on My Trail: The Afterlife of Robert Johnson* **(Winstar video)** Talkers and players gathered at the Rock & Roll Hall of Fame for a celebration of the '30s Mississippi bluesman, and this documentary includes too many fat white guys with nothing to say. But there are lucid, stirring passages from keynote speaker Peter Guralnick; there is Johnson's childhood friend Willie Coffee, crying over his memory of "Sweet Home Chicago" ("I don't like to talk about him too much"). Alongside any number of sclerotic or florid readings of hallowed Johnson tunes by singers black and white, there's skinny white guy Chris Whitley's queer, atonal revision of the previously uncoverable "Hellhound on My Trail," ludicrous in its first notes and a dead man walking, a thing in itself, by its end. And in the power trio Gov't Mule there are fat white guys slamming their way through a don't-let-it-end-yet assault on "If I Had Possession Over Judgment Day"—

with the Rolling Stones' "Stop Breaking Down" and Cream's "Crossroads" the most exciting claim on a Johnson song I've ever heard. Don't go looking to Gov't Mule's own records, or Chris Whitley's, for anything similar; their performances here take place outside their careers.

6 ▪ Chumbawamba, "Tony Blair" (Activator) The chest-thumpingly anarchist English amalgamation recently put out "The Passenger List for Doomed Flight #1721," in which it gleefully fantasizes the deaths of, among others, Bill Clinton, Tony Blair and Gerhard Schroeder—apparently not considering Joerg Haider sufficiently evil to be worth mentioning. Infinitely more interesting is Chumbawamba's fan-club single "Tony Blair," which the band should make generally available before it chokes on its own righteousness. Following the Clash's 1979 *London Calling*, the sleeve mimics the left-to-bottom pink and green lettering on Elvis' first album, the 1956 *Elvis Presley*: in place of the delirious Presley of the original jacket, though still placed right next to Elvis' bassist Bill Black, is Blair. His face split by a smile, he's lightly picking on an acoustic guitar—as if backing up the sweet-voiced young thing on the record, who steps lightly over sock-hop piano triplets while pining away for the dreamboat who promised her "something new" but dumped her as soon as he got what he wanted. "Now you date/ All the girls you used to hate," she sighs; "oo-wah-oo-wah-oo," says the chorus. Even though she says, "I'm not that kind of girl," you just know she'd fall for him all over again. That's not the message Chumbawamba means to send, but it's what happens with good records: they say what they say, not what they're told.

7 ▪ *Clambake* revisited, in William Plummer, "Sensing His Moment" (*People* magazine, Jan. 31) In a recent column, Molly Ivins argued that no one can be elected president without an Elvis component, and confessed she could find no such thing in Bill Bradley, whom she nevertheless spent the rest of her space adoring. Bradley apparently got there ahead of her: "A notoriously

dozy speaker," Plummer reported, "he once studied Elvis movies at the Library of Congress to get a clue to the King's charisma." And still couldn't win New Hampshire: I admit I haven't tried it, but watching Elvis movies at the Library of Congress sounds like eating ribs with a fork.

8 ▪ Eternal return on *The Sopranos* (HBO, Jan. 30) The episode kicked off with a jumping piece of old, East Coast, for all I know New Jersey-specific doo-wop pulsing through a pizza joint run by a man in his 50s; it ended with teenage Meadow Soprano and her friend Hunter cooking at home and singing along to New Jerseyan Lauryn Hill. As events, the songs were more than 40 years apart; in the way the words of both were more interested in themselves than in addressing any listener, in the way they slid off of each other's sounds, the songs were almost the same.

9 ▪ Bob Dylan, "Things Have Changed," from *Wonder Boys—Music from the Motion Picture* (Columbia) Taking phrases out of the air (from the Carter Family's "Worried Man Blues," Duane Eddy's "Forty Miles of Bad Road") to completely inhabit "I been all around the world, boys," a line from scores of old mountain songs and white blues, Bob Dylan the person thus begs leave to inhabit a fictional construct in which he imagines what it would mean to outlive oneself: to retain all of one's faculties and decline to use them. Melville created his clerk Bartleby to define rebellion as withdrawal, his manifesto "I would prefer not to"; using all of his faculties, Dylan guides the receding narrator from the 1997 *Time Out of Mind* into a long step back, letting him look over the whole landscape of that work with an expression composed of a querulous grin.

10 ▪ Bill Clinton, State of the Union address (Jan. 27) "We remain a new nation," Clinton said. "As long as our dreams outweigh our memories, America will remain forever young." "Could Reagan have said it better?" asked a friend, and the answer is, No, he couldn't have said it better, or half as well. Reagan couldn't have brought off the Dylan reference as if it were his own. And I

doubt if Reagan would have done what Clinton did just a paragraph earlier—when, caught in the coded metaphors of American speech, he had a Founding Father ("When the framers finished crafting our Constitution, Benjamin Franklin stood in Independence Hall and reflected on a painting of the sun, low on the horizon. He said, 'I have often wondered whether that sun was rising or setting. Today,' Franklin said, 'I have the happiness to know it is a rising sun'") naming a brothel in New Orleans. Or, as another friend put it, "Cue the Animals."

FEBRUARY 22, 2000

SPECIAL ALL-BEATLES EDITION!

1–3 ▪ The Beatles, "A Day in the Life" from *Sgt. Pepper's Lonely Hearts Club Band* (Capitol, 1967); The Handsome Family, *In the Air* (Carrot Top) and *Down in the Valley: A Treasury of Their Most Willowy and Haunted Songs* (Carrot Top, 1994–2000) Thirty-three years ago, the Beatles marshaled every studio trick to form a collage meant to enclose all modern existence in the arms of absurdity and alienation; the result was stupendous. It made those already passé '50s shibboleths seem so new you couldn't tell the threat from the thrill. The Beatles excavated the habitual in a car crash and the routine in art. They revealed the visionary possibilities of a commute. They threw in what sounded like complete symphony orchestras, echo chambers, electronic distortion and, to end it all, the return of the lost chord. Two-thirds of a century's worth of avant-garde experiments from cubism to futurist noise to Eduardo Paolozzi's post-war "Pop!" assemblages were boiled down into a pop song meant to last forever. The world reeled, then; today, when the seams and stitches of the piece may be more immediately apparent than the whole, it still sounds like a miracle, or an accident.

The Handsome Family, aka Brett (music, vocals) and Rennie (words) Sparks of Chicago, work the deep mines of fundamentalist American music, from the pre-blues and proto-country shouts and ballads where it is presumed that there are no experiments or accidents. In this valley, all thoughts and sounds (here made with guitar, bass, banjo, melodica, piano, drum machine and autoharp) are somehow pre-ordained. There are no seams or stitches, but only a reach toward a secret that enclosed existence before human beings learned to write and will enclose it when they have forgotten how.

The Handsome Family's music is meant to seem discovered, not made; fated, not willed, but when fate is altogether out of your hands absurdity translates as guilt. Across the three albums mostly drawn on for *Down in the Valley*—*Odessa, Milk and Scissors* and *Through the Trees*—the songs that begin as murder ballads in the recognizable line of "Omie Wise" or "Tom Dooley"—the 1994 "Arlene," the 1996 "Winnebago Skeletons"—reach the verge of the 1998 "My Sister's Tiny Hands," which is the "A Day in the Life" of folk music.

Like the Beatles, the Handsome Family use everything they have, everything they can find; the difference is, the effects seem less to have been imposed on a composition than to be circling around a story like vultures. Shadowy clouds pass over the drama of twins so close in the womb and then in life you know neither will ever find another mate; when they are separated by a snake that leaves one dead and the other mad, winds blow through the tale so fiercely you can't tell them from baying hounds, chasing the singer through the swamp as he seeks to kill every snake on earth with a stick. But you don't have to hear the shadows, the wind, the howling. It's all subsumed into Brett Sparks' already-dead narrative tone, his refusal to give up the ghost just yet (over there, over there, one more snake!). The oldest truly common American folk song is the snakebite epic "Springfield Mountain," which is sardonic, mocking and social, a joke for the whole town to share. The aloneness that is the final subject of "My Sister's Tiny Hands" is about a much older, more notorious snake, and in this case Adam is cast out of Eden without Eve; he buried her in the garden. And it's all his fault. If he had never been born, she wouldn't have had to die.

In the Air, the Handsome Family's new album, takes many steps back from this high Gothic—from haunts Edgar Allen Poe might have envied, never mind Bob Dylan. This is like Dylan's soft-footed *Nashville Skyline*—with the portents and warnings of *John Wesley Harding*, of "All Along the Watchtower" and "The Wicked Messenger" hiding inside it. You can miss the murders, the torments of an isolation that is far beyond the help of a mere idea like alienation, because, as the record promises, you are in the air: floating on the airs of flattened melodies, calmed orchestrations, lowered voices. The music might be all about weather, no rain in sight. Outside of the quiet spell the music casts, though, the weather may have to change many times before the songs give up what they hold.

4–9 ■ Astrid Kirchherr & Klaus Voormann, *Hamburg Days* (Genesis Publications / Govinda Gallery) In concert with a "Hamburg Days" exhibition—a show running through March 18 of paintings by original Beatle Stu Sutcliffe, who died in Hamburg in 1962; the early-'60s photographs of the Beatles made by his lover Kirchherr; and new Hamburg-days paintings by Hamburg Beatles discoverer Voormann—the Govinda Gallery of Washington, D.C., is distributing *Hamburg Days*, a two-volume, boxed, Genesis art book, available in a limited edition of 2,500 copies for $480, shipping included. It might be recalled that in 1980 Genesis issued a similarly limited $356 edition of George Harrison's *I Me Mine*—which showed up not long after in a $12.95 version published by Simon & Schuster.

No matter how augmented, dressed up or padded with sketches, scene-setting documentation and everything else anyone can think of, as a painter Voormann remains an ordinary commercial artist and Kirchherr's photos remain unforgettable, more severe than they are playful. In line with the way her pictures were restaged and she was interpreted in the fine 1993 Ian

Softley movie *Backbeat*—interpreted as a postwar Mona Lisa by Sheryl Lee, who put her Laura Palmer prettiness into her eyes— her posed portraits of the Beatles as a group or as individuals, or her own self-portraits, communicate more than anything a moment that is about to vanish. As the Beatles played all night in the worst strip club in town, Kirchherr and Voormann glimpsed them as the true avatars of the postwar world they had been trying to make for themselves in bohemian, art-school Hamburg. Her pictures say that in an instant these determined-looking young men are going to leave not only Kirchherr but themselves behind as they are transformed into figments of the common imagination of the entire world.

Beyond the photos—which can be seen elsewhere, though not so gorgeously— what makes *Hamburg Days* uncanny is the way it functions as a collective Kirchherr-Voormann memoir. As they remember growing up under the Nazis, you're reminded how close to the Nazis they and the Beatles all were in 1960, and how close the Nazis remained to them. "We had to say 'Heil Hitler' when we got to school in the morning, and it was the standard greeting when you met someone in the street," Kirchherr says. "When the war was finished and the English came, my mother took me aside and warned me, 'Now you must never say that again,' and I didn't know why. I'd thought it was like saying, 'How do you do?'" She is explicit that her and her friends' attempt to create their own culture, really a kind of secret society, out of Cocteau, the Marquis de Sade, Oscar Wilde, Sartre, and Villon—all combining into something much closer to present-day Goth than '60s existentialism—was an attempt to negate their identity as people who would have grown up as Nazis if Hitler had won: "So even before we met the Beatles, we were creating our own little innocent revolution." It was the success she saw coming for the Beatles, not the guilt of the past, that would take away whatever innocence that revolution had; once you help change the world, innocence is the last thing you can claim.

On his recent Hamburg-days album, *Run Devil Run* (Capitol), Paul McCartney acts as if he never did change the world. The lack of anguish and authority in his bash-and-split renditions of such old Beatles favorites as Carl Perkins' "Movie Magg" or Larry Williams' "She Said Yeah" is as weird as the 1999 picture inside the box, where he looks more like his own child than himself. The music is alive—but nothing close to the anarchy of the music the Beatles actually made in Hamburg. You can find it on various official and legally-contested Live-from-the-Star-Club albums; it was never more raw than on a tape bootlegged as *The International Battle of the Century: The Beatles vs. The Third Reich*. This was a take-off on a real album, in which Vee-Jay Records of Chicago recycled the early EMI Beatles recordings to which they briefly held rights: *The International Battle of the Century: The Beatles vs. the Four Seasons*. On the back was a checklist, where you could award between 10 and zero points to, say, "Baby It's You" vs. "Big Girls Don't Cry." The *Third Reich* version was far more inspired: the likes of "Matchbox" and "Little Queenie" vs. audience noise titled "Arbeit Mach Frei," "Schweinehund," "Your Papers, Please" and "Vhere Ist Pete Best?" Starting tepidly with "A Taste of Honey" and "Till There Was You," the band, with Paul doing most of the singing and John taunting the crowd, soon goes absolutely elsewhere, into sounds so rough the songs barely retain a shred of recognizability. On "Talkin' 'Bout You" 1977 London punk is discovered, not as style but strictly as form, with a disorientingly atonal one-note guitar solo—here, as on "Where Have You Been All My Life" and "Roll Over Beethoven," impossible to credit as the work of sober, worried George. A tame Carl Perkins ditty like "Everybody's Trying to Be My Baby" goes over the edge into a kind of war—or right into the secret society into which Kirchherr and Voormann had already initiated the Beatles, and vice versa.

10 ■ **Ringo Starr, TV commercial for Charles Schwab** As drummer for Rory Storm and the Hurricanes, Ringo often sat in with the Beatles in Hamburg; now he sits up straight in an office delivering investment-counsel gobbledygook to up-and-comers as the menacing piano line of "Money (That's What I Want)" bangs in the background. Of all the Beatles' official recordings, their 1963 cover of Barrett Strong's 1959 original (the first Motown record; there's a blood-and-guts account of the making of the Detroit template in Raynoma Gordy Singleton's *Berry, Me and Motown*, often translated as "Bury Me in Motown") was perhaps the only one to capture the spirit of the Hamburg cauldron—capture it, and heave it at the world. Whenever I hear the Beatles' version, aiming, it seems for its whole length, at John's scream "I WANT TO BE FREE!" I know that nothing could ever be better. I hope Ringo made a good deal: the commercial is a reminder, or, for those who haven't heard the record, a clue.

MARCH 6, 2000

1 ■ **Mary Lou Lord, "Aim Low," on *Mary Lou Lord/Sean Na Na* (Kill Rock Stars)** After the who-cares kick of Janis "The Female Elvis" Martin's old rockabilly twirl "Bang Bang" and the shtick mournfulness of Lucinda Williams' "Hard Road" (could there be any other sort of road in a Williams song?), Lord ends her half of this EP with real indie soul music: a version of the Bevis Frond's pretty, painful account of someone afraid of the sound of her own voice, somehow combined with the momentum of Trisha Yearwood's "She's in Love With the Boy." That one song says "You got no target, it's impossible to miss it" and the other says "reach for the stars" turns out to have nothing to do with why both are good.

2 ■ **Julien Temple, director, *The Filth and the Fury* (Fine Line)** Temple, who made the much-fictionalized Sex Pistols film *The Great Rock 'n Roll Swindle* for impresario Malcolm McLaren in 1980, returns with a documentary for the surviving band

members—all of whom, for present-day interviews, are presented in silhouette, either because they don't want to look old or, as Temple has said, because it makes them look like criminals. How cool. Like the opening Collapse of England montage, which is supposed to set the Pistols' eruption in a causative social context, the device is a distraction. As Johnny Rotten makes clear, he wasn't fighting unemployment or corruption or racism or Pink Floyd—he was fighting resignation, in all its forms. He thinks he lost: "Yes, I can take on England," he says of himself and Sid Vicious. "But I couldn't take on one heroin addict."

"They are the antithesis of human existence," says a London council member. What comes across in the still-shocking, irreducible performance footage, often fitted to studio recordings, is Rotten's absolute seriousness—the sense that he's on some suicidal mission, that he has no choice—and the unprecedented, unfollowed power of the songs he used. Perhaps most riveting is a segment (shot in a small venue, from below the stage, in blue tint) of "God Save the Queen." Rotten is in a conventional, unripped suit jacket and bow tie. The clothes accentuate him not as a juvenile delinquent but as a speaker in the public square, dressed respectfully to address his fellow citizens—with the rain of frogs that 16th century artists showed spewing from the mouth of the Antichrist now issuing from his. "At least when I die," guitarist Steve Jones says today, "they can say, I did something."

3–4 ▪ **Will Oldham, *Guarapero—Lost Blues 2* (Drag City), and Byrds, "Lover of the Bayou," on (*Unissued*) from (*Untitled*)/(*Unissued*) (Columbia Legacy)** Oldham, in Louisville in the 1990s, and Roger McGuinn, in Hollywood in 1970, heard something glamorous and unkillable in old American music. To Oldham, it might have been music that was altogether forgotten, so that to remember it would require a voice that could leave its body. To McGuinn, it was a Technicolor movie starring none other. "I'm the lover of the bayou!" he crows, mak-

ing a complete fool of himself, except that the crossing rhythmic lines of a band exploding into a song—the guitars, the voice and the leading harmonica pulling away from each other—open the story to the point where you can see the singer turning into a Louisiana Paul Bunyan, striding from Lafayette to Baton Rouge in a single step.

Oldham sings like the kid McGuinn's hero took into the swamp to raise and then forgot. His voice cracks opens fissures of doubt in everything he says. At his most vehement he sounds the most frightened. "Johnny Ace was drunk, was fucked, was NOT ON STAGE" he insists of the spectral R&B singer who shot himself playing Russian roulette on Christmas Eve 1954—as if the fact that Ace did it in his dressing room is what's really important, though Oldham will never be able to explain why. Unless it's because he believes the old story that it was really Ace's label boss Don Robey who pulled the trigger.

5 ▪ **Milla Jovovich, "Satellite of Love," on *The Million Dollar Hotel—Music From the Motion Picture* (Interscope)** Intense, clumsy, convincing—who'd have guessed that if you put the actress who wore the adhesive-tape dress in *The Fifth Element* behind an old Lou Reed song she'd sound just like Macy Gray?

6 ▪ **David Thomas and Foreigners, *Bay City* (Thirsty Ear)** Bay City—a.k.a. Santa Monica—was the nice little mob town where Raymond Chandler's private eye Philip Marlowe went to get beat up in the '40s. In Denmark, the brooding leader of Pere Ubu tries to walk its streets, but they might as well be water under his feet. Read *Farewell, My Lovely* instead.

7–8 ▪ **Beachwood Sparks, *Beachwood Sparks* (Sub Pop) and Broken by Whispers, *Trembling Blue Stars* (Sub Pop)** Sub Pop was once the arm the Seattle scene reached out to the rest of the world. By way of London and Los Angeles it's now offering two of the wimpiest records you'll ever hear—or, if the times are better than this music is betting they are, won't. As the critic Mark Shipper imagined the perfect James Taylor lyric back in the early '70s: "The wind blows/I fall down."

9 ■ **Steely Dan, *Two Against Nature* (Giant)** You might think it's against nature for Donald Fagen and Walter Becker to return with music precisely as airless as that offered on their last studio album, *Gaucho,* which came out in 1980. But maybe inside the not-very-clever tunes is an argument: I'm Rip van Winkle! I slept for 20 years and missed nothing! As the more interesting Steely Dan "Timeline/Bio" wheel included in the press packet says of 1947, the year before Fagen's birth: "Charlie 'Bird' Parker records 'Klacktoveedsedsteen' for an obscure jazz label. This is the last significant work of the classic period. Nothing very important happens from this moment on."

10 ■ **On Feb. 21 at 63rd Street and College Avenue, Oakland, Calif.** "Heard anything important to you on the radio today?" asked a radio commercial. No: just *Morning Edition*'s false concern, filmmakers bragging about how smart they are on *Fresh Air,* no music worth the time it takes to change the station. Then at Royal Coffee, where neighbors' complaints have put severe limits on what employees can play, a shock: Etta James' fabulously girly 1963 "Two Sides to Every Story" ("There's always his side, and yours too!"), with the women in the shop singing under their breath to the frantic scratchy chorus. "They're always two sides to every story!" James shouts as her two backing singers, little devil and little angel perched on her shoulders, go "TWO SIDES!" and then swoon together into a sighing "Yeahhhhh"—it just fades, slides, there's nothing like it—when James meets a new guy. In the sister shop next door: Hank Williams' "I Saw the Light," the morning suddenly so unfixed you could imagine everyone in the place converting on the spot.

MARCH 20, 2000

1 ■ **Ernest C. Withers, *Pictures Tell the Story* (Chrysler Museum of Art, Norfolk, Va.)** In this companion volume to the exhibition running through May 7—the first collec-

tion of work by a Memphis, Tenn., photographer best known for his 1950s shots of Memphis musicians looking as if they own the world—the most notable pictures are from the civil rights movement. There is *"Tent City" Family,* from Tennessee in 1960, evicted from their home for voting; the smile in the father's eyes is devastating in its pride. There is the well-dressed young protester carrying a sign reading, "Communist Can Eat Here Why Can't We?" There is *First Day of Memphis Integration,* 1961, three young children looking out a car window, one of them a girl of perhaps 7 with eyes so bright you can't believe the future she sees isn't real, and a scared woman in the front seat covering her face. There is a filthy toilet, a sink and a rotting wall, an image so stark, ugly and composed you can read it as an art photograph aestheticizing squalor until you read the caption: "Boarding House Bathroom from Which James Earl Ray Shot Dr. King, 422 South Main Street." And there is King's funeral procession, moving down Main Street in Memphis, past the State Theater advertising "ELVIS PRESLEY AT HIS BEST: 'STAY AWAY JOE.'"

Despite the fact that Withers' 1956 and '57 photos of the Hillbilly Cat smiling backstage with B. B. King and Brook Benton are pictures of brotherhood, this is the most complete image there is of the irrelevance, and the silence, of Elvis. After that, the shot of the Bobby Bland band onstage in about 1950—in essayist Daniel Wolff's description, traveling "in a one two three beat from Bland to his hot guitarist to the blissful young sax player, with a final rim shot provided by the portrait of W. C. Handy on the wall behind"—is a relief you may think you have no right to feel.

2 ■ **Cadallaca, *Out West* (Kill Rock Stars)** In this side project, organist "Dusty" (Sarah Dougher of the Lookers), guitarist "Kissy" (Corin Tucker of Sleater-Kinney) and drummer "STS" (Junior of the Lookers) nail what Lesley "You Don't Own Me" (But) "That's the Way Boys Are" Gore would have done in 1980 if she'd blown off

her age and formed a punk band with ? and the Mysterians. That is, as Kissy she'd get all Frankie and Johnny on her cheating lover ("Out West"), but dropping Frankie's regrets for Mili Avital's "I never loved you anyway" in *Dead Man*; as Dusty she'd sing about sex in a car to the one she did it with so that the bad memory will last longer for the other person than for her.

3 ▪ **Cat Power, *The Covers Record* (Matador)** Chan Marshall is precious and arty. She can also make "(I Can't Get No) Satisfaction" sound like a version of "Boys Don't Cry" and Moby Grape's 1967 walk down Haight Street, "Naked If I Want To," feel as if it's chiseled on a tombstone. Which it probably is, somewhere.

4 ▪ **Sarge, *Distant* (Mud)** Last words from the defunct Illinois punk quartet, with both new tunes ("Detroit Star-lite") and live old ones ("Fast Girls") jumping with singer/writer/guitarist Elizabeth Elmore's singular leaps from desperation to amusement to confusion to gritting her teeth. Plus a "These Boots Are Made for Walkin'" that should have been recorded as karaoke, not in a studio with horns.

5 ▪ **Robert Frank, *US 285 (1956)* outside "Walker Evans" (Metropolitan Museum of Art, New York, through May 14)** The comprehensive retrospective of the Evans photographs—the first, it said there—was in truth pretty skimpy and suffered from overfamiliarity. The countless outtakes from the 1936 Alabama work known from Evans' and James Agee's *Let Us Now Praise Famous Men* were completely ignored in favor of the official images. Making a stronger claim, in a lead-in gallery devoted to photographs that influenced Evans and were inspired by him, was a single picture from Robert Frank's 1958 collection *The Americans*, the most ordinary and mythic shot imaginable, just a flat road in the middle of the night in the middle of nowhere, white line down the middle, one black car approaching. Evans' comments on the piece, from 1958 *US Camera Annual*, more or less a Theory of the Springsteen Road Song, appeared next to it: "In

this picture, you instantly find the continent. The whole page is haunted with American scale and space, which the mind fills in quite automatically—though possibly with memories of negation or violence or of exhaustion with thoughts of bad cooking, extremes of heat and cold, law enforcement, and the chance to work hard in a filling station."

A few lines from Ishmael Reed's 1972 novel *Mumbo Jumbo* should have been there, too: "'Deluxe Ice Cream, Coffee, 1 cent Pies, Cakes, Tobacco, Hot Dogs and Highways,'" says a Haitian to 1920s Harlem hoodoo detectives PaPa LaBas and Black Herman. "'Highways leading to nowhere. Highways leading to somewhere. Highways the [U.S. Marines'] Occupation used to speed along in their automobiles, killing dogs, pigs and cattle belonging to the poor people. What IS the American fetish about highways?' 'They want to get somewhere,' LaBas offers. 'Because something is after them,' Black Herman adds. 'But what is after them?' 'They are after themselves. They call it destiny. Progress. We call it Haints.'"

6 ▪ **"Rock Style" (Metropolitan Museum of Art)** A Tommy Hilfiger production, with co-sponsorship from Condé Nast and Estée Lauder, it made you feel like you'd dreamed your way into a *Vanity Fair* ad supplement and would never wake up.

7 ▪ **Randy Weeks, "Madeline," on *Madeline* (Hightone)** The composer of Lucinda Williams' "Can't Let Go" digs himself into a very dark, very convincing seduction song in a town where there's nothing else to do. Weeks' voice isn't strong enough to make the recording stand up for long, but while it lasts there's a cruel, alluring shadow of Larry Clark's *Tulsa* in the background.

8 ▪ **Hillary Clinton at Riverside Church, New York (March 5)** What's disarming about Hillary Clinton is the way she stands up in front of a crowd and speaks at length in paragraphs, without notes, without seeming to have memorized anything, simply as if she knows her own mind. She's that organized and that fierce. But this day, addressing the not-guilty verdict in the trial of the

police who shot Amadou Diallo without mentioning it, she was, one by one, reading the sort of words ("To hunker down instead of reaching out. To shut doors instead of opening them") nobody speaks without counting the cost of each.

9 ▪ Chloë Sevigny gets lucky in love in *If These Walls Could Talk 2* (HBO, March 5) After getting HIV in *Kids* the first time she has sex, V.D. in *The Last Days of Disco* the first time she has sex, falling in love with a man who turns out to be a woman and then gets shot in front of her in *Boys Don't Cry*, it's about time. Interesting music, too—faraway, smoky soul—as opposed to the horrifying washing-machine melodies of the Ellen De-Generes/Sharon Stone episode.

10 ▪ Washington Phillips, "I Had a Good Father and Mother," on *Storefront and Street-corner Gospel (1927–1929)* (Document, Austria) A heavy-set, unsmiling man in his 30s, Phillips had a sense of humor ("Denomination Blues," a deadpan account of the endless antipathies Christian orders find in a message of love). He played an instrument that sounded like an electric zither run through a Leslie speaker cabinet, showing you a heaven populated by ghosts. In 1929, at his last recording session, he sang the saddest song in the world, thanking his parents for putting him on the right path. You listen and you know the world is poorer because he is not in it.

APRIL 3, 2000

1 ▪ Lou Reed, "Possum Time," from *Ecstasy* (Reprise) It's 18 minutes long and you can play it all day long. A huge fuzztone that sounds more like a construction site than a guitar sets an implacable, unsatisfiable zigzag line in play. "It's possum time!" a slightly demented, definitely pleased man announces. "I feel like a possum in every way!" In fact he sounds like a man who won't back down, and you follow him, at a distance, on a nighttown walk. When it ends it's as if the sun is coming up—so soon? Already? You've seen nothing that isn't ugly, but the walk has its own rewards.

"The only one left standing," Reed says, sounding tired. He's grown all the way into his role as bad conscience—his own and the nation's. He may even grow out of it, but not yet. When, in the Velvet Underground, in another era, a young man who sounded old sang with fright and nausea of "all the dead bodies piled up in mounds," who'd have thought that more than three decades later he'd still be prowling the streets looking for more of them, more bodies, more mounds, like a detective of the obvious?

2 ▪ Phil Collins, "You'll Be in My Heart," best original song (Academy Awards, March 26) Given that as an original song "You'll Be in My Heart" barely exists, Collins sang the hell out of it—while wearing the night's best-looking suit.

3 ▪ Nick Tosches, *The Devil and Sonny Liston* (Little, Brown) This short, clean book about the St. Louis Stagger Lee who in 1964, in one of the most shocking upsets in boxing history, lost the heavyweight championship to Cassius Clay (Muhammad Ali, soon enough), is a keen reminder of the limits of biography—limits biographers almost never respect. That is: the biographer's subject has no inner life. No matter how many letters, diaries or suicide notes the subject leaves behind, all you have are lies. You can't know what goes on in someone else's head—unless you are a novelist, and are willing to imagine another's inner life, at which point biography ceases and fiction begins. So as you pass through this account of a man whose notoriety probably bought him only a few more years than he could have expected from a life on the street, don't wonder what, in the depths of his soul, he really thought. As Tosches tries to decide why Liston was found dead in his house in Las Vegas in 1971—dead, probably, for a week—think about what Tosches calls "the unseen sediment, detritus, and sludge beneath the course of this book." He means the world of manipulation and enforcement, murder and fraud, that the biographer's illusion that we can know what makes a person tick allows us to ignore.

4–5 ■ **Patti Smith, *Gung Ho* (Arista) & Angie Aparo, *The American* (Arista)** Two albums from the same label with the American flag imprinted on the discs. Aparo is a shaved-head guy who poses in front of urban wreckage but sings like a sensitive '70s troubadour; Smith bleeds for all humankind, but she's noisier. On "Strange Messengers" she condemns slavery. Just as she once confidently declared herself a "Rock 'n' Roll Nigger," now she slumps to the ground as the whip cuts her flesh and her children are sold down the river. "History sends such strange messengers," she announces: guess who? With her band just a megaphone and her singing merely a flag to wave, she pulls out all the stops, shouting: "My people!/I speak to you!/I burned, I swung, I toiled for you and your children!" But now all her people do is "burn out your lives on crack and sorrowful stories," betraying their ancestors, betraying *her*. (By the way, what's wrong with sorrowful stories?) She hasn't even gotten to Vietnam yet, or the sneering twist she gives the words "Colonial-*ism*, imperial-*ism*," as if the real purpose of history were to confirm the hipster's superiority to it. "Donna, donna, donna/I'm the world's Madonna," National Lampoon's *Radio Dinner* once had Joan Baez warble; Smith has taken over, but somehow lost Baez's fab sense of humor along the way.

6 ■ **Dennis Miller, "Rant on Patriotism," *Dennis Miller Live* (HBO, March 24)** "You want to dwell on this country's fuck-ups? Be my guest . . . But you might want to remember that when you stomped into CIA headquarters waving your Freedom of Information Act permission slip you were not summarily hustled into a damp sub-basement where a jackbooted sadist with one eyebrow and tinted aviators Elvis wouldn't even fucking wear is smoking unfiltered cigarettes that smell like a skunk getting a perm as he clamps jumper cables on your nipples and starts humming the love theme from *Midnight Express*." Too true. On the other hand, there's that scene in *Top Secret!* where Val Kilmer is being tortured by East German secret police. Delirious, he sees himself wandering the empty halls of his all-American high school: he registered for a class, he forgot all about it, now he's trying to get to the final, but school was over last week, and . . . and then he comes to. The East Germans crank the juice on the jumper cables, but a satisfied smile spreads over Kilmer's face: it was only a dream.

7 ■ **Surveillance Camera Players, *1984*, on *Surveillance Camera Players*** This small troupe stages plays in front of surveillance cameras, often in subways, then films the action off public monitor screens. Here, with four actors, eight minutes (out of a 45-minute video) and a pidgin comic-book script (signs held up by a man in a grinning death's-head mask, I.D. placards around the necks of Winston and Julia), the story comes across: because it's so familiar a few slogans and the right setting can call the whole thing back, especially when weird organ-like music is leaking in from another corridor, people pass by the show as if it's invisible, and the primitivism of the dramaturgy reduces Orwell's prophecy to the scale of litter. "WE ARE THE DEAD" reads the lovers' sign; Death's Head holds up the novus ordo seclorum Masonic pyramid from the dollar bill. "Can I ask you what you're doing here?" says a man with a security guard's menacing politeness. "Taping this," says a woman. "Do you have a permit for this?" Death's Head holds up "ROOM 101." "You don't need a permit to do this," the woman says. "You don't?" "Why are you guys doing this?" says a second man. "To show that surveillance cameras are everywhere," says the woman. "Yeah," the man laughs, "but who doesn't know that?" Death's Head shoots Winston in the head; from somewhere, there's applause.

8 ■ **"They Can't Sing . . . But They Can Play" (Oakland Athletics TV commercial)** The team's youngest ballplayers take turns on a ratty high school auditorium stage where a bored, smiling, middle-aged music teacher is playing the organ. With cracking voices and expressions of absolute sincerity they apply themselves to a song that was a hit well before any of them were born: Simon and Garfunkel's "Scarborough Fair," here killed deader in under a minute than countless karaoke bars have managed in decades.

9 ■ **Rosie and the Originals, *The Best of Rosie and the Originals* (Ace)** For the 1960 "Angel Baby"; a lovely, previously unreleased cover of the Students' 1958 "I'm So Young" ("Can't marry no one"); and a study of how a group with one perfect moment in it tries to stave off the inevitable.

10 ■ **Ass Ponys, "Swallow You Down," from *Some Stupid with Flare Gun* (Checkered Past)** This is what the Twin Cities Twin-Tone sound of the 1980s was for—the Replacements, Hüsker Dü, Soul Asylum and Babes in Toyland using guitars to render ordinary stuff heroic, tragic, a thrill—but now it's 20 years later in Ohio and the guys in the band are promising a suicidal friend they won't walk away, not ever. They build the music until it's too good to let loose, so they let it sweep them up, riding a sunny, rising melody for "I won't let them swallow"—and then crashing hard for "you down," paying off the loan the first five words took out on a pledge easier to make than to keep. This is what it's all for.

APRIL 17, 2000

1 ■ **Marah, *Kids from Philly* (E Squared/Artemis)** I haven't heard a band sing so convincingly from the inside of a bad neighborhood since the Youngbloods' "Four in the Morning," and that was a long time ago. Marah works with a small, tight sound, as if they have nothing they can afford to waste, but they're far-seeing. Their best pieces seem at once cramped—as cramped as the room the singer rents—and infinitely expansive: you have no idea how far the songs will go before they'll let go of you. For a moment you might wonder why the Vietnam tune "Roundeye Blues" begins with castanets and a radio-familiar three-stroke drum pattern, but after that you're too caught up in the story to care. The sudden density of the music and the cruelty of the ideas inside it shoot up on the chorus, burning off the romanticism of some young guy's war fantasy. "Don't smoke the Bible," the singer warns. The last verse ends with a stinger; it's so harsh, so unpolished, you can't accept it as the last word. You want the story to go on. But by then the singer is trailing away, musing over the Ronettes' "Be My Baby," and you find out what those castanets and that drum pattern were for.

2 ■ ***Down and Out—The Sad Soul of the Black South* (Trikont)** This extraordinarily sophisticated anthology focuses on obscure singers and strange records. It begins with George Perkins and the Silver Stars' 1971 "Crying in the Streets," a purposeful negation of Martha and the Vandellas' 1964 "Dancing in the Street" and a eulogy for the Civil Rights Movement. "I see somebody marching," Perkins cries, but he doesn't; he's crying in the street because all he sees are ghosts. Then there is Bill Brandon's "Rainbow Road," a generic voice telling a generic tale, but with such pathos it seems that without the existence of a genre, which allows men and women to disappear into anonymity, some would never have the nerve to speak at all. And there is Dicky Williams' "In The Same Motel," an adult version of the Rays' 1957 "Silhouettes," where a guy comes home from work and behind the shade of his big picture window sees his wife kissing another man—except it isn't her, because he lives in one of the new subdivisions where all the streets and houses look the same and he's "on the wrong block." This time the guy's out of town in a motel with thin walls; he's just settling down for a lonely night on the road when he picks up the sounds the man and woman in the next room are making. "Oh," he says in a way you wish he wouldn't, "I got so tired of hearing my woman scream." "I am a forgotten lover/That is, if you have time to hear," Virgil Griffin and the Rhythm Kings sing so modestly from Greensville, Miss., speaking not only for everyone here but for the genre itself.

3 ■ ***Sinners and Saints (1926–1931)* (Document)** Early commercial recordings of

pre-blues song survivals, from the T.C.I. Section Crew's very smooth railroad-gang number "Track Linin'"—a cappella gospel in form, a day's first cup of coffee and train whistles inside of it—to the Nugrape Twins' odes to a drink that will make you a better person and bring you closer to God.

4 ▪ Sarah Dougher, The Walls Ablaze (Mr. Lady) Organist for the cheapo-punk trio Cadallaca, Dougher sings and plays out of doubt here, dropping hints all over the place that happy endings are elsewhere. The women in her songs might be kin to the character Samantha Morton plays in *Jesus' Son*, all brains and fatalism, contemptuous of the obligation to explain herself even as she does exactly that.

5 ▪ Down to the Promised Land—5 Years of Bloodshot Records (Bloodshot) There are more gems among these 40 previously unheard tracks by bands on or about the Chicago country label than the Handsome Family's cover of Bill Monroe's "I Hear a Sweet Voice Calling," Rico Bell and the Snakehandlers' bitter "Money to Burn" or Hazeldine's dark, damned "Unforgiven." That's merely all I've found so far. But if there's anything better than Amy Nelson and Eddie Spaghetti of the Seersuckers mooning about what they did on the floor I'll be surprised.

6–7 ▪ J. Bottum, "The Soundtracking of America" (Atlantic Monthly, March) & Philip Roth, The Human Stain (Houghton Mifflin) There are many reactionary propositions in critic J. Bottum's manifesto—notably the idea that there was once a common "belief in the intellectual coherence of human beings and the world," that "Music used to have a purpose: to express and, indeed, to perpetuate this shared sense of coherence." Now, that coherence is lost and music has no purpose. It is empty, nothing more than a soundtrack, interference, static, aural caffeine.

What this actually means is that once upon a time only certain people needed to be taken into account as "human beings and the world"—*that's* what's gone. Any future shared sense of coherence will have to be based on something more than the hegemony of a single, and singly gendered, ethnic group. But Bottum doesn't hear it this way. He hears only the emptiness of music as such, the muteness, and with the great goal of social coherence—or, in reality, social domination—missing, he hears the danger of music. Bottum hears it as an irrational art form; it cannot contain ideas. It grants false but overwhelming credence to sentiments of utter vapidity and banality: "Even in, say, Vivaldi's 'Four Seasons'—in, that is, a deliberate effort to make music express something rational—the ideas it takes 45 minutes to convey amount to little more than winter is cold and summer is hot." Music convinces us we know what we don't, understand what we've never thought about. Worst of all—my characterization of Bottum's thesis, not his—music makes ordinary people feel heroic, as if they can do anything and be anyone. But it's all a lie: "What can a genuinely tragic folk song tell us, except that we no longer know what to make of tragedy?"

As Sgt. Joe Friday used to say to his partner in the *Mad* magazine *Dragged Net* parodies, "How's your mom, Ed?" Coleman Silk, in Philip Roth's new novel, a 71-year-old classics professor, can explain. Banished from the college he once transformed, he's caught up in a transforming affair with a 34-year-old janitor. Now every Saturday night he tunes in the local Big Band show and, he says, "Everything stoical within me unclenches and the wish not to die, never to die, is almost too great to bear. And all this from listening to Vaughn Monroe." He goes on: "Let anyone born in 1926 try to stay alone at home on a Saturday night in 1998 and listen to Dick Haymes singing 'Those Little White Lies.' Just have them do that, and then tell me afterwards if they have not understood at last the celebrated doctrine of the catharsis effected by tragedy." Who do you trust, a real-life critic or an imaginary professor? One whose true demand on art is that it offer not ideas but arguments, or one who believes that music less contains ideas than finds them in those who hear it, and then says what those ideas are worth?

8 ▪ Melvins, "Smells Like Teen Spirit" and "Ramblin' Man," from *The Crybaby* (Ipecac) Buzz Osborne of the Melvins was Kurt Cobain's first mentor in punk, so he has as much right as Tori Amos to cover Cobain's best song. Hey, it's a free country, so he even has a right to ask '70s flesh-crawlingly rock-bottom teen idol Leif Garrett to sing it on the Melvins' guest stars album. Fruit of perhaps the most perverse singer-to-song match since Bert Parks sang Bob Dylan's "Maggie's Farm" in *The Freshman* (and he was *great*), the track begins so pristinely, with such punch, it suggests a terrible possibility. What if Garrett, currently heading a band called Godspeed and looking like the sort of person who'd paper his walls with pictures of the sort of person he used to look like, rises to the occasion? What if he's *good?* The world remains on its axis; Garrett is completely effete. You can hear all the words, and without Cobain's mumbles, his swallowed lyrics, the fear of being understood, there is no music. Then Hank Williams III takes his grandfather's spookiest tune. The hesitation in the way the melody opens up—the curling finger, then the fading smoke, of the first notes on the steel guitar—make it Williams' most cloven-hoofed. The band never pushes the song, and never loses it, but after two verses the young singer falls behind, which only makes the drama more believable.

9 ▪ Common, *Like Water for Chocolate* (MCA) If the cover art—a 1956 Gordon Parks photo of a young black woman in Alabama, dressed for church, drinking from a "Colored Only" water fountain—is the music, and the record's title the words, nothing on the record itself comes close. I don't know what would, though.

10 ▪ Bruce Springsteen and the E-Street Band, *Land of Hope and Dreams* (Crystal Cat bootleg, Barcelona, April 11, 1999) It's stirring to hear the old sanctified train that don't carry no gamblers turn into a train that carries whoever most needs a ride: "Losers and winners, whores and gamblers, broken-hearted, souls departed." And it's stirring to hear them all lift their glasses together and sing their own song. Caveat emptor: the fans in Barcelona couldn't clap on the beat to save their city from Franco.

MAY 1, 2000

1 ▪ *American Psycho*, directed by Mary Harron (Lions Gate) This really is Katrina Leskanich's moment. In 1985 with Katrina and the Waves she scrubbed the airwaves clean with the horrifyingly bright "Walking on Sunshine." ("Soon to be a major floor-wax commercial," one reviewer wrote at the time.) Now the gruesome thing is leaking out of Patrick Bateman's headphones as he heads into his office, serves as a hideous wake-up call in *High Fidelity*, and chirps from your TV in incessant ads for Claritin allergy pills while fresh-faced folk frolic on the grass and little kids pick up the chorus. No wonder everybody has to die.

2 ▪ Sleater-Kinney, "Is It a Lie," from *All Hands on the Bad One* (Kill Rock Stars) With guitarists Carrie Brownstein and Corin Tucker now joined by drummer Janet Weiss as singers, the music of the band no other group is even chasing is easier to hear and harder to keep up with, especially on this trickily constructed death song—which despite its description of a traffic accident might one day fold into the tradition of 19th-century murder ballads like "Omie Wise" or "Banks of the Ohio." The piece is all questions, and when "Was it a lie?" is asked for the last time, a plain tone exchanged for a who-cares fade, it's not a single person but a whole way of life that seems to have been run down. It's a mystery, but perhaps nothing compared to the one in the cover photo, which looks like documentation of a performance-art piece staged in a union-hall-cum-nightclub circa 1943—or the one in the leading guitar figure on the last cut, "The Swimmer," which is much closer to David Lynch's *Twin Peaks* than John Cheever's river of pools. The meaning of the glamorous photos in the booklet or Brett Vapnek's sparking video for "You're No Rock 'n' Roll Fun" is not mysterious: good clothes can make you happy.

3 ▪ **Green Velvet, *Green Velvet* (F-111)** Techno, very playful, very accessible, very funny when dubbed with dank, deadpan monologues and the multivoiced "Answering Machine," where any number of people, all of whom I like to think are DJ Curtis Jones (otherwise known as Cajamere or Green Velvet), helpfully call up to inform the guy screaming "I! Don't! Need! This! Shit!" that, for example, "I hate to do this over the phone, but I sort of can't do it in person, I want to thank you for the engagement ring, I know you probably gave it to me after I told you I'm pregnant and stuff . . . but the baby's not yours, so you don't have to worry about it, I'll always love you."

4 ▪ **White Town, "Duplicate," from *Peek & Poke* (Parasol)** A man surrounded by two women floats through what could be Human League's "Don't You Want Me Baby" with all the fear, fury and self-hatred removed. At under four minutes it's over far too soon, as if music-maker Jyoti Mishra didn't trust himself. "Inspired by," among others, Monkee Michael Nesmith, late physicist Richard Feynman, preening role model bell hooks and onetime silent movie actor Lev Davidovich Bronstein.

5 ▪ **Hanson, *This Time Around* (Island)** Fine: nothing as catchy as "MMMBop," but eager, jumping, edging up to the territory marked out by the Indigo Girls' "Shame On You."

6 ▪ **Bruce Conner, "Dead Punks and Ashes," Curt Marcus Gallery (578 Broadway, New York, through Saturday)** In 1978 at the Mabuhay Gardens in San Francisco, filmmaker-collagist-sculptor Conner—who more than a decade before orchestrated light shows at the Avalon Ballroom across town—stood at the lip of the stage photographing punk bands for *Search and Destroy*. What he liked most was to catch a group's first gig; after that, he's said, something, some measure of fear and a refusal to give into it, is lost. New York Eye, aka Emily Marcus (related to me, not the gallery), reports: "The few dozen black-and-white photos of actual punk people look like pictures of punks—costumed, rowdy and drunk, including a stoned and skinny Toni Basil (who 12 years before performed in Conner's film *Breakaway*). Weirder are the memorial collages for three local musicians who died, carefully but sparely decorated and surprisingly moving. *Ricky Williams: Dead Punk* (of the Sleepers) stands out (among *Will Shatter* of Negative Trend and Flipper and *Frankie Fix* of Crime) for its draped hospital tubing, catheters still attached, but the pieces work best as a group; it's nice thinking of the three of them hanging out together, and I get the feeling Conner sees himself in their eventual company.

"In the second part of the show Conner brings the doom home. Black-and-white photos of motel TV screens, caught in the middle of the late-night creepshow, welcome and deceive, but the real point of the room is a collection of immodest and unattractive photocopy collages of the artist's decline into illness, pain, old age and cynicism—autobiographical records that are not so much morbid as mundane. It's a dismal room, half full of distracting, barking TVs, with one wonderful exception, and the only piece in the show with a sense of humor: a brick neatly wrapped in an Ace bandage. Brings a smile to my lips."

7 ▪ **Sarah McLachlan, "I Will Remember You," in Columbine High School Massacre video (Jefferson County, Colo., Sheriff's Department)** With her tune running under April 20, 1999, footage of pools of blood in emptied, shattered rooms, McLachlan sounds unspeakably facile and insincere. "I hope that just didn't destroy that song for me for the rest of my life," a cop viewing the video said to a reporter for KRON-TV in San Francisco. But what song wouldn't collapse under this weight? The Rolling Stones' "Gimmie Shelter"? Ice Cube's "Dead Homies"? Of course they would. Nirvana's "Come as You Are" probably would not—but maybe only because Kurt Cobain, too, is dead.

8 ▪ **Neil Young,** *Silver and Gold* **(Reprise)** Given that Young works on a pendulum, this hilariously vapid collection of acoustic musings (might want to get Buffalo Springfield back together, "give it a shot," why not, why not row row row your boat down the L.A. River) presages great things in the future. For the time being, as an old National Lampoon *Radio Dinner* spot had it, "The last half-hour of No Neil Young Music was brought to you by . . ."

9 ▪ **Bad Livers,** *Blood and Mood* **(Sugar Hill)** The quirky backroads duo digs deep into the country that opens up out of Harry Smith's *Anthology of American Folk Music* in order to . . . get really cute.

10 ▪ *Velvet Goldmine,* **directed by Todd Haynes (Miramax, 1998)** I rented this paean to the Ziggy Stardust era to see what Christian Bale was doing before he turned into Norman Bates, and came away touched: by Toni Collette's impersonation of broken down Susan Alexander in the *Citizen Kane* interview scenes, by Ewan McGregor's heedless merging of Iggy Pop and Kurt Cobain, by the dream their characters shared of a world redeemed by style. "We set out to change the world, ended up just changing ourselves," McGregor's washed-up star tells Bale's reporter long years after the glam utopia has vanished. "What's wrong with that?" Bale asks reasonably, but as if he knows exactly what's wrong with it. "Nothing," says McGregor without bitterness, "unless you look at the world"—and the camera pulls back to show the bar they're sitting in, a place devoid of color, flair or self-invention, of Corin Tucker shouting, "Culture is what we make it" on the new Sleater-Kinney album, so roughly it sounds like she's saying "cut your ears."

MAY 15, 2000

1 ▪ **The Holy Childhood,** *Up With What I'm Down With* **(Gern Blandsten)** There's a cracked vision in this sprawling music— some drunk in his 20s conducting the Band with a few female friends to loosen the choruses, maybe—that reaches a pitch of experi-

ence and desire so expansive the whole thing seems to have been recorded outdoors.

2 ▪ **Richard Belzer as Detective John Munch,** *Law and Order: Special Victims Unit* **(May 5)** For once, no joke, no conspiracy mongering, just a case that sucks him in and breaks over his head, leaving his nihilism boiled down to the coldest professionalism, rewriting his ruined skin, wire glasses and dark beady eyes into the most complete deadpan imaginable, so that the suspect has two choices: fall into the black hole of this man's face, or confess, fast.

3 ▪ **Wire at Great American Music Hall, San Francisco (May 2)** Formed in 1976, they were from the start the most severely arty of all British punk bands, and it was their severity that saved them: their pursuit, it always seemed—as over the decades Colin Newman, Robert Gotobed, B. C. Gilbert and Graham Lewis went their own ways and reformed, dumping an all-but-unsolvable confusion of LPs and CDs off the charts—of form before and after anything else. Despite Newman's cutting accent ("London suburban art-school sarcastic," according to critic Jon Savage), or the fact that in 1991, lacking Gotobed, the group recorded as Wir, their humor was all in their melodies, playing against the sense of espionage in their lyrics, against the harsh, absolutely self-contained bass drums guitars rhythms of their ridiculously brief songs. In a word, they were perfect.

For the sold-out first show of an eight-date American tour they were instantly up to speed: terrifically loud but precise, with Newman's staccato delivery for "Pink Flag" letting every word stand out clearly. They were pure punk in shape and attack—punk as wish, as what it could be, as an ideal— but without any baggage as to clothes, attitude, history. Never big stars, they carried nothing more than their old or young-looking selves and their sound onto the stage. Nothing was mythicized; nothing happening in the music referred to anything that wasn't present, except to the degree that the music referred to, or in its way reformed, the world at large. Expressions were dour. Movement was minimal. The four played as if they had invented punk— or had stumbled upon it the day before, as if their project was so conceptual it was completed before it was begun. Doubt and nervousness underlay every tune. The cryptic invitations of the words suggested code. That made the momentary release of the melodies in the likes of "Dot Dash" or "French Film (Blurred)" unbearably pleasurable, because even as you felt the pleasure, you felt it being taken away.

Remaining tour dates: May 15, Irving Plaza, New York; May 26–28, the Garage, London.

4 ▪ **Wire, *Third Day*** Five indistinct rehearsal cuts recorded last fall. Forget the "first edition: 1 of 1,000" printed, not stamped, on the sleeve (as I read it, that means there can be 1,000 first editions of limitless pressings each) and look for *On Returning (1977–1979)* (Retro/EMI, 1989), *Behind the Curtain: Early Versions 1977 & 1978* (EMI, 1995), *Chairs Missing* (Harvest/EMI, 1978, their best) and *Document & Eyewitness* (Rough Trade, 1981), in whatever configurations you might find, plus Ian Penman's fine "Flies in the Ointment" in the March issue of *The Wire*.

5 ▪ **Richard Shindell, *Somewhere Near Patterson* (Signature)** I bought this glossy folk recording because of a fulsome *New York Times* review ("What does it mean to say a singer-songwriter is the best?") trumpeting "the vocal equivalent of Shaker furniture." Bet you didn't know "Shaker" was a synonym for "florid."

6 ▪ **Ben Shahn, Farm Security Administration photo, Oct. 1935** From the FSA home page, go from Subject Index to United States-West Virginia-Welch, from there to United States-West Virginia-Scotts Run, from there to No. 30, and you'll find Shahn's picture of a businessman or government man—dressed in fedora and three-piece suit—sitting in a clearing next to a very handsome guitarist: "Love oh, love, oh keerless love," someone wrote down, at-

tempting to capture the player's mountain dialect. His expression is at once wistful and impassioned, and his face is delicate, almost effete—there's nothing of the weathering of Appalachia in his features—which only makes the caption more odd: "Doped singer relief investigator reported a number of dope cases at Scotts Run." No audio, but listen to Lead Belly's 1935 recording of "Careless Love" (on *Midnight Special*, Rounder) if you want to hear the morphine—in the song, if not the singer.

7 ▪ **North Mississippi Allstars, *Shake Hands With Shorty* (Tone-Cool)** In this juke joint, the old—sometimes very old—blues are part of the atmosphere. With the guitars, even a mandolin and a washboard, buzzing off the walls, you don't have to notice that the vocals are stuck in neutral, or if you do you can tune them out.

8 ▪ **U. S. Postal Service, "1990s Celebrate the Century"** Sure, if you really want your letters celebrating cellphones and SUVs, virtual reality, computer art, *Titanic* ("A James Cameron Film"—did they, which is to say we, have to pay extra to say that?) and a visual and conceptual vagueness that beggars the imagination: take "New Baseball Records," which neither on the front of the stamp nor the explanatory back bothers to say what the records are or who set them. As for the *Seinfeld* number: no Elaine crawling out of somebody's bed, just—a doorway.

9 ▪ **Belle and Sebastian, *Fold Your Hands Child, You Walk Like a Peasant* (Matador)** Myself, I'd prefer they walked like an Egyptian—at least they couldn't maintain their coy folk melodies, their arch pre-Raphaelite narratives, if they had to do it at right angles.

10 ▪ **Merce Cunningham Dance Company, *Interscape*, with music by John Cage (*One 8*) and décor and costumes by Robert Rauschenberg (Zellerbach Hall, Berkeley, Calif., May 3)** After his molecules-in-motion pointillist backdrop for a dance set to Morton Feldman's 1958 *Summerscape*, for the new *Interscape* Rauschenberg offered a typically bullshit collage—disassociated images that connected to nothing, generated

no tension, merely sat on their screen mute and still. In place of his *Summerscape* leotards, which in their lightness left the illusion of nakedness, he came up with outfits decorated with more meaningless images. It didn't matter. The music was rendered on what one might call a distressed cello (all scratching and dying chords, like John Cale's viola at the end of the Velvet Underground's "Heroin") and broken—or, somehow, extended—by long periods of silence, in which the dancers continued to move without hesitation, in the same stutter-step they used with the cello. The effect was no sense of mime, but an unnatural suspension of one element of life, which made life itself feel like a construct, invention or accident. At the end, Cunningham came out for a bow, appearing as the complete happy bohemian: Carl Sandburg mop of white hair, dark coat, dark shirt and striped baggy pants he might have bought off a village fool somewhere in central Europe in 1547.

MAY 30, 2000

1 ▪ **Eminem, *The Marshall Mathers LP* (Interscope)** Why is he so much more believable, funnier, scarier and for that matter whiter—a realistic voice—on Dr. Dre's *2001* than on his own record?

2 ▪ **John Gutmann, *The Photography of John Gutmann: Culture Shock* (Merrell Publishers)** Gutmann (1905–98) left Germany for San Francisco in 1933, and thereafter let the California light bleach the irony out of his avant-garde eye even as what the native-born took for granted remained thrilling and odd to him. He moved around his new city like Robert Frank with a sense of humor. He loved signs, especially crowded, overwritten signs—the 1938 *Yes, Columbus Did Discover America* (a sedan screaming from "AND HOW THESE COYOTES HOWL" on the hood to "THE TRUTH MARCHES ON" on a back fender) or the 1988 *Che Guevara, Malcolm X, Rosa Luxemburg, et al. at the 'Militant Forum' Bookshop*—that communicate like citizens driven mad by their times.

There are fabulous shots of Count Basie Band dancers, women on the street, repeated intimations of leftist culture as a Theosophical cult: the past in the pictures dares you to imagine the world has changed. "Exposi of NAZI AGENTS in San Francisco" reads a poster advertising a Jan. 30, 1938, meeting at Eagles Hall—who was there, who was exposed, where are they now?

3 ▪ **Berkeley Liberation Radio, 104.1 FM (May 11, 8:30 a.m.)** Sometimes you can pick up this pirate station, sometimes you can't. This day the radio seemed to stick on a faraway soul production, though it was more like an emanation: the style was 30 years ago, but the feeling was as old as the world. As if from the top of a mountain, a man chanted: "Why does my heart/Feel so bad?/Why does my soul/Feel so bad?" A highly pitched orchestration bridged the distance between him and the woman who shared the song. A specter of exile and banishment overwhelmed any sense of genre. The woman departed for the desert, the man floated off his mountain top and disappeared.

The record ended—or rather fell into a long, staticky silence. Transfixed, I drove around in circles for the next half hour, trying to stay within range, hoping for someone to I.D. the tune, through a couple of minutes of a Noam Chomsky lecture on the U.S. as the Great Satan, more silence, Metallica from *S&M*, more silence, more Chomsky, the civil-rights movement jailhouse anthem "Ain' Gonna Let Nobody Turn Me 'Round," more silence, then Chomsky dithering over the introduction of another lecture only to be cut off cold by the 9 a.m. DJ, one "Sunny Day." That strange soul record, it turned out, was Moby, who dies on my stereo and gets me on the radio every time.

4 ▪ ***Forever Dusty: Homage to an Icon—A Tribute to Dusty Springfield* (R&D)** A set that soars when people you may not have heard of sing songs you may not have heard. It begins with the Laura Love Band's stultifying note-for-note version of "Son of a

Preacher Man"—and then dives into street-level pop heaven with "What's It Gonna Be" by the Butchies, catches SONiA's cool and dreamy "I Just Don't Know What to Do with Myself," lets you imagine yourself on the disc with Lord Douglas Phillips and Gretchen Phillips' utterly straight, guileless, nearly karaoke "Yesterday When I Was Young," and former Gang of Four bassist Sara Lee's absolutely karaoke "I Only Want to Be with You." Best of all might be Jennifer Kimball's "Chained to a Memory," where every note seems pressed down like a dead flower in a book of bad poems.

5 ▪ **Mary Gaitskill, "Folk Song 1999" (www.nerve.com)** Gaitskill starts this short story with news items, as if the daily paper is where you can now find the everyday perversity, the gothic portents, of the old ballads: here a murderer on a talk show with relatives of his victims, turtles stolen from a zoo, a woman aiming for the record books with a thousand-man gang bang. By the end, she turns into "John Henry," the folk hero who died in a race with a machine. She's no Tralala; she's going to win, but while she won't fuck herself to death, she may erase herself. Or she may simply be acting out a drama that was already in some versions of "John Henry," say J. E. Mainer's Mountaineers' "John Henry Was a Little Boy," collected on the new *Harry Smith's Anthology of American Folk Music, Volume Four*: "John Henry had a lovely little woman/Her name was Polly Ann/John Henry got sick and he had to go home/But his Polly drove steel like a man/Polly drove steel like a man (Some woman, boys!)"

6 ▪ **Don Henley, *Inside Job* (Warner Bros.)** While it's well known that as one gets older, one tends to find changes in the world at large unsettling, confusing, fucking irritating, *a rebuke to one's very existence*, it's generally not a good idea to make a career out of saying so.

7 ▪ ***The Filth and the Fury—A Sex Pistols Film* soundtrack (Virgin)** Everything of the pit (and I don't mean the mosh pit) you can hear in the theater—the unknowable, the unspeakable—is translated into clean speech by the magic of digital housekeeping. The sound isn't bad, it's evil.

8–9 ▪ **Rian Malan, "In the Jungle" (*Rolling Stone*, May 25) and Solomon Linda's Original Evening Birds, "Mbube," on *Mbube Roots—Zulu Classical Music from South Africa, 1930s–1960s* (Rounder)** From Malan, the capitalist odyssey of a 1939 song its creator sold for "about one pound cash" and which to this day has made tens of millions for others: the song generations of campers know as "Wimoweh." In the annals of theft and fraud that make up at least half the story of popular music, what's astonishing is not that Linda (1909–62) reaped so little, but that, today, his family receives anything at all; what's uncanny is that the Evening Birds' dignified, stately original is instantly recognizable as "The Lion Sleeps Tonight," the cheesy 1961 No. 1 by the Tokens. I heard it three times in one day recently; the voices on the verses are still embarrassing, but after Malan's piece, the chorus sounded glorious.

10 ▪ ***Her Bright Smile Haunts Me Still—The Warner Collection, Volume I* (Appleseed)** There is old and there is old. On this 58-cut anthology of field recordings made between 1935 and 1966 by folklorists Frank and Ann Warner, you sometimes hear the sound of people living in an old-fashioned manner—living according to a frame of reference that is at once familiar and defunct, like an old brand of soda pop, or for that matter the term "soda pop." When "Yankee" John Galusha of New York sings "Days of 49," though, you are in another world, just a few years after the Gold Rush; when Lee Monroe Presnell of North Carolina sings "Farewell to Old Bedford" and the plain but undeniably mystical "Sometimes in This Country," you hear the society that was here before the Founding Fathers met to turn it into a nation.

JUNE 12, 2000

1–2 ▪ **Aislers Set, *the last march* (Slumberland) & Young Marble Giants, *Salad Days* (Vinyl Japan)** Those who know the Young

Marble Giants of Cardiff, Wales—including Courtney Love, who covered their "Credit in the Straight World" on Hole's *Live Through This*—treasure the minimalist three-piece's 1980 *Colossal Youth* as proof that punk meant cutting back to essentials, including, one would think from the sound of the thing, stuff like furniture, heat, more than one change of clothes. The 1979 demos collected on *Salad Days*—"recorded in the rundown heart of student bedsit land"—prove something else: that to pull off a concept that strict you need perfect execution.

Alison Stratton's ultracool YMG vocals might have been picked up from the screen—from Anna Karina in '60s Godard movies. The Bay Area combo Aislers Set catch the same casual vehemence, the sense that while you can read your fate in dust motes you can also sweep them up. Recorded "either in Amy's garage or Wyatt and Alicia's living room," they make dream pop feel as easy to make as a can of soup, and as dangerous: watch that jagged edge. A woman singing, "I cut my teeth on dirty looks" isn't what you're supposed to find in dream pop, but here the line goes by like a smile: watch those smiles.

3 ▪ *Sam Phillips: The Man Who Invented Rock 'n' Roll* (A&E, June 18, available on home video in July) Directed by Morgan Neville, written by Peter Guralnick, narrated by Billy Bob Thornton, this 90-minute documentary again and again trumpets the magical ear of the great Memphis producer and Sun Records founder—but the words that explain how Phillips captured varieties of American speech at their fullest, through such mediums as Howlin' Wolf, Elvis Presley, Jerry Lee Lewis, Junior Parker, Pat Hare and countless more, don't make it into the film. Instead there are the results, and wonder.

Visiting the ruins of the penitentiary where, at the age of 17, in 1943, he was sent to serve 99 years for rape, Johnny Bragg of the Prisonaires—the group he formed in prison—describes the genesis of his lovely R&B hit "Just Walking in the Rain." Now

he's very old, nattily dressed, and, talking about what it meant to glimpse the rain from the inside, he begins to sing. He's absolutely glorious. The song expands, taking in anyone's aspirations for what they can never have. "I always had hope," Bragg says. "Of getting out. You know why? I was innocent." Phillips got him down on tape in 1953, 10 years into the 24 Bragg would eventually serve.

Shaking their heads in awe are, most notably, R&B singer Roscoe Gordon (Phillips "could reach the soul of man through that board"), Sun producer Jack Clement ("He scares the heck out of some people. He's telling you something, and you know he's full of . . . prunes, but it's profound, whatever it is. He can have you believe in something and you know it's not true. For a while") and Memphis musician Jim Dickinson. With typical eloquence he sums up Phillips' achievement by describing a 1954 show at Memphis' Overton Park Shell, where with one "Ellis Presley," billed below country ham Slim Whitman, the crowd found itself faced with the future. "It forced the listener to make a choice, simply to accept it or reject it, if nothing else. What followed that choice was freedom, because of course that's what follows a choice."

4 ▪ Sonya Hunter, *Finders Keepers* (Innerstate) Good title for an album of mostly other people's songs, but Hunter doesn't get to keep them: she's a terrible singer. Except on Jeb Nichols' "GTO," where the hot '60s Pontiac is celebrated as if it were a horse in the Virginia mountains in 1885.

5 ▪ Tarbox Ramblers, "Third Jinx Blues," on *Tarbox Ramblers* (Rounder Select) Ordinarily the folkies at Rounder can't tell a rock 'n' roll band from a tree, but this Boston four-piece can play from the shadows. A wrong-side-of-the-bed blues catches the mood of a man who wants only to tell the world the bad news, but who refuses to be rushed. It's like Canned Heat or the Beat Farmers at their best; it's so good you wonder why the group fills up the rest of its album with old-timey warhorses (to the point of piling "Jack of Diamonds" on "The

Cuckoo"—they're the same song) that at best are B-plus college papers and at worst copied off the Internet, if not old Kaleidoscope albums.

6 ▪ David Johansen, *David Johansen and the Harry Smiths* (Chesky) Johansen, aka the dread Buster Poindexter, equates shtick with being, and on this dive into prewar blues the shtick is that to sing very old songs you must sound as if you are very old. There are Amos 'n' Andy vocals, and despite his many protestations, I don't believe Johansen has ever been to Memphis. But on Rabbit Brown's ineffable 1927 "James Alley Blues" he gets lost in the song. Covering Bob Dylan's "World Gone Wrong" rewrite of "Delia," Johansen seems sorrier about what happens there than anyone before him.

7 ▪ Bob Dylan, "Blowin' in the Wind (live)," on *The Best of Bob Dylan, Volume 2* (Sony UK) A friend in 1963, when we first heard this song: "Kinda ersatz." He meant it was written by the times, not by anyone in particular. But in this seven-minute, undated 1990s "field recording"—right out of the crowd, like a bootleg—the song is less a message than an occasion for music, with a lot of guitar. The song itself is now blowing in the wind, and has long ago blown away from its author; on this night people have momentarily attached themselves to it, the author with little more claim to the composition than the audience. The confidence and condescension of a younger man—*Don't you get it?*—have turned into the regret of an older one. The song is no oldie, though. Singing alongside Dylan, Charlie Sexton and Larry Campbell take the tune to a new, higher register, and suddenly "Blowin' in the Wind" is not only an occasion for music, not when it's daring the future to shut it up.

8 ▪ Stanley Booth, *The True Adventures of the Rolling Stones* (A Cappella Books) The 1984 epic on the epic year 1969, back in print. From the new afterword: "The last time I heard the Stones, I went in like a civilian, with a ticket. Inside the entrance just past the ticket-taker a girl was passing out

applications for Rolling Stones Visa and MasterCards with the tongue logo. I had a vision of NATO leasing the tongue to put on helicopters, tanks, bombs. In the sixties we believed in a myth—that music had the power to change people's lives. Today people believe in a myth—that music is just entertainment."

9 ▪ The Haggard, *A Bike City Called Greasy* (Mr. Lady) Two women from Portland, Ore.—guitarist Emily Kingan and drummer sts—playing what is by now very formal hardcore, but with monsters-from-the-deep mythical undertones: in the sound of the voices, not the words they use.

10 ▪ Dusty (Sarah Dougher), "Cadallaca Meet the Backstreet Boys" (*Puncture* #46) Bumped from their date at a Portland studio by the BBs, the women in the punk trio "started conjecturing about their sexuality in song form, penning the bluesy number 'One Night with a Backstreet Boy,'" available soon or never as a hidden track on the next Sleater-Kinney single ("pending outcome of slander suit").

JUNE 26, 2000

1 ▪ Oval/Markus Popp, *ovalprocess* (Thrill Jockey) Techno as surf music: blips, buzzes and hums, with a dream in the background and moving like water.

2 ▪ Don Asmussen, "The San Francisco Comic Strip: On Microsoft, Monopolies and Breaking Up" (*San Francisco Examiner*, June 11) "What Judge Jackson did took guts," Asmussen began in a panel featuring the *Examiner* headline "JUDGE JACKSON SPLITS UP MICROSOFT." "But then the power got to him . . ." Second panel: "JUDGE JACKSON ALSO SPLITS UP 'JOURNEY' Annoying '70s Band Has Gone on Long Enough, Says Jackson. Judge vows to 'never hear that lovin' touchin' squeezin' song ever again.'"

3 ▪ Chris Isaak and Kelly Willis on *Sessions at West 54th* (PBS, June 3) Isaak was his usual diffident self until he cut out with rockabilly guitar on "Baby Did a Bad Bad Thing." Willis, in a simple, gorgeous red dress, melted the walls from the first notes

of "What I Deserve." The words of the song wound into each other; nothing stood in the way of Willis' expanding voice, which seemed to seek out all the corners in the room that other voices might not reach. She got more out of a word than some people get out of a career. With Willis digging into "that" or "happy" with no sign of pushing you could hear, just the grimace on her face, it was real soul singing—not the mindless melisma, the vocal equivalent of an Eddie Van Halen guitar solo, that rules female singing on the radio today. "I Have Not Forgotten You" is a hurting song that in the almost thrown away "So many got it tougher than I do" makes room for the whole world without identifying the singer's suffering with the world's. This is Willis' most striking number, but it wasn't allowed to speak for itself, as it does on her 1999 album *What I Deserve*. It had to get bigger: BIGGER, as if you might mistake the showcase for a mere tune. It was an insult to the listener: no one needs cues to understand how much is at stake in this melody, but three lines in the drums fell on the song and nearly toppled it. There was a guitar solo the song didn't want and didn't need. And then Willis sang a verse almost a cappella, time stood still, and the world could have ended for all you'd have noticed.

4 ▪ 'N Sync at Network Associates Coliseum (Oakland, Calif., June 11) Kayla D'Alonzo: "I had been waiting two months for June 11th. My dad got press passes for my friends and me. Since we are only 11 years old my dad went with us. We got to the concert at 7:30, it was really crowded. Pink was on stage when we arrived, it was really loud. After she was done a huge poster came down of 'N Sync, that's when the screaming began. Finally at 9 'N Sync came out, on strings like puppets, it was cool. Smoke and fireworks were coming out from the stage, it was so loud, all the girls around me were screaming and jumping up and down. They were screaming 'We love you Justin, Joey, Chris, Lance and J. C.' J. C. looked the best because he had the best clothes and he rocked the concert. My favorite song

they sang was 'It Makes Me Ill.' They were dressed like patients in a hospital. They sang 12 songs; I wish they had done more songs. They are pretty good dancers. They ran all over the stage. My eyes never left the stage."

Pete D'Alonzo (48): "The most important experience was scrutinizing my youngest daughter and her peers chanting/ gazing wild-eyed at the icons of rock music of their time. The time wasn't right before, during or after the concert to relate to them what the experience was like for me during my rock extravaganza of years past. It was their moment to cherish, and I'm not one to remove that time they will remember for a lifetime . . . My overall view? The band was giving the audience the most their money could put out, with all the rigid guidelines they must conform to. It was definitely a memory that will be etched in my mind for a lifetime."

5 ▪ Les Primitifs du Futur, *World Musette* (Sketch Studio) Featuring Dominique Cravic (writing, vocals, guitars) and two dozen others, among them proud moldy fig R. Crumb, this is old-timey music, with Paris in the '20s and '30s standing in for Memphis or Mississippi at the same time. The feeling is impossibly romantic—and as pretentious as a postcard. "Robert Johnson on the radio," mutters an American voice in "Portrait d'un 78 tard" ("Belated Portrait of a 78"). There's a tribute to Louise Brooks with lyrics so corny ("I saw your face/ And heard your voice/ Which sang only for me") you can imagine someone crooning them while strolling along the Seine. There's "Kid Chocolate," a sentimental cartoon of Jack Johnson. There's even music that, while all about Paris, doesn't seem to depend on America, though it probably does.

6 ▪ No Rest in Peace for Chester Burnett (1910–76) or, Can White Men Sing the Blues, Part #4789 "Today is the birthday of blues great Howlin' Wolf," read the chirpy DJ. "He's celebrating his 90th today. And today the House of Blues is . . ." Putting him on display, stuffed?

7 ■ **Favorite Albums of Senatorial Candidates in Minnesota, from "So You Want to Be a Senator" questionnaire (*City Pages*, Minneapolis, May 31)** Mike Ciresi (Democratic-Farmer-Labor, 54): "Ann's Favorites" (wife's compilation of his favorites); David Daniels (Grassroots—party, not group—45): Bob Marley & the Wailers, *Natty Dread*; Leslie Davis (Independence, born 1937): *Janis Joplin's Greatest Hits*; Mark Dayton (DFL, 53): Jefferson Airplane, *Volunteers*; Dick Franson (DFL, 71): "All of Frank Sinatra's albums"; James Gibson (Independence, 47): "my wedding album"; Jerry Janezich (DFL, 50): Meat Loaf, *Bat Out of Hell*; Steve Kelly (DFL, 47): Mary Black, *Collected*; David Lillehaug (DFL, 46): Kansas, *Greatest Hits*; Steven Miles (DFL, 50): Bob Dylan, *Time Out of Mind*; Erik D. Pakieser (Libertarian, born 1969): Beastie Boys, *Paul's Boutique*, Ice Cube, *Death Certificate*, Beatles' "white album"; Ole Savior (DFL, 50): Rolling Stones, no album named; Rebecca Yanisch (DFL, 47): Van Morrison, *Moondance*; Rod Grams (Republican, incumbent): did not respond.

8 ■ **Posters for More Than Food restaurant (Jung von Matt an der Isar Agency, Munich)** "Guttes Essen statt bvser Krieg" ("Good eating instead of evil war") is the slogan: airbrushed archival graphics show soldiers on the battlefield. While one waves a huge wooden soup stirrer instead of a rifle, two others, with Nazi insignia transformed into neutral striped epaulets, carefully study a menu in a bunker. Maybe Germany is taking Gerhard Schroeder's "New Start" business too far.

9 ■ **Steve Earle, *Transcendental Blues* (E Squared/Artemis)** Anyone singing with this much growly insularity wants not to tell you how much he doesn't know but how many times he's seen it all before. For the King of Dirt Road PC, every breath goes back to the breather. Atrocity: "The Boy Who Never Cried."

10 ■ **John Garst, "Delia" (e-mail postings, June 10 & 14, courtesy John Dougan)** Two weeks ago I was praising David Johansen and the Harry Smiths' cover of Bob Dylan's rewrite of the traditional "Delia," from Dylan's 1993 *World Gone Wrong*—a song so seemingly generic it sounds more written by its genre than rooted in any facts. The number appeared in print as "One More Rounder Gone" in 1911; early research was done in 1928 by Robert W. Gordon of the Library of Congress (who "supposedly traced the song's origins to Savannah," Michael Gray writes in his inexhaustible *Song and Dance Man III: The Art of Bob Dylan*). Blind Willie McTell recorded it, as have Johnny Cash, Waylon Jennings, Bobby Bare and Ronnie Wood, not to mention Mr. Acker Bilk; Dylan first taped a living-room version in St. Paul in 1960. "Seems to be about counterfeit loyalty," he wrote in 1993. "the guy in the courthouse sounds like a pimp in primary colors . . . does this song have rectitude? you bet. toleration of the unacceptable leads to the last round-up."

Garst, of Georgia, recently went looking for the story behind the song—someone is passing for white, a woman is murdered ("You loved all those rounders, never did love me") and the killer is calm and humble—"and within two hours I had it." With interpolations: "Delia Green, age 14, was shot and killed by Moses 'Coony' Houston, age 15"—Dylan uses "Cutty"—"in the Yamacraw section of Savannah (characterized for me by a local historian as 'poor, black and violent') at about 11.30 PM on Christmas Eve, 1900. She died Christmas day in her bed at home." ("Wouldn't have been so bad/If the poor girl died at home," Dylan has Delia's mother lament). "Delia and Coony had been 'more or less intimate' (newspaper) for several months and Coony said something to the effect that he would or wouldn't let her do this or that. Delia reacted with strong words to the effect that he had no control over her whatever. He then shot her. All accounts, from the very beginning, emphasize how calm, cool, deliberate and polite Coony was. . . . He appeared in court wearing short pants (on the advice of his lawyer, I suspect). The jury asked the judge for a clarification at one point, 'What would be the sentence for a murder conviction with a recommendation of mercy?' The judge replied that the law specified life imprisonment. Shortly thereafter the jury returned with that verdict and the judge sentenced Coony to 'life.' He replied, 'Thank you, sir.'" In other words, a Savannah murder that was no mystery when it happened, as a song turned into one, and which has already lasted longer than *Midnight in the Garden of Good and Evil* has any chance to.

JULY 10, 2000

1 ▪ Ace Atkins, *Leavin' Trunk Blues: A Nick Travers Mystery* (Thomas Dunne/St. Martin's) Following last year's *Crossroads Blues*, in which Travers, a white Tulane musicologist, uncovered both a cache of unreleased Robert Johnson recordings and the murders behind them, this tale of an aging Chicago gangster who uses the street name "Stagger Lee," a long-dead South Side record producer named Billy Lyons and a forgotten singer rotting in jail takes time to escape the corniness of its premises. When it does it's because Atkins gets inside his detective's skin as a trespasser: "Why," Travers hears Johnson asking him in a dream, "do you believe in a world that doesn't believe in you?" "I don't want to be in no paper," Ruby Walker tells the professor—also a former New Orleans Saint and sometime blues harmonica player—when he interviews her in prison, and she doesn't mean the newspapers. As the book grinds to its end and the bodies pile up, you realize that all the investigator can do is hope someone else will pull the trigger, not because he can't but because it's not his story to end.

2 ▪ Amanda Ghost, *Ghost Stories* (Warner Bros.) "Welcome to my filthy mind," Ghost says to introduce herself, and she sounds like she's singing from the basement of a nightclub long after whoever locked up thought it was empty—but then she changes her clothes and gets all wistful instead. The result is a really great Spice Girls album.

3 ▪ Sinéad O'Connor, *Faith and Courage* (Atlantic) Ever since "Mandinka," O'Connor has worked hard to disguise the fact that she can sing rock 'n' roll like she's cracking a whip. There are moments of that here on "Daddy I'm Fine," a fast pop autobiography in which O'Connor celebrates her teenage hairstyles, boot styles and what it felt like to "wanna fuck every man in sight." Otherwise this highly praised comeback is all sanctimony, albeit cosmic sanctimony.

4 ▪ Sarah Vowell, "On Patriotism and 'The Patriot,'" *open letters*, July 4 "I think about the Declaration of Independence and the Constitution all the time. Mainly because I watch a lot of TV. I keep a small, 95-cent copy of the two documents handy so that I can fact-check the constitutional interpretations in the shows of David E. Kelley and Aaron Sorkin. In my little booklet, the Declaration and the Constitution are separated by only a blank half-page. I forget that there are eleven years between them, eleven years of war and the whole Articles of Confederation debacle. In my head, the two documents are like the A-side and B-side of the greatest single ever released, recorded in one great drunken night."

5–6 ▪ Colson Whitehead, *The Intuitionist* (Anchor) and Bob Dylan, "I'll Keep It With Mine," from *the bootleg series, volumes 1–3 [rare & unreleased] 1961–1991* (Columbia) Dylan's weary 1966 piano demo is about whether or not to get on a train; Whitehead's novel is a metaphysical mystery about elevator inspection; and these lines, from Whitehead's gnostic textbook "*Theoretical Elevators, Volume Two*, by James Fulton," could have been written to translate the song: "You are standing on a train platform. A fear of missing the train, a slavery to time, has provided ten minutes before the train leaves. There is so much you have never said to your companion and so little time to articulate it. The years have accreted around the simple words and there would have been ample time to speak them had not the years intervened and secreted them. The conductor paces up and down the platform and wonders why you do not speak. You are a blight on his platform and timetable. Speak, find the words, the train is warming towards departure."

7 ▪ **"Germaine Krull—Photographer of Modernity," at the San Francisco Museum of Modern Art (through July 30)** In Munich and Berlin, Krull (1897–1985) staged incandescent nude lesbian tableaux and angled new buildings as godheads. But her most striking pictures are of friends and associates, notably S. M. *Eisenstein (1930)*, cropped so that only below the chin is there any air, the rest of the face overwhelming the frame, allowing the filmmaker's big, beady eyes to leave the present-day viewer an impression of the sexually repressed madman, the Ed Gein, the Jason whose hockey mask is his own face; *Etude (1931—portrait of Wanda Hubbell)*, stunning both because Hubbell is so beautiful and because, tears on her face, eyes down, she has lent herself to a generic portrait of the film actress, not remotely mistakable for anything else, that is, a real person; and *Walter Benjamin (1926)*, where, despite a reddish-brown tint added to the critic's mustache, light seems to glow behind this black-and-white image, in the long and tousled hair, until you see a Jewish Elvis, if not a 1920s Lou Reed.

8 ▪ **America, *Highway: 30 Years of America* (Rhino)** "Spanning three decades and nearly all of America's 23 albums," says the press release, "*Highway* contains 64 tracks in a three-CD boxed set that features the classic rock staples 'A Horse With No Name,' 'Sister Golden Hair,' and 'Ventura Highway,'" and, if one is writing on Independence Day as Gerry Beckley and Dewey Bunnell are performing at Wellesby Park in Sunrise, Fla., one must ask two questions: what does it say about this country that this group has gotten away with recording 23 albums? And, to paraphrase Walter Benjamin, could even the dead listen to 64 straight America songs?

9–10 ▪ **Dave Alvin, *Public Domain* (Hightone) and John Lee Hooker, *The Unknown John Lee Hooker: 1949 Recordings* (Flyright)**

Rockabilly rootsman Alvin bids for the ultimate Americana album, with fabulous colored old photos (a black cowboy in what looks to be a sheep herd's worth of chaps) and a matching set of p.d. hits: "Shenandoah," a variant of Mississippi bluesman Tommy Johnson's "Maggie Campbell," "Railroad Bill," "Delia," "East Virginia." Just over half a century ago, in Detroit, Hooker—a variant of whom appears in *Leavin' Trunk Blues* as Elmore King—did something similar, responding to a Czech cartoonist and record collector's wish for the old country stuff no one wanted to hear anymore with solo versions of "Two White Horses," "Rabbit on the Log," "Six Little Puppies and Twelve Shaggy Hounds," "John Henry," "Jack O'Diamonds," the ancient ring shout "Old Blind Barnabus" and a variant of what would become "Mystery Train." The difference is absolute. Alvin sings every commonplace tune in a plummy, unquestioning manner that suspends whatever is uncertain, unfinished or threatening about any of the unkillable songs; Hooker addresses artifacts of the local culture of his Mississippi childhood, which were in fact emblems of a vernacular national culture, as if they threaten him directly, and as if he has the ability to stare them down and wait them out. The whole point of commonplace music is to take up a song everyone knows, that everyone is sick of, that everyone was *born* sick of, and then to sing it and make it be heard as if the singer is creating the song on the spot, drawing on familiarity and dissolving it in the same motion. Alvin does the opposite. He sings like the musical director of a summer camp; he's going to teach you these songs, and exactly how to sing them. Hooker's the guy telling ghost stories after lights-out, stories so laconically offhand you can never get them just right when you try to tell them to somebody else.

JULY 24, 2000

1 ▪ **Dido, "Thank You," from *No Angel* (Arista)** What's most interesting about the

way this piece now emerges from Dido Armstrong's 1999 debut album is how completely its first minute and a half—the material sampled by Eminem on his recent "Stan"—now seems definitively appropriated. On *No Angel*, an otherwise dulled record that begins in dance clubs in London and might as well be on the beach at Ipanema by its end, you're listening to a number about a woman with a hangover. The drifting, fatalistic quality of the melody seems all out of proportion to its insistently ordinary payoff—with an insistently ordinary melody stretched over the remaining two minutes—which is that the singer is grateful to her boyfriend, whose love redeems bad days. This does not quite match what Eminem does with Dido; using her music to place beauty in between the pages of an awful story, he makes her into the angel of death.

2 ▪ Dick Slessig Combo, presented by Jessica Bronson, "Rock Your Baby," at the Portland, Ore., Art Museum (July 7) Carl Bronson, bass, Steve Goodfriend, drums, and Mark Lightcap, guitar—the Dick Slessig Combo, as in dyslexic—were playing on L.A. conceptual artist Jessica Bronson's internally lit bandstand for the Portland opening of "Let's Entertain," a motley assemblage of glamorous art statements first staged at the Walker in Minneapolis. They were at least a half-hour into a performance that would eventually cover 90 minutes before I realized the nearly abstract, circular pattern the trio was offering as the meaning of life—it was all they were playing, anyway—was from George McCrae's effortlessly seductive 1974 Miami disco hit. Or rather the pattern wasn't from the tune, it *was* the tune, the thing itself. Variation was never McCrae's point (the big moment in his "Rock Your Baby," the equivalent of the guitar solo, is when he barely whispers "Come on"); finding the perfect, self-renewing riff was. "I could listen to that forever," I said to Bronson when he and the others finally stepped down for a break. "We'd play it forever if we were physically capable," he said. The bandstand is empty now, but a

50-minute edit of the number will be running in the air above it, over and over, through Sept. 17.

3–4 ▪ Billy Bragg and Wilco, *Mermaid Avenue Vol. II* (Elektra) & *'Til We Outnumber 'Em* (Righteous Babe) *Mermaid Avenue Vol. II* is Bragg and Wilco's proof that the light touch of last year's astonishing completions of lyrics Woody Guthrie never got around to making into songs was a fluke. Compared to the blanket of piety enveloping a Guthrie tribute from a 1996 Rock & Roll Hall of Fame conference—featuring Bruce Springsteen, Ani DiFranco, the Indigo Girls and more, every speaker droppin' his g's (never has plain-folks talk sounded more affected)—it's Little Richard's "Ready Teddy."

5 ▪ Shalini, *We Want Jelly Donuts* (Parasol) The singer lives in North Carolina, and you can imagine her small songs, pushed forward in a flat, conversational voice, as a fantasy of knocking the acronym made by her title off the top of her local charts, where it means "What Would Jesus Do?"

6 ▪ "The Life Casts of Cynthia Plaster Caster: 1968–2000," Thread Waxing Space, New York City (through July 29) New York Eye reports: "Though I've never liked the word 'groupie' and am not inclined to embrace my inner slut, I am a rock 'n' roll girl and it's not as if I don't appreciate wanting to sleep with rock stars. But up until a couple of weeks ago, I was only vaguely aware that there had been a Cynthia Plaster Caster—I didn't know her name or even if she was fact or fancy—so I was delighted to discover that not only is she real, so were her casts, and I could go see them. It seemed like a cause for celebration, that in the midst of ubiquitous *Behind the Music* marathons, reissues, box sets, exposés, redolent praise and idealized recapitulation, autobiographies, celebrity gossip and endless reruns of *Rock and Roll Jeopardy*, there was this little show that simply and without fluffy fanfare was exhibiting 67 actual rock people's plaster-casted cocks. I invited all my friends.

"Cynthia Plaster Caster never stopped casting, and many of the rigs are recent casts, but I think it's fair to say that the absolutely weirdest and most titillating among them—and they're all weird and titillating—must be the balls-attached, slightly off-kilter monument of Jimi Hendrix. Fun facts: Jimi, we're told, was uncommonly able to sustain his erection for longer than the required 60 seconds, and Cynthia, exuberant and impatient, prematurely burst open the mold, causing it to break apart. (It was later glued back together.)

"A guy friend asked if 'The Life Casts' was a fair sampling and I'd say it was. Identified and unadorned, often hilarious, perfectly plain white plaster penises belonging to people we know or know of, listen to and watch—it was fun and it was art. I'm going back."

7 ▪ John Hiatt, "I Wanna Be Sedated" (KFOG-FM, San Francisco, July 16) The singer-songwriter who usually doesn't trust rock 'n' roll, weird clothes or showmanship, from a 1996 live broadcast, just acoustic guitar, pounding, audience handclaps and a gleefully demented old-codger vocal. If he put this out he might not have to do those earnest PBS musician-interviews anymore—or get away with them.

8 ▪ Fall Time, directed by Paul Warner (Live Entertainment Video, 1993) So obscure it's not even in Leonard Maltin: a sub-Coen Bros./Murphy's Law crime drama set in a small Wisconsin town in 1957, with Mickey Rourke, Stephen Baldwin, and David Arquette, but the point is Sheryl Lee as a mousy bank employee who turns out to be the only one with brains, and the only winner. Here as elsewhere, from Twin Peaks to This World, Then the Fireworks, but perhaps most expansively here, Lee's more of a silent movie actor than anyone else of her time. "We had faces then"—and they knew what to do with them, how to act from inside the face, and so does Lee. She says everything about doubt, longing, lust or worry in a single look, a look you can't read to the bottom; the only thing she can't do, hopping a freight with the money, leaving four bodies behind in a shack, is wistful. Probably be-

cause that was the one thing the director was able to tell her to do.

9 ▪ Lillian Gish and Robert Mitchum, "Leaning," on Oxford American Southern Sampler 2000 (included with the July/August issue of Oxford American) A gospel song from the end of the 1955 Night of the Hunter, and the ultimate battle of the bands: good vs. evil.

10 ▪ Slobberbone, Everything You Thought Was Right Was Wrong Today (New West) Cover: Photo of "Dust storm approaching Spearman, Texas, April 14, 1935," and it's too late to run. That's the spirit of everything good from this Texas quartet: the big, loser blues of "Josephine," the title "Placemat Blues" (a protest song: "Where's the place at the table for folks like us?") and especially the back-country "Gimme Back My Dog." Feedback, a simple count on a banjo, a light sound except for the rough growl of Brent Best asking for his dog back. Then the stops come loose from the music: the dog, it turns out, is the singer's true self, there's almost nothing of it left after the years he's spent with the woman he's talking to, and the only way he can get it back, the only way he can look in the mirror and see anything at all, is to beg. Meaning every word, he never goes too far; he never says anything he can't take back. And no, he doesn't get his dog back either.

AUGUST 7, 2000

1 ▪ Forever Mine, written and directed by Paul Schrader (Telluride Film Festival, Sept. 1–4) In this deliriously romantic version of The Count of Monte Cristo, it's 1973 at a glamorous Florida resort. Catching a glimpse of Gretchen Mol stepping out of the surf like Botticelli's Venus—all she's missing is the shell—cabana boy Joseph Fiennes knows his life will never be real without her. Soon he's talked her into bed, and it was like the discovery of gold for both of them, but she's only been married eight months and the pain of what she's done is ripping her apart. "Stop talking like an

adult," Fiennes says oddly. "Tell me why." "Why what?" Mol says. "What do you think?" Fiennes says. "Why do birds sing so gay? Why does the rain fall from up above? *Why* did you get married?"—and the old words from Frankie Lymon and the Teenagers' "Why Do Fools Fall in Love" slip in and out of Fiennes' speech as if he thought up the words on the spot. Because of many kinds of misfortune, the film is slated for a Nov. 4 showing on the Starz cable channel rather than a theatrical release; until distribution catches up with the picture the Telluride screenings will be the only chance to see it on a screen as big as its reach.

2 ▪ **Trailer Bride at the Great American Music Hall (San Francisco, July 28)** At the head of America's least obvious country band, Melissa Swingle could have escaped from a 1936 Walker Evans photograph; she doesn't make eye contact. For that matter, she looks at the floor, as if she has something to say but doesn't want to have to stand up in front of people to get it across. In tune with her sardonic, self-effacing waitress' *I get off at 10 and then I go home* drawl, she offers a few splayed-leg dance steps in lieu of arm gestures or head fakes. *Whine de Lune*, the band called its album; that's the sound Swingle, who plays everything but drums and bass, gets from a saw while guitarist Scott Goolsby, carrying what could be 8 inches of pompadour, puts hard, dead-cowboy notes in the air and then makes them dissolve, so slowly it's as if you could watch it happen, and so definitively it's hard to believe you heard what you heard.

3 ▪ **MasterCard commercial** Cognitive dissonance sighting, as reported by Charlie Largent: "Various 'Priceless' descriptions of family bonding ('For everything else there's MasterCard'), all set to the tune of 'Lolita's Theme' from the 1962 Kubrick film . . ."

4 ▪ **Salon Table Talk (July 27)** Hazel Shade: "I keep thinking that Lorillard and Brown & Williamson, et al., should simply start a cigarette campaign like the Apple and the Gap khaki ads. Think of it, a sexy picture of every interesting person since the inception of photography: 'Bob Dylan smoked.' 'FDR smoked.' 'Albert Einstein smoked.' 'Greta Garbo smoked.' 'Miles Davis smoked.' 'Albert Camus smoked.' Wouldn't it be great?"

William Ham: "A few years ago, I wanted to pitch the American Psychiatric Association an ad featuring that classic picture of Lou Reed with the Iron Crosses shaved into his tonsure with the legend 'Lou Reed Had Shock Treatment.' I really think it could have touched off an electrode renaissance."

5 ▪ **CBS Radio News (July 27)** For a spot on Federal District Judge Marilyn Hall Patel's decision, later stayed, mandating suspension of Napster operations, an interviewer found guitarist G. E. Smith, late of the *Saturday Night Live* band and Bob Dylan's "Never Ending Tour" and famed for his ability to combine obsequiousness with self-glorification: "It costs money to get our product out there," Smith said, then complaining that people take it off the Net for nothing and "it's not fair." As if anyone would pay money for a record because his name was on it—with Napster he might get heard by accident. So score one for the judge.

6 ▪ **René Magritte, *La lectrice soumise* (The Subjugated Reader), 1928, in "Magritte" (San Francisco Museum of Art, through Sept. 5)** Very vulgar, with heavy lines and none of the stylized stillness of a typical Magritte: a woman with dark hair, brown eyes, thick eyebrows, yellowish skin, gray sweater, black skirt, seated against a blue background and holding a book. The shock and horror on her face, her bugged-out eyes, make you wonder: why didn't Alfred Hitchcock buy this and use it as his logo?

7 ▪ **Onedia, *Steel Rod EP* (Jagjaguwar)** A Brooklyn combo with an avant-garde rep leaves no hint of it here, and leaves little enough of an impression with the five songs listed. It's the untitled hidden track, which pops up less than a minute after the official program ends, that pulls you in: a trash rehearsal, a 15-minute organ riff the rest of the band takes up as the meaning of life for lack

of any better suggestion. Not the sort of thing one can publicly release these days, and not in any way distinctive, just what thousands of bands have done for 50 years when a lack of inspiration struck them, as complete a version of What Seemed Like a Good Idea at the Time as you'll find anywhere.

8–9 ▪ **John Fahey,** *How Bluegrass Music Destroyed My Life* **(Drag City Books) and** *The Essential Bill Monroe & the Monroe Brothers* **(RCA)** In his recent collection of stories the experimental guitarist recalls the day in the mid-'50s that a record on the radio changed—or, maybe, took—his life: "Then I heard this horrible, crazy sound. And I felt this insane, mad feeling . . . I went limp. I almost fell off the sofa. My mouth fell open. My eyes widened and expanded. I found myself hyperventilating. When it was over I tried to get up and go and get a paper bag to restore the correct balance of power between oxygen and carbon monoxide. I screamed for help but nobody was around and nobody came. I was drenched with sweat. It was like I had woken up to a new and thrilling and exciting horror movie." The disc that occasioned this response—and Fahey is just warming up; wait 'til he gets to the record store—was Bill Monroe and His Bluegrass Boys' 1941 cover of Jimmie Rodgers' 1930 "Blue Yodel No. 7." Play it now: can you hear what a teenager heard one day when he, oh, had the flu or something, if he isn't making the whole thing up? Enough to keep you listening. There's something off about the rhythm, something somehow not right.

10 ▪ **Bob Dylan: The American Troubadour, directed by Stephen Crisman, written by Ben Robbins (A&E, Aug. 13)** This two-hour documentary is a thrilling exercise in the legal doctrine of fair use. With no permissions forthcoming for any material controlled by its subject, let alone a contemporary interview, the drama proceeds according to occasional fragments of old recorded Q&A's, enough panning of still photos to make you think the career in question predated the invention of motion

pictures, never more than a single chorus of any given song and a great deal of time devoted to the pronouncements of not very many talking heads, during which Todd Gitlin, in the '60s a head of Students for a Democratic Society and currently a sociology professor at NYU, emerges as his generation's David Halberstam. Around the edges are traces of an untold story: a circa-1958 tape of Dylan's Hibbing, Minn., high-school combo the Golden Chords harmonizing on a piece of original doo-wop ("I'll be true, I love you, yes I do"—after a moment it sounds more like Fargo's Bobby Vee's earliest Buddy Holly imitations) is really not that far from the 1967 Basement Tapes Dylan tune "Dontcha Tell Henry" as performed now by Levon Helm of the Band. At 60 he's been through cancer and looks it. He sounds it: his barely audible rasp, mandolin clutched to his chest, calls up a simple music that will outlive its singers, not that people like Helm or Dylan seem likely to grant that death's mortgage on their bodies ought to take priority over the music's lien on their souls.

1 ▪ **Walter Ruttmann,** *Weekend Remix* **(Intermedium)** Tricky, tricky, tricky. In 1930 filmmaker Walter Ruttmann (1887–1941) premiered an 11-minute, 10-second radio play: a sound collage depicting an ordinary Berlin weekend. Ruttmann used street sounds, speeches, a cat meowing and children playing, and what he got were changes in mood and meaning every time you listen. Heard now, the cadences of men engaging in public address inescapably call up the cadences we know from Hitler: that was the time, and those were the rhythms of that time's speech. So doom and portent are coded into the piece after the fact, and you can't get rid of them. Simultaneously, though, you hear people out for a good time: you hear free time. The work is absorbed by the history that followed it; then it escapes that history, and your own sense of what happened, the knowledge you bring to the work that it doesn't have, sucks you in. You are listening to what life was like in one place before that place would force a change in what life was like, all over the world.

Barbara Schäfer and Herbert Kapfer of Bayerischer Rundfunk in Munich—a radio station responsible for the most ambitious and inventive radio plays being produced today—invited six contemporary sound artists to take on "Weekend," lost until its rediscovery in New York in 1978. Here, bits of sound that are peripheral on the original may come to the center; bits of contemporary songs weave in and out of tones and mechanics that are undeniably far away; new rhythms are made with the sound of cellphones and computers at work. DJ Spooky and John Oswald achieve the most extreme displacement—a sense that we remain right where Ruttmann found his century, 70 years ago. Or should have. Or could have.

2 ■ **Jason Starr, *Nothing Personal* (Four Walls Eight Windows)** Crime fiction: panic as a complete version of ordinary life. No special effects. Plus, a happy ending, if only for the least deserving characters.

3 ■ **Submarine, *Skin Diving* (Kinetic/Reprise)** In demeanor, tone and the way they rush a phrase or a beat, this London trio catches a genre-scrambling but time-specific combination: '6os Italian go-go movies where nothing can go wrong and late-'5os French new-wave movies where nothing can go right. For the first few numbers—"Sunbeam," "Heartfailure"—singer Adaesi Ukairo, drummer Richard Jeffrey and guitarist Al Boyd are in the imaginary Europe conjured up not long ago by Hooverphonic of Belgium. A high, female voice working through a simple techno structure suggests a new world that never appeared, not 40 years ago and not five: what makes this world so alluring is also what leaves you stranded. After that, the band loses focus—but the opening cuts may bring you back again, certain you are missing something, which I'm sure I am. In a perfect world the press release would be

the liner notes: the anonymous writer reports that while Boyd, listed as an M.D. as well as a guitar player, "ceased any meaningful dialogue with other humans at about the age of seven when he first heard Boston's 'More Than a Feeling,'" the band as a whole is so fixated on da Vinci's *The Last Supper* that "in 1999 they launched a (so far unsuccessful) campaign to have a reproduction of the painting mounted in every public access building in England and Wales."

4 ■ **Jill Scott, *Who Is Jill Scott?—Words and Sounds Vol. 1* (Hidden Beach)** You're supposed to say, "No one will have to ask after *this*," and this debut by the writer who has worked with the ambitious hip-hop group the Roots is utterly expert and assured: soul nouveau without received mannerisms or borrowed style. It's also as self-congratulatory as a magazine piece by Wendy Wasserstein or an obituary by Christopher Hitchens.

5 ■ **Joan Osborne, *Righteous Love* (Interscope)** Finally, after five years, a follow-up to *Joan Osborne* and "One of Us." What's new: every '8os neo-hippie Hollywood studio cliché known to humankind (you can see the tie-dye on the walls), plus some no one ever thought of before—as neat a trick as Osborne's vocal attack, a unique combination of bombastic and coy. What's strange: a cover of Bob Dylan's bombastic "To Make You Feel My Love," the one atrocity on his 1997 *Time Out of Mind*. Osborne sings it in a small voice, with no flourishes, no big gestures, so that even the most pretentious phrases ("the highway of regret") sound like something someone might actually say.

6 ■ **Quills, directed by Philip Kaufman (Telluride Film Festival, Sept. 1–4)** It's in the last 45 minutes or so of this blazing fiction about the end of the Marquis de Sade—due for general release in November—when the film begins to move like a piece of music, gathering its rhythms and concentrating them into a force that takes on a life of its own. In the Charenton asylum, Geoffrey Rush's Sade has been stripped of his pen

and paper, but he can't not create stories. From his barren cell he begins to shout a new tale through the walls, each sentence carried by a bucket brigade of inmates and workers until, garbled but not lost, the words reach Kate Winslet's laundress, the devoted reader who writes each fragment down—and then all hell breaks loose. After that there is only madness on all sides, libertines and censors, lunatics and doctors. It's no small irony that Sade's nemesis, Michael Caine's Dr. Royer-Collard, was famous as the leader of the Doctrinaires, who were not the first French doo-wop group but should have been. The result is a horror movie about the rights of man.

7 ■ **Kim Gordon, Ikue Mori & DJ Olive** (SYR) A Kim Gordon noise project, with its strength in her singing. At times Gordon's meandering lines are just finger painting; more often there are hints of trouble her band Sonic Youth hasn't touched in years.

8 ■ **Sally Timms & Jon Langford, *Songs of False Hope and High Values*** (Bloodshot) On leave from the Mekons, why are they wasting their precious time with Willie Nelson's "Blue Eyes Crying in the Rain" or Dolly Parton's "Down in Dover" when they have songs of their own as fragile as "I Picked Up the Pieces" to play?

9 ■ **Elvis Costello, "Brilliant Disguise"** (Warner Bros., 1996) "A demo for George Strait," the DJ said of this extra track from Elvis Costello's "It's Time" single. (Thoughtful of him to be pitching Bruce Springsteen copyrights rather than his own, but never mind.) With Costello's acoustic guitar leading and bare bass and drums muffled in the background, the number comes across as a folk ballad, leaving the original overstated and unsure of itself. This seems to go on and on, as if it were "Barbara Allen," and you can hear how subtle the song really is, if it is.

10 ■ **Keith Bradshaw, "G.M. Has High Hopes for Vehicle Truly Meant for Road Warriors" (*New York Times*, Aug. 6.)** A clarion call for the George W. Bush era, at least up to Nov. 7 (reading the *Times*' political coverage, you'd think he'd been elected

months ago): "The rugged individualists," says division manager Michael DiGiovanni on the marketing of the H1 model of the Hummer, the latest in personal tanks—guaranteed higher pollution, lower gas mileage, greater visibility obstruction and higher other-to-self roadkill ratio—"are people who really seek out peer approval."

SEPTEMBER 4, 2000

1 ■ **Eleventh Dream Day, *Stalled Parade*** (Thrill Jockey) This Chicago trio got it right a long time ago: the sound of fate (taking its time) on the guitar, vocals that seem like whispers no matter what their volume, an overwhelming sense of displacement combined with a refusal to leave. They first found their voice under George Bush; here guitarist Rick Rizzo, drummer Janet Beveridge Bean and bassist Doug McCombs act surprised that after eight years under Clinton their old language of dramatic fuzztone and bitter jokes no one thinks are funny still speaks so clearly.

2 ■ **Domenic Stansberry, *The Last Days of Il Duce*** (St. Martin's Minotaur) A murder mystery that's creepily convincing in its plot, which concerns lingering traces of fascism in San Francisco's North Beach; completely convincing about the energy of sexual obsession that drives the plot; and, around the edges of the plot, utterly suggestive about the way immigrants lose their freedom as Americans when the hyphen drops away. A man who once might have been called an Italian-American and who is now merely an American looks into the face of his dead brother's Hispanic wife: "'How are you and the kids set?' I asked. 'Maybe I could help out.' It was a lie of course. I didn't have any money in the world and she knew this. Besides, she had her friends and the community around her, and after the funeral she and her two kids named Julia and Juarez Jones would disappear into that great other population of California the newspapers and television always mentioned but seemed to know nothing about. . . . I wished I could dis-

appear into that other world too, but the magic hour for people like me had long since passed."

3–4 ▪ Aug. 22: The Radio Speaks out of Both Sides of Its Mouth KALX, the Berkeley college station, is playing "Anna-Letmeinletmeout," from the minimalist-repetitive German band Trio's 1982 *Trio and Error*. As a dumb love song it seems so fresh, paradoxical, intelligent, the few syllables it bothers to use reaching the level of, say, the Beach Boys' "Barbara Ann"—but that high plateau reached not in spite of sophistication and art theory but because of them. Then *click click click* across the stations into the middle of Wet Wet Wet's version of the Troggs' "Love Is All Around." It's the opposite of Trio: mindless, a big, stupidly overblown arrangement, phony nightclub singing, and still it's moving: you can't hurt this song. Axl Rose or Lucinda Williams or Fred Durst or Lauryn Hill could do this song and sound sincere.

5 ▪ *Great Moments of the 20th Century* (Rhino Word Beat) The century as sound bite, and over three CDs it's a game to see who will return to the ether and who will get under your skin. Winners: Andrew West of KRKD, on the air reporting the assassination of Robert F. Kennedy as it happens ("Oh my God . . ."), pure panic, diving into the event itself ("The gun is pointed at me right this moment . . . Hold him, Rafer!"); California Gov. Ronald Reagan on Arthur Bremer's assassination attempt on presidential candidate George Wallace. Handed a dispatch as he was speaking at a fundraiser, then breaking the news to the audience, Reagan is absolutely calm, like the radio pro he'd been; he speaks in an unsurprised, reflective tone, wondering what, really, could be happening to the country, as if for once he didn't know.

6 ▪ The Band, "Don't Do It," from *Cahoots* (Capitol) Remastered versions of the original albums by the Band are coming out, each with extra tracks. This is the best of them, from the early '70s: a rather laconic Marvin Gaye number pulled inside out until all that's left is speed and heat.

7 ▪ Nell Dunn, *Up the Junction* (Counterpoint) In 1963 Dunn, then in her mid-20s, published this book of stories about women in London's Battersea slums. The dialogue and the action are blunt, cruel, pointless, life as one big non sequitur. What's most striking, now, is the way Dunn describes a world so class-bound it is absolutely impervious to change: either the events Dunn, a reporter, drew on took place before the Beatles arrived to change the world ("Sonny fiddled with the jukebox, which suddenly burst forth 'Rambling Rose, Rambling Rose/Why she rambles no one knows . . .'"), or else nobody noticed.

8 ▪ North Mississippi All-Stars, "KC Jones (On the Road Again)," from *Shake Hands with Shorty* (Tone-Cool) A standard collage made out of a few of the countless versions of the 100-year-old song, not well-sung, not particularly well-played—but on the radio, in the Colorado Rockies, it sounds so in time, as if it has all the time in the world to get to the mysterious lines you can imagine are what the song is really about, no matter how many other songs they turn up in. Never mind heroic engineer Casey Jones and his train wreck—what's that against "I told her my name was on the tail of my shirt / Natur'l born Eastman don't have to work"? The first phrase is easy enough to translate: Kiss my ass. But the natural born Eastman is still on the loose. And speaking of which—

9 ▪ Bill Clinton on "The Second Year of a Process of Trying to Totally Rebuild My Life from a Terrible Mistake I Made," Willow Creek Community Church, South Barrington, Ill. (Aug. 10) Howard Hampton: "Bill's happy, discursive visit to the evangelical lion's den was remarkable, not least for the format and the seated body language, which could not help recalling Elvis '68 sitting and addressing the audience during the taping [of his comeback TV special] with the Rev. Scotty Moore as interlocutor. (I'm referring to the full session that ran on C-Span, not just the confessional stuff that made "Nightline" and the headlines.) God only knows what he'll say or do [at the convention] but after this performance, if he strode out in leather jacket with Rosa Parks on one arm and the Playmate of the Year on the other, I wouldn't be entirely surprised."

10 ▪ Lynn Harrell and Caitlin Tully, Aspen Music Festival (Aug. 12) Acting as master of ceremonies for a special benefit day, the renowned cellist Harrell, in his 50s, played in busker's street clothes with 12-year-old violinist Tully during an intermission. After introducing Tully as someone the audience would be listening to for decades to come, Harrell turned to her and said, "I have to ask you—do you listen to the Backstreet Boys?" "No," said Tully hesitantly, as if suddenly and definitively embarrassed by her own age. Too bad she didn't say, "No, but have you heard Eminem's 'Stan'?"

SEPTEMBER 18, 2000

1–2 ▪ Telluride Film Festival Diary: Shadow of the Vampire, written and directed by E. Elias Merhige (Sept. 1) and Boomtown Rats, "I Don't Like Mondays" (Columbia, 1979) Everybody loves vampire movies; let's just say that with this, on the making of F. W. Murnau's 1922 *Nosferatu*, you get more than you bargain for. It's a comedy with a terrible payoff. I walked out of the theater thrilled, queasy, wondering what art is worth and how much an artist—in this case, not Merhige but John Malkovich's appallingly convincing Murnau—can charge for it. I went down a stairway into a basement sandwich joint where "I Don't Like Mondays" was playing, and though there was nothing in the place for sale I wanted, I couldn't leave. That record all about a girl shooting up her high school just made me smile. Those big, dripping piano notes, that effete Bob Geldof delivery, punk as "You Can't Always Get What You Want"—both the movie and the song were asking the same questions, but, just as the movie was made to ensure you couldn't answer them, the song did.

3 ▪ Wallflowers, Breach (Interscope) The tunes on this follow-up to the huge *Bringing Down the Horse* flow along with-

out stumbling, Jakob Dylan's voice at once hoarse and smooth. But there are lines that don't fit—don't fit here and wouldn't fit in anyone else's music: "Look at you with your worn out shoes / Living proof that evolution is through" is intriguing, not that I have a clue what it means, but "Sam Cooke didn't know what I know"—Dylan's teeth clench on the line, as if he'd rather he didn't know but, given that his sound is all fatalism, he has no choice. Moral: this record is far more hoarse than smooth.

4 ▪ Bratmobile, Ladies, Women and Girls (Lookout!) "I'm old, and Croatian," Allison Wolfe, singer for this Olympia, Wash., trio, said from the stage of the Fillmore in San Francisco in June. Since they started out in 1991 the Bratmobile women have learned nothing (or cast off all superfluous knowledge); they still come off as if they just now realized that systemic oppression and bad manners deserve the same *nyah-nyah-nyah*.

5 ▪ Jackie Leven, "You've Lost That Loving Feeling," on Defending Ancient Springs (Valley Entertainment) Leven is a bland, poetic singer—singing at the words, not through them—but with Pere Ubu's David Thomas playing Little Bobby Hatfield to Leven's Big Bill Medley, the old Righteous Brothers classic is twisted from plea to complaint. Won't mean a thing to anyone not already seduced by Thomas' Gyro Gearloose-as-Nobel Peace Prize winner act (where, as on his *Meadville*, a cover of "Can't Help Falling in Love" fits right in with a lecture on Charles Fort), but he's so—*monkey time*.

6 ▪ Badlands: A Tribute to Bruce Springsteen's "Nebraska" (Sub Pop sampler) The complete set isn't due till November, but there's no need to wait on this shocking discovery by bighearted and/or leftist singers: the 1982 Springsteen album had social content! So it's cool to sing the songs! But the performances are square. Chrissie Hynde might be up to the dead-man-talking inhabitation of teen mass murderer Charles Starkweather on the title song—but not by treating it as a prayer. Billy Bragg wants you to know that Woody Guthrie could have written "Mansion on the Hill." Ani DiFranco comes up with an interesting entree into "Used Cars," singing as if through a string and a tin can, but she's all smugness for the last, kiss-my-ass-goodbye line. Aimee Mann and Michael Penn (who proves definitively that Mann did not marry him for his voice) are predictably pleased with themselves for "Reason to Believe"; the results are unspeakable. But look, *Bruce* is a bighearted, leftist kind of guy, usually ready to pay tribute to people who deserve it: why isn't *he* here, taking on "State Trooper" or "Open All Night" as if he didn't get them right the first time around? That's what he does on his own stage.

7 ▪ **James Lee Burke, *Purple Cane Road* (Doubleday)** Perhaps the most interesting aspect of current fiction is the way President Clinton is beginning to make his way into it. It may be some time before anyone goes beneath Philip Roth's dazzling surface skating in *The Human Stain*, but Burke has nothing to apologize for. Here the Bayou crime novelist comes up with one Belmont Pugh, governor of Louisiana. As he runs for a second term, word gets out that he's both a drunk and the father of twins—by his mulatto mistress. He appears on TV to beg forgiveness; the Jimmy Swaggart move doesn't work. So he steps up at a Fourth of July rally: "His face was solemn, his voice unctuous. 'I know y'all heered a lot of stories about your governor,' he said. 'I won't try to fool you. They grieve me deeply. I'm talking heartfelt pain.'" Pugh pauses: "'But I'm here to tell you right now . . . that *any*time, *any*where, *any*body . . .' He shook his head from side to side for emphasis, his voice wadding in his throat as if he were about to strangle on his own emotions. 'I mean *any*body sets a trap for Belmont Pugh with whiskey and women . . .' His body was squatted now, his face breaking into a grin as wide as an ax blade. 'Then by God they'll catch him every time!'" He's "reelected in a landslide," of course; more to the point, it's Burke's version of Clinton not as Swaggart but as Earl Long, Huey's damned, heroic brother.

8 ▪ **Rick Shea, *Sawbones* (Wagon Wheels/AIM)** As dirt-eating country troubadours go, Shea is notably plummy, but here and there the beat slows and the sky clouds over. Best number: Don Wayne and Bill Anderson's casually vengeful "Saginaw, Michigan," which would die if the singer showed his hand a note too soon.

9 ▪ **Regarding a Sept. 4 item on Nell Dunn's *Up the Junction*, about working-class women in London in the early '60s, Mark Sinker writes from the U.K.** "I still own my mum's 1966 Pan paperback edition, complete with pulp cover painting of a blonde girl in jeans and leather. The blurb says that, yes, 'In 1959, Nell Dunn, then 23 and newly married, crossed the bridge from fashionable Chelsea and bought a tiny house in Battersea . . .'—and the stories were first published in the *New Statesman*, so must have been written pre-Beatles. But what always fascinated me (since the early '80s, newly arrived in London) was the sense the book captured of London (and thus the U.K. as a whole) as a series of landlocked villages, mutually invisible to one another. Colin McInnes's Soho is a galaxy away from Dunn's Clapham. I think that a great deal of this U.K. somnolence survived the Beatles upsurge, which really operated globally rather than locally—like bombsites, some bits of the city remained quite undisturbed into the mid-'70s. (Jon Savage is good on this in *England's Dreaming*: Steve Jones and John Lydon, from West and North London respectively, are all but foreigners to each other.) South of the Thames really only woke up with punk and after: Squeeze actually wrote a song called 'Up the Junction' (and mined similarly landlocked/timelocked lives, in some ways). There was a TV drama and a 1967 or 1968 film, directed by Ken Loach (soundtrack by Manfred Mann), by which time the datedness was showing badly: they tried to update it, and it comes across as Boulting Brothers meets *Day of the Triffids*. The scene that lingers is set high in a ruined building with the wall blown out, looking out over a luridly painted cityscape."

10 ■ **Telluride Diary: Paul Schrader (Sept. 2)** The director as ontologist: "Once you go back to 1974, nothing else matters." Even if he was talking about his movie *Forever Mine*.

OCTOBER 2, 2000

1–4 ■ **Campaign events (September)** With Al Gore recently citing "He not busy being born is busy dying" as his favorite Bob Dylan quotation, David Hinkley of the *New York Daily News* suggested a contest on what Gore's favorite Dylan line *should* be.

"Bury the rag deep in your face/ Now's the time for your tears," sneered Nader supporter Dave Marsh. But Marsh also volunteered that perhaps more to the point would be a question recently raised by Berkeley, Calif., photographer Liz Bordow: "Everyone remembers where they were when they heard that Kennedy was shot; I wonder how many people remember where they were when they first heard Bob Dylan's voice. It's so *unexpected*."

Marsh: "Gore's answer? Bush's?" Yes, that would settle it—assuming Bush *has* heard it. On the other hand, the recent Radio City Music Hall benefit for the Gore–Lieberman ticket, where, at the end, Bette Midler, Sheryl Crow, Don Henley, Timothy B. Schmidt, Glenn Frey, Lenny Kravitz, Matt Damon, Paul Simon, Julia Roberts and Salma Hayek came out to sing "Teach Your Children," would have raised an even more awesome question, had Dylan been there too: When was the *final* time you heard Bob Dylan's voice?

5 ■ *Nurse Betty*, **directed by Neil LaBute, written by John C. Richards & James Flamberg (Gramercy Pictures)** This hilarious and affecting movie is remarkable in that after two unrelentingly cynical films (*In the Company of Men* and *Your Friends & Neighbors*) LaBute has exchanged realistic stories and utterly contrived emotions for an unbelievable story that turns up real emotions. One result: in a dark bar in Williams, Ariz., empty except for the middle-aged bartender and the regular drunk, Ricky Nelson's beautifully underplayed 1958 No.

1 "Poor Little Fool" is on the jukebox. The song doesn't fill up the room, it simply lives in it. The message is that nothing ever changes here, nothing ever happens, and for a moment the tune takes the scene outside of the violence of the plot, which has just pulled into the parking lot.

6 ■ **Telluride Film Festival Diary: to name the movie would be to give away the ending, so . . .** It's an almost generic scene: after an increasingly edgy buildup following a beginning that promised little more than a comedy of skits, there's a terrific payoff in the form of a double killing by a hitman. As the bodies tumble in a basement, rising up on the soundtrack are the Dells, from 1956: "Oh What a Night," still a lot of people's favorite doo-wop song. Playing over a scene of really convincing carnage, the music is sweet, confirming, and most of all complete. Which made me wonder: why does it work? The same association is all over Martin Scorsese's movies, starting with *Mean Streets* and Johnny Ace's "Pledging My Love."

The director stood up for a question-and-answer session; "Why does doo-wop seem so appropriate for killings in movies?" I asked him.

"Well, doo-wop *is* Joe. And it's his night, so—'Oh What a Night.'"

That couldn't have been the whole story. There is something about the simplicity and directness of the emotionality in doo-wop that speaks to the lack of complexity in the desire to see bad people who are troubling your life *dead*—and which, on screen, confirms that desire: confirms it, makes it beautiful, for the moment.

The director: "But he committed a crime. He'll get caught." But not that night, and not on *his* screen.

7 ■ **Anthony Frewin, *Sixty-Three Closure* (Four Walls Eight Windows)** A cool, then panicky book about a man and a woman in a small town in England stumbling on an anomaly in the who-killed-Kennedy story: photos collected by a dead friend seem to say Lee Harvey Oswald was in the U.K. when he should have been in the Soviet

Union. What makes the story work is the confidence it gives you that the couple will get out of the story sadder but wiser, not with the discovery of who-killed-Kennedy but that, after a lifetime palship, they were meant for each other, that the past really is another country, and a valid passport will get you home.

8 ▪ Waco Brothers, *Electric Waco Chair* (Bloodshot) It seems certain now that on record the self-proclaimed Last Dead Cowboys will never get close to their live sound, where a vehemence that seems to come out of the ground is summoned to overwhelm any mere songs, and so burns the songs into your heart. On record they're closer to the '70s English country band Brinsley Schwarz, which is nothing to be sorry about, unless you want to judge all those you find wanting, which dead cowboys tend to do. Here the vocals alternating between Jon Langford and Dean Schlabowske produce the sense of a conversation between friends who see the world in the same way and feel everything differently. Defeat is the primary condition of their lives, but while for Langford defeat is the only condition of life he trusts, and so in a way he loves it, can trust himself only when he's looking up from the bottom, Schlabowske will never be at home in his misery, even if he's never lived anywhere else. He's Hank Williams, still singing about hope long after he should have learned it'll never knock; Langford is Williams' biographer, saying all those things Williams could never say out loud.

9 ▪ Telluride Film Festival Diary: Wilkinson Library Dedication Stone, 2000 (Telluride, Colo.) "Access to knowledge is the superb, the supreme act of truly great civilizations. Of all the institutions that purport to do this, free libraries stand virtually alone in accomplishing this mission."—Toni Morrison

OK—but it's a library. How about access to syntax?

10 ▪ Minimalist poet found hiding in *New York Times* daily TV log listing of *Law and Order* repeats (Sept. 21)

A&E, 6 P.M. "The Troubles." Violence. A&E, 11 P.M. "Silence." Murdered.

OCTOBER 17, 2000

1 ▪ P. J. Harvey, *Stories From the City, Stories From the Sea* (Island) There are dead spots: the helpless Patti Smith impersonation in "A Place Called Home," the deadfish handshake Thom Yorke of Radiohead gives Harvey in their duet on "This Mess We're In." But with "Kamikaze" and "This Is Love," one number pounds on top of the other, thin sounds building until a wall you can't climb is staring you in the face. The plain fact that Harvey never uses all she has, never tells the secret, makes what she is willing to say a tease, a dare, a threat. But all of that seems far away on the first number, "Big Exit," which could have come off the Band's second album if she'd been around to play on it. Along with the hammering beat she gets on her guitar, the verses scratch at the memory, until finally the Band's basement-tapes tall-tale "Yazoo Street Scandal" comes out of hiding. But the chorus is all Harvey, and Harvey in the air, circling the globe like Superman. "Baby, baby, ain't it true / I'm immortal / When I'm with you," she wails, not a crack or a tear in her tone, and, yes, she sounds like she has been here for a thousand years.

2 ▪ *Invasion of the Body Snatchers* returns to San Francisco 22 years after Kevin McCarthy is run down in the street screaming, "They're here! They're here!": Natalie Jeremijenko, *One Tree*, at "Picturing the Genetic Revolution—Paradise Now" (Exit Art, 548 Broadway, New York, through Oct. 28) The installation ("Mixed Mediums Courtesy Postmasters"): eight putatively identical shrublike saplings in green containers. From explanatory material: "Cloning has made it possible to Xerox copy organic life and fundamentally confound traditional understanding of individualism and authenticity . . . 'One Tree' is actually one hundred tree clones of a single tree micropropagated in culture. These clones were originally exhibited together as plantlets at Yerba Buena Center for the Arts, San Francisco, in 1999. This was the only time they were seen together. In the Spring of 2001,

the clones will be planted in public sites throughout the San Francisco Bay Area, including Golden Gate Park, 220 private properties, San Francisco school district sites, Bay Area Rapid Transit stations, Yerba Buena Performing Arts Center, and Union Square. A selection of international sites are also being negotiated."

3 ▪ *Croupier/Sing-a-Long Sound of Music* (Waverly Theater, New York, Sept. 30) Where the warning label on the marquee reads "PG," not "R."

4 ▪ David Margolick, *Strange Fruit: Billie Holiday, Café Society, and an Early Cry for Civil Rights* (Running Press) With lyrics by Lewis Allen (aka Abel Meerpol, adoptive father of the sons of convicted atomic bomb spies Julius and Ethel Rosenberg after the latters' execution), the anti-lynching song was both a hit and a scandal in 1939, when Holiday recorded it: "Black bodies swinging in the Southern breeze / Strange fruit hanging from the poplar trees." Margolick somehow fails to mention this early version, regarding a lynch frenzy in Vicksburg, Miss.: "From gamblers to negroes, from negroes to white citizens, and from these to strangers: till, dead men were seen literally dangling from the boughs of trees on every roadside; and in numbers almost sufficient, to rival the native Spanish moss of the country, as a drapery of the forest."

—Abraham Lincoln, "On the Perpetuation of Our Political Institutions," 1838.

5 ▪ *Almost Famous*, **written and directed by Cameron Crowe (DreamWorks)** The scene in the movie where lightning hits the band's plane and guitarist Billy Crudup happily starts singing "Peggy Sue" is fine; so is the whole crew picking up "Tiny Dancer" on their bus. But the acting by heroes Patrick Fugit and Kate Hudson is excruciatingly self-conscious—and so, in a way, is the script. That a midteen Cameron Crowe was able to chronicle the adventures of musicians so vividly that many of them refused to allow coverage by *Rolling Stone* unless Crowe was the writer is remarkable; the notion that Crowe did it by means of warts and all is absurd. Crowe's ability to convinc-

ingly portray rock stars as thoughtful, honest, fun-loving, caring, decent—and nothing else—had a great deal to do with changing the magazine he worked for from a journal that could throw the realities of Altamont in the faces of both its readers and its namesake to a magazine that would let cover boy Axl Rose pick his own writer and photographer. I don't doubt that Crowe wrote what he saw—or, rather, that he wrote about what he found most real—but there's more to reality than the belief that, as Anne Frank didn't put it, people are basically nice.

6 ▪ John Mellencamp, "Gambling Bar Room Blues," from *The Songs of Jimmie Rodgers—A Tribute* (Egypt) Top performances come from Dicky Betts, Iris DeMent and liner-notes essayist Bob Dylan (it's his label), but John Mellencamp is in another country, where the song is sung as if for the first time. To the inexhaustible melody of "St. James Infirmary," a road bum in a good mood revels in cynicism, in a belief life doesn't get any better than this even if anybody else would call this shit. With an amazingly loose, '20s street-blues arrangement and cracked fiddle from Miriam Sturm.

7 ▪ Tom Perrotta, *Joe College* (St. Martin's) After the perfect-pitch *Election* (forget the bludgeoning movie version), this coming-of-age novel, set in 1982, is a trifle—and no novelist, no matter what age he's coming of, can be allowed to present "If Ted and Nancy were a plausible couple, why not Polly and I?" as if it were English. Still, there are moments when the reflections of the working-class Jersey-Yalie narrator turn him into someone you'd like to meet: "I remember watching the debate between Reagan and Carter and feeling a huge abyss open up at my feet when the commentators began declaring Reagan the winner, even though he'd seemed to me to have performed a fairly plausible imitation of a twinkly-eyed village idiot. I wondered if it was Yale that had made me such a stranger to my own country or having smoked too much pot as

a teenager. In any case, it was unnerving to find myself dwelling in a separate reality from the majority of my fellow citizens, my parents included. I was enough of a believer in democracy—or maybe just safety in numbers—to not be able to derive much comfort from the stubborn conviction that they were wrong and I was right."

8 ▪ Hooverphonic, *The Magnificent Tree* (Epic) The insinuating, vaguely diseased moods that singer Lieske Sadonius brought this Belgian techno-exotica combo caught the nervousness that lay beneath the earliest Paris new wave movies. With Geike Arnaert in front, they've moved on to catch the very essence of the cheesiest *La Dolce Vita* knockoffs, which is to say Italian vacation films.

9 ▪ ®™ARK, *Biotaylorism*, at "Picturing the Genetic Revolution" (as above) A hilariously detailed, deadpan video heralding the application of Frederick Taylor's principles of modern industrial organization to bioengineering—but ending with a brief prescription for sabotage, notably sneaking into toy stores and attaching warning labels to Barbie dolls regarding the cosmetic and genetic surgery those adopting a Barbie self-image might face somewhere down the line.

10 ▪ Speaking of "Yazoo Street Scandal," a correspondent writes: "I was playing some music for my 9-year-old daughter the other day: 'Lo and Behold,' 'Yazoo Street Scandal,' a few other lo-fi favorites. 'These sound like they were recorded in somebody's house,' she said. 'Yes,' I told her. 'A pink house. On a tape recorder. In the basement.' She pondered this and said, 'This music sounds so good. Why does Britney Spears spend so much money getting everything perfect-sounding in the studio?'"

OCTOBER 30, 2000

FORWARD INTO THE PAST: SPECIAL
ELECTION EDITION!

1 ▪ Pere Ubu 25th Anniversary Tour (Knitting Factory, New York, Oct. 14) Too cool: not the homemade theremins, or the feed-

back apron singer David Thomas wore, or the dedications ("A song written for men going through their midlife crises, who have punk roots. If there's ever a time for punk, it's when men have their midlife crises"—a dedication followed, a few minutes into the song, with "the pogo section," with the enormous Thomas moving to the beat less like Sid Vicious than Sidney Greenstreet), but the fanfare music the band used to set itself up for a night of confusion: Max Frost and the Troopers' "Shape of Things to Come." From the 1968 AIP trash classic *Wild in the Streets*—produced by Mike Curb, with a never-known Billy Elder impersonating youth Führer Max Frost (in the movie, would-be James Dean Christopher Jones)—it was a song that 32 years ago somehow sounded as stirring as it did embarrassing, just as it did three weeks before the nation was to go into its booth to decide the shape of things to come. Which, the song reminded everyone, "nothing can stop." More next column.

2 ▪ Richard Pryor, . . . *And It's Deep Too! The Complete Warner Bros. Recordings (1968– 1992)* (Rhino) A big box of CDs of a black man onstage turning everyday life upside down. You listen and think, "How, why, was this voice silenced? What, how much, was lost?" Among other things, the voice of the white square, squared: our next president.

3 ▪ Telluride Film Festival Diary, *Turbulent*, Shirin Neshat, director (Telluride, Colo., Labor Day Weekend) Should you have the chance, do not pass up even the most inconvenient fringe-festival, museum or cable opportunity to see this shocking short film. No sex, no violence, just, in present-day Iran, a man—co-producer Shoja Azari—singing to an all-male audience. He turns his back; his tone is full, rich, but infinitely supple. There are no affectations; sound is everything. And as he shows he can go anywhere he seems to be holding something back. And then the film cuts to Sussan Deyhim, a woman singing, but this time facing the seats—of an empty auditorium. She could be singing in five voices at once; the untrained ear hears overdubs, but in fact it's what Yoko Ono always thought she sounded like, doubled, tripled, with a musicality you can't translate not because Deyhim is singing in Farsi but because she is singing over your head, hitting some notes only certain human beings can hear, which is to say whoever might be excluded from her illegal concert: in Iran, everyone.

4 ▪ Randy Newman, "A Fool in Love," "Poor Me," "Got My Mojo Working," from the soundtrack to Meet the Parents (Dream-Works) The one-time "King of the Suburban Blues" offers a typically craven movie song, a dead cover of a Fats Domino tune and the sort of paint-by-numbers white-boy blues bash that in other hands was already a national skin crawler in 1967, the year before Newman issued his first album, . . . Creates Something New Under the Sun, which he did. The nadir of his career.

5 ▪ Caitlin Macy, The Fundamentals of Play (Random House) A frighteningly expert first novel—set a decade back, a rewrite of The Great Gatsby as filtered through a Whit Stillman lens. Here irony is the essence of all human life, only the gross, vulgar Gatsby character doesn't know it, which makes him less than human. But then how do you decipher the Daisy character, who except for this exchange is so insulated she barely lives on the page? "At some point," says the male narrator, "I made another brilliant contribution to the conversation by asking what she had majored in. Still, I was curious to know."

> "American studies."
> "How'd you pick that?" I said.
> "Same as anyone." But of the other couple hundred students who had graduated with that degree, I doubt a single one would have given the same reason Kate did. "I love this country," she said. I thought at first she was being disingenuous, but she got a look in her eye then which I have never forgotten. It was a look of highly intensified complacency—if that's possible—which I was sure no feast or threat of famine would ever shake.

6 ▪ Larry Clark, Tulsa (Grove) From the director of Kids and Another Day in Paradise, his first work: a 1971 book of photos from the junk world of his long-extended youth. Deservedly legendary: if Robert Frank's The Americans was a picture of the roads that '50s teen mass murderer Charley Starkweather, the voice of Bruce Springsteen's "Nebraska," might have taken if he'd gotten away, this is much worse—what if Starkweather had just stayed home?

7 ▪ From liner notes to Nothing Seems Better to Me: The Music of Frank Proffitt and North Carolina—The Warner Collection, Vol. II (Appleseed) In 1940 folklorists Frank and Anne Warner taped hill singer Frank Proffitt's offering of a local ballad called "Tom Dooley," about a 19th century murder of a young woman by her former lover. The song traveled, and in 1958 a collegiate trio from Menlo Park, Calif., made it No. 1 in the nation. (For the whole, rich story, see Robert Cantwell's When We Were Good: The Folk Revival.) Proffitt, in a letter from 1959:

> I got a television set for the kids. One night I was a-setting looking at some foolishness when three fellers stepped out with guitar and banjer and went to singing Tom Dooly and they clowned and hipswinged. I began to feel sorry sick, like I'd lost a loved one. Tears came to my eyes, yes, I went out and balled on the Ridge, looking toward old Wilkes, land of Tom Dooly. . . . I looked up across the mountains and said Lord, couldn't they leave me the good memories. . . .
>
> Then Frank Warner wrote, he tells me that some way our song got picked up. The shock was over. I went back to my work. I began to see the world was bigger than our mountains of Wilkes and Watauga. Folks was brothers, they all liked the plain ways. I begin to pity them that hadn't dozed on the hearthstone. . . . Life was sharing different thinking, the different ways. I looked in the mirror of my heart—You haint a boy no longer. Give folks like Frank Warner all you got. Quit thinking Ridge to Ridge, think of oceans to oceans.

Isn't this a little too good to be true?

8 ◼ **Wallflowers on *Saturday Night Live* (NBC, Oct. 21)** I wrote about it weeks ago, but I still don't know how Jakob Dylan gets away with "Sam Cooke didn't know what I know," let alone four times in one song. He does, though, and it's one of the weirdest accomplishments in pop-music history, and it's not his looks. I don't think.

9 ◼ **"Crossroads of American Values," Toyota commercial (NBC, CBS, ABC, beginning October)** Presumably thanks to Robert Johnson estate controller Steve LaVere, one can now enjoy the work of one of America's greatest artists merely by turning on the TV. It's the worst cover ever of a Johnson song, in this case the 1936 "Cross Road Blues," featuring a horridly hyped-up white blues voice—compared with this, Randy "Mojo" Newman *is* Johnson. "*Down* to the crossroads / Tryin' to flag a ride," the piece begins; cars are streaming, people are engaging in transactions, it's just full of busyness. "Goin' *down* to the crossroads," the voice finishes up: "I believe I'm goin' down," which means, *down* to the Toyota dealer's. Never mind the line from the song itself, about a black man about to be caught alone on a public road after dark, where he's as good as dead: "I believe I'm sinking down," on his knees, in terror and surrender to his fate. The surrender part still works; only the fate has changed.

10 ◼ **Waco Brothers at Brownie's (New York, Oct. 21)** "This is a much more *likable* Waco Brothers than last year," singer and guitarist Jon Langford announced from the stage at the end of an all-day Bloodshot Records showcase at the CMJ Music Marathon. "That's what we're all about," added guitarist and singer Dean Schlabowske, "likability." "We don't play no *alt country*," Langford continued. "That's a *Washington* word! We play real music for normal people!" True to their adopted George W. Bush "all things to all people" posture, they started off with "Fox River," a celebration of a river that flows where it wants to flow, and ended with guest Sally Timms swaying to the irresistible melody of "Seminole Wind," an ode to flood control. Otherwise the pol-

itics were up to the music, and vice versa, with Langford proposing "W." as an all-purpose obscenity for the next four years ("'W. off,' 'W. you,' 'That last song was pure W.,' 'They really W.'d us over that time'") and introducing mandolinist Tracey Dear—like the rest of the Wacos, save token American Schlabowske, from the U.K.—as "a man who pays his taxes and can't vote! That's what your country was founded on: taxation without representation! Underpaid foreign workers like the Waco Brothers!" The sound fell apart heroically for Neil Young's "Revolution Blues," put itself back together for Johnny Cash's "Cocaine Blues," came home for the anti-Clinton "Coo Coo" rewrite "See Willy Fly By" ("Clinton's looking pretty good right now," Langford said after the show) and rose as high as Waco Brothers music goes with Schlabowske's indelible "If You Won't Change Your Mind," broken in half by a guitar solo that turned the word "bereft" into a physical sensation—a gorgeous sensation.

NOVEMBER 13, 2000

1 ◼ **Ethan and Joel Coen, *O Brother, Where Art Thou?* (Touchstone Films, due for release Dec. 21)** Three white prisoners escape from a Mississippi chain gang in the middle of the Depression and run straight into a series of blackouts about old-time music—starting when they stop their jalopy to pick up a young black man in suit and tie, bluesman Tommy Johnson, fresh from selling his soul to the devil for guitar prowess and ready to rock. Unlike the younger Robert Johnson, Tommy Johnson ("Cool Drink of Water Blues," 1928, though here he's given Skip James' music to play) actually bragged of the transaction. (What could be cooler?) When in the Coen brothers' version he's seized by the Ku Klux Klan for ritual sacrifice, he figures it's just payback coming sooner than he bargained for.

It's a scene that recalls *The Birth of a Nation*, but it's so culturally blasphemous there are really no precedents for it. In a clearing in the dead of night, hundreds of Klansmen in pure white robes whirl about like a college marching band at halftime, executing lightning moves as if they were born to them. They come to rest in formation, facing a red-robed Grand Master. Johnson is brought before him—and then, from a high platform, from inside the Master's mask, issues the most horrifying, the most full-bodied, the most perfect rendition of the ancient plea "Oh Death" ("Won't you spare me over for another year?") imaginable. As the long, tangled song goes on, with no accompaniment but the audience, the victim and the night, a lynching becomes a philosophy lesson—and the slapstick escape that follows takes off none of the chill.

2 ▪ *O Brother, Where Art Thou?* **soundtrack (Mercury)** Typically, the dynamism of the film doesn't translate into disembodied recordings—if, as with the torrential "Man of Constant Sorrow" the cons-plus-Johnson cut in a radio station, it's even the same recording. Pick to click, among the modern re-creations by the likes of Ralph Stanley, Alison Krauss, Gillian Welch, Emmylou Harris, the Cox Family and the Whites: running under the titles, Harry McClintock's 1928 version of the hobo jungle anthem "The Big Rock Candy Mountain."

3 ▪ **Nov. 8, From the Ether:** A friend writes: "I went to sleep when the networks called Florida for Bush, woke up 90 minutes or so later to see they were recalling it again, down to 500 votes at that point—and, shortly, someone cut to a shot of an Elvis impersonator (in black street clothes, but with the sideburns/hair/aviator glasses), presumably in Nashville, clasping his hands in silent prayer. It was that kind of night."

4 ▪ **Al Gore, Huntington, W.Va., Nov. 4** Lest we forget, as we will, at the close of the campaign, with Gore taking up George W. Bush's truthful but (simply because of, in Bush's mouth, the accidental nature of its truthfulness) bizarre claim that "The people in Washington want to treat Social Security like it's some federal program,"

Gore finally hit the note that had eluded him for so long: "It wasn't a slip of the tongue. It was an expression of ingrained hostility, a preference on the other side for a dog-eat-dog, every-person-for-himself mentality that—" And here the words vanish into the next four years.

5 ▪ **Bono, "Foreword" in "Q Dylan" (*Q Magazine,* U.K.)** "The best way to serve the age is to betray it," Bono says of Bob Dylan, quoting Brendan Keneally from *The Book of Judas.* He goes on: "The anachronism, really, is the '60s. For the rest of his life he's been howling from some sort of past that we seem to have forgotten but must not. That's it for me. He keeps undermining our urge to look into the future."

6 ▪ **Richard Carlin and Bob Carlin, *Southern Exposure: The Story of Southern Music in Words and Pictures* (Billboard Books)** Mostly pictures, from the 1850s to the 1950s—pictures of musicians who made the music that in the 1920s was already the last word of another world. It's the real world of *O Brother, Where Art Thou?*—especially on the cover, in a shot also reproduced inside. The photo is mottled, degenerating: it shows a dashingly handsome, dark-haired man with dark, hooded eyes looking you in the face under a broad-brimmed hat. Foulard tie, jacket, vest, watch chain: holding his five-string banjo, he is the dandy, the woman stealer. You wake up next to him and he's already gone. In Warren Smith's irresistibly slow, beckoning 1957 rockabilly tune he's the man with a "Red Cadillac and a Black Moustache," but all through Lee Smith's 1992 novel *The Devil's Dream,* back from her to the Carter Family in 1940, forward again to Bob Dylan's 1992 *Good As I Been to You,* he's Black Jack Davey. Given what stories, regrets, laments, fond memories or erotic dreams he might have left behind in Hope, Ark., where he stands as his picture is taken, sometime in the 1890s, he is also Bill Clinton.

7–8 ▪ **Kasimir Malevich, *Dynamic Suprematism,* 1915/16 and Bill Woodrow, *Twin-Tub with Guitar,* 1981, at the Tate Modern (London, to January)** In a huge, insistently conceptual long walk through 20th century art, these pieces jumped out. In the Manifesto Room of the "History/Memory/Society" sector, the old broadsides covering the walls shout and stamp their feet, announcing Futurism, the Bauhaus, Kandinsky's New Theater, Suprematism itself, while off in a corner Wyndham Lewis is Blasting England to bits. Among a few other paintings is the Malevich, a tilted but upright triangle; it's quiet, modest. From somewhere in Russia it pulls all the noisy declarations of the future into its own abstraction and silences them. In its abstraction, the piece at least seems to speak clearly—about the *ease* of remaking and rearranging the world, its constituent elements of life. If you keep looking, though, the triangle begins to look like a figure, an idea, a person, someone with a name. With the bars and squares that score the triangle now arms, eyes and hats, the figure gestures. It is now obese, absurd, threatening, its identity so obvious: Alfred Jarry's loathed and loved Pere Ubu, in Jarry's own woodcuts the same shape, the same fascist trod across whatever might be in his way—and now, with Ubu on the march into the New Day, somehow morally cleansed.

Ivan Chtcheglov, 1953, "Formulary for a New Urbanism": "Given the choice of love or a garbage disposal unit, young people all over the world have chosen the garbage disposal." Not so fast, says Bill Woodrow, born 1948 in the U.K., in his own room in the "Still Life/Object/Real Life" sector. For his piece he'd cut the outline of an electric guitar out of the grimy metal casing of a post-war Hotpoint washing machine but not removed it, so the two remain attached like a parasitic twin still part of its host. The curators comment: "The sculpture wittily combines two potent symbols of Western consumerism." Not so fast: why not art out of functionalism, or the art hiding in objects of utility, the desire hiding in need? Woodrow himself: "The guitar was a pop icon and the washing machine was an everyday, domestic item. So it was bringing the two things together like a slice of

life." Not so fast: why not the urge to create sneaking out of the wish for comfort, and superseding it? There's no trouble imagining this as Pete Townshend's diddley bow, his first guitar.

9 ▪ **Middle-aged man shaking a cardboard coffee cup full of change like maracas (6th Avenue and 13th Street, New York, Nov. 5)** He was hammering out a tremendously effective R&B number that sounded halfway between anyone's "C. C. Rider" and almost anything by Bo Diddley, and it wasn't until I'd added my change to his and was halfway down the block that the song revealed itself out of its own beat: Elvis Presley's first record, "That's All Right."

10 ▪ **Pere Ubu 25th Anniversary Tour (Knitting Factory, New York, Oct. 14)** "The long slide into weirdness and decay," leader David Thomas announced. When synth player Robert Wheeler moved his hands over his two homemade theremins—to play the theremin you can't look like anything but someone casting spells—the small pieces of metal seemed less like musical instruments than UFOs, and the high-pitched sounds coming from them, drifting through the rest of the music like swamp gas, nothing but the cries of the creatures trapped inside. Like any number of people other than myself must feel as I write, the day after the election.

NOVEMBER 28, 2000

SPECIAL BIZARRE ALL-QUOTATION EDITION!

1–2 ▪ **Alan Berg and Howard Hampton on Election Eve and after** Berg, Nov. 6: "I am trying to cope with my jitters by listening to the five CDs of Dylan's Basement Tapes bootlegs and nothing else till it's over." Nov. 9: "I didn't think I'd have time to listen to all *five* CDs. When things got rough, right before Pennsylvania came in, 'Clothes Line Saga' came on and that took care of Pennsylvania. Right now it just went to 'We carried you / In our arms / On Independence Day.' No question about what this will be resolved on: 'I'm Not There.'"

Hampton, Nov. 18: "Today I played the only appropriate song I could find: 'I Was in the House When the House Burned Down.'"

I called Warren Zevon to find out where he was on Election Night, but he wasn't home.

3 ▪ Fran Farrell, "I Want to Be Teeny-bopped: Teen Star Sex Fantasies" (*Nassau Weekly*, Princeton, N.J., Oct. 19) "Jordan Knight, of the New Kids on the Block, was the first person I ever masturbated about.... While my friends were playing with Barbie, I was imagining having sex with Jordan, and sometimes a threesome with Joey, on their big tour bus. See, I met Jordan when I was 10; it was downhill from there. Fast forward 10 years, to London, England. I'm walking down the street when I see a sign, the most beautiful sign I've ever seen—Jordan Knight, performing at 4 o'clock today. I couldn't believe my luck. Then I thought, this isn't luck, it's fate. We met 10 years ago, but now it's legal for him to have sex with me!!!! So I wait in line for FOUR HOURS. Yes, four hours for that has-been. The line was full of 15-year-old girls with thick British accents, acne and very bad teeth. I was squished in the middle of a crowd of sweaty, ugly girls screaming for a washed-up '80s pop star. But when he came onstage . . ."

4 ▪ Sen. Joseph Lieberman, Fiftieth birthday greeting for Bob Dylan (U.S. Senate, May 24, 1991) "Twenty-five or 30 years ago, I would have had a very difficult time imagining Bob Dylan, whose music was so much a part of my life at the time, being 50 years old, an age he attains today, his birthday. I would have had even greater difficulty imagining me taking note of his achievements in remarks in the Senate of the United States.

"Back in 1963, it is hardly likely any member of Congress would have been talking about Bob Dylan, at least not on the floor of either chamber; at least not in favorable terms. After all, it was he who said of them, 'Come senators, Congressmen, please heed the call / Don't stand in the doorway, don't block up the hall.' So times have changed, though Dylan's sentiment still holds true when we consider how many problems we still have to heed. I am sure he sings those words with the same spirit and intensity today as he did 28 years ago.

"There is a mystery to Bob Dylan, which is surprising, in a way, given how freely he has expressed himself through his music. But the mystery results, I think, from Dylan's refusal to play roles society might seek to assign him—roles like superstar, rock idol, prophet. 'I tried my best to be just like I am / But everybody wants you to be just like them.'"

5 ▪ David Thomson, *The Big Sleep* (BFI Publishing) On Lauren Bacall, director Howard Hawks and *To Have and Have Not* (1944): "Betty was born in 1924, and grew up looking like nothing else on earth. I mean, how does one describe that young woman who could look like a Jewish teenager, a Eurasian doll, a Slav earth mother and the smoke that gets in your eyes—and all that before Hawks got hold of her? Add to that the allegation that she was only 17, and you can see what a wide-open country America was then."

6 ▪ Ishmael Reed on the dance mania "Jes Grew," sweeping the nation after the election of Warren G. Harding, "the first race president," in 1920, and the conspiracy of the "Antonist Wallflower Order" to stop it (*Mumbo Jumbo*, Scribner, 1972) "It has been a busy day for reporters following Jes Grew. The morning began with Dr. Lee De Forest, inventor of the three-element vacuum tube, which helped make big-time radio possible, collapsing before a crowded press room after he pleaded concerning his invention, now in the grips of Jes Grew: 'What have you done to my child? You have sent him out on the street in rags of ragtime to collect money from all and sundry. You have made him a laughingstock of intelligence, surely a stench in the nostrils of the gods of the ionosphere.'"

Tycoon Walter Mellon: "Jes Grew tied up the tubes causing Dr. Lee De Forest to cop a plea at the press conference. . . . At the rate of radio sales, $600 million worth will be sold by 1929, correct?"

Hierophant of the Wallflower Order: "That is true, Mr. Walter Mellon."

"Suppose people don't have the money to buy radios. It will be an interesting precaution against this Jes Grew thing, isn't that so?"

"I don't get what you're driving at, Mr. Mellon."

"The liquidity of Jes Grew has resulted in a hyperinflated situation, all you hear is more, more, increase growth. . . . Suppose we shut down a few temples. . . . I mean banks, take money out of circulation, how would people be able to support the appendages of Jes Grew, the cabarets juke joints and the speaks. Suppose we put a tax on the dance floors and get out of circulation J[es]. G[rew]. C[arriers].s like musicians, dancers, its doers, its irrepressible fancy. Suppose we take musicians out of circulation, arrest them on trumped-up drug charges and give them unusually long and severe prison sentences. Suppose we subsidize the hundreds of symphony orchestras across the country, have government-sponsored waltz-boosting campaigns . . ."

"But wouldn't these steps result in a depression?"

"Maybe, but it will put an end of Jes Grew's resiliency, and if a panic occurs it will be a controlled panic. It will be our Panic."

7 ▪ **Hal Foster, Election "Diary," on a word soon to disappear from our lexicon (*London Review of Books*, Nov. 30)** "'Chad' . . . For some reason I think of Troy Donahue, and imagine him dimpled, pregnant, hanging or punched."

8 ▪ **Colin B. Morton on Metallica and Napster in "Welsh Psycho: Extracts From the Teenage Diary of Colin B. Morton" (*Clicks and Klangs* #3, Oct./Nov.)** "William Hague, leader of the U.K. Tory Party, has recently come out in defence of a man who shot dead a youth who was trespassing on his private property. Even more recently, the Tory Party has used, without permission, the music of Massive Attack to help promote the idea that we shouldn't have to pay tax or care about the sick. Hague's own logic dictates, therefore, that Massive Attack's Daddy G and 3D should have the right to shoot all members of the Tory Party for trespassing on their Intellectual Property. Either Intellectual Property doesn't exist, or they can have that right. Hague can't have it both ways. (Well, he can, but that's another story entirely.)"

9 ▪ **Seminar on Harry Smith's *Anthology of American Folk Music* (Princeton University, Nov. 17)** One person at the table, on the notion of the panoply of farmer-miner-laborer-domestics or itinerant professional entertainers such as Dock Boggs, Sister Mary Nelson, Frank Hutchison, Uncle Dave Macon, Blind Lemon Jefferson or Bessie Johnson, as their 1927–32 78s were assembled by Smith in 1952, as a "town" or "community" (following, among other comments, "Hattie Stoneman ought to be drowned" and "Uncle Dave seems much too satisfied about the prospect of apocalypse"): "If it is a community, it's not one I'd want to be part of." "Of course no one wants to be part of it," another participant said later. "All these people are poor!"

10 ▪ **Special "Forward Into the Past" Election Update—Francis Russell, *The Shadow of Blooming Grove: The Centennial of Warren G. Harding* (McGraw-Hill, 1968), quoting Progressive newspaper editor Brand Whitlock on the Republican Party's nomination of Warren G. Harding as its candidate to replace Woodrow Wilson** "I am more and more under the opinion that for President we need not so much a brilliant man as solid, mediocre men, providing they have good sense, good and careful judgment, and good manners."

DECEMBER 18, 2000

1–2 ▪ **Eleventh Dream Day and Come at Mercury Lounge (New York, Nov. 25)** Thalia Zedek and Chris Brokaw of Come sat with electric guitars for a short set of down tunes built around high notes—tunes that came most to life in the instrumental passages, with words less messages than structures. Zedek carries the world-weariness of a Slavic Anna Magnani (having flown into New York that day, she apologized for the rawness of her voice, blaming it on the fact that she couldn't smoke on the plane); for her last number, she picked the first couple of notes of "California Dreamin'." I took it for a joke, a false beginning to a song that would turn out to be the opposite, but she continued on with an absolutely lethal version of the Mamas and the Papas' first hit, taking it into Puritan graveyards, the death's head angels on the tombstones staring back at the singer as she left the song on the ground.

Eleventh Dream Day—guitarist and main singer Rick Rizzo, drummer and sometime singer Janet Bean, bassist and sometime guitarist Doug McCombs, joined by friend Mark Greenberg on organ, bass and drums, and by powerful guitarist Tara Key on two numbers—play infrequently these days, especially outside of Chicago. You'd never know it. With their first song Rizzo drove the music to levels of intensity it takes the best bands five or six numbers to approach. It seemed impossible that the band would ever get back there, but again and again it did. Rizzo has an insistently ordinary, mild-mannered, reasonable, amiable demeanor; what comes out of his mouth as he sings, his voice on an even keel, avoiding almost all dramatics, is a creature of decency and desperation. But as a guitarist Rizzo is without limits, and if the lines he plays have definition, the creature pumping them out has none. He's a well without a bottom, a creation of fury, resentment, revenge, someone who gives his songs no reason to stop. Bent over to the breaking point, leaning back on his heels, he still looked ordinary, like Bill Paxton—not the good, sort of dumb Paxton of *Twister* and *Titanic* but the friendly, class-clown killer vampire Paxton of *Near Dark*. From beginning to end the band found the song within the song, some core of rhythmic momentum, building on itself, that the song didn't have to give up, and Eleventh Dream

Day seemed to take it not as theirs but as something to be used and then put back in the song. One jarring note: among the many talismans on Key's guitar was an old reflector campaign button, showing a profile of John F. Kennedy from one angle, "The Man for the 60's" from another. I don't recall "the '60s" being referred to as "the '60s"—that is, conceptually—in 1960, which means some adman, or maybe Arthur Schlesinger Jr., if not Andy Warhol, was way ahead of his time.

3–4 ■ **Cannanes and Steward, *Communicating at an Unknown Rate* (YoYo) and Cannanes, *Electro 2000* (Insound Tour Support)** This Australian combo is playful before it is anything else. The long "Savage" certainly is, with its bright little synth notes, and Frances Gibson's sunny, thoughtful voice asking herself questions and a guitar chiming in like a particularly considerate friend. But it keeps on, until the repetitions in the small riffs that build the tune unsettle the notion that it's headed for a happy ending, like the way that Charlize Theron, in most of her movies, sparkles like a spring and then ends up dead. I don't know where "Savage" ends up, except that it's nowhere near where it started, even if, on paper, the notes would say the two places are exactly the same.

The five-song *Electro 2000* is even sunnier, a dream-pop manifesto, but has anyone ever woken up from a dream as gorgeous as "You Name It"? This is Gibson again, walking through fields of flowers while the Northern Lights spread salacious rumors about her and she plays the Go-Go's "Our Lips Are Sealed" in her head. In 1983 it might not have seemed so striking, but today you won't hear anything this band is doing anywhere else.

5 ■ **Nick Talevski, *The Encyclopedia of Rock Obituaries* (Omnibus)** Four hundred ninety pages of dead people, even including writers, and not just Lester Bangs. Too much about the lives, not enough about the deaths, but it's a start.

6 ■ **Drive-by Truckers, *Alabama Ass Whuppin'* (Second Heaven)** The name of this country-rock band and the title of its live album sum up the attitude the Drive-by Truckers mean to substitute for whatever else they might need. But halfway through, even they seem tired of it.

7 ▪ **Neil Young, Friends & Relatives,** *Road Rock* **(Reprise)** As an apparent stopgap in lieu of the long-awaited many-CD first installment of his multi-many-CD career retrospective, Young offers a recent tour document: note-for-note cover versions. Of his own songs.

8–9 ▪ **"Amazons of the Avant-Garde" at the Guggenheim (New York, through Jan. 7)** Context revealed the second-spookiest work in this show of mostly promiscuously colored pre- and immediately post-revolution paintings by female Russian artists, which runs in galleries alongside the big, superpopular Armani retrospective. (Sponsored by *InStyle*: "My favorite magazine!" my companion said. "When people ask me if I'm looking forward to anything, I always say, *InStyle!*") Nadezhda Udaltsova (1885–1961) might not have spoken so clearly anywhere else, but here, with her 1915 *Red Figure*, she was a mediator between commerce and the eternal, which is one of the things an artist is supposed to be. In the frame an orange-red cubist woman, slight and slim like the Armani mannequins, sat in a mostly cubist room of infinite style—a room that, with a half-circle of a back window letting in the light, took in the styles to follow, from de Stijl to art deco to '50s moderne. In its predictiveness, the picture had a harsh, dismissive authority; I mean, you can feel stupid looking at it. Yet the woman is casual in her all-encompassing modernity, on top of the century as if it had already happened and she's thinking it over.

The No. 1 spookiest piece was Natalia Goncharova (1881–1962) in *Grimaces in Art*, a futurist poster from a 1913 number of the journal *Teatr v Karrikaturakh*. She posed in a peasant's headdress, with her face painted so violently that the woman then in her early 30s looked 80—a comment, perhaps, on how old Russian peasant women in their

30s actually looked. But the picture was less historical than primeval: Goncharova's cheeks, chin and forehead were scored with heavy black lines, cuneiforms, signs, unreadable Paleolithic cave symbols or proto-writing. What you see, along with the heroic shout of modernism, are wrinkles so deep you could stick your fingers in them, unless you see the marks of badly healed scars cutting down and across the face so brutally you can almost feel the knife that would have put them there.

10 ▪ **Bijou Market hot sauces (1015 Decatur St., New Orleans)** Along with the vast array of submissive Bill and dominatrix Hillary postcards, and the usual do-you-dare hot sauce brands—Open Grave, Capital Punishment, Last Rites, Sudden Death—there was, this year, Bubba's Best ("As Usual Comes Up a Little Short"), Hillary's Diet Sauce ("Made From Pure Whitewater—for Use in Place of Health Insurance") and, among various Lewinsky products, the Monica's Down on Your Knees hot sauce, with the label picturing what seemed to be permanently attached versions of what Lewinsky herself once hopefully called her "presidential knee-pads." Compared with last year, when Decatur Street shops displayed T-shirts printed with photos of a joyously smiling Monica with semen dripping down her chin, this was a big step toward national reconciliation. Or something.

JANUARY 8, 2001

1 ▪ **Arliss Howard,** *"The Human Stain by Philip Roth"* **(Houghton Mifflin audio books)** Album of the year? This is it: unabridged, eight cassettes, 14 1/2 hours and a tour de force by an actor less known for his roles in *To Wong Foo, Thanks for Everything, Julie Newmar!* and *Tales of Erotica* than for his marriage to Debra Winger. Winger has a small role in *The Human Stain*; all it does is throw Howard's performance into relief. He contrives different voices for different characters, and many different voices for different incarnations of the same character,

without ever seeming to do so, without ever losing an overall narrative authority. It's as if, somewhere behind all the acting, Howard himself were the real author of Roth's novel. With not a word missing, this means a lot of ruminating, a lot of philosophy, repetitions that on the page can seem like a whisper and that spoken out loud can sound stupid. With Howard speaking, the same phrases, the same ideas coming up again and again, work in the listener's mind not as irritations, but as reminders, as part of the listener's own memory. This is the perfect companion for a long, long driving trip—but be sure to time the end of the trip to the end of the story. Otherwise you'll be left stranded, wondering what you're doing so many miles from home, no place to be when, as at the end of Howard's reading, all of life comes crashing down.

2–3 ▪ PJ Harvey at Bowery Ballroom, New York (Dec. 11) and at Daddy-O's, 44 Bedford St., New York (Nov. 19) Harvey was very glamorous at the Bowery Ballroom; she ran the band with her guitar. Still, she's so self-composed that when she offered a few conventional words to the crowd it seemed unnatural, out of place—or as if the audience weren't needed at all. There were moments when doors you didn't know were there opened, moments when you might see yourself across town at the Museum of Modern Art, gazing into Jackson Pollock's 1950 *One* and realizing you could be looking at a 30,000-year-old cave painting or wall engraving, looking into an image redrawn or scored by hundreds of hands over hundreds or thousands of years. But mostly her performance was a series of songs—and it was surprising to find the new "Big Exit" already a standard crowd pleaser. The audience's cheers made the song seem like a finished thing, already known.

A few weeks before, at a Village bar, a guy was shouting into his cellphone. The bartender cranked his Rolling Stones *Let It Bleed* CD higher and higher; the guy just upped his own volume. But when "Midnight Rambler" and "Monkey Man" and "You Got the Silver" yielded to "You Can't

Always Get What You Want," you realized it wasn't simply some self-important jerk with his Nokia that was killing conversation, or even the ever-rising loudness of the music, but the music itself. This was, after all, merely the best rock 'n' roll album ever made, and when it's playing it's kind of hard not to listen to it. The bartender proved his touch was perfect by following with Harvey's just-released *Stories From the City, Stories From the Sea.* "Big Exit" is the first cut, and it immediately raised the question, Why isn't *she* in the Rolling Stones? It's not as if they don't need her help, or as if she's not already standing in their shoes.

4 ▪ Gossip, *That's Not What I Heard* (Kill Rock Stars) From Arkansas: very tough, very grimy, very Southern—all dirt and spit, with a feeling Pussy Galore once found, probably on an old copy of *The Rolling Stones, Now!*

5 ▪ Val Kilmer on *Saturday Night Live,* Dec. 9 (NBC) Before applying himself to a startling impression of Jeb Bush being spurned by former lover Katherine Harris (and you haven't lived until you've seen her in the "Fashion Police" pages of the Dec. 25 issue of *Us*), at the end of his monologue Kilmer said, "U2 is actually on the show tonight." As a violation of *SNL*'s most hardened cliché—the hideously tiresome "[Name of musical performer] is here!"— it was right up there with Kilmer's "Shoot him in the face" advice to Christian Slater in *True Romance.*

6 ▪ "Dearly Departed: Remembering those in the arts who died in 2000," *San Francisco Chronicle* Datebook (Dec. 31) Average age for the 20 entries under "Pop Music," including Roebuck Staples, 84; Lord Kitchener, 77; Edward "Tex" Beneke, 77; and Screamin' Jay Hawkins, 70: 54. Average age for the 47 entries under "Classical Music," including Neil Wilson, 44; David Shallon, 49; David Golub, 50; and Michael J. Baker, 51: 77.

7 ▪ Peter Loge, "Comment," on *Morning Edition,* NPR (Dec. 20) Big question for the nation, according to Loge, director of Washington's Justice Project, an anti–death penalty group: figuring out a future for Al Gore, especially with the possibility that he might have to subsist on "Tipper getting the Wildcats back together for one last VH1 special." Noting that Gore seemingly had "no marketable skills," and that traditional opportunities for ex-vice presidents— motivational speaking or writing a book— raised specters of boredom beyond hope (the Spiro Agnew–Gerald Ford tradition of lobbying, fixing and introducing corrupt foreign businessmen to influential members of Congress and the executive branch went unmentioned), Loge proposed that Gore, drawing on his years of experience showing up at state funerals and second-rank fundraisers, offer himself as an "event stand-in." Gore could rent himself out to family reunions, charity events, Little League games or whatever function someone else wanted to avoid, Loge announced somberly—and he could be just as stiff and wooden as he wished. After all, what could be more polite at such gatherings than a robot that says "Yes," "Thank you" and "More punch would be delightful" better than any human? In other words, calls for national unity, "putting hard feelings behind us" and acknowledging George W. Bush's legitimacy as president (as, according to a December *New York Times* poll, 40 percent of the public, as opposed to 99.5 percent of the media, do not) are all very well, but what's really necessary to establish Bush as the landslide winner he has pretended to be since Nov. 7 is the transformation of Gore into the automatic punch line of every loser joke—no matter that he plainly won the election, in Florida as in the nation at large.

8 ▪ *Leni Riefenstahl 2001 desk calendar* (Taschen) Speaking of legitimacy ("Riefenstahl's current de-Nazification and vindication as indomitable priestess of the beautiful," Susan Sontag wrote in 1974, when Riefenstahl, who will turn 99 this year, could still pose as a nymph, "do not augur well for the keenness of current abilities to detect the fascist longings in our midst"), this is going too far—or coming too close.

9 ▪ **Johnny Cash, *American III: Solitary Man* (American)** "I" and "II" in the Cash revival—put old man together with new songs—did nothing for me; here an inner depth combines with the deep voice to take some of the songs to places neither they nor Cash have reached before. Neil Diamond's "Solitary Man" was always a great record, but also a kind of whine; here it's a testament. Will Oldham's "I See a Darkness" is creepy as Oldham himself does it as Bonnie "Prince" Billie; now it's a premonition of death that lets you see through death's eyes. The thriller is U2's "One": with Bono's bellowing gone it's revealed as a perfect tune. As the singer waltzes with himself in the studio apartment no one else has entered for months, only the pop lightness of the melody convinces you the song is something other than an old mountain air.

10 ▪ ***The Suburbans*, directed by Donal Lardner Ward, written by Tony Guma and Donal Lardner Ward (Tristar 1999, HBO, Dec. 7)** Ultra-adorable record company rep Jennifer Love Hewitt facing terrified one-hit-wonder '80s band now on tour for the first time in over 15 years: "So! We beat on, boats against the current, ceaselessly into the past!" Her telling the Suburbans she's quoting F. Scott Fitzgerald doesn't make them feel any better.

JANUARY 22, 2001

1 ▪ **Don Asmussen, "San Francisco Comic Strip": "This Week: President-Elect George W. Bush's Cabinet Nominees" (*San Francisco Chronicle*, Jan. 14)** For the first panel, a *Chronicle* front page: "ASHCROFT: 'I'LL ALLOW BLACK ABORTIONS.' Bush's Attorney General Nominee Meets Halfway: Nominee's openness to compromise shows that Bush's promise of a new era of bipartisanship is heartfelt."

2–3 ▪ **Snoop Dogg, "County Blues," from *Dead Man Walking* (Death Row) and Honeyboy Edwards, *Mississippi Delta Bluesman* (Smithsonian Folkways)** "The county gives plenty blues"—in a piece on police harassment with vocal and harmonica samples that put it right back in the South of 70 years ago, the man with the smooth, trickster drawl walks the rhythm slowly down the street, looking back and forth to see which direction his ancestors are coming from. "They got me wearing county blues," sings an old man again and again, as women's voices swirl around his like caressing hands, like snakes. "They got me wearing / Penitentiary shoes." As for Edwards, who as a young man hung around with Robert Johnson, this handsome reissue of a 1979 session is proof the country blues can be as dull as anything else.

4 ▪ **Pere Ubu, The Shape of Things (Hearthen, available through Ubutique)** Recorded from the crowd at the Mistake in Cleveland on April 7, 1976—when guitarist Peter Laughner, who would soon leave both the band and his life behind, steps out of the first number, "Heart of Darkness," you understand why people who knew him still testify he heard things they never would. Just as memorable, though, are the two poseurs in the audience trying on British accents: "Band seems to be lacking a bit of *energy* this evening." "Bit of *something*." They're so callow, and it's easy to laugh— but then, you wouldn't have known it was a historic night, either. Where are they now?

5 ▪ **Atmosphere, Ford One & Ford Two (Fat Beats, vinyl only)** A set of raps and dubs from Slug, a Midwesterner who shares Eminem's accent but moves as slowly as the Detroiter moves fast. The hard, cold, northern Minnesota autobiography "Nothing But Sunshine" isn't that far in mood from the Barbarians' 1966 "Moulty," which you can find on the original *Nuggets* collection— until, with a sucker of a fan stuck in the throat of a sardonic, bitter man who's been fooled too many times, Slug starts warbling the Temptations' "My Girl" ("I've got sunshine / On a cloudy day . . ."), and no better than you might. The intrusion of the sound of ordinary life into the performance is as startling as it is when the woman starts telling her story in the middle of Human League's "Don't You Want Me."

6 ▪ **Robert Storr, Gerhard Richter: October 18, 1977 (Museum of Modern Art)** As I write, one-time Frankfurt revolutionary Joschka Fischer, now Germany's foreign minister, is testifying in the trial of one-time Red Army Faction member Hans-Joachim Klein, who is accused of complicity in the murder of three people in a terrorist raid on an OPEC meeting in 1975. Not long after, three of Klein's comrades—Ulrike Meinhof in 1976, Andreas Baader and Gudrun Ensslin on Oct. 18, 1977—were found dead in their cells in the maximum-security prison that had been built to house them. Richter's 1988 paintings of images of the Baader-Meinhof Gang alive and dead— crepuscular, black-white-gray underwater paintings derived from news photos—seem exploitative in the MOMA exhibit (which closes Jan. 30) this book explores; as big as 6 feet by 7 feet, they seem like absolute appropriations of another's being, like grave-robbing. This doesn't belong to you, you want to say to the artist—it doesn't belong to *me*. The display is indecent. But what about the indecency of how these people were treated in life, deprived of sleep, subjected to constant white noise, all the forms of torture that leave no marks? Well, what about it? That's not the question; that's just to use word magic on the walls. But in the book, you can look into the pictures. Just as the paintings themselves took their subjects over, in book-size reproductions they seem to capture real people, people retreating from the artist's eye as from yours.

The most modest, unsensational painting in the exhibit—Baader's phonograph, with an LP on it, though in the painting there's no hope of identifying the record— is the most arty of the pictures on the page. But if you dismiss it you'll miss the book's most interesting footnote: "An inspection [of the original prints] involving careful scrutiny with a high-powered microscope as well as computer-enhanced re-imaging" revealed "that the record on the turntable in Baader's cell was Eric Clapton's 1974 release *There's One in Every Crowd*." Storr goes on to relate the music and lyrics to the event, but the event doesn't bring the born-dead music to life.

7 ▪ **Caroline Sullivan, *Bye Bye Baby: My Tragic Love Affair With the Bay City Rollers* (Bloomsbury USA)** There were many 1977s, of course; this unapologetic fan's memoir by a nice Jewish girl from New Jersey is powered by one question: will the author, pushing 20 in those days, ever lose her virginity? To one of *them*? Halfway through the book it seems she does. Seventy pages later it seems she didn't. I think she did, but I wouldn't bet the farm on it.

8 ▪ **Dean Santomieri, "crude rotation" (Archipelago)** Musique concrète, beginning with echoes of marching music so faded they might be from the First World War.

9 ▪ **Kelly Harrell, "The Cuckoo She's a Fine Bird," from *Kelly Harrell: Complete Recorded Works in Chronological Order, Volume 2, 1926–1929* (Document)** For perhaps the most commonplace of all Appalachian ballads, a normally canny Virginia singer offers a primitive, self-effacing vocal orchestrated between verses not by mountain fiddle but Central European nightclub violin. Plus a real cuckoo clock. You want weird, this is weird.

10 ▪ ***The First Family's Holiday Gift to America: A Personal Tour of the White House* (Fox, Dec. 15)** Bill Clinton walks you into his Music Room, set up both for playing and remembering. On a wall there's a picture of him jamming with Kenny G, a poker hand's worth of gold "Don't Stop Thinking About Tomorrow" discs from Fleetwood Mac, and Herman Leonard jazz photos, lovingly described, including the famous one of tenor saxophonist Dexter Gordon wreathed in smoke. There's Elvis onstage, pensive off it, and on a shelf a ceramic version waving from a pink Cadillac. Last shot before the tour moves on: a litter of saxophones, real and jewelry size, brass, gold and silver, scattered randomly, like junk for the country to throw out.

1 ▪ **Vladimir Mayakovsky/El Lissitzky, *For the Voice* (MIT Press)** In 1923, in Berlin, the futurist poet and the suprematist designer made a thrillingly Soviet book: poems that flew off the page as signs broke out of pictures and letters severed themselves from words, then regrouped in lines and paragraphs, so that each poem was forever in contest with itself, the ante upped every time you came back to the same black-and-red page. In this stunning edition, there are 5 1/4-inch-by-7 3/8-inch facsimiles of the original edition, in Russian and, translated by Peter France, English, plus *Voices of Revolution*, a volume of critical essays edited by Patricia Railing.

You start with the noise the pictures make, and in that language nothing that follows really matches the second poem, with "beat out our march" pounding across two pages, the last two words standing up to a suprematist red square only by refusing to stay in formation. Then you start to read, and after the fourth poem, "Scum," the other voices in the book can feel silenced. "Give me a rich man," you can almost hear Mayakovsky chanting in his rumbling voice (as you can hear him for real in the 1914 and 1920 recordings collected on the anthology *lunapark 0,10* [Sub Rosa], "the fattest / the baldest. / By the scruff of his neck I'll haul him / in front of the Famine Committee. / Look." What you're now looking at is the cannibalism that swept through parts of the countryside during the civil war that followed the revolution. People posed for pictures of themselves with the remains of people they'd killed to eat; Mayakovsky doesn't flinch. Like a true early-20th century avant-gardist, he goes for the jugular: "Son? / Father? / Mother? / Daughter? / Whose turn." In London, he sees a banquet: "May / savages, / eaters of human flesh, / from the colonies come scavenging." He travels to Paris, Berlin, revolution following him across the map, and the curse on the bourgeois world begins to seem automatic, until he returns to Soviet Moscow:

"May your fat steak be turned into scissors / and cut your stomach apart." In 1930, face to face with the murder of the revolution as since the first decade of the century he had written it out, he shot himself. He was 35.

In 1918 Mayakovsky and others had called for poets to take up brushes and paint whole towns. "This seemed to be utopian," El Lissitzky said in 1922, "and yet subsequently it came to pass." "You know, this is a most interesting piece of work," Lenin said of Mayakovsky's 1921 "150 Million." "A peculiar brand of Communism. It is hooligan Communism." But by the end of the decade Mayakovsky stood accused of bohemianism and social parasitism. In her essay "A Revolutionary Spirit," Railing quotes Russian critical theorist Ramon Jakobson's 1931 "On a Generation That Squandered Its Poets": "We strained toward the future too impetuously and avidly to leave any past behind us . . . as for the future, it doesn't belong to us either. In a few decades we shall be cruelly labeled as products of the past millennium. All we had were compelling songs of the future; and suddenly these songs are no longer part of the dynamic of history."

Tall, robust, with a threatening shaven skull and even more threatening eyes, Mayakovsky entered legend as part of the first crop of glamorous, inscrutable 20th century performers to be harvested young, joining in his own time Rudolph Valentino and Bix Beiderbecke, then as the years went on James Dean, Charlie Parker, Patsy Cline, Marilyn Monroe, Robert F. Kennedy, Jimi Hendrix, Jim Morrison and Kurt Cobain. But he was from another country, one that he partly invented and that in any case no longer exists. You look at *For the Voice* and struggle to believe its 1923 ever happened: that the book was ever published, made, thought up, even a notion abandoned as soon as it came into view. Even that stretches credulity. All that power, packed into a few small pages, a rebuke to the future we live in.

2 ■ **Butchies, *Butchies 3* (Mr. Lady)** A trio from Durham, N.C., that manages to combine vocal ache and prettiness, majestic chords and tiny drum sounds, "woo-hoo-hoos" and ugly stories, speed and what seems like a dead stop, until you realize they never stop moving.

3 ■ **Paul McCartney, *Liverpool Sound Collage* (Capitol)** In the footsteps of Walter Ruttmann's 1930 Berlin *Weekend* (covered here Aug. 21, 2000), for the Peter Blake show "About Collage," at the Liverpool Tate through March 4, the Cute One excavated his old town according to noise-music experiments the mop-tops first pursued in 1968 with "Revolution 9." The difference for these pieces, made to play in the exhibition space, is that the 1965–69 voices of the Beatles McCartney mixes into his own ambient street recordings sound only vaguely familiar. John, Paul, George and Ringo sound not only as if they came from these streets but as if they went back to them, to live.

4 ■ **E-Trade Super Bowl Halftime Show (CBS, Jan. 28)** As Aerosmith and 'N Sync ran onto the field for their all-star revue, soon to be completed by neo-soul queen Mary J. Blige, rapper Nelly and Britney Spears as Miss American Fuck, the sound system pumped out the first chord each of "Start Me Up" and "Hard Day's Night." Never mind the parade of the Lines 'Round My Eyes Are Protected by a Copyright Law gestures of Aerosmith or the animatronic Michael Jackson moves and constipated singing of 'N Sync: according to the script viewers were supposed to follow, Aerosmith are the Rolling Stones and 'N Sync are the Beatles. Don't like it? Hey, as they say in D.C., get over it. Justin Timberlake says the Beatles were once dismissed as a "boy band," too. Paul McCartney doesn't remember that, but he's 58 years old, and probably doesn't remember what he's doing in his own living room.

5 ■ **Tim Easton, *The Truth About Us* (New West)** The insert to this singer-songwriter's much-praised step away from alt-country shows a guy lolling on a couch, his eyes cast and an arm raised toward what must be light streaming in through a window. He never gets up, though.

6 ▪ Aislers Set, "Attraction Action Reaction"/"Clouds Will Clear" (Suicide Squeeze) It's the B-side of this 7-inch single from the cool, calm and collected Bay Area quintet that's the charmer: a woman warbling about getting someone's attention, and so simply you all but tune out. And then an even simpler but much deeper guitar part lets you feel how her heart beats when she gets what she wants. Plus the best label name of the season.

7 ▪ Jon Langford, "PainTings," at Other Music (New York, Dec. 6, 2000) The paintings hung on the walls of this avant-garde record store were part of Langford's long-running "Death of Country Music" series, many of them renderings of Hank Williams, but the one that stood out bore no musician's name. With talismans of doom scattered inside the frame—a skull, a Masonic eye—for *Forgotten Cowboy Singer* Langford recast an old publicity still, adding to the would-be star's 10-gallon hat, western shirt, huge guitar and bigger smile a blindfold over his eyes. The plumminess of the pose made the picture as Langford finished it very creepy: this cowboy didn't know that he couldn't see, let alone that now, likely half a century after his photo was taken, he was dead.

8 ▪ Richard Pryor, . . . And It's Deep, Too! The Complete Warner Bros. Recordings, 1968–1992 (Warner Archive/Rhino) What's most shocking about listening to the nine CDs in this set straight through, which is easy to do, is that by the time Pryor gets to the incident where he set himself on fire free-basing, on the 1982 *Live on the Sunset Strip*, he's turned into the same character he pinned so mercilessly on *That Nigger's Crazy* 12 years before: the one who, in "Wino & Junkie," can barely talk.

9 ▪ Object in cluttered NPR studio (New York, Dec. 15, 2000) In an apartment rigged up for remotes but with so much stuff piled so randomly you half-expected someone to come in, announce a pledge drive and start selling every cracked book and discarded piece of clothing, stood an Elvis figure I'd never seen before: lithe, gold lamé, holding a mike stand, frozen in mid-jump-step, sly grin on its face, mounted on a silver base. I pushed a button marked "Demo"; the Elvis began to dance, fast, and a loud, powerful "Hound Dog" came roaring out of a hidden speaker. "It's a telephone," said an engineer passing by—"Elvis Presley Telephone," to be precise, courtesy Telemania, division of Tilbor-Hetman Enterprises. "That's what it does instead of ringing."

10 ▪ George W. Bush's inaugural cowboy boots (Jan. 20, all networks) Black, with "GWB" engraved on the sides and the presidential seal imprinted on the front—which is to say that in his personal appropriation of the symbols of the presidency, Bush made it clear he is not president merely in the constitutional sense but also in a corporate sense. The presidency is a logo, and he owns it.

FEBRUARY 20, 2001

1 ▪ Ja Rule, "Put It on Me" (Murder Inc./Def Jam) Something like Barry White without the subtlety, this inescapable radio hit reaches depths of degradation most gangsta music never hints at. More tuneless than Fred Schneider of the B-52's but in his way just as fey, Ja Rule slobbers as females swirl around him like a harem, melismatizing their brains out, their sound so far removed from actual human sexual response it becomes the vocal equivalent of breast implants.

2 ▪ Bryan Ferry, "Where or When" and "Falling in Love Again," from As Time Goes By (Virgin, 1999), also included on Ferry's Slave to Love—The Best of the Ballads (Virgin, 2000) Of the standards that make up *As Time Goes By*, it's "I'm in the Mood for Love" that's in the air today, thanks to the film of almost the same name. But these are the heartbreakers. Despite the between-the-wars tuxedos 'n' long dresses art on the CD insert, the material doesn't signify the old glam rocker's progression to a more mature, reflective—that is, decadent—state of mind. If anything, the demands Ferry is making on his music are more extreme than ever.

Here the songs are tragic: it's impossible to imagine they've ever been sung with such delicacy, with such an awareness that the slightest false move would break them. The sensibility might have first surfaced on Ferry's cover of John Lennon's "Jealous Guy" (included on *Slave to Love*), cut just after Lennon's murder, but that recording now sounds merely personal compared with songs that, as Ferry sings them, seem to bleed all across the changing map of 20th century Europe. "Where or When" (1937) opens with a theme that suggests nothing so much as a Berlin cabaret where the bohemians who've been there every night for 15 years accept that the Nazis aren't going away, and make their peace. The singer, though, won't give up, so he imagines himself into the future, turning into Cary Grant in *Notorious*—meeting the same enemy around the next turn, but with the odds changed. "Falling in Love Again" (1930) is if anything more blasted; Ferry could have retitled the tune "Slitting My Wrists Again" and you wouldn't even notice. He might be picturing Gabriel Byrne in *Miller's Crossing*, as Byrne realizes that no matter what good he does for others, no matter whom he loves or who loves him, the story will shut him out.

3 ▪ Twin Princess, *The Complete Recordings* (Hidden Agenda/Parasol) An arty duo from Seattle—arty right down to their not-weird version of Frank and Nancy Sinatra's 1967 "Somethin' Stupid"—but with enough charm to make you want to walk through the galleries where the stuff is playing. No. 1 this week: "Deep Sleep," repetition as its own reward. Moving up: "Gimme a Kiss."

4 ▪ The Incredible Moses Leroy, *Electric Pocket Radio* (Artemis) Long ago, a big, sloppy-looking man called Larry "Wildman" Fischer used to stand on street corners in Berkeley and Los Angeles and importune passersby: "Hey, you want to hear a new-type song for a dime?" If you said yes, something indescribable came out: flat and toneless, but weird enough (Fischer's sidewalk hit was about his mother committing him to a mental hospital) and sweet

enough to make you wonder—and, if not cough up another dime, hang around to listen if anyone else did. In 1968, during his freak-show period, Frank Zappa put out a Wildman Fischer double LP on his Bizarre label; it got great reviews. A follow-up did not; outsider artists are supposed to temporarily overcome their psychoses, not have careers.

Ron Fountenberry of San Diego—who as a performer takes the name of his great-grandfather Moses Leroy (1900–90), a Houston civil rights activist who, from the '30s to his death, spoke, sued, demonstrated and finally, in his last years, as a voter registrar, sat behind a desk to change his city and his country—stands somewhere between Larry Fischer and Brian Wilson. You can't tell the studio genius from the kid fooling around in his bedroom. Leroy's cutting and pasting, as unpretentious as a strip mall, results in songs that throw you off: sunny, disconcerting, glowing with the smiles of benign phantoms. Absolutely nothing seems to be at stake in this music other than amusement. Leroy works at it, and singer Camilla, taking a number every few tracks, gets to enjoy it. You take Leroy's radio out of your pocket whenever you remember it's there, to see what's on; always, it's something you've almost heard before.

5 ▪ Bastard Sons of Johnny Cash, *Walk Alone* (Ultimatum) More from San Diego: for getting away with (or licensing) the name, the phrase "dead soldier" and the hearty male chorus on "Texas Sun"—which might remind you of the beginning of the cattle drive in *Red River*, when Howard Hawks cuts from one cowboy face to another, and you know that whatever's coming next, it won't be as good.

6–7 ▪ Taj Mahal, *Taj Mahal* (Columbia Legacy, recorded 1967) When you listen to *Rising Sons Featuring Taj Mahal and Ry Cooder* (Columbia Legacy), a collection of unreleased demos recorded in Los Angeles in 1964, you can't believe Taj (né Henry Fredericks) ever made it to *Taj Mahal*—even if it took three years and a trip around the block. The country blues from the earlier sessions are as dead as the dog the man pokes with a stick in Bruce Springsteen's "Reason to Believe" ("Like if he stood there long enough / That dog'd get up and run"). On *Taj Mahal,* the former member of the Pioneer Valley Folklore Society and the rest of, as the *New York Times* embarrassed its members into saying, Mr. Mahal's band, with Cooder still in tow, took momentary title to songs that had been sung by hundreds before them. Hammering his harmonica, Taj pulls Sonny Boy Williamson's "Checkin' Up on My Baby" inside out— *that's* where she is, right inside the song!— and on the long stroll he takes through "The Celebrated Walking Blues" he suspends the more than three decades between its first recording and his own, between the more than three decades since his recording was first heard and today. "Heh-heh," he says, in what might be the most lascivious half-second in blues, until a few minutes later, when he says it again: this, you're sure, is the sound everyone who came before was looking for, and that everyone, Taj included, has been looking for since. The big, bulging notes on his slide guitar flap in the air like wash on a line, then billow up in the wind of Cooder's mandolin; the rhythm makes all the time in the world, and when the recording ends, you know the song doesn't.

8 ▪ **Levon Helm & the Barn Burners at Biscuits and Blues (San Francisco, Feb. 6)** They went into Muddy Waters' "I'm Ready." "They're using that in Viagra commercials now," said Maria Muldaur, leaning across the table. You've seen it: guy prancing around his apartment, dressing sharp, because now the song doesn't mean he's ready ready ready to fuck. It means he's ready ready ready to see the doctor to talk about why he can't.

9 ▪ **Taj Mahal, "The Celebrated Walking Blues," on *Taj Mahal* (Columbia Legacy)** Not that Viagra wasn't already in the song, or anyway its ancestors: "Got to go to Memphis, baby / To have my hambone boiled / You know I done laid around here in Clarksdale, baby, until my / Little old ham-

bone was spoiled." And if that doesn't work, you go see the gypsy. That always works. And always costs.

10 ▪ **Nick Bromell, *Tomorrow Never Knows—Rock and Psychedelics in the 1960s* (University of Chicago Press)** A short, passionate study written from inside the story it tells, and less about drugs, perhaps, than the way adherents of a music and a culture came to recognize that the ground beneath their feet had turned into air. Bromell, a professor of English at the University of Massachusetts at Amherst, sums up in a passage of surpassing cruelty: "Just four years earlier, *yeah, yeah, yeah,* they were taking to the dance floor because *something was happening.* Now they found that they could not, after all, escape from history. Nor could they make it. How, except with 'Tombstone Blues' or 'Yer Blues,' could they name this condition—one in which the earth's most privileged cohort was also powerless, radicalized for nothing, fated to wait for decades on the watchtower, listening to the wind rise and watching the approach of two riders who knew their destiny yet would never, it seems, arrive?"

MARCH 5, 2001

1–3 ▪ **Oh Susanna, *Sleepy Little Sailor* (Catamount), *Johnstown* (Stella/Square Dog, 1999) and *Oh Susanna* (Stella, 1997)** Oh Susanna is singer, guitarist and songwriter Suzie Ungerleider of Toronto. There's the echo of the North Carolina mountains in her voice, but on *Sleepy Little Sailor,* the first record she hasn't put out herself, you can also hear Sarah McLachlan. You can also hear someone with nothing to prove: no one else would have the nerve to take up Otis Redding's "I've Got Dreams to Remember" and then sing from inside the song as Redding did not; Ungerleider puts you on the street as she sees her lover with someone else, letting you feel his tongue in her mouth. And you can hear Tanita Tikaram's unexplainable "Twist in My Sobriety," from 12 years back, as Ungerleider moves into "All That Remains" and "Forever at Your Feet," as elegant musically as they are unstable as stories— *What happened?* they leave you asking. *Is he, is she, already dead?*

For all that, nothing on *Sleepy Little Sailor* or the EP *Oh Susanna* comes within miles of "The Bridge," from *Johnstown*. Very little released in the past three years by anyone comes close to it. This is the sort of song the tradition of the Appalachian murder ballad should have written by itself: a ballad that tries to be about suicide and ends up being about murder anyway, "Barbara Allen" without love, with a graphic bluntness that's absolutely modern and a dream logic that's absolutely Brontëan. Perhaps the tradition did write it; maybe Ungerleider can so lose herself in other singers, other songs, that she has no need to sing as if she has written the songs she did in fact write. Piano, violin, guitar and especially the quiet shifts of a Hammond organ enclose the story Ungerleider is telling, finishing it, leaving it as frightening as it is gorgeous. I played the song all day, over and over, trying to make it turn out differently.

4–5 ▪ **Robert Nighthawk et al., *And This Is Maxwell Street* (Rooster) and Levon Helm and the Barn Burners at Biscuits & Blues (San Francisco, Feb. 6)** *Maxwell Street* is a triple CD—two discs of "dime in a cigar box" performances recorded in 1964 at Chicago's open-air market by Mike Shea for his film *And This Is Free*, one disc of guitarist Mike Bloomfield interviewing guitarist Robert Nighthawk—and some of the most incendiary blues jams ever caught on tape. There is Big John Wrencher, leading Nighthawk and guitarist Little Arthur through "Lucille," the heat from his harmonica wilting every weed in earshot; there's Nighthawk himself, a dull singer, lifting whoever's gathered around off their feet with "Peter Gunn Jam," "Take It Easy, Baby" and "Back Off Jam," hitting notes the citizens don't suspect are there. But there is also an archaic, less obviously crowd-pleasing music, as if sneaking out of Chicago shacks like repressed memories: Arvella Gray's long "John Henry," merely a snippet of a song he

could sing for hours; the James Brewer Gospel Group's "When the Saints Go Marching In," lifted up as if the hoary chestnut has been forgotten for 100 years and the sheet music has just been discovered under floorboards; and Fannie Brewer's "I Shall Overcome," the source of the civil rights anthem, here as real as a single body. "I'll see his face, today," Brewer promises the congregation she's made of the people gathered on the street to listen. "I do believe, I'll see his face someday." As music it's a smaller promise than the one she makes to herself as she ends her song: "I'll be alright, I'll be alright/I'll be alright someday."

The Barn Burners could be one of the white blues bands that were forming across town as Shea ran his tapes—the material is not very different. It might be the same stuff Levon Helm of the Band was playing with his teenage Jungle Bush Beaters in Marvel, Ark., in 1958. More than 40 years later, Helm, his voice burned to a rasp by radiation treatments for throat cancer, sounds 100 years old but looks like Porter Wagoner; sitting behind his drums, he is the center of gravity in this six-piece combo, just as saxophonist Bobby Keys of Lubbock, Texas, said to have played with Buddy Holly, best known for his solo on the Rolling Stones' "Brown Sugar," is its face of nothing-to-prove. The two of them about 60, everyone else, including singer Amy Helm, about 30—it felt right. Every note was in place, but too often every note stayed in place. The musicians were drawing a blues picture; they weren't quite in it.

Frontman Chris O'Leary carries the group: with a huge shout to open "Hey Porter," a force-of-nature harmonica sound on "Wang Dang Doodle," his blocklike smiling face and linebacker's body, he generates what authority the group has, but they need more. Like O'Leary at his best, they have to trust the music to generate their authority. They are steps away.

6 ▪ **43rd Annual Grammy Awards (CBS, Feb. 21)** During the Barcelona Olympics, when synchronized swimming first became an official event, a sportswriter caught what was wrong: "astonishing," he said, and "faintly repugnant." That was Destiny's Child, maybe because they might as well have been wearing swimsuits, because they move so well and because they seem so corporate. As the night went on, the parade of dyed blond hair, plastic surgery, bare midriffs and flattened stomachs that do not occur in nature turned sickening. No, neither Ricky Martin nor Britney Spears, who don't look even slightly human, took the stage, but they weren't needed. Disassociation ruled. Listening to Best New Artist Shelby Lynne's album, the coldy formal re-creation of '6os soul music *I Am Shelby Lynne*, you might have responded, "No, you're not—from the evidence of this record, *nobody* is Shelby Lynne"; here, either duetting with Sheryl Crow or accepting her award, her attitude of bemused disdain didn't really square with the big "Please Buy My Breasts" sign she wore on her chest. Highlights: Discover Card's fabulous Danger Kitty commercial, a Los Angeles '8os hair band *Behind the Music* segment in under a minute, with nothing left out; the Jesus and Mary Chain smeared into the background of a Chevy commercial; the McDonald's commercial with Kobe Bryant and the "We Love to See You Smile" tag line, more money for Randy Newman, a regular on the Oscars, excluded from the Grammys; Macy Gray performing her overaired "I Try," sounding like an actual person in a sea of purple wigs, ending her spot sitting in a chair; Eminem's shockingly hard, heaving "Stan," which reached new territory as he took the voice of the crazed fan on a suicide run with his pregnant girlfriend screaming from the trunk of his car, the stakes raised high above any played for on record. It was shattering, and likely the strongest performance the show ever let itself in for.

7 ▪ **James F. Smith, "Rebels on Rugged Road to Peace" (***Los Angeles Times***, carried in the** *San Francisco Chronicle***, Feb. 25)** On the beginning of the 2,000-mile Zapatista caravan from Chiapas to Mexico City to seek constitutional amendments expanding the rights of indigenous Mexicans: "Last night,

surprised tourists mingled with hundreds of Zapatista supporters in front of San Cristobal's cathedral, waiting for the rebels. Roaming vendors sold small dolls of the Zapatistas, even T-shirts with a photo of [Subcommander] Marcos on the front and the words 'Zapatour 2001' on the back. 'This could be a Rolling Stones tour,' said Jack Jones, a 58-year-old visitor from Austin, Texas, who bought two of the shirts. 'Somebody needs to support these people. What a great story for the 21st century.'"

8 ▪ **Michael Janofsky, "For Ex-Student Protestor, a Pardon Without the Spotlight" (***New York Times***, Feb. 24)** Disgraceful as the pardons of Marc Rich, Pincus Green and the Hasidic swindlers may be, that the story has been trumpeted in mainstream media with far greater force than and sustained many times over that of the Supreme Court's nullification of the presidential election is an infinitely greater disgrace. Conspicuous by its absence, the purloined election is like the purloined letter: the fact and means of its erasure must be hidden in plain sight. Janofsky's piece on Bill Clinton's pardon of Howard Mechanic is a signal example of how it's done—how one story is used to hide the other.

In 1970 Mechanic was given a five-year federal sentence for throwing a cherry bomb during an antiwar demonstration at Washington University in St. Louis—an act he did not commit. He fled. After 28 years of hiding in plain sight in Phoenix as one Gary Robert Tredway, Mechanic was exposed and sent to prison. To little notice, as Clinton left office he granted Mechanic a pardon; nearly a month later, it becomes a story. "A path to freedom on the backs of ordinary citizens," announces the teaser box in the piece, the line matched in the second paragraph: "Mr. Mechanic walked a path to freedom on the backs of ordinary citizens, thousands of them." To "walk on the backs" of others is to exploit, traduce or oppress them—who, one might wonder, are these thousands of ordinary Americans exploited, traduced or oppressed by Howard Mechanic? G.I.s in Vietnam in 1970, placed in even greater jeopardy by protesters undermining America's will to fight? Not exactly, as it turns out, seven paragraphs later: "Old friends in St. Louis and new ones in Arizona . . . created a Web site to collect petition signatures—nearly 3,000 at last count, said Bruce M. Rogers, a college classmate of Mr. Mechanic's—and to urge supporters to contact elected officials." One would think such a fact would call for a characterization along the lines of "a path to freedom with the helping hands of ordinary citizens, thousands of them"—but that would be to assume that the *Times'* treatment of the Mechanic story was about something other than keeping a very different story alive, until, presumably, Bill Clinton and Hillary Clinton take the place of Marc Rich, or Howard Mechanic, as fugitives from justice.

9–10 ■ John Fahey, 1939–2001 (Feb. 22) and Jon Langford at Johnny Foley's (San Francisco, Feb. 22) An acerbic man who suffered no fools, the experimental guitarist was his own equal as a writer. "It's great," he said of J. P. Nestor's 1927 recording of "Train on the Island." "But what is it?" Recalling Hank Williams' last concert in 1953—or, rather, making it up—he caught what should have happened in *How Bluegrass Music Destroyed My Life*, a book of fabulist autobiographical pieces he published last year: "First thing Williams did was curse and swear at us. 'Why dontcha all go home?' he yelled into the mike. 'I hate every damned one of ya.'" In Fahey's story it was just a setup for capturing a song: "At some point in the show he sang 'Alone and Forsaken' and while he did that many of us almost died of grief and fright."

Fahey calls it "the greatest song of despair ever written" and quotes the first line: "We met in the springtime." He makes you pause. "By the fifth word," he says, "you know it's all over."

It was by chance that Jon Langford of the Mekons, accompanied on Hawaiian guitar by Jon Rauhouse, closed a vibrant solo show with a harsh, syncopated version of "Alone and Forsaken." (The posthu-

mously released 1949 original can be found on the recent Williams album *Alone With His Guitar*, with cover art by Langford). Langford hadn't read Fahey's book. Sometimes the right time creates the right place.

MARCH 19, 2001

1–2 ■ *The Sopranos*, Alan Coulter, director; David Chase, writer; Kathryn Dayak, music editor (HBO, March 2) and *Peter Gunn: "Death House Testament" and "Skin Deep"* (Rhino Video) As orchestration for the FBI bugging scheme that dominated this season's first episode, the combination of the *Peter Gunn* theme—from the 1958–61 private-eye TV series; Henry Mancini won the 1958 album of the year Grammy for his soundtrack—and the Police's 1983 "Every Breath You Take" was quite brilliant. Too brilliant—the stalker-quiet second song creeping out of the car-chase noise of the first, so that both seemed to have precisely the same beat, was uncanny, but once, not three times. It got me wondering how *Peter Gunn* itself might play today. It was the opposite of *The Sopranos*—the least nervous crime show imaginable, despite the fact that when Gunn got beat up, which happened at least once every half-hour, he got completely stomped.

Craig Stevens, who died last year at 81, played the hipster detective as a slightly more Jewish version of Cary Grant in *North by Northwest*; Herschel Bernardi played Lt. Jacoby as a very Jewish version of Tonto. Ethnically, only the villains were straight—and, at best, or worst, straight out of film noir slime. In "Death House Testament," directed by series creator Blake Edwards, the alcoholic mob croaker Dr. Alford could be moonlighting from *Kiss Me Deadly*; the camera is so tight on his face as he puts Gunn out you can feel his sweat dripping through the screen. When Gunn tries to escape from Alford's clinic, Stevens gets as close to Raymond Chandler forcing Philip Marlowe to stand up ("'Okey, Marlowe,' I said between my teeth. '. . . You've been shot full of hop and kept under it until you're as crazy as two waltzing mice. And what does it amount to? Routine. Now let's see you do something really tough, like putting your pants on'") as any movie actor— and once Stevens' version of Marlowe gets his pants back on and can act cool again, he doesn't even need the best lines. "Please, give me an excuse," he says, holding a gun on Alford and his boss. "No, thanks," the doctor says, "I'm drinking." Gunn doesn't even offer a comeback. He just smiles. He's a watcher, a listener, wary but amused, not a talker. The '50s were psychoanalysis central; you can't imagine Stevens taking Tony Soprano's place in Dr. Melfi's office, but you can see him taking hers.

3 ■ Book of Love, "Boy," from *I Touch Roses—The Best of the Book of Love* (Reprise) "Uh-huh." "Uh-huh." "Uh-huh." In 1986 it sounded like Trio's "Da Da Da," but without apology; today it sounds like a conversation. It was not much more than an opening bid from a three-woman, one-man modern-world synth 'n' harmony outfit that never made a bad record.

4–5 ■ Low, *Things We Lost in the Fire* (Kranky) and Peter S. Scholtes, "Hey, We're in Duluth," Minneapolis *City Pages* (Feb. 7) "When they found your body / Giant Xs on your eyes / And your half of the ransom," Alan Sparhawk sings in "Sunflower," "The weather hadn't changed"—I made the last line up, but it wouldn't be out of place. From Duluth, where 42 years ago Bob Dylan stood in the audience at the National Guard Armory as Buddy Holly played his third-to-last show, this notoriously unhurried trio captures the insignificance of human desire as opposed to the fact of a Minnesota winter even as they suggest they might prefer that the weather never change at all. Or, as Scholtes puts it in his Minneapolis visitor's piece on "the emerging sense among Duluthians of an emerging sensibility among Duluthians"—that is, signs of a termite culture going public—"if there is one certainty at the heart of Duluth's mystique it is Lake Superior. The lake is always there and it is always cold. It will

always be there and it will always be cold. Nothing about the physical landscape of the lake's corner should make a visit this spring more pressing than one the next."

6 ■ Johnny Dowd, *Temporary Shelter* (Koch) Featuring mover Dowd and hairsalon proprietor Kim Sherwood-Caso of Ithaca, N.Y., this is the bad conscience of country music as surely as the sheriff in Jim Thompson's *The Killer Inside Me* is John Wayne's—though the people in Dowd's songs are more like Thompson's most humiliated characters, and in their most profound moments of embarrassment. With Sherwood-Caso's voice going far past the song in "Hell or High Water" and Dowd's guitar scraping the paint off its darkest corners, or in the bad hotel room called up by the unclean '50s white jazz in "Cradle to the Grave," it's the sound of "the joke's on me"—the somehow pristine sound of even that kind of joke failing to get a laugh out of the crowd.

7 ■ *When Brendan Met Trudy*, directed by Kieron J. Walsh, written by Roddy Doyle (Collins Avenue/Deadly Films 2) As culture—as the picture it draws of what it means to live happily, almost fully, in a funhouse of representations—the writing in this movie is as sexy as the smile in Flora Montgomery's eyes. "He makes movies," Montgomery's young thief says to her warden, describing her young schoolteacher boyfriend, and he does: home movies, as scripted by Godard, Iggy Pop, Kevin Spacey, Jean-Claude Van Damme starring in *Remedial Action*. As when he runs into one of his teenage students, whose names he can never remember, in a supermarket. "Dylan," the boy reminds him, as his parents beam at the one remaining sign of a hipness long since erased by the class system. "Mr.— Tambourine Man," the teacher says, having already forgotten the student's name again but translating the reference into a bigger story. The kid has no idea what he's talking about.

8 ■ Saks Fifth Avenue, *Caribbean Lifestyles— Live a Little Volume 2* (Sony Special Products) An in-store giveaway CD: 12

Caribbean lifestyles, but only one of them offered by an actual Caribbean, Ini Kamoze of Jamaica, which I guess makes him the poster and the likes of Men at Work ("Down Under"), Blondie ("The Tide Is High") and Mungo Jerry ("In the Summertime") travel agents. There are the unavoidable tourist-trap disasters (Bobby Bloom's "Montego Bay," Buster Poindexter's "Hot, Hot, Hot") but also that moment when the tropical storm breaks into a sky unlike any you've seen before. I mean, nothing with Johnny Nash's "I Can See Clearly Now" on it is a waste of money, and this one's free, at least if you buy something else.

9 ■ Corrs, "Breathless" (Atlantic) Surveys show most Americans aren't getting enough fluff in their diet. This radio hit, up there with Maxine Nightingale's "Right Back Where We Started From," so good on the team bus in the 1977 hockey movie *Slap Shot*, is the perfect cure. Already in heavy rotation on Patrick Bateman's Walkman.

10 ■ *Pola X*, directed by Léos Carax (Arena Films) Based on Herman Melville's *Pierre, or the Ambiguities*, about a young man and a young woman, Isabelle, who appears out of nowhere and claims to be his sister, set in contemporary France, and, as the lives of the two become ever more entwined, starring Guillaume Depardieu as Kurt Cobain. Pierre leaves comfort, mother and fiancée behind and with Isabelle finds a hiding place in an abandoned Paris factory that's been taken over by a terrorist cell-cum-noise music orchestra (music provided by Scott Walker, one-time member of Righteous Brothers imitation the Walker Brothers, in later years a Jacques Brel disciple). Already famous as someone he isn't—as "Aladin," pseudonymous author of a cult novel—Pierre hunches over his desk in his bare room, scribbling endless pages in red ink. Desperate for a publisher and an advance, he appears as himself on a literary talk show; when he freezes up in terror at the interviewer's asking him who he really is, he becomes the person hiding in so many Nirvana songs, able to speak

only through the screams of the choruses, retreating into the near silence of the verses almost instantly. "Impostor!" someone shouts from the studio audience. It's the shout Cobain always heard, just as the publisher's response Pierre's new manuscript finally receives—"A raving morass . . . reeks of plagiarism"—is the judgment Cobain always pronounced on his own work. It can't be an accident that Depardieu, who begins the film cleanshaven, with neatly trimmed blond hair, looks just like Cobain by the end (a wig and a fake beard, Depardieu says)—or that he exits the plot in the back of a police van, a shot that all too closely echoes the famous photo of Cobain in an ambulance in Rome, Courtney Love looking at the camera with her face a smear of determination and fear. I have the feeling that even if Cobain were still alive, he would have entered the vocabulary of other people's work just as fiercely as he has as a dead man.

APRIL 2, 2001

1–2 ■ Linda Gail Lewis, *The Devil, Me, and Jerry Lee* (Longstreet) & Van Morrison/Linda Gail Lewis, *You Win Again* (Mercury) If you're sick of the broken-arm school of memoir writing, in which self-criticism is magically transformed into self-congratulation— Adair Lara's *Hold Me Close, Let Me Go: A Mother, a Daughter, and an Adolescence Survived* is a recent example—this frank ("It's a miracle we're not all more fucked up than we are"), funny ("Jerry Lee would probably not do a double take if he were seated at the Last Supper"), fatalistic ("In Ferriday I could have married a cousin and not even known it") and short (166 pages with big print) look back by Jerry Lee Lewis' little sister is like a good drink at the end of a long day. She can tell a story; she can get out of the way and let a story tell itself. "When I was very young, my mother was always commenting about what pretty little hands I had," she says. "I think it finally got to the point where [older sister] Frankie Jean really had heard enough about my beautiful hands, so naturally, she took me over to the oven and helped me to place them directly on the hot grates inside"— it's that "to" in "helped me to place them," slowing the description, making it more formal, that makes the moment perfect.

It's too bad Van Morrison doesn't know how to get out of the way. He hooked up with Linda Gail at a Jerry Lee convention (she was performing, he was there as a fan)—but mainly, it seems, to walk all over her. For the blues and rockabilly standards on *You Win Again,* he's like the husband at a party telling everyone how great his wife is and then finishing every sentence she tries to start. Maybe someone— Elvis Costello? Laurie Anderson? Peter Guralnick?—will hear how good this woman is, as quick and economical as a singer as she is on the page, and find her the time and place to make her own record.

3 ▪ Shaver, *The Earth Rolls On* (New West) From 1993, with the undeniable *Tramp on Your Street,* Shaver was country singer and writer Billy Joe Shaver and his guitarist son Eddy; the younger Shaver died of a drug overdose on New Year's Eve. He was a serious guitar player, and on "Evergreen Fields" he ran loose. He counts off the "We Will Now Tell the Terrible Tale" beat, then opens up a solo that gets out of the terrible tale alive, and makes you want to hear it again.

4 ▪ *Hellhound on My Trail—Songs of Robert Johnson* (Telarc) Despite notes from Lawrence Cohn, who knows whereof he speaks, this tribute album, a set of tunes written by the '30s bluesman and performed by David Honeyboy Edwards, Clarence "Gatemouth" Brown, Pinetop Perkins, Keith Brown, Robert Jr. Lockwood, Robert "Victim of Love" Palmer and more, more, more, starts dull and gets worse until, with Eric Gales' "Me and the Devil Blues," it gets to horrible—plummy, empty, incompetent, glib. Like "Louie Louie," "Dust My Broom" is hard to ruin; Joe Louis Walker pulls it off. Chris Thomas King, who played the older Mississippi singer *Tommy* Johnson in *O Brother, Where Art Thou?* is a high-

light, and he's just OK. The only real exception is Susan Tedeschi, who offers a spare, distracted, Trailer Bride–style version of "Walking Blues"—you can see right through her shift, just because it has been washed so many times. You realize what the difference is: she's singing the song as if what happens in it happened to her.

5 ▪ *The Early Blues Roots of Bob Dylan* (Catfish) The tribute album backward— assembling the originals, the set makes the present-day man pay homage to his forebears, whether he wants to or not. But Bob Dylan is not at issue—right off, with the Mississippi Sheiks' 1931 "I've Got Blood in My Eyes for You," you hear how completely 62 years later he entered the song and changed it from the inside out. The structure remains the same; only the soul is different. Rather, it's the wide range of the compiler's ear—picking up Booker T. Sapps' obscure "Po' Lazarus," Will Bennett following the melody of "Railroad Bill" in 1929 like a man going downstream in a canoe, the Rev. J. C. Burnett chanting "Will the Circle Be Unbroken" in a black church in 1928—that makes you realize what an undiscovered country remains to be found. When, just before the end, in the Parchman Farm Penitentiary in Mississippi in 1939, Bukka White begins to hammer the high, ringing chords of "Po' Boy," his voice an eternal whine, as if he knows this is the only way to get God's ear, you reach that country, and you can't believe you have to leave. You can; he couldn't.

6 ▪ Maria Muldaur, *Richland Woman Blues* (Stony Plain) Yet another sort of tribute album—the quilting-bee version, when friends and neighbors gather to help stitch up the music. Some of the same people from the Robert Johnson session, as if in another life (Taj Mahal, huge and ancient on "Soul of a Man"; Alvin Youngblood Hart, terrific adding scratches and scrapes to "I'm Going Back Home"), some of the same songs as the Dylan collection (Lead Belly's "Grasshoppers in My Pillow") and, as Muldaur's voice gets bigger and bigger for Memphis Minnie's "In My Girlish Days," as

big, it seems for a few minutes, as Bessie Smith's, a sound that could not be less girlish.

7 ▪ **16 Horsepower, *Hoarse* (Checkered Past)** A live recording of original-sin rock from a Denver quartet that can separate the wheat from the chaff, especially when leader David Eugene Edwards straps on his banjo. Unfriendly, unforgiving—their version of "Bad Moon Rising" makes the Creedence Clearwater original seem like an open question.

8 ▪ **Julie Lasky, *Some People Can't Surf— The Graphic Design of Art Chantry* (Chronicle Books)** The most striking pictures in this handsome, well-written appreciation of the work of the former Seattle punk poster artist (whose own *Instant Litter* collection appeared in 1985) might be those of Chantry and Sir Francis Chantry—real separated-at-birth stuff, except that one was born in 1954 and the other in 1781.

9 ▪ **Jon Carroll, "The Faith-Based Presidency" (*San Francisco Chronicle*, Feb. 22)** The moderate way to dissent from Bush's presidency is to complain that he acts as if he had been elected in a landslide, rather than not elected at all. Like Thomas Friedman's March 13 *New York Times* column on faith-based air-traffic control, Carroll's picture of the unreality of present-day governance is a ghost story: "We now have a faith-based presidency. We need to have faith that we have a president. We have a person in the White House who is called the president, but it is hard to imagine him doing the job. Faith is the evidence of things not seen. We do not see him working, and yet we believe he is. We do not see him thinking, and yet we believe he is. We believe he is in charge. Our rational minds may waver. Always there is doubt. It is the challenge of the faith-based path to move beyond doubt. We cannot reason ourselves closer to the reality of the Bush presidency . . . we have the faith and he has the presidency."

10 ▪ **Heike Baranowsky, *Auto Scope,* in "010101: Art in Technological Times" (San Francisco Museum of Modern Art, through July 8)** In a not-overburdened show of am-

biences, recombinations, scans and a photo maze was this video, shot from a vehicle traversing the periphery of Paris and projected in four identical feeds. Speeding along, the assembled double-double images collapse into each other, so that each image is a mirror of itself—when trees come into the field of vision, the city becomes a series of Rorschach blots. There are moments of color, of ads and the bodies they feature, but mostly it's road, walls, apartment buildings, factories, overcast. "This is Paris?" someone in the room said. "It looks like Poland."

APRIL 17, 2001

1 ▪ **Ben Harper & the Innocent Criminals, *Live From Mars* (Virgin)** This is the worst album I've ever heard. Not because it's more than 137 minutes long—it was the worst album I'd ever heard after 10 minutes. It begins with thick waves of insensate cheering (track by track, you can hear the engineer pushing the volume up at the end of every number)—and then, out of the maelstrom, comes this pathetic, strangled, self-pitying, self-righteous, melisma-crazy bleat, the voice of a sensitive man alone in a world where, as he puts it, "I'm not as afraid of dying / As I am of getting old." It's an unsingable couplet, with that first "as" dissolving the first syllable of "afraid," but who needs rhythm when your heart's in the right place, when you're against pollution and stuff like that? How low can you go when what you really want is to be the new Richie Havens? This record proves that no one knows, but I'll bet Ben Harper wouldn't have dared do "Sexual Healing" if Marvin Gaye were still alive.

2 ▪ **Daft Punk, *Discovery* (Virgin)** The masked French techno duo makes oceanic dance music—music to dance to in your dreams. The 1997 *Homework* seemed to have no bottom to it; this has endless warmth, an openness of spirit that asks only that you melt. Try to resist: the opening "One More Time" begins with a tinny sample, as if from an old, old radio. The radio begins to play a naive melody, and soon enough you remember Kool & the Gang's "Celebration" never felt anything but good. With a bigger, deeper drum sound, the '80s are all over this record, in the thrilling "Superheroes," a pounding Pet Shop Boys march with a big, uplifting finale, the Pet Shop Boys' cover of the Village People's "Go West" without the sadness, without the trick AIDS played on the song; in the endless wildness of "Veridis Quo." This is the one. It's loud but never rushes; it reimagines George McCrae's already abstract Miami soul classic "Rock Your Baby" alongside the Italian disco group Cetu Java's gorgeous, somehow sinister "Adonde." The pace is cool, but a sense of mission is never muffled, never hedged. The theme running over the drum sound seems to double back on itself, to generate its own accompaniment, to step back and listen to itself, to approve, to rejoin the gathering of tones and declare itself: Give me a riff and I'll save the world!

3 ▪ Duets, directed by Bruce Paltrow (United Airlines in-flight entertainment) Maria Bello is very good at saying, "I'd be pleased and honored to fuck your brains out"; this PG edit of the horrible Karaoke World picture dubs in a car revving its engine so you can't hear her. There is, though, a moment of instruction, when hustler Huey Lewis and recently met daughter Gwyneth Paltrow team up on Smokey Robinson's "Cruisin'." Dion, speaking of Hank Williams in a *Fresh Air* interview last fall: "His commitment was so total. He'd bite off the end of words: 'I got it now!'" This is the opposite: the definition of plumminess, where a song exists only as a vehicle for the singer's vanity, where if the word "forever" appears it can only mean "So long, sucker." So here "forever" is not bitten off but stretched out, into "Fou-ahhh-evvvvahhhh," the singers forcing the melody to carry more than it can bear, until it can produce only lies. Time stands still: the commonplace effect becomes an absolute, raising insincerity to a transcendental value. The crowd goes as wild as a Ben Harper applause track, as it does for everything in

the movie—except for Andre Braugher's weird, heart-rending reversal of the guy in the crowd screaming for "Free Bird."

4 ▪ Milarde (Mediaset TV, March 18) On the Italian version of *Who Wants to Be a Millionaire* (a milarde is a billion lire, about $500,000), a woman faced the final question: Albert King—Writer? Formula 1 driver? TV journalist? Musician? She chewed her lips, her fingers, twisted in her seat, and an aura of the fix came off of her in waves. "Well, I know B. B. King is a musician," she said—as if, confronted with somebody named King, one would automatically think B. B. and not, say, Martin Luther. "Ah, yes," said the host, "B. B.— 'Blues Boy.'" One would have thought this promised an early resolution, but no. Angst, despair—finally the woman was led away, as if to perdition. Ten minutes of commercials followed. The woman returned. Over 15 minutes, she struggled with inner demons. Writer? Musician? It could have been *Sophie's Choice* for all you could tell from her face. It was fake—if it wasn't it was pornographic—and then, the answer. Yes, she will plunge into the abyss: "Musician."

The result was a truly religious deliverance. The woman seemed ready to kiss the host's feet, to pledge to him her unborn children. By the logic of her performance, had she lost they would have had to put her down, like Jane Fonda at the end of *They Shoot Horses, Don't They?*

5 ▪ Persona Grata (17, rue du Temple, Paris 4e) Just across the Pont Neuf on the Right Bank is Conforama, a household furnishings department store. What's inside— items guaranteed to put you to sleep on your feet—seems to translate the name of the place: a play on *confort* (comfort), to an English speaker it reads Conform-o-rama. But small stores offering typical French design—simplicity combined with uniqueness, a lack of ostentation with flair—are all over the city, and this one stood out. Persona Grata is divided into sections, each with its own manifesto—"Good Taste? Bad Taste?" "Design? Child's Play!" "Objects: Stories without Words"—and a Princess toaster, all gleaming silver except for a black base and handles, paid off on the last one. Without a single anthropomorphic feature it was nonetheless a face. It grinned, saying, "Good morning. Click me." It was welcoming, but it also suggested it had a mind of its own—that as much as it was there to serve you, it would wait for you to go to sleep, and then get up and wander all over the house, moving things.

6–7 ▪ Cat-Iron, *Cat-Iron Sings Blues and Hymns* (Smithsonian Folkways) & 15.60.75, aka the Numbers, *Jimmy Bell's Still in Town* (Hearthan) Cat-Iron was a blues singer from Natchez, Miss. In 1958 Frederic Ramsey Jr. recorded him and wrote him up in the prestigious *Saturday Review*. All through Ramsey's interesting piece—the liner notes to the original Folkways release, included on the custom cassettes or CDs you can now order through Smithsonian Folkways—run the lyrics of "Jimmy Bell," Cat-Iron's signature number. Otherwise second- or thirdhand, here Cat-Iron's guitar takes on its own voice, stating no theme, only dropping hints, pulling you closer; as he sings, he seems less to be telling a story than promising he'll tell you later. No wonder: Jimmy Bell, with "greenbacks enough to make a man a suit," has come to drive the women from the church. "All you need," he tells his sister, "is not to shout." The sense of some enormous transformation is in the air. What it is you can't tell.

In 1975, opening for Bob Marley, singer-guitarist Robert Kidney took his seven-piece, three-sax band from Kent, Ohio, onto the stage of the Agora in Cleveland. "Jimmy Bell" was the Numbers' wipeout piece, as much Bobby Darin's "Mack the Knife" as Cat-Iron's cryptic crusader. Picking up on the bare syncopation in the Cat-Iron version, the Numbers press the rhythm right away, the bass slithering over the beat like a snake, then rhythm guitar, then Kidney's thin voice, insisting on that greenback suit until you can see it walking down the street as his lead guitar picks up the bass's theme and flails it like a whip. Across nearly 11 minutes, the performance is all play and

menace, all here and now, all origins erased, a reach beyond the story to the willfulness in which it begins, a willfulness only a long, mean solo will turn up. By the time Kidney returns to words Jimmy Bell has come and gone and come back again, and you're on the next train out. "Up the road I'm going," Jimmy Bell tells his wife. "She said," Kidney shouts for her in terror, "She said, 'What road?'"

8 ▪ Reuters, "British Sequel to 'The Omen'" (*International Herald Tribune*, March 20) "London—The Labour Party will use a spoof video based on the cult 1970s horror movie 'The Omen' to assail its rivals in approaching elections. . . . The video [uses] imagery and music from 'The Omen' to liken Conservative leader William Hague to the character Damien, the son of the devil, and former Prime Minister Margaret Thatcher to the anti-Christ."

Too bad the Democratic Party won't have the nerve to come up with its own version, even though it might put a crimp in GOP plans to rename the entire country after Ronald Reagan.

9 ▪ Debbie Geller, producer of the Arena documentary *The Brian Epstein Story* and author of *In My Life: The Brian Epstein Story*, visits the 31st Annual Beatlefest (March 17) "I don't know if you've ever been to one of these things. I never have and assumed it would be full of obsessive Beatle collector types and there certainly were a lot of those. But what really struck me were the middle-class, middle-aged and younger clean-cut suburbanites there, virtually all of whom were having a great time. The vast floor of a chain motel in true Nowheresville, N.J., was broken up by ad hoc groups of guys with guitars and lots of people standing around them singing with unselfconscious enthusiasm and energy. Lots of them had their kids with them, who didn't seem embarrassed by mom and dad and were even singing with them most of the time.

"I'm only telling you this because I think you might understand, or maybe not, the sense of loss I felt in the face of this enthusiasm. Not that they've ever been anything less than the most popular group ever, but this current re-renaissance of interest in the Beatles has meant that my own original relationship to the group is becoming more and more distant. I can talk about the importance they had to me and all, but I can't remember what it felt like anymore. It's hard to remember a time when everyone didn't know all the words to all the songs, when the Beatles were doing unexpected things, when you couldn't predict what was going to happen, when a Beatle record being released was a major event and when they were so glamorous and their world was so glamorous, you could barely imagine what it was like.

"Rather than feeling a sense of commonality with people as I watched them singing the songs I've known the words to as well for at least 30 years, I felt like they were singing songs sung by a different band."

10 ▪ *The Rutles: All You Need Is Cash,* **Directors Guild of America Theatre Complex (Los Angeles, March 9)** After a screening of the 1978 TV film about the Bizarro World version of the Beatles, Rutles Neil Innes, Eric Idle and Rikki Fattar came out for a panel discussion and questions from the audience. Idle was asked if it was true that Jermaine Jackson had bought the rights to all the Rutles songs. He didn't get it right away.

MAY 1, 2001

1 ▪ **Ass Ponys, "Kung Fu Reference," on** *Lohio* **(Checkered Past)** The voice is pained and passionate, the voice of a fan of the TV series who, the melody convinces you, wants more than anything in this world for the show to mean as much to you as it does to him. Why? Because, you find out in a verse you'd rather not have understood, this man has nothing in his life but a choice between *RoboCop* and *The Bride of Frankenstein*—whatever's on tonight. The chorus seals the song: "If you ever gave a damn for Sonny Jim / I know you will—remember him." It's in the rise and fall, the

shining light that, for some reason, 26 years after the show went off the air, isn't out, even if like me you never watched it, or heard of Sonny Jim. A heroic guitar solo seems to carry its own double inside itself; it's uncanny, and like all great guitar solos not an interlude, but the story translated, elevated, pushed out in front of itself like a life the singer will never live.

2 ▪ **"No Depression in Heaven—An Exploration of Harry Smith's** *Anthology* **of** *American Folk Music,***" produced by Hal Willner (Getty Center, Los Angeles)** The '60s Cambridge folkie Geoff Muldaur led the assemblage. He looked like the kindly town pharmacist; when he opened his mouth a dynamic version of Noah Lewis' 1928 "Minglewood Blues" came out like a tiger. "You're going to be killing a lot of people tonight, aren't you?" fiddler Richard Greene asked Rennie Sparks of the Handsome Family, who was one of only four or five people under 40, or maybe 50, on the stage. "That's what I do best," she said sweetly. Sparks writes lyrics about murder and clinical depression for her husband, Brett, to sing; she introduced the Blue Sky Boys' 1936 "Down on the Banks of the Ohio" as a song in which "a woman is slaughtered to ensure the river remains full." "This record sounds like it came from Mars," Greene said, kicking off Floyd Ming and His Pep Steppers' 1928 "Indian War Whoop" (a new version orchestrates Baby Face Nelson's arrest in *O Brother, Where Art Thou?*). It sounded just like Slim Whitman's "Indian Love Call," which in *Mars Attacks!* makes all the Martians' heads explode.

The 14-person band was heading toward cuteness when Garth Hudson, late of the Band, began to play. He was everywhere at once. As soon as you thought you caught a tune—"Home Sweet Home," "Shenandoah"—it vanished. He was an avant-garde pianist in a 1915 grind house, forgotten girlie flicks and "In a castle dark" epics turning profound under his fingers. And then, like a sermon, came a low, thick, unbending voice from the back of the stage, insisting on the Great Depression as God's will, punishment for sins unknown, even uncommitted, and insisting on the only solution, which was suicide. "I'm going where there's no Depression," as the Carter Family sang in 1936, on their way to heaven. "There'll be no hunger, no orphan children crying for bread / No weeping widows, toil or struggle." The singer was Maud Hudson, and when, with absolute dignity, she reached the lines "No shrouds, no coffins / And no death," you realized the song was calling for nothing so small as the end of a life, but for the end of the natural order: the end of the world. The end of the singer, and the end of you.

3 ▪ **Britney Spears and Bob Dole for Pepsi-Cola (April, all networks)** Britney cocks her hips and implies she's about to burst out of her top. The 1996 Republican nominee for president, sitting in a comfortable chair with a comfortable dog at his feet, checks her out. A teenage fast-food cook stares at a TV with his mouth hanging open. The Dole dog barks; "Easy, boy," Dole says. He's stupefied, but you can tell the Viagra is no longer doing the trick for "erectile dysfunction, what we call 'E.D.'"—and that the other E.D., Elizabeth Dole, is out of the picture. Sex was never in the picture; they were a power couple. But now there's no power and E.D. ("America's Most Influential Woman") is doing *Success Magazine*'s "Success 2001," opening for "William Jefferson Clinton." No matter what you think of Britney Spears, you can be happy she doesn't have to do this yet. As if anyone has to.

4 ▪ **Martin Luther King Jr. for Alcatel (April, all networks)** ". . . live out the true meaning of its creed," says the man standing in front of the Lincoln Memorial on Aug. 28, 1963—by the magic of digital technology, or a stand-in, speaking to an empty plaza. The racist dynamic in the United States resulted in the construction of King as an iconic figure whose function was to marginalize and silence all other actors and voices in the civil rights movement. His posthumous function was to marginalize and silence the movement itself, either as part of the nation's true history—as opposed to Black History Month—or future possibility. But the emptying of King as even a symbolic figure, literally deprived of his audience until, it's suggested, Alcatel can round it up, can be credited only to his legal heirs. I like seeing what songs can stand up to being made into commercials; the song King sang that day in Washington can't. The contradiction is too great.

5 ▪ **Ralph Ellison, "On Bird, Bird-Watching, and Jazz," in *Living With Music—Ralph Ellison's Jazz Writings*, edited by Robert O'Meally (Modern Library)** The late novelist and critic vs. punk, in 1962: "For all its velocity, brilliance and imagination there is in [Charlie Parker's music] a great deal of loneliness, self-depreciation and self-pity. With this there is a quality, which seems to issue from its vibrato-less tone: a sound of amateurish ineffectuality, as though he could never quite make it. It is this amateurishness-sounding aspect which promises so much to the members of a do-it-yourself culture; it sounds with an assurance that you too can create your own do-it-yourself jazz. Dream stuff, of course, but there is a relationship between the Parker *sound* and the impossible genre of teenage music which has developed since his death." Following that, Ellison takes up the question that really interests him: if Parker was "Bird," what kind of bird? A robin, he decides, as in the old, impenetrable, happily sadistic song "Pick Poor Robin Clean," best heard in the 1931 version by Geeshie Wiley and Elvie Thomas (on *Mississippi Blues—Vol. 1, 1928–1937*, Document).

6 ▪ **Howard Sounes, *Down the Highway—The Life of Bob Dylan* (Grove)** Sounes is a graceless writer with no point of view, but he's talked to most of the people who've talked to everyone else and a number of people who haven't. Such as William Zantzinger, the drunken Maryland landowner who in 1963 caned a 51-year-old black hotel worker named Hattie Carroll.

She died; he got six months and, thanks to Bob Dylan's "The Lonesome Death of Hattie Carroll," a name to live in infamy, if not a story to dine out on the rest of his life. "He's a no-account son-of-a-bitch," Zantzinger says of Dylan. "He's just like a scum of a bag of the earth."

7 ▪ **Kasey Chambers, *The Captain* (Asylum)** It's no wonder the young Australian singer can "reduce Lucinda Williams to tears," as it says on her album; on "Cry Like a Baby," she sounds just like her. But on this tune, which trailed the April 15 "He Is Risen" episode of *The Sopranos*, Chambers leaves you stranded, unsure what the song is about—not a problem Williams has ever had. A little-girl voice pulls against a dark, quiet, jagged guitar hiding in the deliberate beat, and the music turns up innocence, self-loathing and corruption—and the face of, as you listen, daughter Meadow, wife and mother Carmella, and finally husband, father and boss Tony.

8 ▪ **Mark Knopfler, *What It Is* (Warner Bros.)** There's nothing here that wasn't on Dire Straits' *Making Movies*, and that was more than 20 years ago. Not even the claim to experience in the laconic, thrown-away title phrase, the claim to have seen too much. It's that there isn't anything like it on the radio, and won't be until the next time Knopfler digs these sighs and riffs out of his basement.

9 ▪ **Fred Eaglesmith & the Flying Squirrels, *Ralph's Last Show* (Signature Sounds)** On a two-CD live album, "Mighty Big Car." "Elvis had one, so did Hank / That don't look like money, that look like a bank."

10 ▪ **McSweeney's No. 6 (McSweeney's)** The inclusion in the literary journal of a CD with 44 tracks, most by They Might Be Giants, is more than apt; TMBG take *McSweeney's* to places mere writing could never get. "This CD was going to be left blank," it says right on the disc, "because it was a pretty thing when blank, but then we remembered how likely you were to leave it atop your stereo, uncased, and thus how likely it was that you would then forget what

this CD was, exactly whose music was on it (in it?), and then you would maybe even go and *record over it*—songs by *other bands even*—using some terrible new software, and in doing so make us all feel sad. So we put some words on it. This. Hi." This is, in fact, the opposite of writing, just as TMBG, whose concept is the word "clever," is the opposite of rock 'n' roll. This is posing within seven layers of irony, which is to say it means exactly what it says: Aren't I adorable?

MAY 14, 2001

SPECIAL ABSURDITY OF WORLDWIDE COMMEMORATION OF BOB DYLAN'S MAY 24 60TH BIRTHDAY EDITION!

1 ▪ This column has been unable to confirm a report that at his May 1 concert in Asheville, N.C., Bob Dylan performed his Oscar®-winning song, "Things Have Changed," with the Thing Itself prominently displayed on a speaker cabinet. True or false, the story doesn't touch the night Michael Richards showed up on *The Tonight Show* wearing his new *Seinfeld* Emmy as a necklace.

2 ▪ **Bob Dylan, "Return to Me" on *The Sopranos: Peppers & Eggs—Music from the HBO Original Series* (Sony)** Listening to his startlingly gentle version of "You Belong to Me" on the *Natural Born Killers* soundtrack, you could figure that Jo Stafford would have smiled at Dylan's cover of her 1952 smash, her biggest record. And you can imagine what Dean Martin would have to say about this cover of his 1958 smash—and his best record. Probably he wouldn't say anything, just give Dylan the same sneer Robert Mitchum gives Johnny Depp in Jim Jarmusch's *Dead Man*. A look that says, "Are you still here?"

3 ▪ ***A Nod to Bob: An Artists' Tribute to Bob Dylan on His Sixtieth Birthday* (Red House)** Suzzy and Maggie Roche can't help letting you know how clever they were to choose "Clothesline Saga," one of Dylan's coolest songs—and their bohemian posing stands out as rock 'n' roll raunch on this

collection of bored and pious folkie tributes, most of which somehow project condescension through the veil of homage. But if you've ever yearned to hear "I Want You" done as a prayer, this is for you.

4 ▪ New Dylan Alert! Robbie Fulks, *Couples in Trouble* (Boondoggle) Fulks has an uncanny ability to write songs as if they were remembered from a previous life—a life lived in England in the 17th century. This album leads off with "In Bristol Town One Bright Day"—"a stranger he came calling," that other person says through Fulks. It's a new—or unfound—version of "The Daemon Lover," dripping blood: "And on his lips the strangest words seemed so meek and common." You want a warning? That's a fire alarm. This is the sort of song Dylan would be sneaking into his shows next week, if he hadn't already recorded it as "House Carpenter" (1962, on *the bootleg series, volumes 1–3*) and "Blackjack Davey" (in 1992, on *Good As I Been to You*). As for Fulks, the rest of the record is Don McLean in loud clothes.

5 ▪ David Hajdu, *Positively 4th Street— The Lives and Times of Joan Baez, Bob Dylan, Mimi Baez Fariña and Richard Fariña* (Farrar Straus and Giroux) This disagreeable book contains a connection I've never seen anywhere else: between Dylan's 1965 "Subterranean Homesick Blues" and the Woody Guthrie/Pete Seeger song "Take [or "Taking"] It Easy." First verse: "Mom was in the kitchen, preparing to eat / Sis was in the pantry looking for some yeast / Pa was in the cellar mixing up the hops / And Brother's at the window, he's watching for the cops."

6 ▪ *Duluth Does Dylan* (Spinout) Bands who still live where Bob Dylan was born dive in with no respect and come out sounding as young as they are. Not all of it is good, and some of it's horrible, but little is predictable—not Chris Monroe's deep winter cover drawing, the First Ladies' wasted "Father of Night," or the way the chorus of "Like a Rolling Stone" keeps surfacing in the Black Labels' "Where did you say we are? And who are you, anyway?" reading of "Rainy Day Women #12 & 35."

Everybody must get stoned, like a *rolling stone*—why didn't anyone think of that before?

7 ▪ Old New Dylan Alert! Bob Marley & the Wailers, *Catch a Fire: Deluxe Edition* (Tuff Gong/Island) Before releasing the Jamaican sessions that made up this 1972 album—songs included "Stir It Up," "Kinky Reggae," "400 Years," "Slave Driver" and "Stop That Train"—producer and label owner Chris Blackwell had some overdubbing done in London. This set presents the originals—including two numbers left unrevised and unissued—on one disc, plus, on a second, *Catch a Fire* as it almost, but not quite, caught fire around the world.

"Concrete Jungle"—available in its first form as a Jamaican single—was always the test between the real thing and its adulteration. This profound protest against the specific political and economic realities of Jamaica in the moment, and against the weight of history, of slavery, pressing down like an elephant's foot every time the singer tried to think, speak or act, is smaller as the Wailers made it on their own—spare, the sound open, the backing vocals word-by-word clear. Despite the backing singers, and the careful, impeccable rhythm of the band, this is one man's testament, a work of dignity.

In London, John "Rabbit" Bundrick of Texas added organ, and Wayne Perkins of Alabama added guitar; the backing vocals were muffled—and somehow given even greater presence. There is a long, slow introduction, Perkins edging his way into the theme like a stranger trying to walk into a bar without anybody noticing, though after one turn into the music he's got his money out. Aston Barrett's bass, a counter in Jamaica, is huge here; as much as Bundrick's Garth Hudson-like tentacles, it's this that makes a mood in which you can't tell curse from judgment, the future from too late. Straight off, the sound puts everything in doubt, and everyone on the record in jeopardy.

As the song goes on, the backing singers seem to circle Marley's lead, pointing at him, smiling, frowning, offering approval, withholding it, and soon the prosaic has vanished from the performance: the crying chorus is made up of the "many thousands gone" of "No More Auction Block," the indelible slavery song first heard by whites from black Union soldiers. Odetta sang it in the 1950s, and no one ever went farther into the song than Bob Dylan, singing it in the Gaslight Café in New York in 1962 (on *the bootleg series, volumes 1–3*)—much farther, that night, than when he took some of the song's melody, and some of its spirit, for "Blowin' in the Wind." *Where Dead Voices Gather*, Nick Tosches calls his forthcoming book on 1920s blackface minstrel artist Emmett Miller—this remixed "Concrete Jungle" is one place they gather.

All through the progression of the song, Perkins has been waiting, offering up a sign or a riff, a comment or a counterpoint, like the man in the bar looking a split-second too long at the guy who seems to own the place, holding his glass in a way not quite the same as anyone else, calling another drink with words that are English but sound like Spanish. As Marley steps back, then, Perkins steps in. The solo he plays is so restrained in form, and so passionate in tone, it translates the pain of Marley's story into a dream beyond words or even images. It is a dream of flight, of the running man trapped, escaping only to be trapped again, until, in a shocking moment, the solo turns over, and turns back on itself, as if to say: this record will end, but the story can't end. Not well; not even badly. And you can't wait it out. "400 Years"? You thought that meant from then to now, but it means from now to then. And then turned over, and run backward.

8 ▪ **Bob Dylan, *Bob Dylan Live: 1961–2000* (Sony Japan)** Sixteen tracks, from "Wade in the Water," taped in 1961 in Minneapolis, to "Things Have Changed," from Portsmouth, England, last year. Killers: the old ballad "Handsome Molly," from the Gaslight in 1962, and "Dead Man, Dead Man," studio version on *Shot of Love*, 1981. Taped in New Orleans that same year, "Dead

Man" is a textbook warning against the devil, if you listen as if you're reading; if you hear it, it's a poker game, and the singer's winning.

9 ▪ **Pre-Dylan Alert! Robert Cantwell, "Darkling I Listen: Making Sense of the 'Folkways Anthology,'" talk at "Harry Smith: The Avant-Garde in the American Vernacular" (Getty Center, Los Angeles, April 20, 2001)** About old American music, as first recorded in the 1920s and assembled by Smith in 1952 as the six-LP anthology *American Folk Music*—which, given the degree to which he absorbed it, in the late '50s and early '60s might have been Bob Dylan's pillow. The records were not quite the songs, and the performances of the songs were not quite the songs either, Cantwell argued: when seven decades ago those who Dylan once called "the traditional people" faced new machines, what resulted were "thought experiments, science fictions—newer than new, as it were, and older than old. They lead us, finally, to the *Anthology*'s central mystery: How can *these* performances have found their way to *those* records? Or better, these records to those performances?—questions that would not arise at all were it not for the still deeper question with which Harry has confronted us: *What is a record?*"

With the strange old sounds ("It is the *sound* of the old records we have, not the records themselves"), Cantwell said, Smith "placed us roughly where the listeners to Edison's phonograph were, phenomenologically speaking, in the early weeks of its public unveiling, when, according to the editor of the *Scientific American*, 'the machine inquired as to our health, asked how we liked the phonograph, informed us that [it] was very well, and bid a cordial goodnight.' At succeeding demonstrations young women fainted; eminent scientific heads were convinced it was a trick of ventriloquism; a Yale professor pronounced it a flat-out hoax. What was this machine that could steal the human voice? That could make absent people present—or was it that it rendered present people absent? That immortalized the human voice, but at the same time abolished it? What can one say of a machine that brings the dead back to life, but in the same instant buries them again?" No one has ever come closer to rendering Smith's selections—the likes of the Alabama Sacred Heart Singers' "Rocky Road" or Blind Lemon Jefferson's "See That My Grave Is Kept Clean"—in mere words, as opposed to, as with Dylan's versions of the latter, on his first album in 1962, and in the basement tapes sessions five years later, more recordings.

10 ▪ **Anonymous Dylan fan (e-mail, May 7)** "Bob birthday blast of coverage reminds me of fifties country song—*I forgot to remember to forget*—except updated—*I forgot, then remembered then forgot then remembered then remembered why I never should have forgotten in the first place.*"

MAY 29, 2001

1 ▪ **Michael Sergio, director/writer, *Under Hellgate Bridge* (Cuva Pictures)** One baroque scene in this worthless New York mob 'n' junkies movie: evil low-level mobster Vincent and noble pretty boy ex-junkie Ryan, one-time rivals over ex-junkie Carla, now married to Vincent, give each other dirty looks in the local bar. Vincent's thugs have Ryan pinned to a chair; Vincent, in a fancy suit, waltzes Carla around a table gleaming with blue stemware. Wearing a matching blue cocktail dress, Carla, who Vincent has shot up "for old time's sake," flops on his shoulder as the jukebox plays Terry Cole's rendition of Bobby Bland's 1959 "I'll Take Care of You," one of Bland's most delicate and painful recordings. "I know you've been hurt / By somebody else," Cole sings as Vincent lays Carla on a table and sodomizes her, grinning at Ryan until his face breaks up in orgasm: "I can tell by the way you carry yourself." "This really takes me back," Vincent says.

2 ▪ **Trailer Bride, *High Seas* (Bloodshot)** Melissa Swingle, singer and multi-instrumentalist leader (saw, guitar, banjo, harmonica, piano) of this country band, which sounds like an old motel on Route 66

looks, is going to have to change her "I Used to Be Disgusted, Now I Try to Be Amused, But Usually It's Not Worth the Effort" T-shirt sooner or later. But not just yet.

3 ▪ **John McCready, "Room at the Top," *Mojo* (May)** The story of Joe Meek, the UK's first real independent record producer. The Tornadoes' 1962 "Telstar," which alone among period pop songs playing in the "Les Années Pop" show at the Pompidou Centre in Paris this spring came across as a match for the best of the pop art on the walls, was his biggest hit; he killed himself in 1967 after shotgunning his landlady to death. McCready on Meek's work with songwriter Geoff Goddard: "Like Joe, Goddard was an amateur spiritualist with a Buddy Holly obsession. Goddard's interests pushed them to attempts at contacting dead stars—Al Jolson, Mario Lanza, and even Buddy. The sessions prompted Geoff to pen Mike Berry's 'Tribute to Buddy Holly.' Joe and Geoff decided to call up Buddy and see if he thought the record would be a hit. His reply? 'SEE YOU IN THE CHARTS.'"

4 ▪ **Colson Whitehead, *John Henry Days* (Doubleday)** Anthropologist Harry Smith found the ballad "John Henry"—or the story of the ex-slave and spike driver who dies in a race with a steam drill—bottomless. No less than four versions are included on the four volumes of Smith's *Anthology of American Folk Music*—by the Williamson Brothers and Curry ("Gonna Die With My Hammer in My Hand," 1927), Furry Lewis ("Spike Driver Blues," 1928), J. E. Mainer's Mountaineers ("John Henry Was a Little Boy," 1936) and the Monroe Brothers ("Nine Pound Hammer Is Too Heavy," 1936). Scattered through this novel about a young journalist on a junket for the release of a John Henry stamp are Whitehead's versions of the way the song generates versions of itself: tales of how singers find the song, or how the song finds its singers, be they a present-day crackhead or a Jewish song-plugger a hundred years ago. Whitehead's hero stands in the way of a story trying to tell itself, but there is deeper

writing here than in novels that have nothing wrong with them.

5 ▪ **Jonathan Franzen, "Freeloading Man," review of Colson Whitehead, *John Henry Days*, New York Times Book Review (May 14)** Novelist Franzen leads with the declaration that he was "irritated" by Whitehead's having made the hero of his first novel, *The Intuitionist*, a woman: "Although it's technically impressive and theoretically laudable when a male novelist succeeds in inhabiting a female persona, something about the actual practice makes me uneasy. Is the heroine doing double duty as the novelist's fantasy sex object? Is the writer trying to colonize fictional territory that rightfully belongs to women? Or does the young literato, lacking the perks of power and feeling generally smalled"— *smalled?*—"by the culture, perhaps believe himself to be, at some deep level, *not male at all?*" Leave aside the assumption that women are by definition "smalled," or, for that matter, the case of Henry James (who, some have argued, was, you know, not exactly male at all, at least as Franzen seems to define male). By the lights of Franzen's argument, Whitehead, who is black, should also not attempt to inhabit white characters, which he does throughout *John Henry Days*, and Franzen, who is white, should certainly not be judging the work of a black novelist. But since he is, we can fairly ask: is he using Whitehead as his fantasy sex object? Is he trying to colonize territory that rightfully (at least as Franzen defines "rightfully") belongs to black writers? Does he perhaps believe himself to be, at some shallow level, not white at all? Or is he simply a moron who should never write about anyone but himself?

6 ▪ **Lucinda Williams, "Angels Laid Him Away," on *Avalon Blues—A Tribute to the Music of Mississippi John Hurt* (Vanguard)** More proof that Williams has taken the fawning reviews of her *Car Wheels on a Gravel Road* to heart, and is now ready to bestow her genius on anyone dead enough to keep quiet about it. Too bad Joe Meek isn't around to deal with this.

7–9 ▪ **"Vermeer and the Delft School," Metropolitan Museum of Art (New York, closed May 27)** "The baddest painter since God's Jan Vermeer," Jonathan Richman proclaimed on "Vincent Van Gogh." ("Bompabompadomp ramalangadangdang bompabompadomp oo-wah-oo," went the chorus.) A banner with those words should have hung over Vermeer's *The Procuress* (1656). On the right side of the large, florid painting is a man flipping a prostitute a gold coin while resting his other hand on her breast; on the left is a dandy, by consensus a Vermeer self-portrait, his eyes sparkling in a ravenously privileged male grin.

It's not characteristic. All through the Delft work, especially that of Vermeer (1632–75) and Pieter de Hooch (1629–84), there are quiet rooms, courtyards, streets. There is the emergence of bourgeois life as "a new idea in Europe" (as Saint-Just, at the height of the French Revolution, named happiness)—as a new idea of harmony, simplicity, domestic art, leisure, neoteny (children are dressed as miniature adults, but their faces are their own, and the faces of adults retain childlike features). There is a stillness, a peace of mind that rules even as tales of colonial adventure bring drama into the home. There is a complete absence of decadence or pretentiousness—or, most of the time, even anxiety. (Vermeer's 1662–63 *Woman With a Lute* is a glaring anomaly: a girl with hollow eyes in a bird's face, her blonde hair receding as if she's suffering from malnutrition, could be a London punk in 1976.) A whole way of being can be summoned in the luminous possibilities of a single flower or a commonplace bowl.

If you'd left the exhibit and walked across the museum to the William Blake show, you'd have passed van Gogh's 1888 *Madame Roulin and Her Baby*, which measures the real distance between the Netherlands in the 17th century and France in the 19th: between a new idea and an old one. The mother is on the right, her head downcast, her yellow face fading into the yellow background as she holds up her baby with its ugly adult's face, with its grimace of one who has already apprehended and understood the ugliness of the world into which it has so recently been born. The mother's age can't be told from her face, but her hands are old and arthritic; she looks down in shame from her monster.

10 ■ **Soundbreak.com, advertisement (Prince & Mulberry streets, New York, May 9)** Down the side of a building, the head of a pleasant-looking middle-aged man; your accountant, pharmacist, hardware store clerk. "Their music drowns out the evil voices in my head," he's saying.

JUNE 11, 2001

SPECIAL OUT OF TOWN OUT OF MIND SUMMER EDITION!

1 ■ **Monkees, *Summer 1967—The Complete U.S. Concert Recordings* (Rhino)** Proof that the economy is still humming: market calculations indicate there remains enough disposable income to ensure a positive return on the release of a double live CD collecting, in their entirety, four shows consisting of the same 17 songs. Played in the same order. By the same people.

2 ■ **Advertisement for U.S. Trust (*Los Angeles* magazine, June) & David Leonhardt, "If Richer Isn't Happier, What Is?" (*New York Times*, May 19)** This column does not credit the existence of political conspiracy or coordinated propaganda. Therefore the simultaneous appearance of a news story about how "money really cannot buy happiness" and how "even though income [has] risen dramatically since World War II, Americans say they are no happier" and an ad headed "Money Is Not the End of Worry. It Is the Beginning" can have nothing to do with deflecting resentment over the unprecedentedly regressive character of the recently passed tax bill. "You have more dependents, more possessions, more investments," says copy under a stark painting of a 40-ish woman who looks like Daria without a sense of humor. "Yet you're still expected to fight your way through a zillion e-mails and voice mails each day, just trying to hang on to your sanity, your ideal weight, and your quality time with your family. How can you explain to other people the fear that your children might never need to work?" "Who would believe all that money could ever feel like a burden rather than a blessing?" the ad asks. It answers not just for U.S. Trust, but for the person idly reading along: "We would." Wouldn't you?

3 ■ **Quasi, *The Sword of God* (Touch and Go)** Earnest playing, uninteresting singing—of a certain strain, indie music of absolute purity.

4 ■ **Nick Lowe, *The Convincer* (Yep Roc)** From the last of the rock 'n' roll pranksters, songs too dull even for parody.

5 ■ **Scott Miller & the Commonwealth, *Thus Always to Tyrants* (Sugar Hill)** Nothing here—not the cravenly self-conscious rewrite of Charles Frazier's *Cold Mountain*, especially not the even more cravenly self-conscious rewrite of the Band's "The Night They Drove Old Dixie Down"—suggests this *isn't* an homage to John Wilkes Booth. Except that Scott Miller's declamatory style isn't going to scare anyone.

6 ■ **Love, Janis: The Songs, the Letters, the Soul of Janis Joplin (Columbia Legacy)** She didn't mean it. Whatever it was.

7 ■ **Bonnie "Prince" Billy, *Ease on Down the Road* (Palace)** Going nowhere, particularly on the swooning chorus of "Just to See My Holly Home," where it doesn't matter.

8 ■ **Yayhoos, *Fear Not the Obvious* (Bloodshot)** A foursome with bad teeth in a fearless stumble into the Faces' *A Nod Is as Good as a Wink . . . to a Blind Horse*, which pays off on "For Crying Out Loud." And on "Dancing Queen," where the three-sheets-to-the-wind band turns its roadhouse into a karaoke bar.

9 ■ **John Carman on *Bad News, Mr. Swanson* (*San Francisco Chronicle*, June 1)** On a comedy about a man diagnosed with terminal cancer, which will or won't appear this fall on FX cable: "The medical death sentence emboldens Whaley to seize control of his life and become more assertive with his

estranged wife, his overbearing father and his bosses. He also finds himself in a fantastical relationship with Death, a spike-haired, beer-swilling reaper played by John Lydon, the erstwhile Johnny Rotten of the Sex Pistols." Wow, death! What's next, the Antichrist?

10 ▪ **Joe Queenan,** *Balsamic Dreams: A Short but Self-Important History of the Baby Boomer Generation* **(Henry Holt)** The BBG defined not by the conventional 1946–62 but by 1943–60 ("Randy Newman, one of the few famous Baby Boomers who is not a thoroughly revolting human being, was born in 1943. I need him in this book"), and including an "Are You a Full-Fledged Baby Boomer" quiz with good questions and bad answers. For example: "On August 3, 1962, Lee Harvey Oswald and Sirhan Sirhan are paddling a canoe down the Potomac at 12 miles an hour. Meanwhile, Charles Manson, James Earl Ray and Mark David Chapman are hurtling toward them in a motorboat cruising at 75 miles an hour. If the two boats collide just south of the Jefferson Memorial, which Baby Boomer hero will still be assassinated in the next few years: (A) Martin Luther King, (B) Bobby Kennedy, (C) John Lennon, (D) John F. Kennedy."

Real Life Rock Top 10 answer: A, B, D.

JUNE 25, 2001

SPECIAL DEAD PEOPLE EDITION!

1 ▪ **Baz Luhrmann, director, Luhrmann and Craig Pierce, writers,** *Moulin Rouge* **(20th Century Fox)** Part *Showgirls*, part Dennis Potter's *Lipstick on Your Collar*, this delirious musical has the courage of its own ridiculousness. It never goes soft, never backs away from its commitment to the constantly trumpeted "bohemian revolution," presented as a new religion of art, love and to thine own self be true, in practice a proof that you can get away with anything so long as you never admit there's anything the least bit odd about what you're doing. After half an hour, the appearance of "Smells Like Teen Spirit" in a 1900 Paris chorus line or

"The hills are alive with the sound of music" as avant-garde poetry is so liberating, so obliterative of a century's worth of cultural piety, that you start rewriting the movie to fit your own heart. I couldn't understand why doomed lovers Ewan McGregor and Nicole Kidman were duetting on David Bowie's "Heroes" when they could have been singing "That's My Desire"—a scandal in 1947, when it was first recorded ("To spend one night with you" is the opening line), then turned into a dream by countless East Coast vocal groups in the 1950s, most indelibly by Dion and the Belmonts.

2 ▪ **Bobbettes,** *The Best of the Bobbettes* **(Crash)** In 1957 five young girls from P.S. 109 in New York wrote a song about their cool principal: "Mr. Lee" was a top 10 hit. Still, the edge in the swift, gleeful piece of street doo-wop—jailbait lusting after a grown-up authority figure—made sense of the 1960 follow-up: "I Shot Mr. Lee." The girls didn't say why; they didn't have to. By this time the Bobbettes were barely into their midteens.

Heard today, "I Shot Mr. Lee" ("Ah, shot him in the head, boom boom") is totally wild. It's funny; it's almost believable. The surprise is that a group as one-hit marginal as the Bobbettes can so easily sustain a collection of more than 30 tracks: the slow, gorgeous "The Dream," which bridges the gap between the Chantels' "Maybe" and Rosie and the Originals' "Angel Baby"; the witty "Rock & Ree-Ah-Zole (The Teenage Talk)"; the "Party Lights"-like tragedy of "Mama Papa," where the singer turns on the TV only to see her boyfriend dancing on *American Bandstand*—with someone else.

3 ▪ **Rennie Sparks,** *Evil* **(Black Hole Press)** Despite the accurate jacket description of Sparks as "lyricist for the gothic country duo the Handsome Family," her short stories are unspectacularly prosaic accounts of angry, isolated, confused young women and the trouble they get into. They live on the rotting edges of a big city; everyone seems to know someone who's been murdered. The notion of any of Sparks' characters growing up is where

the tension comes from: that is, you can't imagine it. One who's on her way is the narrator of "4-Piece Dinette Set $799.99": "I'm a good worker at least no worse than the rest, except for Post-its. I like to steal them. Everyday I grab a pad or two off someone's desk as I head out to my car. Driving back to the city, I toss Post-its out my car window and watch them through the rearview mirror, skidding and rolling in the dirt. I don't know why I do it. I guess I don't really want to know why."

4 ■ **Ben Harper, blurb for** *Avalon Blues: A Tribute to the Music of Mississippi John Hurt* **(Vanguard)** "If it wasn't for Mississippi John Hurt, I would not be making music at all," he says. It's always a good idea to put the blame on someone who isn't around to defend himself.

5 ■ **Kelly Vance, review of Herschell Gordon Lewis'** *1968* **She-Devils on Wheels** **(East Bay Express, June 15)** "It has everything you look for in a drive-in movie: cheap production values, rotten acting, stupid writing, inept direction—the works. Think 'Faster, Pussycat! Kill! Kill!' In fact, take practically any biker flick you have ever seen and turn it up a notch on the Dumb-O-Meter. This film defines the word 'nadir.' And yet, somehow, abstract concepts appear much more clearly when glimpsed from the rock-bottom of human experience."

6 ■ **Chris Walters,** *The Ghost of Jim Thompson Stalks L.A.,* **collage of title and excerpt from letter from Bonnie Bakley to Robert Blake before the signing of a prenuptial agreement in October 2000 (letter from** *New York Daily News,* **May 9)** "I think psychologically it helps me get even with mankind," Bakley wrote to her soon-to-be husband and, after Bakley's unsolved shooting May 5, widower (he went back to the restaurant where the two had had dinner to get his gun, Blake told police, then returned to his car and found her dead), of her life as a grifter. "My father tried to get fresh with me when I was seven, while my mother was in the hospital having Joey [her brother]. He died before I could grow up and kill him."

7 ■ **KFRC-FM (San Francisco, June 17)** "Father's Day Superset," featuring Marvin Gaye, who on April 1, 1984, gave his father the ultimate Father's Day present. On the air, Bob Dylan immediately followed, though not with "Highway 61 Revisited," which begins, "God said to Abraham, kill me a son—"

8 ■ **Joy Division,** *Les Bains Douches 18 December 1979* **(Factory)** The severe, serious, nevertheless thrilling sound of young men walking all night in the Manchester rain—thrilling because, in the course of that long walk, anyone can find out what he really wants, anyone can fall behind, anything can happen—as captured mostly at what sounds like a very underattended show in Paris. As with other severe, serious post–Sex Pistols groups—Wire, the Cure—there's the chilly feel of postwar espionage films, the voices of people who have no idea how they found themselves in jeopardy, let alone how to get out. There's no balance in the performance, no obvious match between Ian Curtis' singing, Peter Hook's bass, Bernard Albrecht's guitar and Stephen Morris' drums: As soon as you think of the Velvet Underground you think of the Doors, and then realize that, compared with this band, they were all about order.

The most brutal and beautiful numbers here are taken from January 1980 live recordings in Holland. "Digital" is too strong, too hard, too much; on "Atmosphere," the distant, silent-movie organ sound that would give the band that went on as New Order, after Curtis' suicide on May 18, 1980, a claim to the deepest dives of the new decade and, along with Foreigner's "I Want to Know What Love Is," its best singles: "Temptation" and "Bizarre Love Triangle." Joy Division's second, 1980 album was called *Closer*; this could have been called "Close Enough."

9 ■ **Eddie Cochran,** *The Town Hall Party TV Shows 1959* **(Rockstar Records video)** The rocker remembered in his own country mostly for "Summertime Blues," and beloved in the U.K. because he toured there and died there (in a car crash in 1960), ap-

pears on a Los Angeles country music show with his band Dick D'Agostin & the Swingers, who are much better than their name. Seemingly taking his visual cues from Edd "Kookie" Byrnes of the L.A. private eye hit *77 Sunset Strip*, Cochran is short, compact, well-dressed and absurdly good-looking, his pompadour so big and glossy it just begs for Byrnes to show up and lend Eddie his comb. But he doesn't need it until "Money Honey," the second-to-last song of the night. Cochran is singing, playing guitar, chewing gum and rotating his shoulders all at the same time, and every element seems necessary for the spell he casts. "Whenever we put this on," said the counterman at Down Home Music in El Cerrito, Calif., as he and everyone else in the place tried to keep doing what they'd been doing, "I never get any work done. I might as well take the rest of the day off."

10 ▪ **Roger McGuinn, *Treasures From the Folk Den* (Appleseed)** Given McGuinn's startlingly warm, open work on old American music with Jeff Tweedy and Jay Bennett of Wilco (see *The Harry Smith Connection*), this should have been, as Dikembe Mutombo recently put it, a walk in the cake. Thanks to contributions by worn-out Judy Collins, Joan Baez, Odetta, Jean Ritchie and Josh White Jr., the result is an earnest workshop, with the main lesson being How Not to Do It. This comes courtesy of excruciating performances in which Pete Seeger, who for six decades has accepted that he cannot sing blues, does. "I realize I'm used to slightly different chords," he says in the most refined voice imaginable. "They're not logical chords."

JULY 16, 2001

1 ▪ **Unitas, *Porch Life* (No Idea)** They could have called it "Blood on Our Sleeves"—on this rough set of songs about being fans in a band, everything is familiar, nothing fits and anything is an occasion for passion. "What's your favorite Uncle Tupelo song?" says the singer to you or the other three guys in the group; his is "Screen Door."

(From *No Depression*, 1990, Rockville Records—the lyric sheet is footnoted to discographical information on the music everyone on the porch is talking about, that everyone loves, that everyone feels oppressed by.) The sound is tear-away; you can almost feel the pieces pulling apart. The band ram through their songs as if they don't want to give you time to talk about what's wrong with them, or for that matter what's right—say, the fierce, double-back riff in "Unitas (Picks A) Fight Song" ("The only thing more boring than you is your audience"—quick, think of a comeback for *that*). There's even a manifesto. "I'm not about to advocate forming a committee to go out and confiscate copies of Start Today and the Minor Threat discography, but it almost sounds like a good idea." The manifesto ends with a question: "'How is this a punk rock record?' If you don't know, I'm not telling." It's a punk rock record because the people who made it have been around the block too often to care whether they look cool this time around. Which doesn't answer the question of why this Gainesville band named itself after the quarterback for the Baltimore Colts.

2 ▪ **Clarence Ashley, *Greenback Dollar—The Music of Clarence "Tom" Ashley, 1928–1933* (County)** Ashley (1895–1967) was one of the greatest of the "old-timey" singers—those who, in the first third of the 20th century, sang as if the new century was a trick that would disappear soon enough, as if only songs made long before you were born would hold your interest for more than a season. He was born Clarence and recorded under that name, but everyone knew him as Tom; when the bottom fell out of the old-timey market in the '30s, the recording artist Clarence Ashley disappeared and the performer Tom Ashley kept on. In 1960, at a fiddler's convention in North Carolina, he and guitarist Clint Howard and fiddler Fred Price were approached by folklorist Ralph Rinzler, who asked if they had knowledge of a Clarence Ashley, whose bottomless recordings of "Coo Coo Bird" (1929) and "House Carpenter" (1930) had

been collected on Harry Smith's 1952 *Anthology of American Folk Music.* "Clint Howard recalls the moment," one can read in the *Greenback Dollar* notes: "Fred and me had known Tom all our lives, but we just knew him as Tom. So I said, 'No, I don't. Do you know a Clarence Ashley, Tom?' Tom started to say, 'No,' but he had a second thought: 'Hell, I'm Clarence Ashley!'" As a public artist, he began a second life, but musically there was really no change from his first.

Even as a young man, Ashley had a squeaky, baffled old-codger's tone. He reveled in the deadpan mysteries of "Haunted Road Blues" and "Dark Holler." But those songs, like "Coo Coo Bird" and "House Carpenter," are the high culture of old-timey. On *Greenback Dollar,* drawn from Ashley's various string bands as well as his solo recordings, low culture pulls harder: hokum rules. Ashley performed in blackface on the minstrel-show, medicine-show circuit; you can hear the blackface snigger in Ashley's amazingly obscene "My Sweet Farm Girl," which gets both cunnilingus and analingus into a single verse. You can hear the common, secret culture of the south in Ashley's detailed versions of the true-crime ballads "Frankie Silvers," "Old John Hardy" and "Naomi Wise." And in an extremely vicious reading of "Little Sadie" you can hear a man who might have reason to forget his own name.

3 ▪ Julien Temple, on *The Great Rock 'n' Roll Swindle* (1980) and *The Filth and the Fury* (2000), Fresh Air (NPR, July 3) The director on why *Swindle* was just that—his and Sex Pistols manager Malcolm McLaren's attempt to force fans to confront their worship of idol-smashers—and on how *Filth* was his attempt to give the surviving band members the chance to tell their own stories, all of them "scarred for life" by a process in which Temple was not innocent: helping to drag them through "the chemotherapy of fame."

4–7 ▪ David Gray, *Flesh* (EMI reissue, 1994), *Sell, Sell, Sell* (EMI reissue, 1996), *White Ladder* (ATO) and *Lost Songs* (ATO) For those

who think memoirs written by white people in their 50s or younger are true.

8 ▪ White Stripes, *White Blood Cells* (Sympathy for the Record Industry) As the disc unwinds, the smart, bashing punk offered by a Detroit ex-husband (guitar, vocals) and ex-wife (drums) opens into the near nursery rhyme of "We're Going to Be Friends" or the INXS slickness of "I Think I Smell a Rat." Maybe Jack and Meg White really do have sympathy for the record industry. But for the moment the heart of their music seems to be in "Offend in Every Way," a harsh, expert storm of old guitar riffs, old curses and the steady, disinterested beat of someone who sounds as if she learned the story in the womb. The sound starts in Memphis, where the music was recorded, and then heads for the hills.

9 ▪ Amir Bar-Lev, *Fighter,* Minneapolis/ St. Paul International Film Festival (April 4) After escaping the Nazis in his native Czechoslovakia, a man returns after the war to help remake his country. The Stalinist government sends him to prison, where every day loudspeakers blast "that optimistic socialist music" (period footage shows a robust, bright-faced young couple in traditional Czech dress dancing a traditional Czech dance; they look just like Ricky Martin and Britney Spears)—"the kind of music my father always called organized farts."

10 ▪ Nick Hornby, *How to Be Good* (Riverhead) The narrator tells her husband of 20 years she's "been seeing someone."

"I'm presuming that you'll be moving out in the next couple of days," he says.

"The affair's over," she says. "As of this minute."

"I don't know about that," he says. "But I do know that no one asks Elvis Presley to play for nothing."

1 ▪ Club 8, *Club 8* (Secret Agenda) From a Swedish duo (Karolina Komstedt, vocals; Johan Angergard, instruments and writing), dream pop with the undertow dream pop needs. "Love in December" plays off the phrase "I'll be there for you," but where the Rembrandts' *Friends* theme song promises that the singer will make jokes when you can't decide what to wear, here the singer might be promising she'll sit by your deathbed, and the promise is sweet; in the rolling tones of "Say a Prayer" light shades and dark swirl like ye-ye singers entertaining Bateau-Mouche passengers on the Styx, not the Seine. It's a love-and-espionage sound that's been missing since the Belgian band Hooverphonic's 1996 *A New Stereophonic Sound Spectacular*—apparently a sound only Europeans can make, or hear.

2 ▪ **Allan Ball, producer, *Six Feet Under*** (HBO, July 8) Thirty-ish Nate, on the trail of his late father's hidden life, discovers his secret hideaway: a grimy four walls behind a restaurant, fitted out with ratty couch, dirty coffee table, big TV, a phonograph and a rack of LPs. It looks just like Beavis and Butt-head's video room. Nate pulls out an album and cues it up: the Amboy Dukes' 1968 psychedelic horror *Journey to the Center of the Mind*, Ted Nugent's first big moment. Nate imagines his father in the place: doing the frug in his three-piece undertaker's suit, smoking dope with bikers, bringing in a prostitute for a blow job, picking off people on the street with a sniper's rifle. Nate falls asleep on the couch; in a dream, he turns to his dad as the queasy '67 sound of "Spooky" fills the dead air: "What the hell is this place, this music? Since when do you listen to the Classics IV? Who the hell are you?"

3 ▪ **Mary Gauthier, *Drag Queens in Limousines*** (In the Black) A self-consciously dark, would-be Gothic set of songs—so self-conscious, as with the miserabilist autobiography of the title song ("I hated high school, I prayed that it would end / The jocks and their girls, it was their world / I didn't fit in"; Janis Ian's "At Seventeen" was more than anyone needed to hear about this, and that was a quarter-century ago), that there's no room for Gauthier to move to her own rhythms. But on "Our Lady of the Shooting Stars" she doesn't

press, doesn't worry that you might miss the point. Her voice makes shadows; the music unwinds slowly, and you have no idea where she's taking you. To the miserabilist "Karla Faye," as it happens, about Karla Faye Tucker, executed in Texas. (*"Please don't kill me!"* laughed then Gov. George W. Bush over her letter asking for clemency.) It doesn't matter. The voice in "Our Lady" is singular, beyond anything classy country singers like Emmylou Harris and Gillian Welch would ever reach for.

4–7 ▪ **Go-Go's, *God Bless the Go-Go's*** **(Beyond);** *Return to the Valley of the Go-Go's* **(IRS, 1994); "Belinda Carlisle Rocks Naked" (*Playboy*, August); Jane Weidlin,** *Dear Weirdos* **(Experience Music Project, Seattle)** The reformed band is more alive on the new *God Bless the Go-Go's* than it was on a few dull 1994 cuts tacked onto *Return to the Valley of the Go-Go's*, its "half dive into the unknown, half heard it all before" retrospective. Lead singer Belinda Carlisle sounds more alive than she looks in *Playboy*, smoothed and inflated beyond nature. But of the new songs (which include "Daisy Chain," a three-minute, 45-second *Behind the Music* mea culpa), only "Insincere" even hints at the fierceness and ambition that took the group out of the new world of late-'70s Los Angeles punk and into the hearts of young girls all over America when *Beauty and the Beat*, their 1981 debut album, hit No. 1. All of that is present on the first CD of *Return*: dirty, late-night performances and rehearsals from 1979 and 1980, with Ventures-style guitar snaking through the noise so distantly it's as if Charlotte Caffey were playing from the back of the room; the bitterness in "This Town," which after 20 years is still unsatisfied; the defiance and delight in "Our Lips Are Sealed," which after 20 years is still undeniable. All that's missing, really, is an enhanced track with a clip of Carlisle's nervous, hard-nosed interviews in Penelope Spheeris' 1980 film *The Decline . . . of Western Civilization*, and guitarist Jane Weidlin's 1978 fan letter to Los Angeles punk heroes the Weirdos: a fantastic collage that, beginning on a roll of toilet paper with an ad for the Fruit-of-the-Month Club pasted onto the first sheet, proceeds from manifesto ("Who needs fruit when you can be a weirdo?") to P.S. ("John I think you're really keen") while taking in Alka-Seltzer tablets, a vinyl belt, photographs of the author, a rubber glove and instructions on how to brush your teeth.

8 ▪ Cyndi Lauper, "Money Changes Everything," at Boston Pops (Independence Day) Boston Blackie, aka Lindsay Waters, reports on a live performance of Lauper's greatest recording: "In 1984 I rushed to the TV when called to see Cyndi Lauper sing on national television. This was in Minneapolis and we were just about to move to Boston. We listened to 'She's So Unusual' all the way across the country as we cried because we were leaving the Twin Cities: she with her downtown manners from New York and some songs from Uptown Minneapolis from Prince. Now on the Fourth of July I found myself called to the TV again.

"Seeing her now, packed into her skimpy silver dress with the super-short skirt, was strange. There she was, doing the bump with Mr. Conventional Keith Lockhart, in the most conventional city in the U.S. The Boston Pops threatened to give us Cyndi Pops. She sounded good and fresh and peppy, but the scene put me in mind of how time and place change things as absolutely as money. In the 18 years since she first sang the song, the city of Boston, and especially the area around the Hatch Shell on the Charles River, has changed because money has poured into the city. Downtown Boston has gone and is going through a major reshaping. Boston is a city of old money, of people who would rather sit on their money than spend it. Luckily the taxpayers of the U.S. can be called on to make up the difference when the locals are frugal, so all the new bridges, roads and high-rises can be paid for by new money. The place Lauper was playing encouraged one to see her performance in the most cynical light, but she bopped so hard you could almost imagine that Boston was on the verge of the change it has resisted for at least a hundred years."

9 ▪ Michael Mann, producer, *Crime Story* reruns on A&E (Mondays) On July 16 it was Chicago, 1963: a 1986, first-season episode about a psycho killer who's a dead ringer for Stiv Bators. It was graphic beyond anything on network television before or since, and from beginning to end there were great cars, shot from street level, great clothes and great hair, especially the bizarre flattop pompadour on mob comer Ray Luca (Anthony Denison). But the truest moment came in the opening scene: a party for Lt. Mike Torello (Dennis Farina) and his Major Crime Unit, the whole hipster crew and their wives and girlfriends dancing slow and cool to the hometown Impressions' 1963 hit "It's All Right."

10 ▪ Flier for Gossip show at 7th St. Entry (Minneapolis, July 8) For the unkempt Arkansas threesome, Sharon Stone crossed her legs in *Basic Instinct*. The near white-out glow the artist had imposed over the too-familiar image erased the role Stone played in the picture as the object of gossip, replacing it with something sexier: the suggestion that she's about to whisper it in your ear.

AUGUST 20, 2001

1 ▪ New Pornographers, *Mass Romantic* (Mint) Put five guys from Vancouver in a band that would rather be Oasis or even the Small Faces in their arty period—or the Beach Boys topping "Good Vibrations" or, why not, the Beatles—together with someone doing a good imitation of Phil Spector crinkling up tinfoil, bring in Bloodshot country singer Neko Case and watch a smile spread through the room, and then watch it soar into the sky like a balloon, and Case fly through the air like Supergirl, or anyway Helen Slater, who will do. "The song, the song, the song that's shaking me," Case warbles off her feet in "Letter From an Occupant"; I couldn't make out the next line, but the boys' "woo-woo-woo-woo, wee-ooo's" were clear as day. Then came the

opening shots of "To Wild Homes," and I found myself applauding. In the car, in the fast lane. From last year, and for good.

2 ■ Bobby "Blue" Bland, *Two Steps From the Blues* **(MCA)** From 1961: the first full album by the strangest-looking and most original postwar blues stylist—a man whose sense of tragedy was as carefully cut as his sharkskin suits. Never too much drape, never a fold showing, with so many different threads running through the material the result is a glow, the glow of despair and loss at twilight, be it the gentle "Lead Me On" or the horrifying "St. James Infirmary." On the front: Mr. Bland himself, jacket slung over his shoulder like Frank Sinatra, mounting the two steps that will take him inside the blue-paneled building where, you can bet, he will inquire about his royalties. "What royalties?" Duke Records president Don Robey will ask him. "I don't see your name on any of those songs."

3 ■ David Rakoff, *Fraud* **(Doubleday)** Rakoff's embarrassed stories are mostly funnier and creepier on *This American Life* than on the page, where you can begin to think he went begging for his Wrong Guy for the Wrong Job assignments. Thus the center of gravity here is not Rakoff at all, not as our guide to the absurdities of contemporary speech and mores or weird cool person. "The Best Medicine" is a report on the Sixth Annual U.S. Comedy Arts Festival in Aspen, Colo., where the self-congratulation of the event—Eric Idle: "They are the finest people in the world, aren't they, comedians?"—leads Rakoff to question the legitimacy of his own birth: "Yes, not like those pushy, conceited Doctors Without Borders, and don't get me started about that bitch Daw Aung San Suu Kyi." "There's really no arguing with Preston Sturges," he says, referring to *Sullivan's Travels* and its insistence that all people want out of art is something to take their mind off life, "but it bears repeating that even though laughter may well be 'the best medicine,' it is not, in point of fact, actual medicine." This won't win Rakoff cheers from the positive-attitude crowd, but he's already had cancer.

4 ■ Katastrophywife, *Amusia* **(EFA/ Almafame)** In 1990 Babes in Toyland of Minneapolis—singer and guitarist Kat Bjelland, drummer Lori Barbero, bassist Michelle Leon—released *Spanking Machine* on the local Twin/Tone label. It was as free and fierce a sound as anyone found in the post–Sex Pistols era—and there was nothing like Bjelland screaming, as an effect, as an event, an event taking place in one of her songs or off the record, in the street outside wherever the group was playing that night. Neal Karlen's *Babes in Toyland: The Making and Selling of a Rock and Roll Band* chronicled what happened next: a lifeless, overworried album on a major label, a "triumphant spot on the 1993 Lollapalooza, the most prestigious tour in rock and roll," and that was that. Now Bjelland has a new trio with at least three puns in its name, and how her head stays on her body I have no idea.

5 ■ *Oxford American* **No. 40** The bad news is that the passionately edited bimonthly literary magazine from Oxford, Miss., is going quarterly. It's not a shock. To take nothing away from Roy Blount Jr. and his "Gone Off up North," when the hardest bite in your pages comes from your humor columnist, too many other people are biting their tongues. The good news is that the Fifth Annual Music Issue is probably the best so far. Witness after witness steps forth to testify in favor of an ignored, forgotten, misjudged or misunderstood pioneer, obscure genius or contemporary prophet without honor. From James Hughes on the Gants ("Mississippi's Beatles") to Robert Bowman on Linda Lyndell ("The Woman Who Saved Stax") to Bill Friskics-Warren on Bill Nettles ("protorockabilly" from the late '30s) to Billy Bob Thornton on his new album to David Eason on country singer-songwriter Steve Young and more, more, more, the reader can't wait to hear what the writers are talking about, and the 22-track CD included with the magazine gives you instant access to crushing disappointment. Mississippi's Beatles are really Mississippi's Beau Brummels (but odd enough to send me to the record store in search of *Road Runner! The Best of the Gants* on Sundazed). Billy Bob Thornton's "Ring of Fire" is absolutely terrible. Steve Young is still a bore. In other words, the CD will save you the money the writers had almost convinced you to spend. Not that they would take a single word back: these are fans ripping off their shirts to show you who's really tattooed on their chests. They don't care if you agree with them, they just want you to look, and why not? Why shouldn't the writing be more convincing than the music? But then you come across something as emotionally tricky, as musicologically intense, as Tom Piazza's "A Light Went on and He Sang," on country blues founder Charley Patton, and even if you've been listening to Patton for years, you know that when you close the magazine you'll cue up a disc and hear the man for the first time.

6 ▪ **Gin Blossoms, "Found Out About You," from *New Miserable Experience* (A&M, 1992)** "Yes, the Blossoms are still broken up," reads the Unofficial Gin Blossoms Home Page, "but you can follow the former members in their new efforts . . ." Do they hold up so well because singer Robin Wilson still sounds not only miserable, but as if nothing could possibly have changed, including the world? Or because songwriter Doug Hopkins included his 1993 suicide in his 1992 songs?

7 ▪ **Clash, *Take It or Leave It* (Wise/P.F.P. vinyl bootleg)** Recorded May 8, 1977, in Manchester. Awful sound. And when they go into "J.A."—the Maytals' "Pressure Drop"—you can hear the world stand up and change.

8–9 ▪ **Maggie Greenwald, director, *Songcatcher* & *Music From and Inspired by the Motion Picture "Songcatcher"* (Vanguard)** The movie never gets out of its clothes, thanks to Janet McTeer, whose imperious Lily (When can I take a *bath*? McTeer seems to be asking every five minutes) is loosely based on Maud Karpeles, who with Cecil Sharp in 1916 to 1918 collected more than 1,600 variants of 500 songs from 281 singers in the Appalachian highlands. One

remarkable scene: country singer Iris DeMent as a mountain woman offering the collector "When First Unto This Country"— the words are prosaic, the feeling loaded into them otherworldly—just after her husband has sold their farm for 50 cents an acre to oily Earl Giddens (David Patrick Kelley), local representative of McFarland Coal. Another: after a brawl at a dance, Giddens, beaten to a pulp by hero Tom Bledsoe (a comfortably beefy Aidan Quinn), pulls himself to his feet, closes his coat over his pistol and launches into "Oh Death." He walks off into the night, leaving the song to whoever wants to finish it—not, luckily, the red-robed Klan leader who declaims it like a speech in the Coen Brothers' *O Brother, Where Art Thou?* What are the chances of this ancient, bottomless song turning up in two general-release movies in one year?

DeMent's performance, as thin and brittle as anything she's ever recorded, is listed as "Pretty Saro" on the soundtrack album; "Oh Death" is sung by Kelley, Hazel Dickens and Bobby McMillon as "Conversation With Death." There are other fine moments, among them Rosanne Cash's "Fair and Tender Ladies" and, from Emmylou Harris' florid "Barbara Allen" to Allison Moorer's horrid "Moonshiner," too many songs sung to the mirror. For a better song-catching film, seek out David Hoffman's early-60s *Music Makers of the Blue Ridge* (Varied Directions) if you can find it; for the songs behind the story from people who never left where the songs came from, walk into any good record store and look for Doug and Jack Wallin, *Family Songs and Stories from the North Carolina Mountains* (Smithsonian Folkways), which has no flies on it.

10 ▪ **David Thomas, David Johansen, Steve Earle and Philip Glass, "Kassie Jones," from Hal Wilner's Harry Smith Project (Royce Hall, UCLA, April 26)** The big all-star jam to close the all-star concert, and thanks to Glass, who sounds as if he's playing underwater, and as if he grew up doing it— "Mr. Boogie," Thomas says disdainfully, after announcing the supergroup as Crosby,

Stills, Nash & Young and trying and failing to figure out who's who ("Love the one you're with, baby!" someone shouts)—the singers disappear right into the song. You can sense them attempting to hold back, to maintain some shred of individuality while exploring how a railroad man who actually lived turned into a figment of the common imagination, but the only way to tell the story is to let it tell itself.

SEPTEMBER 4, 2001

1 ▪ Great Pop Moments (That Should Have Happened Even if They Didn't Division): Valerie Mass, "People" column (*Denver Post*, Aug. 6) "**Elton John** spilled the beans about his former liquor-soaked, drugged-out life in an interview with *The London Mirror*. . . . John said he met **Bob Dylan** and **George Harrison** at a party he was hosting in Los Angeles but was unable to talk any sense to them. 'I'd had quite a few martinis and [God] knows how much cocaine. So I started babbling on about how [Dylan] had to come up to my room and try on my clothes . . .'"

2 ▪ Bob Dylan, "Summer Days," from *Love and Theft* (Columbia) Speaking of trying on new clothes—four years ago, Dylan's celebrated *Time Out of Mind* mapped a country of abandoned roads and emptied cities, and nothing like what's happening here could have happened there. "*Waaaal*"—in this song, "Well" is always "Waaaal," "Yes" is always "Yaaaaaaassss," pure minstrel diction, as befits an album seemingly named for Eric Lott's 1993 study *Love and Theft: Blackface Minstrelsy and the American Working Class*—"Waaaaal, I'm standing on a table, I'm proposing a toast to the King," the singer shouts from inside a roadhouse where a Western Swing band is running a jitterbug beat as if it's twirling a rope. On the dance floor women are flipping in the air and couples snap back at each other like towels in a locker room. The singer high-steps his way across the room, Stetson topping his Nudie suit. How much proof do you want that the night can't go wrong? "Why don't you break my heart

one more time," he says happily to the woman at his side, "just for good luck?" He stretches out the last word as if he can't bear to give it up.

3 ▪ Erase Errata, *Other Animals* (Troubleman Unlimited) This four-woman San Francisco combo sings and plays in the clipped, impatient manner of the 1980s Leeds punk outfit Delta 5—until at the end of this first album, with "Dexterity Is #2," they're breaking up their sound in the manner of Gang of Four, which sparked Delta 5. The difference is that Delta 5 and Gang of Four premised their music in their leftist-feminist milieu while Erase Errata's sound comes free of any political context— anything a listener could assume as a premise of what they're impatient about, or what the break-up of their sound might signify. With borrowed voices they're beginning their own story from the beginning, and it's a bright, scratchy experiment—with one eyebrow raised in sardonic doubt.

4 ▪ Gillian Welch, *Time (The Revelator)* (Acony) New old-timey singer Welch had the Walker Evans FSA look down from the start. Now, with sententious, self-absorbed singing, in a tone that sounds weirdly like David Baerwald—though God knows without his passion—she comes forth as barefoot seer, offering oddly abstract songs about Elvis' death and Lincoln's assassination. The idea is that both events are best understood, or felt, as folklore: the Elvis song is put to the tune of "Casey Jones," while Welch's second Lincoln song, "Ruination Day Part 2," explicitly compares Lincoln to both Casey Jones and the *Titanic* and for good measure rewrites "500 Miles" to shoehorn Lincoln's funeral train into the number as well. This might be interesting if Welch didn't sing as if she figured all this out a long time ago and can't be bothered to get excited about it now.

5 ▪ Thalia Zedek, *Been Here and Gone* (Matador) Or, for her band Come, "Came and Went." There's a dead spot for a Leonard Cohen song, Zedek's own tunes in Marianne Faithfull/Weimar cabaret mode when she seems bored, but mostly you might hear a singer-guitarist wondering what would happen if she followed the Rolling Stones' "Moonlight Mile" to the very end.

6 ▪ Madonna, "La Isla Bonita," from *Madonna: Drowned World Tour* (HBO, Aug. 26) In her Eva Peron getup, but looking more like the love child of Marlene Dietrich and Leni Riefenstahl, finally she came up with an oasis in a desert of strutted shtick: a good beat everyone could actually dance to.

7 ▪ Heavenly, *Heavenly Versus Satan* (K reissue) This column shamelessly worships the Oxford ground Amelia Fletcher floats above, be it with Talulah Gosh from 1986 or Heavenly since 1990, when this album, never before released in the U.S., was made. "Shallow" is the perfect moment: a modest guitar pulse, no high notes, a sweetness that can't last and wouldn't be worth the time if it could.

8–9 ▪ "The Presidential Pen" (*New York Times*, Aug. 8) & "Satan Gets 2-Year, $6.8 Million Deal" (*New York Times*, Aug. 9) And speaking of Satan, why is it that the latter headline led a mere two-inch item, while Bill Clinton's book deal was covered like a new pardons scandal, with padded news reports followed by arch Op-Ed page lampoons and an editorial that for all of its schoolmarmish distaste ("The one thing that would be most helpful now, to all of us, is candor") had already collapsed into gibberish? "It's hard to tell just what Mr. Clinton will sound like in print," the editorialist wrote. "The man is most himself when winging it in front of a crowd, which means that this may be one of the few presidential memoirs ever written before a live audience." Monty Python had Thomas Hardy doing that years ago with *The Return of the Native*, but somehow I don't think that's the reference here.

10 ▪ John Moore, "Lucinda Williams Gives Stellar, if Subdued, Concert" (*Denver Post*, Aug. 9) "Williams was genial but somber, and not as talkative as usual. Ironically, it was when she began dedicating songs to her favorite dead musicians that the pace picked up . . ."

1 ▪ Handsome Family, *Twilight* (Carrot Top) As he sings the words Rennie Sparks has written, the fatalism in Bret Sparks' voice now comes in a deeper drone than ever before. He sits in a diner watching the crowds gather across the highway. He tells you why. It's a terrible story, but for the moment the way he's telling it is worse: is he even alive? That one song later he turns up living in a park is no shock. But "I Know You Are There" is a shock. Enveloping the stalker in the lyrics, walking right over the suicide who's singing, is the voice of another singer, crawling out of the others and leaving their bodies by the road like old clothes: a man speaking in waltz time the way you might imagine a president late in the 19th century would deliver a patriotic address. It all feels right, clear, heroic, simple, everyday.

2–3 ▪ Terry Zwigoff, director, *Ghost World* (United Artists) & *Ghost World: Original Motion Picture Soundtrack* (Shanachie) Clomping in her Doc Martens, Thora Birch as self-consciously outsider high school graduate Enid finds out what's on the other side of outside when she lets Steve Buscemi's old-timey culture fetishist Seymour sell her an LP at a garage sale. As the warped vinyl spins on her little box—and you can pick up the whispery sound of the warp on the soundtrack album—she hears Skip James' 1931 "Devil Got My Woman," hears the high, otherworldly voice from Mississippi promising "Nothing but the devil, change my baby's mind," believes it, and, lying back, staring at the ceiling, moves only to put the tone arm back on the same track, all night long.

Missing Britney Spears' "Oops! . . . I Did It Again" and the Backstreet Boys as examples of the "horribly contrived commercial slop" Zwigoff couldn't afford ("I wanted this music to heighten the alienation and fit into the general feeling of paranoia and cynicism I was attempting to create"), the soundtrack offers surprises: Mohammed Rafi's "Jaan Pehechaan Ho," the fabulous rock 'n' roll dance number from the 1965 Indian film *Gumnaam* that's running on Enid's TV as the movie opens, or "Pickin' Cotton Blues." In a sports bar, after a legendary ancient black bluesman has been ignored by the crowd, a young white trio comes on, announcing it's going to jam on the real authentic true-life Delta sound, then leaps into a ridiculous number written by Zwigoff, which doesn't come off as remotely so awful as it's supposed to.

What does: the end of the film, when, with both Enid's life and his in shreds, Seymour speaks earnestly to his therapist, hoping he's turned the corner, that he won't have to see her anymore. "Let's start with that next week," she says. He leaves, and as the therapist closes the door her face falls in disgust.

4 ▪ **Bobbie Ann Mason, "Three-Wheeler,"** from *Zigzagging Down a Wild Trail* **(Random House)** A woman has let two vaguely threatening young boys talk her into letting them clean up her yard; Mason slides her down the situation until it opens into what's really on her mind.

"'How much dirt have you boys moved? I'm not paying you for Sunday-school lessons.'

"'We need your riding mower to pull our wagon, so it'll be faster.'

"'That's silly.'

"'We can make twice as many loads.'

"The idea tempted her. She could get the mower out. She had filled it with gas before the yard-man's two-hour visit. A two-hour yard man ought to be twice as good as a sixty-minute man, she thought, remembering the raunchy old song. She always thought it should be the theme song for *Sixty Minutes*. Her mind was flying around loose."

5 ▪ **Alison Krauss & Union Station, *New Favorite* (Rounder)** Not only does she continue to get thinner and blonder with each new release, now the accompanying photos have her braless in a red lace top and hanging out in a diner with her all-male band—yes, we get the idea. When the songs are good she continues to drift away from what-

ever's obvious in a tune, but the numbers that might stick hardest—Bob Lucas' "Momma Cried," the traditional "Bright Sunny South" and "The Boy Who Wouldn't Hoe Corn"—are sung by guitarist Dan Tyminski, perhaps best known, or unknown, as the voice George Clooney lip-synchs for "Man of Constant Sorrow" in *O Brother, Where Art Thou?* Sounding weathered and beefy, he relaxes into the age of the songs, shakes hands with Dock Boggs, then disappears back into the band like a trick of the light.

6 ▪ **Morgan Neville, writer and director,** *The Hitmakers: The Teens Who Stole Pop Music,* **in "Pop Goes the Music Week" (***Biography,* **A&E, Aug. 27)** In a dream tour of the Brill Building, you saw a lot of stories about assembly-line songwriting and the invention of the girl group told as they've been told before, though they've never been told better. What you hadn't seen before: Mary Weiss-Stokes, lead singer of the Shangri-Las, her hair still straight and blonde, her eyes fiery through wire-rimmed glasses, speaking with pride and dignity of how, 35 years ago, she put everything she had and more into "Remember (Walking in the Sand)," "Leader of the Pack," and "I Can Never Go Home Anymore"—and then Shangri-Las' producer and songwriter Shadow Morton, who as he looked back seemed to be looking around corners. He was Mohair Sam: as a smile played on his lips, behind tinted glasses his eyes were lying even when his tongue told the truth. Weirder: *Biography* host Harry Smith, looking too much like the high school principal and secret rock 'n' roll demon Michael Ironside played in the great *Hello Mary Lou: Prom Night II.*

7 ▪ **World Trade Organization/International Monetary Fund/World Bank/Group of Seven, *Junichiro Koizumi Presents My Favorite Elvis Songs* (BMG Funhouse)** The super-cool, super-popular, super-nationalist prime minister of Japan wants it known that Elvis' voice "eases my fatigue," that "these days, I feel a sort of healing power from his gospels," and that he and Elvis share the same

birthday. For the cover of *Presents*, he's digitally posed right next to the Big E circa 1956, looking for all the world like a Washington tourist posing next to a life-size cutout of an American president. The song selection—which does not include "King of the Whole Wide World," but which does include "Are You Lonesome Tonight," Boris Yeltsin's favorite Elvis song—is true fan's work. With "Wear My Ring Around My Neck" the closest thing to a rocker, which is not very close, the Big J goes for such glorious but ignored ballads as "I Was the One" (flip side of "Heartbreak Hotel"), "Don't" and "You Gave Me a Mountain," not to mention the Martin Luther King Jr. tribute "If I Can Dream," "Can't Help Falling in Love" and "Hawaiian Wedding Song." So where's the karaoke disc?

8 ■ **Randy Newman, "The Beehive State,"** from *Randy Newman Creates Something New Under the Sun* (Reprise, 1968) Given Salt Lake City's purchase of the 2002 Winter Olympics, this song is sure to get more airplay than it's ever had before, which is none: as the singer says, speaking to the nation and sure he will never be heard, "We gotta tell this country about Utah, because nobody seems to know." Which may not change: as *San Francisco Chronicle* sportswriter John Crumpacker put it on Sept. 7 in his "Olympic Beat" column, "Utah is known as the Beehive State for the archaic hairdos worn by waitresses in time-warp coffee shops."

9 ■ *Old Time Texas String Bands, Volume One: Texas Farewell* (County) Opening with Jim Tate's high-stepping 1929 title tune, the set makes it to the back room of the worst bar in Dallas by the fourth cut, the 1928 "Blues in the Bottle" by Prince Albert Hunt—a sometime blackface fiddler who was shot to death at the age of 30 for stealing another man's wife. He growls through dirty teeth, rolls on the floor, punches his fist through his stovepipe hat, passes out, gets up, falls down, and after every verse kicks up a dance-call with a single downstroke so fat and sweet you're ready to hire him to clean up your yard.

10 ■ **George W. Bush, "Address to the Nation" (Sept. 11)** "The American economy will be open for business," he said. In his brief, poorly written speech there was no empathy, no outrage, only a nervous attempt to project competence, to assume his own legitimacy, but behind the big desk he grew smaller with every word. Compared to this Rudolph Giuliani seemed like Churchill.

OCTOBER 1, 2001

1 ■ **Steve Weinstein, e-mail, Sept. 15** "Incredibly bad taste, or just another radio station on autopilot? Driving I-89 into Vermont today, I heard the local oldies outlet playing Petula Clark's 'Downtown.'"

2 ■ **Shangri-Las,** *The Very Best Of* **(Goldenlane)** The Sept. 17 edition of this column noted the striking present-day interview in the Aug. 27 A&E documentary *The Hitmakers: The Teens Who Stole Pop Music* with Mary L. Stokes—in the mid-'60s, as Mary Weiss, the lead singer of the Shangri-Las. Stokes is now a project manager for Furniture Consultants in the Flatiron district of Manhattan. "I don't know why anyone would be interested in my experiences of September 11, 2001," she wrote me on Sept. 22 in response to a query. "So many people shared these experiences. I don't understand why anyone would care to hear my story." Maybe because Stokes writes in a voice you can hear echoing from the songs she sang, which people still carry with them.

"On the morning of September 11th I was downtown walking to a meeting a few blocks north of the Trade Center. As I crossed the street I heard a sound that I had never heard before. It was a jet airliner, lower than I have ever seen except for being on the parkway near LaGuardia when a plane comes in for a landing. It was so close to the surrounding buildings that everyone just stood still and stared, as the sound echoed off the stone walls. It all happened so fast. We watched the plane hit the first tower. At first everyone thought it was some kind of bizarre airline accident. There was so much debris spilling into the air, and fireballs exploding.

"I just stood there frozen in my tracks. I could not believe what I was seeing, and I kept pinching my cheek to wake up. (I have since heard this same reaction from many other people following this disaster.) I could not believe that there were 18 minutes between the first and second plane. It seemed to be a much shorter time. There were young women crying. I tried to console a few of them. Only when the second plane hit did everyone realize that New York was being attacked by terrorists. As I kept staring at the building, I was aware of many structural uprights now missing, and had a strong gut feeling to get out of the area. Another fireball shot out, and people started running. I held onto a street post in order not to be trampled by the crowd, then began walking uptown. There was no cell phone service. All the pay phones had long lines. There was no bus or subway service.

"While I continued walking, I heard a loud crack, turned around and saw one of the buildings coming down. People were crying, screaming and running everywhere. The cloud of debris from the collapse just missed me. I walked to my office uptown. Only when I saw my co-workers did I start to cry and shake.

"Everyone that I know is alive. Many people I know were not that fortunate. There are so many people dead. So many people hurting. So many businesses ruined. All of the people I speak to in New York are on some kind of roller coaster ride. It is so hard to focus on anything, much less conduct business. The nation is wounded, and it will take a very long time to heal. I know that America grew up on September 11, 2001. Where is our national security? How in the world could a plane ever fly directly over the Pentagon or White House?

"The fire department, police and EMS workers are so brave. No human being should ever have to see the things that these men and women have viewed during this catastrophe. They are extraordinary human beings.

"New York will never be the same. The United States will never be the same. For that matter I will never be the same person.

"We all want to go to sleep, and wake up and realize it's been a bad dream.

"It's not."

3 ▪ Karlheinz Stockhausen on art for art's sake (*New York Times*, Sept. 19) "Mr. Stockhausen responded to a question about the attacks on the United States by saying: 'What happened there is—they all have to rearrange their brains now—is the greatest work of art ever. That characters can bring about in one act what we in music cannot dream of, that people practice madly for 10 years, completely, fanatically, for a concert and then die. That is the greatest work of art for the whole cosmos. I could not do that. Against that, we, composers, are nothing.'" Creepy, in its privilege, its insulation—but not more so than novelist Rick Moody on the massacres as "a web of narratives" (*Salon*, Sept. 18) or critic John Leonard's insistence that no terrorist could possibly have a mind as interesting as that of a novelist writing about one (*Salon*, Sept. 21).

4 ▪ *Mulholland Dr.*, directed by David Lynch, written by Joyce Eliason and Lynch (Universal, opening Oct. 12) Early in the picture, a movie director with a teen-theme project is running auditions, dressing sophisticated, tough-as-nails stars up in chiffon to lip-synch to Connie Stevens' 1960 "Sixteen Reasons" and Linda Scott's 1961 "I've Told Every Little Star." Though at this point *Mulholland Dr.* still seems like a regular story with different characters, you already get the feeling that there's something off, that the pieces aren't fitting together: that there's more happening, more at stake, than what's on the screen would seem to justify.

How the pieces don't fit together is the story the film tells. In an astonishingly controlled, extremist performance, Naomi Watts (previous credits include *Children of the Corn IV*) plays Betty Elms, a cute blonde from a small town in Ontario who arrives in Los Angeles with hopes of becoming an actress; how Elms leaves, or as who, if she leaves at all, is the mystery. At the start, she walks out of LAX with stars in her eyes. The shot is both iconic and clichéd, silly and scary, because the radiance in Watts' face, communicating the depth of her character's commitment, or insanity, pushes the shot almost into abstraction.

That's true for every scene Watts is in—most shockingly, her first reading. We've just seen her stumble through the dumb soap-style script with mystery woman-cum-roommate Rita, played by Laura Harring; they can barely get through the lines for laughing at them. Elms shows up at the studio and is paired with a bored, middle-aged actor; within seconds, with the crew standing around and trying to pretend their eyes aren't bugging out of their sockets, Elms has taken the man to levels of sexual tension so delicate and intense you can barely stand to watch. Where did this come from? What's next?

It came from a cute blonde arriving at LAX with stars in her eyes and pages from *Hollywood Babylon* flying through her brain—and what's next is a night at the Club Silencio. Rita wakes up at two in the morning speaking in Spanish; she wakes Betty, and insists they leave for what turns out to be an all-night lip-synch palace. The dank, rotting theater is pure Hollywood: street-level, scag Hollywood. A few junkies, alcoholics and other insomniacs dot the seats. A man appears and announces the concept—everything is taped. But he and another man move so convincingly to the sounds behind them it's as if they've called them into being. The sense of displacement hits Elms like a disease: suddenly she is shaking in her seat like a spiritualist's table, shaking as if her bones are about to come out of her mouth, her skinny body invaded, close to bursting. Rita holds her still, and then a honey-haired woman with yellow eye makeup comes onto the stage and begins to move her lips to Rebekah Del Rio's "Llorando," a transcendent Spanish version

of Roy Orbison's "Crying." She will collapse before the song is over—it goes on—but by then the song has already done such damage to the women listening they don't even notice that she's on the floor.

5 ■ **Leiber & Stoller Present the Spark Records Story** (Ace) Try-anything Los Angeles R&B from 1954–55, when two East Coast Jews who thought they were black were writing, producing, hustling. Many treasures if you love the style, and lost classics even if you don't: the Honey Bears' fast and hard "One Bad Stud," Big Boy Groves & Band's "I Gotta New Car"—until the bank takes it back. Disappointment: Gil Bernal's "King Solomon's Blues," just because it doesn't live up to its title. I think Taj Mahal's "The Celebrated Walking Blues," cut in the same town 12 years later, would, somehow.

6 ■ **Elizabeth Elmore, "You Blink," on the Elmore/Robert Nanna Split EP (Troubleman Unlimited)** "I knew enough to keep my mouth shut"—from the leader of Sarge, her voice smaller than ever, its demands on the world as big.

7 ■ **Firesign Theater, *The Bride of Firesign* (Rhino)** The surrealists loved the Marx Brothers; the four Angelenos of the Firesign Theater are what the Marx Brothers might have been if they were art theorists, or what the surrealists might have been if they had an American sense of humor. In the late 1960s and early '70s, they made comedy records that exploded the genre, infinitely layered stacks of commercial noise, unproduced TV shows, old radio plays and real elections, moving so fast that a stray pun could open up an entire new subplot, or drop the bottom out of whatever plot you thought you were following. But it was the Vietnam War, Firesign member Peter Bergman once said, that was at the root of it all. Did he mean the group's instinct for confrontation, their understanding that they too were at war, at war against the war, with whatever weapons they had? Or did he mean the absurdity that comes with the most justifiable of wars along with the most criminal? After the disarmingly low-key

Just Folks . . . A Firesign Chat in 1977—an
album that, like all of their true work,
could take years to reveal itself—the troupe
went into the wilderness; they didn't pull
themselves out of the swamp of self-parody
until *Eat or Be Eaten* in 1985, and even
that evaporated after a few plays. That they
have now made a record that doesn't immediately explain itself may be a very bad
sign.

8 ■ Luna, "Going Home," from *Bewitched*
(Elektra, 1994) Michael J. Kramer writes
from Chapel Hill: "I can't get the lyrics of
this dumb Luna song out of my head: 'The
Chrysler Building is talking to the Empire
State; the Twin Towers are talking to each
other; saying, "All is forgiven, I love her
still"; and we're home, home, goin' home.'
I don't quite know if it fits, but it was always
in my head walking down toward the Knitting Factory with those two big towers hovering above, back when I was living in New
York. And it's still in my head now."

9 ■ *America: A Tribute to Heroes,* telethon for families of Sept. 11 victims (Sept. 21,
all networks) On a very middle-aged, anti–
rock 'n' roll show, Fred Durst of Limp Biz-
kit came across with Pink Floyd's "Wish
You Were Here," as did guitarist Mike
Campbell inside Tom Petty's "I Won't Back
Down." Playing a pipe organ in the background as Eddie Vedder found his way into
"Long Road" as if he didn't know everything
the tune had to say, Neil Young looked so
old you could imagine he'd crawled to the
stage all the way from the Oklahoma Dust
Bowl in the '30s—though that was also the
impression he gave onstage at Woodstock in
1969. But it was Wyclef Jean and the Dixie
Chicks who hit the high notes. Natalie
Maines has a gorgeous voice, but with
the new "I Believe in Love" it was also questioning, wondering what its own beauty
was worth. It was one voice carrying the
whole of the country style from the 19th
century into a present that no longer
existed, bringing a momentary peace of
mind into a present that was now all future.
Jean caught the heart of "Redemption
Song," Bob Marley's greatest composition;

it's the melody that sweeps you up, because it's the melody that holds the song's
immeasurable pain. But this night Jean also
found the bravery in the music, and that
became the music: the sense that to stand
in public this night, in this way, for this
purpose, might indeed be to risk your life.

Earlier, Jim Carrey spoke of evacuees in
the World Trade Center carrying a woman
in her wheelchair down flight after flight of
stairs. "We found a courage," Carrey quoted
one of them, "we didn't know we had." It
was, Susan Sontag said in an ice-cold comment in the Sept. 24 *New Yorker*, "a morally
neutral virtue." She was speaking of "an attack on the world's self-proclaimed super-
power, undertaken as a consequence of
specific American alliances and actions"
(some people can read minds, some people
can't), stressing the courage of the attackers
as opposed to those who, like American
bombers over Iraq, or Belgrade or Kosovo,
"kill from beyond the range of retaliation."
Presumably she meant that courage can be
put to the service of purposes morally good
or morally evil—as can sex, the accumulation of wealth, the equitable distribution of
resources, or rhetorical eloquence. What
virtue for Sontag would not be morally
neutral? I can't read minds, but I'd bet on
something like, you know, the literary
imagination. Sept. 21 was just songs, rich
and impoverished, dead and alive.

10 ■ Cecily Marcus, report on United Airlines Flight 522 from Chicago to Buenos Aires
(Sept. 16) "On United's third day of flying
after the attacks the movies showing were:
Shrek, Crocodile Dundee, A Knight's Tale
and *The Manchurian Candidate.* Can you
believe that? I was too afraid to watch it."

OCTOBER 15, 2001

1 ■ Media crisis logos (Sept. 11–Oct. 7)
CNN: "America Under Attack," "Target:
Terrorism"; MSNBC: "Attack on America,"
"America on Alert," "America Strikes
Back"; Fox News: "America's New War,"
"America Strikes Back"; *Newsweek*: "War on
Terror"; *New York Times*: "A Day of Terror,"

"After the Attacks," "A Nation Challenged"; the *Onion*: "Holy Fucking Shit."

2 ▪ New Order, *Get Ready* (London) What a dull title. What a great record. When Ian Curtis of the dark-end-of-the-street Manchester combo Joy Division killed himself in 1980, guitarist Bernard Sumner, bassist Peter Hook and drummer Stephen Morris decided to "keep the band together." Instead of riding their already sainted name they changed it, added keyboard player Gillian Gilbert and set out to redefine dance music as a love unto death, as a merging of disco, romance and apocalypse. From "Temptation" through the seemingly countless remixes of "Bizarre Love Triangle" they soared through space and time. But that was all a long time ago.

Get Ready is an album of muscle, with Sumner's old guitar-as-bass sound underpinning rhythms that feel as untested as a new car. In the jumps and changes, though, are moments of beauty so full and yet hard to catch they are more ominous than promising, more fleeting than present. When you go back to find them again, you can't: the churning "Turn My Way" is less a composition, or a jam, than a glimpse into something that can't be described, only pointed to. The songs don't hold still, don't hold shape—until "Rock the Shack," which is the romantic apocalypse banged out in a garage, the teenage musicians trying out their sneers and volume, imagining a battle of the bands with the Swingin' Medallions.

3 ▪ *Come Together: A Night for John Lennon* (TNT, Oct. 2) Compared to this—from Yolanda Adams plus 12th Beatle Billy Preston turning "Imagine" into a mugging to Dustin Hoffman's crinkly insecure-superstar grin—the Sept. 21 *America: A Tribute to Heroes* telethon was "Sympathy for the Devil."

4 ▪ Macy Gray, *The Id* (Epic) This is seductive, entrancing: a spangled and physical follow-up to Gray's one-woman soul explosion of the 1999 *On How Life Is*. But that record communicated both mastery and desperation. Here the entitlement of the diva begins to sneak in—no matter how threatening or weird *The Id* is, or self-consciously tries to be. There's a quality in Gray's music that's reminiscent of the heroine of Gayl Jones' stone-hard 1975 first novel, *Corregidora*, about a mutilated blues singer—it's in the constriction in Gray's throat, the sense of something essential always held back, something it would be death to reveal, something that's none of your business. It's that refusal to come across—to offer the "I love you, I'm yours" that every real diva throws to her audience like a handful of petals—that song after song pulls against the alienation of the role Gray is now playing, or anyway trying out.

5 ▪ Scott Leeper/Clear Ink, *Behind the Opera* (KDFC-FM, San Francisco, Oct. 4) ". . . on 'Behind the Opera,'" intoned the familiarly concerned, therapeutic voice, promising folly, ruin and redemption. "Floria Tosca had it all: looks, fame and the love of painter and political activist Mario Cavaradossi. But . . ." Wow, I thought, VH1 is *franchising* this stuff! I almost missed the first cut-in, a woman speaking with disdain: "She was convinced Mario was cheating on her. And . . ." And then this guy with a gravelly voice came on: "First she sells herself to Police Chief Scarpia to save her boyfriend. Then she turns around and stabs the chief with a dinner knife! Not your classic career move." I couldn't wait for the rest—which turned out to be *"Tosca*. Now at the San Francisco Opera."

6 ▪ Dr. Cornel West, *Sketches of My Culture* (Artemis) Pictured on the front of his CD clutching a mike while emoting so deeply he may be slightly wrinkling his three-piece suit, the academic celebrity (that's not a description, that's his profession) raps: "In all modesty," one can read on his Web site, "this project constitutes a watershed moment in musical history." Better than his books.

7 ▪ Firesign Theater, *The Bride of Firesign* (Rhino) It's not the Philip Marlowe meets postmodern architecture joke ("Frank Gehry has ruined my building!" cries the private eye. "He climbs the 13 chain-link steps to his work place," says the narrator fatalistically). It's not the rerun of the recent Los Angeles mayor's race, which pits a career criminal against a career cop. This time through, it's the obscure, perfectly tossed off Nervous Norvous reference, which is to the 1956 all-time car-crash song "Transfusion" (you can find it on the Rhino set *Hot Rods & Custom Classics: Cruisin' Songs & Highway Hits*): "Pass the chalice to me, Alice."

8 ▪ **Wedding Present, "Falling," from** *hit parade 1* **(First Warning, 1992)** Heard on Radio K, Minneapolis ("Real College Radio"): the occasionally necessary reminder that punk exists, as a principle of deconstruction from the inside of a sound. You can pick up a tune that's already something else, as with this originally delicate, elegant Julee Cruise number (lyrics by David Lynch, music by Angelo Badalamenti): one gorgeous ache. Or you can simply listen to "Smells Like Teen Spirit" and hear the principle applied not to an extant composition but to a whole music, a whole culture, a whole world. Drenched in *Twin Peaks* mysticism, "Falling" is about the acceptance of death, the death wish that's the real secret hidden in *Twin Peaks*, but the prettiness of Cruise's singing, her restraint in the face of an absolute, allows you to forget what the music is saying. David Gedge's Velvet Underground riff repetition tribute band Wedding Present batters and smashes at the tune like thugs kicking a drunk on the street. They don't cover the tune, they cover the title: everything in the music falls down, falls to ruin. How does the melody survive the wreckage? By using itself to rebuild the song.

9 ▪ **Louis Menand, "Holden at Fifty"** **(*New Yorker*, Oct. 1)** "Once, you did ride a carousel. It seemed as though it would last forever," Menand concludes, trying to add a graceful, elegiac note to yet another of his screeds against youth culture and its diseased adult residue, nostalgia. But he can't get past received ideas: "You go to a dance where a new pop song is playing, and for the rest of your life hearing that song triggers the same emotion." Thoughtless and

reductionist, assuming that pop songs are by definition so vapid they are incapable of acquiring new meaning, or revealing new tones in the face of new events, new times, changed listeners—and assuming that any listener stupid enough to be caught by a song is incapable of thinking, or of responding to a changed world in a different way— Menand only digs his hole deeper.

"It comes on the radio and you think, *That's when things were truly fine.* [Gentle Reader: Have you ever thought this?] You want to hear it again. You have become addicted. [This happens the first time you hear a song? That is, nostalgia, a.k.a. thatswhenthingsweretrulyfineism, is present as soon as a song appears? Or do you become addicted only *after* the song first appears on the radio? Discuss.] Youth culture acquires its poignancy through time, and so thoroughly you can barely see what it is in itself. [As opposed to real culture, which is transparent?] It's just, permanently, 'your song,' your story. When people who grew up in the nineteen-fifties give *The Catcher in the Rye* to their kids [Gentle Readers of a Certain Age: Have you ever done this?], it's like showing them an old photo album: *That's me.*

"It isn't, of course," Menand finishes. "Maybe the nostalgia of youth culture is completely spurious. Maybe it invites you to indulge in bittersweet memories of a childhood you never had, an idyll of Beach Boys songs and cheeseburgers and convertibles and teenage crushes which has been constructed by pop songs and television shows and movies, and bears little or no relation to any experience of your own." But it's not the fault of, say, the Beach Boys' "I Get Around"—which for California teenagers in 1964 did not construct but reported—that Menand, an Easterner ("I transferred to Berkeley, didn't like it, went back," he says of his university days), apparently did not experience what the song describes, or that for more than a quarter of a century he has made a career out of writing as if he, unlike most people who have been young, has never been embarrassed.

10 ▪ Henry Flynt, "Picket Stockhausen Concert!" in *In The Spirit of Fluxus*, ed. Janet Jenkins (Walker Art Center) Regarding composer Karlheinz Stockhausen's Sept. 16 pronouncement in Hamburg that the Sept. 11 terrorist attacks on New York City constituted "the greatest work of art for the whole cosmos": Sarah Vowell recalls that in 1964 Henry Flynt—the musician/theorist who for two weeks replaced John Cale in the early Velvet Underground, and who in the 1968 Realists handbill "OVERTHROW THE HUMAN RACE!!" would call for, among other things, "Starting a thermonuclear 'spasm' war that will decisively transform human consciousness (and possibly biology)"—issued a flier announcing a demonstration against an upcoming Stockhausen performance in New York. "Jazz [Black Music] is primitive . . . barbaric . . . beat and a few simple chords . . . garbage [or words to that effect]," Flynt quoted a 1958 Stockhausen lecture at Harvard. Flynt attacked intellectuals who promoted "The Laws of Music" ("Common Practice Harmony, 12-Tone, and all the rest, not to mention Concert etiquette"—"'Music' Which Will Enoble You to Listen to It'") and condemned Stockhausen precisely for his talent: "He is a fountainhead of 'ideas' to shore up the doctrine of white plutocratic European art's supremacy." "BUT THERE IS ANOTHER KIND OF INTELLECTUAL," Flynt insisted: "Maybe they happen to like Bo Diddley or the Everly Brothers." He concluded: "STOCKHAUSEN—PATRICIAN 'THEORIST' OF WHITE SUPREMACY: GO TO HELL."

Henry Flynt, 2001: finally released 1970s recordings *Graduation and Other New Country & Blues Music* (Ampersand). The theory was alive; the music wasn't. Stockhausen, Sept. 19: "The journalist in Hamburg completely ripped my statements out of a context."

OCTOBER 29, 2001

1 ▪ Kaleidoscope, "Please," from *Infinite Colours, Infinite Patterns—The Best of Kaleidoscope* (Edsel) It's no fun, the specter of—

the specter of SPECTRE stepping out of James Bond movies and into everyday life, leaving postal workers dead in Washington, the vaporized thousands brought back to life for a few paragraphs and then returned to nowhere each day in the *New York Times*, and whoever is next by whatever means are next. Songs that cut all the way down are too painful to put on when you know that's what's coming, and too real to take off when they're spinning. "*Please*," sing this 1960s Los Angeles psychedelic country-blues band, digging so far down into the mine of the word you can feel as if you'll never have the will to escape it. But the New Pornographers' "Letter to an Occupant" is still No. 1 on my chart.

2 ▪ A friend writes: "*People* magazine, 10/22: *Cuttin' Heads*, John Mellencamp (Columbia), reviewed by Chuck Arnold: 'Now that American flags are adorning every front porch, it's time to dust off the old John Mellencamp discs—mostly the ones where Cougar was still a part of his recording name. In the '80s he carried the banner for Americana, with a string of hit albums including . . .'

"Sorry—I just can't transcribe more. Flags on 'every front porch'? Even Mellencamp's 'little PINK houses'? Shouldn't John Ashcroft be looking into musicians by now? Mellencamp carried the 'banner' for the meretriciously titled radio format 'Americana'? This will probably come as a shock to—well, come to think of it, Gillian Welch and Wilco could use a shock. By the way, this is the same 'Johnny Cougar' whom I interviewed one night in L.A. at the Starwood Club in the '70s and who told me, 'This country has a big ol' heart, but it's also got politicians who'll break it every time.'"

3 ▪ Evelyn Nieves, "Bastion of Dissent Offers Tribute to One of Its Heroes" (*New York Times*, Oct. 22) Regarding a testimonial at the Oakland City Hall for Rep. Barbara Lee, "for being the only lawmaker in the House or the Senate to vote against granting" George Bush "the authority to use military force against terrorism": "Few here would argue that Ms. Lee would have re-

ceived this hearty a celebration anywhere in the country." Not that to the *New York Times* anywhere in California has ever really been part of the country.

4 ▪ William A. Shack, *Harlem in Montmartre: A Paris Jazz Story Between the Great Wars* (California) It's at the very end of this short book, in "Le Jazz Cold: The Silent Forties," that the late Berkeley anthropology professor gets to the Zazous: "By December 1941 these young people began appearing in cafes off the Champs-Elysées and the Latin Quarter. . . . In the metro you might see a young man or woman board a car, raise a finger in the air and say or cry 'Swing' and take a hop, before shouting 'Zazou, hé hé hé, za za zou.' Then three slaps on the hip, two shrugs of the shoulder, one turn of the head. Finished!"

They weren't serious jazz fans—with their flamboyant hairstyles and zoot-suit clothes, they were jitterbuggers. Soon the collaborationist press was calling for their heads—wasn't getting rid of scum what the Nazis were *for?*—and weren't a lot of these degenerate cosmopolitans obviously *Jews?* When in 1942 all Jews in Occupied France were forced to wear Yellow Stars, Shack writes, "Many non-Jews abhorred the decree and themselves wore a star on which they wrote BOUDDHISTE, GOÏ, or VICTOIRE"—Zazous wrote "SWING." Thugs cut their hair off. They had songs, like the 1943 "Ils Sont Zazous," written by Johnny Hess and M. Martelier, where a country notary arrives in Paris dressed in the formal business attire of about 1900, which in the provinces has never gone out of style—and in Nazi Paris finds himself the epitome of cool: "Hair in wild curls, eighteen-foot-high collar . . . a jacket that drags on the ground." "There resides the spirit of all Zazous," the tune ended: how many perished? How many went on, in the streets or watching from the cafés, to cross the line of the mid-century, to ride the next wave?

5 ▪ Jean-Michel Mension, *The Tribe: Conversations with Gérard Berréby and Francesco Milo*, translated from the French by Donald Nicholson-Smith (City Lights) A man swims back through rivers of alcohol to the Paris of the early 1950s, when he was a teenage delinquent with borrowed ideas in his head and cryptic slogans painted on his pants. As an intense and subjective account of the creation of a subculture, this is also a true work of bookmaking, with illustrations and marginalia so completely contextualizing the story it doesn't matter if you have no idea who any of the characters are or why anyone is talking about them now. With a passage like this—just a man in his mid-'60s sitting in the same café that today is just across the street from the Mabillion Métro station—you don't stop: "The real neighborhood was here, at the Café de Mabillion, on the Boulevard Saint-Germain. Not the Dupont-Latin. The Dupont-Latin was the port, or the beach, before the great departure; and you had to cross the Boul' Mich'—leave the Latin Quarter, was the way we put it—and make the voyage from the Dupont-Latin to the Mabillion: that was the initiation. Most people got lost, got drowned, on the way over. There were some even who went back home right away, but the vast majority of the people from the Dupont drowned crossing that ocean."

6 ▪ Hoarding, rue de Seine, Paris (Oct. 7) Posters and leaflets, announcements and ads, glued to the board, ripped, decaying, pasted over, new, photocopied, expensively printed, mostly in multiples: for an Andy Warhol gallery show, job listings, a chamber music concert, city and country tours, more gallery shows, museum exhibitions, real estate agencies and, always only partly visible from under something else, readable whole only by putting the pieces from three different places together, a big black-and-white square with block letters in English: "I WAS HONEST."

7 ▪ Steve Erickson, "L.A.'s Top 100" (*Los Angeles Magazine*, November) Records made in Los Angeles from 1930 (Jimmie Rodgers) to 2000 (Eminem), and perhaps only a novelist could write a list that so fully tells a tale you don't even think about what's been left out. Certainly only a native Angeleno would include such hidden touchstones as the Premiers' 1964 "Farmer John," Charlie Parker's 1946 "Lover Man," the Mamas and the Papas' 1967 "Twelve-Thirty," the Jewels' 1954 "Hearts of Stone" or Ray Charles' 1963 "That Lucky Old Sun." No one but the author of *Amnesiascope*, though, could have written "snapping the beat to set the tempo, [he] was upstaged by his own fingers" (Tennessee Ernie Ford, "Sixteen Tons," 1955), "Phillips probably didn't notice that the young girls coming to the canyon were named Kasabian and Krenwinkle" ("Twelve-Thirty"), "Robert Johnson by way of Marilyn Monroe" (Julie London, "Cry Me a River," 1955), "holding his own soul hostage" (Percy Mayfield, "Please Send Me Someone to Love," 1950), "Their record company decided it would bring this Ann Arbor band out to L.A. to keep it under control, which was like bringing the Black Death to 14th-century Europe to control the world's rodent population" (the Stooges, "Loose," 1970) or turn Los Lobos' 1984 "A Matter of Time" into an account of how Ritchie Valens actually got up and walked away from that plane crash that killed Buddy Holly and the Big Bopper.

8 ▪ **James Mathus & His Knockdown Society,** *National Antiseptic* **(Mammoth)** The Squirrel Nut Zippers have their old-music cabaret act down, but they're too cute. So the North Mississippi Allstars, who are not cute but don't sing as well as Mathus, shove the Zippers' leader face down into the dirt and he comes up spitting it out, but not all of it. Charley Patton's "Shake It and Break It" turns into rubber band music, but there's a rhythmic undertow to all the best tunes here, pulling back against the dominant rhythm, the players questioning the voice and vice versa. "Spare Change" ("Ain't worth a dime today") is dark, deadly, the blues as Chuck Berry once defined them: "When you ain't got no *money*." It's a modest version of Otis Rush's deep-blues "Double Trouble," all on the surface, as deep as it has to be.

9 ▪ **Fastbacks, "Waterloo Sunset," and Heather Duby, "The Way Love Used to Be,"** from *Give the People What They Want: The Songs of the Kinks* **(Sub Pop)** Aren't tribute

albums terrible? There isn't a performance on *Hank Williams: Timeless* (with Bob Dylan, Sheryl Crow, Mark Knopfler with Emmylou Harris, Emmylou Harris with Mark Knopfler, Keith Richards, Beck and Johnny Cash on hand) worth playing twice. *Give the People What They Want* features mostly performers who wouldn't know how. But here—with the two most uncoverable songs Ray Davies ever wrote—two singers, faced with exquisite melodies they cannot in fact sing, humble the songs before the flatness of their own voices. Duby doesn't even try to make "The Way Love Used to Be"—a reach into a past that never existed that is so passionate you can imagine it was composed by Jack the Ripper—her own; she merely lets it carry her. Can she keep the song's promise? Yes, because while Davies was singing to himself, Duby is singing to another person, a person she has herself made real. "Terry and Julie" in "Waterloo Sunset" might have been Davies' wave to Terrence Stamp and Julie Christie, but as Kim Warnick looks out the window of the song's old man, she is both of the people she gazes at; she owns the world.

10 ▪ **Wayne Robins writes:** "20 Oct: I'm riding the subway this afternoon down from Times Square. Three black men with plenty of mileage on them get on unobtrusively at 34th St. One of them says to a woman in a loud voice: "Ma'am, do you know what time it is?" The elderly man sitting across from me looks at his watch and yells back, 'One o'clock.' 'No!' one of the trio shouts gleefully. 'It's doo-wop time!' At which time the three men begin singing one of the most beautiful a cappella versions of 'In the Still of the Night' I've ever heard. As I reach into my wallet to put a dollar in the contribution bag, I realize my face feels turned inside out from smiling. It was the happiest I've been for 60 seconds in the last five weeks."

NOVEMBER 12, 2001

1 ▪ **Beth Orton, "Stolen Car,"** from *Central Reservation* **(Arista, 1999)** A guitar plays

like a cello, straight through to the end, through feedback, as if nothing can change. That sense of rootedness, of permanence, drives this broken-voiced ballad of no way out. The woman who steps forth—as opposed to the younger person who sings the smooth tunes that follow this opening cut—is a familiar face in certain parts of London, Manchester, Birmingham, Coventry, Leeds. She's in her 40s, in her 50s, still beautiful, her face longer than it was, her eyes piercing, her jaw a warning. Like the heroine of Alison Fell's 1984 novel *Every Move You Make,* she's been through feminism when it was a closed, even Stalinist movement; unlike the heroine of Rod Stewart's "You Wear It Well," the radical blues have left marks all over her. Now she lives alone. She teaches or runs a gallery or works in publishing. Everything she left behind, everything that left her behind, is in her voice, which says there was no other choice, and that it was a choice.

2 ▪ **Bob Giraldi, director, *Dinner Rush* (Worldwide)** Though it opens with a mob execution right in the street, within minutes the film is all laughs: in Tribeca, in a one-time trattoria that's now the latest genius-chef hot spot (the real Gigino, a trattoria on Greenwich St. between Duane and Reade), everything goes wrong. Taking time out to place one last ruinous bet, and taking time out from that to fuck the receptionist who the chef thinks is his girlfriend, the sous-chef is throwing the kitchen out of whack. A famous food critic arrives and raises her eyebrow in doubt while the chef panics. A gallery owner blows in with a huge party and within minutes has bugs crawling over everyone's flesh. The power goes out. Gangsters show up with no intention of leaving until the place is in their name. John Corbett (Sarah Jessica Parker's boyfriend in *Sex and the City*) sits at the bar, amused at the human comedy—and at some invisible point everything that was funny is suddenly not.

3 ▪ ***Good Rockin' Tonight—The Legacy of Sun Records* (London/Sire)** Aren't tribute albums terrible? Here, for a TV documentary,

everyone from Paul McCartney to Bob Dylan to Sheryl Crow to Bryan Ferry add nothing to Memphis explosions, from Charlie Rich's deep "Who Will the Next Fool Be" to Warren Smith's dark-hollow "Red Cadillac and a Black Moustache" to Elvis' slow-walking "Don't Be Cruel" (yes, a Sun recording—by Jerry Lee Lewis), while Johnny Hallyday and Elton John massacre Carl Perkins' "Blue Suede Shoes" and Lewis' "Whole Lotta Shakin' Goin' On." Only one man escapes to tell the tale: Kid Rock, with the Howling Diablos of Detroit, leaping onto "Stick" McGhee and His Buddies' "Drinkin' Wine Spo-Dee-O-Dee" (a hit on Atlantic in 1949, and a Lewis touchstone from that day to this) as if it's a horse he can ride all the way into the present, which he does, shouting "NO FLIES ON ME, SUCKERS!" all the way home.

4 ▪ **Michael Guinzburg, *Top of the World, Ma!* (Cannongate)** Pure raunch—which turns into pain and suffering, which turns into a reader's empathy for people you can hardly believe exist: Willem de Kooning cured of Alzheimer's by a miracle drug and fucking his brains back, a teenager cheating on her mother, a man with a world-historical case of acne, a young hustler chasing a rumor that Jackson Pollock ended his life as a pedophile and, near the end, a new board game, "The American Dream," where you win by parlaying immigrant identities and attendant handicaps into money—that is, the American Dream. "Mariah's a Guatemalan midget with cooking skills but no English at Georgetown Law," says one player of her opponent, "and I'm a Lithuanian prostitute with AIDS just off the boat working in a *Dunkin Donuts.*" No happy ending.

5 ▪ **Hissyfits, "Baby," on *Letters From Frank* (Top Quality Rock and Roll)** Standing out on a disappointing album from Brooklyn's sunniest, trashiest, most worried guitar-based rave-up girl group, a floater: a small voice that takes on deeper textures with every phrase, a simple pulse that goes in circles even as it rushes toward the finish line.

6 ■ *"Give Me Your Hump!"—The Un-speakable Terry Southern Record* (Koch/Paris) It was a great idea, readings from the works of the late black humorist—author of *Candy, The Magic Christian, Blue Movie* and "You're Too Hip, Baby," the perfect short story about a white man on the Paris jazz scene in the 1950s—and the result is a dead fish. What comes off the page as unlikely, unstoppable—No, he isn't going to go *farther*, is he?—seems smugly obvious coming out of anyone's mouth. Marianne Faithfull, Michael O'Donoghue, Allen Ginsberg, Southern himself: they're too hip.

7 ■ A friend who works in theater writes: "I just finished teaching a class as a 'guest artist' at the local hoity-toity private school, which is trying to fashion itself into an arts magnet. I asked the students to pick a question they wanted to explore, and they picked (drumroll) 'What is love?' and I thought Oh God no. They are so completely surrounded by money and the 'correct' answers and the giant stick that their whole world has up its ass. It's hard to feel sorry for them, but still there's a lot of pressure to be perfect or they will not be 'invited back'—and the school has had a rash of suicides. Two of my students were on suicide watch and had to leave rehearsal early every day to go to counseling. The students spent three-quarters of the class trying to do things 'right' and giving very safe answers and doing safe things and they're all incredibly bright—maniacally so.

"They each came up with 10 things they always wanted to do on stage. As soon as the lists were made they asked 'We're not really going to do this, are we?' but you could immediately see them thinking 'Oh my God, we actually could do this stuff.' They ended up smashing guitars and screaming the lyrics to 'Wish You Were Here' and banging the gazillion dollar baby grand for all they were worth. Dogs were coming on stage running all over, one kid tried unsuccessfully to vomit, and at the end they had a giant food fight with peanut butter and jelly sandwiches and just generally acted their age as hard as they could. The audience was all dressed in fancy black dresses and suits and after the curtain call the students spontaneously charged into the audience and started sliming them with peanut butter and jelly. It was god-awful, but they made a little Cabaret Voltaire for themselves and I got to watch them let themselves be 15 for half an hour.

"It's sad to know that's probably the extent of it. They wouldn't wash the peanut butter off—they were still running around all slimy when I left half an hour later. I'm pretty sure I'm 'not invited back.'"

8 ■ David Lynch/Angelo Badalamenti, *Mulholland Dr.* (BMG/Milan) This is not like the movie. There is no imperative to keep you interested, entertained or following the story. Rather there is so much silence on this soundtrack album, or waiting, that you can forget you are listening to anything, so that when the sound comes back—creeps back, usually—you don't know where you are. In the movie you always know right where you are—Hollywood, which, as one viewer put it, signifies the real message of the movie: Stay away.

9 ■ Bertha Lee, "Mind Reader Blues" (1934), from *Screamin' and Hollerin' the Blues: The Worlds of Charley Patton* (Revenant, 1929–34) This amazing set—a tribute both to records as repositories of national memory and to records as fetish objects—is just what it says it is. Patton, the central progenitor of Mississippi Delta blues, recorded in Wisconsin and New York in six different sessions, under different names, in different styles, traveling and performing with different compatriots; the seven CDs here, presented in the form of an album of 78s, with the equivalent of two full-length books, collections of original advertisements and record labels and much, much more, present the full results of each recording session, whether by Patton or others, so that in fact not only the will of a single performer but the air he breathed is captured whole.

Part of that air is the very last performance from Patton's last session, from his wife Bertha Lee. You stick the word "blues" onto the right phrase and it's as if you've never heard the phrase before, and that's what happens here (Mike Watt of the Minutemen: "A good title is worth a thousand lyrics"). A woman with an undistinguished voice and an ordinary sense of timing starts out with the claim that she can read her man's mind; she proceeds to do it with no more emotion than you'd expect her to use on the dishes—maybe less. "Baby, I can see / Just what's on your mind"—what spouse can't do that? But you don't live every minute of the day with that kind of knowledge—or do you? "Well, I'm worried now / But I won't be worried long," Lee ends her song; usually the words mean the singer's life is about to end. It's only death that takes care away. But in this moment it isn't her trouble that's on her mind.

10 ■ **Street scene, Canal & Bourbon streets, New Orleans (Nov. 3)** Next to a mailbox, a young woman with a baby on her hip was wearing a black T-shirt with a homemade "EVIL" spelled out in silver sequins; a middle-aged woman with three young children was shaking a white bucket and chanting "Help our church, please help our church"; a huge man walked by in a black-and-silver T-shirt with "Good/Evil" running over a picture of a man in a cowl; on the back of the mailbox, under the headline "RESISTANCE IS FERTILE," was a poster picturing a young Hispanic/Indian woman with a baby at her breast and a rifle on her back, the logo "Crimethinc." and a text: "The greatest illusionist spectacle in the world no longer enchants us. We are certain that communities of joy will emerge from our struggle. Here and now. And for the first time, life will triumph over death." Looming over it all, a billboard: "LARRY FLYNT'S HUSTLER CLUB. TWO GIRLS FOR EVERY GUY."

NOVEMBER 26, 2001

1 ■ **Strokes, *Is This It* (RCA)** Fast, expert, hanging-out sounds from a young New York five-piece with a guru—not the so-named older guy with the comb-over pictured with the band on the insert, but, wow, Lou Reed. Julian Casablanca's vocals may be filtered so that their tinny sound matches the group's skinny-tie beat, but that doesn't save the Strokes' "Modern Age" from dissolving back into the Velvet Underground's "Beginning to See the Light"—and "Modern Age" is the best thing here. The cover of the import version offers a white woman's naked ass cupped by a black gloved hand: "So 1983," said one disappointed fan.

2 ■ **Yeah Yeah Yeahs, *Yeah Yeah Yeahs* (Shifty)** As slick as the Strokes are, this ill-named New York trio (can you imagine yourself saying, "Hey, let's go see the Yeah Yeah Yeahs"? It's like saying "Let's go see Who's on First") are abrasive. They're so heedlessly tough that the arty touches at the end of "Miles Away" can seem like a relief, a promise that the music is an effect, not reality. But the first four songs on this EP are as good as they have to be; they might be a way of your getting used to Karen O's small, pressured voice, until with "Our Time" you're ready to actually listen to her. Announcing "I—may be dead, honey," over a stop-time orchestration of the band's single-guitar and drums wall of sound, O could be Melissa Swingle of Trailer Bride as easily as she calls up Mary Weiss of the Shangri-Las: you don't question for a second that she knows what she means. Her voice curls, like a finger beckoning you into the music. "It's the year to be hated," she says, then leading a chant: "OUR TIME! It's our time! OUR TIME! To—be—hated—" The music rises like a flag blowing. "C'mon, kids," O says—and there is nothing so modest, so defiant, so hopeless, so much of a smile, short of the Who's "The Kids Are Alright." But this song has its own place and time, even if it didn't make its time, but fell into it—even if 19 men came from elsewhere and destroyed thousands to make the song's time. Three musicians standing up to attest with the crowd they gather around themselves that they're ready to be hated, that they've waited all their lives for the chance—I can't believe people in New York aren't singing this on the street.

3 ■ **www.findagrave.com** It was Connie Nisinger, a high school librarian in the

Midwest, who decided that this interesting site needed a picture of the final resting place of Billy Lyons, shot dead in St. Louis on Christmas Day, 1895, his corpse kicked through time ever after in the countless versions of "Stag-o-lee," "Stacker Lee" and "Stagger Lee." Click "Search by name," type in "William Lyons," and there is Lyons' plot in St. Peter's Cemetery in St. Louis, sec. 5, lot 289. The site allows you to "Leave flowers and a note for this person": keep clicking and you can leave a cigar or a beer instead. Advertising bars include "Contact Your High School Classmates"—to find their graves?

4 ▪ Hanif Kureishi, *Gabriel's Gift* (Scribner) Screenwriter for the socially commonplace and artistically unique London romances *My Beautiful Laundrette* and *Sammy and Rosie Get Laid*, writer and director of the stupidly dismissed *London Kills Me*, author of *The Buddha of Suburbia*, *The Black Album* and *Intimacy*, Kureishi is a born storyteller, but he is not a natural novelist. On the page, his dialogue can seem perfunctory, looking for another medium, a way from one place to another, not what a person would say: "'Talent might be a gift but it has to be cultivated. The imagination is like a fire or a furnace; it has to be stoked, fed and attended to.'" The man talking, speaking to a teenage boy, is a great rock star from the 1970s, still worshipped; far more alive on the page than the star or the boy—or dead on the page, which here amounts to the same thing—is Rex, the boy's father, who once played with the star. Save for his moments in that man's sun, he has been a nobody, and he has stoked, fed and attended to his failure until, after nearly 30 years, he can almost live off of it.

There are thousands upon thousands of middle-aged men like Rex, each one the butt of every musician joke, their delusions of glamour inseparable from their resentment of almost everyone they meet, men for whom aging means only helpless self-parody. Yet while Kureishi's version contains them all, gives off the smell of fear they carry, Rex is not only a version, a type

or a joke. Even though you may not want to, you can see him, imagine the way he talks, the way he moves, and even if you know too many people whose lives he is living out, he doesn't look or move like they do. In that sense Kureishi, if not a natural novelist, is a real one.

5–6 ▪ Ernest C. Withers, *The Memphis Blues Again: Six Decades of Memphis Music Photographs*, selected and with text by Daniel Wolff (Viking Studio) & *American Roots Music*, edited by Robert Santelli, Holly George-Warren and Jim Brown (Abrams) While not as rich as Withers' *Pictures Tell the Story*, in which music was one element in the great social drama of the Civil Rights movement, there is a reminder of Withers' true vision in a portrait of Aretha Franklin at a Southern Christian Leadership Conference event two months after the assassination of Martin Luther King Jr., her face swollen—from tears or a beating you can't tell. Otherwise there's merely fabulousness, everywhere you look: Louis Jordan and his father in matching 10-gallon fedoras, the Moonglows in action, a crowd waiting outside the Club Ebony in the rain, B. B. King accompanied on facing pianos by Jerry Lee Lewis and Charlie Rich, a Hollywood Elvis back in town and posing as if he's already slept with everyone in it. It's history as rumor, as a story you know can never be nailed down, proven, finished, only forgotten, until someday people will find these pictures and disbelieve everything they say.

American Roots Music—the book of the PBS TV series—is very nearly a miracle: it makes the twisted tale of American music, its strands intertwined like lovers hiding from the light, seem bland. Worse, it makes the tale seem obvious. And, as it is obvious, it has nothing new to say, which means that as a tale it was over before it began.

The Withers book is $14 cheaper, too.

7–8 ▪ *Britney Spears Live from Las Vegas* (HBO, Nov. 18) & *Jennifer Lopez Live* (NBC, Nov. 20) Howard Hampton writes: "In case you missed it, I can tell you that I watched Britney Spears' concert and I missed it too. It's as if she's made of flesh-colored Teflon.

You can look, but your gaze just slides right off the surface. It's not simply that she lacks imagination, personality, charisma, or stage presence" (hosting *Saturday Night Live* last year, she had it all) "but that this absence is the structuring principle of her act. There's not even the pretense that those different voices are really coming out of her body, to the point where her piped-in vocals were like canned fetish objects, floating over the stage like props. It comes across like a Vegas Club Silencio converted into a vocational junior high school for strippers." Two nights later, Gary Radnich of San Francisco NBC-TV affiliate KRON ended his nightly sports report with detailed comparison footage of the Spears and Jennifer Lopez specials, naming Lopez the clear winner because she had more costume changes—and because while "When Jennifer Lopez crawled on the floor she acted like she meant business. When Britney Spears crawled on the floor you wanted to say, 'Get up.'"

9 ■ Mick Jagger, *Goddess in the Doorway* (Virgin) Reviews are saying this isn't really terrible. It's really terrible.

10 ■ Berkeley, Calif., Contra Costa Ave. (Nov. 17) On our woodsy street, the mail carrier walks with dignity, handling dogs, obstructions of foliage and hanging gardens of huge spider webs with determination, humor and a pith helmet. After watching her negotiate a particularly steep and slippery walkway, a neighbor offered encouragement: "All this, and then the *anthrax* terrorists. I'll bet when you went to work for the post office you didn't realize you'd be a, a—" The neighbor couldn't find the right word. "A warrior!" the mail carrier said.

Thanks to Andrew Hamlin

DECEMBER 10, 2001

1 ■ Jim Borgman, editorial cartoon (*Cincinnati Enquirer*, Dec. 1) In 1963, for the sleeve of *Meet the Beatles* (*With the Beatles* in the U.K.), photographer Robert Freeman pictured John, George and Paul from left to right on top, with Ringo directly below

Paul: the left sides of the faces white, the right sides in shadow, then-shockingly long black hair and black turtlenecks isolating the faces against the starkest black background imaginable. All Borgman did was black out the two faces on the left. On the occasion of George Harrison's death, nothing I read, heard or saw came close.

2 ■ Paula Frazer, *Indoor Universe* (Birdman) The former singer for Tarnation—which always seemed to imagine itself as the lounge act at Heartbreak Hotel—still can't crush a fly in her fist. It's not that she won't; she can't close anything all the way. Her orchestrations might be made out of swamp gas; the closer she gets to the objects of her desire, the less substantial they are. Making her way into the vampirish "Stay as You Are" as if she's pushing cobwebs out of her face with every step, she flats on her words as they end a phrase, hesitating, almost stopping. Patrick Main's organ carries her forward like a stick on a stream. You can play the song again and again, waiting for the melody to exhaust itself, to reveal why something so familiar sounds less obvious each time you hear it—though you might also play it again and again because only three songs later Frazer is singing with a rose clenched in her teeth, which sort of ruins the effect.

3 ■ *Flying Side Kick—Home Alive Compilation II* (Broken Records) For this set in support of the self-defense group formed after Seattle musician Mia Zapata was raped and killed while walking home from a show, no quarter is asked and none is given. The Gossip's "I Want It (To Write)" is pure heat, as primitive as an early Rolling Stones track. Amy Ray of Indigo Girls, here with the Butchies, is as always preaching to the converted—but my God, can she sing! Carrisa's Wierd can't spell "weird" but they can make it, playing male and female voices through a violin until something very distant, very dead, something vaguely pre-Raphaelite, rises out of the music. Every one of the 15 bands here comes up with something unexpected, pushing a little

harder, maybe digging into its pile of tapes for something rejected just because, at the time, it didn't seem like anything anyone would want to hear.

4 ▪ Hadacol, *It's All in Your Head* (Slew-foot) This is "Rio Bravo"/Ricky Nelson "So tough he doesn't have to prove it" country from Missouri. The music is warm, unadorned, corny, naked, until a tune beginning "I was standing in the corner / Feeling just like Gerald Ford" opens up like a murder mystery. So of course they drop it right there. You don't listen to Hadacol's songs so much as pass them by, like road signs.

5 ▪ Jennifer Saunders, producer, *Absolutely Fabulous* (Comedy Central, Dec. 3) In a diet-induced delirium, God appears to Edina as Marianne Faithfull, wistfully mooning over what fools these mortals be. But then the Devil arrives—in the person of Anita Pallenberg in a black-red wig and upholstered horns. It's the siren of *Performance*, the absolute '60s ice queen, now looking lined, weathered and wonderful, and plainly having the time of her life—or eternity, as the case may be. "*You* gave them vanity," God says of Edina's weight-loss panic. "No," says the Devil. "*Self-loathing.*" As they go for a drink you can tell they were always in it together.

6 ▪ Sprint commercial on cellphone dyslexia (Fox, Nov. 26) "I said on a cellphone we need a 'backup for O'Neill.' What we got," says a football coach, as amid linebackers and ends running their drills a middle-aged man in a yachting outfit plays a Farfisa organ and a matronly blond woman in a long black gown warbles "Do That to Me One More Time" into a hand mike, "was the Captain and Tennille."

7 ▪ Gov't Mule, *The Deep End Vol. 1* (ATO/BMG) The Southern power trio comes back from the death of bassist Allen Woody with a double disc of grinding blues, aided by a virtual benefit concert of bassists—Jack Bruce of Cream, Flea of Red Hot Chili Peppers, Mike Watt of the Minutemen, Bootsy Collins, many more—plus another 13 utility players from Gregg Allman to Chuck Leavell. Everything's going along

fine until Little Milton, who made blues records for Sam Phillips in Memphis in 1953 before moving on to Chicago, takes over on "Soulshine." The trick to making albums with guests is keeping people who're too good for you off the guest list.

8 ▪ *New York Times Book Review*, "Editor's Choice: The 9 Best Books of 2001" (Dec. 2) As offered by a friend, "A Translation":

- *Austerlitz* by W. G. Sebald: "As so often in Sebald's fiction, direct connections are never highlighted in the vast loops and sudden knottings of his rhetoric." Translation: "You can't tell what's going on."
- *The Corrections* by Jonathan Franzen: "The important thing to know about Jonathan Franzen's novel is that you can ignore all the literary fireworks and thoroughly enjoy its people." Translation: "You have to ignore what a prick Franzen is in order to read the book."
- *Hateship, Friendship, Courtship, Loveship, Marriage* by Alice Munro: "As Alice Munro gets older, the challenges faced by her characters get darker." Translation: "This is even gloomier than most Canadian fiction."
- *John Adams* by David McCullough: "There will always be some readers who feel that the historian's subduing of Adams's noisy feistiness in this account—his rashness, stubbornness and sometimes bizarre behavior—makes him a little less himself." Translation: "McCullough knew that if he was too honest he could kiss the miniseries deal goodbye."
- *John Henry Days* by Colson Whitehead: "The ambition of Colson Whitehead's second novel is to define the interior crisis of manhood in terms of the entire pop-mad consumer society." Translation: "Somebody on the *Book Review* staff is thinking about buying a red Jag to alleviate his midlife crisis."
- *The Metaphysical Club* by Louis Menand: "The approach also gives his thesis a kind of theatrical excitement that no severe intellectual history could engender." Translation: "Reading this stuff bores us as much as it does you."

• *True History of the Kelly Gang* by Peter Carey: "That alone would make this novel the most compelling reading on the list." Translation: "We're above just reading for pleasure."

• *Uncle Tungsten* by Oliver Sacks: "As charming as his prose always is, Oliver Sacks cannot write for long without finding a subject outside himself." Translation: "He's a rambling old geezer."

9 ■ Velvet Underground, *Bootleg Series Vol. 1: The Quine Tapes* (Polydor) A modest three-disc box of recordings guitarist Robert Quine made at shows in St. Louis and San Francisco in 1969, featuring a furious "Foggy Notion," a 17-minute "Follow the Leader" and 24-, 29- and 39-minute performances of "Sister Ray." The sound is perfect: you can hear through the smoke, the grime, the enthusiasm or indifference of the crowd, the 32 years.

10 ■ Cameron Crowe, director, *Vanilla Sky* (Dreamworks/Paramount) Charles Taylor writes: "In *Vanilla Sky*, the Cruisesuzs, Tom and Penelope, re-create the cover of *The Freewheelin' Bob Dylan*. May God have mercy on us all."

JANUARY 7, 2002

1–2 ■ *The Concert for New York City* (Columbia) Aren't tribute albums terrible? From the Oct. 20 event where Sen. Hillary Clinton was booed and Melissa Etheridge wasn't, there are surprises. "Providing aid to New Yorkers victimized by the attack on September 11, 2001," Destiny's Child offers a "Gospel Medley" that kicks off with Beyoncé Knowles' revelatory proof that with melisma there is no beginning and no end. "Glopglopglopglopglopglopglopglopglop" is the closest I can get to the momentum she generates—it sounds like she's gargling with olive oil. For God.

With Mick Jagger and Keith Richards' "Salt of the Earth," the feeling is desperate in a contrived way, but still desperate; the rhythm is much richer than in the distracted version of the song the Stones left behind when they closed their 1968 "Rock and Roll Circus." Who can say that Jagger didn't mean it then, that "the faceless crowd / A swirling mass of gray and black and white" didn't look real to him, or that he doesn't mean it when he says that now the crowd does look real? To hear Richards change a line from "Let's drink to the good and the evil" to "the good not the evil" is stirring. Is it like Jagger changing "Let's spend the night together" to "Let's spend some time together" (or, as he has always insisted, "Let's spend some mmmugh together") for the Ed Sullivan Show? It's not completely different. Does that mean Jagger and Richards are practicing self-censorship? Or that as songs move through time and time works on songs, there is no reason for songs to stay the same?

3 ■ Selby Tigers, *Charm City* (Hopeless) You can learn a lot about a town by listening to what it doesn't show. You don't see what you hear on this disc while walking the streets in St. Paul, for example. You see the trees, the Mississippi, the houses—you can even see the seasons change, but not a face that, like guitarist Arzu D2's voice, sends out Howard Devoto's 1977 Buzzcocks fuck you (from Manchester, the "Boredom" phrasing and snarl), Kathleen Hanna's 1991 Bikini Kill fuck you (from Olympia, the "Suck My Left One" disdain) and Penelope Houston's 1977 Avengers fuck you (from San Francisco, the "American in Me" glee). Here all that sounds as if it's in the St. Paul air. Plus you get Dave Gardner as Sammy G's bass, running rings around the songs as if he showed up from somewhere else and will be somewhere else tomorrow.

4 ■ *Intimacy*, directed by Patrice Chereau (Pathé) In a ratty two-story apartment, you hear the Clash's "London Calling" in dank background; it feels old and undiminished. This is where a divorced man and a married woman meet once a week for anonymous sex. It's less graphic than real: grimy, clumsy, then achieving a drive it seems nothing could stop—fucking that seems to exist outside of any movie. But as remarkable as the sex—with an almost unbearably intense good-sex scene followed by an almost

unbearably intense bad-sex scene—is what happens when the man and the woman try to follow each other into the world at large: what happens when they come between each other. The lucidity of flesh turns into the incoherence of speech. They can't hear; you can't hear.

5 ■ Sarah Dougher, "Keep Me," from *The Bluff* (Mr. Lady) Dougher's music on her own is different from the music she makes in the Portland trio Cadallaca because there's no back door in her own songs, no moment when they even suggest someone might be pulling your leg. (With Cadallaca, it's all back door—the front door is when you figure they mean what they say.) Here the contrast between the measured pace of Dougher's singing and the get-it-over-with beat makes you want to get out of the way, but both doors are locked.

6 ■ David Menconi, *Off the Record* (Writers Club Press) As a rise-and-fall-of-a-rock-band novel—here about a Nirvana-like trio from Raleigh, N.C.—*Off the Record* is distinguished by thrilling accounts of songs coming together and songs coming apart: Menconi, who writes for the *News & Observer* in Raleigh, can get music on the page. He can get his words off the page: a producer compares recording a note or a phrase at a time "to filming car wrecks by leaving cameras running on street corners." On signing with Gus DeGrande, the Don King of the music business: "Ken could only assume that, with Joseph Stalin and Colonel Tom Parker unavailable, Tommy had settled for the next worst thing." But then comes the first show of the band's tour behind their smash album, which the Kurt Cobain figure opens and closes with his version of the Sex Pistols' "Holidays in the Sun." Played once.

7 ■ "Lesley Gore: It's Her Party," on *Biography* (A&E, Dec. 7) When I tried to tell people how good this program was the day after it ran, everyone I spoke with had already seen it, sometime during the night. "I could have gone back to school," says the pre-Beatles hitmaker (four straight in the top five in 1963), "and become a lawyer or a

doctor"—that's not how the rock 'n' roll story goes, and this is a rock 'n' roll story. Quincy Jones is part of it, from "It's My Party," the No. 1 first record, to today, speaking as if this nice Jewish girl from Tenafly, N.J., is his god-daughter. The nice Jewish girl who could have become a lawyer gets cheated out of all her royalties. The girl who couldn't be stopped becomes a woman no one wants to hear. The edge in her voice—no metaphor, but a physical grate, something that scratches at the listener— and the real misery she put into high-school lyrics turn a teenage girl into Miss Lonelyhearts, as people with problems that cannot be solved write her for help. You can see it all in her face, now, and you break when she tells her sweetest, most hurtful story: that when her "You Don't Own Me" was used in the 1996 *First Wives Club*, Gore would time her daily walks so she could pass by a theater where the movie was playing, so she could hear people singing the song as they came out.

8 ■ *Vanilla Sky*, directed by Cameron Crowe (Dreamworks/Paramount) What's most creepy about the scene where a hologram of John Coltrane plays at Tom Cruise's birthday party—before the morally vacuous hero is sent on his journey of discovery—is that you suspect whoever came up with the idea was wondering if he could afford something like that for his own birthday party. And now he can.

9 ■ *There Is No Eye: Music for Photographs—Recordings of Musicians Photographed by John Cohen* (Smithsonian Folkways) I shouldn't write about this, because I wrote the introduction to Cohen's photo collection, which carries the same title. But nobody else is. There is a lot here that shouldn't get lost—but what, before now, was barely found is the great folklorist Alan Lomax's 1967 recording of "Love My Darling-O." Lomax's earlier field recording of the tune, as sung by a prisoner named James "Ironhead" Baker, is described as a "Negro version of a Scots ballad"; in Lomax's hands it's a dangerous song about adultery sung to the tune of "Which Side

Are You On?" Lomax is partly Burl Ives here, part Jean Ritchie; his tone is plummy. But he lets the song take him, until he is as much the sort of coal miner or holiness church member he himself would record as he is a member of a collegiate folk trio with matching madras shirts. The mystery of his performance, its timelessness and its depth, is precisely its inauthenticity.

10 ▪ **Overheard in a hospital waiting room (Palo Alto, Calif., Dec. 4)** "As a former Deadhead—" "Is there really such a thing as a former Deadhead? Shouldn't it be re-covering Deadhead?"

JANUARY 28, 2002

1 ▪ **Mendoza Line, *Lost in Revelry* (Misra)** From Georgia, the sound of people who expect nothing, don't even necessarily think they deserve more and nevertheless want everything: a lifetime guarantee and an airtight alibi, as the Tubes once put it; "A damn good disguise to live this one down," as they put it. With Shannon McArdle rising bar by bar out of the perfect picking of "Whatever Happened to You?" there is the sweetness of Brinsley Schwarz; there is the doubting undertow of Richard and Linda Thompson. The sound of people in love with each other and not trusting each other: on "We're All in This Alone" you could be listening to the Mekons, if the Mekons had come out of the U.S.A. At its unpolished best, as on "Red Metal Doors," the music moves by like traffic. Male and female voices throw the songs back at each other— "Mistakes were made tonight," as they warble over fuzztone—but there's no end to the game. And there is, on the back of the press release, in the form of a look back over the last few years, a manifesto:

"The seller," the band writes, "could not sell without guilt, the buyer could not buy without shame. . . . And after a certain period of buying, day after day, at the most exorbitant prices, all that we would never have wished to be given as a gift, the relationship between our shopkeepers and us began to seem surprisingly antagonistic.

Were our merchants, it crossed our minds more than once, actually trying to kill us?" Then the band turns into the sellers, selling its music: "From the sad sacks who made it, to the sad sacks who bought it . . . or has anyone doubted that the consumer has been viciously and systematically tricked all these years? Really? And did you really believe that the consumer himself didn't know?" The band finishes: "We must accurately reflect the real burden and real struggle of America, the essential question which only an American asks and only an American can answer: namely, what have you done with the relatively limitless freedom and prosperity which you've been given as a gift?" For people who named themselves for the batting average beneath which one sinks into oblivion to become one with, as Dostoevski put it in "The Grand Inquisitor," "those God forgets" (i.e., .200), they are beginning again from the beginning; the heartland may be wherever they happen to be playing tonight.

2 ▪ **Christopher Hitchens, "For Patriot Dreams" (*Vanity Fair*, December)** After describing his attachment to New York and his return, following the destruction of the World Trade Center, to lecture "newly enrolled New School students, some of whose parents wanted them back in the heartland, that they'd be sorry forever if they abandoned the city at such a time," the British journalist, for whom "heartland" is only English for "unserious place where rubes live," turned his readers into just those rubes, asking himself, or rather asking his readers to ask him, "Shall I now take out the papers of citizenship? Wrong question. In every essential way, I already have." Or, as the guy with an American flag flying from his SUV and an FDNY cap on his head said when a kid asked him, "Gosh, mister, are you really a New York fireman?": "Son, in every essential way . . ."

3 ▪ **Loudon Wainwright III, *Last Man on Earth* (Red House)** Over these many years, a little of Wainwright has gone a long way.

Inside his funny upper-middle-class folk music he's so naked about his embarrassments his forced rhymes can embarrass the listener—maybe that's what goes a long way. But here gruesomely autobiographical tunes dig in, until you want more than anything for the singer to find his way out of his misery. You root for him to escape his loneliness, the shadow of his mother's death, his failures, his dodgy cult audiences, to get out of bed.

4 ▪ Neal Pollack & the Pine Valley Cosmonauts, *The Neal Pollack Anthology of American Literature* (Bloodshot) The idea is good: in a package designed as a parody of the hallowed Harry Smith *Anthology of American Folk Music*, Kelly Hogan, Sally Timms and Jon Langford spin old-timey fiddle spells as *McSweeney's*-designated parody of the great American writer reads his parodies of great American writer blather—from the sound of his voice, because he had nothing better to do after being turned down for a part in *Swingers*. Unbearable.

5 ▪ Robert Salladay, "Media Pack Keeps Condit on Tightrope" (*San Francisco Chronicle*, Jan. 12) On Rep. Gary Condit's appearance at a candidates' forum at the Branding Iron Restaurant in Merced, Calif.: "Condit offered only his now-famous Chiclet smile and silence to reporters' questions about the Levy controversy. . . . It had been another strange hour for Condit, who sat quietly during most of the luncheon, occasionally suppressing a smile at the assembled competition. That included Paul Yonker, a very intense-looking Vietnam veteran carrying a folded American flag. 'I believe it's time to go back to the moon,' said Yonker, a Republican rancher from Mariposa, which is outside Condit's 18th congressional district. 'They had a biosphere. It worked in the Southwest. Let's go to the moon. I believe in the flag amendment.' Others included Elvis Pringle, a Los Angeles record producer who said he wanted to build a space center in the Central Valley but offered absolutely no details; a college professor who talked so fast that he was almost unintelligible; a San Jose gas station manager who

read . . . his . . . speech . . . very . . . slowly; and a former state assemblyman whose remarks consisted of quoting the Constitution and singing Lee Greenwood's 'God Bless the USA' in its entirety."

6–7 ▪ Buddy & Julie Miller, *Buddy & Julie Miller* (Hightone) Country singers and writers, currently the toast of New York, and striking—especially for Julie Miller's shredded punk vocals, which can keep the slickness of the arrangements at bay for only so long.

8 ▪ Mirah, "Cold Cold Water" (K single) and *Advisory Committee* (K) Mirah, a Pacific Northwest singer who used to go by the unwieldy but untoppable name Mirah Yom Tov Zeitlya, is as modest as Chan Marshall as Cat Power, and more insinuating—her high voice makes it unnecessary for her to spend the first moments of each number burning off her own pretentiousness. "Cold Cold Water" is haunting, but it could also be someone looking out the window and thinking of the Temptations' "I Wish It Would Rain." The song leads off *Advisory Committee*, which is full of experiments with tone, tempo and orchestrations that leave their songs behind—a record that feels as if it were recorded too soon.

9 ▪ J. F. Bizot, *Underground: L'Histoire* (Editions Denoël, Paris) The strangest item in this oversize compendium of mostly '60s–'70s lore—mostly drawn from the pages of the magazine *Actuel*—has to do with pictures the late Dutch photographer Ed van der Elsken made in Paris in 1952 and collected in his classic 1957 photo-novel *Love on the Left Bank*. He frequented a bar called Moineau's, where then assembled a group of sometime artists and would-be revolutionaries who named themselves the Lettrist International: the "provisional microsociety" chronicled in Jean-Michel Mension's recent memoir *The Tribe*. On the edges of their tiny milieu—their table—was an Australian siren named Vera.

Like many other men, van der Elsken was obsessed with her, shooting her dancing with Africans in nightclubs, undressing, looking at her breasts in a mirror. As in the picture of her on Page 21 of *Underground*, her head thrown back theatrically, everyone looking at her as if she's crazy, van der Elsken dramatized Vera as the ultimate bohemian, saint of her own self-destruction, doomed to forever wander the paths of desire and folly—until 1960, anyway, when as Bizot's puckish research proves she turned up on the cover of an album by ultimate professional San Francisco bohemian Rod McKuen. His *Beatsville* featured not only "The Co-Existence Bagel Shop Blues," "What Is a Fabian" and the fabled "The Beat Generation" (which in 1977 Richard Hell & the Voidoids turned into "The Blank Generation"), but also a painting of van der Elsken's Vera beaming her kohl-rimmed eyes at the would-be purchaser as an existentialist version of McKuen stared into his wineglass. She deserved better—an appearance sometime in the '70s in the stunning van der Elsken photo of a naked couple fucking on their farm as, on a side road, a motor scooter rolls by obliviously, a picture that takes up all of Page 142 of Bizot's book. Which, for all you can tell, she got.

10 ▪ **Cable TV in Hampton Inn & Suites, Columbus, Ohio (Jan. 8)** On nearly 100 channels there's no hint that it's Elvis Presley's 67th birthday (I missed the evening news, where Gov. Bob Taft, also born on Jan. 8, would have been mugging with Elvis impersonator Prentice Chaffin). But there is everything else. It's a utopia of repetition and reversal, repeats and revision, a nirvana of self-referentiality where you've long since committed half of what is set before you to memory, word for word, and are ready for everything else: a never-seen *Law and Order* starring Harris Yulin as a thieving physicist *click* a *Seinfeld* I can't tell if I've seen or not *click click click* one painful scene after another from *Saturday Night Fever click* the cliff-jump and *click Cheers click* N.Y.P.D. *Blue click* the final shootout from *Butch Cassidy and the Sundance Kid* ("For a moment I thought we were in trouble") *click* a relentless *Mad TV* trailer for *Leaving Metropolis*, with Nicolas Cage playing

Superman as a stinking drunk *click* Faith Hill searching for her birth mother *click* to the void: Shania Twain, surrounded by thousands of screaming fans and perhaps half a dozen cameramen, barking out "Rock This Country," cantering from one circus-like ring to another. Like a horse, she can count her steps but she has no sense of rhythm; she can't sing, but she can tease; she isn't pretty, but she appears representing so much money the idea is hard to form. To call the production cynically organized is to beg the question; sealed in silver Spandex, Twain's body is organized even more cynically—but not as cynically as her brace of fiddlers. Sawing away on bodiless, digitalized instruments, they appear in the midst of this extravaganza of trickle-down glamor merely as a sign of the traditional: to prove that the old ways are the best, if that's all you can afford. By then it was past 2, I was ready for *Videodrome*, but it wasn't on.

1 ▪ **A. J. Albany, "Low Down," in *Tin House* (Winter 2002)** The music issue of this adventurous literary magazine leads off with the extraordinary memoir of a now 40-year-old woman who grew up as the daughter of Los Angeles jazz pianist Joe Albany ("Albany's jumbled, idiosyncratic sense of time is almost all his own, and his solos are cliff-hanger explorations," Richard Cook and Brian Morton write in *The Penguin Guide to Jazz*) and Sheila Boucher ("She was responsible for some of the best parts in *Howl*, something Ginsberg confessed to my father years after the fact," Albany writes). Both were heroin addicts; Boucher was a prostitute who walked out when Albany was 6. "They were both bright and talented," Albany says in her first published writing, "but always competing to see who could fall the furthest and the fastest down the ladder to hell. I have a photo of myself at one and a half years old, with my very pregnant mother. When I asked her about the fate of the baby, she was dismissive and said that had definitely been

some john's kid, who she ended up selling to a wealthy doctor and his wife in Bel Air." Out of this Albany recreates a landscape, that of her childhood and of the small-time L.A. jazz junkie, where misery is a faraway sound floating above a voice speaking in tones of affection, terror, rage, love and, most of all, a hipster's defiance.

Not a word is pushed. Albany goes back to the fleabag hotel where she and her father lived when she was 7. Her best friend there was a 9-year-old named LaPrez. "One night LaPrez came to our room and asked my dad if he could give him some help with his mother. When he opened the door to the room, she was sitting straight up in her Murphy bed, eyes wide and staring at us, scarf still tied around her arm. She was blue, dead at least an hour. In the hotel lobby, there was a TV set that three of the resident rummies had total control over, twenty-four hours a day; usually horse races or cop shows were on, but for this one fucked-up night, they sat us down on their smelly old-man sofa and let us watch cartoons." Throughout, Albany pins her parents' crimes against her; when she forgives them, one by one—or, really, brushes them off, with a gesture that seems to freeze in the air—you believe her.

Nothing else in *Tin House* touches Albany, though in the course of a piece on Brian Wilson built around the 1966 John Frankenheimer movie *Seconds* Andrew Hultkrans comes up with one of the two or three best lines in the history of rock criticism ("Nietzsche would have hated *Pet Sounds*") and Robert Politio's proposal that Bob Dylan's shadow career on bootlegs is richer than his official career on Columbia albums needs at least 100 pages, not 10 (the idea that the traditional ballads collected on the bootleg *Golden Vanity* might be more truly Dylan's music than, say, "Memphis Blues Again" is intriguing, but would anyone seek out Dylan's bottomless versions of "When First Unto This Country" or "Trail of the Buffalo" without having heard "Memphis Blues Again" first?). More characteristic are Shusha Guppy's deadly "La

Chanson Française" and Lawrence Joseph's "The Music Is: The Deep Roots of Detroit R&B," an unbelievably pedestrian essay that only occasionally rises to the level of soppiness. But unless Amy Jo Albany writes a book this is the only place you can hear her.

2 ▪ **Britney Spears on *Saturday Night Live* (NBC, Feb. 2)** In her second turn as host she was smart, funny, shameless and fast—a step ahead of anyone around her. Playing a Barbie daughter, the latest third of Gemini's Twin or a doper Hampshire College student who can hold smoke in her lungs for six and a half minutes, she was closer to Jean Harlow or Uma Thurman than the body-snatched performer the world has grown to love and fear; as her own musical guest her IQ seemed to drop 100 points as soon as she opened her mouth to sing.

3 ▪ **Cat Power, "Come on in My Kitchen," on Sonic Youth curated *All Tomorrow's Parties 1.1* (ATP)** The Robert Johnson composition—from 1936, not 1932, as it says here—is one of the most delicate and unusual of all country blues pieces, and performers take it up at their peril (*The Best of Johnny Winter* includes a particularly ham-handed example from 1973). Chan Marshall sucks the song into her own drifting, solipsistic notion of the blues, and the tune emerges stripped of any association with the past, sounding more like a white, middle-class young woman embellishing her troubles in a very good writers-workshop story than a story once told by an itinerant young black man. You can hear that as a travesty, or you can just get lost.

4 ▪ **Katha Pollitt, "$hotgun Weddings," *The Nation* (Feb. 4)** After considering federal and state projects to push poor women with children into marriage—everything from $100 a month welfare bonuses to propaganda campaigns to "huge funding of faith-based marriage preparation courses" to "fatherhood intervention programs"—the colmnist and divorced single mother asks herself what it would take for her "to marry against my own inclination in order to make America great again." Answer: "If the government brings Otis Redding back

to life and books him to sing at my wedding, I will marry the Devil himself. And if the Devil is unavailable, my ex-husband says he's ready."

5 ■ **North Mississippi Allstars, *51 Phantom* (Tone-Cool)** On the rough blues trio's debut album *Shake Hands With Shorty* there was casual proof that a hundred years had not begun to exhaust "Casey Jones," but here old-time seems to mean the '60s. The cover shows a Highway 51 sign, but from the embarrassingly poor lurch into the Allman Brothers' "Blue Sky" in "Lord Have Mercy" to the cover-band Hendrixisms of "Circle in the Sky," this band is running on fumes.

6 ■ **Never Mind Bono at the World Economic Forum in New York, Here's the Edge at "The Future of Theoretical Physics and Cosmology" in Cambridge (Jan. 11)** Real Life Rock science correspondent Steve Weinstein: "The Edge was seen chatting with astrophysicist Sir Martin Rees following Rees's talk at the recent 60th birthday party for Stephen Hawking at Cambridge University. Hawking is known as the Keith Richards of theoretical physicists, and indeed remarked to one bystander that despite his recent brush with death while speeding in his new wheelchair, he 'wasn't lookin too good but [he] was feelin' real well.'

"The Edge has recently been collaborating with Hawking on a bold new idea intended to make sense of the ill-defined Euclidean path integral that plays a central role in Hawking's 'no-boundary' proposal for the initial state of the universe. Later in the evening, the U2 guitarist was spotted with cosmologist Neil Turok in the VIP 'behind Hawking' area, with a rare view of the screen on which Hawking's communications appear. The Edge reportedly needled Turok for stealing U2's 'Unforgettable Fire' title for his recent paper with Khoury, Ovurt and Steinhardt on what they call 'The Ekpyrotic ("out of fire") Universe.'

"The evening concluded with a song to Hawking written by general relativity expert Bernard Carr, and performed by Hawking's students and The Edge (vocals, not guitar).

This was the high point of the evening to that moment, but it was eclipsed by the appearance of a Marilyn Monroe impersonator and then the Can-Can Dancers, six women in 'Moulin Rouge' costumes displaying what some characterized as 'a lot of leg.' "

7 ■ **Jim Roll, *Inhabiting the Ball* (Telegraph Company)** With an album sponsored by the literary journal *McSweeney's*, the Ann Arbor singer offers educated folk music. The music is precious before it's anything else: the whole affair exists in quotation marks. The gimmick is that eight of 13 songs feature lyrics by novelists Rick Moody or Denis Johnson, the most interesting being Johnson's version of a 19th century murder ballad, "Handsome Daniel." I've never heard Johnson sing, but I have seen him with a knife sticking out of his head in the movie of his *Jesus' Son*, and I'd bet he could put more into this song than the person who's singing it now.

8 ■ **Bill Keller, "Enron for Dummies," *New York Times* (Jan. 26)** "How cool was Enron? About two years ago a *Fortune* writer likened utilities and energy companies to 'a bunch of old fogies and their wives shuffling around halfheartedly to the not-so-stirring sounds of Guy Lombardo. . . . Suddenly young Elvis comes crashing through the skylight.' In this metaphor, the guy in the skin-tight-gold-lamé suit was Enron. The writer left out the part where Elvis eats himself to death."

9 ■ **Bill Clinton, "Globalization," Zellerbach Hall, University of California at Berkeley (Jan. 29)** The opening theme music was about 30 seconds of James Taylor crooning Stephen Foster's "Hard Times," but the real music came from the speaker. There was a slide in Clinton's talk that is never present when he's using a teleprompter; here, for a well-organized, detailed, quietly passionate speech, which no doubt he's given many times but seemed made up on the spot, he wasn't even using notes. The rhythm was that of a man at ease with himself and not at ease with the world, which made it possible for him, unlike his replacement,

to speak as if the world was real, and not a construct of publicity. "You've seen him on television, you know what he thinks, he's a serious person," Clinton said of Osama bin Laden. "'Don't tell me about my common humanity, the only thing that matters about me is my difference,'" he said, characterizing bin Laden and others who work from a position of absolute truth.

It was only a small step from one tribe of true believers to another: "I wouldn't have believed it if I hadn't experienced it," Clinton said of the refusal of the Republican Party, from Jan. 20, 1993 to Jan. 20, 2001, to accept the legitimacy of his presidency. The parallel drawn between Republicans and Islamicists—between those who know the world is theirs by right, and not yours—was unspoken, and unmissable.

10 ■ **Mary Chapin Carpenter and Anne Lamott, Royce Hall, UCLA (Jan. 26)** Both gave the adoring audience "the same glow of buoyant optimism," Marc Weingarten reported in the *Los Angeles Times.* "However," as Howard Hampton noted, "the DJ Shadow/Philip Roth show was postponed on account of darkness."

FEBRUARY 25, 2002

1 ■ **Electrelane, *Rock It to the Moon* (Mr. Lady)** A dog barks quietly, holding time at bay; a Farfisa organ traces a small circle. A guitar breaks the stasis, voices complain from a distance, drums neatly set the first tune on its track. Before you know it you're on a deserted beach in some European spy novel with DJ Shadow providing the fog and ? and the Mysterians the chase music. By the second cut this four-woman instrumental combo from England has gone back to "Batman Theme," which takes them into the same "Endless Tunnel" the forgotten San Francisco band Serpent Power got lost in in 1967, though here it opens into an amusement park. Deep in the background, you begin to pick up people talking. In the indecipherability and allure of what they're saying, the specter of Julee Cruise floating by seems like the most natural thing in the world. You realize you have no idea where the band will go next, or what unresolved 20th century image it will turn up—a Hans Bellmer doll under a police spotlight, Lauren Bacall walking out of a room, Bobby Kennedy waving to a crowd with that somber look he'd get, as if he knew.

2 ■ *The Executioner's Last Songs: Jon Langford and the Pine Valley Cosmonauts Consign Songs of Murder, Mob-Law & Cruel, Cruel Punishment to the Realm of Myth, Memory & History to Benefit the Illinois Death Penalty Moratorium Project, Volume 1* **(Bloodshot)** Aren't tribute albums terrible? Even when they're for a good cause? Could it be that the finer the cause—and the Illinois Death Penalty Moratorium Project is not only a good cause, it has shocked the state and the nation with its success, which is to say with its proof of the inherent corruption of capital punishment—the worse the tribute album? Steve Earle's florid "Tom Dooley" is par for his course, but with Neko Case, Jon Langford and Sally Timms, Brett Sparks of the Handsome Family and Dean Schlabowske of the Waco Brothers, how else to explain why such imaginative and inventive performers fall so short of the likes of "Knoxville Girl," "Poor Ellen Smith" and "Gary Gilmore's Eyes"—songs that are in their blood?

3 ■ *Birthday Girl,* **directed by Jez Butterworth (Miramax)** To a soundtrack that draws deeply from music for personal hygiene commercials, Nicole Kidman turns into Meg Ryan.

4–5 ■ **Dave Van Ronk, *The Folkways Years, 1959–1961* (Smithsonian Folkways) and *No Dirty Names* (Verve Folkways, 1966)** When he died Feb. 10 at 65, Van Ronk left behind a well of generosity and affection. Many of those who passed through the Greenwich Village folk milieu in the 1960s, perhaps most, learned the classics from him—"In the Pines," "Careless Love," "Spike Driver's Moan," "Betty and Dupree"—but as *The Folkways Years* makes plain, what set Van Ronk apart from those with whom he shared his place and time was not his ability to bring the old music to life. Only rarely, as on the shattering "Zen Koans Gonna Rise Again" from *No Dirty Names,* one of his few original compositions—the sardonic title instantly dissolving into a chant of self-loathing as "The Mayor of MacDougal Street" looked down from his railroad flat at the junkies hustling their women in the doorways—did he sing anything you couldn't have heard someone else sing better. Van Ronk was different because he was what so many people think they want to be, if only they could find the time: a man whose life was a gesture of welcoming, a storyteller whose stories allowed those who were listening to imagine that they themselves were in the story, at the same time sitting back in the warmth of Van Ronk's presence, listening to their own adventures.

6–7 ▪ **Big Bad Love, directed by Arliss Howard (IFC) and** *Big Bad Love: Music From the Original Soundtrack* **(Nonesuch)** As director, co-writer and actor, Howard takes Larry Brown's 1990 short story collection and finds a single tale, or quest: the attempt of a fucked-up middle-aged man in Mississippi to turn himself into a writer without betraying . . . no, not his inviolate self, but the people he loves and who love him. Beginning with Howard, who as the male lead has the rare talent of disappearing into his own skin, the cast is extraordinary: Debra Winger as the writer's bitter ex-wife, Angie Dickinson as his disappointed mother, Paul Le Mat as his let's-party best friend, Rosanna Arquette as Le Mat's girlfriend, alive on the screen as she hasn't been since long before the black hole she hit with *Desperately Seeking Susan,* the passionate woman of *The Executioner's Song* and *Baby It's You* stepping out of a 20-years-older version of herself. The direction is all about sunlight and bar shadows, so naturalistic that when what looks like a spear flying the flag imbeds itself in the writer's wall and naturalism flips into surrealism, you accept it without thinking. But Brown's book, the material that drew Howard to the movie, is not as strong as what Howard and others brought to it. Watching, you know there's

more to the people in his picture than its story will let them say.

As the film moves on, you hear Fat Possum blues—Asie Payton, T-Model Ford, Junior Kimbrough—the way you notice the film's kudzu, as part of its landscape. There's an ugly confrontation between Howard and Winger in a juke joint; what I took away from the scene was a blond woman in a beehive hairdo dancing gracelessly and soulfully as R. L. Burnside's band hammered out "Snakedrive." But Burnside's version of Bob Dylan's "Everything Is Broken" is a man dressing up in someone else's clothes—and not such great clothes, either. It takes you out of the movie. The few seconds of Dylan's "License to Kill" coming out of Billy Bob Thornton's Jeep in *Monster's Ball*—it's just a long scratch on the soundtrack—has more bite than any number given full shape in *Big Bad Love,* maybe because Howard respected the music too much, and his own prerogatives as an artist too little.

8 ▪ *Evangeline Made: A Tribute to Cajun Music* **(Vanguard)** Aren't tribute albums terrible? John Fogerty, Linda Thompson, Linda Ronstadt, Nick Lowe, David Johansen and Richard Thompson really love cajun music. It's "hand made." It "comes from the heart." It sounds slick.

9 ▪ **Catheters,** *Static Delusions and Stone-Still Days* **(Sub Pop)** Hard noise from Seattle: one step into the fast takeoff of "Search and Destroy" Stooges, two steps past the cruelty of Eater's "1977 original punk" (as Thora Birch puts it in *Ghost World*) and out the other side, into a momentum that is its own reward, the kind of thrilling punk drive Green Day never quite caught. The first notes sound like a revival, an homage, but it doesn't take more than a few minutes to be sucked into this maelstrom as if it's happening for the first time.

10 ▪ **Josh Ritter,** *Golden Age of Radio* **(Signature Sounds)** On the front of the disc you're looking from the rear of a schoolbus, every seat filled with a young teenager with long brown hair sitting straight and still. "Golden age of radio," it says along the

bottom, and you wonder: what song on the bus's radio was it that froze these kids? What song would break the ice? But except for "Harrisburg," with a bad-news melody worthy of Will Oldham, the songs here are all words, and they wouldn't know.

Correction: In the Feb. 11 item about Jim Roll's *Inhabiting the Ball*, I wrote that, regarding the performance of the song "Handsome Daniel," the lyrics of which were written by novelist Denis Johnson, "Johnson could put more in this song than the person who's singing it now." The verses were in fact sung by Roll, his guitarist and his drummer.

MARCH 11, 2002

1 ▪ **"Paula Jones Replaces Fisher in *Celebrity Boxing*" (CNN.com, March 4)** Yes, it was all about her reputation: "Amy Fisher is out and Paula Jones is in as Tonya Harding's *Celebrity Boxing* opponent, Fox announced Saturday. . . . Jones, who lives in Cabot, Arkansas, told the Arkansas *Democrat-Gazette* she's not concerned about the notorious skater. Her only fear: the safety of her new nose job."

2 ▪ **Manic Street Preachers, *Know Your Enemy* (Virgin)** This fiercely unpretentious record features Christopher Wool–style lettering, an epigraph from Susan Sontag ("The only interesting answers are those which destroy the questions"), abstract art by Neale Howells and a host of expertly produced songs that allow you to imagine what the Beatles might be doing if they were still together and hadn't lost their edge. (If the singer on "Miss Europa Disco Dancer" isn't Paul McCartney—McCartney today, in his ragged rockabilly clothes—he could be.) But the music reaches its height with "Epicentre," an unbreakably stirring piece of 1970s-style guitar rock that calls back such dead heroes as Paul Kossoff of Free and Rory Gallagher of Taste. One chord after another, the song climbs its own steps, a leap from the top of the tower preordained. "Feels like / There's / No escape," James

Dean Bradfield says in a harsh cadence, breaking up his line like Wool breaks up words. "Except through / Our hate."

3 ▪ **Elvis Costello, *This Year's Model* (Rhino reissue, 1978)** No album ever has to sound better, but God help us if any album ever sounds more under pressure. With "This Year's Girl," "The Beat," "Hand in Hand" and "Lipstick Vogue," both the singer and the band are so swept up in the cruelty of the music it's hard to credit the multitude of choices shuddering out of every note, word or riff—what can come across as pure emotion can also communicate as craft. What feels like spew one day will feel like someone biting his tongue the next. No wonder that "Radio, Radio" and "Night Rally," both burning on their own terms, feel contrived by comparison; next to numbers that can scare you because they cut the ground out from under your feet, they're just protest songs. In sum, a world-historical statement—plus, as with all the new double-CD Costello reissues on Rhino, an extra disc of junk.

4 ▪ **Caitlin Cary, *While You Weren't Looking* (Yep Roc)** Big, chiming guitars are one of the corniest devices in rock 'n' roll, but sometimes there's no better way to say that no matter how bad the story you're telling, you're coming out of it like Timi Yuro with "What's a Matter Baby (Is It Hurting You)"— as pure vengeance. That's the feeling the fiddler from Whiskeytown gets on "Thick Wall Down," despite the fact that her words tell a story about how bad turns into good. It's one more proof that the refugees from the never-so-hot band are better off on their own— Ryan Adams with glory-rock success, Cary, unafraid to sound too much like Sarah McLachlan, with tunes that might stick.

5 ▪ **44th Annual Grammy Awards (CBS, Feb. 27)** The only highlight, from a very diminished Jon Stewart: "In Afghanistan, they were ruled by a totalitarian regime for five years, and when Afghanistan was liberated, the first thing that happened was that *music* was played on the streets there. (Applause from the hall, but somberly; this

is a tribute.) And three days later even they were sick of Creed." (Rumbles of protest from at least a few in the seats: that wasn't very nice, especially after Stewart had set them up to act patriotic.)

6 ▪ **Dennis Miller Live (HBO, Feb. 22)** Since Bush assumed the presidency, the one-time gadfly has become an administration cheerleader and his audience a gang of chanting dittoheads (this night people laughed mockingly over attorney Gloria Allred's assertion that the Supreme Court decision that made Bush president was "wrong," as if to say, "That's just *so* 2000, you cunt"). There's still room for good writing, though Miller has trimmed his famous blind references with I.D.s, perhaps because he thinks his new crowd might be a bit slow on the uptake. "We're not living in a police state," he said during his rant. "The only people longing for 1984 are the original members of the band Whitesnake"—and it's that "the band" that bleeds the line dry.

7 ▪ **24 (Fox, Feb. 26)** As it begins to emerge that presidential candidate Sen. David Palmer (Dennis Haysbert) is being run by forces unknown to him, his wife, Sherry Palmer (Penny Johnson Jerald), tries to keep him focused—by insisting that Palmer's asking who he's actually working for can wait until after the California primary. "We're almost there," she says reassuringly—and more like Angela Lansbury in *The Manchurian Candidate* every week. The premise of this show from its first episode was that you can't trust anyone; you, the viewer, really can't. It's stunning that the level of tension hasn't simply been sustained over three months, but deepened.

8 ▪ **Daniel Wolff, co-author of You Send Me: The Life & Times of Sam Cooke and editor of Ernest C. Withers' The Memphis Blues Again,** considers a White House photograph officially titled *The President and Presley Examine Documents,* and initiates a caption contest. The results so far:

Wolff: "So, if I read this correctly, you're saying that if I can dream of a better land, where all good people stand hand in hand, then why can't that dream come true?"

"Yes, sir."

Dave Marsh: Kissinger (listening through keyhole) "Damn! Adorno swore this was impossible!"

Anonymous staffer at the Clinton Presidential Library, Little Rock, Ark.: "I'm sorry, Mr. Presley, but what you're asking is just not feasible."

"Thank you, Mr. President. I'll be back."

9 ▪ **Low and Dirty Three, In the Fishtank (Konkurrent)** Premise: the Dutch label "invites bands to whom they are strongly related"—in this case the Duluth crawlers and the Australian instrumental trio led by Warren Ellis' violin—"to record while touring Holland." So every number, including what might be the first version of Neil Young's "Down by the River" cut by a woman, Low's Mimi Parker, seems 10 minutes long, and not too long. Drifting in and out of "When I Called Upon Your Seed," Parker turns the music into a church; it's as unnerving, and as lacking in doubt, as the scratch of Ellis' fiddle in "Cody." You can almost hear the water freeze—the canals in Amsterdam, Lake Superior, the Bass Strait.

10 ▪ **Law and Order (NBC, Feb. 27)** Trying to nail a company that sells personal information taken off anyone's computer, Elisabeth Röhm's young assistant D.A. Serena Southerlyn does a little research on her boss, Sam Waterston's crusty Jack McCoy, just to see how hard it might be. "You listen to a lot of Beatles and fusion jazz," she says, confirming the clichés of the character. "And you have what I can only describe as a very weird obsession with the Clash."

MARCH 25, 2002

1 ▪ **Pink, "Don't Let Me Get Me" (Arista)** This is a heartbreaker, and it makes every one of the male loser hits of the last decade—Radiohead's "Creep," Offspring's "Self Esteem," Beck's "Loser"—come off like pickup lines. The snap of Pink's rhythm sense makes you almost certain the woman whose story this is will get out of it—out of her own skin—but around every sharp turn is the voice of self-hate, the only thing her

parents ever taught her, and then you just don't know.

2 ▪ Reputation, 924 Gilman, Berkeley (March 15) Elizabeth Elmore led the tough, self-lacerating punk combo Sarge in the second half of the '90s; her new group, playing ahead of the April release of *The Reputation* (Initial Records), Elmore's strongest recording, was fourth on a five-act bill. You don't expect an opening band to have it all, to make the territory of a small, foreign club their own, to blow off the setting and make you see only them, but Elmore burns the stage—she singes it, she doesn't burn it down. There's fright behind the determination in her warbling voice, and she plays lead guitar like Elvis Costello: rhythm, then a lift that suggests rather than describes, then back to rhythm, as if the theme that suddenly shifted the song was an illusion. Watching this woman in her mid-20s, on a year's leave from law school at Northwestern, fronting three men who seemed either distinctly older or younger than she is, I wondered what sort of lawyer she'd make. Her performance carried an atmosphere of ordinary life; it was as easy to imagine her as a 40-year-old bandleader as to see her as a 30-year-old attorney. What the two would have in common might be someone who knows how to focus, to bear down, someone as hard on her client as on the other side, someone you wouldn't hire lightly.

3 ▪ Steve Almond, *My Life in Heavy Metal* (Grove) Most of the stories in this first collection originally appeared in such prestigious quarterlies as *Missouri Review*, *Ploughshares* and *New England Review*; that the two best, the title piece and "How to Love a Republican," were first published in *Playboy* is no accident. "This, it would turn out, is the main thing we had in common: a susceptibility to the brassy escapism of myth," says the narrator in "Run Away, My Pale Love." Almond's first-person narrators are always saying embarrassingly arty things like that. Though they're not the same people, they talk as if they are, one character after another indulging in the same effete verbal tics ("taking" lunch or

"supper" rather than eating it, the implicit entitlement in the phrase not fitting the people talking). Almond can't write dialogue by instinct, and he doesn't think his language through. When the narrator of "The Body in Extremis" describes a woman with "Behind this posed sangfroid, of course, was the inner panic nurtured by ambitious immigrant families," Almond doesn't seem to realize that his "of course" turns what's supposed to be a character into a type, and that he's just dismissed the person who's going to have to carry the story. But "My Life in Heavy Metal," the memoir of a cheating love affair carried on by a newspaper rock critic in El Paso, is always alive ("Jo looked like she'd been struck in the back of the head with an eel," he says of his girlfriend at a Mötley Crüe concert), and "How to Love a Republican" starts off creepy and only gets worse. It's 2000, and a bearded liberal working for Citizen Action meets a blond McCain volunteer who works for the Heritage Foundation. She takes him to hear George Will speak on "the deracination of moral authority" and to meet her mentor ("It occurred to me that Trent had served in the Armed Forces," the narrator says of shaking hands with the guy, "possibly all four of them"). She ends up in the Bush camp; he votes for Nader. What happens next may stand as one of the truest nightmares of the post-election, when sex dissolves into events and lovers into the public choices they thought they could keep separate from their private lives. For the only time in the book, Almond pulls no punches. He comes to life as a writer, not as an orchestrator of attitudes and skits, and the reader goes down with his hero.

4 ▪ Rosalie Howarth, back-announcing "Friday I'm in Love" (KFOG-FM, San Francisco, March 1) "The Cure! The Antidepressant Years!"

5 ▪ "Young Elvis: The Man and the Movement," with Michael Anderson, Peter Guralnick, William P. Kelly and Camille Paglia (Graduate Center, City University of New York, March 18) Sarah Vowell reports: "What a pleasure to listen to those who know things. Peter Guralnick knows things about RCA engineer Steve Sholes or how the archival record makes clear that Vernon Presley always paid his bills, and Camille Paglia can answer a question about Elvis impersonators by bringing up 'ancient mystery religions' in which 'the devotee becomes the god.' Walking into this panel discussion on the early Elvis, I think I was afraid the notoriously chatty Paglia might bully the mild-mannered Guralnick, but it was more than a real conversation. They were the million-dollar duet. In blue shirts and black blazers, from the waist up, they were even dressed alike. She recalled being a teenager in the '50s calling in to a radio station to vote for Elvis against Pat Boone; he reminded her that Elvis loved Pat Boone. She thanked him for researching the costume design of Elvis' 1968 black leather suit; he grinned big as she riffed on the eroticism of Elvis' Southern diction, 'Dropping off the consonant at the end was so sensuous. Eating, drinking, talking, sex—it's all the same thing.'

"Guralnick, it turns out, was the shocking one, surprising Paglia twice. Since the panel is part of a [*New York Times*–sponsored] series on the 1950s, there was a lot of talk about James Dean and Marlon Brando and the parallels between the pared down recording methods of Sam Phillips and method acting. After Paglia had returned again and again to the subject of Elvis as a 'method singer,' Guralnick informed her, 'Elvis read Stanislavski.' To which Paglia girlishly replied, 'For heaven's sake!' Guralnick added that, 'Unfortunately, you don't see anything that bears that out in his future [film] performances.' Then Paglia practically fell out of her chair when Guralnick said that the so-called '68 Comeback Special leather pants had to be dry-cleaned because Elvis, who 'told June Juanico that being onstage was better than sex,' climaxed at the show's climax. I'm sure my mother would be so proud, that I actually stood in the book signing line afterward to ask Guralnick why he edited this juicy tidbit out of his book *Careless Love*, and he

said that he didn't, it's just subtle. I looked it up, and he's right: the book quotes a crony who says, 'After he finished singing, he was literally spent.' When I read that the first time around I must have thought Elvis was just real tired. I did, for purely journalistic purposes, pop in the tape of the special and carefully watch all the leather segments to see if I could find the exact moment when Elvis peters out, but that damn guitar is in the way the whole time."

6 ■ **Selby Tigers, *The Curse of the Selby Tigers* (Hopeless)** Despite such all-American titles as "Cheerleading Is Big Business," the St. Paul quartet, in moments the truest rock 'n' roll band on the planet, reinhabits the music the Adverts and X-ray Spex left behind in London a quarter-century ago more fiercely than ever—until on the '50s-style teen-dream "The Prom I Never Had," they take off their black clothes to reveal the rented pastel tuxedos and gowns they've been trying to get out of since high school.

7 ■ **Suzzy and Maggie Roche, *Zero Church* (Red House)** Prayers set to music, and unspeakable, especially on the Shaker song "This Gospel How Precious." The version recorded in the 1960s by Sister Mildred Barker of Sabbathday Lake, Maine (collected on *Early Shaker Spirituals*, Rounder), is all you need to know: it's distinguished from the Roches' version precisely by not being precious. Barker's unaccompanied singing doesn't call attention to its own perfection—which is what the Roche sisters have been about since the release of *The Roches* in 1979, for which New York critics unanimously creamed in their jeans. Barker's performance is unpretty but anything but artless; it's an event, and it's hard to picture anyone singing the song the same way. The words "I know how to pray / I know how to be thankful," are scary, because Barker makes you realize what a huge thing that is to know how to do. The Roche sisters sing as if they know how to sing prettily, and as if that will suffice to get God's ear. After all, as they insist on their 9/11 special, "New York City," "New York City is down on her knees," and guess

what it's doing there? "Prayin' / Together with you," whether you are or not.

8 ■ Robert Warshow, *The Immediate Experience: Movies, Comics, Theatre and Other Aspects of Popular Culture* (Harvard) Warshow (1917–1955) was the popular culture man in the milieu of the postwar New York intellectuals, and this book, now augmented with eight previously uncollected essays and worshipful new commentaries from film critic David Denby and cultural theorist Stanley Cavell, is a legendary manifesto. Today it's also dull. Famous–by–reputation pieces such as the 1948 "The Gangster as Tragic Hero," which at seven pages smacks of get-it-over-with, may have had its influence on Pauline Kael's 1955 "The Glamour of Delinquency," but only the latter still has any blood running through it. Much is made of Warshow's "immediate experience" credo—"A man watches a movie, and the critic must acknowledge that he is that man"—but there is no man in the seat in these pages. Warshow pointedly rejects irony as a mode of both experience and criticism, but it is all too telling that his writing is littered with scare quotes—with countless crudely ironic references to the likes of "'typical' American experience," "the operation of 'simple' and 'American' virtues," "a 'typical' American town" where "all 'real' Americans live." *I am not fooled*, this man says, and critics have to be willing to be fooled. That is what being "that man" is all about.

9 ■ Shocker of the Week (from "Lucinda Williams: What I've Learned," interview with Brendan Vaughn, *Esquire*, April) "Some of my best friends are music critics."

10 ■ "Enronomania!" (American Folk Art Museum, New York, opening April 1, 2009) There's the short con, which is no more than claiming the 10 you gave the clerk was a 20, and then there's the long con, a true native art form. "Enron had its own myth-making machinery, recruiting employees as actors to fake out Wall Street analysts when they came to call," Frank Rich wrote in the *New York Times* on March 2. "The hoax even extended to the building of a

Hollywood-style 'trading room' set in Enron's Houston skyscraper." But a reading of linguist David W. Maurer's 1940 *The Big Con* (republished in 1999 with an introduction by Luc Sante) makes plain that the Enron scam was merely a billion-dollar revival of "the rag," a con Maurer traced to Cheyenne, Wyo., in 1867, when a three-card monte dealer named Ben Marks opened the Dollar Store, with trinkets in front to draw the marks to the barrels in the back. Not long after the turn of the century the innovation had led to the Big Store: the phony fight club, the phony horse-race parlor and then the rag—the sham brokerage.

"The victim first bets with money furnished by the con men, is then sent home for a large sum of money and is fleeced," Maurer wrote. "For the rag the store depicts a broker's office complete with tickers, phone service, brokers, clerks and customers. The same board which did duty for the races is often turned over to reveal a set-up for recording stock prices." The Big Stores were "manned and furnished" with such realism "that the victim does not realize that everything about them—including the patronage—is fake. In short, the modern big store is a carefully set up and skillfully managed theater where the victims act out an unwitting role in the most exciting of all underworld dramas. It is a triumph of the ingenuity of the criminal mind." Or, really, of the American mind: "For mere money, a thing useless and meaningless in itself," Jim Thompson wrote in 1963 of Cole Langley, the tragic hero of *The Grifters*, "he traded great hopes and a new perspective on life. And nothing was ever managed so that the frammis would show through for what it was. Always the people were left with hope and relief."

APRIL 8, 2002

1 ■ Cassandra Wilson, *Belly of the Sun* (Blue Note) The great jazz singer recorded this album in a converted shack in her native Mississippi, not, as music business rumors have it, in a grave where a blues singer

whose name no one can remember was buried before he was temporarily exhumed to allow for Wilson's makeshift studio. The extraordinary range of material includes, along with Wilson's own compositions, covers of songs made famous by the Band, Fred McDowell, Glen Campbell, James Taylor, Bob Dylan and Robert Johnson. Wilson's way with these numbers recalls nothing so much as Narcissus, gazing into a pool of water and falling in love with his reflection, and the result is the same: falling in.

2 ▪ **Heather Nova, *South* (V2)** Seven years on from the still unsettlingly frank "Walk This World," there's a breathy shiver in Nova's voice, which otherwise is smooth enough for TV commercials, that shoots her into realms of uncertainty. The story she acts out is that of a woman who has constructed a life of propriety solely to allow her fantasies to take on flesh. As you pass her on the street, she knows you can't tell. Electricity comes off of her in waves, but you can't be sure she's where it's coming from. So you play the album again.

3 ▪ **Puta-pons, *Return to Zero* (Vinahyde)** By way of Chicago in 2000, return to Liliput, anyway—which in punk terms (Zurich noise, 1978–83) may amount to the same thing. Except on the stunningly fast ride of Shelly Kurzynski Villaseñor's guitar solo in "(You Need a) Shot in the Arm," which delivers it.

4–5 ▪ **Eva Hesse, *Untitled 1970*, in "Eva Hesse" (San Francisco Museum of Modern Art, through May 19; Weisbaden Museum, Germany, June 15–Oct. 13) and *Eva Hesse*, edited by Elisabeth Sussman (SFMOMA/Yale)** Also known as *Seven Poles*, this work, coming at the very end of the exhibition, and of the German-American sculptor's short life, speaks in many voices. Seeming to bulge and swell, the yellowed, L-shaped wire-polyethylene-fiberglass constructions vary in height from 6 to 9 feet; they might have been inspired, Robin Clark writes in the catalog, by Olmec figurines or Jackson Pollock's 1952 *Blue Poles*. As Elisabeth Sussman arranged it for the exhibition, working from photos of the piece in Hesse's studio, but not

academically, allowing the poles their implicit freedom to move, the feet of most of the poles turn toward each other, and the thing looks like a version of Stonehenge, made out of Martians. Even as it played with eternity, it was laughing at itself.

6 ▪ **Dickel Brothers, *The Recordings of the Dickel Brothers Volume Two* (Empty)** Fans of the *O Brother, Where Art Thou?* soundtrack and its *Down From the Mountain* live follow-up can test their affection for old-time Appalachian string band music played by new-time people against this quintet—who, unlike some of the *Brother/Mountain* performers, honor tradition and laugh off piety with equal rigorousness. Performances of songs recorded in the 1920s and '30s by such masters as Charlie Poole, Riley Puckett, Gid Tanner & the Skillet Lickers, Dick Justice and Earl Johnson's Clodhoppers are reminiscent of the early versions, but not exactly remakes. They seem to come from somewhere else, a place of greater delight and less guilt: present-day Portland, Ore., or at least Portland a couple of years ago, when this record was made. The dead-cat-swinging invention of the sound is caught best in the group's own liner notes, in their Story of the Band, which is certainly better than the Ramones': "It's been three and a half years since Matt and Clancy Dickel realized they were brothers. They wagered there were probably more knowing how Pa Dickel was such a, how shall we say it, free spirit. It wasn't long before they unearthed three more just from looking up Dickel in the phone book . . ."

7 ▪ **Van Morrison, "He Ain't Give You None," "Linden Arlen Stole the Highlights" and "Snow in San Anselmo" (KALX-FM, Berkeley, Calif., March 11)** The nearly hysterical blues monologue from *Blowin' Your Mind!* (1967) yielded to the painfully hesitating piano opening of the tune from *Veedon Fleece* (1974), which faded into the inconclusive weather report from *Hard Nose the Highway* (1973), raising the question of whether or not Morrison had, in fact, just died—why else does anyone get three songs played in a row these days? I

remembered the writer Jonathan Cott calling the beginning of "Linden Arden" a "prayer"; I realized that for all the times I'd played the cut in my own house, wanting nothing more than to get lost in its forest, I'd never listened to the words, which in a car came across directly. The story was about men sent to kill the man the song was named for, and how he killed them instead: at the foot of all the pre-Raphaelite sunbeams in the music, blood on the floor. I also realized how little distance separated "Linden Arden" from Elton John's "Your Song."

8 ▪ **Neil Young, *Are You Passionate?* (Reprise)** Clink, clink, clink—it might happen between Young and Booker T. Jones and Duck Dunn of Booker T. & the MGs onstage, but not in the studio. No wonder Crazy Horse had to come in and juice this long afternoon nap with nine minutes of "Goin' Home," by-the-numbers but still bottomless grunge. The Flight 93 song, "Let's Roll," starts off with chills down your spine, but they come from what you carry within yourself, not what the singer's giving out. This is no "Ohio"; by the second verse your mind is already wandering.

9 ▪ **Rocket From the Tombs, *The Day the Earth Met Rocket From the Tombs: Live From Punk Ground Zero, Cleveland 1975* (Smog Veil/ Hearthan)** Not to be confused with Rocket From the Crypt—not in this life, not in the next—the band that became Pere Ubu puts down demos, gets up on stage, throws what they have at the crowd to see if any of it will come back. This is part of the history of guitarist Peter Laughner, who died in 1977 at 24, used up by himself, a shocking legacy behind him: sounds no one else would ever make, from the jittery lead to "What Love Is" to the deliberate, suicidal cadence of "Ain't It Fun." Here you can't tell if Laughner's sardonic attitude is covering up the pain or if the pain is just there to root the attitude—until he underlines breaks between verses with what can seem like four versions of himself, too many guitars speaking different languages and no translator needed, and you don't care. He hammers

away at a fuzztone, again and again, convincing you he's said what he has to say, that he's used up the song. Then he steps into a stately, Clapton-like solo, and you can see him holding his instrument the way Errol Flynn held a sword.

10 ▪ **Bruce Conner, *2002 B.C.* (Available through the Michael Kohn Gallery, Los Angeles)** This DVD collects eight 16mm films made by the San Francisco experimental artist, including the 1966 *Breakaway* with Toni Basil and the 1981 *Mea Culpa* for David Byrne and Brian Eno's *My Life in the Bush of Ghosts*. But the time-stoppers are in the 1967 *White Rose*, a seven-minute mystical documentary, scored to Miles Davis' *Sketches of Spain*, about the removal of Jay DeFeo's huge painting *The Rose* from her San Francisco apartment, and two found-footage pieces on Conner's Kansas 1940s childhood, the 1976 *Take the 5:10 to Dreamland* and the 1977 *Valse Triste*. From inside a high school science film, or a training film for animal husbandry majors, or a Chamber of Commerce promotional film, you see another movie beginning: David Lynch's *Blue Velvet*. At the least, this is surely where Lynch saw it beginning. And that, for the few minutes these films last, is just the beginning.

APRIL 22, 2002

1 ▪ **Elvis Costello, *When I Was Cruel* (Island)** This always surprising work reaches into the netherworlds of such long-ago Costello compositions as "I Want You," "Pills and Soap" and "Green Shirt." More than that, it conjures up the displacement— the weird sense of privileged resentment— of the overlooked "My Dark Life," made in 1996 for the *X Files* tribute *Songs in the Key of X* (now included on the Rhino reissue of Costello's *All This Useless Beauty*, from the same year). And with Steve Nieve, keyboards, and Pete Thomas, drums, *When I Was Cruel* is a redrawn breath of Costello's 1978 voice, the thuggishness thickened in the throat like a certain thickening of the body. The tunes are rough, hard, inventive,

moving too fast: "Like a Jewish figure revolving on a music box." Really? Did I just hear that coming out of the song, or did I write it in myself?

The heart of the album—across years of experiments, Costello's best since *All This Useless Beauty*, if not far better—may be "When I Was Cruel No. 2" ("When you were cruel?" cry the fans. "When weren't you?"). The slow performance has the languid feel of post–*La Dolce Vita* movies, everybody passed out in their Pucci outfits and only the singer walking through the gilded room, deciding what to take. The music is built around a tiny sample "from a '60s italian pop record by the great singer, mina," repeated every six seconds: "Oh, no," she seems to be saying. It's an indelible bit of rhythmic punctuation, and like Eminem's use of Dido's "Thank You" in his "Stan" but infinitely more subtle, a commentary on the story the singer is telling, insisting on doubt, melodrama and bad news.

2 ■ **Christian Marclay, *Guitar Drag*, in "Rock My World: Recent Art and the Memory of Rock 'n' Roll" (California College of Arts & Crafts Wattis Institute for Contemporary Arts, San Francisco, through May 11)** It's not clear from the works on display here—grounded in their existence as visual or mixed-media works, rather than as visual referents to musical events, and thus combining into a much more successful show than any of its many forgotten rock 'n' art precursors—whether "The Memory of Rock 'n' Roll" means the present-day memory of a finished thing or the memory of the music carries within itself. That's especially true of turntablist and collage artist Marclay's video, made in Texas in 2000: 14 minutes of an electric guitar dragged behind a pickup truck. The guitar is attached to an amp in the truck bed, so that as it's scratched and battered over rocks, brush, road and dirt it howls with noise. Shot from a comfortable distance, then very closely, then too closely, as if you're only an inch from the action, the guitar is self-evidently a solid-body version of James

Byrd Jr., as he was dragged to death by Texas racists in 1998. Part of what is horrible, and fascinating, about *Guitar Drag*, though, is that most viewers will know that Byrd came to pieces, and the guitar doesn't. Long before the video is over, the guitar stops emitting sound; it loses its guitarness, and even its metaphor. It turns into stuff, junk, something someone tied to a truck for lack of anything better to do with it. Still, at the end, you wonder if it might be fixed—and, if it could be, what it would sound like. People can be killed, Marclay's piece says; rock 'n' roll may be dead, which means you can't kill it.

3 ■ **Dirty Vegas, *Days Go By* (Capitol)** A sampler for a forthcoming album makes it plain that the way this modest piece of London dance music daft punks its way out of the Mitsubishi commercial where most Americans first heard it—with a sense that, in the right car, on the right road, with this song on the radio, you really could disappear into an eternal pop memory, shared by all—is in the electronically distorted vocal, reaching for what's already behind it. That is, an acoustic version of the song is a complete zero.

4 ■ **Paul Butterfield Band, *An Anthology: The Elektra Years* (Elektra)** 1964–71, in no hurry. With heartbreakingly beautiful photos of handsome young men.

5 ■ **Paul Butterfield with the Band, "Mystery Train," from *The Last Waltz* (Rhino reissue)** From 1976, and inside the perfect count, faster than sound.

6 ■ **John Ashcroft & the Paul Shaffer Band, "Can't Buy Me Love" (*Late Night with David Letterman*, CBS, April 9)** Ken Tucker writes: "Pressed by the host to sing his biggest hit, 'Let the Eagle Soar,' the Attorney General declined. Instead, Ashcroft—who is, says one of his aides quoted in the April 15 *New Yorker*, 'in a great mood all the time these days'—used his time to chat about why he'd just arrested lawyer Lynne Stewart (Letterman maintained a patriotic silence; the audience applauded), and then got behind the keyboard to assay a stiffly-pounded instrumental version of the Beatles

hit. If he'd wanted to make extra-sure he'd never achieve a rhythm that might have tempted him to dance, which he believes is against his religion, he should have covered McCartney's more recent, Super Bowl stupor-inducing 'Freedom.' Or, to be on the safe side, simply arrested Paul."

7 ▪ **"Secrets of Investing 2433" (unsolicited e-mail from trading@micron.net, April 10)** It's in the quick setup, the whiplash turnaround:

"Are you angered by the mess in the Middle East? Feel helpless?

"Since you can't change the situation, at least find out how it can change the quality of your life for the better.

"Click in the link below to quickly take a look on how turmoil in the Middle East could affect US oil prices and how you can counteract it."

But wait—if "you can't change the situation," how can you counteract it? Or does the "it" refer to your quality of life? And what about the grammatical impossibility of "take a look on how"? Who wrote this? And from where?

8 ▪ **"Didn't Ask to Be Born" on *This American Life* (WBEZ/NPR, March 29)** After a divorce, Debra Gwartney moves to Oregon. Her two oldest daughters, Amanda and Stephanie, 14 and 13, pull away, hard, and take a long, hard fall. "When I first started getting into the punk rock scene in Portland," Amanda says, "I got into it purely for the angry, drunk violence aspect of it. That's what really spoke to me at first." About 50 minutes later, at the close of the program, host Ira Glass read the credits, ending up with thanks for funding from various sources, and especially "from the listeners of WBEZ Chicago, WBEZ management overseen by Tobey Malatia, who explains what attracted him to National Public Radio this way," and there was a cut right back to Amanda Gwartney: "I got into it purely for the angry, drunk violence aspect of it. That's what really spoke to me at first."

9 ▪ *Bandits,* **directed by Barry Levinson (MGM Home Video)** The songs Jim Steinman writes may sound phony on the radio,

and worse at home; in the movies they march across the screen like rock gods. That was heroically true in Walter Hill's *Streets of Fire*; it's modestly true here. You believe Cate Blanchett's housewife mouthing along to Bonnie Tyler's "Holding Out for a Hero" while whipping up an elaborate dinner for her husband to be too busy to eat. You believe her even more when she apologizes to thief-on-the-run Bruce Willis for loving Tyler's "Total Eclipse of the Heart." "It's a sappy chick song," she says. "It's not sappy," he says, and you don't know whether to believe him. The line seems like a quick way into her pants, until he tops her with an all-time sappy guy song: his "Total Eclipse of the Heart," he says, is Michael Murphey's "Wildfire"—which, fortunately for the viewer, Blanchett is spared. You don't see Willis getting lucky with that on the soundtrack.

10 ▪ **Patti Smith,** *Land (1975–2002)* **(Arista)** With notes by Susan Sontag. "To the conquered!" she writes. Isn't that Ralph Nader's line? And where's "Pumping (My Heart)"?

Thanks to Howard Hampton
and Cecily Marcus

MAY 6, 2002

1 ▪ **Wilco,** *Yankee Hotel Foxtrot* **(Nonesuch)** The cover features photos of Chicago skyscrapers, and the first four words, "I am an American," are the same as those of Saul Bellow's 1953 *The Adventures of Augie March*: "Chicago born," Bellow said after a comma; "aquarium drinker," Wilco leader Jeff Tweedy says without one. But Augie March knew how to walk against the wind on the streets, to go right past you with such force you turned around and watched his back, wondering who he was—while Tweedy's singing, never strong, here recedes into a dithering miasma apparently meant to signify thinking it all over, plus sound effects apparently meant to signify the modern world. In other words, it isn't against the law to redo *Revolver*, but that

doesn't mean it's a good idea. Especially if you're an American.

2 ▪ **Sheryl Crow, "Soak Up the Sun" (A&M)** Money, fame, cheesecake photos, and on this song she still sounds like someone making her first record without the slightest interest in whether it will go anywhere at all.

3 ▪ **Warren Zevon, *My Ride's Here* (Artemis)** And the black stretch takes off like a shot, with a determination that seems to want nothing more from life than proof it can only get worse. "Do everything I tell you," says the singer in "Sacrificial Lambs," gritting his teeth inside his hipster smile. "Then we'll talk." The driver rounds a corner and picks up Carl Hiaasen, Mitch Albom and Hunter Thompson. The bestsellers and the guy whose songs don't sell scribble lyrics, grinning over all the great lines. The writers are wondering how cool this is; the singer is wondering how big their names should be on the front of the CD. Sparks fly. It's the back end of the limo, dragging the pavement.

4 ▪ **Grateful Dead, *Postcards of the Hanging: Grateful Dead Perform the Songs of Bob Dylan* (Grateful Dead/Arista, 1973–90)** "Totally supplants 'Peter Yarrow Sings Rage Against the Machine,'" writes Howard Hampton.

5 ▪ **Party of Helicopters, *Space . . . And How Sweet It Was* (Troubleman Unlimited)** From Kent, Ohio, and for anyone who loved Bush—the band, not one or the other occupant of the White House. With more ferocity, more art, less time, the same thrill.

6 ▪ **Blasters, *Testament: The Complete Slash Recordings (1981–1985)* (Rhino)** The Los Angeles rockabilly combo could nail it; with "No Other Girl" and "American Music," the songs leaping with syllables drawn out over their own rhythms, words snapping back on themselves like rubber bands, they nailed it shut. But except for a cover of John Mellencamp's "Colored Lights," there's nothing here anyone needs that wasn't on *The Blasters Collection*, and at least an hour's worth of stuff nobody needs.

7 ▪ **"Enronomania!" (American Folk Art Museum, New York, opening April 1, 2009)** Back in 2002, James L. Swenson and Daniel R. Weinberg began their extensively illustrated *Lincoln's Assassins: Their Trial and Execution* (Arena) with Lew Wallace's striking *Conspirators' Tableau*—what they called "a fanciful painting of John Wilkes Booth and his associates on the grounds of the U.S. Capitol as they watch Abraham Lincoln deliver his Second Inaugural Address on March 4, 1865." (Booth was definitely there; others of the eight convicted co-conspirators may have been.) Wallace got around—as a Union major general he served on the military tribunal that tried the surviving assassins, and after that, as territorial governor of New Mexico, befriended and then ordered the murder of Billy the Kid, and then wrote *Ben Hurr.* But what was it that led him to picture the conspirators leaning or standing on huge blocks of granite, one of them carved into an exact precursor of that tilted E true fans still remember as the Enron logo?

8 ▪ **American Magus: Harry Smith—A Modern Alchemist, directed by Paola Igliori (Inanout Digital Productions), at the IV Buenos Aires International Independent Film Festival (April 18–28)** Southern Tip writes: "If Argentina is a country that loses everything (the peso loses more than half its value, the National Library loses a big part of its collection in the course of a move, films are barely preserved and personal collections have to be thrown out when it's politically dangerous to hold on to them), then seeing a movie about Harry Smith, the weirdest collector who ever lived, may make no sense at all. But the wildness of Smith's curiosities, from ancient phonograph records to paper airplanes to string sculptures to painted eggs, might be a shot in the heart to someone living out their own no-future—because suddenly everything is possible and anything might matter. It's hard to assimilate a man whose endless, diverse collections teetered in piles above his bed but who could also distill hundreds of years of dread into a headline for someone's worst

nightmare, as he did in the handbook for his 1952 *Anthology of American Folk Music, Volume One: Ballads* (though most Argentines would have no problem getting the everyday devastation of 'Young Agriculturist Neglects Seed—Loses Both Crop and Fiancée'). Igliori, editor of a book that carries the same title as her film, doesn't fit Smith into the mold of a genius or an eccentric, an anthropologist or a student or a savior, though the people she interviews call Smith all of these things. Her movie is less a balanced portrait of a peculiar person who did exceptional things than something you can imagine seeing at Coney Island's freak show, right after the Snake Lady and before the Unbelievably Strong Tattooed Twins swallow their swords."

9 ▪ Michael Rutschky, on "Americanization? Popular Culture Abroad," at the conference Democracy and Popular Culture (John M. Olin Center for Inquiry Into the Theory and Practice of Democracy, University of Chicago, April 20) "I remember him saying we should never listen to noise," Rutschky, author of *Berlin: Die Stadt als Roman* (The City as Novel), said of studying with Theodor Adorno in the 1960s. "The noise of Heidegger or the noise of the Beatles, it was the same."

10 ▪ Pizzeria Uno, Wabash and Ohio, Chicago (April 20) On a cold, blustery night, a little speaker on the outside of the building was playing "Hound Dog." The original, sung by Willie Mae Thornton, from Los Angeles in 1953. It sounded about as old as the weather, and also like an accident of place and time—then and there, here and now.

MAY 28, 2002

1 ▪ Laurie Anderson, *Live at Town Hall New York City September 19–20, 2001* (Nonesuch) An exquisite piece of work in a situation that had to be close to impossible to navigate: straight off, Anderson offers a brief, inhumanly effete little homily on the eight-day-old ruins of New York and the blood fear of what comes next. It's unbear-

ably precious—until, somewhere into the first or second of these CDs, you realize Anderson's whole performance is an exercise in breath control, and that introduction comes back as a stifled scream, a swallowed curse, whatever *you* think you might have said in the same circumstance, which Anderson pointedly didn't say in your place.

Song after song becomes perhaps more of a song than it ever was before—"Let X = X," "Strange Angels," "Coolsville." But how Anderson managed to get through "O Superman" without losing the strict, science-fiction beat is beyond me. Dating from 1979, the composition, it's now clear, is Anderson's "Gimmie Shelter," her "Anarchy in the U.K.," her Book of Amos, her "Sugar, Sugar"; it's the end of the world, and it's catchy. It was always terrifying; it was always cute. But now, instead of predicting the future, the song is looking back at a future that has already taken place. Who, what wrote such lines as "Here come the planes / They're American planes / Made in America / Smoking, or Non-Smoking?"—and how did Anderson sing those lines after it had been revealed that "Smoking" was the answer the song had always contained? These nights were a great patriotic speech, with, scattered through the audience, the dead: Allen Ginsberg, Langston Hughes, Emily Dickinson, Abraham Lincoln.

2 ▪ New York's a Lonely Town When You're the Only Surfer Boy Around, Vermont Dep't. The Magic Rat (aka Steve Weinstein) writes from Norwich: "This is the kind of thing we have for entertainment up here, if we're LUCKY:

"'GANDY DANCER CAFE Presents: HUBCATS, Saturday, May 25 @ 9.00, $5 cover, 39 Main Street, Historic Downtown White River Junction, VT

"'The HUBCATS are an acoustic duo from the Burlington, VT area. The duo is comprised of Stewart Foster and Fred Bauer. A mix of acoustic guitar, mandolin, bass, vocal harmonies and a diverse song list that tends to stray from the mainstream gives this duo a unique appeal. Stewart's . . . early influences have been James Taylor, Jim Croce, Jonathan Edwards and others. While those influences are still noticeable in his style, influences that have played a bigger role in more recent years are such artists as Lyle Lovett and David Wilcox. Brauer has been reviewed by some as a combination of John Paul Jones & Peter Townshend. . . . The HUBCATS has just released a CD titled *FIRST SNOW."*

"Feel my pain."

3 ▪ Gossip, *Arkansas Heat* (Kill Rock Stars EP) Not as sharp a title as *That's Not What I Heard,* the trio's debut, but absolutely accurate. You can hear the whiplash of outsiders' hate as readily as you can imagine you're listening to a punk Rolling Stones—which is to say, Stones rehearsals, and so roughly that 20-something singer Beth Ditto can stick "1965" in the title song as if nothing that's happened since has fooled her for a minute.

4 ▪ Isabelle Huppert in *The Piano Teacher,* directed by Michael Haneke (Kino International) Marketing consultants vetoed the original title: *Let It Bleed.* As well as promoting it as a version of *Pandora's Box.* My God, where does Huppert go after the last shot?

5 ▪ *About a Boy,* directed by Paul Weitz and Chris Weitz (Universal) There's a dull soundtrack of new songs by Badly Drawn Boy; the musical high point of this fine picture comes near the end, when the hopelessly nowhere 12-year-old stands alone for a school "Kidz Rock" talent show and attempts to croak "Killing Me Softly With His Song," his mother's favorite. He's dying a thousand deaths—until his friend and protector Hugh Grant strolls onstage strumming an electric guitar. Missing his floppy hair, looking at once slightly embarrassed and as if he's realizing a lifelong dream, Grant gets just enough melody under the tune to make the boy's effort seem passable, if only barely, and that's what makes the scene—the refusal of the triumphant finish coded into the moment by countless movie moments like it. It's a combination of Michael J. Fox's pseudo-invention of Chuck

Berry's duckwalk in *Back to the Future* and Jennifer Jason Leigh's excruciating but undeniable nine-minute performance of Van Morrison's "Take Me Back" in *Georgia*—brought way, way down to earth.

6 ▪ Permanent city history exhibition, McCord Museum (Montreal, May 11) While the delights of the Montreal city museum are many—especially an extensive, multimedia presentation of all the different ways the place gets really cold—the stopper was the surrealism-in-action display on wealth and poverty circa 1900. A photomural of an all-but-collapsing hovel and five siblings looking about three years apart handled the latter part of the story. The former was, properly, in a glass case. It contained a Japanese lacquered screen, a set of china, a gilt chair, an oil painting of the Honourable Mrs. Hugh Graham and Her Daughter Alice, and two life-size mannequins of same, clad in lovely purple dresses, a silver teapot where Mrs. G's head should have been, a serving dish for her little girl's.

7 ▪ Bratmobile, *Girls Get Busy* (Lookout!) The now venerable riot grrrl originals have more fun—more experience they don't need. Allison Wolfe may be the flattest singer this side of Fred Schneider, but it's a far side. What she does with her limits makes her part of her audience; what Schneider does with his makes his audience an object of contempt. Hot shot: "What's Wrong With You?" where the plaintive "Baby, I don't hate men / Maybe I just hate you" is followed by cheerleader chants.

8 ▪ Pet Shop Boys, *Release* (Sanctuary) The comeback, or anyway the return—but despite "London," which may stand with their best, they could have called it "Vaguely."

9 ▪ Diann Blakely, "Duets With Robert Johnson," *BOMB* (Summer issue) Blakely is an Alabama-born poet and author of *Farewell, My Lovelies* (Story Line Press, 2000—start with "Reunion Banquet, Class of '79"). Here she weaves a very few lines from songs written in the 1930s into her own reveries, and the result is that Johnson joins a greater history than that to which he

is usually consigned, which is to say that of Mississippi country blues. In Blakely's "Crossroads Blues" the only person named is Ashley Wilkes; in her "Little Boy Blue" Johnson's teacher Ike Zinnerman "sings, but history shakes with louder sounds," and the modern sound of the country blues is suddenly the sound of the Battle of Vicksburg, and the little blue boys are dead Union soldiers. In her "Ramblin' on My Mind" it truly is Blakely who lets her mind wander: one of her ancestors appears like a haunt, her wounds still open, "the first woman killed by Nat Turner's gang," then fades past a slave owner into the evils Blakely hears Johnson "claimed for songs / Which foretold more bad news: factory stockyard closings / King shot in Memphis, schoolkids selling crack / By fallen tractor sheds. All great migrations done." Like a songwriter—like Bob Dylan—Blakely trusts a line that cannot be pinned down by time or place, by history ("All great migrations done"), to suck those that can ("schoolkids selling crack") into its instability, where all things are possible.

10 ▪ **Stephen M. H. Braitman, "Letter to the Editor"** (*San Francisco Chronicle*, **May 18**) "I love the idea of Lucas John Helder's alleged art project of creating a smiley face out of pipe-bombing patterns in the Midwest. It seems that Stockhausen's comments about the World Trade Center attack [have] borne fruit. No more limits on creativity! 'Terrorist Art' is a new genre, and has just begun to inspire the work of artists throughout the world."

JUNE 10, 2002

1 ▪ **Elvis Costello & the Imposters, Berkeley Community Theatre** (**May 23**) He played for well over two hours, and he needed the time. With original London Attractions Steve Nieve on keyboards and Pete Thomas on drums, plus Davey Faragher, a bassist from California, Costello looked sleek and ready, his voice was seamless, and for more than half of the show little came across whole. "When I Was Cruel No. 2" and

"Dust," terrific songs from last month's album, *When I Was Cruel*, lost shape to visual fussiness, missed connections between musicians, lazy rhythms. New tunes "15 Petals" and "Spooky Girlfriend," along with "Man Out of Time," "Clowntime Is Over," "High Fidelity" and others of the older songs Costello chose lack shape as compositions, and the quartet had none to give them. Endings were often pointlessly extended with parodic extravaganzas; Costello played to the crowd, asking for singalongs or eliciting the slow, barely-on-the-beat clapping that has as much to do with music or performance as the Wave does with baseball. ("I liked it better when he was an angry young man and acted as if the audience wasn't there," said a friend.) As if searching for the spines of the songs, Costello's tone turned into a bleat.

With three sets of encores, everything changed. There was no "Alison," no "(The Angels Wanna Wear My) Red Shoes." There was, first, the new "Alibi." It went on and on, rebuilt from the ground up with radical shifts in pacing, silences yielding to shattered guitar notes, pantomime as words dropped out of the song or reached their limits. "Stop me if you've heard this but," Costello added to the recorded version, like a sadist who is also a flagellant: "Papa's got a brand new / Alibi." That last word began to work as the clincher of any argument, a one-word summation of the human condition. As the song stretched, so did the idea.

"Lipstick Vogue" has been a heart attack on stage since 1978, but the lines "Sometimes I almost feel/Just like a human being" always stop the song dead even as it rushes on. Regardless of his demeanor, weight, hair, Costello has always been able to put that version of the human condition—feeling almost human—across, and its sulfurous residue carried over into the new "Episode of Blonde," made into a stand-up comedy act, the sung parts breaking off for something close to a Lord Buckley routine with vaudeville moves and Nieve, his hair flying in full Professor mode, playing his theremin like a wah-wah pedal. Again, the performance seemed impossibly long. Not too long, but as if the recorded version was merely a template of what the song could be onstage, where there was room to move, to disappear, to come back as somebody else.

The finale was "I Want You," first heard on the 1986 album *Blood & Chocolate*. It's Costello's epic, a template for so much more, including the best songs on *When I Was Cruel*, but more than anything an irreducible thing in itself. The piece is all darkness, threat, death and punishment—suddenly, that was the human condition, and no breath of any other air could make it into the music, or out of it. Now the silences in the performance were black holes, sucking in any intimations of only-kidding, of take-it-back. The jagged guitar notes that figured in "Alibi" were bigger, more unstable—huge discords calling up Neil Young's improvised soundtrack to Jim Jarmusch's *Dead Man*. *I cannot get to the bottom of this*, Costello seemed to say with every two lines, *but will not stop trying*.

There was no bottom; there simply came a point where, for the moment, there was nothing more to say. Filing out music: Roy Orbison, "It's Over."

2–4 ▪ **DJ Shadow,** *Live From Austin* **(Mothers Milk, 1999), DJ Shadow with Cut Chemist,** *Brainfreeze* **aka** *Dance the Slurp* **(Pirateria Fonografica, 1999) and** *The Private Press* **(MCA)** *Live From Austin*: scratching. *Brainfreeze*: humor. *The Private Press*: vision, by means of a ready-made remake of "Dead Man's Curve."

5 ▪ **Bryan Ferry,** *Frantic* **(Virgin)** At first the latest solo album by the great fan-as-artist feels tired. By comparison to Ferry's outrageous version of Bob Dylan's "A Hard Rain's A-Gonna Fall" on *These Foolish Things* in 1973 (an album that also featured a hysterical take on Lesley Gore's "It's My Party"), new covers of Dylan's too-familiar "It's All Over Now, Baby Blue" and "Don't Think Twice" seem pro forma. It can take a while to catch how noisy, how vulgar the strings and harmonica make "Baby Blue,"

or how cutting the instrumentation on "Don't Think Twice" to piano reaffirms what the song really is: a melody. Then a few seconds of "Ja Nun Hons Pris," credited to Richard the Lion-Hearted and sung by soprano Mary Nelson, opens onto the gorgeous "A Fool for Love," where Ferry takes the king's cloak and nobody cares. After which "One Way Love"—a melancholy, utterly obscure single by the Drifters in 1964, slightly more prominent that same year in a bouncy version by the Paris ye-ye singer Ria Bartok—is the sun coming out.

6 ▪ **Kills,** *Black Rooster* **(Dim Mak EP)** Press release: "A smoking 23 yr old American girl, a 'don't look at me' London boy with a thousand yard stare"—and both of them with a thousand pounds of attitude worn like a slip. You might hear the Kinks or the Rolling Stones from 1964, Blondie's "Rip Her to Shreds" from 1976, X's "Los Angeles" from 1980, but that doesn't mean the Kills duo have heard them; they sound as if they're starting from scratch. There's a fierce guitar undertow on "Cat Claw" and a crunch in the male-female singing on "Dropout Boogie." Not to mention "Gum," a monologue.

7–8 ▪ *CQ,* **written and directed by Roman Coppola (MGM and Outrider), plus coming attraction** The best thing about this preening vanity project was a trailer for Jonathan Parker's *Bartleby*, starring Crispin Glover. From *Back to the Future* to *River's Edge* to *Dead Man*, Glover developed a persona of passive loathing at once so weird and recognizable it verged on obscenity—but here he seems to have put everything he has into the barely different ways his precise, bland office worker can quietly deliver a five-word anarchist manifesto, "I would prefer not to." Too bad Herman Melville isn't around to hear him.

9 ▪ **American Hi-Fi, Berkeley Community Theatre (May 23)** "Robert Johnson sang primitive blues about women," the producer Frank Driggs wrote in 1961 in the notes to *Robert Johnson: King of the Delta Blues Singers*, and the manner in which the words fell together made them toll like a bell. Opening for Elvis Costello, this self-proclaimed "rock 'n' roll band from Boston!" sang whiny songs about girlfriends.

10 ▪ **Joel Selvin, "A Life With Rock Royalty," obituary for Sharon Sheeley (San Francisco Chronicle, June 2)** Sheeley wrote Ricky Nelson's 1958 "Poor Little Fool," his first No. 1 hit; with Jackie DeShannon she wrote the Fleetwoods' delicate 1961 "(He's) The Great Impostor." She died May 18 at 62. In 1959 she wrote "Somethin' Else" with Eddie Cochran, the most handsome of early white rock 'n' roll singers and, according to Nik Cohn's founding pop history *Awopbopaloobop Alopbamboom*, the most perfect. Sheeley was also Cochran's fiancée, injured in England along with Gene Vincent in the 1959 car crash that took Cochran's life. "Although Sheeley lived 42 more years, she never got over Eddie," writes Selvin, author of *Ricky Nelson: Idol for a Generation* and the unforgiving *Summer of Love*. "She was never able to stay with another man for long. Cochran loomed over her life. She will be buried in a plot next to him."

"'Poor Little Fool' provided a modest annual stipend," Selvin concluded. "She lived quietly with her grown son, across the street from her sister. She entertained visitors with hilarious anecdotes and reminiscences, peppered with sly humor and innuendo. Sheeley was the original Riot Grrrl, even if those in her debt never knew. One young music business secretary sighed to Sheeley about Cochran's good looks a few years ago. 'Honey,' Sheeley said, 'you should have seen him when he was breathing.'"

JUNE 24, 2002

1 ▪ **Chumbawamba, Readymades (Republic/Universal)** With a picture of Berlin dadaist John Heartfield shouting on the cover, you might think the Leeds righteousness brigade would be back with another set of finger-wagging dark prophecies: Even their 1997 get-drunk, get-really-drunk hit "Tubthumping" was about how getting drunk only postpones a confrontation with hegemony. That's certainly what the sleeve

notes offer, carefully explaining which particular social injustice each song addresses. The performances, on the other hand, are rich, layered, musically finished, emotionally unresolved. Often built around tiny vocal samples from U.K. folk musicians—the repetitions are like bird calls, or sounds in a dream that you can recognize but not name—the best numbers seem to float back to a time when their promises were made, to escape our time, where everyone knows the promises were never meant to be kept. That sense of regret, or damnation, is never erased; it's suspended. The longing from the late Lal Waterson in "Salt Fare, North Sea" is about betrayal, but also about a refusal to give up; "All in Vain" is about defeat, but too beautiful to be final. All across this record, the band sets snares for itself, but the musicians they have appropriated to valorize their quest for what Berlin dadaist George Grosz called "the big no" refuse to let them step in their own traps.

2 ▪ **Cherish, directed by Finn Taylor (Fine Line)** Or, Last Night a DJ Took My Life. With Robin Tunney as the life, Brad Hunt as the DJ and Liz Phair as the meanie you always knew she was.

3 ▪ **Randy Newman, Good Old Boys (Reprise/Rhino reissue, 1974)** Newman's elegant album about the white South in a time of confusion: Martin Luther King was dead and Richard Nixon was president; people could still convince themselves nothing would ever change, even though they understood nothing would ever change back. Newman's original idea was an entire album in the voice of one white Birmingham steelworker. That is here as a second disc, a solo demo session called "Johnny Cutler's Birthday," recorded in early 1973. It is rough and blasted. "Louisiana 1927" is like a comic strip by Vermeer on "Good Old Boys" and like an editorial from the *New Orleans Times-Picayune* as part of "Johnny Cutler"—and more convincing. Newman sits at his piano, talking to his producer; what comes across is an artist in a bad mood, his misanthropy and self-

loathing undisguised, his sense of humor something to use and throw away, like a cigarette butt.

4 ▪ **Peter Bradley, MP (Labour, The Wrenkin), Early Day Motion, House of Commons (May 22)** Motion: "That this House pays tribute to the legendary Arthur Lee, also known as Arthurly, frontman and inspiration of Love, the world's greatest rock band and creators of *Forever Changes*, the greatest album of all time; notes that following his release from gaol he is currently touring Europe; and urges the honourable and especially Right honourable Members to consider the potential benefit to their constituents if they were, with the indulgence of their whips, to lighten up and tune in to one of his forthcoming British gigs."

5 ▪ *The Passion of Joan of Arc* **(1928), directed by Carl Theodor Dreyer, original score played by the Buenos Aires Symphonic Orchestra with the National Polyphonic Chorus of the Blind, conducted by Santiago Chotsourian, Teatro Colón, Buenos Aires (June 2)** Southern Tip writes: "For the second time this fall, the grand Buenos Aires opera house turns into the best movie theater imaginable—velvet box seats, a quiet audience and a chance to see restored prints of G. W. Pabst's *Pandora's Box* and Dreyer's *The Passion of Joan of Arc* with live orchestral accompaniment. The conductor must have a little screen in the pit with him because every time someone opens a door or strikes a bell, the sound from below is right on the mark. In *Joan of Arc* it's Renée Falconetti's gorgeous face that is so astonishing. Even before they cut all her hair off—an act that in this film is as shocking and violent as burning her alive—you wonder how Falconetti (who died in Buenos Aires in 1945) survived her own performance. It makes complete sense that she never made another movie again. How could she when I can barely imagine seeing another movie?"

6–7 ▪ *Bartleby*, **directed by Jonathan Parker (Outrider) and Ralph Rumney,** *The Consul: Contributions to the History of the* *Situationist International and Its Time— Conversations with Gérard Berréby,* **translated from the French by Malcolm Imrie (City Lights)** Yes, Crispin Glover is believable as the clerk whose purposeful withdrawal from work, passive resistance to termination and finally refusal to vacate his office even after the concern that hired him has vacated the premises slowly drives his boss David Paymer mad—as he is as Adolf Hitler, as Bartleby appears in one of Paymer's nightmares. Not that the tale, which in its present-day setting owes as much to Mike Judge's 1999 film *Office Space* as to Herman Melville's 1856 short story, can't play differently in real life. "One evening, during our time at Canterbury when I taught art, I was a bit worried because one of my students had barricaded himself inside a kind of shelter he'd made out of his canvases," the late painter Ralph Rumney (1934–2002) recalls in ruminations over his travels with the European avant-garde. "He refused to come out or to communicate. Despite my superiors' wanting to call the police and the student psychiatric services, I got an agreement that we would do nothing until the next morning on the grounds that he might see things differently after a night's sleep. Michèle [Bernstein, with Rumney and others a founder of the revolutionary artists' group the Situationist International in 1957, and Rumney's second wife], had told me the solution was simple: I had only to give him Melville's 'Bartleby' to read and everything would sort itself out during the day. Which is exactly what happened." Bernstein knew how terrifying the story really is.

8 ▪ **Charley Patton (1891?–1934),** *Screamin' and Hollerin' the Blues: The Worlds of Charley Patton* **(Revenant), con't.** Sausalito Slim writes: "I'm avoiding trying to totally rewrite yet another piece for the Great Metropolitan Newspaper (they now want only 'interview-based' record reviews, whatever that's supposed to mean. Me: 'So, Neil Young, how come your new album sucks?' NY: *click*). They held on to my Charley Patton piece for six months, then rejected it after the box set didn't win a Handy Award, because it wasn't 'newsworthy.' And Revenant said they couldn't set up a phoner with Patton because he's been hanging with Mingus lately, and he's convinced him that letting the white man call him 'Charley' is demeaning."

9 ▪ **Hobart Smith, "The Coo Coo Bird," from** *Songcatcher II: The Traditions That Inspired the Movie* **(Vanguard)** These selections from 1960s Newport Folk Festival performances make it plain that Doc Watson was one of the dullest traditional singers ever to record and that Hobart Smith, a Saltville, Va., banjo player who died in 1965, was one of the most fierce. Surrounded here by Dock Boggs, Clarence Ashley, Fiddlin' Arthur Smith and Roscoe Holcomb, he sounds as if someone or something has set him on fire, as if his only chance to escape is to run right out of his own skin.

10 ▪ **"R. Kelly, R&B Star, Is Indicted on Child Sex Charges" (***New York Times***, June 6)** "Chicago, June 5—R. Kelly, the Grammy-winning R&B singer, was indicted today on 21 counts of child pornography after the authorities said he made a sexually explicit videotape with an underage girl that has been selling in bootleg versions on street corners across the country. . . . In a statement released this afternoon by his Los Angeles lawyer, Mr. Kelly said, 'Even though I don't believe any of these charges are warranted, I'm grateful that I will have a chance to establish the truth about me in a court of law.'" "Smacks of a desperation ploy," writes one correspondent: "his one and only chance to be mentioned in the same breath with Chuck Berry."

Thanks to Perfect Sound Forever

JULY 8, 2002

1 ▪ **Jennifer Love Hewitt, "BareNaked" (Jive)** Not that the actress who once noted that the real message of the posters for *I Still Know What You Did Last Summer* was "I Know What Your Breasts Did Last Summer" is playing off her body or anything. To

start off this co-written single, the Queen of Televised Adorableness moves into a melody seriously picked out on acoustic guitar, then twists a line just like Sheryl Crow: "Didja ever have that dream where you're walking naked down the street?" Another terrific moment: "Didja ever feel so deep that you speak your mind, you put others right to sleep?" sung matter of factly, like someone shaking hair out of her face, and then a chord change hands the number over to the Britney factory. The song fights back, but it never gets out of that hole. Or that cloud. Or whatever that prison of vagueness is.

2 ▪ **Nicolas Guagnini,** *30,000* **(1997–2000), in "Ultimas Tendencias" (Latest Directions), Museo de Arte Moderno de Buenos Aires (June 16)** As you approach the piece in its gallery, bits of black paint on 25 wooden rods, 1 centimeter wide, 45 centimeters high, give the impression of many fragmented faces. Close up, as you circle the work, moving from right to left, the splotches resolve themselves into a single male face: dark hair, dark circles under the eyes, a neatly knotted tie. As you continue to circle, the face begins to dissolve until, when you arrive at the left side of the construction, it's a complete blank. What it was was a model for a proposed monument in a proposed Garden of Memory: a memorial to those executed, tortured to death or disappeared during Argentina's barbaric 1976–83 military dictatorship, a regime that announced itself as El Proceso Reorganización Nacional; Guagnini, born in Buenos Aires, was 10 when it began.

The feeling the thing gave off was this: you're walking down the street, now, 20 years after the fall of the generals, who today live among you, perhaps under house arrest, perhaps free. You think you see someone, someone you've assumed is dead. Like Dr. Zhivago glimpsing Lara from the bus, you rush toward the person—no, it's not who you thought it was. But then you see another one. And another. And another.

3 ▪ **Nazareth Pacheco,** *Untitled 1997–98,* **in "El Hilo de la Trama" (The Thread Unrav-**

eled), **Museo de Arte Latinoamericano (Buenos Aires, June 12)** For an exhibition subtitled "Contemporary Brazilian Art," Pacheco, born in 1961, was working on the world as it was when she was a little girl, fashioning a severe cocktail dress out of black and white beads and safety razors. There was nothing punk about it. Hanging in the air, it was very nervous, very thin, very Warhol Party at the Factory, very neurasthenic, very future lung cancer.

4 ■ **Alvin Youngblood Hart, *Down in the Alley* (Memphis International)** Hart's previous re-creations of old American music—country blues, especially, but also his own songs, draped in the must of the past—seemed both felt and forced. You could imagine him in a time machine, dropping in quarter after quarter, the thing buzzing and smoking, giving off mood but never actually going anywhere. But here, as part of the first offering from a modestly ambitious new label—other releases include *The Missing Link*, previously unknown 1979 recordings by the cranky and very dirty hobo singer Harmonica Frank (1908–84), and a live album by Memphis soul singer Carla Thomas—Hart wears the old blues like clothes, kicking up a storm of banjo notes on "Deep Blue Sea" for the pleasure of the sound, clattering around "Broke and Hungry" as if it's his own apartment.

5 ■ **Robert Plant, *Dreamland* (Universal)** It happened in 1971 in "Rock and Roll," "Stairway to Heaven" and "The Battle of Evermore" on ZoSo. With visionary versions of '6os chestnuts ("Morning Dew"), scattered country blues themes ("Win My Train Fare Home") and originals ("Last Time I Saw Her"), it happens now. It's a leap through time—back in time, it seems, until the aura of the unlikely takes over. The freedom in the music is the freedom of rehearing old songs as if they had been imagined by other people, but never written, never recorded. If the songs are to be put into the world someone else will have to do it, so the singer volunteers. In this suspension, everything is in harmony and no possibilities of rhythmic force, of momen-

tum generating more of itself ("Skip's Song," from the late Skip Spence), are foreclosed. Since Led Zeppelin broke up Robert Plant has been much more a fan than a performer, but here the distinction is meaningless. He'll be 54 on Aug. 20, his skin is creased like tinfoil, but inside it he sounds completely at home.

6 ■ **Percival Everett, *Grand Canyon, Inc.* (Versus Press, 1999)** The birth of an American con man, or, President Truman attends a flood in Iowa by way of President Coolidge's attendance at a flood in Randy Newman's "Louisiana 1927": "Daddy Tanner drove his son to southern Iowa one spring to see the devastation caused by a major flood. There was a huge crowd of people standing near the edge of the sandbag dike and they joined in and it turned out that President Truman had come down to see the devastation too. The great man kept saying things to a little fat man beside him and the little fat man would write those things down on his notepad.

"The sight of pigs, cows, barns and a sleigh bed floating away did not impress young Tanner, but he was impressed by the idea of having a little fat man with a notepad by his side."

7 ■ **Syd Straw, Village Underground (New York, June 28)** The Magic Rat writes: "At a show from the unclassifiable downtown singer, you're apt to get funny, rambling stories punctuated by dialogue with the audience and interspersed with drink requests ('I'm the thinking man's drinking woman'). Straw's voice is wry, then yearning—and the struggle to reconcile the two lends cohesion to sets that can run from the jazz standard 'Bewitched, Bothered and Bewildered' to Straw's blasted, desperate 'CBGB's.' This time, accompanied only by pianist Joe Ruddick and bewildered last-minute addition Dave Schramm on guitar, she ran through her 'Madrid,' the Magnetic Fields' 'The Book of Love,' Shania Twain's 'You're Still the One' (with novelist Rick Moody on vocals and guitar), culminating in a beautiful performance of Peter Blegvad's 'Gold,' which, like all great interpretive

singing, left you unable to separate the singer from the song."

8 ▪ Handsome Family, *Live at Schuba's Tavern* (DCN) On this December night in Chicago last year, Brett and Rennie Sparks' Gothic songs—which owe as much to Emily Dickinson as to "The Wagoner's Lad," as much to "Apache" as to Edgar Allan Poe—take on a new drama. The sense of an alcoholic Shakespearean actor reciting *King Lear* for an underattended tent show audience in a Colorado mining town somewhere around 1880, always present in Handsome Family music, is heightened. With unexpected deep breaths, with a deepened voice, the singer is suddenly 10 feet tall. Lyric writer Rennie makes jokes between numbers ("If we're over $5,000 in debt that means you're off your medication, right?"); they seem to push her husband out of the nightclub, into the streets, until within minutes he's wandering the prairie like Brigham Young with no one behind him.

9 ▪ Verónica Longoni, displays at Salsipuedes Condimentos, Calle Honduras 4874, Salispuedes, Calle Honduras 4814 and O'D. A (Objetos de Artistas), Calle Costa Rica 4670 (Palermo Viejo, Buenos Aires, June) The 31-year-old Longoni makes dolls of various sizes, from life-size to 8-inch amulets (a woman holding an aspirin between her legs to ensure virginity on her wedding day). But her best new work, recently in the window of Salispuedes Condimentos (an accessories shop down the street from the parent clothes store), is a whole population of 4-inch figures. They look like dada dolls: like variations on the "magical bishop" cardboard costume Hugo Ball assumed in Zurich in 1916 to pronounce his sound-poems, with wings for arms, claws for hands, a striped tube almost replacing his head.

None of Longoni's dolls look precisely like Ball's costume, but all carry the same suggestion of an absolute transformation, which isn't necessarily willed. Beginning six years ago, Longoni's project came out of her journeys through Argentina and elsewhere in South America, researching the

way images of local saints migrated into local popular culture. It was a process of desacralization, where explicit or literal religious connotations were lost and the imagery was freed, even though in new objects vestiges of ritual power remained. Thus in the Condimentos window you could see a froglike creature with three red roses sprouting from its featureless head; a white body with faint black circuits traced on its trunk and a head of two wired light bulbs; women giving birth; a person made of typescript clutching a blank black book; a torture victim in a straitjacket; someone with horns or knives protruding from the chest like the spikes of a stegosaurus' tail, many more.

With Argentina's economic collapse, Longoni explained, there is little gallery or institutional space for young artists. But with no formal art world to work in, a show in a shop window is as much of a show as one in a gallery. More people see the work, with the spell of art's own sanctimony absent and the notion of buying something ordinary. In that sense Longoni's work is itself part of the process of desacralization it fools with. Just as Hugo Ball migrated from dada blasphemy to his own kind of sainthood, dying a devout Catholic, here art migrated out of arthood. The size of the dolls demanded that the passerby lean forward and peer into each figure, its details too small for anything to be obvious, each one seemingly silenced and speaking, damned and telling the same joke.

10 ▪ Julio Cortázar, *Hopscotch*, trans. from the Spanish by Gregory Rabassa (Pantheon, 1963, 1966) In Paris in the late '50s, the Serpent Club—various not-young expatriate bohemians—lay around an apartment, listening to old 78s. "Two corpses," the narrator says of Bix Beiderbecke and Eddie Lang "clinching and breaking" on cornet and guitar "one night in 1928 or 29," and over the next 25 pages more corpses clinch and break with the living. Bessie Smith's "Empty Bed Blues" goes on, on a disc made of Bakelite: "The needle made a terrible scratch, something began to move down deeper as if there were layers of cotton between voice and ears, Bessie singing with a bandaged face, stuck in a hamper of soiled clothes." "The intercessors," the narrator thinks, "one unreality showing us another, like painted saints pointing towards Heaven. This cannot exist, we cannot really be here, I cannot be someone whose name is Horacio. That ghost here, the voice of a Negro woman killed in an automobile accident twenty years ago: links in a nonexistent chain." After Jelly Roll Morton and Duke Ellington the narrator calls for "Stack O'Lee Blues" by Fred Waring and His Pennsylvanians—he doesn't say if it's the 1924 or 1928 version.

In the late '50s Fred Waring wasn't a corpse; he had his own TV show, peddling white-out jazz and standards, the safest music imaginable. But in Paris the narrator doesn't know that. He or Cortázar himself is trying to figure out why "Every so often the dead fit the thought of the living." Like no one else I've read, the great Argentine novelist (1914–84) gets to the oddity of the fraternity that comes together when one is listening to and feeling at one with the dead, who on records are more physically present than in any other medium: on the page, on the screen, even in a personal memory of a night when you were there to see the singer, alive.

JULY 23, 2002

1 ■ **Tommy Lasorda on Ted Williams (***San Francisco Chronicle***, July 6)** "He had a great pair of eyes. They say he could watch a 78 record go around and tell you what's on the label." Normal people can't do it with a 45.

2 ■ **Jill Olson, *My Best Yesterday* (Interstate)** The jingle-jangle of the Searchers in the guitars, their "Needles and Pins" bite in this young woman's voice, a warmth and a feel for loss that the Searchers never got around to—and a sense of place that makes Olson, who sings far less convincingly in the San Francisco country band Red Meat, at once familiar and someone you haven't yet met. "I hope these pop tunes remind you of the sounds that might have blasted from the radio of a brand-new 1966 Ford Ranchero," Olson says, "way back before you were born." Or perhaps before she was.

3 ■ **Subway commercial for Dijon Horseradish Melt (Fox Sports Net, July 13)** One "Jim" ("a Dennis Miller–type of guy who tells it like it is," says Subway publicist Les Winograd) pulls up to a burger joint in a car full of buddies. He's about 40, tall, well-exercised: "Turkey breast, ham, bacon, melted cheese, Dijon horseradish sauce," he says in the drive-through, exuding an aura of Supermanship all out of proportion to the situation. "That's, like, not on our menu," says the young, pudgy, confused person taking orders. "It's not only not on your menu," Jim says, "it's not on your radar screen!" "Do we have a radar screen?" the clerk asks a supervisor as Jim peels out. "Think I made that burger kid cry?" Jim says to his pals, all of them now ensconced in a Subway with the new Select specials in front of them.

It seems plain that, finally, George W. Bush is making himself felt in culture. The commercial takes Bush's sense of entitlement—which derives from his lifelong insulation from anything most people eat, talk about, want or fear, and which is acted out by treating whatever does not conform to his insulation as an irritant—and makes it into a story that tries to be ordinary. But the story as the commercial tells it is too cruel, its dramatization of the class divisions Bush has made into law too apparent. The man smugly laughing over embarrassing a kid is precisely Bush in Paris attempting to embarrass a French-speaking American reporter for having the temerity to demonstrate that he knew something Bush didn't. (*Real Americans don't speak French.*) Even someone responsible for putting this talisman on the air may have flinched at the thing once it was out there in the world at large, functioning as public discourse, as politics—the last time I saw the spot, the final punchline had been dropped.

4 ■ **Counting Crows, *Hard Candy* (Geffen)** After the tied-in-knots *This Desert Life*, a return to form: songs about endless free time, a fortune under the couch cushions not to mention in the bank, nothing to do and nowhere to go. Played with all hearts on sleeves. With angst. ANGST. *ANGST*. And it works: It describes a real terrain where people without endless free time or too much money to count actually live. Even if Adam Duritz's hair has reached the point where it looks ready to fly away with him.

5–6 ■ **Phil Collins, Shirley Bassey, Bryan Adams, Queen, Annie Lennox, Cliff Richard, Elton John, Brian Wilson, Eric Clapton, Steve Winwood, Tom Jones, Rod Stewart, Joe Cocker, Ozzy Osbourne, et al., *Party at the Palace: The Queen's Jubilee Concert*, Buckingham Palace (Virgin) and Furry Lewis, Bukka White and Friends, *Party! At Home—Recorded in Memphis in 1968* (Arcola)** Aside from Tom Jones' "You Can Leave Your Hat On"—a Randy Newman ode to fetishism for which I somehow doubt the queen was present, done in full *Mars Attacks!* mode—the package is as worthy of all the performers joining hands onstage at the end of the concert to commit mass suicide as you might expect. I was looking forward to the conceptually irresistible set-up of comparing *Party* to the similarly titled release by blues singers who had the advantage of being already dead. But then I did the honest thing and listened to it.

7 ■ **Bill Moody, *Looking for Chet Baker: An Evan Horne Mystery* (Walker)** Moody's idea of adding a brooding intensity to his jazz detective is having him say "Don't go there" over and over—or having him tell us that to catch a very special moment he "punched the air and said Yes!"

8 ■ **Mark Zwonitzer with Charles Hirshberg, *Will You Miss Me When I'm Gone? The Carter Family & Their Legacy in American Music* (Simon & Schuster)** It's shocking, but aside from John Atkins' obscurely published 1973 *The Carter Family*, this is the first book about a trio that from the 1920s through the '30s made what remains as profound and influential a body of American song as can be found anywhere. It's also shocking that even though it is more than 400 pages long, *Will You Miss Me When I'm Gone?* is not a serious book. Zwonitzer, who makes documentaries for NPR (Joe DiMaggio, Mount Rushmore), acknowledges his dependence on interviews by Hirshberg (author of undistinguished books on Elvis Presley and the Beatles), on 1960s interviews by folklorists Ed Kahn and Mike Seeger, on research by the scholar Charles Wolfe, and more. But not a quotation or a fact in the book is sourced, which makes it worthless for anyone who might want to pursue routes Zwonitzer might be opening up. Even the many photos are undated. There is no bibliography or discography.

As writing, the book is cute when it isn't tone-deaf. Hardly a page goes by without Zwonitzer attempting to convince a reader that, as a Northerner, he's down-home with the Carter Family's Virginia mountains, juicing the narrative with countless versions of "mighty fine," "pretty fair" or "flat out." "When the crop was good—and, tell the truth, even when it wasn't so good—there was always corn to spare for liquor," he says in his rangy voice. Oh, those hillbillies!—always going around saying things like "tell the truth." As for the music, Zwonitzer has no sense of how to get a song into prose. Other people will have to tell whoever might want to know why the Carter Family needs a book, not that the Carter Family has ever ceased to do it.

9–10 ■ **"Reimagining July 4," *New York Times* (July 4) and "Dissent: The American Way," *San Francisco Chronicle* (July 4)** The contrast between these two unsigned editorials could not have been more complete. The *Times* writer spoke of the "breathtaking" renewal of "the principles behind" the country, adding that, "As principles go, they are generous to a fault"—whatever that means. The writer went on to speak of the difficulty of "feeling one's freedom" ("a little like trying to feel the rotation of the earth"), while finding the notoriously resistant idea of freedom itself not at all difficult to define: "Freedom is the ability to choose whom and what you will become according to your own lights." How very New Age or, rather, Republican: it's up to you, you're on your own, and there is no such thing as society, let alone politics. Freedom certainly has nothing to do with citizens attempting to determine the nature and purpose of their community, their common predicament, their more perfect union.

The great historical struggle to create that union was the subject of the *Chronicle's* broadside, which one can hardly imagine running in any other major daily in the country. It pulled no punches. "Ever since Sept. 11," the writer began, "President George W. Bush and Attorney General John Ashcroft have tried to quash dissent by questioning the patriotism of people who seek to protect our civil rights and liberties." The writer went on to trace the history of our best-known patriotic traditions, rituals, sayings and songs, from the Pledge of Allegiance to the motto on the Statue of Liberty to "America the Beautiful," noting that the latter was written in 1883 by Katherine Lee Bates, a feminist professor of English at Wellesley who lived "for decades" with "her life partner Katherine Coman, an economist and social historian. It's unlikely that those who sing the stirring words 'and crown thy good with brotherhood, from sea to shining sea' know that a progressive lesbian who agitated for a more democratic America authored these words." In other words, the writer was saying, the story of the country is a continuing story, and it starts again when you lift your eyes from the paper.

AUGUST 5, 2002

1–3 ▪ **David Johansen and the Harry Smiths, "Death Letter," on *Shaker* (Chesky Records); White Stripes, "Death Letter," on *De Stijl* (Sympathy for the Record Industry, 1998); and Son House, "Death Letter," on *Son House: Father of the Delta Blues—The Complete 1965 Sessions* (Columbia Legacy, 1992)** Son House (1902–88) was the most melodramatic of the great Mississippi Delta blues artists, and when he sat in New York City in 1965 to record "Death Letter," he pulled out all the stops—just as he'd done with the sardonic "Preachin' Blues" in 1930, when he first recorded. In 1965 he wasn't the musician he'd been as a young man, but the drive to thread a song through six minutes or more was still there. The guitar playing is splayed, but it cuts to the bone; the man recalling the death of the love of his life takes satisfaction from the fact that he will never get over it.

White Stripes Jack and Meg White attack "Death Letter" as Steve Miller might have, a couple of years after House cut it: Miller on stage at the Fillmore in San Francisco, determined to prove that disrespect—a tone more mordant than wounded, an orchestration less elegant than simply loud—is the surest route to the truth. With their band still coming together in 1998, the Detroit punk combo is as stumbling as House was, and they care as much as he did: that is, not at all. Again and again they climb the spine of the song, leaping off like little kids diving from a rock into a pond. They climb out, shake the water out of their hair and the song is theirs.

Punk progenitor Johansen—New York Dolls frontman in the 1970s, lounge lizard Buster Poindexter in the decades that followed—takes a different tack in his current incarnation as tramp folklorist. He shambles into the tune as if it's obvious, as if its tale wouldn't even be worth telling if he weren't already drunk. Against House's more than seven minutes, or the White Stripes' branding-iron sound, Johansen needs only four laconic minutes to make the dead woman in the song perhaps more dead than she's been before. There's something about Johansen's sense of humor—his weird way of communicating that even as he's getting his story across he's forgetting something more important—that allows him to relax into songs a contemporary white man should be ashamed to even consider singing.

4 ▪ **Comet Gain, *Réalistes* (Kill Rock Stars)** Three in the morning in someone's London

apartment, unattached men and women not giving up on the night: at first you hear blithering, then the smartest blithering you've ever heard. Then shots in the dark: "There's no security in purity." Then anguish and hope, forgiveness and curses, and a heartbreaker from its title to the last note: "Why I Try to Look So Bad." By this point you're hearing people you'd like to meet.

5 ▪ Bernard Weinraub, "*Six Feet Under* Leads Emmys with 23 Nominees" (*New York Times*, July 19) "*Six Feet Under* was not shown to a test audience, as it would be at a network," series creator Alan Ball tells Weinraub. "Nobody ever suggested bringing people from a mall to get their opinion of the show"—and can you imagine? *Mall people* judging the work of the man who wrote *American Beauty*? The man who unmasked American suburbia as a land of moral hypocrisy and spiritual decay as not more than three or four hundred other movies had ever done before?

6 ▪ Anything for Art, or You Will Know Those Who Turn Self-Deprecation into Self-Congratulation by Their Trail of Dead (Shoreline Media press release, July 25) "Two days ago, while in Philadelphia to tape Fresh Air, Linda Thompson found out that Lucinda Williams was playing that night, and then scored tickets to the show. Williams, who was tipped off that Thompson was in the crowd, stopped midway through her set and explained that 'I feel really self-conscious Linda Thompson's in the audience.' She was, however, able to finish the show."

7 ▪ X-Ray Spex, *The Anthology* (Sanctuary) With Poly Styrene's screech prophesying the London Hanif Kureishi would begin to write out in the mid-1980s, an affirmation of life no less fierce than Son House's affirmation of death, and a setting that burned with the same intensity. The songs tumble down one after the other, each whole, each bursting its skin: "The Day the World Turned Day-Glo," "Let's Submerge," "Identity." On the first disc, collecting the 1978 *Germfree Adolescents* album, Rudi Thompson's sax rolls over the music like a storm, but he holds the shape

of each number; with the eight tunes cut in the Roxy nightclub in 1977, the sound splitting in half a dozen directions at once, original saxophonist Lora Logic (who in 1995 combined with by-then Hari Krishna sister Styrene for a few new tunes) is utterly elsewhere. She seems to be playing from a nightclub in Saigon, as if punk was as likely to first raise its head there as anywhere— and as Poly runs her songs to ground, it's Lora who gives every performance its smell of the uncanny, the unreal, the sense that the performance this recording documents could never have happened.

8 ▪ Uncle Tupelo, *89/93: An Anthology* (Columbia Legacy) Dull, but as Jeff Tweedy proves in a previously unreleased number that begins as a plaintive love ballad, there is no such thing as a bad version of "I Wanna Be Your Dog."

9–10 ▪ On Louis Armstrong: Julio Cortázar, from *Hopscotch* (1963, translated from the Spanish by Gregory Rabassa, Pantheon, 1966) and Percival Everett, from *Glyph* (Graywolf Press, 1999) In Paris in the late 1950s, in an apartment where every jazz 78 seems deeper than the last, an Argentine in his 40s lets his mind drift back to "Storyville nights, where the old only really universal music of the century had come from, something that brought people closer together and in a better way than Esperanto, UNESCO, or airlines, a music which was primitive enough to have gained such universality and good enough to make its own history, with schisms, abdications, and heresies" and most of all "Satchmo, everywhere, with that gift of omnipresence given him by the Lord, in Birmingham, in Warsaw, in Milan, in Buenos Aires, in Geneva, in the whole world, is inevitable, is rain and bread and salt, something that is beyond national ritual, sacred traditions, language and folklore: a cloud without frontiers, a spy of air and water, an archetypal form, something from before, from below, that brings Mexicans together with Norwegians and Russians and Spaniards, brings them back into that obscure and finally forgotten flame, clumsily and badly and precariously he delivers them back to a betrayed origin."

In *Glyph*, his hilarious novel about the games language plays with people, Percival Everett brings Aristophanes together with Ralph Ellison, and has them put it somewhat differently. Aristophanes: "All war is unnecessary and finally ruinous for all parties, but yet I find that the notion of sincere reconciliation doesn't appear as an option for humans, or for politicians either." Ellison: "Perhaps. But the condition you call war is often the condition of life for many. We have in our time a musician who clowns before kings and queens, wipes down his sweating brow with a rag between creating the sweetest music with the same lips and breath that make a graveled growl of a voice. He is at war. Necessarily and perhaps forever. And his weapon is irony. The enemy loves what he does, but when they imitate him, try to make it themselves, they hate him because, not only do they fail to recreate his music, they are terrified of becoming the one they mimic."

Or, as Melissa Maerz of *City Pages* in Minneapolis described Holly Golightly's show at South by Southwest in Austin last March 27, "Little white singer-songwriter snarls the blues like a one-woman White Stripes. Somewhere, indie rockers torn between folk and garage are discovering the next big thing. Somewhere else, Son House is laughing his ass off."

AUGUST 26, 2002

1 ▪ **Jaime O'Neill, "It's only rock 'n' roll, but it's enough, already" (*San Francisco Chronicle*, Aug. 4)** After dismissing the notion of the teenager as "a marketing construct" and seemingly regretting that, at 58, he ever was one, rejecting all forms of youth culture as manipulations, frauds and posing, O'Neill hits the clincher: "The anthems of the '60s anti-war movement have killed more of us than the war itself." Inarguable, of course, but we need details: how many people did Bob Dylan's "A Hard Rain's A-Gonna Fall" kill as opposed to Freda Payne's "Bring the Boys Home"? Country Joe and the Fish's "I-Feel-Like-I'm-Fixin'-to-Die Rag" vs. Edwin Starr's "War"? Barry McGuire's "Eve of Destruction" vs. Sgt. Barry Sadler's "Ballad of the Green Berets"? Oh, right, wrong question, that was a pro-war song—how many lives did it save?

2 ▪ **Bruce Springsteen, *The Rising* (Columbia)** It's too long—at 72 minutes, longer than the Rolling Stones' storied *Exile on Main Street*. The poorer songs—"Into the Fire," "Let's Be Friends (Skin to Skin)"— seem to go on forever. The set may well be what the film critic Manny Farber defined as "white elephant art": as an indirect but inescapable picture of the world in which Americans have lived since a New York headline proclaimed "U.S. ATTACKED," it is certainly "an expensive hunk of well-regulated area."

It is also less like any sort of pop music album than a speech—maybe a speech given without an audience, like Lincoln out in the woods declaiming to the trees. The speaker tries on many voices, rhetorical devices, exercises in repetition or metaphor. As with Martin Luther King's 1963 address to the March on Washington, neither the classical passages ("Further On [Up the Road]") or gratuitous grace notes ("Empty Sky") make it obvious that what the speaker is doing is building a platform to support the weight of what, in fact, he has to say— and for the grandeur with which he means to say it.

That is the title song. As "The Rising" begins you can hear the speaker stand with his feet planted on the platform, which may be no more than a tree stump; the music his voice summons tips him off the stage and out of the forest, off to search for his audience, to see his face in others' faces. The song is at once enormous and simple, an act of will and a ready-made. It has room in it— room for the dead and for those who mourn them, for those who care and those who don't, for those who believe they can't be touched and those who already have been.

It may be that the song actually has room for the enormity of the event it means to enclose. It may be that the song speaks the language of the event: not the language of those who perpetrated it, but the language of people trying to make sense of it, to translate it, to at once accept and resist its reality. The song seems much too short, so when it's over you play it again.

3–4 ■ Elvis Presley, "Elvis Talks About His Career," on *Live in Las Vegas* (RCA) and "Hound Dog" on *Roots Revolution* (Tomato) or *Good Rockin' Tonight: The Evolution of Elvis Presley—The Complete Louisiana Hayride Archives* (Music Mill) If you want to know who he was and where he came from ("From my side of the story. There's a lot that's come out about what happened, but never from my side"), listen to the astonishing onstage monologue that ends the first disc of this four-CD set. It's August 24, 1969, three weeks into the engagement at the International Hotel in Las Vegas that brought Presley back to life as a performer, and he feels happily naked, sly, sardonic, coolly nailing his enemies, one by one: "So they arranged to put me on television. At that particular time there was a lot of controversy— you didn't see people moving—out in public. They were gettin' it on in the back rooms, but you didn't see it out in public too much. So there was a lot of controversy . . . and I went to the *Ed Sullivan Show*. They photographed me from the waist up. And Sullivan's standing over there saying, 'Sumbitch.' I said, 'Thank you, Ed, thank you.' I didn't know what he was calling me, at the time."

To hear the controversy as a thing in itself—the event from which half the country was fleeing while the other half was running right for it—listen to the version of "Hound Dog" Presley offers on the December 15, 1956, broadcast from the No. 2 country radio show ("They've been looking for something new in the folk music field for a long time, and I think you've got it," the host says hopefully to Elvis at his first *Hayride* appearance, in 1954). On *Roots Revolution*, new musicians have done note-for-note re-recordings of the original, very distant backing parts from guitarist Scotty Moore, bassist Bill Black and drummer D. J. Fontana (not Jimmy Day's steel guitar), but the difference is marginal—the sound is still bad, the performance is still shockingly fast, hard and mean, and the screams from the crowd comprise the most excited sound you'll ever hear in your life.

5 ■ Emry Arthur, "Man of Constant Sorrow," on *Man of Constant Sorrow and Other Timeless Mountain Ballads* (Yazoo) Arthur backed the Virginia mountain singer Dock Boggs on guitar in 1929; "he couldn't reach the chords," Boggs remembered. "He'd been shot through the hands. Bullets went through his hands." From the year before, you can hear those shots on the first recording of a song that during the folk revival of the 1960s would be sung by Bob Dylan, Judy Collins and countless others, and that in *O Brother, Where Art Thou?* Dan Tyminski (vocals) and Soggy Bottom Boy George Clooney (lead lip-synch) turned into a rave-up you had no trouble believing could sweep the South. Arthur maps the same territory, but as an exile. Singing haltingly, in a high voice, testifying shamefully that he has no lover, no friends, no home and deserves no better than an unmarked grave ("You're dreaming while you're slumbering / While I am sleeping in the clay"), he might as well be hitting the strings with blunt instruments.

6 ■ Sean Wilentz reports on Bob Dylan's return to the Newport Folk Festival after 35 years (Aug. 5) "The thing that was most apparent to me was how ghostly it was— because they're all dead. All the people the young folk artists were drawn to in 1965 or before; they're all dead. Mississippi John Hurt is dead. Son House is dead. Geoff Muldaur was funny: He asked who had been to Newport before; he asked who had been born in 1965. Maybe half had. He told a story about Mississippi John Hurt: 'He'd just do a little finger-picking—and we'd all collapse.' There were a lot of ghosts around. At the same time it was a very conscious passing on of that tradition to something new—on the part of the older folks. Dylan did that very intentionally. Songs that he was singing in 1965, and songs that recalled that tradition.

"There was a roots stage—[but] given the explosion of interest in [old-time] music, there was too little. Most of the music was personal song-stories. In a funny way, what with *O Brother, Where Art Thou?,* Alison Krauss, the festival seemed to be out of step with where folk music now *is.* It was largely virtuoso self-indulgent adolescent angst. It was Shawn Colvin.

"Dylan walked out on stage with [Orthodox Jewish] earlocks—and a ponytail, and a fake beard. He looked like a guy who was on the bus to Crown Heights and got lost. From another angle, not really seeing the beard, he could have been in a girl group—he could have been in the Shangri-Las. Then he looked like Jesus Christ. He was putting on a show, and he was donning a mask—because he's a minstrel. A Jewish minstrel. And an American minstrel.

"There came a point when he could have said something—when he was introducing the band. I looked at him very closely then—but he just sort of smiled. He twitched. And then he went into the last song, 'Leopard-Skin Pill-Box Hat.' Then he goes away, and comes back, and does a sizzling Buddy Holly, 'Not Fade Away,' the Grateful Dead arrangement. Again it was ghosts. That was Bob Dylan. He was the whole fucking tradition. He was a one-man festival."

7 ▪ **Kelly Willis, *Easy* (Ryko)** The devastatingly clear-voiced country singer can walk on melodies as if they're water. The first number, Willis' "If I Left You," has that kind of melody, but the words are inescapable, and they make no sense: if the singer left the guy who left her, she'd worry about him all the time and love him forever. The best number here is Paul Kelly's "You Can't Take It With You," a brilliantly slick putdown ("You might own a great big factory, oil wells on sacred land"—"sacred land" is a priceless touch) Willis sings with barely a hint of malice.

8 ▪ *Me Without You,* **directed by Sandra Goldbacher (Fireworks/Goldwyn)** As we follow best friends Marina (Anna Friel) and Holly (Michelle Williams) from 1973 (jumping rope) to 2001 (watching their children play), pop eras come and go. In 1978, when the girls can't be more than 15, they crash at a punk non-party where Holly lets Marina's brother make love to her and Marina lets a guy shoot her up with heroin; a few years later their apartment wall features dead Ian Curtis of Joy Division, clutching his mike stand like a cross. You hear all the right period music, from the Clash to the Stranglers to Echo and the Bunnymen—and nothing sounds half so right as, in a scene shot in a club where half the men seem to be wearing Adam Ant pirate hats and skirts, a DJ pumps out Depeche Mode's "Just Can't Get Enough."

9 ▪ **John Paxson, *Elvis Live at Five* (Thomas Dunne/St. Martin's)** On a Dallas TV station looking for a new angle on the 25th anniversary of the death of Elvis Presley, a producer and a computer genius create a virtual Elvis and, making no pretense that it is anything but the image of a dead man, turn him into a talk show host. Then the station owner takes over and turns Elvis into a demagogue, taking on homosexuals, immigrants, Hare Krishnas, his denunciations backed by footage created by means of the same technology that keeps Elvis talking. Soon homicidal mobs roam the land, their victims driven before them: "Thousands of men, women and children in a long snaking line of misery and fear stumbling through the winter snows of Nebraska."

Very convincing. No happy ending.

10 ▪ **Bruce Springsteen, "The Rising," on *Late Night With David Letterman* (CBS, Aug. 2)** With Steve Van Zandt singing into Springsteen's mike along with Patti Scialfa as the song hit its last choruses, it was impossible not to see his dimwitted *Sopranos* thug Silvio Dante there too. And that made it feel as if the song meant, among other things, to kill somebody.

1 ▪ Scott Ostler, "Insincerity Taken to New Levels" (*San Francisco Chronicle*, Aug. 31) On baseball's new labor-management agreement: "At the news conference, ever-hip Commissioner Bud Selig quoted the Beatles, saying of the negotiations, 'It's been a Long and Winding Road.' And as the Beatles noted in that song, 'We've seen this road before.'

"Unfortunately, Selig did not quote from the Beatles' tune 'Money (That's What I Want).'"

2 ▪ Holiday Inn School of Hospitality and Resort Management, University of Memphis (Aug. 16) A blond woman approached the desk at this training hotel: "I'm checking out: Linda Evans." "Linda Evans?" said a man standing next to her. "From *Dynasty*?" "A long time ago," she said. "But I killed all my husbands."

3 ▪ *Here Is New York: A Democracy of Photographs*, conceived and organized by Alice Rose George, Gilles Peress, Michael Shulan & Charles Traub (Scalo Books) A compendium of more than 1,000 pictures drawn from the evolving downtown exhibition that, beginning about a week after last year's terrorist attacks, opened itself to photographs from professionals and amateurs, until it seemed everyone in New York was taking part. Some 5,000 photos were scanned, filed and printed, and, within the limits of the makeshift space at 116 Prince Street, hung like laundry.

There is no telling what image will break down all defenses, erase the year's time, open the hole in the ground and in your memory. For one person I know it was the man in a T-shirt that read "I'VE GONE TO PIECES," the splayed fingers of his right hand over his face. For me it was a young woman holding an American flag during a vigil or memorial gathering in Washington Square Park: the flag as if billowed by no more than the expression on her face, some combination of stoicism, sadness and an absolute inability to read the future.

4 ▪ Sleater-Kinney, *One Beat* (Kill Rock Stars) "Turn on the TV," the second cut, "Far Away," begins, and the singer does: from Portland, Oregon, she sees the World Trade Center, and then what's left of it—nothing. But this opening moment doesn't carry over into the rest of the song, and guitarist Corin Tucker's high, hard shouts miss the moment even as she calls it up. Across the rest of the album, Tucker, guitarist Carrie Brownstein and drummer Janet Weiss seem to miss their targets, even if their targets are each other. What's missing is a certain spark, that dimension of expectation and desire that previously made so many songs outrun themselves. Except perhaps in the rolling and rumbling choruses of "Light-Rail Coyote," here the band is in front of its songs, looking back at finished things. Years after they appeared, "Dig Me Out," "Little Mouth," "Jenny" and "Was It a Lie?" are not finished things.

5 ▪ Bruce Springsteen and the E-Street Band, Compaq Center (San Jose, Aug. 27) One of Springsteen's talents is in bringing his biggest numbers down to earth. He opened with "The Rising," which immediately set the show on a high plateau, looking down on the ruins of the World Trade Center, from the perspective of what writer Homi Bhabha named "the Unbuilt." Much later, Springsteen introduced the band. "The Goddess of Love," he said of his wife, singer and guitarist Patti Scialfa. "I like to call her mental Viagra. Come on up for the risin'," he said.

6 ▪ Peter Wolf, "Growin' Pain," from *Sleepless* (Artemis) Peter Wolf has been around long enough to show up in Robert Greenfield's 1982 novel *Temple*, drunkenly fronting the J. Geils Band in a Cambridge club in the late '60s and explaining the meaning of "L7" to the hero. With J. Geils he went from blues and soul to the '80s hits "Love Stinks" and "Centerfold"; on his own he married Faye Dunaway and made albums. None came close to the shuddering blasts of cold air that stormed all over the J. Geils Band's 1970 cover of John Lee

Hooker's "Serve You Right to Suffer"—or the smile in "Love Stinks."

"Growin' Pain" has every year of that story in it—that story as ordinary life unmarked by stardom. It moves on a sharp, bouncing beat, but lost bets and blown chances pull against it, filling the tune with the likelihood that the dead ends of the lives chronicled in the song will never open onto any better road. Wolf gets stronger as the number goes on, but even as the sound rises he seems to sing more quietly, as if to offer old friends a respect the world they live in denies them.

Sleepless will get momentary attention for Mick Jagger's "You're So Vain"–style vocal on the banal "Nothing But the Wheel" or Steve Earle's cowboy shtick on "Some Things You Don't Want to Know." But this song may keep coming back.

7 ▪ **Robert Greenfield, *S.T.P.—A Journey Through America with the Rolling Stones* (Da Capo)** A reissue of the 1974 account of the Rolling Stones' 1972 return to the U.S.A.—with tickets, at least in San Francisco, to make amends for the 1969 horror at Altamont, a flat $5. This is the same tour followed in Robert Frank's film *Cocksucker Blues*—named for the song Mick Jagger sings as the picture begins—and Greenfield's book exposed how much of the movie was staged, and how much of the tour, crowded with celebrities from Truman Capote to Marisa Berenson to Dick Cavett and other rock gods, was not. Again and again the book took its readers into dark rooms, then woke them up in time to make the bus—or would have, had the book had readers. In 1974 it was, as Greenfield notes in a new foreword, "the very first full-length book ever published about the rock 'n' roll tour. Those times being what they were, though, no one expected those who loved the Stones to rush out and buy this volume. They were too busy getting high and listening to *Exile on Main Street*. Which is why only fifteen hundred hardback copies and thirty-five hundred trade paperback copies were ever printed." It entered oblivion as a classic.

Today the book is confusing. What Greenfield describes is happening so fast no sense of in-the-past holds; the action seems to be taking place in the present moment. And then, on the last page, with the tour running into the next year: "Michael Jagger had his whole life in front of him, with several already left behind. The Stones would go on as long as he needed them to. . . . For Jagger was a young man, just thirty." At this point the book falls on the reader like a building, carrying all the weight of what the Rolling Stones so purposefully accomplished in the few years before Greenfield drew what he seems to have suspected might not have been an arbitrary line, along with the weight of what they didn't bother to do in the many years that, now, bring us to the band's latest swing through the economy.

8 ▪ **Dixie Chicks, *Home* (Open Wide/Columbia)** With all the publicity about rebel girls with big smiles taking on the Nashville machine and taking country music back where it belongs, you expect more than . . . dobros.

9 ▪ **Hall Robinson Choir, "St. Louis Blues," from *Walk Right In—When the Sun Goes Down: The Secret History of Rock 'n' Roll, Vol. 1* (Bluebird/RCA)** There are endless riches in archivist Colin Escott's new excavations in the Bluebird and RCA vaults, and imaginative, non-canonical programming: here the classically trained baritone Paul Robeson's 1926 "Sometimes I Feel Like a Motherless Child," the Carter Family's 1930 "Worried Man Blues" and Mississippi blues singer Robert Petway's unnervingly simple 1941 "Catfish Blues" seem to come from the same radio station. But there is an odd displacement in "St. Louis Blues," the last cut: 20 professional male and female voices with a repertoire of spirituals recording in Hollywood in 1939 and here led by an exuberant woman singing as if from the soundtrack of Vincente Minnelli's 1943 all-black musical *Cabin in the Sky*. It might take only a moment to realize that Ike and Tina Turner's 1966 "River Deep, Mountain High" is a rewrite, and that its producer and co-writer

Phil Spector had to have heard the Hall Robinson Choir's version—and that when he took Ike and Tina into Gold Star Studios in Hollywood his goal was to top it. Which he did.

10 ▪ 24 Hour Party People, directed by Michael Winterbottom (United Artists) Manchester, England, late '70s: There are passages in this droll dramatization of a long episode in pop history that show Joy Division finding their sound, then what seem like huge crowds in tiny nightclubs finding and losing themselves in the now stark, now all but dreamed songs, and they are the most powerful and mysterious musical sequences I've ever seen on film. Actor Sean Harris looks little like Joy Division singer Ian Curtis, but the nervousness of his dancing—a trance you wouldn't want to enter and may barely stand to watch—makes David Byrne in *Stop Making Sense* look like Daffy Duck. Harris' Curtis is on to something, he hasn't decided whether he can say what it is, when he hangs himself the movie goes from Olympus to a parking lot, and you no more than the people in the movie will believe that neither you nor they will ever make it back.

SEPTEMBER 23, 2002

1 ▪ Press release, D. Baron media relations (Sept. 12) "Los Angeles, CA—Celebrated recording artist composer Warren Zevon, one of rock music's wittiest and most original songwriters, has been diagnosed with lung cancer which has advanced to an untreatable stage." Playing: "Mohammed's Radio," the churchy live version from the 1982 *Stand in the Fire* ("Even Jimmy Carter's got the highway blues"); the delirious rising in the 1978 "Johnny Strikes Up the Band"; the regret in the melody of "Looking for the Next Best Thing" in 1982; the shared dread of "Run Straight Down" in 1989; the delicacy of "Suzie Lightning" in 1991 and "Mutineer" in 1995. From 1976, when he went public with "Desperadoes Under the Eaves" on the album *Warren Zevon*, it has been more than a quarter century of gun-

play and bravado, not for a moment concealing Zevon's loathing for his own betrayals and those of the world around him. "I was in the house when the house burned down," he sang in 2000. From afar he has been a good friend.

2 ▪ Music in Balthazar (New York, Sept. 5) For a still-hot restaurant with a reputation for cool to uphold, either a new concept of cool or real problems with the concept. Playing indistinctly in the background as we come in after 11—can it be, no, it can't be, why *is* it? It's Scott McKenzie's "San Francisco (Be Sure to Wear Flowers in Your Hair)" from 1967, one of the sappiest songs of all time. Then a lot of terrible *Saturday Night Live*–style fake jazz. Then finally, loud, every note standing out: "Gimme Shelter" by the Rolling Stones, probably the greatest pop recording of the last 50 years, and not dinner music. Not even walking-out music. Not even cool. Far beyond cool, in a realm where the concept is an embarrassment.

3–4 ▪ Slobberbone, *Slippage* (New West) and Plastic Mastery, *In the Fall of Unearthly Angels* (Magic Marker) On "Springfield, IL.," the first track of Slobberbone's *Slippage*, the hard, loose, fast band from Denton, Texas, combines a desperate country vocal that's all over the room with a guitar playing off its own promises, never quite paying off, replacing each moment where the music falls just short with a greater promise. You get the feel of a terrible place the musicians want only to escape—why is it so full of life? In a much more punk manner, with floating chords and vocals lifting away from their songs, Plastic Mastery of Tallahassee catches the same fear, the same hurry. It's a queer sound: the sound of people almost but not sure there is no place for them.

5 ▪ Sinéad O'Connor, "Lord Franklin," from *Sean-Nós Nua* (Vanguard) The traditional ballad Bob Dylan recast in 1963 to look back at his youth as if he were already dead—and, in O'Connor's hands, never more gorgeous, never more accursed. O'Connor's disdain for sustaining a career makes it possible to forget her; this is a reminder of why it is impossible to write her off. She will be around, harrying everyone into their graves.

6 ▪ Bernie Woodall, "Book Says Grateful Dead Has Grand Place in History" (Reuters, Sept. 4) An interview with Dennis McNally, on his bestselling *A Long Strange Trip: The Inside History of the Grateful Dead* and his plans for a follow-up, on the Mississippi: "I want to write a book about the river and Highway 61 and Bob Dylan, Mark Twain, Robert Johnson and a jazz player to be named later." To be titled "Whatever."

7 ▪ Vito Acconci at the Aspen Institute (Aspen, Colo., July 19) Speaking in conjunction with the recently closed Aspen Art Museum exhibition "Vito Acconci/Acconci Studio," Acconci, now in his 60s, combined a brief run-through of his career from the 1960s to about 1980 (his life as a gestural/performance artist and sculptor) with a thrilling account of his work with his own architectural studio: a nearly two-hour talk that was at once galvanizingly visionary and completely down to earth.

He said many things, even most things, twice. Returning to a phrase or an idea almost as soon as its first version left his mouth, it seemed less that he was unsure you understood than that, nearing the end of a thought, he had already reconsidered it, and so put it into words again to see if they still worked. There was a great physical presence in his speech, especially when he moved away from his lectern and turned his back on the slides he was working with, leaning forward, rocking back on his heels.

He was mapping the work of his New York–based Acconci Studio—a crew of architects and others who since 1988 have been working on the redesign of extant buildings and the part-closed, part-open spaces that adjoin them, from an entryway in the Philadelphia International Airport to corporate complexes all over Europe, from a roundabout in London to small household objects. Most of the projects have never been built—and despite Acconci's accounts of commissions or competitions for commissions, it was hard to believe, looking at drawings and models as they appeared on the screen behind him as he speaks, that they were ever meant to be built. They are so blatant in their refusal to accept the claim of form on content—and thus when Acconci showed slides of actually completed projects, some in the audience gasped. They had already grasped the careful, patient but anarchic utopianism inherent in whatever the studio does, its absolute reach for another city in another life—for elsewhere, wherever that might be.

While the fundamental premise of almost every project had to do with bringing the outside of a building in or the inside of a building out, to break boundaries between space and people, to unregiment work and confuse the borders between work, respite and leisure, that doesn't speak to the driving force of play in the projects: the desire to bring the outside in or the inside out just to see what happens when you do. The realization of the simplest project—the roundabout that expands into a ziggurat and folds up like a flower according to the flow of traffic around it—carried the ambitions of the most grandiose. No space, no building, was *for* anything; as the Acconci Studio ethic became clear, you began to see as the studio does, to see that no building is fated, none is fixed, none, no matter how old or insured, was ever more than a whim, a bribe, an idea, good or bad, whose time had come.

As Acconci spoke, every slide he projected dovetailed with fragments of a personal manifesto, flying through descriptions and anecdotes like a memory interrupting a sales talk: "I see art as an exchange, a meeting, where the person in the role of the artist comes face to face with a person in the role of the viewer." "Actually building projects is a problem, because it screws up the theory." "My work began in an art context as a kind of resentment toward the do-not-touch of museums and galleries: 'The art is more expensive than you are.'" The equation doesn't hold with the Acconci Studio projects: even when built, you can't believe anyone ever funded them. But there are more of them, out there in the world, all the time.

8 ■ **Steve Earle, *Jerusalem* (Artemis)** The supposedly heretical "John Walker's Blues"—on the page, a puerile self-justification from inside the heart or mind of "the American Taliban"—has brought Earle the biggest boost of his career, press coverage everywhere, right up to a respectful interview in the *New York Times Magazine*. The album carries not just a lyric sheet, but a statement: "Lately I feel like the loneliest man in America," Earle begins, trumpeting his courage. He goes on to discuss hysterical patriotism, the Vietnam War, domestic repression, race riots: "Well, we survived all that—and I believe that we'll survive this, as well." By "this" he means the Bush administration's drive toward autocracy and secret government—not the actual physical jeopardy of the USA. There is no acknowledgment that the country faces a real enemy, that the country itself, not a few buildings, has already been attacked, that it has been shown to be more vulnerable than its enemies ever imagined it was. "God bless America, indeed," he says finally, in that sarcastic, self-congratulatory trope of bad critics everywhere.

The music is not bad. It's missing Earle's usual smarm; his singing is less mannered than it is on all the records by other people he's been popping up on lately. "John Walker's Blues" is a real song.

9 ■ **Sarah Vowell, *The Partly Cloudy Patriot* (Simon & Schuster)** On why Al Gore should have had the producer of *Buffy the Vampire Slayer* running his show instead of the people who blew it: "High school is the most appropriate metaphor for the 2000 presidential campaign, since high school is the most appropriate metaphor for life in a democratic republic. Because democracy is an idealistic attempt to make life fair. And while high school is the place where you read about the democratic ideal of fairness, it is also the place where most of us learn how unfair life really is." The best book I've read about patriotism since

Charles L. Mee Jr.'s *A Visit to Haldeman and Other States of Mind*—and that came out in 1975, just after Watergate.

10 ■ **Wire, "The Afgers of Kodack," from *Read & Burn* (Pink Flag)** They were on stage at the Roxy in London in 1977 when punk gave birth to itself; they were always ridiculously smart, always interested in espionage, and no less so here—with a furious negation ending an EP of otherwise indistinct and pointless tunes. "Read and burn?" The band burns up its own footprints.

Thanks to Chris Walters

OCTOBER 7, 2002

1–2 ■ ***Igby Goes Down*, written and directed by Burr Steers (United Artists) and trailer for *The Man From Elysian Fields*, directed by George Hickenlooper (Goldwyn)** Movie logic: at the end of *Igby Goes Down*, Jason Slocumb Jr., played by Kieran Culkin, visits a catatonic man in a mental institution: his father Jason Slocumb. It's Bill Pullman, who we've seen in flashbacks willfully driving himself out of his family, out of society, out of his mind. The Western-hero face was still there, some years back, the features sharp, but even then this once-strong, silent man was silent because he had nothing to say. It's one bad step past the familiar: the father's sardonic smile, when he still recognized his son, is from the chump Pullman played in *The Last Seduction*, the deadness in his eyes now from the terrified man he played in *Lost Highway*—it's as if he's stepped out of those roles only to complete them.

The same confusion between art and life—are Bill Pullman's previous roles part of his filmography or his biography?—is at work in *The Man From Elysian Fields*, where Mick Jagger looks at once like the gangster he played in 1970 in the "Memo From Turner" sequence of *Performance* and a desiccated version of a 60-year-old Jennifer Love Hewitt. Here he appears as the pimp Luther Fox, which is to say that he is also playing a version of James Fox, who in *Performance* played the real gangster, and for whom Jagger's *Elysian* character is half-named. Far more deeply, though, Jagger is appearing as a fantasy version of himself, 35 years after the Rolling Stones, last hitting with the 1965 "(I Can't Get No) Satisfaction," were definitively erased from public consciousness by the San Francisco sound of the Jefferson Airplane, the Grateful Dead and It's a Beautiful Day. After decades as the highest paid gigolo in Europe, what else would he be doing but running an escort service?

3 ▪ **Thalia Zedek, *You're a Big Girl Now* (Kimchee EP)** "I got tired," are the first words the relentlessly thanatopic singer and guitarist offers—but except on Bob Dylan's title song, not tired enough.

4 ▪ **Justin Timberlake, "Like I Love You" (Jive)** 'N Sync update: while Joey Fatone takes Broadway in *Rent*, Lance Bass "remains hopeful" that his backers will come through with the $20 million for his Russian space flight (His backers? He didn't have the dough himself? And what do they get? Product placement?), Chris Kirkpatrick weighs a bid for the Republican nomination to take on Sen. Bob Graham in '04, and J. C. Chasez considers trying to save the Devil Rays, Justin Timberlake has gone for the solo career. He's got the Neptunes at the board, the *Thriller*-period Michael Jackson hat, the *Bad*-period Michael Jackson yelps, the George Michael "Faith" arrangement, and a paint-thinner voice.

5 ▪ **Dave Morey, "Ten at Ten" on KFOG-FM (San Francisco, Sept. 11)** The matchless daily show that usually interpolates "10 great songs" and sound bites from "one great year" made a one-day switch, airing listeners' request messages and then the songs they wanted played to commemorate the attacks of the year before. Many of the messages were singular. A man noted that "Sept. 11 was always a happy day for me," because it was his father's birthday, then told how his father, a crisis manager in Iowa, immediately flew to New York to do what he could. Another man spoke of playing Billy Joel's "New York State of Mind" on a jukebox in a bar, upsetting the other

patrons—"but that was a time when you felt you could go up to anybody and start talking," and so he did. But of all the songs chosen—from Don Henley's "The End of the Innocence" to U2's "Walk On" to the Corrs' "When the Stars Go Blue"—only Dire Straits' "Brothers in Arms" reached the event, and then only in Mark Knopfler's guitar playing, a hurtful funeral oration for a funeral that, you might have sensed, could take place only in the arc of the oration's own music.

6–7 ▪ **Bert Berns, *The Heart & Soul of Bert Berns* (Universal) and Solomon Burke, *Don't Give Up On Me* (Fat Possum)** Berns, a legendary New York record man, was 38 when he died in 1967. Collections honoring such a figure usually come in boxes; ignoring Berns' pop hits with Van Morrison and the McCoys, this is a single disc of nine deep-soul numbers that Berns wrote and produced, plus one misguided homage. Some of the tracks here were big—Solomon Burke's "Everybody Needs Somebody to Love" and "Cry to Me," Garnet Mimms & the Enchanters' "Cry Baby," Irma Franklin's "Piece of My Heart," the Isley Brothers' "Twist and Shout." Some—the obscure Hoagy Lands' heart-stopping "Baby, Come On Home," Freddie Scott's "Are You Lonely for Me, Baby" and the Drifters' "I Don't Want to Go On Without You"— might never have existed at all. But together these records make a picture so delicate you can almost hear the performers' fear that anything they do will break it. You hear strange, astonishingly delicate bits of instrumentation—guitar triplets, a hesitating piano, room to breathe all through the arrangements—that produce the feeling that the great voices Berns recorded were not quite of this earth.

"If everybody sang this song, I believe it would save the whole world," Solomon Burke announced in 1964 as he moved into "Everybody Needs Somebody to Love." Today, singing new songs by Van Morrison, Elvis Costello, Bob Dylan, Dan Penn, Tom Waits, Nick Lowe and Brian Wilson, he sounds most of all unsure of himself. He can dominate the material, but just from the outside. Only on producer Joe Henry's "Flesh and Blood"—deathly slow, every moment felt through and then left behind with regret, the next step taken without an intimation of hope—does he sound like he's wearing his own clothes.

8–9 ■ **"Absolut Pistols" (Absolut Vodka ads, available in postcard form at Tower Records) and the Sex Pistols at Inland Invasion, Devore, Calif. (Sept. 14)** Absolut used the *Never Mind the Bollocks Here's the Sex Pistols* art, with the pink "Sex Pistols" in a lumpy version of the bottle. Not quite as nervy as the online Dos Equis "Viva la Revolucion" ad from a few years ago that featured lifelong alcoholic Guy Debord of the Situationist International ("Made his own dead time," Dos Equis said, rewriting situationist-inspired graffiti from the May '68 revolt in France, "Live without dead time"), but Dos Equis didn't have to ask permission to use Debord's name, because he'd already killed himself. The Sex Pistols—Johnny Rotten, Paul Cook, Steve Jones and Glen Matlock, which as a functioning commercial enterprise last month played for 52,000 people at a punk festival in Southern California—charge and approve, and more power to them.

10 ■ **Sleater-Kinney, Fillmore Auditorium, San Francisco (Sept. 22)** Jane Dark reports: "Having seen Sleater-Kinney four or five times, I'm not sure I've ever seen them do a cover. And never wanted to—they're too good at sounding like themselves. They sounded like themselves last night, except more so: Where I was standing, Carrie Brownstein's vocals and Corin Tucker's guitar both seemed low, so the band resolved to axioms: Corin's voice ripping open the complicated, angular spaces of Carrie's shifting figures. Janet Weiss has grown into a tremendous drummer, beyond tremendous—undeniable.

"The Fillmore seemed a little large, and swallowed up the songs from when they were small: 'I Wanna Be Your Joey Ramone,' which I still believe is their greatest (if not in fact *the* greatest) song, seemed at-

tenuated, a perfect little bomb that couldn't blow up the whole room. But the new songs were better than on record, and 'You're No Rock n' Roll Fun' and 'Words and Guitar' were better than ever, particularly for what they didn't do—for all the ways, no matter how massively compelling, they would never be rawk anthems.

"They did do a cover. They did an anthem. It was Bruce Springsteen's birthday and they hauled off and played 'Promised Land' to start the encores. They played it tight and fast with no fooling around, with close harmonies in the chorus, and at the beginning of the third verse where there's that part about 'desert floor' it sounded to me like they were saying 'Desert Storm' and suddenly you understood that these women singing a guy's coming-of-age song weren't just taking liberties, they were talking liberties: that 'Mister I ain't a boy, no I'm a man' wasn't an illusion of independence, of the dream of getting out of your hometown, like so many Bruce songs. It was about the inseparability of that particular swagger and being draft age. Bruce's 'desert floor' was a different desert altogether, so far outside your hometown that the people had names you couldn't pronounce. A couple of minutes later Corin was howling 'Dig me out' over and over, and it seemed like the hole was the whole world."

Thanks to Howard Hampton and Jason Gross of Perfect Sound Forever

OCTOBER 21, 2002

1–3 ■ **Mekons, Mercury Lounge (Sept. 21, New York City)** Swinging east on their 25th anniversary tour, the old punks added a special show by popular demand—"a concept," singer and guitarist Jon Langford said from the stage, "with which we are not that familiar"—at 6 p.m. Noting that one fan praised the idea as "a Mekons dream come true—home by 9!" Langford announced the door policy to the crowd already crammed into the small room: "Nobody under 40." Nobody left. The band, from accordion on one side to fiddle on the other, ranged from the primitive rant "The Building" to singer Sally Timms' dreamy bombscapes of a ruined London, but it was when various members began to read from the group's just-published *Hello Cruel World: Selected Lyrics* (Verse Chorus Press) that the performance transcended the night. Elegantly printed, illustrated with photos and Blakean cartoons, the book doesn't read like a conceit—that is, you actually can read it—but that was no preparation for what happened when the words were read out on stage. The idea seemed an utter contradiction: why have someone step out of a band and read song lyrics when the band was present and ready to play them? In truth, the first reading, Langford with "Funeral," came off as a clichéd political speech. But then the lyrics truly began to change shape, to lift off on such flights of rhetoric they became unrecognizable as songs. When non-singing drummer Steve Goulding stepped to the front of the stage and raised the book, the words rang like Shakespeare.

"Failure in the short run guarantees success in the long run," Neil Young once said. The Mekons' run, not exactly toward success, a quarter-century of small clubs, small labels, day jobs and a calling that has not worn out, has been a long one in itself. So long that later that night, as Langford, Timms and accordionist Rico Bell broke for dinner at a Chinese place called Kam Chueh, the fortune that turned up in one cookie did not quite communicate as a portent: "The seeds of success lie in your last failure." On the terms of success, every Mekons show is a failure.

4 ■ **The Great Crusades,** *Never Go Home* **(Glitterhouse/Germany)** When this Chicago foursome set off on their third album, with "Hand Grenade Head" and "Out of Our Little Town" ("They don't sell sleeping pills over the counter," Brian Krumm sings, and you know that's as hopeful as the song will get), they carry themselves like Midwestern gangsters: with the determined, bitter nihilism of Tom Hanks in *Road to*

Perdition, but also the gleeful nihilism of Billy Zane in *This World, Then the Fireworks*. But as the road out of town gets longer, you hear a guitar player putting a south-of-the-border melody on *The Wild Bunch*, surf combos tuning up in Southern California in 1962, a steel-guitarist clocking in in Nashville, a banjo player picking for himself somewhere in Virginia in the 1920s, and the band never hurries a step.

5 ■ **San Francisco Giants vs. St. Louis Cardinals, National League Championship Series, Game 3 (Fox, Oct. 12)** At Pac Bell Park in San Francisco, as a man in the bleachers had a home run bounce off his hands for the second time, a camera picked up a shirtless man sitting behind him, his mouth hanging open. One announcer speculated that the shirtless guy was dumbfounded that rubberhands had blown two chances in a row. A second announcer noted that shirtless was wearing headphones, and the camera pulled in: the guy wasn't surprised, he was completely zonked. "He must be listening to the Grateful Dead," said the announcer. Someone back at Fox World Domination put on an impossibly vague Dead track (Deadheads would call it abstract), with Jerry Garcia whispering "odelay" over and over as guitar notes struggled to take shape and then died like minnows and the tune went on and on and the face of the man in the headphones never changed.

6 ■ **Jim Jocoy,** *We're Desperate: The Punk Rock Photography of Jim Jocoy, SF/LA 1978– 1980* **(powerHouse Books)** At first Jacoby's full-length posed color portraits of people on the scene seem to owe everything to the black-and-white pictures in Isabelle Anscombe's 1978 *Punk*—for that matter, the SF/LA punks seem to owe everything to the Londoners in the Anscombe book. But the longer you look—and not, particularly, at the shots of Joan Jett, Exene Cervenka of X, Johnny Thunders or other stars—the more you begin to see what it took to remake yourself as a freak, as a social idiot, as someone you weren't meant to be. A woman with short black hair in a short black vinyl skirt who looks like a follower

of the early San Francisco punk band Crime; a blond woman wearing red, black, blue, yellow, white and green stripes and squiggles, smoke drifting over her face like a small cloud; a small woman dressed demurely in black and blue and something in her eyes that seems to be daring the world to fuck with her, and not because she knows what will happen if it does—soon enough, you're seeing real people everywhere.

7 ■ **David Gates, "Everybody Must Get Sloshed" (New York Times Book Review, Oct. 13)** On Tim O'Brien's novel *July, July*, about a class of '69 30th-anniversary college reunion and how dreams of a better world turned to dust, gold dust that still shines with the pain of hopes abandoned and hearts that even under a carapace of corruption beat on to the music the man can't bust even though he did. Choosing among requisite "uptight Republican housewife," "draft-dodger who split for Canada" and "still-traumatized Vietnam veteran" with "a voice in his head," Gates homes in on the latter, or rather his "imaginary friend," one "Johnny Ever." "Talk about cynics!" says Gates. "'Seen it once, seen it a zillion times,' this hard-boiled internal parasite tells his host. 'We're talkin' grand illusion here. Fairy tales . . . "Hair." Your whole wacked-out generation, man, it got turned around by all that tooby ooby walla starshine crud.'" "Edgy stuff," Gates says. "If you can't believe in 'Hair' anymore, what can you believe in?"

8–9 ■ **Ed Ward on Domino Records, Fresh Air (NPR, Sept. 3) and The Domino Records Story (Ace)** Resident pop historian Ward told the story of an odd little label launched in 1957 in Austin, Texas, by a team of solidly middle-class white entrepreneurs who met at a business seminar called "How to Market a Song." They experimented. Their strangest record was Joyce Harris' New-Orleans–style chant "No Way Out": no way out from your love, was the concept; it wasn't the feeling, which was life and death. A male voice begins the song with "I gotcha! I gotcha! And there's no way out—" twisting the last word into a drawl so menacing you can't believe anyone can answer

him; Harris does, if only by sounding as if she's tearing snakes out of her hair.

The label's stars were the Slades, especially with their original version of "You Cheated"—a reworking of the Penguins' 1954 doo-wop classic "Earth Angel"—which became a national hit when in 1958 it was covered by the Shields, who as they were black and the Slades, whose passionate, close-harmony rehearsal tapes are the hidden treasure of *The Domino Records Story*, were white, turned the vitally important American tradition of whites strolling to riches on the backs of blacks on its head. Or anyway sideways: Jesse Belvin, who wrote "Earth Angel," was the lead singer of the Shields, and as with white covers of black records, compared to the Slades the Shields were slick.

Ward played the Slades' "You Cheated"—rough but reaching, for just what you couldn't quite tell. The soul music that was just around the bend? A transparency in the tune the singers couldn't quite find? Hollywood? The humid last notes hung in the air, as if they were ready to burst into rain. "It was a magnificent record," Ward pronounced, as if stunned at his own story, at the glory a marketing seminar could turn up, just like that.

10 ■ *Law and Order: Special Victims Unit* **(NBC, Oct. 4)** "That's another 25 years," Detective Ice-T says to a murder suspect, setting up a line that for a moment left film noir heroes from Humphrey Bogart to Guy Pearce in its dust. "Your parole officer isn't born yet."

NOVEMBER 4, 2002

1 ■ **Sam McGee, "Railroad Blues," from the anthology Classic Mountain Songs (Smithsonian Folkways)** McGee (1894–1975) played guitar with Uncle Dave Macon in the 1920s, with Fiddlin' Arthur Smith in the '30s and '60s; in this 1964 recording he blows holes through the idea of "country music," the "breakdown," the "guitar solo." Long, thin notes stretch into the air until you think you can't hear them anymore,

but you can; bass strings swoop down to rescue the melody from the silences that are almost left behind. It's a workout, a cutting contest—but more than anything an acting out of the pioneer spirit, of America as experiment, as, "Hey, there's always something better over the next hill," but deep down not really caring if there is or not, not if to get from one place to another you can move like this.

2 ▪ **Don DeLillo, Belknap Lecture, Princeton University (Oct. 16)** DeLillo read from his forthcoming novel, *Cosmopolis*, due next spring, about a day in the life of one Eric Packer, a 28-year-old billionaire currency trader. As the book opens he's in his white limousine, on his way to get a haircut. Refusing to dramatize, letting the words carry the story, DeLillo read quietly, and the result was a dreamlike rhythm. As Dave Hickey says of *Chet Baker Sings*, there were "no range dynamics, no tempo dynamics, no expressive timbre shifts, no suppression of extant melodics, no harmonic meandering, no virtuoso high-speed scales." Later there were questions from the audience. "What do you know about being fabulously wealthy?" a woman asked. "I can spell both words," DeLillo said.

3 ▪ **"Piss off Ryan Adams, win a prize!" (Oct. 17)** The tale of Ryan Adams' response to a fan who shouted out for Bryan Adams' "Summer of '69"—Adams screaming, demanding the house lights be turned on, identifying the offender, paying him $30 as a refund for his ticket and refusing to play until the guy left the hall—even made it into *Time*. But not the response of songwriter Robbie Fulks, on his Web site: "Any reader on this site who attends a Ryan Adams show and disrupts the show with a Bryan Adams song request will receive in return merchandise"—T-shirts and autographed CDs—"of his or her choice equal to the cost of the ticket, from my online store . . . please provide the date and location of the show, what you yelled, and what Ryan's reaction was."

4–5 ▪ **16 Horsepower, *Folklore* (Jetset) and Woven Hand, *Woven Hand* (Glitter-**house/Germany)** In its best work, as with the 2000 *Secret South*, the Denver combo 16 Horsepower calls up the specter of itinerant preachers you can't tell from thieves. It's scary to believe David Eugene Edwards' voice—it can be scarier not to. But *Folklore* lacks all conviction—and no one can get away with sounding bored with a song as good as the Carter Family's "Single Girl," let alone with Hank Williams' "Alone and Forsaken." Edwards could have been saving it all for his solo project Woven Hand— here, from the first notes, a banjo clattering as if the distant past is rushing forward so fast the future will be defenseless against it, nothing is certain. You understand what it means to wander in the desert, abandoned by God and hating every human face, and you wonder why such a life sounds so rich.

6 ▪ **Ramsay Midwood, *Shoot Out at the OK Chinese Restaurant* (Vanguard)** Whether Midwood has a degree in creative writing from Harvard or was born in a graveyard in Alabama, he's selling weirdo country shtick. But he's also got Skip Edwards playing organ. "Monster Truck" is going nowhere until a descending wash of sound takes you out of the performance, and suddenly you're floating down a river on a raft; nothing is happening in "Fisherman's Friend" until there's this odd little squeak, and then a new, wordless voice is singing the song, with humor and depth, and a momentum that seems to have come out of a need or a desire nothing in the music has even hinted at is burning off the pose. Strange.

7 ▪ **Yeah Yeah Yeahs, Irving Plaza, New York (Oct. 15)** On their 2001 EP this New York trio was rough, sardonic, pulling an anthem, "Our Time," out of the ground: "Our time / To be hated!" singer Karen O chanted. This night, opening for Sleater-Kinney, all they had were gestures, and by the time they got to "Our Time," the last song, it felt like not even the band believed a word it said.

8 ▪ **"Ferus," at Gagosian Gallery, New York (Sept. 12–Oct. 19)** In a celebration of the revolutionary Los Angeles Ferus Gallery, which from 1957 to 1967 showed many of the most surprising works by Wallace Berman, Bruce Conner, Jay DeFeo, Richard Diebenkorn and Ed Keinholz, the most powerful piece was an unusual Andy Warhol *Triple Elvis* from 1963. Back then, Ferus mounted a whole show of Warhol Elvises, using the giant panels to make a labyrinth the visitor had to find a way through. Unlike most *Triple Elvis* works, the one in the Gagosian showed not three separate versions of Elvis from the movie *Flaming Star*—Elvis in cowboy gear, pointing a gun out at the world, his body hunched, his black-rimmed eyes falling into his face—but only two. On the right side of the piece there was a single, stable image. On the left there was a single image with a shadow breaking out of it, as if the Elvises were shaking, about to come apart. As Elvis' body separated from itself, the terrified blankness in his eyes was more alive than ever.

9 ■ Chieftains, *Down the Old Plank Road: The Nashville Sessions* (RCA) Backing such outsider-country names as Alison Krauss, Lyle Lovett, Martina McBride, Vince Gill, Buddy and Julie Miller, Gillian Welch and Patty Griffin, plus Earl Scruggs, Bela Fleck and John Hiatt, the hallowed Irish quintet leads them through the thickets of such great numbers as Dock Boggs' "Country Blues" and Uncle Dave Macon's "Way Down the Old Plank Road," into a land of such blandness you can barely tell you're listening, let alone to who or what. It's an acting out of America as, "Well, whether or not there's always something better over the next hill, you're probably better off not knowing." I blame the Chieftains; no one else here has ever been so dull.

10 ■ Bob Dylan, "Train of Love," from *Kindred Spirits: A Tribute to the Songs of Johnny Cash* (Lucky Dog) Aren't tribute albums terrible? Dylan almost never does good work on them, but here, surrounded by Dwight Yoakam, Steve Earle (it's against the law to make a tribute album without him), Travis Tritt, Keb' Mo', the unspeakable Hank Williams Jr., Bruce Springsteen, Mary Chapin Carpenter, Sheryl Crow, Emmy-lou Harris and Rosanne Cash, he gets real, real gone, though not before pausing to wave goodbye: "I used to sing this song before I ever wrote a song," Dylan says before "Train of Love." "I also want to thank you for standing up for me, *way* back when." Way back in 1965, onstage at the Newport Folk Festival, where, as the current revisionist line has it, nothing actually happened.

NOVEMBER 18, 2002

1–2 ■ *8 Mile*, directed by Curtis Hanson (Universal) and Eminem, "Lose Yourself," on *Music From and Inspired by the Motion Picture "8 Mile"* (Sony/Interscope)
The picture is alive to Eminem's presence, and he is alive to the picture, seeming to withdraw from the camera even as he pulls its eye toward him. Taking the viewer through a few days in the life of a white Detroit rapper in a black milieu—the adventures of a young man whose attempts to step out of oblivion are at best wary and at worst, and most believable, terrified—Eminem gives a performance that is all gravity. When the movie ends, there is a sense that it has, in fact, ended—that the movie has caught its own story.

Then "Lose Yourself" begins to play under the closing credits, and in an instant it blows the film away. The music dissolves the movie, reveals it as a lie, a cheat, as if it were made not to reveal but to cover up the seemingly bottomless pit of resentment and desire that is the story's true source. Again and again the piece all but blows up in the face of the man who's chanting it, Eminem lost in his rhymes until suddenly people are shouting at him from every direction and the music jerks him into the chorus, which he escapes in turn. The piece builds into crescendos of power, climbing ladders of refusal and willfulness step by step, rushing nothing, never reaching the top because it is the music itself that has put the top so high.

It's Eminem's greatest single recording, but it's more than that. As with Jerry Lee Lewis' "Whole Lotta Shakin' Goin' On,"

Aretha Franklin's "I Never Loved a Man (The Way I Love You)," the Miracles' "The Love I Saw in You Was Just a Mirage," Bob Dylan's "Like a Rolling Stone," Grandmaster Flash and the Furious Five's "The Message," the Rolling Stones' "Gimmie Shelter" or Nirvana's "Smells Like Teen Spirit," it's one of those moments in pop music that throws off everything around it, setting a new standard, offering a new challenge, proving that, now, you, whoever you are, can say anything, and with a beauty no one can gainsay. That's what's happening here. The cutting contest at the end of 8 *Mile* is a small thing compared to the cutting contest "Lose Yourself" throws down on pop music as such.

3–5 ▪ Goyard, 233, rue St. Honoré, Paris (Oct. 27) You hear postwar jazz in any even vaguely expensive place in Paris. An otherwise painfully quiet restaurant features an entire Johnny Hodges live album; a hotel on the site of the fabled Tabou nightclub, once the haunt of Boris Vian, Juliet Gréco and Miles Davis, now offers a live trio, or disembodied voices determined to simultaneously mine the legacy and smooth it away. But in a posh luggage shop, empty except for a customer and a salesman, someone had programmed jazz chart toppers—though, really, it was only Peggy Lee's 1958 "Fever" that allowed you to hear Tennessee Ernie Ford's 1956 version of the Merle Travis folk song "Sixteen Tons" as jazz.

With both recordings the orchestration was so spare it was almost spectral, something you imagined rather than heard. You could picture each performer lit by a single spot, otherwise in complete darkness on his or her nightclub stage, moving so minimally that the slightest gesture would communicate as a promise or a threat. Except for Ford's big final chorus, nothing was even dramatized. The recordings were about bringing out a single, unique taleteller, removing everything else from the world the song made, leaving nothing but the hipster smile in the first word and the orgasmic smear of the last of Lee's "Daddy-O don't you dare," nothing but the throwaway

snap in Ford's "A lotta men didn't, a lotta men died." The songs stayed in the air; after these one-of-a-kinds, Bobby Troup's 1946 "Route 66" was just sweeping up.

6 ▪ Bubblegum Babylon (VH-1, debuting Nov. 24) From west of Philadelphia, Widmerpool reports on a "'history' of pop pop-music," which the show seems to think began with David Cassidy and culminated in Britney": "At one point, Danny Bonaduce says that at the height of the *Partridge Family's* popularity, on tour, 'It was like Saddam Hussein—you had to keep moving from safe-house to safe-house.' After this context was placed in my mind, I wondered what stopped the producers from spirit-gluing a beard onto the also-interviewed Monkee Peter Tork, so he could do his uncanny Osama bin Laden impersonation. The repulsively casual pop-group/Hussein comparison gave a new perspective to the *Dick Van Dyke* episode in which Van Dyke and Mary Tyler Moore provide a 'safe-house' for British invasion hitmakers Chad and Jeremy. Except C & J didn't ask DVD or MTM to kiss their armpits in fealty; I bet Peter and Gordon would have."

7 ▪ Varin Frères (Amédée and Eugène), *Reims, cathèdrale, gargouille et jeune homme en casquette, vers 1854,* in "Chefs d'Ouevres de la Collection Photographique de la Musée d'Orsay" (Paris, through Feb. 23) In a passageway high in the cathedral, near a gargoyle, a man in a white shirt, dark pants, a scarf around his neck and a dark cap with a big bill slouches against a wall, right hand on his hip, left hand on his knee. It's perhaps the earliest photograph ever made of '50s cool—of Marlon *Wild One* Brando-James *Rebel Without a Cause* Dean-Elvis leaning-against-a-motorcycle Presley cool. *Eighteen-fifties* cool.

8 ▪ *Invasion of the Body Snatchers* (1956), directed by Don Siegel (Ojai Playhouse, Ojai, Calif., Oct. 19) Muzot (Genevieve Yue) writes: "Stars Dana Wynter and Kevin McCarthy were there for a brief Q&A session at the end. The screening itself was disappointing—a DVD instead of 35 mm, a false start in the Spanish language option and an uncomfortable shoebox theater preserved as a historical landmark—but I had the great experience of watching the movie with a group of junior high school students, a few rows in front of me, who were seeing it for the first time. No real fright, but plenty of giggling and cheering. When the actors stepped up, Dana Wynter looked blankly at the audience and declared herself a card-carrying pod. Kevin McCarthy scanned the theater suspiciously, everything about him gruff, and, speaking to no one in particular, said, 'Are they all pods? No! We have to do it again.' Not everyone knew how to react; it stung like an accusation, a familiar panic that wasn't so easy to laugh at. I got the feeling this had become his line, worn not like the flat joke of an aged actor but a reminder of what made his warnings in the film so powerful to begin with, a sounding of the voice from the hills."

9 ▪ Northern State, *Dying in Stereo* (Northern State) I wouldn't say a word against a Long Island hip-hop trio with an MC who calls herself Hesta Prynne—except that with that name she's going to have to deliver stronger stuff than the charming "The country's getting ugly, and there's more in store / But don't blame me, 'cause I voted for Gore." Something like—

10 ▪ Election flyer, www.moveonpac.org (Princeton University, Nov. 5) "REGIME CHANGE BEGINS AT HOME—VOTE"

DECEMBER 9, 2002

1 ▪ Announcement (Madison Square Garden, Nov. 11) For years, the same voice has opened every show with the same phrase, squashing the name at the end into one word: "Ladies and gentlemen, please welcome, Columbia recording artist, BOB DYLAN!" Last Aug. 9, though, a piece appeared in the *Buffalo News* in anticipation of a Dylan date in Hamburg, N.Y. It led with a paragraph recapitulating Dylan's career. As print it was boilerplate—but to hear that paragraph now, appropriated as Dylan's official new introduction, was pure media shock. It's the displacement that takes place

when the conventions of one form are shoved into the conventions of another form: "Ladies and gentlemen, please welcome the poet laureate of rock 'n' roll. The voice of the promise of the '60s counterculture. The guy who forced folk into bed with rock, who donned makeup in the '70s and disappeared into a haze of substance abuse, who emerged to find Jesus, and who suddenly shifted gears, releasing some of the strongest music of his career beginning in the late '90s. Ladies and gentlemen, Bob Dylan!"

2 ▪ "Masters of War" (MSG, Nov. 11) In 1991, with the Gulf War underway, Dylan stepped onto the stage at the Grammys telecast with his band. They were to play before Jack Nicholson presented Dylan with a Lifetime Achievement Award. The combo dove into a blithering, all-stops-out piece of rhythm, Dylan smearing every word into a single sound. It was "Masters of War," from 1963, Dylan's best, and most unforgiving, antiwar song—but you couldn't necessarily tell. The song was buried in its performance, as if history were its true audience.

With a second Gulf War looming, there was no disguise when, seven songs into the first of two New York shows, Dylan gathered his small band into a half-circle for an acoustic, almost chamber-music version. Played very slowly, very deliberately, the performance made you understand just how good the song is. It wasn't a matter of relevance. You could imagine that if the last war on earth had occurred 39 years ago—if the song had, by its very appearance, ended war—the song would still speak, just as a 7,000-year-old god excavated in Jordan and recently installed in the Louvre is still speaking, reminding you of what you came from, of who you once were.

3 ▪ Cover: Elvis Costello's "(The Angels Wanna Wear My) Red Shoes," 1977 (MSG, Nov. 11) He didn't sing about the shoes; having apparently invested more wisely than the angels, he wore them.

4 ▪ CD: *The Bootleg Series, Vol. 5: Live 1975—The Rolling Thunder Revue* (Columbia)

Confusion in almost every vocal, a pound of sugar in almost every arrangement. Right, the famous "donned makeup in the '70s" period.

5 ▪ **Paul Muldoon, "Bob Dylan at Princeton, November 2000," from "Do You, Mr. Jones?"—Bob Dylan With the Poets and Professors, ed. Neil Corcoran (Chatto & Windus, U.K.)** Muldoon is a poet (author most recently of *Moy Sand and Gravel*), co-author of Warren Zevon's recent "My Ride's Here" and a professor at Princeton. Leading off this new essay collection with a new poem, Muldoon goes back to the show Dylan played at Princeton in 2000— which took place in Princeton's Dillon Gym. " 'You know what, honey? We call that a homonym,' " the narrator of the poem says to the woman he's with as the concert starts. Then Dylan's only previous appearance at Princeton enters the poem—in 1970, when Dylan was present not to play but to accept an honorary degree. " 'He wouldn't wear a hood,' " the narrator of the poem remembers. " 'You know what, honey? We call that disquietude.' "

6 ▪ **Cover: George Harrison's "Something," 1969 (MSG, Nov. 13)** A final encore, done very straight. Musicians love this song; they admire the ability to craft anything that's at once generic, anonymous and likely to generate income for a hundred years.

7 ▪ **"Summer Days" (MSG, Nov. 11)** In a perfect world, this would be the turnaround cut on a live album called "Having a Rave-Up With Bob Dylan!"

8 ▪ **"Yea! Heavy and a Bottle of Bread" (MSG, Nov. 11)** Dylan's first performance of the song since he recorded it with the Hawks in a basement of a big pink house in upstate New York 35 years ago. Two of the five who were there then are dead. The house was recently on the market as a prime Dylan collectible. The tune still blew the air of pure American fedupness: "Pack up the meat, sweet, we're headin' out."

9 ▪ **"It's Alright, Ma (I'm Only Bleeding)" (MSG, Nov. 11)** From 1965. The audience always waits to cheer for "Sometimes even the president of the United States must have to stand naked." By now the song has outlasted almost as many presidents as Fidel Castro: Lyndon Johnson (no problem, for a man who liked to receive guests while sitting on the toilet), Richard Nixon, Gerald Ford, Jimmy Carter, Ronald Reagan, George Bush, Bill Clinton (who as president was stripped naked, and who you can imagine singing the line to himself) and now George W. Bush. The line took nothing away from the last man on the list; he lives in the armor of his own entitlement.

10 ▪ **"All Along the Watchtower" (MSG, Nov. 11)** The second of two encores, it began very strangely, with guitarist Charlie Sexton rolling a few spare notes that seemed to call up a distant western—Jim Jarmusch's *Dead Man*, maybe, with Neil Young's improvised and timeless guitar soundtrack. It was in fact the opening of Ferrante & Teicher's 1961 twin-piano hit "Theme From *Exodus*," from the movie based on Leon Uris' 1958 novel about the creation of the state of Israel. Whether you caught the reference or not, it took the song about to emerge from its own history—one of Dylan's most world-ending, from 1968, a year that over and over again felt like the end of the world—out of itself. Now the song was going to speak with a new voice: that was the promise that little introduction made.

It was impossible to imagine that Dylan ever played the song with more vehemence, or that, this night, six days after the midterm congressional elections, the performance was not utterly political, as much a protest song as "Masters of War." Not when, after Dylan, Sexton and guitarist Larry Campbell led an overwhelming instrumental climb through the tune's themes following the closing verse, Dylan came back to the mike to sing the opening verse again in a wild voice, throwing the last lines across the seats and out of the hall like a curse: "Businessmen they drink my wine, plowmen dig my earth / None of them, along the line, know what—any—any of it—any of it is—worth."

JANUARY 2, 2003

1 ▪ **Mendoza Line, "Sleep of the Just,"** from *Almost You: The Songs of Elvis Costello* **(Glurp)** Aren't tribute albums terrible? This one is really terrible—and the Atlanta band's view all the way into one of Costello's greatest recordings ranks with Eminem's "Lose Yourself" and DJ Shadow's *The Private Press* as the most undeniable sound of the year.

Maybe it was always obvious that the song is about the gang-rape of a local girl at an army base, with the woman looking back: "The soldier asked my name and did I come here very often / Well, I thought that he was asking me to dance." Maybe the song was always about the woman cherishing his death when his company's transport vehicle is blown up: he's getting the sleep of the just, all right, the big sleep. In Costello's performance, though, the beauty of the composition makes the story into a fable, and the people in it float like ghosts.

Shannon McArdle is all flesh, still trying to wash off the stains after all these years. She makes her voice small and flat for the difficult shifts in timbre, removing any hint of professionalism. She's as off-the-street as the woman in the middle of the Human League's "Don't You Want Me," and the naturalism of the performance—carried from the beginning by a solemn church organ that is even more damning when it plays pop changes—is almost unbearable. The woman has her satisfaction over the soldier's death, but that's all she has. He and the rest took everything else.

That a woman is singing makes all the difference. Costello himself could go all the way into the song, but McArdle goes out the other side.

2 ▪ **Boomtown Rats, "I Don't Like Mondays" (Columbia, 1980)** Southern Tip reports from Tierra del Fuego, Argentina: "'I Don't Like Mondays' was playing in a cab in Ushuaia. It sounded better than ever. I asked the driver to turn it up and told the person I was with he couldn't talk. It made me think that radio is the farthest reaching, most democratic medium for art there is. How bad can it be to live in the southernmost city in the world, which is on an island—a city that to reach by car you have to cross the Straits of Magellan and twice cross the Chilean border—how bad can it be when the DJ plays 'I Don't Like Mondays'?"

3 ▪ **Dennis Haysbert as President David Palmer, 24 (Fox, Tuesdays)** If Bill Clinton was not, as Toni Morrison famously claimed, the first black president, then Dennis Haysbert—who has, for reasons not unrelated to the racism that is the deep subtext of the Palmer character, received far more praise for his Sidney Poitier turn in the lifeless *Far From Heaven* than for his work here—is playing the first black Bill Clinton. It's in his apparent naiveté, the way he carries his size, and most of all in the angry self-control in his face as he realizes once again that he's been betrayed by one of his own, whatever "his own" means. As his estranged wife Sherry has been arguing since halfway through the show's first season, there's no such thing.

4 ▪ **New Order, *Retro* (Warner Bros., 1980–2002)** Across four CDs of hits, remixes and live recordings, it doesn't matter that the Manchester dance band's 1983 "Blue Monday" remains the biggest selling 12-inch single ever. Compared to the Shep Pettibone mix of the 1986 "Bizarre Love Triangle" (where again and again, in moments memory can't hold, the sound shifts faster than a fast cut in a film), "Blue Monday" remains a soap jingle. And compared to the full, 8 minute 41 second version of the 1982 "Temptation," probably the best 12-inch single ever made (a journey comparable to the Boz Scaggs/Duane Allman version of "Loan Me a Dime," moving from delirium to contemplation and, so violently, back again), the Shep Pettibone remix of "Bizarre Love Triangle" is very nice.

5 ▪ **Touré, *The Portable Promised Land* (Little, Brown)** The author bio promises the Brooklyn writer's first novel, *Soul City,* "soon enough," but the best of the stories in this first collection are pieces of a novel reaching for each other, then backing away. There's a lot of padding—credibility lists of negritude on the order of "The African-American Aesthetics Hall of Fame," or "101 Elements of Blackness (Things That'll Make You Say: 'Yes! That There's Some Really Black Shit!')" that were done better in Darius James' *That's Blaxploitation!* There are stories that don't take off. But the book drops all pose for the mystery of what happens when the borders between black and white begin to dissolve. In "Attack of the Love Dogma," "The Playground of the Ecstatically Blasé," the three-part "Black Widow Story," "The Commercial Channel" and "They're Playing My Song" Touré stops moving characters like toy soldiers and lets them move him. "The Black Widow Story" is a superhero comic book, a trash race novel, Chester Himes influenced by Lester Bangs—you have no idea what will come next. Is Charisma Donovan, high-school queen turned femme fatale turned porn star, a version of the Black Widow, a white woman who becomes the female Tupac "on a dare after drama class," or are they the same person—and could either tell if either were? "You remember," Touré says as he sets the scene, "how things were last summer when Jamais was brand-new and like, the only thing the city was talking about. The French Bistro décor. The barefoot girl in the glass case behind the bar sitting on a pillow reading *Paradise Lost*, all night every night . . ."—and somehow you do remember. You're right there. And you don't like it when the author lets you go, too soon.

6 ■ Joshua Clover, "Modest $100 Million Proposals, for Better or Verse" (*Village Voice*, Nov. 27–Dec. 3) On the $100 million-plus gift by rejected amateur poet Ruth Lily to *Poetry Magazine*: after three sensible notions on what to do with the money ("lobby for pro-education candidates," "buy a million poetry books every year and give them away," "free medical coverage to every poet accepted for publication"), Clover pulls out the stops. Such ideas, he says, "would burn a tiny fraction of the bequest: Instead of in-vesting the remainder, *Poetry* could secede from the Union, purchase the Republic of the Marshall Islands (GDP: $99 million), and appoint their very own poet laureate, who would then meet the U.S. laureate in a battle to the death, wreaking unfathomable destruction across the landscape."

7 ■ *The Jimmy Show*, written and directed by Frank Whaley (First Look Pictures) Whaley as a New Jersey man with a dead-end job who lives for open-mike nights at local comedy clubs, where the heartfelt cry "YOU SUCK!" is the most response he ever gets. Or, Bruce Springsteen, the Bizarro Years.

8 ■ Johnny Cash, *American IV: The Man Comes Around* (American/Lost Highway) The fourth time around for the Old Man Sings New Guy Songs concept is not too many, especially when so many old songs are part of the show: could anyone else let the line "Sometimes in the saddle, I used to go gay" from "Streets of Laredo" slip by without a hint of self-consciousness? There are stunning duds, most notably a version of Ewan MacColl's "The First Time Ever (I Saw Your Face)" that reveals how horrible the song actually is (though there's no footnote about how it inspired "Killing Me Softly," which is even worse). Cash does best with a strong melody and a light, insistent beat—and here, with Nine Inch Nails' "Hurt," he goes deeper into the composition than Trent Reznor ever did. As with U2's "One" on his *III*, Cash understands the piece as a weight; he assumes it, and then, as you listen, lets it crush him. When *V*, *VI* or *VII* comes out posthumously, it won't sound any more posthumous than this.

9 ■ Duke Mitchell, "The Lion," from *"Gimme Dat Harp Boy!"—The Roots of the Captain* (Ozit Records) On a label named for the leading lights of London's 1960s underground press, a heroically diverse collection of strange records that prophesied Captain Beefheart—a word like "influenced" is just too paltry—a very hot late '50s–early '60s fuzztone stomp. With the fuzztone played by saxophones.

10 ■ **Homer Quincy Smith, "I Want Jesus to Talk With Me" ("Tangled Roots," Princeton University, Nov. 23)** At a conference on old-time music, Dean Blackwood of the "raw musics" reissue label Revenant talked about the idea of "phantom artists": people whose names can be found on the labels of old 78s, but about whom nothing is known, including whether the names on the labels are real. He played a 1930 recording by Elvie Thomas, and the 50 or so people in attendance (including Brett and Rennie Sparks of the contemporary country Gothic duo the Handsome Family, whose performance would close the conference, and Tony Glover and John Koerner of the 40-year veteran Twin Cities roots band Koerner Ray & Glover, who had opened the event with their last concert—guitarist Dave Ray would die six days later) shook their heads in wonder.

Blackwood played a 1926 Paramount release by Homer Quincy Smith and mouths dropped open in shock. "I want Jesus to walk with me"—a man sings in a slow, measured cadence, making it plain he understands how much he's asking for. The performance begins with the tinny sound of a calliope, which as Smith's voice goes down to the bottom of a mine turns into a huge pipe organ. At the end, Smith lets his voice rise, until it seems a thing in itself, on its way to Jesus, leaving the singer behind. Another participant had prepared a response to Blackwood's presentation, but as an instance of the great game of "Follow that, motherfucker!" I never saw anything like it.

JANUARY 20, 2003

1 ■ **The Best News of the Week: "Arrest in Punk Singer's '93 Slaying" (Associated Press/San Francisco Chronicle, Jan. 12)** "SEATTLE—A Florida man has been arrested and charged with murder after DNA linked him to the death of rising punk-rock star Mia Zapata in 1993, police said.

"Police said Jesus C. Mezquia, 48, was arrested late Friday in the Miami area. His DNA profile matched a sample taken from the crime scene more than nine years ago, police said.

"Zapata, the 27-year-old lead singer of The Gits, was last seen alive July 7, 1993, in Seattle's Capitol Hill neighborhood. Her beaten body was left on a street curb more than a mile away. She had been strangled with the drawstring of her Gits sweatshirt.

"Police had no leads in the slaying. The Seattle music community—including its biggest names, Pearl Jam, Nirvana and Soundgarden—raised $70,000 to hire a private investigator, but eventually the funds dried up."

2 ■ **Donnas, Spend the Night (Atlantic)** "Faster than sound," as Big Brother and the Holding Company put it 35 years ago in San Francisco, up the Peninsula from the Donnas' Palo Alto. But Big Brother didn't have Skyline Boulevard in their blood. Speedshifting on the Skyline turns at midnight, way above the Stanford hills, is just what the Donnas' new music feels like—except when it feels like X in 1980, the punk band burning their song "Los Angeles" into the pavement like rubber. Today "You Wanna Get Me High" jumps off the radio, as familiar as weather, as much of a shock as lightning hitting your house. "Take It Off" is right behind. This is what rock 'n' roll never forgets—or rather it's what rock 'n' roll always forgets, until people like Brett Anderson, Maya Ford, Torry Castellano and Allison Robertson find it.

3 ■ **Alison Krauss and Union Station, Live (Rounder)** Fine, fine, but across two discs it's the smallest sound that cuts the deepest: "Forget About It," sung as if the singer's walking out on a fight at 4 a.m., her tiredness indistinguishable from her contempt.

4 ■ **Michael O'Dell, letter to the editor, City Pages, Minneapolis (Dec. 4)** Among pages of letters praising City Pages editor Steve Perry's Nov. 27 cover story "Spank the Donkey," in which Perry argued that people of good will should abandon the Democratic Party in favor of generations of Republican rule sufficient to produce conditions conducive to the election of

Ralph Nader: "You should go back to singing for Journey."

5 ▪ Mark Halliday, *Jab* (University of Chicago Press) Ken Tucker writes: "Pop and rock have inspired some of the worst poetry ever, from Patti Smith to Tom Clark to Jim Carroll to Exene to Jewel to Amiri Baraka (New Jersey could have avoided the controversy over Baraka's anti-Semitism if they'd just gotten an advance of the Roots' *Phrenology* and heard him 'perform'). But Mark Halliday consistently makes music work for him as subject matter. In *Jab* he imagines a session trumpet player during the recording of Jan and Dean's 'Surf City' in 1963:

" 'I see this trumpet player (was there even a horn section in that song? / Say there was) / I see this one trumpet player with tie askew / or maybe he's wearing a loose tropical foliage shirt sitting on a metal chair waiting / for the session to reach the big chorus / where Jan and Dean exult / "Two girls for every boy" / and he's thinking / of his hundred nights on his buddy Marvin's hairy stainy sofa / and the way hot dogs and coffee make a mud misery / and the way one girl is far too much . . . / Surfing—what life actually lets guys ride boards / on waves? / Is it all fiction? Is it a joke? / Jan and Dean and their pal Brian act like it's a fine, good joke / Whereas the trumpet player thinks it's actually shit / If anybody asked him, a tidal wave of shit / Nobody's asking'."

6 ▪ Esperanto Cafe, Christmas night (114 MacDougal St., New York) In this place that never closes, there are many volumes of *The History of Philosophy*, but no evident traces of Esperanto, the language invented in the late 19th century by a man who believed that if all people spoke the same tongue— "manufacturing a Tower of Babel in reverse," as Lester Bangs put it—there would be no more war. As snow fell heavily outside, the Rolling Stones' 1969 "You Can't Always Get What You Want" was playing. Then came the killingly original blues line that opens their 1964 cover of Irma Thomas' "Time Is on My Side," and time really did begin to slide. It was only 107 years before, to the night, that in a saloon in St. Louis a

man named Billy Lyons snatched the Stetson hat off the head of a man named "Stag" Lee Shelton, and Shelton, who some called Stagolee, shot him, retrieved his hat, and walked out the door.

7 ▪ Richard Avedon, "Portraits" (Metropolitan Museum of Art, New York, closed Jan. 5) Overfamiliar work, but in the room featuring pictures from Avedon's "In the American West" series there was a stopper. Some of Avedon's shots of highway bums are so lurid they're unforgettable, in the worst, freak-show manner; *Clarence Lippard, drifter, Interstate 80, Sparks, Nevada, August 29, 1983* was different. Instead of the lantern jaw and killer's eyes of the other men on the walls, Lippard held himself in reserve. The countless big, dark freckles— or skin cancers—that covered his face and hands spoke for a life lived out of doors; his dark blazer and clean white shirt made it seem as if he were a gentleman farmer out for a stroll. Very handsome, in a moneyed East Coast way, with a full head of sandy hair, Lippard appeared in two photos. One—as if shot from below, showing Lippard from the waist up—softened his features, weakening his chin and turning his nose bulbous; he looked something like Kevin Kline in one of his good-guy roles. But the other picture, shot head-on and cropped at midchest, presented Lippard gazing straight out, his chin strong, his nose hard: in the way he carried himself, daring you to judge him.

His face now suggested Gregory Peck or Robert Ryan; the disease on his skin deepened his face, until you could see Lincoln along with the movie stars. And then another movie star who is not, really, a star: Bill Pullman, in the desert in *Lost Highway*, and then in *Igby Goes Down*, in the asylum.

8 ▪ *La Bohème*, directed by Baz Luhrmann (Broadway Theatre, New York, Dec. 22) The 1896 Puccini opera updated to 1957, complete with cool Marlon Brando references and "Let's go, cats!" dialogue, but with dying heroine Mimi looking like a leftover from a World War II movie, the men not remotely convincing as either Europeans or artists and the big Rive Gauche set altogether 19th century fin de siècle. Which didn't matter. The change from garret apartment for Act 1 to Left Bank street for Act 2 was made in half light; when the stagehands, costumed as Paris workers, had everything in place, the audience thought the action would proceed in the shadows. Then the lights were flicked on, the tableau lit up like a firecracker, and a collective "Ah-hhhh!" filled the theater. There were prostitutes draped over balconies, a patriotic parade, urchins and clochards, little rich kids in fancy coats, an English millionaire in tails with not-dying heroine Musette on his arm. The scene paid off with Musette's (Jessica Comeau, this afternoon) long, increasingly passionate "Quando e'n vò"—which in 1959 was turned into Della Reese's great hit "Don't You Know." It was a pure pop spectacle, which made the shift to Act 3, from Let's Party to Tragedy, seem a little glib.

9 ▪ John Doe, "Employee of the Month," from *Dim Stars, Bright Sky* (Im/BMG) There's something of the feel of Randy Newman's "Vine Street" here, and as a loser's song it's convincing. But it's not half as convincing as losers John Doe plays in the movies, from Amber Waves' ex-husband in *Boogie Nights* to Mr. Werther in *The Good Girl*: characters so depressed they can barely summon the energy to look away from the camera.

10 ▪ Joe Strummer, Aug. 21, 1952–Dec. 22, 2002 "You know what they said? Well, some of it was true!"

FEBRUARY 3, 2003

1 ▪ White Stripes, *Elephant* (V2/Third Man) Before my turntable broke (the vinyl version was all I could find), this sounded like the Detroit guitar-and-drums combo's *Rubber Soul* at least as much as Pussy Galore's "Pretty Fuck Look."

2 ▪ *The Murder of Emmett Till*, directed by Stanley Nelson, written by Marcia A. Smith and narrated by Andre Braugher (PBS, Jan. 20) This documentary on the 1955 lynching of a black 14-year-old Chicago boy near

Money, Miss., opened with a lovely shot of the meandering Tallahatchie River—where Till's body, weighted down with a cotton gin fan, was dumped after he was killed for supposedly whistling at a white man's wife. Later there were images of a bridge, and I couldn't help thinking of Bobbie Gentry's 1967 "Ode to Billy Joe." A girl tells the story of how her boyfriend, Billie Joe McAllister, jumped to his death from the Tallahatchie Bridge, into the Tallahatchie River—and how, her family has heard, she and Billie Joe were seen throwing something from the same bridge, into the same river, just days before. What was it? Bobbie Gentry has never said, but isn't there a memory of Emmett Till's murder in whatever it was?

3 ▪ Lucinda Williams, *World Without Tears* (Lost Highway) The first song, the modestly titled "Fruits of My Labors," begins with a shimmering, subtle progression played on a Leslie guitar. Then comes a slurred, dragging, unbelievably affected voice to tell you how deeply its owner feels: so deeply barely a single word is actually formed. Every little touch—brushes on the snare, say—is mixed up high, to let you know how carefully everything has been done. There is irony in "American Dream": despite the title, the song is about how bad things (poverty, drug addiction—because of Vietnam—and black lung) take place in America. But the singer will press on. "Bay swee bay 'f's alla same," Williams promises, "tay th' glore en day ov' the fame." Not due til April, but why wait? It's not getting any better.

4 ▪ Robin Williams, *Live 2002* (Columbia) Nowhere near the action of last year's HBO roller coaster, but it only takes him a few minutes to hit his stride—with the tragedy of the Supreme Court's striking down the execution of the retarded. Here and there, glimpses of a man whose *no* could do more to change the country than any words from Tom Daschle, Joe Lieberman, Nancy Pelosi or John Edwards.

5 ▪ *Rolling Stones Live* (HBO, Jan. 19) Mojave Sam (Howard Hampton) writes:

"They've been worse. I thought of William Cody and his Wild West Show, fancifully reenacting Little Big Horn. Buffalo Bill preening in time-honorific Custer'd fashion, Sitting Bull on rhythm guitar (sporting traditional headdress, but what happened to his voice—is it changing back?), Annie Oakley guesting on 'Honky Tonk Women,' etc.; I believe 'Can't You Hear Me Knocking' was their tribute to the building of the transcontinental railroad, in real time. In any case, they gave the people what they wanted, and no one was any the wiser." Except that on "Gimmie Shelter," backing singer Lisa Fischer, otherwise as florid as Patti LaBelle, looked Mick Jagger in the face and opened up the doors of the song.

6 ■ **Ann Charters, editor, *The Portable Sixties Reader* (Penguin)** At more than 600 pages, a definitively clueless anthology ending with bad poems about the deaths of the decade's top 10 dead people. Count down! Ten! Hemingway! Nine! Marilyn Monroe! Eight! John F. Kennedy! "When I woke up they'd stole a man away," says Eric von Schmidt—hey, who's "they"? As Donovan used to say, "I really want to know," but never mind, Seven! Sylvia Plath! Six! Malcolm X! Five! Martin Luther King Jr.! Four! *Robert* F. Kennedy! Three! Neal Cassady! Two! Janis Joplin! And topping the chart: Jack Kerouac! With a straight obit from the *Harvard Crimson*! Solid! But Janis died in 1970. If she can get in, why not Jimi Hendrix? Captain Beefheart played a soprano sax solo for him the day his death was announced that said more than anything here.

7 ■ **Bonnie "Prince" Billy, *Master and Everyone* (Drag City)** In his current incarnation as Billy, Will Oldham looks like Nietzsche on the cover of this disc, and that's as far as it goes. What used to be Southern Gothic is now Southern hospitality—depressed, but very polite.

8 ■ **Pretty Girls Make Graves, *Pretty Girls Make Graves* (Dim Mak)** Hot punk from Seattle—and with every move in place, dispiritingly third-hand.

9 ■ **"Rude Mechanicals Financial Advisors answer the most frequently asked questions of investors and patrons alike," fund-raising letter (www.rudemechs.com)** After advising "FULL DIVESTMENT" from the stock market and the bond market ("As long as Pierce Brosnan is cast as James Bond in the 007 movies WE CANNOT RECOMMEND ANY BONDS whatsoever. Madonna is doing the theme song for the new movie. Have some self-respect") and answering "Is ART really a sound investment?" with a definite yes ("If you had given Emily Dickinson five dollars in 1864, your investment would now be worth more than 'this new Value in the Soul—Supremest Earthly Sum'"), the Austin theater group concludes with a set of irrefutable graphs: "Verizon stock value over the past five years vs. Patrons of Rude Mechs Spiritual Satisfaction," "ImClone stock value over the past five years vs. Rude Mechs Artistic Growth," "WorldCom Market Valuation vs. Increase in Overall Artistic Fulfillment brought to Patrons of Rude Mechs," and, bringing it all back home:

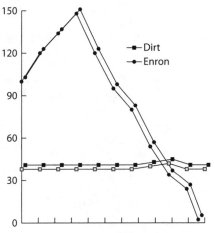

Enron stock value over the past five years - vs. - value of a handful of dirt

10 ■ **Helen Thomas at White House press briefing, Jan. 6** In his 1972 study *The World Turned Upside Down: Radical Ideas During the English Revolution*, Christopher Hill,

poring through the annals of the 16th and 17th centuries, tried to reconstruct the beginnings of a heresy that by the 1650s was making itself known across England. There would be a document noting that a certain craftsperson had questioned the divinity of Jesus; 20 years later there would be a record of a woman denying the need to work. Across a page or so, a dozen examples of seemingly stray people claiming that all true spirits were God and that all authority was false took on a huge charge, less from the power of any given fragment than from one's sense of how much was missing between the fragments. Reading the transcript of the exchange between 82-year-old Hearst News Services columnist Helen Thomas and White House spokesman Ari Fleischer, what was so shocking was not what she said, but, given the socialization produced by the news writing and even editorial writing in the likes of the *New York Times*, how bizarre it seemed—because in the context of contemporary political discourse Thomas spoke not as a reporter but precisely as a heretic:

Thomas: At the earlier briefing, Ari, you said that the president deplored the taking of innocent lives. Does that apply to all innocent lives in the world? And I have a follow-up.

Fleischer: I refer specifically to a horrible terrorist attack on Tel Aviv that killed scores and wounded hundreds. And the president, as he said in his statement yesterday, deplores in the strongest terms the taking of those lives and the wounding of those people, innocents in Israel.

T: My follow-up is, why does he want to drop bombs on innocent Iraqis?

F: Helen, the question is how to protect Americans, and our allies and friends—

Thomas and Fleischer went back and forth in several more exchanges. The president is only interested in defense against Iraq, Fleischer reiterated.

T: And he thinks they are a threat to us?

F: There is no question that the president thinks that Iraq is a threat to the United States.

T: The Iraqi people?

F: The Iraqi people are represented by their government. If there was regime change, the Iraqi—

T: So they will be vulnerable?

F: Actually, the president has made it very clear that he has no dispute with the people of Iraq. That's why the American policy remains a policy of regime change. There is no question the people of Iraq—

T: That's a decision for them to make, isn't it? It's their country.

F: Helen, if you think the people of Iraq are in a position to dictate who their dictator is, I don't think that has been what history has shown.

T: I think many countries' people don't have the decision—including us.

Thanks to Chris Walters

City
Pages
2003·2004

1 ▪ **A.R.E. Weapons,** *A.R.E. Weapons* **(Rough Trade)** New York City, very self-mocking about their street smarts, very anguished about the street, and utterly expert in a way that hides all craft. Guys come hunching down the sidewalk in their leather jackets: "Let's hear it for America," says the singer, sarcastic and completely straight. As a heartfelt adolescent plea for parental forbearance, "Hey World" has the defiant lift of the Yeah Yeah Yeah's "Our Time" and the regret of the Clash's "This Is England"—you can imagine it coming out of Claire on *Six Feet Under*, and it's stirring. "You're either part of the problem," you hear as the band sets you up to ignore its clichés, "or you're part of the fucking miserable solution we call life."

2 ▪ **The Kills,** *Keep on Your Mean Side* **(Rough Trade)** The U.S./U.K. duo starring in a very hot version of their song "Fuck the People"—and very casually. And not so casually on a primitive punk rewrite of Lead Belly's "Don't You Leave Me Here." There's a cold bravado: "Don't you leave me here/Got my name stitched on your lips so you won't dare." But the performance collapses now into a then. You're back in a time and place where someone left behind might never get out—no trains, no cars, no busses, no horses, no maps.

3 ▪ **Bob Dylan for Victoria's Secret (Fox, March 4)** "Only two things in this world worth botherin' your head about and them's sex and death," says a "debauched Midwestern businessman" in Michael O'Donoghue and Frank Springer's 1968 comic serial "The Adventures of Phoebe Zeitgeist." That's the only explanation for the commercial that uses B.D.'s suicidal 1997 "Love Sick" to orchestrate a montage of underwear models looking dour under their hooded eyes. But it's a better Dylan setting than the nearly four-hours-long God-blessed-the-Confederacy film *Gods and Generals*, which features his "Cross the Green Mountain." I haven't seen the picture, but I have seen the TV trailer featuring Robert Duvall sitting in a chair as Robert E. Lee and opining through a mouthful of molasses, "'s in Gawd's han's naw," as if to say, "Hey, don't blame *me*." On the other hand, "Love Sick" is an actual song. At more than eight dying minutes, "Cross the Green Mountain" might as well be the movie.

4 ▪ **Randy Newman for Ford (Fox, February 18)** For the first time in recent memory, a Newman tune was not nominated for an Oscar, and Randy must be feeling the pinch—or decided *Fuck it*, once and for all. Instead of merely licensing, say, "I Love to See You Smile" to McDonald's to rewrite and rerecord into eternity, he's writing from the ground up and selling his own voice. "It's right there in front of your eyes," he sings with exuberance and shame. "If you haven't looked at a Ford lately—look again."

5 ▪ **David Lynch and John Neff,** *BlueBob* **(Solitude/Ryko)** Lynch on words, drums, guitar, Neff on guitar, drums, vocals: Link Wray opening for Pere Ubu. "I Cannot Do That" is the musical equivalent of an outtake from *Lost Highway*, furiously sustained; out of the all-directions-at-once noise of "In the Pink Western Range" comes a dog, "barking like Robert Johnson." But the hit is "Thank You, Judge," an R&B divorce-court novelty.

6 ▪ **The Raveonettes,** *Whip It On* **(The Orchard)** Forget the Danish twosome's advertised Buddy Holly homage. In moments—"Chains," "Cops on Our Tail," "Beat City"—they make it into the film noir they're watching. *Gun Crazy*, probably.

7 ▪ **AFI,** *Sing the Sorrow* **(Dreamworks)** San Francisco goths with a cast of thousands don't know the meaning of pretentious, but you wish they did.

8 ▪ **Eva Cassidy, "Fields of Gold," from** *Songbird* **(Blix Street)** You hear this slow cover and you want to know who it was who made the Sting song feel as if it were hundreds of years old; that the singer has been dead since 1996, the year she recorded it, has nothing to do with it at all.

9 ▪ **New Orleans, March 9** All sorts of music comes out of the doors in New

Orleans: Bob Seger and disco in souvenir shops, the Drifters and the Young Rascals in the big, high-ceiling Rue de la Course coffeehouse at 3128 Magazine Street, Billie Holiday's greatest hits one day and Sisters of Mercy the next in CC's Community Coffee on Royal. It's rare to find music so quiet you have to be still to notice it—and when you do, it sticks. In what was previously the morning madhouse of Mothers at 401 Poydras, Robert Johnson's 1936 "Ramblin' on My Mind" now got lost in the dim light of the new, half-empty backroom—and in Luigi's muffaletta joint at 915 Decatur, in the middle of the sleaziest block on the sleaziest tourist street in town, you could barely make out a plinking banjo and a hesitating vocal in a crude version of "Spoonful." At first I was sure I'd heard it before—the feel and the style of the piece were somehow implied by the song. But there was too much space between the notes, too much air in the sound. "Do you know who's singing?" I asked the counterman. "It's WWOZ! 90.7!" he said. "It's Will Slayden, recorded in 1952," said the WWOZ DJ a few minutes later. "It's new: *African-American Banjo Songs from Western Tennessee.* Do you want the address? It was put out by the Tennessee Folklore Society, MTSU Box 201, Murfreesboro, TN 37132. Isn't it great?"

10 ▪ Associated Press, March 14: "Dixie Chicks singer criticized for anti-Bush comments" For the record, Natalie Maines, on stage, London, March 10: "Just so you know, we're ashamed the president of the United States is from Texas." Maines was born in Texas—in Lubbock, Buddy Holly's hometown. George W. Bush was born in New Haven, Connecticut, and to run for office adopted a tough-guy version of what he took to be a Texas accent. On September 21, 2001, in New York City, for the *America: A Tribute to Heroes* broadcast, Maines introduced the Dixie Chicks' "I Believe in Love" in a deep performance; Bush posed at Ground Zero with his arm around a New York City worker, promising aid he later withheld.

1 ▪ Nineteen Forty-Five, *I Saw a Bright Light* (Daemon) The first time you hear this, it might sound ordinary; the third or fourth time it can be shattering. There is the heart-on-our-sleeves heedlessness of the Mendoza Line's "We're All in This Alone"—but with Nineteen Forty-Five guitarist Hunter Manasco's scared leads and bassist Katharine McElroy's handholding backing vocals, none of the Mendoza Line's irony. In the kind of apartment that's too small to get clean, Eleventh Dream Day's "It's Not My World" has been played so many times that the glory you can only get by opening the window and the self-affirmation you can only get by closing it are in the walls—and so is the lift of the Feelies' "Raised Eyebrows," the feeling of going flat-out in a car that has a day left to live. Manasco, McElroy, and drummer Will Lochamy are from Birmingham, Alabama; they look familiar, but you haven't seen them before.

2 ▪ Don DeLillo, *Cosmopolis* (Scribner) This compact day-in-the-life novel has been savaged by critics from *People* to the *New York Times* as obvious, cheap, empty, and backward. The line is that the hero is a soulless 28-year-old billionaire financial manipulator, and that's just so three years ago, isn't it? But he isn't soulless. Like the detective in Paul Auster's *City of Glass*, he's holding himself together with string and gum, and then he isn't. The 2000 setting isn't in the past. It's the country blowing up in its own face, as it does whenever the individual's realization of the American dream erases America—a nation that, here, comes together only in the last pages, in the middle of the night, with 300 naked movie extras sprawled in the street.

3 ▪ Madonna, "American Life" (Warner Bros.) Question, 1956: "Will I be pretty, will I be rich?" Answer: "Que sera, sera." Response, 2003: "'Whatever will be, will *be?*' You call that American? Can't somebody fix this shit?"

4 ▪ Reese Witherspoon in *Freeway* (1996, Republic Pictures Home Video) Why you can never remember who won the Oscar a year later: because compared to an unnominatable performance like this, America's pre-sweetheart as all-time juvenile delinquent, the performances that are nominated (for *Freeway*'s year, Brenda Blethlyn, *Secrets and Lies*; Diane Keaton, *Marvin's Room*; Frances McDormand, *Fargo*; Kristin Scott-Thomas, *The English Patient*; Emily Watson, *Breaking the Waves*) barely exist. Southern Tip (Cecily Marcus): "Not even Reese Witherspoon is allowed to be as good as Reese Witherspoon was in *Freeway*."

5 ▪ Luc Sante, "The Birth of the Blues" (Yeti #2) Inside this words 'n' graphics journal (plus 30-track soundtrack CD) is a displacing argument from underworld historian Sante: that just as geneticists now claim that all living people are descended from a single woman who lived perhaps 140,000 years ago, the blues—"a particular song form made up of 12 measures of three-line verse, with a line length of five stressed syllables and an AAB rhyme scheme" (Charley Patton, 1929: "Hitch up my pony, saddle up my black mare/Hitch up my pony, saddle up my black mare/I'm gonna find a rider, baby, in the world somewhere")—did not emerge, evolve, develop, or come to be in any folk sense. Sometime in the 1890s, in East Texas or the Mississippi Delta, the blues, which surprised everyone, black and white, "could only have been invented," by a "particular person or persons," just as "the x-ray and the zipper and the diesel engine were invented in the same decade" by particular persons. We know their names, though; if the blues was invented, why by 1910 at the latest did nobody know by whom, when, where? Illiteracy, poverty, racism—but also because the blues was so portable that once the first blues singer sang the first blues song to the first blues listener, "it is easy to imagine that within 24 hours a dozen people had taken up the style, a hundred inside of a week, a thousand in the first month. By then only ten people would have remembered who came up with it, and nine of them weren't talking."

6 ▪ Cursive, "Staying Alive" from *The Ugly Organ* (Saddle Creek) A one-foot-in-front-of-the-other beginning, then a slow, ten-minute slide into sleep. The band slips into a military march rhythm near the end, and then falls into Angelo Badalamenti's arrangements for Julee Cruise in *Twin Peaks*, where the deaths that occur in the music are never final, even if the bodies are buried.

7 ▪ KBSG-FM, Seattle (February 25) Barry Franklin writes: "Yesterday I was standing in the checkout line at a small retail shop on Mercer Island. On a clear day, one can see the Cascades from its window, just 20 miles to the east. Due to the rain clouds, though, the mountains weren't visible. Talk, among the clerk and those waiting in line, centered on the dark gray clouds and the imminent rain. The radio was tuned to an oldies station, airing the song 'Rhythm of the Rain' by the Cascades. I pointed out the exquisite beauty of this moment of synchronicity to my fellow humans who, I think, didn't quite get it."

8 ▪ Rosanne Cash, *Rules of Travel* (Capitol) Great Harlequin Romance cover.

9 ▪ Porch Ghouls, *Bluff City Ruckus* (Roman/Columbia) Great *God's Little Acre* trash-paperback-jacket-style cover. A song called "Nine Dollars Worth of Mumble" that's worth four minutes of your time. And "Girl on the Road (Ford Fairlane)," which goes right over a cliff. Or rather the bluff, which is to say out of Memphis and into the drink.

10 ▪ "Eating It" comedy showcase, Luna Lounge (New York City, January 20) Sarah Vowell writes: "As part of MLK day, they asked the audience to sing along with 'Ebony and Ivory,' the white people doing McCartney's part and the black people Stevie Wonder's. This meant a whole room drowning out Paul, followed by maybe one sheepish black guy, the only one in the audience, singing along with Stevie. The point being, even us smart, good-hearted New York wiseacres who cringe at the thought of segregation find ourselves socially segregated by default. I had started out the day reading King's speech to the Memphis sanitation workers, marveling at the way he could call for togetherness without a hint of icky, sappy fakery, and there I was hours later, singing sap. Yet when I was singing my part, singing along with Paul, even though there's hardly a lamer song, I found myself singing embarrassingly loud."

MAY 14, 2003

1 ■ The New Pornographers, "The Laws Have Changed," from *Electric Version* (Matador) Neko Case pipes in the background like an organ. Then, as a multiple exposure, she's high above the music, singing down to a single image of herself. Male voices take over the blips in the background as Case goes back to the sky. "So all hail—What will be revealed today," she trills, but, as on the New Pornographers' *Mass Romantic*, she's the revelation, and coming out of this band there's no sound richer than hers abroad in the land today.

2 ■ The White Stripes, Warfield Theatre (San Francisco, April 28) The unbelievable brazenness of the Betty Boop cartoons that preceded the band fit right in with the drama that followed: every tune seemed to have its familiar, and not in the restagings of Lead Belly's "Boll Weevil" or Son House's 1965 "Death Letter." How can they seem to get Herman's Hermits' "I'm Henry VIII, I Am" and Pussy Galore's "Cunt Tease" into—or maybe out of—the same song? Where did Vicki Lawrence's "Night the Lights Went Out in Georgia" come from? Or more to the point, where did it go?

3 ■ Christopher Logue, *All Day Permanent Red: The First Battle Scenes of Homer's 'Iliad': Rewritten* (Farrar Straus Giroux) Logue's *Iliad* project is not to retranslate it, but to rewrite other translations. The innovation is the rampant use of modernisms ("The Uzi shuddering warm against your hip") or neologisms ("Greekoid scum!"). It can seem gimmicky. And then you are right there, in the action, less reading than listening: "Think of raked sky-wide Venetian blind./Add the receding traction of its

slats/Of its slats of its slats as a hand draws it up./Hear the Greek army getting to its feet."

4 ■ The Folksmen, "Never Did No Wanderin'," from *A Mighty Wind: The Album* (DMZ/Columbia) Christopher Guest's movie lives up to its title; comparisons of this set of overmilked gags with Guest's loving neurot-o-rama of *Best in Show* are as self-congratulatory as its worst songs. Are reviewers really that pleased they get the joke? But on the radio, Michael McKean and Harry Shearer's frighteningly accurate parody of a Kingston Trio "whalin' song" comes off as very nearly the real thing: catchy, faintly embarrassing, stirring.

5 ■ The Be Good Tanyas, *Chinatown* (Nettwerk America) Speaking of faintly embarrassing, there is that name—but by the second track on their second album, this Vancouver trio is long gone, setting up house in the late Townes Van Zandt's "Waiting Around to Die." With the foreboding melody, they call up "Streets of Laredo" (hear it on Johnny Cash's *American IV*) or "Hills of Mexico" (hear Roscoe Holcomb on *Mountain Music of Kentucky*). Frazey Ford and Samantha Parton sing as if they're already dead; Trish Klein's high, slow harmonica solo, drifting across the years from Country Joe and the Fish's "Bass Strings," seals the coffin. And then there is a version of Kid Bailey's 1929 "Rowdy Blues," as light, sweet, and unhurried as Canned Heat's "On the Road Again"—which, suicidal as it is, takes you right back to "Waiting Around to Die." And then it's hard to listen to anything else for the rest of the day.

6 ■ Scott Amendola and Carla Bozulich, "Masters of War" (*www.protest-records.com*) Bob Dylan's hardest antiwar song: over nine minutes, it gets bigger, and noisier. There are moments when the storm in the music makes it difficult to remember what you're listening to. Bozulich's voice, never so convincing with the Geraldine Fibbers—never convincing you so much is at stake—is thick, considered, like Anna Domino's in Snakefarm. In moments it can be arty in its

strangled effects—and then Amendola's drumstick comes down in a manner so artless it's scary. But it's Eric Crystal's shredding saxophone solo that nails the song to the ground, that takes it somewhere it hasn't been before, not on *The Freewheelin' Bob Dylan* in 1963, not when Dylan smeared it into the 1991 Grammy show, during the first Iraq war. The hectoring self-satisfaction of speakers at antiwar rallies begins to creep into Bozulich's voice after that (the tone that lets you know the last thing such people want is for the powerful to do good; if that happened, how could they feel superior?)—but then, for the final verse ("And I'll stand over your grave till I'm sure that you're dead"), the instrumentation drops to almost nothing, bare taps and silences, and you hear someone speaking for herself.

7 ▪ Patricia Tallman in *Night of the Living Dead*, directed by Tom Savini (STZ, May 2) The lone woman to escape the plague of cannibal zombies—mute with shock in the beginning, by the end she's ready to shoot anything that moves—wakes up to find the sun shining and the spell broken. She watches as a crowd of yahoos torment a zombie in a corral while others use lynched corpses for target practice; she flinches as the bodies jerk in the air. "They are us and we are them," she says. "Say what?" says a hunter. "Nothin'," she says, afraid again. I suppose this shot-for-shot 1990 remake isn't as good as George Romero's 1968 original, but it was still too much to take: too close to home, which is to say to the picture the country has been offering itself on the nightly news.

8 ▪ James Mathus Knockdown Society, *"Stop and Let the Devil Ride"* (Fast Horse) If the appropriation of old country blues by the White Stripes or the Be Good Tanyas bothers you, here's what it sounds like when it's done without wit, imagination, or a decent beat. The devil wouldn't be caught dead riding with these guys.

9 ▪ Yeah Yeah Yeahs, *Fever to Tell* (Interscope) The feeling of people pushing through a crowd, when there's no crowd.

10 ▪ Charles Taylor, "Chicks Against the Machine," *Salon* (April 29) A steely, cant-destroying account of how and why, after their *Primetime* interview with designated patriot Diane Sawyer and their naked *Entertainment Weekly* cover, the Dixie Chicks can now open their shows with "I Won't Back Down"—and close them with Natalie Maines announcing "Our final encore tonight is gonna be 'Dixie.'" "After all," Emily Robison or Martie Maguire can say, "it was Abraham Lincoln's favorite song."

JUNE 4, 2003

1–10 ▪ David Thomas, "Disastodrome!" (Freud Playhouse, UCLA, Los Angeles, February 21, 22, 23) It was a version of a Raymond Chandler mystery, with tough, cool, and fooled detective Philip Marlowe written out in favor of the bit characters hanging around the corners of the plot, and it brought forth a large cast. There was (1) impresario-writer-director-actor-singer-musician Thomas himself, since 1975 leader of the avant-Cleveland band Pere Ubu, a huge man leaning on a cane, letting himself down into a chair and seeming to fall asleep as others moved around him, (2) poet Bob Holman, (3) Frank Black, late of the Pixies, (4) Robert and Jack Kidney of 15-60-75, a combo from Kent, Ohio, that goes back before the last number in its name, (5) composer Van Dyke Parks, (6) the Two Pale Boys, trumpeter Andy Diagram and guitarist Keith Moliné, plus Yo La Tengo drummer Georgia Hubley, (7) singer Syd Straw, (8) actor George Wendt, and (9) the current incarnation of Pere Ubu itself, along with (10) a reunited Rocket from the Tombs, the spectral pre-Ubu band in which Thomas's story began: a rocket on its way back to the tomb, featuring not only the living—Thomas, bassist Craig Bell, and guitarist Cheetah Chrome—but also, with Richard Lloyd of Television standing in for guitarist Peter Laughner (1953–77) and singer Stiv Bators (1949–90), the specter of the dead.

It was a queer assemblage, and the noisy crowd that gathered for the three-night performance festival wouldn't have been surprised that the show passed under the radar of the national music press, the art press, the theater press. The crowd knew it was lucky to be in the right place at the right time.

The stories Thomas spread across the three nights—about bands forming and breaking apart, people meeting and separating, the interstate highway system, the towns the interstate left behind, the way elements of speech, commerce, and culture disappear, and how, after those things are gone, people like those on Thomas's stage appear to reenact them—were most of all suggestive. As the tale unfolded, the cast grew even larger, drawing familiars and doppelgängers. On the second night, for the increasingly nervous, so-called improvisational opera *Mirror Man*—part sermon, part rant, part minstrel show, part lecture on spiritual uplift—the scene opened in a diner. Off to the side was a bus-stop bench with an ad for a wax museum. With musicians spread across the back of the stage, Frank Black walked out of the crowd in an aloha shirt, looking less like himself than John McCain, communicating the same sense of solidity and frustration. George Wendt, Black, and Thomas sat down together on the bench, and as the audience waited for it to collapse under their seven or eight hundred pounds, Wendt was Babe Ruth and Thomas was Fatty Arbuckle. But when Thomas took the microphone—Panama hat on his head, his cane like chemotherapy, a sign of both debilitation and a will not to die—the character who came out of his body was, someone said, more like Orson Welles as Father Mapple in the movie version of *Moby Dick*—or Welles as Hank Quinlan in *Touch of Evil*.

Earlier, when the curtain came up, Syd Straw stood at the diner table, dressed in an aquamarine uniform, holding a pot of coffee, but she didn't seem to move. Black and Georgia Hubley sat down and Straw took their orders. The stillness of the scene—as off to the left Bob Holman recited a broken narrative, sounds bounced off the walls,

and songs were begun and sometimes finished—pushed the scene even farther into the background than it actually was; Edward Hopper's *Nighthawks* drifted into your mind as easily as it drifted out of it.

David Lynch was the missing actor, if he really was missing. When on the first night Robert Kidney held the stage like a bad dream, he could have been Dennis Hopper's "well-dressed man" from *Blue Velvet*. "Look for me down at One-Eyed Jacks," he said, gesturing toward the whorehouse in *Twin Peaks*. Kidney wore a dark suit, dark shirt, dark tie, a fedora pulled down over his face so that all you could see of his features was that they were creased and old; he sang in a mellifluous, weirdly unaged voice, his guitar stopping the rhythm inside the likes of Robert Johnson's nearly seventy-year-old blues "Last Fair Deal Gone Down" and turning the tunes into fables: "Nobody really wants to hear the blues, because it's too slow, it's boring, it's tedious—like life, like my life." For an encore he and his brother played Bo Diddley's "Who Do You Love," and it squirmed the way Roy Orbison songs squirm in *Blue Velvet* and *Mulholland Dr.* changing as it twisted: "Tell me hoodoo you love."

Moment to moment, incident to incident, song by song, others stepped into Kidney's, or Lynch's, shoes: Syd Straw, sitting at the diner table alone, her head in her hands, the weight of her fatigue capsizing the theatrics of the men on the stage like Peggy Lipton's *Twin Peaks* waitress at the end of her shift; Thomas sitting at a desk with a manual typewriter, crumpled paper, and what looked like a week-old sandwich as if he were Jack Nance in *Eraserhead*, clenching his teeth as if that would force thoughts out of his clotted brain; and, everywhere, a sense of time as something used up somewhere in the past, by someone else.

The difference between Lynch's American towns and the decaying towns on and off Thomas's Lost Highway—the phrase repeated so often it finally fell somewhere between a prayer and a brand name—was that in the darkest, most dead-end actions Thomas orchestrated in Los Angeles, there was always the sense that they were a setup, that all together they made a story which, when you heard the punch line, you would understand as a joke. When on the last night the 49-year-old Thomas gave his all to Rocket from the Tombs' adolescent lament "Final Solution," it didn't end up so far from Dion and the Belmonts' "Teenager in Love." But the punch line never came, unless it was the last line of "Nightdriving," somewhere in *Mirror Man*, I think, as if Thomas was floating across all the chanting voices, incantations, and reverb guitar of the night before and the night to come: "See ya *around*, sucker!"—the second syllable of the third word cracking like a whip, like a grin as big as the room.

JUNE 25, 2003

1 ■ **John Mellencamp, *Trouble No More* (Columbia)** Old songs, old singer, fresh sound: Mellencamp turns Dicky Do and the Don'ts' obscure 1959 doo-wop "Teardrops Will Fall" into stupendous backwoods rockabilly, with fiddle playing by Miriam Sturm that shoots up from inside the music like the wind Toni Marcus blew through Van Morrison's "Full Force Gale." Taken up in the last few years by David Johansen as well as the White Stripes, Son House's "Death Letter" is now some kind of subterranean pop hit; in Mellencamp's version there's a shift halfway through its six minutes—Michael Ramos's organ coming in to let you know that the reality of death is setting in, that the singer too is now sliding toward death—that is so sure, so unafraid of itself musically and so terrified of itself morally, that the song leaves the pop world and goes right back to the dead man who wrote it. And yet, with good covers of compositions by Robert Johnson, Hoagy Carmichael, or Willie Dixon flashing by, it's "To Washington"—a modest rewrite of "White House Blues," a 1926 Charley Poole number about the McKinley assassination— that may cut the deepest. The first verses,

setting the scene of the last presidential election, seem timeless, as if they're taking place far in the past; the final verses, about the Iraq war, are the sort of protest lyrics that don't outlast the time it takes to sing them. But it's the melody, picked out on mandolin by Mike Wanchic—the traditional power of the melody, the way it anchors the theft of Florida in 2000 in a murder that took place in 1901—that makes the tune hurt, filling it with sadness, loss, betrayal, defeat.

2 ■ ***Wisegirls*, directed by David Anspaugh (Lions Gate)** Made in 2001, starring Mira Sorvino, Melora Waters, and Mariah Carey as waitresses in a Staten Island mob joint, this film went straight to video. Is that because Carey is faster, more obscene, and tougher than any woman in *The Sopranos*?

3 ■ **William Burroughs, *Junky: The 50th Anniversary Definitive Edition* (Penguin)** Modern pre-history from Burroughs in Mexico in about 1950, learning "the new hipster vocabulary" from "refugee" junkies: "'Cool' [is] an all-purpose word indicating anything you like or any situation that is not hot with the law. Conversely, anything you don't like is 'uncool.' From listening to these characters I got a picture of the situation in the U.S. A state of complete chaos where you never know who is who or where you stand."

4 ■ **Alan Garthright, "No-Fly List Ensnares Innocent Travelers" (*San Francisco Chronicle*, June 8)** "In their efforts to prevent a repeat of the Sept. 11 tragedy, the U.S. government and the airline industry are relying on software so outdated it can't distinguish between the last name of Osama bin Laden and punk rocker Johnny Rotten Lydon. . . . Many airlines rely on name-searching software derived from 'Soundex,' a 120-year-old indexing system first used in the 1880 census. It was designed to help census clerks quickly index and retrieve sound-alike surnames with different spellings—like 'Rogers' and 'Rodgers' or 'Somers' and 'Summers'—that would be scattered in an alphabetical list. Soundex gives each name a key using its first letter

and dropping the vowels and giving number codes to similar sounding [consonants] (like 'S' and 'C'). The system gives the same code, L350, for 'Laden' and all similar-sounding names: Lydon, Lawton, and Leedham."

In other words, it's right on target for Antichrists.

5 ▪ The New Pornographers, Bimbo's (San Francisco, June 9) The songs—"It's Only Divine Right," "Letter from an Occupant"—were rockets. On "The Laws Have Changed," as Carl Newman boosted Neko Case's somersaulting lead singing with falsetto chirps, flags flew. The band—with keyboard player Blaine Thurier twirling his left arm when he just couldn't stop himself and Kurt Dahle smiling over the hardest bass drum sound you'll ever hear—was its own air raid siren, and the message was *All Clear.*

6 ▪ The Riverboat Gamblers, *Something to Crow About* (Gearhead) From Denton, Texas: Beatle-era punk—the Knickerbockers with "Lies," say—with a thrash follow-through, like the Descendents' "Weinerschnitzel." On "Ice Water" or "Catch Your Eye" they can make you believe the style was invented yesterday. That they take it all back on the last cut, with what starts off as a rewrite of Santo and Johnny's 1958 "Sleep Walk," only means they'll do slow dancing if you ask politely.

7 ▪ The Squids, Tracy Hall (Norwich, Vermont, May 30) The Magic Rat (Steve Weinstein) reports: "Prominently noted on poster advertising a benefit show: 'Alcohol and Smoke Free. Please bring a clean pair of shoes to protect the dance floor.'"

8 ▪ Ben Harper, "With My Own Two Hands" from *Diamonds on the Inside* (Virgin) People used to attack Sting for his fake Jamaican accent; how does Harper get away with it? First by coming on like the god Denis Johnson said Bob Marley would turn into, then playing the Joan Osborne slob-like-the-rest-of-us Jesus.

9 ▪ Larry Clark, *Punk Picasso* (Luhring Augustine Gallery, New York; through June 28) New York Eye (Emily Marcus) writes:

"Clark made his name with the speed-freak photos in *Tulsa* in 1971 and the film *Kids* in 1995; his first gallery show in five years is a collection of mementos that illustrate his life with embarrassing intimacy. There's no wall text or labels for correspondence and talismans (for Roger Maris, Sonny Liston, Bruce Lee), for old records (Billie Holiday's *Lady Sings the Blues*, Bob Dylan's "George Jackson") both mounted and playing through the gallery speakers. A torn piece of paper with a quote from Blake shares space with a clipping about the execution of three Arkansas serial killers and shots of a young Clark and his Tulsa friends giving each other blow jobs and shooting up. What makes Clark's photos and films powerful is the clarity of his voyeurism: his palpable lust. On the walls, the uncoordinated elements of Clark as kid, family man, and shock-artist go a long way toward depicting the whole man—and still do little to lessen the primary affront of his work."

10 ▪ A wedding at Gale Mansion, Minneapolis (May 25) DJ Joel Stitzel's repertoire went back and forth between classic soul (Betty Banks's 1964 original of "Go Now," Aretha Franklin's 1967 "I Never Loved a Man (The Way I Love You)") and older group sounds: the Chantels' 1958 "Maybe" never sounded richer. And as the music for the bride and groom's first dance "Love Theme from *The Godfather*" never sounded stranger. "Just this one time, I'll let you ask me about my affairs," said one guest after another.

JULY 16, 2003

1 ▪ Patti Smith at Martin Luther King Jr. Park, Berkeley (June 15) Smith and Boots Riley of the Coup were performing in support of International A.N.S.W.E.R., a group affiliated with the Workers World Party, the left-fascist sect that uses Ramsey Clark as its dummy and the Palestinian Intifada as its true cause. It being Father's Day, Smith dedicated "People Have the Power" to her father. He was gone, she said—but there was still Ralph Nader, "father to us all." Or, as Paul Berman, author of the recent *Terror and Liberalism*, wrote two days earlier in *Salon* of the Nader cult, "I interpret the Green Party as a movement of the middle and upper-middle class, as actually having a certain satisfaction with the way things are—which is to say, the reason you should vote for the Greens is because you want to feel the excitement of political engagement, the adventure of it, but you don't really care what it's going to mean for other people if the Republicans get elected." You're voting not as a member of a polity, where each citizen is presumed tied to every other; you're voting to place yourself above not only your fellow citizens, but above the democratic ritual that presumes to make a republic. You're voting to affirm your own purity—like voting Republican, as Krist Novoselic put it when Nirvana was first accused of selling out, "so you can get tax breaks. Now *that's* sold out."

2 ▪ **Bob Dylan in *Charlie's Angels: Full Throttle* (Sony Pictures)** Widmerpool (a.k.a. Ken Tucker) writes in: "Not on the KICK-ASS soundtrack album to this KICK-ASS movie—who needs him there, when you've got Nickelback and Kid Rock collaborating on a KICK-ASS version of Elton's 'Saturday Night's Alright for Fighting'? No, Dylan sneaks in during the scene in which a KICK-ASS Drew Barrymore gathers her belongings to leave Angel headquarters, and we clearly see that one of her few cherished possessions is a vinyl copy of *Bringing It All Back Home*. So the real mystery of the movie is, who wanted that product placement in a film filled with shots plugging Cingular Wireless and Body By Demi? My guess? Crispin Glover had been using the album on the set to get himself in the mood to play a bitter, religion-warped mute, and director McG did what he does best, which is stealing cultural totems and reducing them to throwaway junk-jokes that make the viewer feel as though the ASS of anything in life that matters has been KICKED."

3 ▪ **Trailer Bride, *Hope Is a Thing With Feathers* (Bloodshot)** When Melissa Swingle,

leader of this country band, plays her saw, it sounds like a theremin. Brief snatches of psychedelic guitar by Tim Barnes are like an opening into another world. As on the modest, painful 1999 *Whine de Lune* and the 2001 *High Seas*, Swingle is laconically miserable. But she no longer sounds convinced she's saying anything anyone needs to hear.

4 ▪ **Liz Phair, "H.W.C." on *Liz Phair* (Capitol)** When in the only tune here that raises itself above water Phair puts what might as well be spam porn (you know: "OUR SLUTS CAN'T WAIT TO DRINK YOUR HOT WHITE CUM") on top of candy-cane sound, it's like watching Barbies fucking. You can call that radical displacement, or you can call it spam.

5 ▪ **DJ Shadow, *Diminishing Returns Party Pak* (bootleg)** For the second of two discs drawn from BBC jockey John Peel's March 29 show: a 40-minute collage of apparent examples of 1965–73 California pop, Fairport Convention–style folk rock, and British post-Beatle-isms. It's all so stylistically third-hand and discographically obscure that you imagine only Shadow can still name the tunes—even if anyone can hear the desire and idealism that seem coded in their forms.

6 ▪ **David Carr, "Major Stars Not So Crucial as Concept Trumps Celebrity" (*New York Times*, June 23)** "Musical stardom has always been a very calculated affair," Carr writes. "Elvis might have been just another hillbilly if it were not for Col. Tom Parker." It's been true for decades that white male Southerners are the last class one can denigrate in polite company, but would this sneer have appeared in the *New York Times* if Alabamian Howell Raines were still the editor?

7 ▪ **Jeff Tamarkin, *Got a Revolution! The Turbulent Flight of Jefferson Airplane* (Atria)** "Moby Grape chugged along only for a couple of years before circumstances did the band in." From the *Whatever* school of rock history.

8–9 ▪ **Sly and the Family Stone, "Thank You for Talkin' to Me Africa" (1971) on *The**

Essential Sly and the Family Stone (Epic Legacy) and Skip James, "Cypress Grove Blues" on *She Lyin'* (Genes, 1964) or *Complete 1931 Recordings in Chronological Order* (Document) The Mississippi bluesman and the San Francisco dandy, speaking the same language: the high, faraway moan of one man calling out from the dead, telling the other not to join him.

10 ■ **Penelope Houston, "The American in Me" and "Scum" at "Stand Up and Be Counted: Howard Dean Declaration Celebration Party" (Hyatt Regency Hotel, San Francisco, June 23)** In 1977 "The American in Me" was the torn flag flown by the Avengers, the best punk band in San Francisco and probably the nation. With a teenage Houston at the mic, you can hear the song on *Died for Your Sins* (Lookout!). It's scabrous, self-loathing, crude, undeniable, a thing in itself, with "Kennedy was murdered by the FBI!" slamming into "It's the American in me that makes me watch TV!" as if one was the other. Twenty-six years later, Houston, now a folk singer, was asked to sing "The American in Me" by a Dean worker she met at a protest against the new FCC regulations on media consolidation. Performing with guitarist Pat Johnson, she dropped the Kennedy line: "Here I am at a presidential rally singing about the assassination of a president—what if something happened to Dean later? How would that feel? It's all red, white, and blue—mostly white and blue—and I've got this inverted soundbite about Kennedy." She also left out a verse about live television coverage of the Symbionese Liberation Army hideout burning to the ground in Los Angeles in 1974: "It seemed dated—but it's happening now more than ever. People numbed by an image. An image seen over and over until it becomes meaningless." But this night "The American in Me" was a statement of pride—with "Scum," from Houston's 1999 *Tongue* (Reprise—included on Houston's *Eighteen Stories Down* retrospective), dedicated to the man Howard Dean hopes to oppose.

1 ■ **Hem, *Rabbit Songs* (Dreamworks reissue)** From Brooklyn, this set of nihilist love letters—originally released independently in 2001—keeps company with Van Morrison's *Astral Weeks*, Denis Johnson's novel *Jesus' Son*, Sarah McLachlan's "Sweet Surrender," and the old American ballads in which the singer narrates his or her own death. In a clear, sweet, altogether assured voice, Sally Ellyson sings Dan Messé's songs of abasement and ruin less as if she's looking back on folly than helplessly anticipating it. Violin, viola, cello, and piano carry her into the songs like a stream carrying a piece of wood—there's no will here, no struggle, not even a wave as again and again the people in these tunes go down, somehow rising to the surface every time.

2 ■ **Richard Powers, *The Time of Our Singing* (Farrar, Straus, & Giroux)** "Maybe it could work after all, this act of total madness," thinks a young black woman in her parents' home in Philadelphia in 1939; to their horror, she is about to marry the German-Jewish refugee physicist she met in the crowd at Marian Anderson's historic concert at the Lincoln Memorial that same year, arranged by Eleanor Roosevelt after the Daughters of the American Revolution barred the black contralto from their Constitution Hall. "Maybe they could make an America more American than the one the country has for centuries lied to itself about being." *The Time of Our Singing* is the story of these two people and their three children—the tale of the evanescent success and crushing defeat of the America the parents want by the America they mean to transcend—and the most ambitious and fully realized novel I've read since Philip Roth's *American Pastoral*. After Powers's last several novels—increasingly airless, didactic tracts about science and social wrongs—it's a shock.

3 ■ **Pearl Jam with Corin Tucker, "Hunger Strike," Sports Palace (Mexico City, July 18)** Eddie Vedder leads, and then Tucker sub-

sumes him. As she pushes the words of the old Temple of the Dog number in front of her in a deep, thick voice, the performance finds its feet somewhere between Guns N' Roses' "Civil War" and Robert Plant and Sandy Denny's duet on Led Zeppelin's "Battle of Evermore."

4 ▪ "John F. Kennedy Jr.'s Life Was Cut Short Four Years Ago in a Plane Crash. *What If He Had Lived?*" (headlines for a cover story by Edward Klein, *Parade*, July 13) The bad faith, the lies, the corruption—all of it would be gone, of course.

5 ▪ Fleetwood Mac, Oakland Coliseum Arena (Oakland, July 23) They'll never escape *Rumours*, but new songs didn't sound new or old. "What's the World Coming To" brought the night to life; "Say You Will" sealed it. The words are trite, it'll make millions when it's franchised, and the chorus is a whirlpool, pulling you in. "Someone once said, 'When love is gone, there's always justice, and when justice is gone, there's always force,'" Lindsey Buckingham said, introducing "Peacekeeper," which comes off as a middle-of-the-night meditation on the Iraq war. I don't think Laurie Anderson is going to mind his turning "O Superman" into folk wisdom.

6 ▪ "The Pinko Behind Little Richard"— or Your Freedom of Information Act at Work (e-mail from Dave Marsh, July 21) Bumps Blackwell (1918–85) was a founder of rock 'n' roll. He produced Sam Cooke's early pop records, Guitar Slim, Lloyd Price, Little Richard's "Tutti Frutti"; co-wrote "Reddy Teddy," "Rip It Up," and "Long Tall Sally"; in 1981 he co-produced Bob Dylan's "Shot of Love." Dave Marsh writes: "His FBI file identifies him as a member of the Young Communist League in Seattle c. 1943. He joined because he was fired from the Seattle Tacoma Shipyards on the grounds that he was a Negro; in essence, the Communist Party got him his job back: the campaign included a benefit dance called 'Jive Bombers Swing into the Second Front Stomp.' 'On Blackwell's return to his job,' the file reads, 'many white young workers personally approached him expressing their sup-

port and welcoming him back to his job.' Blackwell was already a musician and is further alleged to have been attending CP 'hootenannies . . .'"

7 ▪ Warren Zevon, *The Wind* (Artemis) Last fall it was announced that Zevon had been diagnosed with terminal lung cancer. Nothing on the old rounder's putative farewell album can erase his version of "Knockin' on Heaven's Door," which is not a joke.

8–9 ▪ Jeff Bridges in *Masked and Anonymous*, directed by Larry Charles (Sony Classics) and *Masked and Anonymous—Music from the Motion Picture* (Columbia) Bridges's rock critic Tom Friend is trying to get an interview with Bob Dylan's half-forgotten troubadour Jack Fate. Looming over Dylan like a rain cloud, Bridges has a list of questions but instead of asking them spins his own theories of what it all means without letting Dylan get a word in—except that the words coming out of Bridges's mouth are words Dylan wrote: *Woodstock, man. You weren't there, were you? I was there. Hendrix, man, what he did. The mechanics. What he did to "The Star-Spangled Banner." Was that treason? I don't think so. You could hear the tears in every note: "Love me, love me, I am a native son." He was reaching back to his Founding Fathers. To the Pilgrims . . .* Dylan stares at him and turns away, but what happens to Dylan's own music in the film—with, say, Articolo 31's "Come una pietra scalciata," an Italian cut-up that's no less violent or loving a treatment of "Like a Rolling Stone" than Hendrix's version of the national anthem—is what happens here, what nearly all of the characters in the film are trying to do: in an America that has collapsed into dictatorship and racketeering, to connect with a way of life that has gone into the past, that no longer makes any sense.

10 ▪ Summer travel tips (e-mail, July 22) Michele Anna Jordan writes from Dallas: "The back of the ticket to the Sixth Floor Museum at Dealy Plaza offers $2 off your purchase of $15 or more at the Spaghetti Warehouse on North Market St."

AUGUST 27, 2003

1–4 ■ **Lady J on KALX-FM (Berkeley, August 18)** Mondays 9 to noon is Lady J's shift at the same college station that figures in Jonathan Lethem's new novel, *The Fortress of Solitude*; this morning, she outdid herself. There was the Delmonas' blitheringly happy version of the Premiers' 1964 "Farmer John"—covered by Neil Young on *Ragged Glory* in 1990, but not before this all-female mid-'80s U.K. outfit got their hands on it. You can imagine the Slits at the mic and the crowd on Johnny Rivers's "Secret Agent Man" as the audience, the singer telling Farmer John she's in love with his daughter, the women in front of the stage holding their breath for the chance to scream "wheee!" for every "the way she walks," not to mention every "the way she talks." Then the Larks' "Honey from the Bee," gussied-up doo-wop from 1955, and the Aaron Sisters' weird 1932 "She Came Rollin' Down the Mountain," from *Flowers in the Wildwood: Women in Early Country Music, 1923–1939*. Singing unaccompanied, in a farm-girl accent so sharp you could hitch it up behind a mule and plow with it, the Aaron Sisters offer the tale of Nancy Brown, who throws over one suitor after another until she finds the man she's been waiting for: "A city slicker with hundred dollar bills." They live happily ever after, but Anny Celsi doesn't, not on Lady J's choice "'Twas Her Hunger Brought Me Down," a song inspired by Dreiser's *Sister Carrie* and released this year on *Little Black Dress & Other Stories*. Celsi is Hurstwood, narrating his own downfall; the singing is just past ordinary. The backing, except for a few archaic passages from a banjo, is perfunctory. The music is all in Celsi's writing, which is direct, killing—"I took twenty thousand dollars/Where it went I can't explain/I'd be richer if I'd thrown it from the train"—needing no ornamentation and getting none. What the DJ offered was her taste, a reach for oddity, a faith that each song would somehow sing every other.

5 ■ **Sinéad O'Connor, "Big Bunch of Junkie Lies," from *She Who Dwells in the Secret Place of the Most High Shall Abide Under the Shadow of the Almighty* (Vanguard)** This surfaces from a two-disc set ("rare and unreleased" plus a 2002 concert) like a corpse in a mountain lake. The clear-voiced sainted victim ruling the music is replaced by an avenger, the snarling rocker O'Connor has almost always tried to hide, and the performance is devastating, a curse in the form of a prayer. She breathes out the words slowly in front of an acoustic guitar; the blows land when a single word is sung full-throated, followed immediately by a dead drop to a bone-dry whisper. "You sucked the life out of my true friend," O'Connor says, but the truth of the song is that she knows the man she's singing to couldn't care less.

6 ■ **Graham Roumieu, *In Me Own Words: The Autobiography of Bigfoot* (Manic D Press)** This unassuming rant would be hilarious even without the primitive Ralph Steadman–like drawings, and the guts of the story aren't found in Bigfoot's tale of how he abandoned his career as a junk bond trader to form a Seattle grunge band, or what he thinks of Sam Donaldson ("Me like man's hair. Me take him hair and eat man"). They're in the prosaic: "What happen world me ask? Me once believe in good. Now, no. World go shit."

7 ■ **The Kills, *Fried My Little Brains* (Rough Trade EP)** Their own "Jewel Thief" ought to work as an answer to the last cut, a cover of Dock Boggs's deathly 1927 "Sugar Baby." But "Jewel Thief" is all attitude, and "Sugar Baby" is a drone. The singers keep their bodies away from the words coming out of their mouths, a fatal abstraction.

8 ■ **The Cutters, "(Back in the) 20th Century," from *In the Valley of Enchantment* (Blackjack)** From Humboldt County, California, best known for marijuana plantations in national forests, guitarist Mike Wilson, drummer Ray Johnson, and bassist Tad Sutera use London punk inflections on Angela Brown's American voice for a message no different from that of their neighbor Bigfoot. It's pissed off, it's funny, it's sharp (Brown drops comments on her own lines like Johnny Rotten muttering to Clio), it's alive to its own momentum (the last "No!" following "Nancy Reagan just said" nearly pulls Nancy's size two over her head). As a song about exile in your own hometown, not to mention your own country, or your own century, it can be a stone in your shoe.

9 ▪ **Sarah Vowell writes in from the blackout (New York, August 15)** "I went for a walk in the dark last night for a little, marveling at the stars. Walked past people on a stoop blaring 'Smells Like Teen Spirit' on a boombox and everyone was giddy, singing along: 'With the lights off, it's less dangerous, here we are now, entertain us.'"

10 ▪ *Christian Marclay,* **catalogue organized by Russell Ferguson (UCLA Hammer Museum/Steidl, for an exhibition closing at the Hammer August 30, at Bard College September 28 through December 19, at the Seattle Art Museum February 5 through May 2, 2004)** Marclay is an American with European avant-garde credits, a pioneering turntablist (his 1983 Phonoguitar allowed him to scratch a vinyl LP while performing guitar-hero gestures), an irrepressible investigator of the record as talisman (with countless cut up and reconfigured discs, album covers, sculptures made of melted or chopped vinyl albums and singles), a social critic (his 2000 video *Guitar Drag* is a complex and visceral version of the 1998 dragging murder of James Byrd in Jasper County, Texas), and a prankster with a bottomless appetite for trash: as for so many art punks, "Batman Theme" was his ground zero. His work doesn't come off the pages of a catalogue: you have to go where it is and look at it, listen to it, laugh at it, let it laugh at you. Still, there is one stunner here, in sound historian Douglas Kahn's essay "Surround Sound," regarding the 1930s experiments of neurologist Wilder Penfield, "the first bio-turntablist": "When Penfield lowered [a] wire instead of a stylus onto the grooves of . . . one patient's exposed brain, the patient, still conscious and alert, was

convinced that there was a gramophone playing in the operating room." "Everybody grew up listening to all this stuff," Marclay responds, "and all this music is, in a way, already sampled in our heads."

1 ▪ **Neva Chonin, "Sex Pistols' Lydon tries, but can't revive rage on reunion tour at Warfield"** (*San Francisco Chronicle*, Sept. 5) "What can you say about a 25-year-old legend that died? That it changed your life, changed music history, hated the Beatles?"

2 ▪ *Paul McCartney in Red Square* **(a documentary on A&E, Sept. 18)** It was last May 24, with an audience of 100,000, the camera picking up one honey shot after another, and often Paul can't hit the notes: "We Can Work It Out" and "The Two of Us" are as painful as "I Saw Her Standing There" is true. Musicians, critics, government officials talk about how the collapse of the Soviet system was unthinkable without the Beatles—without their embodiment of a secret or inaccessible culture people desperately wanted to join. You hear the memory of imprisonment: "We lived on a separate planet and they could never come here," says the leader of the Soviet-era band Aquarium. But if the story makes you think of Lou Reed inducting Dion into the Rock and Roll Hall of Fame, describing how the Belmonts sent him "the sound of another life," soon enough the film will give you Mikhail Gorbachev, looking diminished and blank, and you can't gainsay his dutiful testimony that the Beatles told "the young people of the Soviet Union there was another life"—what else could they have heard? On stage, "Live and Let Die" is big and gets bigger in front of a video-screen montage of Russian peasants, Leonid Brezhnev and Vladimir Putin, folk musicians in traditional dress, and more honey shots. "I could fulfill one of my wishes only in 1984 when I bought *all* of the Beatles LP records," says Sergei Ivanov, the Russian minister of defense. A commercial comes on: Davy Jones or a lookalike promoting

A&E's *Meet the Royals* (Camilla and Charles appear in two-shot) while he or someone else chirps "Hey, hey, they're the royals!" Back to the stage: "Maybe I'm Amazed," and then "Back in the U.S.S.R." The instant leap in the crowd tells you this is what they came for, what they wouldn't leave without. You see a cool-looking guy in the audience, looking right at the camera, with a deep, knowing smile. The song was supposed to be a joke, as in *Who'd want to go back to the U.S.S.R.?*, and today the U.S.S.R. doesn't even exist. But the people in Red Square do, and the song does, and now the people present to hear it played change the unspoken negative of the song into an affirmation of their own existence. Yes, it was a script, and everyone was playing a part, but you'd have to be a truly great cynic not to smile over this tale.

3 ▪ Rolling Stones, *Sympathy for the Devil Remix* (Abkco) By Full Phatt: zero. By Fatboy Slim: less than zero, dragging the band behind its own beat, plus stupid sound effects. By the Neptunes: with the ending, they open a door in the song not even the song knew was there. From "Lay your soul to waste" on, they layer Western-movie strings and a thin, chopping guitar sound to create a sense of isolation and abandonment, until the last "Woo-woo"s fade away into a desert of loss and despair.

4 ▪ Team Doyobi, "Team Doyobi's Remix," from *O <S>*, compiled by Radboud Mens (staalplaat.com) Out of nine otherwise dullard versions of "O Superman" ("O Hyperman," "O Super Mom," etc.) comes utter displacement from the U.K.—those "ah-ah-ah"s running all through Laurie Anderson's little play about terrorism as an orgasm.

5 ▪ Seth Borenstein, "EPA: CO2 No Pollutant–Ruling Made on Clear Act" (*Denver Post/Knight-Ridder*, Aug. 29) "'Refusing to call greenhouse-gas emissions a pollutant is like refusing to say that smoking causes lung cancer,' responded Melissa Carey, a climate policy specialist for Environmental Defense, a moderate New York-based environmental group. 'The earth is round.

Elvis is dead. Climate change is happening.'"

6 ▪ Anonymous blurb on *Bubba Ho-Tep*, *New York Times* fall movie preview (Sept. 7) "Two residents of an East Texas nursing home—one believes himself to be Elvis Presley (Bruce Campbell), the other John F. Kennedy (Ossie Davis)—team up to defeat a soul-sucking mummy who has risen from the local swamp." Howard Hampton writes: "In other words, the Clinton-with-Two-Heads beats back Bush—draining *his* swamp."

7 ▪ "Classic Blues Artwork from the 1920s" 2004 calendar (Blues Images) On the cover: the single extant photograph of Mississippi blues progenitor Charley Patton, previously known only from the neck up. Yes, he was straight off the plantation. Though it turns out he was wearing spats.

8 ▪ Michael Corcoran, "Exhuming the Legend of Washington Phillips," in *Da Capo Best Music Writing 2003*, edited by Matt Groening (Da Capo) The story of how a man who left behind some of the most unusual gospel recordings of the 1920s (and, with "I Had a Good Father and Mother," perhaps the most heartbreaking) was not who music historians thought he was, but someone else with the same name. Which is fitting, given that in *Best Music Writing* Michael Corcoran's piece ended up credited to someone named Michael Cochran.

9–10 ▪ Soundtracks: *Martin Scorsese Presents the Blues: Red, White and Blues—A Film by Mike Figgis* and *Martin Scorsese Presents the Blues: The Soul of a Man—A Film by Wim Wenders* (HIP-O Records) I haven't seen the blues documentaries running on PBS—Scorsese served as executive producer for the series, and directed one episode—but I have heard the accompanying CDs, and I can tell you that Tom Jones's "Goin' Down Slow" (in the Figgis film) shows a deeper recognition of Howlin' Wolf than Lucinda Williams's embarrassing "Hard Time Killing Floor Blues" (in the Wenders) does of Skip James—and that Jones has infinitely more of himself to bring to the song. These two albums in particular are a study in weird contrasts, with *Soul of a Man* filled with ridiculous performances by Shemeika Copeland, Cassandra Wilson, Lou Reed, Bonnie Raitt, and Nick Cave, and *Red, White and Blues* mixing small masterpieces from Louis Armstrong (1947), Miles Davis (1957), and Big Bill Broonzy (1956) with famous and obscure recordings from the British 1960s (Cream's runaway-train version of Robert Johnson's "Crossroads," the Spencer Davis Group's impossibly sure, bone-chilling "Hey Darling") and grounded, present-day pieces by Jones, Lulu, and Jeff Beck. The shocker is the Lonnie Donegan Skiffle Group's more cited than heard 1954 cover of Leadbelly's "Rock Island Line." Donegan is so excited he runs right out of the studio and into the street, shouting, dancing, and you can almost hear thousands of British teenagers—among them four named John, Paul, George, and Ringo—saying to themselves, "I could do that! I have to! Now! This is the sound of another life!"

OCTOBER 22, 2003

1 ▪ **The Fiery Furnaces, *Gallowsbird's Bark* (Rough Trade)** Brooklynites Eleanor and Matthew Friedberger offer hilarious sibling-loathing liner notes and songs that seem to come from an alternate universe: "Up in the North" and "Don't Dance Her Down" make instant sense and also make you feel as if you've never heard anything like them before. There's a cover of Virginia mountain banjoist Dock Boggs's 1929 "Old Rub Alcohol Blues" that is both utterly contemporary and not a cover at all: Eleanor Friedberger sings as if she's worked out every idea in the words for herself, fingering her own scars, and at first the instrumentation is simply big, gonging piano notes. Boggs's version is dead-man-walking; the Friedbergers are walking very carefully, but they fall anyway. "My mind, my mind," Eleanor says as the song seems to get away from her, or perhaps it's that she doesn't want it anymore.

It all comes together in the chorus of "Two Flat Feet": passion, anger, contempt,

melody, sardonicism, fear—like Blondie's "Rip Her to Shreds" without the comic-strip wink. Like the best and least obvious album I've heard this year.

2 ▪ **Metric, "Combat Baby," from *Old World Underground, Where Are You Now?* (Everloving)** Emily Haines sounds very well-educated, and very tired of being so pissed off. The result is a severe, fast little pop song about not getting what you want—not even seeing what you want on the street, no matter what reflection you see in the shop windows, no matter what's on sale on the other side, even though you never wear anything but black.

3 ▪ **Randy Newman interview with Bob Edwards, *Morning Edition* (NPR, Oct. 8)** The day after California voted to smash its government, Newman was discussing *The Randy Newman Songbook, Vol. 1*, solo piano recordings of 18 of his tunes. Edwards brought up the new version of the 1972 "Sail Away," noting that its premise of a con man sweet-talking Africans onto his slave ship with promises of ease and abundance back in the U.S.A. wasn't exactly in the historical record. "What am I supposed to say," Newman said, "'Slavery is bad?' It's like falling out of an airplane and hitting the ground, it's just too easy. And it has no effect."

"But the contrast is so strong," Edwards said. "That beautiful melody . . ."

"It worked out well," Newman said. "It ended racism in this country. Kids today don't remember, now that it's gone away."

4 ▪ **Goldfrapp, "Lovely Head," from *Bande originale du film 'Demonlover' de Olivier Assayas* (SND)** New Crime Jazz: wet Paris streets whistling, harpsichord, a Shirley Bassey–style vocal—plus a high trick voice that could have come from the Skyliners' "Since I Don't Have You." And then into "Dirge" by Death in Vegas, featuring the same mood and what feels like the same voice. Weird.

5 ▪ **Paula Frazer, *A Place Where I Know: 4-Track Songs 1992–2002* (Birdman)** Frazer did her best work in San Francisco in the mid-'90s, but it's all of a piece: Roy Orbison

is god, but Frazer can't hit his notes, so she makes a world in a much smaller, more confined space. After a time you wonder how she keeps singing, since it feels as if there's no more air to breathe. She keeps singing by letting the quietly harsh sound she gets from her guitar slow down old folk melodies—secrets she knows but Roy Orbison didn't. Or didn't tell, as she does.

6 ▪ Culturcide, "They Aren't the World," from *Stay Free's Illegal Art Compilation CD*, free at "Illegal Art: Freedom of Expression in the Corporate Age," Nexus Gallery, Philadelphia (Oct. 3–Nov. 2) Keeping company with the likes of the first rock 'n' roll sample hit, Buchanan and Goodman's 1956 "Flying Saucer," as well as Negativland's legendary 1991 "U2" and Invisible Skratch Piklz's 1996 "white label edit," this 1987 revision of USA for Africa's self-congratulatory 1985 mandatory number-one hit "We Are the World" by a troupe of Houston dadaists is still ridiculously funny—Culturcide records itself right on top of the original—not to mention brutally cruel. Bruce Springsteen sounded like Joe Cocker the first time around; here he sounds like he's undergoing throat surgery without anesthetic. And he's nothing compared to Culturcide's Cyndi Lauper: one woman as three Chipmunks.

7 ▪ Placebo, *Sleeping with Ghosts* (Astralwerks) Music: Bush-league Bush. Cover: spectral woman's naked body merging with corporeal half-naked male figure—an image that still carries some of the charge of the version left behind by Cro-Magnons 15,000 years ago, traced in stone in what is now La Marche, France.

8 ▪ Joe Strummer and the Mescaleros, *Streetcore* (Hellcat) If Strummer hadn't died at 50 last year, the rough versions of the Wailers' "Redemption Song"—a melody that seems capable of redeeming anyone who comes near it—and "Silver and Gold," earlier recorded by co-composer (with Fats Domino and Dave Bartholomew) Bobby Charles in 1972 on his *Small Town Talk* as "Before I Grow Too Old"—would still bleed, and still make you smile. It would have been so easy to find some studio goof

on an old Clash number to stick on at the end.

9 ▪ Charles Peterson, *Touch Me I'm Sick* (Powerhouse) One difference between this big book of black-and-white photographs of Seattle punk in action and Peterson's 1995 *Screaming Life*, which collects a few of the same shots, is that here the sense of movement is much stronger. It's a vortex. Sometimes you can hardly believe anyone got out of it, and you know some didn't. Another difference is that the bands in the photos are not identified with captions. All that information is on a chart in the back—which means that as you look, you don't necessarily know what you're looking at. The two guitarists with John Brown beards—one of them looking mean enough to be John Brown—who are they? Do you really want to know? On page after page, flying hair heavy with sweat fills the image, and for once there is no difference between people on the stage and people in the crowd.

10 ▪ *Blues Poems*, edited by Kevin Young (Everyman's Library Pocket Poets) Dozens of poems, from the Harlem Renaissance to the present, not too many songs. Rhythms are sometimes forced, but when they're not—as with Gayl Jones's "Deep Song," or Langston Hughes's "Song for a Dark Girl," a rewrite of "Dixie" as a lynching lyric—it's like a whole literature exhaling. And there are continual surprises, like half-cast spells or whispers of forgotten curses, as with Melvin B. Tolson's late '30s "Sootie Joe," where a minstrel speaks through a chimney sweep: "Somebody has to black hisself up/For somebody else to stay white."

NOVEMBER 12, 2003

1–2 ▪ Brooks & Dunn, "Red Dirt Road" (Arista) and Martina McBride, "Independence Day" (RCA, 1994), on *The Bear*, 95.7 FM (San Francisco, Oct. 20) As melody, orchestration, the way the arrangement shows its hand, these two country hits are almost the same song. They're both about small towns and independence, making your own way, becoming yourself—etc. upon etc.

The Brooks & Dunn version is strictly personal, but set in terms of experiences all real guys have: "That red dirt road" is where the singer "had my first beer," "wrecked my first car." The McBride version is about a woman who takes a stand—and raises the flag for others. A woman who, by her solitary action in a community where everybody knows what's going on and nobody does anything about it, raises the promise of a more perfect union, or any kind of union. A woman performs an act—burns down her house and kills her husband— that forces everyone to pay attention, which requires that everyone have an opinion, even if one's real opinion is not what one says in public. The act creates a real community by dividing a false one. And through the metaphors used to portray it, this act draws on national ethics, on the history of the country for motive and justification and explication—and in the process extends or changes those national ethics, that patriotic history. None of the Revolutionary generation equated Independence Day with "the day of reckoning"— Judgment Day, the day when "the guilty pay"—as McBride does, but when you hear this song (written by Gretchen Peters), the connection seems to have always been there, hiding somewhere in the Declaration.

"Independence Day" is sung full-throated, but with odd, harsh snaps at the ends of lines, cutting them off, throwing you off, personalizing the song: no one else would think to sing it this way. "Red Dirt Road" is cuddly-growly, with words curling back on each other, creating an impression of modest regular-guyness. "Independence Day" is plain: the father is "a dangerous man." In a "small, small town" "word gets around." Everyone knows this guy is beating his wife. In "Red Dirt Road" the song turns, or falls, on its euphemism-by-omission: while the fact that this is where the "had my first beer" guy had his first girl is implicit, you're made aware that the singer won't say this, and it feels like a cheat.

One is a song that anyone could sing and almost everybody in country music has. One is a small story waiting in the greater American story for that greater story to give it meaning and ennoble it, or for the greater story to fall to pieces by failing to come through.

3 ▪ *Elephant,* **directed by Gus Van Sant (HBO Films)** The Columbine shootings, or the feel of high school life, and what happens when what everyone has reasonably taken as reality becomes something else.

4 ▪ **The Strokes,** *Room on Fire* **(RCA)** This bright set of tunes about nothing is a leap past the celebrated/backlashed *Is This It?* The band sounds like a band, not a set list of precursors. On those moments in "Reptilia" and "I Can't Win" when guitarists Nick Valensi and Albert Hammond Jr. step out of the machine-stamped song structures, there's a great lift. You can forget that, as with bassist Nikolai Fraiture's "War Is Peace" T-shirt, for singer Julian Casablancas hot means cold.

5 ▪ *School of Rock,* **directed by Richard Linklater (Paramount)** It's interesting that the 1950s rock-movie plot—forces of authority try to stop music, end up tapping feet— is still serviceable. Why does the lead outraged parent look just like neo-con talking head William Kristol? The kids in the theater where I saw the picture went completely bananas for exposed fake teacher Jack Black's inadvertently pedophilic mea culpa "Your kids have touched me—and I think I can honestly say that I touched them." But all that pales next to Maryam Hassan as Tomika, telling Black she wants to sing, doing "Chain of Fools" with the camera tight on her face as it begins to slide into a trance, just slipping around the eyes.

6 ▪ **Handsome Family,** *Singing Bones* **(Carrot Top)** Featuring what ought to be a double-sided smash by the folk duo: "If the World Should End in Fire" backed with "If the World Should End in Ice."

7 ▪ **Richard Thompson, "A Love You Can't Survive,"** **from** *The Old Kit Bag* **(Cooking Vinyl)** A peace-corps-to-prison-to-drug-lord tale you could have expected from Warren

Zevon. At the end, there are notes so huge they come out of Thompson's mouth and wrap him up like a shroud.

8 ▪ **Randy Newman, "The Great Nations of Europe," Bimbo's 365 Club (San Francisco, Oct. 26)** "A song that sums up better than anything else ever written the last 400 years of Western civilization," Newman said to introduce his chronicle of expansion and extermination, starting with the Canary Islands—according to some anthropologists the last redoubt of the Cro-Magnons, at least until the Portuguese got there. "Didn't he enunciate more clearly than with other songs?" said the man next to me. "He wanted people to hear the words."

9 ▪ **Mad TV Kobe Bryant skit, "Consensual" video, with director's credit to Michael Jordan (CBS, Sept. 27)** Neo-soul vocal as Bryant (Aries Spears) seduces women in the jury box and high-fives the judge. You know he'll walk.

10 ▪ **Press release on CMJ Music Marathon in New York City (Seattle, Oct. 25)** "200 years ago Lewis and Clark, after learning of the Louisiana Purchase, left the East Coast to explore the rest of the New Land. Bringing a Newfoundland dog named 'Seaman' and Lewis' slave 'York,' the two set out on a historic journey that is still marveled at today. Their now legendary voyage reveals the natural desire of man to explore the world around him.

"This month Sub Pop Records will follow the same path of William Clark and Meriwether Lewis (except totally in reverse!) to CMJ in New York. Accompanying us will be our Chihuahua Vito and our intern 'York.'"

DECEMBER 3, 2003

1 ▪ **Johnny Cash with Joe Strummer, "Redemption Song," from Johnny Cash, Unearthed (American/Lost Highway)** The title of this five-CD set—four discs of outtakes from the 1996–2003 "American Recordings" sessions, plus a best-of—is weird at best: poor Johnny's less than three months in the ground and already they've dug him up? But from versions of "Big Iron" to "Salty Dog," from "The Banks of the Ohio" to "Chattanooga Sugar Babe," songs find their ghost, and nowhere more than on Bob Marley's testament. The weight Cash brings to the very first lines, "Oh pirates, yes they rob I/ Sold I to the merchant ship"—a physical weight, a moral weight, the weight of age and debilitation—is so strong it floats the song as if it were itself a ship, sailing no earthly ocean. The reversal of what would be Cash's "me" for Marley's "I" makes a crack in the earth, a man stepping into another time, another place, entering fully into another history. Then Joe Strummer comes in, plainly nervous, rushing the words precisely as he does not on the shivering version of "Redemption Song" on his own posthumous release, Streetcore: He's tight, blank, and the performance never recovers. By the end it's all but dead—and those first moments will bring you back again and again, trying to make the recording come out differently. Five CDs don't come cheap, but the radio does, and a song like this is what the radio is for: to shock whoever's listening.

2 ▪ **The Volebeats, Country Favorites (Turquoise Mountain)** With tunes from famous country songwriters Roky Erickson, Abba, Serge Gainsbourg, and George Clinton, the York Brothers' sexy-then-and-sexy-now 1949 "Hamtramck Mama" plus six of their own songs, not a false note.

3 ▪ **"Edith Piaf, la môme de Paris," Hôtel de Ville, Paris (through January 31, 2004)** In a room where the walls are covered with song lyrics, words highlighted in lavender: "bleu," "mourir," "destin," "ciel," "rose," "non," "enfer," "lumière," "rue," "rêve," "pleurer," "coeur," "chagrin," "homme," "heureux," "amour," "ivresse."

4 ▪ **Ida Lupino in Road House, directed by Jean Negulesco (1948)** Playing a nightclub singer in a bar over a bowling alley, she talks her way through "One for My Baby" until it feels like a Shakespearean tragedy rendered by the Dead End Kids. "That's the best singing without a voice I've ever heard," says an astonished Celeste Holm.

5 ▪ **Oliver Hall writes in about subliminal censorship (Nov. 4)** "Something I overheard tonight at a coffee house: 'It's a race dog owner's worst dream, that the dog'll catch the white rabbit. The dog'll be destroyed, he'll never race again. Kurt Cobain caught the white rabbit, and he realized it wasn't all it was cracked up to be. And he shot himself.' I loved the odd lyrical way she put this—she'd just been gabbing about her anemia to an uninterested date—and hated what she said. It's been so odd watching Kurt Cobain's transformation over the past decade, from yelping sewer rat to cautionary tale; as I recall, for five years after he died, the only Nirvana songs you heard on the radio were 'All Apologies' and 'Come as You Are.' When I was sixteen some other teen broke into my house and stole all my Nirvana CDs. I replaced them when the insurance check came and was shocked to find the liner notes to *Incesticide* deleted, as I was shocked, watching the rerun of the band's first *Saturday Night Live* appearance, that the French kiss between Cobain and Krist Novoselic had been edited out of the end credits, and shocked every time I have to remind my friends of the Michael Jackson impersonator Nirvana sent up to accept their MTV award. Sometimes I feel like Charlton Heston in *The Omega Man*, the last person on earth, who knows every line of dialogue in *Woodstock*."

6 ▪ **Grandpaboy, *Dead Man Shake* (Fat Possum)** Fat Possum has branched out from old southern black men self-consciously playing blues to younger northern white men self-consciously playing self-conscious blues, as if it's, you know, all music, whatever that means. Jon Spencer is enough of a jerk to pull this off, but Paul Westerberg isn't.

7 ▪ **Bobdylan.com store** Featured items: "Self-Portrait Throw Blanket," "Masked & Anonymous Tee," "Jonny Rock 'I'll Be Your Baby Tonight' Corset."

8 ▪ **John Humphrys, review of Lynne Truss's *Eats, Shoots & Leaves: The Zero Tolerance Approach to Punctuation* (*The Sunday Times*, London, Nov. 9)** "Truss writes: 'The confusion of the possessive "its" (no apostrophe) with the contractive "it's" is an unequivocal sign of illiteracy and sets off a simple Pavlovian "kill" response in the average stickler.' I think she probably understates the case when she argues that people who persist in writing 'good food at it's best' deserve 'to be struck by lightning, hacked up on the spot and buried in an unmarked grave.' Lightning strikes are altogether too random. There should be a government task force with the single duty of rooting out such barbarians and burning them at the stake."

9 ▪ **Brian Morton, *A Window Across the River* (Harcourt)** From the author of *The Dylanist*, a quiet third novel about the revival of a love affair that by the end of the book will likely strike the reader as more of a mistake than its protagonists can bear to admit—and also a revival of so-called K-mart fiction, where brand names and pop songs, now taken out of Bobbie Ann Mason's mid-south and given a literary Manhattan twist, take over the imaginations of people who are trying to think. Here there's *NYPD Blue*, Mumia Abu-Jamal, and, in the 35-year-old heroine's panicked reaction to a doctor's recommendation that her last living relative be moved to a hospice, Christopher Hitchens attacking Mother Teresa "because some of the people she cared for in her hospice could have been cured" but for her belief "that it was best for them to die and go to heaven" ("I'm not thinking right, Nora thought. I shouldn't be thinking about Christopher Hitchens at a time like this") and not knowing "what irony was anymore—not since Alanis Morrissette put out that song 'Isn't It Ironic?' and all the reviewers pointed out that the things she was referring to as ironic, rain on your wedding day and so on, weren't actually ironic at all.

"Probably, she thought, I shouldn't be thinking about Alanis Morrissette right now.

"Alanis Morrissette and Christopher Hitchens.

"Together at last."

10 ▪ **Atmosphere, *Seven's Travels* (Epitaph)** Slug still wears his heart on his sleeve, and as smart noises and off-stage interjections come together as context, chorus, and audience, its beat is as true as it ever was. Especially on the gorgeous "Always Coming Back Home to You," an ending so emotionally clear it's no surprise Slug, Ant, and DJ Mr. Dibbs couldn't rest with it, adding a hidden track as if to take the edge off a language they're not altogether comfortable speaking.

DECEMBER 24, 2003

1 ▪ **Natalie Merchant, *The House Carpenter's Daughter* (Myth America)** The songs are from Fairport Convention, *The Anthology of American Folk Music*, protest-song handbooks, an 18th-century hymnal, a one-time Ithaca, New York, folk band called the Horseflies. With her thick, heavy voice, Merchant hangs over the tunes as if, in the infinitely suggestive words of so many other songs, she's letting her hair hang down, covering the songs in every meaning of the word. Fiddle from Judy Hyman (of the Horseflies) is the instrument that most often takes the lead, shaping the songs— "Down on Penny's Farm," a worker's complaint that Bob Dylan turned into "Maggie's Farm," is taken as a country stomp—but what Merchant does is plainly uncanny. "House Carpenter's Daughter": that makes Merchant the child abandoned when her mother left her carpenter husband for a demon lover, so Merchant sings these songs from the inside, from a distance, sneaking up behind them, looking up at them like a child, looking back at them like an old woman. A dance unreels like a memory more than an event; a story becomes not a memory but an account of an event that is sure to take place tomorrow.

You don't know where you are. "Which Side Are You On?" written by Florence Reece during a miner's strike in Harlan County, Kentucky, in 1932, doesn't come off like a protest song. Though the lyrics remain specific—"You'll either be a union man/Or a thug for J. H. Blair"—the setting of the song, the time and place it makes, is not. With a ghostly chorus—you can see the dead saying, *I see living people*— Merchant leads the performance as if into a battle that was lost before she was born, and that will be fought when she's gone. When she sings the Carter Family's "Bury Me Under the Weeping Willow," you're at the funeral, and then you're drunk at the wake. Each is less a memory or an event than a ceremony—as is almost every song here, high-stepping or barely moving at all.

2 ▪ **Highlights from the Rock & Roll Hall of Fame and Museum (a.k.a. Rock Hall), #1 (Cleveland, Dec. 7)** Poster for the fourth-to-last appearance of Buddy Holly, Ritchie Valens, and J. P. "Big Bopper" Richardson:

WINTER DANCE PARTY
Laramar Ballroom
Fort Dodge, Iowa
January 30, 1959
Dancing for Teenagers Only—Balcony Reserved for Adult Spectators

3–5 ▪ **Ryan Adams, *Love Is Hell, pt. 1, Love Is Hell, pt. 2, LLOR N KCOR* (Lost Highway)** Adams seems to have stepped into the void left by the disappearance of the audience for Counting Crows, by far the best straight-ahead rock 'n' roll band of the last decade. Unlike Counting Crows' Adam Duritz, whom *San Francisco Chronicle* critic Aidin Vaziri, reporting on a recent local show, described as "looking like a barefoot bus driver with an octopus strapped to his head," Adams appears to be a regular guy—sensitive, all heart, gets angry because he feels so much, but no serious hang-ups or a need to act out. Adams looks more like the successful nonentity John Mayer, for whom Counting Crows had to open on their last tour, or for that matter Josh Groban. And underneath his clatter and angst, what he has to offer is different mostly in style from what Clay Aiken and Ruben Studdard are selling.

6 ▪ **Dixie Chicks, *Top of the World Tour— Live* (Open Wide/Columbia)** One big grin. Not included: "My mother always said, when you can't say something nice, go to

London and say it in front of 20,000 people"; "I Believe in Love."

7 ▪ Rock Hall Highlights, #2 (Cleveland, Dec. 7) Poster: along the top, "E. J. Recreation Center, Johnson, N.Y." Then: "Direct from Nashville, Tenn." Then, in enormous type: "HANK WILLIAMS." Details of lesser acts follow, culminating at the bottom, in the biggest letters save for the headliner's, with "CARL PERKINS 'Mr. Blue Suede Shoes.'" But Hank Williams died on New Year's Day, 1953, three years before Carl Perkins released "Blue Suede Shoes"—how could they be on the same bill? Because, just above "HANK WILLIAMS," in type so small it almost isn't there, you can just make out "Audrey (Mrs.)."

8 ▪ 24 (Fox, Dec. 9) When temporary Counter Terrorism Unit command Michelle Dessler (Reiko Aylesworth)—previously notable this year for an embarrassingly low-cut top and push-up bra—confronts apparent mole Gael (Jesse Borrego), it's in a head-on, full-face close-up, and suddenly you're seeing someone you haven't seen before. There was a toughness in the stillness of the moment; you could sense a real character beginning to emerge. Given the rhythm of the show, that means you have no idea where she'll go, or be taken.

9 ▪ Joe Strummer and the Mescaleros, "Redemption Song," video directed by Josh Cheuse (Epitaph) On a downtown New York street, a man spray-paints a memorial portrait of the onetime Clash frontman; the portrait of Strummer covers an entire wall. People of different ages gather to watch it go up, or gaze seriously as they pass by. Others pose in front of it, proudly, giggling, some as if they're humbly (Steve Buscemi) or defiantly (Jim Jarmusch, Cara Seymour) putting their handprints into the picture, joining it. At the end there's performance footage, just strong enough to make you say, *Ah, shit.*

10 ▪ Rock Hall Highlights, #3 (Cleveland, Dec. 7) "Steven Tyler Bust. 1997. Fabricated by Kevin Yagher Productions"—in a Lucite cube, a replica of the Aerosmith singer with hair flying, eyes bulging, mouth all but swallowing the microphone clutched in disembodied hands. A visitor: "This is the best. I think this is what we all want for Steven Tyler: to have his head cut off and put in a box."

1 ▪ Mr. Airplane Man, *C'mon DJ* (Sympathy for the Record Industry) A Boston duo—Margaret Garrett, guitar, Tara McManus, drums and organ—recording in Memphis, then calling out from the Memphis murk. They go back, past Mazzy Star, Robin Lane, the Spikedrivers, to young white men playing blues in the Sun studio in the mid-fifties, then back from there, to a bar where the customers are so drunk they can't even tell what color they're supposed to be. The result sounds as contemporary as anything by such like-minded outfits as the White Stripes, the Kills, the Fiery Furnaces: an insistence that the present is a con, the past a myth, music a mask. You don't think about that in the stomp of "Red Light" or the haze of "Don't Know Why," but in "Wait for Your Love" the vocals are buried, and so are the guitar and the drums. Everything takes place behind a curtain, until with a final whamwhamwham the band hits and runs.

2 ▪ *Kill Bill Vol. 1—Original Soundtrack* (Maverick) Not that there's anything less than fabulous here, but the eleven minutes plus of Santa Esmeralda's mariachi version of the Animals' "Don't Let Me Be Misunderstood" is almost beyond human intent.

3–4 ▪ *Cold Mountain—Music from the Miramax Motion Picture* (DMZ/Columbia) and *Goodbye, Babylon* (Dust-to-Digital 6-CD reissue, 1902–60) The sensibility that producer T Bone Burnett brought to the *O Brother, Where Art Thou?* soundtrack doesn't work for *Cold Mountain*; Jack White and Alison Krauss seem to be looking over the horizon at something else, something that actually interests them. The new recordings of Sacred Harp singers—people following a primitive notation system as the means to bring a whole community into a complex song—have spirit, but there's no ground in the sound. To hear what the form, or philosophy of life, can be, seek out the country-religious music collection *Goodbye, Babylon*. Pressed into the tinny confines of commercial 78s from the 1920s or '30s, people stand and deliver themselves to God, as if by pure will they can make him listen. If he can turn away from the Huggins & Phillips Sacred Harp Singers' 1928 "Lover of the Lord," with the lead voice of a nerdy teenage girl deep inside the sound, he's not worthy of them—not worthy of the dead. As an all-night DJ shouts in Geoffrey O'Brien's forthcoming book *Sonata for Jukebox*, "Alabama gospel records from before recording was invented"—that's the feeling.

5 ▪ **Spam e-mail (Jan. 3)** Why is it that the words "Young Goodman Brown"— referring to the 1835 Nathaniel Hawthorne story where a devout Puritan is drawn into the devil's forest ("On he flew, brandishing his staff with frenzied gestures, now giving vent to an inspiration of horrid blasphemy"), toward a coven of Satanists and, at its center, his wife, Faith—keep popping up in the upper-left corner of Paris Hilton video ads?

6 ▪ **Hootie & the Blowfish, video for "The Goodbye Girl," from the TNT original movie** *Neil Simon's "The Goodbye Girl"* **(Jan. 16, 18, 20)** It runs on *Law & Order* central as an endless commercial: the musicians playing in the rain plus Patricia Heaton of *Everybody Loves Raymond* as a wan middle-aged woman acting mainly with her nose job and Jeff Daniels offering come-hither eyes in a sad-puppy face—compared to this, his *Dumb and Dumber* character was Sean Connery in *Robin and Marian*. Cutting in and out of the movie, the band seems inspired, risking anything, even electrocution, to pay homage to David Gates, who first recorded this terrible song, back in 1978, right about the time Bread stopped fooling anybody.

7 ▪ *American Blues Festival 1962–1966*, **2-DVD set (HIP-O Records)** Sonny Boy Williamson, Otis Rush, Victoria Spivey, Memphis Slim, even Howlin' Wolf, and

more, in Germany, in hokey but appealing stage sets or before polite audiences, and all giving at best 10 percent of the minimum they could have gotten away with back in Chicago. Except for T-Bone Walker on "Don't Throw Your Love on Me So Strong," plainly too much of an artist to think he's more the owner of the music than it is of him.

8 ▪ *The Cooler*, **directed by Wayne Kramer (Gryphon Films)** There's nothing happening here but Alec Baldwin's performance, pushing far beyond his 1992 role as the sales-force executioner in *Glengarry Glen Ross*. The scene where Baldwin's Old Vegas casino boss explains his values to Ron Livingston's New Vegas business-school mobster is supposed to dramatize passion and experience against callowness and training, and it does—as a display of what it means to disappear into a character, to let him walk without the puppet strings the director is so obviously using on Livingston. Also featuring an unsurprisingly convincing turn by 'N Sync's Joey Fatone as craven lounge singer Johnny Capella.

9 ▪ **Arthur Moore, *Security Service Individually Watermarked* (Maverick)** A letter accompanying this pre-release CD stated that for security reasons the object in question could not itself carry the information that (1) Arthur Moore was in fact Alanis Morissette, (2) *Security Service* was really an album titled *So Called Chaos*, (3) "By accepting this CD" one was agreeing not to copy it, play it in a computer, put it on the internet, lend it to anyone, or play it for anyone, and (4) that any such use of the object in question could somehow be traced. So I can't tell you anything about it. Or wouldn't be able to even if I had listened to it, which I was much too scared to do.

10 ▪ **Sarah Vowell reports from Pearl Harbor, Hawaii (Dec. 21)** "Went to visit the *Arizona* this morning. What really got me was the little marker to the lower left of the wall of names: the vets who survived but wanted their ashes sprinkled in with those of their comrades. Two of them died just this year. Then I took the bus up to the North Shore

to watch the surfers. My sister and I always had a thing for surfer movies. There was one called *North Shore* that came out when we were teenagers in Montana about a kid from Arizona who learned to surf in a wave pool and moved to Oahu where the real surfers looked down on him but then he won them over and got the cute Hawaiian girl.

"Off to watch the sunset and listen to Warren Zevon. Last night I was doing that and the sun dropped below the horizon line just as his version of 'Knockin' on Heaven's Door' was ending, thereby proving that if there is a God, he directs really hack videos."

FEBRUARY 11, 2004

1 ▪ **Electrelane,** *The Power Out* **(Too Pure)** In 2001 these British women released the almost all-instrumental *Rock It to the Moon*, and you couldn't begin to say what it was. This time, working with professional reprobate Steve Albini, the result is almost a narrative: a series of embarrassing misfires and experiments (a poem by Siegfried Sassoon done with a choir) followed by a long, long chase. With "Take the Bit Between Your Teeth," the band does: it's an all-stops-out grunge jam, about nothing but getting through the forest to the clearing—or the feeling of not caring if you ever get anywhere else. "This Deed" is very European film music, very sexy, very where's-the-gun; "Love Builds Up" is syncopated in a way that's all suspense. Cheap organ and drifting voices have made their own place, as unlikely as the Pre-Raphaelite party of Donovan's "Bert's Blues" or the locked room of Joy Division's "Love Will Tear Us Apart," and no less irresistible. This is as rich a record as you'll hear this year, and almost certainly the least obvious.

2 ▪ **Butchies,** *Make Yr Life* **(Yep Rock)** These three punk musicians will probably call their next album *The L Word*, which will be to the TV show as the homemade PRADA T-shirt one of them is wearing here is to the trademarked version. For the moment what they're after is pop craft—from

echoes of Elizabeth Elmore's Reputation to a doo-wop guitar figure running through a love song.

3 ▪ **David Denby, "Living in America,"** *New Yorker* **(Jan. 12)** Last fall, Denby, a film critic for the *New Yorker*, published "My Life as a Paulette," as in an acolyte of the late *New Yorker* movie critic Pauline Kael. It was his exorcism of the spell the witch cast on him even in death: an account of how Kael befriended him, encouraged him, praised him, and one day called to tell him he wasn't really a writer and that he ought to do something else with his life. Well, he showed her—he got her job!—but as a critic Denby remains dead weight. His style is the equivalent of someone clearing his throat. On those rare occasions when he assays an argument, it's indisputable that nothing will ever rescue him from mediocrity.

In "Living in America," pumped by his liberation from Kael and at the same time helplessly but perversely imitating Kael's sense of herself as an American writer, Denby takes on Vadim Perelman, the Russian/Canadian director of *House of Sand and Fog*, Jane Campion, the New Zealander director of *In the Cut*, and Alejandro González Iñárritu, the Mexican director of *21 Grams*. These people should not be making movies for American audiences, Denby says: "They don't really get America right . . . they miss the colloquial ease and humor, the ruffled surfaces of American life." They insist on the ugliness, horror, obsessiveness, and vengeance in American life (like Denby's hero, the Clint Eastwood of *Mystic River*, which apparently also pulses with the ruffled potato chips of American life, though I must have slept through those parts), but they "may be complacent in their own ways. Perhaps they accept tragedy too easily . . . Dolorousness"—yes, Denby is free; that's not a word Kael would have used at gunpoint—"is becoming a curse in the more ambitious movies made in America by foreign-born directors." "We don't need other people's despair," Denby concludes;

plainly, foreigners can get down with it like John Woo or they can shut up. Kael didn't know the half of it.

4 ▪ **Townes van Zandt, "Coo Coo," on** *Acoustic Blue* **(Tomato)** A 1994 concert version from the late country songwriter: never has "Coo Coo"—or "The Cuckoo," or "The Coo Coo Bird," or "Jack o' Diamonds"—taken on such detail, such melodrama. Two minutes in and it's not a song at all, it's a western.

5 ▪ **Barry Gifford,** *Brando Rides Alone* **(North Atlantic Books)** A very short account of the 1961 *One-Eyed Jacks*, the only movie Marlon Brando ever directed. You can squint trying to find more than attitude in Gifford's critical method and confuse yourself trying to figure out why that's all he needs.

6 ▪ **Joshua Beckman and Matthew Rohrer, "Hillbillies," from** *Adventures While Preaching the Gospel of Beauty* **(Verse Press)** "Hillbillies" is only the most notable of the 19 often improvised poems included here, all of them recorded on the spot in clubs, on roadsides, in front of signs, etc. It instantly elevates Beckman and Rohrer—a Huey-Dewey-and-Louie duo of New York tourists—to the top of whatever chart it is that ranks artists who should be shot.

7 ▪ **Henry Flynt and the Insurrections,** *"I Don't Wanna"* **(Locust Music)** 1966 Fluxus protest music from Flynt, an experimental troublemaker (he subbed with the Velvet Underground and denounced Karlheinz Stockhausen as a racist who didn't understand the Everly Brothers) with a reedy, old-timey voice and a hot, hard-to-follow guitar style. On the cover, he looks like he's submitting a high school science project; song by song he chants cut-up denunciations of the Vietnam War and Wall Street and hits atonal Carl Perkins notes while drummer Walter de Maria, who would go on to erect the celebrated land-art work *Lightning Field* in New Mexico in 1977, runs around the room hitting things at random, and in time.

8 ▪ **Tarbox Ramblers, "Country Blues," on** *A Fix Back East* **(Rounder)** Producer Jim Dickinson gets a big, echoey *Time Out of Mind* sound, which makes it feel as if everything here is taking place inside the not altogether sane head of the singer. But Michael Tarbox is so growly he might as well be a bear, and when he applies himself to Dock Boggs's 1927 testament to a wasted life, the startling boogie arrangement makes his voice feel like a put-up job. But his slide guitar makes another voice—and when Tarbox comes back singing in an almost delirious mode, he takes the song out of his head and into some ugly bar, where new people keep turning up even if no one's left for years.

9 ▪ **Carole King for John Kerry (caroleking.com, Feb. 2)** King was all over New Hampshire before the primary, singing "I Feel the Earth Move" at house parties and "You've Got a Friend" at benefit concerts—but has she played "The Locomotion"? "One Fine Day"? Or redone Bobby Vee's "It Might as Well Rain Until September" as "It Might as Well Rain Until November"—whatever that would mean?

10 ▪ **Steve Weinstein passes on news of the "Hell Freezes Over Tour" (New England Ticketmaster Ticket Alert posting, Jan. 29)** Events included Rufus Wainwright at Toad's Place in New Haven, Carrot Top at the State Theater in Portland, Maine, Lynard Skynyrd (or imposters who can't spell) and 38 Special (wonder if they can still pull off their great "If I'd Been the One"), Barenaked Ladies, and "An Evening with Christ . . ."—which a click on the link revealed to be cheap at the price, $25, even if "Christ" turned out to be Christine Lavin.

MARCH 3, 2004

1 ▪ **Michael Pitt and the Twins of Evil, "Hey Joe," from** *The Dreamers: Original Motion Picture Soundtrack* **(Nettwerk America)** This movie about three young people making a whole world out of movies, sex, and parental allowances in a Paris apartment as the near-revolution of May '68 takes place outside is not as good as it should be. It pulls its punches; it doesn't go far enough. It may

also be that when the trio finally run out into the street, the demonstration that sweeps them up feels fake not only because it's poorly staged, but because the world that's been left behind was so complete—and, at just that moment, so dangerous. Lead actor Michael Pitt's thuggishly casual reading of the '60s non-classic "Hey Joe"—not to mention the amazingly precise '60s guitar playing by (presumably) half of his backing band, which cuts the tune down to its molecules—seems to have nothing to do with this or anything else in the film, but it sounds right.

2 ▪ **Pink Nasty, *Mule School* (Fanatic)** From Wichita, a young woman who acts like Maggie Gyllenhaal's characters and sings with the restraint of country artist Kelly Willis—with occasional slips into the floridness of Lucinda Williams. There's a wonderfully thrown-away ditty called "What the Fuck"; there's "Missing the Boat," a disconcerting piece that takes two minutes to find its shape and when it does breaks into a realism that makes "I'll drink beer for you, I'd have sex with you, I'll drink beer for you" feel like a letter to someone the singer will never write to again.

3 ▪ **Debbie Geller, "America's Beatlemania Hangover" (BBC News, Feb. 7)** The only 40th-anniversary-of-the-Beatles-on-Ed-Sullivan tribute worth noting. As a girl in a "left-wing, atheist, divorced family" in Levittown, Long Island, "the archetype of American suburbia," Geller has no answer when kids ask her what religion she is: "I had never even heard the word before." She isn't "so much bullied as barely tolerated." But then suddenly everyone has to have a favorite Beatle, and everyone wants to know who everyone else's is: "A girlish democracy was created." Watching on February 7, 1964, she realizes it's George: "During the postmortem at school the next morning, I announced my discovery with confidence. Although Paul was the undisputed favorite, my choice was accepted with respect. And no one ever made fun of me again."

4 ▪ **Bonnie "Prince" Billy, *Bonnie "Prince" Billy Sings Greatest Palace Music* (Drag City)**

Aren't tribute albums terrible? And this is a self-tribute album—smug versions of great Palace songs by Will Oldham, a.k.a. Palace—a whole new terrible genre.

5 ▪ **Old Crow Medicine Show, *O.C.M.S.* (Nettwerk America)** Why people hate folk music.

6 ▪ **Negatones, *Snacktronica* (Melody Lane)** Why people hate smart alecks.

7 ▪ **T. C. Boyle, *Drop City* (Penguin)** Almost impossible: a novel about a 1970 hippie commune in which the author embarrasses neither his characters nor himself.

8 ▪ **Bob Dylan, "It's Alright Ma (I'm Only Bleeding)," from *Live 1964: Concert at Philharmonic Hall—October 31, 1964* (Columbia)** Everyone who's heard Dylan perform this number in the 39 years since it appeared on his *Bringing It All Back Home* knows what will happen when the line "Even the president of the United States sometimes has to stand naked" (as it's sung here) comes up: the crowd will stomp and cheer to show what side they're on, or rather what messy choices they're superior to. But on this night Lyndon Johnson had yet to be demonized. Nixon had not been elected. Ford had not replaced Nixon, or Carter Ford, or Reagan Carter, or Bush Reagan, or Clinton Bush, or Bush Clinton. No one had heard the song before—and it's so strange to hear the line produce only silence, as if it's not obvious what the line says.

9 ▪ **"The Fog of War: Robert S. McNamara and Errol Morris in Discussion," University of California at Berkeley (Feb. 4)** Throughout a long talk arising from Morris's 2003 documentary *The Fog of War*, moderator Mark Danner pressed the former Secretary of Defense—under Kennedy and Johnson the tribune of the Vietnam War—to apply his conclusions from that time to the present day. Again and again, McNamara—at 88 in frightening command of his faculties, vehement, direct, lucid, at times even monomaniacally focused—ignored the question, dodged it, refused it, denied it. Finally Danner announced that he would read the "Eleven Lessons" from McNamara's 1995 *In Retrospect: The*

Tragedy and Lessons of Vietnam: "I'll ask you while I do so," he said, "to keep the present situation in mind."

One by one, the items went off like small bombs: "'We failed to . . . We failed to . . . We failed to . . . We failed to draw Congress and the American people into the pros and cons of a large-scale military action before it got underway. . . . We did not realize that neither our people nor our leaders are omniscient. . . . We do not have the God-given right to shape other nations as we choose . . .'"

"When I read these lessons again I felt a chill go through me," Danner said. "I was in Iraq. In October, reporting . . . they seemed to reflect with uncanny accuracy—it's for that that I've tried to push you, not only about—" McNamara cut him off.

"What he has done," he said to the audience, "is extract those lessons from this book. The lessons are in there. . . . I put them forward not because of Vietnam, but because of the future!" He turned to Danner: "You want me to apply them to Bush. I'm not going to do it." He turned back to the audience, full of people who decades ago fought him with everything they had. "YOU APPLY THEM TO BUSH."

10 ■ **New York Times, "Music Albums Chart, Billboard/Soundscan, February 9 through 15" (Feb. 23)** #1 Norah Jones, #2 Kenny Chesney, #5 Josh Groban, #6 Harry Connick Jr., #7 Evanescence, #10 *2004 Grammy Nominees* compilation—it's probably pointless to read anything into this sudden domination of comfort, balm, reassurance, and acceptance at the start of an election year. At least I hope it is.

MARCH 24, 2004

1 ■ **Mendoza Line, "It's a Long Line (But It Moves Quickly)," on *Fortune* (Cooking Vinyl)** From people hiding in present-day America—just as the Mekons of *Fear and Whiskey* and *The Edge of the World* were all but moles in Margaret Thatcher's Britain—a swift, irresistible put-down song ("She called you a cab and they brought you a hearse"). Debbie Harry had her finger on this trigger in Blondie's "Rip Her to Shreds," but Shannon McArdle makes you think she didn't pull it.

2 ■ **The Bear, 95.7 FM, San Francisco, music criticism (Feb. 24)** I.e., following Toby Keith and Willie Nelson's 2003 lynch-mob ode "Beer for My Horses," where everybody who's not swinging from a tree meets "up back at the local saloon," with Reba McEntire's 1992 version of "The Night the Lights Went Out in Georgia," where the judge rushes off to dinner and "they hung an innocent man."

3 ■ **"In other news," official Sleater-Kinney website (Sleater-Kinney.com, March 3)** "Urban Outfitters, the store dedicated to reselling your childhood back to you via nostalgia and irony-based fashion, is selling a T-shirt that says: 'Voting Is For Old People.' Unless you are under the age of 18, this shirt will be banned from all Sleater-Kinney shows."

4 ■ **Sons and Daughters, *Love the Cup* (Ba Da Bing!)** Except for an edge of restraint, the edge of not telling all they knew, there wasn't anything on this Glasgow quartet's folky 2002 EP *The Lovers* to suggest the snaking tension—or the pounding fury—of the tunes here. "Fight" begins slowly, then blows up in the singers' faces; "Johnny Cash" opens as the murder ballad "Pretty Polly" taken at a fierce pace, the curses of the words chasing David Gow's drums until Adele Bethel, Ailidh Lennon, and Scott Paterson are screaming for the tune's last minutes as if they've already killed whoever it is the song wants dead.

5 ■ **"Lee Greenwood puts heart into his pre-race performance to kick off this year's Daytona 500" (Pollstar, Feb. 15)** Heart may not be the word: as passed on by Steve Weinstein, who provided his own caption ("Lee Greenwood and choir giving quasi-Nazi salute at NASCAR rally—while presumably singing 'God Bless the USA' in Aramaic"), the photo, shot just before George W. Bush proclaimed, "Gentlemen, start your engines!" showed Greenwood raising his right arm, high, stiff, and forward, while four

women dressed in blazing red clerical gowns and two men draped in yellow lifted theirs with at least a slightly ambiguous bend in the elbow. Or, as one could have read a month later in the program for the annual convention of the National Association of Evangelicals in Colorado Springs, which Bush addressed on closed-circuit TV ("You are doing God's work with conviction and kindness, and on behalf of our country I thank you"), "What Can 30 Million Evangelicals Do for America? Anything We Want."

6–7 ▪ Lou Reed, *Animal Serenade* (Reprise) & *Live: Take No Prisoners* (Arista) If you don't like Lou Reed, double live albums won't convince you. Whether onstage in New York in 1978 for the biting *Take No Prisoners* or in Los Angeles last year for the reflective *Animal Serenade* (what, an animal serenade without "Possum Time"?), he's not selling anything, and he takes whatever time he needs: 17 minutes for the relentless stand-up comedy routine that's the *Prisoners'* "Walk on the Wild Side," nine minutes for "Set the Twilight Reeling" on *Serenade*. The highlight of the latter might be "Tell It to Your Heart," which would fit David Lynch's *Mulholland Dr.* even better than Reed's version of "This Magic Moment" did *Lost Highway*; the benchmark for *Prisoners*, if not for Reed's entire presence over the decades, is "Street Hassle"—also included on *Animal Serenade*, and in a performance that seems complete until what Reed did with the song 26 years ago makes you realize the drama in the number can never be complete. Reed lets the scene where the singer is telling another man to get his dead wife out of the singer's apartment dictate the rhythm; with the bouncy Waltzing Matilda beat suddenly stripped back, it's a long, jittery moment of absolute naturalism. You forget that the lines Reed is speaking rhyme, that these are lyrics in any kind of song. It's a play, not a song, and the Brando in Reed is all the way out, walking back and forth across the stage. There is no stylization you can hear.

8 ▪ Walter Hopps at "Jay DeFeo and The Rose: Myth and Reality" (San Francisco Mu- seum of Modern Art, Feb. 28) It was a symposium on the San Francisco artist's painting *The Rose*. DeFeo (1929–89) began working on it in 1957; in 1965, the work having long since taken over her life, she and her husband were evicted from their apartment, and the unfinished painting, which by then had grown to more than 10 feet by eight feet and weighed nearly 2,000 pounds, was removed to the Pasadena Art Museum where Hopps, then its director, planned to show it—though it wasn't until 1969, when Hopps was gone, that it finally appeared. Before long it disappeared, walled up like a corpse in the San Francisco Art Institute. In 1995 it was broken out and restored; the next year it was at the Walker as part of the touring exhibition "Beat Culture and the New America: 1950–1965."

This day in San Francisco, Hopps, now curator of the Menil Collection in Houston, remembered a night at the Fillmore Auditorium in the late 1950s, when he and DeFeo had gone to see Count Basie: DeFeo loved his "Hello Central, Give Me Doctor Jazz." DeFeo was dancing alone in front of the stage; when the band took a break, Basie motioned her over. She came back to Hopps: "He wants me to go backstage!" She went. When the band returned, DeFeo reappeared, blushing. "Well, what on earth went on?" Hopps asked. "He asked me to go away with him," DeFeo said. "What did you say?" "I told him there's this big painting I have to finish."

9 ▪ Joe Rathbone, *I Can Hear the Windows of Your Heart Breaking* (Zakz) First winner of the Rod McKuen Prize for Gross Metaphorical Elaborationism. And the music sounds just like the title.

10 ▪ Oliver Hall writes in: "L.A. is having one of its occult fits of meaning again. Driving back from the polling place this afternoon in the lower-middle-class neighborhood where I've lived for the last 14 years, I found a street I'd never seen before: Barbara Ann Street. It only seems to go about a block, and there was nothing on it but an abandoned couch, a torn-up Camaro, and something covered in a blue tarp."

370

APRIL 14, 2004

1 ▪ *Salon,* **"Letters," regarding the pending removal of Bob Edwards as host of NPR's** *Morning Edition* **(March 30)** The bemusement Edwards has for 25 years offered ordinary important events is of a piece with the *What seems to be the problem?* tone he adopts for absolute catastrophes. Neither is more than a genteel version of standard D.C. cynicism. But familiarity with anything on the air breeds resistance to change—that is, it breeds "All is for the best in this best of all possible worlds"—far more readily than it does contempt. "For me," one Edwards follower wrote *Salon,* "Bob Edwards has become the Mister Rogers of my adult life. His ability to report and explain all facets of news stories in an even-keeled, compassionate manner has allowed me to accept and understand even the most difficult and horrific events of the world with a sense of optimism."

2 ▪ **TV on the Radio,** *Desperate Youth, Blood Thirsty Babes* **(Touch and Go)** This New York experimental pop band—credited as Tunde Adebimpe, vocals and loops; Kyp Malone, vocals, guitars, and loops; David Andrew Sitek, music—is never obvious. Some songs are too vague to notice, and they hide the ones that aren't—until a slowly building storm ("Dreams") or a dragging but determined walk home in the middle of the night ("Wear You Out") makes it clear this music comes out of a real city: an invisible city. Getting there is easier than reporting back, but these people are inventing a new language to pull it off.

3 ▪ **Tom Perrotta,** *Little Children* **(St. Martin's)** The *New York Times* is pumping this diverting, evaporating novel about young couples with children in suburbia—probably because some *Times* writers who still think John Cheever and John Updike had something to say are thrilled to have their own suburbs reauthenticated in fiction. But this book doesn't touch Perrotta's high school novel, *Election,* which is nothing like the every-punch-telegraphed movie version, or for that matter *Joe College,* Per-

rotta's college novel. The new book *is* just like a movie, and you can hardly read a page without seeing Eric Stoltz and Maura Tierney as the leads.

4 ▪ **Beyoncé, Baaba Maal, et al.,** *46664: Part 1—African Prayer* **(46664)** The first of three albums collecting performances from the November 29, 2003 Cape Town concert that inaugurated Nelson Mandela's "46664" campaign against AIDS. "46664 was my prison number," Mandela said in his speech that day. "For the 18 years that I was imprisoned on Robben Island I was known as just a number." Highlight: Bob Geldof, "Redemption Song." Perhaps done as badly as Bob Marley's greatest composition can be, but that melody can keep any singer alive.

5 ▪ **Queen, Ladysmith Black Mambazo, et al.,** *46664: Part 2—Long Walk to Freedom* **(46664)** Highlight: Corrs, "Breathless." Even if they act as if what makes the song wonderful is that it's supposed to be taken seriously.

6 ▪ **Eurythmics, Ms. Dynamite, et al.,** *46664: Part 3—Amandla* **(46664)** Highlight: Bono and The Edge, "One"/"Unchained Melody." The great thing about U2's "One" is that if they hadn't recorded it, Johnny Cash would not have sung it. The good thing about Bono's version of "Unchained Melody" is that it can remind you of Bobby Hatfield of the Righteous Brothers, who last November dropped dead just before he was to go onstage and sing the song one more time. Still, when you hear Mandela say, "46664 was my prison number," you might wonder why the Maytals weren't there to perform Toots Hibberts's song about his own time in prison: two years for marijuana possession. As he first sang more than 30 years ago, on the indelible Jamaican chant "54-46 Was My Number": "Right now someone has that number." The song was recently redone with Jeff Beck on the stars-galore Toots and the Maytals self-tribute album *True Love*—yet another example of this terrible new craze for repetition as a first principle of modern life.

7 ▪ *The Sopranos* **(HBO, March 28)** Tony and Carmella are at a conference about their fuck-up son with his school counselor, played by David Strathairn. "So, he called the English teacher Daddy-O?" Tony says, quoting the Coasters' 1959 "Charlie Brown." The counselor doesn't get it, which is a mistake—Strathairn's characters always get it.

Later, at a high-stakes poker game, David Lee Roth is playing himself, looking a few hundred years past his Van Halen days, and also looking human. The mobster played by Robert Loggia tells a joke about the first Jewish CPA in heaven; "I used to be able to write off condoms," Roth says wistfully. But anyone who knows Roth's autobiography will have trouble believing he didn't ask the director to give him a chance to throw the joke back in Loggia's face. "Every step I took on that stage was smashing some Jew-hating, lousy punk ever deeper into the deck," Roth wrote in *Crazy from the Heat*. "*Every step.* I jumped higher 'cause I knew there was going to be more impact when I hit those boards. And if you were even vaguely anti-Semitic, you were under my wheels, motherfucker. That's where the lyrics came from, that's where the body language came from, that's where the humor came from, and that's where the fuck you came from."

8 ▪ **Iron and Wine, *Our Endless Numbered Days* (Sub Pop)** Sam Beam's version of folk music has received enormous praise. Is that because he combines Gothic lyrics with a voice that insists he long ago saw through all their mysteries? Or because his beard looks like it weighs 10 pounds?

9 ▪ **Spam e-mail from jaysonblair_th@ stgl.gr.ch (March 20)** "The only solution to Penis Enlargement." No, his book isn't selling, but who knew he'd fallen this far?

10 ▪ **The Doors, *Boot Yer Butt!—The Doors Bootlegs* (Rhino Handmade)** This four-CD box of 1967–70 live performances is not drawn from soundboards or well-made audience tapes, but from absolutely horrible recordings made with damaged equipment and originally pressed onto illegal vinyl that warped and splintered as soon as you tried to play it. Here, Jim Morrison can

sound miles and miles away from the little handheld microphone that's picking up his messages—messages that feel like they're coming from a void, because you may not be able to make out a single instrument behind Morrison's voice. The band can emerge and disappear, as if it's playing a séance, not a show. But if you're willing to crawl through the black caves of this set, the result is a treasure chest.

Strange things happen on these discs, and especially strange things seem to have happened at the April 18, 1970 show at the Honolulu Convention Center. "Mystery Train" starts out as "This Train" (you know: "You don't need no ticket, just get on board"). After a buildup, the vocal sound overwhelms everything around it, and Morrison seems lost in the possibilities of the song, inventing words, ignoring the band's rhythm, erasing it with a huge scream. "Light My Fire" unfolds over 20 minutes. Guitarist Robbie Krieger starts it off as "My Favorite Things"; Morrison finds "Fever" hiding inside the big hit. "Love comes when you least expect it," he says as the music slows almost to a stop—but after that everything is harsh, wild, rough, unforgiving.

Throughout there is the sense that anything can happen, that the songs are less pieces to perform than opportunities for vision—usually banal visions of other songs, occasionally visions of music made with intent and found only by chance.

MAY 5, 2004

1–2 ▪ **Eagles of Death Metal, *Peace Love Death Metal* (AntAcidAudio) and Dock Boggs, *Country Blues: Complete Early Recordings (1927–29)* (Revenant)** Featuring a member of Queens of the Stone Age but starring the singer and guitarist Jesse "The Devil" Hughes (credited throughout as J Devil Huge), *Peace Love Death Metal* is an uncompromisingly inflamed but deep-down wimpy stomp through an American high school: a high school defined on one hand by Gus Van Sant's film *Elephant*—

his version of the Columbine mass murders—and on the other hand by Daniel M. Pinkwater's novel *Young Adults*, where the endemic jocks-versus-brains conflict takes the form of a struggle between two conflicting theories of art (and, of course, life), with the two-man Dada Ducks gang going up against the conformist goons of Heroic Realism.

Some of the Eagles' song titles are better than the songs—the George Clinton tribute "Whorehoppin (Shit, Goddam)," "San Berdoo Sunburn"—but "Bad Dream Mama" pays off from first note to last, and still falls short of "Kiss the Devil." "Who'll love the devil? Who'll kiss his tongue? Who will kiss the devil on his tongue?" Huge growls, and answers himself: "I'll love the devil! I'll kiss his tongue! I will kiss the devil on his tongue!" "Kiss the Devil," it turns out, is a very light rewrite of Virginia banjoist Dock Boggs's "Sugar Baby": a mountain-symbolist masterpiece that, hinting at a man's wish to murder both his wife and his child ("Who'll rock the cradle, who'll sing the song? Who'll rock the cradle when you gone?"), is more demonic than these Eagles—not to mention the other Eagles—would ever dare to be. And that's why the rewrite works. Jesse Hughes heard Boggs, understood him, and also understood that the only way he could ever sing Boggs's song was to turn it into a joke. It's a good joke, but that's not all it is.

3 ▪ Loudon Wainwright III, "Presidents' Day" (www.lwiii.com) By November 3 this anti-Bush song may seem as pathetic as a Wesley Clark campaign button. For the moment it's as sharp as an Oliphant editorial cartoon, with that little bird talking at the bottom.

4 ▪ Mendoza Line, *Fortune* (Cooking Vinyl) The CD booklet here is full of words, but like ballplayers who fall below the line the band named itself for (.198: Mario Mendoza's 1979 full-season batting average with the Seattle Mariners), some of the band's best words are doomed to be forgotten because they're wasted in press material. For *Fortune*, they're in a couple of

anonymous, first-person pages titled "About the Songs," with the back story of "Fellow Travelers" (which in the 1950s meant traitors) described directly: "As recollections of the 2000 presidential election dissolve into a hazy, melancholic fugue, they stopped to wonder if it had all really happened that way: was our country really given away to a small coterie of unprincipled Fortune 500 acolytes. . . . Were these men really assisted in their ascendancy by a group of so called 'liberal activists' whose self-aggrandizing exercise in 'protest' helped set the real cause of progressive politics back forty years . . . and who will ever have enough money to buy our country back now? Additionally: Wasn't that the year my every aspect of the social and emotional fabric of my life unraveled utterly? Could it be that this is more than a coincidence? I have a bad feeling this might all be my fault . . ." Out of that mix of rage and fear, self-ridicule and guilt, come country songs with vowels dragged into the next county and rave-ups about the national debt compounded daily by private failures. In a number where the sweet trill of a steel guitar coming off the last word gives almost nothing back to what a fiddle has already taken away, the simple heartbreak of singers whose loss of faith in their country has made it impossible to trust the people they love can break your heart as well. "Make every day count," the press release says, "even if it can only count to three."

5–7 ▪ Leslie Bennetts, "Not Across My Daughter's Big Brass Bed You Don't, Bob" (*Los Angeles Times*, April 16); Mel Gibson, producer, *The Passion of the Christ—Songs Inspired by* (Universal South); Mirah with the Black Cat Orchestra, "Dear Landlord," from *To All We Stretch the Open Arm* (YoYo) Bob Dylan Sellout Alert! Bennetts, who made her name attacking Hillary Clinton in the pages of *Vanity Fair*, again raises the flag of moral outrage. This time it's because of the way "an artist who once had a profound effect on American culture" can now be found in a Victoria's Secret commercial. There he is in the city of gondolas and Ti-

tian; as his suicidal "Love Sick" plays, he squints across the Grand Canal at a montage of underwear models, thus giving a whole new meaning to "See Venice and die." But what about "Not Dark Yet"—like "Love Sick" from the wasteland of Dylan's 1997 *Time Out of Mind*—appearing on a collection of mostly old recordings that Mel Gibson has put to work celebrating his very own movie to the point of claiming that he himself is somehow responsible for their creation? Bennetts thinks an underwear commercial is pedophilia, Gibson thinks a song following a man down a dead road is about Jesus, and they may be right—but not as right as the one-time riot grrrl chanteuse Mirah Yom Tov Zeitlyn, who, like so many before her, understands that a profound Bob Dylan song can, in other hands, sound like anybody's common sense.

8–9 ▪ **Penelope Houston with Pat Johnson, "The Pale Green Girl," from** *The Pale Green Girl* **(DBK Works) and Nancy Sinatra, "Bang Bang (My Baby Shot Me Down)" (Reprise)** A slow, hesitating song with a quick, poppy chorus, right up to that point where guitarist Pat Johnson makes you lean forward and wonder what his few broken, abstract notes are saying, and Houston, in her most powerful moments since she broke up the Avengers in 1979, cracks the punk whip that's been hiding in the tune all along. I heard it on the radio immediately after Nancy Sinatra's shockingly avant-garde 1966 version of a Sonny and Cher hit, from the *Kill Bill, Vol. 1* soundtrack. The *Vol. 2* set would be better off with "The Pale Green Girl" than anything that's actually on it.

10 ▪ **Jan Berry, 1941–2004** He treated everyone around him like something to kick out of the way, including the truck he crashed into 38 years ago and never really walked away from. He never apologized, except perhaps in that perfect moment in "Dead Man's Curve," after the Jag he's been racing has been totaled; a hand runs across the strings of a harp, and Jan finds himself not in his Stingray in heaven, playing a lute, but in the hospital, putting on a convincing

show of humility—"Well, the last thing I remember, Doc, I started to swerve . . ."— but you can bet he's secretly grinning over every word.

JUNE 30, 2004

1 ▪ **Leah Garchik, June 14 (***San Francisco Chronicle***)** Regarding George W. Bush declaring the day of Ronald Reagan's funeral a national holiday, bold-faced names columnist Garchik cited a report of signs on the D Street post office in San Rafael, just over the Golden Gate Bridge in Marin County, on Friday, June 11: "Post Office Will Be Closed Today in Memory of Ray Charles."

2 ▪ **Ratatat, "Seventeen Years," from** *Ratatat* **(XL)** Two guys in a bedroom studio in Brooklyn make what sounds like the instrumental B-side of "Hey Ya"—the music is about half that inventive, which is to say very inventive, and never calls attention to itself. But then the glee of trading one piece of sound for another fades, and you're floating on a lullaby. The movement draws you in, quiets your mind, and then, whatever this is, you're swimming through it.

3 ▪ **Lucinda Williams, "Love That Mystic Hammering" (***New York Times Book Review***, June 13)** "I sure don't pretend to be no intellectual," says the adored tribute-album contributor in her piece on Bob Dylan lyrics. Her father was a college professor, but she spent her childhood out by the barn eating dirt, which is why her own songs ring so true today.

4–5 ▪ **PJ Harvey,** *Uh Huh Her* **(Island) and Nick Catucci, "Carnal Fission" (***Village Voice***, June 9)** Harvey rubs, scrapes, drags chairs around the room; sometimes it feels as if her music comes from her guitar applying pressure to her skin rather than her fingers applying pressure to her guitar strings. Each album seems to gravitate toward the point where a certain state of mind and body will flare up into a single image—which will then burn out and disappear, leaving you incapable of remembering what the image was, only that you glimpsed it. Here, you're on the way with the pulse of "Shame," only the second song; you can feel the destination has been reached with the next, "Who the Fuck?" which combines a Lenny Kravitz beat with an extremist, primitivist Sheryl Crow vocal—an affinity that lets you hear Harvey listening to Crow, lets you hear Harvey hearing something in Crow's voice nobody else hears, maybe including Crow herself.

That's the problem with artists: They know things other people don't. They feel compelled to say what those things are, and to conceal the strangeness and alienation of the act. If there is an "I" in their work, it ceases to refer back to the person writing, painting, singing; the person whose name is on the work has momentarily replaced herself with a made-up person who can say or do anything. This is what makes such a person an artist, and it's why critics who try to reduce an artist's work to her life are cretins. Thus we have Nick Catucci in the *Village Voice*, assuring his readers that *Uh Huh Her* is "a break-up album"—"as all save her last have been," he adds, in case you think there might be something out there that doesn't fit into a thimble. Forget that situations everyone goes through might go through Harvey differently than they do through you or me; don't worry that there might be anything here that isn't immediately obvious; after all, Catucci says, she's "an easy read" and "she's got a one-track mind." "We know she's been fucking and fighting, probably in equal measures, and maybe in the same moments." You can almost smell him, can't you?

6–7 ▪ **Patti Smith, "Radio Baghdad," from *Trampin'* (Columbia) and Michael Kamber, photo accompanying Edward Wong's "Deputy Foreign Minister Is Fatally Shot in Baghdad" (*New York Times*, June 13)** Smith has been selling death for years—but now mere husband, brother, friends, and poet comrades take a backseat to a whole city, a whole civilization: civilization itself! That's what was destroyed when the U.S. took Iraq. For Smith it's a chance to gas up the piety boilers, and remind us that we (or,

rather, "they," which is us, but not her, unless we accept her vision, in which case we can be her, gazing with sadness and disgust at those who remain "they") destroyed a perfect city, the center of the world, where once walked "the great Caliph." How does it sound? Silly. The Aloha-Elvis wall hanging you could see in the background of Kamber's photo—captioned "American soldiers searched a suspected stronghold of the Mahdi Army, the militia loyal to Moktada al-Sadr"—was infinitely more interesting. Why doesn't Smith write a song about what Elvis was doing there: about a "we" that even she might not be able to make into a "they," unless the "they" included Iraqis, too?

8 ▪ **Blue Sky Boys, *The Sunny Side of Life* (Bear Family)** A five-CD box set of songs recorded between 1936 and 1950 by Bill and Earl Bollick of West Hickory, North Carolina, who look like the nicest insurance salesmen you'll ever meet. Their music creates a simple, innocent, white small town, all calm and pastoralism, and the calmest, most pastoral tunes are the murder ballads.

9 ▪ **Evan Eisenberg, "Bushido: The Way of the Armchair Warrior" (*New Yorker*, June 7)** A single page, and, with a quietly implacable rhythm, one word to the next, the most frigid, frightening, and complete portrait of the current occupant of the White House I have read. Machiavelli could have written the following lines, and in slightly different form he did: "The Chinese word for 'crisis' combines the characters for 'danger' and 'opportunity.' For the armchair warrior, the significance of this is clear. Every crisis is an opportunity, and the lack of crisis poses a grave danger." But even Machiavelli's ghost might flinch at the smile of evil to which Eisenberg appends his last period.

10 ▪ **Shangri-Las, City Hall Park, New York City, June 19** In the May 17, 2001, edition of this column, then running in *Salon*, I included an item, written more than a week earlier, on an A&E documentary that featured an interview with Mary L. Stokes—

formerly Mary Weiss of the Shangri-Las, the lead singer with long, straight blond hair. She was talking about why the 1964–65 tragedies of "Remember," "I Can Never Go Home Anymore" or "Leader of the Pack" were not difficult for her: because, she said, she had enough pain in her own life to stand up to the songs. A few days after the destruction of the World Trade Center, I heard that Stokes, now a manager for a furniture company, was present when the towers were hit and when they came down; I contacted her and asked her to write about that day for this column, and she did. When I read that the Shangri-Las would be performing in New York City, I asked my friend Robert Christgau to cover the show; as this will be my last column in *City Pages* for at least a year, the idea of tracing that circle, if not closing it, seemed right.

Christgau reports: "This may be the oldest crowd I've been in anywhere short of the Metropolitan Opera (and a beatnik poetry reading I attended a few years back). Intros by Randy Davis of WCBS-FM, 'New York's oldies station,' promising to 'walk you right down memory lane' in the 'real heart of New York City.' 'They were known as the bad girls of rock and roll . . .' Backing band all in black, three ladies in black slacks with V-cut red satin tops. Stage left a brunette in her twenties, stage right a well-preserved forty/fiftysomething, also brunette. But there's no Mary Weiss in sight—unless she now has brownish hair in a curly frizz,

which would be bad for business. Four or five dozen onlookers come up in front of the stage in the sun, those on benches stay there, most of the crowd of perhaps 200 hangs back in the shade, including senior latecomers who really need to sit. The band vamps, sounding way too perky, and they are: the opening number is 'You Can't Hurry Love,' followed by 'Give Him a Great Big Kiss,' the nicest hit in the Shangri-Las' repertoire, which is also too perky. It's a generic oldies set ('Johnny B. Goode,' 'The Loco-Motion,' 'Be My Baby,' etc.) with three Shangri-Las tunes."

It turns out the Shangri-Las are the Shangri-La: Marge Ganser, "the twin who didn't die of a barbiturate overdose," accompanied by her daughter Mary and a friend. Christgau: "Five blocks from Ground Zero, we're told (well, not 'we,' but the younger fans Marge was looking down at; we 'survivors'—yes, the term was adduced, by young Mary—know enough to stay out of the midday sun) we're going to have 'a hell of a history lesson.' And the lesson is that although the Shangri-Las live (except for the dead Ganser) their individual-collaborative achievement does not; the lesson is that the past is already smooshed together into one perky playlist."

Bye-bye.

Note: We were all fooled, and none of us had done our homework: the show was a fake. Marge Ganser died of breast cancer in 1996.

Interview
2006·2007

1–2 ■ **Neko Case,** *Canadian Amp* **(Lady Pilot) and** *Fox Confessor Brings the Flood* **(Anti)**
With the New Pornographers, Case shoots cries of passion and glee into the air until she towers over the band like a waterspout. On her own albums, pitched toward country, she has always sung too carefully—except on the EP *Canadian Amp*, released as an Internet-only item in 2001 and now available in stores. There, she took Neil Young's "Dreaming Man" so soulfully Young evaporated from the music; with Hank Williams's "Alone and Forsaken," Case herself almost disappeared into the song, which is as far as anyone should go into that most blasted of American suicide notes. But with Case now in her mid-thirties, something like aging is taking place. On *Fox Confessor* she sings as if she knows more—or doubts more. There's a warmth here, as if drawn from a deep well, that she didn't have to give before. Song by song, stories swirl. With "Hold On, Hold On," Case leaves a party at 3 A.M. ("Alone, thank God"); she turns her car west, with Duane Eddy as a guide, ghost riders in her sky.

3 ■ **Stephen Colbert,** *The Colbert Report* **(Comedy Central, Dec. 1)** He interrupted himself to muse over Rick Springfield's great 1981 hit "Jessie's Girl." "I have not been able to get the song out of my head," he said. "I wish that I had Jessie's girl. I wish that I had—what's that next line?" he asks the stage manager, who probably wasn't born when the song topped the charts. Colbert swivels his head. "Rick, what's the next line?" And then Springfield, holding a guitar, happily responds. "Where can I find a woman like that," he bangs out and immediately stops. "That's it. Thanks, babe," Colbert says, moving right along, as if Springfield were a prop man.

4 ■ **Cat Power,** *The Greatest* **(Matador)** For a decade, Chan Marshall has dedicated herself to tempos that stop and a voice that courts silence. Here, playing with Memphis soul musicians, she fools with strange new tools: coming down hard on a word, a rumble on guitar, hints of melodrama. But what's at stake is the search for a darker hollowness, a more complete nowhere; with "Hate" she meets Neko Case somewhere in Arizona and in a battle of the bands, sucks her up like dust.

5 ■ **Rubettes, "Sugar Baby Love," from** *Breakfast on Pluto: Music from the Motion Picture* **(Milan)** From 1974, and the most deliriously happy sound imaginable. No wonder Cillian Murphy's character Kitten can smile in the face of horror; this never goes off the charts in her head.

6 ■ **Ameriquest Commercial (Aug. 21)** Weirder by far than the Rolling Stones' performance at the Super Bowl was this spot, where, as an unbelievably desiccated and self-parodying (*until* the Super Bowl) Mick Jagger prances onstage, a young, properly dressed Ann Coulter look-alike emerges from the crowd to explain that Ameriquest is underwriting the band's 2005 tour because they want to help you with your mortgage. "Mick! I love you!" she screams as the crowd lifts her into the air. Back on her feet, disheveled, replacing her glasses, she nevertheless has the self-control to explain that Ameriquest is not only sponsoring the tour but is the registered owner of the slogan "Proud Sponsor of the American Dream." Or, as the Firesign Theatre once put it, speaking of a company they named U.S. Plus: "We own the idea of the idea of America."

7 ■ **Black Angels,** *Passover* **(Light in the Attic)** A drone band looking for the sound of paranoia and dread: the vortex comes in the slow, rotting noise of "The First Vietnamese War." And the second? And the third?

8 ■ **Dion,** *Bronx in Blue* **(Dimensional Music Recordings)** He sings Robert Johnson songs in his own voice, but he plays guitar as if he's making the songs up on the spot.

9 ■ **Ken Tucker,** *Fresh Air* **(WHYY/NPR, Dec. 20)** On Bob Dylan at the Beacon Theater in New York: "He sang 'I'll Be Your Baby Tonight,' and he just bit off the words—'Shut the *light*/Shut the shade.' It was as though he was about to direct a porn film, the way he said those words."

10 ■ **Cat Power, "Paths of Victory," from** *North Country: Music from the Motion Picture* **(Columbia)** Taken from her 2000 *The Covers Record*—and somehow the throaty intonations, the deliberate pacing, are a perfect match for Charlize Theron's performance. Even though I knew the recording, when it played behind the credits I thought it was Theron singing.

MAY 2006

1 ■ **Dana Spiotta,** *Eat the Document* **(Scribner)** In 1972 a bombing meant as a protest against the Vietnam War goes wrong; a young woman and a young man go underground. Twenty-six years later they turn up under new names in the same town; inevitably they will meet. But in the meantime the most interesting character in this pitch-perfect novel—with references to Shulamith Firestone and Dock Boggs tossed off so lightly that even if the names mean nothing, they help create the frame of fictional reference and make their own sense—is the woman's teenage son. It's 1998; he's obsessed with *Smile* bootlegs composed entirely of "10, 15, 20 takes that are nearly identical to each other." This is a portrait of how smart a 15-year-old can be: "You are in the recording studio when they made this album. You are there with all the failures, the intense perfectionism, the frustration of trying to realize in the world the sounds you hear in your head." The lines don't come off the page as a metaphor for the story the novel tells; the boy's voice is too intense for it not to claim his own story.

2 ■ **The Fever,** *In the City of Sleep* **(Kemado)** Geremy Jasper's pretentiousness is his strength; he'll try anything. What makes the music move is the strangeness filtered into familiar landscapes. In "Eyes on the Road," it's 4 A.M. somewhere in New Jersey. The police-radio voice-over is funny, and so present you feel yourself looking over your shoulder to see if you hit someone back there. Keep your eyes on this road and soon enough you'll be seeing eyes on the road as well.

3 ■ **Rosanne Cash,** *Black Cadillac* **(Capitol)** One after the other she lost a stepmother, a father, and a mother. She sings as if she never got a chance to settle anything with any of them, so instead of crying at the funerals on this album, she says inappropriate things. On "The World Unseen," she moves slowly, as if from room to room in an empty house, all the action in her hesitation. "I will look for you between the grooves of songs we sing," she says, and finally the other mourners begin to relax. Then, with a deepening of her voice so unmistakable the people around her can see her shut the door, she walks away, rewriting Lead Belly's "Goodnight, Irene" in head. She'll look for them, all right: "in morphine and in dreams."

4 ■ **Honda, "This Is What a Honda Feels Like" commercial** In a parking garage, a conductor assembles a chorus to outdo the Human Beatbox and the Human Orchestra. With nothing but their mouths they start the car, drive through a tunnel, around turns, over cobblestones. They close the sunroof with the newest new-car sound you've ever heard. But the sexiest moment comes when they turn on the windshield wipers.

5–8 ■ **The 48th Annual Grammy Awards (CBS, February 8)** Best Smarm: John Legend, who will be a Grammy hero for decades. Best Legend: Sly Stone, who in a gold lamé topcoat and a blond Mohawk looked like a cross between Wesley Snipes in *Blade* and a sea monster. Best Monstrosity: as a concrete sign of emotion, post-Mariah Carey melisma is a sign of insincerity; what is meant to appear as a loss of control is its imposition; a woman projecting autonomy is practicing a pimp aesthetic. There was Kelly Clarkson, Mary J. Blige, Christina Aguilera—but what the hell, let's give the prize to Joss Stone. Best Dressed: Keith Urban, head-to-toe in Nicole Kidman.

9 ■ **The Raveonettes, "Twilight" and "Somewhere in Texas" from** *Pretty in Black*

(Columbia) Western ballads that would have been perfect for the soundtrack to *Kill Bill: Vol. 2*—a queer combination of serenity and menace.

10 ▪ The Fiery Furnaces, *Bitter Tea* (Fat Possum) For their fourth album, the most interesting and perplexing of all the two-person male-female bands offers a funny-noises record. There are squeaks and scratches, Beach Boys effects, and between-the-wars cabaret. When Eleanor Friedberger's vocals are run backward, she sounds Russian, when brother Matthew's are, he sounds Hungarian. And nothing is lost: when the singing goes back in the right direction, the feeling of not caring how you got where you are is so musical, you may not even notice the change. But most of the time the feeling is that of a smart kid with a chemistry set—or a three-CD *Smile* bootleg—experimenting on his sister, who knows more than he does. Best song: "Benton Harbor Blues," a rewrite of "96 Tears."

JUNE 2006

1 ▪ Sarah Bernhardt, *L'Aiglon*, from *In Performance* (no label) At the Jewish Museum in New York, near the end of the exhibition "Sarah Bernhardt: The Art of High Drama," which closed April 2, there was, after rooms of posters, costumes, books, photographs, and silent film clips, a listening station. What you heard was four minutes from Rostand's *L'Aiglon*, starring Bernhardt (1844–1923) as the son of Napoleon, recorded for Edison in 1910—or rather what you heard was a wire being drawn through a body as its voice refused death: *Not yet, not yet*, Bernhardt seems to say, *not until I have said what I have to say, and what I have to say is, Why? Why?* I played it over and over; I couldn't believe I would have to walk out of the building and never hear it again. In the museum gift shop, they were sold out of almost everything, including "Who Do You Think You Are, Sarah Bernhardt?" T-shirts. But they still had copies of this CD.

2 ▪ Frank Black, *Honeycomb* (Back Porch) The Pixies' singer; he recorded in Nashville, but he made a Memphis album—with, among many more Bluff City musicians, Reggie Young, guitarist on Dusty Springfield's "Son of a Preacher Man." A highlight is "Song of the Shrimp," one of the most reviled Elvis movie songs, which with a laconically inebriated voice Black turns into a surreal folk ballad on the order of "Froggy Went A-Courtin'." Before that comes "Go Find Your Saint," with a rough voice riding a melody so sweet the singer's dirty coat seems to shine, and before that, with Black's voice high and slipping, is the most defenseless version of "Dark End of the Street" ever made.

3 ▪ The Wallflowers, "God Says Nothing Back" from *Rebel, Sweetheart* (Interscope) Occasionally this single resurfaces on the radio out of the murk of last year, and everything around it feels cheap. With a stoic backbeat and Jakob Dylan's fatalistic way of biting off his words, this is the sound of someone thinking—about insignificance, in the pop world, in the real world.

4 ▪ Cindy Bullens, *Dream #29* (Let's Play/ Blue Lobster) In 1978, at 23, she made "High School History": If you pull out all the stops you can do stuff in high school they'll be talking about for years, but they stopped talking years ago. Now she's in her early fifties—and on an album about self-delusion, divorce, and pulling out all the stops, she concedes nothing.

5 ▪ IBM Commercial, "What Makes You Special?" You see armies of determined men and women in suits like armor, in crowded elevators, marching down corridors, every one of them mouthing the Kinks' absolutely ferocious 1966 "I'm Not Like Everybody Else"—and, my God, for an instant nobody is.

6 ▪ Yeah Yeah Yeahs, *Show Your Bones* (Interscope) All you read about them is how soon they'll be huge. The music is judged according to whether or not it will make that happen, and despite the fact that Karen O has a voice as human as it is urgent, she seems to judge herself on the same terms. Better than all that here: "Cheated Hearts"; the "Telstar" guitar solos in "Turn Into."

7 ▪ **Amazon.com, editorial reviews** "Who writes this stuff?" asks my friend Steve Weinstein, passing this on, typos and all: "Jewel is about to deliver her most personal and autobiographical record so far—*Goodbye Alice in Wonderland*. Not content to relegate herself to a traditional music areana, or to be typecase, Jewel has established herself as a culturally significant and relevant brand."

8 ▪ **Prince, *3121* (Universal)** His version of "The *Playboy* Philosophy," circa 1962.

9 ▪ **Derek McCulloch & Shepherd Hendrix, *Stagger Lee* (Image Comics)** On Christmas night 1895, in Bill Curtis's saloon in St. Louis, "Stag" Lee Shelton shot Billy Lyons; by the time Shelton died in prison in 1912, he was more legend than flesh. In this blazing graphic novel—part folklore, part love story, part thrilling *Law & Order* episode with a deadpan denouement— Shelton hears a guitarist in the next cell playing the "Stackalee" song: "That song about me." No, says the singer: "I think Stackalee from Memphis." There are endless subtleties here—taken from the historical record when it's there, invented with the lightest touch when it's not—and, somehow, no resolution at all. Not after more than a hundred years, thousands of singers, and likely thousands more to come.

10 ▪ **Devin McKinney a.k.a. Declan MacManus, Popwithashotgun.blogspot.com, March 21** Too perfect: "I had a vision after watching *The Sopranos* the other night that the last show would end with Tony dying in Carmela's arms, and that the last song of all would be 'Poor Side of Town,' by Johnny Rivers."

JULY 2006

1 ▪ **Kanye West, Coachella Valley Music and Arts Festival (April 29)** Solidifying his position as One of the Best People on the Planet, he switched from singer to DJ and announced he was going to play "one of my favorite songs": a-ha's "Take on Me," the most deliriously irresistible hit of 1985. Doing either the "Carlton dance" or the "Molly Fucking Ringwald," as uploads on youtube described his moves, West high-stepped across the stage while the crowd sang the song en masse, going up all the way—and it's a long way—for the impossible high notes that dissolve the chorus into air.

2 ▪ **KT Tunstall, "Other Side of the World," from *Eye to the Telescope* (Relentless/Virgin)** It's all about Tunstall's seemingly endless drift through the second word in "You're on the other side of the world to me." In that moment this woman from Scotland could be the great Bermudan-Canadian singer Heather Nova, and not in the world at all.

3 ▪ **Mandy Moore, *American Dreamz* (Universal)** Almost too good on her numbers in the hard-nosed *American Idol* parody where she'll do anything to win, but she'll live in film history for the way she delivers a single line: "I'm not physically attracted to other people, but . . ."

4 ▪ **Chris Walters** From a friend, a haiku for Gene Pitney, 1941–2006, who in the early '60s, with "Town Without Pity" and "(The Man Who Shot) Liberty Valance," caught the voice of the outsider too bitter to shake anyone's lying hand: "Can't cut my own throat / Before I tell this whole town / To go fuck itself."

5 ▪ **The Handsome Family, "All the Time in Airports," from *Last Days of Wonder* (Carrot Top)** From the surrealist Albuquerque folk duo, slow power chords behind the details that can make an airport the black hole of everyday life: late at night, "the cages pulled across the stores," and in the morning, "when they drive the waxer across the floor." It's dead air you don't want to breathe, but you can't help it.

6 ▪ **B. Molcooli and Band, "He Don't Love You," Berkeley Farmers Market (March 4)** A toddler walked up to the soul singer and an accompanist and held one hand to each of their guitars, letting the sound go right into his skin.

7 ■ **The King, directed by James Marsh, written by Milo Addica and Marsh (Think-Film)** One Elvis Valderez (Gael García Bernal, Che Guevara in *The Motorcycle Diaries*) gets out of the Navy and sets forth to remake the family of the father who left him a bastard, the father he's never met, now a middle-class fundamentalist preacher (William Hurt, so good you may not recognize him). The movie is a version of the demonic Elvis who emerged in the popular imagination after the real Elvis's death—demonic because, as a king, he holds absolute power over others' hearts—but pushed farther than ever before. With Pell James as Elvis's half sister, indelible when she realizes she's going to hell.

8 ■ **The Doors, *"Doors Ride Again—box set, movie, and Vegas show in the works for the band's 40th anniversary"* (Rolling Stone, May 4)** That's not all. When Jim Morrison died, Evan Serpick reports, organist Ray Manzarek and guitarist Robby Krieger wanted to go for commercials, but drummer John Densmore said no: "Onstage, when we played these songs, they felt mysterious and magic. That's not for rent." Now he's saying yes: "We might consider something technology-oriented, or some hybrid car or something, but it's gotta be right." And for the movie, they'll only do nudity if it's absolutely necessary to the script.

9 ■ **The Sopranos, "Live Free or Die," April 16 (HBO)** Vito, the only loyal man Tony has left, is exposed as a homosexual. He flees, planning to kill himself before anyone in the mob can do it for him. In a New Hampshire diner, the cook, seeing him for who he is, makes him feel at home as he never has in New Jersey; other gay men come in. In an antique store run by a gay man, Vito stares at a license plate: "Live Free or Die." Can he? Doesn't that promise apply to him, too? Coming up behind him, playing in full under the credits: X's desperate, depressed version of Dave Alvin's "4th of July," and the promise and heartbreak of American democracy goes right to your chest.

10 ■ **Sleater-Kinney, "Jumpers," Great American Music Hall, San Francisco (May 3)** Guitarists Carrie Brownstein and Corin Tucker pulled a thread that unraveled the music and tied it in a knot, but it was Janet Weiss who caught the drama. "She's got the best drummer's hair ever," said a friend.

AUGUST 2006

1 ■ **Jon Langford, "Lost in America," from *Gold Brick* (ROIR)** This summer Bruce Springsteen will be getting thousands on their feet with "John Henry," cheering the tale of a man who in the years after the Civil War died proving he could hammer through rock faster than a steam drill. In October, Oxford will publish Scott Reynolds Nelson's *Steel Drivin' Man*, where John Henry is real-life prisoner number 497 in Virginia's Richmond Penitentiary. But in Jon Langford's leaping "Lost in America," John Henry is the country itself. He's there when the last spike is driven into the Transcontinental Railroad, walks away from the fight with the drill, dies in the "Wreck of Old 97," turns up as a soldier at Abu Ghraib—and, just possibly, takes the September 11 planes back from their hijackers and breaks Columbus out of Guantánamo. It's as rousing as Springsteen's version, and absolutely heartbreaking, which for some reason the actual "John Henry" folk song never is.

2 ■ **The Lovekill, *These Moments Are Momentum* (Astro Magnetics)** Cleveland by way of Omaha, and more exciting than driving the 800 miles at 100 mph.

3 ■ **Gang of Four, "Natural's Not in It," from *Entertainment!* (EMI)** "The problem-uh, of-uh leisure," Jon King chanted uncertainly on the band's first album, in 1979; he made the notion sound like a black hole. Now the song will kick off Sofia Coppola's *Marie Antoinette*. "Andy and I thought it was a fantastic idea to use this song for the film, when we heard it was a new take on the costume drama," King says of himself and Gang of Four guitarist Andy Gill. "It seems to have shook up the audience

in Cannes. It could easily be French paro-
chialism about a Yank taking on this
iconic figure without due deference. It's the
only developed country where there'd be a
prosecution of a rapper for criticizing Napoleon and de Gaulle."

4 ▪ **Peter Carey, *Theft* (Knopf)** "We had
been born walled out from art, had never
guessed it might exist," says an Australian
painter in Carey's new novel, "and then we
saw what had been kept from us." The resentment is patent, but still it's a shock
when fragments of pop songs—art the man
wasn't born walled off from—explode in his
mouth as he rails against a 16th-century art
critic: "You went to the finest schools all
right but you are nothing more than a gossip and a suck-up to Cosimo de' Medici. I
was a butcher and I came in through the
bathroom window."

5 ▪ **Ronnie Dawson et al., *Rockin' Bones:
1950s Punk & Rockabilly* (Rhino)** Across 101
tracks from 1954 through 1964, the trash
(Dwight Pullen's "Sunglasses After Dark")
is so giddy it makes the masterpieces
(Elvis's "Baby Let's Play House") feel like
folk music.

6–9 ▪ **Irma Thomas, Dr. John, Elvis
Costello, Allen Toussaint, Bruce Springsteen**
In the work Thomas and Dr. John did last
fall for the collection *Our New Orleans*
(Nonesuch), you could almost hear Katrina
blow away decades of complacency. Now
they walk blankly through their paces on
the formally similar package *Sing Me Back
Home* (Burgundy), credited to the no-doubt
already disbanded New Orleans Social
Club. On Thomas's own *After the Rain*
(Rounder), the songs are classy, the arrangements contrived, and once past a tense,
every-breath-I-take remake of the Drifters'
1960 "I Count the Tears," the singing is
confused. Costello and Toussaint's *The
River in Reverse* (Verve Forecast)—recorded
last November and December in Los Angeles and New Orleans—is tedious. But in
Concord, California, on June 6, Springsteen's update of Blind Alfred Reed's 1929
complaint "How Can a Poor Man Stand
Such Times and Live" rang true even

through the self-congratulatory stomp of his
huge "Seeger Sessions" band. It was his
verse about George W. Bush's first visit to
New Orleans after the flood; "He took a
look around, gave a little pep talk, said 'I'm
with you,' then took a little walk," Springsteen sang.

10 ▪ **Jon Langford, *Nashville Radio* (Verse
Chorus Press)** Almost any one of these
photo-based paintings of old country singers would serve as a grimy, plastic-covered
image on a tombstone. But there's so
much hidden-in-plain-sight detail in the
pictures—mottos, slight facial distortions,
quotations—that by page 120 Hank Williams
as St. Sebastian (in a cowboy hat but otherwise naked from the waist up, from a photo
taken after an arrest) seems obvious. All
the graves are open.

OCTOBER 2006

1 ▪ **Weegee, "Heartbreak Pillow" c. 1945,
in *Unknown Weegee*, International Center of
Photography, New York City** The street photographer, here shooting a small bed in a
small room: a headboard, what looks like a
gilt bedspread, and a heart-shaped pillow
that might be covered in heavy fabric, big
enough for only one head. A decade before
the fact, it's the clearest glimpse ever of the
inside of Heartbreak Hotel.

2 ▪ **Peter Spiegelman, *Death's Little Help-
ers* (Vintage Crime)** A private eye is trying to
get information out of his client, who just
wants to bite his head off. The Ramones on
her stereo aren't helping. Then she puts on
Roxy Music, which stops the action the way
a sap on the back of the detective's head
would in a normal crime novel. "She sat at
the drafting table, stubbed out her cigarette,
and rubbed her eyes with the tips of her fingers. . . . I watched her and listened to the
music and we sat that way for what seemed
a long time." Four minutes, thirty seconds:
The song is "More Than This," never sounding more true than it does in the silence of
a page.

3 ▪ **The Blow, *Paper Television* (K)** You get
the feeling Khaela Maricich's voice can go

anywhere without her leaving her room in Olympia—even, as in "True Affection," 20,000 leagues under the sea. "You were out of my league," Maricich sings, bringing the old story back to dry land, maybe making you care more about how her story turns out than you ever did about Jules Verne's.

4 ▪ Pere Ubu, *Why I Hate Women* (Smog Veil) On the inside sleeve: "This is an irony-free recording." Which refers to . . . the album title? The songs (including "My Boyfriend's Back," which is not a cover of the 1963 hit by the Angels)? Or how to live?

5 ▪ Bill Fitzhugh, *Highway 61 Resurfaced* (William Morrow) A lost-tapes mystery—all blues mysteries are lost-tapes mysteries—but unlike the rest, this pays off with a climax so rich you want to hear the tapes as much as the people hunting them down.

6 ▪ The Pine Box Boys, *Arkansas Killing Time* (Trash Fish) Murder ballads one after the other, and, not halfway through, enough to make you queasy. Especially the indelible little number "The Beauty in Her Face," which goes as far into the mind of a killer as anyone needs to. You know how it's going to end before the first verse does, and you spend the rest of the song trying to make it come out differently.

7 ▪ Paul Muldoon, "Sillyhow Stride," *The Times Literary Supplement,* May 31 From the Pulitzer Prize–winning poet, guitarist for the Princeton band Rackett, and sometime song-writing partner with Warren Zevon ("My Ride's Here," from 2002, one year before Zevon's death at 56), a long elegy for the old California rounder. It starts off straitjacketed with song titles and lyric quotes; then the ground of the poem begins to slip, the room grows close, and more than anything you want a breath of fresh air. Which you get: "Every frame a freeze-frame/Of two alcoholics barreling down to Ensenada/In a little black Corvette, vroom vroom."

8 ▪ Michelle Polzine, Chosen Best Pastry Chef by *San Francisco* magazine The former guitarist in Special Agents of Her Majesty's Secret Cervix, now at Range, a gem in the Mission District: "If people like what you're

doing when you're playing punk, you're doing something wrong. As a pastry chef, I can please people and still retain my integrity."

9 ▪ "Marin Center Presents: Ian Anderson Plays Jethro Tull," Advertisement, *San Francisco Chronicle* "Ian Anderson, founding member of the legendary rock band Jethro Tull, has long been considered to be the foremost and to many, the only exponent of rock-style flute"—and God knows being the only is a sure way to being the foremost. Not to mention appearing as your own tribute band.

10 ▪ Hem, *Funnel Cloud* (Waveland) Chamber folk music from Brooklyn, but where the 2002 *Rabbit Songs* could get under your skin like a disease, here Sally Ellyson's singing is all but willfully pallid, and the music goes nowhere. Except in the instrumental "The Burnt-Over District"—named for the section of western New York that in the 1820s was so inflamed by revivalism that by the time Joseph Smith led his flock west there was hardly anyone left to save—which weaves the theme to *The Manchurian Candidate* into "Shenandoah" and goes all over the country, from then to now.

1 ▪ The Drones, *Gala Mill* (ATP/R) I was attracted to this solely because the title of the band's last album, *Wait Long by the River and the Bodies of Your Enemies Will Float By,* echoes two of my favorite band names: When People Were Shorter and Lived Near the Water and And You Will Know Us by the Trail of Dead. How could *Gala Mill* be anything but great? Sure, dull title, but according to the press release, this Australian four-piece, led by singer-guitarist Gareth Liddiard, recorded on "an isolated 10,000-acre farm" in Tasmania. Eat your heart out, Nick Cave.

None of that—and none of the band's earlier music—is any preparation for what happens here, from the first moment. "Jezebel" is a long, delirious song that seems to suck all the chaos and horror of the present moment into a single human being, who struggles to contain that world inside himself. Especially on the choruses, when a drone comes up, hovers, waits—and it's unnerving, waiting for the sound to break—you can't tell if the singer succeeds or not, or if it would be better if he succeeded or failed. Better for who? You are dragged into this song as if you were a prisoner. The performance is a shocker—and the album, casting off its echoes of Neil Young and Eleventh Dream Day, staking out its own territory in song after song, can hardly recover from it. Not until the final number, a nine-minute reenvisioning of a traditional Australian convicts' ballad—and after that, you really will know this band by their trail of dead.

2 ■ **Someone Still Loves You Boris Yeltsin, *Broom* (Polyvinyl)** Okay, but they don't do "Are You Lonesome Tonight?"—Boris's favorite song.

3 ■ ***Clerks II*, written and directed by Kevin Smith (The Weinstein Company)** Last line of the film: "Today is the first day of the rest of our lives." Immediately jettisoned by Soul Asylum's suicidal "Misery."

4 ■ **The Grates, *Gravity Won't Get You High* (Dew Process)** For "Inside Outside"— fast, desperate, cool, absolutely unafraid of how smart it is. "I might live to tell the tale," says singer Patience, "of how young girls once rode a whale."

5 ■ **Ellen Barkin, "It's nighttime in the big city . . ." *Theme Time Radio Hour With Bob Dylan* (XM Radio)** Every week, before Dylan as disc jockey begins spinning his discs and telling his tales, Barkin, the woman who so long ago in *Diner* couldn't put her husband's records back in the right order, now stands back and lowers the boom. After her opening line, what by now amounts to a poem in progress unfolds: "A woman walks barefoot, her high heels in a handbag . . . A man gets drunk, he shaves off his moustache . . . A cat knocks over a lamp . . . An off-duty cop parks in front of his ex-wife's house." Is he stalking her, or do they still sleep together?

6 ■ **Cat Power, *Live on KEXP* (eMusic exclusives)** Four numbers recorded on the air with only guitar and piano, and likely a more complete summation of who this woman is and what she does than can be found anywhere else. It's all so quiet you don't know whether to hold your breath or scream.

7 ■ **Robert Plant, *Nine Lives* (Rhino)** In 1982 the ex-Led Zeppelin dervish drifted in a sea all his own, a surfer on a wave that never reached shore. That was "Far Post," then a B-side, nearly impossible to find since. It's here. You can play it all day long.

8 ■ **Bob Dylan, *Modern Times* (Columbia)** Inside the sometimes slack rhythms and the deceptively easy lines, a deep longing. For a trail of dead.

9–10 ■ **Peter Stampfel: Karen Dalton, *It's So Hard to Tell Who's Going to Love You the Best* (Koch, 1997) and Holy Modal Rounders, *Alleged in Their Own Time* (Rounder, 1975)** On *Gala Mill*, the Drones cover "Are You Leaving for the Country," a song learned from a recording by the '60s Greenwich Village folk-scene jazz singer Karen Dalton. She had an acrid voice, and she lived an acrid life: caught like a purse-snatcher in Stampfel's song "Sally in the Alley." He uses the lyrics to "Sally" to end his notes to the reissue of Dalton's 1969 album; he recorded it on the Holy Modal Rounders' *Alleged in Their Own Time*, nearly 20 years before Dalton died. You'll forget the Drones' "Are You Leaving for the Country"; you may forget Dalton's (on her just-reissued 1971 album *In My Own Time*). You won't forget "Sally"—a nursery rhyme about a junkie.

FEBRUARY 2007

Special Four Item Edition (It was a Lousy Month)

1 ■ **Brian Morton, *Breakable You* (Harcourt)** Sometimes, as in his first novel, *The Dylanist*, Morton has perfect pitch—and especially writing about parties, where people have to think of something to say, a kind of discomfort that takes away one's

sense of the novelist having to think of things for them to say. This time it's a literary party in New York: "E. L. Doctorow, remote behind his air of suave imperturbability, was talking to Laurie Anderson, who was, as always, carefully disheveled, and Lou Reed, who had the pruny monkeyish face of somebody's grandfather, but who was imperishably hip—the hippest man in the room, in any room, by definition." What's so effective about the passage is how casually it distinguishes hip—or cool, the better word—from Doctorow's act. Cool is beneath the action, looking up; the air of smugness that surrounds every picture of Doctorow like smoke speaks for someone working much too hard to look as if he hasn't worked for years.

Reed demonstrated how it works not long ago, in an "in-conversation" night with the critic Anthony DeCurtis at the 92nd Street Y in New York City. On *Berlin*: "One of those career-ending moments" (though Reed later announced he'd be performing *Berlin* at St. Anna's Warehouse in Brooklyn, with a set by Julian Schnabel). On work: "When I can't write it's so impossible it's a joke, and I can't even imagine how it's done." He broke character only when asked about "the stature of rock 'n' roll in the culture today": "I just love a good rock band. Always have. . . . The first time I heard Out-Kast do 'Hey Ya' for the first 15 seconds I was saying 'Oh man, I could listen to this forever'—and then you kind of had to." And when a woman in the audience asked him a question in a mall-rat accent so heavy he had to ask her to repeat it twice.

2 ▪ **TV on the Radio,** *Return to Cookie Mountain* **(Interscope)** Before the election last November, the sense of dread loaded into this dark cloud—the way the group sounds as if it's been hiding out with Ralph Ellison's Invisible Man at least since the start of the second Bush presidency—was inescapable. Now the feeling—echoing Frankie Lymon's doo-wop cry, the punk gloom of Sisters of Mercy and Joy Division, the clatter on the streets of Jonathan Lethem's *The Fortress of Solitude*—is just

slightly less immediate. People are still running down one street, hiding in the corners of another, but you no longer have to feel as if that's the only possible way to live.

3 ▪ **Chris Smither, "Diplomacy," from** *Leave the Light On* **(Signature Sounds/Mighty Albert)** The same shift of real time onto music takes place with the old blues guitarist's song about the Iraq war—which it doesn't have to mention by name. The song is so what-the-fuck, so stuff-happens ("Slip-slidin' away," Smither sings, apropos of nothing, or everything) that if it sounded brazen last fall, when Smither was knocking it out for Scott Simon on NPR's *Weekend Edition* or at Joe's Pub in Manhattan, today it sounds as if a good part of the country is singing along: "Take it or leave it, it's the deal of the day," go the lines, the American sticking out his hand for the whole world to shake. "And if you leave it, you get it anyway." It's as if millions of people actually heard this song—and as if this verse has, now, an extra line: *Hey—what kind of deal is that?*

4 ▪ **Murray-Dodge Hall, Princeton University** I'm sitting in the courtyard of this small Gothic pile, reading Lester Bangs's 1971 rant "James Taylor Marked for Death" for a class I'm teaching, coming on his mini-generational history about the way counter-cultural messianism "sent us in grouchy packs to ugly festivals just to be *together* and dig ourselves and each other, as if all of this meant something greater than that we were kids who liked rock 'n' roll and came out to have a good time, as if our very styles and trappings and drugs and jargon could be in themselves political statements for any longer than about 15 stoned seconds, even a threat to the Mother Country!"—and there in front of me, courtesy of the class of 1969, commemorating its 25th reunion in 1994, is a large granite cylinder with a yin-yang symbol and, engraved in block letters, lyrics from Joni Mitchell's insufferable "Woodstock": "We are stardust, we are golden, and we've got to get ourselves back to the garden." All I could think was

how remarkable it was that they both ended up here, still arguing.

1 ■ **Pink Nasty, *Mold the Gold* (pinknasty .net)** A singer and guitarist from Wichita, Kansas, she doesn't even try to live up to her name. "We could go to Starbucks/And talk a lot of shit about people/We don't know, now/Who probably live in New York"—you get the feeling that the borders of the life described are Starbucks over here and *Seinfeld* reruns over there. Whether the songs are full of rhythmic stop signs (the gorgeous, almost doo-wop ballad "Hot Pink House") or move so fast you can't imagine them stopping for anything ("Dirty Soap"), there's a pugnacious, resentful depression all over the music, but it's a depression alive to itself: it might be one person's way of taking revenge on the world.

2 ■ **The Moaners, *Blackwing Yalobusha* (Yep Roc Records)** Speaking of depression— Melissa Swingle, who can play anything, and Laura King, who plays drums, sound as if they long ago disappeared into the black hole and came out completely unimpressed.

3 ■ ***Shut Up & Sing* (The Weinstein Company)** Barbara Kopple, co-director here with Cecilia Peck, is still best known for *Harlan County, U.S.A.*, her 1977 documentary about a miners' strike; this film, about the Dixie Chicks trying to come up with the nerve to spit in the hurricane of abuse that followed lead singer Natalie Maines's 2003 denunciation of George W. Bush, isn't altogether different. The women are millionaires, but a memory of destitution, or a sight of it somewhere in the future, is present in the bones of their faces. The passion and fear that drive a strike are present in "Not Ready to Make Nice," which, as it takes shape and then emerges as a finished thing—calm, resolute, and hard—is like a woman watching her own autopsy: whatever it said to you on the radio, the song here, with real-life death threats behind it, holds as much terror as defiance. "Now

that we've fucked ourselves anyway," Maines says at one point, "I think we have a responsibility to . . . continue to fuck ourselves."

4 ■ ***Law & Order: Criminal Intent* (USA)** You're the devil!" a man says to Kathryn Erbe's Detective Alexandra Eames, in the episode called "Cuba Libre," after she's tricked him into giving himself away. "You should see me in a blue dress," she says flatly—and given the resolute plainness of Erbe's character, the line would work almost as well if she said, "You should see me in a dress." But then it wouldn't have that Detroit snap, right back to Shorty Long's 1964 "Devil With the Blue Dress," and Detective Eames wouldn't get to walk off with the barest curve of a smile on her face.

5 ■ **Paula Frazer and Tarnation, *Now It's Time* (Birdman Records)** After years of silence the female Roy Orbison returns, shrouded in swamp gas as always—with the sense that what you're hearing isn't quite there; with her syncopated yet faraway melodies or a spectral wail deep in the sound, every hesitation in Frazer's voice says she isn't telling you a fraction of what she could.

6 ■ **Michael Tolkin, *The Return of the Player* (Grove Press)** The Hollywood insider panicking, keeping his head down, his mouth forming nothing but *yes*; he's learned "to give up his own taste . . . and to surrender to the audience. He consoled himself with the example of Eric Clapton, a brilliant musician who might have been as difficult for the masses as Bob Dylan, or Hendrix if he had lived, but Clapton pursued the middle way."

7 ■ **Pet Shop Boys, *Pop Art: The Hits* (Capitol Records/EMI)** A great career for Neil Tennant and Chris Lowe, and all of it might fit in Dusty Springfield's mouth as she breathes "Ah-ha-*ha*" in her guest spot on the 1987 "What Have I Done to Deserve This?" lifting the last syllable just slightly, perhaps the sexiest wave goodbye in all of pop music.

8 ■ **Jerry Lee Lewis, *Last Man Standing* (Artists First)** Because he's frozen solid.

9 ■ **Chris Estey, writer, and David Lasky, artist, "Critical Mass: A Story of the Clash," in** *Hotwire Comix and Capers* **(Fantagraphics Books)** Beginning and ending with Joe Strummer at 50, at his kitchen table on December 22, 2002, about to drop dead. Best panel: future Clash bassist Paul Simonon on the tube one day, two people reading newspapers crowding him on either side, his eyes catching the headlines "Police and Thieves Clash at Notting Hill" on his right, "European Clash in—" on his left. Estey and Lasky leave out the lightbulb going on over his head.

10 ■ **Randy Newman, "A Few Words in Defense of Our Country" (Nonesuch at iTunes)** Iraq as the end of America—and maybe a hidden track on the next Dixie Chicks album.

MAY 2007

1 ■ **Electrelane, *No Shouts, No Calls* (Too Pure)** Singer Verity Susman could hardly sound more English than her name—loose, flighty, constantly surprised, with an innocence that can re-create itself after every shock—despite a darkening shade. Since their debut in 2001 with *Rock It to the Moon*, this quartet has made music that seems to take place in the air—not flying, just barely off the ground. That lends a sense of abstraction to guitarist Mia Clarke's delirious search for the sublime through repetition, or the rhythms of bassist Ros Murray and drummer Emma Gaze. The lines they trace are straight, but all cut up, out of order, a hopscotch music where you never quite know where you are.

2 ■ **Jonathan Lethem, *You Don't Love Me Yet* (Doubleday)** His eighth novel, and his best since *Gun, With Occasional Music*, his first. The oddness there, with the lines between humans and animals a thing of the past, is still present in this apparently ordinary-life tale about a band (you get their whole story in one rehearsal, one gig, and one radio showcase)—present with a con artist who claims to be the guy who thinks up all those senseless-acts-of-beauty bumper-sticker/T-shirt/coffee-mug slogans. The premise is rich; what makes the book sing are Lethem's accounts of what happens when a crowd on the street hears a band inside a building, the way the whole of a song is present in four words of a four-line chorus, or when for a moment four musicians understand each other better than any one of them understands him- or herself: "Denise met the call, ticked the beat double-time. The sound was sprung, uncanny, preverbal, the bass and drum the rudiment of life itself, argument and taunt, and each turn of the figure a kiss-off until the cluster of notes began again. Who needed words? Who even needed guitars, those preening whiners?"

3 ■ **John C. Reilly, "My Son John," from** *Rogue's Gallery: Pirate Ballads, Sea Songs & Chanteys* **(Anti)** The highlight of a set featuring Nick Cave, Bryan Ferry, Gavin Friday, Lou Reed, Robin Holcomb, and dozens more, the Irish ballad (better known as "Mrs. McGrath," as on Bruce Springsteen's *The Seeger Sessions*) about a sailor who lost his legs to a cannonball takes on an unearthly cast when the not-the-star of *Boogie Nights* and *The Good Girl* barrels into the mystic: when he chants the chorus, *Timmy roo dun-dah, foddle riddle dah, whack for the riddle timmy roo dun-dah*, it feels like a thousand-year-old curse.

4 ■ **Paolo Nutini, "New Shoes" (Atlantic)** The whole world may soon be sick of this— every shoe company on earth had to be bidding on it the day after it was released— but for the moment it's as irresistible as irresistible gets.

5 ■ **Marnie Stern, *In Advance of the Broken Arm* (Kill Rock Stars)** Want to hear little girls screaming on a beach for 45 minutes? No? This might change your mind.

6 ■ **Peter Hartlaub, "Lies, lies, lies, they're going to get this geeky guy,"** *San Francisco Chronicle* **(March 2)** Much of the best current film criticism is in the "advisory" daily papers run at the end of the supposedly real reviews, as in this one for the PG-13 teen comedy *Full of It*: "This film contains sexual situations, profanity, mild violence, and

several references to the band Poison, which may lead to 'Every Rose Has Its Thorn' getting stuck in your head during the ride home."

7 ▪ Joe Boyd, *White Bicycles: Making Music in the 1960s* (Serpent's Tail) He was there, with the British avatars of today's fey freak-folk movement: with the Incredible String Band, Fairport Convention, Anne Briggs, Nick Drake, Vashti. What happened in those halcyon days? One thing after another.

8 ▪ Warren Zevon, *Stand in the Fire* (Rhino/Asylum) Loud in the Roxy in Los Angeles in 1981—with "Mohammed's Radio," a night that turns its back on the dawn; plus four performances not included when the album was originally released. They aren't as good as the ones that come before—but since there will be no more, they come across, one by one, from "Johnny Strikes Up the Band" to "Hasten Down the Wind," as heartbreakers.

9 ▪ Mary Weiss, "I Just Missed You," from *Dangerous Game* (Norton Records) A staircase, climbed to the top, and you can feel every step.

10 ▪ Howard Fishman, "I'm Not There (1956)," on *Howard Fishman Performs Bob Dylan & The Band's "Basement Tapes" Live at Joe's Pub* (Monkey Farm) Not an interpretation but, for as long as it plays, an irrefutable translation of a legendary song that seems beyond human ken, and not only because half of its words are missing and you can't quite be sure if the other half are there or not. Soon to be a major motion picture.

JUNE 2007

1 ▪ Michael Thomas, *Man Gone Down* (Black Cat) In this stupendously jittery novel, the narrator, with no idea how to make it to the end of the week when the bills come due, walks into a Brooklyn club on amateur night. Al Green is on the sound system, singing "Tired of Being Alone"— cut off to make room for Ed and Peter, a folk group, who before they can do their song about the day "we started bombing

Afghanistan," have to explain it—and the scene as Thomas lets it play is so perfect you can hardly bear to stay in the room. Even as your skin crawls over "It's a song about war, I guess. . . . But it's about the sadness of it all, which is something people don't really see," you can't wait to find out how much worse it will get.

2 ▪ The Avett Brothers, *Emotionalism* (Ramseur) Employing mainly guitar, banjo, and inferior recording equipment, two brothers from Greenville, North Carolina, listen for the Beatles. That opens the door to the house their songs make—a place where the doors stick and the floors aren't level. There's an odd, shifting light and folk-art knickknacks in the bedrooms, not to mention Buddy Holly 45s and a warped copy of the Band's second album in the attic.

3 ▪ The Polyphonic Spree, "Lithium," from *Wait* (Good) If you thought Kurt Cobain sounded psychotic on this, wait till you hear it sung over a tinkling piano by the president of your high school science club.

4 ▪ R. Crumb, *R. Crumb's Heroes of Blues, Jazz & Country* (Abrams) Why are the faces of the blues and country performers weathered, while every jazz man's is smooth?

5 ▪ Samuel L. Jackson, "Stack-O-Lee," *Music From the Motion Picture Black Snake Moan* (New West) This is the prison version. Jackson stamps out the words as if he learned them there.

6 ▪ The Death of a Party, *The Rise and Fall of Scarlet City* (Double Negative) Four people from Oakland, California, gulping, shouting, delirious, only occasionally pulling back to gain an inch of perspective, running right over a cliff ("She's too young to be sleeping with a married man, but you're too old to care"), and then scrambling back up to try it again. The songs are all mysteries, hard to penetrate, full of allure, demanding you solve them.

7 ▪ Jean Baudrillard (1929–2007) "The French critic and provocateur Jean Baudrillard, whose theories about consumer culture and the manufactured nature of reality

were intensely discussed both in rarefied philosophical circles and in blockbuster movies like *The Matrix*, died yesterday in Paris," Patricia Cohen wrote on March 7 in *The New York Times*. That same day a photo of an elderly Baudrillard reading on stage while accompanied by a very tall blonde got up as a queen from outer space popped up in my e-mail box. He was dressed in what appeared to be a gold lamé jacket. The Elvis costume came across as, yes, a critique of consumer culture, and also as an inadvertent admission that Baudrillard's intellectual glamour was that of a media player—one whose philosophy always fit snugly into the sound bites he deplored.

8 ▪ Rufus Thomas, "Stop Kicking My Dog Around," from *Can't Get Away from This Dog* (Stax) Thomas (1917–2001) claimed that Sam Cooke wrote this song for him, "backstage at a theater off Broadway that I was working with Sam, Jackie Wilson, and Lesley Gore," and as Thomas recorded it sometime in the mid-'60s, it did have that Sam Cooke glide. But the song goes back to the minstrel shows—and so did Rufus Thomas. Could it have been that Cooke, even if he was only 2 when he left Clarksdale, Mississippi, where he was born in 1931, remembered hearing Thomas sing the old piece as he passed through with the Rabbit Foot Minstrels, and that Thomas forgot?

9 ▪ Larry Kegan, Howard Rutman, Robert Zimmerman, "Let the Good Times Roll," "Boppin' the Blues," "I Want You to be My Girl," "Lawdy Miss Clawdy," "Confidential," and "Ready Teddy."

10 ▪ "Bob Dylan's American Journey, 1956–1966" (Frederick R. Weisman Art Museum, University of Minnesota) On Christmas Eve 1956, three boys, two 14 and one 15, pooled their quarters for the record machine at Terline Music in St. Paul, Minnesota. You put in a coin and got about 30 seconds, so with the 15-year-old pounding a piano they rushed to harmonize on whatever they could until the machine cut off, and then started up again with another tune. It sounds like a slumber party, and what's surprising is not that one of these kids turned into Bob Dylan, but that less than a year later he was—as pictured in a recently discovered photo featured in the Weisman show—singing the same songs in a band called the Golden Chords, commanding a stage with fervor and confidence, dressing pretty much as he dresses now: flash coat, dark pants, dark shirt, white tie.

The
Believer

2008·2014

SEPTEMBER 2008

1 ■ *Prime Suspect 7—The Final Act*, directed by Philip Martin, written by Frank Deasy (Acorn Media, 2006) You suspect the father of a missing schoolgirl until he puts his head inside her backpack as if he knows this is as close to her as he'll ever get again. "Did you ever hear that song, 'Smells Like Teen Spirit'?"

2 ■ Bonnie "Prince" Billy, *Lie Down in the Light* (Drag City) For years Will Oldham—traveling under variations of the name Palace, as himself, as a figment of his own imagination, no doubt under names I've missed—has written and sung from an Appalachian highlands that may as well be his own imagined country. But in his music Oldham gets to live there, and there he does what he wants; even as you might swoon at their delicacy, the songs give off the smell of perversity. Here he sings as the sole member of his own religion—and you can't tell if the faith has all but died out or if the prophet has yet to find his first follower. He can call up a company of selves at will, to watch, to witness, then make them disappear before the revelation comes: "Kneel down to please me," he says, as caught between sex and adoration as Madonna in "Like a Prayer," but his voice tells you he's the supplicant. From song to song the feeling is more abstract, harder to hold on to, beauty flashing like an animal in the forest you can't be sure you saw at all, just as in the moment you're convinced this person will never make a record this good again.

3 ■ Howard Hampton writes (June 11, 2008) "I stumbled on Dylan's endorsement of Obama (*London Times*, June 5: 'Right now America is in a state of upheaval. Poverty is demoralizing. You can't expect people to have the virtue of purity when they are poor. But we've got this guy out there right now who is redefining the nature of politics from the ground up—Barack Obama. . . . Am I hopeful? Yes, I'm hopeful that things might change. Some things are going to have to'). Makes sense that there would be that spark of

recognition—the thing that amazes me is that the Clintons never seemed to get that they were dealing with someone more formidable than a Howard Dean in blackface. So they wound up looking like Baez and Seeger, the Old Regime, undone by the sound of a greater sense of possibility than they were willing to entertain—hence the whole 'Electability' issue would frame the election as 'No We Can't' (elect a black man) vs. 'Yes We Can' (dream a better country, as MLK or poor tortured RFK did once upon a time)."

4 ■ Shannon McArdle, *Summer of the Whore* (Bar/None) Late of the Mendoza Line, for the title song McArdle summons a slow shame ballad, full of portent and dread, a pop form that goes back to the early '60s ("Suspicion," "Endless Sleep") and has never worn out, maybe because so few have had the nerve to try it. It's a self-lacerating heartbreaker ("A little filth for my record," the singer snaps over a dead marriage)—with the reverb on the guitar making each note a warning, the voice seems to grow thinner and stronger at the same time.

5 ■ Counting Crows, *Saturday Nights & Sunday Mornings* (DGC) Why is it so uncool to like Counting Crows? Because Adam Duritz has made so much money that he can wear his heart like a coat instead of merely sticking it on his sleeve? "1492," the first thing you hear, is Jon Langford's "Lost in America" with Columbus standing in for John Henry, relentless, ridiculous, embarrassed, defiant, and despite hilariously pretentious song titles as the album winds on ("When I Dream of Michelangelo," "On a Tuesday in Amsterdam Long Ago"), its echo never really dies out.

6 ■ Hoagie's Restaurant, Hopkins, Minnesota A family place filled with placards and metal ads, some original (Uncle Remus Syrup: "Dis sho' am good," says an old black man), some reproductions, and one bizarre anachronism: a go-getter dressed in '50s suit and tie and a sly grin holding up an LP under a banner: EDUCATION: THE NEXT BEST THING TO A RECORD DEAL.

7 ▪ **Robert Plant and Alison Krauss,** *Raising Sand* **(Rounder, 2007)** The old rocker and the bluegrass queen: very nice people. Very polite. To each other, to the songs, and to you. But all the singing is whispering and it was the dullest album of the year.

Onstage, though, fervor comes out— especially for Led Zeppelin songs that go back to the woods. On YouTube videos from this year's New Orleans Jazz and Heritage Festival, the Druids in "Battle of Evermore" take to the skies: two final minutes of furious mandolin slashing and Plant's snaggletoothed hair bucking ("Bring it back! Bring it back!" My God, are you sure? Bring what dragon back?) as if the notes have him on a trip wire. For "When the Levee Breaks," with Plant quieting Krauss's keening fiddle to let lines from Bob Dylan's "Girl from the North Country" float through to be lost in the flood, the song sweeps up Memphis Minnie and Kansas Joe McCoy, who recorded it in 1929, and walks their ghosts across the stage.

8 ▪ **Carolyn Jessop with Laura Palmer,** *Escape* **(Broadway Books, 2007)** "I was born into a radical polygamist cult. At eighteen, I became the fourth wife of a fifty-year-old man. I had eight children in fifteen years. When our leader began to preach the apocalypse, I knew I had to get them out." In case you were wondering what she's been doing since *Twin Peaks*.

9 ▪ **Randy Newman, "A Few Words in Defense of Our Country," from** *Harps and Angels* **(Nonesuch)** It's been clear for some time that the theft of the 2000 election laid the foundation for the Bush administration as such: if they could get away with that— with the Supreme Court having discredited itself to get Bush into the White House, the last check was gone—they could get away with anything. And, says Newman's unmade bed of a song, the bed of someone who hasn't gotten out of it for days, they did.

The number was first floated on iTunes in 2006, then adapted as an op-ed piece for the *New York Times*; now, to shards of the tune to "Columbia, Gem of the Ocean," Newman runs through the worst leaders in history, from Stalin and Hitler back to King Leopold of Belgium and Torquemada, trying to convince himself they were worse than our own, but who cares if they weren't? In a verse the *Times* left out, he thinks about the curse of history: "You know it pisses me off a little / That this Supreme Court is gonna outlive me." "Get over it," Justice Antonin Scalia said in April of *Bush v. Gore*. "It's so old by now." He'll get the last word, but to sing even a clumsy song in the face of that knowledge is not nothing.

10 ▪ **What I really want to do is be Edmund Wilson, or "Interview with the Doors,"** *Mojo Navigator* **#14, August 1967, collected in** *Bomp! Saving the World One Record at a Time*, **edited by Suzy Shaw and Mick Farren (Ammo)**

JIM MORRISON: "Interviews are good, but . . ."

MOJO: "Oh, they're a drag."

JM: "Critical essays are really where it's at."

OCTOBER 2008

1 ▪ **I'm Not Jim,** *You Are All My People* **(Bloodshot)** A songwriting collaboration between the novelist Jonathan Lethem and Walter Salas-Humara, singer-guitarist for the Gainesville, Florida, band the Silos— and from the first track you're somewhere utterly familiar where nothing quite fits. "Mr. October" is the title, but you might have to listen a long time before you catch Reggie Jackson flashing across the TV screen in the bar, just as the singer (Salas-Humara, as on every number) is having trouble putting the bits of memory the tune assembles together. Hangover music—*Did that really happen?*—but the first reason you might miss Mr. October is that the melody, running down descending lines on the guitar, breaking up as the lyrics aim for the last line of a verse, is almost too sweet to bear. It carries regret for the fact that neither you nor the singer can come away from this song with any certainty. Did the singer ever see any of the people he's singing about again?

The half-light of "Mr. October" is filtered through everything that follows: the noir one-liners in "Missing Persons" ("a bum tries to sell you his hat"), catchy bubble gum ("Amanda Morning"), a depressed ballad that would have fit in Lethem's *Men and Cartoons* if baseball cards count as cartoons ("The Pitchers Gave Up"), and, maybe with more sticking power than anything else, three shaggy dog stories, spoken-word pieces that could have come off of a 1950s Beat comedy LP by Ken Nordine, one of which actually features a dog. A man with a talking dog walks into a bar, where the old routine immediately shatters. The guy telling the story keeps a level head, but he can't keep the story straight. The bartender's comebacks don't fit the lines he's handed. It's a *Twilight Zone* episode that can't find its way out of the first act. "I've been in every bar in every joke in this country," the guy says, as if he deserves to know how all this comes out as much as you do.

2 ■ Robert Altman, *Santana, Altamont Speedway, Livermore, CA, December 1969,* in *The Sixties* (Santa Monica Press) Everyone knows Carlos Santana's the-pain-of-the-universe-is-in-my-fingers grimace, and this is one of the best shots ever made of the guitar god hitting that note. Except that he's playing maracas, which kind of takes the edge off.

3 ■ Miranda Lambert, "Famous in a Small Town," from *Crazy Ex-Girlfriend* (Sony) From last year, not the hit, still floating around the country stations, an expert number about truth, lies, and gossip: "Everybody dies famous in a small town," and, even in your grave, you'll never hear the end of it. "We heard he was caught red-handed with her mama," Lambert sings querulously. "So that's just what they let us all believe." You mean that with-her-mother story was a cover-up? For *what*?

4 ■ Rolling Stones, "Gimme Shelter," in "The Dark Defender," on *Dexter,* season two (Showtime) Dexter walks into a bar . . . to find the bartender who killed his mother with a chain saw thirty-four years before, in front of him, when he was three. Slow motion, tilted image, with a red filter, and as Michael C. Hall opens the door, the song comes up on the jukebox; at the end of the long lead-in, when the last guitar note breaks over the rest of the music, he sits down at the bar. The music moves on. The suspense that is generated is the suspense the piece has gathered to itself over all these years, never sounding like the past, still sounding like the future.

5 ■ James Lee Burke, *The Tin Roof Blowdown* (Simon & Schuster) The ten-minute egg: Detective Dave Robicheaux and his boss, Sheriff Helen Soileau, approach Detective Lamar Fuselier at a crime scene, a hut holding the rotting bodies of two men shot to pieces. ("Their viscera was exposed, their facial features hardly recognizable. Their brain matter was splattered all over one wall. Both men wore sports coats, silk shirts, and expensive Italian shoes with tassels on them.") Fuselier throws tough-guy repartee at Robicheaux, who once saw him cheating on a police exam. "'Mind if we take a look?' Helen said. 'Be my guest,' he said, finally taking notice of her. His eyes traveled up and down her person. 'We got barf bags in the cruiser if you need one.' 'Give it to your wife,' she said."

6 ■ Bob Dylan, "32–20 Blues" from *Tell Tale Signs: The Bootleg Series No. 8* (Sony) Robert Johnson recorded it in 1936, Bob Dylan in 1993 for his *World Gone Wrong*, lines from it traveled the South through the first decades of the twentieth century before turning up in 1956 in the Crickets' "Midnight Shift"—and here, on a three-CD set made up mostly of footnotes to official releases from the last twenty years, it breaks the pace. The dominant tone of the thirty-nine performances is reflective; this is a search for a groove. The syncopation Dylan finds on acoustic guitar at first lags behind his singing; before he's a third through, the fluttery beat has made room for the voice to slide right off the lines, until you can follow the last words of verses ("none"—"nuhhhhnnnn"—"come," "right," and a "hell" so faint it might not be that at all) as if they're rabbits running through the brush.

7 ▪ **Dario Robleto, Military issued blanket infested with hand-ground vinyl record dust from Neil Young's "Cortez the Killer" and Soft Cell's "Tainted Love," in "Neo-Hoodoo: Art for a Forgotten Faith" (Menil Collection, Houston, June–September; P.S.1, New York, October 19–January 26, 2009)** Beige-cream, with light red stripes, thin on the sides, thicker in the middle: a true army blanket from the mid-1880s. Yes, it calls up soldiers passing out blankets infested with smallpox during the Indian wars after the Civil War—if it's not the thing itself—but it's also a swirl of confusion. "I understand 'Cortez the Killer,'" I said to Robleto in Houston, "but why 'Tainted Love'? Because the blankets were tainted?" From his response it didn't seem as if that notion had even occurred to him. "Soft Cell, *soft sell*," he said—hey, says the Army, we just want to warm up our Indian brothers and sisters on those chilly Plains nights. "But also because of all that '80s synth-pop," Robleto said. "It was like another British invasion"—more like the one in the seventeenth century than the one in the twentieth. Or, as Memphis bandleader Jim Dickinson once put it, turning the story inside out, "Giving synthesizers to the British was like giving whiskey to the Indians. Their culture never recovered."

8–10 ▪ Anton Corbijn's film about Joy Division really should have been titled after the band's "Atmosphere"; in *Control* (Genius DVD), from the emergence of the post–Sex Pistols band to the suicide of singer Ian Curtis in 1980, the dark skies and darker streets of Manchester overshadow any story. Even rooms have clouds in them. The second half of the film is predictable, tiresome, like real life, or the biopic version of a real life, but the first hour is like a storm, like a perfect punk show: when the band takes the stage for the first time, when they finished "Transmission"—the actors playing and singing—I realized that half a minute had gone by and I hadn't taken a breath. What Sam Riley as Curtis does with the song ("No language, just sound")—what he does with his face even more than his voice—and what Corbijn

does with his camera are as shocking as anything I've seen on a screen. On *The Factory, Manchester, Live 13 July 1979*, included as a second disc with the recent reissue of Joy Division's first album, the 1979 *Unknown Pleasures* (Factory), Curtis sounds as if he were twenty feet tall; Bela Lugosi, passed on by Bryan Ferry, is coming out of his mouth. The performance of "Transmission," the last number, is what was channeled for *Control*, and it's a frenzy, itself seemingly channeling Sarah Bernhardt in one of her tear-my-heart-from-my-own-breast speeches—until, near the end, Curtis lets loose. It's impossible to say what he lets loose with: nothing so commonplace as a scream or a shout, nothing so earthly as a cry of rage or anguish or frustration. It was nothing the band could summon at will. With *University of London Live 8 February 1980*, on the reissue of the 1980 *Closer* (Factory), the music is already freezing, trapped in contrived arrangements meant to frame Curtis's increasingly jittery song structures; the band has become its own prison. People don't kill themselves for reasons; they kill themselves to end the story.

With thanks to Chris Walters

1 ▪ *The Gits,* **directed by Kerri O'Kane (Liberation Entertainment)** They were Mia Zapata, vocals; Matt Dresdner, bass; Andrew Kessler, a.k.a. Joe Spleen, guitar; and Steve Moriarty, drums. They formed at Antioch in 1986 and moved to Seattle in 1989, in time to catch the second wave of Northwest punk. The first half of this long-after-the-fact documentary is the band coming together, finding its music, and the pace is frustrating. You get only tiny snatches of songs, onstage, on the sound track, and what little is there is so alluring, so full of the spirit of someone driving herself through a storm of her own making, so delicious ("Another Shot of Whiskey," "Here's to Your Fuck"—they took Dennis Hopper's rants in *Blue Velvet* and

made a language out of them) that you can barely stand it when the film moves back to exposition, interviews, scene-setting. Inside the band's velocity, the sound has grandeur; as Moriarty pounds shirtless and Dresdner and Kessler leave the action to Zapata, she is shockingly alive onstage, breathing the band's tremendous, unpredictable rhythms like air. But as the band members tell you how they began to come into their own, you are there, and, bit by bit, whole songs begin to assemble themselves, in complete performances, in cutups of many performances, in costumes (street clothes, Medieval court jesters), in haircuts: "While You're Twisting, I'm Still Breathing," "Bob (Cousin O.)," "Second Skin." It's a great thrill to watch a whole creation take place in full before you, a song as a life lived. I've never seen the special quality of liberation punk offered people brave enough to take the stage and hold it put across so powerfully onscreen—and as the band members talk years later, they don't hide the sense of privilege they still retain, the privilege of, once, making their own drama.

Zapata was raped and strangled to death sometime after 2 a.m. on July 7, 1993, on a deserted Seattle street. The second half of the movie is a funeral and a cold-case police procedural, the long story of a small community shattered, paranoia replacing comradeship and rivalry: *It could have been any of us*, a fear that cuts both ways. Selene Vigil of 7 Year Bitch is a quiet, bitter, dignified presence: "She was missing in action." The case gets nowhere; Joan Jett fronts the three men to sing Gits songs and raise money to hire a detective: they "found out a lot of dirty about a lot of people"—about people they knew, that is—but no leads. You see the tombstone:

MIA KATHERINE ZAPATA
AUG. 25, 1965–JULY 7, 1993
CHERISHED DAUGHTER-SISTER-ARTIST-
FRIEND-GIT

Ten years later, a DNA match pulls up a felon in Florida. He's returned to Seattle to stand trial: a huge thug with death all over his face. Vigil: "This is the last person that she saw. She was looking into this guy's eyes." O'Kane trusts her story; she never embellishes, never tells you something you've already heard. She's not afraid of her story, either; there's not an unearned look on any face she found.

2 ▪ **Lucinda Williams, *Little Honey* (Lost Highway)** The very first track ends with a flourish so drawn-out and self-congratulatory she might as well have dubbed in applause over the last note.

3 ▪ **Hanif Kureishi, *Something to Tell You* (Scribner)** In London, a middle-aged psychoanalyst tied in knots tries to untie himself. "I guess I'd been something of a snob before, wondering whether it was healthy to be so moved by Roy Orbison and Dusty Springfield."

4 ▪ **All Girl Summer Fun Band, *Looking into It* (AGSFB Music)** Not as funny as the Portland combo's 2002 debut, with "Car Trouble" and "Cell Phone," but on top of a beat that snaps like a pencil there are gorgeous harmonies floating over no-nonsense lead vocals relating how nothing works out the way you thought it would. The day Jen Sbragia, Kim Baxter, and Kathy Foster describe is all-American: getting in the car, driving all over town running errands, looking at the signs, wondering if the person who just passed you on the left is someone you went out with two years after high school, the radio on, imagining it's you.

5 ▪ **Fucked Up, *The Chemistry of Common Life* (Matador)** It's glorious, the lyricism buried beneath the crumbling mountains of sound the Toronto hardcore band makes here: a wall of noise that's not so hard the complexity of the singing—its doubt—can't break through. Mostly that's Pink Eyes, a.k.a. Father Damian, real name Damian Abraham, who growls, roars, rends his garments. But it's the backing vocals of lighter voices that give the vision of social collapse and moral panic a kind of serenity. Repeating one phrase over and over in breaks between Abraham's rages in "Black

Albino Bones," Dallas Green appears as a second mind, saying what Abraham won't, what he can't, what might make him seem weak, afraid, though Green never sounds remotely weak or afraid. One song later, in "Royal Swan," instead of trading pieces of time, Katie Stelmanis-Cali floats like a queen in a costume epic behind Abraham's increasingly harsh chorus, until finally they're walking through the ruins shoulder to shoulder. It may not match the eighteen-minute single "Year of the Pig," where Caitlin Starowicz, Katherine Pill, Visnja Jovanovic, Lauren Moses-Brettler, and Alison Griggs stroll through the forest of the music like a whole tribe of Little Red Riding Hoods to Abraham's Big Bad Wolf—by the end, with the band fighting off its own feedback, you realize they've been in cahoots all along—but it's not certain anything this group can do would, or should.

6 ■ **U.S. Army, "Army Celebrates 60 Years of Integration" (television commercial)** The spot was all over the airwaves in July, marking the day in 1948 when, as a front-page featured in the spot showed, PRESIDENT TRUMAN WIPES OUT SEGREGATION IN ARMED FORCES. "Celebrating sixty years of a unified armed forces," says a voice that might be Dennis Haysbert's, over a montage of soldiers then and now: "A diverse army is a strong army." We know the word *integration* has disappeared from the language, but this makes it seem as if (first clause) we used to have two armies (which of course we did, during and after the Civil War) and that (second clause) it's good to have people from different backgrounds in the army. What's interesting is that the very fact of the message implies that this is still an open question.

7 ■ **Pipettes, "Pull Shapes," from *We Are the Pipettes* (Cherrytree, 2007)** Whenever this comes on—I heard it on *The L Word*—it'll be a surprise. Smiles as good as the one that breaks all over the chorus always are.

8 ■ **Ruth Gerson, *Deceived* (ruthgerson .com)** Death ballads, those first sung by people who've been dead for more than a century ("Butcher's Boy," "Banks of the Ohio," "Delia's Gone") and some first sung by those still living (Bobbie Gentry's "Ode to Billie Joe," Dolly Parton's "Down from Dover"), getting under the skin every time.

9 ■ **Vladimir Feltsman, conductor and piano, Shostakovich's *Piano Concerto No. 1 in C minor, op. 35,* 1933 (Aspen Music Festival, August 7)** In-your-face, thumb-up-your-nose drive, crazy-quilt rhythms, cool breezes blowing through spare piano notes followed by clashing and banging and a runaway train to nowhere. It was futurism both as ethos and musical practice—a movement that had a huge impact on the Russian avant-garde in the 1910s and '20s, and that in the early '30s was still traveling under the Stalinist radar. As a conductor, Feltsman was unpretentious, very physical, but in the sense of someone at home in his own skin, never drawing attention to himself, no violent maestro's head shakes or arm wrestling with invisible demons. He gestured like a man having a conversation with the musicians—the Sinfonia, the student orchestra—just someone trying to make a point.

10 ■ ***Rock 'n' Roll Camp for Girls,* edited by Marisa Anderson (Chronicle Books)** It's a week in Portland when girls from eight to eighteen form bands with strangers, write songs, learn to play, and make themselves heard—or, in other words, stand up in the public square, not alone, and speak to the crowd: "Bold," Carrie Brownstein of Sleater-Kinney writes in a foreword, "is learning how to play the drums on Monday and performing in front of five hundred people on Saturday." A lot of this wonderfully illustrated book (shadowy photos and bright cartoons) is friendly, point-by-point how-to, but there's also Sarah Dougher's history lesson "Real Girls Rock," Jodi Darby's "Self-Defense," in which Mia Zapata is a presence in her absence ("No matter how spirited and strong we might be, we are all potential victims of violent crimes"), and, perhaps most indelibly, "How I Got Out of My Bedroom (in eleven lessons)" by Mirah Yom Tov Zeitlyn, who records as Mirah. (Seek out Mirah with the Black Cat Or-

chestra, *To All We Stretch the Open Arm* [yoyo], recorded "in Larry Barrett's basement in Seattle, WA, in January 2003, as the world braced itself for another war.") "In 1993, I was a student at Evergreen State College in Olympia, Washington," Zeitlyn writes. "I remember going to a Bikini Kill show downtown, standing outside the Capitol Theatre and looking through the open door at all the girls inside and then deciding to just walk home. It should have been a very inclusive situation. I was a girl, I believed in the power of like-minded people gathering together, I was starting to make music, too. But I went home instead of joining in. I didn't feel cool enough to stay." Or, as the late novelist Alexander Trocchi once put it, "We have to attack 'the enemy' at his base, within ourselves."

JANUARY 2009

1 ▪ **Fiery Furnaces,** *Remember* **(Thrill Jockey)** Present-day New Yorkers by way of Oak Park, Illinois, Eleanor Friedberger, who does almost all of the singing, and brother Matthew Friedberger, the guitarist-organist-pianist who writes most of the songs and composes the train-wreck arrangements, plus whoever is playing bass and drums with them at any given time, are the most unpredictable band in the country. Or rather their songs are the most unpredictable. They start in one place and moments later they're looking back at themselves from the other side of the street without giving you a hint of which side you're on. This is a double live album, and their best—or, anyway, the album that takes their music further than any before it: *Gallowsbird's Bark, Blueberry Boat, Bitter Tea*, the notorious *Rehearsing My Choir*, about the Friedbergers' grandmother. The song structures might be jazz, in the same way that Steely Dan made rock and roll out of jazz, except that Steely Dan songs actually have structures, and Fiery Furnace songs often seem to have trapdoors and banana peels; the themes ("Single Again") might come from the Carter Family.

The package carries an unusual warning: "Please do not attempt to listen to all at once." No kidding: after only the first disc—twenty-four cuts, with twenty-five on the second—I was exhilarated, spinning, and would have played it again immediately if I hadn't been completely exhausted. I have no idea how the band keeps up with itself. There's Hendrix all over the guitar, but calliope in the organ. Sometimes the vocals drop so far back they seem to be off-stage. Arrangements are too complicated to be made up on the spot, but you can hardly credit people patient enough to craft them before the fact. Eleanor Friedberger's style is conversational but frantic, racing through domestic horror stories and Hong Kong crime films, the music pulling her like a marionette, an arm flailing here, a leg buckling there, her head whipping around in circles. She's exasperated, she's got to get it out, she has to tell you the story, but the phone is ringing and she has to take this call but there's another call coming in OMG someone just cut her off and oh, right, where were we? "And then they drove me to an Albertsons outside of Boise," she relates in the hubbub of "Oh Sweet Woods," deliberately, to make sure you can follow this, "and took me into a back room. And they said they wanted to balance my checkbook," a sexual reference you might not have heard before, but the innuendo is unmistakable, *Hey, baby, how'd you like me to balance your checkbook?* except that doesn't seem to be it at all, "and they said they wanted to organize my receipts," which doesn't exactly have the same ring to it, "and itemize my expenses and that I had the key to a safety deposit box with treasury bonds and the key to another safety deposit box where I'd stashed away the only pewter pocket watch that ever belonged to Joseph Smith's great-great uncle's brother-in-law—and I said, You've got the *wrong* Eleanor Friedberger."

"Half the record is from actual shows and half is the hourlong set from our *Bitter Tea* tour recorded totally live in my apartment," Eleanor wrote when I asked how the album was made. "As Matt says, it's a live album about live albums." "Did you have people over to make an audience?" I asked. "There wasn't enough room to have people over!"

2 ▪ **Doors, *Live at the Matrix* (Rhino)** It's March 1967 and you've wandered into this supposed folk club on Fillmore in the Marina in San Francisco and there's a four-piece band onstage with a tall lead singer who flops all over the place. They have an album out, *The Doors*, and maybe you've heard a few tracks on KMPX, the FM station that's still alternating music you never imagined hearing on the radio with shows in Chinese and Tagalog. Now they're six or seven minutes into, not exactly anything that fits the word *song*, but some Freudian psychodrama that somehow never loses its musical moorings, and—and, listening to this double CD, as opposed to the countless Doors live albums dumped on the market over the last few years (Philadelphia! Boston! Even *Boot Yer Butt!*, the cavernous, almost mystically fuzzy set of bootleg recordings compiled by Rhino in 2003), you can feel yourself as you might have been then, born or not, looking at the stage, at the few people at the tables in the room, trying to take in even a fraction of the sound, and wondering, *What the hell is going on?*

3 ▪ *Frozen River,* **Shattuck Theatre, Berkeley (March 6, 2008)** An oddly noisy audience for an art film about a destitute woman in upstate New York who turns to smuggling illegal immigrants over the border: a man boos the preview for *A Girl Cut in Two*, presumably to let everybody else know he disapproves of girls being cut in two. What's shocking is the way people snigger at the heroine's poverty when the cheap cord she tries to use to tow a car snaps, or when there's nothing in the house—her trailer—for her kids to eat but popcorn and Tang.

4 ▪ **KT Tunstall, "Little Favours" (Virgin, 2007)** Tunstall hits high notes by letting her voice break; as it does, you hear someone questioning herself, her motives, what she wants. The spectral presence that hovers somewhere in the sound—part Sarah McLachlan, part Dion, a presence made of will and doubt—has been generated by the radio itself. When it comes on, it seems to have drifted in from another country, another time, more likely the future than the past, as in the day after tomorrow.

5 ▪ **Brenda Lee, "Break It to Me Gently," on *Mad Men*, "The Gold Violin" (Season 2, Episode 11, AMC)** Closeout music after the episode ends with January Jones throwing up in the car on her way home from the party where she finds out her husband is sleeping with the comedian's wife. It's 1962, when the song would have been on the radio, but it never sounded so threatening when it was.

6 ▪ **Shawn Colvin, "Viva Las Vegas," on *Till the Night Is Gone: A Tribute to Doc Pomus* (Forward, 1995)** If you make a movie where nobody is anything but stupid, does that make you smart? Feeling unclean after the Coen Brothers' *Burn After Reading*, *The Big Lebowski* was like discovering an enclave of democratic spirit in, say, the Department of the Interior: Jeff Bridges thinks he deserves respect, so he treats everybody else with respect. But this slow, twilight version of the old Elvis song, running under the closing credits, picking up a motif carried in the film itself in predictable fashion by T-Bone Burnett and Carter Burwell, contains a landscape that the L.A. of the picture never touches: a whole city of dead ends.

7 ▪ *Classic Blues Artwork from the 1920s—2009 Calendar* **(Blues Images)** Ads made for the Negro press by the old Paramount label—Kokomo Arnold's 1934 "Milk Cow Blues" gets a light boost as "The Greatest Record Ever Made"—and taking off into the ether with a tableau for Blind Lemon Jefferson's 1928 "Worried Blues." In a room with cracking plaster and a potbellied stove, a man in a suit, suspenders, and glasses is asleep on a bed; even passed out, he looks like a lawyer. A barefoot woman in a shift sits up straight and eager, smiling at the door, where a well-dressed man carrying a box labeled SHOES stands grinning—and you get the feeling what she really wants from her outside man is . . . shoes.

8 ▪ **Scott Simon, "Ole Miss: Presidential Debate Host, Cultural Treasure," on *Weekend Edition* (NPR, September 27, 2008)** The day after the first McCain–Obama debate, reflections on how Oxford, Mississippi, has changed from the time when James Meredith arrived on campus in 1962 as the first black student in the University of Mississippi's history: the student body rioted, members of the mob killed two people, and every student stood up and walked out when Meredith entered his first class. "I'm glad that in these times it may be hard for us to imagine the *courage* of James Meredith," Simon said, in his typically flat, soothing way, which is usually a setup for something blunt: "He walked across campus, went to class, and put his head down to sleep in a place where he *knew* that there were people nearby who wanted to kill him." Forty-six years later, there's a statue of Meredith on campus and Oxford is a sophisticated town with "visible integration"; it was only two years ago that the old-time music band Crooked Still, which can dive very deeply, felt a need to redo Bob Dylan's 1963 "Oxford Town," but they're from Boston. "For years," Simon said, "Mississippi was considered a state that was only *barely* a part of the country"; now it "played a role in electing the next president." Simon paid tribute to the sacrifices of those who had lived and died to make it so, and then cued Robert Johnson's 1936 "Cross Road Blues." In Johnson's Mississippi, to be caught on the road after dark could mean death for a black man; Simon's implication was that Mississippi had crossed over. Johnson's recordings have been remastered so the sound is full and complete, but this began tinnily, from a distance. Then Johnson hit a loud, quivering note on his guitar and you were in a barn, the note was a shot, and the story wasn't about James Meredith at all, it was about Emmett Till.

9 ▪ ***The Exiles*, directed by Kent McKenzie (Milestone) and Revels, *Intoxica!* (Sundazed)** Last year saw the first-time commercial release of this 1961 film about American Indians wandering through life in the Chavez Ravine sector of Los Angeles—a Los Angeles that was wiped away for Dodger Stadium. As people gather in apartments, go out to bars, pile into cars, there's a constant, real-time sound track by the Revels of San Luis Obispo ("Six Pak" and "Church Key" were California hits in 1960): wherever there's a jukebox or a radio in the movie, the Revels are on it, a pseudo–surf band distinguished by the unrelieved crumminess of its sound, which turns every echo of something distinct, unique, contingent, unlikely—moments in the music that might remind you of the Everly Brothers, Jack Scott, Don and Dewey, the Champs, Santo and Johnny—into the same cheap, grimy insult the film itself follows in every frame, as if to say, as the film won't quite allow itself to do, *I don't care, I don't care if you care, so why should you? Give up!*

10 ▪ **Paul Beatty, *Slumberland* (Bloomsbury)** A novel in the voice of DJ Darky, a.k.a. Ferguson Sowell, an African American from Los Angeles who hangs out at the Slumberland bar in Berlin in the years before and after the wall came down. Searching-for-the-perfect-beat plot aside, what makes this book sing on every page is the fact that you're in the presence of someone who's so smart you don't want to miss a word he says. I don't mean Beatty. Our DJ with his phonographic memory—he never forgets a sound—has opinions on everything, and every one of them, tossed out as punch lines and wisecracks and putdowns and tears in his beer, seems the result of hours of thinking it over: the rebuke, the pose, the atrocity, the psychopathology of everyday life in the form of what's on the jukebox. We meet Lars Papenfuss, a "master spy who used his cover as a pop-culture critic to prop up dictatorial movements like 'trip-hop,' 'jungle,' 'Dogme 95,' and 'graffiti art' instead of puppet third-world governments." "I hate Wynton Marsalis in the same manner Rommel hated Hitler," DJ Darky says, pushing his German-historical hangover for lack of anything better to do. "Whenever I hear Marsalis's trumpet playing I feel like the Desert Fox forced to come

to grips with the consequences of totalitarianism after the war has been all but lost."

1 ▪ Frank Fairfield, "Darling Corey" / "I've Always Been a Rambler" (Tompkins Square 7" / myspace.com/frankfairfield) A young Californian who sings and plays as someone who's crawled out of the Virginia mountains carrying familiar songs that in his hands sound forgotten: broken lines, a dissonant drone, the fiddle or the banjo all percussion, every rising moment louder than the one before it.

2 ▪ *There'll Always Be an England: Sex Pistols Live from Brixton Academy* with *The Knowledge of London: A Sex Pistols Psychogeography,* directed by Julien Temple (Rhino/ Freemantle DVD) At the show, from 2007, there seems to be almost as much footage of the audience as of the band, and what's odd, if you've been anywhere recently where fame is on the stage, is that you see almost no one holding up a cell-phone camera, taking a picture of an event instead of living it out, even if a thirtieth-anniversary show is a picture of another show before it is anything else. Instead, people are shouting, jumping up and down, shoving, and most of all singing their heads off. Johnny Rotten, Steve Jones, Paul Cook, and Glen Matlock ("You're a lucky cunt," Rotten says near the end, "because this is the best band in the world") find moments they might not have found before. The old British tourist song "Beside the Seaside" is sung in full as a lead-in to "Holidays in the Sun"; in the fiercest passages of "God Save the Queen" and "Bodies" a true dada vortex opens up as words lose their meanings and seem capable of generating entirely new ones. But the real fun is in the "psychogeography" ("The study of the specific effects of the geographical environment, consciously organized or not, on the emotions and behavior of individuals"—*Internationale Situationniste* #1, June 1958), which is the band minus Rotten taking us on a tour of its old haunts. Cook and Matlock look the same as they did in 1976, merely older, but Jones is unrecognizable. Onstage he looks like one of his own bodyguards; here, wrapped in a heavy coat, with dark glasses and a cap pulled down, he could be a mob boss or merely a thug with money in his pocket. The three are touring Soho, checking the hooker ads in doorways. (Jones goes up, comes down: "That was great! But she made me wear a johnny.") "It's like a fuckin' Dickens novel," Jones says, surveying the sex shops, the dubious hotels, the strip clubs they once played (the El Paradiso, they remember, was so filthy they cleaned the place themselves). "I feel like a bucket of piss is going to come flying out the window." They visit pubs, search for old performance spaces ("Do you know where Notre Dame Hall is? The Sex Pistols did a show there—ever heard of the Sex Pistols?"), and like spelunkers they navigate dank hallways until they reach their old rehearsal space and crash pad off Denmark Street. Rotten's caricatures of the band members are still on the walls, plus "Nanny Spunger" (Sid Vicious's Nancy Spungeon) and "Muggerade" (manager Malcolm McLaren by way of Malcolm Muggeridge). And there is the outline of a manifesto, words running down a wall:

AWFUL
HEARTACHE
STUPID
MISERY
ILL BOOZE
END DEPT ILL
SICK
DISMAL

"This is where we began to take it seriously," Glen Matlock says. "If there was half an idea floating around, we was in a position to do something about it."

3 ▪ Tom Perrotta, *Bad Haircut: Stories of the Seventies* (Berkley, 1994) Perrotta's ongoing chronicle of men and women moving through the last decades (*Election, Joe College, Little Children, The Abstinence Teacher*) is no secret. But until a few months

ago I'd completely missed this first book, a collection of stories following one Buddy, of Darwin, New Jersey, from Cub Scouts to the summer after his first year in college. There doesn't seem to be a moment Perrotta doesn't get right, or more than right: "On Friday, Mike was holding hands with Jane. On Monday he had his arm around a hot sophomore named Sally Untermeyer, while Jane drifted through the halls, looking like she'd just donated several pints of blood."

4 ■ *Ty Segall* (Castle Face) Away from the San Francisco punk combo the Traditional Fools, Segall dives into one-man-band bedroom classicism. Very mid-'60s—with the Seeds, the Standells, and Bo Diddley smiling down from the walls—until "Oh Mary," a leap into the crazed undergrowth of the '50s, where you never knew what you'd find when you turned over a rock: most likely some guy screaming about "Oh Mary" while chasing a beat as if it's a snake and he's on a horse.

5 ■ Eugene Carrière, *Two Women* (Minneapolis Institute of Art, Minneapolis) Though the painting is from the late nineteenth century, the mood is shockingly modern—a picture where the present is already the past. In a portrait that calls up Margarethe von Trotta's *Marianne and Juliane*, about two sisters, a ghostlike face hovers over the shoulder of a woman in a red dress holding her chin in her hand, her eyes looking off to the right, into the future, toward death. This is a picture of a woman thinking—and the feeling is that by some chance the painter has caught something that has never happened before.

6 ■ Serena Ryder, "Sweeping the Ashes," from *is it o.k.* (Atlantic) A twenty-five-year-old from Peterborough, Ontario, Ryder presses hard, and over a whole album the feeling can go soft. But this is the first track; it hasn't yet worked as a warning a listener might take to the rest of her songs, and so a simple angry love song rises up like an epic. The tie to ordinary life is never cut—not with a banjo running the rhythm—but all Ryder has to do is take a deep breath to

open up the song, to blow the clothes off the floor of her bedroom and reveal how much territory the performance actually claims. If you heard this on the radio you might come away feeling bigger, stronger, defiant.

7–8 ■ TV Smith, *In the Arms of My Enemy* (Boss Tuneage) and Jamie Palmer, video for "Clone Town" (vimeo.com/1945972) In 1978, Smith led his band through the perfect London punk album, *Crossing the Red Sea with the Adverts*: the sleeve showed the title on a billboard and the ugliest public housing in the city behind it. Now he looks like someone you'd cross the street to avoid, old, beaten down, muttering to himself, consumed by his own fury. "Clone Town" isn't even Smith's best new song, but it presents the character he's made fully: a crank, unwilling to keep his mouth shut, the man with the bad news, even if that makes him someone you'd cross the street to avoid. "You don't really want to know how they get those prices so low!" he sings in a battering closing refrain, the phrase taking on another exclamation point with every repetition—but you do, you do.

9–10 ■ Lawrence Frascella and Al Weisel, *Live Fast, Die Young—The Wild Ride of Making Rebel Without a Cause* (Touchstone, 2005) and *Rebel Without a Cause*, directed by Nicholas Ray (Warner Bros., 1955) Even without a single distinctive sentence—note the tripping-over-its-own-feet syntax of the subtitle—this book is irresistible. With all of the principals other than writer Stewart Stern dead—James Dean (1955), Sal Mineo (1976), Ray (1979), Natalie Wood (1981), a wipeout, as if Dean came back in that Porsche Spyder to get them—Frascella and Weisel rely mostly on actors who in the film played gang members (Corey Allen, Frank Mazzola, Steffi Sidney, Beverly Long, Dennis Hopper) to reconstruct it. But because the movie changed the way the world looked, how it felt, they only have to apply a bit of pressure to a tiny matter—the sixteen-year-old Woods's simultaneous affairs with Ray (on his urging) and Hopper (on hers), the fate of Dean's red jacket—to find their own drama. Today the gravity in the picture belongs wholly to Dean, and the gravity is a matter of an intellectual energy so bright the man carrying it seems constantly on the verge of bursting into flames.

MARCH–APRIL 2009

1 ▪ **Cat Power, *Dark End of the Street* (Matador)** Six numbers left over from *Jukebox*, her deadly covers collection from 2008, but with every song here—most deeply with her version of Brendan Behan's "The Auld Triangle"—the slow ache of Chan Marshall's voice comes through like a promise that might take her a lifetime to keep.

2–3 ▪ **KT Tunstall, "Little Favours," from *Drastic Fantastic* (Virgin, 2007) and "Mr. Fritter," "The Tunstallator" (YouTube)** So fierce on its own terms, as Tunstall's voice wraps itself around her own body; in another life it opens up into a bizarre video, credited to an "ex-teacher," a slightly balding man of about thirty-five who'll turn out to be a cross between Terence Stamp in *The Collector*, whoever killed the Black Dahlia, and your everyday bondage fetishist. "I just want to show you something I've been building for the last few months," he says before he beckons you into his house to show you a life-size puppet topped by a rotating box of Tunstall faces with an ugly slashed mouth. After jerking the strings on the mouth, on the metal hook that serves as the hand on the plastic guitar, and the body, all in sync to the music—precisely, which only makes it worse—the man, silently singing along with the drumbeat that opens the record, ties the strings around his own face as he kneels before his idol, just like Ed Gein draping the faces of the women he killed over his own. And the song still sounds glorious.

4 ▪ **Irma Thomas, "Wish Someone Would Care," from *Soul Queen of New Orleans* (Mardi Gras) or *Swamp Dogg Presents Two Phases of Irma Thomas* (S.D.E.G.)** Not the quiet original, from 1964, the saddest song that ever hit the Top 40, but a shouting version cut in 1973 with the eccentric soul singer Swamp Dogg at the controls, reproduced by him twenty years after that—turning up now late in *The Curious Case of Benjamin Button*, for a few moments in a diner late at night, as if from somewhere in the back, maybe a dishwasher singing to herself and keeping time off the beat by banging on the counter with a fork.

5 ▪ **Orioles, "Crying in the Chapel" in *Revolutionary Road*, dir. Sam Mendes (sound track album on Nonesuch)** Hidden in this adaptation of a 1961 novel about spiritual death in the suburbs of New York in 1955—a book that would never be mentioned today if it had been set in Michigan or California—is one strange scene. Leonardo DiCaprio's self-loathing business-machine promotion man Frank Wheeler sits in his cubicle late at night, speaking into a Dictaphone. "Knowing what you've got," Wheeler says deliberately. "Knowing what you need," he says. "Knowing what you can do without"—all with the Orioles' ethereal harmonies about peace and redemption drifting somewhere behind him, as if from another building. "I live from day to day," they sing, their words aimed right at the office drudge Wheeler has become. But the group sets an inescapably poetic mood, and for a moment you can believe that the artist that Wheeler and his wife know sleeps somewhere inside of him is about to break through. "That's inventory control," Wheeler says.

5 ▪ **Beyoncé, "All I Could Do Was Cry," in *Cadillac Records* (Sony Pictures)** The Chess Records story, with Muddy Waters, Little Walter, Howlin' Wolf, Etta James, Chuck Berry: one thing after another and no sense of having gone from one place to another, with a finale listing the date of each of the principals' inductions into the Rock and Roll Hall of Fame, as if they needed that validation. The reason to see it is Beyoncé, singing James's songs with such drama, conviction, and simultaneous mimicry and invention you can hardly credit her own musical career as anything

but a marketing strategy. Yes, she's a businesswoman: after getting under the skin of this music, why else would she still be out there twirling in her own melismatics, over-souled and overdressed? What happens here happens most completely with James's early "All I Could Do Was Cry." It's the first song we see her cut in the studio—off to the side, you see Jeffrey Wright's Muddy Waters shut his eyes and lift his eyebrows in admiration as Beyoncé comes down hard on a line, and you know just how he feels. Omitted from the soundtrack album in favor of one of Beyoncé's own songs—but you can find the whole scene on YouTube, where you can also hear James herself.

6 ▪ **Teddy Thompson, "Down Low," from** *Upfront & Down Low* **(Verve Forecast, 2007)** Hidden in his collection of dull versions of country standards is a single original: the cruelest, most self-pitying, least overstylized, and best Chris Isaak ballad in years. Minus only Chris Isaak.

7 ▪ **Alvin & the Chipmunks, "Don't Stop Believin,'" from** *Undeniable* **(Razor & Tie)** Finally, the supposedly most downloaded song of the twentieth century gets the singer it always needed.

8–9 ▪ **Stanley Booth, "Triumph of the Quotidian," in** *William Eggleston: Democratic Camera, Photographs and Video, 1961–2008,* **ed. Elisabeth Sussman and Thomas Weski (Whitney Museum/Yale) and** *Eden,* **dir. Declan Recks (Samson Films)** On the white gallery walls of the Whitney, in a show that closed in January and is now at the Haus der Kunst in Munich, Eggleston's deadpan color photos didn't hold their places; they got lost in the crowds looking at them. In the catalog, though, each image on its own page, you can hear what Eggleston is after: silence. As in his 1972 picture of shoes under a bed, creating the atmosphere of a room no one has entered for years, nearly everything he processes through his camera and his darkroom looks abandoned. That makes room for Stanley Booth to tell stories, and one started me thinking about how songs travel. In *Eden*, a film about a

miserable Irish couple's tenth anniversary, Aidan Kelly's Billy Farrell leaves his wife in a disco for a party, chasing a girl he thinks has eyes for him, though all she sees is an old man. He passes out drunk; in a room behind him, people start singing "House of the Rising Sun." Farrell wakes up, automatically singing along, sees the girl, stumbles to his feet, and as he grabs her, forcing himself on her as she tries to push him away, the song continues, but now the voice you hear belongs to Sinéad O'Connor, an avenging angel who seems to be singing from inside Farrell's heart, which she's turned against him. The song has gone from its commonplace beginnings somewhere in the American South, somewhere in the late nineteenth or early twentieth century, to Bob Dylan's first album, in 1962, to the Animals' epochal 1964 worldwide hit, to countless versions by street singers and karaoke belters, to a party in an Irish town in the early twenty-first century, where if nothing else it's a song everybody knows, and from there into the spectral hands of a woman who could stare down anyone on the planet—and who's to say where its true home is, who owns it, whose singing most rings true? "A number of years back," Booth says of Eggleston, "he was honored by the Photographic Society of Japan at a Tokyo ceremony on the occasion of photography's sesquicentennial anniversary. When he accepted his award, Eggleston, who speaks little Japanese, sang, in English, 'Heartbreak Hotel.' Still singing—'I been so lonely, baby'—he went out to the sidewalk, where a Japanese woman he remembers as 'very beautiful' looked into his eyes and said, 'Oh so lonely.'"

10 ▪ **Tallest Man on Earth, "It Will Follow the Rain," 7" with** *Shallow Grave* **(Mexican Summer)** A.k.a. Kristian Mattson of Dalarna, Sweden, the Tallest Man on Earth sounds the way he wants to: as if he's stuck his head out of his hole in east Kentucky just long enough to make you wonder if you shouldn't crawl in after him. The guitar picking is of that seductive, mysterious strain that goes back to "The Coo Coo," a

calm inside the bluegrass nervousness. "Have you ever"—that's all he needs to say to make you feel as if you have.

MAY 2009

1 ■ Caroline Weeks, *Songs for Edna* (Manimal Vinyl) An "English Rose" (so described in a press release) setting Edna St. Vincent Millay to music? On the sleeve a leafy, garlanded Ms. Weeks holds a conch shell to her ear—the better to hear the glowing girl-poet of "Renascence" in 1912, a dead alcoholic in 1950? There's a swan, for the 1921 "Wild Swans," pressed onto the disc. I put it on, betting the music would be worse than the packaging.

That was a while ago, and I haven't taken it off. Weeks sings Millay's words slowly. She sings Millay's rhythms, or dowses for them. "Her poetry, you soon found out, was her real overmastering passion," her old Greenwich Village friend Edmund Wilson wrote in 1952. "She gave it to all the world, but she also gave it to you." A reader entranced by Millay's lyricism—not yet catching the way a blunt nihilism would reach up out of the ether of a poem and scratch its face—can always convince herself she's the "you," and read Millay as if she were Sylvia Plath or J. D. Salinger, which is to say as if Millay is *her*. But Weeks sings—high, fingering her guitar, maybe with clarinetist Peter Moyse singing wordlessly behind her—as if she's heard something others haven't heard.

Death—anticipated, remembered—is all over the songs. The album breaks after its first five pieces (among them "Renascence," "What lips my lips have kissed," "Wild swans"), beginning again with "The return," from 1934, and you can almost sense an anchor being dropped.

Weeks will nearly stop, letting a piece breathe. When she moves back into it you can hear that she's hearing something she herself hadn't heard before. This rhythm of encounter makes it all but impossible to follow the tracks as tributes, or homages, even if you're reading along as Weeks puts her mouth around Millay's words, or her body.

"It was difficult for the romantics of the twenties to slow down and slough off their youth, when everything had seemed to be possible and they had been able to treat their genius as an unlimited checking account," Wilson wrote. "One could always still resort to liquor to keep up the old excitement, it was a kind of way of getting back there." As Weeks heads to the end of her project, the pace seems to slow even more, but more seems to be at stake. Each step carries the voice closer to a last word, whatever it might be—you'll know it when you find it. The sulfurous air of David Bowie's profoundly creepy "The Bewlay Brothers," from his 1971 *Hunky Dory*, seeps into Weeks's songs as if under their doors. There's a sense of violation, of salvation as a joke, and a pagan self-destruction—getting *lost*, in a forest where priests can't go—the only destination worth seeking.

There's no resolution in any single one of Weeks's pieces. There's no progression. Each song leaves the singer where she found it, or it found her. Maybe that's why I keep going back to it.

2 ■ Bob Dylan, *Theme Time Radio Hour: Madness* (Sirius XM, February 5) "Here's a man, that some call the William Faulkner of jazz. Now, I've got to tell you. I've heard this guy play since the sixties, and I've never heard anybody *call* him 'the William Faulkner of jazz'—but there it is in a book. I mean, somebody just *wrote* that. I can't imagine anybody calling him 'the William Faulkner of jazz.' I mean, that'd be like calling Garnet Mimms the Gabriel García Bernal of soul music," Dylan said, apparently introducing Gael Garcia Bernal to Gabriel García Márquez. "It's just not *done*.

"I'm getting excited over *nothing*. Let me just play the record. By the way—I consider William Faulkner to be the Mose Allison of literature. Here they are, together again, Mose Allison and William Faulkner, singing the Percy Mayfield song 'Lost Mind . . .'"

3 ■ The Drones, *Havilah* (ATP/R) Gareth Liddiard could come from the far side of a Clint Eastwood western—set in his own

Australia. There's a desperation in his whole demeanor that speaks for some titanic struggle—resignation versus justice, or justice versus peace of mind. The tired way Liddiard sings "to be nailed to a door" ("Luck in Odd Numbers") could be translated by any of those words. There are echoes of Neil Young or Rick Rizzo of Eleventh Dream Day in his guitar playing—a manic ditch-digging. There's nothing here to match the death march of "Jezebel" on the 2006 *Gala Mill*—but what if there were?

4 ■ Flyer, Portland, Maine (January 28) The Obama that those of little faith dream of and that Obama refuses to be—the avenger, not the advertised Jesse Ray Carter, an OK Chris Smither-like bottleneck player—but where did whoever put Obama's head onto the famous Jim Marshall photo of Johnny Cash find that scowl?

5–6 ■ James Tate, "The Wine Talks" and Charles Harper Webb, "The Secret History of Rock & Roll," in *Third Rail: The Poetry of Rock and Roll*, edited by Jonathan Wells (MTV Books, 2007) Tate is aiming for a sting, and even though he moves from a pleasant moment to a cruel joke, you're still blindsided when it comes. As a technical performance

the poem carries its own thrill. Webb begins with what you can take as a joke—

> Elvis Presley, Bo Diddley, Bill Haley & the Comets
> were lies created on recording tape by the same Group
> who made The Bomb, with the same motive: rule the world

—but after three pages he's made his case.

7 ■ Allen Toussaint, *The Bright Mississippi* (Nonesuch) Mostly solo piano, looking for the right elegy. But the opening "Egyptian Fantasy" lets you think there might be a pyramid under New Orleans where they have parties only on February 29, accounts of which are kept in a special copy of Ishmael Reed's *Mumbo Jumbo*.

8 ■ Sometymes Why, "Glorious Machine" on *Your Heart Is a Glorious Machine* (Signature Sounds) Ruth Ungar Merenda of the Mammals, Kristin Andreassen of Uncle Earl, Aoife O'Donovan of Crooked Still—and it's O'Donovan who has the gift of atmosphere, who can change the temperature of a room. You can hear that on Crooked Still's erotic embrace of old folk songs on its 2006 *Shaken by a Low Sound*, and how it all somehow vanished last year on *Still Crooked*—as if the cute title wasn't a giveaway. You wouldn't necessarily expect better from a group that spells *sometimes* with a *y*. But one soft deep breath into the title song and all resistance crumbles. "If you give me one reason not to leave, I'll show you all the tricks up my sleeve"—as O'Donovan sings the words they find a circular pattern. They draw a circle around the people in the song. Anybody else, you can think, would repeat lines that good. O'Donovan lets them hang over the song, leaving you aching to hear them again.

9 ■ William Hogeland, "American Dreamers" in *Inventing American History* (MIT Press) On the lies surrounding two figures no one else would think of as political doppelgängers: Pete Seeger as a Stalinist, and William F. Buckley Jr. as a racist. Hogeland writes quietly, carefully, never letting his knowledge of the entire frame of reference of his argument make the reader feel ignorant, but he can hit. Pete Seeger's having "inherited communism from his father," the musicologist Charles Seeger, was a "decisive event in the history of American vernacular music." Buckley's 1957 *National Review* editorial calling for the suppression of black voting on the grounds that, as Buckley put it, "the claims of civilization supersede those of universal suffrage," was, Hogeland shows, never disavowed, only smoothed away; it was of a piece with Buckley's whole career as "the leisure-class warrior-philosopher, provoked to militancy by ubiquitous barbarism . . . battling to push back both the mob and the weak-willed mob enablers who were ruining the civilization that had produced his own gorgeousness." Reaching the end of this forty-page essay, you can imagine such scores are there only to prepare the ground for a passage that is more damning for its apparent affection: "Seeger and Buckley were public romantics. When they were young, and without regard for consequence, they brought charisma, energy, and creativity to dreaming up worlds they wanted—possibly needed—to live in. Because they made those worlds so real and beautiful that other people wanted to live in them too, they became larger-than-life characters, instantly recognizable a long way off, not quite real close up, and never quite grown up even when old."

10 ▪ **The Land Beyond the Sunset (Google Films/YouTube)** A fourteen-minute film from 1912, directed by Harold Shaw, about the *New York Herald Tribune*'s Fresh Air Fund—and the furthest thing from a documentary imaginable. There are the shadows of spirits on a shed, a magic book, and a child stealing a boat so that he can float off the end of the earth, just like Enid boarding her bus at the end of *Ghost World*.

NOTE: *In my last column, I said that the Adverts' perfect 1978 album,* Crossing the Red Sea with the Adverts, *featured a sleeve that "showed the title on a billboard with the ugliest public housing in the city behind it."*

The Adverts were much sharper than my memory. The billboard read LAND OF MILK AND HONEY.

Thanks to John Coleman, Tom Denenberg, and Tom Luddy.

JUNE 2009

SPECIAL FOREIGN CORRESPONDENT EDITION

1 ▪ **Miguel João (Chiado Square, Lisbon, April 6)** A street singer with an early Springsteen look and an unusual style. Most people trying to sing songs on the order of the Wailers' "Concrete Jungle" or Bob Dylan's "Like a Rolling Stone"—songs that are like whales in their power to displace everything around them—act at least slightly embarrassed. João strummed sharply, with silences, and sang as if he'd written the tunes the night before—as if, with great seriousness, he was fooling with them, experimenting, working them out as you watched.

2 ▪ **A Canção da Saudade, directed by Henrique Campos (1964)** At Leão d'Ouro in Lisbon, the literature professor Américo António Lindeza Diogo pulled out his iPod to pass around a perfect print of "the first Portuguese rock-and-roll movie." Starring pop star Vitor Gomes and Ann-Margret lookalike Soledad Miranda, it's a parable of cross-generational conflict as expressed through—and ultimately resolved by!—music: traditional fado v. the new sound, which ultimately blend into a new new sound. What's so gripping about the film is that you may have already seen it a dozen times: with the same plot, the same faces, the same gestures, the same contrived, spontaneous songs and dances, the picture was made between 1957 and 1965 in the US, the UK, Germany, France—for all I know Canada, Mexico, South Africa, India, Brazil. All except for one stunning shot: the cast ringing a stairwell and looking down to the camera on the distant bottom, just like the Beatles on the cover of their first album.

3 ▪ **"William Eggleston, Paris" (Fondation Cartier, Paris, through June 21)** From At-

get to Brassaï to van der Elsken and beyond, in photographs Paris has always been a black-and-white city. The approach the Memphis color photographer takes is to all but escape Paris as a subject. His intent is not to capture a unique city but to let his eye move toward whatever attracts it, and the result is that the strongest images might have been made in Chicago, Beijing, Berlin, or Buenos Aires. One picture showed a tableau that could have come from any city where technology is advertising before it's anything else. Oozing confidence, health, and freedom, a man and a woman walk down a corridor of an ultramodern (which thus already looks out of date) gallery or mall or office building. But they appear superimposed, as if they're projections, not people—and seemingly superimposed over them is an Asian man on a cell phone, bigger, and if anything more confident. In the background, an older couple walks away from our gaze; they seem both symbolic and dropped in. In the middle, shadows of two men in an office discussing something in a relaxed way communicate almost subliminally. Was this picture *taken*, in the vernacular sense, or was it in a literal and not photographic sense *made*—and never actual at all? That's precisely not how Eggleston works, which makes you wonder what, if anything, this is a picture *of*.

4 ▪ **"The Jazz Century: Art, Film, Music and Photography from Picasso to Basquiat" (Musée du quai Branly, Paris, through June 28; Centre de Cultura Contemporània de Barcelona, July 21 through October 18)** A huge, very popular exhibition, with an overemphasis on visual art with a capital A instead of, say, a Billie Holiday dress or Duke Ellington's tuxedo. But despite a black hole almost before the show gets under way—positing 1917 as the year of the birth of jazz, when it had been all over New Orleans since the end of the nineteenth century, led by Buddy Bolden's band, of which there survives one photograph, because in 1917 the all-white Original Dixieland Jazz Band made the first record with the word *jass* in the

title, and the Navy shut down the Storyville red-light district (once upon a time purists would have called this the year of jazz's death, not birth)—there were highlights around every corner:

• In an opening wall of pre-jazz sheet music—coon songs, minstrel standards—a full-color illustration for E. T. Paull's 1899 composition "A Warmin' Up in Dixie": black men and women dancing around a fire in the woods. It's where slaves would go to sing forbidden songs, which might be coded spirituals—"Daniel in the Lion's Den," for one—but here it's a Devil's Sabbath, with the firelight reflected in the dancers' eyes turning each one demonic. Racist, but not about nothing.

• Sheet music for Bert Williams's "Nobody," in 1906 a number one hit for nine weeks. "Latest Oddity Successor to 'I May Be Crazy But I Ain't No Fool,'" reads a tagline. Is it jazz? As music, no. As heart, all the way.

• A first edition of F. Scott Fitzgerald's *Tales of the Jazz Age*. A little band and lots of dancers on the jacket—it should have been a curio. But it was the thing itself, and it had an aura you could have touched if it wasn't in a glass case.

• Illustration by Aaron Douglas for the "Charleston" chapter of Paul Morand's 1929 jazz novel *Black Magic*: a black jazz club, in smoky grays. In the foreground, people at tables, dominated by a long arm and a hand resting on a chair, from the left; in the background, a saxophonist seated in a chair, a pianist behind him; in the middle, hanging down almost to the empty dance floor, a noose: more suggestive and shocking—because it was inside a jazz image—than the pictures of actual lynchings that bracketed the exhibition's illustrated time lines this artifact was part of.

• Cover story, *Etude Music Magazine*, August 1924: "The Jazz Problem: Opinions of Prominent Public Men and Musicians."

• *Jazz Magazine*, October–November 1954, sidebar to an article titled "Bird Lives! Bird Lives! Bird Lives! Bird Lives! Bird Lives! Bird Lives!" (and he wasn't even dead yet): the poet Ted Joans reporting on a "dada-surrealist party (poems by Breton, Prévert, Péret, etc.)" in Greenwich Village: "Parker arrived without a costume . . . but he improvised one": taking off his shirt and shoes, rolling up his pants, and whiting up his face into a mau-mau mask. Who was this joke on? Who got it?

• And, among many film clips, perhaps the most explosive moment of all: the "Come to the City" sequence of F. W. Murnau's 1927 silent *Sunrise*, with the flapper seducing the married country man with tales of thrills, glamour, *jazz*: she kisses him in the marsh where they've been lying, and suddenly it all appears, with a pounding band right in your face, the conductor throwing his arms into the air, all of it overwhelming, with lightning superimpositions and tilted frames that perhaps more than anything in all of cinema say, This is what movies were for, this is why they were invented, to catch this movement.

5 ▪ **Walter Mosley, *The Long Fall* (Riverhead Books)** On I'm Not Jim's *You Are All My People*, the Jonathan Lethem/Walter Salas-Humara collaboration "Walks Into" is an infinitely complex stand-up routine on the opening line of the all-all-American joke—and out of this cradle endlessly rocking comes a Mosley version, in his first novel featuring a black New York City private eye named Leonid McGill. One tricky, unstable theme of the book is that racism isn't what it used to be—but, McGill says as he walks into Oddfellows Pub, a white man's bar in Albany, "it wasn't 2008 everywhere in America. Some people still lived in the sixties, and others might as well have been veterans of the Civil War. In many establishments I was considered a Black Man; other folks, in more genteel joints, used the term 'African-American,' but at Oddfellows I was a nigger where there were no niggers allowed."

6 ▪ **Bonnie "Prince" Billy, *Beware* (Drag City)** " 'My Life's Work' would be his 'My Way,' " Will Oldham says in the April issue of *Mojo*, speaking of Elvis Presley and one

of his new songs; on the cover of the album he looks just like Friedrich Nietzsche. "That's my dream. When I meet him I'll say, I've got this tune, man, you wanna see if you can get behind it? I'm sure he would, because he's already sung it so many times. In my mind, I hear him." I don't hear it, but I'm still trying.

7 ▪ **Neko Case, *Middle Cyclone* (Anti)** People seem to be reviewing Neko Case's hair more than her music.

8 ▪ **Van Morrison, *Astral Weeks Live at the Hollywood Bowl* (Listen to the Lion)** Listen to "Madame George"—that's what Morrison is doing.

9 ▪ **Standard Hotel (Los Angeles, March 8)** Phone buttons: FRONT DESK, ROOM SERVICE, VOICE MAIL, HOUSEKEEPING, MOTIVATIONAL SPEAKER. And also FLUFFER, though that might mean more in the San Fernando Valley than in L.A.

10 ▪ **Lisbon, April 6** A friend on her apartment overlooking the Cemitério dos Prazeres (the Cemetery of Pleasures): "I have a great view of eternal life."

JULY–AUGUST 2009

1 ▪ **Bob Dylan, *Together Through Life* (Columbia)** Casual, to the point where the clumsiness comes to the surface—except with "Forgetful Heart," where a shadow passes over the singer's face. But nothing here quite carries the weight of a scene from last season's *In Treatment*, when Mia Wasikowska's smart, sarcastic, suicidal teenage gymnast Sophie turns the tables on Gabriel Byrne's fifty-something psychologist Paul Weston, as if once she was so much older but she's younger than that now and he's too old to know what she's talking about. " 'The times they are a-changing,' " she says as a session is ending. "It's from a Bob Dylan song. My gift to you."

2 ▪ **P J Harvey and John Parish, *A Woman A Man Walked By* (Island)** From "Sheela-Na-Gig" on her first album, in 1992, Harvey has never made any secret that her music is meant to make a home for an avenging pagan goddess. Any song called "Pig Will

Not" all but promises that figure will appear in a great snout mask, making inhuman sounds, and that is what happens: "WILL NOT!" she shouts in acrid fury, making a sound Fucked Up would pay for if they could get Harvey to sell it. "I WANT YOUR FUCKING ASS!" she yells in "A Woman a Man Walked By/The Crow Knows Where All the Little Children Go," the latter part of the title turning Harvey into a witch. You step back before these moments, and go back to them when you think you're equal to them, not just because nothing else here is.

3 ▪ **"American Letterpress: The Art of the Hatch Show Print" (Experience Music Project, Seattle, Washington, through July 19; Durham Museum, Omaha, Nebraska, October 31, 2009, through January 10, 2010; Austin Museum of Art, Austin, Texas, February 13 through May 9, 2010)** The Nashville company's blunt, colorful block designs haven't changed much from movie posters in the '30s ("She's the WOMAN behind the KILLER behind the GUN! J. EDGAR HOOVER tells her amazing story in 'PERSONS IN HIDING'") to concert promotions for the likes of Beck or the Strokes today. A walk through the show brings a sense of repetition most of all. But there are ghosts on the walls, and suspense even in the captions. As with the very first Hatch bill, for a lecture in Nashville in 1879 by the Reverend Henry Ward Beecher, brother of Harriet Beecher Stowe, as both a social reformer and an adulterer at the time likely the most famous preacher in the United States, now speaking on "The Reign of the Common People": "Parquet and Dress Circle, 1-, Family Circle, 1-"—and, for the onetime fire-breathing New England abolitionist, no doubt a concession to local custom: "Colored Box, 50¢." As with these lines, below a wall of '50s prints: "Imagine the scene at Hatch. Two men are setting type for posters on tables side by side. One is a poster for the Rabbit Foot Minstrel Show . . . the other is a poster for someone named Presley."

4 ▪ **Levon Helm, *Electric Dirt* (Vanguard)** Born in 1940, growing up in Arkansas,

Helm saw the Rabbit Foot Minstrels and he saw Elvis, both before he was fifteen. You can hear those events in this music, especially on the call-and-response in Larry Campbell's "When I Go Away," with Helm pounding his voice as if it were his drums as others shout back at him as if he were a mountain and they're in it for the echo. Helm's 2007 *Dirt Farmer*, which won a Grammy for Best Traditional Folk Album, is pale compared to Allen Toussaint and Steven Bernstein's sliding New Orleans horn arrangements, especially for "Kingfish," Randy Newman's ode to Huey P. Long. With throat cancer behind him, and most recently on-screen as a very convincingly dead Confederate general in Bertrand Tavernier's *In the Electric Mist*, Helm now sounds most of all robust, perhaps with his best music since the Band's *Last Waltz* ahead of him.

5 ▪ **Liechtenstein, *Survival Strategies in a Modern World* (Slumberland)** Three young women from Sweden take less than twenty-three minutes to skip from Liliput grinning through their punk songs in Zurich in the 1980s, to the Teddy Bears mouthing doo-wop in Los Angeles in 1958, for that matter picking up next-door neighbor Jorgen Ingmann in Copenhagen in 1961 before they're in the air. You never miss when you kick it off with "Apache" guitar.

6 ▪ **Andrew Britton, *Britton on Film: The Complete Film Criticism of Andrew Britton*, edited by Barry Keith Grant (Wayne State University Press)** Britton (1952–94) was a critic who took nothing at face value and nothing for granted. Writing in the British and Canadian journals *Movie* and *CineAction*, he interrogated pictures under a third-degree light, but as if he were Philip Marlowe and the movies were cops, and sometimes it seemed like a put-up job. But not in the 1986 "Blissing Out: The Politics of Reaganite Entertainment," nearly sixty pages that will leave you feeling as if you've just read a movie version of the Justice Department's report on torture under George W. Bush—and as if the era the essay describes has not even begun to end.

7–8 ▪ The Kills, *Keep on Your Mean Side* (Domino) and Dead Weather, *Horehound* (Third Man) Alison Mosshart and Jamie Hince had so much fun trying to live up to their name on the Kills' 2003 debut album—and, on this reissue, with numbers from the EP *Fried My Little Brains* and elsewhere, including their graveyard version of Dock Boggs's "Sugar Baby"—it didn't always sound like an act. But they never caught up with themselves, and now Mosshart's singing with the White Stripes' Jack White in Dead Weather, where it sounds as if nobody ever leaves the house.

9 ▪ Andrei Codrescu, *The Posthuman Dada Guide: Tzara and Lenin Play Chess* (Princeton) Marked by a gigantic, repeating error—the Cabaret Voltaire in Zurich, where dada was discovered, opened in 1916, not 1915—this is a book of endless riches and complexity. Cutting wit is everywhere: "In Germany, antiwar demonstrations by tens of thousands of people gave way to tens of thousands of corpses who had obviously changed their minds." No good writer can resist the language of the dada manifesto— though maybe it's more a gesture, a certain James Dean slouch, than a language—and Codrescu doesn't try. In an age when bad writers are afraid most of all of their own voices, then putting every word that might mean anything at all in self-protecting scare quotes, "No art in its right! Mind (i.e., for sale) can possibly *mean* what it says. Therefore, Dada is not art," is a first step toward a cure. But "Dada is a tool for removing parentheses and removing the world from between quotes with the forceps of inspiration" slams the door so hard it opens onto a country where people are not afraid. The whole affair is rooted in an apocryphal chess game between founder of dada Tristan Tzara and founder of communism V. I. Lenin, and two more-than-open questions: Who won? And is the game over?

10 ▪ Bob Dylan, video for "Beyond Here Lies Nothing" (YouTube) A montage of photos from Bruce Davidson's 1959 series "Brooklyn Gang"—Larry Clark's *Tulsa* as made suitable for *Vogue*—with the Jokers getting tattoos, hanging around, taking their shirts off, going to Coney Island, trying to look as if they don't care. Near the end a woman with lank black hair and black eye-makeup comes into the story. She carries experience the boys don't, desires they couldn't fathom, but she has nowhere else to go and so she's here. She's a dead ringer for Amy Winehouse, and you miss her more than ever.

SEPTEMBER 2009

1 ▪ Fiery Furnaces, *I'm Going Away* (Thrill Jockey) Musicality in speech is a common theme; the peculiar delight in the Fiery Furnaces' eighth album in their six years is the realism of speech in their songs. The music is a given, so if you catch, say, the way Eleanor Friedberger turns her words, "Well, I thought I was thinking, but apparently not," whatever context the words might inhabit in their narrative drops away, and you might be transported to a city street and enveloped by the feeling not of listening to a performance but of hearing a woman on her cell phone as she strides past you, with precisely the intensity and surprise of a smell taking you back to a face or a voice you haven't thought of for years.

2 ▪ Robert Cantwell, "A Harvest of Illth," in *If Beale Street Could Talk: Music, Community, Culture* (University of Illinois Press) Cantwell is a subtle writer, and his collection of essays on the transformation of everyday life by art that resists disappearing back into the ordinary and the predictable is full of paradox ("The disc renders the performance silent, as the photo renders its subject invisible, each not merely representing, but replacing the other"). But in "A Harvest of Illith"—John Ruskin's word for a form of wealth that "as it leads away from life, it is unvaluable or malignant," here naming Mississippi blues 78s made in the '20s and '30s as accumulated by a few young men in the '40s and '50s—Cantwell finds his way into a kind of frenzy. If Beale Street could talk it might say this: "Like a bus driver caught in a skid"—imagine a tourist bus, with the driver on his intercom, "That's where they had the Palace Amateur Nights, they say Elvis sang there before anyone knew his name, *Oh shit, hold on!*"—"the Delta blues thrusts the musician into a swiftly proliferating emergency that tests not only his competence as a musician but his grasp of the whole nature of his body and his instrument in the midst of the wider context of natural laws of which he and it are parts."

3–4 ▪ David Thomson, "After Citizen Kane—A New Socratic dialogue" (*McSweeney's* 31) and Adam Lambert, "A Change Is Gonna Come" (*American Idol* final, Fox, May 19) Thomson has Susan Sontag trying to get Franz Kafka, Virginia Woolf, Charlie Chaplin, and Ernest Hemingway to vote against *Citizen Kane* in the 2012 *Sight & Sound* poll on the greatest movies ever made. "I always vote on *American Idol*," says Woolf. Would she have voted for Adam Lambert, who for the season's final face-off placed his bet on Sam Cooke's civil rights anthem, the greatest soul record ever made? Ken Tucker of *Fresh Air* has compared what Lambert does to other people's songs to the outrageous and inspired operations David Bowie performed on the likes of British Invasion hits on *Pin Ups*; he played Lambert's version of "Burning Love" to prove his point, and it did. But this night Lambert began as if soul music were a picture in a magazine; every note and gesture was a referent to a referent that the picture had rendered invisible. So much alienation was built into the performance, where according to *Idol* precepts all emotions are absorbed into *I want*, that Lambert became his own impersonator. After thirty seconds of hitting notes ("Not singing, or vocalizing," said a friend. "Vocaling"), he screamed, to show that he could really hit a note, and the performance went to a rank hysteria, which was meant to stand for actually hearing one's own words, for being moved by what one was singing about. And then the coup de grâce, as Lambert turned a song about a change that had to come because it would affect a whole people, a

whole country, perhaps even the whole world, into a pitch for votes, magically replacing a common history with solipsism. "*I know my change is gonna come!*" he sang, leaving Cooke's inescapably shared "a change is gonna come" in the dust—making the song his own, the ultimate *Idol* praise phrase, in the most absolute way, erasing everyone, dead or alive, that the song truly contained. The judges were beside themselves. Lambert lost to Kris Allen, in the word of the day Pat Boone to Lambert's Elvis, but he will be closing his act with "My change is gonna come" until Sam Cooke returns in the common imagination to claim it, and for Lambert the song will fall away from him and he will be the last to know. Up in heaven, trying to negate eternity, probably Virginia Woolf would have voted for him: "That show can cheer me up sometimes better than a Cornish cream tea."

5 ▪ Tom Meyer, "Back Page" cartoon (*San Francisco Chronicle*, May 17) There's an older man shouting at his unhappy daughter: "Hey—we had to pay for our parents' Social Security, you have to pay for ours!" "Your parents were part of the Greatest Generation that delivered us from the Depression and the Nazis. . . ." she says, shoving her finger into his potbelly: "*Your* generation gave us Iraq, the Great Recession, trillion-dollar deficits, and Duran Duran!"

6 ▪ Ed Zuckerman, writer, "Rock Star" episode of *Law & Order: Criminal Intent* (USA, May 3) The first show with Jeff Goldblum as Detective Zach Nichols. "I have a Grammy!" says Daniel Gerroll as old washed-up British rock star Philip, now landlord, sexual blackmailer, band manager, and killer, when Goldblum sneers at him. "Milli Vanilli had a Grammy," Goldblum says mordantly, turning himself back into the crotchety rock critic he played in *Between the Lines* in 1977.

7–8 ▪ Jerry Leiber and Mike Stoller with David Ritz, *Hound Dog: The Leiber and Stoller Autobiography* (Simon & Schuster) and Josh Alan Friedman, "Jerry Leiber: Kiss My Big Black *Tokhis!*" in *Tell the Truth Until They Bleed: Coming Clean in the Dirty World of*

Blues and Rock 'n' Roll (Backbeat) With Ritz, who's been ear and pen for autobiographies by Ray Charles, Aretha Franklin, Etta James, and more, the songwriters who from the beginning of their partnership in 1950 defined rhythm and blues and rock and roll talk their tales one after the other, back and forth: tales told before, in many cases, but not with such a sense of satisfaction and reflection, with such a lack of guile or resentment. Leiber speaks of deriving the words for "Is That All There Is?," eventually an indelible hit for Peggy Lee in 1969, from Thomas Mann's "Disillusionment," while Stoller says he went for the spirit of Kurt Weill for the music; together they recount trying to sell the song to Marlene Dietrich ("The song you just sang is who I am," she tells Leiber, "not what I do"), then Barbra Streisand. What about Lotte Lenya? Ultimately they take Lee into the studio, she sings the song again and again, and they settle on take thirty-seven, because, for take thirty-six, when the three got it all—"Peggy had done it. We had done it. The enormous potential in this strange little song had been realized"—the engineer forgot to press the RECORD button. Leiber relates a lot of the same stories in Friedman's profile; with the gentlemanliness of Ritz's presentation replaced by Friedman's insistent street-grit milieu and tough-guy narration, they aren't half so convincing.

9 ▪ Eliot Ross, *Passover at Jake's: The Rosenbloom Seder Plate,* 2008, in the "Dorothy Saxe Invitational: New Works/Old Story—80 Artists at the Passover Table" (Contemporary Jewish Museum, San Francisco, February 27–June 2, catalog available through the museum) "An assemblage of objects memorializing my father and his brothers who never took time off to celebrate a Jewish holiday," Ross says: on a blue and white Pabst serving tray, with WHAT'LL YOU HAVE? emblazoned on the edge, there's a snapshot of the four Rosenbloom brothers posing in front of a bar, and before them an ashtray with a few butts, a cigar stub for a lamb shank, a shot glass, the whole thing held up with a Budweiser bottle.

10 ▪ Elvis Presley, "That's All Right" (Cole Coffee, Oakland, May 23, 8:30 a.m.) For a minute, the little coffee spot had no customers. As I walked in I caught the first strum of Elvis Presley's first record. "That's nice," said one of the three twentyish women behind the counter. Another took my money and began dancing as the first one starting singing. A feeling of freshness and confidence rang through the music and into the air of the room.

OCTOBER 2009

1 ▪ Worst News of the Month: CRIME LEADERS KRAY TWINS SCHEMED TO TAKE OVER AS THE BEATLES' MANAGERS (*Entertainment Daily,* June 21) The scheme the Krays supposedly hatched was simple: instead of cutting up Brian Epstein with swords, threaten to expose him as homosexual—never mind that Ronnie Kray was gay himself. You can imagine that John Lennon might have found the prospect of being managed by the scariest people in London cool beyond cool—for about five minutes.

2 ▪ Ettes, *Do You Want Power* (Take Root) With guitarist Coco Hames in front, drummer Poni Silver in back, and bassist Jem Cohen in the middle, this is a punk band— and depending as much on your mood as on their intentions, you might pick up the swooping grandeur of the Adverts' "Great British Mistake," the speed of the Clash, the distance and space the Rolling Stones found in rhythm and blues. Songs can take off so fast they all but leave you behind. But the oddest notes might be the most compelling, a few months or years down the line: the way the I-Can-Wait-Forever Appalachian voice of "O Love Is Teasin'" or "The Cuckoo" winks out of the verses of "While Your Girl's Away," the Cheshire-cat smile in "Keep Me in Flowers."

3 ▪ *Bad Lieutenant: Port of Call New Orleans,* directed by Werner Herzog (Saturn Films) Nicolas Cage's lieutenant walks into a surveillance room across the street from a house detectives are checking out, hallucinating his head off from crack and coke.

"What are these fucking iguanas doing on my coffee table?" he says, as one of the lizards only he can see begins to rotate an eye while Johnny Adams's New Orleans version of "Release Me" comes out of its mouth— or its nose, or whatever it is that iguanas sing out of.

4 ▪ **Nicholas Rombes, *A Cultural Dictionary of Punk, 1974–1982* (Continuum)** You can't use this for reference, and not because there's no table of contents. Jumping all over the place is too much fun. A typical entry is the faux-referential "Ongoing force of *me*, the," which cites a 1987 Johnny Rotten response to an "interviewer's statement that there had not been anything as revolutionary as the Sex Pistols": "There has been something as revolutionary as the Sex Pistols. The ongoing force of *me*." You might laugh as you skip backward or forward to *Dhalgren* (1975 novel by Samuel R. Delany, news to me) or "Punk, influence on something other than music or fashion"; you might also be stopped in your tracks by phrase-making I doubt could have been produced by anyone else on earth.

5 ▪ **Charles Taylor writes in on seeing Sonic Youth for the first time (United Palace Theater, New York City, July 3)** "How do you explain the difference between volume that is pulverizing and volume that's liberating? At one point during the first encore, Kim Gordon, who was wearing a silver sheath dress, was doing her go-go-dancer moves and looked as if she was actually surfing the waves of sound. Visually and in attitude, she's the steady center of that band. At times, she and Thurston Moore and Lee Ranaldo and Mark Ibold would form a loose circle, facing each other, and they had the deadly precision of a group of hired killers in a Leone western. And the music seemed to me perfectly pitched between songs and guitar freak-outs, the latter of which never— never—lost discipline or structure. Maybe only Neil Young has that sense of physical expansiveness at his most slashing.

"Part of what moved me, and this may sound trivial, was that for the first time in memory I was at a rock show watching people older than myself, and people not playing at anything, not posing, but doing what they love without feeling they have to resort to rock-star clichés of bad behavior to do it. Did you see Gordon in *Last Days*? I hated that movie. I thought it treated Kurt Cobain the way generations of college girls have treated Sylvia Plath (though there it fits): as the fetish object at the center of a death trip. When Gordon walks in, she shows the entire movie for the lie it is. Here's someone who is as rock and roll as rock and roll can be, and she's not self-destructive or frantic or foolish. She's an adult. That's why I loved her as the gangster snapping off orders in Cantonese in *Boarding Gate*. She is such a cool, self-possessed professional. Jean-Pierre Melville would have adored her."

6 ▪ **Fiery Furnaces press release (Thrill Jockey Records, July)** On the follow-up to the summer's *I'm Going Away*: "The band is very optimistic—despite or because of it all—and will continue its 'Democ-Rock' efforts by releasing a fully-fledged 'Derocmacy in America' limited edition vinyl box-set. It might be called something like *Your Cashier Today Was ACM CASHIER 96....*" Misreading "Derocmacy" as "Deromacy," I asked Furnace Matthew Friedberger if it was a typo, and if so, or not, what it meant. His reply: "It's meant to be the equally idiolect-ed 'Derocmacy.' 'Roc' as in 'Rock'.... But that's neither here nor there. And maybe 'Deromacy' is one of those fruitful sort of typos. It might therefore have—unknowingly—been derived from 'derivo'—meaning the derive or divert. So 'Deromacy' might refer to an imagined, or real, Diversionary Republic.—Or from 'derogo'—the Derogatory or Critical Republic.—Or from 'derosus,' which apparently means 'gnawed away'—so, the Eaten-Away Republic.

"'Derocmacy' has to do with the 'Democ-Rock' thing, which started as a lark on our tour last year during the primaries. We had people vote on what we'd play and held a 'caucus' to determine what our next album would be. And I was to write songs, or put together songs, based on or determined by whatever printed ephemera fans had on them and put down on the stage (along with their song-votes). Receipts, mainly (So the cashier number on a receipt would provide the intervals for the tune, and so on). The slogan was 'Make the details of your life the sound track to your life.'"

7–10 ▪ Megan Pugh, "Who's Bad? How the King of Pop changed the course of American dance by transforming its past" (*FLYP*, July 3). Michael Thomas, "I Was Not Michael Jackson" (*New York Times*, June 28). Bob Herbert, "Behind the Façade" (*New York Times*, July 4). Bill Wyman, "The Tragedy of Michael Jackson" (*Wall Street Journal*, July 15) These are a few of the few pieces on Michael Jackson's death where writers had the heart or the nerve to dig out from under the endless stream of cant about the "sound track of my life" and "his gift to the world" and "now perhaps he can rest in peace." In a scintillatingly linked essay on the website *FLYP*, Pugh set the scene with the spontaneous explosion of dance, not merely speech, that first greeted the news ("Fourteen-hundred prison inmates in the Philippines performed a massive, synchronized dance tribute in bright orange jumpsuits," as you watch), and then moved out to trace Jackson's debt to (and, clearly, study of) Bill Robinson, the nineteenth-century moonwalker Billy Kershands, Gene Kelly, and more, not diminishing Jackson's work but allowing it to take on its full dimensions by expanding its context. Thomas, author of the novel *Man Gone Down*, a perfectly conventional realistic novel that can at times make you feel as if you're reading *Ulysses* or *Invisible Man*, begins as harshly as he can, hearing the news on the radio, thinking about how he'd already left not only Jackson but his own brother behind: "He knows I don't care about him." He goes back to the 1970s and the Cousin 5, the living-room singing group he, his brother, his sister, and his two cousins formed in thrill and homage, and proceeds to twist his heart and yours. Herbert writes about a man who bought the world:

about meeting Jackson in the mid-1980s, when he carried Emmanuel Lewis around "almost as a pet"—with Lewis, "probably 13 at the time, but he looked much younger, maybe 7 or 8," a symbolic stand-in for the children in Jackson's bed. Wyman presented Jackson as a man sustained only by his fame—sustained in the sense of Jackson himself feeding off his own renown. Wyman did not shy away from the hideousness of the face Jackson presented to the world, and not the face he got with plastic surgery: rather how, after inventing the previously unknown throne of the King of Pop and awarding himself the crown, "he developed a fondness for walking around in front of a large band of what seemed to be Central American military personnel; this was in the '80s, the era of Salvadoran juntas and assassinations of priests and nuns. One album, *HIStory*, featured an enormous Soviet-style Jackson statue on the cover. Replicas of it were set up when he made public appearances."

Unlike the thugs he liked to dress up as, Jackson didn't have people killed. He enacted a complex drama that implicated millions of people in labyrinthine ways. With the avalanche of biographies and biopics to come, it will be hard to see even the curtain behind which that drama took place, but gathering these pieces and others as tough-minded in one place would be a first step.

NOVEMBER–DECEMBER 2009

1 ▪ Mike Seeger, 1933–2009 August was a wipeout in American music: the rockabilly original Billy Lee Riley, dead at seventy-five on the second; the punk flash Willy DeVille at fifty-eight on the sixth; the electric guitar pioneer Les Paul at ninety-four on the thirteenth; the Memphis termite Jim Dickinson, a.k.a. leader of Mudboy and the Neutrons, at sixty-seven on the fifteenth; Ellie Greenwich, cowriter of "Da Do Ron Ron," "Be My Baby," and "Leader of the Pack," at sixty-eight on the twenty-sixth. But the cruelest note may

have been struck with Mike Seeger, the folklorist, producer, filmmaker, and scholar-on-his-feet, dead at seventy-five on the seventh. He died beloved and respected, but also bitter—over the fact that as a singer and player in his own right, those whom Bob Dylan once called the folk police never accepted him as a peer of those he helped rescue from obscurity and bring into the light: Dock Boggs, Clarence Ashley, Roscoe Holcomb, and countless more—great artists who themselves had no trouble accepting him at all.

2 ▪ **Drones, Bell House (Brooklyn, September 9)** Having flown in that day from Australia, complaining of jet lag and offering to share bronchitis with the sparse crowd, they threw out one ferocious song after another. "Sitting on the edge of the bed crying," Gareth Liddiard sang over and over, with storms of noise whirling around his head, the words muttered, chanted, shouted, whispered, until the piece seemed less about a broken heart than the human condition. Guitarist Dan Luscombe said they'd be doing songs from their 2005 album . . . *Wait Long by the River and the Bodies of Your Enemies Will Float By*. It was a prosaic promise: the embattled *us* the band enacts against the empowered *them* waiting outside the club that was itself the shelter from the storm the Drones were dramatizing. But it didn't come off that way. The music was so strong, so full of loose wires twisting through the air in a spastic dance, that you could imagine that yes, you were the "you" in "your enemies"—and that Liddiard, Luscombe, bassist Fiona Kitschin, and drummer Michael Noga were your enemies, and that as they floated by this was the song they sang.

3 ▪ *Mad Men*, **"My Old Kentucky Home" (AMC, August 30)** It's the wedding party for Roger Sterling of Sterling Cooper, the white-haired dandy who's dumped his wife for a secretary, now offering the guests his rendition of "My Old Kentucky Home"—in blackface. It's 1963, the height of the Civil Rights movement; the refusal of the history that's being made elsewhere in America

magnifies the gruesomeness of the act. It can stay in your mind like an overheard insult: the presumption that the subjects of Sterling's performance will be excluded from its audience, unless they're maids or houseboys, in which case they're invisible anyway.

4 ▪ **Thomas Pynchon, *Inherent Vice* (Penguin)** In the late '60s and early '70s, people used to talk about the great hippie detective novel. About a dope deal, of course, with an outsider/outlaw version of Philip Marlowe or Lew Archer—and Roger Simon's Moses Wine, starting out in 1973 with *The Big Fix* and still on the case thirty years later, wasn't it. Hunter Thomson played the role well in *Fear and Loathing in Las Vegas*, and then dissolved in his own hype. Pynchon's Doc Sportello somehow realizes the fantasy.

There's lazy writing—the repeated use of the screenwriter's "a beat" to signal a pause, neologisms ("At the end of the day") that weren't there then, set pieces lifted from the likes of *The Little Sister* or *The Chill* (the visit to the big mansion, the hero doped up in the locked room)—but Pynchon's affection for Sportello's time and place, Los Angeles circa 1970 with the shadow of the Manson murders still hanging in the air, is overwhelming, and it's this that powers the book. What's new is Pynchon's depiction of the economy of the hippie utopia as altogether heroin-driven; Sportello himself, a one-time skip tracer who's graduated into the world of the licensed PI, beach bum division, who at twenty-nine could be a former member of the Charlatans; and Sportello's nemesis, the infinitely manipulative LAPD homicide detective Bigfoot Bjornsen. "The whole field of homicide's being stood on its ear," he says, "—bye-bye Black Dahlia, rest in peace Tom Ince, we've seen the last of those good old-time L.A. murder mysteries I'm afraid. We've found the gateway to hell, and it's asking far too much of your L.A. civilian not to want to go crowding through it, horny and giggling as always, looking for that latest thrill. Lots of overtime for me and the boys I guess, but it brings us all that much closer to the end of the world"—and you can almost see Squeaky Fromme, not to mention generations of Los Angeles psychics and mystics, perched on his shoulder, smiling like the Mona Lisa. There is a line that in any other hands would be ridiculous but here feels exactly right—a line that to get off the ground needs a whole book behind it, that hits the note the book itself needs to lift off into the air. "He waited until he saw a dense patch of moving shadow, sighted it in, and fired, rolling away immediately, and the figure dropped like an acid tab into the mouth of Time"—a moment that fades into an ending nearly tragic in the gorgeousness of all that will soon pass away. Doc Sportello would be about seventy now—there's a whole series of stories behind him or, for Pynchon, ahead of him.

5 ▪ **The White Ribbon, directed by Michael Haneke (Telluride Film Festival, September 5)** In 1913, a series of disasters overtakes a small German village, and the events come most starkly to life in two linked shots in this black-and-white film. A woman, a worker, has been killed in an accident. Haneke places the camera to take in a rough, crumbling room where her naked body has been set on a bed. The camera waits. The woman's husband walks into the room. He covers the body. He leaves the room. The camera eye remains in place; you wait. Not long after, two children are about to be caned by their father, the town minister. With the camera positioned to take in a carefully decorated hallway, the epitome of bourgeois propriety, they pass into the next room. The door is closed; the camera remains focused on the hallway. The camera waits; the viewer waits.

In both cases, with these long and stationary shots, the action, either on camera or off, ceases to matter. It is the places that come to life, that witness, that hear, and that translate what has occurred for the viewer, which is to say they lead the viewer to imagine what else these walls have seen—or, perhaps more particularly for Haneke, since the movie is a parable about

the emergence of Nazism, what they will see. The dread and foreboding in these waiting images, with ambient sound, the sound of the rooms breathing—they are not only part of a greater drama, but visually its black holes—can load the same qualities into the seemingly more benign images from which they are so directly drawn: Walker Evans's 1936 photos of tenant family shacks in Hale County, Alabama.

6 ▪ **Jean (Hans) Arp, Birds in an Aquarium, c. 1920 (Museum of Modern Art, New York)** In Richard Powers's 2003 novel The Time of Our Singing, Delia Daley, an African American pianist from Philadelphia, and David Strom, a German-Jewish refugee physicist from New York, meet in the crowd at Marian Anderson's 1939 performance on the steps of the Lincoln Memorial. "The bird and the fish can fall in love," is the line that runs through the book, "but where will they build their nest?" "The bird can make a nest on the water," one reads on the last page. "The fish can fly." With this small assemblage of wood cutouts—in beige and black, what could be a neolithic mother figure as background; in grey, two schematic bird goddesses on the figure's chest, a red heart in one, a black heart in the other; and at the base, or the belly, rolling waves in red, brown, and blue—Arp made the fable come true.

7 ▪ **Mekons, "Thee Olde Trip to Jerusalem," Great American Music Hall (San Francisco, July 28)** With his cadaverous sunken eyes, Lu Edmonds, who plays such ancient instruments as the saz, had the look of one of the seventeenth-century heretics the song is about: the look of one of them as he might have been then, and as he might be today if he'd never died. I thought I heard someone call out for "I Wish I Was a Mole in the Ground," which in this context was "Free Bird."

8 ▪ **Deer Tick, Born on Flag Day (Partisan)** There's great depth here, rooted in folk tunes many generations older than the musicians. The way John McCauley can mock himself and still convince you he means every word he says lifts lines out of

the burgeoning Providence noise. "Smith Hill" is a sardonic song about nihilism so moving I had to stop it, then play it again to hear McCauley sing "I could drink myself to death tonight, I could stand and give a toast." Perhaps best is "Friday XIII," a duet with the Providence singer Liz Isenberg, whose readiness to find a laugh anywhere brings back Townes Van Zandt's "Waiting Around to Die"—without any death. "I can drink a lot better than I could in my teens," the guy promises; "*oooooo*" goes the girl. Hidden track: "Goodnight Irene"—party version.

9 ▪ *The Texas Sheiks* (Tradition & Moderne) Even with shimmering cover art by Ed Ruscha, there's something inherently hokey about old-time old-time music mavens—led by Geoff Muldaur, who came out of the Club 47 in Cambridge nearly fifty years ago—going back to the well one more time. The bet is that the allure in tunes first recorded in the '20s and '30s—"The World Is Going Wrong," "Poor Boy, Long Ways from Home," "Traveling Riverside Blues"— remains a treasure to be found, no matter how many times you might have thought you touched it. It pays off most improbably in Johnny Nicholas's vocal for his revision of Skip James's 1931 "Hard Time Killing Floor Blues." The imitation of James's growl, his cadence, the weight of a tramp wearing all the clothes he owns on his back—it's embarrassing, and then it's a trance. And then it's a sting, as Nicholas shows his hand and explicitly tips a song composed in the trough of one depression onto the edge of another one.

10 ▪ Richard Powers, *Generosity: An Enhancement* (Farrar, Straus and Giroux) In this novel, a T-shirt: DADA: IT'S NOT JUST FOR UMBRELLAS ANYMORE.

JANUARY 2010

1 ▪ Gossip, *Music for Men* (Columbia) After years living off the novelty that singer Beth Ditto is bigger than female singers are supposed to be, this trio has produced an album as cool and impassioned as any-

thing since the heyday of Book of Love. Everything that might get in the way of put-you-on-the-spot vocals and slap-back rhythm has been pared away; the songs breathe and snap. That you might hear Roxy Music's "Love Is the Drug" or Fine Young Cannibals' "She Drives Me Crazy" in "Heavy Cross" doesn't mean the band is recycling someone else's hits; the musicians have a jukebox in their collective head, just like anybody else. That turns up an "I Heard it through the Grapevine" quote in "Love Long Distance" so graceful it can almost make you doubt you've heard it before—and even if you know you have, the Bronski Beat beat, thin, clean, and swirling, will make you forget. With "Spare Me from the Mold," as strong an image as you can ask from a song title, they head out into a rave-up so hot they can turn it into a breakdown with the twist of a neck. Sometimes craft gives as much pleasure as vision; sometimes vision sneaks right out of craft.

2 ▪ Dion, "Daddy Rollin' (In Your Arms)," in *Big Fan*, written and directed by Robert D. Siegel (Big Fan Productions) Near the end of a film that in the pitch meeting you can see Siegel trying to sell as a cross between *Buffalo '66* and *The King of Comedy* ("What about *The Fan?*" "It's '*Big Fan*,' and who remembers *The Fan* anyway?" "Me?"), there's a no-ambient-sound slow-motion bar scene where the hero, the schlub "get a life" was invented for, walks through the place like Robert De Niro in his Mohawk, all sorts of conflicting and repressed desires flooding him like a bad cold; the only sound you hear is the flipside of Dion's 1968 "Abraham, Martin & John," the most threatening record he ever made. Somebody knows their stuff.

3 ▪ Bill Pullman in *Oleanna* (John Golden Theatre, New York, October 20, 2009) Immediately after the final, violent "cunt" scene, Pullman, the professor, and Julia Stiles, the student, the only characters in this revival of David Mamet's 1992 play about sexual harassment and feminist conspiracy, return to the stage with copious distance between

them—"The curtain call is as directed as anything else," said a friend—and he looks haggard, confused, shaken, as if he truly has been somewhere else and isn't back.

4 ▪ **Catherine Corman, *Daylight Noir: Raymond Chandler's Imagined City* (Charta)** It seems like an unassailable idea: matching original dialogue or descriptions to new photographs, stalk Los Angeles as if scouting locations for remakes of all the Philip Marlowe movies, for every building he ever walked into or out of—the exits, so often leaving a body behind, usually being more memorable than the entrances. But as the pages turn, it becomes clear Chandler's writing never needed illustrations—or that a picture of a city hall is not going to stand up to "He had my wrists now, instead of me having his. He twisted them behind me fast and a knee like a corner store went into my back. I can be bent. I'm not City Hall," never mind that a picture of an expensive Moorish tower sucks the irony out of the last line. But there's one plain and ghostly exception, a version of the house where, in *The Little Sister*, Orrin Quest found a room. In Corman's hands it's a rickety wooden staircase leading to a door topped by a crude English sunrise motif, with two palm trees hovering over the building like giant undertakers: an image that carries so much suspense the quote facing it dies on its page.

5 ▪ **David Lang, original music in *(Untitled)*, directed by Jonathan Parker (Goldwyn)** Lang won the 2008 Pulitzer music prize; I can't imagine it would work on the soundtrack album, but on screen his avant-garde conceptual noise music parodies, which include a musician popping bubble wrap but usually focus on a bucket, have a glamour that deepens scene by scene— especially when, to pay the rent, Adam Goldberg's fearless composer takes jobs playing piano at a supper club or a wedding and still can't help dumping the likes of "Night and Day" or "Wonderful World" for atonal minor chords that shout "Death, death, death!" at the fleeing crowds. It makes sense that Marley Shelton's ice-queen New York gallery owner falls for Goldberg the first time she hears him, and that he's so self-consumed he doesn't notice that her own clothes, apparently all made out of metal-based fabrics, generate sounds as alluring as his (cellophane packages being opened in movie theaters, wood being sanded, wrenches unscrewing bolts)—whenever she walks, turns, or tries to take them off.

6–7 ▪ **Raincoats and Viv Albertine, Knitting Factory (Brooklyn, October 16, 2009)** I hadn't seen the Raincoats, one of the UK's original all-female punk bands, for just short of thirty years. Original members Gina Birch (bass, guitar) and Ana da Silva (guitar, bass) looked precisely as they did when they started out, merely older. Anne Wood (violin, kalimba, bass), who joined the band in 1994, replacing original violinist Vicky Aspinall, looked like Molly Shannon and carried herself like the lead in Abel Gance's *Napoleon*. The young drummer, Vice Cooler, from San Francisco, who records as Hawnay Troof, added a drum sound so big, and so light on its feet, that each song seemed to start a few inches off the ground and stay there. Viv Albertine, guitarist of the Slits, *the* original all-female UK punk band, opened the show solo; she joined the Raincoats for their version of the Kinks' "Lola," a signature crowd-pleaser, but the second-to-last song, "In Love," from the band's first single, from 1979, was, in the words of th Faith Healers, "everything, all at once, forever." I was waiting for that one song, and when it began I realized I'd altogether forgotten it, remembering only the impact it had when I first heard it: remembering the shock. It blew up the jammed little room, half filled with people half as old as the other half: shouts and cries and curses and pleas, all coming as if from a single throat, a wild, unsatisfied, unsatisfiable celebration of the discovery that, in someone else's eyes, you exist, you cannot be erased, even if in the next moment you're hit by a car and all you leave is a stain on the street.

Albertine played only new songs; they're better with a band, as on her Myspace page, but they still seem contrived. Her stage talk, which took up at least half of her time, was if anything more practiced, and moved with all of the passion, humor, and daring her music lacked. Her ruminations took her through the breakup of her fifteen-year marriage over her wish to go back to music after not touching a guitar for a quarter of a century; her terrible sex life then and now; the beginnings of punk and the Stalinist tinge among the small, insular group that made up the first wave, a few friends who really did mean to change the world by embodying a new way of life. She told tales of being shouted down on the street for holding hands with her punk boyfriend, Mick Jones of the Clash, and of being forced to get rid of all her T-shirts ("from Biba, the best store in the world"), because they had scoop necks. Then, as if relating a fairy tale, putting down Mother Goose and picking up the Brothers Grimm, she told the story of the arrival in London, just as the scene had found itself, of the Heartbreakers, from New York: "They brought Nancy Spungen, but what they really brought was heroin." Within weeks, she said, the same Stalinism that made her get rid of her favorite clothes meant that if you weren't using heroin you weren't cool enough to speak to: "Really rigorous people, questioning everything, and now all they cared about was finding the next fix." "I succumbed," she said. "I let Johnny Thunders shoot me up. My arm turned black for three weeks. I was living with my Mum and had to hide it. Luckily I didn't go down that road. I never did it again. I wouldn't want my daughter to know about it." A smile never left her face; at fifty-four she looked thirty at most. "The curse of the Slits," she said, leaving everyone to wonder what she meant.

8 ▪ **Coen Brothers, *A Serious Man* (Focus Features)** The scene where the ancient rabbi quotes from the Jefferson Airplane's "Somebody to Love" as if the lyrics came straight from the Talmud is its own double take. But why does the song sound so terrible on the soundtrack?

9 ▪ **Kay West, People.com (September 21, 2009)** "Before a packed house of 1,500 fans and a balcony filled with invited guests, Grammy-winning rock-folk singer Lucinda Williams said, 'I do,' to her boyfriend and manager Tom Overby on Friday. The couple, who have been together for three years, tied the knot onstage at First Avenue, a music club in Minneapolis. The audience was in the dark about the pending nuptials until Williams, at the end of her performance, told the crowd that like country legend Hank Williams, she was going to share her happiness and her wedding with fans. Hank Williams married his second wife onstage in New Orleans." Ken Tucker comments: "Williams also announced that she'd recently decided she wants to be referred to hereafter as 'the daughter Hank never knew he had,' rather than as 'the daughter of poet Miller Williams,' because 'the whole poetry angle really isn't working out for me anymore now that folks have actually examined my lyrics.'"

10 ▪ **Josh Lieb, *I am a Genius of Unspeakable Evil and I Want to Be Your Class President* (Razorbill)** This first novel, featuring twelve-year-old Oliver Watson, a fat Captain Beefheart fan who rules the world but not his Omaha middle school, seems powered by the same malignant spirits that fester in Fletcher Hanks's completely unhinged comic strips of the late '30s and early '40s, lately collected by Fantagraphics as *You Shall Die by Your Own Evil Creation!* and *I Shall Destroy All the Civilized Planets!* This is funnier, because you can usually forget that the story would actually be worse if you took it as Oliver's fantasy instead of his real life.

FEBRUARY 2010

1 ▪ **Kelly Clarkson, "Already Gone" (from *All I Ever Wanted*, Sony BMG)** Sometimes you want singers to wear their hearts on their sleeves. Especially when they sound like Sarah McLachlan.

2 ▪ *The Missing Person*, **written and directed by Noah Buschel (The 7th Floor)** Matching its center of gravity—the way that with every scowl directed outward at the

world Michael Shannon's private eye pulls more deeply into himself, as if he can make himself his own black hole—the movie itself is dark and muffled. It's hard to see and hard to hear. The plot is full of dead ends. But there is one moment of clarity, so full of unguarded warmth it seems to be from another film altogether, or another life: the detective and a woman who's picked him up in a bar dancing in a crummy Los Angeles hotel room as the radio plays the Jive Five's 1961 "My True Story." "But we must cry, cry, cry," Eugene Pitt sings, going up high, turning the swamp of the past into at least a hint of a future, and you think, yes, tell *this* story—while at the same time you're wondering, OK, a thirty-five-year old Jive Five fan, he's from New York, I can believe that, but how did he find a doo-wop station in California?

3 ▪ **Punk shoes from Giovanna Zanella (Castello 5641, Calle Carminati, Venice)** Six-inch heels on black pumps with a Doc Martens sole and a red Mohawk that looks more like a weapon than a haircut coming out of the back.

4 ▪ **Herbert Bayer, *Design for a Multimedia Building*, in "Bauhaus 1919–1933: Workshops for Modernity" (Museum of Modern Art, New York, through January 25)** It's all Regina all the time: on one face of the rectangular box, a film projected from inside showing Ms. R. pulling her lips apart in a happy if brainless smile; on another, a huge gramophone horn protruding, broadcasting the new hit "Regina." On the roof, a smoke hole emitting small black clouds that spell out . . . you guessed it. To the side of the horn, under an overhang, a man exiting, while the diagram helpfully indicates the In and Out. The whole looks like a valentine from Bayer to his girlfriend Regina, a modernist treehouse, or a De Stijl–influenced mock-up of an ad for a freestanding one-woman brothel. The playfulness and glee of the design perfectly catches the thrust of the exhibition as a whole: the story of adventurous, questing, ambitious people with their lives and a world to change before them, about to be crushed.

5 ▪ **Jenny Diski, *The Sixties* (Picador)** If you liked *An Education* and were wondering what happened next . . .

6–7 ▪ **Bob Dylan and Dion, United Palace Theater (New York, November 17, 2009)** The stage was pure House of Blue lights before Dylan came on: deep velvet background, upside-down electric candles ringing the top of the stage. In that setting "Beyond Here Lies Nothin,'" from *Together Through Life* last spring, was a sultry vamp from a '40s supper club. Clearly the song was still opening itself up to Dylan; he sang with heart, as if looking to find how much it might tell him. "Dedicated to our troops," Dion had said earlier, for "Abraham, Martin and John," and the mood Dylan was creating was already too fine for "Masters of War"; instead he sang the mom-sends-son-off-to-glory-and-then-he-comes-back folk song "John Brown" in a hard-boiled voice, the Continental Op running down the murders in *Red Harvest*. Most striking of all was "Ballad of a Thin Man." In Todd Haynes's film *I'm Not There*, Cate Blanchett, as Dylan in London in 1966, acts out the song standing alone behind a mic stand like a nightclub singer, no protection of a guitar between performer and audience. It was something Bob Dylan had never done, but that was precisely the posture he assumed now, as if the movie had taught him something new about his own song: how to make it more intimate, more direct, so that it was the audience, not the singer, that was left more naked, more defenseless.

For all that, Dion stole the show. He opened with Buddy Holly's "Rave On"— and that had to be to remind both Dylan and the crowd of the night in early 1959, just days before Holly died, when a seventeen-year-old Robert Zimmerman sat in the Duluth National Guard Armory, Holly himself sang "Rave On," and Dion was an opening act at that show, too. Now he was seventy, and his voice grew, opened, gained in suppleness and reach with every song. One by one, he put the oldies behind him, so that it all came to a head with "King of the New York Streets," from 1989.

It's a gorgeous, panoramic song: a strutting brag that in the end turns back on itself, a Bronx match for the Geto Boys' "Mind Playing Tricks on Me." It opens with huge, doomy chords, wide silences between the notes, creating a sense of wonder and suspension, and you don't want the moment to break, for the music to take a single step forward—just as, after the song has gone on and on, you can't bear the idea that it's going to end. From that almost-frozen beginning, the pace seemed to speed up with every verse, but it wasn't the beat that was doubling, it was the intensity and the drama. Dion's wails were as fierce as ever, but never so full of wide-open spaces, the voice itself an undiscovered country, and it was impossible to imagine that he had ever sung better.

8 ■ **Gov't Mule, "Railroad Boy," from *By a Thread* (Evil Teen)** Upsetting a trainload of expert grind-it-out, the centuries-old melody and story of "Railroad Boy" (a.k.a. "The Butcher's Boy"), which sounds like the precursor of the Teen Death Song: "Tell Laura I Love Her," "Last Kiss," "Teen Angel," but perhaps more to the point, "I Don't Like Mondays," "Endless Sleep," and most of all "Ode to Billie Joe." Ruth Gerson made the connection explicit in 2008 with her *Deceived*; in Gov't Mule's hands, or hooves, it sneaks up on you like a villain in a *Scream* movie. Which makes the name of their label all too perfect.

9 ■ **Malcolm McLaren, "Shallow" (Pennsylvania Academy of the Fine Arts, Philadelphia, October 24, 2009–January 3, 2010)** Twenty-one "musical paintings"—which is to say, loops of found footage depicting people gearing up to have sex with soundtracks made up of smeared pop songs, snatches of interviews or spoken-word performances, and swirls of movie tunes. "No matter how shallow people say pop music is," McLaren writes in his exhibition note, "it continues to confound, astound, and seduce something deep in all of us—the desire to change the culture and possibly, if

it be only for a moment, change life itself. No matter how shallow people say sex is, it continues to occupy and post-occupy everyone's thoughts, forcing us to be irresponsible, childish and everything this society hates, and why not?" A topless blonde woman descending a staircase and dragging a fur coat behind her as Joy Division's "Love Will Tear Us Apart" answers Captain and Tennille's "Love Will Keep Us Together" is a joke that never comes to life. There's a shaggy, fleshy guy with his arm draped around a grinning beanpole; they don't seem to be listening to the bits of the Staple Singers' "Respect Yourself" floating in and out of a disco version of an old country blues, and when the camera pulls back to show a handgun jammed into the front of the second man's pants, you don't hear the music either, because now the man's faraway resemblance to Timothy McVeigh is undeniable. Best of all is a dressed-up seventies couple, seated on a couch, apparently watching a movie on TV, both smoking, with fragments of the Zombies' "She's Not There" circling their heads. It's super-slow motion; the slightest change in expression becomes an event that you follow in a state of suspense. As the man steals glances at the woman with a self-satisfied smile crawling over his mouth, her eyes widen in an expression of surprise or fright that imperceptibly but definitively changes into arousal, and then the sequence begins from the beginning. You watch them again and again—and then finally McLaren allows the film to go a step further. The man is still contemplating his conquest, the woman is still lost in her own world, until she turns her head and sees him, her eyes as clear as if she were speaking out loud: Who is this guy? Where did *he* come from?

10 ■ ***Ed Sullivan's Rock and Roll Classics: The 60s* (PBS, November 29)** Fund-raising break commentary by host TJ Lubinsky: "Public television has always been there as an alternative to"—the Ed Sullivan Show?

Thanks to Liz Bordow, David Bordow, David Ross, and Peggy Ross

1 ▪ Yellow Fever, *Yellow Fever* (Wild World) From Austin, Jennifer Moore and Isabel Martin play guitar, bass, and sing; Adam Jones plays drums and bass; and the early '60s meet the early '80s, neither of which anyone in the band is likely old enough to remember, which is simply to say that despite oldies formats there is no time on the radio. The band's music is full of air, with brittle Young Marble Giants rhythms—and its humor (quotes from the Jaynetts' 1963 "Sally, Go 'Round the Roses" and Ben E. King's 1960 "Spanish Harlem," plus sexy organ right out of Freddy Cannon's 1962 "Palisades Park") is sometimes muffled by Young Marble Giants archness, which has its own charms.

2 ▪ Stephen Thompson, "'American Idol' and the Making of a Star" (*Morning Edition*, NPR, December 23, 2009) For Thompson's own ideal *American Idol* song, "On the Wings of Dreaming Eagles," which you'll swear you've already heard, even if you can't remember whether it was Clay Aiken or Adam Lambert on season four or season seven.

3 ▪ Woods, "Born to Lose," from *Songs of Shame* (Shrimper) There's a broken, incomplete quality on every song here—something unknowable. But on this number—odd, incomplete, and, at 1:59, unsettlingly short—the name of the album comes into play. The tempo is slow, with bare guitar notes and distantly echoed backing vocals that come across less as voices than as memories, or wind. From Brooklyn, Jeremy Earl's croaked, pleading singing is as spectral as anything else: the testimony of someone whose time has already run out, and who doesn't think he deserved a minute more than he got.

4 ▪ Ken Maynard, *Ken Maynard Sings The Lone Star Trail* (Bear Family) With close to a hundred pictures between 1923 and 1945, Maynard (1895–1973) was the first singing Hollywood cowboy. Perhaps because of his high voice, he made only eight recordings, in 1930, with five—"Sweet Betsy from Pike," "Fannie Moore," "When the Roundup's Done this Fall," "Jesse James," and "A Prisoner for Life"—released here for the first time, and not one is less than haunted. He could be listening now to Woods's "Born to Lose," smiling and saying, too bad they left that off my album.

5 ▪ *Gigante*, written and directed by Adrián Biniez (Ctrl Z Films) A very quiet movie about a surveillance worker at a huge Montevideo supermarket who falls in love with a floor cleaner while watching her on one of his video screens. He's enormous and moonlights as a bouncer at a nightclub; she's not pretty but endlessly appealing; he follows her all over town and beats up people who make catcalls at her. They finally meet, and you know it's a match made in heaven, because they both love Metallica and Biohazard.

6 ▪ DeSoto Rust, "Calgary," from *Highway Gothic* (DeSotoRust.com) There's nothing Gothic here, just the thirty-seven-thousandth ride down the American road, not a line escaping its cliché or even trying to. You can imagine Philadelphian Ray Hunter gargling dust to get the right sound in his throat. And somewhere inside the play between Dave Reeve's drums and David Otwell and Steve Savage's guitars, there's the kind of satisfaction you can only get if you're behind the wheel, alone, for a moment forgetting where you are, maybe because Marshall Tucker's "Can't You See" is on the radio.

7 ▪ Absolut Vodka, The Rock Edition (Absolut Spirits Co.) More like the Black Metal Edition—except that with the zipper on the side, the thick studded black casing looks less like a guitarist's wrist guard than a sex slave's S&M mask.

8 ▪ Georgia O'Keeffe, "Abstraction" (Whitney Museum of American Art, New York, September 17, 2009–January 17, 2010) Anyone can be forgiven for thinking, but I've *seen* Georgia O'Keeffe; the work in this great show has been hidden behind the flowers and skulls. This is bedrock, as much painted by the American landscape as it is about it. *Wave, Night* (1928: desert, a lake bed in the foreground, at the top, in the middle, a

single white spotlight, which only barely illuminates the shadow of a road reaching diagonally from middle-right down to far-left) is as much an anticipation of Robert Frank's highway pictures in *The Americans* as the 1919 *Abstraction* is of Batman's Gotham City—or as the very early charcoal drawing *Train at Night in the Desert* (1916: clouds billowing up at either side, almost black on the left, gray at the right, the train in the center, but in a way that while a sense of movement is undeniable the train is itself a cloud) is of Elvis Presley's "Mystery Train."

9 ▪ **Kevin Bradley, Robert Johnson (Chelsea Market, New York City, December 16, 2009)** One of a series of letterpress posters on the walls of the meandering hallways, this stood out: for the backlit eyes, the filed teeth, and the caption: "They say he sold his soul, but he tricked Saten by putting his soul in his music."

10 ▪ *Pirate Radio*, **directed by Richard Curtis (Universal Pictures)** Set in the mid-'60s, this movie about illicit rock 'n' roll broadcasting from a ship in the North Sea into bedrooms and offices all across the UK lines up *Don't Knock the Rock* (1956), *Animal House* (1978), *American Hot Wax* (1978), *Pump Up the Volume* (1990), *Titanic* (1997), and finally *Dunkirk* (1958), and plays them like a xylophone. It sounds wonderful, it's hilarious, and it features Rhys Ifans as the coolest DJ in screen history. But when the ship begins to sink and the thousands of LPs and 45s in the station library are swept away (never mind what Walter Benjamin said about the artistic products of mechanical reproduction lacking the aura of art—as they're carried off by thousands of pounds of water, these records *are* aura), a deeper analogue appears. That's Tom Stoppard's 2006 play *Rock 'n' Roll*, for the horrible scene when the Czech hero discovers that the secret police have smashed his albums, every one.

MAY 2010

1 ▪ **Ellyn Maybe, Rodeo for the Sheepish (Hen House Studios)** I heard half of the long,

quietly mesmerizing "City Streets" on the radio—what was this? A woman with a poem, with music and a sung chorus not behind her but circling her, and the poem neither exactly recited nor sung, but spoken with such a lilt, in a voice so full of miserabilist pride—at forty, a woman is still getting high-school insults tossed at her ("Hey Mars girl," a man shouts on the street, "get off the Earth")—that it's music in and of itself. There is no bottom to Maybe's inventiveness, to her adoption of Nirvana's *Oh well whatever never mind* as an artistic tool, to a confidence that allows her to toss off a bedrock statement on the American character ("There are people / who know the cuckoo is the state bird / of most states of mind") in a throwaway voice so that its humor hits you not as a joke but as an echo. There is nothing like this album except for the real life it maps.

2 ▪ **Train, "Hey, Soul Sister" (Sony)** A perfect fan's letter, with the high, light sound of someone madly in love with the idea of being in love. You can see the singer dancing in circles in his bedroom, waving his arms in the air. Could the soul sister who inspired this record make one half as good?

3 ▪ **Lady Gaga, "Bad Romance" (Interscope)** When she turns *Love* into *Lahv, lahv, lahv*, as if she could care less, the inhuman edge of this semiological construct— the performer, not the song—can open up a hole in your soul. When it feels as if Kiki and Herb are smiling down at her from the heights of their "Total Eclipse of the Heart" she's Robert Plant, lost in communion with the ancestors, like Medusa or Gene Vincent.

4 ▪ **Keri Hilson, "Knock You Down," featuring Kanye West and Ne-Yo (Interscope)** The swirl.

5 ▪ **Carolina Chocolate Drops, Genuine Negro Jig (Nonesuch)** "Fragments of humble and cryptic work songs appeared," Constance Rourke wrote of how the voice of the slave made its way into blackface minstrelsy before the Civil War. "Defeat could be heard in the occasional minor key." In

the hands of this string-band trio, taking up "Genuine Negro Jig," popularized by Dan Emmett in the 1840s, you can hear that sense of defeat stretched so far from the ordinary facts of life that it begins to turn into what was hiding in Rourke's choice of the word *cryptic*: into resistance, or, if not that, escape. And when Justin Robinson's autoharp surfaces a few songs later, in "Kissin' and Cussin'," which takes off from Rabbit Brown's 1927 "James Alley Blues," the aura of the uncanny—of time travel as a version of walking out your front door—is almost as strong.

6 ■ Handsome Family, "Jenny Jenkins," on *Face a Frowning World: An E. C. Ball Memorial Album* (Tompkins Square) Aren't tribute albums terrible? This one, celebrating a traditional Virginia singer who died in 1978, features mostly bland vocals and the happy-go-lucky accompaniment by the Health & Happiness Family Gospel Band, which might as well be Hippie Heaven circa 1971. In that house, it feels as if the Handsome Family, picking a children's nonsense song off the floor—*Will you, I won't, Will you, I won't*—came in through a window. Asking the questions, Brett Sparks sounds like a preacher trying to save a child from perdition; throwing them back in his face, or rather over his shoulder, at a horizon only she can see, Rennie Sparks sounds like a talking goth doll.

7 ■ *Who Do You Love*, directed by Jerry Zaks (Alexander/Mitchell Productions) In the 1930s, two Jewish Chicago boys, Leonard and Phil Chess, hear a black street singer going off about motherfucker this and motherfucker that, and they walk off playing with the word, almost chanting it, trying to catch the man's inflection, because somehow it just sounds so good, feels so good: "What does this mean?" one kid says to the other.

The second movie in two years about Chess Records, this one tells the story from 1946, when the Chess brothers decided to open a blues club, to 1955, when Bo Diddley arrived to change the tune. Partly because of the short time span, it's a chamber piece

compared to *Cadillac Records*, a shapeless movie that never got off the ground. This has so much movement it's like one long gasp, and yet its dynamics are always controlled, its scenes intense, its humor snapping, its pain ugly and ineradicable, its flair for the startling moment unending. The performances are never showy; each actor seems to be searching for his or her center of gravity, and when they find it, the movie comes out of itself: when at the beginning and the end Robert Randolph as Bo Diddley serves up the title song, his white socks flashing like stars and his feet moving too fast to credit, it's like a dream of the birth of rock 'n' roll come true. David Oyelowo as Muddy Waters is a well of dignity: "You know that ain't no good to me," he says without embarrassment when Chi McBride as the songwriter Willie Dixon hands him a lyric sheet. Megalyn Ann Echikunwoke's Ivy Mills, a fictionalized version of Etta James, is nothing as a singer; as a woman looking Leonard Chess in the face, seeing right through him but wanting what she sees, she is as much will as fear. Alessandro Nivola's Leonard Chess is a businessman first and last, but he's also still trying to figure out what *motherfucker* means. "Dix is my mentor," Leonard Chess says at one point to Muddy Waters, who wonders why Willie Dixon is always looking over the boss's shoulder, but who has no idea what *mentor* means. "I am his guide to the exotic Negro world," Dixon says, honey dripping from his mouth.

8 ■ Tommy James with Martin Fitzpatrick, *Me, the Mob, and the Music: One Helluva Ride with Tommy James and the Shondells* (Scribner) Nice kid from Ohio walks into the big time in New York in 1966 and then the door slams behind him. He doesn't mind, because "Hanky Panky" goes to number one on Roulette, his music gets better, and he's almost never out of the top ten. In 1968 he campaigns for Hubert Humphrey (who tells James his secret plan to end the Vietnam War), and then the vice president of the United States writes the liner notes to *Crimson and Clover*—and if

the Jewish gangster running his career is owned by the Genovese family, isn't that what America's all about? "He saw the world as a crime family," James says of Morris Levy, whom he clearly loved. "And most of the time he was right." Maybe it all goes back to the folk process, to the way Tommy James and the Shondells, teenagers in Dayton, found "Hanky Panky" in the first place—the song traveling from the "B-side of a record nobody ever heard" to James's friends the Spinners' Sunday-afternoon show to a rehearsal where all any of the Shondells could remember was "My baby does the hanky panky" and they had to make up their own words. "We were actually doing an imitation of the Spinners' imitation, and who knew how far the chain stretched?" Was that really any different from Morris Levy putting his name on your songs?

9 ▪ Martin Amis, *The Pregnant Widow* (Knopf) Out of the cradle, endlessly rocking, or why this novelist's best days may be ahead of him: "As the fiftieth birthday approaches, you get the sense that your life is thinning out, and will continue to thin out, until it thins out into nothing. . . . Then fifty comes and goes, and fifty-one, and fifty-two. And life thickens out again. Because there is now an enormous and unsuspected presence within your being, like an undiscovered continent. This is the past."

10 ▪ James Wolcott, "A Certain Acoustic Quality in the Air" (VF.com, March 3) On the street, with the temperature in New York not yet reaching into the low 40s, Wolcott was struck by a sense less of déjà vu than of rightness, "reminding me of something, but what?—what? Then the picture liquidly surfaced in my brain like a print in a developing tray. It's like the album cover of *The Freewheelin' Bob Dylan* out there today! . . . I wouldn't be surprised if I turned the corner and saw Bob and Suze Rotolo, arm in arm, stepping out of folk history and heading my way." Summed up as a weather report, and they should all be so suggestive: "Early Bob Dylan Album Cover, with a chance of precipitation."

1 ▪ Club 8, *The People's Record* (Labrador) You know that Dire Straits song "Twisting by the Pool"? If a whole album of twisting-by-the-pool music by a demi-ABBA—Karolina Komstedt and Johan Angergård, Swedes with a bossa-nova collection—sounds appealing, this is for you. Especially on "We're All Going to Die."

2 ▪ Alfred, "Like a Rolling Stone," in *Bob Dylan Revisited: 13 Graphic Interpretations of Bob Dylan's Songs* (Norton) Almost everything here is destructively literal, to the point that most of the pictures meant to illustrate the songs are accompanied by matching lyrics that instead illustrate the pictures—or reveal the complete lack of imagination behind them. By stunning contrast—and in stunning use of shifting color schemes, where each chapter in the story of a woman attempting to escape into a life of her own and continually finding herself imprisoned by the life she was born to is governed by shadings of blue, taupe, yellow, olive green, brown, gray, and finally a bright, light-filled page that is scarier than anything darker—Alfred trusts abstraction. Until the very last of his sixty-seven panels there isn't a word to be seen. The story he tells isn't obvious, isn't clear. It doesn't match Dylan's soaring, heat-seeking-missile crescendos and choruses—it brings them down to earth. It isn't a social allegory. It's one person's odyssey, a lifetime that returns her to precisely the place she first flees. And the Siamese cat isn't a symbol of evil, or anything else. It's the woman's conscience, or what, all along, has been singing the song that has been playing deep in the farthest back corners of her mind. Following the tale as Alfred sees it, it's as if you've never heard the song at all, and now you must.

3 ▪ Scott Ostler, "Bay Area Sports Scene Is Giants and Disasters" (*San Francisco Chronicle*, April 1, 2010) On the so-far futile attempt of the Oakland A's to move to San Jose, with disaster rating by tornado: "The A's (three tornadoes) are Running Bear, the American Indian in a 1960s novelty song of the same name by Johnny Preston. Running Bear is in love with Little White Dove. In our local drama, Little White Dove is played by the city of San Jose.

"Bear and Dove can't get together because their respective tribes are at war. All they can do is gaze longingly at one another across a big river.

"That's the A's. Their very existence depends on finding a way to overcome politics and hook up with San Jose. Frankly, most of us wish the two would get a room.

"The song, by the way, ends with Running Bear and Little White Dove jumping into the river from opposite sides, and 'the raging river pulled them down.'"

4 ■ Hanoi Janes, *Year of Panic* (Captured Tracks) Almost-one-man band Oliver Scharf, from Saschen, Germany, near Dresden. Caspian Sea Surf Music, suggests the press release, which is close enough—song titles include "Beachkids," "Surfin' KMC," and (note the surfin' variation on the album title) "Summer of Panic"—but Scharf is closer to Jan and Dean than Brian Wilson, and a lot closer to Jonathan Richman than either of them. Except on "Good Bone," when he's closer to Buddy Holly. Gloriously.

5–6 ■ Hugh Brown, *Allegedly: The Hugh Brown Chainsaw Collection* (Grand Central Press) and Caitlin Williams Freeman, "Confections" (San Francisco Museum of Modern Art) What if Matisse, Duchamp, Man Ray, Pollock, Lichtenstein, Cornell, and more, more, had incorporated chainsaw motifs into their work—not to mention Arbus (she didn't?), Warhol, Ruscha, Kruger, Holzer, Prince, Hockney, and Mapplethorpe? It's not likely many of them would have come up with anything as coolly subtle as Brown's constructions, fruit of a project decades in the making. Least convincing: a phallic remake of Meret Oppenheim's *Object*. Blink and you'll miss it: a perfectly rendered version of Walker Evans's 1936 Farm Security Administration photograph of a New Orleans movie theater, which instead of Bert Wheeler and Robert Woolsey's *The Nitwits* is now featuring *The Texas Chainsaw Massacre Part 2*. Brown's work is also a gallery

show (at the Robert Berman Gallery, Los Angeles, July 24–August 21), which were it to be installed at SFMOMA you could walk through and then go up to the rooftop coffee bar and try to chose between Caitlin Williams Freeman's Jeff Koons White Hot Chocolate with cup and saucer slathered with gold leaf; Frida Kahlo Mexican Wedding Cookies; a blue, red, yellow, and white Mondrian Cake; and, most perversely, Build Your Own Richard Serra—where standing in for the iron walls are a Swedish gingersnap, a chocolate sable cookie, a graham cracker, and, as the bar to hold the mini-Stonehenge in place, a citrus tuille cookie. Plus a napkin complete with instructions to keep the thing from falling down while you set it up.

7 ■ *Surveillance*, directed and cowritten by Jennifer Chambers Lynch (2008, Magnolia DVD) For nightmare performances by Pell James and Ryan Simpkins—with Simpkins, in her fearlessness and lack of affect after seeing her entire family massacred, presented, by way of her blond braid, as Patty McCormack in *The Bad Seed*, which means a sequel in which she will either kill Bill Pullman and Julia Ormond or join their gang. With David Lynch's crawl song "Speed Roadster" in his high, come-into-this-alley-with-me psycho rap over fuzzed blues.

8 ■ *Kiss Meets the Führer of the Reich* (YouTube) In 1966 Woody Allen bought rights to a Japanese James Bond imitation called *Kagi no Kagi*, dubbed in his own dialogue, and released the thing as *What's Up, Tiger Lily?* As Allen's first and funniest movie, it made an increasingly unhinged kind of sense—and so do the slew of uncredited videos that with English subtitles play the same trick on a four-minute section of the 2004 German film *Der Untergang*. It's April 20, 1945, Hitler is in his bunker, surrounded by his staff, raging, despairing, then reflective, almost wistful—and then it's June 25, 2009, for *Hitler Finds Out Michael Jackson Has Died*, or three months later, for *Hitler Finds Out Kanye West Disses Taylor Swift*. But the killer is June 8, 2008. Poring over charts, plotting strategy

to the end, as head of the German division of the Kiss Army, Hitler is preparing for the band's big concert. He will stop at nothing to get Peter Criss and Ace Frehley to add their signatures to his buttocks—he's already got Gene Simmons and Paul Stanley. Then an officer steps forward, trembling, to deliver the bad news: Frehley and Criss are not touring with the band. There is a silence no one dares break. Another officer, grasping at straws, suggests that all may not be lost: the substitutes are said to be "competent musicians." "What do Kiss fans care about competent musicians!" Hitler explodes. Again, silence. Again, the remaining officers looking desperately at each other, knowing the wrong word could mean their deaths. Hitler backs himself into a corner, shrinking into himself, cursing wildly, but then fury turns to acceptance. It's over: "I can't even rest my hopes on Mr. Ace Frehley's new solo album." And it's all in the timing—the camp timing of the original transformed by the bizarrely human timing of the subtitles, catching nuances the real movie never dreamed of.

9 ▪ *Assassination of a High School President,* directed by Brett Simon (2008, Sony DVD) *Scream* was a parody of the high-school slasher movie, and for most of its length this increasingly creepy exercise— with Reece Thompson as the school paper reporter Bobby Funke ("Funk!" he keeps correcting everyone) and Mischa Barton as the femme fatale—is a parody of *Scream.* But step by step, in emotion if not plot, it moves toward the believable. At the end, with the hero distraught and refusing to accept the whole truth, when his editor turns to him and says, "Forget it, Funke, it's high school," the moment sticks harder, seems less of a screenwriter's gloss, than it did in *Chinatown.* Plus Cat Power's "Speak for Me" running over the credits, and capturing the chaos of high-school life as well as anything on the screen.

10 ▪ Penelope Houston at Library Laureates presents Urban Legends (San Francisco Public Library, April 16) The great Avengers singer, a longtime SFPL staff member,

came up: "I'm dressed as a *literary* urban legend," she said. Perhaps 5′ 2″, moles pasted on each cheek, streaked blond hair over one eye, goggle-dark glasses—she *was* JT Leroy. Or as much as anyone impersonating someone who existed only as an impersonation could be.

Thanks to Jeff Gold

JULY–AUGUST 2010

As a compiler, Allen Lowe is the music historian's equivalent of David Thomson with his ongoing editions of *A Biographical Dictionary of Film* (the latest will be out this fall). In 1998 Lowe produced the nine-CD *American Pop: An Audio History—From Minstrel to Mojo: On Record, 1893–1946;* in 2006 the thirty-six-CD *That Devilin' Tune: A Jazz History [1895–1950].* Now he is unrolling a thirty-six-CD *Really the Blues? A Blues History 1893–1959* in four installments; the first nine-CD box, covering 1893 to 1929, appeared this spring from West Hill Radio Archives. With at least twenty-four numbers to a disc, *Really the Blues?* is a cornucopia; it's a swamp. It's a forest to get lost in, tree by tree or even leaf by leaf. It's a grand and overarching story—though that ? at the end of his title marks Lowe's doubt as to whether with the blues such a story is possible, or even a good idea. It's a flurry of fragments, leaving you grasping for a way to follow the trail.

As his free-swinging liner notes make clear, Lowe is a radical pluralist; as a synthesizer he's completely idiosyncratic. He may love disjunction far more than unity— but what others hear as disjunctions may be unities to him. Thus along with late-nineteenth-century black quartette singing, Bert Williams, W. C. Handy, early gospel, vaudeville blues, minstrelsy survivals, New York City productions featuring the likes of Mamie Smith, Sarah Martin, and then Bessie Smith, Louis Armstrong, King Oliver, and the lone-traveler-with-guitar of the country blues, there is also Paul Whiteman, Jimmie Rodgers, white mountain singers, Billie Holiday, bluegrass, Sacred Harp chanting, Frank Sinatra, Doris Day, and a Charles Ives piano piece from his *Symphony no. 1*. In Lowe's hands, the blues is not a feeling ("A good man/woman feeling bad," in the classical phrase, or, in Buzzy Jackson's recent revision, "A bad woman feeling good"). It's a language: something one can draw from the times and the landscape, or out of oneself; it's a language one can learn. As a language, it gives whoever can speak it a certain purchase on the world, allowing one to present it or oneself in a light different from the light that falls on you without your will or desire coming into play. That is why it takes so many, even infinite, forms.

In the world of the blues as Lowe affirms it, any attempt at summary, let alone a critical assessment of what his crafted world is worth, of whether it's a spinning globe or a pile of feathers, would demand far more time than it takes to listen—and given the shape of his production, constantly calling you back to play a given piece a second or a tenth time, to make it fit, to hear how it doesn't, summary may be beside the point. For that matter, while Lowe covers every conceivable genre, style, form, and fashion, the recordings he chooses are almost never generic, an example of something as opposed to a thing in itself. Within any genre he is drawn to its anomalies, not the master chord but the broken cord. I hope to take up each of his four boxes as they arrive; here are ten echoes from the first.

1 ▪ Bert Williams, "Nobody" (1906) "Not a blues, but—" it's always said: it's a spoken piece about being treated as if you don't exist, or as if you never should have been born. ("Coon Song. Baritone Solo" was the notation on the original release.) As philosophy it's a straight line from this to Ralph Ellison's *Invisible Man*, two world wars, a Great Depression, and forty-six years later. But in its cadence and in the melody of its speech it's a leap to Muddy Waters's "Rollin' Stone" two years before that, and to Elvis Presley's "Heartbreak Hotel" four years later.

2 ▪ Fisk University Jubilee Quartet, "Poor Mourner" (1911) Formal gospel by trained singers—but in the highs and lows, the irreducibly spooky tones of a different voice, eyes without a face, a face without a name: what John Fahey meant when he said that inside certain gospel records you could hear "a cloven hoof beating time."

3 ▪ Prince's Band, "St. Louis Blues" (1915) The big, bouncy, so-called first blues: "A terrible song, melodically bland and formally vulgar, a middle-class state of the blues," Lowe says. "But the blues was a form Handy could not tame." You can catch it here, in the half-lights in the verses, the spectre of a haunt already reaching to take the form back.

4 ▪ Roosevelt Graves and His Brother, "I'll Be Rested" (1926) So modern sounding, with air between every word and every note.

5 ▪ Hendersonville Double Quartet, "I Want My Life to Testify" (1926) Lowe writes of the dignity of this recording. It's the dignity of the scorned, the illiterate, the worthless, eight people speaking as a group to affirm that none of them is like anybody else, that if they're worthy God will see each for who he or she really is, which means that if you don't, you sin.

6 ▪ Blind Willie Johnson, "Motherless Child" (1927) Compared to Johnson's "Dark Was the Night—Cold Was the Ground," one of the great works of American art, a pop song: "Blind man's bluff," Lowe says. That's the echo. What does that mean?

7 ▪ Moses Mason, "Molly Man" (1928) In the 1890s in St. Louis, the street singer Bill Dooley may have written both "Stagolee" and "Frankie and Albert," on the spot. You can imagine that this is what he sounded like.

8 ▪ Frank Stokes, "Take Me Back" (1928) From Memphis, all but turning cartwheels, Stokes always had his tongue in his cheek, and his tongue was like a whip.

9 ▪ William Moore, "One Way Gal" (1928) When Moore looked out at the world, he never saw it end. The sun dropped down to the horizon, but it never set.

10 ▪ Furry Lewis, "Judge Harsh Blues" (1928) Black man, white justice. I was going to say Judge Harsh is forgotten, and Furry Lewis's name is spoken in a hundred languages, but that is glib. Judge Harsh will never die, and not because Lewis made him immortal. In this modest performance, made up of commonplace lines from a score of other songs ("My woman come a-running, with a hundred dollars in her hand / Crying Judge, Judge, please spare my man / One hundred won't do, better get your three"), you can, as always when Lewis tells his stories, feel that he has thought them over for a long time, and that he's still thinking as he sings.

1 ▪ Laurie Anderson, *Homeland* (Nonesuch) "Only an Expert" is not anything anyone could have expected from Laurie Anderson: a pop song. It moves quickly on a stuttering and unpredictable beat. The verses are like a stand-up comedy act where the comic is constantly winking at the audience, but not exactly to indicate everyone in the privileged room is in on the joke. You can't tell what the wink is saying, and it exerts its own pull of fascination. The chorus is pure pop, the singer taking pleasure in the momentum of a few words that quickly cease to mean anything—they could be doo-wops. The music is that cool, that unafraid of itself. The bits of Lou Reed's feedback running in the deep background of the piece as it moves on, each fragment curling in on itself like paper in fire, suggest that there's a lot to this song that isn't being said, even though it has over nine hundred words.

Like a lot of this album, with its Department of Security title—the Nazi word Homeland saying that everywhere else is Empire—"Only an Expert" moves quickly into the traducing of the Constitution and the morals of American history by George W. Bush and his administration. But as such it's a novelty song, which I once heard defined as a song that was funny and not about love. This song is very funny for more than seven and a half minutes, and it gets funnier the more you listen to it. Its currency is disbelief: everything it describes is presented with an expression of well-what-did-you-expect acceptance, which in every other moment turns into you-must-be-kidding, which, as you listen, over and over, can change into nightmare, hate, fear, self-loathing, and fantasies of murderous revenge.

Except perhaps on *The Ugly One with the Jewels and Other Stories*, from 1995, Anderson's best album until this one, her voice has been a raised eyebrow: arch, knowing, sometimes sneering, even smug. It's no different here. What is radically different is that here Anderson has built a context—on an expanding, old-fashioned Zeitgeist album that means to translate everything into its own language, to replace a diffuse and fugitive frame of reference with one the singer has built herself—in which everything she says, her every tone of voice, is suffused with such regret and pain over what has happened to the country the singer has to describe that the arch, the knowing, the sneering, and the smug are revealed as hopeless, worthless masks. Song by song, through play, surprise, tunes that drift like dreams in and out of the words and textures of "O Superman," that soft-spoken jeremiad that across nearly three decades has lost none of its prophetic gravity, Anderson heads toward the center of her story, a more than eleven-minute spoken piece—with movie-like music behind it, maybe calling up *Lost Horizon*, a better title than Anderson's "Another Day in America," music suggesting that you've been here before, even if here has never been more than a figment of someone else's imagination—performed, by means of a filter, in a male voice.

Out of his slow, heavy, I-used-to-be-disgusted-now-I-try-to-be-amused growl, it's impossible not to picture the man speaking. I see him as tall, heavy set, a one time prep-school Ivy Leaguer who's worked in the State Department for forty years. He's seen it all. He's seen presidents, senators, secretaries of state come and go, and now he's seen too much. He tells jokes as if they're parables; he offers parables as if he can tell them as jokes, but they fall flat, a whole country falling flat on its face. As he goes on, with Antony Hegarty coming in behind him, floating around his head like the ghost of his dead, younger self, he gives up even trying to be amused; every word he says turns sour in his mouth. We've come too far, he's saying; nothing is going to change back to what it was, or what we thought it was, or what we hoped it could be. When the song ends—and it doesn't fade out; it stops with a last, self-silencing note—it's horrible. You feel the story, the country, has outlived itself.

2 ■ Jay-Z & Mr Hudson, "Young Forever" (Roc Nation) In a small drama where the land of eternal youth sounds a lot like the Islamist martyr's paradise, what makes the performance so gripping is the way Jay-Z plays against the British R&B singer Mr Hudson's gorgeous re-creation of Alphaville's 1984 "Forever Young." He's testifying off to the side, then going silent for Mr Hudson as if listening to what he's saying, waiting in the alley of his own song for that moment when he'll dash out and jump the train of the old one, then running his own train of words straight through the melody, jumping off with perfect timing when Mr Hudson takes the music back.

3 ■ Hockey, "Song Away" (Capitol) The Portland band is dynamite on the air, when you're not expecting it, when you tune right in to the middle. Despite the fast pace, the speechifying vocals, there's a hint of the languor of Sheryl Crow's "All I Wanna Do." The muscle in the guitar-bass-drums rhythms is so arresting that on the radio it can erase the video from your mind, and the video, by Skinny—kin to Samuel Bayer for Nirvana's "Smells Like Teen Spirit," with the ordinary horror of being a nerd at a gym dance replacing the *Prom Night* menace of Nirvana's pep rally—is one of the funniest, warmest, and most socially accu-

rate (the way the geeky kid looks at a row of the coolest girls in school as if they're from another planet) high-school movies ever made.

4 ■ Flotilla Choir, "We Con the World (Turkish 'Aid to Gaza' Song with Captain Stabbing & Friends)" (YouTube) Contrived almost overnight after the May 31 attempt of the *Mavi Marmara* to break the blockade of Gaza, this Israelis-in-Arab-drag video is the most outrageous parody of "We Are the World" ever devised. And, except for "We Are the World 25 for Haiti," recorded in February by Justin Bieber et al.—in the *very same studio* where Michael Jackson, Lionel Richie, and so many more once checked their egos at the door!—the most effective.

5–6 ■ Matt Diehl interviews Joni Mitchell (*Los Angeles Times*, April 22) "Bob is not authentic at all," Mitchell said. "He's a plagiarist, and his name and voice are fake. Everything about Bob is a deception." Charles Taylor comments: "In protest, Chelsea Clinton changes her name to Hibbing."

7 ■ KFOG-FM (San Francisco, May 14) A deep, sonorous radio voice: "Back in the Stone Age, this song was used to repel dinosaurs." Then the DJ played Dramarama's "Anything, Anything," which sounded as if it would have worked.

8 ■ Tom Jones, *Praise and Blame* (Lost Highway) The seventy-year-old-onetime Welsh R&B stomper goes back to his blues and gospel roots, digs them up, tosses them in the fireplace, and with John Lee Hooker's 1959 "Burning Hell," burns down the house.

9 ■ Crooked Still, "Henry Lee" from *Some Strange Country* (Signature Sounds) A carefulness, a flinching hesitation, has boxed in Aoife O'Donovan and everyone else in this sensual old-timey band since their *Shaken by a Low Sound* four years ago. But on this ancient, mystical murder ballad, they make a labyrinth, and don't even try to get out.

10 ■ Bret Easton Ellis, *Imperial Bedrooms* (Knopf) His second book named after an Elvis Costello song: a sequel to *Less Than Zero*. "Our reunion tour," says E. C.

OCTOBER 2010

1 ▪ **Corin Tucker Band, *1,000 Years* (Kill Rock Stars)** There are strings on the first music to be heard from Tucker since Sleater-Kinney left itself behind in 2006; on "Riley," which seems to dig down farther with every deep, slowly exhaling breath, all the strings do is emphasize. In moments you might hear Christine McVie in Fleetwood Mac—the clear voice of "Spare Me a Little of Your Love" and "Over My Head"—but the toughness you could miss with McVie remains the motor of Tucker's music. The trouble can come at any time, and it does, over and over.

2 ▪ **Elizabeth Cook, *Welder* (31 Tiger)** Country is not supposed to be this frankly salacious, whether about quaaludes or sex, or the difficulty of telling one from the other—but Cook was probably not raised to become the woman she is, writing and singing about "making love in the disco era," which somehow summons up the specter of a single act of intercourse lasting at least five years and a joke the singer will be telling for the rest of her life. "My hands were in his mullet," she laughs, at the time, the guy, and herself, but why not? She bends around the corners of her stories until her voice cracks, and her nostalgia is inseparable from her pride. That's what anyone might most carry away from this record: you couldn't find regret with a Geiger counter.

3 ▪ **Carlene Carter, "Me and the Wildwood Rose" (YouTube)** Her grandmother Maybelle sang it with the Carter Family; her mother, June Carter, sang it. After wonderful records long in the past, a lost career, arrests for heroin, a marriage to Nick Lowe that must seem like someone else's Hollywood movie, the death of her mother and her stepfather, Johnny Cash, Carlene Carter plays the song as if it's the home where when you come back knocking it has to let you in.

4 ▪ **John Mellencamp, *No Better Than This* (Rounder)** Mellencamp had a ridiculously precious idea: record a set of new songs in the Sun studio in Memphis, where Howlin' Wolf and Elvis once walked the few square feet as if it were the earth; in the First African Baptist Church in Savannah, Georgia, a stop on the Underground Railroad; and in Room 414 of the Gunter Hotel in San Antonio, where in 1936 Robert Johnson faced a wall and sang "Cross Road Blues"—and not just put the thing out on CD and vinyl, but do it all in *mono*.

Slowly, tune by tune, and so imperceptibly that each time you play the album it might seem to shift at a different time, the muffled sound of the music begins to work on the ear as something not old, but looking back at the singer from a future he may not reach. Nothing is rushed; in "Save Some Time to Dream" (Memphis), "Thinking About You" (Savannah), and "The West End" (Memphis), Mellencamp's voice sounds like something he had to scrape off the back of his throat. And then comes "Love at First Sight" (Savannah). The singer passes someone on the street, and glimpses their whole life together. It takes him four and a half minutes to tell you everything that happened, the music bouncing lightly up and down, back and forth, like hopscotch, but with every detail—a smile, a kiss, her getting pregnant, them getting married, her leaving him for another man—you never don't know that the singer saw it all in an instant, and you know that on any given day, you could, too.

5 ▪ **15-60-75, a.k.a. the Numbers, "Matchbox Defined," from *The Inward City* (Hearthan)** Formed as a blues band in Kent, Ohio, at the end of the '60s, the Numbers have ground on ever since, as if searching for the end of time, or a solution to the mysteries of the songs they still can't get out of their heads. Here the guitarist, Robert Kidney, who now uses a cane, takes up a song that made its way from Blind Lemon Jefferson in the '20s to Carl Perkins in the '50s to the Beatles in Hamburg in the early '60s to, you can be certain, the Numbers not long after, and which, regardless of how many times Kidney has sung it, still makes no sense. So with a harmonica solo that could

have come off of the first Cream album and a train-whistle guitar solo that summons up the Yardbirds at the Fillmore in 1968, Kidney takes up the tune as a philosophical investigation. It was a lifetime ago, he says, when an old blind man asked him if a matchbox could hold his clothes—"And I shook my fist and I said, old man, how could a matchbox hold my clothes?" But almost every word is its own line as Kidney relates the tale, Jefferson stepping out of the grave to taunt him—"The old / blind / man / asked me"—and the almost violent hesitations churn up drama. "And I / thought / about it / for / *ten years*"—you know he's never going to get out of this. But then comes a hangover, when everything is slowed down, every thought the lifting of a house, and everything is clear. The singer sees his wife watching TV; he could walk out the door right now, "with *nothing*"—the nothing of her not even noticing he's gone. Kidney tells the story as if he's opened that door a thousand times and closed it and walked back into the kitchen for another beer just as many. But it doesn't matter; he's seen through his life, and now he can sing the song as if he owns it, instead of the other way around. If he ever could close that door behind himself, "And where you're going nobody knows / Then a matchbox will hold your clothes."

6 ▪ **Eminem, *Recovery* (Aftermath)** What makes Eminem different is a sense of jeopardy: a bedrock conviction that whatever there is in life worth having, and whatever of that you might have, you don't deserve it. Maybe in anyone else's hands that would translate into self-pity, fake panic, hair-pulling desperation—but not here. In these songs, it translates into a kind of ethics, where the person speaking tries more than anything to see every possible point of view, every conceivable response, every missed chance, all at once.

7 ▪ **Leah Garchik, *San Francisco Chronicle* (June 29)** Dep't. of Lest We Forget: "I got my hands on that issue of *Rolling Stone* with the interview that caused the firing of Gen. Stanley McChrystal, the cover of

which was particularly interesting because its main focus was on Lady Gaga with a pair of guns (borrowed, I assume) and a pair of buttocks (her own, but probably airbrushed). The story about 'Obama's General' was mentioned in the smallest cover line of anything else, indicating the editors didn't think it would cause much fuss.

"Surely all the trouble it did cause must have been the result of a simple mistake: an editing mix-up in interviews. Obviously, someone mistakenly put McChrystal's lines in Lady Gaga's mouth and vice versa.

"What McChrystal really said about the commander-in-chief: 'I've really never loved anyone like I loved him. Or like I love him. That relationship really shaped me. It made me into a fighter.' About his relationship to the soldiers: 'I'm really good to the people around me. . . . I'm not a diva, in any sense of the word.' About the war in Afghanistan: 'I committed myself to my heartbreak wholeheartedly. It's something that I will never let go. . . . As artists, we are eternally heartbroken.'

"What Lady Gaga really said about the obligations of being a star: 'How'd I get screwed into going to this dinner? . . . I'd rather have my ass kicked by a roomful of people than go out to this dinner.' About her social life: 'All these men, I'd die for them. And they'd die for me.' On dressing for the stage: 'It's shirts and skins, and we'll kill all the shirts.' And on current events: 'Even Afghans are confused by Afghanistan.'"

8 ▪ **Philip Kerr, *If the Dead Rise Not* (Putnam)** In Kerr's now six-book Bernie Gunther series—following the onetime Berlin cop and private detective through the Nazi era, to postwar Vienna and Perónist Argentina, now book-ending Berlin in 1934 and Havana twenty years later—the whodunnit, or even the why-dunnit, has never been the point. The battle Gunther fights is against his own sense of oppression, miasma, nihilism. Here Kerr has his hard-boiled wisecrack machine revved up to high—"Don't get me wrong," Gunther says, in lines that bounce off the screaming faces at Tea Party rallies, "I just love Nazis. I've a sneaking sus-

picion that ninety-nine point nine percent of Nazis are giving the other point one percent an undeservedly bad reputation"— but as 1934 fades out in a horror of murder and blackmail, and 1954 takes shape as a game of love and blackmail Gunther can't win, the wisecracks dry up. You want Gunther to end up with the woman he's been in love with for twenty years as much as he does, but you don't have to pay the price— until the last pages, which make the most depressing ending to any novel I've read in years.

9 ▪ *Cabaret—The Adult Entertainment Magazine* (August 1956) A friend passed on this nightclub trade publication, devoted mainly to strippers; the headlines were, with unbelievably garish cover photo, I TAUGHT JAYNE MANSFIELD ABOUT SEX (inside comedown: "I taught her about sex as it is manufactured in Hollywood") and WHO THE HELL IS ELVIS PRESLEY? (inside surprise: aside from a few obviously made-up quotes—"I'd like to study dramatical acting. I don't care nothing whatsoever about singing in no movie"—a smart and accurate profile). But the most displacing tidbit came on the last page, in the "Backstage" column by one Arch Ayers, where you could find the real Jayne Mansfield: "PUBLICITY MAD Jayne Mansfield will do anything to make the papers. Shortly after telling Winchell and three other columnists that she had broken off with her current flame, Robbie Robertson, she was heard on the phone telling her boyfriend: 'But Robbie, you don't believe all that stuff you read in the columns.'" Reached in New York, Robertson had this to say: "Don't you just hate it when one of those bombshell chicks blows your cover. I was only twelve at the time, but I knew how to make a woman feel special."

10 ▪ Elvis Presley, **"Stranger in My Own Home Town"** In truth, "Who the hell is Elvis Presley?" is a question that has never been answered—or, as Nick Tosches once put it, "Elvis Presley will never be solved." Here he is in 1970, spinning out songs in the studio, grabbing on to an old Percy Mayfield number, taking it slowly, languidly, until the pres-

sure just barely increases, and suddenly you know you're hearing the sort of plain truth Elvis almost never permitted himself: he knows the envy, the resentment, the hate behind every smiling face. The performance appeared only in 1995, on *Walk a Mile in My Shoes: The Essential 70's Masters*, but with lines missing the Internet now gives back.

"I'm going back down to Memphis," Elvis sings, though plainly that's exactly where he already is. "I'm going to start driving that motherfucking truck again." You hear a defiance inseparable from self-loathing, a man who sees the envy, the resentment, the hatred in every smiling face: "All those cocksuckers stopped being friendly / But you can't keep a hard prick down." There's no sense of obscenity or provocation as he sings. It's plain speech, but with that last line he's gone, off into a country only he can enter, into the utopia of his own gifts, where not even a song as good as this one can tell a fraction of what he knows. As he turns his back and walks away, he's "just standin' here wonderin,'" as he himself had to have sung out loud more than once, "if a matchbox would hold my clothes."

Thanks to Doug Kroll, Nick Tosches, and Jim Marshall

NOVEMBER–DECEMBER 2010

1 ▪ Bryan Ferry, *Olympia* (Astralwerks) Want to hear a whole album of "Slave to Love"—or a whole album about hanging around in bars, pretending you're younger than you are, an undercurrent of lounge-lizard ooze bringing everything to . . . life? Thanks in part to Roxy Music guitarist Phil Manzanera and saxophonist Andy Mackay, there's not a false note—especially when a deliriously romantic, regretful, deep-soul embrace of Traffic's it's-too-late ballad "No Face, No Name, No Number" takes the singer out of *Olympia's* incandescently sleazy paradise, stranding him within sight of a real-world home he'll never reach.

2 ▪ *Biutiful*, directed by Alejandro González Iñárritu, at the Telluride Film Festival,

September 5 Javier Bardem as a father dying of cancer, trying to raise two children while keeping his head above the sewage of the criminal underground economy in Barcelona—and as misery accumulates, in his body, in his family, on the streets, in the basement where illegal Chinese workers sleep, his panic increases, and he begins to slow down, because he can't keep up. The movie captures the look and feel of Barcelona as a place where people live, not just as a theme park—imagine Woody Allen's *Vicky Cristina Barcelona* in this cauldron, and it vaporizes in a second. At nearly two and a half hours, the picture, the story, is not a minute too long; like the lives it describes, it's too short. It's draining; when I walked out I felt as if I'd just given blood.

3 ▪ Frazey Ford, *Obadiah* (Nettwerk) For Ford, the most distinctive voice in the Be Good Tanyas, "Bird of Paradise" is not an image, it's a lilt. The words as she sings them are wings. It's that "San Diego alley," sneaking out the darkness of the song and returning to it almost before you can register it, that's the image, and you can't see to its end.

4 ▪ *Carlos*, directed by Olivier Assayas, at the Telluride Film Festival, September 4 In a conversation about his film on the terrorist Carlos, who from his murder of French police in Paris in 1975 to his capture in the Sudan nearly twenty years later was a one-man spectre haunting Europe, Assayas at first said that he had thought of scoring it to classic orchestral movie music throughout. "But the film did not want it. The film laughed in my face." So from scene to scene—Carlos preening naked in a mirror, the takeover of the OPEC oil ministers' conference in Vienna in late 1976, after that the shooting of a military policeman at a Swiss checkpoint, a weapons delivery, a breakdown in communications—the movie is less scored to than invaded by post-punk songs so romantic and tough they create empathy for situations even as the film withholds it from its characters. New Order, the Feelies, the Dead Boys' "Sonic Reducer," most viscerally Wire's "Dot Dash,"

a song that seems to terrorize itself—not in any way keyed to the scenes in chronological, soundtrack-of-our-lives banality, they raise the question of whether the best and most adventurous music of the late 1970s and early 1980s was as animated by international terrorism, by the spectre of a world where at times it could seem that only a few armed gnostics were in control of anything, as by anything else.

5 ▪ David Thomson, *Humphrey Bogart* (Farrar, Straus & Giroux) There are passages in each of Thomson's recent short biographies—Bogart, Bette Davis, Gary Cooper, Ingrid Bergman—that frame a classic film in terms no one else would choose. Here, on Bogart's Roy Earle, in the 1941 *High Sierra*: "Earle was a killer, a thief, a loser—sure, he had a kinder side to him, and he got along in a strange tough way with Marie. But he never stopped the film and said, look, folks, I'm a reformed character. I'm a nice guy. Honest, I am. He never asked for anything. Maybe that's what Huston saw and maybe he guessed how it could fit in a new moment in American history when all of a sudden the real heroes didn't have to wear labels but could act as mean, as hard-bitten and as unsentimental as . . . Sam Spade or Rick Blaine or Philip Marlowe (or Tom Joad)"—the difference is Thomson's claiming a movie not for film history, which is what anyone else would have done, but for American history.

6 ▪ Cyndi Lauper, video for "Money Changes Everything," from *The Body Acoustic* (Sony, 2005) Who knew Tom Gray's 1978 "Money Changes Everything" (which five years later Lauper ripped up as a lament and stitched back together as vengeance) was all along looking for life as a fatalistic Appalachian stomp, something the grownups who are now singing it—playing it on fiddle and harmonium, swirling to it—absorbed as children like a lullaby or a slap?

7 ▪ Robert Plant, *Band of Joy* (Rounder) Much is made of Plant's working with Nashville musicians under the name of the band he played in before he joined Led Zeppelin, back in the blimp age. But against the free, unencumbered stroll through "Cindy, I'll Marry You Someday," a commonplace song Plant learned from a recording by the great North Carolina folklorist Bascom Lamar Lunsford (1882–1973), everything else—new songs, covers of numbers by Townes Van Zandt, the Minnesota duo Low, Los Lobos, Richard Thompson, Barbara Lynn, even the gothic spiritual "Satan Your Kingdom Must Come Down"—feels contrived. "When I found Bascom Lamar Lunsford," Plant said recently, "I was born again"; the true roots he's getting back to are those he's yet to find.

8–9 ▪ Washington Square Park, New York City, 10 p.m., August 30 It was a hot night and the park was jammed; there were a lot of people with guitars out, under the arch, around the fountain, wherever there was an open space under the lights. But sitting on the ground in the dark, yards away from any other person, was someone singing and playing Rod Stewart's "Maggie May." He sang it very slowly, as if he was still working it out—as on *The Rod Stewart Sessions 1971–1998*, a box set released last year on Rhino, you can hear Stewart working it out in the studio, plugging in nonsense lines, trying to get a hold on the melody, as if the song were coming out of the air, as if it wasn't simply his world-historic 1971 rewrite of the old Liverpool folk song about a prostitute and a sailor.

It was odd, and, if you were in the mood, heart-stopping. The man in the dark was in public, as if he had a need to make himself heard, to an audience as spectral as he had made himself. As a public performer, he had withdrawn into himself, where only his sound drew any listener to the dim outline of his body. So the strain of loss and regret that's one part of Stewart's original was now the whole song, but staged as if it were a play. The man was singing Stewart's words, following his tune, all the way back to the docks, and, as the song played out, Rod Stewart might never have been born.

10 ▪ Justin Sullivan and Friends, *Tales of the Road* (Attack Attack, 2004) Looking around the Internet for odd Tom Jones songs, I stumbled on a video from this album and was stunned by as unforgiving a performance of "Masters of War" as I'd ever seen. Here the front man for New Model Army, along with the drummer and guitarist from the London punk band—who with Jones rammed their way through "Gimme Shelter" as if it were a collapsing building—begin a set recorded around Europe, mostly, it seems, in Germany, with the title song, apparently about the most tiresome subject in the annals of rock 'n' roll. But that's not it.

As with the music throughout the album, a darkness pervades everything, and with echoes of elements in rock 'n' roll most resistant to borrowing, even homage—Bruce Springsteen's harmonica in "Nebraska," the reach of the Doors' "The End," the primitivism of the Mekons' "The Building"—the very first minutes are the spookiest of all. In the place called up with "Sitting in the all-night café in a curl of smoke, telling tales of the road," you might glimpse not a few aging musicians in a Greek restaurant in Soho but anarchists from the late nineteenth century meeting up in a Whitechapel tavern to pass secrets, then disappearing in the night. This isn't sorry-babe-the-road-is-calling-me. If it's a rock 'n' roll road then it's a different rock 'n' roll.

1 ▪ Scott Shepherd in *Gatz*, directed by John Collins, produced by Elevator Repair Service (Public Theater, New York, October 29, 2010) At the very end of this partly dramatized reading of *The Great Gatsby*—with various people working in and around a somewhat ratty 1980s office, here and there turning into Gatsby, Daisy, Tom Buchanan, and anyone else who appeared in Fitzgerald's pages eighty-five years ago—Shepherd puts down the book he's been reading from since he came across it in a desk compartment nearly eight hours before, and begins a drift all the way into the Nick Carraway he's only intermittently portrayed, a drift into the canonized reverie of the final pages.

From "I see now that this has been a story of the West" to "ceaselessly into the past," they comprise some of the most gorgeous American writing, words suspended in their own air—sentences that have been so relentlessly quoted, memorialized, worshiped, and declaimed that they are now clichés preserved in their own amber. It's not easy to read these last paragraphs, but it's far more difficult to say them out loud: to make it feel as if you haven't heard them before, to bring the words down out of the clouds and into the mouth of someone who can convince you he's talking to you when he's saying them.

I can't tell you exactly how Shepherd did it. He sat at a desk and moved, as if he were thinking with his arms and shoulders as well as his mind, his memory, as the thoughts he was relating came to him. It wasn't a reverie. He did seem to be looking at the big houses as he spoke of them, to see the trees that weren't there. He seemed almost on the verge of tears, and to change his demeanor, his manner of speaking, in order to protect the words from his own emotions—his, Nick Carraway's, or his, Scott Shepherd's? But as I listened in a small theater suddenly so still the quiet was its own kind of loudness, I noticed that I was tapping my foot.

If there's a rhythm in that ending as Fitzgerald wrote it, it's spectral and complex—something it might take an Ives or a Satie to find. In Shepherd's hands it was a beat. Slow, measured, a ragtime ghost.

2 ▪ **John Legend and the Roots, *Wake Up!* (Columbia)** When Legend first appeared, he seemed spontaneously generated by the Grammy Awards: as bland, contrived, and smarmy as his name. He's never been so convincing, so flesh-and-blood, as on this recasting of 1970s political soul music as a manifesto for the end of the first decade of the twenty-first century, and the Roots, who wear musical history like clothes they picked up that morning off the floor, have

a lot to do with that. Guitarist Kirk Douglas cuts the bottom out of Bill Withers's 1973 "I Can't Write Left-Handed"—about Vietnam on Withers's record, about Afghanistan on this one—leaving Legend to make his way through the moral wilderness of the song on his own, and he sounds as if he's been waiting years for the chance.

3 ▪ **... *Next Stop Is Vietnam—The War on Record: 1961–2008* (Bear Family)** A daunting package—thirteen CDs of music and documentary inserts, one of song lyrics, and a more-than-three-hundred-page illustrated hardbound book—organized thematically: disc 2, "Proud to Serve," is mostly   dead-soldier-serves-the-cause-of-freedom songs, mostly performed with a really bottomless insincerity. The set reaches its apotheosis with Bob Braun's appalling 1966 "Brave Men Not Afraid": "Someone may die for me tonight," he says happily, smugly, as if he's on his third drink. The most bizarre note is struck with Lee Hazlewood's 1968 production of "The Warrior" by Honey Ltd.—a female quartet from Detroit, previously known, one learns, as the Mama Cats, whose first single, "My Boy," about a soldier on his way to Vietnam, was produced by Bob Seger. "The Warrior" is presented here as "a terrifying anti-war song," but we've just heard them introduced by Bob Hope, "on tour in Vietnam," performing for our troops, presumably offering our boys this weird *Playboy* fantasy, this complete eroticization of war and death: "It's good, it's so good . . . We must kill more people . . . This body is precious, as it's lowered to the grave . . . Oh God! It's so good!" And the ending: "Da da da da da," just hopping down the street.

4 ▪ **"Prints: Now in 3-D!" at the Minnesota Center for Book Arts (Minneapolis, July 9–October 31, 2010)** A show of objects and print works, including a ravishing red/pink prom dress and pumps, a set of clothes to be presented at an ER for a rape kit, and Jonathan Stewart's *Let-Go* series—a set of boxes with boxy, LEGO-like cartoon characters acting out Stewart's theme: "I am

primarily concerned with how history, experiences, and emotions are packaged for consumption. My boxes point toward a marketplace where these characteristics are bought and sold." So there are five bright boxes that look like they ought to contain animal crackers, red and blue, pink and yellow: *Leaving with the Kids* (walking out on the husband, 4×6 in.), *Nowhere Else to Go* (homelessness, 7×5 in.), *Panhandling for Change* (6×4 in.), the hard-to-read *Pregnancy Test* (3×4 in.), and, most striking, the tiny (1½×2½ in.) *Rejection Letter*, just about big enough for one small cookie inside, or a small piece of rolled-up paper. On the front: a man holding a letter by his thigh. On the back, you read it over his shoulder as he reads it, as any rejection letter reads to whomever gets it: "To whom it may concern—We regret to inform you that you are not the best at what you do. We have decided to go with somebody else. They are much better than you in every way."

5 ▪ Joe Posnanski, "# 23: Tom Cheek on Joe Carter's game-winning World Series homer in 1993," from "Thirty-Two Great Calls" (SI.com, October 14, 2010) Posnanski:

"I see Joe Carter every now and then. He lives in Kansas City and every so often we will be at the same event and we'll make some small talk. I've never asked him—making me one of four people in American [*sic*] who has not—but I do wonder what it does for the rest of your life to hit a home run that wins the World Series. How often do you think about it when no one is around? How does it make you feel to talk about it every single day?* At some point does it feel like someone else hit it, someone you aren't anymore?

"Anyway, Tom Cheek's call was memorable.

" 'Touch 'em all Joe, you'll never hit a bigger home run in your life!' "

*"*I think about this with musicians. You write a song, and you work on the words ('Wait, what else rhymes with heaven?') until it's exactly what you want it to sound like. You bring it to the band, and maybe they collaborate, add a guitar thing here, a drum thing there. You record it, then record it*

again, and again, and maybe again. And when you finally get it down, through production, you really like it. You think it might become a hit.*

"Does it occur to you while you are doing it that it really might become a hit? And if it does, yes, of course, it will make you a lot of money. But you might have to play this song FOR THE REST OF YOUR LIFE? Does it occur to you that you may end up traveling city to city, for years and years, and every time you start this song people will go crazy and they will sing along, and after a while the song may become used up for you, but it will NEVER become used up for them? They will never get tired of it, not ever. When you are old and retired, and you show up somewhere, they may STILL want you to sing that song. In fact, for them this song actually IS you.

"Every time Bruce Springsteen pours his heart into Born To Run, my admiration for him doubles."

6–8 ▪ Sam Amidon, *I See the Sign* (Bedroom Community, 2010), *All Is Well* (Bedroom Community, 2007), "The Only Tune" on Nico Muhly, *Mothertongue* (Bedroom Community, 2008) A twenty-nine-year-old folk singer, Amidon is wispy, indistinct, insinuating, at his best suggestive of something he can't quite get across. He has his own style, his own approach, but he seems most of all to be listening to himself, and even on *All Is Well*, dedicated to Dock Boggs, his hero and mine, it wasn't enough to keep me listening. But across nearly the last fourteen minutes of Nico Muhly's *Mothertongue*, otherwise operatic translations of English heresies, there is more than a glimpse of why Amidon may someday turn his voice into a language.

He takes up an old folk song, or simply an old folk phrase, the sort of thing that has migrated from tune to tune for hundreds of years: "The cruel wind and the rain." He begins with an odd hesitation, as if in a recital he can't push through a mirror, the words coming out one at a time: "There, there, there were, there were, there were two, there were two, there were two sis, there were two sis, there were two sisters. . . ." And then a murder.

It's incalculably spooky, the way the action comes out of nowhere, the way Amidon has prepared you to expect nothing. His light voice is weightless here, which is not the same thing; retelling this fable, he sounds as if he heard it only once removed from the actual event. Now he's lying in his bed late at night, wondering how much of the story he believes, turning it over and over in his mind, trying to make it hold still, trying to decide if he wants to believe it or not.

Then his voice changes—it's bent, deeper, insistently unmusical, unpleasant. Now he's trying to enter the story, almost as a character, and the ululations in the background bring forth a whole chorus of cemetery spirits. They'll let Amidon into the story, but not out of it ("I do not believe the rage the dead experience can be contained by the grave," says Detective Dave Robicheaux in James Lee Burke's *The Glass Rainbow*); Amidon is right at the doorstep of the song. His voice stretches, you hear objects fall in the background, a piano tinkles atonally, and he seems to walk away.

Then he's floating through the verses again, back in the story: "He made fiddle pegs from her long finger bones." You can hear her breathing in the background, as if she's not dead, as if she can feel herself being cut up, like Uma Thurman buried alive in *Kill Bill*. The tone never changes. Does the singer believe any of it, now? Is he just playing with the story, which he heard just yesterday? The woman behind him believes it.

The production is very formally avant-garde, yet somehow implied by the song itself—a version of the song the song itself wanted to hear. And that is true folk music if anything is.

9 ■ **Gang of Four, *Content* (Yep Roc)** Just as *The King's Speech* is an action-packed thriller about speech therapy, the Gang of Four's 1979 debut album *Entertainment!* was an action-packed thriller about false consciousness and commodity fetishism. There was resistance—a strangled *no* inside almost every moment of panic.

The feeling on *Content*, the first album of new songs in sixteen years by singer Jon King and guitarist Andy Gill, with bassist Thomas McNeice and drummer Mark

Heaney as new members, is that of a kind of frantic longing. It's the metallic sound of people caught in the trap of modern capitalism—wanting what they can't have and, worse, what they don't even want, people consumed by a sense of a loss every time an ad appears or a purchase goes into the computer. It's a music of confusion, until the tone shifts with "A Fruit Fly in the Beehive," where the person running through his own nightmares wakes up, the dream still in front of his eyes, and begins to think, and the result is a moment of calm surrounded by a sense of jeopardy. Gill counts off the rhythm circling each line, each idea.

10 ■ **U.S. Senator Russ Feingold, Democrat of Wisconsin, concession speech (November 2, 2010)** Feingold came into the Senate in 1992 with Elvis at his back— to counter negative ads against him in the Democratic primary, he ran a don't-believe-everything-you-read spot with the banner headline ELVIS ENDORSES FEINGOLD. The next day everyone in the state knew who he was, and that he had a sense of humor. He went out with the same flair. "So—so—so, to all of you," he said finally. "In the words of, who else, Bob Dylan: 'But my heart is not weary, it's light and it's free / I've got nothin' but affection for all those who've sailed with me.'" He quoted Dylan's "Mississippi" as if the words were old and familiar, from Wordsworth, maybe; it was all in the lift, the barest hint of surprise, he gave to "not weary"—something Dylan, for all the times he recorded the song (for *Time Out of Mind* in 1997, for *Love and Theft* in 2001), never found. "So," Feingold said finally, "it's on to the next fight. It's on to the next battle. It's on to 2012! And—*and!*—it is on to our next adventure. *Forward!*"

Thanks to Ken Tucker and Ben DeMott

FEBRUARY 2011

1 ■ **Jeffrey Foucault, *Cold Satellite* (JeffreyFoucault.com)** A collaboration with the poet Lisa Olstein, who wrote the words for

Foucault's drawl—a drawl that sometimes grows a tail so long it curls around itself, with a country feel that puts the people who live in the Nashville charts to shame. Then a deep-ditch electric guitar takes a country song into the blues, and lets it go back where it came from. Nothing is pressed, to the point that sometimes the way the voice pulls away from a word or a guitar from a phrase is its own kind of preciousness—but not in "Twice I Left Her," which shifts the music into a more resolute kind of quiet, a bigger emptiness in a single room. An acoustic guitar figure comes up against drums buried far away, like a memory. The story creeps out, and stops well short of its end, though you can glimpse it. Foucault drifts over the words so lightly that they seem to fade as they're sung, and you might stop trying to hear them as words, let them come as sounds.

2 ■ Cee Lo Green, "Fuck You," from *The Lady Killer* (Elektra) The emotions in these three minutes and forty-two seconds are so wonderfully scrambled—I hate you, I hate your money, I hate her for loving your money, I love her anyway, you can keep your money, just let me have her back, but following you both around all over town is better than staying home and hating myself—that every time the singer gets to the chorus, you can imagine that he's never felt better in his life.

3 ■ Gary Kamiya, *Shadow Knights: The Secret War Against Hitler* (Simon & Schuster) From the new Pulp History series, Kamiya's startlingly immediate text plus documentary photos, maps, and blazing war-comics illustrations by Jeffrey Smith. With crisscrossing stories from Norway, Paris, and London, the tension, the excitement, and the glamour build until you feel like you're trapped inside of every good antifascist movie ever made. Until the end, in a torture chamber in Dachau, when you are trapped by history.

4 ■ KT Tunstall, "Uummannaq Song," from *Tiger Suit* (Virgin) "Hold your fire—I'm coming out and I'll tell you the truth": in

the front, her voice is pop, singing harmlessly defiant lines, reaching for a hit and a spread in *GQ*. But in the back, her shouts are pulling in another direction, where she's running for her life even though she's the last person on Earth.

5 ■ Paul Auster, *Sunset Park* (Henry Holt) Moving through this tale of Brooklyn squatters are the themes Auster has been pursuing since his first novel, *City of Glass*, appeared in 1985: the way a ghost can come out of nowhere and leave everything changed. Life is a field of unlikelihood: "That is the idea he is toying with, Renzo says, to write an essay about the things that don't happen, the lives not lived, the wars not fought, the shadow worlds that run parallel to the world we take to be the real world, the not-said and the not-done, the not-remembered." That is philosophy, but in real life lives actually lived can become so spectral they disappear back into the not-lived. Unlikelihood turns into forgetting and facts into fables, as with a character catching the news of the death of a pitcher who, on the mound in 1976, talked to baseballs before throwing them past baffled hitters: "First Herb Score, and now Mark Fidrych, the two cursed geniuses who dazzled the country for a few days, a few months, and then vanished from sight."

6 ■ Rod Stewart, *Once in a Blue Moon: The Lost Album* (Rhino) From 1992. For his covers of Stevie Nicks's "Stand Back," the Contours' "First I Look at the Purse," and more—but especially for "Shotgun Wedding." Stewart's hero Sam Cooke didn't do this? Why *not*? Yes, he was already dead when Roy C wrote it, but for a song this right he could have climbed out of the grave.

7 ■ Daniel Lanois, *Soul Mining: A Musical Life* (Faber & Faber) A producer looks back. And remembers how much better *Time Out of Mind* would have been if Bob Dylan hadn't interfered.

8–9 ■ Keith Richards, *Life* (Little, Brown) and *Dangerous Minds,* "Deconstructing 'Gimme Shelter': Listen to the Isolated tracks of the Rolling Stones in the Studio" (dangerousminds.net) "I wrote 'Gimme Shelter' on a stormy day," Keith Richards says, and even with the Bulwer-Lytton cloud floating over the words, they can send a chill through your skin, because you are about to hear—maybe: who knows what he'll say?—the story of the rock 'n' roll song that, from "Mystery Train" to "Ready Teddy" to "Whole Lotta Shakin' Goin' On" to "A Change Is Gonna Come" to "Like a Rolling Stone," the form itself was asking for all along. "I was sitting there," Richards says a few pages later, "just looking out of Robert's window and looking at all these people with their umbrellas being blown out of their grasp and running like hell. And the idea came to me. You get lucky sometimes. It was a shitty day. I had nothing better to do . . . I wasn't thinking about, oh my God, there's my old lady shooting a movie in a bath with Mick Jagger. My thought was storms on other people's minds, not mine."

That's one version. When you hear the pieces of the song on their own, each part—separate tracks for Richards's two guitar lines, the vocals, bass, and drums—is so strong it becomes not a part but a version of the whole. With each track four minutes, the length of the full song, so that there are silent periods whenever the given element isn't present, there's nothing that isn't thrilling on its own terms. Richards is so thoughtful, and at the same time such a master of instinct—he knows what he's going to want, and uses that knowledge as a guiding hand when pure desire seems the engine of his playing—that you could listen for hours without beginning to get to the bottom of the work. The shocker is in the vocal track—Mick Jagger and the soul singer Merry Clayton in tandem. There's a dank, hollow echo behind every word, as if they were recording in a mine shaft. It's not apparent if you listen to the song as it has played on the radio for the last forty years, but here it's overwhelmingly present: the source of the depth of the sound of the whole.

Whether or not Jagger and Clayton recorded separately, at different times, even in different places, as you listen you hear them singing face to face. With the first "Rape, murder, it's just a shot away," Clayton soars, dives down, in complete control, like an eagle surveying the whole territory of the song, and suddenly her voice almost breaks. As Jagger shouts in the background, she seems to hesitate, falling behind the beat, the song itself, then rushes back, finding her footing in the maelstrom: "It's—just—" And then all the way back, reclaiming the song with its hardest, most desperate moment, with the cadence of the last three words like someone throwing herself down a flight of stairs in a harsh and perfect rhythm: "A shot away." It's one of those panicky instants in the creation of a piece of music that could never be predicted or planned, and that only the best record-makers hear for what they are and leave in, letting the mistake define what will be left behind. "What key? What key?"

10 ■ Lisa Olstein, "Radio Crackling, Radio Gone" (lisaolstein.com) This poem could be about Katrina or any other natural disaster, and Olstein's own reading is a flat, conversational, unpretentious, ordinary recitation: a young person's voice, American and modern, accentless, without attitude or pose, picking its way through the ruins piece by piece.

Thanks to Joshua Clover

MARCH–APRIL 2011

1 ■ Eminem and Lil Wayne, "No Love" on *Saturday Night Live* (December 18, 2010) In a performance that reduced the original collaboration for Eminem's *Recovery* to a stiff rehearsal, Lil Wayne was the carpenter, with enough conviction in his hesitating syllables to cause pain: "No love lost, no love found" cut. Then Eminem takes the song, walking the boards Lil Wayne nailed down, clumsily, with no ability to create a rhythm out of physical movement, and it doesn't matter: the staccato beat he makes, then rides, that shoots his words out in front of him is jaw-dropping. The momentum he generates between the walls of each beat

seems almost beyond the ability of a body to produce it. On record, the number isn't so far beyond its sample of Haddaway's somewhat cheesy 1993 "What Is Love (Baby Don't Hurt Me)"; here, it touches "Lose Yourself," the shocker that ran under the credits for *8 Mile*—when you thought the movie was over, and the real story was just starting.

2 ▪ **The Fiery Furnaces, "I'm Not There," Le Poisson Rouge, New York (December 5, 2010)** Over the last few years, Howard Fishman and Sonic Youth have translated and recorded this once-almost-incomprehensible Bob Dylan song. This night, it seemed to have drifted into Eleanor Friedberger's mind unbidden, and she told its tale as if, now, it was her life to lead.

3 ▪ **Anika, *Anika* (Stones Throw)** The Nico-like face, the Nico-like voice—for that matter the Nico-like consonants—it reeks of concept. But Skeeter Davis's 1963 "End of the World" always had something uncanny—something from beyond the grave—beneath its lost-love lyrics, and the twenty-three-year-old Anika Henderson—she's English, her mother is German—brings it to the surface. And there's something deeply displacing, and gripping, about hearing "Masters of War" sung with a German accent. Suddenly, all sorts of people who weren't in the song before are now crowding its stage: Nazis, yes, but also Marianne Faithfull with her "Broken English," inspired by Ulrike Meinhof, and the female German terrorists who in Olivier Assayas's *Carlos*—Julia Hummer's Nada, Nora von Waldstätten's Magdalena Kopp, Katharina Schüttler's Brigitte Kuhlmann—are more fearsome than the men, maybe because they seem so eager to be consumed by the fire they're trying to make.

4 ▪ **Peter Hujar, *Thek Working on Tomb Effigy 8, 1967*, in "Paul Thek: Diver, A Retrospective," Whitney Museum of American Art, New York (October 21, 2010–January 9, 2011)** One of a series of photos in a slide show, this leaps out. It's tall, thin, blond, long-haired Thek standing at a work table, with his "Dead Hippie" sculpture lying flat on a

platform—a sculpture of himself, or almost. The figure is Thek, but inhumanly incomplete, the features rough and crude, the right arm missing a hand, and the positioning of the figure is pure déjà vu. It's the artist in the intermediate stage of growing his own pod: a one-man remake of *Invasion of the Body Snatchers*.

5 ▪ **Sheryl Lee in *Winter's Bone*, directed by Debra Granik (Lionsgate)** Somehow, teenage Maddy Ferguson didn't follow cousin Laura Palmer into the river. She ran off into the woods, all the way across the country, changed her name, and twenty years later turned up in the Ozarks as a forty-year-old woman (not quite looking or speaking as if she was born there, though it's hard to believe anyone in the film's mountains wasn't), just for the chance to look Jennifer Lawrence's sixteen-year-old in the eye, to see herself, to give the girl the kind of loving, no-hope smile she could have used herself, back before she was dead.

6 ▪ **Allo Darlin', *Allo Darlin'* (Fortuna Pop!)** Breathy, small-voice pop that makes a world of ease and nimbleness, leaping over tall buildings or anyway garden fences in a single bound. ("I've got no money to burn but I'm going to burn what I've got," Elizabeth Morris sings in "Silver Dollars," and you don't exactly believe her; "I know this band is awful but I like them an awful lot," she goes on, and you absolutely do.) Funny, breezy, smart: references include Max von Sydow, Woody Allen, Johnny Cash, old "I'd Rather Fight Than Switch" cigarette ads, and Weezer, the latter to derisive laughter, which could be the most perfect moment here.

7 ▪ **Allen Ruppersberg, *A Lecture on Houdini* (1973), in "Houdini: Art and Magic," Jewish Museum, New York (October 29, 2010–March 27, 2011)** Easy to miss in this thrilling survey of the career and afterlife of the unforgotten escape artist is a small video cut into a large screen that's showing footage of Houdini hung upside down and freeing himself from a straitjacket. On the small screen, you see Ruppersberg in a straitjacket, seated at a desk, twisting

and stretching as he reads from a type-script of his own Houdini biography. Near the end, his efforts to wriggle loose become more desperate, and his reading more strangled, out of breath—and suddenly the real events he's describing are suspended. As each sentence takes you closer to the end, the feeling is that if Ruppersberg can somehow escape before he reaches the description of Houdini's death, Houdini won't die.

8–9 ■ Carolina Chocolate Drops, "Sitting on Top of the World," from *Things About Comin' My Way: A Tribute to the Music of the Mississippi Sheiks* (Black Hen, 2009) and *Dona Got a Ramblin' Mind* (Music Maker Relief Foundation, 2006) Aren't tribute albums terrible? Yes, but with Rhiannon Giddens's fiddle keening so distantly in the background, you can imagine that the Chocolate Drops are slowing the Memphis combo's 1930 blues standard down almost to a stop as a way of slowing down the world, so they won't have to get off—just as, five years ago, on a first album that said hello to almost everyone in the old-timey neighborhood, from "Little Sadie" to "Sally Ann," "Tom Dula" to "Black-Eyed Daisy," they nevertheless jumped the train of "Old Cat Died" as if the same thing would happen to them if they couldn't ride out of town on the rail of their own strings, so fast that moment to moment you can't tell Giddens's and Justin Robinson's fiddles from Dom Flemons's harmonica, which might be the whole point.

10 ■ YOU CAN CHECK OUT ANYTIME YOU LIKE, BUT YOU CAN NEVER LEAVE, headline, *Wall Street Journal* (January 4) Over a picture of then-governor Jerry Brown with Linda Ronstadt and Glenn Frey of the Eagles, 1976, on the left, and Brown being sworn in as governor of California, 2011.

Thanks to Chris Ohman

MAY 2011

1 ■ PJ Harvey, *Let England Shake* (Vagrant/Island/Def Jam) It's shocking to real-ize that her first album appeared nineteen years ago. While from one record to the next radical leaps alternate with at least one step back, from *Dry* to *Rid of Me* to the quicksand of *4-Track Demos*, from *To Bring You My Love* to the bottomless *Stories from the City, Stories from the Sea* to *Uh Huh Her* to *A Woman a Man Walked By* with longtime collaborator John Parish—never mind the bootleg *Blind Peggy Death*—her sound has traveled with such immediacy, such an insistence that what you're hearing is happening now, that notions of time, career, progress, or decline are meaningless.

Here her voice feels higher, damaged. The back-and-forth with Parish (guitar and percussion, saxophone and trombone) is more delicate than ever; notes feel as if they're reaching for each other and barely missing. But the deep-blues pessimism that has driven Harvey all along finds a field so stark you can't not picture it. The terrain the songs claim—a country used up, "damp filthiness of ages," acres of corpses, "arms and legs were in the trees"—lets you imagine Harvey started out to create a soundtrack after the fact to *Children of Men*—the sounds coming out of her mouth feel like Clive Owen's face looked—and then decided to remake the whole picture instead. While ending one song with a line from "Summertime Blues."

2 ■ Kathleen Hanna, "Smells Like Teen Spirit," Joe's Pub, New York (December 15, 2010, YouTube) As she goes on at length with the story of how she named the song, which she later found herself stripping to—it's a stand-up routine, starting with graffiti on a fake teen-pregnancy center, graffiti on a bedroom wall, and then "one of those hangovers where you think that if you walk in the next room there could be a dead body in there?"—both glee and suspense take over the room. It's the suspense of someone describing how history was made, which is to say describing how it might not have been; it's the glee of having been in the right place at the right time, and for once saying exactly

the right thing. When Hanna finally begins to sing the song itself in her little-girl voice, and the hairs rise on the back of your neck, you can feel them one by one.

3 ▪ **Low Anthem, *Smart Flesh* (Nonesuch)** A lot of people hear worry and trouble in Arcade Fire and the Decemberists, but all I find are bland, warming voices reassuring the listener that somebody cares. On their fourth album, this Providence quartet—whose Myspace profile lists its genre as "Comedy/Minimalist/Psychedelic," which is as helpful as "Harry Reid/Patsy Cline/Humphrey Bogart" might be—goes for the nihilism of real art: saying what you want to say without wondering if it's going to do anybody any good. "Boeing 737" opens with a flurry of thrilling noise and a tale so lacking in piety you start playing the movie it calls up before the first verse is half over. "I was in the air when the towers came down / In a bar on the 84th floor," the singer says, like a drunk in another bar who's told this story so many times he actually believes it. But two tracks earlier, in "Ghost Woman Blues," the singer has already convinced you that the ghost he saw in the cemetery wasn't a ghost at all, that both the woman and the song might be two hundred years old, and by now you're ready to believe anything.

4 ▪ **Vladimir Putin, "Blueberry Hill" (December 11, 2010, YouTube)** Phil Bronstein, *San Francisco Chronicle*, January 10: "In front of a fawning crowd, including Hollywood celebrities, Putin charmingly sang 'Blueberry Hill.' It reminded me of those Adolf and Eva home movies at Berchtesgaden, laughing and playing with their German shepherds." Or, as Eva, a big Al Jolson fan, liked to do, dressing up in blackface.

5 ▪ **Gang of Four, First Avenue, Minneapolis (February 12)** In front of an unfawning but enthusiastic crowd whose ages, from twenties to sixties, matched those of the four onstage—founding members Andy Gill and Jon King in their mid-fifties, new members Tom McNiece and Mark Heaney in their forties and thirties but appearing much younger—the strongest performances were physical epics. Compositions that were once tied to specific social or political circumstances—"Armalite Rifle," about torture in Northern Ireland in the 1970s, or the stop-time, spoken "Paralysed," about mass unemployment and forced redundancy under Margaret Thatcher in the 1980s—reemerged as basic, general, borderless tales, to be told around the campfire of a show like this one. "Do As I Say," from the band's recent *Content*, was a hysterical, then implacable acting-out of an all-pervasive tyrannical madness. These songs and others went on and on, as if for each number the writers had forgotten to include a way out. It was one long analysis; the cheering was loud after the first encore and louder after the second.

6 ▪ **Antietam, *Tenth Life* (Carrot Top)** As the leader of this undefeated New York trio, singer and guitarist Tara Key has never pulled her punches, but never have they landed so fiercely, and with such grace, as they do here, six songs in. "Clarion" is an instrumental, a melody building on its own lyricism, all sunsets and sunrises, until it fades into "Better Man," where it reveals itself as a fanfare, because this is the song—relentless, confident, triumphant, every swagger earned and paid for a hundred times over—you didn't know you were waiting for.

7 ▪ **Social Distortion, *Hard Times and Nursery Rhymes* (Epitaph)** Over nearly twenty years this Southern California punk band—led by Mike Ness, who sometimes comes across as the bad seed of namesake Eliot—hasn't come close to making a poor record. This is staggering.

8 ▪ **Howard Jacobson, *The Finkler Question* (Bloomsbury)** "After more than a dozen years roaming the ghostly corridors of Broadcasting House in the dead of night, knowing no one was listening to anything he produced—for who, at three o'clock in the morning, wanted to hear live poets discussing dead poets, who might just as well have been dead poets discussing live poets?—he resigned."

9–10 ■ Platters, "Smoke Gets in Your Eyes" (Mercury) Released in 1958, just months after Eddie Cochran's "Summertime Blues," it's drifted through its own haze ever since, now for a long moment hovering over Michelle Williams and Ryan Gosling for the awful sex scene in Derek Cianfrance's *Blue Valentine*, until the music fades away and dies as the sex does. Bryan Ferry covered the Platters' version—the composition goes back to the 1930s—in 1974 for *Another Time, Another Place*, trying to get underneath the Platters' soaring, heroic embrace of the song, to find a smaller song inside of it. Sneaking in behind the closing credits in Sofia Coppola's *Somewhere*, his version is gorgeous, threatened, a heart exposed, and for a verse or so he's allowed to say everything the movie can't, or more likely won't.

Thanks to Daniel Marcus

JUNE 2011

1 ■ Gareth Liddiard, *Strange Tourist* (ATP) The film critic Mick LaSalle, in the *San Francisco Chronicle*, recently answered a reader's query as to why the superb film *Never Let Me Go*—the movie about an English boarding school attended exclusively by boys and girls destined to be harvested for their organs—failed to receive an Oscar nomination as one of the ten best films of the year. ". . . a movie's chances go down if viewers feel like killing themselves after an hour," LaSalle replied. *Strange Tourist* is like that: a man sitting in a room, hitting notes on an acoustic guitar, meandering through tales of one defeat after another, with alcohol leaving tracks on the songs like a snail. But Liddiard leads the Drones, who with far more drama, dynamism, and fury can also make you feel like killing yourself, or anyway wishing the world would end, or wondering if, in one symbolically complete event at a time—a school shooting here, a successful Republican filibuster there, a new Lucinda Williams album on the horizon—it hasn't already. Here, in a quiet, art-

less, shamed, constricted way, a person emerges: a fictional construction, someone without a flicker of belief or, for that matter, interest in redemption, cure, or another life. Against all odds, especially across the more than sixteen minutes of "The Radicalisation of D," the final track, he makes you want to know what happens next.

2 ■ Jay-Z, *Decoded* (Spiegel & Grau, 2010) An old-fashioned artist's book—thick, gorgeous, a collage of memoir, rhymes, photos, newspaper front-pages, drawings, paintings, and so dense in mass and swift on the eye that you have no idea what might appear each time you turn a page. For me the book lit up when I stumbled on the page with an old picture of Ronald Reagan—from the '40s or '50s, looking ingratiating and slick—with the shadow of Osama bin Laden peering over his shoulder. The little superimposition swirled: Jay-Z's point was that Reagan was happy to see New York turn into Crack City, that we've forgotten the "historical amnesia and the myth of America's innocence that led us into the war in Iraq." But to me, Reagan came right out of the book, smiling over Jay-Z's shoulder, handing him a Medal of Freedom, telling him that he, like all of the other people on the stage, was an American hero for proving that in this great country anyone can make himself so rich democracy is beside the point.

3–4 ■ *Mildred Pierce*, directed by Todd Haynes, written by Haynes and Jon Raymond (HBO) and Michal Grover-Friedlander, *Operatic Afterlives* (Zone Books) At the end of the fourth episode, Kate Winslet's Mildred, Brian F. O'Byrne's Bert (Mildred's ex-husband), and a few others gather excitedly at one of Mildred's restaurants; someone brings out a 1930s box radio and places it on a table. They're going to hear the radio debut of Mildred and Bert's daughter Veda: a "coloratura soprano," though they're not sure what that is. Mildred and her daughter, played by Morgan Turner as a child, and by Evan Rachel Wood as a near adult, are more than estranged; her daughter considers her mother, a successful business-woman, little more than a peasant. There's nervousness all over Winslet's face.

The radio show is vulgar, all noisy ads and smarm: Veda banters icily with the idiot announcer. There's a fanfare-commercial, and then Veda begins to sing. On the sound track, it's the Chinese color-atura Dilber, performing "Bell Song" from Léo Delibes's 1881–82 opera *Lakmé*—but we've already seen Evan Rachel Wood, a woman with a screen presence so fierce and delicate that we picture her face on the face of the radio as the sound comes out, and the tension on Winslet's face is re-placed by terror.

In *Operatic Afterlives*, the Israeli musi-cologist Michal Grover-Friedlander argues that, at its most extreme, opera, "founded as it is on the myth of Orpheus," is "an at-tempt to revive the dead with the power granted to singing." This is what we are hearing, if not something more. Opera may be about the production of sounds of such purity, transcendence, and force that they deny the fact that they could be made by mere human beings—and thus the audi-ence and the singer herself can be ab-sorbed into the notion that the singer is not human, but other than human, or inhu-man. As one cannot imagine a mere mor-tal making such sounds, she ceases to be mortal. It's not that she becomes immortal; she was never born, and therefore she can-not die. It's the emergence of a monster of grace; as Mildred and Bert look on, they realize they have created this monster. Haynes shows the faces of the people listen-ing, and then there's a slow pan across the radio, with sound coming out of the deco mouth of the speaker, as if the monster could turn into an inanimate object, or bring it to life—as if the radio is itself alive, or as if a deadly homunculus lives inside it.

5 ▪ **Attachments, *Go Away* (attachments .bandcamp.com)** Jonathan Richman is back! In the shape of an Oakland quartet having too much fun to be embarrassed by any-thing, just like the man himself.

6 ▪ **Secret DJ, Philadelphia International Airport (March 13)** Playing as you got off the plane, as you walked down the terminal, into the baggage-claim area, music to—soothe your nerves? Wake you up? Torture your brain? What is that? And it was Bob Dylan's 1966 "Rainy Day Women #12 & 35," Bill Deal & the Rhondels' obscure 1969 "What Kind of Fool Do You Think I Am?", the Beach Boys' glorious 1963 "Be True to Your School," and, with a crack, a surge, the kind of urgency that was not in music before rock 'n' roll, the Animals' 1964 "I'm Crying." I don't think I've heard a set that good on an actual radio station in twenty years.

7 ▪ **Gil Scott-Heron, "Me and the Devil," from *I'm New Here* (XL)** The song commu-nicated resignation when Robert Johnson sang it in 1937, and it communicates resig-nation now. The difference is that Johnson's devil was specific; here it seems to be life it-self.

8 ▪ **Dana Spiotta, *Stone Arabia* (Scribner)** From the author of *Eat the Document*, a new novel about a musician and his sister, both of them in their late forties. The book maps a post-punk milieu where the sense of completeness punk offered, in this case in Los Angeles, never goes away. Spiotta can capture whole lives in the most ordinary transaction, and make it cut like X's "Los Angeles" or the Avengers' "Car Crash," as when the brother comes to his sister for money, for gas, for food: "I pulled open a drawer. I riffled through the papers until I found a credit card offer that included some low-interest-rate checks attached to a piece of paper upon which many caveats, warnings, catches, and asterisks (which I supposed meant risks of a sidereal nature) were printed in the classic credit-card tiny faint print. The first time you actually read the words printed on these things was to feel the last connection to your childhood die. I filled one out for a thousand dollars."

9 ▪ **Randy Newman, *The Randy Newman Songbook Vol. 2* (Nonesuch)** The second of his solo piano recordings of old songs reaches its height with the first of them,

"Dixie Flyer," about Newman's mother leaving L.A. for her native New Orleans during World War II, when Newman's father was overseas. The regret in the opening notes as he looks back is awful: as he sings now, his father is dead, his mother is dead, this is his attempt to feel for himself the dilemma the world dropped on them like a bomb, and they will never hear him, never understand how fully he understands. The train crosses the country, Newman is barely born, but he feels the journey, hears what it means to be Jewish in the South. He flinches, he pushes harder, takes a stand, draws a line in the sand, and he leaves who he is behind that line, because he knows he would have made the same choice his mother did. It all happened in 1988 on *Land of Dreams*, but not with this depth of compassion, this hate: "Trying to do like the gentiles do / Christ, they wanted to be gentiles too / Who wouldn't down there, wouldn't you? / An American Christian / God damn!"

10 ▪ **RaveUps, "You Can't Judge a Book by Its Cover" (Eagles Hall, El Cerrito, California, April 9)** As a Yardbirds tribute band, they hit their stride with a cover of the Yardbirds' cover of Bo Diddley. "I look like a farmer, but I'm a lover / Can't judge a book by looking at the cover," Dave Seabury sang—wiry, balding, coat and tie, a used-car dealer's mustache, thirty years ago the drummer in the East Bay punk band Psychotic Pineapple. Until the last chorus, when you couldn't read his face or his tone: "I look like an insurance salesman, but I'm a male prostitute!"

JULY–AUGUST 2011

1 ▪ **Robert Johnson, *The Centennial Collection* (Columbia Legacy)** Johnson's 1936 and 1937 recordings—to quote the late Wilfrid Mellers in his unsurpassed study *Music in a New Found Land*, "the ultimate, and scarifying disintegration of the country blues. . . . The expression of loneliness—the singer speaking with and through his guitar—could be carried no further"—have

been reissued in countless formats since they were first collected, in 1961. They have been remastered, reengineered, rebalanced, all but reamed to bring out the sound you can't hear but should. But never like this. For this celebration of the hundredth anniversary of Johnson's birth, on May 8, 1911, in Hazlehurst, Mississippi, there are new liner notes by the blues historian Ted Gioia and by Johnson copyrighter Steve LaVere—but what the music now needs is a full technical report. LaVere's praise for digital transfers and noise reduction by the engineers Steven Lasker and Seth Winner is not adequate. What they've done is a revelation: they have stripped the past from Johnson, the nearly three-quarters of a century from then to now, and placed him and you in the same room. He's playing to you, trying to get across. You are trying to tell him that you've never heard anything like this before, even though you have his records, even in a half dozen redundant editions, played to death, the covers of the original LPs instantly memorized for the drama of the first, the ordinariness of the second, which, coming in the wake of the first, was more dramatic still: the idea that some individual with a name and a face could be responsible for music that, no less than the forgotten playwright Aeschylus stole from, rewrote the human spirit. You're trying to tell him all this; he's listening.

You may have listened to Johnson through each successive improvement, each set of new sonic clothes; you haven't heard these notes, these words, these leaves trembling on the trees.

2 ▪ **Elvis Costello and the Imposters, "Jimmie Standing in the Rain" (Fox Theater, Oakland, California, May 8)** Near the end of the show, when he'd dropped the Spectacular Spinning Songbook format, he stepped into this tune from his 2010 *National Ransom*. It's about a man in a British coal town, getting nowhere in his attempts to get by with cowboy music—because this is also a song about the Great Depression, and

there's no work, anywhere. The man in the song seemed to sink lower, down to his knees, the more expansive and delicate Costello's voice became. The sound in the hall had been one impenetrable echo from the start—at one point Costello stepped away from the mike stand and sang without any amplification at all, and for a moment you could hear a real person on the stage— but finally the clouds cleared. And then, without any change you could catch, he was singing the last, desperately smiling verse of Bing Crosby's 1932 "Brother, Can You Spare a Dime?" For a moment, many things just out of reach for the rest of the night were present: beauty, terror, a curl in the words, a naked soul, shame. The sounds in Costello's throat grew bigger even as they seemed to scurry away from him, back into history, out into the street. "Mr. Harburg's song," Costello said the next day, speaking of Yip Harburg, who wrote the words Crosby sang, "is sadly back in vogue."

3 ▪ **Alison Krauss and Union Station, *Paper Airplane* (Rounder)** You could say there's nothing new here in New Bluegrassland. Krauss and guitarist Dan Tyminski still trade tunes. Their approaches are so different—he's funny regardless what story he's telling, she's a fatalist (the way she says "Save your breath" in "Sinking Stone") no matter how happy an ending—they seem more like people who say hello when they pass each other on the street every day than members of the same band. If you want something new you might as well bulldoze the town.

4 ▪ **Rainy Day, "I'll Keep It With Mine" (YouTube)** Someone took Susanna Hoffs's 1984 version of this 1966 Bob Dylan demo—a song that, as far as I know, has never been done badly, by anyone—Nico, Fairport Convention, Bettie Serveert (behind the crawl in *I Shot Andy Warhol*, maybe the best)—and used it as a sound track for excerpts from the rigorously formalist avant-garde filmmaker Guy Debord's 1961 movie *Critique de la séparation*. In a Paris travelogue, the camera is madly in love with a young girl: a round,

trusting face, very short hair, a gamin from central casting. As it follows her down the street, pauses over her outside a café, stops her in still photos, Hoffs, recording almost a quarter century later—former L.A. punk in the Bangs, in 1984 a glamour girl in the Bangles—seems to have been there and gone. She could be that same person, all those years later, facing the fact that all the wrong turns in her life started here.

5 ▪ **Steven Brower, *"Breathless Homicidal Slime Mutants": The Art of the Paperback* (Universe)** There are many collections of lurid paperback covers. This book makes gestures toward bibliographic seriousness, but it's really about the necklines, when there are any: I mean, where would modern painting be without Erskine Caldwell? Still, it's the nighttown cover for *The Catcher in the Rye* that might be the most unsettling: this thickset guy with what looks like a backward baseball cap on his head holding a heavy suitcase and walking with determination straight into a New York grotto of bad news, a look of utter suicide on what little you can see of his face.

6–7 ▪ **Perry Lederman, "Impressions of John Henry" and Debbie Green, "Who's Going to Be My Man?" on *Hear Me Howling! Blues, Ballads, and Beyond as Recorded by the San Francisco Bay by Chris Strachwitz in the 1960s* (Arhoolie Records)** An illustrated, 136-page book with a fine text by Adam Machado, four CDs of mostly unreleased work cut between 1954 and 1971 by the German-born folklorist and notoriously honest record man Strachwitz on the blues singers Skip James, Big Joe Williams, Lonnie Johnson, Bukka White, and Lightnin' Hopkins, the Berkeley folkies and rock 'n' roll singers Country Joe and the Fish and Joy of Cooking, the R&B shouter Big Mama Thornton, the Zydeco King Clifton Chenier, and many, many more—it's unquestionably historic stuff. It can tingle. But it's not their best stuff, and while I listened, fascinated, I was more moved by the unknown early '60s performances by the guitarist Perry Lederman, dramatizing the John Henry story by trading off between taking the parts of both the steel-driver and the steam drill, and Debbie Green, the Cambridge folk-singer who—so pretty people found it easy not to take her seriously—spent a good part of a lifetime accusing Joan Baez of stealing her music and borrowing her soul. On a version of "In the Pines," her playing is as ragged, self-conscious, and convincing as her testament is elegant and enraged: "By the time I got to Berkeley toward the end of 1960, she had recorded all the songs that I taught her. All my arrangements, and learned all the inflections and facial expressions. She's a mime. So anyway, then I couldn't do any of that material because I was a Baez imitator."

8 ▪ **"Dreamweapon: The Art and Life of Angus MacLise" (Boo-Hooray Gallery, New York, May 10–29)** Robert Polito reports: "Memorialized often only as the first drummer (polyrhythmic bongos and tablas) of the Velvet Underground, Angus MacLise was the speeding Wagner of New York's '60s downtown: a guy from the suburbs, by way of Paris and India, who intended to scramble poetry, music, dance, theater, art, religion, and film into a total spectacle. Drolly curated by Johan Kugelberg and Will Cameron, the broadsides, posters, handwritten notes, and calligraphy of Dreamweapon suggest the post-cataclysmic totems of a vast, irretrievable civilization—Petra, Pompeii, or Z—if the residue of that civilization consisted of nothing besides ink and a hundred radiant pieces of paper. Collectors tag such stuff ephemera. The wonder is that most of this survived at all, never mind that decades later we still wander the ruins. A 1966 flier for the Film-Makers Cinematheque proposes that you see 'in the person, or just in the film' Harry Smith, the Gato Barbieri Quintet, Andy Warhol, Larry Coryell, Jack Smith, D. A. Pennebaker, Bob Neuwirth, Gerard Malanga, Jonas Menkas, Don Snyder, Marie Menken, Barbara Rubin, Weegee, '& ANGUS MACLISE & THE VELVET UNDERGROUND in THE DENTAL DE-STRUCTION OF THE CHAIRS a MASS MENTAL CONCENTRATION AGAINST FURNITURE BY MOVIES MOVIE MOVIES SLIDES & LOOPS & BURNING PROJECTORS MUSIC WOVEN FOR 12 DAYS ONLY IN THE MASS LOVE CONTEST "SMOTHER ME" FREE FORM WALKING BOO LOVE HISS n' COME COSTUMED.' If that's an advertisement for Paradise Lost, a 1979 pencil draft of a poem (MacLise would die that year in Nepal) is a postcard to the next world—'Enjoying life I look forward to death with the eagerness, of a lover. The stars will be mine!—and the final depths of poetry.'"

9 ▪ **Dolores Fuller, 1923–2011** In the 1953 *Glen or Glenda*, she gave Ed Wood—"the cross-dressing writer and director of films so awful they have a stupefying, apocalyptic beauty," Margalit Fox wrote in her *New York Times* obituary for Fuller—the angora sweater he craved beyond all flesh. Then she became a songwriter, cowriting the Elvis numbers "Rock-a-Hula Baby" and "Do the Clam"—compositions so awful it's embarrassing to type their names. Whatever Ed Wood got from her, she got back.

10 ▪ **Robert Johnson's Hellhound on My Ale (Columbia Legacy/Dogfish Head Craft Brewery, dogfish.com)** As a promotional tie-in, I figured this had to be terrible: all concept ("Brewed with Lemons," the front label reads, with the second label explaining the flavoring "as a shout out to Robert Johnson's mentor Blind Lemon Jefferson"), no beer. It comes only in a twenty-five-ounce bottle, there was no one to taste-test it with, but I opened it anyway.

It was rich without noise, with a huge head. Flavors swam through the glass. It was so smooth it was like drinking a sunset. I reached for the bottle and it was empty.

SEPTEMBER 2011

1 ▪ **Fucked Up, *David Comes to Life* (Matador)** "If you want a picture of the future," George Orwell wrote in 1984, "imagine a boot stamping on a human face—forever. And remember that it is forever." Fucked Up is a little like that. There must be few forces in the universe as unrelenting as the singer Pink Eyes' hardcore slam of words,

slogans, chants; at first listen he's one single giant battering ram. At more than seventy-five minutes, the lifelong love story of *David Comes to Life* might as well go on forever. That's all there as the album opens, but by the end it's gone. I can't speak for the subtleties of the story: it's hard to catch a reading of *The Sorrows of Young Werther* in the middle of a riot, and a short novel's worth of lyric sheets is not music. But as a work where words less tell a story than signify that, somewhere, a story is present, this is a gorgeous, invisibly layered, extraordinarily ambitious, and fully realized testament to how far, in the present moment, pop music can go. Throughout, female voices sweep in to undercut Pink Eyes' male stomp, and every time you hear those voices, they seem to be coming from different people, from different times. There's never a lessening of speed, frenzy, of action-movie *action*, but as the songs go on, all eighteen of them, an emotional if not narrative clarity begins to take over. Near the end, with "A Little Death," "The Recursive Girl," and "One More Night," the numbers feel increasingly fresh, new, invigorating; the musicians sound as if they, too, are about to seize a new life.

2–3 ▪ Eleventh Dream Day, *Riot Now!* (Thrill Jockey) and the Coathangers, *Larceny & Old Lace* (Suicide Squeeze) The Coathangers are a casual female punk band that's been hanging around Atlanta for five years; Eleventh Dream Day is a Chicago group led by Rick Rizzo and Janet Bean for almost a quarter of a century—and just as a ninety-year-old is more likely than a fifty-year-old to live to a hundred, chances are Rizzo and Bean will still be pounding—Rizzo's guitar playing can be more percussive than Bean's drumming—when guitarist the Crook Kid Coathanger, drummer Rusty Coathanger, bassist Minnie Coathanger, and keyboard player Bebe Coathanger have gone on to other names. The Coathangers start off their third album with "Hurricane," and they live up to the title in an instant. Just as you can see Patty McCormack in *The Bad Seed* in their "Hurricane" video (on You-Tube), you can hear Sleater-Kinney in the blunt insistence of the singing, Delta 5 in the displacing bass breaks, and, most of all, Kleenex in the playground shouts of the chorus. And you can feel a glee, a sense of both escape and arrival in the right place at the right time, that makes where the band learned its tricks irrelevant. And after that it's like a show where the costume changes are more compelling than the music. The group tries on one style after another, until, well before the record ends, each song sounds more contrived than felt. *Riot Now!* is Eleventh Dream Day's tenth album, but there's no pose struck anywhere on it; almost every track is infused with discovery, doubt, unease. The songs feel less like songs than jagged, almost random pieces of the same bad day. "Tall Man" is a moment of panic boiled down into a few words and a riff from Dramarama's "Anything Anything": you can imagine Rizzo and Bean seeing a guy on the street, saying, "He sure is tall," then, half-jokingly, "He's too tall," then, not joking at all, "He's too fucking tall to fucking *live*," then the two of them imagining a building falling on him. With Bean shouting behind Rizzo's everyman leads, there's a core of ferocity in every number, and, with the way Bean's voice sometimes seems to be suspended above Rizzo's, a question mark to his exclamation point, a core of fatalism. There's no hint in their music that life is ever going to get any easier, or any less interesting.

4 ▪ Lydia Loveless, *Indestructible Machine* (Bloodshot) On her second album, this twenty-one-year-old country singer from Ohio shows herself drinking white lightning or gasoline (cartoon on the front cover) and smoking a cigarette (photo on the back). She and her band are weirdly disconnected, as if the band was playing on one side of the street and she was recorded walking by on the other side and making up songs as she went. Moments of truth leap out of sarcasm and disdain ("They get away with shit / That I never will," Loveless says in "More Like Them," a grown-up version of Claudine Clark's teenager's "Party

Lights"). In "Can't Change Me," which is a blast of pain, not bravado, there's a weight, a grounding, that allows Loveless to ignore meter and come across as if she's seen everything twice. What you're left with is a big, warm, open, sometimes desperate voice.

5–6 ▪ Rave on Buddy Holly (Fantasy) and Buddy Holly, Not Fade Away: Complete Studio Recordings and More (Hip-O) Aren't tribute albums terrible? Yes, and from Paul McCartney's Screamin' Jay Hawkins imitation on "It's So Easy" to Karen Elson's flattening of Holly's swirling melody in "Crying, Waiting, Hoping" to Patti Smith's benediction on "Words of Love," this celebration of Holly's would-have-been-seventy-fifth birthday lives up to the genre—save for the Black Keys' modest, spooky "Dearest," Modest Mouse's offering "That'll Be the Day" as if they're remembering some other song the title just happens to remind them of, and Lou Reed, with Laurie Anderson on electric violin, turning Peggy Sue into a grunge queen. Holly has to be smiling; he's heard this all before. As you can hear on *Not Fade Away*, people were revising his music before he was barely cold in the ground. You listen to the six CDs, collecting performances from 1949 to the first days of 1959, as if to a novel unfolding—until the end, when it all goes to hell. You hear the quiet, soulful, fiercely ambitious demos Holly made in his last months in his Greenwich Village apartment; no sooner did his plane go down in that Iowa cornfield in 1959 than his producer Norman Petty got the tapes, fixed them up, and, again and again, put them on the market. The contrast between the music as Holly made it and Petty's successive dubbing sessions—featuring strings, the clueless New Mexico band the Fireballs, and nameless hacks—is so stark it suggests not greed but resentment: a producer's desire to dissolve an artist's singular intelligence into a product cheesy enough to prove that his music could have been done by anyone, and wasn't worth doing. So go back and listen again to Holly alone:

"Love Is Strange," "Dearest," "Peggy Sue Got Married."

7 ▪ The Jet Age Compendium: Paolozzi at Ambit, edited by David Brittain (Four Corners Books) Eduardo Paolozzi (1924–2005) was perhaps the first and certainly one of the best pop artists—a magpie who could pass a newsstand, come away with a movie of headlines and images playing in his head, then go home and burn it down to a single collaged frame—as he did in 1947 with *I Was a Rich Man's Plaything*. Twenty years later he began working with the London arts magazine *Ambit*, and for seven years after that he let the Vietnam War invade his mind the way he'd once made room for sex magazines and soft-drink ads. He wrote absurdist essays and fractured plays, layered photographs, cut pictures out of magazines to make new magazines, and even produced his own newspaper: a one-page broadside called *Bad News at the Breakfast Table*. Aside from an obscene two-panel comic strip in the bottom right corner, a list of corporations on the left border, and sex ads bottom left, it consisted entirely of reports of mid-1960s American riots and murders. It had to have been devastating then, because it's devastating now: a portrait of a country where anyone can be killed at any time. News item: MAD SNIPER KILLS 15, WOUNDS 31 FROM U OF TEXAS TOWER. News item: PERCY'S DAUGHTER IS SLAIN IN CHICAGO. The specter of Charles Whitman firing down into the campus plaza in Austin is part of the national consciousness, but who remembers that Valerie Jean Percy, daughter of soon-to-be U.S. senator Charles Percy, was killed in her own "palatial suburban home"?

8 ▪ Department of Counterhistory In 2000, Al Gore was considering a running mate. He came close to picking John Edwards, then the number one rising-star fresh face of the Democratic party. Instead, most likely to distance himself as far as possible from Bill Clinton, he chose Joe Lieberman, a tribune of sanctimony so pious in his condemnation of Clinton during the Lewinsky scandal that Philip Roth gave him a cameo in *The Human Stain*. As a candidate, Lieberman—who in 2008 was John McCain's first choice as a running mate, until McCain's campaign managers told him no—is best remembered for his vice-presidential debate with Dick Cheney, whom he graciously allowed to run all over him as if Cheney were a pickup truck and Lieberman Lucinda Williams's gravel road. Which didn't stop him: In 2003, Lieberman announced that he himself would seek the Democratic nomination for president. But there was a road not taken. Eighteen years before, in 1975, Bob Dylan had gathered figures from all across his career—Joan Baez, Jack Elliott, Allen Ginsberg, Bob Neuwirth, countless more—for a traveling minstrel show. WHO IS JOE LIEBERMAN? ran the headline of an ABC News story on January 2, 2003. "Lieberman has spent most of his professional life in politics," the piece ran in part, "but there's perhaps one aspiration he might have enjoyed pursuing. 'I went through a Bob Dylan phase,' he said. 'One of his tours was called The Rolling Thunder Review—when Joan Baez was with him and people would come and go. It would have been fun to have spent a few months with Dylan on The Rolling Thunder Review.' " It might not have saved the country, but Joe Lieberman banging a tambourine for "Bob Dylan's 115th Dream" is something I would have paid money to see.

9 ■ Jaan Uhelszki, "Off the Charts," *California* magazine (Summer 2011) On KALX, Berkeley's college radio station, and its tradition of recruiting guests to tape station IDs (number one on the charts, from the Reagan years: "This is Attorney General Ed Meese on KALX in Berkeley. It's a *crime* if you don't stay tuned"): "In February 1985, an emissary of Charles Manson called the station to arrange an interview. His one stipulation: He only wanted to talk about music. Reporters Arnold Woods '84"—*California* is the Berkeley alumni magazine—"and Kevin Kennedy taped the convicted serial killer at the state medical facility in Vacaville, and for a brief time afterward you could tune into the station and

hear, 'Hi, I'm Charlie Manson and you're listening to KALX in Berkeley.' "

10 ■ **Frank Fairfield, *Out on the Open West* (Tompkins Square)** With his first album, the young California traditionalist seemed as if he was on his way to becoming his generation's Mike Seeger: an oldtimey musician who knew everything and could play anything, a librarian with such empathy for his archive of archaic styles that in moments he might stand alongside the old singers and players, as ghosts or in the flesh, singing with them like a brother. This album, made up mostly of songs that appear handed down but aren't, is proof that Fairfield is someone else: a wicked messenger passing through town and leaving everything slightly frayed, damaged, unfixed, every gaze deflected toward an object just barely out of sight. This happens in "Haste to the Wedding/The Darling True Love," with one foot in the twenty-first century and the other in the eighteenth, neither foot staying in one place for more than a few measures at a time, and in "The Winding Spring," where a banjo is its own reward. But with the first notes of "Poor Old Lance," you know you're in different territory. The melody, really a fanfare, is bent, stretched, curved, seems familiar and teasingly out of reach—you could spend a day playing the song over and over, searching for the place you once heard that melody before giving up and admitting that probably you never did. The orchestration is glorious. Three fiddles, Fairfield, Justin Petrojvic, and Josh Petrojvic send the tune into the air and keep it there. Deep, slithering undertones from Brandon Armstrong's bull fiddle, played with a bow, keep it rooted to the ground, and sometimes pull the song under it. There is tension from the first. The words are hard to make out, because Fairfield's elisions, slides, slurs, and halffinished phrases are as much music as anything coming off the strings. But you catch enough: something about a man going down; a jailhouse, ten years. As this little play unfolds, chorus by chorus, the whole country comes into view, glimpsed as if over

a ridge: a place of discovery, joy, despair, defeat, "a land of peace, love, justice, and no mercy," all enacted in a single prison cell.

OCTOBER 2011

1–2 ▪ Amy Winehouse, *Back to Black* (Republic, 2007) and the Shangri-Las, *Myrmidons of Melodrama* (RPM, 1964–66) Again and again after Winehouse died, on July 23, you could read her talking about how she'd written the self-mocking, self-loathing, unflinchingly fuck-you songs for *Back to Black*: "I didn't want to just wake up drinking, and crying, and listening to the Shangri-Las, and go to sleep, and wake up drinking, and listening to the Shangri-Las." But she did. That's why she would let their deathly "Remember (Walking in the Sand)" drift into "Back to Black"—there is a stunning montage of her gorgeous performances of the two-pieces-in-one on YouTube. That's why, in "Rehab" and especially in her irresistible, unreadable 2008 Grammy performance of "You Know I'm No Good," Winehouse was her own leader of the pack, but without a pack, without even girlfriends to ask her if she was really going out with him, if she was really going all the way, on her own, perhaps with nothing but the satisfaction of getting it right, saying what she had to say, adding something to the form that brought her to life as an artist, adding her name and face to the story it told. Yes, she wrote "You Know I'm No Good," and like any work of art it was a fiction that bounced back on real life, maybe the author's, maybe not; as she sang it on the Grammys, you could hear her listening to the song as well as singing it, hear the song talking to her, hear her asking herself, as she sang, "Is that true? Is that what I want? Is that all I've got?"

"She could not stand fame any more than I could," Mary Weiss, the lead singer of the Shangri-Las, said after Winehouse died. "I wish I could have helped her, even if she never sang publicly again. My hairdresser told me that is just ego, thinking that maybe you could possibly make a difference when others could not. I thought about it, long and hard. I do not think so. I would have only spoken about her pain, not drug usage, until (if ever) she was ready. I related to her so much it is a bit scary. . . . I will never understand why people get off kicking people when they are down and need help. How could that possibly make you feel better about yourself?"

With anyone else but Mary Weiss as a lead singer, the doom in Shangri-Las songs might have turned into a joke, but it never happened: every time, whether in "Remember," "Give Us Your Blessings," "Out in the Streets," "I Can Never Go Home Anymore," or "Past, Present, and Future," the singer was a different person, starting from the beginning, telling her story as far as it would go, which was never very far. Their songs, like Winehouse's, were all locked doors, doors that locked you out or that you locked yourself from the inside. But maybe because she is still here and speaking plainly, inside Weiss's words you can imagine other lives for Amy Winehouse: a junkie on the street like Marianne Faithfull, who finally walked away, back into the career she never really had the first time around, first recording in the same year the Shangri-Las first recorded, this year covering their ghostly "Past, Present, and Future" on a new album; a grimy singer with a guitar case open at her feet, like anyone in your town; a social worker with years of shock treatment behind her, like June Miller; a music teacher for kindergarteners; an old woman with stories nobody believes.

3 ▪ Amen Dunes, *Through Donkey Jaw* (Sacred Bones) The music here—less abstract than vague—may be trying to live up to its cover photo by Deborah Turbeville, which could have appeared in Michael Lesy's *Wisconsin Death Trip:* a dark-haired woman with glasses, a hand held to her open mouth in alarm, and frightened eyes—eyes frightened by something behind them, not in front of them.

4–5 ▪ McCabe and Mrs. Miller, "Nebraska," from *First Person Singular Presents*

Debts No Honest Man Can Pay (Pegasus Books, Berkeley, July 20) and *Debts No Honest Man Can Pay* (Veritas, mccabeand-mrsmillerband.com) Taking part in a performance series that means to redefine not only the literary event but the literary as such, the duo—guitarist and singer Victor Krummenacher, late of Camper Van Beethoven, and pianist and singer Alison Faith Levy, once of the Sippy Cups—stepped up to perform, or rewrite, Bruce Springsteen's 1982 album *Nebraska*, and they hit a vein right from the start, with the title song. As a murder ballad, Springsteen's account of Charley Starkweather and Caril Fugate's 1958 teenage murder rampage is as stark as a Robert Frank highway photo—a song so severe in its conception and performance it could have been made to deny anyone else the chance to sing it. Krummenacher and Levy, who later recorded all the songs from the show, with "Highway Patrolman" as the clear, soul-deep standout, seized Springsteen's song by doubling down, with Krummenacher as Starkweather and Levy as Fugate trading verses and sharing lines that in Springsteen's original had been Starkweather's alone. He was executed in 1959; Fugate, who claimed to be a hostage, was paroled in 1976. Since then she has never spoken of the eleven bodies she and Starkweather left across Nebraska and Wyoming, but she was speaking this night. She was there as Levy sang, "Me and him, we had us some fun"—and she came in without flinching to sing Starkweather's real-life line about what he wanted when he went to the electric chair, "Make sure my pretty baby / is sitting right there on my lap."

6 ▪ **Woods, *Sun and Shade* (Woodsist)** There's a little of Velvet Underground's "New Age," more of the Kinks' "Waterloo Sunset," a lot of the Beatles and more of the Beach Boys, but the feel of the bedroom is stronger: from the high, high voices of "Pushing Onlys," the primitive, fully realized pop song "Who Do I Think I Am," the tunneling playing in "Out of the Eye," this is the band the fifteen-year-old music obses-

sive Jason in Dana Spiotta's novel *Eat the Document* would have formed, if only in his head.

7–8 ▪ **Diann Blakely, "Dead Shrimp Blues," with comment by Lisa Russ Spaar, *The Chronicle of Higher Education* (July 15)** For years, Blakely has written what she calls "duets" with Robert Johnson: her poems visiting his songs, his songs breathing in her poems. Here she has Tennessee Williams and Maggie from *Cat on a Hot Tin Roof* cross paths with the blues singer in Clarksdale, Mississippi, so she can address him directly, circling around the imagery in one of at least two Johnson songs built around a metaphor for impotence. She writes like a window-peeper: "I'll undress / Down to my humid white-girl slip." Spaar follows the way Blakely's words curl around Johnson's until it can seem as if Johnson's are curling around hers; she rescues the phrase "posted out" from the murk of Johnson's song so you can hear it crack in Blakely's.

9 ▪ **Eleanor Friedberger, *Last Summer* (Merge)** Jittery—someone talking too much, for a moment gritting her teeth if that's what she has to do to squeeze out the five or six words that matter. That's the story, until near the end the tension begins to break—with Friedberger's own piano running the music in "I Won't Fall Apart on You Tonight," her harmonica breaking "Early Earthquake" open with a huge laugh, her distantly doo-wop guitar chording letting the last song end the album miles away, and lives away, from where it began.

10 ▪ **Mekons, *Ancient and Modern 1911–2011* (Sin/Bloodshot)** This is a treasure chest, and what it contains is the whole of the band's thirty-four-year stumble-and-fall career: Tom Greenhalgh's no-hope chronicles, Sally Timms's icy X-ray gaze, Jon Langford's rousing odes against all odds—odes to defeat, because the game is fixed. But across eleven songs, none of that touches the delicacy, the detail, the tiny gestures that make the music new: the quiet, measured, rock-hard spoken interludes by Susie Honeyman and Sarah Corina in the

title song; the intimations of plague, carried by fleas or ideas, in "Warm Summer Sun," mapping the same blasted terrain PJ Harvey is crossing in *Let England Shake*. And then there is "Geeshie": a dive into Geeshie Wiley's uncanny 1930 "Last Kinds Words Blues." "Lu and I," Jon Langford says of Mekon Lu Edmonds, "became obsessed with the unpredictable insanity of the chord progressions, the length of the bars. Then we tried to play an instrumental version, cut it up into pieces"—and then let Sally Timms walk the tune from a Mississippi juke joint to a Weimar cabaret, turning Geeshie Wiley into Kurt Weill, though the tune in its new form moves so lightly on its feet it could be, to Weill's endless delight, the other way around.

Thanks to Andrew Hamlin

NOVEMBER–DECEMBER 2011

1 ▪ **David Lynch, *Crazy Clown Time* (Sunday Best)** Lynch has written songs before, most memorably for Julee Cruise. He's recorded, notably with John Neff for the 2003 *Blue Bob*. But he has never tried anything like this: singing and playing lead guitar on a full-out set of songs. By its end, he has mapped a version of America—an America bordered on one side by teenagers getting drunk and on the other by perverts insisting they're just like anybody else, *fuckhead*—a picture of ordinary life as funny and unsettling as you can find in *Mulholland Dr.* or *Lost Highway*. There is terrific psychedelic Duane Eddy guitar—a slow, seductive rhythm, reverb as big as a house. Again and again, there is a talking voice playing with syllables, stretching them out, bending them, curling them, until you become altogether attuned to the musicality of every inflection. But most of all, there are scenes you can visualize as you listen. For "Football Game" there is dramatic, gonging guitar, and the feel of the Top 40 death ballad brought up to date. "I went down . . . to the football game," says a beaten-down character missing half his teeth (he's not that far

from David Thomas in "Nowheresville," telling a story about the guy who thought his wife was going to leave him, how he had this great idea to build a motel on the new interstate, but then they put the interstate on the other side of the valley . . .), and you don't take him seriously until "I saw you / with another man," and the stakes go up.

"Good Day Today" plays with '60s yé-yé, Hooverphonics' synthesizer lounge ambience, cheesy French movie music, with tiny background synthesizer *uh-uh-uh-uh-uhs*, all so someone you do not want to meet can tell you, "I want to have a good day today," which is to say he'll do whatever he has to do to get it—don't pedophile serial killers deserve one too? There is "Speed Roadster," Bruce Springsteen's "Stolen Car" as a stalker's reverie, and "These Are My Friends," where the singer tells you, "I got a truck," that he's "got two good ears, and my eye on you"—it's a high-school love song, Marty Robbins's 1957 "A White Sport Coat (And a Pink Carnation)" crossed with Larry Clark's *Tulsa*, a creepy, moving version of Rosie and the Originals' 1960 "Angel Baby" slowed down to a crawl: "These are my friends, the ones I see each day / I got a perscription fer a product, keep the hounds at bay."

These are rich, sometimes tricky studio assemblages; after a few listenings you're only scratching the surface, but with "Crazy Clown Time" you might get everything the first time. It's Lynch in his high, thin voice, the old man suddenly reinhabiting his teenage self, Frank from *Blue Velvet* stopping you on the street to tell you *just how it was* when "Susie, she ripped her shirt off, completely"—and it's that *completely* that still has him shaking his head in wonder after all these years. "Calling Little Richard," the song begins, and he's right there, the parents are gone, and while the party gets increasingly out of control ("Then he poured beer all over Sally . . . Danny spit on Susie"), nothing really terrible happens. But the tempo slows, the atmosphere goes heavy and dark, as if the party has moved from Fred's house to the roadhouse in Twin

Peaks. "Susie had hers off completely," the man keeps saying, as if he's trying with everything he has to remember exactly what that looked like, and just can't. It would have been interesting to hear this on the radio in 1965, a dank, gothic, blues version of "Double Shot (Of My Baby's Love)." "It was really fun," the old man says finally.

2 ▪ Sometymes Why, "Too Repressed" (YouTube) Aoife O'Donovan of the Boston traditionalist band Crooked Still in a side project with Kristin Andreassen and Ruth Merenda—though apart from background laughter this club performance is really all O'Donovan, with her angelic face, her soft, probing tone, and a new song which starts off like any other hand-me-down ballad she might take up. Until she gets to the chorus. "I want to *fuck* you," she sings, "but I'm too repressed / I want to *suck* you / But I can't take off my dress." She's as convincing on the first lines as she is unconvincing on the second.

3 ▪ Martin Scorsese, *George Harrison: Living in the Material World* (HBO) A three-and-a-half-hour documentary on George Harrison, the Quiet Beatle, otherwise known as the Dull Beatle? Yes, and when it's over you'll want more. Never has Harrison's music sounded so rich; never has his story been told with less pomposity and more grace. And, after Harrison's years of seeking a higher truth, a purer life, a moment of shock, what he said after he and his wife, Olivia Harrison, fought off the man who broke into their house determined to exterminate the Beatle "witch": "I never tried to kill anyone before."

4 ▪ James Gavin, *Deep in a Dream: The Long Night of Chet Baker* (Chicago Review Press) Across a lifetime of ruin, the persistence of "My Funny Valentine."

5 ▪ Veronica Falls, *Veronica Falls* (Slumberland) Maybe out of season, this is warm-weather driving music, airy and determined, with more than a hint of the Jamies' "Summertime, Summertime," as it plays in James Toback's 1978 *Fingers*, with Harvey Keitel in a café with his boom box playing when a man at the next table complains. "Do you believe this?" Keitel says. "This is the Ja-

mies, man! 'Summertime, Summertime'—the most musically inventive song of 1958!"

6 ▪ Percival Everett, *Assumption* (Graywolf Press) "I was tired of being a good guy," says small-town New Mexico deputy sheriff Ogden Walker, not quite all there in the three detective stories that make up this book. Coming at the end of the last one, this simple line sends you back, mentally rewriting the ones that preceded it to try to make them work out differently, but they are not quite all there either. These are murder mysteries where the holes in the plot undermine all the apparent facts.

7 ▪ Michael Pisaro, *asleep, street, pipes, tones* (Gravity Wave) Pisaro is a minimalist composer whose music—here, a more than hour-long piece—reaches for what can feel like nearly absolute abstraction. The abstraction, though, is so complete that you soon begin to feel at home with it. It begins to feel like a landscape, and you begin to inhabit it, to feel your way through it, to recognize features, even to remember landmarks. What begins as a kind of industrial noise turns into industrial wind, and you have the feeling of being taken into a vast desert, which after a long traverse opens up onto a city, one of Anselm Kiefer's abandoned, after-the-apocalypse ruins, and you can imagine yourself living there. Or, as the title implies, at least sleeping there.

8 ▪ Alan Jackson, Norah Jones, Patty Loveless, Jack White, et al., *The Lost Notebooks of Hank Williams* (Egyptian) Aren't tribute albums terrible? Yes, and for a collection of Hank Williams lyrics now set to music, Lucinda Williams goes so far around the bend of her own mannerisms she vaporizes like the Wicked Witch of the West. Everyone else is merely earnest and competent, except for Jakob Dylan, whose "Oh, Mama, Come Home" finds a quick beat, then slows the song behind it, then looks past it. Two-line verses, a four-line chorus: you feel someone walking a circle around his day, trying to find a way out, then not caring if he does, in love with the rhythm of his loneliness. It's the most modest track on the album, the only one with nothing to prove, and you could play it all day long.

9 ▪ Steven Greenhouse, "Examining a Labor Hero's Death: Letter Emerges in 1915 Case against Joe Hill (New York Times, August 26) "A new biography makes the strongest case yet that Hill . . . executed by a Utah firing squad in 1915 . . . was wrongfully convicted of murdering a local grocer, the charge that led to his execution at age 36. . . . The book's author, William M. Adler, argues that Hill was a victim of authorities and a jury eager to deal a blow to his radical labor union, as well as his own desire to protect the identity of his sweetheart."

There was powerful if circumstantial evidence against Hill: on January 10, 1914, the same night John G. Morrison and his son were shot to death in their grocery, Hill, an organizer and songwriter for the IWW, the "one big union" which before 1920 was spreading like fire among the miners and loggers in the west, was himself shot in the chest. Prosecutors argued Hill had been hit by a shot Morrison's son had gotten off before dying, and though Hill had supposedly mentioned a woman and a jealous suitor to the doctor who treated him, at his trial he refused to say anything at all. But for his book *The Man Who Never Died*, Greenhouse went on, Adler found a "long-forgotten letter from Hill's sweetheart that said he had been shot by a rival for his affections"—and, Greenhouse reported, Adler had been inspired to dig up the bones of the case "after reading Bob Dylan's *Chronicles*, which argued that the Hill case was a miscarriage of justice."

In 1968, Dylan based "I Dreamed I Saw St. Augustine" on the old labor song "I Dreamed I Saw Joe Hill Last Night" ("Alive as you or me," it went; "'I never died,' said he"). "The more I thought about it," Dylan says in the three pages in *Chronicles* he devotes to Hill and the question of the protest song, "'Long Black Veil' seemed like it could have been a song written by Joe Hill himself, his last very last one"—but who knew that wasn't poetry but detective work?

10 ▪ Brighton Rock, written and directed by Rowan Joffe (IFC) On the Brighton pier in 1964, at a "Make a Record of Your Own Voice" booth, Pinkie Brown—played by a terrifying Sam Riley, who four years ago in *Control* gave a shattered performance as Ian Curtis of Joy Division—cuts the first punk 45. Luckily, the stuff they use for the discs is really cheap.

JANUARY 2012

1 ▪ Yael Bartana, Entartete Kunst lebt! (Degenerate Art Lives!), as part of "Germany Is Your America," curated by Michael Bracewell and Anke Kempkes (Broadway 1602, September 13–December 15, 2011) An animated five-minute 16 mm film—which ought to be playing now not solely in galleries but as an art-house short, a film-festival gem, an online sensation—derived from Otto Dix's still-shocking 1920 painting *War Cripples*, which was seized and shown by the Nazis at the 1937 Munich Degenerate Art exhibition. Bartana begins with silhouettes in a hobbled march across a dim screen, which is soon filled by an ever-increasing parade of four hideously maimed war veterans from Dix's picture, figures that in Bartana's hands turn into countless different people. In a parade of wooden legs and prostheses, all are in uniform, each one is seemingly more cut-up than the last, with the sound hammering and clattering from the tap dance of the artificial limbs to the screech and cranks of mechanical jaws and other body parts, until the centerpiece seems to become the jaunty man with dark glasses and a cigarette and no arms or legs, being pushed in a cart. More and more and more of them, sometimes shot from above, so you see only massed lines of hats—by the end spelling out the title of the piece like a college marching band as led by Leni Riefenstahl. What's most striking is the image of *happiness* on the faces of the men—not pride, really, but smugness: "Look at what *I* gave for the Fatherland."

2–3 ▪ Mekons at Bell House (Brooklyn, October 7, 2011) and City Winery (Manhattan,

October 8, 2011) At Bell House, before a surging, stand-up throng, they opened with "Thee Olde Trip to Jerusalem"—the trip the heretic takes, so that at the end any place can be the New Jerusalem. In the frenzy of the performance, everyone was a crusader, a Templar knight, a Ranter, a Familist, a Shaker, a Muggletonian. It was Norman Cohn's *Pursuit of the Millennium* boiled down to a chant and blown up into "Hey Bo Diddley." Later, with the Zuccotti Park occupation in its first month, guitarist Jon Langford announced he was "going to Wall Street." There were cheers. "To see my investment banker," he went on. "Play golf with Hank Williams Jr. and Hitler." Sally Timms stepped forward to sing "I love a millionaire," and you could see her crooning it at the head of a march, the song now a manifesto of ambivalence, self-hatred, whoredom, money, surrender, and rage. The next night at City Winery, with the band seated in a minstrel-show half circle for an audience of chattering texters, except for Rico Bell sacrificing his firstborn son for "Hard to Be Human Again," the band did not quite come across—but in a place that a few nights before had hosted a "Music of Sting Wine Pairing" (twenty-five songs, seven wines, with "tasting notes placed at your table" to "reveal why we think each wine flight goes with the particular songs it's paired with"), who could?

4 ▪ Deep Dark Woods, *The Place I Left Behind* (Sugar Hill) The band is from Saskatoon; their music comes from the Appalachian highlands. Burrowing inside the ambience of Clarence Ashley's "Dark Hollow Blues," and summoning the menace of half-forgotten local legends, they live up to the cool suggestiveness of their album title. But what's new is swooning lead guitar from Burke Barlow: an expansive, keening, thrillingly modern sound old-timey music almost never gets.

5 ▪ Tony Bennett and Amy Winehouse, "Body and Soul," from Tony Bennett, *Duets II* (RPM) Put this in your computer and iTunes will tell you it's Easy Listening. Not anymore. You can hear Bennett forming the words, one by one; Winehouse was speaking her own language.

6 ▪ Kim Criswell, "One," in *Happy Days in the Art World,* written by Michael Elmgreen and Ingar Dragset, directed by Toby Frow, NYU Skirball Center for the Performing Arts (November 1, 2011) Two men, once a couple, now just collaborating artists, wake up in a bunk-bed limbo; after about a hour of *Waiting for Godot*–like freaking out, making sardonic jokes, and wondering if they still have a career, Criswell shows up as a blind hysterical postmodern Federal Express delivery person and steals the show like Jim Brown breaking into a Woody Allen drawing-room comedy. And then at the end, when she's apparently dead, she lifts herself off the floor on one elbow and in a full, clear voice sings the U2 song.

This is the great modern melody, a match for the Wailers' "Redemption Song." U2's original is stiff, bellowing, but they left a treasure on the road for anyone to find. The song actually seems to ennoble whoever sings it: Johnny Cash, Warren Haynes, Kim Criswell, so many more to come.

7–8 ▪ Steven Bernstein's Millennial Territory Orchestra, *MTO Plays Sly* (Royal Potato Family) and Sly Stone, *I'm Back! Family and Friends* (Cleopatra) Aren't tribute albums terrible? Yes, and Sly Stone dives into the quicksand with his first new music under his own name since the Treaty of Versailles: old songs featuring Ray Manzarek, Ann Wilson, Jeff Beck, Johnny Winter. Actually, it's not terrible; there's just no reason to listen to it. But Steven Bernstein's downtown New York assemblage is another story. Very little is obvious: not Martha Wainwright diving into "Que Sera, Sera" as if it were a well, the disturbing moans all through "Sly Notions 2/Fun," the Dean Bowman and Vernon Reid rediscovery of the blues in "Time." The musicians and singers seem to be chasing the music down, not remotely sure they'll catch it, or that they deserve to.

9 ▪ Washington Phillips, "A Mother's Last Word to Her Son" (1927), in *We Need to Talk About Kevin,* directed by Lynne Ramsay (BBC Films) In the ultimate bad-seed picture,

a Texas gospel singer with a tragic voice emerges to say that from the day Tilda Swinton and John C. Reilly's son was born there was no hope.

10 ■ Bo Diddley, "Hey Bo Diddley," on *Shindig*, 1965 (YouTube) Around the time this show aired, well-meaning people were making films in which one could see first-rank blues singers offering European audiences approximately 5 percent of what they'd need to get over in a South Side bar. In a sort of TV-studio-as-night-club setting, with well-dressed couples at his feet, the Great Reverberator smashes out of the box with the first note, handsome, powerful, flashing an outrageous rubber-legged strut, his band steaming, and a horn section that looks like it was recruited out of a Delta Sig house at the University of Myrtle Beach. "If this were any better," John Jeremiah Sullivan writes in, "I think my head would burst into flames."

Thanks to Steve Weinstein

FEBRUARY 2012

1 ■ *Rid of Me*, written and directed by James Westby (Phase 4 Films/Submarine Deluxe) In 2002—though it looks earlier: people can still smoke in bars—a woman is kicked out of her marriage and stranded in a small town somewhere in the Pacific Northwest. All she wants is revenge: on her ex-husband, his old girlfriend/new wife, his worthless friends, on herself for buying into the scam in the first place. Katie O'Grady walks her character through her dead-end room, into a job in a candy store, down supermarket aisles, and then, as a formerly nice middle-class genteel housewife in her thirties, straight through punk, until she ends up lying down drunk on a sidewalk in the middle of the night. It all rings so true you don't really believe she's going to get up; the movie could end right there, but it doesn't. Because there's still this subplot about a Cambodian rock song the director wants to get in.

2 ■ Bonnie "Prince" Billy, "Quail and Dumplings," from *Wolfroy Goes to Town* (Drag City) Will Oldham brings you into the tune slowly, picking his mandolin in and out of an old mountain pattern, with Angel Olsen following his words in the background, then barely stepping past him with soft *ooos*. You relax into the song. Then someone claps hands, and Olsen grabs the song and, at first sounding as if she's going to expire on the spot, stands up and demands that the song give up truths it hasn't even hinted it might contain. Her voice breaks the pleasant folk spell Oldham has cast; there's something stentorian and cruel in her cadence, in the way she hits back at the song as if it's an enemy, a lie. And it's this moment of drama that gives the song the power to tell whatever truth it knows. When Oldham comes back, after a rough, harsh electric-guitar break from Emmett Kelly, with "Weather ain't judgment and money ain't love," he can stop you cold, the banality of the second phrase brought down by the uncertainty of the first.

3 ■ Jonathan Lethem, *The Ecstasy of Influence—Nonfictions, Etc.* (Doubleday) There's a stiffness in many of the essays on fellow novelists, reputation, career, book tours, and literary theory; four pieces on the terrorist attacks on New York in 2001 doggedly say nothing. But when Lethem writes about music, there's an unencumbered energy flowing through his sentences, a sense of discovery. The seemingly tossed-off, priceless notion that "pop was a trick, a perverse revenge against the banality of daily life dreamed up collectively by ten or fifteen Delta bluesmen and a million or a hundred million screaming twelve-year-old girls" conflates effortlessly with the idea that "little-girl screams" were "the essential heart of the Beatles' true sound, the human voice in a karaoke track consisting of the band itself." "The Genius of James Brown," from 2005, is the hit: three days in the studio and a night backstage in London a week later as a version of Moby-Dick, with a seventy-two-year-old Brown as Ahab and his band members as his grumbling, awestruck crew. As Lethem follows Brown through a remake of his 1971 "Soul Power," he falls into a theory of James Brown as a

time traveler, "like Billy Pilgrim in Kurt Vonnegut's *Slaughterhouse-Five*"; it sounds cute, even trivial. But it takes Lethem only a page to march from the claim that Brown somehow "saw, or, more exactly, heard the future of music"—a line that sounds like a cliché even if the idea is new—to something so rich Lethem becomes a juggler of ideas, keeping six of them in the air at once, and making the reader feel the thrill: "If the man was able to see 2005 from the distance of 1958, he's also prone to reliving 1958—and 1967, and 1971, and 1985—now that 2005 has finally come around. We all dwell in the world James Brown saw so completely before we came along into it; James Brown, in turn, hasn't totally joined us here in the future he made." You can shake your head in wonder over that, and then turn a few pages and run smack into Lethem running a little word-association game—

Analyst: James Brown. Please say the first thing that comes to mind.
Patient: I feel good!
Analyst: Stay with that thought.
Patient: Uh, just like I knew that I would?

—and realize that this would sound better on Brown's tombstone than all of his heroic titles scrolling down.

4 ▪ **Shailene Woodley in *The Descendants*, directed by Alexander Payne, written by Payne, Nat Faxon, and Jim Rash (Fox Searchlight)** Playing Alexandra King, daughter of George Clooney's Matt King, at the door of her mother's lover, verbally driving nails into his forehead as his eyes pop out—a moment that catches just how quick and tough a seventeen-year-old can be.

5 ▪ **Loretha Z. Smith on "Ike Zimmerman," Alabama State Council on the Arts/ Alabama Arts Radio Series (July 24, 2011)** The story has long been told that, sometime in the 1930s, Robert Johnson of Mississippi spent a year or more with an unrecorded blues singer from Alabama, and under his tutelage changed from an incompetent guitar banger to someone you could imagine the guitar had been waiting for since some-

one first tuned its strings. Johnson's mentor's name is usually given as Isaiah "Ike" Zinnerman, or Zinneman; it was Zimmerman. That opens a spectral connection to a singer from Hibbing, Minnesota, who, when he first heard Robert Johnson, "immediately differentiated between him and anyone else I had ever heard." But as Zimmerman's daughter Loretha filled in her father's life, one also learns that he later presided over his own Pentacostal church in Compton, California. That opens up the possibility that his parishoners included the parents of kids who went on to form N.W.A—the possibility that Ike Zimmerman could also have passed something on to Dr. Dre, Ice Cube, and Eazy-E, or that we might see them as much Johnson's progeny as Muddy Waters, Eric Clapton, Walter Mosley, Bob Dylan, or Cat Power. Loretha Smith described her father taking Johnson to a cemetery (owned by white people, she said gleefully) to play, sitting on gravestones—a Johnson-lore ghost story related here as plain family fact. "He learned Robert so *good*, how to play the guitar, that he was telling him he was ready to leave, and go back, to where he came from," Smith said. "And my understanding, now, he came from Tennessee, where he was tryin' to play the guitar, but when he went back he could play better, than any of those. And so they named my daddy the *devil*, because, they felt like no human being could teach a person how to play the guitar like that. But my dad, he wasn't the devil. He was a good man. Very good man."

6 ▪ **Charles Taylor reports on Fucked Up at Le Poisson Rouge (New York, November 14, 2011)** "Le Poisson Rouge is a strange place to see a rock 'n' roll show: a medium-sized basement room in a piss-elegant club that looks like it thinks the basement is where that kind of show belongs. The performers stand on a low-rise stage near the front of the room, surrounded by the crowd on all sides, standing in a circle. Fucked Up had to fit all five members on that stage plus a string quartet. It didn't matter much to Pink Eyes, who spent the whole show facing the

crowd, holding the microphone out so we were hearing the audience's vocals (most of them knew every word), roaming around to different parts of the room, at one point jumping up on the bar, and then, when the song ended, politely shaking hands with the bar staff before taking a candle and pouring hot wax on his chest while singing Madonna's 'Erotic.' This is a guy who clearly believes the fans are part of the band. He thanked ones he'd recognized who had come distances to see the show, offered profuse and heartfelt thank yous after each number, gently *shhhed* the crowd so they listened when the string quartet played. It was lovely, and it was also the problem. You can't tell moshers, 'This is your show, too,' because they just take that to mean that they're cool for acting like assholes. It was no surprise when the most persistently obnoxious of the moshers, a little bastard with a ridiculous 'fro that made him look like Leo Sayer inducted into the MC5, climbed onstage and was handed the mike. I was about ten feet from the edge of the mosh area. I saw some girls in there, and the ones who were held aloft weren't being manhandled. But it's still male in the worst sense. (I loved the riot grrrls for getting rid of this shit at shows.) These adolescent boys—most of them well past adolescence—would never think of themselves as frathouse thugs. But I kept thinking that there was no difference between them and the cretins out supporting Joe Paterno. Essentially, they're all fascists who believe their traditions are sacred and fuck anyone who's hurt by it. Maybe this is generational. But you can't get swept up into FU's sweaty, loving camaraderie if you're worried about getting your glasses shattered, or that someone's foot is going to smash an overhead light or set that hanging speaker swinging one too many times. Given the hardcore genre Fucked Up works in, I don't know what the answer is. I do know that the majesty of *David Comes to Life*, which the band played in its entirety, was lost. It wasn't a bad show. The band put their heads down and powered through the music. The sound

had the steeliness and flexibility and hypnotic shimmer of vibrating sheets of metal. Eighty minutes of that kind of force can feel hypnotic. What was missing was the sense that the record gives of something being fought for and hard-won and of your having had some part in the outcome. I think Fucked Up's hearts are in the right place. This is a band I could love and not just admire. But they've got to resolve how to stay true to a belief in community when your community sweeps up bullies along with everyone else who's willing to listen."

7 ▪ Snakefarm, *My Halo at Half-Light* (Fledg'ling) A follow-up to the 1999 *Songs from My Funeral*, or the second chapter in Anna Domino and Michel Delory's techno book of traditional ballads—"Little Maggie," "Staggerlee," "Omie Wise"—music that turns into its own kind of dream pop, picking up echoes of Portishead, Bryan Ferry, the Cranberries, Kate Bush, and Pauline Murray along the way. "Darlin' Corey"—the wellspring of a whole school of songs of faithless lovers that has tangled through the southern forests since the time of Daniel Boone like a rat king—is the most deadly. The melody is transposed from "The Streets of Laredo," the mood is that of someone fingering memories like rosary beads, and by the end of "Darlin' Corey"'s few minutes—"Corey," Domino calls her plainly, with an intimacy the song may have never permitted before—whole lives seem to have been lived and ruined.

8 ▪ "Viggo Mortensen: Hollywood's Grungy Antihero," *New York Times Style Magazine* (December 4, 2011) Inside, accompanying a profile by Zoë Heller, Mortensen has a fifty-three-year-old's lines cracking his face when he grins. In the retouched cover photo, all pensive and fey under a watch cap, he looks exactly like Justin Bieber.

9 ▪ Carolyn Hester, "Lonesome Tears," Teatro Bibiena, Festivalettertatura, Mantua, Italy (September 9, 2011) and on Hester's *From These Hills* (Road Goes on Forever, Outpost, 1996) Hester, a Greenwich Village folkie from the late '50s and early '60s, recorded her first album in 1957 at Norman

Petty's studio in Clovis, New Mexico, with Buddy Holly chipping in on guitar during rehearsals; one of the songs she cut was "Black Is the Color of My True Love's Hair." When Holly and the Crickets played London the following year, the show began with a ghostly organ sound, but no organ, no musician; then a platform rose from beneath the stage, revealing Holly alone at the keyboard, playing "Black Is the Color" as if it was the only song anyone needed to hear. In Mantua, in a severe, steep eighteenth-century theater where Mozart once performed, Hester took the stage with her two daughters and, before running through a set of wasn't-that-a-time chestnuts, stilled the room with Holly's "Lonesome Tears," the song as she played it at once earthy and delicate, sounding both like a handed-down ballad and a perfectly crafted pop song. "The day before yesterday was his birthday," she said, with a tone that made you think not a week had gone by since his death in 1959 that she hadn't thought about him.

10 ▪ **"Regifting: Songs My Mother (or Some Other) Gave Me," hosted by Joe Christiano and Theresa Kelly, St. Alban's Episcopal Church, Albany, California (December 4, 2011)** "Cover songs only!" was the first of a list of rules for a hootenanny of "passed on" tunes ("This Land Is Your Land," went a list of suggestions, "Up on the Roof, My Yiddishe Momme")—along with the disclaimer that original songs would be permitted only if they were "credited in performance to Paul Anka."

Thanks to Diann Blakely

MARCH–APRIL 2012

1 ▪ **Roots, *Undun*** Even if you catch only a phrase here and there, the story this shape-shifting album tells is plain. Just through the feel of the music, you know you are following the story of a single person, as he slowly pulls himself out of simple questions and simple answers and into a sense of self that throws off anyone else's idea of who he's supposed to be, even if he's drowning in confusion, conflict, voices hammering in his head, all answers to any questions far behind him. The voices telling his tale continually change—on "Lighthouse," the sound couldn't be more toothpaste, but it's also a relief from the street life swirling around it. There's a reason the Geto Boys' "Mind Playing Tricks on Me" is quoted early on: the same humility, the same sense of struggling to know what you don't know, runs through the songs like a river to cross. The rapping is close to ordinary speech—the bravado, the sneer, that makes so much rapping one-dimensional and tiresome isn't in this music. But the more you listen the more you hear—stray echoes of Dion & the Belmonts, Coolio's "Gangsta's Paradise," the ambition and the willingness to slow down, not to rush, of Sly and the Family Stone's *There's a Riot Goin' On*. You don't want this to end, and not only because of dread at what the ending will be.

2 ▪ **A Place to Bury Strangers, *Onwards to the Wall* (Deep Oceans)** From New York, the spirit of Joy Division—until the riptide of the title song, when the band all but changes places with New Order. But New Order never had a singer like Alanna Nuala—a.k.a. Moon—who as she rides through the middle of the number could be a horsewoman riding a ghost.

3 ▪ ***Pina*, directed by Wim Wenders (HanWay Films)** An unforgettable moment in this gorgeously vivid tribute to the late choreographer Pina Bausch, as performed by members of her Tanztheater Wuppertal, from her 1978 piece "Kontakthof," with Peter Dennis's delirious 1975 version of Jimmy Dorsey's 1946 "T. D.'s Boogie Woogie" pushing them on. A line of men seated in chairs, dressed in suits, hammer their way across the floor toward a line of women in slinky dresses rubbing themselves against the wall behind them—a routine that in its aura of trance and violence seems to capture the ambitions of every avant-garde nightclub from the Cabaret Voltaire on down. As a 3-D movie *Pina* ought to be on a double bill with Werner Herzog's *Cave of Forgotten Dreams*.

4 ■ Comet Gain, *Howl of the Lonely Crowd* (What's Your Rupture?) Formed in 1992, this British group appears here stuck in the Beat past of the '40s and '50s, with the references to Allen Ginsberg and David Riesman followed by "Herbert Huncke, Pt. 2," a tune about the Times Square junkie celebrated by Jack Kerouac in *On the Road* that the Velvet Underground forgot to record; "The Ballad of Frankie Machine," pushed wonderfully by singer Rachel Evans; and the last track, "In a Lonely Place," which lets Humphrey Bogart's damned face look back over all the wasted years. It doesn't seem like a concept, merely people in the band wrapping themselves around things they like, and nothing gets in the way of a vocal diversity, of the surprise eruptions of feeling (the guitar break in the lovely, soulful "After Midnight, After It's All Gone Wrong," the thrill of "Thee Ecstatic Library") that make you want to see the band opening for the New Pornographers.

5 ■ Rocket from the Tombs, *Barfly* (Fire) The group formed in Cleveland in 1974; now, almost buried behind singer David Thomas's self-questioning, crooning croak, is the most subtle and quietly passionate guitar band in the land. A land perhaps defined by the faces on the back of the CD sleeve that the musicians key their names to: Vachel Lindsay (drummer and organist Steve Mehlman), Edgar Allen Poe (guitarist Cheetah Chrome), Mark Twain (bassist Craig Bell), Herman Melville (guitarist Richard Lloyd), and Stonewall Jackson (Thomas).

6 ■ Robert W. Harwood, " 'Stack O'Lee Blues'—the first sheet music (and more)" (iwentdowntostjamesinfirmary.blogspot .com, December 20, 2011) From 1924, the first publication of the true-crime bad-man ballad that came out of St. Louis in 1895, reduced to a lame tune and lyrics about a new dance craze keyed to a racist playground chant. The sheet-music art is what's uncanny: in red, blue, pink, white, and black, a swirling abstraction, in circles and rectangles, that calls up the dada experimental films being made at exactly the same time.

7–8 ■ "Sanford Biggers: Sweet Funk—An Introspective" (Brooklyn Museum, through January 8) and Billie Holiday, "Strange Fruit" (1959, YouTube) A big room, centered by *Blossom* (2007), an installation with a huge tree growing through a piano with its bench knocked over and lying in dirt: a prepared piano that plays a slow version of "Strange Fruit." Nearby is *Cheshire* (2007), a video showing a large tree with black men climbing it, a lynching tree reclaimed with the smile of the Cheshire cat when one man reaches the top, where when black screen-breaks appear you hear "Strange Fruit" by Imani Uzuri. Here "Strange Fruit" is fixed, a reference point, unlike the 1959 footage of Holiday, old and ravaged, singing the song in a nightclub with unparalleled vividness, so that every word makes a separate scene you are forced to visualize, that she is forced to visualize—you can see and hear her resisting the song, as if she can barely stand to sing it. The piece by Biggers that lives up to this performance is *Bittersweet the Fruit* (2002), where a tree branch with leaves, installed horizontally, has a two-by-three-inch video screen cut in. It's described as an allegory of the pickup-truck lynching of James Byrd Jr., in Jasper, Texas, in 1998—one of the killers, Lawrence Brewer, was executed on September 21, 2011, two days before Biggers's show went up—you see, in a wooded area like the scrub forests Byrd was dragged through, a naked black man with gray dreads seated playing a piano. The sound plays backward, slow, fuzzed, then frantically speeding up and clattering— and the sense is that of the man trying to go back in time, to when he wasn't dead.

9 ■ Randy Newman, "A Few Words in Defense of Our Country," from *Live in London* (Nonesuch) It can be hard to hear the world catch up with Newman's misanthropy.

10 ■ "Gaga Constellation" Christmas windows, creative direction by Nicola Formichetti, directed by Tim Richardson (Barney's Workshop, New York, December 14, 2011) Various Gaga fantasies—and the one that works is *Gaga Machine*, with LG's body painted gold and transformed into a Futur-

ist motorcycle. Passing by, Marinetti would have broken the glass and climbed on.

1 ▪ **Alison Faith Levy, "Itsy Bitsy Spider," from *World of Wonder* (Mystery Lawn Music)** On an album of children's songs, this glorious recording—with startling new verses pitting a mouse against a cat, a monkey against a tiger, a hippo against a snake, and the spider against a bumblebee—comes forth huge, pounding, with a passionate vocal from Levy and, from producer Allen Clapp, the most convincing re-creation of Phil Spector's Wall of Sound anywhere. Precisely, it's "Itsy Bitsy Spider" as the Ronettes' "Be My Baby," the feeling bigger with each chorus, and each chorus more ambitious, more deliriously affirming Levy's animal-kingdom moral fables.

But Spector, now serving nineteen-to-life for second-degree murder in the 2003 shooting death of the failed actress and House of Blues hostess Lana Clarkson, remains as much an author as Levy. Released in 2009, Vikram Jayanti's trial documentary, *The Agony and the Ecstasy of Phil Spector*, can leave you almost certain that Spector did not kill Clarkson (after watching his attorneys present forensic evidence at his first trial, which hung the jury, you can imagine Spector bringing out a gun, showing it off, listening to Clarkson talk about how worthless her life had turned out to be, and then handing it to her: "Go ahead and kill yourself, I don't care"). On February 21 the Supreme Court refused to review the case; as Spector waits out his time, I hope this puts a smile on his face.

2 ▪ **Eleanor Friedberger at the Independent, San Francisco (February 4)** Appearing with Friedberger were a drummer, a bass player, and guitarist John Eatherly, who's likely in his mid-twenties, looks sixteen ("That song was about fun times," the thirty-five-year-old Friedberger said at one point, "back when I was his age"), and has the fastest hands I've ever seen. He reminded me of Tim Lincecum: he seems to invent melodies as he plays others, and he can shred. His face is always quiet; there's a lyrical slide in his attack that takes the coolness off what might seem like technique for its own sake, and if his lyricism is still a step or two away from soul, it will come. Friedberger herself is impossible to fix, a singer who at her most distinctive comes across like someone arguing over the phone. A rambling, seemingly scattershot set turned on a dime with the unreleased "When I Knew." It's the kind of bouncing, emotionally blunt song the radio was invented to play, a song you hear once and then play over and over in the radio of your memory, hoping that when it is released it'll sound half as right. For an encore, Friedberger came out alone and sang "(Ummm, Oh Yeah) Dearest," recorded by Buddy Holly on acoustic guitar in his Greenwich Village apartment the month before he died, when he was younger than Eatherly. The song is so perfectly written (by Ellas McDaniel—Bo Diddley—Prentice Polk, and Mickey Baker) that it doesn't seem written at all, and Friedberger let it sing itself, as if she were following a step behind, in love with the way every barely sung "Ummm, yeah" opened into catacombs of affection and regret.

3 ▪ **Jennifer Castle, *Castlemusic* (No Quarter)** From Toronto, Castle was one of the Siren voices on Fucked Up's *David Comes to Life*. Here she wanders like a pilgrim through the desert once crossed by Paula Frazer of Tarnation, Hope Sandoval of Mazzy Star, Julee Cruise, and, maybe most of all, Kelly Hogan's "(You Don't Know) The First Thing About Blue." Two-thirds of the way through, with "Misguided," Castle reaches a pitch of mystical transport so gorgeously ethereal she seems about to drift off into lands that don't appear on any map. But then everything gets tougher, and the desert turns into Duane Eddy's forty miles of bad road.

4 ▪ **Dave Bickler on *The Colbert Report* (Comedy Central, February 2)** As an answer record to Newt Gingrich's unauthorized use of Survivor's "Eye of the Tiger" at campaign rallies, Survivor lead singer Bickler took the stage and made a heroic, without-a-breath dash through what could have been an entire page of Gingrich's *A Nation Like No Other*—to the tune of "Eye of the Tiger." "A nation explicitly Christian!" he declaimed: "Of the tiger!" When Bickler got to Gingrich quoting Patrick Henry, he made "Give me liberty or give me death" sound like a power ballad.

5 ▪ **Big Brother and the Holding Company, "Light Is Faster Than Sound" (June 23), from** *Live at the Carousel Ballroom, 1968* **(Columbia Legacy)** Six minutes. Total riot. Punk shamed. Desperation, release, fear and driving right through it, hitting a wall, climbing over it, falling into a swamp. As Jim Thompson wrote in 1952 in *The Killer Inside Me*, "A man is hanged and poisoned and chopped up and shot, and he goes right on living." There are screams that seem to come from other than ordinary bodies, *wow-wow-wows* that sound like hurricanes chafing at the starting block, a feedback solo that breaks up as it's played, or as it *arrives*—can you go faster than sound, on your own two feet, with the wind of a nightmare at your back, a nightmare you can't bear to wake from because you want to know how it turns out?

6 ▪ **Deborah Sontag and Walt Bogdanich, "8 Guilty for Prison Massacre in Rare Trial of Haiti's Police" (***New York Times***, January 19)** Or Judge Dread lives. In 1967, the Jamaican ska songwriter and producer Prince Buster took on the mantle of an Ethiopian judge come to Kingston to rid the land of its scourge of thugs; across three historic singles—"Judge Dread," "The Appeal," and "Judge Dread Dance" (a.k.a. "The Pardon")—he piled hundred-year sentences on teenage murderers, jailed their lawyers, left them weeping and pleading for mercy, then set everybody free and left his seat to lead a cakewalk through the court: "I am the judge, but I know how to dance." Judge Dread reappeared on January 19, in Haiti, in the person of Judge Ezekiel Vaval, when, in an act that broke the culture of im-

punity that had always surrounded Haitian government officials of any sort, he sentenced eight police officers to prison for a jailhouse massacre they had perpetrated and covered up. "The decision of the judge is his expression of the truth," said Judge Vaval, as in cadences that matched Prince Buster's in both spirit and form he handed down sentences of two to thirteen years of prison and hard labor, giving police chiefs the longest terms. "There are other versions that exist but this is mine. And that is the law."

7 ▪ **Gaslight Anthem, "Changing of the Guards," on** *Chimes of Freedom: The Songs of Bob Dylan* **(Amnesty International/Fontana)** Aren't tribute albums terrible? Yes, especially when they're for a good cause, and *four CDs long*—but Gaslight Anthem, from New Jersey, puts so much humor and dread into this *Street Legal* number, unrealized in Dylan's own hands, that you forget it's a Dylan song. Elsewhere, even on the few tracks worth hearing more than once (Diana Krall's "Simple Twist of Fate," Ziggy Marley's "Blowin' in the Wind," Miley Cyrus's "You're Gonna Make Me Lonesome When You Go," Bryan Ferry's steely "Bob Dylan's Dream"), words generally come out more clearly than on the originals, because so little is going on musically, either in terms of playing or singing—there's nothing else to listen to, to be distracted by. "People have a hard time believing that Shakespeare really wrote all of his work because there is so much of it. Do you have a hard time accepting that?" Dylan was asked in 1991. "People have a hard time accepting anything that overwhelms them," he said.

8 ▪ **Barack Obama, "Sweet Home Chicago," White House Blues Night (February 21/PBS, February 27)** In what would have been Robert Johnson's hundred–and–first year, one of his songs was sung by the president of the United States. After a command from the guitarist Buddy Guy ("I heard you singing Al Green—you have started something, you gotta keep it up now"), he started out flat on "Come on, baby don't you want

to go / Come on, baby don't you want to go," and then with a rounded, lifting tone just barely swung "Chicago" into the night. He couldn't have taken the tune from the band more casually; he must have heard this song all his life.

9 ▪ *Venus in Fur,* **written by David Ives, directed by Walter Bobbie (Manhattan Theatre Club, New York, December 18; now at the Lyceum)** "Like the Lou Reed song?" says Nina Arianda's Vanda as this storming, shape-shifting two-person comedy gets going. An actress shows up late to try out for a part, only the director is there, he says they might as well get it over with, and then the battle begins. It's Naomi Watts's audition scene in *Mulholland Dr.* with a subtext out of Camille Paglia's *Sexual Personae*— translated by Betty Hutton in *The Miracle of Morgan's Creek* and by Martha Raye in *Monsieur Verdoux.* Unless Vanda is the lost sister of the Marx Brothers crossed with Lady Gaga and Helen of Troy, who after more than three thousand years has a lot of scores to settle.

10 ▪ **"King's Court," Super Bowl Pepsi commercial (NBC, February 5)** After dispatching various miserable contestants for a single can of Pepsi, King Elton John is faced with *X Factor* queen Melanie Amaro, who, packaged as a stand-in for the Queen of Soul, steps up to perform a hideously over-souled and oversold version of Aretha Franklin's "Respect." After Elton sheepishly awards her the coveted red, white, and blue can, she zaps him into a dungeon and gives everyone in the court a free drink. In a better world, Elton would have sent her back to her TV show: "Lady, I *served* with Aretha. I know Aretha. Aretha is a friend of mine. Lady, you're no Aretha."

JUNE 2012

SPECIAL OVER-SEVENTY EDITION!

1 ▪ **"Robert Johnson at 100," Apollo Theater, New York (March 6)** Charles Taylor reports from the scene: "The trick to feeling comfortable in Sunday clothes is to make sure that Sunday isn't the only day you wear

them. The famous 1930s picture of Robert Johnson looking sharp in his three-piece suit was projected over the stage for much of the centennial celebration, and the casual ease of everything about Johnson in that picture acted like a judgment on the parade of supplicants, posers, pretenders, and mediocrities who passed beneath. The ones who stood up to Johnson's gaze were confident enough to sport their own style. Taj Mahal, walking out with the calm familiarity of a beefy working man approaching a job he long ago mastered, played and sang 'Hell Hound on My Trail' with a sound rooted to the earth while moving with the lightness of Jackie Gleason. Sam Moore's high vocal was at first lost in 'Sweet Home Chicago' but the sweetness of his voice gradually drew you in like a beckoning finger. Elvis Costello, striking an unconscious echo of Johnson's crossed-knee posture, performed a charming 'From Four Until Late' as if the evening's honoree were George Formby, master of the English music hall. The Roots, who bend their knee to no one and do tradition the honor of never treating it as tradition, unleashed a staccato 'Milkcow's Calf Blues' that was flabbergasting in its confidence. With ?uestlove's drumming controlling singer-guitarist Kirk Douglas like a puppet master's strings, the number grew into a duet recalling the unexpected and joyous rapport in *Diner* when Timothy Daly shakes up a lagging strip-club duo by taking over the empty piano, finding allies in the suddenly knife-sharp drummer and in the tired dancer out front, who responds as if she were once again the youngest girl on the bill. No one was more at home in his style than James Blood Ulmer, who followed Taj's 'Hell Hound' with his own, never leaving his seat in the house band, using his voice and guitar to emit a series of yelps and moans and mutterings that could have been devil dogs at the crossroads, or the spirits of Stonehenge. The other ghost present, the faint smile on Ulmer's face, suggested that the phantoms of the ages were all his familiars."

2 ▪ **Mariee Sioux, *Gift for the End* (Almost Musique)** Not as immediately arresting as Lana Del Rey's "Video Games," but mapping the same nowhere, and without the metallic smell of early death. That isn't to say death is missing. Sioux, from the California Gold Rush country, sings softly, strums and picks, and you can't get a fix on her in any way. Even as she seems to come right up to you, you sense a distance that can never be bridged. That may be because the eight songs here carry the feeling of Grimms' fairy tales. "We've learned our lessons," plead young girls, and you don't want to know what schooled them. In her most uncanny moments, Sioux is less playing her songs than swimming through them: "No rest, no rest, no rest, no rest."

3 ▪ **Jay Leeming, "Desolation Row," from *Miracle Atlas* (Big Pencil Press)** The whole place has been torn down and "replaced / by the new civic center, a gigantic white building / funded by a Norwegian greeting card company." No one remembers all those strange characters who used to roam the place, "though now and then their names / turn up on the newspaper's last pages: Doctor Filth / found strangled to death in the Brazilian jungle."

4 ▪ **Werner Herzog, *Hearsay of the Soul*, video installation, Whitney Museum of American Art, New York (through June 10)** A highlight of the 2012 Biennial: in a separate room, in a five-channel, five-panel projection, landscapes of stone valleys and terraced stone mountains—manipulated seventeenth-century etchings by Hercules Seghers—frame the cellist Ernst Reijseger. Moonfaced, his head shaved, he plays hard, his mouth open like an electric guitarist writhing in the agonies of being moved by his own sounds, his eyes closed—when at the end he opens them, it's a shock. The landscapes, at first all panorama, are slowly explored so that nearly infinite detail begins to emerge. Where once there was only landscape, now there are rocks; where there were only rocks, there are solitary human figures, who look as accidental as the rocks. To Herzog, the Biennial curator Elisabeth

Sussman said, Seghers's etchings are "the beginning of modernity"; with Reijseger, at the end of his piece sliding his fingers down the strings as if he's playing slide cello, time slides off.

5 ▪ **?uestlove, "Put the Needle on the Record," EMP Pop Conference, New York University, New York (March 25)** On his record collection, now reaching seventy-five thousand LPs, and the fetishism that goes with it: "I hated the orange Capitol label. I wouldn't listen to anything with it. So I missed *Pet Sounds* and post–*Rubber Soul* Beatles." He started as a child: "Album covers I was scared of, logos I was scared of, they'd go to the bottom of the collection." "What was the first record you bought with your own money?" asked moderator Harry Weinger. "I had an adult's knowledge of music at the age of five," ?uestlove said, "but I didn't have a job." Then in 1979 "Rapper's Delight" came out and he had to have it. "I had three hours in school to borrow a dime," ?uestlove said, "—from thirty-seven people." That, he said, was the first record he bought with his own money, "borrowed money." "Did you pay everybody back?" Weinger asked. "No," ?uestlove said, as if it still bothered him, a little bit.

6 ▪ **Bruce Springsteen, "Wrecking Ball," from *Wrecking Ball* (Columbia)** "I don't know how you write something so affecting from the point of view of a concrete bowl," a friend said of this song about Meadowlands Stadium, "but there you go."

7 ▪ **Penelope Houston, *On Market Street* (Devoted Ruins)** When not touring with the Avengers, her reformed and still-fierce late-'70s San Francisco punk band, Houston makes quiet records; here, a smoothly keening organ leads her through tired San Francisco bars and ugly San Francisco streets. The small voice is all knowledge, with the fatigue of not believing tomorrow is going to be any different from today. The bill comes due with "On Market Street," where three violins and a cello stop all the other stories cold. Houston sings like someone watching, not a singer at all, warbling about the human wreckage she passes on her way to work,

composing a song in her head as she shows her ID to the guard, sits down at her desk, picks up a stack of papers, and hums.

8 ◾ **"Bibliophilia: Collecting Black Books— The Archie Givens, Sr. Collection of African American Literature," Elmer L. Andersen Library, University of Minnesota, Minneapolis (February 6–April 20)** It's displacing to come face to face with the tiny first editions of Phillis Wheatley's 1773 *Poems on Various Subjects, Religious and Moral*, the 1845 *Narrative of the Life of Frederick Douglass, an American Slave*, the 1850 *Narrative of Sojourner Truth: A Northern Slave*, Paul Laurence Dunbar's privately published 1892 *Oak and Ivy*, or countless other treasures you might never have imagined you would ever actually see. Along with LeRoi Jones tapes, Kirby Puckett memorabilia, toys, children's books, LPs, Black Panther newspapers, there are surprises everywhere you look: the blazing dust jacket of Zora Neale Hurston's 1934 novel *Jonah's Gourd Vine*, which seems to take its power not from the fervor of the gesticulating preacher but from the very few worshippers around him, as if they're the first or the last of a cult about to vanish. And all this can fade against the September 7, 1937, letter from Clara E. Stokes, a Federal Writers' Project administrator in Jackson, Mississippi, to Carrie Campbell, a field-worker about to conduct her first interviews with former slaves, and then three fragments of interview transcriptions on yellowed paper that look as if they'd crumble at the touch—the Dead Sea Scrolls of the New Deal. Two are in pencil, one in typescript, and while the edges of lines are folded or broken, the voice and the history it stands for come through: "She sure was good to us. And even so much as gave us a cow. If it hadn't been for that KuKlux. Lord how they did scare us. They had a song [unreadable]"—and it breaks off. Everyone I've spoken to who's seen this show has said the same thing: *This has to travel.*

9 ◾ **Tom Jones, "Evil" (Third Man)** Howlin' Wolf recorded this song in 1954. Jones sings it as if he's calling 911.

10 ◾ **Dion, "Ride's Blues (For Robert Johnson)," from *Tank Full of Blues* (Blue Horizon)** Why wasn't he at the Apollo? As he moves ever more surely into blues, the man who gave up his seat on Buddy Holly's death plane has lost nothing of his voice, but his guitar speaks even more eloquently. This piece, coming after the three cool, expert, casual love-and-trouble numbers that open this superb album, is immediately elsewhere, a place where all is menace, and a queer, complete sense of fatalism settles over the trees. "He told me on the way there / He was born in sin," the man telling the story mutters. "Huh. What else is new?"

Taj Mahal, born 1942; Sam Moore, 1935; Elvis Costello, 1954; ?uestlove, 1971; Kirk Douglas, 1972; James Blood Ulmer, 1942; Mariee Sioux, 1985; Jay Leeming, 1969; Werner Herzog, 1942; Hercules Seghers, circa 1589; Ernst Reijseger, 1954; Bruce Springsteen, 1949; Penelope Houston, 1958; Tom Jones, 1940; Dion, 1939.

Thanks to Steve Perry

JULY–AUGUST 2012

1 ◾ **Laura Oldfield Ford, *Savage Messiah* (Verso)** From 2006 through 2009, Ford produced the issues of the fanzine collected here: hundreds of pages of text, maps, bland drawings of vague faces, and cumulatively riveting photos of architectural detritus— roads, graffiti, housing blocks, filthy courtyards, storefronts, overgrown building sites, almost all of them utterly depopulated— chronicling a long walk through the back alleys and abandoned patches of a London remade through Thatcherist and New Labour gentrification and the evictions and new constructions of the looming 2012 Olympics. Read straight through, Ford's work is the most convincing follow-through there is on the project of poetic urban-renewal inaugurated by the situationists Guy Debord, Ivan Chtcheglov, and Michèle Bernstein. In the early '50s, they and a few other young layabouts began an

exploration of Paris as a city that ran according to its own backward-forward-spinning
clock, where a drift down the streets might
so scramble time that 1848 would exert a
stronger spiritual gravity than 1954. In
places Ford echoes Nan Goldin's *The Ballad of Sexual Dependency*, her slideshow of
sex and death in bohemian New York in the
1980s, and the cityscape in Andrea Arnold's
2006 film *Red Road*, where in a decaying
Glasgow foxes dart around the base of apartment buildings that are corroding from the
inside, almost as strongly. On any given page,
Thomas De Quincey, from his 1821 *Confes-
sions of an English Opium-Eater*, might be
holding Ford's hand: "I could almost have
believed, at times, that I must be the first discoverer of some of these *terrae incognitae*,
and doubted whether they had yet been laid
down in the modern charts of London."

Number by number, *Savage Messiah* is
a delirious, doomstruck celebration of
squats, riots, vandalism, isolation, alcohol,
and sex with strangers, all on the terrain of
a half-historical, half-imaginary city that
the people who Ford follows, herself at the
center, can in moments believe they built
themselves, and can tear down as they
choose. The past is a shadow, an angel, a
demon: most of what Ford recounts seems
to be taking place in the '70s or the '80s or
the '90s, with the first decade of the twenty-
first century a kind of slag-heap of time—
of boredom, enervation, despair, and
hate—that people are trying to burrow out
from under. "1973, 1974, 1981, 1990, 2013,"
she chants on one page. "Always a return.
A Mirror touch. A different way out."
"Queen's Crescent is the nexus of knife
crime, a flashing matrix of Sheffield steel,"
Ford writes in *Savage Messiah #6*, ". . . suspended somewhere between 1968 and 1981,
and I sense my darling there, on the corner
of Bassett St. and Allcroft Road. I'm searching the brickwork with dusty fingertips for
the first Sex Pistols graffiti of 1976. He was
here then, and possibly now, we drift in circles around each other"—and answering
herself on the facing page: "In the fabric of
the architecture you can always uncover

traces and palimpsests, the poly-temporality
of the city. As I lay my palm flat against the
wall I grasp past texts never fully erasing the
traces of earlier inscriptions."

The aura of a mystical quest hovers over
even the most sordid incidents, the ugliest
photos of belongings piled up at the foot of
an apartment block. John Legend's "Ordinary People" is on the jukebox: "And all the
guilt I harboured, all the shame, the walk
around Highbury with so much hanging in
the balance, tyranny of choice and the
crashing cruelty of desire, it was all locked
into that one anodyne song."

**2 ▪ Evans the Death, *Evans the Death*
(Slumberland)** Dream pop, casting back to
Pauline Murray and the Invisible Girls in
London in 1980, coming into perfect focus
on "Letter of Complaint," where Katherine
Whitaker dances so delicately, with such a
sense of pleasure, she leaves a light behind
with each step.

3 ▪ Levon Helm, 1940–2012 Watch him
at what might as well have been the end, as
the blind, cursing desert rat in his friend
Tommy Lee Jones's 2005 movie *The Three
Burials of Melquiades Estrada*; listen to him
at the beginning, in 1961, roaring through
Bobby "Blue" Bland's "Further On Up the
Road" (collected on *The Band—A Musical
History*, or on *Ronnie Hawkins and the
Hawks: The Roulette Years*) as if he's not the
driver but the car. And then, in the Band's
"Chest Fever," as he marshals what Tom
Kipp, once of the Montana punk band De-
ranged Diction, calls "THE BACKBEAT OF
GOD" to summon a sound that feels far more
like a civil war than "The Night They Drove
Old Dixie Down," let Helm describe an
American epic of love and madness, home
and flight—a sound so rich you can listen
and watch at the same time. That was 1968.
The music had no temporal frame of reference clinging to it then, and it doesn't now.

**4 ▪ Peter Stampfel in conversation with
RJ Smith, "'We're Gonna Rise When the Sun's
Going Down,'" at the EMP Pop Conference,
NYU, New York (March 23)** He loved rock 'n'
roll and he loved old-time music—but they
were "incompatible," the cofounder of the

Holy Modal Rounders said of his dilemma in the Greenwich Village folk scene in the late '50s and early '60s. Then in 1961 he heard Bob Dylan singing "Sally Gal." "His phrasing was so *clearly* rock 'n' roll-influenced. He was *already* combining folk and rock 'n' roll. I thought—what if we could bring Uncle Dave Macon, Charlie Poole, back, now, set them right here in the middle of rock 'n' roll—what would they do?"

5 ▪ **Jack White, *Blunderbuss* (Third Man Records)** Regardless of the passion in the music White made with the White Stripes—a harsh, at times almost frightened passion—there was always something cold about it. Whatever was happening, it was happening not here but over there—and to someone else. The best performances on White's first solo album are those where this isn't true, and in each case it may be because White's ownership of the sound, his ability to look down on his own creation, is weakened, because other people are making themselves felt, and with such heart: Brooke Waggoner's parlor piano on "Hypocritical Kiss," Ruby Amanfu's comradely backing vocals on "Love Interruption," most of all Ryan Koenig and the mandolin player Pokey LaFarge singing not behind White but around him on "I Guess I Should Go to Sleep," a reverie so entrancing that by the end the sense is that the singers slipped away well before they started singing, and what you're hearing is the dream.

6 ▪ **Bo Diddley, *Road Runner: The Chess Masters, 1959–1960* (Hip-O Select)** I recently saw the first volume of this archival project, *I'm a Man: The Chess Masters, 1955–1958*, priced at $200 at Amoeba Records in Berkeley; Amazon had it at $255.99. I have no idea why. A few years ago it was just another reissue, if, as with anything the late strange character produced, full of twists and turns no one else would ever think of. Here, on an at least for the moment normally priced set, you can find the most formally primitive and the most formally avant-garde music refusing to acknowledge any difference. "Bucket" strings folk-lyric fragments

over the Bo Diddley beat, but there's nothing generic, nothing automatic in the improvization—the thing is like a hand made of swamp gas, reaching out of the past, crooking its finger. "Mumblin' Guitar" ("Whatchyu say, man? Quit mumblin', and talk out loud," Diddley opens it) is a swarm of insects dancing on his fretboard; you can see him throw the guitar away to get them off his face, and then stand back grinning as the guitar plays itself.

7 ▪ **Julyan Davis, "Dark Corners: The Appalachian Ballad—Paintings of the South" (Greenville County Museum of Art, South Carolina, through July 1; Morris Museum of Art, Augusta, Georgia, opening September 1)** Davis's talents are those of an illustrator—his faces have no life and his bodies have no movement. But he can see places—and in two paintings in this series of images he's attempted to draw out of the likes of "Little Maggie" and "Barbara Allen," he sees places no one has seen before. For "Pretty Polly," instead of the hills and valleys of the murder ballad it's a huge, ruined barn, covered with the wreckage of abandoned artwork, as if vandals broke in and destroyed the place with buckets of paint, canvases, stretchers, and unfinished images; the place looks dangerous, and you don't need to see the woman inside or the man approaching from outside to feel that. With "Darling Corey," the tale of a faithless lover, there's a pastoral scene, a Currier and Ives print: winding dirt road, bare trees, melting snow, spring about to burst, and, in the distance, set in a meadow at the foot of a mountain, a family home, with smoke that at first comes into the landscape like fog billowing out of the windows, the hint of red so faint that at first, as you come up the lane singing, "Wake up, wake up, Darlin' Corey, what makes you sleep so sound?" you might think everything's all right.

8 ▪ **DJ Shadow, *The Less You Know, the Better* (Island)** What made the sampling artist's 1996 *Endtroducing . . .* and *The Private Press*, from 2002, so spooky—what let the person born Josh Davis live up to his

chosen name—was a mood of clandestin-ity, of subterranean communication, the way he could make you feel as if you were listening in on a conversation you were never meant to hear. On *The Less You Know, the Better*, that happens only once, with "Give Me Back the Nights." Shadow wraps film-noir tones around "The Night," a frantic, all-but-suicidal lost-love rant by one C. E. Rabinowitz that Davis found in a thrift store—a 45? From an LP? In the least readable credits sheet I've ever seen, he doesn't say—until the singer loses his performer's body and be-comes a figment of anyone's nightmare. And that's better than thinking that the singer's nightmare is still going on. You can wake up; with Shadow pressing down on him, you know he can't.

9 ■ *Black Clock* no. 15 (CalArts) A special issue of this adventurous literary quarterly on imaginary cinema, filled with clumsily executed posters for, say, *Casablanca* star-ring Ronald Reagan and Hedy Lamarr, who were up for Rick and Ilsa; *Intolerance* remade by Baz Luhrmann and starring Sasha Grey; *Kill Bill* directed by Russ Meyer and featuring Marilyn Monroe, John Wayne, Robert Mitchum, Dorothy Dain-dridge, Natalie Wood, Takashi Shimura, and Machiko Kyô, and each one all the more frustrating because the pictures were never made. The highlights might be Mi-chael Ventura's "Lou 'n' Charlie," the story of an eighteen-year-old Louise Brooks's af-fair with Charlie Chaplin in the form of a memoir by Brooks's lesbian roommate, and Howard Hampton's "Breakaway: Summer of '69," a scholarly piece about how the San Francisco avant-garde filmmaker Bruce Conner took over *Easy Rider* when Dennis Hopper abandoned the project, complete with footnotes to nonexistent passages in real books, and so convincing that even the last paragraph, referencing "the McGovern interregnum and the Reagan backlash" and a final, post-credits mini-sequence where "a television announcer is heard introducing a car dealer ('and now here's Cal Worthing-ton and his dog Spot') as Conner injects

Un chien andalou's famous scene of a straight razor slicing a human eye," rolls by without a blink. And both seem modest next to Anthony Miller's "A History of the Cinema 1920–2014," first in a ten-page chro-nology ranging from *Das Cabinet des Dr. Caligari* to an all-female remake of *The Maltese Falcon* starring Lindsay Lohan as "Sam(antha) Spade" and Patricia Clarkson as Kasper Gutman, and then ranging in pop-ups through the journal's more than 190 pages, in which all of film history re-volves around successive biopics on the late-Victorian adventurer Richard Burton (Lon Chaney plays him in *The Mecca Mas-querade*, Harry Reemes in *Dick Burton's Kama Sutra*) and the infinitesimally slow emergence, over nearly one hundred years, of an underground pseudo-masterpiece called, at least at first, *The Zoo*, "a work of undetermined length and origin by a filmmaker known only as 'Darc' (some-times misidentified in studies of early film as 'D' arc')."

10 ■ Van Morrison, "Sweet Thing," in *The Five-Year Engagement*, dir. Nicholas Stoller (Apatow Productions) If you're going to fall in love at first sight to a song, nothing could be more complete than the Richard Davis bass pattern that opens this one: a lifetime unfolding in fifteen seconds flat.

SEPTEMBER 2012

1 ■ Corin Tucker Band, *Kill My Blues* (Kill Rock Stars) Starting at nineteen with Heav-ens to Betsy in Olympia, Washington, moving on with Sleater-Kinney in Portland, Oregon, for more than twenty years Corin Tucker has been ripping up the pop land-scape with the hurricane of her voice—a hurricane of subtlety, pauses, a sense of thinking it all over inside the maelstrom. On Tucker's second album under her own name, the music is so fast out of the box, so relentless and fierce, that the doubt hiding in the sound—*This way, that way, now, not now, never?*—might not surface right away. Sooner or later it will, and the music will take shape less as sound than drama. And

then, if you're pulled back to the avalanche that begins with "Neskowin," the third number, and only lets you go two songs later, at the end of the fifth, with Tucker's banging the signature riff of "Smells Like Teen Spirit" as if her own "Constance" simply told her that was what it wanted, you may wonder how anyone could hold her breath as long as Tucker seems to.

2 ▪ **"State of Disconnect" (State Farm)** Thirty-second spot: State Farm agent on the phone, selling, in a clipped tone: "You name it, we're here, anytime, anywhere, any way you want it." Customer, in his kitchen, flatly: "That's the way I need it." "Any way you want it?" "All night?" "All night." "Every night?" "Any way you want it." "That's the way I need it," the customer says, then pausing, as if replaying the conversation in his head: "We just had ourselves a little Journey moment," he says. "Yep," says the agent. "Saw them in '83 in Fresno," the customer says. "Place was crawling with chicks." His wife comes into focus at the other end of the kitchen and gives him a dirty look. "I gotta go"—and as much as I loathe Journey, this was a perfectly crafted little fiction about pop music as real life. The agent and the customer aren't proud or embarrassed or fannish, but kind of weirdly stoic: *We're fated to share this stuff to the end.*

3 ▪ *God Bless America,* **directed by Bob Goldthwait (Darko Entertainment)** A middle-aged man facing oblivion and his *Juno*-hating Ellen Page-like teenage sidekick saving the country from itself, one bullet through the head at a time, starting off with a reality-show star complaining about the car she got for her sixteenth birthday, loudmouths in a movie theater ("Thanks for not talking during the feature. Thanks for not using your cell phone," says the man to the lone survivor. "You're welcome," she says, as if she's just learned a valuable lesson). With Tea Party thugs beating up a man with Parkinson's because he supports the Affordable Care Act, it's American culture as a madhouse, a lot broader and a lot more convincing than *Nashville,*

bodies everywhere, blood all over, with the whole show ending with a staging of the "Eat Flaming Death, Fascist Media Pigs" section of the Firesign Theatre's *In the Next World, You're on Your Own,* scored to the Kinks' "I'm Not Like Everybody Else." That's taste.

4 ▪ *The Technical Impossibility of Dyslexia in a Mind Afflicted by Autism: The passage of a few people through the Damien Hirst retrospective at the Tate Modern between 3.52pm and 4.49pm on Tuesday, 24 April 2012,* **Observed by Fred Vermorel (YouTube)** With a title referencing Guy Debord's 1959 Paris film *On the Passage of a Few Persons Through a Brief Moment in Time,* Vermorel (author of, among other books no one else would have written, *Vivienne Westwood: Fashion, Perversity and the Sixties Laid Bare,* with Westwood naked from the waist down on the jacket) wanders the galleries with his video camera. He layers dialogue and sound from mystery films or radio plays over footage of people at the exhibition, until the camera goes into a darkened screening room, and we're hit with an homage to Debord's 1952 feature-length film *Hurlements en faveur de Sade,* most of which is black screen and dead silence (the rest is dialogue and a white screen), ending with the oddly loud, metronome-like sound of the footfalls of people walking through one room after another, trying to get engaged with objects, and not really succeeding. There's a sadistic, nearly endless putative voicemail message from the Damien Hirst International Foundation— at first believable, then pure surrealist poetry, about sponsorship, surveillance, vandalism, the decomposed body of a black woman, and a businessman found hanging from a tree in a bondage mask—in other words, things you might someday encounter at a Damien Hirst exhibition. It's a piece of phone art akin to the story in Nicholas Kristof's May 31 column in the *New York Times:* "Does it bother you that an online casino paid a Utah woman, Kari Smith, who needed money for her son's education, $10,000 to tattoo its Web site on her

forehead?"—which, like Vermorel's piece, is a version of what, in 1985, in *Zone*, Michel Feher and Eric Alliez called "The Luster of Capital," in this case, the humiliation of capital, the ability of capital to pay people to abase and debase themselves before it. The casino isn't advertising its product, but advertising that it can get people to sell themselves to it for a price, and the Hirst voicemail is speaking the same language.

5–6 ▪ **PiL, *This Is PiL* (PiL Official) and Oliver Hall, "John Lydon: I Am Folk Music," *L.A. Record* (June 18)** The first song on the first album in twenty years by the band John Lydon formed after the demise of the Sex Pistols is "This Is PiL"—and it doesn't matter what your cachet, when you were born, or even if you're dead: you can't do a name-of-the-band song without sounding like the Monkees. But the second song, "One Drop," is a version of the first—and it's staggering, a manifesto that the once-and-future Johnny Rotten has given up nothing and never will. You can ignore him, or shake your head in wonder at the way he can ram the lines "We are the ageless, we are teenagers" through the history he shares with his audience, which includes people who weren't born when he and the Sex Pistols were rehearsing on the Monkees' "(I'm Not Your) Steppin' Stone"—and come out the other side with his best album since *Metal Box*, and that wasn't twenty years ago, it was thirty-three. "I am a member of the folk, I am one of the folk, I am folk music, and that's how it is," Lydon told Oliver Hall this spring, speaking of this record. "And *we will con-tin-ue*. And there will be folk to follow me, and music will continue to progress in a very positive and steady way, always with the voice of rebellion. And no touch of découpage, is it? Is that what they call it? Or faux painting? Rustic? Fuck off. I leave rustic up to Neil Young—you know when he wrote *Rust Never Sleeps*, that cheeky monkey? 'Oh, this is the story of Johnny Rotten, the king is gone but he's not forgotten.' So we ring him up, don't we, for the VH1 show, right? 'I never heard of Johnny Rotten,' says Neil Young."

7 ▪ **Neil Young and Crazy Horse, *Americana* (Reprise)** Too much of what's here, from the listless, condescending cover of the Silhouettes' 1957 "Get a Job" to the pallid version of "Wayfaring Stranger," a song so ghostly it's almost impossible for a singer not to be swallowed by it, is dead air. But the opening blast of folk songs—more than five minutes of "Oh Susannah," nearly six of "Clementine," and more than eight of "Tom Dula," that last simply hammering away at the standard Kingston Trio lyrics as if there weren't so many other ways to tell the story—gives these old texts a life neither they nor anyone who's ever sung them have remotely suggested. The Crazy Horse sound, with Young's lead guitar snaking through it like a sardonic curse, is battering, rough, big, then bigger, then so complete you can believe the story that Johnny Rotten wanted Young to produce the Sex Pistols. But with "Clementine"—which makes it clear that when Billy Talbot, Ralph Molina, and Poncho Sampedro break through the wall of their own sound Young could sing the telephone book and make you think you were listening to the end of the world—what comes out of the old summer-camp singalong is not just a lament for the poor drowned girl, but a murder ballad. The unforgiving slam of the music leaves you as shaken as the way the singer, ending the song with a smile, confesses between the lines.

8 ▪ **Patti Smith, "This Is the Girl," from *Banga* (Columbia)** A tribute to Amy Winehouse. From the Madame Defarge of rock 'n' roll.

9 ▪ **Hemingway and Gellhorn, directed by Philip Kaufman, written by Jerry Stahl and Barbara Turner (HBO)** The reviews were dismissive at best—as they were for *The Right Stuff*, nicely setting people up to be surprised at how tough it was. This is the same. What were reviewers watching, what were they thinking, what sense of discomfort or ingrained disdain was behind the refusal to see what's on the screen? As the war correspondent Martha Gellhorn, Nicole Kidman has never been harder to look

away from, and her looks—fire in her cheekbones, intelligence in her eyes—are part of why it's her most convincing part and performance since *Malice*.

This is a historical drama, taking the protagonists from the Spanish Civil War to the Japanese invasion of China to the Soviet assault on Finland—the 1930s before the world war had come together, when it was one fireball after another—and the most startling element in it is the way Kaufman drops his characters straight into historical documentary footage. When he did the same thing with the 1968 Soviet invasion of Czechoslovakia in *The Unbearable Lightness of Being*, it was gimmicky, jarring, taking the viewer—really, the characters—out of the story rather than integrating them more fully into it. I don't know if it's a matter of changes in technology, a deeper sense of history, or the faces and body language of the actors, but the technique is a miracle here. Most of the time I couldn't tell what, when the actors were present, was historical footage and what wasn't, when a scene was unfolding or was constructed, and quickly didn't care. Something shocking and revelatory was going on. The first instance comes with Gellhorn, Hemingway, and the photographer Robert Capa covering a firefight in Spain. We see men moving on a hill and then, flash, there's the Capa shot of the Loyalist soldier, caught in the instant he takes a bullet. OK, you might think, signal moment in twentieth-century iconography, check. But then the body behind, or inside, the iconic, preregistered image tumbles out of the image and onto the ground, and Clive Owen's Hemingway kneels down next to him. The sense of reality, of contingency, of lived, subjective experience flooding into objectified history and wiping out its received imagery is stunning—but it's nothing compared to the Newsreel Wong moment, the moment when, in a bombed-out Shanghai railroad station on August 28, 1937, H. S. "Newsreel" Wong filmed a blasted, burned, crying baby. A frame was taken from the footage and published all over the world, and even today it makes you want to go through the picture and save the baby, as if it has been screaming for these seventy-five years, and always will be. To see, now, that horrifying, soul-withering footage unwinding through Kaufman's movie like a river, to see the baby placed on the platform, then Kidman's Gellhorn lurching toward it, being pulled back—again, the feeling that this was not a Moment in History but a moment in someone's life, the baby's, is crushing. And as horrible as the moment is, you don't want it to end. You want to see a life, that baby's, removed from its historical heaven and lived out on earth. Which you don't get.

10 ▪ **Brother and sister Nat Wolff and Elizabeth Olsen arguing in the back seat in *Peace, Love and Misunderstanding*, directed by Bruce Beresford, written by Joseph Muszynski and Christina Mengert (BCDF Pictures)** "What about the time when your Barbies tried my toy soldiers for war crimes and had them all decapitated?"

OCTOBER 2012

1 ▪ **Woods, *Bend Beyond* (Woodsist)** It's hard to believe that this small Brooklyn band is on its seventh album: everything they do seems experimental, half-finished. You hear ideas as much as music. It can make you shiver to be brought so close to people working over old themes, probing for ancient songs and melodies, forgotten images. The high, keening voice sounds like whispering; a wah-wah pedal sounds like an old folk instrument, which maybe it is. What makes this record different is Jarvis Taveniere's drumming, which is always human, a voice, a stance, a refusal to cross a line or back down—dramatic, not functional, unless cutting down the sometimes-fey tones of Jeremy Earl's singing is functional. The first seven songs—of twelve—can feel as if they're fading into each other, nice jangly folk rock, so that when "Wind Was the Water" looms up, shoots right out of nowhere and in a minute and a half has gone right back you have

no idea what happened. It's as if those first seven songs were a setup.

2 ▪ *Take This Waltz,* **written and directed by Sarah Polley (Magnolia Pictures)** On the soundtrack, at the end, Leonard Cohen's title song versus the Buggles' "Video Killed the Radio Star." And no contest.

3 ▪ *A.K.A. Doc Pomus,* **directed by Peter Miller and Will Hechter (Clear Lake Historical Productions)** Jerome Felder, who died in 1991, was born in Brooklyn in 1925; at six he contracted polio, but by the late 1940s he was performing in New York clubs as Doc Pomus, a Jewish blues singer on crutches. The records he made were distinctive, but they went nowhere. He had been composing songs for himself; now, writing alone or with partners, he offered his tunes to others, and wrote history: "Lonely Avenue" for Ray Charles, "Young Blood" for the Coasters, "Viva Las Vegas," "Little Sister," and "Suspicion" for Elvis Presley, "There Must Be a Better World Somewhere" for B. B. King, and most memorably, for the Drifters, "Save the Last Dance for Me," "I Count the Tears," and "This Magic Moment."

There is nothing remotely ordinary about this film. It can't be compared to any other music biopic or documentary. There is just too much flair—the directors have a visual imagination that makes the cutting-together of historical footage, album covers, movie posters, vintage interviews with the main subject, and a voice-over of someone reading his journals (Lou Reed, as it turns out), talking heads of people now looking back, still photos, and home movies seem like a revelation instead of a formula— and too much love. The result is countless people—Pomus's ex-wife, his girlfriend, his children, musicians, friends—laughing through tears, and soon enough you're one of them.

Again and again you're pulled up short by a moment too right to take in all at once: you hold it in your memory or stop the DVD and run it back. There are dozens, but I have two favorites. First, a hand goes to a car radio, and the critic Dave Marsh is talking: "You've got a radio on, right? And what's coming across, most of the time, frankly, is static and nothing. And then, this *thing*—and that's the Drifters." It's 1960; Doc Pomus is thirty-five years old. The swooning strings of "This Magic Moment" come up on the soundtrack, and Ben E. King, twenty-one, begins to sing, but with an odd, stentorian hesitation in every phrase, as if he's giving a speech, as if what he has to say is so important he's as much nerves as heart. There's a close-up of the Atlantic label with the song title and the writers' names, then head shots as Marsh goes on: "And that's Doc Pomus, that's Mort Shuman, and it's Jerry Wexler and Ahmet Ertegun, Leiber and Stoller, and Tom Dowd, and all the people who recorded it, and then ultimately, that's you and me." By this time you are following the words swimming upstream against the melody, the delicacy of the story being told; you can hear the fear behind the desire. If you've heard the song before, you'll feel as if you're hearing it for the first time. If you've never heard the song before, you'll have to hear it again: that the film then moves on will seem like a crime.

Almost an hour later, the movie is over. Pomus has died. You've attended his funeral. The credits begin to roll. In a box on the right, people who you've heard tell the story are now singing or talking the words to "Save the Last Dance for Me"—and you recall the footage from Pomus's wedding, when his new wife danced with everyone but her new husband, who found a way to put it all down on paper. A phrase at a time; you're surprised how well writers can sing, or that Ben E. King, who took the lead vocal, speaks the words like talk. Five, eight, twelve, seventeen, twenty, including, just before the end, the songwriters Jerry Leiber and Mike Stoller, Leiber looking terribly debilitated and frail, but hitting all the notes—it goes on and on, until the whole song has been declaimed, and you're caught up in a kind of musicality the film hasn't shown before, not merely putting Dave Marsh's words on the screen, but turning them into a kind of perfect life.

4 ▪ Kim Baxter, *The Tale of Me and You* (kimbaxtermusic.com) Baxter was the most noticeable voice in the wonderful Portland punk quartet All Girl Summer Fun Band. They never pushed too hard. On her first album under her own name, Baxter does. "Oval Frame" is Nirvana with radio distortion around the sides. "Arc de Triomphe," not that far from Freddy Cannon's "Palisades Park," is a celebration of an I'll-do-anything-for-you love that you know won't last, except in memory.

5 ▪ Jacob Mikanowski of State College, Pennsylvania, writes in on the Penn State scandal "State College is a bucolic, tranquil town. The 'Happy Valley' nickname isn't a joke. I saw the *Red Riding* movies last year, and I thought they were well made but that the overarching premise—that there was a conspiracy to protect a child sex ring in a North English town—was basically preposterous. But when the story broke in November, it was like going to bed in Mayberry and waking up in Twin Peaks."

6 ▪ David Byrne, *How Music Works* (McSweeney's) A complex musical autobiography and investigation into the question of how music talks—with an opening scene on Telegraph Avenue in Berkeley in the early 1970s, when Byrne and his Rhode Island School of Design classmate Mark Kehoe, busking their way around the country—Kehoe on accordion and Byrne on ukulele and violin—tried to get people to pay attention to "Pennies from Heaven" and "The Glory of Love"—"as well as our arrangements of more contemporary fare, like '96 Tears'" And that really does tell you all you need to know about what Talking Heads was aiming for all along.

7 ▪ Cathi Unsworth, *Weirdo* (Serpent's Tail) A London private detective arrives in a seedy British town to reopen a twenty-year-old high-school murder mystery. Half of the story is told in flashbacks, and it's the story he doesn't discover: a swamp of sexual degradation, a few people of decency, and a clue that turns on the cover of the second Echo and the Bunnymen album.

8 ▪ James Luther Dickinson and the North Mississippi Allstars, *I'm Just Dead I'm Not Gone* (Merless) "When I leave here, just hang crepe on your door," Frank Hutchison of West Virginia sang in 1928 in "Worried Blues." "I won't be dead, just won't be here no more." Dickinson, a storied bandleader and producer, died in 2009—"Three hundred pounds of barbeque," as one of his friends lovingly said at the time. All that's missing from the spooky show he recorded in Memphis in 2006—with humor in every performance, resentment and regret coming up behind it, especially in a harrowing, last-will-and-testament version of Buffy Sainte-Marie's "Codine"—is a cover of the Hutchison song, with his "won't be dead" turned on its head.

9 ▪ Pussy Riot, "Punk Prayer," Cathedral of Christ the Savior (Moscow) One day in February, several Russian women—reenacting both Johnny Rotten's "I am an antichrist" in "Anarchy in the U.K." and the action of one Michel Mourre, who, in 1950, dressed as a Dominican monk with his head in a Dominican tonsure, in Notre Dame in Paris, stepped up during a break during Easter High Mass to deliver an address on the death of God—momentarily seized a church. They were dressed in bright red-and-pink shifts, blue leggings, and yellow, mauve, orange, and turquoise-colored balaclavas. They genuflected, stood up, began to stomp and prance. They shouted, shrieked—attacking Vladimir Putin, attacking the Church, crossing themselves as they were pulled off by guards—and from the sound they made, clipped, sharp, harsh, joyful, the sound of people feeling, if only for a minute, completely free. Singing in Russian, they could have been the all-women Zurich punk band Kleenex (a.k.a. Liliput), singing in Swiss-German more than thirty years ago.

Charged with hooliganism motivated by religious hatred, Pussy Riot members Yekaterina Samutsevich, Maria Alekhina, and Nadezhda Tolokonnikova were held in prison until August 17, when, after attending their trial while confined in a box, they were found guilty and sentenced to two years in a penal colony; Tolokonnikova's defiant closing statement will be read in public squares and tiny apartments all over the world for years to come. But that's not enough. When the Plastic People of the Universe were mercilessly harassed and its members jailed under the Soviet puppet regime in Czechoslovakia, people smuggled their music out on homemade LPs. Today for Pussy Riot, you can go right to YouTube—but for a lot of reasons, something more tangible, an object, a physical fact, is called for. Kill Rock Stars, which reissued Kleenex and Liliput, not to mention their labelmates and punk comrades Essential Logic and Delta 5, has destiny waiting. Download their performance from the cathedral, put it on a CD, and send it out into the world.

10 ■ **Posting, Hammersmith, London (Jubilee Week)** In the early 1970s, Jamie Reid, by 1976 the designer for the Sex Pistols, put up little pink stickers in London supermarkets: OFFICIAL WARNING—CLOSING DOWN SALE, they read. LAST DAYS BUY NOW WHILE STOCKS LAST—THIS STORE WILL BE CLOSING SOON OWING TO THE PENDING COLLAPSE OF MONOPOLY CAPITALISM AND THE WORLDWIDE EXHAUSTION OF RAW MATERIALS. "God save the Queen / the fascist regime," Johnny Rotten sang in 1977: "Your future dream is a shopping scheme." Thirty-five years later, Danny Boyle, director of *Slumdog Millionaire*, now directing the opening and closing ceremonies for the London Olympics, included the Sex Pistols' "God Save the Queen." But on a wall in London two months before, there was a better homage: either an ironic celebration of Queen Elizabeth's Diamond Jubilee, or just another ad. Or the Sex Pistols' latest trick: a poster screaming "GOD SAVE THE QUEEN AND HER SHOPPING REGIME," promising a "free draw" for a £500 diamond. With graphics precisely mimicking Reid's mimicking of signs just like this one.

1 ■ **Robert Pattinson in *Cosmopolis*, written and directed by David Cronenberg (Alfama Films/Prospero Pictures)** This slight figure, in ill-fitting clothes, no matter how expensive they might be—he's supposed to be a financial titan, or monster, twenty-eight and worth far more billions than that, about to embark on a journey of systematically destroying everything he has. Can he carry a whole movie? It doesn't look like it. But as the film goes on, his face becomes at once more expressive and withdraws more completely into itself, and an Elvis ghost emerges around the smudged eyes, to the point that you half expect someone, maybe the cream-pie guerrilla, to say, "Hey, you're the Elvis of money!" But then the sun goes down, Pattinson sits across the table from his nemesis, and as his eyes go glassy—not blank, but a milky pool with no refection—you could be watching *The Manchurian Candidate*, with Laurence Harvey sitting across from Frank Sinatra as red queens cover the table between them and Harvey remembers what he's done. Except for Keira Knightley, Cronenberg's last picture, *A Dangerous Method*, seemed cast on autopilot, with Viggo Mortensen as Freud and Michael Fassbender as Jung; this, from Juliette Binoche's bouncing art dealer to Paul Giamatti reaching all the way down into his bag of losers, is displacing from the first moment to the last.

2 ■ **Cat Power, *Sun* (Matador)** There's always been an acrid, suspicious edge behind Cat Power's tone of voice; except with other people's songs, where she might drift, get lost, and not care, she doesn't let herself go. What's new here, as the songs, which are indistinctly outlined, slowly take shape, is what I can only call womanliness: a certain warmth, an undeniable lack of fear.

3 ■ **Matthew Friedberger, *Matricidal Sons of Bitches* (Thrill Jockey)** This is the other half of Fiery Furnaces' twelfth solo album, and the fifth this year. ("I'm supposed to make two records this fall," the one-man orchestra Friedberger writes,

"one home made one and one 'proper' studio one—I think of *those* as being from 2012. But they won't be out till next year. In other words, I'm confused by this.") And that's not even counting the "Table" series, which is said to include one album for each of the 118 elements in the Periodic Table. For the meantime, this is described as being inspired by Hollywood's Poverty Row, the no-budget fly-by-night letterhead studios that churned out countless B to Z pictures in the 1930s and '40s. You get a feel for the people hanging around the lots in Nathanael West's 1939 *The Day of the Locust*; you can see what the style (form?) (junk heap?) produced at its most intense in Edgar G. Ulmer's 1945 *Detour*. There's an undertow implicit in both the idea and the fact of Poverty Row, a sense of just-shoot-me surrender, people pressing on to the next shot because it would be too much trouble to stop, and Friedberger catches that, as a kind of memory still present around the edges of even today's most glamorous movies, as in the scene in *Mulholland Dr.* where Naomi Watts hires her hit man. There are forty-five tracks here; go to "I'm Sure It's . . . for the Best," number ten, and "Disappointed Dads," number twenty-four, first.

4 ▪ Beloved (*Les Bien-Aimés*), directed by Christophe Honoré (IFC) Frenchwoman walks into a London bar and hears a band playing a bloodless version of Bo Diddley's "Who Do You Love?" but it moves her—and then she sees the drummer, who moves her more. A year later, after she finds him in another bar with another combo, they head out to the street, singing at each other: *"Qui aimes-tu?" "Qui aimes-tu?"* The song has turned into a little French street ballad—with an urgency all over it that the bar band never imagined.

5 ▪ Mary Davis reports from Manhattan (August 16) "'Is there a concert here tonight?' That was the first question I overheard as I joined the long line for entry to the free event in Liberty Hall at the Ace Hotel, which was explicitly not a concert, but a 'Reading of the Letters, Poetry, Lyrics, and Trial Statements of the Jailed Members of Pussy Riot'—held the night before Maria Alekhina, Nadezhda Tolokonnikova, and Yekaterina Samutsevich were convicted of hooliganism and sentenced to two years in prison.

"The mostly young and stylish crowd seemed attentive as the speakers—poet Eileen Myles, actress Chloe Sevigny, artist K8 Hardy, musician Johanna Fateman, and performance artists Justin Vivian Bond and Karen Finley—took to the spare stage without introduction to read statements and transcripts from the trial, and letters written by the band members to Patriarch Kirill and Prime Minister Medvedev. As the evening wore on, a gaggle of waifish young women wearing trendy shorts, airy blouses, and high heels—models?—appeared in the front of the house, where they whispered among themselves, checked out the room, then slipped away as a group. Meanwhile, Sevigny calmly read Alekhina's March 5 prison letter: 'It's so cold in the cell our noses get red and our feet are ice cold . . . we sleep in our street clothes.' Myles seemed emotional as she recited the rousing letter the band wrote to Patriarch Karill: 'What troubles us is that the very shrine you consider so defiled is so inseparably linked to Putin . . . In the prayer in question we express our grief, shared with million of Christians, that you allowed the church to become involved in a dirty political campaign.' Finley's fiery reading of Alekhina's closing statement honed the message: 'The church loves only those children who believe in Putin. . . . I never thought the Russian Orthodox Church's role was to call for faith in any president. I thought its role was to call for faith in God.'

"Such clarity was not a hallmark of the band's statements, which tended toward exaggeration and self-aggrandizement: should the reference points for Pussy Riot be Brodsky, Kafka, Debord, Solzhenitsyn? Maybe that was the intention: the formal but über-hip setting heightened the sense that the event itself was an extended Pussy Riot provocation, simultaneously earnest and ironic—a dual sensibility likewise suggested by the colorful CBGB/FREE PUSSY RIOT T-shirts sported by many in the audience. The show trial may have been in Russia, but there was a spectacle in Liberty Hall."

6 ▪ **Randy Newman, "I'm Dreaming" (Nonesuch/YouTube)** No matter what happens, Mitt Romney will not fall below 45 percent in the election because 45 percent of the electorate cannot abide a black president. "I think there are a lot of people who find it jarring to have a black man in the White House and they want him out," Randy Newman said of his new song, his little intervention, or witnessing, partly sung to the tune of "I'm Dreaming of a White Christmas," this time "of a white president." "You won't get anyone, and I do mean anyone, to admit it." The performance is quiet, cool, unashamed, the singer disappearing into his character, until he might suck you in, too, whoever you are.

7 ▪ **David Segal, "You Had to Be There: Amid the Wonder, Some Wondering," Olympics wrap-up, the** *New York Times* **(August 13)** "WORST MUSICAL CLICHÉ: The theme to 'Chariots of Fire' played time and time again during medal ceremonies. MOST WELCOME MUSICAL SURPRISE: Joy Division's 'Love Will Tear Us Apart' played in the Olympic Stadium during track and field events." Especially the Draw-and-Quarter.

8 ▪ **Bumper sticker, Berkeley, August 18** "FORGET WORLD PEACE—VISUALIZE USING YOUR TURN SIGNAL." Just above it: a version of the Shepard Fairey Obama HOPE poster with a face that could have been Herbert Hoover's.

9 ▪ **Bob Dylan,** *Tempest* **(Columbia), and at the Capitol Theatre, Port Chester, New York (September 4)** On the surface of this album and far beneath it, a rewriting is going on—a rewriting of what, in his book *Chronicles*, Dylan called "a parallel universe . . . a culture with outlaw women, super thugs, demon lovers and gospel truths . . . streets and valleys, rich peaty swamps, with landowners and oilmen, Stagger Lees, Pretty Pollys and John Henrys—an invisible world that towered overhead with walls of gleam-

ing corridors." In the most intense and ambitious songs here, Dylan takes the folk standards "Barbara Allen," "The Titanic," "Black Jack Davy," "Matty Groves," and more, and guides them to places they have never been—places, you can imagine, the songs always knew were there, but that they couldn't reach. "In Charlotte Town, not far from here," Dylan began his performance of "Barbara Allen" at the Gaslight Café in New York in 1962, changing the usual "Scarlet Town"; the eight minutes it took him to say what the song said then are matched now by the seven minutes of "Scarlet Town." Here, fifty or five hundred years later, the suicides of Sweet William and Barbara Allen have left a curse on the town, a kind of ugly, alluring gravity, each step lifting a leg of a thousand pounds, a force, a specter one can neither accept nor reject—and you don't want to get to the end of it any more than the singer does. "The streets have names / that you can't pronounce," Dylan sings in a slow, considered manner, as if to get you to believe it, to weigh the fact as he does; is it that as soon as you learn how to pronounce the name of a street, it changes? The lines may be as ominous and intriguing as any Dylan has ever sung—and while I fully expect someone to trumpet the discovery that they were taken from Sherwood Anderson, Tacitus, or the sixth-century C.E. Arabian poet Imru' al-Qays, if not Carl Barks, in this music they sound like a gong.

At the Capitol Theatre, Dylan did not play any songs from *Tempest*—which had gone up on iTunes that day, a week in advance of the album's official release—but he offered music that was just as new, if nothing like so old. With the acoustics of the less-than-two-thousand-seat hall shockingly bright—inside the storm of texting, flashbulbs, filming, phone calls, and constant chatter, you could hear every note of Dylan's piano, follow every curling riff on Charlie Sexton's lead guitar—the most effective performances were sly, insistent, rough, syncopated, harsh, and even scary: "Highway 61 Revisited," "High Water (For

Charley Patton)," and "All Along the Watchtower" were sent out in staccato bursts, with stinging, isolated rockabilly notes that were like flashbulbs in the sound. The most carefully written passages in the songs seemed to bring out the most in Dylan as a pure singer, alive to the way a word might call for a hesitation, a moment of doubt, a dive forward. Just as often he put the pressure not on words but on syllables, each one carrying an exclamation point, which suspended the ideas or dramas in the songs—the sardonic dread and idealistic cynicism in "All Along the Watchtower," the Englishman, the Italian, and the Jew at the bar in "High Water"—even as the pace picked up with every chorus. Finally, the whole show was a matter of cadence—with "All Along the Watchtower" moving from! ! ! to a kind of slow, doubting abstraction, the song dissolving into the miasma of a noir film like *In a Lonely Place,* where no one could tell who to be afraid of. Dylan has played this song at the end of shows for years; this was the best performance of it I've ever heard.

10 ▪ *2 Days in New York,* directed by Julie Delpy, written by Delpy, Alexia Landeau, and Alexandre Nahon (Magnolia) Chris Rock's Mingus to Julie Delpy's Marion: "He's mildly schizophrenic? What's mildly schizophrenic? He hears nice voices? He would have killed Ringo and not John?"

JANUARY 2013

1 ▪ Favorite election film: "You Don't Own Me" PSA (YouTube) "I'm Lesley Gore," says the sixty-six-year-old onetime pop star, "and I approve this message." It's powerful to see dozens of women and girls lipsynching to the song that, so long after its moment on the charts (produced by Quincy Jones, #2 in 1964), has become such a touchstone—here, for abortion rights. As there is in the final-judgment almost–*Law & Order* bang! bang! of the music, there's a sense of menace in the pacing of the quick but somehow hesitating cuts from one woman, duo, or trio to the next—directed

by Sarah Sophie Flicker and Maximilla Lukacs, the little movie has the feel of Nan Goldin's *The Ballad of Sexual Dependency.* With the men in the "Top Comments" section hitting back ("Who would want to make love to the unlovable women hating men that open their big yaps on here?"), the spot, which is sure to be back, or remade, for all foreseeable elections to come, was an election in and of itself.

2 ▪ Corner Laughers, "(Now That I Have You I'm) Bored" from *Poppy Seeds* (Mystery Lawn Music) Led by singer and ukulele player Karla Kane, this San Francisco combo has its feet in the pool of the *Smiley Smile* Beach Boys—the supposedly throwaway music ("Vegetables," "She's Goin' Bald") they made after they gave up on Brian Wilson's *Smile* masterpiece. It's sometimes sun-blindingly bright, never less than sweet. It may not wear any better than the singles of another San Francisco band, the long-forgotten Sopwith Camel of "Hello, Hello" fame. But for bringing new life to the dying art of parenthetical titling, this song would make my chart anyway.

3 ▪ Brokeback, *Brokeback and the Black Rock* (Thrill Jockey) Douglas McCombs is focusing the textures of Tortoise, his better-known band, into something close to pure concept, but a concept so formally open there's never a feeling of aesthetic claustrophobia. In other words, after the opening track, the harsh "Will Be Arriving," this slips away into desert surf music, all guitars and reverb, a fantasy soundtrack to *Kill Bill: Vol. 3*—or, if Quentin Tarantino ever finishes it, who knows, the real thing. It's slow, relentless, unforgiving, all landscape and bad weather—music so quietly grand it hardly needs the puny figures acting out the plot.

4 ▪ *Andrew Loog Oldham Presents the Rolling Stones 'Charlie Is My Darling—Ireland 1965,'* directed by Peter Whitehead (ABKCO Films) An expanded version of a film that played briefly as a short and then went on the shelf—and though the concert footage can be hot (especially an ugly,

onstage fans' riot for "I'm Alright") and the interviews with smiling girls and dour boys sometimes odd ("Did you enjoy it?" then-manager Oldham asks one. "No," he says, as if he was determined not to, "the screaming was a bit much." "In the next house we'll turn the screaming off," Oldham promises), the real action is backstage. After talking throughout about his discovery of the fallacy of the supposed ephemerality of pop music, Mick Jagger takes the long view: "In the last two or three years, young people have been—this especially applies to America—instead of just carrying on the way their parents told them to, they've started a big thing, where they're anti-*war*, and they love everybody, and their sexual lives have become *freer*. The kids are looking for something *else*, or some different moral value, because they know they're going to get all the things that were thought impossible fifty years ago. The whole sort of basis of society and values which were accepted could be changed, but it's up to them to carry on those ideals that they have, instead of just *falling* into the same old routine their parents have fallen into. So it's not until the people of twenty-one now reach the age of seventy-five—those kids actually have to be grandfathers before the whole thing is changed." In a way, he and Keith Richards take an even longer view when in a hotel room they start working their way back through "Tell Me," a song from their first album that I once read was "doo-wop trash." It is doo-wop—elsewhere, they fool around with deep-voiced pseudo-Elvis versions of "Santa Bring My Baby Back to Me" and "Are You Lonesome Tonight?" ("This number has been for me," Jagger says for the narration in the middle, "maybe what your father and mother were to you.") But here, with Oldham keeping time by patting his hands on a nightstand, the echoes Richards is fingering out of his acoustic guitar are dark-hollow folk chords, taking the progression of the song—a step-by-step build toward a declaration of love declaimed from a balcony—into a stumble through the sublime, as if the song were not made but found.

5–6 ▪ Corin Tucker Band, Mercury Lounge (New York, September 27, 2012) and Public Image Ltd. at the Hammerstein Ballroom (New York, October 13, 2012) Tucker came onstage featuring Veronica Lake's peekaboo hairstyle, her blond hair draped over one eye. It's an easy look to copy; given how strong Lake was on screen from 1942, in *Sullivan's Travels*, to 1946, in *The Blue Dahlia*, it's a lot harder to live up to. With bassist Dave Depper, guitarist Seth Lorinczi (he and Tucker traded leads, he with feedback and shredding, she with the more lyrical lines), and drummer Sara Lund, a marvel on *oo-oo-oos*, behind her, Tucker pulled no punches, and one eye was all she ever showed.

John Lydon, too, called up an icon from another era. Early on came "Albatross" (from 1979, about "the spirit of '68") and "One Drop" (from 2012, a fifty-six-year-old man declaring, "We are teenagers . . . We are the last chance, we are the last dance"), both staggeringly fierce, one the tale of someone fighting his way through a miasma as thick as quicksand, the next a triumphant refusal ever to give up, both two sides of the same theme: how do you get out from under the shadow of the past and make your own history? Lydon's singing style is close to speechifying: chanting, exhorting, warning. I was thrown by a familiarity in his manner I couldn't immediately fix—but halfway into "One Drop," it fell into place. The intentionally pompous expressions, in a face tilted up, the facial muscles seemingly locked into place, until for a crescendo they were twisting into an expression of anguish and challenge; the harsh, bleating tone; the flat palms held inches apart, just below the neck—those were all elements of Adolf Hitler's speaking style. With all of it put together, as it was this night, it was more than a style. It was a way of drawing on the collective unconscious of the west to get songs about history across.

7 ▪ A history walk in Little Rock, Arkansas (September 25, 2012) In the Clinton Library, from a hallway away from the gallery noting Hillary Clinton's mother's crush on

Keith Richards, there was a waft from another gallery of the 1992 victory speech on the steps of the state capitol: that line about "the mystery of our democracy." Far down the street, after President Clinton Avenue turned back into Markham Street, just across from the capitol, there was a plaque on a stand, FREEDOM RIDERS IN LITTLE ROCK: "On 10 July 1961 five Freedom Riders from the St. Louis Branch of the Congress of Racial Equality (CORE)— Benjamin Elton Cox, Annie Lumpkin, Bliss Ann Malone, John Curtis Raines and Janet Reinitz—arrived at the Mid-West Trailways bus station at Markham and Louisiana Streets. A crowd of between 300 and 400 people watched as they were arrested. The Riders were later released from jail and continued their journey to New Orleans. The Freedom Rides led to the desegregation of bus terminals in Little Rock and other cities by order of the Interstate Commerce Commission (ICC) on 1 November 1961."

Heading toward the Clinton Library again, one would have passed the Butler Center for Arkansas Studies, with a banner announcing a new exhibition: "The Civil War in Arkansas—Invasion or Liberation?" On the next block there was another plaque, this one commemorating the 1880s site of the Concordia Association, a social club for Jews, part of Little Rock since 1830, but barred from all other city clubs and citizens' groups. And then at 511 Clinton Avenue there was the Flying Fish Restaurant, where, had it existed in 1961, black people would not have been allowed. Painted on a window was a quote from "Fishing Blues," a signature song for Henry "Ragtime Texas" Thomas (1874–1950?). When in 1952 Harry Smith compiled his epochal *Anthology of American Folk Music*, he made it the last number, the last word. As Thomas recorded it in 1928, it featured the most joyous pan-pipe playing since the devil put it down, and the most salacious line in American blues: "Any fish bite if you got good bait." Presented as the wisdom of the ages, an absolute truth.

8 ■ **Ralf Paulsen, "Tom Dooley," in** *La Paloma* **(YouTube)** In 1958, the Kingston Trio made the post-Civil War murder ballad "Tom Dooley" an international hit and the Army stationed Pvt. Elvis Presley in West Germany; a year later future West German cowboy actor Ralf Paulsen appeared in this strange movie. Dressed as a GI, with a high Elvis pompadour, seated in a nightclub with two Army buddies, he begins to sing in English, somewhat haltingly, in a dank, somber tone: "Hang down your head Tom / Dooley, hang down your head . . ." The old waiters stare at them. They rise from their table, still singing, staring back at the waiters and the other patrons, staring at the musicians in the nightclub band who are trying to pick up the tune, all of them—it's plain—old Nazis, now confronted with their American liberators—or avengers. The three GIs go through the door, closing it behind them, singing, "Poor boy, you're bound to . . ." and then Paulsen opens the door, sticks his head through, straight at the old man on the other side, pushing the last word of the song right into his face: ". . . die." Shot when Elvis, in uniform, was hanging out in West German nightclubs, resisting the constant calls from other patrons that he get up and sing, Paulsen's scene plays as the most outrageous fantasy of what might have happened if Elvis had done just that—the killer Tom Dooley, in the person of another Southern boy, back from the dead to lay his curse.

9 ■ **Iris Dement,** *Sing the Delta* **(Flari-ella)** Country, old-time, quiet, unassuming, all home truths. With one sting after another.

10 ■ **Second favorite election film (once removed): Jeremy W. Peters, "Strident Anti-Obama Messages Flood Key States" (***New York Times,*** October 23)** On *Dreams from My Real Father*, a DVD purporting to prove that Barack Obama's actual father was an American Communist Party activist and that his mother posed nude for a bondage magazine: "The film is the work of Joel Gilbert, whose previous claims include having tracked down Elvis Presley in the

Witness Protection Program and discovering that Paul McCartney is in fact dead."

Thanks to Virginia Dellenbaugh

FEBRUARY 2013

1 ▪ Percival Everett, *Percival Everett by Virgil Russell* (Graywolf Press) "Two black men walk into a bar and the rosy-faced white barkeep says we don't serve niggers in here and one of the men points to the other and says but he's the president and the barkeep says that's his problem. So the president walks over and gives the barkeep a box and says these are Chilmark chocolates and the barkeep says thank you and reaches over to shake the president's hand. The president jumps back, says what's that? And the barkeep says it's a hand buzzer, a gag, get used to it, asshole." And in this novel, that's just the first chapter.

2 ▪ Bikini Kill, *Bikini Kill* (Kill Rock Stars, 1992) The hurricane riot grrrl band will be reissuing all of their 1990s records. After their demo cassette, *Revolution Girl Style Now!* this five-song EP was their first formal release. With "Liar," a snakepit redo of "Give Peace a Chance," and "Suck My Left One," which is both a declaration of independence and a girl's account of how her big sister protects her by giving herself up to their father every night, it's funny and harrowing, sometimes with no line, and no time, between the two. But it's also only a hint of how radical the group was on-stage. A YouTube clip—"Bikini Kill wdc 1992"—shows lead singer Kathleen Hanna, bassist Kathi Wilcox, guitarist Bill Karren, and drummer Tobi Vail as Hanna stamps out "Girl Soldier," the word *fuck* used for percussion as much as anything else. And then Vail—from her haircut to her T-shirt to her skirt looking exactly as Thora Birch's miserable punk Enid would in *Ghost World* almost ten years later—gets up from behind her drums as Karren sits down at them. She strides up to the mike, grabs it as if it's the only thing left to hold on to in the midst of a storm, and then she makes the storm. She

releases a flood of glossolalia, or dada sound poetry, or a rage beyond language so fierce you can barely believe what you're seeing. Then she goes back to her drums as if what she just did was merely a passing moment of everyday life—which was the Bikini Kill argument about what life is.

3 ▪ Rihanna, "Stay," on *Saturday Night Live* (November 10, 2012) Torch song: small to start with, even on the big notes her voice thins as the song goes on, but the moral force behind it seems infinite.

4 ▪ Tracy K. Smith, "Alternate Take (for Levon Helm)," from *Life on Mars* (Graywolf Press, 2011) A slowly building poem in which the writer ("I've been beating my head all day long on the same six lines") wants nothing more than to feel like the singer must have felt as he sang—what would it have been? "Chest Fever"? "The Weight"? "You know how, shoulders hiked nice and high, chin tipped back / So the song has to climb its way out like a man from a mine."

5 ▪ Jess, "Tricky Cad" in *O! Tricky Cad & Other Jessoterica*, ed. Michael Duncan (Siglio Press, 2012) Jess (1923–2004) was a San Francisco painter and collage artist. From 1952 to 1954 he clipped *Dick Tracy* comic strips out of the Sunday papers and cut them up and scrambled them, until people changed heads and dialogue fractured. This marvelous book—full of more conventional collages made of advertisements and nudie magazines so detailed it would take weeks to decipher them—collects all five extant *Tricky Cad* casebooks (three are lost). *Dick Tracy* itself, Jess said, was "dramatic serious nonsense of the highest order, like *Krazy Kat*"; *Tricky Cad* was "a demonstration of a hermetic critique self-contained in popular art." As in Case 1, the page titled TRICKD, with Tracy running a lie-detector test on a middle-aged woman with a white ponytail. She's furious and hysterical by turns; "TELL THE LION AND THE SHIP TO COME IN," Tracy says. Two panels later her face is doubled by a younger version of herself, with another older version in the background, as she

shouts, "WHERE DID YOU FIND IT?" at Tracy—over a severed hand, still in its shirt cuff, lying on a steel table. "A CROSS DIDN'T DO IT!" she screams from a jail cell. "LET'S HEAR IT ALL, PUNY," says a cop. "I'M SCARED TO QUESTION YOU ABOUT ANOTHER SUBJECT, EVER!" says Tracy. Followed by a series ("KIT CARY," "CRACKY I," "IKICK ART") involving a woman smothering a man with a pillowcase, broken teeth, a missing baby, and a woman, the murderer, sentenced to a year in prison not for the killing but for "living at home." And then it gets complicated.

6 ■ **Cleve Duncan, July 23, 1935–November 7, 2012** Soaring over the skipping piano triplets as if he didn't hear them, Duncan was the lead voice in the Penguins' "Earth Angel," in 1954 one of the first Los Angeles doo-wop singles—a record that has proved as enduring as anything else America has turned up over the last sixty years, including Martin Luther King's address to the March on Washington, which was its own kind of music, the legend of Sylvia Plath, or James Dean in *Rebel Without a Cause*. The song came down to earth—and lived as true a life as in any other place or time—in Philip Roth's 1962 *Letting Go*, when it played behind what might be the saddest line he ever wrote, and this time you could imagine that Duncan did hear Roth's young woman, just the sort of person who would have loved the song: "She could not believe that her good times were all gone."

7 ■ **Michael Robbins, *Alien Vs. Predator* (Penguin, 2012)** Robbins's poetry is quick as thought, as Constance Rourke might have put it, if he'd been around in 1931 for Rourke to include him in her *American Humor: A Study of the National Character*. With Davy Crockett–Mike Fink brags brought up to date ("I clear the jungle with the edge of my hand. / I make love to an ATM. I enrich uranium," followed by the perfect capper: "I'm uninsured") and pop songs bouncing off a nineteenth-century novel (in "Self-Titled," I can't tell if I like "This is Uncle Tom to Ground Control" more than "I just died in my arms tonight"), it might be more true to say Robbins's poetry is thought, or

rather a mind alive but not thinking at all, a jumble of memory and stimuli and distractions and it's-on-the-tip-of-my-tongue, never mind, a roaring in the head of someone talking to someone else while what he's really doing is talking to himself, but barely listening, and having the time of his life.

8 ■ *Nick Cave and Warren Ellis Present Lawless Original Motion Picture Soundtrack* **(Sony Classical)** On covers of Link Wray's 1971 "Fire and Brimstone" and the Velvet Underground's 1968 "White Light/White Heat," Mark Lanegan, leader of the 1990s Seattle band Screaming Trees, might be acting out the titles. He dives headlong over words, chords, rhythm changes as if speed is its own reward—and for a 2012 bootlegging movie set in the 1920s, music from forty years later couldn't hit harder. On the other hand, the bluegrass icon Ralph Stanley was born in the Virginia mountains where the movie is set, in the '20s, when the music that later made his name was already old—and his covers of the same songs sound like shtick, because he's a shtick singer.

9 ■ *On the Road,* **directed by Walter Salles, written by Jose Rivera (IFC)** Jack Kerouac was casting the movie of his novel before it was published (he would star); finally, fifty-five years later, with the book still selling 100,000 copies a year and Kerouac dead since 1969, here it is. Except for Kirsten Dunst, who has nothing to do but act pissed off, the women—Amy Adams, Elisabeth Moss, Kristen Stewart—hold the screen, even if they have only walk-through parts. The men flop. Sam Riley, so fierce as Ian Curtis in *Control* and Pinkie in *Brighton Rock*, is vague and scattered as Sal Paradise (Kerouac); Garrett Hedlund as Dean Moriarty tries hard, throwing himself at the story, but his features are too soft and rounded to give even a hint of why Kerouac and Allen Ginsberg couldn't take their eyes off Neal Cassady. There is one killing scene, at the end. In New York, Moriarty comes out of the night, approaching Paradise, who's dressed in a coat and tie and surrounded by friends; they haven't seen each

other for a long time. Hedlund reaches out, but he seems addled, damaged; you can almost smell his desperation, his loneliness, and you can see Riley smell it too, and step back. "Duke Ellington won't wait," says a voice behind Riley, and he turns away. "I love you as always," Hedlund says, and he's left in the shadows, like Paul Muni at the end of *I Am a Fugitive from a Chain Gang*, slipping into the dark after seeing his one-time lover Helen for the last time. "How do you live?" she asks him. "I steal," he says.

10 ▪ **Rick Perlstein, "The Long Con: Mail-Order Conservatism," the** *Baffler* **#21 (Fall 2012)** "It's time, in other words, to consider whether Romney's fluidity with the truth is, in fact, a feature and not a bug: a constituent part of his appeal to conservatives. The point here is not just that he lies when he says conservative things, even if he believes something different in his heart of hearts—but that lying is what makes you sound the way a conservative is supposed to sound, in pretty much the same way that curlicuing all around the note makes you sound like a contestant on *American Idol* is supposed to sound."

Thanks to Allison Kirkland

MARCH–APRIL 2013

SPECIAL POST-ELECTION WHAT IS
AMERICA EDITION

1 ▪ **Amy Winehouse, "To Know Him Is to Love Him," from** *At the BBC* **(Republic)** A DVD traces her 2006 appearance at the Other Voices festival in the remote Irish town Dingle: a set of exquisite performances, Winehouse singing in a church, tiny under her bouffant, dressed in black jeans, trainers, a low-cut sleeveless top, two face studs, and her tattoos, accompanied only by bass and guitar. In interview footage intercut between songs she talks earnestly about the people from whom she learned to sing—Mahalia Jackson, the Shangri-Las, Ray Charles, Dinah Washington, Carleen Anderson, Sarah Vaughn, and Thelonious Monk, and the film lets

you watch them as Winehouse might have. A CD collects fourteen BBC performances, most of them live, and as she moves through her own songs "Back to Black," "In My Bed," "You Know I'm No Good," and "Tears Dry on Their Own," and the torch singer Julie London's 1955 "I Should Care," you're pulled into the impeccably edited and lit black and white film noir she acted out on the two albums she made while she was still alive. And then, on the last track, after you've admired her sense of style, her commitment to craft, the way her professionalism was inseparable from her fandom, comes the heartbreaker: a 2006 radio-station cover of the first record by the Teddy Bears, with Phil Spector on guitar and contributing the song, a vocal trio that came out of Fairfax High School in Los Angeles to score a number one hit in 1958. Then it was simpering, pious: Spector never failed to mention that he took the title phrase from his father's grave ("From the words on my grave," he once said before correcting himself). Now it's full, rich, gorgeous, and slow, with a step from one word, one idea, to the next, the journey of a lifetime, which neither the singer nor the listener is willing to see end.

2 ▪ **Kanye West at 12-12-12: The Concert for Sandy Relief (New York, Madison Square Garden, December 12, 2012)** Emerging from a sea of sludge—the critic and musician Tom Kipp's term for the way rote rock riffs and gestures, in this case uncountable raised arms, brandished guitars, and drawn-out finales, can accumulate until the entire form can seem like the aesthetic equivalent of landfill—the only hip-hop performer to have been called a "jackass" by President Obama and coincidentally the only hip-hop performer on the bill broke the night open. First high-stepping, then bending low and all but tiptoeing, he made a drama of assault and stealth, upending the parade of stars for twenty solid minutes, raging through parts of twelve songs—from "Clique" and "Jesus Walks" to his lines in Jay-Z's "Run This Town" and Rihanna's "Diamonds"—he brought down the storm everybody else was

only talking about. Suddenly, there was a doubling, art and jeopardy facing off as enemies and leaving arm in arm.

3 ■ George Bellows, *Preaching (Billy Sunday)*, in "George Bellows" (Metropolitan Museum of Art, November 15, 2012–February 18, 2013; Royal Academy of Arts, London, March 16–June 9, 2013) Bellows is best known for his 1909 boxing painting *Stag at Sharkey's*, where the bodies of the two fighters seem to stretch beyond themselves. This 1915 pen-and-ink drawing is even more extreme. The evangelist Billy Sunday started out as a major-league outfielder, and you can see that here. Addressing a huge crowd in an enormous hall—the high roof supported by wooden pillars that look like trees, giving the impression of a camp meeting, though person to person the well-dressed crowd is appreciative, ecstatic, stony-faced, despairing—Sunday stands on top of a jerry-built pine platform, his legs spread, his right arm shooting out, his index finger pointing like a knife, his left arm cocked with his hand in a tight fist, his body so tensed it's as if he's physically daring the whole world to doubt a word he's saying. The picture is thrilling, frightening: an unparalleled portrait of American movement. And seated at Sunday's feet on the platform are four clerks, carefully writing down his words, or entering figures.

4 ■ Adam Gold, "Q&A: T Bone Burnett on 'Nashville,' Elton John's Comeback and Retiring as a Producer," *Rollingstone.com* (December 18, 2012) "Listen, the story of the United States is this: One kid, without anything, walks out of his house, down the road, with nothing but a guitar and conquers the world."

5 ■ Simone Jackson, "The Cuckoo," in *Wuthering Heights*, directed by Andrea Arnold (Ecosse/Film4) Playing the servant Nelly, Simone, cooing to Hindley's baby, sounds like the '60s British folk singer Anne Briggs. Other folk tunes float through the film: "The Cruel Mother," "I Once Loved a Lass," "Barbara Allen." "In the most extraordinary way," the critic Peter Bradshaw wrote in the *Guardian*, "Arnold achieves a kind of

pre-literary reality effect. Her film is not presented as another layer of interpretation, superimposed on a classic's frills and those of all the other remembered versions, but an attempt to create something that might have existed before the book, something on which the book might have been based, a raw, semi-articulate series of events, later polished and refined as a literary gemstone. That is an illusion, of course, but a convincing and thrilling one"—or not an illusion. The movie itself is like a folk ballad whose origins can't be traced, a ballad for which there's no original, and thus no copy.

6 ■ *Son of Rogue's Gallery: Pirate Ballads, Sea Songs & Chanteys* (Anti-) The New York producer Hal Willner is again drawing on his wide circle of rock legends, actors, and moderately obscure downtown Manhattan musicians. There are duds, mostly from the big names—Iggy Pop trying to be hipper than the songs he's declaiming, Patti Smith and Johnny Depp making Real Art out of Old Folk Song. There are shots in the dark no one but Willner could have thought of, let alone pulled off: Macy Gray scratching her way through "Off to the Sea Once More," so believable you can see her on deck with a peg for a leg, Anjelica Huston stepping through "Missus McGraw" as if it were a garden, Tom Waits with Keith Richards letting the melody of "Shenandoah" crawl out of his encrusted throat, Tim Robbins with Matthew Sweet and Susanna Hoffs embracing "Marianne," Robin Holcomb and Jessica Kenny's subtle, faraway "Ye Mariners All," the Americans—a New York foursome, led by Patrick Ferris, whose deep voice doesn't sound like Richard Manuel's but feels like it—on "Sweet and Low," a small essay on the way a regretful mind doubles back on itself forever.

The glowing coal at the heart of all this—there are thirty-six performances—is the New York singer Shilpa Ray, with Nick Cave and Warren Ellis, on seven minutes of Kurt Weill and Bertolt Brecht's "Pirate Jenny." Everyone has done this, from Lotte Lenya in *The Threepenny Opera* to Nina Simone to Bob Dylan rewriting it as "When

the Ship Comes In" to Nicole Kidman using it to massacre the population of Lars
von Trier's *Dogville*. As the song's scullery
maid, Ray rushes into the piece as if her
broom will be her ride when the song is
over. Behind her, a sound somewhere between an accordion and a church organ
sweeps up the music and holds it as one
note. She's enraged, contemplative, funny,
wistful, throwing you back, lost in fantasy:
"This whole fuckin' place will be down to
the ground." Growling, she could be a female hobo who's drunk too much Sterno;
letting her voice smooth itself out over a
string of words, she's a schoolteacher giving
her third-grade class a music lesson. The
kids sing along, and then their parents call
up the principal and want to know where
their children learned this song about "Kill
them now or kill them later."

7 ■ The Acting Company, *Of Mice and
Men*, written by John Steinbeck, directed by
Ian Belknap, Baruch Performing Arts Center
(New York, December 7, 2012, on tour March/
April) With Bob Dylan's defeated, fatalistic, dream-in-the-past 1961 version of "This
Land Is Your Land" as exit music, just after
Lennie (Christopher Michael McFarland)
can finally see the land he and George (Joseph Midyett) will own, just before George
shoots him in the back of the head. What
makes this version of the song so different
from any other, so jarring and hard to take,
is put across in Dylan's understated, hard
cadence, in the way each line of the song is
sung as a single, complete sentence, isolated from any other, so that they are pieces
of an idea calling out to each other, each in
its own exile, long since scattered, ideas that
will never connect again: *This land is your
land. This land is my land. From California,
to the New York Island. From the redwood
forest, to the gulf stream waters. This land
was made for you and me.* It reaches the
heart as "This land is not your land, this
land is not my land, and it never was."

8 ■ The Babies, *Our House on the Hill*
(Woodsist) In this Brooklyn combo, Cassie
Ramone's acrid voice, full of thought,
comes in behind Kevin Morby's compla-

cent leads as a dose of realism, not an attitude. When she takes a verse, especially on
the duet "Slow Walkin," it's as if you've just
passed her going the other way on the
street, caught a snatch of conversation, and
turned your head—Who was that talking?—
half-recognizing the voice but unable give
it a name.

9 ■ Neil Young and Crazy Horse, Barclays
Center (Brooklyn, December 3, 2012) From
passage to passage in a single song, they
were Paul Bunyan, purposeful and determined, felling whole forests with a single
swing of his ax, then Frankenstein's monster, plummeting forward with the thrill of
pure destruction. Some people might say
it's the same thing.

10 ■ Barrett Strong, "Money (That's
What I Want)" (Tamla, 1959), in *Killing Them
Softly*, written and directed by Andrew
Dominik (The Weinstein Company) You can
watch the whole final sequence on YouTube:
it's November 4, 2008, and Brad Pitt's hitman walks into a bar to meet mob fixer Richard Jenkins to collect for the three people
he's killed. Jenkins is trying to stiff Pitt on the
price; on the TV above them, Barack Obama
is giving his victory speech. "We have never
been just a collection of individuals or a collection of red states and blue states," he says.
"We are, and always will be, the United
States of America." "Next he'll be telling us
we're a community, one people," Pitt says—
he hasn't been this convincing since *True
Romance*. "In this country," Obama says,
"we rise or fall as one nation, as one people."
"This guy wants to tell me we're living in
a community?" Pitt says, after shredding
Thomas Jefferson as "a rich wine snob . . .
who allowed his own children live in slavery." "Don't make me *laugh*." With the
scene picking up momentum, force, his
voice quiets: "I'm living in America, and in
America you're on your own. America's not a
country. It's just a business. Now fuckin' pay
me." And then a black screen and Barrett
Strong's ferocious song, written by Berry
Gordy, his first hit, and his last word.

Thanks to Genevieve Yue

1 ▪ *Django Unchained—Original Motion Picture Soundtrack* (Republic) Quentin Tarantino's soundtrack albums are as rich as his movies—with the two *Kill Bill* discs, more so. This is a swamp where hip-hop, Jim Croce, dialogue going on just long enough, spaghetti western classics, and John Legend all rise to the surface, one head bobbing up as another one sinks out of sight. The album creates its own drama, and as you listen, music that in the theater you only heard in snatches or didn't register at all reshapes the story. But Anthony Hamilton and Elayna Boynton's "Freedom" is the fire on the water. It's ominous, menacing, stirring—so much so that it's almost corny. And then the music seems to swoon over itself: time is coming to a stop, and every note seems so rich, so full of suggestion, portent, danger, and desire that you are willing time not to move, because you don't want the moment to get away, even if the song promises that the next moment will hit even harder. The performance is at once a functional piece of movie music and a soul classic that, somewhere back in the '70s, when Isaac Hayes first recorded with Sojourner Truth, got lost in a time warp.

2 ▪ *Girls*, "It's About Time," directed by Lena Dunham, written by Lena Dunham and Jenni Konner (HBO, January 13) Speaking of time warps, or the way that in culture time is a Möbius strip: Dunham's Hannah and Andrew Rannells's Elijah are kicking around ideas for a theme party. "OK," says Hannah, "so it's like the Manson family before they committed any murders? And Squeaky Fromme was just like the Mary of a Peter, Paul and Mary?"

3 ▪ Christian Marclay, *The Clock* (San Francisco Museum of Modern Art, through June 2) Speaking of Möbius strips, you start out watching this twenty-four-hour compilation of film clips as a game, identifying the movies—you walk into the screening room at 5:15 p.m., whatever's happening on the screen is happening at 5:15 p.m. You relax into the jokes in the scenes, into the punning cuts. Then you realize, especially as the clocks approach the hour, no matter what the hour is, that all of the pieces are actually going somewhere: toward suspense as a cinematic value that overrides all others. Marclay goes back and forth between shots of a woman waiting in line with mounting anxiety and a spaghetti western, and it's the shots of the woman where the suspense is at its most intense, even if in the western somebody dies. Ralph Meeker carefully opens a door in *Kiss Me Deadly* and from another film Ingrid Bergman turns her head in shock.

4 ▪ Kelly Clarkson, "My Country 'Tis of Thee," at the Inauguration (January 21) Speaking of shock, she had to follow Aretha Franklin, who performed the song at Barack Obama's first inauguration, and Clarkson didn't shame herself. As she slowly turned the song toward a bigger and bigger presence, she was both a star and self-effacing, heroic and modest. Moving into the forgotten third verse, then the fourth, she made the country look up, saying, *There is so much we don't know, there is so much to remember.*

5 ▪ Kelly Willis and Bruce Robison, *Cheater's Game* (Thirty Tigers) Speaking of Kellys, as a country singer Willis seems to look at the form—the genre, the style, the radio stations, the industry—from a long way off, something she remembers, and misses, but knows her music would be dead if she ever went back to what country music is supposed to be. So she slides on the melodies that drift out of what she remembers, bends to the words, and the feeling that comes out of the songs is like what you feel when you bend a sapling right up to the point where it breaks.

6 ▪ Eddie Money for Geico (YouTube) Speaking of bending till it breaks, a horror movie: four nice people are seated in a travel agency office and in comes travel agent Eddie Money, looking like a sixty-year-old woman carrying a hangover that's already lasted since 1978. "I've got—two tickets to paradise," he sings. "Whoa-ah, whoa."

7 ■ George Packer, "Loose Thoughts on Youth and Age," the *New Yorker* online (February 8) Speaking of paradise, there are certain people who, in respectable circles—such as the *New York Times*—are beyond criticism: Patti Smith, Christopher Hitchens, Nora Ephron, Susan Sontag, among others. Packer might have found another. "American culture belongs to the young, and, for that reason, it isn't really mine any more," he wrote; he's fifty-two. "My favorite album of 2012 was Neil Young's 'Psychedelic Pill,' featuring a twenty-seven-minute meditation, 'Driftin' Back,' about the deterioration of musical sound due to digital technology. Yet, I still live in the culture, experience it, react to it. For example, during the Super Bowl halftime show a friend and I exchanged e-mails (not texts, though they've been making serious inroads on my phone) about Beyoncé's performance. We agreed that it left us a bit cold—a highly polished combination of corporate marketing and pole dancing. But I instinctively sensed the danger in going public with this view, on, say, my Twitter feed (if I had one)."

8 ■ *The Return of the Stuff That Dreams Are Made Of* (Yazoo) Speaking of the deterioration of musical sound due to digital technology, in the notes to this joyous celebration of Record Collecting OCD—a set of ultra-rare blues and country records from the 1920s and '30s—there's a story about one of the pioneers, Harry Smith, who in 1952 turned his twenty thousand 78s into the eighty-four-track anthology *American Folk Music* and set the stage for countless performers to come. "I would hear from Harry when he was short of money, and I would buy some records from his collection," the collector Pete Kaufman writes of a man who was perhaps more of a trickster than anything else. "Finally I heard from Harry and he was down to his last nine most prized records in his collection, and he offered to sell them to me for $50. We met at a bar in the East Village and exchanged money for records. Harry was drinking a beer. He asked the waiter how much it would cost if he dropped the mug

on the floor. The waiter said five dollars and Harry dropped the mug on the floor and Harry gave the waiter five dollars from the money I'd given him. Then he lit a match and burned a twenty-dollar bill."

9 ■ B. F. Shelton, "Oh Molly Dear," from *The Return of the Stuff That Dreams Are Made Of* (Yazoo) Speaking of *The Return of the Stuff That Dreams Are Made Of*, there has always been something terribly creepy about the Appalachian standard "East Virginia," which begins, "I was born / in East Virigina. / North Carolina / I did roam. / There I courted a fair young maiden. / What was her name / I did not know." It's that missing name: it turns the song into a stalker's confession. Or worse: maybe only barely below the surface, it's a murder ballad. Except that in this version, recorded at the Bristol Sessions at the Virginia-Tennessee border in 1927, there's no maybe, and so convincingly it's a secret you might rather not have been told.

10 ■ Christophe Gowans, "The Record Books" (ceegworld.com/the-record-books) Speaking of untold secrets, "If best-selling albums had been books instead," reads a tag line to this site, and then you see, say, Sonic Youth's *Daydream Nation*: an elegant book jacket where the art seems to suggest a British judge in a white wig looming like weather over a tiny skiff. But the true action is in the little book-catalog summaries: here, "6os radical thinker Kenton 'Sonic' Youth's polemic about the refusal to embrace the tide of West Coast philosophies in his native country, Papua New Guinea." And then you can't stop. *Blood on the Tracks* returns as a twenty-five-cent '50s romance thriller, New Order's *Power, Corruption and Lies* as a business manual, *Abbey Road* as a Penguin Classics reprint of a minor novel by Graham Greene, and, perfectly, Van Morrison's *Astral Weeks* looking like a mildewed tract found in the basement of some foreclosed country manse: "This appears to be either a learned book of astrology or a misinformed book of astronomy, written in an impenetrable ancient Dutch dialect. There are many amendments and

corrections—in a rough hand—peppered with large quantities of swearwords still in use today. Peculiar."

1 ▪ **Blind Lemon Jefferson in *Lore*, directed by Cate Shortland, written by Shortland and Robin Mukherjee (2012, Music Box Films)** Germany, 1945, immediately after the surrender: the older sister in a Nazi family tries to lead her siblings to safety. At an American checkpoint, a scratchy old song that in the next years will be recorded by Carl Perkins and then the Beatles is playing on a portable phonograph; the sound rises, then seems to fragment in the air. It's "Matchbox Blues," from 1927. Whatever the idea behind its use in the film—literally, working as a refugee song: "Standing here wondering, will a matchbox hold my clothes"—it waits on the screen as a harbinger of the postwar world these children will be entering. The sound is archaic, the specter is modern.

2 ▪ **Nomi Kane, *Jingle Bell Rock*, SXSW 2010 and *Namaste, Home Is Where the Boss Is* in *Wings for Wheels* and *Sugar Baby* (brewforbreakfast.com)** Kane is an autobiographical Berkeley comix artist. Her thin, plain lines and utter refusal of caricature or exaggeration produce a pathos and sweetness that capture the pain of children that parents can't touch. That's true even when the child and the adult who can't save her turn out to be the same person—as with *Home Is Where the Boss Is*, the chronicle of an entire life, from five or six ("For a time I was convinced Bruce and the Big Man lived behind the speaker grate in my Dad's Honda hatchback") to adulthood. And there is *Sugar Baby*, the diary of a little girl diagnosed as diabetic. Her doctor gives her "an old friend to help [her] practice injections"; it looks like a Raggedy Ann inflatable sex doll. In "Family Restaurants," the girl goes into the restroom to inject herself in the stomach; two older girls come in, see the needle, and walk right back out. "This place has really gone downhill," one of them says.

3 ▪ **Hollis Brown, *Ride on the Train* (Alive)** Presumably named for the Bob Dylan song about a South Dakota farmer who kills his five children, his wife, and himself, this four-piece guitar band from Brooklyn is keeping forgotten Lynyrd Skynyrd promises. The title song, the first track, goes far enough, but with "Walk on Water," near the end, the stops come out, the rivers are crossed, and you can see all the way to the Pacific.

4 ▪ ***Phil Spector*, written and directed by David Mamet (HBO)** This isn't about Phil Spector. It's about Al Pacino, and the way actors carry their roles with them all across their careers. At the end of *The Godfather: Part III*, Michael Corleone's daughter is shot, and then, years later, we see him as an old man, sitting in the Italian sunlight, toppling off his chair dead. This is what happened in between: in a mansion that feels like a haunted house, caution has turned to paranoia, pride to megalomania, resentment to rage, intelligence to suspicion. All of Pacino's awful tics and jerks and shouting find their vessel, and you can't bear to miss a word he says.

5 ▪ **Mark Fisher, "Eerie Thanatos: Nigel Kneale and Dark Enlightenment," in *The Twilight Language of Nigel Kneale*, edited by S. S. Sandhu (Texte und Töne/Colloquium for Unpopular Culture)** In this collection dedicated to the British screenwriter Kneale's *Quatermass* TV and film project, which through the 1950s and 1960s pushed the theme of alien invasion ever more steadily as a threat not from outer space but from within human beings themselves, Fisher takes on the final, 1979 installment. Here the scientist Bernard Quatermass, now an old man after his battles to save the world in *The Creeping Unknown* (1955) and *Five Million Years to Earth* (1967), is bent on rescuing his daughter from a millenarian youth suicide cult: "In place of the hippie dream of a renewed Earth, his trance-intoxicated postpunk proto-crusties—the Planet People—long for an escape into another world, another solar system." The analogue in 1979, Fisher goes on, wasn't *Star*

Wars or *Close Encounters of the Third Kind* but Joy Division, in Manchester, acting out the collapse of the Industrial Revolution in the city where it was born: "The breathtaking audacity of *Unknown Pleasures*, after all, lay in its presumption that youth culture was essentially thanatoid. Maybe only the Stones had made that equation so starkly, but even they had only hinted at it, returning to more familiar hedonic territory. Joy Division were unremitting: a black-hole effect, an inversion and terrible turning back against itself of rock's exhilaration and energy."

6 ▪ **Kacey Musgraves,** *Same Trailer, Different Park* **(Mercury)** When a young performer receives ecstatic coverage all at once in toney outlets—in this case, "Kacey Musgraves's Rebel Twang" by Carlo Rotella in the *New York Times Magazine*, a rave in the daily *Times* by Jon Caramanica, a celebration on NPR by Will Hermes indistinguishable from a press release, with the adjective *beautiful* applied to conventional song structures and accompaniment—chances are there's less there than listening is likely to turn up. When Melissa Swingle called her country band Trailer Bride, you could hear that story in her voice; all you hear in Musgraves's is confidence, as a stance or a marketing strategy. Musgraves has staked out a position as a fearless opponent of country-music piety ("Ms. Musgraves's assault is full-frontal," Caramanica writes), but something else is going on. "If you save yourself for marriage you're a bore," Musgraves sings in "Follow Your Arrow," sounding sick of the hypocrisy she's lived with all her life. "If you don't save yourself for marriage you're a whore"—"-ibble person," she dribbles off. Cool way to say what you mean while playing by the rules of country music and mocking them at the same time, or flattery of the listener cool enough to get the joke, which is everyone? It's not the rebellion that sells the song, it's the coyness.

7 ▪ **Swamp Dogg,** *Total Destruction to Your Mind* **(Alive)** In 1970, Jerry Williams was a very odd, very funny, very catholic

soul singer who sang protest songs—his, Joe South's, whatever moved him. He sang about racism, pollution, alienation, and he never held still; with his crying voice and a lot of wah-wah guitar, he could make the corniest conceit into a true heartbreaker. "Synthetic World" is convincing simply on the basis of its melody, but "The World Beyond," a very slow ballad about nuclear holocaust, takes every cliché to the edge of tragedy. A man dreams about a little boy listening as his father tells him "of the world that used to be." But the father never says a word. The song is all the boy's questions, and each one is more painful than the one before it, sometimes less for the words ("Did concrete cover the land? / And what was a rock 'n' roll band?") than for Williams's voice, so deep with a plea for understanding, comfort, physical contact, a random smile, that you want to reach through the speakers and tell him it will be OK. Except he's already convinced you it won't be, and that you can't reach him: "What was a dog, and what was a shoe?"

8 ▪ **John Parish,** *Screenplay* **(Thrill Jockey)** An album drawn from pieces composed for various contemporary movies (*Sister, Little Black Spiders, Plein Sud*), but that's not how it plays. What you're hearing is the soundtrack to an imaginary European film noir set in the mid-'60s—maybe the 1965 *Symphony for a Massacre*, which has disappeared so completely it might as well be imaginary. You watch your movie as you listen, wondering which of the characters you've cast will make it to the end.

9 ▪ **Nicolas Rapold, review of** *Love and Honor* **(New York Times, March 21)** "The setting is that tragic time in our nation's history" when "federal law apparently mandated the playing of 'Magic Carpet Ride.' Predictable consequences unfold when . . ."

10 ▪ **Daniel Wolff, "Postcards of the Hanging,"** *Oxford American* **(spring)** The best art criticism I've read in ages: a short, plainly written walk-around in Bob Dylan's "Desolation Row," teasing out why the end of the song is the beginning and the begin-

ning the end—and why it is, like so many other tunes that seem like something else ("Bob Dylan's 115th Dream," "Highlands," "Ain't Talkin'"), a protest song. "A bluesy harmonica replaces the voice. It smears across the other instruments, almost knocking the lead guitar off-rhythm. Like a blackout after a string of scenes. Or like speech when speech doesn't work anymore."

1 ▪ Eleanor Friedberger, "I Am the Past," from *Personal Record* (Merge Records) The song doesn't just get under your skin, it seems to emerge from under your skin, a memory lost a lifetime ago, but somehow now speaking in its own, full voice. On her second solo album, Friedberger is bright, light, taking pleasure from the softly bouncing melody, the muted trombone, the skipping flute, letting the darker shadows of her character—alluring, beckoning, irresistible, unnameable and unknowable—rise up and disappear. Is the sprite really singing only a nursery rhyme, as she says before she turns into something else? You could play this song all day long and not get to the bottom of "I am the past. . . . You have no idea what happened before me"—of the way Friedberger floats through the words, turning them into a wave goodbye, Audrey Hepburn, her hair in a scarf, in a skiff, smiling as she slips over the horizon.

2 ▪ Jo Jackson, lettering; Chris Johanson, pictures; cover art for *Last Kind Words 1926–1953* (Mississippi Records, 2006) This collection of blues and gospel, an out-of-print LP from a few years ago, is named for and leads off with Geeshie Wiley's 1930 "Last Kind Words Blues," a song that carries the singer from a man's death to her own, and takes the uncanny as a walk down the street. The sleeve shows the walk down the street. It's a colorful folk-art grid of a pleasant, sunny, orderly American place, and all the people going from here to there, looking out the window, sitting on the pavement, and what they're saying, what they're thinking. Back cover, in a neighborhood of apartment houses: "I am like some kind of a log rolling." "That's ok is it a fish I don't know what the hells going on anymore." "It is hard to leave you." "Death is only a dream." "Ding dong." "It was so careless so very careless." "I'm going." "I see you." Front cover, downtown: "That is no way to get along don't now." "Don't let nobody turn you round." "Money can't buy your soul." "Salvation." "No kind words nowhere." "Death is only a dream." It's a portrait of nearly complete isolation (a woman on the phone saying, "I called you this morning" might be talking to an actual person, or leaving a message), each phrase its own kind of last word, with no sense that anyone is listening, and most of the music—from Blind Willie and Kate McTell, the Mississippi Moaner, Robert Wilkins, Lulu Jackson, Cannon's Jug Stompers—falls just short.

3 ▪ Lightning Dust, *Fantasy* (Jagjaguwar) On a third album, Amber Webber and Josh Wells let their music float just off the ground, the sometimes-harsh consonants or quick shifts in tone from *Lightning Dust* (2007) and *Infinite Light* (2009) falling away like clothes. What's left is a kind of séance. Webber's voice—bigger than that of Mazzy Star's Hope Sandoval, less self-regarding than Lana Del Rey's, the closest analogue maybe Brit Marling's demeanor as the quietly terrifying cult leader in *Sound of My Voice*—hovers somewhere between life and death. It's not limbo, it's a country to explore. What happens there? People think they recognize each other as they pass in the air, but names arrive only in the mind after the other person has disappeared. How do people talk there? In incomplete sentences, with a tone that's unstable, that threatens to evaporate as you listen. With Cris Derksen's cello giving the music muscle and bone, it all comes to a head with "Agatha." It's just over four minutes long; depending on your mood, it can feel like nine, it can feel like two. It won't hold its shape, it won't hold still.

4 ▪ Anaïs Mitchell and Jefferson Hamer, "Tam Lin," from *Child Ballads* (Wilderland

Records) Deep down, this is the tale biding its time inside Lightning Dust's sound: a ghost lover makes a woman pregnant, then turns into a wolf, a bear, and a lion before he appears naked in her arms as himself. In the full text of the ancient ballad, it's because he's cursed by a fairy; in Mitchell and Hamer's version, as they explained on the Scott Simon program on NPR, getting rid of the supernatural lets in the subconscious—the real home of fairies and ghosts. Mitchell steps through the song as if she's walking on water lilies, alive to the thrill of telling the best bedtime story in the world.

5 ▪ Rihanna, "Stay" (SRP) It was stunning on *Saturday Night Live* months ago. On the radio, played constantly, the daring of the performance, its challenge to everything around it—the refusal of melisma, the singer not owning the words but letting them capture her, almost no accompaniment but a simple, chording piano—stands out so plainly you can hear the more extreme record the singer, the writers, and the producers might have wanted to make: Rihanna, a melody, a lyric, and absolutely nothing else.

6 ▪ *Twenty Feet from Stardom*, directed by Morgan Neville (Tremolo Productions) A documentary about black female backup singers that owes its life to producer Gil Friesen, who died last December. Darlene Love is the heroine, but every woman here reads from her own book. Most confounding is Lisa Fischer, so wrapped up in her own language as she hums and scats into a microphone today, so one-dimensional as she tried for a solo career in the 1970s with the likes of Crosby, Stills, Nash and Young's "Southern Man." Most dignified, and the most fun, is Merry Clayton, talking about the third verse of "Gimme Shelter." It's the middle of the night in Los Angeles, and the phone rings—there's some group, "The Rolling—the Rolling Somethings," they need a singer. "They picked me up with silk pajamas on," she says, "a mink coat, and a Chanel scarf." "I didn't know her from Adam," Mick Jagger says; he still can't be-

lieve she showed up in curlers. She can't believe what she's supposed to sing. "I said, what? 'Rape—murder—it's just a *shot* away'?" They run through it once. Jagger asks if she'll do another take. "So I said to myself," Clayton says—and you can see her setting her mouth, tensing her body—"I'm going to do another one—I'm going to blow them out of this room." You hear the naked track, just her in dead air; you hear how she did it, her voice breaking, the near-stop just after the last "it's" in "It's just a shot away" that makes all the difference. And it's not even her best story. "Many years ago, when I was singing with Ray," she says of her time as one of Ray Charles's Raelettes, "I saw this guy *contorting* in the front row of the concert. I'm saying to the rest of the girls through my teeth, 'Who *is* that guy? What's *wrong* with him?'" She ended up singing behind Joe Cocker, too.

7 ▪ *The Company You Keep*, directed by Robert Redford, written by Lem Dobbs (Voltage Pictures, 2012) Thirty years after a Weatherman robbery that left a bank guard dead, the whole crew comes up from underground as Redford crisscrosses the country to get Julie Christie to clear his name. It's a good movie. At seventy-one, Christie is Friedberger's "I Am the Past" in the flesh; she has a pull the woman in *Billy Liar, Darling*, or even *Don't Look Now* only hinted at. And what's altogether remarkable, what keeps the story clean, what keeps it whole, is that there is no soundtrack-of-their-lives. No "It's Alright, Ma (I'm Only Bleeding)." No "Turn! Turn! Turn!" No "War." No "Bad Moon Rising." Not one song.

8 ▪ *The Canyons*, directed by Paul Schrader, written by Bret Easton Ellis (IFC Films) A New Poverty Row Productions project, starring a glass house high in the L.A. hills and rotting cinemas in abandoned strip malls. "About kids who got in line for a movie and the theater closed, but they stayed in line anyway, because they had nowhere else to go," Schrader says—and a Los Angeles where film culture consists of people in their twenties with money from

their parents financing "run-of-the-mill slasher movies in Arizona." Starring Lindsay Lohan, who goes all out, and porn star James Deen, who's believable until he has to kill someone, which he didn't really have to do.

9 ■ **Levon Helm, "Kingfish" (Rollingstone .com)** A clip from the documentary *Ain't in It for My Health: A Film About Levon Helm.* On *Electric Dirt*, the Randy Newman tribute to Huey Long seemed like a setpiece about two professional Southerners. Here it's so relaxed, the singer as satisfied as the listener, and the song something Helm could have been singing since he was ten.

10 ■ **Julie Bosman, "Judging 'Gatsby' by Its Cover(s)," the *New York Times* (April 25)** Boycott independent bookstores? In a story about new editions of *The Great Gatsby*— that is, about which stores are stocking only the Baz Luhrmann movie tie-in with Leonardo DiCaprio on the cover (Walmart) and which only the one with the original spooky-eyes art—Kevin Cassem of McNally Jackson, a beloved independent in New York, told Bosman that the movie version was beyond the pale: "'The Great Gatsby' is a pillar of American literature, and people don't want it messed with. We're selling the classic cover and have no intention of selling the new one." Bosman apparently caught the genteel fascism in Cassem's attitude; she asked him "whether the new, DiCaprio-ed edition of 'Gatsby' would be socially acceptable to carry around in public." "I think it would bring shame to anyone who was trying to read that book on the subway," Cassem said. So it's better not to read the book at all than to read it with the wrong cover? Or is Cassem going to be the literary Bernie Goetz?

SEPTEMBER 2013

1 ■ **Counting Crows, *Underwater Sunshine (Or What We Did on Our Summer Vacation)* (Collective Sounds/Tyrannosaurus)** After five top-ten albums on a tony major, the last in 2008, Counting Crows have put out a set of covers on their own label, some

of them from little-known or never-heard bands they came up with in Berkeley in the late 1980s and early '90s. "Every last bit of it," singer Adam Duritz writes, "felt utterly unique and every last bit of it was being repeated somewhere else, lived by somebody else, experienced by a thousand 'someone else's' in places all over like Minneapolis and Seattle and Boston and New York City and, of course, in a little town called Athens, Ga., not to mention London and Dublin and Glasgow." As in those words, and as in all of Counting Crows' best work, Duritz is sentimental, nostalgic, pleading, shameless; he wears his heart on his sleeve while the band, especially guitarists Dan Vickrey and David Immerglück, do their best to tear it off and throw it around the room. It becomes clear that with no period affectations, no genre inflections, Duritz is a soul singer; he sings to plumb the depths. Whether on Kasey Anderson's 2010 "Like Teenage Gravity" or Fairport Convention's 1969 "Meet on the Ledge," he demands the songs explain themselves to him—why this word leads to that one, why the melody curves away from him when he thought he had it in his grasp, why the song cries out for something he can't give but the musicians can, must— and the only way to make the songs do that is to sing them. It happens most acutely with Dawes's 2010 "All My Failures." In the original, the vocal is thin to the point of preciousness; you can hear the singer listening to himself. You can hear vanity, the way the song may not need you at all— and, for that matter, you don't necessarily believe the singer believes he ever failed at anything. Counting Crows pushes hard from the start, and in the play that's instantly under way, Duritz is a witness—to his own failures, sure, but also to yours. And then you are a witness to his, and to your own. And then you play it again, wondering why it sounds so good.

2 ■ **Philip Kerr, *Prague Fatale* (Penguin)** There are probably a number of reasons Kerr wrote this book, the eighth Bernie

Gunther thriller, this one set in Berlin and Prague in 1941: to keep the series running, to fool around with an Agatha Christie parody that turns out to be too self-parodying for its own good, and—with a few pages on a dank room, a woman's head, and a Nazi's foot on a basin that are so harrowing you wish you could stop reading—to finish the argument over whether or not waterboarding is torture.

3 ▪ **Keith Richards on Robert Johnson, from "Love and War Inside the Rolling Stones,"** *Rolling Stone* **(May 23)** "Robert Johnson, there's fear there, yeah. A fear of what? If you've faced fear yourself, you want to tell other people that it's faceable. There's no point in ignoring it. That's an element of the expression in what we've done, in, say, 'Gimme Shelter.' Fear is just a viable element, an emotion to use in a song as any other emotion."

4–5 ▪ **Tom Jones,** *Spirit in the Room* **(Rounder)** In Jones's gnarled hands, Leonard Cohen's 1988 "Tower of Song" is so pure in tone it can make you think of the Tower of Babel before God scattered the single human language into thousands: it's that gorgeous. His version of Blind Willie Johnson's 1930 "Soul of a Man" has its feet in the earth. But too much of the album misfires: "Just Dropped In" isn't half as threatening as First Edition's 1967 original, where the parenthetical that Jones's titling omits brought the song home even before it started: "(To See What Condition My Condition Was In)." The world doesn't need another pious journey to the grave of the "Lone Pilgrim." As Charles Taylor reports, the real story may be playing out onstage: "On May 18, at New York's Bowery Ballroom, Jones opened the show with Cohen's song and here it was a declaration of principles, Jones's astounding confidence a statement of a craftsman's undiminished pride in the face of time. In the 100 minutes of the show he did only one hit, 'The Green Green Grass of Home,' and that tucked into the encore. Jones covered the jubilant spiritual 'Didn't It Rain' but sounded as if he were powerful enough to take sustenance

from the desert, which is why it made sense when he sang about trees springing from rock. No longer needing to prove himself as a showman, Jones now seems to care only about proving himself to the music, which is why the peak of the show—an unexpected version of George Jones's 'He Stopped Loving Her Today'—hit with the quiet devastation of Sinatra's 'Cottage for Sale' or Dolly Parton's 'Down from Dover,' songs that, a few lines in, you don't know whether you'll have the strength to get through. A story of devotion unto death, Jones made it a memorial for Jones's great, ragged career, and made the devotion of the man in the song for the woman he has lost the story of his own dedication to the music before him."

6 ▪ **Barack Obama, speech at National Defense University, Fort McNair (Washington, D.C., May 23)** At one point in Barack Obama's lucid defense of his administration's terror war policies—when he got to the congressional refusal to permit the closing of Guantánamo—Medea Benjamin of Code Pink broke in from the audience: "Excuse me, Mr. President—" "Let me finish, ma'am," he said. They went back and forth, his "To the greatest extent possible, we will transfer detainees who have been cleared to go to other countries" answered by her "—prisoners already. Release them today." His statements, her numbers. The crowd clapped for the president to show which side it was on—but there was nobody dragged from the room, held in protective custody, arrested for disorderly conduct, all of the presidential thuggery so familiar from the Reagan and Bush presidencies that when it doesn't happen you think you must have missed something. "I'm willing to cut the young lady who interrupted me some slack," Obama said, "because it's worth being passionate about." If that was meant to mollify her, it didn't work. She would not quit—and finally the president backed off and, for nearly a minute, waited as Benjamin replaced his speech with hers. He ended with a Norman Rockwell painting—one that had, no doubt, been

painted in advance, with one square erased at the last minute and filled in on the spot: "Our victory against terrorism won't be measured in a surrender ceremony at a battleship, or a statue being pulled to the ground. Victory will be measured in parents taking their kids to school; immigrants coming to our shores; fans taking in a ballgame; a veteran starting a business; a bustling city street; a citizen shouting her concerns at a president."

7 ▪ **The Trajectory of Cinema, #746.** 1942: *Les visiteurs du soir*, directed by Marcel Carné: "Two strangers dressed as minstrels . . . arrive at a castle in advance of court festivities—and are revealed to be emissaries of the devil, dispatched to spread heartbreak and suffering. Their plans, however, are thwarted by an unexpected intrusion: human love" (Criterion.com). 2013: *The History of Future Folk*, directed by John Mitchell and Jeremy Kipp Walter: "Sent to earth to plan for a future invasion, a space alien (Nils d'Aulaire) lands in Brooklyn and instead decides to become a bluegrass musician" (*New York Times*, May 3).

8 ▪ **Felice Brothers, "Dream On," from** *God Bless You, Amigo* (thefelicebrothers.com) The Felice brothers are from the Catskills, not another planet, but they did form their bluegrass band in Brooklyn—and over five albums they have never come up with anything more affecting than this rewrite of the now almost 120-year-old Stagger Lee ballad. Most often it's been a celebration of the African American badman, sometimes it's been a cautionary tale, but rarely if ever has it been a dream of regret. The music moves like a quietly turning stream, carrying the killer farther and farther away from the life he could have lived if, just that once, he hadn't pulled his gun. At the same time, the dream pulls back, so that you see Stagger Lee in the moment before his act, seeing all the way into the half-life he will live: the half-life of exile and prison, the half-life of a real person, one Lee "Stag" Shelton, who disappeared into legend years before he actually died; you can imagine him forgetting his own name.

9 ▪ **Moreland & Arbuckle, 7 *Cities* (Telarc)** A song cycle about Coronado's search for the Seven Cities of Gold on the band's own Kansas home ground—but you don't need any backstory to respond to the muscle and heft on this album, especially the broken-shackles guitar on "Bite Your Tongue," the bursting harmonica on "Time Ain't Long," or to realize that the group's whole reason for being might be to set a scene where covering "Everybody Wants to Rule the World" would make perfect, glorious sense.

10 ▪ **"Izzy Young Reads Bob Dylan's Unpublished Poem 'Go Away You Bomb'"** (soundcloud.com) In 1963, Izzy Young, proprietor of the Folklore Center in New York, asked various people for contributions to a book of anti-war poems that was never published; this year, he traveled from his home in Sweden to auction off what Bob Dylan came up with: "Go Away You Bomb." To a small crowd, Young read it out, sounding more like Allen Ginsberg than anyone else. At first it was laughably phony, or so phony you were supposed to be in on the joke: "My good gal don't like you none. . . . I don't like it none too good." Then there were a few lines about how the bomb was bad. Then it got clever: "'orrible. You're so 'orrible the word drops its first letter and runs." And then it went elsewhere, as the writer turned himself into his own enemy— be that the villains of "Masters of War" or John Wayne or Lyndon Johnson or even Cowboy Slim Pickens, yahooing his way to oblivion at the end of *Dr. Strangelove*, which wouldn't happen until a year later. "I wish that for just one time you could stand inside my shoes, and just for that one moment I could be you," Dylan sang two years later, when he had gone from Greenwich Village phenom to world face; empathy has always been the key to his songwriting, but the turn this doggerel takes is still a surprise. "I want that bomb," Dylan wrote, and Young read evenly, enjoying it as much as he might have flinched from it fifty years ago. "I want it hanging out of my pocket and dangling from my keychain. I want it

strapped to my belt buckle . . . I want that bomb. I want it sticking out of my mouth like a cigar . . . I want to get up in the morning and scare the day right out of its dawn. Then I walk into the White House and say, *Dig yourselves!*"

NOTE: *In my previous column, regarding the new film* Twenty Feet from Stardom, *I mistakenly attributed the performance of "Southern Man" to Lisa Fischer. It was by Merry Clayton. My apologies.—*G. M.

OCTOBER 2013

1–2 ▪ Stephen Burt, *Belmont: Poems* (Graywolf Press) and Breaking Circus, "Driving the Dynamite Truck" (Homestead, 1986) "Yes, another / poem about flowers and kids," Burt says early on in this collection, but the ruling themes are age and how to stave off cowardice—how to keep rage alive. "We have task force reports, // but no tasks, and no force" could be a sentimental definition of poetry as such, but that's not how it works here. Rather, it's a question: of course we have tasks, of course we have force, but what are they, and where is it? "You realize that you have become the person you are—/ not who you were, not who you want to be, / but something close to them, in exactly the way / the new low-intensity streetlights come close to the moon." It may all come to a head in two poems that could not be more different: the searing, all-but-evaporating "There," which can leave you stranded in abstraction and disconnection, and "In Memory of the Rock Band Breaking Circus." "We barely remember you in Minnesota we love // our affable Replacements," Burt, late of Macalester College, in St.Paul, writes of a mid-'80s Chicago and Minneapolis group—but Breaking Circus played "as if you knew you had to get across / your warnings against all our lives as fast / as practicable before roommate or friend / could get up from a couch to turn them off." It's that "them" that sticks: it's the warnings that had to be turned off, not merely a record. And while

it's impossible to hear the band's "(Knife in the) Marathon" today on its own terms, "Driving the Dynamite Truck" remains a weirdly balanced paean to destruction: a clipped, spoken vocal over a melody that comments on itself, a harsh, seemingly one-dimensional pulse that as it moves across the minutes picks up the back-and-forth dynamics of a Gang of Four record from five years before. There's no warmth, no flattery of the players or whoever might be listening.

3 ▪ David Lynch, *The Big Dream* (Sacred Bones) On Lynch's first album, *Crazy Clown Time*, you were listening to an old man who never got over high school—who could never get his pornographic fantasies of Sue and Darlene and Diane out of his head. Here the voice is more that of an old codger unwilling to bring anything into too tight a focus, and the record rides on its music. "The most significant event of the twentieth century?" Kristine McKenna asked Lynch back in the twentieth century. "The birth of rock 'n' roll," he said, and now, in a different language than he spoke in *Blue Velvet* or *Wild at Heart* or *Twin Peaks*, he's taking his place in that story. Like Nina Simone and the Stooges before him, he goes up against Bob Dylan's deadly "Ballad of Hollis Brown" as if it were a test, and from the first two words you know you're hearing about a real person, even if Dylan made him up.

4 ▪ "The Genoa Tip," *The Newsroom* (HBO, July 21) Jeff Daniels meets Emily Mortimer in a bar and she throws his drink into his lap. She's trying to argue with him when Willie Nelson's version of "Always on My Mind" comes on and Daniels turns his back, lost in the self-pity of the performance: "A hundred covers of this song," he says like a penitent contemplating the philosopher's stone, "and nobody sings it like him. Not even Elvis." And something tells you that, deep inside the scene, he knows he's lying, because Nelson gives himself and the listener a way out, and Elvis doesn't, because he's so gorgeously lying: he never thought of her once.

5 ▪ **Bob Dylan, "Suzie Baby," Midway Stadium, St. Paul, Minnesota (July 10, minnpost.com)** In a setting one attendee described as "totally Midwestern—when 'All Along the Watchtower' began, the train running past the stadium blew three perfect whistles"—Dylan went back to 1959. It was then that Buddy Holly's plane went down, on February 3, just days after Dylan (then Bobby Zimmerman of Hibbing, Minnesota) had seen Holly play in Duluth; that, the next morning, Bobby Vee, then Bob Velline, the singer for a just-past-fantasy Fargo Central High School band called the Shadows, answered a promoter's call for someone to fill in for Holly that night in Moorhead, Minnesota; that, in the summer, Zimmerman, calling himself Elston Gunn, briefly joined the Shadows on piano in North Dakota; that, in the fall, the renamed Bobby Vee and the Shadows went into the Soma Records studio in Minneapolis to record their first single, Vee's own "Suzie Baby." A subtle weave of doo-wop and rockabilly, it was a regional hit; picked up by Liberty Records, it made number seventy-seven on the national charts. Vee went on to become a teen idol, with six top-ten hits between 1960 and 1967, including the number one "Take Good Care of My Baby" and the gothic "The Night Has a Thousand Eyes"; by 1970 he was off the charts for good. Bob Dylan went on to become Bob Dylan; in his *Chronicles, Volume One*, he writes affectionately of taking the D train from Greenwich Village to the Brooklyn Paramount in 1961 to see Vee "appearing with the Shirelles, Danny and the Juniors, Jackie Wilson, Ben E. King, Maxine Brown," and more. He went backstage: "I told him I was playing in the folk clubs, but it was impossible to give him any indication of what it was all about." Last year, Velline, now seventy, having reclaimed his given name in 1972 with a singer-songwriter album called *Nothin' Like a Sunny Day*, announced he had Alzheimer's; this night in St. Paul he was in the audience to hear Dylan, seventy-two, dedicate his song to him. "I've played all over the world, with all kinds of people, everybody from Mick Jagger to Madonna. I've been on the stage with most of those people," Dylan said musically. "But the most beautiful"—or did he say "meaningful"?—"person I've been on the stage with is a man who's here tonight, who used to sing a song called 'Suzie Baby.' I want to say, Bobby Vee is actually here tonight." With border-town guitar underlying every phrase, the tune came forth so delicately, suspended in time, as if Dylan, walking on eggshells and not cracking a single one, were glancing back to the past not from the present moment but from well into the future, where the song was, against all odds, with Velline dead, Dylan dead, still sung.

6–7 ▪ **Alfred Hayes, *In Love* (1953) and *My Face for the World to See* (1958) (New York Review Books)** These two short novels, the first set in Manhattan, the second in Los Angeles, might remind a reader of a John O'Hara story, Nathanael West's *The Day of the Locust*, Jean Rhys's *After Leaving Mr. Mackenzie*, Ross Macdonald's *The Chill*, but soon comparisons burn off, the settings float away, and you are in a swamp of sexual obsession where all places and all values melt down to worthless egotism: clenched fists or suicide. "There was nobody anywhere I could miss enough for it to matter and the terrible thing for me was that even when I missed them I knew it was not important and that nothing had been really lost for me," says the man in *In Love*. "That was why she wanted it to be over. That was why she had gone back to him"—cue Elvis Presley, "Always on My Mind." The books feel much longer than they are, because they are so dense, and their density comes from a relentless self-questioning, the first-person narrators locking themselves into their own torture chambers, making themselves talk, and never giving up everything, because then the torturer would turn away in disgust.

8 ▪ **Michèle Bernstein, *The Night* (Book Works)** Clodagh Kinsella's translation of a novel first published in Paris in 1961 as *La nuit* gives full purchase to the unflinching coldness inside this superficially cool

parody of the nouveau roman hiding inside a parody of *Les liaisons dangereuses* inside a parody of the author's life with her then husband, Guy Debord. In a new preface, Bernstein writes that, as a situationist and a member of "the lumpensecretariat," she wrote strictly for money. "Lots of fashionable novels came my way," she says. "I saw how I could write one that would immediately satisfy editors whilst deploying all the rules of the game. The protagonists would be young, beautiful and tanned. They'd have a car, holiday on the Riviera (everything we weren't, everything we didn't have). On top of that, they'd be nonchalant, insolent, free (everything we were). A piece of cake." The cynicism shapes the characters, who revel in it, until it turns into nihilism, and then Bernstein lets them walk away, if they can. "For three weeks, Léda will sing in a cabaret near the Opéra: just long enough so that she isn't forgotten, and can maintain her artistic reputation. Afterwards she'll want to take a role in a film in Japan, and she'll plan on taking Hélène, so they can eat raw fish together and assimilate a trimillennial culture. Hélène will write a letter to Bertrand, who will never reply. Waiting for Léda, she'll head off alone on a health retreat in an isolated farmhouse in Provence. And then later she'll die, on the way home, not far from Hauterives, where Postman Cheval's Palais Idéal is an essential detour, at the wheel of a Porsche that will coil around a plane tree, as generally happens with this type of car in such encounters." Bernstein and Alfred Hayes would have had fun killing a bar together.

9 ▪ **Lady Gaga, "The Star-Spangled Banner," Gay Pride Rally (New York, July 28, YouTube)** Two days after the Supreme Court struck down the central section of the Defense of Marriage Act in *United States v. Windsor*, Lady Gaga appeared as an American version of Marianne, cool as an iceberg in a flaring black dress, holding a small rainbow flag. "My LGBT fans and friends always said to me, I knew Lady Gaga *when*. Well," she said, gesturing at the crowd, "look who the star is now! Now I get to say that I knew *you* when. Now I get to say I knew you when you suffered. When you felt unequal. When you felt there was nothing to look forward to. I knew you then—and I knew you when, but I really know you now." Then she sang ten Super Bowls' and four Inaugurations' worth of the national anthem a cappella, with all of the blessings of the song in the full, clear tone of her voice and all of the war the song now celebrates in the ferocity in her face.

10 ▪ **Ruby Ray, *From the Edge of the World: California Punk, 1977–81* (Superior Viaduct)** Some of Ray's photographs are typical musicians' poses that anyone could have caught. But slowly the apocalyptic tinge in the title begins to pay off. Faces darken. Suspicion rises off of them like steam from the ground. There's a sense of calm, and you can begin to feel as if you were watching a movie with the sound turned off, which in turn gives the impression that everything is happening in slow motion. A picture of Mick Jones of the Clash, leaping across a San Francisco stage in a posture of pure rock cliché, momentarily breaks the mood, because he's acting like a star, his movement choreographed by people he's never met, and in the best pictures here that's not even a possibility: as in *Greg Ingraham (The Avengers)*, you see people doing what they can to be insolent and free in a low-ceilinged room made of grime, heat, glare, and a queer sort of anonymous urgency most of all.

NOVEMBER–DECEMBER 2013

1–2 ▪ *Radio Silence: Literature and Rock and Roll*, **issues 1 and 2, edited by Dan Stone** Published in the form of a literary quarterly, but with a design that promises both seriousness and surprise, this Bay Area journal is something people have been waiting for for fifty years: writing in, through, beside, around, and about music, where the first criterion is writing. There is Fitzgerald sharing pages with Geoff Dyer. There's Ted Gioia trying to bury the myth of Robert

Johnson selling his soul to the devil and finding that it can't be done; there is Jim White trying to explain to an old man that a character in a Cormac McCarthy novel isn't real, only to find Suttree's ghost tapping him on the back. There is Rick Moody, who apparently never met a question he didn't already know the answer to. But favorites or their opposites are not the point. What it is is a radical overturning of the whole notion of what music is, what it's for, where you find it, where it goes, and one issue contains not a hint of what another one might have to offer.

3 ■ **A mother takes her five-year-old daughter to see "PUNK: Chaos to Couture" at the Metropolitan Museum of Art, as related by Deborah Freedman (New York, August 14)** Daphna Mor: "This fashion breaks the rules. They did things that other people thought were ugly, provocative—" Alona Mor Freedman: "I like acupuncture fashion!" Daphna: "It is not acupuncture, it is punk." Alona [*excited that she is wearing tights and a pink shirt herself, and pointing to a contemporary dress inspired by punk*]: "Ima, this is not acupuncture—it is too pretty." Daphna: "I know! This one is not real punk, and anyway—it is not acupuncture, it is punk. Acupuncture is what your uncle does with the needles." Alona: "Ah, they didn't use needles in punk?" Daphna: "They did, but a different kind . . ."

4 ■ **Typhoon, *White Lighter* (Roll Call Records)** This massed and layered music from Portland, Oregon—eleven band members are named—isn't going to reveal itself quickly. Moodily considering the fate of the universe, Kyle Morton sings with unlimited self-importance—"Every star is a possible death," he announces at the start of one number, and then, singing sometimes from behind where the song seems to be, from one state over, from years before it was written, he turns a tone that at first felt pompous into pure urgency. The music might be taking place in the sky—and then, near the end of a song, female voices come in and pull the rug out from under the whole edifice. The big voice is replaced by a little

one—high voices, sometimes unnaturally high, Betty Boop after she's seen it all and is ready to tell at least some of what she knows. And then the record begins to speak in its own tongues. There's a banjo passage in "Possible Deaths" that can stop you cold with its embodiment of regret; doo-wop chords at the beginning of "Prosthetic Love" that promise a sweetness the song turns away from as soon as you feel its pull. Again and again, there's a sense of something missing, something withheld. You're almost there, you can practically touch it, and then you're not sure that what you heard was there at all. "The Lake" might be the most compelling number; certainly it's the loveliest. But it only suggests how bottomless the pools at the heart of these songs are.

5 ■ **Aimee Bender, "Americca," from *The Color Master* (Doubleday)** A story about a household where gifts arrive out of nowhere—"We've been backwards robbed," says one daughter. With an ending set precisely to the rhythm of "Ode to Billie Joe."

6 ■ **Hugh Laurie on *The Colbert Report* (Comedy Central, August 5)** It began with Stephen Colbert taunting Laurie about his professed love for the blues as opposed to the more-appropriate, for an Englishman, Gilbert and Sullivan: "Do you have to live the blues to play the blues—'cause I always heard [*in a growly whisper*] *You gotta live the blues—to play the blues!*" Laurie: "Well, obviously I'm going to say, nooooo, because that's the sort of position I'm in." Colbert: "You're an international star, who was until last year the highest paid man in a drama. OK? That's not exactly sharecropping." Laurie: "No, you're absolutely right. I was handsomely compensated." Colbert: "And a handsome man as well." Laurie: "Well, thank you for that. But here's what I would say. My point is that to me this music—I would hate for this music to be just put in a box of a sort of sociological category of American folk music that is only—it only has meaning because of the experience and the period from which it grew. I think of this music as high art, as high as some bloke singing *Don Giovanni* down the road."

7 ▪ **Walter Mosley, *Little Green* (Double-day)** It's 1967 in Los Angeles and Easy Rawlins is looking for a young black man who has gotten mixed up with hippies and acid. In a commune he meets a runaway who sleeps outside a window and calls herself Coco. She doesn't seem to notice or care that he's black. She doesn't seem to notice or care that she's naked. The detective listens to her talk, watches as she smiles, and for the first time in the ten novels that have tracked Rawlins's secretive life from just after the Second World War to now, he is face-to-face with something he wasn't prepared for, and doesn't understand. It's a queasily thrilling tale as it unfolds: he believes, at least for a moment, that he is glimpsing the fresh green breast of a new world, and, for a moment, so do you.

8 ▪ **Girls Names, *The New Life* (Slumber-land Records)** A Belfast dream-pop four-piece, with, as it happens, only one girl's name in its lineup, and that's appropriate. There are words in guitarist and singer Cathal Cully's songs, but sometimes there don't have to be, and at their most effective—"Projektion," elegant, unpretentious Old World surf music—the occasional human-voice sounds are just another instrument. You can hear Barbara Gogan's Passions, from London, and the Young Marble Giants, from Cardiff, in the late 1970s; the Chantays' "Pipeline" from 1963; but most of all Alphaville, that lovely, bitter German synth combo from the mid-1980s, whose "Forever Young" has so far lived forever at high-school graduations. Girls Names lives in a more-abstract forever.

9 ▪ **Crockett Johnson, *Barnaby, Volume One: 1942–1943*, edited by Philip Nel and Eric Reynolds (Fantagraphics Books)** Johnson is best known for the children's book *Harold and the Purple Crayon*, in which a round-faced, apparently bald little boy creates the world with a single crayon—just like God. But that little boy first appeared, in the early 1940s, in a daily grown-ups' comic strip in the pages of the left-wing New York tabloid *PM*, as Barnaby. He lives in a nice house with his nice parents in a nice suburb. His world is also inhabited by a beer-drinking, cigar-smoking, permanently hungry, profoundly irritating fairy godfather in a pork-pie hat and gossamer wings named Mr. O'Malley, who manages to fuck up every conceivable patriotic, virtuous, charitable, unselfish, necessary wartime endeavor—a neighborhood blackout, a scrap-metal drive—while somehow maintaining an uncanny ability to help Barnaby expose Nazi spy rings. Until, at the end of this big, smiling collection, the House Un-American Activities Committee comes along, and O'Malley, who previously sabotaged a mayor's radio speech with a Duke Ellington record, takes over with an investigation of a man in a red suit. It's wonderful the way Barnaby ignores his parents' attempts to humor him about his delusion, to talk him out of it, to prove that fairies don't exist, and lucky it's the '40s, not the '50s, when they would have packed him off to a child psychiatrist. There's no way Jack Kerouac, along with every other self-consciously cool person in New York, wasn't reading this. O'Malley turns into Neal Cassady, the guy who's not quite human, who never shuts up, who drives you crazy, and who can make anything happen, just like that. There will be a *Volume Two*; in the meantime, there's also Nel's lively, inspiring *Crockett Johnson and Ruth Krauss: How an Unlikely Couple Found Love, Dodged the FBI, and Transformed Children's Literature* (University Press of Mississippi).

10 ▪ **Lester Chambers, "People Get Ready," Hayward Russell City Blues Festival, Hayward, CA (July 13):** For the record: on the day George Zimmerman was acquitted of murder, Chambers, seventy-three, of the Chambers Brothers, dedicated the Impressions song to Trayvon Martin, saying that if its composer, Curtis Mayfield, had been alive he might have changed the line "There's a train a-comin'" to "There's a change a-comin.'" Dinalynn Andrews-Potter, forty-three, then leaped onto the stage and knocked him to the ground. One week later, on August 19, Chambers, who had to cancel shows because of injuries

caused by the attack, announced that he would file a five-million-dollar suit against the city of Hayward, Andrews-Potter, the concert promoter, and those responsible for concert security, saying he was left unable to perform for at least the rest of the year—but his main complaint was that Andrews-Potter, who was charged with felony counts of assault and elder abuse, was not charged with a hate crime. Her attorney said she was a victim of post-traumatic stress disorder—and, NBC Bay Area reported, claimed that "the beat of the song triggered the attack." Presumably, if the case goes to trial, Andrews-Potter will have to name the song that caused her original trauma. And then, if there is any justice, at least in the realm of people coming up with really great excuses for horrible acts—and Andrew-Potter's is much better than the one Zimmerman's lawyer provided for him, charging that the unarmed Martin was indeed armed, "with a sidewalk"—whoever owns the copyright will be able to sue her. For libel. Or slander. Defamation. Loss of earnings due to fear that the song might cause harm to others. Or just for the pleasure of watching Rush Limbaugh, Sean Hannity, Laura Ingraham, Ann Coulter, Michael Savage, and others defend her defense. I mean, you can already hear them saying: *Have you ever heard "A Change Is Gonna Come"? I mean, really heard it?*

Thanks to Linda Mevorach, Deborah Freedman, and Charles Taylor

JANUARY 2014

1 ■ **Pearl Jam and Sleater-Kinney, "Rockin' in the Free World," Tampa, Florida, 2003 (YouTube)** This is no all-star jam. This is rock 'n' roll celebrating the human spirit, a good song, and itself. It's two bands touring together, but now one band, six men, three women, Janet Weiss hammering stand-up percussion next to Jack Irons's drums, Carrie Brownstein facing off with Stone Gossard, Mike McCready soloing joyously while Corin Tucker and Eddie Vedder throw verses

back and forth as if each is the other's all-time teen dream and they're going to make this senior prom last forever, even if the Neil Young number they're dancing to is really Carrie's bucket of blood.

2 ■ **Stanley Crouch, *Kansas City Lightning: The Rise and Times of Charlie Parker* (HarperCollins)** There's a moment in this stirring book when Crouch, homing in on the first Joe Louis–Max Schmeling fight, in 1936, links the three minutes of a prizefight round to the three minutes of one side of "a 78-rpm record, all a jazz band needed to make a complete musical statement." It's part of a plain and poetic argument about the effect of recording technology on both fighting and jazz. It's part of a rewriting of the legacy of Jack Johnson, the first black heavyweight champion, and of how he "almost instigated an interior ethnic riot" when "he chose to go through Harlem bragging about how much money he'd won by betting on the German." Page by page, the book is unpredictable before it's anything else. It ends in 1940, with Parker taking his first steps in New York, still a teenager, but the sense of an odyssey completed, the wind of history at one man's back as he begins to blow it out ahead of himself, is overwhelming.

3 ■ **Rosanne Cash, *The River and the Thread* (Blue Note)** A soul-music travelogue, taking in Memphis, Faulkner, Dockery Farms, the Civil War, Robert Johnson's gravesite, Bobbie Gentry's Tallahatchie Bridge, and Money, Mississippi, the town where Emmett Till was lynched and thrown into the river that runs under the bridge. You don't have to hear any of that; the words don't point to places on a map. What you hear is time passing.

4 ■ **Rachel Harrison, *Fake Titel* (D.A.P.)** An elegant catalog for an exhibition (beginning in Hannover, Germany, in 2013, and ending at the Municipal Museum of Contemporary Art in Ghent, Belgium, on January 4, 2014) most notable for a series of unflinchingly rough 2011–12 colored-pencil portraits of Amy Winehouse—Winehouse

as a Picasso model, or maybe a muse. Winehouse is juxtaposed with Picasso's harlequins, his Gertrude Stein, or his cubist nudes; as she seems to be using her handheld mike as a spray can to conjure *Guernica* out of the air, her own features crack and bend, one eye sliding below the other, her skin bruising in greens and purples. With her beehive seemingly bigger with each picture, her mouth bigger, she begins to resemble a rotting inflatable sex doll—or a junkie decomposing before she's even dead. Yet you are never free of Winehouse's presence, power, desperation, defiance, or need. The tension between her self-presentation as a cartoon and the tragedies enacted in her music is patent here—and finally, with Winehouse sharing an image with Marie-Thérèse Walter, you can see her not as some sort of doppelgänger for Picasso's women, models from life or specters from history, but as their voice.

5 ■ Body/Head, *Coming Apart* (Matador) From singer Kim Gordon, late of Sonic Youth, and guitarist Bill Nace, this is a fierce, sustained fun-house ride with the lights off. Over long stretches, sheets of noise fuse like concrete and then, as a rhythm builds or a melody opens before it disappears, they begin to crack. The music is all undertow. With the folk song "Black Is the Color (Of My True Love's Hair)" emerging at the end of more than thirteen minutes of "Black," you're somewhere in one of the Doors' half-improvised onstage versions of "The End" and Gordon's own harrowing "Shaking Hell," from Sonic Youth's first album, *Confusion Is Sex.* And you're not ready to leave.

6 ■ The Clash, *Sound System* (Sony Legacy) A box set packaged as a facsimile of the boom boxes people used to carry on their shoulders in the '80s, the monster contains the first five Clash albums, obscurities and rarities and B-sides, fanzines and posters and buttons, film clips and outtakes, early sessions and DVD footage of interviews and performances and videos. But not "This Is England," from *Cut the Crap*, the last Clash

album, in 1985, because that album, made after Joe Strummer and Paul Simonon kicked Mick Jones and Topper Headon out of the band, isn't supposed to exist, even if "This Is England" is the band's ethos, its mission, its triumph, and a confession of its failure: its "Streets of Laredo," its "I'm shot in the breast and I know I must die."

7 ■ The Libertines, "Don't Look Back Into the Sun" (2006), as crawl music for *Kill Your Darlings*, directed by John Krokidas (Killer Films) Running under the credits—and finally, a feeling of release. Release from the claustrophobia of the tiny little world created by Daniel Radcliffe's Allen Ginsberg, Dane DeHaan's Lucien Carr, Michael C. Hall's David Kammerer (a weird cross between his Dexter and David Fisher, his *Six Feet Under* character), Jack Huston's Jack Kerouac, and, most quietly and most deeply, as if playing out his own, almost-silent film within a film, Ben Foster's William Burroughs.

8 ■ Neko Case, *The Worse Things Get, The Harder I Fight, The Harder I Fight, The More I Love You* (Anti-) With Case's cool, clear tone—never a burr, a break, a hesitation—*fucking* as an adjective at first seems out of place. Until it comes up again, and you hear it as Case, on her solo albums so often swaddled in overwriting and decorative arrangements, singing in her own voice: her own tired, fed-up voice, the voice of someone who refuses to quit.

9 ■ Jay Z, *Picasso Baby: A Performance Art Film*, directed by Mark Romanek (HBO/YouTube) Not counting exit footage and credits, this six-minute movie, made from a six-hour performance at the Pace Gallery in New York, and most notable for Jay Z's dances with groupie-for-a-day Marina Abramović—not to mention an eclectic crowd of painters, gallery owners, impresarios, actors, schoolchildren, and film directors, all clearly having a great time—answered the question of what hip-hop, celebrity, and contemporary art have in common: they're forms of money. You get the feeling all of the people here could walk out of the gallery and into any other

place and buy whatever they want with the currency of their mere existence.

10 ▪ **Lou Reed, "Street Hassle" (1978), processional at a wedding in Beacon, New York (October 12)** The cellos and violas never sounded more glamorous, never sounded like more of a portent, but the setting didn't immediately match the music: could this actually be what it sounded like? Were they really going to walk down the aisle to *that*? A DJ faded down the song before the second verse, where a woman OD's and the rest of the people at the party throw her body out the door, after which Reed delivers a soliloquy for which he ought to be remembered as much as for anything else: "You know, some people got no choice / and they can never find a voice / to talk with that they can even call their own. / So the first thing that they see / that allows them the right to be, / why, they follow it. You know, it's called—bad luck." RIP, 1942–2013.

FEBRUARY 2014

1 ▪ **Lana Del Rey, "Young and Beautiful," in *The Great Gatsby*, directed by Baz Luhrmann (Warner Bros.)** I've seen this deeply empathetic translation of the novel—where you absolutely believe that people in the '20s were going wild for hip-hop: what *else* would they be dancing to?—every chance I've had (Paris, Berkeley, airplane), and I expect to be going back to it for years. I always see and hear something new, as with this song—gorgeous, but also acrid, like a rotting flower—or less the song itself, maybe, than the way it's threaded through the film, fading deeper into the background each time it surfaces, but never less than indelible, recasting whatever scene it inhabits, moving the characters closer to death each time.

2 ▪ **Finney Mo and His West Dallas Boys live at the River Club in Dallas, 1976 ("Finney Mo / River Club 2," YouTube)** He had the noticeable "Shake That Thing" in Texas in 1963, but this underwater performance from 1976 is worlds away from any sort of

conventional rock 'n' roll or R&B—it sounds like a secret tape Van Morrison kept as a magic lantern to rub when the spirit left him. The musicians slither along the riverbed; Finney rises every minute or so to call out what sounds like "blind robber blind" over and over. You realize there's going to be no story, except that the story—someone going nowhere, forever—is completely present in the slow scratching on the guitar, the thin, unspectacular sound of the saxophone. Does he really shout "Stackerlee!" at the end? The ordinariness of the life that's been described would be the real hell for the old legend.

3 ▪ **Neil Genzlinger, "Kids These Days: They're All Older Than 50" (*New York Times*, November 20, 2013)** On a wave of unfunny sitcoms based on putative adults acting like sniggering thirteen-year-olds (*The Millers*; *Brooklyn Nine-Nine*; *The Crazy Ones*; *Mom*; *Dads*; *Back in the Game*; *2 Broke Girls*; *The New Normal*): "Could it be payback for years of baby boomer boasting and self-glorification?

"Boomers have been boring every generation younger than they are for decades with their constant babble about Woodstock, Vietnam, flower power. They have, subtly or overtly, let every subsequent generation know that its music, books, movies and life experiences are inferior," Genzlinger writes. "The younger generations have choked this down quietly, biding their time. As these generations take over the making of television and become the desirable demographic for advertisers, boomerage characters are paying the price, and older-than-boomer ones are also being swept up in the retaliation frenzy, a sort of collateral damage. It's open season on anyone 55 and above.

"This is the ultimate revenge. Because while someday everything this older cohort holds dear will have been forgotten or undone by revisionist historians, television portrayals will live forever on DVDs and in cyberspace. A century from now, youngsters in history class will sum up the lives of everyone who had gray or graying hair in the second decade of the 21st century with: 'Oh, yeah; those were the people who were obsessed with their bowels and couldn't work a smartphone.' Then, after a pause, they'll add, 'Kind of sad, really.'"

Or, as Howard Hampton reported a week after Genzlinger's piece appeared, "I came upon a listing for Jon Anderson, formerly of Yes, playing a solo gig in Miami Beach—the early show, being 6 p.m. Immediately the *Seinfeld* episode came to mind: Jerry goes to dinner with his parents in Boca at 4:30 so they can get the 'Early Bird Special.' That's apparently where all the old Yes fans have retired . . . Pre-concert dinner with the Seinfelds and Costanzas: Frank Costanza: 'I'm tellin' ya, damn it, "Owner of a Lonely Heart" was the BEST THING THEY EVER DID!!' Morty Seinfeld: 'Get outta here, you're crazy, *Tales of Topographic Oceans* still rules!'"

4 ■ Angels in America, "The Corpse," from *Split Cassette* with Weyes Blood (Northern Spy) Scary, beautiful, with the mood pushed by the tinny sound of a woman laughing only seconds in, then electronically lowered male and female voices: the dreams of the undead. It goes on for nearly seven minutes, words taking shape only occasionally. Odd, decaying sounds trace melodies in washes of echo and distortion. Until a trackable rhythm— which in this context might as well be from a Disney cartoon—takes over after five minutes, you float on this music. At least one person has heard it as a perfect soundtrack to Michael Lesy's *Wisconsin Death Trip*; for me it's playing behind Charlotte Gainsbourg stamping naked through the blasted landscapes of Lars von Trier's *Antichrist*.

5 ■ Lady Gaga, "Do What U Want" with R. Kelly, from *Artpop* (Streamline/Interscope Records) Not as fierce on record as on *Saturday Night Live* last November—less abandoned, with less of a sense of drowning in pleasure, the pleasure you could see in her face of having made it to the top and knowing she belongs there, plus there's no aural equivalent of watching Gaga and

Kelly acknowledging each other as equal sex gods—but this may echo on the radio, in the ether, for a long time.

6–7 ■ Vania Heymann/Interlude, "Like a Rolling Stone" video (bobdylan.com) and Øyvind Mund of *Gylne Tider*, "Let It Be" video (sabotagetimes.com) Jay Lustig of New Jersey's *Star-Ledger* got it right on the Dylan production: "A concept right out of 'The Twilight Zone.' You're watching TV, but no matter what channel you turn to—a news show, a cooking show—whenever someone speaks, all you hear is Dylan singing 'Like a Rolling Stone.'" There's something faintly repulsive about it, something inhuman, something that would never occur in real life, like synchronized swimming. But the "Let It Be" video, a Norwegian tribute to '80s and '90s TV stars mouthing various renditions of the Beatles song as they're gathered on some computerized beach— what seems like scores of them, starting off, in some semblance of rationality, with the likes of Roger Moore, Jason Alexander, Josie Bissett, Corbin Bernsen, and George Wendt, then edging into the less-likely with a hideously mugging Katarina Witt, then going straight over the cliff with a demure Tonya Harding, identified as "Skater in Trouble" and wearing a T-shirt reading CAN YOU SEE ME NOW—is a horror of a very different order. At nearly six minutes it's an invitation to suicide: what other rational response is there to watching Philip Michael Thomas as the most embarrassing air-guitarist in creation? Or Judd Nelson doing nothing at all? Or Peter Falk brought back from the dead to stand on the beach with Kathleen Turner, Sheryl Lee, and Daryl Hannah, none of whom should ever have had to sink so low?

8 ■ Cat Power, Masonic Temple, Brooklyn (November 14, 2013) Eric Dean Wilson writes from New York: "It was a raw-nerve performance. Everything suggested a ritual undoing of the 2012 *Sun* album and its tour, which left Cat Power—aka Chan Marshall—awash in an electronic, beat-driven sound. Here she bounced between what she called a Craigslist-buy guitar and

a candlelit piano, and the shuffle caught the atmosphere of the night: halfway between a basement and a chapel. She flowed from song to song without any intentional break, except to adjust the monitor levels, which never satisfy her, or to ask the audience whether they worked in education. The audience clapped wildly at that, but Marshall insisted: 'I'm not talking about parents who have children—is anyone in education?' A few people laughed. When she didn't get an answer she picked up without any further comment, playing the neck of her guitar with one hand so it appeared to hover in midair while she crooned. She rambled broken anecdotes with no beginning or end, and suddenly spun herself and the audience into a trance. Without announcing her final song, she muttered a few unintelligible words, bowed, and was walking offstage before anyone realized it was over."

9 ■ David Cantwell, *Merle Haggard: The Running Kind* (University of Texas Press) A clear, unflinchingly critical hearing of the songs—that is, in Cantwell's pages they are creative acts, not real, disguised, or fake autobiography—and that lets the songs go anywhere: a subtle yet flesh-and-blood class analysis, an argument against the authenticity argument, and when the focus is precisely on how a song felt its way into its own skin, its own body, you always want more. "The recording Merle and his Strangers made of 'Hungry Eyes,'" Cantwell writes, "is a musical adjunct to, and the artistic equal of, 'Migrant Mother,' the photograph that Dorothea Lange took of Florence Thompson in 1936. The women in both works, Lange's 'Migrant Mother' and Haggard's 'Mama,' document an internal war between pride and inferiority, dignity and shame." If Cantwell often can't get music onto the page, he can make you need to hear every song he writes about.

10 ■ Sundown Songs, *Like a Jazz Band in Nashville* (Sundown Songs, 2008) This is a New Orleans street band that may or may not still exist: the flood song "Here It Comes," from their 2009 album *Far from Home*, might be their truest testament. But

the earlier album cuts more deeply. With irresistibly pretty acoustic guitar playing throughout, and sometimes a clumsy, strummed guitar that's just as evocative, it calls up an Old West people carry with them after the Old West is gone: "Let Em Talk" has the feeling of Butch Cassidy in a Wyoming bar sometime in the 1920s, or Neal Cassady in a bar in San Pedro in the 1990s, trying to get people to believe he's who he says he is. "I've stained the world, in ten thousand ways. / I've stained up your sofa, for ten thousand days," the guy testifies, holding himself up with both hands, as if that's enough work for anyone.

Thanks to Ashawnta Jackson,
Anna Witiuk, Ari Spool, and Luke Wiget

MARCH–APRIL 2014

1–2 ■ *The Rise and Fall of Paramount Records, Vol. 1* (1917–1932) (Third Man Records and Revenant Records) and the Bladensburg High School Video Jukebox (1959bhsmus-tangs.com/VideoJukebox.htm) The Paramount set calls itself a "cabinet of wonder," and it is. You pay your money, a large, elegant wooden box arrives in the mail, and you open it. You stick a thumb drive into your computer, and one of eight hundred songs, the most recent dating to 1927—volume two will appear later this year—begins to play. You finger a set of LPs, marveling at the labels. You glance through a big paperback discographical history. You pry open a heavy, clothbound volume and begin to follow the story of how a Wisconsin chair company figured out it could make money producing cheap records for people to play on its expensive phonograph cabinets, and how, after clueless executives set about recording anything with a pulse, a visionary African American producer and opera follower named Mayo Williams began to move the label into what was called race music—and then you begin to page through dozens and dozens of advertisements so daring, and at times so odd, you can't believe the music will live up to them. Such as one for Ethel Waters's 1922 "That Da Da Strain" ("It will shake you, it will make you, really go insane," wrote a couple of Tin Pan Alley tune-smiths, eager to get a dance-craze tune on the market even if they had to name it after a European art movement): "The Only Genuine Colored Record. Others Are Only Passing for Colored." The price is $400, which, compared to the recent Clash *Sound System* ($249.99 list) or Bob Dylan's *Complete Album Collection, Vol. 1* ($279.98), is not so much a bargain as a gift.

But there are all kinds of wonder cabinets, and the Bladensburg High School Video Jukebox—from the class of '59, culled from YouTube, also featuring just about eight hundred songs, not counting full-length oldies shows and countless more embedded videos—is free. You click the button that lets each selection "drop the coin right into the slot," as Chuck Berry put it, and then you have no idea where to begin, so you hit, say, Dion and the Belmonts' "I Wonder Why—THEN"—a 1958 TV clip with dance moves so complex they might have taken months to work out—and then the same song "NOW," from an oldies show, Dion and, let's say, two of the Belmonts, with hats or scarves hiding their bald heads, and singing with a soul, a yearning, an accumulation of decades of disappointments that the kids three decades before never would have believed, and with vocal dynamics you won't. And then you're off, lost in a labyrinth where, say, Senator Everett Dirksen's sonorous recitation "Gallant Men" rubs up against Johnny and Joe's "Over the Mountain." It's 1957 on Milt Grant's Record Hop, with two black teenagers lip-synching for an all-white dance floor and subtitles running on the screen, as if Johnny and Joe were singing in a foreign language, and then it's "FIFTY YEARS LATER" and piano notes open the doo-wop song, a song that was tragic even in its day, because you could hear, you could feel, that the boy and the girl singing would never get over that mountain, would never cross that sea, are so weighted with experience that when you see Johnny's white hair and white

mustache he looks as if he's grown into the song, that he's finally ready to say what it says.

3 ▪ **"Christopher Wool," Guggenheim, New York (October 25, 2013–January 22, 2014)** A rich, deeply tactile retrospective from the 1980s to the present. As you wind your way up the circular galleries, near the top you find what Wool calls his gray paintings, a pursuit he took up in the middle of the last decade. Most are untitled. Made partly with a spray-painter, they look like any city's urban scrawls, all loose lines reaching for the edges of rectangles and squares. You begin to notice what seems like over-painting, though it's the mark of a rag scrubbing away part of the image that has yet to come together, whiting out, or graying out, whatever cryptic message someone else has left before. Sometimes there are lighter, less-clear revisions, as if someone caught a hint of an idea, a message, and tried to bring it out, to make it talk. The graffiti language at the root of the work breaks down the apparent abstraction of the pieces: they refer to something specific, even if you can't locate it on a map. The pictures are big, unstable, unfixable, lucid, steely, and gorgeous, and the longer you look, the more you see. From 2005, the scrubbing of a piece is not so much an erasure as the creation of a cleared space, a new field of action to be occupied and then abandoned in turn, or even forgotten.

4 ▪ **John Chamberlain, *Pigmeat's E flat Bluesong* (1981), Dia Art Foundation, Beacon, New York (on long-term view)** Chamberlain made his first auto-parts sculpture in 1957; here there are twelve, from 1979 through 1988. It's David Cronenberg's *Crash* played out in single objects, but especially in this 72″ x 75″ x 61″ lump. With fenders wrapped around chrome side strips and remnants of grilles, with yellow dominating red, orange, and cream over splattered surfaces, more than any other piece spread out through a long, open gallery it was a believable auto-auto-assemblage: something that put itself together, either what you might have seen after two or three cars merged into one in a

single crash, or after Chamberlain rescued the thing from a compactor halfway through the job. What's so immediate about it, so real, is that still and fixed as the object is, speed is still present all through it. You can feel the rush that made this.

5 ■ *The Jacksonian*, **written by Beth Henley, directed by Robert Falls, the New Group, Acorn Theatre, New York (November 5–December 22, 2013)** A hotel drama set in Jackson, Mississippi, in 1964, with Ed Harris as a disgraced dentist, Amy Madigan as his disgusted wife, and Juliet Brett as their miserable teenage daughter, and featuring Bill Pullman as what Elvis would have ended up as if "That's All Right" had never gotten out of Memphis: an alcoholic bartender with a thing for jailbait who has no problem shooting a woman for a ring he doesn't even want and letting a black man go to the electric chair for it. "I was a performer for a while," he says under a huge pompadour, sideburns snaking down the sides of his face, but now his whole life is stage fright.

6 ■ **"Vermeer, Rembrandt, and Hals: Masterpieces of Dutch Painting from the Mauritshuis," Frick Collection, New York (October 22, 2013–January 19, 2014)** A small show of rarely seen works, starring *Girl with the Pearl Earring*, which despite its celebrity—you can buy a GIRL ON TOUR T-shirt with, just like a band T-shirt, all the exhibition dates listed on the back (starting in Tokyo, in 2012, finishing up this year in Bologna and the Hague)—you can still actually see. The painting is so luminous it burns off the haze of its publicity; there are countless unwritten books in the eyes. You sense that if you could touch the canvas, you'd feel flesh.

7 ■ *The Past*, **directed by Asghar Farhadi (Memento Films)** In a holiday season of movies whose nonstop *fuck yous* might as well be directed at the audience—*The Wolf of Wall Street* and *August: Osage County* are only the noisiest—this was displacing: a sophisticated picture about decent, intelligent people caught up in a dilemma they are incapable of resolving. Almost every scene brings a secret, or an untold story, but

the movie is like a set of Chinese boxes: inside each secret there's always another one, until the end. A man is about to tell a woman one last thing, you can feel that the film is a step away from turning into gimmickry, and she says stop—she doesn't want to know. For its realism, and its relief, it was the most satisfying movie moment of the year.

8 ■ *The Life and Death of Marina Abramović*, **directed by Robert Wilson, Park Avenue Armory, New York (December 12–21, 2013)** The first true scene opens on a room bare except for a very freaked-out young girl, her even more freaked-out grandmother, and a 1950s washing machine; it's explained that the Abramović household was one of the first in Belgrade to have one. As Paul Anka's "Diana" plays, the girl throws herself onto the machine and begins to kick her legs as if she were trying to swim on it. The grandmother turns her face to the audience and sends electricity through her already *Bride of Frankenstein* hair by the force of her eyes, which seem to be rolling around in her head like cherries in a slot machine. It was the most vivid, in-the-flesh equivalent of the man-made chicken sequence in *Eraserhead* I ever want to see.

9 ■ **Crooked Still, "New Railroad," from** *Shaken by a Low Sound* **(Signature Sounds, 2006)** Oscar Isaac has received universal praise for his performance of "Hang Me, Oh Hang Me" in *Inside Llewyn Davis*. Listen to that, and listen to this.

10 ■ **Maria Alyokhina of Pussy Riot, on her early release from prison under a new amnesty law (December 23, 2013)** "This is a lie."

Thanks to Doug Kroll, Reenee Gregg, Kathy and Larry Thompson, and John Rockwell

MAY 2014

1 ■ **Tacocat, *NVM* (Hardly Art)** Like Seattle's Fastbacks and Portland's All-Girl Summer Fun Band, this group from Longview, Washington—singer Emily Nokes, bassist Bree McKenna, drummer Lelah Maupin, guitarist Eric Randall—are boiling over

with the thrill of writing a song, making it into something that can be played, and discovering that as it happens you love the people you're playing with. The voice is jaded, the sound anything but, and the world that comes into view is a trick, but you can slip its grasp and take off—through the bubbling warmth of "You Never Came Back," the surge of "Bridge to Hawaii," so sweet you can't believe it still hasn't been built, and "Snow Day," which soars to the sun. "Crimson Wave" might be the door that flies open first. You don't have to catch that it's a protest against menstruation ("All the girls are surfin' the wave / surfin' the crimson wave today"): when Randall's whomping guitar solo kicks in it's just punk surf music, shooting the same curl as the Forgotten Rebels' unforgotten "Surfin' on Heroin." The song explodes with its own conceit, with the way there's absolutely no end to what you can find when you take an idea, a riff, a single pissed-off thought, and run with it—something like the tossed-off "Sew a scarlet letter on my bathing suit," or the matter-of-fact "There are communists in the summer house," a line that leaps out as such a perfect non sequitur that it doesn't even have to be a metaphor that can drop right back into the song. I love this band.

2–3 ■ **James Agee, *Cotton Tenants: Three Families*, with photographs by Walker Evans (Melville House Books) and Alana Nash, "Elvis as a Teen? See a Never-Before-Published Photo from His Hometown in Tupelo, Mississippi," *Vanity Fair.com* (January 8)** *Cotton Tenants* collects the recently discovered thirty-thousand-word essay that turned into Agee and Evans's 1941 *Let Us Now Praise Famous Men*. In contrast to the sweep and scope of that book, which rides the same American wind as *Moby-Dick* once the *Pequod* ships off, the piece—a never-printed 1936 assignment by *Fortune* magazine—pitches between fastidiousness and rage, coldly matter-of-fact summaries of infant mortality and flatly reported accounts of family economies, snide dismissals of individuals turned into types, and, for individ-

uals who for a moment escape all typology, an awestruck respect that Agee seems almost desperate to suppress. Agee never finds an even keel, because he doesn't want one. But Evans did want a stable perspective, a certain distanced, confident stance that allowed his subjects—men, women, children, their houses, their beds, their walls decorated with advertisements—to appear as both iconic and ordinary, as individuals and as objects, as poor people smashed by the cotton economy, and as art. It was this—as Agee, in the more than four hundred pages of *Let Us Now Praise Famous Men*, dove so far down into the lives he chronicled it's not clear he ever came up—that has allowed Evans's pictures to enter the common American imagination as images that were not made but found, and that allows you to see them everywhere, as if Evans's eye were not his at all but that of the country itself, dreaming its fractured, free-associating dream. For example: the 1936 picture made of the farmer and three children in Hale County, Alabama, that appears on the cover of *Cotton Tenants*, the man leaning with casual dignity against a support beam of his shack, the kids with their wet hair slicked back to look nice for the camera, and a recently surfaced photo, by an unnamed photographer, of a thirteen-year-old Elvis Presley, alone with his bike on a Tupelo street in 1948, his blond hair also slicked back, his face proud, and what might as well be exactly the same man in the first picture just to the boy's right, the same hat, maybe slightly better clothes. You don't have to know that Evans took photos of soil erosion in Tupelo in 1936—or to imagine that he came back years later to follow up and had his eye caught by a boy on the street who reminded him of children he'd shot before—to know that in the deepest sense he made both pictures.

4 ■ **Pete Seeger, 1919–2014** He sang for union rallies and children, at civil rights meetings in fields and in concert halls. He defied the House Un-American Activities Committee. He was blacklisted and never backed down. He saved the Hudson River.

He lived in a log cabin he built himself and his seventy-year marriage was ended only by death. He was also Arthur Dimmesdale, with all of the moral rectitude and none of the guilt.

5 ▪ **Anna Ostoya, *Adad Good Spirits* (2010), in "*New Photography 2013*," MoMA, New York (September 14, 2013–January 6)** Ostoya is a Polish artist working in New York; this supremely modest piece is a small, rolled-up scroll of the photograph of Hugo Ball in what he called his "magical bishop" outfit from the Cabaret Voltaire in Zurich in 1916, and, next to it, in a placement that mirrors Man Ray's 1926 *Black and White*, is an even smaller conical scroll reading "OS-TOYA íst politicisch" ("Ostoya Is Political"), which is to argue that Ball was, or is, too. It's a lovely dada three-way, quietly punk, blank and yet full of shifting meaning, and, with the white in the piece and its spare setting dominating the grays of the photo and the black of the words, above all coolly delivering its uncool message, which is now cool, too.

6 ▪ **Kevin Young, reading and talk, NOMMO African American Author Series, University of Minnesota (February 12)** Young, author of *The Grey Album: On the Blackness of Blackness* (2012) and eight collections of poetry, reads with delight: not with drama but with deadpan humor, a musician's sense of timing that brings out the seductive economy of his writing. Not a word is wasted, and every word seems to perform at least two jobs at once. He talked about thinking he'd finished with the blues form after his 2003 book, *Jelly Roll*, and how, for the poems in the 2008 *Dear Darkness*, "blues came back and got me." He writes from deep in the tradition and escapes it, as with "Last Ditch Blues": "Tired of digging / my own grave." The killer is "Flash Flood Blues." "I'm the African American / sheep of the family," he says, then, wending his way through six subtly whiplashing couplets to find lines Robert Johnson would have been more than happy to use: "Even my wages of sin / been garnished."

7 ▪ **Joel Selvin, *Here Comes the Night: The Dark Soul of Bert Berns and the Dirty Business of Rhythm & Blues* (Counterpoint Press)** Berns was a songwriter and a record producer; he died in 1967, at thirty-eight, leaving behind such epochal hits as the Isley Brothers' "Twist and Shout," the Drifters' "Under the Boardwalk," Them's "Here Comes the Night." He was also a man of the street, putting people together, avoiding others, looking over his shoulder, making deals that returned howling at his back. Selvin walks through his story with a Broadway swagger that at first feels contrived, third-hand, and after a hundred pages or so feels not only earned but musical, and a rhythm begins to count its way through the story. The songwriter Ellie Greenwich haunts the last part of the book like the ghost of a woman who doesn't know her life is already over; Berns courts death like a man singing Bo Diddley's "Who Do You Love?" under his breath. Again and again, Selvin brings forgotten recording sessions that any other chronicler would have ignored to such stirring life that they validate not only the story he has to tell but the worth of Berns's own life. In 1963 he went into the studio with a neophyte named Betty Harris, who recorded two of his songs: "Cry to Me," already a huge hit for Solomon Burke, and "I'll Be a Liar." Selvin lets you feel the contingency of the moment, how everything that happened—this inflection, that hesitation—could have turned out completely differently, and led to nothing. You probably don't know the performances, but the suspense that Selvin is building is too strong for you to turn to YouTube—and you know that what's there won't match the picture Selvin is drawing: "She didn't know Berns wrote 'Cry to Me' when she auditioned for him by singing the song. She didn't know that he originally envisioned the song the way she sang it, slowed down to a crawl . . . from the first sob that bursts almost involuntarily from her throat, Betty Harris slowly, deliberately picks her way through the pathos," Selvin writes. It's the word *picks* that throws the

scene into relief, producing images both of a woman walking with care and fright and of her picking at her own skin, her own heart.

8 ▪ **Masha Gessen, *Words Will Break Ce-ment: The Passion of Pussy Riot* (Riverhead Books)** An incisive and powerful account of the desires, instincts, decisions, strategies, actions, and punishments of a few people who committed themselves to living as if they were free in a society built to ensure that they were not. The Russian American Gessen, author of *The Man Without a Face: The Unlikely Rise of Vladimir Putin* (who will not say "Pussy Riot" aloud), is first of all a reporter, and she traces the story of a performance-art collective that turned into a "fictional group" that turned into a real group, recording the playground shouts of "Kill the Sexist" at a playground, and then everything that happened, and didn't, when they took their next step, bringing their act into a cathedral. The tone can be sardonic, from the inside, not the outside: "They were ready. Sort of. Maybe. Almost." Gessen also writes like a novelist, preternaturally attuned to the way the perpetrators of an action can lose control of it—"Something felt off among them, and each of them sensed it, the way each partner in a romantic relationship senses when it has started to crack, even though neither can say what went wrong and when"—and to the feelings of loss, missed chances, and abandonment that sometimes accompany even events that, in their small or enormous way, can leave a nation, or the world, or only a single person changed. "There is that moment in every action," Gessen says of a woman who did not go into the cathedral, but might have, "when you have handed over your personal belongings to whoever is helping and you know exactly why you are there and you know what you are about to do and you feel that you can do anything at all and at the same time it is as though you could see yourself, so lithe, so young, so bright in every way, climbing up onto that platform—it was this moment she remembered."

9 ▪ **I Break Horses, *Chiaroscuro* (Bella Union)** Maria Lindén is from Stockholm; through the haze of this shimmering album you can see her playing both the middle-aged La Dolce Vita parties in *The Great Beauty* and the funeral scene in Baz Luhrmann's *The Great Gatsby*, if he'd shot it. You can see her spinning Alphaville's "Big in Japan" over and over in her teenage bedroom, and a few years later watching Julee Cruise swim her way through "Questions in a World of Blue" in *Twin Peaks: Fire Walk with Me* and realizing that was what she wanted to do with her life. This is synthpop draped in Gothic mystery so thick it would be corny if there were a single element in the music—vocals, melody, rhythm, texture most of all—that seemed fixed, settled, seen as a fact by the woman who made it. You could play this record all day long, and I've never played it less than twice in a row.

10 ▪ **Sly and the Family Stone, "Stand," from *Higher!* (Epic Legacy)** On this career retrospective, a moment from a show at the Isle of Wight Festival in 1970: it's 7 a.m. The band is following Miles Davis, the Doors, the Who, and Melanie. The crowd is dead but the group somehow brings it to life; then someone hits Freddie Stone on the head with a soft-drink can and they leave. Before that there is Sly Stone, with a few sentences and a few notes that capture the best of what he left behind: "People believe in a lot of different things—though our universal thoughts, in general. . . . I mean, the people who believe that what's up is up and down is down, simple things, you know. It's very easy to be fair, and don't kill nobody, and those things—hurts if you step on my toe: 'Ouch.' A lot of things happened in the sixties"—and it's so displacing, to hear someone barely halfway through 1970 referring to "the sixties" as an already completely historicized past—"a lot of people *stood* in the sixties. A lot of people went down in the sixties—for standing. That's unfair." He begins a clear, calm, floating a cappella "Stand," as voices come in behind him, then instruments creep in as nothing but

the most distant, quiet vamp, and you can see a small band of people, dressed in white, as they were that morning, gathered in a circle, and then you hear a single drumbeat.

Thanks to Cecily Marcus and
Andrew Hamlin

JUNE 2014

1–4 ▪ Gina Arnold, *Exile in Guyville* (Bloomsbury/33 1/3); Liz Phair, *Exile in Guyville* (Matador, 1993); Pussy Galore, *Exile on Main Street* (Shove, 1986); Rolling Stones, *Exile on Main Street* (Rolling Stones, 1972)

Arnold is a wonderful writer: fearless, precise, full of doubt, never taking anything for granted. She's one of the few people left on the planet who uses *presently* correctly, which can create its own thrill. Going back to Liz Phair's once notorious, now often forgotten, absurdly in-your-face ambitious first album—"a story about a girl and a time and a place," the indie-rock world of Wicker Park, in Chicago, in the early 1990s, but in Phair's hands a story told with such heart that you need no such details to catch every shade of meaning and emotion—Arnold has written a book about the past ("when dinosaurs, as personified by Dinosaur Jr., ruled the earth"), its follies and crimes ("Every past is worth condemning," Arnold quotes Nietzsche, and then puts the words to work), and the idea of an imagined community that the past leaves behind ("Often I think I am a better informed citizen of Middlemarch, Bartsetshire," Arnold says, "than I am of San Francisco"). And it's about what it means for a young woman to simultaneously take on both everyone in her town and take down the album that sums up everything that everyone in her town would like to sound like, look like, act like, be—to take down a whole way of being in the world. "At one point we had felt like misfits or we had felt like 'others,'" Carrie Brownstein recently said of the time she shared with Phair—in her case, in her own indie-rock community, in Olympia, Washington. "It was supposed to be come

one, come all, you know? Freaks gather round and we'll provide you with shelter. And you get in these scenes and you realize, no, I've gone from one set of rules and regulations and codifications of how you should dress and what you should know to another. . . . What should have been inclusive felt very exclusive . . . there were times when I felt very flummoxed by the rules, very alienated, and I was trying way too hard to figure out not just what band to like, but am I liking the right album from that band. And then, am I liking the right band member in that band? Am I liking the right song on the right record? Have I picked the right year to stop liking the band?"

Phair wasn't the first person in the post-punk community to take on the Rolling Stones' *Moby-Dick*. Fourteen years after the release of *Exile on Main Street*, the hilariously obscene Pussy Galore covered the whole double album, all eighteen songs, in what sounded like a single all-nighter, hammering out the tunes until they lost all definition, people shouting back and forth at each other in impatience, frustration, and pure fed-upness, putting the thing out in the most obscure format possible, a five-hundred-copy grimy cassette (though today you can find it all online). It works; you're drawn in by a band's epic refusal to quit. But Phair did something much harder. Writing her own eighteen songs—Arnold, in her own way of playing, or singing, *Exile in Guyville*, makes a case for the pairing of each track of each album—Phair came up with just under an hour of music that today sounds as personal, unique, and yet socially necessary as it did more than twenty years ago. It was a dare: someone no one's ever heard of can say as much, can say more, than someone everyone's heard of, whom everyone *listens* to, and in her own voice. Such a story is always new, and it's new now.

Because it never received enough air-play to be overexposed, because it carried no obvious influences and did not, musically, obviously influence anyone—the spiritual influence of the album, the way it inspired others to take the kind of dare Phair took, was enormous—the music on *Exile in Guyville* has not become dated in any way. "Fuck and Run" is if anything more painful, more defenseless, than it was when it was first heard, because the pain is not only a matter of, in Arnold's words about everything on the album, "what it was like to feel voiceless and powerless in a nightclub, on a road trip, or during sexual intercourse," but it is in the melody, in the way the melody pulls back on itself, and in the rhythmic drive Phair's guitar puts into the story, the sense of inevitability, so that you don't even need the singer to tell you "I can feel it in my bones, / I'm gonna spend my whole life alone."

Arnold is betting on the right horse. Liz Phair's album today sounds completely fresh. It feels completely fresh in the way that it feels completely worn-out, because, when the album ends, you feel as if the person you've been listening to has been through a hard day. That fatigue, that sense of being too tired to care but too blasted not to, gives what Phair did an odd realism that, in her place and time, no one else seemed to know was there, or to want to know.

The obvious thing to say now is that the realism of Liz Phair's version of the Rolling Stones' *Exile on Main Street*—her translation—makes the real thing sound phony, fake, contrived, every gesture postured, not lived, makes it sound not real at all. But if anything, Phair lets you hear how unlikely, how desperate, what a long, long night the Rolling Stones' album really was. Pussy Galore bash their heads off, but the Rolling Stones sound more primitive. The songs are dribs, drabs, fragments, pasted together with spit (the words to "Ventilator Blues," Arnold says, "sound like the Moldavian entry in the Eurovision Song Contest"), and yet, as if they're betting against themselves, they take shape, burrow under the ground, change shape, and come into the light as if they were just getting out of bed. You don't hear production, money, skill, or even intent. You feel

as if you've stumbled onto the scene of an accident where, for some reason, people pitched a tent.

It became a legend, and other people made the tent into a temple and insisted that everyone live in it. Liz Phair was one of those who lived in it. In Gina Arnold's telling, she didn't cast out the money changers; they're still there. Again, she did something more difficult. She walked out, pitched her own tent down the road, and then left that behind, too.

5 ■ **La Sera, *Hour of the Dawn* (Hardly Art)** The spirit here is of people rushing through city streets so fast you can feel the wind they make, but their minds are just as quick: from song to song there's a hint of Eleanor Friedberger's relentless questioning of every moment as it passes. "You go on and on about the things you believe," Katy Goodman says in "Running Wild"—the person she's talking to might be chasing the singer, but she's already turned the corner. With endless invention and flair, the guitarist Todd Wisenbaker gives the former member of the always overrated Vivian Girls space, purpose, and most of all pace.

6 ■ **Umberto Tozzi, "Gloria," in *Gloria*, written and directed by Sebastián Lelio (Roadside Attractions)** At the end of the picture, in present-day Santiago, Chile, in a nightclub for people in their fifties, a woman dances alone to what, inevitably, is her song: she's named Gloria, too. Laura Branigan had the huge English-language hit; the Italian original is only slightly less cheesy. Yet something begins to happen. Played by Paulina García, Gloria has just perpetrated a spectacular breakup with a man who always disappears on her. There's the vaguest suggestion that his dishonesty is of a piece with the likelihood that he once perpetrated disappearances under the Pinochet dictatorship. No one Gloria's age could have missed the hint dropped in the script, but she doesn't seem to care—we don't know what she was doing then, and what she wants is not justice but sex and affection. But she doesn't get much of either,

and now, in the nightclub, going back and forth to the beat, the staircase in the rhythm of the song begins to assemble itself, and she climbs it. You can feel her body lift with each step. No, she doesn't get anywhere. There's no deliverance. Her life doesn't change. The affair is just one more thing to put in the past. But the song has given her far more than the man ever did.

7 ▪ **Season 2, Episode 4,** *House of Cards*, **Netflix** After a CNN interview exposing a newly promoted general as a man who raped her in college, Claire Underwood is at home with Vice President Francis Underwood. There are hints he used to be a folkie: "'Dark Was the Night,'" he says at one point, "gets me every time." Now they're smoking a cigarette they've forbidden each other. "Sing me something," she says. "What do you want to hear?" "Anything." "Pretty Polly, Pretty Polly, let me tell you my mind. / My mind is to marry, and never to part. My mind is to marry, and never to part," he sings, in a deeper voice than the song usually carries. "Before we get married, some pleasure to see, before we get married some pleasure to see"—and as banjo and dobro come up behind him on the soundtrack, the camera pans right, right out of the shot and into black. You don't hear him sing the rest of the song—where he kills her.

8 ▪ **Dex Romweber Duo,** *Images 13* **(Bloodshot)** A rock 'n' roll equivalent of lounge music. Very dumb and very fun.

9 ▪ **David Kinney,** *The Dylanologists: Adventures in the Land of Bob* **(Simon and Schuster)** This could have been a condescending, for that matter sneering, portrait of cultists, monastics, gnostics, and fools: people who can not only name every song on *Empire Burlesque* but also tell you their secret meanings. Instead it's warm, open, discerning. You encounter people who'd be death bending your ear at a bar, but others whom you might want to meet.

10 ▪ **Stephen Colbert, "Happy Birthday,"** **on** *The Colbert Report*, **Comedy Central** **(March 6)** Stephen Colbert had a news report about the ninetieth anniversary of the publication of the song that probably tops "Row, Row, Row Your Boat," the first verse of "The Star-Spangled Banner," and "Guantanamera" on the Everybody Knows It chart. The difference is that thanks to a revolution—or really a counterrevolution— in intellectual property law, "Happy Birthday" is still under copyright, and if you don't protect a copyright, it dissolves into the common square of public domain, so Warner Music does everything it can to make sure that if "Happy Birthday" is sung in any public place or forum—in a movie, on the radio or TV, but also to celebrate the birthday of a cast member at the end of a Broadway show or a Cabinet member at a Cabinet meeting, in a YouTube video, even in a restaurant—you're supposed to pay.

Sure. Like you're going to take your grandmother to Geno's for *her* ninetieth and when the whole family starts up the proprietor's going to run over and tell you to stop or Warner Bros. is going to shut him down. "Don't believe these people are protective of their intellectual property?" Colbert said. "Marilyn Monroe sang it to President Kennedy, and in one year they were both dead."

JULY–AUGUST 2014

1 ▪ **Kim Gordon with Nirvana, "Aneurysm," Rock and Roll Hall of Fame induction ceremony, Barclays Center, Brooklyn (April 10)** That Nirvana used its time onstage to have only women take Kurt Cobain's place was the deepest kind of tribute to a man who in his music did everything he could to, in Camille Paglia's words, "escape our lives in these fascist bodies." But Joan Jett ("Smells Like Teen Spirit"), Lorde ("All Apologies"), and St. Vincent ("Lithium") were karaoke. Late of Sonic Youth, Kim Gordon was the singer her song was asking for, whether it was Cobain or someone else, even if now the song was getting more than it asked for. In a gray dress—"a dress by Theory I found. It reminded me of the dress I wore on that 1991 tour with Nirvana, just about a foot longer"—she was fierce, her head down, her

eyes hooded. As she charged across the stage, the song might have been trying to run away from her, scared to death, but it didn't make it.

2 ▪ Woods, *With Light and With Love* (Woodsist) Jeremy Earl's Brooklyn band sounds less like Brooklyn—or anywhere, or any time—with each new record. The nine-minute title song is the sort of have-guitar-will-travel excursion you don't hear anymore—John Andrews's organ keening in the background, Earl's high voice breaking the pace, then increasing the pressure until only another guitar can stand up to it. Serpent Power did it with "The Endless Tunnel," Neil Young with "Cowgirl in the Sand," Steely Dan with "Do It Again" and "Reelin' in the Years"—while this is playing, you won't care. At the end, with "Feather Man," Earl twists a single tiny theme on an acoustic guitar and suddenly you're hundreds of years in the past, hiding out in the Scottish highlands, waiting for the invaders from the south. How did the band get from one place to another as if all they had done was move from one chair to another? With the sense that in the time it takes to move from one chair to another, the room might disappear.

3 ▪ Bikini Kill, *Yeah Yeah Yeah Yeah* (Bikini Kill Records) For the seven 1991 live performances and practice sessions on the B-side: a band that can barely play discovering itself and realizing that getting better is the worst thing they can do.

4 ▪ Bryan Ferry, the Fox Theater, Oakland, California (April 14) With a six-piece band, not counting his own keyboards and two backing singers whose outfits made them look like shimmying layer cakes, the music was mostly sludge, drowning in an echo broken only by the kind of paint-by-numbers big-move guitar solos that Ferry's music doesn't need and that Roxy Music was made to escape. The air cleared only for "Oh Yeah," a lace curtain that's been blowing in its window for thirty-four years without ever fraying, and John Lennon's "Jealous Guy." Roxy Music began playing it just after Lennon was shot; Ferry commu-

nicated all of the pathos he made the song shoulder then, and he made the song carry it now. You felt the way that death can swallow life, and how at least one song escaped.

5 ▪ Secret Cities, *Walk Me Home* (Western Vinyl) Wonderful press-release lead for a group that, after *Strange Hearts*, recorded in 2011 over email, now steps out with an album made in an actual studio, albeit Tiny Telephone, in San Francisco, which I like to think is actually a telephone booth under the freeway, where the three got a sound somewhere between the two-girls-one-guy Fleetwoods, from Olympia, Washington, in 1959, and a barely existing female punk band like the Anemic Boyfriends, from Alaska in 1980: "Charlie Gokey delved into Roy Orbison's ballads about losers in love while becoming a civil liberties attorney in Washington, DC. Alex Abnos locked into New Orleans soul masters like King Floyd & Dr. John as he became a journalist in New York City. And Marie Parker became a teacher in the band's spiritual home of Fargo, North Dakota." And Gokey has passed his new muse to Parker: in "Bad Trip," "Playing with Fire," and "The Cellar," she recalls Paula Frazer of Tarnation, whose "Big O Motel"—"Heartbreak Hotel" but cheaper—remains the truest Orbison homage there is. She drifts through the songs, not as if she were walking down the street but as if the streets were walking by her, and she were watching.

6–7 ▪ Kronos Quartet, "Last Kind Words Blues," arranged by Jacob Garchik, in John Jeremiah Sullivan, "The Ballad of Geeshie and Elvie," *New York Times Magazine* (April 13) and Nat Baldwin, *In the Hollows* (Western Vinyl) Sullivan tells a long tale of Geeshie Wiley and L. V. Thomas, two women from Houston who in 1930 recorded six inimitable sides for Paramount in Wisconsin and then disappeared. At the end of the online version—which also features videotaped interviews and all of the Wiley-Thomas recordings—the Kronos Quartet appears with a startling performance of Wiley's most distinctive number. As Sunny Yang on cello, John Sherba on violin, and Hank

Dutt on viola map the territory solely through pizzicato, making a setting where David Harrington's violin follows Wiley's original vocals like a second mind, as if Wiley would have sung the song without words if she could have gotten away with it, they rebuild the song from the first note up.

Best known for his playing with Dirty Projectors, Baldwin, leading on double bass and vocals, works with his own version of Kronos Quartet: Rob Moosre on violin, Nadia Sirota on viola, Clarice Jensen on cello, and Otto Hauser on drums. The attack is completely different. There's peace of mind in the Kronos Quartet piece, as a goal; here the goal is harshness, bad weather, bad news. The music is precise, defined—nothing, you feel, could have been done any differently—and driven like a horse on fire. The pleasure this brings is bottomless: you're in the presence of people who seem to know exactly what they're doing without any faith that they'll see another sunrise.

8 ▪ **Fairport Convention, "Tam Lin" (1969), in** *How I Live Now,* **directed by Kevin Macdonald (Magnolia Pictures)** Howard Hampton writes in: "Best music cue of last year: the film drops a sullen, insulated American teen (Saoirse Ronan, impressively unsympathetic) into the country of *Children of Men.* She barely registers that the England she has been shunted off to is under siege; picked up at the airport by an underage cousin in a filthy jeep, she doesn't want to make small talk, so he slips a cassette in the tape deck. What *is* this? she asks in dismay: Fairport Convention's variant of the centuries-old 'Tam Lin,' where Richard Thompson's electric guitar chords bring a dark sky to earth and Sandy Denny makes you believe she could turn men into trees. By the film's end, the girl will have witnessed war and rape, shot two men, and dug through piled corpses to find the body of the boy in the jeep. You can never be sure what's going on behind Ronan's blankly piercing eyes, but you have the feeling "Tam Lin' never leaves her head as the world is coming undone."

9 ▪ *Conference at Night* **(2012), directed by Valérie Mréjen, in "Hopper Drawing: A Painter's Process," Walker Art Center, Minneapolis (March 13–June 20)** The late '40s in the United States were a kind of great exhaling: after holding its breath through sixteen years of depression and war, around 1948 the country finally began to breathe again. A new excitement, a sense of release; blasphemy, and possibility changed the way people walked and talked. It came out over the next years as "Howl," *On the Road*, the music that would take the name "The Birth of the Cool," *A Streetcar Named Desire,* Jackson Pollock's Paleolithic splatter paintings, *In a Lonely Place.* But there was also a great letdown, as the country returned to ordinary life, without the hero stories of the war or the horror stories of the Depression, and the letdown is what Hopper painted in 1949 in *Conference at Night*—or it's what, more than six decades later, a French director and three French actors saw in the painting, and caught in a four-minute-and-fifty-four-second film. After all the great adventures, three people talk dispiritedly, but insistently, as if they are trying to convince themselves that something actually depends on them doing something one way as opposed to another way, or doing it at all as opposed to not doing it at all, and about the maintenance strategies, memos, meetings, and accumulation of files, all to be dealt with tomorrow, that will be needed to keep the conversation going. It's *Office Space,* generations away, in the flick of an eyelash.

10 ▪ *Bob Dylan in the '80s: Volume One: A Tribute to '80s Dylan* **(ATO)** Aren't tribute albums terrible? Sure. But they're not usually a threat.

Thanks as always to Barbara
Shelley and Andrew Keir

SEPTEMBER 2014

1 ▪ **Lana Del Rey,** *Ultraviolence* **(Polydor/ Interscope)** The best that could happen to this whirlpool of an album—freezing up only with its last number, "The Other

Woman," a torch song written by Jessie Mae Robinson and a hit for Sarah Vaughan in 1955, which is structured, which is obvious, and which compared to everything else here sounds artificial and fake—is for it to sell its requisite five million copies and then be completely forgotten. Erased from public memory, so that generations from now, when someone opens a closet and finds—along with the Lana Del Rey hologram projector and the Lana Del Rey Barbie—a CD and an old box to play it on, that person will wonder what it is, and hear it at least as clearly as anyone living now, but in a world where our frame of reference is completely gone. Everything I've read about this record is about its words, literal-minded, Philistine readings that assume that the *I* in any song is a real person, and the same real person: *What is Lana Del Rey telling us about herself?* But no good song—no good creative work of any kind—is literal. Even if the artist starts out thinking she knows exactly what she means to say, the rich text, as I once read, resists not only the reader but the writer as well, and intent vanishes into the swirl of the songs. The music is gorgeous, and uncanny—words matter only when they play a musical role. You can hear the singer fall in love with the staircase she makes out of the repetition of "I fucked my way up to the top . . . fucked my way up to the top"—it's not a confession; it's a rhythm. Again and again, a chord comes down, breaks like a wave, flows back, and you keep listening for that moment to repeat itself, but it never quite does. Lana Del Rey knows how to wait out a song, and this album may know how to wait out its time.

2 ▪ **Cyndi Lauper, *She's So Unusual: A 30th Anniversary Celebration* (Portrait/Epic/ Legacy)** The first disc is the original album, with the four top-ten hits. The second is outtakes, and the first of them, an "early guitar demo" of "Girls Just Want to Have Fun," opens back into a career that might never have happened. The recording is stunning—and also dark, doom-struck, absolutely negative, frantic, panicky, the girl all dressed up

to have fun taking one last look in the mirror and reeling from what she sees.

3 ▪ **Cabaret, directed by Sam Mendes, the Roundabout Theatre Company at Studio 54, New York (June 13)** Cecily Marcus reports from New York: "At the end, Nazism has seeped in everywhere. Alan Cumming's Emcee comes back to center stage, wearing the same black leather trench coat that started the show. He starts undoing the buttons, sort of suggestively, but not really. If you saw the movie, you expect him to be just another Nazi. But in a move that is both a total shock and suddenly makes absolute sense, the Emcee is wasted, standing there dressed in concentration camp pajamas with a yellow star and a pink triangle. It's not a costume; it's not entertaining. It's horrifying and real and makes you wonder why you never understood this story before, no matter how many times you have heard it."

4 ▪ **Amanda Petrusich, *Do Not Sell at Any Price: The Wild, Obsessive Hunt for the World's Rarest 78rpm Records* (Scribner)** Mostly focusing on discs from the 1920s and '30s on the Paramount label, this book is so alive to its subject, to the grail of the music, that it pulls the reader through the author's speculations about Collector's Neurosis or her scuba-dive into the mud of the Milwaukee River in search of records discarded there the better part of a century ago. "But the more I thought about why" collectors gave up their lives to the rare, the arcane, the unfindable, Petrusich writes, "the less I cared," and that's the key to her sensibility: she wants to get inside the music she's writing about, and she does. Her best writing is about listening, rooted in her "base, possibly shameful desire to hear someone so overcome by emotion that they could no longer maintain any guise of dignity or restraint," and as she listens the mask drops from her face as well: "I wanted to crack it into bits and use them as bones," she says of Mississippi John Hurt's 1928 "Big Leg Blues"—you don't know if she means the shellac or the song. She quotes James Weldon Johnson's "O Black and Unknown Bards" to catch the breath of Geeshie

Wiley's 1930 "Last Kind Words Blues": "How came your lips to touch the sacred fire?" Charley Patton's sound translates itself into a single image: "Some goon waiting outside." She watches the collector Joe Bussard as he pulls a record from his shelves and puts it on his turntable, listening to him listen, to the way as the record spins he can't hold still: "At times it was as if he could not physically stand how beautiful music was." Petrusich will make you desperate not only to hear the records she's writing about—though only single copies of the actual discs may survive, you can hear everything on YouTube—but to feel the way they make her feel, to feel the mask dissolve on your own face.

5 ▪ **Dave Hickey,** *Pirates and Farmers* **(Ridinghouse)** In a world divided between pirates and farmers, Hickey makes sure you know what he is—but any posturing dissolves when he homes in on Jackson Pollock's *Autumn Rhythm* as a "disobedient object" or pulls the plug on the Hunter Thompson cult ("I found myself, for the first time, feeling sympathy for Johnny Depp"). There's a lot of re-reading in this collection of pieces from 1999 to the present, and it explodes when Hickey goes back to Jack Kerouac's *On the Road*. It's 2007, the book's fiftieth anniversary, and Hickey tells you he read it exactly fifty years before, "when I was in my early teens"; that he bought it "off the rack, in hardcover, because we were a transient family and the title, *On the Road*, seemed to promise some insight into that peculiar gift and affliction"—he wasn't falling for any best-seller hype, no way. OK, cool. But his account of reading it again twenty years later, after finding himself embarrassed by re-reading Sartre or Hesse or Rilke, isn't cool: "It was like being hit by a truck. It was so much better than I ever would have imagined that I wanted to cry." It's that high-art swoon, so you aren't ready for him to argue that the book's closest cultural kin might be *This Is Spinal Tap*: "They both get sadder every time. . . . With each subsequent experience the truth gets tougher; there is more rage in

the lunacy and outrageousness. The folly of vanity and demented hope becomes more excruciating." But that's not all that lasts. "No story in Dickens or Kerouac is so abject that you do not feel the joy of the author who is writing it," Hickey says, and that holds true for him, too.

6 ▪ **Pere Ubu,** *Carnival of Souls* **(Fire)** David Thomas's love for recycled titles pays off in this wave to the 1962 horror movie, which Pere Ubu has accompanied in-theater. "Golden Surf II," the first song, shoots out like a flood, and then you can ride the wave of transmogrification that sweeps over the whole album. "Carnival" is a combination of "96 Tears" and "The Signifying Monkey" on the surface; below it you can hear second and third rhythms and hints of second and third voices everywhere. "Irene" is Lead Belly's "Goodnight, Irene" hammered by "I Put a Spell on You"—but recalling Lead Belly's last lines, which the Weavers cleaned up for their 1950 hit version. "If Irene turns her back on me / I'm going to take morphine and die"—this might be closer to the Handsome Family's modern murder ballad "Arlene." The killer is the last number, the twelve-minute "Brother Ray": a revisiting of the Velvet Underground's "Sister Ray," but also of Thomas's own numbers "Little Sister" and "Runaway." Thomas walks back and forth in front of a weather report of a jangling groove, telling his story about a phone call from the desert, about how Brother Ray—himself a version of the brother in Raymond Chandler's *The Little Sister*, just before, or maybe after, he turns up dead—just *has* to get it across that he's going to play cards with God in heaven, Thomas at first jocular, a medicine-show majordomo, then wistful, then faraway, each voice marveling, in its manner, over the way some songs never stop teasing you with the possibility that, no matter how many times you've heard them or sung them, you were wrong all along.

7–8 ▪ **Rolling Stones,** *Acoustic Motherfuckers* **(Kobra Records, bootleg) and Nicholas Confessore, "Republicans at Romney**

Retreat Search for Focus," the *New York Times* (June 14) For the indelible regret of its opening strum, the standard version of "You Can't Always Get What You Want" is included on *Acoustic Motherfuckers*, otherwise a collection of if not altogether acoustic then quiet, downplayed outtakes, mostly from the late '60s. There are revelations here, and all are a matter of delicacy and restraint: Mick Jagger's vocals in "You Got the Silver," making the official version, with Keith Richards singing, seem coarse and shallow; in "Wild Horses," the acoustic guitar coming up in front of the singer, then falling behind him, the way a single mandolin note can break you, and then the way Jagger, by stepping away from a word as he sings it, can break your heart; Jagger and Richards together hovering over "Sister Morphine" as if they're afraid they'll wake it up. And as for proof that the depths of this music have yet to be plumbed, all you have to do is read the papers: "On Friday afternoon, former Gov. Mike Huckabee of Arkansas delivered a stump speech that was equal parts red meat and rueful political self-improvement. Republicans, he said, need to stand up for working-class voters, while Washington needs more compromise.

"'The Rolling Stones were the greatest political philosophers of all time,' Mr. Huckabee told the crowd, 'and they got it right: "You can't always get what you want."'"

9 ■ Street musician, corner of Fifth Street North and Third Avenue North, Minneapolis (June 7) In a light rain, as we approached Target Field, where the Twins would beat the Astros 8–0, you could make out a high, keening sound that didn't fit. We passed a Latin drum crew; the high sound got more definite if not louder, and as we turned onto a desolate block it did fit. There was a fiddler, and he might have been a hundred and forty years old: that is, he looked fifty, maybe sixty, but his hat, suit, beard, and mustache made an image of him coming up at that age from West Virginia in the 1920s, and his tone was from the nineteenth century if not before. His music, too, smeared time and place: the harsh, up-and-down cadence from his fiddle, "Shenandoah" splintering into what might have been "East Virginia," was shrouded in low, shapeless moans that felt like an argument about the insufficiency of language to tell any kind of truth worth hearing. He was still singing three hours later, looking as if he'd been playing across town outside Nicollet Park when Babe Ruth drove in six runs on a barnstorming tour in 1924.

10 ■ Kara Walker, *A Subtlety, or the Marvelous Sugar Baby an Homage to the unpaid and overworked Artisans who have refined our Sweet tastes from the cane fields to the Kitchens of the New World on the Occasion of the demolition of the Domino Sugar Refining Plant*, Creative Time, Brooklyn (May 10–July 6) Cecily Marcus reports from New York: "Everyone is talking about the massive woman taking up the back of the building. She's worth talking about, but I want to talk about the boys lining the path to the sugar Sphinx. The boy sculptures are life-sized and realistic. They lack any of the exaggerated features that make the woman in the back a showpiece. The boys are field hands, supplicant and abused, cast of molasses that is breaking down at every moment. At their feet are pools of melting molasses blood. Some have lost legs or arms, and in the humid heat inside the sugar factory, the molasses drains the color from the sculptures, leaving them a translucent reddish, or even white in places. Worse, there are sugar parts dropping from the building onto them, dripping, then cooling, then dripping, leaving the boys' backs, arms, chests, faces mottled and disfigured. They have been beaten and sent back into the fields to work. This art will look different every week it's open. Some of it won't live to see the end."

Thanks to Steve Perry

Acknowledgments

My first thanks go to Steve Wasserman at Yale, who went for this book even when it looked as if it would come out at more than a thousand pages. Also at Yale I thank Eva Skewes for her good humor and indefatigable digging, John Donatich, Mary Pasti, Jennifer Doerr, Sonia Shannon, Jay Cosgrove, Brenda King, and Heather D'Auria. Rich Black provided the cover art, and Lyndee Stalter at Westchester Publishing Services helped produce the book. Emily Forland, Emma Patterson, Marianne Merola, and Henry Thayer at Brandt and Hochman were as ready and responsive as ever. And it is a pleasure to thank the people who over the years have contributed to the columns collected here, sometimes by name, sometimes not, and here noted not alphabetically, so that those looking for their names will see what good company they've kept: Ed Ward, Steve Weinstein, Howard Hampton, Chris Walters, Sarah Vowell, Ken Tucker, Genevieve Yue, Emily Marcus, Barry Franklin, Charles Taylor, Mary Weiss, Robert Christgau, Oliver Hall, Kayla D'Alonzo, Pete D'Alonzo, Cecily Marcus, Mark Sinker, Alan Berg, the late Debbie Geller, Lindsay Waters, Wayne Robins, Jenny Marcus, Sean Wilentz, Joshua Clover, Penelope Houston, Dave Marsh, Michele Anna Jordan, Tina Yagjian, Bill Brown, the late Andrew Baumer, Jon Wiener, Betsy Bowden, Steve Perry, Don Filetti, Robert Polito, John Jeremiah Sullivan, Mary Davis, Jon Savage, Rob Symmons, Eric Dean Wilson, and Jacob Mikanowski.

Credits

Index of Names and Titles

This index is an index of top ten columns and is not a comprehensive index of all the names mentioned in the book.